CURRENT
BIOGRAPHY
YEARBOOK
1955

CURRENT BIOGRAPHY YEARBOOK

1955

EDITED BY

Marjorie Dent Candee

THE H. W. WILSON COMPANY

NEW YORK, N. Y.

Sixteenth Annual Cumulation—1955

Printed in the United States of America

International Standard Book No. 0-8242-0121-3

Library of Congress Catalog Card No. (40-27432)

Preface

In this, the sixteenth volume of CURRENT BIOGRAPHY YEARBOOK, are presented 330 biographies (reprinted from eleven monthly issues and cumulated in one alphabet) of personalities prominent in the arts, sciences, industry, politics, government, education and entertainment. Also included in this volume are twenty biographies of authors which were originally published during the year in the *Wilson Library Bulletin.* These are indicated in the **Cumulated Index** by (WLB) and are listed under the classification **Literature.**

On the international scene, ninety personalities are included; among them seven Prime Ministers, two Kings, three Queens, four Presidents and ten winners of Nobel Prizes. The impact of diplomatic conferences such as those held at Geneva and San Francisco during the year is indicated by the number of diplomatic representatives, which include seven Foreign Ministers and twelve Ambassadors. Representing the United States Government are eleven U. S. Senators, ten U. S. Representatives, ten Governors, U. S. Supreme Court Associate Justice John Marshall Harlan, Secretary of Labor James P. Mitchell, Deputy Secretary of Defense Reuben B. Robertson, Jr., and Secretary of the Air Force Donald A. Quarles.

Revised biographies of fourteen individuals whose sketches were published in earlier volumes, some of them out of print, are also included. Among these are Queen Juliana of the Netherlands, U. S. Senators Walter F. George, Herbert H. Lehman, J. William Fulbright, and Harry F. Byrd, First Deputy Premier Lazar M. Kaganovich and Marshal Georgi K. Zhukov of the Soviet Union, Marshal Tito, President of Yugoslavia, and British Foreign Secretary Harold Macmillan.

In the **Classification** section at the back of this volume the heads of fraternal, professional and veterans' organizations are listed under **Organizations.** Fifty women in many fields of activity are included, and listed under the classification **Biographies of Women** as well as in their special field. The classification **Nonfiction** lists not only professional authors, but also those who have written books about their specialties.

The biographies are prepared by research correspondents in London, Paris, New York, Chicago, Boston, Los Angeles, Denver and other leading cities. The material is assembled from many reference sources such as magazines, newspapers, books, Government offices, "Who's Who's", encyclopedias, commercial and educational organizations, and the information bureaus of many nations. Subjects of the biographies are sometimes interviewed, and asked to confirm or correct facts. The result of this painstaking research is biographical information often unattainable elsewhere. Biographies are kept objective by providing various reference sources which present different sides of controversial issues and personalities. Any major changes in a biographee's position in the course of the year have been noted in the Yearbook sketch and last-minute major changes have been included in the **ADDENDA.**

On the pages following are **Explanations, Key to Pronunciation, Key to Reference Abbreviations,** and **Key to Abbreviations.** At the end of this volume are these Indexes:

Biographical References (consulted by Current Biography research staff)

Periodicals and Newspapers Consulted

Necrology (obituary notices include those who died in late 1954 and three-quarters of 1955 whose biographies have appeared in former volumes).

Classification by Professional Field

Biographies of Women

Cumulated Index, 1951-1955 (1940-1950 INDEX is in the 1950 Yearbook).

Addenda

M.D.C.

NOTE: Authors whose biographies do not appear in any CURRENT BIOGRAPHY volume may usually be found in TWENTIETH CENTURY AUTHORS, edited by Stanley J. Kunitz and Howard Haycraft, published by the H. W. Wilson Company in 1942, or in the 1955 FIRST SUPPLEMENT. Authors of books for young people are generally included in THE JUNIOR BOOK OF AUTHORS (Second Edition, Revised), edited by Kunitz & Haycraft, 1951, also published by the H. W. Wilson Company.

Explanations

Authorities for biographees' full names, with some exceptions, are the bibliographical publications of The Wilson Company. When a biographee prefers a certain name form, that is indicated in the heading of the article: for example, Macmillan, (Maurice) Harold means that he is usually referred to as Harold Macmillan. When a professional name is used in the heading, as, for example, Greta Garbo, the real name (in this case Greta Lovisa Gustafsson) appears in the article itself.

The heading of each article includes the pronunciation of the name if it is unusual, date of birth (if obtainable), and occupation. The article is supplemented by a list of references to sources of biographical information, in two alphabets: (1) newspapers and periodicals and (2) books. See the section ***Biographical References Consulted.***

References to newspapers and periodicals are listed in abbreviated form; for example, "Sat Eve Post 217:14-15 S 30 '44 por" means ***Saturday Evening Post,*** volume 217, pages 14-15, September 30, 1944, with portrait. (For full names, see the section ***Periodicals and Newspapers Consulted,*** found in the rear of this volume.) The reference following each obituary notice is to the New York ***Times***; these notices appear for persons whose biographies have been published in ***Current Biography***.

KEY TO REFERENCE ABBREVIATIONS

January—Ja	July—Jl	Journal—J
February—F	August—Ag	Magazine—Mag
March—Mr	September—S	Monthly—Mo
April—Ap	October—O	Weekly—W
May—My	November—N	Portrait—por
June—Je	December—D	Review—R

KEY TO PRONUNCIATION

(Based on Webster's Guide to Pronunciation)*

ā āle
â câre
ă ădd
ă ăccount
ä ärm
ȧ ȧsk
ȧ sofȧ

ē ēve
ĕ ĕnd
ẽ makẽr

g go

ī īce
ĭ ĭll

K German ch as in *ich* (ĭK).

N Not pronounced, but indicates the nasal tone of the preceding vowel, as in the French *bon* (bôN).

ō ōld
ô ôrb
ŏ ŏdd
oi oil
o͞o o͞oze
o͝o fo͝ot
ou out

th *th*en
th thin

ū cūbe

û ûrn; French eu, as in *jeu* (zhû); German ö, oe, as in *schön* (shûn), *Goethe* (gû'tĕ)
ŭ tŭb
ŭ circŭs
ü Pronounced approximately as ē, with rounded lips: French u, as in *menu* (mē-nü'); German ü, as in *grün*

zh azure
' = main accent
" = secondary accent

(*Exceptions : *th* in then ; main and secondary accents.)

KEY TO ABBREVIATIONS

AAA	Agricultural Adjustment Administration
A.A.A.A.	Amateur Athletic Association of America
A.A.U.	Amateur Athletic Union
ABC	American Broadcasting Company
A.C.L.U.	American Civil Liberties Union
ADA	Americans for Democratic Action
AEC	Atomic Energy Commission
AEF	American Expeditionary Force
AFL	American Federation of Labor
A.L.A.	American Library Association
A.M.A.	American Medical Association
A.P.	Associated Press
ASCAP	American Society of Composers, Authors and Publishers
ASNE	American Society Newspaper Editors
AVC	American Veterans Committee
B.A.	Bachelor of Arts
BBC	British Broadcasting Corporation
B.D.	Bachelor of Divinity
B.L.S.	Bachelor of Library Science
B.S.	Bachelor of Science
CAA	Civil Aeronautics Administration
CAB	Civil Aeronautics Board
C.B.	Companion of the Bath
C.B.E.	Commander of (the Order of) the British Empire
CBS	Columbia Broadcasting System
CCC	Civilian Conservation Corps
C.E.	Civil Engineer
CEA	Council of Economic Advisers
C.E.D.	Committee for Economic Development
CIO	Congress of Industrial Organizations
C.M.G.	Companion of (the Order of) St. Michael and St. George
Com.	Commodore
CWA	Civil Works Administration
CWS	Chemical Warfare Service
D.A.R.	Daughters of the American Revolution
D.C.L.	Doctor of Civil Law
D.D.	Doctor of Divinity
D.Eng.	Doctor of Engineering
D.F.C.	Distinguished Flying Cross
D.J.	Doctor of Jurisprudence
D.Lit.	Doctor of Literature
D.Mus.	Doctor of Music
DP	Displaced Person
D.Pol.Sc.	Doctor of Political Science
D.Sc.	Doctor of Science
D.S.C.	Distinguished Service Cross
D.S.M.	Distinguished Service Medal
D.S.O.	Distinguished Service Order
ECA	Economic Cooperation Administration
ECOSOC	Economic and Social Council
EDC	European Defense Community
ERP	European Recovery Program
ESA	Economic Stabilization Administration
FAO	Food and Agriculture Organization
FBI	Federal Bureau of Investigation
FCA	Farm Credit Administration
FCC	Federal Communications Commission
FEPC	Fair Employment Practice Committee
FERA	Federal Emergency Relief Administration
FHA	Federal Housing Administration
FOA	Foreign Operations Administration
FSA	Federal Security Agency
FTC	Federal Trade Commission
G.B.E.	Knight or Dame Grand Cross Order of the British Empire
G.C.B.	Knight Grand Cross of the Bath
GHQ	General Headquarters
G.O.P.	Grand Old Party
H.M.	His Majesty; Her Majesty
HOLC	Home Owners' Loan Corporation
ICA	International Cooperation Administration
ICC	Interstate Commerce Commission
I.C.F.T.U.	International Confederation of Free Trade Unions
I.L.A.	International Longshoremen's Association
I.L.G.W.U.	International Ladies' Garment Workers' Union
I.L.O.	International Labor Office
I.L.P.	Independent Labour Party
INS	International News Service
IRO	International Refugee Organization
I.T.U.	International Typographical Union
J.C.B.	Juris Canonici Bachelor
J.D.	Doctor of Jurisprudence
K.B.E.	Knight of (the Order of) the British Empire
K.C.	King's Counsel
K.C.B.	Knight Commander of the Bath
L.H.D.	Doctor of Humanities
Litt.D.	Doctor of Letters
LL.B.	Bachelor of Laws
LL.D.	Doctor of Laws
LL.M.	Master of Laws
M.A.	Master of Arts
M.B.A.	Master of Business Administration
MBS	Mutual Broadcasting System
M.C.E.	Master of Civil Engineering
M.D.	Doctor of Medicine
M.E.	Master of Engineering
MGM	Metro-Goldwyn-Mayer
M.Lit.	Master of Literature
M.P.	Member of Parliament
M.P.P.D.A.	Motion Picture Producers and Distributors of America
MRP	Mouvement Républicain Populaire
MSA	Mutual Security Agency
M.Sc.	Master of Science
Msgr.	Monsignor, Monseigneur
MVA	Missouri Valley Authority
NAACP	National Association for the Advancement of Colored People
NAB	National Association of Broadcasters
NAM	National Association of Manufacturers
NATO	North Atlantic Treaty Organization
NBC	National Broadcasting Company
N.E.A.	National Education Association
NLRB	National Labor Relations Board
N.M.U.	National Maritime Union
NRA	National Recovery Administration
NRPB	National Resources Planning Board
NWLB	National War Labor Board
NYA	National Youth Administration
OBE	Officer of (the Order of) the British Empire
OCD	Office of Civilian Defense
OEEC	Organization for European Economic Cooperation
OPA	Office of Price Administration
OPM	Office of Production Management
OPRD	Office of Production Research and Development
OSRD	Office of Scientific Research and Development
OWI	Office of War Information
PAC	Political Action Committee
P.C.	Privy Councilor
PCA	Progressive Citizens of America
P.E.N.	Poets, Playwrights, Editors, Essayists and Novelists (International Association)
Ph.B.	Bachelor of Philosophy
Ph.D.	Doctor of Philosophy
PWA	Public Works Administration
Q.C.	Queen's Counsel
RAF	Royal Air Force
RCA	Radio Corporation of America
REA	Rural Electrification Administration
RFC	Reconstruction Finance Corporation
RKO	Radio-Keith-Orpheum
ROTC	Reserve Officers' Training Corps
SAC	Strategic Air Command
SCAP	Supreme Command for the Allied Powers
SEATO	Southeast Asia Treaty Organization
SEC	Securities and Exchange Commission
SHAEF	Supreme Headquarters, Allied Expeditionary Force
SHAPE	Supreme Headquarters, Allied Powers Europe
S.J.D.	Doctor of Juridical Science
SPA	Surplus Property Administration
SSB	Social Security Board
S.T.B.	Bachelor of Sacred Theology
S.T.D.	Doctor of Sacred Theology
S.W.O.C.	Steel Workers' Organizing Committee
T.U.C.	Trades Union Congress
TVA	Tennessee Valley Authority
T.W.U.A.	Textile Workers Union of America
U.A.W.A.	Union Auto Workers of America
UMT	Universal Military Training
U.M.W.A.	United Mine Workers of America
U.N.	United Nations
UNESCO	United Nations Educational, Scientific, and Cultural Organization
UNRRA	United Nations Relief and Rehabilitation Administration
U.P.	United Press
USO	United Service Organizations
U.S.S.R.	Union of Socialist Soviet Republics
U.S.W.A.	United Steel Workers of America
VA	Veterans Administration
V.F.W.	Veterans of Foreign Wars
WAA	War Assets Administration
W.C.T.U.	Woman's Christian Temperance Union
WFA	War Food Administration
W.F.T.U.	World Federation of Trade Unions
WHO	World Health Organization
WLB	War Labor Board
WMC	War Manpower Commission
WPA	Work Projects Administration
WPB	War Production Board

CURRENT BIOGRAPHY YEARBOOK 1955

ABDULLAH, SEIF-UL-ISLAM, PRINCE *See* Seif-ul-Islam Abdullah, Prince

ADRIAN, E(DGAR) D(OUGLAS) Nov. 30, 1889- Neurophysiologist; educational administrator; author

Address: b. c/o The Master's Lodge, Trinity College, Cambridge University, Cambridge, England

One of England's most honored scientists, Lord Adrian, formerly professor of physiology at Cambridge University and now master of Trinity College, was elected president of the British Association for the Advancement of Science in 1954. He is also president of the Royal Society. Among his many laurels for scientific achievement is the Nobel Prize for Medicine and Physiology, awarded to him and to the late Sir Charles Sherrington in 1932 for "their discoveries concerning the function of the neurons." Dr. Adrian's contributions included descriptions of the mechanism of sense organs and motor nerve cells and the nature of nerve messages. A barony was conferred on him in the honors list of Queen Elizabeth II, in 1955. He was gazetted as Baron Adrian, of Cambridge in the county of Cambridge.

In delivering the presidential address before the British Association for the Advancement of Science in Oxford on September 1, 1954, Dr. Adrian warned: "We must face the possibility that repeated atomic explosions will lead to a degree of general radioactivity which no one can tolerate or escape" (*Science News Letter*, September 11, 1954).

Edgar Douglas Adrian was born in London on November 30, 1889, the son of Alfred Douglas and Flora Lavinia (Barton) Adrian. His father was a King's Counsel, a legal adviser of the Local Government Board, and a Companion of the Bath. Young Adrian received education at the Westminster School and at Trinity College, Cambridge, which he entered with a science scholarship in 1908. He studied physiology for Part II of the Natural Sciences Tripos and was awarded a first class in 1911.

After further studies at St. Bartholomew's Hospital, Adrian was made a fellow of Trinity College in 1913. He received the M.D. degree two years later from Cambridge University. He served in World War I with the rank of captain in the Royal Army Medical Corps from 1916 to 1919. Appointed staff lecturer in physiology in 1920, he continued his research work in the physiological laboratory at Cambridge.

British Inf. Services

LORD ADRIAN

In 1923 he was made a fellow of the Royal Society and two years later he began investigating the sense organs by electrical methods. According to *Nature* (December 9, 1950) Adrian's "early training with Keith Lucas and in clinical neurology . . . equipped him to make full use of the opportunities to reinvestigate much of nervous function presented by the advent of the valve amplifier."

In 1925 Dr. Adrian realized that a combination of the capillary electrometer with an amplifier would permit the recording of far smaller potential changes than had been dealt with previously and might enable him to work on the units of the nerve trunk instead of on the aggregate. "The problem was then to limit the activity to only one or two nerve fibers," Dr. Adrian later said. "In this I was happy to have the cooperation of Dr. Y. Zotterman of the Caroline Institute of Stockholm, Sweden."

With Zotterman, Dr. Adrian demonstrated the rhythmic discharge of impulses by a single sense organ in muscle. This discovery was followed by observations which showed that this was the general principle of signaling used in the nervous system, in motor as well as in sensory nerves. This work made possible a better understanding of the physical basis of sensation and the mechanism of muscular control.

(Continued next page)

ADRIAN, E. D.—*Continued*

Appointed Foulerton Research Professor of the Royal Society in 1929, he devoted most of his time to pure research in physiology. In that year he worked with Dr. Detlev W. Bronk, now president of the National Academy of Sciences in the United States; they developed the method for making the work of the nerves and muscles audible by converting the electrical responses into sound. This is now widely used for investigating diseases of the muscles.

Dr. Adrian was awarded the Nobel Prize in Medicine and Physiology with Sir Charles Sherrington in 1932. Sherrington, in addition to other contributions, had isolated the single motor neuron and had shown how nervous impulses act on the central system and interact to produce coordinated muscular activity. Dr. Adrian had, according to Lloyd G. Stevenson in his book on Nobel Prize winners in medicine, "built upon and extended Sherrington's researches and demonstrated their value."

By 1934 Dr. Adrian had turned his attention to studying the electrical changes in the brain, and following the work of Hans Berger, he laid the foundation for electro-encephalography, which has since become an important new branch of neurology. In the calculation and measurement of the electrical impulses emitted by the brain, he could examine the different reactions of an active or quiescent mind. When the mind is completely at rest, there is a regular discharge of electrical impulses at the rate of about ten per second. When an individual thinks and concentrates his attentions, the mind becomes active, and impulses are discharged at the rate of about two thousand per second.

"Stimulating a nerve may be compared to firing a gun," Dr. Adrian once said. "We may pull too feebly on the trigger, but if we pull hard enough to fire the bullet no amount of extra pulling will make it travel any faster. In the same way, we cannot regulate the intensity or rate of travel of the impulse by regulating the stimulus. Again the gun needs reloading before it can be fired again, and in a nerve fiber the passage of an impulse is followed by a very brief interval during which a further stimulus is ineffective. There can be no continuous activity in the fiber—only a succession of impulses" (New York *Times,* December 9, 1934).

In 1937 Dr. Adrian became professor of physiology at Cambridge University. Under the auspices of the National Academy of Sciences, he visited the United States in 1944 to deliver the Pilgrim Trust Lecture in Washington, D.C. He predicted that new techniques would make brain wave analysis more accurate and that "the search for the mechanisms of the brain... may lead us to a new understanding of human behavior—a synthesis of physiology and psychology" (*Science,* May 5, 1944).

Recently Adrian has been working on olfaction and according to *Nature* (December 9, 1950), "has given us objective facts on which further understanding of this most baffling of the sense organs can be built." In 1951 he succeeded G. M. Trevelyan as master of Trinity College and relinquished his duties as professor of physiology at Cambridge University.

In 1950 he was elected president of the Royal Society, of which he had served since 1946 as foreign secretary. In 1954 Dr. Adrian also became president of the British Association for the Advancement of Science. In his presidential address, Dr. Adrian spoke on "Science and Human Nature" and said: "Our predicament is the inevitable result of our curiosity and of the physical nature of the world we live in, but if we make our behavior worthy of our increased knowledge we can live safely. The scientist therefore has a double responsibility. He must apply his science to learn as much as possible about the mental and physical causes which make us behave as we do, he must study human nature to prevent its failures; but he cannot wait for the discoveries which might make us act more wisely: he must take us as we are and make it his task to point out that the human race cannot stand more than a few thousand large atomic explosions whether they hit their target or miss it."

Dr. Adrian is the author of *The Basis of Sensation* (W. W. Norton, 1928) and *The Physical Background of Perception* (Clarendon Press, 1947). His articles have appeared in many medical and scientific journals. He lectured at the University of Pennsylvania in 1931 under the auspices of the Eldridge Reeves Johnson Foundation in Medical Physics (these lectures were published by the Oxford University Press in 1932 under the title, *The Mechanism of Nervous Action*) and at Harvard University's tercentenary celebration in 1936 (this lecture was printed in *Science,* September 25, 1936). He lectured in North and South America during World War II.

Honors conferred on Dr. Adrian, in addition to the Nobel Prize, are the Baly Medal (1929), Order of Merit (1942), Royal Medal (1934) and Copley Medal (1946) of the Royal Society, and Gold Medal of the Royal Society of Medicine (1950). He is a chevalier of the Legion of Honor. He was awarded numerous honorary degrees from English and foreign universities and is an honorary member of the American Academy of Arts and Sciences and the American Physiological Society. Scientific academies in France, Italy, Sweden, Canada, Mexico, Belgium, Holland, Poland, and Mexico have honored him with membership. He is a fellow of the Royal College of Physicians.

Edgar Douglas Adrian married Hester Agnes Pinsent on June 15, 1923; they have a son and two daughters. Lady Adrian is the president of the Cambridge Association of Mental Welfare and a member of the Royal Commission enquiring into the law relating to mental illness and mental deficiency.

Formerly, Dr. Adrian often went mountain climbing; now he enjoys sailing. His interest in modern art stems from his student days at Cambridge when he and a group of friends presented a post-impressionist exhibit of their own paintings and deceived art critics by the professional quality of their work. He is known as a friendly person and as a "polished and witty" speaker.

According to *Nature* (December 9, 1950), "Dr. Adrian's work has been characterized by simplicity in conception, going straight to the fundamental point where the new techniques could supply the missing links in the older knowledge. This has led him far afield in comparative neurology, from the optic ganglion of the water beetle to the auditory nerve of the alligator; the cortex of the pony, ape or himself have all provided material for his experiments. . . . Whether he speaks to a learned society or to a class of medical students, his audience are made to understand matters they thought too difficult for them."

References

Nature 166:978 D 9 '50
Science 76:427+ N 11 '32
Stevenson, L. G. Nobel Prize Winners in Medicine and Physiology, 1901-1950 (1953)
Who's Who, 1954
Who's Who in America, 1954-55

MCA Artists, Ltd.
ANNA MARIA ALBERGHETTI

ALBERGHETTI, ANNA MARIA (äl"bâr-gĕt'ĭ) May 15, 1936- Singer

Address: b. c/o MCA Artists, Ltd., Beverly Hills, Calif.

A little Italian girl named Anna Maria Alberghetti, who sang for candy, supplied by admiring GI's during World War II, came to the United States when she was thirteen and made her debut as a coloratura soprano at Carnegie Hall. By early 1955 she had been in three films, including Gian-Carlo Menotti's musical play *The Medium,* and had been a guest on nation-wide television shows. During 1954 she gave concerts at the Lewisohn Stadium in New York City and at the Red Rocks Auditorium in Denver, Colorado. When her American visa expired, special legislation was passed by the U.S. Senate in April 1955 granting permanent residence in the United States to Miss Alberghetti and her family.

Born May 15, 1936, in Pesaro, Italy, Anna Maria Alberghetti is the eldest of three children of Daniele and Vittoria Alberghetti. Both parents are musicians. Her father, a graduate of the Conservatory of Pesaro, is a cellist and a baritone; he sang with a number of famous Italian opera companies, including La Scala, and was concert master of the Rome Opera Company. Her mother was formerly a pianist with the Scuola Reggia Musicale on the Island of Rhodes.

Anna Maria began singing at the age of six. From the beginning, her father has been her only teacher. During World War II the Alberghetti family was on the beleagured Island of Rhodes, but the governor, after hearing the child sing, arranged for their transportation by bomber out of the danger area. By 1942 the young singer, with her father as coach and mentor and her mother as accompanist, was appearing in concerts in various European cities.

When Anna Maria was only thirteen, she made her American debut in Carnegie Hall in April 1950. "It was just like the story books," *Time* (May 8, 1950) reported. "Before a concert in Carnegie Hall one night last week, almost nobody in Manhattan had ever heard of thirteen-year old Anna Maria Alberghetti. When it was over, the audience stood up and cheered, famous singers stepped forward to congratulate her, and surprised music critics for the Manhattan press dashed off to write enthusiastic pieces for the morning papers." The New York *Times* critic referred to Anna Maria's singing as "some of the purest, loveliest sounds that have been heard all season."

In June of the same year, now turned fourteen, the child coloratura appeared as soloist with the Philharmonic Symphony Orchestra at Lewisohn Stadium before an audience of 13,000, singing arias from *Lucia, Traviata,* and *The Barber of Seville.* For encores on this occasion she sang three Italian songs for which her mother accompanied her at the piano.

Arthur Berger in the New York *Herald Tribune* (June 30, 1950) credited the young singer with being "capable of tossing off, with a winning air of unconcern, the difficult coloratura arias that give our most experienced singers more than a few jittery moments," and spoke of "an unmistakable musicality, good training in pitch and a certain tenderness of feeling," while commenting also on a needed development in breath support. "There were the slides and the tentative breathing, and if it had been otherwise it would have been unnatural for her age."

ALBERGHETTI, ANNA MARIA—*Cont.*

The young soprano returned to Italy for the making of Gian-Carlo Menotti's film version of his musical play *The Medium* in which she was cast in the role of Monica, the medium's daughter. Of her fulfillment of the role, Olin Downes, music critic of the New York *Times* (September 16, 1951), wrote that it was "all that could be desired and more than it is customarily possible to obtain," praising both her singing and her "highly intelligent acting." The reviewer for *Cue* thought the cast for the picture, including Miss Alberghetti, "could not have been better chosen." *Variety*'s critic said that the part of Monica was played "with grace and distinction." Otis L. Guernsey, Jr., of the New York *Herald Tribune* thought the young soprano "uncertain in pronunciation of the English lyrics, but convincing in action," while the critic for the *Saturday Review of Literature* wrote that "the fourteen-year old prodigy who stirred Carnegie Hall audiences last winter, sings Monica with pure and childlike beauty."

Returning to America, Miss Alberghetti went to Hollywood for the filming of *Here Comes the Groom,* a Bing Crosby comedy produced by Frank Capra and presented by Paramount, in which the coloratura was featured, although appearing in only one scene. Playing the part of a blind little war orphan, Miss Alberghetti rendered the "Caro Nome" aria from *Rigoletto.* *Variety*'s report on the picture spoke of the coloratura's single scene as "a standout."

Both films, *The Medium* and *Here Comes the Groom,* were shown in the fall of 1951. Reportedly, Paramount had offered the young singer a seven-year contract, but according to Miss Alberghetti, as quoted by A. H. Weiler in the New York *Times,* no papers had been signed because her father felt such an arrangement would not allow her time for the concert and television engagements his gifted daughter was filling. However, it was stated in the New York *Herald Tribune* (May 10, 1952) that a contract with Paramount was signed in 1952, and, as is usual with minors, was approved by the Superior Court of Los Angeles. The terms of the contract, which expires June 1956, provide that she will make no more than five pictures, and no more than two in one year.

Miss Alberghetti's next picture, also a Paramount offering, was *The Stars Are Singing,* released in January 1953. Co-starred with Rosemary Clooney and Lauritz Melchior, she portrayed the central character in the plot, that of a young Polish refugee who has entered the country illegally. For this vehicle, she sang an aria from *La Traviata* as well as some lighter numbers. "The singing is something to hear," commented Joe Pihodna in the New York *Herald Tribune* (March 12, 1953), "the plot and the acting are something else again.... It is that gifted fifteen-year old Italian girl... who gives the film a small portion of excitement with a true and strong voice." Other critics were of much the same opinion.

Miss Alberghetti's concert appearances continue and include one at the Red Rocks Auditorium in Denver in 1954. She also accepts engagements which bring her into the entertainment world; it was while filling such an engagement at the Sahara in Las Vegas that, according to Louella O. Parsons writing in the Washington *Post,* the singer persuaded her father to let her sing a popular song, "Ricochet Love." Another such engagement at the Italian Village in San Francisco was filled in July 1954 with Miss Alberghetti as the star attraction, her mother accompanying her at the piano, her father directing the band during her act. On this occasion, *Variety*'s Rafe reported that she "displays a powerful set of pipes, a flair for dramatic presentation and a gift for milking a melancholy song of every bit of pathos. . . . She gets a heavy mitt for almost everything she does." The same critic commented, however, on her rendering of three juke-box tunes, that "she does them like a longhair slumming and displays no gift discernible to any pop fans in the audience."

Miss Alberghetti has also been seen as a guest star on several television shows, appearing with Ed Sullivan, Bob Hope, Eddie Fisher and Red Skelton. It was on Ed Sullivan's *Toast of the Town* that she made her first TV appearance, on May 7, 1950. Among the other programs on which Anna Maria has performed are *Cavalcade of Stars* and the *Arthur Murray Show.*

On April 25, 1955 the Senate passed a bill granting permanent residence to Miss Alberghetti and her family. This special legislation (now pending in the House of Representatives) was necessary since Mr. and Mrs. Alberghetti had testified that they were "involuntary members" of the Fascist party in Italy during the war. The Alberghettis had returned twice to Italy since coming here, once for the making of *The Medium,* and in 1952 for a vacation. On all three entries their status had been that of temporary visitors.

Miss Alberghetti, now nineteen, is slender, dark-haired, dark-eyed. She has been described as "a pale, graceful girl who promises to grow into a beauty." It is her ambition to sing at the Metropolitan Opera House in New York and at La Scala Opera House in Milan, Italy. She lives with her family in Hollywood. It is a musical family, for in addition to father, mother, and Anna Maria, there is the younger girl, Carla, fifteen, who is studying to be a pianist, and the boy Paolo, ten, whose ambition is to be a conductor. Anna Maria hopes to live in a house that will have an outdoor swimming pool, for swimming is one of her hobbies. Asked if she liked to cook, she said, "My mother is a wonderful cook, and I help her with spaghetti and Italian dishes I shouldn't eat."

References

N Y Herald Tribune p12 Je 30 '50; p30 Mr 29 '53 por
N Y Post p20 Je 30 '50 por
N Y Sunday News p2 S 2 '51 por
N Y Times II p9 S 16 '51
Variety 186:30 Mr 12 '52
Washington (D.C.) Post p6T Jl 25 '54

ALBRIGHT, WILLIAM F(OXWELL) May 24, 1891- University professor; orientalist; archaeologist

Address: b. c/o Johns Hopkins University, Baltimore, Md.; h. 4 W. 39th St., Baltimore 18, Md.

In the opinion of Professor William F. Albright, who is recognized as "one of the greatest living Biblical archaeologists," the ancient manuscripts, mosaics and religious relics which have been unearthed during the past two decades have "revolutionized our understanding of the Bible." Dr. Albright is chairman of the Oriental Seminary at the Johns Hopkins University, Baltimore, Maryland, and professor of Semitic languages there. For twelve years he headed the American School of Oriental Research in Jerusalem and directed or advised numerous archaeological expeditions in Palestine and other parts of Southwestern Asia.

He is the author of numerous scholarly articles and books including *From the Stone Age to Christianity*, and *The Archaeology of Palestine*, which have appeared in several American and Continental editions. His analysis and interpretation of the Biblical scrolls discovered by a Bedouin boy in a cave near the Dead Sea in 1947 have provoked much interest among scholars and laymen. "All handbooks on the Bible," he wrote in *American Scholar* (Winter 1952-53), "early Christianity and the history of Judaism will be in need of drastic revision." Albright is the second scientist—after the late James Henry Breasted—in the field of archaeology and ancient history of the Near East—to be elected to membership (in 1955) in the National Academy of Sciences since its establishment by Abraham Lincoln in 1863.

William Foxwell Albright was born in Coquimbo, Chile on May 24, 1891, the son of the Reverend Wilbur Finley and Zephine Viola (Foxwell) Albright. His father was a Methodist missionary, the son of an Iowa farmer of German-French-Northern Irish ancestry. His mother's father was a Cornishman who emigrated to the United States and settled on an Iowa farm close to the Albrights.

A self-portrait included in *American Spiritual Autobiographies*, edited by Louis Finkelstein (Harper, 1948), told of Albright's early childhood in the small Chilean town of La Serena, where Protestants and foreigners were in the minority, thus beginning his keen interest in minority groups. When the family moved to Antofagasta, a larger town, he felt safer. From the age of six he constructed imaginary worlds which covered centuries of time and thousands of miles of space, while he attended a small private school run by British subjects and later a school run by his mother. He read history and theology at home and at the age of eight became interested in archaeology and Biblical antiquities.

The family returned to Iowa when young Albright was in his early teens. His father had six children to support on an income of $400 yearly, and they moved from one drab parsonage to another. The bright spots during these years for William were visits with his grandparents, who owned many books which he read avidly.

When he was sixteen years old he entered the preparatory school attached to Upper Iowa University at Fayette and began studying Latin, Greek, Hebrew, and Assyrian, ancient history and related subjects. He worked his way through five years of preparatory school and college, and received the A.B. degree from Upper Iowa in 1912. For a year he taught in the High School of Menno, South Dakota; a fight with one of the huskiest students brought an end to Albright's high school principalship at the close of the year. He spent a summer as a "tramp farm laborer, riding on top of passenger trains and under freight trains in approved hobo style."

He applied to Professor Paul Haupt, head of the Oriental Seminary at Johns Hopkins University and was granted a fellowship. He received his Ph.D. degree in 1916 and continued at the university on a Johnston scholar fellowship for research. He had begun a study on the ancient Near East, when toward the end of World War I, he was drafted into "limited service."

After the war, he spent a year in Jerusalem (1919-1920) on a Thayer fellowship at the American School of Oriental Research, where he studied modern Arabic and Hebrew. He was made acting director of the school in 1920 and its director in 1921. During the years that followed, Dr. Albright directed the excavations at Gibeah (Tell el-Ful), Tell Beit Mirsim, Bethel, and Ader.

He returned to Johns Hopkins University in 1929 as a W. W. Spence professor of Semitic languages, a position which he still holds. A series of lectures he presented in 1931 at the University of Virginia and the Hartford Theological Seminary were compiled in *Archaeology of Palestine and the Bible* (Revell, 1932). He also wrote a book published in a paper-bound edition by Penguin Books under the title *The Archaeology of Palestine* (1949).

In his article, "Palestine in the Light of Archaeology" (*Annals of the American Academy of Political and Social Science*, November 1932), Dr. Albright credited John D. Rockefeller, Jr., with the gift of $2,000,000, which made possible the existence of the Archaeological Museum in Jerusalem. After civil government was established in Palestine in 1920, Protestant, Catholic and Jewish groups vied with one another in supporting archaeological projects in the Holy Land. The Mandatory Power set up a Committee on Mediterranean Antiquities and Albright was named chairman. He resumed his post as director of the American School of Oriental Research in 1933, and later was made vice-president of the school.

In 1937 Albright's analysis of the Nash Papyrus was published in the *Journal of Biblical Literature* (LVI, No. 3). This is a small fragment containing the *Shema* and the Ten Commandments, and was bought fifty years ago from an Egyptian dealer. It is now in the Cambridge Library in England. The Papyrus

Johns Hopkins Univ.

WILLIAM F. ALBRIGHT

was dated by Albright as from some time early in the second pre-Christian century to some time toward the end of the first century A.D.

During the next few years, Albright continued his writing and lecturing in the United States and Europe. His book, *Archaeology and the Religion of Israel* (Johns Hopkins University Press), was published in 1942. He was visiting professor at the University of Chicago in 1946, and the following year, returned to the Holy Land as chief archaeologist of the Sinai phase of the University of California African Expedition. In 1950 and 1951 he was chief archaeologist of the South Arabian Expedition of the American Foundation for the Study of Man.

As an authority on Biblical languages, Professor Albright's opinion was sought when some scrolls sealed in clay jars were discovered by a Bedouin goat-herd in 1947 in a cave near the Dead Sea. In his article, "The Dead Sea Scrolls" (*American Scholar,* Winter 1952-53), he described these scrolls of leather and parchment which included the manuscripts of the Book of Isaiah and Habakkuk as well as original books from the Essene sect which rivaled the Pharisees and Sadducees in their influence on early Christianity. Arguing from the paleographical evidence, Albright dated the Isaiah scroll at about 100 B.C. (this was later confirmed by radiocarbon dating).

The finding of these scrolls and the controversy among scholars and archaeologists which has raged since the discovery was announced has been described by Edmund Wilson in his article, "The Dead Sea Scrolls" in the *New Yorker* (May 14, 1955), who quoted Dr. Albright as saying that he believes them to be the oldest known Biblical writings in the Hebrew language. Many theologians do not accept this opinion.

The Dead Sea scrolls were among the 1,500 items assembled by the American Fund for Israel Institutions from museums and private collections all over the world for the Smithsonian Institution exhibition (January 10 to 27, 1954). At a preview, Dr. Albright told reporters that newly discovered treasures had added "fresh conflict to the old controversy of science versus religion" (New York *Times,* December 22, 1953). The ancient scrolls will be permanently housed in Israel in a museum to be called the Shrine of the Book.

Writing on "The Judeo-Christian View of Man" in *Man's Right To Knowledge* (Columbia University Press, 1954), Dr. Albright traced the history of the Hebrew and Christian religions and concluded: "During several decades of war against the Nazi, Shinto and Communist worship of the state, Jews and Christians have staunchly defended human freedom. The Judeo-Christian tradition of the intrinsic worth of the individual remains the most solid bulwark of the rights of man."

An outstanding defender of minority groups, Dr. Albright's life work in archaeology has been guided by his desire to overcome prejudices. Professor Albright wrote: "Any nation which has organized national or religious minorities within its territory possesses assets of extraordinary value. As a rule, members of such minorities find life harder than do members of the majority. . . . Under such difficult conditions they react according to Toynbee's principle of 'the stimulus of penalization.' Energetic minorities form an invaluable source of stimulation for the majority, which tends to stagnate unless it receives such stimulation from the outside. . . . As soon as minorities become targets for open persecution and repression, democracy is imperiled. The continued presence and relative prosperity of minorities is thus the best possible test of the viability of a democracy" (*American Spiritual Autobiographies*).

Dr. Albright has received honorary doctorates from the universities of Utrecht (The Netherlands), Upsala (Sweden), Oslo (Norway), St. Andrews (Scotland), Dublin (Ireland), and from Yale, Georgetown, the College of Jewish Studies (Chicago) and others in the United States. Dr. Albright is a member of the national academies of Denmark, Flanders, Ireland, France, the German Archaeological Institute, the British Society for Old Testament Study, and the Asiatic Society of France. He has served as past and present officer of many American and European learned organizations, and of the International Congress of Orientalists.

William Foxwell Albright was married on August 31, 1921 to Dr. Ruth Norton. They have four sons, Paul Norton, Hugh Norton, Stephen Foxwell and David Foxwell. Albright is a Methodist.

References

Directory of American Scholars (1951)
Finkelstein, L. ed. American Spiritual Autobiographies (1948)
International Who's Who, 1954
Who's Who in America, 1954-1955
World Biography (1954)

ALDRICH, RICHARD (STODDARD)
Aug. 17, 1902- Theatrical producer
Address: b. c/o Aldrich & Myers, 22 E. 60th St., New York 22; h. 17 W. 54th St., New York 19; Dennis, Mass.

A theatrical producer with "many strings to his bow," Richard Aldrich has produced more than thirty plays on Broadway including the long-run hits *The Moon is Blue* and *Goodbye, My Fancy.* He has brought to New York such noted professional groups from abroad as the Old Vic Theatre Company of London, the Habimah Players from Tel Aviv, and the Dublin Gate Theatre from Ireland. Likewise a successful summer theatre producer, for the past twenty-nine summers he has operated the Cape Playhouse at Dennis, Massachusetts; he also owns the Falmouth Playhouse at Coonamessett and the Cape Cod Melody Tent at Hyannis. His biography of his wife, *Gertrude Lawrence as Mrs. A,* which first appeared in the *Ladies Home Journal* (July-November 1954), received very favorable criticism and has been high on the best seller lists since it was published by Greystone in January 1955.

On April 28, 1955 the Foreign Operations Administration announced that Aldrich had been appointed deputy director of the FOA mission in Spain with headquarters in Madrid. His partner, Richard Myers, will carry on his theatrical activities during his absence.

Richard Stoddard Aldrich was born in Boston, Massachusetts on August 17, 1902 to Edward Irving and Mary Pickering (Joy) Aldrich. His father, an executive of the Hood Rubber Company, was "a pillar of the Congregational Church [at Northfield, Massachusetts] and an ardent supporter of the Northfield Movement led by the evangelist Dwight L. Moody." Aldrich's paternal grandfather was Thomas Bailey Aldrich, author of *The Story of A Bad Boy;* his uncle, James Joy, was for many years editor of the *Christian Advocate;* another relative, Henry B. Joy, was founder of the Packard Motor Company; he is related to Winthrop W. Aldrich, U.S. Ambassador to Great Britain.

Richard attended Noble and Greenough School near Boston, graduating in 1921. He entered Harvard University and was graduated *cum laude* in 1925. While an undergraduate he wrote for the *Dramatic Mirror* (a position, he has written, which gave him free tickets to shows which opened in Boston).

During the summers of 1923, 1924 and 1927 he worked as business manager of the Jitney Players, which was "an *al fresco* operation," Aldrich recalled, "rain our greatest enemy. Operating in a Ford truck, one night we would play on the Parade Grounds at West Point, the next in the Harvard Yard, one night on a village green, the next in a sunken Italian garden in Southhampton" (New York *Times Magazine,* July 5, 1953). In 1926 he was general manager for Richard Boleslavsky and his American Laboratory Theatre.

At his mother's insistence young Aldrich put aside his undergraduate interest in the theatre ("a dangerous virus which Mother attributed to Professor George Pierce Baker's celebrated 47 Workshop") and became a "fledgling banker" in New York. The first time he saw Gertrude Lawrence act was in Noel Coward's *Private Lives.*

Fabian Bachrach

RICHARD ALDRICH

By 1930, "the Depression had cast a gloom over banking," Aldrich wrote in *Mrs. A.* "Compared to the stagnation downtown, Broadway appeared more and more enticing. Like a timid but persevering bather, I began to dabble in the waters I had always wished to swim in. I began in 1930 to produce plays with Kenneth MacGowan and Joseph Verner Reed."

He presented or co-produced *Art and Mrs. Bottle* (1930), *Lean Harvest* and *The Lady with a Lamp* (1931), *Springtime for Henry* (1931), *Three-Cornered Moon* (1933), *By Your Leave* and *Pure in Heart* (1934), *Petticoat Fever* (1935), and *Fresh Fields* and *Aged 26* (1936).

In the summer of 1935 Raymond Moore, who had founded the Cape Playhouse at Dennis, Massachusetts in 1927, engaged Aldrich to be his production manager. "I shocked him by proposing that we pay Jane Cowl $1,000 for a week's engagement in *Romance.* Miss Cowl justified her then unheard of fee. . . . Fourteen years later, to inaugurate the Falmouth Playhouse, I paid Tallulah Bankhead $5,000 for a week's toil in *Private Lives,"* Aldrich wrote.

Through playwright Samson Raphaelson and producer John Golden, Aldrich arranged in the summer of 1939 for a tryout of *Skylark,* starring Gertrude Lawrence, in his Cape Playhouse. At first he recalls being annoyed and terrified by the glamorous actress. When he learned that she loved working with her hands, and walking in the rain, and soaking up sunshine, he admits that he changed his opinion and their friendship developed all through the following winter.

(Continued next page)

ALDRICH, RICHARD—*Continued*

Despite many misgivings about marrying a star, Aldrich was married to Gertrude Lawrence on July 4, 1940 and in *Mrs. A* he relates how he broke the news to his eighty-year-old mother by telephone from Dennis to Groton. His mother's voice came sharply: "Certainly, I hear you, Richard, but *who* is Gertrude Lawrence?" How his English wife won the affection and confidence of his Puritanical mother is told by Aldrich "with an affectionate detachment both human and warming" (New York *Times Book Review,* January 9, 1955). He has two sons, Richard Stoddard and David Beals, by his marriage to Helen Beals on November 5, 1927, from whom he was divorced in 1936.

With Richard Myers he produced *Margin for Error* (which ran 264 times) in 1939 and *My Dear Children* (117 performances) in which John Barrymore made his final stage appearance in 1940. Aldrich's first association with Myers was in 1937 when they presented *Tide Rising.*

Shortly after his marriage to Gertrude Lawrence, Aldrich became a lieutenant in the U.S. Naval Reserve and was advanced through grades to the rank of commander. They were separated during much of the war years, while Aldrich was executive officer at amphibious bases in England, at Fowey, Southampton, and Plymouth. During 1944 and 1945 he was attached to the staff of Admiral H. R. Stark in London as public relations officer for the U.S. Naval Forces in Europe. He received the Commendation ribbons for the American area and European-African campaigns, the Occupation Medal and the Admiral's Letter of Commendation.

At the end of World War II Aldrich returned to the theatre world to become managing director of Theatre, Incorporated which presented *Pygmalion* starring Gertrude Lawrence and Raymond Massey. The revival ran longer in New York than any other previous production of the Bernard Shaw play (179 performances) and Miss Lawrence played the role of Eliza Doolittle on the successful coast-to-coast tour. (See *C. B.* 1952, Gertrude Lawrence.)

He arranged the six-week engagement of the Old Vic at the Century Theatre, starting May 6, 1946, offering productions of Shakespeare's *Henry IV,* (Parts I and II); *Œdipus; The Critic*; and *Uncle Vanya.* "If I am to have an epitaph," Aldrich once said, "I would want that to be it." The costly venture made a small profit for its sponsors and vindicated Aldrich's judgment that "culture" can be profitable, for the public paid over $300,000 to see the plays. Four of the Old Vic productions were broadcast over the Columbia Broadcasting System television network.

In 1948 Richard Aldrich became a partner with Richard Myers when with Michael Kanin they produced *Goodbye, My Fancy* by Fay Kanin. The play, which starred Madeleine Carroll, in which Shirley Booth had an important role as the Congresswoman's secretary, ran for 226 performances and was also successful with Ann Harding in the stellar role. Subsequent plays which the partners have presented with Julius Fleischmann include; *Caesar and Cleopatra,* starring Sir Cedric Hardwicke and Lilli Palmer (1949) and *The Devil's Disciple* (1951).

On March 8, 1951 Aldrich and Myers with Julius Fleischmann presented Barbara Bel Geddes, Donald Cook and Barry Nelson in *The Moon is Blue* by F. Hugh Herbert, staged by Otto Preminger, at the Henry Miller Theatre. The comedy of young love in the big city proved so winning that it ran for 924 performances, and five road companies toured the United States and a motion picture was made in 1953.

Affectionately known as "Cape Cod's benevolent czar," Aldrich thoroughly enjoys his dual role of country and Broadway impresario. He prepares "package" productions of a few plays which he distributes to his own summer theatres on Cape Cod, but also to a few others in select theatres in the "straw-hat" circuit. His list includes Ogunquit, Fitchburg, Newport, Easthampton, Westport, Ivoryton, Mountainhome, Bucks County and Olney. It was Aldrich who supported the move to pay straw-hat performers the Equity minimum salary.

"If I had the money," said Aldrich, "I'd like to do nothing else but develop new talent for the theatre." In his three Cape Cod theatres he employs about 150 staff members and about thirty apprentices "who neither paid nor were paid for the privilege of drudging about the theatre." He explained that he delegates all the responsibility to the people on his staff, "which leaves me with no worries except whether or not I have picked good people."

In his article "150 Broadways in the Hills," published in the New York *Times,* July 5, 1953, Aldrich estimated that "Where there used to be four summer theatres operating on weekly budgets of less than $1,000 there are now more than 150 and the budgets of some of them are as high as $15,000 each week."

Aldrich's Cape Playhouse observed in 1955 its twenty-ninth season. Among the stars to appear, were Constance Bennett, Shirley Booth, Katharine Cornell, Joan Crawford, Maurice Evans, Helen Hayes, Audrey Hepburn, Mel Ferrer, Jennifer Jones, and Grace Kelly. The Cape Cod Melody Tent, which he started in 1950 as the Musical Circus opened on July 1 at Hyannis for a nine-week season and among the musical shows presented were *Wonderful Town, Guys and Dolls* and *South Pacific.* His Falmouth Playhouse also had a nine-week season in 1955. Some of the Playhouse "graduates" include one-time usher Bette Davis, former apprentice stage-manager Henry Fonda, Robert Montgomery, and Gregory Peck.

He is a stimulator of "The Road" as operator of the National Theatre in Washington, D.C., since 1952 on which he holds a ten-year lease. His production of *Dear Charles* starring Tallulah Bankhead, is touring the United States after a successful Broadway season. He is a director of the American National Theatre and Academy and the New York City Center of Music and Drama. He is also a director of the newly organized Friends of Richard III, Inc., formed in March 1955 to clear the name of the English King now believed to be innocent of the murder of his nephews as related in Shakespeare's play.

In *Mrs. A* Aldrich wrote: "I think I have said enough about Gertrude's character and mine to make it clear that the tempo of her life was the exact antithesis of my own. The law of my nature is to progress steadily, as one mounts a stair—a single step at a time . . . but not Gertrude. Her movement through life resembled the flight of a bird which soars. . . ." The biography of Miss Lawrence (who died on September 6, 1952) has to date sold more than 50,000 copies.

Aldrich is a member of the Society of Colonial Wars, Society of Mayflower Descendants, and Sons of the American Revolution. Among the clubs in which he holds membership are the Union, Harvard, Players, and Dutch Treat in New York; the Metropolitan and Army and Navy in Washington, D.C., the International, Sportsmen's and Buck's in London.

Aldrich is six feet four inches in height, "lean and rangy," with gray eyes and graying dark hair. John S. Wilson described him as "a gracious, unhurried man." In explaining the air of calm efficiency with which he works, Aldrich once said, "I like the theatre. It's both a business and a pleasure to me. Fortunately, I don't get too hysterical. I don't get nervous breakdowns. If I have a flop, I try to forget about it and go on" (*Theatre Arts,* June 1953).

On June 19, 1955 Aldrich was married to Miss Elizabeth Boyd of Louisiana.

References

N Y Times Mag p18 Ja 12 '47; p13 Jl 5 '53
Sat R 35:24 S 6 '52
Theatre Arts 37:72+ Je '53 por
Aldrich, R. Gertrude Lawrence as Mrs. A. (1955)
Who's Who in America, 1954-55
Who's Who in the Theatre (1952)

ALEXANDER, ARCHIE A. May 14, 1888- Former Governor of the Virgin Islands of the United States; contracting engineer

Address: b. Frankel Bldg., Des Moines, Ia.; h. 2200 Chautauqua Pkwy., Des Moines, Ia.

The American-owned Virgin Islands group, including St. Thomas, St. Croix and St. John, is governed by the first Republican to hold this post and the second Negro Governor. Sworn into office on April 9, 1954, Archie A. Alexander, was appointed by President Dwight D. Eisenhower and recommended by both the Democratic and Republican senators from his home state of Iowa. By profession he is a successful civil engineer, contractor and builder.

On August 17, 1955 President Eisenhower accepted the resignation of Governor Alexander who asked to be relieved of "the physical strains of carrying on my administration" because of "urgent admonitions of my medical advisers." He was succeeded by Walter A. Gordon.

"Governor Alexander has undertaken a tremendous task in his dedicated efforts to bring good government to the Virgin Islands," stated Orme Lewis, Assistant Secretary of the Interior (New York *Times,* April 16, 1955). The Governor's recent veto of appropriation bills has caused some members of the legislature in the islands' capital at Charlotte Amalie to demand that President Eisenhower recall him, but the majority of Virgin Islanders have commended his efforts in their behalf during his first year in office.

Archie A. Alexander was born in Ottumwa, Iowa on May 14, 1888. He attended a local country grade school until his father, a janitor, moved his family to a farm on the outskirts of Des Moines. Young Alexander was graduated in 1905 from high school.

He entered the University of Iowa in 1908 to study engineering, despite a warning that "a Negro could not hope to succeed as an engineer" (*Negro Year Book,* 1952).

Although he had to work his way through college, he found time to become a three-letter football tackle and was pledged by the Kappa Alpha Psi fraternity (he later served as president of its national chapter). He received the B.S. degree in civil engineering from the University of Iowa in 1912 and in the same year began work as a designing engineer with the Marsh Engineering Company of Des Moines.

In 1914 he formed his own general contracting firm, A. A. Alexander, Inc. His professional record was recognized by the State University of Iowa in 1925 when he was awarded an honorary degree in civil engineering. Three years later he received the Spingarn Medal, given annually by the National Association for the Advancement of Colored People for the "highest achievement of an American Negro." Specifically, he was cited as "the second most successful Negro in business" for that year.

With a former classmate, M. A. Repass, he organized in 1929 the engineering firm of Alexander & Repass. The partners built an $80,000 concrete tunnel for the State University of Iowa; various bridges for the Chicago, Rock Island and Pacific Railroad in western Iowa and Missouri; a $1,000,000 sewage disposal plant at Grand Rapids, Michigan; a power plant at Columbus, Nebraska; and a civilian airfield at Tuskegee, Alabama. In the District of Columbia and vicinity, Alexander & Repass built the $1,000,000 Tidal Basin Bridge and the K Street Freeway. "We have a $6,000,000 outfit," Alexander told a Senate committee in 1954.

Alexander has been president of the Cedar Hill Construction Corporation, secretary-treasurer of the Douglas Glen Gardens Corporation, and a member of the board of the Supreme Liberty Life Insurance Company of Chicago. He was awarded an honorary Doctor of Civil Engineering degree by Howard University in Washington, D.C. in 1946, and at Iowa's Centennial Celebration in 1947 he was named "one of the first one hundred citizens of merit" among his university's 30,000 alumni.

(Continued next page)

ARCHIE A. ALEXANDER

Alexander's interest in the Virgin Islands was first aroused when he organized and became the president of American-Caribbean Contractors, which made bids for sewage disposal plant contracts in the islands. No Virgin Islands contract was obtained, but Alexander and his wife began visiting the islands fairly often, and Alexander became interested in improving the educational facilities there.

A Republican, Alexander had become assistant to the chairman of the Iowa Republican State Committee and was active in General Eisenhower's Presidential campaign in 1952. Following the resignation in 1954 of Morris F. de Castro as Governor (see *Current Biography*, May 1950), Alexander was appointed by President Eisenhower to fill the $15,000-a-year post. His nomination was confirmed by the U.S. Senate, after endorsement by Senator Bourke B. Hickenlooper (Republican) and Senator Guy M. Gillette (Democrat) of Iowa, on February 18, 1954.

President Eisenhower late in March 1954 sent Charles Kenneth Claunch (Assistant Usher at the White House) to serve as government secretary, a post equivalent to lieutenant governor of a state. On April 9, 1954 Governor Alexander took the oath of office in Charlotte Amalie's Emancipation Garden, where the Danes had freed their slaves in 1848.

Summing up the inaugural address, *Time* (April 19, 1954) noted that Alexander promised to be "Governor of all and every segment of the population. . . . Prejudice is born in ignorance and dispelled by knowledge. . . . We have room on these islands for but one flag, the American flag, and this excludes the Red flag." Alexander pledged himself to work for a bigger tourist trade ("but an economy based on tourist trade alone is not a stable one"), to aid schools, and to help end the islands' water shortage. (The islands' main products are sugar, rum and bay rum, and cattle, but income from exports do not make the inhabitants economically self-sufficient. They are largely dependent upon Federal assistance.)

Acquired by Denmark in the eighteenth century, the fifty-odd small islands or cays now comprising the U.S. Virgin Islands (133 square miles) were known as the Danish West Indies until 1917, when they became a U.S. possession. For strategic reasons the United States purchased them for $25,000,000. The name Virgin Islands was originally bestowed by Christopher Columbus, who discovered the group in 1493. The western islands are British possessions and are administered as part of the Leeward Islands.

The islanders were granted U.S. citizenship in 1927. By 1931 their administration was transferred from the Navy Department to the Department of the Interior. The Organic Act of the Virgin Islands, signed by President Franklin D. Roosevelt on June 22, 1936, gave the islanders greater self-government. The act provided for elective municipal councils of St. Croix and St. Thomas (the latter including representatives from St. John). Joint sessions of the municipal councils, meeting at Charlotte Amalie, constituted the Legislative Assembly. In 1938 a local franchise was given to Virgin Islanders who could read and write the English language. The population is largely Negro, descendants of slaves, and also includes those of Danish, Dutch, French and English ancestry.

In May 1946 President Harry S. Truman (who in his message to Congress in January had recommended "an increasing measure of self-government" for the islanders) named William H. Hastie, a Negro lawyer and educator, as the fourth civilian governor (later he became Judge of the U.S. Court of Appeals, Third Circuit). His successor, Morris F. de Castro, appointed by Truman in 1950, was the islanders' own choice.

During 1953 the replacement of the sixteen-member Legislative Assembly by an eleven-member body was favored in a referendum by two to one; islanders also favored electing their own governor and the return for use in "economic build-up" of taxes collected by the United States on rum exported to the mainland. (The revised Organic Act, 1954, leaves every dollar of Federal income tax, customs duties and other taxes collected in the islands in the treasury of the local government.)

The economic question has been largely the cause of the differences in viewpoint between the Virgin Islands' representatives and that of Congress. The Senate Committee on Interior and Insular Affairs, headed by Hugh Butler (Republican, Nebraska), reported in May 1954 on proposed revisions in the Organic Act of 1936. The revised act became law on July 22, 1954 and required setting up a new unicameral eleven-member legislature, and retained "absolute veto power by the President of the United States over any bills passed by the legislature over the Governor's veto" (*Christian Science Monitor*, September 29, 1954). "Mainland taxpayers," said Butler, "contributed approximately $6,000,000 in 1953 to the government of the 25,000 Virgin Islanders, . . . while no citizen of the Virgin Islands was making any contribution whatever to the Federal treasury" (Washington *Post*, May 31, 1954).

Elections for the new Legislative Assembly were held on November 2, 1954; and at about the same time President Eisenhower named a new commission, authorized by the outgoing Congress, "to study application of Federal laws to the Virgin Islands." The U.S. Supreme Court, by a 5-3 decision on April 11, 1955, declared invalid the Virgin Islands law which had permitted the granting of "quickie" divorces, without requiring husbands or wives to swear that they intended to make their permanent home in the island territory.

Alexander is a past president of the Des Moines Inter-racial Commission and of the Des Moines branch of the N.A.A.C.P. He is a trustee of the Tuskegee Institute in Alabama and Howard University. His church is the Episcopal. His wife is the former Audria Linzey of Denver, Colorado. The Alexanders' only child is deceased.

References

N Y Times p34 F 16 '54
Time 63:38+ Ap 19 '54 por
Negro Year Book, 1952
Who's Who in Colored America, 1950

ALEXANDERSON, ERNST F(REDRIK) W(ERNER) Jan. 25, 1878- Engineer; inventor

Address: b. General Electric Co., Schenectady 25, N.Y.; h. 1132 Adams Rd., Schenectady, N.Y.

General Electric Co.

ERNST F. W. ALEXANDERSON

One of the most prolific geniuses of the electrical age is Dr. Ernst F. W. Alexanderson who, in five decades, has been granted over 320 patents. World-wide fame came to him as a young man in 1906 when he invented the high-frequency alternator which revolutionized wireless telegraphy and telephony. His name must be linked with those of Guglielmo Marconi, Lee De Forest, and Edwin H. Armstrong for his contributions to the science of radio broadcasting. Dr. Alexanderson was acclaimed again in 1927 when he made possible the first home reception of television. In 1955 he received his 321st patent for his invention of a color television receiver for use with the Radio Corporation of America's system of color broadcasting.

During his forty-four years of active service as an engineer for the General Electric Company, he produced numerous inventions in such fields as railway electrification, motors and power transmissions, telephone relays and electric ship propulsion, in addition to his pioneer work in radio and television. He was chief engineer of RCA from 1919 until 1924, while at the same time carrying on his work for General Electric. Dr. Alexanderson today serves as an engineering consultant to both G.E. and RCA.

Ernst Fredrik Werner Alexanderson was born in Upsala, Sweden on January 25, 1878, the son of Professor Aron M. and Amelie (von Heidenstam) Alexanderson. His ancestors include teachers, soldiers, poets, and lawyers. His father taught at the University of Upsala and later held the chair of classical languages at the University of Lund, where Ernst studied from 1896 to 1897, after graduating from Lund High School. Because of an evident aptitude for mechanics, young Alexanderson was sent to the Royal Institute of Technology at Stockholm in 1897 and was graduated as a mechanical and electrical engineer in 1900. He attended the Royal Technical Institute in Berlin, Germany for a year of postgraduate work and studied under Professor Adolf K. H. Slaby, co-creator of the once-important Slaby-Arco system of radio communication.

While in Berlin, Alexanderson read a book entitled *Theory and Calculation of Alternating Current Phenomena* (1897) by Charles Steinmetz, the noted inventor and engineer of the General Electric Company, and was so impressed that he decided to go to America, where such men as Steinmetz and Thomas Alva Edison were at work. He landed in New York City in 1901. After meeting Edison, he went to visit Steinmetz and a close friendship sprang up between them.

At that time, Alexanderson was working for the C. & C. Electrical Company in New Jersey as a draftsman, but in February 1902 he was hired by G.E. to do the same work, on the recommendation of Steinmetz. The next year he took the G.E. test engineering course, and in 1904 he was appointed a member of the company's engineering staff, designing generators under the direction of Steinmetz.

When Alexanderson first arrived in America, radio was limited in use because of the weak transmitters then available. In 1904 Reginald A. Fessenden, a pioneer radio experimenter, asked G.E. to build for him an alternator capable of producing alternate current of high

ALEXANDERSON, E. F. W.—*Continued*

frequency. Alexanderson was assigned to the task and after constructing several models, he devised a practical alternator of the desired frequency which was installed in Fessenden's laboratory at Brant Rock, Massachusetts. From this station a radio program was broadcast on Christmas Eve, 1906, which included a voice and a violin solo. Alexanderson subsequently improved the alternator by substituting iron for wood in the armature.

His work was immediately recognized as brilliant, and when he returned to Sweden on a visit, many industrialists there urged him to remain in his native land. However, his father predicted that the Old World was doomed to revolution and destruction, and advised his son to settle in America. Young Alexanderson heeded the advice, and became a naturalized citizen of the United States in 1908.

Alexanderson soon improved his alternator, which led to the development of reliable transatlantic radio communication. In 1915 Guglielmo Marconi, "father" of radio, came to see a demonstration of Alexanderson's 50-kilowatt alternator at the G.E. laboratories at Schenectady, New York, and one was subsequently installed at the Trans-Atlantic Marconi Company station at New Brunswick, New Jersey. During World War I a 200-kilowatt alternator, installed at this same station, was able to transmit to portable field sets in France and throughout the world. On October 20, 1918 it carried an ultimatum of President Woodrow Wilson direct to Germany. By 1925 there were Alexanderson alternators installed in Sweden, Hawaii, England, Poland, as well as in the United States. King Gustav V of Sweden decorated Alexanderson with the Order of the North Star.

At the end of World War I the British-Marconi Wireless Company renewed negotiations for the exclusive use of the Alexanderson alternator. However, the United States Government favored retention of control of the machine by a domestic company. As a result, G.E. and several other large American corporations organized the Radio Corporation of America in 1919. Alexanderson was appointed chief engineer of this enterprise and spent the next five years dividing his time between G.E. and RCA. He relinquished his chief engineer's post at RCA in 1924, but remained as a consulting engineer with that firm until G. E. liquidated its holdings in RCA in 1932.

Several Alexanderson alternators are still in service in transocean radiotelegraph service. When modern short-wave transmitters and cables break down during magnetic storms, and "sun spots" are prevalent, the Alexanderson alternator at Rocky Point, Long Island is then used to maintain contact with Europe and England.

Dr. Alexanderson has been inventive in almost every branch of radio electricity. His tuned radio frequency receiver system, patented in 1916, provided selective tuning and became one of the basic principles of modern radio broadcasting. This system was soon to dominate the radio industry, but not until after an international legal wrangle in which selective tuning was attacked as "unworkable." While on the witness stand during one of these trials, Alexanderson was confronted with the argument that no one in the court room had ever witnessed a demonstration of the system. The inventor called for a recess, sent out for materials, built a model in the court room and successfully demonstrated the principle, all in the same day (New York *Times*, October 25, 1952).

During World War I he also created the multiple-tuned antenna, the antistatic receiver, and the magnetic amplifier. Together with the alternator and the multi-tuning system, the amplifier established the practicability of transatlantic telephony; in 1919 the first two-way conversation took place between the station at New Brunswick and the steamship *George Washington*, 900 miles at sea, with President Woodrow Wilson on board.

The magnetic amplifier was made obsolete by Alexanderson himself when he invented the highly important electronic modulator, which by applying an improved vacuum tube to radio telephony, made possible the construction of powerful transmitters for high frequencies, another milestone in the history of radio. An unexpected and dramatic use of Dr. Alexanderson's inventions in radio was made in 1923 when his son Verner was kidnapped from in front of his Schenectady home. The six-year-old boy was missing until a caretaker at a lake resort recognized him and the kidnappers from a description broadcast by radio station WGY, and notified the police.

Alexanderson's name will also be recorded in history for his pioneer efforts in television and the transmission of pictures by radio. On June 5, 1924, he transmitted the first facsimile message across the Atlantic, a hand-written greeting to his father. In 1927 he staged the first home reception of television at his own home in Schenectady, using high-frequency neon lamps and a perforated scanning disc. He gave the first public demonstration of television on January 13, 1928.

With the withdrawal of G.E. from the affairs of RCA in 1932, Dr. Alexanderson devoted himself at G.E. to the application of electronics to power. He holds patents on such devices as the inverter, by which direct current can be changed into alternating current through the mercury-vapor arc, and single-phase motors for railway electrification. He has also made important contributions to radiant energy guiding systems for aircraft and the automatic steering of both air and water craft, and has developed countless applications of vacuum tubes in power transmission.

Another electronic wonder with which the name of Alexanderson is associated is the amplidyne—an extremely sensitive and powerful system of amplification and automatic control which he designed in cooperation with other G.E. engineers. While the amplidyne was adapted to the firing of antiaircraft guns in World War II, it was originally designed for use in steel mills and other plants requiring delicate control of continuous manufacturing processes. Applications for the system are said to be practically limitless, since it can be extended to almost everything that moves under power.

Although he retired officially from his full-time position at G.E. on January 1, 1948, Dr. Alexanderson continues to work in the company's laboratories as consulting engineer. In 1952 he renewed his association with RCA as a consultant, and has been working closely with that firm on the development of color television. His color television receiver, to be used with the RCA system of color broadcasting, can also receive black and white programs. Dr. Alexanderson has said, "The novelty of my invention is in the method by which the color selection is accomplished" (New York *Times*, February 12, 1955).

The engineer has received the Gold Medal of the Institute of Radio Engineers (1919), Order of Polonia Restituta (1924), John Ericcson Medal (1928), Edison Medal from the American Institute of Electrical Engineers (1944), Cedergren Medal from the Royal Institute of Technology of Sweden (1945), and Valdemar Poulsen Gold Medal and Royal Danish Medal (1946). He holds the honorary D.Sc. degree from Union College, Schenectady, New York (1926) and an honorary Ph.D. degree from the University of Upsala, Sweden (1938). He is a fellow of the Institute of Electrical Engineers and a member and past president of the Institute of Radio Engineers. He also holds memberships in the Royal Swedish Academy and Sigma Xi.

Dr. Alexanderson was married to Edith B. Lewin on February 20, 1909. She died in 1912. On March 30, 1914 he married Gertrude Robart of Boston, who died in 1948. His third marriage was to Thyra Oxehufwud in June 1949. He has four children: Amelie, Edith, Gertrude, and Verner Alexanderson.

He was elected the first commodore of the Lake George Yacht Club and introduced there a shallow-draft type of Swedish-built boat used by North Sea pilots. In his pocket he likes to carry many keys and a circular slide rule the size of a silver dollar (*Popular Science*, July 1942).

References

N Y Times VIII p12 O 25 '42; p13 Ja 25 '45; p22 F 12 '55
Pop Sci 141:89 Jl '42
American Men of Science (1955)
Benson, A. Will To Succeed (1948)
National Cyclopædia of American Biography Current Volume A (1926)
Who's Who in America, 1954-55
World Biography (1954)

ALLOTT, GORDON (LLEWELLYN)

Jan. 2, 1907- U.S. Senator from Colorado; lawyer

Address: b. Senate Office Bldg., Washington 25, D.C.; 11 Cedar Hills, Lamar, Colo.; h. 110 W. Elm St., Lamar, Colo.

The victory of Gordon Allott (Republican) in the November 1954 election in Colorado for United States Senator came as a surprise since his Democratic opponent had been strongly favored in predictions. Allott had served as lieutenant governor of his state for two terms. He has been active on state and national Republican committees since 1935, when he became the first chairman of the Young Republican League of Colorado. A lawyer by profession, he is a partner in the firm of Allott and Wollbrinck, and has been attorney for Prowers county, the city of Lamar and the towns of Wiley and Hartman.

Gordon Llewellyn Allott was born in Pueblo, Colorado on January 2, 1907, the son of Leonard John and Bertha (Reece) Allott. His father was a Federal meat inspector at the stockyards and his mother was a schoolteacher. Like his sister and older brother, Gordon was interested in music and church activities. He was altar boy in the local Episcopal church and tenor soloist in a boys' choir that toured the state. He later became active in the Y.M.C.A.

Athletics, in which he took part at Central High School, also received his attention at the University of Colorado. He was captain of the university's track team in 1927, high point man at the Rocky Mountain Conference Meet in 1925 and 1926, record holder of the high and low hurdle race in the Rocky Mountain Conference Meet in 1925, 1926 and 1927. In 1929, running under the colors of the Denver Athletic Club, he won the junior and senior national championship in the 400-meter hurdles and a place on the Amateur Athletic Union All-American track team.

At the university he was active in the Players Club, the Masque, and Little Theater productions. He was a member of Delta Sigma Phi and president of Phi Gamma Delta fraternities. During his summer vacations he worked in the Pueblo Steel Mills and during the academic year he waited on tables at the university. He was granted his B.A. degree in 1927.

Receiving his LL.B. degree in 1929, Allott was admitted to practice in Colorado in the same year and in Federal Court in 1930. He returned to Pueblo to enter practice, but within a year he moved to Colorado's Arkansas Valley, settling in Lamar, a wheat-belt trading center with a population of 6,829. He served as a county attorney for Prowers county in 1934 and from 1940 to 1948, city attorney for Lamar from 1937 to 1941, attorney for the towns of Wiley and Hartman, district attorney 1946 to 1948, attorney for the Amity Mutual Irrigation Company, and member of the state board of law examiners from 1948 to 1950. He is now a director and attorney for the First Federal Saving and Loan Association in Lamar.

In politics Allott gained state-wide notice as the first chairman of the Young Republican League of Colorado from 1935 to 1938. He managed the Congressional campaign of Colonel Henry Leonard during the 1938 election and in that year also became national committeeman of the Young Republican League of Colorado, to serve until 1940. During the Presidential campaign of 1940 he was director of the Young Republican Division of the Republican National Committee. In the Young Republican National

Wide World

GORDON ALLOTT

Federation he was general counsel from 1938 to 1941, chairman from 1941 to 1946, and a member of the executive committee from 1946 to 1949. He served on the state board of paroles (beginning in 1951) and on the legislative council (beginning in 1953).

On August 10, 1942, Allott entered the Army Air Forces and fought for nineteen months in the South and Southeast Pacific with the 339 Fighter Squadron, receiving the Distinguished Unit Citation. He participated in seven campaigns and won seven battle stars. After forty-five months of service, he was released in 1946 with the rank of major.

During the war, on New Caledonia, he met Harold Stassen, with whom he formed a close friendship. Allott campaigned vigorously for Stassen in the 1952 Presidential nominating convention. Later Allott became a strong adherent of the Republican candidate, General Dwight D. Eisenhower.

The first of Allott's two terms as lieutenant governor of Colorado began in 1951. Robert Stapp pointed out in *Rocky Mountain News* (May 31, 1954), "Although he has been active in politics for more than twenty years, Allott has been a lone wolf in Colorado Republican circles. In 1950 he was chosen as the running mate for Ralph Carr in the gubernatorial race. When Carr died shortly before election, the party by-passed Allott and handed the top spot to Dan Thornton, a political novice. Since then Allott has bided his time." As *Time* (November 15, 1954) expressed it, Allott's "light, as lieutenant governor, has been hidden under the bushel-basket showmanship and popularity of [the] governor."

Because of the governor's frequent absences, however, Allott was often before the public as acting governor, signing bills and making appearances and speeches. An article in the Denver *Post* credits him with winning as lieutenant governor a reputation as one of the most objective and impartial presidents ever in the Colorado legislature.

When Edwin C. Johnson vacated his post in the U.S. Senate to run for governor of Colorado in 1954, Allott became a candidate in a Senatorial race against former Democratic Representative John Carroll. He campaigned as a strong supporter of the Eisenhower Administration, using as his chief slogan: "Support Ike with his kind of Congress." He was an advocate also of Secretary of Agriculture Ezra Taft Benson's farm program. "The real issue in the Eighty-third Congress, as I see it," Allott said, "was whether prices should be set by government or whether the farmer should be allowed to retain the opportunity of getting a fair price by producing for an effective demand in the market place." He accused the Democrats of spreading "fear of depression, fear of our foreign policy and fear of our farm program" (New York *Times,* November 7, 1954).

Two days before the election, Denver's Research Services, Inc., which has a reputation for accurate predictions, gave Allott's opponent a five to four chance of being elected. Allott received 220,272 votes to Carroll's 210,549.

Allott, who was favored especially in the farm sections of Colorado, stated in an interview for *U.S. News & World Report* (November 12, 1954): "I have worked with water and with agriculture problems for many years, and I think that most of the farmers felt that—even though, whether or not they agreed with what was being done or didn't agree with what was being done—they felt that I could serve them better than my opponent."

Since Dan Thornton retired from politics in 1954, Allott's election to the six-year term in the Senate made him second only to senior Senator Eugene D. Millikin in the leadership of the Republican party in Colorado. Allott was reported in the New York *Times* in December 1954 to be among the Western Senators firmly aligned behind proposed reclamation legislation providing for the Upper Colorado River water storage and the building of the Echo Park Dam. This was expected to come before Congress during the first session of the Eighty-fourth Congress.

When Congress opened in January 1955, Allott was assigned to the Senate's committees on the District of Columbia and on labor and public welfare. As a member of the latter committee he took part in hearings conducted in February on President Eisenhower's controversial school-aid program. His early votes were "yea" to raise Congressional salaries from $15,000 to $22,500 and give comparable increases to Federal judges (February) and "yea" to confirming the nomination of John Marshall Harlan to the Supreme Court (March). He opposed a substitute for the Administration tax bill which had as one provision a $20 tax cut to families with incomes of not more than $5,000 a year (March).

Allott has given much time to community affairs. For six years he has been a director of the Hillcrest Country Club and was a secretary of the Southeast Colorado Livestock Association in 1933, 1934 and 1935. He belongs to the Lamar Chamber of Commerce, is a member of the Recreation Commission and chairman of the Lamar Planning Commission. He is a Mason, a past president of Rotary, a member of the American Legion, the Veterans of Foreign Wars, the Colorado Bar Association, and the Southeastern Colorado Bar Association (president, 1942). He is a senior warden of the Episcopal Church.

The Senator and his wife, the former Welda Olive Hall, who were married on May 15, 1934, have two sons, Roger Hall and Gordon Llewellyn, Jr., both high school pupils at the time of their father's election to Congress. Allott is five feet eleven inches tall and weighs 194 pounds. *Newsweek* (December 6, 1954) pictures him as an "easygoing pipe smoker . . . who relaxes instantly by stretching out on the living room floor."

During the war Allott was a nonflying officer, but he later learned to fly, now pilots a small plane for recreation and belongs to the Flying Farmers of America. He plays the piano by ear, enjoys reading historical novels and biographies, and has an extensive Abraham Lincoln library.

The Allotts own an outboard motorboat and like to spend their holidays fishing, swimming, water skiing or duck hunting.

Gordon Allott has been described by reporters Robert L. Perkins and Robert Stapp in the *Rocky Mountain News* as a "level-headed" man who "indulges in no public acrobatics."

References

N Y Times p50 N 7 '54; p16 Ja 4 '55 por
Newsweek 44:28 D 6 '54 por
Rocky Mountain News My 31 '54; p8 Ag 29 '54
Congressional Directory 1955
Martindale-Hubbell Law Directory, 1952
Who's Who in the West (1954)
Who's Who in United States Politics (1952)

ALONSO, ALICIA Dec. 21, 1921- Ballerina

Address: b. c/o Ballet Russe de Monte Carlo, 64 W. 56th St., New York 19; Ballet Alicia Alonso, 11 Num. 156, Vedado, Havana, Cuba

The artistry of Cuban-born ballerina Alicia Alonso has been acclaimed on three continents. For fifteen years she has been associated with Ballet Theatre, and is also the founder in 1948, of a ballet company of her own, the Ballet Alicia Alonso, which has been granted an annual subsidy by the government of Cuba. She holds the title of "Dama" conferred upon her on August 5, 1947, when she was the recipient of the Carlos Manuel de Céspedes Decoration, this being the highest honor Cuba bestows upon a civilian.

Dama Alonso is a dancer of the classic style whose name today is irrevocably associated with the century-old ballet, *Giselle*, in which she has scored repeated triumphs. In May 1955 she joined the Ballet Russe de Monte Carlo company.

Alicia Ernestina de la Caridad del Cobre Martínez Hoyo, the daughter of Antonio Martínez de Arrendondo, a Cuban army officer, and Ernestina del Hoyo y Lugo, was born in Havana on December 21, 1921. As a child she was responsive to music and dancing and her parents sent her at the age of eleven, to the Sociedad Pro-Arte Musical, where she received ballet training two or three times a week, eventually becoming the star pupil.

On February 19, 1937 she married Fernando Alonso, a member of the newly organized Mordkin Ballet Company, which opened at the Majestic Theatre in New York in the fall of 1937. In New York with her husband, she continued her study of ballet, receiving additional training from Madame Alexandra Fedorova, the Vilzak School, and the School of American Ballet. She and her husband appeared in the Broadway musical comedy, *Stars in Your Eyes*, presented in 1939 and featuring Ethel Merman and Jimmy Durante. She also danced in *Great Lady* (1938).

The young couple next appeared with Ballet Caravan, Alicia touring with the company as a soloist in the years 1939-1940. Entering the ranks as a member of the *corps de ballet*, she began her association with the Ballet Theatre in 1940.

Miss Alonso was appearing as a soloist when her career was interrupted in 1942 by incipient blindness. The dancer then had three eye operations and, for a year and a half was in bed, forbidden to move her head, her eyes covered with bandages. "It was torture for me being still," she told Wallace B. Alig (*Américas*, July 1953), "feeling my muscles lose their power." But she never gave up. She danced "with her fingers, and after a while I could do any step with them" (*PM Magazine*, June 30, 1946). She taught herself to "dance" *Giselle*, and after the bandages were removed and she could see, she had to learn to walk again.

When Ballet Theatre played its New York engagement at the Metropolitan Opera House in the fall of 1943, Alicia Alonso was back in the cast and heading it in her debut in the title role of *Giselle*. The occasion "proved to be one of the most distinguished performances of the season," John Martin wrote in the New York *Times* (November 3, 1943). Commenting that the role "is the richest and the most demanding in the entire classic repertoire," he reported that "Miss Alonso acquitted herself with brilliance."

Her partner in the 1943 offering was Anton Dolin. In 1945, when Ballet Theatre was seen at the Metropolitan Opera House, *Giselle* again served as a vehicle for Miss Alonso, this time with André Eglevsky as her partner. The following year, Ballet Theatre played two New York runs, at the Metropolitan in May, and at the Broadway Theatre in October; in the latter engagement, Igor Youskevitch stepped into the male role, in which he danced opposite Miss Alonso for several successive seasons.

ALICIA ALONSO

When Ballet Theatre opened at the New York City Center in 1947, the repetition of *Giselle* evoked further acclaim for Miss Alonso, the New York *Herald Tribune* critic declaring that the performance "was richer in emotional hues, more exact in pure movement, than even the fine performance of last year." Her dancing of the enchanted queen in *Swan Lake*, her appearance in *Les Sylphides*, and in the première of George Balanchine's *Theme and Variations* all found high favor. John Martin, in summing up the Ballet Theatre season, wrote of "the emergence of Alicia Alonso into the category of the great. . . . The promising young artist had incontrovertibly given place to the true ballerina" (New York *Times*, December 2, 1947).

For its spring season at the Metropolitan in 1948, Ballet Theatre opened with *Theme and Variations*, Miss Alonso and Youskevitch filling the principal roles. Of the ballerina's work, the New York *Times* critic (April 5, 1948) wrote that she "accomplishes with supreme ease what verges on the technically impossible." In the same season she danced the Mexican sweetheart in Eugene Loring's ballet, *Billy the Kid*; substituted for Nora Kaye in *Aurora's Wedding* (also called *Princess Aurora*); took the leading role in *Fall River Legend*, the ballet of Agnes de Mille based on the story of Lizzie Borden; appeared as the ballerina opposite Hugh Laing in *Petrouchka*; and again was seen in *Giselle*.

During one of Ballet Theatre's periods of inactivity, Alonso returned to Cuba, and there, in the fall of 1948, founded the Ballet Alicia Alonso. With Fernando Alonso as general director and Alberto Alonso as artistic director, the company, largely composed of Ballet Theatre personnel, gave its first performances in Havana before undertaking a South American tour. The New York *Times* (January 23, 1949) reported that the Cuban government, through its Ministry of Education, had bought out the house for three performances and had guaranteed the new ballet company an annual subsidy.

The South American tour was a successful one; Miss Alonso is reported to have received forty-seven curtain calls in Buenos Aires. In the spring season of 1951 Ballet Theatre returned to the Metropolitan Opera House, opening with William Dollar's *Concerto*, Alicia Alonso and Igor Youskevitch dancing the principal roles. She also choreographed *Ensayo Sinfonica*, arranged to Brahms' Variations on a Theme by Haydn.

The first attempt to present a major ballet company to a movie audience was in April 1952 when the Ballet Theatre played a four-a-day schedule at the Warner Theatre in New York between showings of a Western picture. Miss Alonso danced the rose adagio from *Princess Aurora* sixty-four times in sixteen days. This was twice as many times as she had danced the role in her entire career.

On September 28, 1952 the Ballet Theatre company returned to the Metropolitan Opera House where Miss Alonso danced "an enormously winning and skillful performance of the soubrettish heroine of *La Fille Mal Gardée*," then stepped directly into "the morbid melodramatics" of *Fall River Legend*. Her performance in *Swan Lake* brought this comment from John Martin: "Her movement is steel and diamonds, of incredible technical beauty, and [she has] a mastery of phrasing that she has never before approached."

A European tour during 1953 brought Miss Alonso further recognition. London hailed her *Giselle*. In Rome, *Il Tempo* described her as an "incomparable Giselle." In New York the company was seen in only a "one-night stand" given at the Metropolitan in May 1954, on which occasion Walter Terry of the New York *Herald Tribune* commented, "For well over a hundred years, *Giselle* has had no rest. Miss Alonso revealed this ballet's lasting glories." On April 12, 1955 Ballet Theatre opened at the Metropolitan Opera House for a three-week engagement. Miss Alonso and Youskevitch danced the "Black Swan" *pas de deux* from *Swan Lake*, and were members of a distinguished cast including such guest artists as Alicia Markova, who appeared in honor of Ballet Theatre's fifteenth anniversary.

On May 12, 1955, the New York *Times* reported that Alicia Alonso would not return to Ballet Theatre next season, but would appear instead with the Ballet Russe de Monte Carlo. Her annual commitment with her own company in Cuba, however, makes her available to the Ballet Russe for only half the season. During July 1955 she appeared as guest artist with Anton Dolin's Festival Ballet during its engagement in Great Britain.

Miss Alonso is five feet three and a half inches tall and weighs 110 pounds. She has dark hair and dark eyes. In comparing her with the great ballerina, Alicia Markova, critic John Martin described Alonso as "more earthy, more crystalline, more Latin, less Gothic." Her seventeen-year-old daughter, Laura, has been associated with the Alonso Company in Cuba. Dama

Alonso once told a reporter that *Giselle* is her favorite role and that she considers *Theme and Variations* the most difficult ballet she has done. "Of course I dance the rhumba and the conga," she admitted. "I love them. They are part of my blood." Because of her gypsy grace, she was nicknamed "Unga," short for Hungarian.

When relaxing from her arduous training as a prima ballerina, Miss Alonso paints landscapes, swims, and sews on her costumes. She collects American Indian pottery, arrowheads, and musical instruments (*Américas*, July 1952).

References:

Américas 4:6+ Jl '52 pors
N Y Herald Tribune p18 Ap 20 '51
N Y Times II p12 D 2 '47
PM p38 D 14 '47 por
PM Mag p 19 Je 30 '46 por

Chujoy A. Dance Encyclopedia (1949)
Davidson, G. Ballet Biographies (1952)
Terry, W. Star Performance (1954)

AMRIT KAUR, RAJKUMARI *See* Kaur, Rajkumari Amrit

ANDERSON, HOWARD (RICHMOND) Oct. 1, 1898- University dean

Address: b. c/o University of Rochester, 19 Catharine Strong Hall, 31 Prince St., Rochester 3, N.Y.; h. 301 University Park, Rochester 20, N.Y.

In the opinion of Dr. Howard Anderson, dean of the University of Rochester's School of Liberal and Applied Studies, students must learn how to weigh evidence, to discuss in their classrooms both sides of issues, and to reach decisions in the light of such evidence (New York *Times*, November 26, 1950). Teachers have an unusual opportunity, he believes, through teaching current events to help students in thinking constructively about important public affairs.

After twenty years of experience in the classroom, Dr. Anderson was director of the School of Education at Cornell University from 1944 to 1946. He then became a curriculum specialist and chief for social sciences in the division of higher education of the U.S. Office of Education in Washington, D.C., where he served until February 1954 when he assumed the deanship at the University of Rochester.

Howard Richmond Anderson was born in New York City on October 1, 1898 to Lars Gustav Anderson, a mechanical engineer, and Charlotte (Johnson) Anderson. Both natives of Sweden, his parents had moved to the United States in their youth and had married in this country. Growing up in Minneapolis, Howard studied until 1916 at the Minnesota Academy, where he also edited the school's magazine and yearbook and played basketball. On April 9, 1917 the young man joined the Army as a private and was assigned to the 332d infantry. During one year he served with

HOWARD ANDERSON

the American Expeditionary Force and was awarded the Italian Croce di Guerra in 1918. He was discharged as a first sergeant on May 3, 1919.

While majoring in history at Augustana College in Rock Island, Illinois, Anderson met a good part of his expenses by working as a millwright's helper. He also found time to maintain an honor student's rating, to participate in debating and to play basketball. After he had taken his B.A. degree in 1922, he taught history for six years at the Theodore Roosevelt High School in Wyandotte, Michigan. Anderson completed requirements for his M.A. degree in education at the University of Chicago in 1928. Two years later, having submitted the thesis "Neutralization of Belgium, 1813-1839," he was granted a Ph.D. degree in modern European history by the State University of Iowa.

After receiving his doctorate, Anderson, who had been a graduate assistant since 1928 at the State University of Iowa, was made assistant professor of history and head of social studies of the university's high school. He held these posts until his appointment in 1937 as assistant professor of education at Cornell University and director of social studies in the Ithaca, New York public schools. In 1939 the educator was promoted to an associate professorship and three years later to a full professorship. Anderson spent his last two years at Cornell, from 1944 to 1946, as director of the School of Education and of the summer session.

During this period Dr. Anderson edited *Teaching Critical Thinking in the Social Studies* (1942), the thirteenth yearbook of the National Council for the Social Studies, and the Cornell University *Curriculum Series in World History*. Beginning in 1936 he prepared, with E. F. Lindquist, a number of bulletins published by the National Council for the Social Studies on selected test items in eco-

ANDERSON, HOWARD—*Continued*

nomics, government and history. He is also the author of *World History* (Houghton, 1942), written with Arthur Boak and P. Slosson.

Anderson in 1946 became a specialist for social sciences in the U.S. Office of Education (since 1953 part of the Department of Health, Education and Welfare) in Washington, D.C. In February of the following year he was sent to Germany with eight other American educators to aid in the reconstruction of a denazified school system in that country. The specialists worked directly in the schools and with the school boards in preparing for the occupation government an outline of educational aims. An article by Anderson on the social studies program for German schools appeared in *School Life* (October 1947).

From 1948 to 1951 Anderson was chief of the section on instructional problems in secondary schools of the Office of Education. He was then promoted to the position of chief for social sciences in the division of higher education and in that capacity remained with the Office of Education until 1954. He participated in the United Nations Educational, Scientific and Cultural Organization's seminar on improvement of textbooks, held in Belgium in 1950, and UNESCO's seminar on the teaching of history, held in France in 1951.

Anderson has frequently contributed articles to educational publications on the work of the Office of Education. Among these are "Geography in the Work of the United States Office of Education" (*Journal of Geography*, May 1947), "Guidance for Active Articulate Citizenship" (*Educational Leadership*, November 1948), and "Trends in Teaching Social Studies" (*School and Community*, February 1951).

One of the articles in which Anderson emphasized the function of schools to prepare youth for democratic living was "Techniques in Teaching Current Affairs" (*School Life*, November 1946). In "Basic Study Skills Are Important" (*National Education Association Journal*, September 1949) he spoke of the need of study skills in social science—such as reading charts and graphs.

Addressing the thirteenth annual convention of the National Council for the Social Sciences in November 1950, Anderson called attention to pressures in recent years to direct thinking in the United States about "certain countries, certain institutions, certain ways of living and social groups." The use of such slanted material in the classroom could be used, he said, in conjunction with material advancing opposite points of view.

Anderson's appointment as dean of the University of Rochester's School of Liberal and Applied Studies was announced in December 1953. The school, which was established under its present organization and name in 1944, grew out of the earlier division of university extension. It is designed to answer the needs for an academic program and to offer degrees to students unable to attend the university's other schools. Anderson began his tenure as dean in February 1954.

Anderson served from 1941 to 1945 on the committee for democratic citizenship of the National Association of Secondary School Principals and of the National Council for the Social Studies (president, 1940). Among the other organizations with which he is affiliated are the National Education Association, American Association of School Administrators, American Educational Research Association, National Society for the Study of Education, and American Historical Association. He is a Mason and belongs to the American Legion and Phi Delta Kappa. The dean attends the Lutheran Church and is a Democrat.

Anderson's wife, a former member of the staff of UNESCO in Paris, is Monica Stewart (Luffman) Anderson. The couple, married on December 22, 1951, has a daughter, Monica Jane. By a previous marriage, on June 27, 1923 to Greta (Karling) Anderson, which ended in divorce on November 20, 1951, he is the father of William Howard and Douglas Gustav. Anderson, who has blue eyes and brown hair, is six feet in height and weighs 190 pounds. He likes to spend his free time fishing or reading historical fiction.

References

N Y Times p6 D 19 '53 por
Leaders in Education (1948)
Who's Who in America, 1954-55

ANGELES, VICTORIA DE LOS Nov. 1, 1923- Singer

Address: b. c/o S. Hurok, 711 5th Ave., New York 22; h. Calvet 31, Barcelona, Spain

The Metropolitan Opera's star-studded roster of singers frequently features the name of Victoria de los Angeles, Spanish lyric soprano who performs as brilliantly in German opera as in French or Italian. She arouses the same audience enthusiasm in America as she did in Europe on the concert and opera stage and over the radio.

The televised opening of the Metropolitan's 1954-55 season on November 8 featured Miss de los Angeles in the first act from *La Bohème*, on stage with Richard Tucker. On November 18 she scored another success as Marguerite in *Faust*. Reviewing Massenet's opera, *Manon*, performed at the Metropolitan Opera House on December 3, 1954, Olin Downes in the New York *Times* wrote of Miss de los Angeles: "Here was the most eloquent, moving Manon we have seen or heard; singularly expressive, in facial play, gesture, irresistible in song."

On her concert tours of the United States, Miss de los Angeles has appeared with the Pittsburgh Symphony, the Chicago Symphony, the Detroit Symphony, and other major American orchestras. For RCA Victor and His Master's Voice she has recorded *Faust*, *The Barber of Seville*, *Pagliacci*, and Falla's *Vida Breve*. She has also appeared on radio and television programs.

The euphonious name of Victoria de los Angeles was adopted for stage purposes. Born November 1, 1923, in Barcelona, she was christened Victoria Gamez Cima, the traditional combined Spanish form derived from the maiden name of her mother, Victoria Garcia Cima, and her father, Bernardo Lopez Gamez. She has a sister, and a brother who became a lawyer.

Reared in her native city, where her father was a caretaker at the University of Barcelona, Victoria studied at the Instituto Balmes. "To the delight of the students and the annoyance of the teachers," reported *Time,* her childish singing could be heard in the classrooms. But the professors recognized her talent and urged her to study at Barcelona's Conservatory of Music. She completed the six-year course in three years.

After five years of independent study she entered the International Contest of Music and Singing held in Geneva in 1947, from which, victorious over 120 other contestants, she emerged with a first prize. Engagements to appear on the concert stage then took her all over Europe, Canada, South America, and South Africa. On the operatic stage, she appeared at La Scala in Milan, at the Grand Opera in Paris, at Covent Garden in London, at the Royal Opera House in Stockholm and in Copenhagen, and at the Teatro Colon in Buenos Aires. Festival audiences heard her at Edinburgh, at the Maggio Fiorentino in Florence, at the Holland Festival, the Switzerland Festival, and Coronation Festival, London.

By the time that Miss de los Angeles made her New York debut at Carnegie Hall on October 24, 1950, her fame had preceded her. Virgil Thomson in the New York *Herald Tribune* appraised her voice as "one of rare natural beauty, the schooling impeccable, the artistry first class." Douglas Watt of the *New Yorker* called Miss de los Angeles "a marvelous singer," and remarked that "an interesting thing about her voice is its dark, solid quality in the lower half of its range: the other night she sounded pleasantly like a mezzo-soprano a good deal of the time."

A more guarded review was given by Olin Downes of the New York *Times,* who found that "Miss de los Angeles gave a series of singularly uneven performances." B. H. Haggin of the *Nation,* covering her second Carnegie Hall recital in November, thought "it was an exciting experience to hear the young soprano produce in her very first phrases notes that were as lovely and secure as those she continued to amaze one with the rest of the evening."

For her Metropolitan Opera debut in March 1951, Miss de los Angeles was assigned the role of Marguerite in Gounod's *Faust,* a particularly felicitous choice, according to Virgil Thomson. On March 20, as Cio-Cio San in *Madame Butterfly,* she impressed Francis D. Perkins of the New York *Herald Tribune* by her "care for both nuance and detail . . . in . . . the vocal and visual aspects." Olin Downes dissented, believing that she did not have "the dramatic brilliancy and impact required for climactic moments," as well as being "inclined to mannerisms, exaggerations of acting and phrase."

VICTORIA DE LOS ANGELES

On the other hand, Irving Kolodin of the *Saturday Review of Literature* stated that "Miss de los Angeles' Butterfly is certainly the most interesting new one we have seen since Licia Albanese first sang the part here in the late 1930's." Rounding off the season in the role of Mimi in *La Bohème,* another Puccini heroine, Miss de los Angeles impressed Robert Bagar of the New York *World-Telegram and Sun* by the authenticity of her interpretations and Arthur Berger of the New York *Herald Tribune* by her beautiful realization of the "lightness and tenderness" of Mimi. His praise was more measured for her performance in *The Marriage of Figaro,* in November 1951, in which he found that at "her best she sang with more elegance than anyone else . . . but vocally she was uneven."

She returned to the New York concert stage, at a November 1952 recital in the Hunter College Assembly Hall. The New York *Herald Tribune* reviewer said that "at all moments Miss de los Angeles showed herself to be one of the few really satisfactory musicians singing today." About a week later, she sang the title role in *Madame Butterfly* at the Metropolitan, in spite of a sprained ankle suffered during the performance. In December she made her first appearance as Micaela in *Carmen.*

Early in January 1953, she sang the role of Eva in *Die Meistersinger,* to the plaudits of Irving Kolodin, writing in the *Saturday Review.* Other critics agreed that she was equally proficient in Wagnerian roles as in French and Italian.

When Miss de los Angeles opened her 1953-54 season at Carnegie Hall, the *Times* critic remarked that her voice was apt to become "a bit metallic and breathy in extended fortissimo passages," while Miles Kastendieck of the *Christian Science Monitor,* noted, on the contrary, "the velvet quality of her voice, so rarely

ANGELES, VICTORIA DE LOS—*Cont.*
heard these days." Admiring her Mozart, Handel, Schubert, and Brahms songs, the *Musical America* reviewer commented: "Her performances of Schubert's 'Wanderers Machtlied' and of Brahm's 'Nachtigall' were among the finest I have ever heard."

Her subsequent appearance in *Faust* in November 1953 brought small praise from the critics for her rendition of the "Jewel Song," although they praised other aspects of her performance. Her *Mélisande,* late in December, met with greater approval, with Jay S. Harrison of the *Herald Tribune* describing it "as musically exact and vocally glorious." The *Musical Courier* critic felt that "her French diction, her musical phrasing, her movements on stage and her spirituelle appearance made her an ideal representative of the role."

Repeating the role of Mimi in *La Bohème* early in January 1954, Miss de los Angeles led the New York *Herald Tribune* commentator to write: "Her Mimi is the best now available to the local public and surely one of the finest anywhere to be heard." Louis Biancolli of the New York *World-Telegram and Sun* caught a slight thinness in her voice in some spots, but "elsewhere the singing was the soft and lovely miracle she has accustomed us to." In her portrayal of Rosina in the *Barber of Seville* she brought to the role "a characterization which is charming, full of humor, arch and flirtatious, and altogether delightful," (New York *Times,* April 8, 1954) a point of view substantially shared by the *Musical America* critic.

Miss de los Angeles' marriage to Enrique Magrina Mir on November 28, 1948 was the culmination of what the New York *Times* called "a long Spanish courtship," for they had met seven years before in a coffee house in Barcelona. That city is still their home, where Miss de los Angeles and her impresario husband, who handles her business affairs, return between engagements. The soprano is five feet four inches tall, brown-eyed and black-haired. At the end of her concerts she usually takes a guitar in hand and gives an encore of Spanish flamenco songs. She enjoys knitting, reading, and cooking.

References

Mus Am 72:15 Ja 1 '52
N Y Herald Tribune IV p13 N 1 '53
Time 56:64 N 6 '50

ANGLE, PAUL M(CCLELLAND) Dec. 25, 1900- Historian

Address: b. c/o Chicago Historical Society, Chicago, Ill.; h. 1802 Lincoln Park W., Chicago, Ill.

The ability of Paul M. Angle to bring to the writing of history the excitement and immediacy of today's news has made him an important chronicler of America's past. A leading authority on Lincoln lore, he has written *The Lincoln Reader,* a 1947 Book-of-the-Month Club selection; *"Here I Have Lived"; A History of Lincoln's Springfield, 1821-1865*; and with Carl Sandburg, *Mary Lincoln, Wife and Widow.* More recent books are *Bloody Williamson; A Chapter in American Lawlessness* and *By these Words; Great Documents of American Liberty, Selected and Placed in their Contemporary Settings* (Rand McNally, 1954).

Since 1945 Angle has been the director of the Chicago Historical Society. Prior to that time he was historian of the Illinois State Historical Library and secretary of the Illinois State Historical Society from 1932 to 1945. He also served as executive secretary of the Abraham Lincoln Association.

Paul McClelland Angle was born in Mansfield, Ohio on December 25, 1900, the son of John Elmer and Nellie Laverne (McClelland) Angle. He was the sixth child in a family of seven, and although money was scarce, his father, a grocer, encouraged him to attend college. After studying at Oberlin College in Ohio in 1918 and 1919, he transferred to Miami University, Oxford, Ohio and majored in history. By working at odd jobs, he earned his tuition. He joined Sigma Chi, was a member of the varsity football team, was awarded the Phi Beta Kappa key, and received the A.B. degree in 1922.

After selling life insurance for eight months in Rochester, New York, he decided to return to studying history. He pursued graduate studies at the University of Illinois, from which he received the M.A. degree in 1924. In the following year he was a salesman for the American Book Company. In 1925 he accepted the position of executive secretary of the Lincoln Centennial Association (which later became the Abraham Lincoln Association) in Springfield, Illinois. During the period in which Angle served in this post (1925-1932), he wrote a series of books on Lincoln's day-by-day activities, which were published by the association.

Among these books were *Lincoln in the Year 1858* (1926); *Lincoln in the Year 1859* (1927), concerning Lincoln's trip to the east, when he attracted attention as a possible Presidential dark horse; *Lincoln in the Year 1860 and as President-elect* (1927); and *Lincoln in the Year 1854* (1928), concerning Lincoln as a successful lawyer in Springfield, Illinois.

With Carl Sandburg, poet and Lincoln scholar, Angle wrote *Mary Lincoln, Wife and Widow* (Harcourt, 1932). While the book received mixed reviews, Angle's arrangement of the letters, documents and appendix was warmly praised. The New York *Post* (November 19, 1932) commented that the letters remained the only trustworthy clue to Mrs. Lincoln's personality. Angle became the historian of the Illinois State Historical Library and secretary of the Illinois State Historical Society in 1932.

"Here I Have Lived"; A History of Lincoln's Springfield, 1821-1865, written by Angle, was published in 1935 by the Abraham Lincoln Association and reissued in 1950 by Rutgers University Press. The New York *Times* (August 13, 1950) reviewer stated that "its return engagement, by request, is a happy event, not only for Lincoln study, but for American social and

PAUL M. ANGLE

cultural history." With Richard L. Beyer, Angle wrote *A Handbook of Illinois History* (Illinois State Historical Society, 1943).

In 1945 Angle was appointed director of the Chicago Historical Society. He edited *A Shelf of Lincoln Books; a Critical, Selective Bibliography of Lincolniana* in 1946 (Rutgers University Press in association with the Abraham Lincoln Association). Professor J. G. Randall of the University of Illinois wrote that the book has the merit of "supplying adequate appraisals of the eighty-one titles included . . . In the author's style there is . . . a sustained attractiveness rarely found among bibliographies" (*Book Week*, July 14, 1946).

The first complete one-volume biography of Abraham Lincoln was completed by Angle in 1947. *The Lincoln Reader* (Rutgers University Press) combines 179 selections from the best writings of sixty authors. Angle included some of Lincoln's own accounts of his life (supplied for a campaign biography), his letters, and the impressions left to posterity by friends and associates.

The Lincoln Reader was immediately acclaimed as a new kind of biography. Lewis Gannett (New York *Herald Tribune*, February 10, 1947) wrote: "Angle . . . one of the great Lincoln scholars, has done an extraordinarily skillful job in weaving this patchwork quilt . . . ." Ira Wolfert in *PM Magazine* (February 9, 1947) commented: "Paul M. Angle has handled [the book] . . . brilliantly, with a depth of scholarship and a breadth of perception that make editing seem creative. . . ."

Charles Poore (New York *Times*, February 8, 1947) wrote: "What is new about Mr. Angle's book is the way he has arranged what is old. . . . Obviously it's not a perfect form of biography. You sometimes have an uneasy feeling that it is a little too close to radio technique, the kind that rounds up a diversity of sources with a running commentary." *The Lincoln Reader* was a Book-of-the-Month Club selection in February 1947.

Bloody Williamson; A Chapter in American Lawlessness (Knopf) was written by Angle in 1952 and was reprinted in 1954 as *Resort to Violence; a Chapter in American Lawlessness* (Lane). It is a history of Williamson county, Illinois from the 1860's to 1951, describing family feuds, labor fights, and Ku Klux Klan attacks. W. E. Wilson (*Saturday Review*, October 18, 1952) wrote that Paul M. Angle displayed "a rare combination of talents: the sharp eye for detail and the vivid, swiftly moving narrative style of a first-class newspaper reporter together with the unimpeachable honesty and the scholarly thoroughness of a fine historian." The historian has also contributed to professional periodicals. He served as a consultant in history to the U.S. Army Air Forces in 1943 and 1944.

On June 17, 1926 Angle was married to Vesta Verne Magee. The couple has a daughter, Paula (Mrs. James E. Lovett), and a son, John Edwin Angle. The author is solidly built and has twinkling blue eyes; he has a warm personality and is soft-spoken. For relaxation he watches baseball and hockey games, and enjoys reading, walking, and the movies and theatre, if they do not deal with historical themes.

Angle belongs to such organizations as the American Historical Association and the Mississippi Valley Historical Association. His clubs are the University and the Tavern in Chicago. Angle received the honorary Litt.D. from Augustana College (1941), LL.D., Knox College (1944) and the L.H.D. degree, Illinois College (1947). Allan Nevins once said that Angle was able to "track down just what Lincoln was doing on a day in 1885."

References

N Y Post Mag p47 F 11 '47 por
N Y Times VI p12 Jl 5 '42; VII F 11 '45
Who's Who in America, 1954-55

ANGOFF, CHARLES (ăn'gŏf) Apr. 22, 1902- Author

Address: b. c/o Beechhurst Press, Inc., 11 E. 36th St., New York 16; h. 614 W. 157th St., New York 32

Reprinted from the *Wilson Library Bulletin* June 1955

When Charles Angoff, fresh from Harvard, was working on a suburban Boston newspaper in the early nineteen-twenties, he thought it would be wonderful to work on the *American Mercury*. So did many other young men eagerly reading the green-backed magazine that was breaking every literary precedent and electrifying postwar America. But Angoff wrote to H. L. Mencken—and got the job.

Barely settled into his new office, he was startled to hear Mencken say: "I'm going away for two weeks. My private astrologer tells me nothing will happen. You run the office." Red-

CHARLES ANGOFF

haired Charles Angoff managed to survive. He observed the one rigid rule those two iconoclasts, Mencken and George Jean Nathan, maintained—that every manuscript should be opened, read, and either returned or acknowledged the day it was received. It was the initiation of the man whom Mencken himself called "the best managing editor in America." Since then, Charles Angoff has written some fifteen books and edited another half dozen.

Charles Angoff was born in Russia on April 22, 1902, the son of Jacob Joseph and Anna (Pollack) Angoff. He was brought with his family to America in 1908. "I began to write quite early," he says. "A sonnet when I was twelve really started me. I've had many poems published but never a collection. My first published work was an article."

Angoff became an American citizen when his father was naturalized, and also took out separate citizenship papers. He is passionately American. His love of his adopted country is reflected in nearly all of his writing, especially in his series of novels of Jewish life, three of which have been published—*Journey to the Dawn* (1951), *In the Morning Light* (1953), and *The Sun at Noon* (1955). "My publisher [Beechhurst Press] calls it a 'marathology,'" he says. "The fourth volume, 'Between Day and Dark,' will appear in the spring of 1956, and I'm at work on the fifth." All three books were selections of the Jewish Book Guild, and in 1954 Angoff won the Harry and Ethel Daroff Memorial Fiction Award with *In the Morning Light,* "the best novel of Jewish interest published in 1953 in the United States."

Angoff earned his way through Harvard University, "working in the market." He began to write for the Boston *Transcript,* where H. T. Parker edited the literary department. Parker was an elderly bachelor who found a kindred soul in the intense young man. "I was the whitehaired, Jewish-American immigrant," Angoff recalls. "He was very kind to me." One day Parker studied his protegé. "We Puritans can see into the future," he said abruptly. "America will remember you in years to come, Angoff. I wish I knew all the ways."

Then came the *Mercury* and the managing editorship, which involved getting out the magazine each month. There were some bitter battles. "I fought with Mencken for weeks," Angoff says, "before he would buy Faulkner's 'That Evening Sun Go Down.' I urged him for months to buy Thomas Wolfe, but he wouldn't. When I became editor I bought Wolfe's 'Boom Town.'"

For a year Angoff ran the *Mercury* single-handed. Then he went successively to the *Nation, Scribner's, North American Review,* and *Living Age.* In 1943 he returned to the *Mercury,* to his former post of managing editor, where he remained until its sale in 1950. In the meantime, he was writing. His first book appeared in 1931, *A Literary History of the American People* (Knopf). *The Handbook of Libel* (Essential Books, 1946) was a monumental work. Two of his plays, *Something To Sing About* and *Moment Musical,* have been produced off Broadway. His two collections of short stories, *When I Was a Boy in Boston* (Beechhurst, 1947) and *Adventures in Heaven* (Ackerman, 1945), were well received. All of the stories appeared in magazines first, while two, "Where Did Yesterday Go?" and "Jerry," were reprinted in Martha Foley's *Best American Short Stories.*

However, it is Angoff's saga of a Jewish immigrant family's integration with American life that has won the greatest critical acclaim. This is not only a remarkable literary achievement from sheer scope, but the novels are written with compassion and beauty. The *Saturday Review* (January 15, 1955) compared his work with that of Thomas Wolfe, saying that the three novels and those to follow are in reality a single book as Wolfe's four novels were part of a larger work. "When he is done," the review continued, "his version of American-Jewish life will stand on a shelf all of its own. He appears to have the stamina, the patience, the knowledge, and the love of his material to produce the truly 'great Jewish fictional work' of our time." Meyer Levin goes even further. In a review in the Portland *Oregonian,* he said: "Mr. Angoff's saga of American-Jewish life is Nobel Prize material."

Charles Angoff was married to Sara F. Freedman on June 13, 1943 and has a daughter, Nancy Carol. He has blue eyes, weighs 155 pounds and is five feet seven inches tall. He is on the staff of the New York office of the radio-TV program *Meet the Press,* as well as associate editor of Mercury Publications. He lectures frequently—in Canada, New England, the South, and the Middle West. Two nights a week he teaches writing and contemporary literature, at New York University and at Hunter College. And after the fifth volume of his saga there will probably be several more, eight or nine in all.

References

Angoff, C. When I was a Boy in Boston (1947)
Who's Who in America, 1954-55
Who's Who in American Jewry, 1938-39
Who's Who in the East (1953)
Who's Who in World Jewry, 1955

ANTOINE Dec. 24, 1884- Hairdresser

Address: b. 5, rue Cambon, Paris 1, France; 1, ave. Paul-Doumer, Paris 16, France

"The hairdresser who has contributed most to artistic hair cutting for women," states the *Encyclopædia Britannica,* "is Antoine of Paris . . . he has given the modern woman's head that sculptured look which makes her classically beautiful." Originator of the twentieth-century version of bobbed hair, of blue-dyed hair, sculptured curls, upswept hairdos, and other original coiffures, he has earned the title of "the world's greatest innovator in women's hair styles." For half-a-century he has dressed the hair of outstanding women of society as well as stars of the theatrical and motion picture world.

Beginning in his native Poland as apprentice to his uncle, he moved to Paris at eighteen and soon rose to top place in the world of *haute coiffure.* In 1925 he opened the first Antoine salon in the United States and has since expanded his enterprises until they now include sixty-two salons in the United States, Canada, Australia, England, and France which were visited by over 5,000,000 women during 1954.

Born on Christmas Eve, 1884, in Sieradz, Poland, Antek Cierplikowski was the fourth son of Antek and Maria Cierplikowski. His father was a shoemaker, his mother a "strong, handsome peasant woman" who recognized and encouraged her son's artistic talents. When he was eight, the boy created his first hairdo. He persuaded his six-year-old sister, Salome, to let him cut and dress her hair, using honey to keep the curls in place. The honey worked like lacquer, but attracted a swarm of bees.

Antek attended the Russian-Polish school in Sieradz from the time he was eight till he was fourteen, when he was apprenticed to a barber-surgeon. His ability with the shears was so apparent that his parents sent him to work for his uncle, Pawel Lewandowski, the leading hairdresser in Lodz. There at seventeen he had his "high day of destiny." Substituting for his uncle, he dressed the hair of a prominent lady of fashion. She was astonished at his skill, told him he was a genius, and urged him to go to Paris.

Taking her advice, he arrived soon afterward in Paris, where he found a job at forty cents a day braiding hair for switches. One evening a crowd of girls came into the shop, all demanding immediate attention. The young

Studio-Iris, Paris

ANTOINE

Pole was asked to help, and from then on Antoine (as he was now called) was much in demand. His employer took him to Deauville, where he created a new style among the international set by arranging hair like a hat.

At Deauville, Antoine became friends with the shop's manicurist, Marie-Berthe Astier. After working for various hairdressers in Nice, Cannes, Biarritz, and Paris, Antoine went to London in 1905 where Marie-Berthe had gone to work. They were married in Hampstead in June 1905. In his autobiography, *Antoine* (Prentice-Hall, 1945), he wrote: "I don't think I would ever have reached any safe place in my career without her French common sense and her gift for saving pennies at the right moment. She has been and is the brilliant business manager of all my enterprises."

After the death of their new-born son, the young couple returned to Paris in 1906 and took an apartment in Montmartre. For five years Antoine went to the houses of his clients by appointment, but in 1911 he and his wife had saved enough to open their own shop at 5 rue Cambon. Sarah Bernhardt, Eleonora Duse, Cécile Sorel and other stars of the stage became customers, as did socially prominent women, including Mrs. Cornelius Vanderbilt, Mrs. Harrison Williams, and royalty such as the Queens of Spain, Romania and Egypt. His fees were about twenty dollars for a hairdressing and frequently went higher. When he was asked to come to London to do a lady's hair for a party, he set the price ridiculously high at $1,000, but she paid it without hesitation.

In Paris Antoine made close friends with the Italian painter (Amedeo) Modigliani and Swiss sculptor, Richard Kissling. The friend who influenced him most was Xavier Dunikowski, a Polish sculptor, who gave Antoine the idea of becoming a sculptor himself and creating "hair-sculpture." "The impulse is the same, whether

ANTOINE—*Continued*

the material is women's hair or clay," Antoine wrote in his autobiography. "What I have in mind comes first. The material comes second."

It was by accident that Antoine originated the hair bob in 1910. He had been asked to dress the hair of actress Eve Lavallière who had been cast as a girl of eighteen. While he was wondering how to make his forty-five year-old client look younger, a child entered the room, her hair cut short and in bangs. Adapting this youthful style, he solved the problem. The result was so successful that women besieged Antoine to cut their hair short and make them look younger, but it was not until 1912 that he consented to bob other women's hair. Within a few years bobbed hair became a world-wide vogue, denounced in press and pulpit, but adopted by women everywhere.

During World War I the hairdresser introduced ornamented wigs of brilliant colors to be worn at the extravagant "charity fêtes" of the period. In more recent years he has created wigs in various styles and colors so that a customer may try them on like dresses and decide what style looks best for her.

Another of his successful innovations was blue-dyed hair. Lady Elsie Mendl asked him to do something about her graying hair. He thought a certain shade of blue would look well, but since hair had never been dyed blue before, he experimented first on his white borzoi. The blue dog created a sensation in Paris, and Antoine concluded that blue hair would do the same for women. In 1924 he dyed Lady Mendl's hair blue and millions of other gray-haired women followed her example.

By 1922 Antoine had shops in Biarritz, Cannes and Deauville, as well as in Paris. His activities were expanded to include dress and hat design, sculpture, the manufacture of beauty preparations and the training of beauty operators. Needing more space, he decided to build a house constructed almost entirely of glass, containing living quarters for himself and his wife and rooms for a hairdressing school. It was completed in 1927. For the housewarming he sent out invitations engraved on crystal. Fifteen hundred guests came. The house was furnished in glass and as a final touch Antoine had a glass coffin which he used as a bed. Always a showman, he appeared at the housewarming in a white satin frock coat. "In this business," he observed, "you have to be part actor, part doctor, part diplomat and part artist."

The New York store, Saks Fifth Avenue, invited Antoine in 1924 to direct its beauty establishment. He redesigned the Saks salons, trained operators, gave hairdressing demonstrations before fashion editors and the press, and staged a gala opening attended by hundreds of celebrities. Five years later he established a school for hairdressers modelled after the one in the Glass House in Paris. He taught them to "master hundreds of ways [to do a wave or coiffure], a different design for every type of face, for every fashion, for every purpose."

"Women come to us shopping for a new personality," he told a reporter in *Coronet* (January 1955). "To a great extent our work is correcting nature's deficiencies. If a woman has bad ears, we hide them. If her forehead is too high, bangs will shorten it. Upswept hair will give a sense of height to the short woman, and a long bob will shorten a woman who is too tall. There is no such thing as a 'standard' hairdo. Every woman is an individual problem."

From 1925 till 1939 Antoine regularly spent at least two months a year in the United States, traveling to his beauty salons established throughout the country, supervising, training and giving special consultations. His greatest expansion came during World War II. Having arrived in New York in 1939 to take care of contracts, he was unable to return to France after the Nazi occupation in May 1940. For the next five years he worked at extending the chain of Antoine salons, setting up a cosmetics manufacturing business, and enlarging his school for training technicians. He became an American citizen in 1946.

There are fifty-two Antoine salons in thirty-eight major cities in the United States; five salons in Canada, one in London, one in Melbourne, Australia, his original salon in Paris, and shops in Cannes and Marseille. He has cosmetics factories in Germany, Spain and Italy. Approximately 10,000 people work in his various establishments which bring in millions of dollars each year.

While expanding spectacularly in the United States, Antoine has continued to hold top place in European *haute coiffure.* In 1937 he took sixty-five operators to London to dress the hair of court ladies for the coronation of King George VI. That same year he dressed the hair of Mrs. Wallis Warfield Simpson for her wedding to the Duke of Windsor. (In 1953 he gave her a "poodle cut.") Antoine supervised the preparation of court ladies for the coronation of Elizabeth II.

He has also influenced hairdressing in Russia, for Madame Molotov, head of the Soviet Cosmetics Trust, visited his salon in Paris to get ideas for beautifying Russian women. Antoine designed Claudette Colbert's bangs, Greta Garbo's long bob, and Mary Martin's short sculptured curls for *South Pacific.* He has staged many pageants and fashion shows.

Among many innovations introduced by Antoine was the streaked forelock of white or blonde hair on a dark coiffure. He was the first to use lacquer to hold hair in place and to develop the idea of sculptured curls and permanent waves molded to fit the contours of the head. He originated the shingle and the upsweep. Among his recent innovations are golden butterflies that can be stencilled on the hair before a party and washed out afterward.

In 1954 he created Flame, short hair brushed forward over the ears and up toward the forehead. In February 1955 he introduced Fireworks, similar to the Italian cut but curlier, with sculptured ringlets designed to bring the shape of the head into the best possible proportions. Working with a headform, pins, curling iron and strands of hair, Antoine creates dozens of new styles each year which his assistants introduce to customers. As in his youth, he still spends many hours in museums.

Antoine commutes between America and Europe, and often flies to London, Cannes or Marseille in his private plane. For relaxation he does sculpture or plays the pipe organ in his Paris home. He no longer lives in the Glass House, but in a modern apartment he designed and had constructed in the fashionable Passy district in 1935. He also has an apartment in New York, a cottage at Fire Island, New York, a villa at Cannes and at Gravigny, France.

Noted for his elegant and eccentric dress, the hairdresser likes to wear dramatic capes, shirts with pleated ruffles on the collar, shoes that add an inch-and-a-half to his height of five feet six inches. He has blue eyes, graying hair worn in a pompadour to add height, and weighs 151 pounds. His favorite sports are ice-skating, horseback riding, and flying. Antoine's religion is Catholic.

In his autobiography, *Antoine,* he wrote: "Every woman is not born with a Grecian nose or golden hair, and old age is without pity. But as the years go by, character and intelligence and beauty of spirit make their mark on the face as on the general bearing. . . . Nearly all women carry within themselves an element of beauty which it is for me to discover and emphasize and this, I believe, is the true function of my profession."

References

Coronet 37:100+ Ja '55 por
Ind Woman 24:269 S '45
Antoine (1945)

AREILZA, JOSÉ MARÍA DE, COUNT OF MOTRICO

(ä-rā"ēl'thä hô-sā' mä-rē'ä dā mô-trē'cô) Aug. 3, 1909- Ambassador from Spain to the United States; author

Address: b. Embassy of Spain, 2700 15th St., N.W., Washington, D.C.; h. 2801 16th St., N.W., Washington, D.C.

When José María de Areilza, Count of Motrico, Spain's new Ambassador to the United States, presented his credentials to President Eisenhower in November 1954, he commented on "the cordial understanding" between the two countries after "a long period of misunderstanding." He was appointed to this post by Generalissimo Francisco Franco to replace José Félix de Lequerica y Erquiza. Since his arrival in Washington, D.C. Ambassador Areilza has urged closer participation for Spain in the United Nations. His request that Spain be allowed to establish a permanent observer at the U.N. was approved by Secretary General Dag Hammarskjöld on January 25, 1955.

Relations between Spain and the United States were strengthened by the signing of an agreement on September 26, 1953 which gave the U.S. the right to use "a number of Spanish air and naval bases for the defense of Western Europe and the Mediterranean." The U.S. government agreed to provide military and economic aid and to furnish a total of $226,000,000 to implement the accord.

José María Areilza y Martinez-Rodas was born in Bilbao in the Basque country of Spain on August 3, 1909, the son of Dr. Enrique Areilza y Arrequi and the former Elisa Emilia Martinez y Arana-Rodas y Mendiolea. His parents were the Count and Countess of Rodas. His mother, because there was no direct male descendant, had inherited the title and in the Spanish tradition, her husband became count. Dr. Enrique Areilza y Arrequi was an eminent surgeon and professor and was internationally known for his experiments in the prevention of tuberculosis.

Young Areilza was educated in private schools, attended Bilbao University and was graduated as a technical engineer. He entered the University of Salamanca and received a law degree in 1932. King Alfonso XIII had fled from Spain in 1931 and the changes in government that followed convinced Areilza that the Falange, the party organized by Franco in 1937, would best govern Spain. He joined the party and accepted the office of mayor in Bilbao. A year later, in 1938, he was named director general of industry in Franco's Cabinet.

Areilza served as director of industry for two years. In 1943 he became a member of the Cortes (Parliament). He had become known for his articles on political issues and was coauthor of the book *Reivindicaciones de España* (1941) with Professor Fernando María Castiella y Maíz of the University of Madrid.

In *Embajadores sobre España* (1947) Areilza analyzed the books written about Spain by the ambassadors of the Allied nations during World War II and praised U.S. Ambassador Carlton J. H. Hayes for his book, *Wartime Mission in Spain, 1942-1945.* Areilza wrote that Hayes understood Spain's position far better than the administration in Washington. He emphasized his own view that it would have been as suicidal for Spain as for Turkey, Sweden or Switzerland to have shown partiality for the Allies.

Appointed Ambassador to Argentina in 1947, Areilza headed the Embassy at Buenos Aires for three years. Sam Pope Brewer reported in the New York *Times* (January 9, 1950) that a "personality clash" had occurred in 1949 between Ambassador Areilza and Señora Eva Perón, wife of President Juan Perón. It was reported that Señora Perón had "insulted" the Spanish Ambassador and he had tried to resign, but Franco had persuaded him to remain. Areilza returned to Spain in 1950, however, and his resignation was accepted.

One of Areilza's editorials in the Falange newspaper *Arriba*, according to the New York *Times* (February 4, 1950), reversed *Arriba's* previous statement concerning Secretary of State Dean Acheson. The editorial pointed out that the Spaniards had been wrong to be annoyed over Acheson's criticism of Spanish affairs, as it had marked the beginning of a new "phase of friendliness in United States relations with Spain."

This comment was regarded by some as an indication that Generalissimo Franco might remodel some of his policies along more demo-

Shelburne Studios

JOSÉ MARÍA DE AREILZA,
COUNT OF MOTRICO

cratic lines in return for "friendlier treatment" by the United Nations and the Western powers, and was borne out by later developments. The General Assembly revoked its 1946 resolution against Spain in November 1950 and thus opened the way for Spanish participation in the international agencies sponsored by the U.N. The resumption of full diplomatic relations between the United States and Spain was also foreshadowed by Congressional approval of a $62,500,000 loan to the Spanish government in August 1950 (See Francisco Franco biography, *Current Biography*, March 1954). On February 5, 1951 Stanton Griffis was sworn in as the new American Ambassador to Spain; the current Ambassador is John Davis Lodge.

During 1953 Areilza took an active part in the campaign for the return of Gibraltar to Spain and gave a series of lectures in which he presented Spain's case. At various periods he has also engaged in industrial and banking activities in Spain.

Following his appointment as Ambassador to the United States in 1954, Areilza visited New York and talked with the U.N. delegates of several nations to learn their attitudes on the Madrid request, which he had presented to General Dag Hammarskjöld, for a permanent observer at the U.N. (New York *Times*, January 14, 1955). He also addressed the Overseas Press Club and described his country as "an uncompromising foe of communism." When advised that Secretary Hammarskjöld had granted Spain's request, Areilza stated: "Spain has always been inclined to cooperate in the task of world justice and peace between the nations."

At the Overseas Press Club meeting in New York City, Areilza was asked to comment on a New York *Times* (December 16, 1954) dispatch which reported that the Spanish government was considering a bill giving government-approved editors full control of the management of daily newspapers. The Ambassador said that what the regime actually had in mind was a "new press code to permit the end of censorship. Responsibility would be left with editors, but the government, while allowing proprietors free choice of the latter, would reserve the right to 'veto' Communist or revolutionary appointments" (New York *Times*, December 17, 1954). He later stated that the draft of the press law had been withdrawn at the request of Franco.

The December 18, 1954 issue of the *Times* reported a Falange decision to reduce the quota of government-controlled newsprint allotted the monarchist newspaper *A.B.C.*, thus requiring it to buy the rest of its newsprint at higher prices on the free market. Areilza denied that the government was thus "fining" the *A.B.C.* and explained that allocations of the less expensive, government-controlled newsprint is made in proportion to a newspaper's circulation.

The Spanish government has been giving signs of dissatisfaction with the amount of aid it is receiving under the 1953 agreement with the United States. According to the *Christian Science Monitor* (February 16, 1955), the Ambassador has been "'exploring'—letting it be known that really something should be done about the agreement. The United States was not getting its bases and airfields quite as quickly . . . as expected, neither was Spain getting the economic help and military equipment it had thought would be pouring in as a result of the arrangement." *Arriba*, according to the New York *Times* (February 14, 1955) credits Areilza with the view that "if the average Spaniard sees that U.S. assistance is not followed by an improvement in his standard of living, the popularity enjoyed by the United States among Spaniards will fade away like a dream." (During the fiscal year—July 1, 1954-June 30, 1955—the United States gave $170,000,000 in economic assistance to Spain, up to February 1955.) On June 1, 1955 U.S. Ambassador John David Lodge said that more than $500,000,000 in military and economic aid had been allotted to Spain since the signing of the United States-Spain agreement in September 1953.

José María de Areilza was married on October 21, 1932 to Mercedes de Churruca, whose full name is María de las Mercedes de Churruca y Zubira-Calbeton y Urezar. She inherited the title Countess of Motrico in 1941 and in accordance with Spanish tradition, shares it with her husband. The Count and Countess of Motrico have five children: Enrique, Mercedes, Juan, Miguel and Cristina.

The Ambassador and his wife speak English fluently. They take a particular interest in the American Friends of Spain Foundation and have been guests of honor at benefit social functions held by the organization in New York and Florida. Ambassador Areilza is six feet tall, weighs 180 pounds and has hazel eyes and gray hair. His religion is Roman Catholic.

Reference

Guía Nobiliaria de España (1944)
N Y Herald Tribune p1 IX Ap 3 '55

ARLEN, HAROLD Feb. 15, 1905- Composer

Address: b. c/o ASCAP, 575 Madison Ave., New York 22

HAROLD ARLEN

The composer of the very familiar tunes, "Stormy Weather," "Blues in the Night," "That Old Black Magic" and other hit songs, is Harold Arlen. His popular "Over the Rainbow," written for the motion picture *Wizard Of Oz* (1939) won an Academy of Motion Pictures Arts and Sciences Award ("Oscar"). A member of the American Society of Composers, Authors and Publishers (ASCAP) for twenty-five years, Arlen has many songs for Hollywood motion pictures and Broadway shows to his credit, the latest being for the films *A Star Is Born,* starring Judy Garland and *The Country Girl,* with Grace Kelly, Bing Crosby and William Holden, and for the musical comedy *House of Flowers,* starring Pearl Bailey. His music is described by John Tasker Howard in *Our American Music* (1946) as "typically an expression of the age he lives in," with "an authentic Negroid flavor that is characteristic of the folk element of jazz."

The composer was born Hymen Arluck in Buffalo, New York on February 15, 1905, the son of Samuel and Celia (Orlin) Arluck. His father was a cantor in the synagogue, where Harold began singing in the choir at the age of seven. In his seventh year, also, he began taking piano lessons, while his brother studied violin. Harold attended the public schools and was graduated from Hutchinson High School in Buffalo.

At the age of fifteen, Arlen began playing professionally in Buffalo cafés and on lake boats as a member of the piano, violin and drum team, the Snappy Trio. As his group progressed to engagements with the better clubs and restaurants, he increased its number to six and called the band the Yankee Six. He played the piano and sang. During 1924 he made trips to New York City to hear Ethel Waters sing and in 1927 he brought his band, then numbering fifteen, to Manhattan, under the name of The Buffalodians.

After working in Arnold Johnson's orchestra as a pianist and arranger in the *1927 Scandals,* produced by George White, Arlen became associated with producer Vincent Youmans, "who liked his pianistic hot licks and interpolations" (*Collier's,* December 9, 1944). He composed his first song hit, "Get Happy," which was sung in 1928 as the finale of Ruth Selwyn's *9:15 Revue.* George Gershwin called it "the most exciting finale he'd ever heard" (*New Yorker,* January 29, 1955).

Harold Arlen joined Ted Koehler in 1930 in a collaboration on songs for the Cotton Club revues. This alliance, which lasted four years, brought him the name of "the foremost writer of Negro tunes." He wrote the music for "I've Got the World on a String" and "Kickin' the Gong Around," introduced by Cab Calloway, and "Between the Devil and the Deep Blue Sea." "Stormy Weather," written for Ethel Waters in 1932, became a nation-wide hit after she first sang it in a Cotton Club revue. Arlen collaborated with Ted Koehler in preparing the music for the eighth and tenth editions of Earl Carroll's famous *Vanities* in 1930 and 1932.

With E. Y. Harburg and Ira Gershwin, Arlen formed an alliance in 1934 to compose the songs for the musical show *Life Begins at 8:40,* in which Ray Bolger danced. *Time* (September 10, 1934) stated that the revue "is graced with good music . . . highly suitable for humming." Among the tunes were "What Can You Say in a Love Song," "Let's Take a Walk Around the Block," and "You're a Builder-Upper." Also in 1934, the composer created the music for J. P. McEvoy's third edition of the Broadway musical, *Americana.* With E. Y. Harburg, he collaborated on the popular song, "Satan's Li'l Lamb." The next year, he moved to Hollywood, California and started to write music for the movies.

Returning East in 1937, he wrote the score for *Hooray for What!,* the Broadway musical starring Ed Wynn. Back in Hollywood, Arlen worked with E. Y. Harburg on the score for the film, *Wizard of Oz,* released in 1939. His Academy Award-winning song, "Over the Rainbow," was removed from the movie three times before it was finally included, and brought fame to its singer, Judy Garland. The composer wrote the first few notes of this tune while hearing noisy automobile horns in heavy city traffic. Another of the movie's songs, "We're Off to see the Wizard," became the "Aussies" (Australian troops) marching song during World War II.

In composing, Arlen has said, "If I have the first four bars, the rest isn't so bad." In his pockets he carries music score sheets on which he can make notes. With his song, "Blues in the Night," composed for the screen film of the same name in 1941, he "made a contribu-

ARLEN, HAROLD—*Continued*

tion to American popular music that established him as one of our most gifted light composers," wrote John Tasker Howard.

Arlen collaborated with lyric writer Johnny Mercer on the songs for the Paramount picture *Star Spangled Rhythm* (1942), including "That Old Black Magic"; for *The Sky's the Limit* (1943), with Fred Astaire, who sang "One for My Baby"; and for *Here Come the Waves* (1944), with Bing Crosby and Sonny Tufts singing "Accentuate the Positive." He collaborated with E. Y. Harburg on songs for the film *Cabin in the Sky* (1943), including "Happiness Is Just a Thing Called Joe," sung by Ethel Waters. With Ted Koehler he wrote the music for *Up in Arms* (1944), starring Danny Kaye and Dinah Shore. In Berlin during 1945 a Russian songstress revived Arlen's Cotton Club revue song "Ill Wind" and it became a big hit with American soldiers.

The Broadway production, *Bloomer Girl* (1944), for which Arlen wrote the music and E. Y. Harburg the lyrics, included the show-stopper "I Got a Song," revamped after being rejected from the score for *Cabin in the Sky.* B. H. Haggin wrote in the *Nation* (October 21, 1944): "In some of his music for *Bloomer Girl,* Harold Arlen uses a gently flowing style that comments amusingly on the 1861 situations it deals with. Most of it, however, is traditional Broadway musical comedy music, no more than routine and competent, but enjoyable, and genuine. . . ." He adds that in the song "T'morra, t'morra," Arlen and Harburg "produce something that ranks with the best of Rodgers and Hart." The reviewer in *Theatre Arts* (November 1944) commented: "Its songs and its movements do not flow inevitably from its story, [but] *Bloomer Girl* has its quota of song hits—"The Eagle and Me," "Right as the Rain," [and] "When the Boys Come Home."

For the Negro musical play *St. Louis Woman* on Broadway in 1946, Arlen wrote tunes to lyrics by Johnny Mercer. In this show, Pearl Bailey had "her first big hit" as the singer of "Legalize My Name" (*Life,* April 29, 1946). Two years later Arlen composed the film music in the Universal-International picture *Casbah* (starring Tony Martin), the third movie dealing with the Parisian rascal, Pepe Le Moko in Algiers.

With Ira Gershwin as his lyricist, Arlen composed the musical scores for the 1954 Warner Brothers remake of the seventeen-year-old film, *A Star is Born* in CinemaScope, and the Paramount movie *The Country Girl.* Of the former, the New York *Times* (October 12, 1954) screen critic wrote: "There is the muchness of music that runs from a fine, haunting torch-song at the outset, "The Man Got Away," to a mammoth, extensive production number . . . "Born in a Trunk." He called the musical numbers "among the finest things in the show." Arlen's songs in *The Country Girl* included "The Pitchman" and "The Search is Through."

For the Broadway musical production *House of Flowers,* Arlen collaborated with author Truman Capote on the lyrics to the fifteen songs in the show and wrote the music. William K. Zinsser in the New York *Herald Tribune* (December 26, 1954) described "The Sleeping Bee" as "a haunting song," and "I Never Has Seen Snow" as "a good bet to be remembered as one of Arlen's masterpieces."

Many of the composer's songs, including "Let's Fall in Love," for the movie of the same name, are heard on jukeboxes and on the radio. His song "Captain of the Clouds" became the official song of the Royal Canadian Air Force. Among his other well-known melodies are "It's Only a Paper Moon" and "Last Night When We Were Young," In *Americannegro Suite,* he created four spirituals. His movie scores include music for the pictures *Strike Me Pink, Stage Struck,* and *Gold Diggers*; and he wrote individual songs for the films *Babes in Arms, Love Affair* and *Rio Rita.*

Harold Arlen is married to Anya Taranda, a former showgirl in Earl Carroll's *Vanities.* His principal recreations are golf, reading, and painting. The *New Yorker* (January 29, 1955) described him as "a worried-looking, friendly man, with thick black hair and sparkling eyes." He prefers to compose tunes before the lyricist writes the words.

When Arlen moved to Hollywood in 1943 he said, "California agrees with me much better than New York" (New York *Post,* June 23, 1943). Moving back to New York in 1955, he commented, "Hollywood did well by me. . . . Now it's time for a change. I'm convinced that New York and the theatre are where I belong" (*New Yorker,* January 29, 1955).

References

N Y Herald Tribune IV p 1+ D 26 '54
N Y Post Mag p43 Je 23 '43 pors
New Yorker 30:18+ Ja 29 '55

ASCAP Biographical Dictionary of Composers, Authors, and Publishers (1952)
Who's Who in America, 1950-51
World Biography (1954)

ARMAS, CARLOS CASTILLO *See* Castillo Armas, Carlos

ARNON, DANIEL I(SRAEL) Nov. 14, 1910- Plant physiologist; educator

Address: b. c/o Division of Plant Nutrition, University of California, Berkeley, Calif.

A team of scientists at the University of California headed by Dr. Daniel I. Arnon, by reproducing the process of photosynthesis outside the living plant cell, solved an "elemental secret of nature" during 1954 which opens the way toward eventually "liberating mankind from his dependence upon crops and animals for food" (New York *Times,* January 2, 1955).

Dr. Arnon's findings include the discovery of a new photosynthetic mechanism and the identification of hitherto unrecognized photosynthetic catalysts (vitamin B_2, K and C). In these experiments it was demonstrated that the chloroplast is a complete photosynthetic unit capable of carrying out the principal reactions of photosynthesis outside the living cells. Dr. Arnon's other work in plant nutrition—the role of micronutrients in plant growth and the study of the participation of soil elements in photosynthesis—has been of great value to farmers and agricultural experts.

Born in Warsaw, Poland, November 14, 1910, Daniel Israel Arnon was reared in the United States. He received his B.S. degree from the University of California in 1932, followed four years later by his Ph.D. degree in plant physiology. In 1936 he was appointed an instructor in truck crops, and six years later he was made an assistant professor of plant nutrition. He became an associate professor in 1946 and is now a full professor.

Dr. Arnon's first research activities were on micronutrients, minerals needed by plant life in extremely small amounts. Other nutrients are needed in larger quantities. Known micronutrients include such minerals as zinc, boron, copper, and manganese, which are necessary to plants in dilutions of approximately one part to twenty million. Other micronutrient essentials have been the subject of research.

In 1939 Arnon (in collaboration with P. R. Stout) conducted a controlled experiment with tomatoes. He grew some plants in a soil containing the elements considered necessary for proper maturation. Other seedlings, which he grew in a soil mixture containing the element molybdenum, thrived better than those grown without it. His later work on micronutrients showed that vanadium is also an essential to the growth of green plants (see *Nature*, December 5, 1953).

Using experiments first conducted by W. F. Gericke, Arnon and a colleague added some essential information about whether crops grown by the water-culture method would be more profitable commercially than those grown in the soil. The water-culture method is a process in which large tanks, filled with water and a nutrient solution, replace soil as a media for crop production. Working with tomatoes again, Arnon, together with D. R. Hoagland, also of the University of California, raised two crops, one in soil and one in a water culture. The conditions were similar for the plants in both media.

In a paper discussing the experiment in *Science* (June 2, 1939), Arnon and Hoagland wrote: "The average yields, as well as the highest yields of individual plants, from soil and water cultures do not justify a conclusion that the potential crop yield is higher in a favorable nutrient solution than in a fertile soil." They suggested that the water-culture method might be reserved for greenhouses specializing in high-priced out-of-season crops or utilized in areas where good soil is not available. They found that soil is still the most profitable means of raising large yields of common crops, because the culture method requires large expenditures for the installation of tanks.

Later, in an analysis of the effect of vitamin B_1 on the growth of plants, Arnon wrote: "Evidence was obtained to show that several widely differing species, when grown from seed under

ASUC

DANIEL I. ARNON

favorable conditions, are not limited in their growth by an inherently low rate of vitamin B_1 synthesis" (*Science*, September 20, 1940).

In 1940 Arnon was honored with D. R. Hoagland by the American Association for the Advancement of Science for their presentation of the most outstanding scientific paper of the year at the 107th meeting of the association. The prize of $1,000 was donated by both scientists to the Berkeley laboratories to continue research activities.

Their work suggested a new theory to explain the method by which plant roots absorb their food from the soil. The committee on awards stated that they had shown "that energy is expended by roots in the absorption of mineral nutrients from [the] soil. The energy comes from the metabolic activity of the root. Absorption, therefore, is not a passive process of diffusion, as formerly thought, but is rather a vital biochemical function in which the root performs work. This contribution is important not only from a fundamental theoretical standpoint, but also from a practical standpoint, especially in agriculture. It emphasizes the fact that absorption is not a static, but a dynamic process" (*Science*, February 7, 1941).

As a major with the U.S. Army from 1943 to 1946, Dr. Arnon utilized his knowledge of crop production by the water-culture method for the benefit of soldiers in the West Pacific. Stationed on Ascension Island (Ponape), where the soil was incapable of producing large quantities of edible plants, he grew crops in gravel and water with chemicals added.

With several other researchers Dr. Arnon began to study photosynthesis in the late 1940's. Photosynthesis is the process by which green plants use the energy from the sun to make carbohydrates (starches) from carbon dioxide and water and release oxygen to the air. The

ARNON, DANIEL I.—*Continued*

particle of the plant that carries on photosynthesis is the chloroplast, which contains the green coloring matter known as chlorophyll.

By isolating the chloroplasts from the plant cells of spinach, the scientists studied photosynthesis without any interference from other cell processes. After six years the photosynthesis discoveries of Dr. Arnon and his collaborators, Dr. F. R. Whatley, Dr. M. B. Allen, John B. Capindale (graduate student), and Lois J. Durham (graduate student), were announced. Their investigation was supported in part by a research grant of the National Institutes of Health, U.S. Public Health Service.

In a paper delivered before the A.A.A.S. convention in December 1954, Dr. Arnon warned of the difficult work still required, but stated: "The achievement of extracellular photosynthesis brings nearer the day when man, after mastering the secrets of the process in green cells, will reduce his age-long dependence on crop plants for food and energy by devising his own photosynthetic reactions driven directly by the energy of the sun. When this proves attainable, it will usher in an era of unlimited abundance for the benefit of all mankind" (New York *Times*, December 30, 1954).

According to Dr. Arnon, extracellular photosynthesis involves three major reactions. In the first, photolysis, water is decomposed by light into "active" hydrogen and oxygen. "The 'active' hydrogen," Arnon wrote, "which is raised to a high energy level by light, is the agent which actually accomplishes the synthesis of organic compounds during photosynthesis.

"Until now it has been assumed that 'active' hydrogen does this only by reducing carbon dioxide. Evidence has now been obtained that in addition to this conventional 'carbon dioxide photosynthesis' there is also a 'phosphate photosynthesis' which proceeds in the absence of carbon dioxide. In 'phosphate photosynthesis' inorganic phosphate is used to form an organic phosphorus compound, adenosine triphosphate (ATP). The process is being named photosynthetic phosphorylation."

The scientist points out that photosynthetic phosphorylation is different from the conventional carbon dioxide photosynthesis in that oxygen is not set free. The "active" hydrogen instead recombines with the "active" oxygen from which it was separated during photolysis. Dr. Arnon wrote that "ATP is not peculiar to photosynthetic organisms, but is a universal constituent of all living cells, plant or animal, and is used as the 'currency' for paying the energy 'bills' of the multitude of chemical reactions necessary for life."

The light-generated ATP is used, wholly or in part, for the third reaction of photosynthesis —that of the reduction of carbon dioxide. In this reaction a portion of the "active" hydrogen formed during photolysis combines with ATP to form first, sugar phosphates and then starch. (See the scientist's articles in *Nature,* August 28, 1954, and *Journal of the American Chemical Society,* December 20, 1954, for further information.)

Dr. Arnon has been editor of the *Annual Review of Plant Physiology* for several years. In 1951 he contributed to *Mineral Nutrition of Plants,* a symposium published by the University of Wisconsin Press. He has written for numerous scientific journals and has served as American editor of the international publication, *Plant and Soil.* He is a member of the Society of Plant Physiologists (he became secretary of the Western section in 1941), the American Chemical Society, and the A.A.A.S.

He was honored with a Guggenheim Fellowship to Cambridge University, England in 1947. The following year he was a guest lecturer at the Belgian-American Educational Foundation in Liége and in 1950 he delivered two papers at the Seventh International Botanical Congress in Sweden. In July 1954 he talked on photosynthesis before an international congress on botany in Paris.

Dr. Arnon is married and has several children. He is a naturalized American citizen. *Business Week* has praised the scientist's new work on photosynthesis: "So far-reaching are the possibilities that—if the first results prove out—it may in time outrank the splitting of the atom as this century's major contribution to mankind."

References

N Y Times p1+ D 30 '54; IV p9 Ja 9 '55

American Men of Science (1949)

ARONIN, JEFFREY ELLIS (ä-rō'nĭn) Aug. 16, 1927- Architect; author

Address: b. c/o Voorhees, Walker, Smith and Smith, 430 Park Ave., New York 22; Reinhold Publishing Co., 330 W. 42d St., New York 36; h. Woodmere Blvd., Woodmere, N.Y.

Speaking before the members of the American Meteorological Society on September 9, 1954, Jeffrey Ellis Aronin, New York architect and author of the book *Climate and Architecture* (Reinhold, 1953), declared: "We ought to try to live with our climate, not against it. We should put our weather to work helping to heat our homes in winter and cool them in summer." Among the methods he advocates "for taking advantage of the weather" are "capturing" the sun's heat directly with chemicals or ray-catching window devices, cooling arrangements which make the most of winds, and overhangs, louvers, sunbreakers, balconies, evergreens, vines and other shading equipment.

During a 3,100-mile trek in the frozen regions of Hudson Bay, Canada, where he slept in igloos, Aronin first became impressed with the way man can make the most of climate. He developed his ideas on the subject after an 11,000-mile trip through Canada, Mexico and the United States, during which he interviewed Frank Lloyd Wright, Richard Neutra and other prominent architects. He forsees that in twenty years or sooner houses will need neither heating nor air-conditioning units. He contends that if the Eskimo can accommodate his igloo to extreme weather conditions, the modern architect can do likewise, even in temperate and tropical regions. The ultimate shortages of fuels, and their high cost, will require the prospective homeowner to learn something of the science of climatology.

Appraising the book *Climate and Architecture* by Jeffrey Ellis Aronin, the *Saturday Review* (February 20, 1954) commented: "He formulates a thought that flings a challenge at the doubtful blessings of climatic gadgeteering, from the chill-shocking air conditioner to the electric blanket: 'Let us learn how to live with the climate, not in opposition to it.'" His book was favorably discussed during 1954 on numerous radio and television programs; he was interviewed by Pegeen and Ed Fitzgerald, Faye Emerson, Maggi McNellis, and many other commentators. On April 17, 1954 the Columbia Broadcasting System presented a half-hour educational program on television entitled *You, Climate and Architecture*, with Aronin's book as the central theme.

An associate of several New York architectural firms, Aronin has designed shopping and community centers, apartments and private residences, offices and banks, schools and libraries, and a variety of other structures. He has also assisted on the designs of a large U.S. Navy Communications Station at Norfolk, Virginia and a U.S. Navy Laboratory and has developed plans for the U.S. Army Corps of Engineers for an Army camp and an Air Force base at Plattsburg, New York.

Born in London, England on August 16, 1927, Jeffrey Ellis Aronin is the son of Joseph and Bertha (Danziger) Aronin. His sister, Isobel Joy Aronin, is a writer. His father, a native of New York City, is a fur merchant; his mother, who was born in Newcastle-on-Tyne, England, was formerly a concert pianist.

Jeffrey evinced an interest in architecture in his early youth. Before he had attained school age, he spent many hours drawing sketches of public monuments and other edifices in and around London.

At the age of six, after attending kindergarten for a year, Aronin entered London's Peterborough Lodge School. During his early teens he achieved prominence in athletics, starring as center-forward of the soccer team, excelling in gymnastics, and winning several trophies for swimming.

When he was seven he was taken on a brief visit to the United States, and, as he wrote recently, he was so deeply impressed by New York's skyscrapers that he vowed someday to "return to the United States to design, as an architect, many fine structures" of his own.

In 1939, with war in Europe imminent, Aronin's parents sent him to New York, where he lived with relatives. He attended Columbia Grammar School until 1940, when his family moved to Woodmere, Long Island. Thereupon he entered Woodmere Academy, winning his letter in soccer there four successive seasons and acting in several school plays. He spent his summers from 1941 until 1943 at Kamp Kohut in Maine; as editor of the camp's weekly magazine he won the Columbia Scholastic Press Association's first prize in its annual competition for school and camp periodicals.

Mario Rosel

JEFFREY ELLIS ARONIN

After graduating from Woodmere Academy in 1944, Aronin entered Hamilton College, Clinton, New York. During a year's attendance there he passed the Red Cross instructor's course and thus qualified to conduct classes in swimming, life saving and water safety for the U.S. Army. In October 1944 he enrolled at the University of Manitoba in Winnipeg in order, as he has said, "to get a perspective of education . . . in another country and to pursue . . . architectural endeavors." He became a regular contributor to the university's newspapers and edited its architectural magazines. In 1946 he participated in the Canadian Army's Exercise Muskox, a three-month, 3100-mile expedition in the far north designed to test how man can live in extremely cold weather. On this expedition he first became impressed with "the way man can make the most of climate not only in these frigid regions" but also "in more temperate and tropical ones."

The following year he developed his ideas on the subject after an 11,000-mile trip through Canada, Mexico, and forty-five of the United States. In 1949 he won his B. Arch. degree from the University of Manitoba; his thesis was the design of a recreation center to be built at Cedarhurst to serve the entire Five Towns of the Woodmere, Long Island area. His plans call for three connected buildings including a swimming pool, gymnasium, library, social wing and auditorium, football and softball fields, an ice hockey rink, tennis and handball courts, and bowling alleys.

For sixteen months in 1949 and 1950 Aronin served in a New York architectural office. In the fall of 1950, desiring to undertake specialized research, he enrolled in McGill University in Montreal, where he investigated further the

ARONIN, JEFFREY ELLIS—*Continued*

relation of climate to architecture. Aronin was awarded the degree of Master of Architecture in 1951, *magna cum laude*.

In the spring of the following year he was nominated for a scholarship of the American Institute of Architects to conduct advanced research. Canada's Director of Building Research asked Aronin in 1952 to advise his committee on certain aspects of Canada's new National Building Code and to assist in its composition. Early in 1953 he was elected a practicing member of the Manitoba Association of Architects, the Royal Architectural Institute of Canada, and the Sociedad de Arquitectos Mexicanos.

Aronin's recent book, *Climate and Architecture*, the product of several years' study, has achieved wide distribution. The author shows in the work how primitive man "intuitively recognized climate in his building designs" and how this recognition can be utilized in modern construction. He demonstrates the influence of the sun, wind, precipitation, lightning and humidity on architecture, discusses their varied effects in a wide range of conditions, and explains how to control them through building orientation, site and town planning, and the use of such devices as *brise-soleil*, trees, wind-breaks and snow fences. To describe his special phase of architectural study Aronin coined the term "airchitecture."

He pays tribute "to the intuitive genius for orientation of the Eskimo and the Indian, of colonial settlers in Mexico and Virginia, and of the Japanese who consult a 'specialist on directions' before planning a house. Climatic ignorance became epidemic [Aronin believes] with the Industrial Revolution and such modern building features as the indiscriminately employed flat roof or picture window, and mass-produced materials. [His] conclusion is that we have to replace our lost instinctual sense of orientation with the new vocabulary of modern man: scientific research and statistical presentation. . . The macroclimate of the total region is established. The microclimate of community and individual shelter follows, [with] outstanding examples of contemporary architecture" (*Saturday Review*, February 20, 1954).

"*Climate and Architecture*, aside from its comprehensiveness, is unique for its scholarly aspect," commented *Progressive Architecture* (May, 1954).

An important factor in using nature, in Aronin's opinion, is in selecting the right place to build. Buildings a block apart can vary greatly in their climate, depending on topography, bodies of water adjacent, trees, rain patterns and terrain. Flat space above roofs of office buildings heats the air above them, causing the air to rise. Air from industrial areas on the fringes of cities rushes into the business district to fill the void. The result is smog and haze over many cities.

"Why don't they plant trees and shrubs on top of buildings and in vacant spaces by the street?" Aronin asked. "Or put awnings over sidewalks the way they did years ago? Window boxes of flowers and shrubs would help, too. All these would catch dust and muffle noise, as well as insulate" (Columbus, Ohio, *Dispatch*, September 10, 1954).

Aronin is affiliated with a number of professional organizations, including the New York chapter of the American Institute of Architects and the Royal Institute of British Architects. He is secretary of subcommittees #6 and #7 of the Mayor's Committee for Better Housing, City of New York.

The architect is unmarried. He is five feet nine inches tall and weighs 160 pounds. He has dark brown hair and brown eyes. He is active in Boy Scout work. He enjoys chess, music and stamp collecting, and his favorite sports are golf and swimming.

Aronin said that most people do not realize how easy it is to conserve heat. In most of his designs the sun's rays warm heating fluids on the roof of the house. Good roof insulation retains the heat at night. Even on cloudy days, he said, 80 per cent of the sun's radiation reaches us. Proper location is also an important factor, and basements can be kept dry all year and snow shoveling can be kept to a minimum.

References

Christian Sci Mon p9 Je 16 '54
Columbus (Ohio) Dispatch p 1+ S 10 '54
Frontpage (Israel) S 16 '54
Gazette (Montreal) My 15 '54
Nassau (L.I.) Review-Star p23 D 1 '49
Newsday p39 N 4 '53 por
South Shore (L.I.) Record N 12 '54

ASWELL, JAMES Apr. 27, 1906-Feb. 23, 1955 Author; worked ten years for King Features Syndicate; wrote *The Midsummer Fires* (1948), *There's One in Every Town* (1951); *The Birds and the Bees* (1953); his novels, all with Louisiana settings, were praised for their realism and theses, but criticized for their plots; his short stories appeared in leading magazines and were collected under the title *The Young and Hungry Hearted*. See *Current Biography* (Yrbk) 1951.

Obituary

N Y Times p27 F 24 '55

BABB, JAMES T(INKHAM) Aug. 23, 1899- Librarian

Address: b. c/o Yale University Library, New Haven, Conn.; h. 389 St. Ronan St., New Haven 11, Conn.

A businessman whose love for books made him a full-time librarian, James T. Babb is the head of the Sterling Memorial Library and all the departmental and school libraries of Yale University in New Haven, Connecticut. These libraries contain about 4,250,000 books, famous recordings, subscribe to over 1,300 scholarly publications, and publish the *Yale University Library Gazette*. The Sterling Memorial Library is noted for having one of the world's largest collections of English and American history and literature.

Babb, who has served at Yale since 1938 and has been the university librarian since 1945, has stated that duplication of little-used books in the nation's many libraries can be avoided by a system of five or six storage libraries strategically located throughout the country. He said: "The libraries should probably be a part of our national library system under the direction of the Librarian of Congress. The development of such a joint storage library will, in itself, stimulate cooperative library activity in a wider area" (*Report of the Librarian,* 1951-1952).

James Tinkham Babb was born on August 23, 1899 in Lewiston, Idaho, the only child of Daisy (Tinkham) and James Elisha Babb, an attorney, who successfully argued several important cases before the United States Supreme Court, and a serious student of the history of the Pacific Northwest. He is a direct descendant of John and Anna Maria (Riel) Babb, who came to Virginia from Germany in 1752.

After graduating from Phillips Exeter Academy in Exeter, New Hampshire in 1920, James entered Yale University, where he received the Ph.B. degree in 1924. From 1924 to 1926, Babb was a student at Yale School of Law. He became an investment banker in 1926 with the New Haven firm of Edward M. Bradley & Company, with which he was associated for twelve years.

While still an undergraduate, Babb became an active book collector and assembled the works of Joseph Conrad as well as early American fiction writers. In 1938 he gave up his business career to devote himself to the world of books, accepting the post of assistant librarian at the Sterling Memorial Library, Yale University. In December 1942 Babb became acting librarian, when the university librarian, Bernhard Knollenberg, took a leave of absence to serve in the U. S. Government. On January 13, 1945 Dr. Charles Seymour, then president of Yale, announced that Babb had been appointed university librarian.

Yale College (first called Collegiate School of Connecticut, and later named for Elihu Yale) was founded in 1701 by ten ministers. Believing that a library was basic to such a school, they each donated their own treasured books for the founding of the institution. Thus Yale began with a collection of books before it had a student body or a faculty. Since that time, the library has played a significant role in the development of Yale. Many prominent Englishmen donated gifts of their works including Edmund Halley and Sir Richard Steele; among the collection Sir Isaac Newton gave in 1713 was a first edition of his *Opticks* and a second edition of his *Principia*; in 1733 (Bishop) George Berkeley sent a gift of nearly 1,000 volumes to Yale.

By 1918, when John W. Sterling (Yale, 1864) left a major part of his fortune to Yale University, space for books was scarce. Part of the Sterling funds was used to build a new library. The Sterling Memorial Library, which

Alburtus—Yale News Bureau
JAMES T. BABB

was completed in 1930, is modern Gothic in style and built of Indiana limestone. In the entrance hall, a decorative frieze illustrates the history of the university, and in windows throughout the building, illustrations from famous manuscripts and books have been reproduced on glass.

The Sterling Memorial Library contains seventeen major collections including the Collection of the Literature of the American Musical Theatre, American Oriental Society Library (about 16,000 volumes), Babylonian Collection, Crawford Collection on the Modern Drama, Benjamin Franklin Collection, Collection of American Literature, James Weldon Johnson Memorial Collection of Negro Arts and Letters, Map Room, Numismatic Collection, and Western Americana Collection. The library also offers special services such as the Andrews Loan Library (which lends textbooks for a term or a year to self-supporting students), the Audio Visual Center, exhibitions, and a typing room.

Among the collections of manuscripts, first editions and letters presented to the Sterling Memorial Library have been those of Teodor Józef Konrad Korzeniowski (Joseph Conrad), given by George T. Keating in 1938; of Walt Whitman, given by Adrian Van Sinderen in 1940; and of George Eliot (Mary Ann Evans), acquired by the library in the 1930's and subsequently augmented to over 800 letters.

G. Robert Vincent, a New York sound engineer, presented to the Yale library in 1942 over 5,000 records. Some of these were of the voices of Queen Victoria, Florence Nightingale, William Ewart Gladstone, David Lloyd George, Georges Clemenceau, and several U.S. presidents. In 1945 Mrs. Samuel H. Fisher gave to the library her collection of playing cards from all parts of the world during the past five cen-

BABB, JAMES T.—*Continued*

turies. During the school year of 1945-1946 Gertrude Stein made a permanent gift of all her manuscripts to the Yale library.

Over a period of six years beginning in 1945, Yale's Western Americana Collection received the William Robertson Coe collection of 10,000 printed items, including early newspapers, a gallery of paintings by the earliest artists of the West, Russian imperial ukases granting rights to the Russian-American Company, and fifty-three manuscript maps drawn by William Clark of the (Meriwether) Lewis and Clark expedition. Babb also contributed to the library's Western Americana Collection many books on early Idaho.

In 1952 Yale received what *Life* (April 21, 1952) called "one of the most important Americana 'finds' in years"—the Pequot Library of Southport, Connecticut. It contains hundreds of valuable New England documents, early histories of the New World, autographs of all the signers of the Declaration of Independence, a pamphlet written by Christopher Columbus in 1493, and two first editions of Richard Hakluyt's *The Principall Navigations*, published in 1589, in which Hakluyt compiled accounts of explorers like Sir Francis Drake and Sebastian Cabot. The value of the Pequot Library, which is on loan to Yale for fifteen years, is estimated at $500,000.

Babb is also in charge of the twenty-eight School and departmental libraries at Yale, including the medical and law libraries. The Historical Library of Yale University School of Medicine was endowed by Dr. Harvey Cushing and dedicated on June 15, 1941. Its collections include those bequeathed by Cushing (which is rich in documents on the anatomy of the Renaissance, and surgery of Tudor England and which contains Andreas Vesalius' books and 165 incunabula) and Dr. Arnold C. Klebs (devoted largely to fifteenth century medical literature), and presented by Professor John F. Fulton (relating mainly to seventeenth and eighteenth century medicine).

The professional organizations in which Babb holds memberships include the Connecticut Library Association (president, 1945-1946), American Library Association, council of the Bibliographical Society of America (former president), and Bibliographical Society of England. He is an associate fellow of Davenport College, Yale. His clubs at Yale are the Fence, Elihu, and Elizabethan; in New York he belongs to the Century Association, Grolier and Yale.

James T. Babb and Margaret Bradley were married on December 21, 1925. Their children are Barbara and James Bradley Babb. The librarian enjoys fishing and reading for relaxation. In 1945 Babb was awarded an honorary M. A. degree from Yale. He has contributed to professional periodicals and compiled *A Bibliography of the Writings of William McFee* (Doubleday, 1931).

In his annual report of 1952-1953, Babb wrote that "the curriculum of our American colleges in the eighteenth and nineteenth centuries was simple. The student read few books and those intensely. Now the curriculum is extensive and the university library must gather material on thousands of subjects, much of it ephemeral and some even bad. . . . With quality the library will be a real help in the instruction of the student; with quantity as our aim, the library would become difficult, if not impossible, for even the exceptional student to use."

References

Library J 70:122 F 1 '45
International Who's Who, 1954
Who's Who in America, 1954-55
Who's Who in Library Service (1955)
World Biography (1954)

BAILEY, L(IBERTY) H(YDE) Mar. 15, 1858-Dec. 25, 1954 Botanist; horticulturist; educator; author; associated with Cornell University for many years; an authority on North American sedges, raspberries and New World palms; collected more than 200,000 plants from all over the world for the Bailey Hortorium (at Cornell), which also has his vast library on plant lore; wrote numerous books. See *Current Biography* (June) 1948.

Obituary

N Y Times p17 D 27 '54

BAILEY, PEARL (MAE) Mar. 29, 1918- Singer

Address: b. c/o William Morris Agency, 1740 Broadway, New York 19; h. 109 Bank St., New York 14

A singer with an insouciant charm, expressive hands, and a lazy way with a song is Pearl Bailey, who arrived on Broadway from the night club circuit. She herself claims that she is not a singer, has never had a singing lesson, and simply tells "stories that are set to music." She has also appeared in vaudeville and in the motion picture *Carmen Jones*. Her first Broadway role as a solo star in the musical *House of Flowers,* she admits was "like closing your fist on the career you dreamed of" (New York *World-Telegram and Sun,* February 5, 1955).

She won the Donaldson Award for the most promising new performer of 1946 for her work in the Negro musical show *St. Louis Woman.*

Her Coral, Columbia and Decca records with "name" bands are best sellers. Wolcott Gibbs in the *New Yorker* (February 11, 1950) called her songs "all too brief exhibitions of comic genius." She has been a guest artist on television programs such as *What's My Line?* and *Toast of the Town.*

Pearl Mae Bailey was born in Newport News, Virginia on March 29, 1918, and started dancing and singing at the age of three. Her father, Joseph James Bailey, is a minister with the House of Prayer, and Pearl claims that the "swaying rhythm" practiced by this group during worship services was "bred" in her. Besides her mother and father, Pearl's family includes two sisters and one brother, all of whom entered show business, except for the oldest sister. Her brother is Bill Bailey, both a tap dancer and a minister.

In 1933 she moved with her family to Philadelphia, Pennsylvania. While she was a student in William Penn High School she entered an amateur song and dance contest and won first prize of a two-week engagement at the town's Pearl Theater at a salary of $35 a week. She left high school, but the vaudeville house closed before the end of two weeks and her salary was not paid. Determined to become a professional singer, she commuted to Scranton, Wilkes-Barre and Pottsville, Pennsylvania, where she sang in night clubs for $15 a week.

While spending the summer with a married sister in Washington, D.C., Pearl won a $12 prize at the Jungle Inn for "a buck and wing dancing act" of her own. She discovered that she could dance as well as sing without formal instruction. She began performing in small night clubs in Washington, where she claims: "I got $18 a week with . . . tips" (New York *Post*, January 16, 1955). She received several offers from popular bands and became vocalist with the bands of Cootie Williams and later with Count Basie, with whom she also made records.

Signed at the Village Vanguard, New York City in 1941, by Max Gordon, Miss Bailey was an immediate hit. This engagement was followed by eight months at the Blue Angel, a smart East-side cafe.

During World War II Pearl Bailey toured Army camps from Texas to California with U.S.O. troupes. Upon her return to New York, she appeared at La Vie en Rose club, owned by Monte Proser. She made her stage debut on March 30, 1946, when she shared top billing in the Negro musical *St. Louis Woman* at the Martin Beck Theatre. Howard Barnes wrote in the New York *Herald Tribune* (April 1, 1946), "Pearl Bailey [in the role of Butterfly] pulls the show up by its shoestrings every time she makes an entrance." Her style is on the order of Ethel Waters, according to drama critic Lewis Nichols (New York *Times*, April 1, 1946). She sang "Legalize My Name" and "A Woman's Prerogative." She also sang in Cab Calloway's band at the late show at the Cafe Zanzibar.

In her first film, a Paramount production, *Variety Girl*, Miss Bailey introduced her famous song "Tired," that she has made into a popular recording. For Coral Records she has made such hits as "Row, Row, Row," "That's Good Enough for Me," and "Takes Two to Tango." While under contract to Columbia Records in 1950, she recorded "Nothin' for Nothin," and "There Must Be Something Better Than Love," which she sang in the Theatre Guild operetta *Arms and the Girl*. She also contributed to a Decca album of songs from this musical, in which she played the role of an escaped Virginia slave.

"My greatest admiration," wrote reviewer Wolcott Gibbs in the *New Yorker* (February 11, 1950), "is reserved for Miss Bailey." Richard L. Coe wrote that she took over the show "the way no other performer manages to do" (Washington *Post*, January 8, 1950).

PEARL BAILEY

When the Broadway revue *Bless You All* opened in December 1950, Brooks Atkinson, drama critic for the New York *Times* (December 15, 1950), called the humor "only tepidly funny," but wrote that "Pearl Bailey . . . can make a ballad take on a piquant personality."

Her engagements between 1950 and 1954 were at the Latin Quarter, Boston; Capitol Theatre, Greenwich Village Inn, and La Vie en Rose, New York; Ciro's, Hollywood, California; the Desert Inn, and Flamingo at Las Vegas, Nevada; and several clubs in London, England.

A critic for *Variety* (June 4, 1952) wrote of her performance at La Vie en Rose, "Gone are those extraneous gestures which used to over-emphasize Miss Bailey's lyrics, and in their place is a more potent comedy effect that she achieves by understatement."

Chosen for the role of Carmen's friend, Miss Bailey was filmed by Twentieth Century-Fox in *Carmen Jones*, which starred Dorothy Dandridge, the screen version of Georges Bizet's opera set in Florida with a Negro cast using colloquial English. Bosley Crowther, reviewer for the New York *Times* (October 29, 1954), called the film "not so much poignant as it is lurid and lightly farcical."

In Truman Capote's Broadway musical *House of Flowers*, which opened at New York's Alvin Theatre on December 30, 1954, Miss Bailey was the star performer in the role of Madame Fleur. The New York *Times* critic wrote that she "has an amusing style but feeble material . . . throwing away songs with smart hauteur and strutting imposingly." Among her songs, a number of which she included in a record album is "What is a Friend For?" The play closed after 181 performances.

Among television programs in which she has been featured are *Colgate Summer Comedy Hour; Toast of the Town*; Milton Berle's

BAILEY, PEARL—*Continued*

show; *What's My Line?* and *The Name's the Same.* Because of her fondness for ad-libbing she admits that she has had "the most fun playing vaudeville" (*World-Telegram and Sun*, February 5, 1955). Harold Arlen, composer of the music in *House of Flowers*, considers that Pearl has one of the great natural voices. On her comic talent, Robert W. Dana (New York *World-Telegram and Sun*, January 12, 1954) commented: "This gal is so loaded with natural wit, which she throws out with no trace of stinginess in rambling asides" that she is "one of the mightiest of song stylists."

Pearl Bailey married Louis Bellson, Jr., a drummer in popular bands, in London, England on November 19, 1952, after securing a divorce from John Randolph Pinkett, Jr., on March 20, 1952, whom she had married August 31, 1948. She likes to read and write verse, enjoys music (especially when sung by Ella Fitzgerald or Frank Sinatra), and hopes to have a dramatic part in a serious play. She has been described as a tall, sylph-like, handsome girl, with a haunting voice.

On March 29, 1955 Pearl Bailey was voted Queen of Columbia University's Show and presented with a plaque for "the outstanding musical comedy performance of the year." Reviewing the Columbia LP record of songs from *House of Flowers,* the New York *Times* (April 10, 1955) commented on "the assured singing of Pearl Bailey, whose clear, calm enunciation must make her the lyric writer's dream."

References

N Y Herald Tribune p19 Mr 21 '52
N Y Post p2-M Ja 16 '55
N Y Sunday News II p2 F 13 '55
N Y World-Telegram Mag p2 F 5 '55
Vogue 108:140 Ag '46

BANNISTER, CONSTANCE Feb. 11, 1919- Photographer

Address: b. 24 Central Park S., New York 19; h. Cold Spring Rd., Syosset, N.Y.

A specialist in photographing babies, Constance Bannister has taken more than 100,000 pictures of the younger generation which have brought her world-wide recognition. Bannister babies, usually accompanied by amusing captions, are featured in books, magazines and pamphlets, and on calendars, billboards and other advertising media. Her latest book is *Puppy and Me* (Rand McNally, 1955). She has made several film shorts and has appeared on numerous radio and television programs. Her comic strip, "Baby Banters," was a popular syndicated feature for six years.

Constance Bannister was born Constance Gibbs in Ashland City, Tennessee, February 11, 1919, the tenth child of Arthur Thomas and Bessie Lorraine (Jackson) Gibbs. There were fourteen children in the family, nine girls and five boys. Her father was engaged in farming and real-estate ventures. Constance—known to most of her friends as "Connie"—attended school in Ashland and wanted to be an artist. After a friend gave her a camera, she became enthusiastic about photography. She went to New York in 1937, determined to earn her way through art school, and enrolled at the New York School of Applied Design.

A few months later, she transferred to the School of Modern Photography, and later studied at the New York Institute of Photography. Her first job with a camera was with the Associated Press as society photographer, and she was sent to Florida during the 1938-1939 season. An opportunity to photograph the cast of *Ice Capades* on the West Coast came soon after Miss Bannister returned to New York, and while in California she worked on several film shorts.

In the 1940's she photographed numerous glamor girls and sold many of her photographs to national magazines. "Glamor Goes To War" by J. C. Furnas (*Saturday Evening Post,* November 29, 1941) was illustrated with photographs by Constance Bannister. Enthusiastic letters-to-the-editor resulted in an assignment to photograph a ballet series.

During World War II, she made photographs for war bond posters and contributed her services to USO by doing camera stories. Many of her glamor-girl photographs became "pin-up girls." No one had thought of "pin-up babies" until Miss Bannister tried a few. One of her baby pictures which had been reproduced in a national magazine was found in the possession of a German soldier captured by a U.S. infantry group. The *March of Time* featured the incident in one of its films, and thereafter, Miss Bannister was firmly established as a baby photographer.

After her appearance in *Babies By Bannister* (Columbia Pictures), a movie short, she was interviewed on the subject of "How To Shoot A Baby" (*American Magazine,* January 1944) and related that she could get almost any expression she wanted by following a baby's antics and waiting for surprise expressions.

She supplied "Bannister Baby" covers to the Chicago *Tribune* Graphic Section for several years, and in 1946, started a comic strip called "Baby Banters" (Transworld Features). The strip ran in about fifty newspapers throughout the country twice a week for about six years. Miss Bannister said that she gave it up because it consumed too much time.

Parents sought studio portraits of their infants because of Miss Bannister's ability to get unusual expressions and paid as much as $500 for a picture. A growing demand for baby covers by national magazines kept her hunting for photogenic babies. Clapp's Baby Food, Heinz, Borden, Hood's Milk, Gerber's, Beechnut and Johnson & Johnson selected Bannister babies to advertise their products, and Bannister Enterprises was established in 1948.

Bannister's Bantering Babies, a movie short, was released by Warner Brothers in 1948, and a series of baby calendars was launched. A week-by-week engagement book (Edward Stern and Company, Philadelphia) with fifty-two baby portraits with humorous seasonal captions written by Miss Bannister has appeared yearly since 1950. A. S. Barnes and Company of New York and Brown and Bigelow of St. Paul, Minnesota have also featured Bannister baby calendars.

Miss Bannister's first book *A Child's Grace* (E. P. Dutton and Co., 1945) was a prayer book for juveniles, and used by churches. *The Baby* (Golden Series, Simon and Schuster, 1950) was captioned as "A photographic inquiry into certain private opinions." A selection of photographs from *Senator, I'm Glad You Asked Me That!* (American Binder Co.), a satire on Senate investigating committees, was reproduced by the *Saturday Evening Post* (May 31, 1952) and presented as "taken during the N I C (Nursery Investigating Committee's) inquiry." Miss Bannister was praised for "outstanding camera work among exclusive members of the Safety-pin Set." *We Were Spies Behind The Iron Curtain* (American Binder Co., 1953), a paper-bound book of grimacing baby pictures, was reprinted in a series of booklets by the U.S. Information Service in Vienna, and caused "repercussions" in Communist countries because of the pert-faced infants and satirical adult captions.

Librari-anna (Columbia University Press), a pamphlet issued for distribution at the American Library Association's 1952 Conference to introduce Columbia's newest publications, displayed twenty-two Bannister babies as librarians and library patrons in distinctive poses with humorous captions by Jeanne and Bob Holmes. *Let's Face It* (Brown and Bigelow, 1954)—another pamphlet—illustrated the hopes and disillusionments of party-givers-and-goers via Bannister babies in whimsical attitudes. In *Puppy and Me* (Rand McNally, 1955) Miss Bannister introduced her two dogs—"Duchess" a female boxer and "Balloon-Head" a poodle—as pals for some of her favorite babies.

Fifty-two Bannister babies, in familiar card-table attitudes decorated a novelty deck of cards, that is expected to be Brown and Bigelow's top "remembrance" item in 1956, after advertisers have filled in the blank TV screens on the backs of the cards. She has patented a true-to-life baby doll, manufactured by the Sun Rubber Company, Barberton, Ohio.

Miss Bannister has made frequent appearances as Baby Editor on the Arlene Frances *Home* show (WRCA-TV). She appeared on Dave Garroway's *Today* program on May 3, 1955, and has often discussed her work on other popular TV and radio shows.

She became Mrs. Stephen Arthur Bannister on January 28, 1937, but the marriage ended in divorce in 1940. Her marriage to Air Force Captain Charles G. Fredericks took place in 1946 and she was divorced seven years later.

Miss Bannister divides her time between an apartment-studio in New York and a studio-home in Syosset, Long Island, which she calls a "miniature country club for children," and was described to Joan Cook (New York *Herald Tribune,* August 26, 1953) as a "former sports cottage on an estate" with a tennis court, swimming pool, a playyard with swings and slides and an indoor squash court. Miss Bannister said that she "discovers" most of her baby models in local stores and nearby Levittown.

CONSTANCE BANNISTER

Described as a "bundle of energy" and a "photogenic photographer," Miss Bannister is five feet four inches tall and a little "plump," has light brown hair and brown eyes and a Southern accent. Although she is a Republican, she says that her interest is in the "right" man, rather than the party. She attends St. Bartholomew's Episcopal Church.

An enthusiastic tennis-player and ball-room dancer, Miss Bannister has won prizes in each of these activities, and is especially proud of a silver trophy tennis award, given by the Bath and Tennis Club, Palm Beach, Florida. She is a member of the Sea Spray Club in Palm Beach, and of the Atlantic Beach Club of Long Beach, Long Island. A keen interest in sewing and design led to several devices to simplify dress and hat-making. She has also invented gadgets for her cameras, and has patented one of them.

"If I had my life to live over," she confided, "I would be an architect and plan simple houses for simple, easy living."

References

N Y Herald Tribune p12 Ag 26 '53
Sat Eve Post 224:120 My 31 '52 por
Who's Who in America, 1954-1955

BARNES, HENRY A. Dec. 16, 1906- Traffic director

Address: b. c/o Department of Traffic Engineering, 413 St. Paul Pl., Baltimore 2, Md.; h. 4904 Woodside Rd., Baltimore 29, Md.

"As the number of automobiles in use increases by the millions every year," said Henry A. Barnes, traffic expert, "cities cannot wait for the costly construction of more expressways and freeways. The traffic engineer must squeeze the last ounce of efficiency out of existing thoroughfares." Since July 1953 he has

HENRY A. BARNES

been traffic director of the city of Baltimore, Maryland, where he has introduced many modern devices and electronic controls for eliminating traffic accidents and automobile congestion.

When director of traffic engineering in Denver, Colorado (1947 to 1953) and in Flint, Michigan (1941 to 1947), Barnes was credited with major improvements in traffic conditions in those cities. He utilized, he says, "the same basic tools: paint (lots of it); signs (many thousands); modern traffic signals; no-parking rules; one-way streets; law enforcement; modern street lighting systems; public relations; and redesign of streets to meet present standards" (*The Lamp*, November 1954).

Barnes firmly believes that "there's more traffic control in a pail of paint than in anything else you can name. Here in Baltimore they used to use maybe 2,500 gallons of paint a year. This year I'm going to use close to 20,000 gallons." He even uses weighted empty paint cans instead of concrete "islands" to help unscramble traffic at intersections (*Business Week*, May 29, 1954).

Henry A. Barnes was born in Newark, New York on December 16, 1906, the son of Herman Myron and Maude Louise (Henion) Barnes. His father, of English ancestry, was a house painter, and his mother, of Dutch descent, had worked as a secretary. Young Barnes was reared in his native town and in Daytona Beach, Florida. He attended Washington High School in Newark, but left school to go to work for the New York Central Railroad as a laborer in its car repair shop in his home town in 1921. During the next year he studied electrical engineering in night classes and later declared: "I practiced in the shop as much as possible of the engineering I learned" (*The Lamp,* November 1954).

While in the electrical contracting business at Daytona Beach, between 1922 and 1926, Barnes began studying traffic problems by driving a taxicab. He was influenced in his choice of a career by Henry Osborne, a traffic engineer in Buffalo, New York, and by D. Grant Mickle, a traffic engineer with the Automotive Safety Foundation in Washington, D.C.

When he moved to Flint, Michigan in 1926 to work for an electrical contracting firm, he continued his night schooling at the General Motors Institute of Technology there. Extending his night school education over more than twenty years, he later took graduate courses at the University of Michigan and Michigan State College.

After two years with the Flint electrical contracting firm, and a similar period with an automobile production concern in that city, Barnes went into business for himself as a cabinet maker in 1930. His next position was with the Flint Chevrolet Motor Company in 1933, working as maintenance electrician in its engine plant, until he was laid off in 1937.

He found temporary work in the Flint Police Department as signal engineer and "learned the policeman's viewpoint, too" (*The Lamp*, November 1954). From 1941 to 1947 he was captain of the police as well as traffic engineer in the department. He was largely responsible for installing a modern street lighting system that was reflected in lowered automobile insurance rates. Between 1942 and 1945 he was Federal war transportation administrator for Genesee county, Michigan.

Barnes left Flint in 1947 to take the post of traffic director in Denver, Colorado for $7,500 a year, 50 per cent more than his previous salary. He raised the city's traffic engineering budget from about $6,000 to $500,000 annually, and increased the traffic capacity on several streets from a few hundred cars to 2,000 automobiles an hour. During his first year there, motor accidents in Denver causing personal injury decreased 40 per cent, and traffic deaths declined 30 per cent.

"A great deal of the improvement came about simply by using paint—ten times as much paint as Denver had used before," Barnes wrote in his article "How To Untie Traffic Knots" (*The Lamp*, November 1954). He also erected 20,000 new traffic signs, and installed 180 miles of through streets and seventy-two miles of one-way streets, replacing a previous number of ten.

Because Barnes believes it is unsafe to mix cars and people at a crossing, he introduced at busy Denver corners what is known as the "Barnes Dance," although he is not the inventor and the "Dance" was originally used in Kansas City. This permits pedestrians to cross in any direction during an interval in which all traffic lights at the intersection are red. In the first year of its use in Denver, it not only created a speed-up in the movement of motor traffic, but reduced pedestrian deaths at crossings from seven to none.

Convinced that "traffic by its nature is unpredictable" and that "the fixed-time signal . . . piles up chaos and more chaos," Barnes instituted signals that continually adjust themselves to the flow and density of traffic in response to an electronic "master" controller. This "cycle-selector" or electronic brain, capable of supervising traffic lights over a large area including 120 intersections, contains five miles of wire and 30,000 electrical connections, and its construction took two years at a cost of $115,000. Previously, the largest such master-built device handled only twenty intersections. Regarding the Denver installation, Barnes observed: "One hundred and twenty traffic cops, even if gifted with extrasensory perception, could not begin to do as well" (*The Lamp*, November 1954).

Barnes is said to have "complete disregard for precedent and red tape" (*Business Week*, May 29, 1954). In accepting the $18,000-a-year post of traffic director in Baltimore (which makes him the highest salaried traffic engineer in the world), Barnes requested and received "freedom from political interference" (New York *Times*, May 26, 1953). He also obtained job security in the form of a minimum four-year term.

"Hank" Barnes took up his duties as traffic commissioner in Baltimore on July 15, 1953, facing the pride and tradition of a more than 200-year-old city, where he described the traffic-signal system as "probably among the most antiquated of any city in the country" (*American City*, September 1954). His traffic engineering department, replacing a former traffic commission, was set up as an independent unit on equal standing with other major departments in the city, and having 129 employees and a Bureau of Special Services that cooperates with the police, school authorities, highway engineers, city councilmen and other public officials.

"Our liaison man with the schools," Barnes advises, "is placing more 'push-button' traffic signals where children can reach the button to give themselves a green light for crossing the street" (*The Lamp*, November 1954). "More efficient mass transportation," Barnes believes, is another solution to city traffic congestion. He contends that congestion in American cities cannot be eliminated "until we help the transit companies to attract more riders and thus take more private cars off the streets at rush hours" (The *Lamp*, November 1954).

In order to modernize Baltimore's traffic system, Barnes raised the traffic budget from $460,000 in 1953 to $2,000,000 a year in 1955. According to *Newsweek* (December 27, 1954), "most Baltimoreans gagged on Barnes' medicine, but then felt better." His requests for the removal of view-obstructing monuments or street-narrowing shade trees, and the replacement of feeble but picturesque gas lamps with adequate street lights produced written complaints from citizens that he lacked "soul." His painting of traffic signal towers a bright yellow, evoked the comment: "Now you can see them a mile away!" (*The Lamp,* November 1954).

Convinced that the success of any traffic program needs public cooperation and understanding, he now conducts weekly television and radio programs in which he interviews members of the public and answers telephone inquiries and complaints. In this way, he finds, citizens recognize the need for changing their driving habits, or surrendering parking privileges and traditions. "Lots of folks who were out of sorts with all Hank's innovating have become his firm supporters just through hearing him talk," reported *Business Week* (May 29, 1954), "and he's never afraid to admit it if he makes a mistake."

In an address on September 21, 1953 to the joint meeting of the United States Conference of Mayors and the Canadian Federation of Mayors and Municipalities at Montreal, Barnes warned that neglect of the problem of city traffic congestion would bring "huge economic losses and material depreciation of United States and Canadian cities" (New York *Times,* September 22, 1953).

The traffic director holds a citation from the Civitan Club, Denver, commending his bringing "order out of chaos in the city's traffic pattern" (*Business Week,* May 29, 1954). He received the Distinguished Service Award for his World War II transportation work from former president Harry S. Truman. Among his organization memberships are the American Institute of Electrical Engineers, the Illuminating Engineering Society, the Institute of Traffic Engineers and the Highway Research Board. He is a Mason and a member of the Methodist Church. Colleagues call him "reasonable, incisive and fair" (*Business Week,* May 29, 1954).

Henry A. Barnes married Hazel Mae Stone on September 1, 1928, and their children are William Henry and Virginia Nancy. The traffic director, who smokes several cigars a day, is five feet nine inches tall and weighs 168 pounds. He has blue eyes and gray hair. "Hank" Barnes enjoys photography, model railroading and cabinet making. He has a fine sense of humor and is a popular speaker at club meetings.

References

Bsns W p150+ My 29 '54
N Y Times p5 My 26 '53
Newsweek 44:20+ D 27 '54
Time 61:28 Mr 16 '53

BARRYMORE, LIONEL Apr. 28, 1878-Nov. 15, 1954 Actor noted for his character parts; brother of John and Ethel Barrymore, with whom he acted on stage and screen; made his stage debut (1893) with Louisa Drew, his grandmother; studied painting in Paris; made his first stage hit in *The Mummy and the Humming Bird* (1903) with his uncle, John Drew; wrote scenarios for D. W. Griffith; started his motion picture career in the Biograph Studio in New York; he played stage role of Colonel Ibbetson in *Peter Ibbetson* (1917); other Broadway successes included *The Copperhead* (1918); *The Jest* (1919); *Macbeth* (1921); won an Academy Award (1931) for his movie role in *Free Soul*; his notable screen roles were in talking pictures: *Grand Hotel*; *Reunion in Vienna*; *Dinner at Eight*; *Treasure Island*; *David Copperfield* and with his sister and brother in *Rasputin*

BARRYMORE, LIONEL—*Continued*
and the Empress; played role of Dr. Gillespie in the *Dr. Kildare* radio series; his interpretation of Scrooge in Dickens' *Christmas Carol* became a yearly Christmas radio feature; also received recognition for his artistic and musical achievements; elected to the Society of Etchers, and in 1944 his symphony, *Partita*, was performed; wrote theme song for radio program, *Mayor of the Town* in which he was starred. See *Current Biography*, (July) 1943.

Obituary

N Y Times p1+ N 16 '54

BAXTER, FRANK C(ONDIE) May 4, 1896- University professor; television personality

Address: b. c/o University of Southern California, Los Angeles 7, Calif.; c/o Columbia Broadcasting System, Hollywood, Calif.; h. 1614 Camden Parkway, South Pasadena, Calif.

Thanks to the popularity of a series of lectures called *Shakespeare on TV*, Dr. Frank C. Baxter "may take the credit for making the entire nation aware of the fact that teaching is being done on television and done highly effectively," stated William Cumming in *This is Educational Television* (1954). Baxter, for many years recognized as one of the world's great teachers, has been on the faculty of the University of Southern California since 1930. His award-winning televised lectures on Shakespeare were first presented over KNXT, a CBS station in Los Angeles, in September 1953 and were later seen elsewhere in the country by kinescope recording.

While *Shakespeare on TV* was still being shown in the East on WCBS-TV, Baxter in August 1954 gave the opening lecture of a new weekly series, *Now and Then*, in which he drew on the literary heritage of the world. Critics, commenting on his wit, enthusiasm and skillful presentation of his subject, have suggested that the TV industry can learn from Baxter on how to stimulate the viewer's imagination.

Frank Condie Baxter, the son of Frank C. Baxter, a salesman and Lillian Douglas (Murdoch) Baxter, was born in Newbold, New Jersey on May 4, 1896. He spent part of his early life in Pennsylvania and was employed from 1912 to 1917 by the Pennsylvania Salt Manufacturing Company in Philadelphia. Following his discharge from the Army Medical Corps at the end of World War I, he was about to return to the salt company; "but," he says, "I decided to do what I had always really wanted to do."

He therefore enrolled at the University of Pennsylvania, and during part of the time he studied for his B.A. degree, he worked as assistant instructor in zoology (1922-1923). In the summers of 1920, 1921 and 1924 he engaged in scientific research in California's Painted Desert area, as assistant to Dr. Harold S. Colton. With Colton he wrote a guide called *Days in the Painted Desert and the San Francisco Mountains*, published in 1932 by the Northern Arizona Society of Science and Art.

Interested also in dramatics, he acted in about thirty plays during his undergraduate years. He was elected to Phi Beta Kappa and was graduated *summa cum laude* in 1923. Remaining at the university as an instructor in English, he took courses for the M.A. degree, conferred in 1925. For the next two years he taught classes in English at both the University of Pennsylvania and Swarthmore College. He then studied and taught for a year (1929-1930) at the University of California in Berkeley before going to England for further graduate courses. He was granted his Ph.D. degree in 1932 by Trinity College, Cambridge University.

Baxter's association with the University of Southern California in Los Angeles had begun in 1930, when he accepted an appointment as assistant professor of English. In 1934 he became associate professor and since 1937 has been full professor. (He served in 1947 as chairman of the university senate.) Aside from Elizabethan literature, particularly Shakespeare's writings, Baxter's special fields of interest have been humor, the novel, and the history of printing. He has made several miniature models of early printing presses.

"I went into teaching because I thought it was the most exciting thing in the world," Baxter told Don Ross of the New York *Herald Tribune* (November 7, 1954). Well liked by U.S.C.'s students, he was voted the man "who should teach all the classes in the university." *Time* (December 26, 1949) in discussing the popularity of his traditional Christmas readings at U.S.C., quoted the university's daily *Trojan*, "If you haven't taken a course from Dr. Baxter, you haven't been to college."

In a program called *Southern California Summer Session*, heard over CBS's station KNXT in Los Angeles, the university in the summer of 1953 began presenting a college-level course which viewers could take for college credit. Professor Baxter appeared on the last three telecasts of the season to introduce his fall credit course. The course that he then gave weekly on TV, in addition to teaching four English classes at the university, began on September 26, 1953. It was filmed in a studio classroom attended by about fifteen of the 332 students who registered for the course for credit. Many other students registered to take the course without credit.

Shakespeare on TV, as the course was named, consisted of eighteen lectures (forty-five minutes long) covering eight of Shakespeare's plays and including discussions of such related subjects as the Elizabethan theatre. The plays considered were *King Lear, Richard II, Romeo and Juliet, Twelfth Night, Henry V, Much Ado About Nothing, Othello* and *Hamlet*. By the end of the first semester, Baxter had an audience of some 750,000 persons (*Life*, December 7, 1953), giving his program a higher rating locally than many popular commercial shows. Los Angeles' educational TV station

KTHE, which went on the air in December 1953, ran kinescopes of *Shakespeare on TV* twice a week, while KNXT was still carrying the live program. It was also made available to other educational TV stations and institutions.

Baxter's lectures on Shakespeare won ten major national and regional awards, including the 1953 Sylvania award for educational television and the Ohio State University award in the field of "systematic instruction: telecourse." The Academy of Television Arts and Sciences awarded an "Emmy" statuette to Baxter in 1954 as best local male performer and another to the program for public service. On April 22, 1955 Baxter received an engraved medallion with a bas-relief of Shakespeare from the American Shakespeare Festival for his television lectures on the times and the work of the bard.

Commenting on the success of *Shakespeare on TV* a few months after its premiere, John Crosby said, "It has always been my theory that great teachers would make wonderful (and popular) TV personalities just like great comedians." Dr. Baxter, he continued, has the two gifts of a good teacher—"an imposing command of his material and a great love of his subject" (New York *Herald Tribune,* November 16, 1953).

When some of the lectures were presented on CBS television network by kinescope recording, in a weekly series beginning June 1954, they were widely praised in the East. "Here is a man," observed Jack Gould, "who takes the curse off the word 'education' itself and shows that learning can be made one of the most stimulating and amusing experiences open to the TV viewer" (New York *Times,* June 20, 1954).

Now and Then, Dr. Baxter's first "live" TV network series, which originates from KNXT, began on August 1, 1954 and was concluded in May 1955. The weekly half-hour Sunday program has been described as "an exploration of the world's literary heritage," in which Baxter talks about whatever has been of particular interest and enjoyment in his lifetime of reading. Scottish and English ballads, the first folio edition of Shakespeare's writings, Anglo-Saxon literature, and the poetry of Donne, Browning, and Whitman are a few of the subjects he considers. He reads as much as possible from the books he discusses, first setting the scene for a passage and often interrupting his reading to comment on a word or line. Among the visual aids that he uses are a model of a Shakespearean theatre, a model of a Viking ship, small figures, maps, pictures and charts. He offers his viewers a reading list to guide them in further study. On July 3 Baxter returned to CBS-TV with a ten-week program, *Shakespeare on TV.*

In seeking to convey to his audience the sense of excitement that the past evokes in him, Baxter "does not over-popularize his material for the sake of the multitudes," Rod Nordell pointed out. "He is aiming not for high-brows, not for the vulgar, but for the middle mass

FRANK C. BAXTER

'who haven't read enough and know it.' On his opening program he warned, 'If you don't invest your imagination, it will be a pretty blank experience' " (*Christian Science Monitor,* August 24, 1954). Harriet Van Horne of the New York *World-Telegram and Sun* (June 29, 1954) remarked, "This is not ersatz education, sugar frosted. This is real!"

Television, Baxter believes, is a great teaching tool, but not a substitute for classroom instruction, which enables students to ask questions." Nor can television replace reading," he says. "Education—which should never stop just because you have left school—is only achieved in our time by reading. Good talk is fine, but conversation and even direct experience can only teach you the history of the moment. They can never give you the depth and perspective that acquaintance with the experience of the past can give" (*Christian Science Monitor,* February 3, 1954).

Dr. Baxter belongs to the American Association of University Professors and to the Phi Kappa Phi and Beta Sigma Tau fraternities. He is chairman of the Democratic Committee of South Pasadena. His church is the Baptist.

He and his wife, the former Lydia Spencer Morris, who were married on May 28, 1927, have two children, Lydia Morris and Francis Condic. The U.S.C. professor has been pictured in the New York *Herald Tribune* as a "tallish, round-faced man . . . with a fringe of sandy hair around a bald head and sparkling blue eyes behind steel-rimmed eyeglasses," and as a "man whose intellectual enthusiasms are infectious."

References

Christian Sci Mon p9 F 3 '54 por
N Y Herald Tribune IV p6 N 7 '54
Time 54:30+ D 26 '49 por
Who's Who in America, 1954-55

BEALL, J(AMES) GLENN (bĕl) June 5, 1894- United States Senator from Maryland

Address: b. c/o Senate Office Bldg., Washington 25, D.C.; h. Frostburg, Md.

As chairman of a subcommittee of the United States Senate Banking and Currency Committee, J. Glenn Beall, the junior Senator from Maryland, headed investigations during 1954 into the sharp rise in coffee prices. Since taking his Senate seat in 1953, Beall (Republican) has served on the committees on the District of Columbia, public works, and banking and currency. From 1943 to 1953 he represented the Sixth District of Maryland in the U.S. House of Representatives.

In the first session of the Eighty-fourth Congress (1955), Beall voted to authorize President Eisenhower to take war action, if necessary, in defense of Formosa (January).

Born in Frostburg, Maryland on June 5, 1894, James Glenn Beall is the son of Olin and Florence (Glenn) Beall. He attended public schools and Gettysburg College in Pennsylvania. In 1918 and 1919 he served in the Ordnance Corps of the U.S. Army and was discharged with the rank of sergeant. For many years Beall has been engaged in the insurance and real-estate business in Frostburg and Cumberland in Maryland.

Interested in governmental activities, Beall served as a member of the Allegany County Road Commission from 1923 to 1930. He was a state senator from Allegany county from 1930 to 1934. In 1938 and 1939 he was chairman of the Maryland State Roads Commission.

Elected to the Seventy-eighth Congress in 1942 from the Sixth District (which includes Allegany, Frederick, Garrett, Montgomery, and Washington counties in Maryland), he was re-elected to the Seventy-ninth, Eightieth, Eighty-first and Eighty-second Congresses. During his career in the House he served on the committees on the District of Columbia, flood control, roads, public works and in 1951 on the Select Committee to Conduct a Study and Investigation of the Education, Training, and Loan Guaranty Programs of World War II Veterans.

During the first session of the Seventy-ninth Congress (1945), Representative Beall favored a permanent Committee on Un-American Activities (January), a resolution to submit to the states a constitutional amendment for House participation in the ratification of treaties (May), continuing the subsidy programs of the Reconstruction Finance Corporation (May), an anti-poll tax bill (June), a second appropriation of $1.3 billion for the United Nations Relief and Rehabilitation Administration (December), and the employment-production bill (December). He opposed the extension of the Trade Agreements Act to 1948 (May).

In the following session (1946) Congressman Beall voted "yea" in regard to reasonable profits under ceilings of the Office of Price Administration (April), draft exemption for boys of teen age and fathers (May), overriding the veto of the OPA bill (June), and an amendment to an UNRRA appropriation bill to prohibit relief in any country which censors news accounts of UNRRA activities (June). Beall voted "nay" on extending the draft to 1947 (April), $400,000,000 in housing subsidies (May), overriding the Case bill veto (June), and the $3.7 billion loan to Britain (July).

His roll call votes in the first session of the Eightieth Congress (1947) indicate that he voted for submitting to the states a constitutional amendment limiting the Presidency to two terms (February), banning portal-to-portal pay suits (February), extending rent control to February 29, 1948 (May), the Greek-Turkish aid bill (May), and overriding the Taft-Hartley bill (June).

The Congressman was recorded in 1948 as favoring the six-billion-dollar foreign aid authorization (April), overriding the tax-reduction bill veto (April), repealing Federal taxes on oleomargarine (April), overriding the veto of a bill to exclude newspaper and magazine vendors from coverage under the Social Security Act (April); he voted for the tidelands oil bill (April), a subversive activities control bill (May), a one-year extension of the Trade Agreements Act (May), and a displaced persons bill (June).

Proposals which Beall supported in the first session of the Eighty-first Congress (1949) included the extension of the Economic Cooperation Act to July 30, 1950 (April), the Wood bill repealing the Taft-Hartley law (May), eliminating the provision for public housing from the long-range housing bill (June), a bill to support farm prices at 90 per cent of parity (July), a bill to increase the minimum-wage rate (August), and a 50 per cent reduction in European arms aid (August). He opposed the extension of rent controls (March) and the long-range housing bill (June).

Among votes cast by Beall in the second session (1950) were those favoring a Fair Employment Practice Commission without enforcement powers (February), reduction of Federal spending by $600,000,000 (May), overriding the veto of the bill to credit to veterans of World War II in the postal service time spent with the armed forces toward promotion and salary increases (June), and overriding the Communist control bill veto (September). He was against guarantees for private capital invested abroad (July) and the Lodge-Gossett constitutional amendment (July).

The Representative favored in the first session of the Eighty-second Congress (1951) a combination draft-Universal Military Training bill (April), cutting the government's civil payrolls (April), a $10,000,000 reduction for reclamation funds (May), prohibiting the duplication of private power lines (May), and prohibiting the control of commodity margins (July). Beall voted against banning the quota system for livestock slaughtering (July) and reasonable profits under all price ceilings (July).

In the following session (1952) Representative Beall voted "yea" on a measure to cut the appropriation for the Tennessee Valley Authority by $14,000,000 (March), a forty-six-billion-dollar military spending ceiling in 1953 (April), using the Taft-Hartley law to halt the steel strike (June), terminating Federal rent controls on September 30, 1952 except in

Wide World

J. GLENN BEALL

critical defense areas or where local authorities request the continuance of the Federal rent control system (June), and overriding the veto of the immigration bill (June). He voted against ending consumer price controls on June 30, 1952 (June).

On November 4, 1952 Beall was elected to the U.S. Senate for the term ending in January 1959, defeating Democratic Representative Lansdale G. Sasscer of the Fifth Congressional District. The Senate roll call in 1953 includes the following measures which Beall favored: the offshore oil bill (May), an across-the-board cut in appropriations (May), reducing soil conservation payments (June), and penalizing nations trading with the Soviet Union (July). He opposed using foreign aid to cut farm surpluses (July), profits tax relief for small businesses (July) and keeping benefits heretofore given by law in a constitutional amendment insuring equal right to men and women (July).

After the price of green coffee beans had jumped from fifty-seven to seventy-four cents a pound from November 1953 to the end of January 1954, Beall was appointed to head a subcommittee to investigate the situation. The Federal Trade Commission charged the New York Coffee and Sugar Exchange with having "contributed to and promoted" the rise in coffee prices (Washington *Post*, October 11, 1954).

Beall's subcommittee held two days of hearings on October 12 and 13 at which both the FTC and the Coffee Exchange were represented. At this time Beall estimated that increases in the price of coffee had cost the American public $293,000,000 in the first eight months of 1954. The subcommittee attributed the high prices to a frost in Brazil in July 1953, inadequate crop reporting and alleged irregularities on the Coffee Exchange.

On January 4, 1955 it recommended that the cost of coffee "be determined by factors of supply and demand in a free economy" instead of putting coffee futures trading under governmental regulation (New York *Times*, January 5, 1955). By the middle of February 1955 prices of coffee had returned to approximately the same level at which they had been in November 1953.

A strong opponent of the St. Lawrence seaway before its approval by Congress on May 6, 1954, Beall said: "The seaway would not contribute to national defense but on the contrary, in time of war, would be a defense liability. With its two dams and some fifteen locks it would be most vulnerable to bombing or sabotage, and could be put out of commission for long periods of time" (New York *Times*, January 12, 1954).

Beall's voting record during 1954 showed that he opposed the Bricker constitutional amendment limiting the treaty-making powers of the President (February), an amendment to the wool subsidy bill maintaining 90 per cent farm price supports (April), adding $35,000,000 to the Rural Electrification Administration's loan authority (June), an amendment to substitute a liberalized three-year trade act for the administration's one-year trade act extension bill (June), an amendment to increase income tax exemptions from $600 to $700 (June), cutting $500 million from the foreign aid bill (August), an amendment to make membership in the Communist party a crime (August), and an amendment attaching a postal rate increase to a bill raising the pay of Federal employees (August).

Among measures favored by the Senator in 1954 were a one billion dollar excise tax cut (March), a constitutional amendment limiting membership of the Supreme Court to nine justices (May), the atomic energy bill (July); he also voted for an amendment to the foreign aid bill forbidding the use of funds to stimulate strategic mineral production abroad (July), the foreign aid bill (August), the farm bill (August), and condemning the conduct of Senator Joseph R. McCarthy (Republican of Wisconsin) on two counts (December).

In the present Congress he was one of thirty-four Senators who sponsored a home rule bill for the District of Columbia. On January 18, 1955 he was named chairman of the business and commerce subcommittee of the Senate District of Columbia Committee.

The Senator is a Mason (Knight Templar), Shriner, Elk, Eagle, Knight of Pythias, and Rotarian. Married to Margaret Schwarzenbach on September 15, 1926, Beall is the father of three sons.

References

Washington (D.C.) Post p1B Ap 27 '52
Biographical Directory of the American Congress, 1774-1949 (1950)
Who's Who in America, 1954-55
Who's Who in United States Politics (1952)
World Biography (1954)

BEARDSLEY, WILLIAM S(HANE) May 13, 1901-Nov. 21, 1954 Governor of Iowa; received Ph.G. degree from Bowen Institute of Pharmacy and Chemistry (Brunswick, Missouri); operated a drugstore in New Virginia, Iowa (1922-1938) and a 900-acre farm there since 1938; member of Iowa State Senate (1932-1940) and Iowa House of Representatives (1947-1948); became governor of Iowa in 1949; planned to retire at end of third term in January 1955; advocated increased state appropriations for the public schools and conservation of soil and water resources. See *Current Biography* (June) 1950.

Obituary

N Y Times p1 N 22 '54

BEAUCHAMP, MRS. ANTONY *See* Churchill, Sarah

BEINUM, EDUARD (ALEXANDER) VAN (bā'nŭm) Sept. 3, 1900- Conductor

Address: b. c/o Columbia Artists Management, 113 W. 57th St., New York 19; h. Joh. Verhulststraat 37, Amsterdam, the Netherlands

A warm welcome was given to Eduard van Beinum, the conductor of Amsterdam's famous Concertgebouw Orchestra, by critics, musicians, and audiences when he made his North American debut with the Philadelphia Orchestra in January 1954. He returned to the United States in October 1954 and brought with him the entire 101-man Concertgebouw for a good-will tour.

American critics were almost unanimous in acclaiming van Beinum, long admired in Europe, as one of the most talented conductors of our time. Winthrop Sargeant wrote in the *New Yorker* that he seems "to be in direct control of more musical detail than any conductor in recent memory except Toscanini."

In describing the Concertgebouw, with which van Beinum has been associated since 1931, American critics compared its "mellow" qualities to those of Rembrandt's paintings and well-aged wine. While in the United States, the orchestra played over forty concerts in the East, South and Middle West and performed at the United Nations in New York at the invitation of Dr. E. N. van Kleffens, president of the ninth General Assembly meeting. Rafael Kubelik also conducted the orchestra during the tour.

Eduard Alexander van Beinum was born on September 3, 1900 in Arnhem, a town in the eastern part of the Netherlands. He is the son of Eduard Alexander van Beinum and the former Antonia Polman and has four sisters and one brother. Young Eduard's father, grandfather and great-grandfather were musicians. His brother, who is a violinist and choir conductor, gave Eduard his first lessons on the violin and piano.

Eduard attended the Arnhem Hoogere Burger School. At seventeen he was playing the violin with the Arnhem Philharmonic Orchestra. A year later he went to the Conservatorium Musick in Amsterdam, where he studied harmony and composition under Sem Dresden and piano under de Pauw.

Van Beinum began his professional career as a pianist, but gradually gave up both violin and piano to concentrate on conducting. He led the Schiedam and Zutphen choirs and then was engaged in 1927 as conductor of the Haarlem Orchestra. He served simultaneously as conductor of the Haarlem Roman Catholic Choir.

In 1931 van Beinum was invited to go to Amsterdam as "second" conductor of the Concertgebouw. The "first" conductor at the time was the famous Willem Mengelberg. Van Beinum was promoted to "first" conductor in 1938, and when Mengelberg retired to Switzerland at the end of World War II, van Beinum was made permanent musical director of the Concertgebouw.

During the years that van Beinum worked under Mengelberg, his reputation grew steadily. In addition to working with the Concertgebouw, he was a guest conductor with other orchestras throughout Europe. In 1937 he made a tour of the Soviet Union with the Leningrad Philharmonic Orchestra.

He is the third full-time conductor the Concertgebouw has had since its founding under the direction of Willem Kes in 1888. (The orchestra is named after the hall in which it plays—Concert Gebouw means Concert Hall—and receives financial aid from the national, provincial and municipal governments.) The Concertgebouw has been host to such guest conductors as Bruno Walter, Pierre Monteux, and Leopold Stokowski. Celebrated composers who have directed their own works with the orchestra include Debussy, Mahler, Ravel, Schönberg, Hindemith, Elgar, and Richard Strauss.

Under van Beinum's leadership, the Concertgebouw has played in many European countries and at the Edinburgh Music Festival. The Dutch maestro is frequently sought after for guest performances. His guest appearances with the London Royal Philharmonic Orchestra were so popular that he was appointed "first" conductor of that group in 1949, a post which he held until the strain of commuting to London between Amsterdam performances became too great.

The Concertgebouw's regular season is strenuous. The orchestra averages a hundred concerts a year, playing three or four times a week during the eight-month season. In recent years the Concertgebouw under van Beinum has made numerous recordings. These are available on London, Decca, HMV, Columbia, and Epic labels.

Van Beinum was a little uncertain how the orchestra members would withstand their 7,000-mile itinerary in the United States. "In Amsterdam," he explained, "the musician who lives farthest from the hall is just fifteen minutes away on a bicycle. Once every three weeks we go to The Hague for a concert—a forty-three minute trip. The next day, the orchestra is very tired" (*Time,* January 18, 1954).

If "barnstorming" was a strain on the orchestra, it was not reflected in their playing. Rarely have the American critics been so much in accord in their enthusiasm. The Concertgebouw's Carnegie Hall debut in October made an auspicious start with what one critic called "the finest performance of the 'Star-Spangled Banner' [he had] ever heard."

In comparing van Beinum's "superb instrument," as Stokowski has called the Concertgebouw, with the best American orchestras, critics noticed in the Amsterdam group "a mellow and well-aged quality our own orchestras seldom achieve," "a more relaxed manner of playing," and a more "meticulous attention to finespun detail." The difference was one of emphasis, between "tradition" in the European group and "showmanship" in this country, Miles Kastendieck concluded (*Christian Science Monitor,* October 23, 1954). *Time* commented: "The Concertgebouw made less noise than the best U.S. orchestras, and its climaxes were never ear-piercing. Rather, it seemed to inhale smoothly, reach its peaks easily, then relax with a sigh instead of an exhausted gasp."

In an interview with Howard Taubman, van Beinum remarked on this difference himself. Speaking of the Philadelphia Orchestra, he observed, "Its members have more flexibility than those of our orchestras in Europe . . . more skill and virtuosity . . . a conductor of character could take such an orchestra and mold it to his heart's desire, whereas units like the Concertgebouw and the Vienna Philharmonic could not have their essential qualities recast even by a conductor of tremendous personality" (New York *Times,* October 10, 1954).

Van Beinum does not use a baton in conducting, and his economy of gesture has been widely noticed. He is a "no-fuss-no-muss sort of musician who gets what he wants with a minimum of exertion," Harvey Taylor observed (Detroit *Times*). Olin Downes called him "one of the most skillful and polished conductors we have heard in seasons . . . he gains his effects without superfluous gesticulation and he is fortunately without the mannerisms of an actor on the podium" (New York *Times*). Winthrop Sargeant commented that van Beinum combined a "meticulous regard for workmanship" with a "great deal of dash and fire" (*New Yorker*).

Although he is partial to the works of Haydn, Mozart, and the modern French, Dutch, and Russian composers, van Beinum is admired for his ability to interpret sympathetically music as diverse as that of Béla Bartók and Anton Bruckner. This accomplishment may reflect in part certain conclusions van Beinum reached when he was ill for some time in 1951.

Confined to his bed, the conductor had time to listen to a great deal of music on the radio. He was "shocked" to discern how many musicians seemed to be projecting themselves rather than the music. Van Beinum had always con-

Godfried de Groot, Amsterdam

EDUARD VAN BEINUM

ducted without a score, but he resolved then that when he went back to work he would always have the printed music before him. Even if he had no need to refer to the music, he felt that its presence would remind the audience, the orchestra, and himself that the prime factor was the composer.

When he led the Philadelphia Orchestra in a Bruckner symphony, a listener marveled that he had never felt so comfortable with Bruckner before. Van Beinum, recalling the comment, said, "That was the best critic I have ever had. Not me—but Bruckner. That is good."

On his arrival in the United States in October 1954, van Beinum was awarded an honorary Doctor of Music degree by Rutgers University, New Brunswick, New Jersey. Previous honors have included designation as an officer of the French Academy, chevalier of the French Legion of Honor and officer of the Netherlands' Order of Orange Nassau. He has also received the Order of the Star of the North (Sweden, 1946) and the Order of the Dannebrog (Denmark, 1946).

Van Beinum, who is five feet nine inches tall and weighs about 150 pounds, has deep-set gray eyes and black hair. He enjoys horseback riding and hunting in his leisure time. He speaks German, French, and English in addition to his native tongue. His reading tastes run to history and books of travel. He is a member of the Roman Catholic Church. He was married on July 12, 1927 to Josepha Antonia Anna Maria Jansen, an accomplished violinist. The van Beinums have two sons, Eduard and Bartolomeus.

References

N Y Times II p9 O 10 '54
Time 51:69 Ap 12 '48; 63:77 Ja 18 '54
Who's Who, 1954

BETHUNE, MARY MCLEOD July 10, 1875-May 18, 1955 Negro educator; co-founder and president (1904-1942) of Bethune-Cookman College (formerly Daytona, Florida, Normal and Industrial School for girls); vice-president of the National Association for the Advancement of Colored People and president of the National Council of Negro Women; was special adviser to President Franklin D. Roosevelt on minority affairs and director of the Division of Negro Affairs in the National Youth Administration; in World War II was special assistant to the Secretary of War for selection of the first Officers' Candidates Schools for WACS. See *Current Biography* (Jan.) 1942.

Obituary

N Y Times p29 My 19 '55

BLAKE, EUGENE CARSON, REV. DR. Nov. 7, 1906- Clergyman; organization official

Address: b. 510 Witherspoon Bldg., Philadelphia 7, Pa.; h. Rittenhouse, Claridge, Philadelphia 3, Pa.

The president of the National Council of Churches of Christ in the United States of America is the Reverend Doctor Eugene Carson Blake, who is known to television audiences since 1953 as the master of ceremonies of the Sunday afternoon half-hour TV religious program, *Frontiers of Faith.* The National Council elected Blake its president to succeed Bishop William C. Martin, on December 2, 1954 for a three-year term. The Council was established in 1950 as a cooperative body (comprised of thirty Protestant and Eastern Orthodox denominations, representing over 35,000,000 adherents) for the purpose of working together in such fields as evangelism, social research, missions, and charity. The group has approved plans for a new $14,000,000 national headquarters on Riverside Drive, New York City.

In its program for peace, Dr. Blake has stated, the National Council of Churches of Christ advocates support for the United Nations, international regulation and reduction of armaments, a workable atoms-for-peace plan, and economic and technical assistance to the world's underdeveloped areas (New York *Times*, January 6, 1955). Its brotherhood month message of 1955 emphasized that "racial prejudice in any and all forms is contrary to the will and the design of God" (New York *Times*, February 5, 1955).

Dr. Blake is also the stated clerk (chief administrative officer) of the General Assembly of the Presbyterian Church in the U.S.A., an office he will hold until 1956. He has held pastorates in Pasadena, California; Albany, New York; and New York City.

Eugene Carson Blake was born in St. Louis, Missouri on November 7, 1906 to Lulu (Carson) and Orville P. Blake. His father held a position on the sales staff of the Inland Steel Company and was an elder in the Presbyterian church. With his brother, Howard, Eugene received Biblical instruction early in life. Eugene attended the Lawrenceville School in New Jersey, where his intellectual interests were stimulated by one of his teachers, Thornton Wilder, who later became a Pulitzer Prize winner.

On entering Princeton University, Blake was active in several undergraduate organizations, played guard on the varsity football teams in 1926 and 1927, winning his letter and the Poe Cup for good sportsmanship. After receiving his A.B. degree, with honors in philosophy, in 1928, Blake was sent by the Presbyterian Board of Foreign Missions as a teacher at Forman Christian College, Lahore (now in Pakistan). The next year (1929-1930) he spent studying at New College, Edinburgh University, the theological college of the Church of Scotland. Returning to the United States, he entered Princeton Theological Seminary to prepare for the ministry. He was awarded his Th.B. degree in 1932.

His first pastorate was an assistantship at St. Nicholas Collegiate Church, New York City, from 1932 to 1935. Blake next accepted a call as pastor of the First Presbyterian Church in Albany, New York, where he remained five years. He also was a visiting lecturer in religion at Williams College, Williamstown, Massachusetts in 1938-1940.

Called to the Pasadena Presbyterian Church, Pasadena, California in 1940, he served for a period of ten years. Under his ministry the church became one of the largest and strongest of its denomination in the country. He also served as pastor of the church's radio station, from which he broadcast regularly. Occidental College in Los Angeles awarded him the D.D. degree in 1941.

When the World Council of Churches was established in 1948, in Amsterdam, the Netherlands, Dr. Blake was a delegate and became a member of the United States conference for the World Council of Churches. The World Council fosters cooperation between 163 different Protestant and Orthodox traditions. Blake also became active in 1950 in the newly created National Council of the Churches of Christ in the U.S.A., the successor to the Federal Council of Churches of Christ in America. He preached at the closing service of consecration of the council's constituting convention in Cleveland, Ohio, and asked for an end of religious competition and denominational rivalries. He later served on several of the council's committees.

The Presbyterian Church in the U.S.A. elected Dr. Blake on May 29, 1951 as the stated clerk of its General Assembly to succeed the late Doctor William Barrow Pugh. Blake, who is serving a five-year term, was unanimously elected at the General Assembly's 163d meeting in Cincinnati, Ohio.

At the meeting the General Assembly also voted against mercy killing as violating the Sixth Commandment and recommended amending its 222-year-old Confession of Faith to allow remarriage by the church of divorced persons "when sufficient penitence for sin and failure is evidenced" (*Pathfinder*, June 13, 1951). This recommendation was later approved by 259 presbyteries, more than the required number necessary for adoption.

As the representative of over 2,500,000 Presbyterians in this country, Dr. Blake sent a letter in November 1951 to Roman Catholic Archbishop Francis Cardinal Spellman of New York City, pledging cooperation with the Roman Catholic Church and people "in our common fight against the inroads of humanistic secularism and the attacks of atheistic communism" (New York *Times,* November 22, 1951). The next month, in reaction to an investigation of officials of the Bureau of Internal Revenue, he appealed for a unity of effort by members of Protestant, Catholic and Jewish faiths against widespread "moral collapse" (New York *Herald Tribune,* December 8, 1951).

Upon his return from a round-the-world tour of distress areas in 1952, he described a "sweep toward Christianity" among North Korean prisoners of war. He termed the 9,000,000 refugees an "explosive problem" in West Germany, called the situation of refugees "complicated" in Pakistan and India by political difficulties over Kashmir, and suggested that Israel withdraw to the border lines established by the United Nations partition plan, in order to create peace with the Arabs (New York *Times,* January 18, 1952).

In defense of a controversial letter sent in November 1953 by the General Council of the Presbyterian Church in the U.S.A. to its 8,000 congregations, protesting "assaults on basic human rights" in the United States, Dr. Blake declared that among the serious threats to the life and work of Protestantism in this country are a wave of "anti-intellectualism . . . which tends to blur all distinctions except that of white and black," and "the forces of totalitarianism, Communist and fascist, which hate the church which holds God, not man, is sovereign" (*Time,* December 28, 1953).

At a meeting of the World Presbyterian Alliance, an organization made up of sixty-five self-governing bodies in forty-six countries, held in Princeton, New Jersey on July 28, 1954, Dr. Blake defined the five "basic" tenets of religious freedom as: "freedom to worship God, freedom to obey God, freedom to learn and to teach the Christian faith, freedom to witness to the Gospel, freedom to determine the internal government and conditions of a church body" (New York *Times,* July 29, 1954).

In March 1954 Blake was chairman of the subcommittee of the National Council of the Churches of Christ in the U.S.A. which drew up the statement which the council adopted, urging eight procedural reforms in Congressional investigating committees and a single joint committee to investigate subversive activities, to insure maintenance of American freedom.

Dr. Blake was elected and installed as president of the National Council in December 1954. The council, which is composed of denominations ranging from the Five Years Meeting of Friends (Quakers) to the Greek Orthodox Church, influences its members by its interpretative pronunciamentos on practical problems, although these declarations are not binding on its members.

REV. DR. EUGENE CARSON BLAKE

After his election Dr. Blake flew to the Far East to take Christmas greetings to GI's and chaplains. He talked with President Syngman Rhee of South Korea, and also visited Honolulu, Manila, Okinawa and Tokyo. Discussing the problems of occupation forces, he advised American churches to develop chaplains, train young people on what to expect in service, and "keep in contact with the boys" (*National Council Outlook,* February 1955).

The clergyman is the author of several articles in theological magazines and is represented in the collection of *Best Sermons* for 1944, 1946 and 1951-1952 (G. P. Butler, editor). Concerning an increase of religious interest in the United States, Dr. Blake warned against the danger of pushing a superficial interpretation of the will of God in social and political affairs into fanaticism and against those who turn religion into "magic—that is, to try to use God for their own purposes rather than to serve God and find His purposes" (*Christian Century,* December 29, 1954).

Dr. Blake holds a number of honorary degrees from American colleges as well as from Princeton University (1952). He is a trustee of the San Francisco Theological Seminary, San Anselmo, California, Princeton Theological Seminary, Occidental College, Lawrenceville School, and Presbyterian Hospital in Philadelphia.

He married Valina Gillespie on September 12, 1929. *Newsweek* (March 28, 1955) describes Dr. Blake as "an affable, broad-shouldered six-footer." He has dark eyes and graying hair. His recreations are swimming, golf, and playing with his Boston terrier; he enjoys watching baseball and football.

References

Christian Sci Mon p6 D 3 '54
Newsweek 45:55+ Mr 28 '55 pors
Time 62:33 D 28 '53; 64:69 D 13 '54
Who's Who in America, 1954-55

BLAKESLEE, A(LBERT) F(RANCIS) Nov. 9, 1874-Nov. 16, 1954 Botanist; geneticist; was associated in various capacities with Carnegie Institution's Station for Experimental Evolution, Cold Spring Harbor, New York (1915-41); visiting professor of botany and director of the Smith College Genetics Experiment Station (since 1942); conducted research on use of colchicine to change chromosome arrangements in certain seeds to produce giant-sized strains; investigated mutation in the jimson weed and genetics of taste and smell. See *Current Biography* (Oct.) 1941.

Obituary

N Y Times p31 N 17 '54

BLISS, HENRY E(VELYN) Jan. 29, 1870-Aug. 9, 1955 Bibliographer; former associate librarian College of the City of New York (1891-1940); one of the foremost contributors to the systemizing of bibliographic classification; his first book, *The Organization of Knowledge and the System of the Sciences* (1929) was introduced by John Dewey as "a monumental work" and an "important and much-needed contribution" to the unification of knowledge; his system of classification was published in four volumes under the title, *A Bibliographic Classification* (H. W. Wilson Co., 1940-1953). See *Current Biography* (Sept.) 1953.

Obituary

N Y Times p25 Ag 10 '55

BLOUGH, ROGER M(ILES) (blou) Jan. 19, 1904- Businessman; lawyer

Address: b. c/o United States Steel Corp., 71 Broadway, New York 6; h. 580 Park Ave., New York 21; Hawley, Pa.

"For the long range, I can't see anything but advancement and increased capacity for the steel industry," said Roger M. Blough in May 1955 after his election as chairman of the board and chief executive officer of the U.S. Steel Corporation, the world's greatest steel-making enterprise. Blough, a lawyer and former schoolteacher, succeeded Benjamin F. Fairless to the chairmanship. He has been associated with the corporation for sixteen years, part of the time as general counsel.

The steel, coal, iron ore, and transportation empire has, according to *U.S. News & World Report* (May 13, 1955), a steel production capacity nearly double that of all companies in Great Britain. Soviet Russia's total steel production "outstrips this single American firm only moderately." In 1955 the total sales of the corporation were 3.5 billion dollars. Clifford F. Hood (see *C.B.*, April 1953) is president and chief administrative officer of U.S. Steel Corporation.

Roger Miles Blough was born in Riverside, Pennsylvania on January 19, 1904, the son of Christian E. and Viola (Hoffman) Blough. His father was a truck farmer. After attending a one-room grade school in Riverside, young Roger took preparatory and college work at Susquehanna University in Selinsgrove, Pennsylvania. During college he was active in sports and was chairman of the student council in his senior year. He was granted an A.B. degree in 1925.

Subsequently he taught history for three years at a high school in Hawley, in the Pocono Mountains in Pennsylvania, and served also as supervising principal during his third year. He then decided to become a lawyer and entered the Yale Law School in New Haven, Connecticut. He was editor of the *Yale Law Journal* and received his LL.B. degree in 1931. He became engaged in the general practice of law with White & Case in New York City and was admitted to the New York bar, the Pennsylvania bar, and to practice before the Supreme Court of the United States.

His association with U.S. Steel, often also called "Big Steel," began during the investigation of the steel industry by the Temporary National Economic Committee (established by the U.S. Congress) in Washington, D.C. in the late 1930's and early 1940's. Irving S. Olds, a member of White & Case since 1917, was appointed special counsel for U.S. Steel in the investigation in 1938 and during 1939 and 1940 Blough acted as associate counsel for the corporation. After hearing the testimony of numerous American businesses and industries, the committee reported its findings and recommendations on economic problems and on monopoly control in the United States in the spring of 1941 (see the summaries in *Newsweek,* April 7, 1941, and *Time,* April 14, 1941).

Leaving White & Case in 1942, Blough went to Pittsburgh, Pennsylvania, where he became general solicitor in charge of all legal matters for the U.S. Steel Corporation of Delaware. When the Delaware firm and three other operating subsidiaries of the U.S. Steel Corporation merged to form the U.S. Steel Company, a steel-producing subsidiary, Blough was made on January 1, 1951 executive vice-president (law), secretary, and a director of the new company. At the beginning of 1953, the company was merged into the U.S. Steel Corporation, when the parent company became primarily an operating company.

Meanwhile, Blough had been appointed vice-chairman of the board of directors (on May 6, 1952), a director (on August 26, 1952), and a member of the finance committee of the U.S. Steel Corporation. Benjamin Fairless, president of the firm since 1938, had been made chairman of the board in 1952. "As Fairless' alter ego on many trips to Washington," *Time* magazine has stated, "Blough helped shape policy." Blough also helped John W. Davis plead Big Steel's case in the U.S. Supreme Court against the seizure of the steel industry by President Harry S. Truman in 1952. The court ruled on June 2 that Truman's action was unconstitutional; the mills were returned to their owners.

After the death of Nathan L. Miller, general counsel to U.S. Steel, Blough in July 1953 assumed this position. He continued to hold his other offices in the corporation. In the spring of 1955, after Fairless retired as chairman of

U.S. Steel, Blough was elected by the board of directors on May 3 to succeed him. He is the seventh chairman, the others being Elbert H. Gary (1903-1927), J. P. Morgan, Jr. (1927-1932), Myron C. Taylor (1932-1938), Edward R. Stettinius, Jr. (1938-1940), Irving S. Olds (1940-1952), and Fairless (1952-1955). Fairless' salary in 1954 was reported to be $259,000; Blough's for that year was said to be $162,000 (New York *Herald Tribune,* May 4, 1955).

The U.S. Steel Corporation was founded in 1901 through an amalgamation of ten companies; the principal persons bringing this about, according to the *Encyclopedia Americana,* were Gary, Andrew Carnegie, Charles M. Schwab, and J. P. Morgan. While in 1901 the corporation produced about two-thirds of all the steel in the United States, it now, in spite of growth in its absolute size, makes about one-third of the steel in America each year (*Fortune,* April 1950 and *Life,* May 16, 1955).

"I fully subscribe to the policies of Ben Fairless," Blough stated after his election. "I intend to do all I can to continue his great program of progress." As chairman he will probably try to achieve a long-term goal set by Fairless: to expand Big Steel's yearly capacity from its present 38.9 million tons to 60.9 million by 1975—in order to keep pace with the growing American population. He will have to find the capital with which to finance the new construction. Further experimentation with different types of steel and synthetics is expected. Another of his responsibilities, according to *Business Week* (May 7, 1955) is to be "steel's No. 1 public relations man." Blough is also supervising the negotiations with the United Steelworkers of America union, which is seeking higher wages. Several 16mm. films sponsored by U.S. Steel are listed in *Educational Film Guide.*

In a speech in Chicago on May 12, 1955 before the National Association of Credit Men, Blough declared that industrial research leads to more jobs and higher wages and that it plays a vital role in leveling out the "dips and even abysses" of the American economy. "Research," he said, "offers the only road to finding out how to produce more and better goods cheaper. And finding out how to produce more and better goods cheaper is the proven way of guaranteeing more and better jobs and wages—contractual devices to the contrary notwithstanding."

During the last nine years, he continued, American industries had spent 13 billion dollars on research, compared to 4.5 billion dollars used from the founding of the nation up to 1946. In the last five years, when U.S. Steel has expanded its research functions five times from what they had been, the company developed and produced commercially 300 new steels. New power lawn mowers, television sets, etc., all the result of research, have provided jobs for thousands of persons and the purchasing power with which they could buy all sorts of goods.

In answer to his question, "Need we fear periods of recurring economic depression?" he said: "We ought to fear them enough not to be smug about our progress. But we ought not to be pathologically frightened so that we reach into the medicine chest of economic quackery every time the slightest quiver runs through production and employment."

U. S. Steel Corp.
ROGER M. BLOUGH

For the U.S. Steel Foundation, Blough announced in May 1955 grants totaling $1,052,000 to about 400 colleges and universities in forty-three states, in its aid-to-education program for 1955. "The financial plight of privately supported education continues to be serious," Blough stated. "The action of the U.S. Steel Foundation emphasizes the mutual interests served by a substantial flow of free funds to colleges and universities. Unrestricted aid evidences confidence in—and helps retain independence for—higher education. Unrestricted funds are especially useful in permitting free choice of the best means for faculty development" (New York *Times,* May 17, 1955).

Commenting on the opportunity for youth today, Blough stated: "We need the constructive sceptics, the close reasoners who are willing to venture, and we need the hard realists who are willing to give weight to the open course as well as the barrier. Opportunities have not dried up. They have expanded. There are large and small chances every day in large businesses and in the thousands of smaller businesses."

Susquehanna University awarded him an honorary LL.D. degree in 1953. He is a member of the American and Allegheny county bar associations, the American Iron and Steel Institute, and the Yale Law School Association (he became a member of the executive committee in 1952). His clubs are the Duquesne, University and Fox Chapel Golf in Pittsburgh; the Pine Valley Golf in Clementon, New Jersey; the Rolling Rock in Ligonier, Pennsylvania; and the Union League in New York City.

(Continued next page)

BLOUGH, ROGER M.—*Continued*

On June 13, 1928, Roger M. Blough married Helen Martha Decker, whom he met in Hawley, Pennsylvania. The Bloughs have twin daughters, Jane Elizabeth and Judith Ann, who are attending Wellesley College in Massachusetts. Blough is almost six feet tall and weighs 188 pounds. *Time* has described him as "a methodical worker with a quiet wit and a knack for getting along with people." It is also reported that he "thinks big" and "talks little."

"I'm just an ordinary guy," Blough has said. "I like to work hard and I like to relax. I go to bed early and I get up early [he usually gets to his office at 71 Broadway in New York City by eight o'clock]. On week ends I like to go to my home in the country and plant a tree or a flower. I like to take over the cooking assignment at home occasionally."

References

Bsns W p26+ My 7 '55 por
N Y Herald Tribune p 1+ My 4 '55 por
N Y Times p41+ My 4 '55 por
N Y World-Telegram p17 My 9 '55 por
Time 59:99 My 19 '52 por; 65:98 My 16 '55 por
Who's Who in America, 1954-55
World Biography (1954)

BOHROD, AARON (bō'rŏd) Nov. 21, 1907- Artist; teacher

Address: b. c/o Associated American Artists Galleries, 711 5th Ave., New York 22; University of Wisconsin, Madison, Wis.; h. 432 Lorch St., Madison, Wis.

Much of the minutiae of American city life has been recorded by the brush of Aaron Bohrod, once called "Chicago's gift to art." A realist, he believes that a painting however faithfully represented, is nevertheless a distillation process, sent through an artist, thus making it different from a photograph. His work is represented in many museums and he has been the recipient of a number of major awards. He was one of the American painters commissioned by *Life* magazine to record World War II, and spent two years at the various fronts. Since 1948 he has been artist in residence at the University of Wisconsin.

Still lifes by Bohrod painted so realistically that visitors invariably try to touch the canvasses were exhibited at the University of Wisconsin during December 1954 and are regarded as outstanding examples of the *trompe-l'oeil* (fool-the-eye) technique of painting, to which he has turned since the war. He has also won a reputation as a designer of ceramics and fabrics.

Aaron Bohrod was born on November 21, 1907, the younger son of George Bohrod, a Russian immigrant who entered the grocery business in Chicago, and of the former Fannie Feingold. He began to draw at a very early age. When his elder brother began to study medicine, he learned something of anatomy from his textbooks. Helen Trieglaff, in a study of Bohrod written for *Parnassus,* reports that he was an honor student at Crane High School. He then spent a year at Crane Junior College, which he was obliged to leave in order to go to work. The Encyclopedia Britannica Collection Catalog states that he was "a printer's devil, broker's messenger, mechanical draftsman and commercial illustrator" at this time.

In 1927 Bohrod was able to begin his studies at the Chicago Art Institute. After two years he became a commercial artist in an advertising agency and a department store to earn money for further study. In New York he enrolled at the Art Students' League, where from 1930 to 1932 he studied under John Sloan—whom he considers his "most helpful teacher"—Boardman Robinson, and Kenneth Hayes Miller.

Taking as his subject the streets and citizens of Chicago, Bohrod captured the Carr Landscape prize of the Chicago Art Institute in 1933 with his *Street.* The following year he received the Institute's Eisendrath prize for *Coal Yards* and the Tuthill prize for his watercolor *Division Street.* The same competition, in 1935, brought him the Watson F. Blair prize of $400 for his *Road in Peoria,* and at the Chicago Artists Ball at the end of the year, he received the group's award of $200 for his *Palos Park Landscape.*

Two Guggenheim awards bestowed upon Bohrod, in 1936-37 and in 1937-38, enabled him to tour the country and make further studies of the American scene. In 1937 he also received a commission to do three mural panels for the United States Post Office, in Vandalia, Clinton, and Galesburg, Illinois.

When an exhibition of Bohrod's paintings opened at the Rehn Gallery in New York in 1937, the New York *Herald Tribune* (October 10, 1937) observed, "It is a thoroughly pleasant group of pictures he has painted, placing a casual and revealing sidelight on American character and customs." His 1939 exhibition at the Association of American Artists brought this comment from the *Art News* reviewer: "He shows again and again his instinct for finding an unusual angle for his subjects so that no matter how worn and commonplace, he sees a scene freshly . . . and reveals on canvas its inner plastic meaning." Of the same exhibition, *Art Digest* remarked: "Bohrod's use of color is unique at the moment. He pitches each tone to its topmost intensity and sometimes to the shrill point where it dances before the eyes."

To the November 1940 exhibition of water colors by contemporary American artists at the Worcester Museum of Art, Bohrod contributed the *gouache Chicago Street in Winter.* Upon showing again in New York, at the Associated American Artists Galleries, in November 1941, Bohrod's work provoked this comment from the New York *Times* critic: "Bohrod has not innovated to any extent but his work gains in strength and sureness. What might so easily be mere social consciousness is in the work of this artist transmuted into understanding of the scene and its people."

Life (November 10, 1941) presented a portfolio of Bohrod's scenes with the remark, "The shabbier the scene, the more Bohrod likes to portray its wistful beauty, especially under the glow of a neon sign . . . [he is able] to romanticize the so-called ugliness of American life, without destroying its essential character or darting too far from reality." Appointed artist in residence at Southern Illinois Normal University in 1942, he held "open studio" for majors in the arts, gave criticism, demonstrations, and lectures.

As a member of *Life's* War Art Unit from 1943 to 1945 Bohrod covered events of World War II in various theaters of war. Reproductions of his paintings of the war in France appeared in the April 30, 1945 issue of *Life;* of the war in England in the March 5, 1945 issue; and of the Omaha Beach invasion, done from sketches made on the spot, in the April 30, 1945 issue.

Moment Musicale, a scene of the South Pacific front, and other of his paintings were shown at the Metropolitan Museum of Art in New York, in the July 1945 War Against Japan Exhibition, sponsored by the United States Treasury Department. *Joan of Arc in Montebourg* (depicting an untouched statue in a devastated town) exhibited in the forty-ninth annual show at the Chicago Art Institute in June 1945, brought him the Logan Art Medal and $500.

Sixteen oils devoted to war scenes were presented at the Associated American Artists Gallery in July 1945 and another group in 1946. "They are not war paintings, however, in the strict sense," wrote the New York *Times* reviewer (March 24, 1946). "The subject values sought are pictorial and human. . . . His brushwork is at once vivid and subtle."

Postwar work by Bohrod appeared in the Ohrbach collection, at the Associated American Artists Galleries in January 1947 and at the Museum of the City of New York in May 1947. His one-man show at the Associated American Artists Galleries in December 1949 received this comment from the New York *Herald Tribune*: "From regional scenes with a suggestion of forcefulness a dozen years ago, Bohrod has progressed toward realism of a more orthodox picturesqueness." The *Times* reviewer was "disappointed" because of a "static quality and a still-tableau-like presentation." His exhibition in March 1952, said the *Times,* "put one directly in touch with the American scene. Direct, because he paints in a straightforward, almost documentary style, romantic because he selects landscapes with overtones of sentiment."

Appointed artist in residence at the University of Wisconsin in 1948, Bohrod there began two years later to collaborate on ceramics with F. Carleton Ball. Together, they were responsible for more than two hundred pieces, formed on the potter's wheel by Ball and decorated by Bohrod. These were exhibited at the Associated American Artists Galleries in New York City in October 1952.

Bohrod's work may be seen at a number of American museums: the Metropolitan Museum of Art, the Whitney Museum of American Art, and the Brooklyn Museum in New York, the

Stephen Deutch

AARON BOHROD

Boston Museum of Art, the Pennsylvania Academy of Art, the Corcoran Museum in Washington, D.C., the Swope Gallery of Art in Terre Haute, the Butler Art Institute in Youngstown, the University of Arizona, the Walker Art Center in Minneapolis, the Norton Art Institute, the Telfair Art Academy in Florida, the Davenport (Iowa) Art Institute, the Cranbrook Academy, the Witte Memorial Museum, and the universities of Nebraska, Illinois, and Ohio. He received the first award of merit in 1940 from the California Water Color Society for his *Jackson Boulevard Houses,* the first prize of the Philadelphia Water Color Society in 1942, the fifth purchase prize of $1000 in the Artists for Victory Exhibition at New York's Metropolitan Museum of Art that year, and the Corcoran second prize as well as the W. A. Clark prize and silver medal in Washington, D.C. in 1943. Bohrod has done a series of scenes for the Missouri Documentary Art Project (1946), the Pennsylvania Documentary Art Project (1947), and the Michigan Documentary Art Project (1947).

Bohrod has illustrated two books—*The Illinois* and *The Golden Watch,* designed fabrics distributed by major department stores, and painted advertisements for Lucky Strike cigarettes. In 1940 he taught painting at Chicago Art Institute. Several paintings have been reproduced in *Time, Fortune, Coronet,* and *Esquire* (the last-named also had an article on him by Harry Salpeter in March 1940).

By his marriage on December 27, 1929 to Ruth Bush, Aaron Bohrod is the father of three sons, Mark, Georgi, and Neil. He is five feet six and a half inches tall, weighs 146 pounds. The Encyclopedia Britannica Collection Catalog has described him as "a shy, blond man who is not overly talkative, but quick-witted and observant to a rare degree." Boh-

BOHROD, AARON—*Continued*

rod's religious affiliation is Jewish. Less preoccupied with baseball than he was as a boy, Bohrod now prefers tennis and table tennis. Book collecting and the violin also provide him with relaxation.

References

Art Alliance Bul O '52
Art Digest 16:21 S 1 '42
Life 11:92+ N 10 '41 por
Mag Art 37:250 N '44
Time 64:94 D 6 '54

Who's Who in America, 1954-55
Who's Who in American Art, 1953

BONNER, PAUL HYDE Feb. 14, 1893-

Author

Address: b. Charles Scribner's Sons, 597 5th Ave., New York 17; h. The Teacherage, Summerville, S.C.

Reprinted from the *Wilson Library Bulletin* Sept. 1955

Paul Hyde Bonner's, *Excelsior!,* which was published in 1955 by Scribner and became a Literary Guild selection, was compared to Galsworthy's *The Forsyte Saga* by Edward Weeks in the *Atlantic Monthly.* Its central figure is a Swiss banker who rules his family with a rod of iron. A quarter of a century ago, Bonner resigned his lucrative post as vice-president and director of his naturalized Swiss father-in-law's firm, Stehli & Co., weaver of silks, and took his wife and four sons to Europe. Bonner has been a singer, a colonel in the U.S. Army Air Forces, an adviser on diplomatic missions, and, since 1952, a novelist.

Paul Hyde Bonner was born in Brooklyn, New York, February 14, 1893, the son of Paul Edward Bonner, a banker, and Theodora Wilson (Hall) Bonner. He attended Adelphi Academy and Polytechnic Preparatory School before going to Phillips Exeter Academy in Exeter, New Hampshire. After a year at Harvard (1911-1912), he opened letters in the Australian department of a New York export firm, Strong and Trowbridge. Joining the tenor squad of the Schola Cantorum, young Bonner impressed its leader, Kurt Schindler, with the bird-like quality of his high notes. Schindler sent him to Enrico Caruso, for whom Bonner sang "Salut demeure" from *Faust,* and Caruso gave him a letter to Giuseppe Campanari, a noted vocal coach. Financed by a doting great-aunt, Bonner studied two years, and auditioned at La Scala in Milan. On June 14, 1914, he signed contracts to sing in Piacenza and Brescia; on August 1, World War I broke out and the contracts were cancelled. Bonner got his first taste of diplomatic service helping the American consul at Milan with stranded tourists.

PAUL HYDE BONNER

On his return to New York, Bonner auditioned for Oscar Hammerstein at the Victoria Theatre, surrounded by caged lions, and won another contract, also cancelled. After two years in his father's bank, he enlisted in the 27th Division, sailed for France, and was commissioned a second lieutenant two days before the Armistice. On April 30, 1917, he had married Lilly M. Stehli, daughter of Emil J. Stehli; they have four sons, Paul Hyde, Jr., John Tyler, Henry Stehli, and Anthony Edmonde. The years 1919 to 1931 were spent in his father-in-law's firm. Alexander Woollcott was a frequent guest in the Bonners' home at Locust Valley, Long Island; many of his *Letters* were addressed to them.

After a disagreement over the firm's policy, Bonner took his family to Europe. They lived at Vaucresson, near Paris; spent three years in England, "the finest and most stimulating a family ever had"; then five years at Rye Center, New Hampshire, to be near the sons who were then attending Exeter and Harvard. Bonner was a colonel in the Army Air Forces, in charge of allocation of aluminum products to the aircraft industry, during World War II, serving in the matériel command at Wright Field and in the Pentagon. He was next appointed central field commissioner of the Foreign Liquidation Commission of the Department of State, with headquarters in Paris, and then was made special advisor to the Ambassador to Italy on matters concerning the Treaty of Peace. In 1949, he was special assistant to the chief of the Economic Cooperation Administration Mission to Italy.

At fifty-eight, Bonner found himself, he says, "in search of some steady, do-it-yourself employment to stave off boredom when I started to write my first novel. There was no evidence that I could write fiction, but there was a trend in the air. Many retired bankers, soldiers, and diplomats (I had a fling at all three) were dabbling in the arts. So why not I?"

John P. Marquand called Bonner's book *SPQR* (Scribner, 1952) "the best novel about Rome that an American has written for many, many years," while William Pfaff in *Commonweal* termed it "a romantic and silly story," and

Fanny Butcher declared in the Chicago *Sunday Tribune* that "it is written with rare sophistication." Charles Rolo in the *Atlantic* praised its sure treatment of the Italian setting, and the portrait of "Monsignor Walsh."

The *New Yorker* thought his next book, *Hôtel Talleyrand* (1953) "shallow and self-assured and sometimes clever"; the San Francisco *Chronicle* described it as "a trenchant moving story of real people," and the New York *Times,* "the wittiest and most entertaining high comedy of the season." *The Glorious Mornings* (1954), twelve stories of hunting and fishing, seemed to the *Times* "a pleasant mixture of weather-wisdom and urbanity." Hollis Alpert of the *Saturday Review* summed up *Excelsior!* as "a quiet, neat story, with all the world-shaking events muted." John Brooks in the New York *Times,* describing the book's subject as "neutrality, its practice and ethics," called it "in the best sense sophisticated." Dan Wickenden in the New York *Herald Tribune Book Review* wrote that while *Excelsior!* attempts "only a surface presentation of emotions and mental processes," the book is "an expert and entertaining novel that also has something to say."

Bonner finds his chief interests in his family, his friends, and his pictures. "The lure of quail and duck shooting," he writes, "made me settle in South Carolina, where my wife and I live from September to June, spending the summer months fishing in Ireland, Canada, or Montana. It is not a bad life, considering that I enjoy writing as much as field sports." Bonner is an "Eisenhower Democrat" who lists his church affiliation as Protestant Episcopal. He is of medium height and weight (five feet eight inches and 150 pounds), with gray hair and brown eyes.

References

N Y Herald Tribune Bk R p3 Ap 20 '52
Sat R 38:15 Je 18 '55 por

BORN, MAX Dec. 11, 1882- Physicist
Address: h. Macardstrasse, Bad Pyrmont, West Germany

Cited for his "fundamental research in quantum mechanics, especially for his application of matrix mechanics to quantum mechanics," a noted German physicist, Dr. Max Born shared the Nobel Prize in Physics in 1954 with Professor Walther Bothe of the University of Heidelberg. Dr. Born is equally distinguished in theoretical physics for his teaching, his contributions to atomic theory, and his written works on the subject. He was formerly a teacher at Göttingen, Cambridge, and Edinburgh universities; he is now retired and lives in West Germany.

Max Born is the son of Gustav and Margarete (Kauffmann) Born of Breslau, Germany. His birth date is December 11, 1882. His father, a medical doctor, taught at the University of Breslau. Following his training in the Kaiser Wilhelm Gymnasium in his home town, Max Born continued his studies at the universities of Breslau, Heidelberg, Zurich, Cambridge, and Göttingen, from which he received his Ph.D. degree in 1907.

Wide World

MAX BORN

In 1909 he became *Privatdozent* at Göttingen (a *Privatdozent* is an unsalaried lecturer whose income is derived from the fees paid by students electing his course), extraordinary (assistant) professor at the University of Berlin in 1915, and ordinary (full) professor at the University of Frankfurt am Main in 1919. In 1921 he returned to Göttingen to head the physics department there, where, under his administration, it became a center of learning in the field of theoretical physics rivaled only by Niels Bohr's famous Institute for Theoretical Physics in Denmark.

In its article in connection with Born's receipt of the Nobel award, *Nature* (November 13, 1954), stated that his work as an inspiring teacher has been as noteworthy as his other distinguished achievements. Recalling that his school at Göttingen had long been the most important center to which young scholars might go "to be infected with that enthusiasm and optimism which characterize Born's own work," the periodical added: "The men who worked with him later at Cambridge and Edinburgh include many who made their mark on modern physics."

The Hitler government, with whose policies and practices Professor Born disagreed, forced him to leave Germany in 1933. He settled in England where he taught at Cambridge University and became Stokes lecturer of mathematics in 1934. He moved to Edinburgh University in 1936 as Tait professor of natural philosophy and remained there until 1953 when he retired to Bad Pyrmont, a spa in West Germany.

Professor Born's scientific work has been confined mainly to the theoretical, as distinguished from the experimental, aspects of modern atomic theory. His early work con-

BORN, MAX—*Continued*

cerned the interatomic forces in crystals, the theory of crystal lattice vibrations, on which he has written treatises. During his later years at Edinburgh he also contributed significantly to the theory of the structure and properties of liquids.

The major part of his fame, however, as the Nobel citation suggests, is due to his work in quantum theory. In the 1920's while the ground work for modern atomic theory was being laid, Professor Born took a leading part in the development of the basic concepts of the new mathematics of the atom.

Following the appearance of Bohr's hypotheses concerning energy levels of the electron in which Max Planck's concept of quanta was associated with the theory of atomic spectra, efforts had been made to interpret subsequent experimental data through the mathematics of classical mechanics with indifferent success. In 1924 the famous French physicist, Louis de Broglie, using the work of Planck coupled with concepts drawn from Albert Einstein's relativity theory, propounded a theory which suggested that the electron is associated with a group of waves.

Within a short time, Werner Heisenberg, who was Born's assistant at Göttingen, stated his famous "uncertainty principle," which demonstrated that the laws of classical mechanics could not be applied to phenomena involving the magnitudes of the lighter atoms and sub-atomic particles because their position and velocity could not be simultaneously known, the very act of observing the one inevitably changing the other.

Because of this circumstance, he recommended that calculations could be fruitful in this area only in so far as they dealt in probabilities. Born took up the problem at this point, formulating a system in which de Broglie's electron wave became a wave of probability, the presence of the wavelike manifestation indicating the probable presence of the electron presumed to be associated with it. This system is called matrix mechanics.

In his book *The Restless Universe* (Dover, 1951), he explains how he came to work it out: "A student occasionally goes to lectures about abstruse subjects just for fun and speedily forgets about them. This is what happened to me with a lecture on higher algebra, of which I recollected little more than the word 'matrix' and a few simple theorems about these matrices. But that sufficed. A little playing about with Heisenberg's physical formula showed the connection. Then it was an easy matter to apply the results."

While Born, in association with P. Jordan and Heisenberg, was working out matrix mechanics, Erwin Schrödinger was working independently on his own wave mechanics which reached the same goal by different means. Finally, Paul Dirac showed that the two systems could be blended into one, the resultant system being the quantum mechanics to which the name is applied today.

Professor Born continued his contributions to atomic theory in the late 1920's and early 1930's. During this period he derived a formula for the description of the phenomenon of "scattering" of streams of particles diffracted by the molecules in a target against which the stream is directed. Born's formula which applies perturbation theory to these events, is called the Born approximation and has remained a standand method of dealing with these phenomena.

About the time he was driven from Germany by the Nazis, Born had begun to consider the problem of the relation of the electron to its field in an effort to relate quantum theory to J. C. Maxwell's equations through the quantization of the electromagnetic field. He continued his work in England in association with L. Infeld, one of his students. Although his unitary field theory did not succeed, Born has not ceased to work on this difficult problem.

Professor Born went to India in 1935 as a guest lecturer at the Indian Institute of Science in Bangalore. He addressed a meeting of the South Indian Science Association in Bangalore on the significance of the number 137 which is often the result of operations among the constants commonly used in atomic theory: Planck's constant, the speed of light, the charge on the electron. Born stated that the explanation of this number is a major problem in physics, and that its significance should help solve the problem to which he had addressed himself in working out his unitary field theory.

He became a British subject in 1939 and continued his teaching and writing. He did not take part in the wartime development of atomic energy for military purposes. "I cannot refrain from saying," Born commented in *Nature* (October 13, 1951), "that I, personally, am glad not to have been involved in the pursuit of research which has already been used for the most terrible mass destruction in history and threatens humanity with even worse disaster. I think that the applications of nuclear physics to peaceful ends are a poor compensation for these perils."

In *The Restless Universe* he pointed out the tremendous responsibility which must lie on the shoulders of those scientists who did take part in it. He notes with regret that not only has some of their skill now been devoted to utter destruction (the H-bomb, unlike the A-bomb with its fruitful concomitant of the atomic pile, being useful only as a weapon), but also the harmful impact of politics on physics has made itself felt through the classification of some scientific data, preventing the free interchange of information among researchers.

The physicist is a fellow of the science academies of Göttingen (1920), Russia (1925), and Prussia (1929); of the Royal Society of London (1939); and of the Royal Society of Edinburgh. He is an honorary fellow of the Indian, Rumanian, Peruvian, and Danish academies of science and was awarded honorary doctorates by the universities of Bristol, Bordeaux, and Oxford. He received the Hughes Medal of the Royal Society of London in 1950.

He is the author of many notable books: *The Constitution of Matter, Modern Atomic and Electron Theories* (Dutton, 1923), *Einstein's Theory of Relativity* (Methuen, 1924), *The Mechanics of the Atom* (Bell, 1927), *Atomic Physics* (Blackie, 1935; 5th edition, 1951),

Experiment and Theory in Physics (Cambridge University Press, 1943), *A General Kinetic Theory of Liquids* (with H. S. Green; Cambridge University Press, 1949), and *Natural Philosophy of Cause and Chance* (Clarendon, 1949). His book *Dynamical Theory of Crystal Lattices* (Oxford, 1954) was written with Kun Huang.

Max Born married Hedwig Emma Martha Ehrenberg on August 2, 1913. They have three children. He is a member of the Lutheran church. His hobbies include music and hiking. At the conclusion of his book *The Restless Universe,* he wrote: "Not everything is knowable, still less is predictable. But the mind of man is capable of grasping and understanding at least a part of Creation; amid the flight of phenomena stands the immutable pole of law."

References

Nature 166:926+ D 2 '50; 172:1082 D 12 '53; 174:907 N 13 '54
Who's Who, 1954
World Biography (1954)

BOTHE, WALTHER (WILHELM GEORG) (bō-tĕ) Jan. 8, 1891- Physicist; university professor

Address: b. c/o Institute of Physics, Max Planck Institute for Medical Research, Jahnstrasse, Heidelberg, Germany ; h. Im Bäckerfeld 6, Heidelberg, Germany

The Nobel Prize in Physics for 1954 was shared by two German-born scientists, Dr. Walther Bothe, professor of physics at the University of Heidelberg, and Dr. Max Born, formerly a professor at Edinburgh University, now retired and living in West Germany. Professor Bothe, who is also director of the Institute of Physics of the Max Planck Institute for Medical Research at Heidelberg, was honored for "the coincidence method [a way of measuring time with extreme accuracy] and his discoveries with this method." Both Nobel laureates have been leaders in the "new physics" which started with relativity and quantum theory.

Walther Wilhelm Georg Bothe was born on January 8, 1891 in Oranienburg, a city near Berlin in Prussia, Germany. His father, Fritz Bothe, was a merchant. After he had completed his elementary schooling, young Walther continued his studies at the University of Berlin under the famous scientist Max Planck and received his Ph.D. degree in 1914. He then served in World War I.

Meanwhile Bothe had become associated with the Physikalisch-Technische Reichsanstalt (Physical and Technical Institute) in Berlin and after the war he continued his association with the institute. In 1925 he became a *Privatdozent* in physics at the University of Berlin, and in 1929 he was appointed extraordinary (assistant) professor of physics.

From 1930 to 1932 he held a professorship of physics at the University of Giessen, moving to Heidelberg next as professor in the physics department of the famous university. He was named director of the physics institute of the Kaiser Wilhelm (now Max Planck) Institute for Medical Research at Heidelberg in 1934 and has remained in that post. From 1934 to 1946 he was an honorary professor at the University of Heidelberg and in 1946 he became again a regular professor of physics there.

Professor Bothe's professional life has been devoted mostly to teaching, writing, and carrying on work in experimental research. He is an authority on cosmic ray phenomena, electron diffraction, and nuclear physics. In 1921 he issued an important paper on the dynamical theory of refraction. His notable work which has earned him the Nobel Prize—was his introduction of coincidence methods into counting techniques and his discoveries using these methods.

In the coincidence method, according to *Science News Letter* (November 13, 1954), "two Geiger-Müller tubes are connected in series, and only those atomic reactions making both tubes conducting simultaneously are recorded." Applying this coincidence method to the study of the recoiling particles associated with the (Arthur H.) Compton effect, he and the late Dr. Hans Geiger showed that "the conservation laws are satisfied in each individual event and not merely on the average." This, wrote *Nature* (November 13, 1954), "was fundamental for the interpretation of atomic processes."

In 1929, in collaboration with Werner Kolhörster, he applied his coincidence method to the study of cosmic rays, devising a sort of cosmic ray telescope so that the behavior of this penetrating radiation might be studied with greater accuracy. Professor Bothe's system has been developed and refined by many workers since, but the basic concept remains as he originally worked it out. In their work on cosmic rays, the scientists, wrote *Nature,* "helped to establish the presence of penetrating charged particles." (See their article, "The Nature of Penetrating Radiation," in *Nature,* April 27, 1929).

In his study of nuclear radiations, Bothe, in 1930, in collaboration with Dr. H. Becker, reported that if certain elements, notably beryllium, were exposed to bombardment by alpha rays, a very penetrating emanation was discharged from the target. It was supposed at first that these new rays were very high energy gamma rays, but repeated experiments by others indicated that this was not the case. Sir James Chadwick (who received the Nobel Prize in 1935 for his work) demonstrated in 1932 that these rays actually manifested the presence of a particle which, since 1920, had been deemed an interesting theoretical possibility, the neutron.

At Heidelberg in 1935, he devised a now widely used notation system for describing nuclear reactions. According to *Nature* (November 13, 1954), Dr. Bothe has also done pioneer work in studying "hard gamma rays and the nuclear photo-effect produced by such rays and the problems of multiple scattering of electrons and of neutrons. On problems of scattering he has not only done experimental work of great importance but has also made valuable contributions to the theory." (An

Wide World

WALTHER BOTHE

article on scattering by Bothe appeared in the *Handbuch der Physik,* Berlin, 1933, by Hans Geiger and K. Scheel.)

During World War II he worked with Nobel Prizewinner physicist Dr. Werner Heisenberg and others in Nazi Germany's effort to develop atomic energy for military purposes and supervised the construction of Germany's first cyclotron, completed in 1944. After the war Professor Bothe continued to work with the cyclotron, engaging in medical research at Heidelberg.

In an interview reported in the New York *Herald Tribune* (September 9, 1949), Bothe, who was at that time attending an International Conference on Experimental Nuclear Physics in Basel, Switzerland, agreed with his colleague Dr. Heisenberg in the prediction that science in the U.S.S.R. would soon fall far behind the West and that the difficulties in the development of the atom bomb there would be immense. Recalling the stifling effect of Nazism on German science, the two physicists compared the influence of dogmatic theories, such as the pronouncements on heredity of T. D. Lysenko (Soviet geneticist) to their own unfortunate experience under Hitler. Dr. Bothe said that it had been impossible to teach in the universities in Germany because the Nazis had said some physics was Jewish and it could not be taught. He maintained that "no physics could be taught intelligently," without the contributions of Jewish physicists.

The Nobel Prize in Physics for 1954 of approximately $35,000 was awarded jointly to Bothe and Max Born by the Swedish Royal Academy of Science. According to the will of Alfred Nobel, the nineteenth-century Swedish inventor, the income from his estate is divided each year into five equal prizes, for work in physics, chemistry, literature, medicine and physiology, and peace. The prizes are awarded irrespective of nationality for outstanding contributions of persons or organizations. Nominations for the prize may be made by former prize winners and by members of recognized institutions of learning or official academies in any country.

Bothe has published numerous accounts of his experiments. With Hermann Wollschitt he contributed a work on calorimeters and calorimetry to the *Handbuch der biologischen arbeitsmethoden* (1920-), edited by Emil Abderhalden. Bothe's book, prepared in collaboration with W. Gentner and H. Maier-Leibnitz and published in 1940, was entitled *Atlas Typischer Nobelkammerbilder* and is an important standard source in its field.

He was senior author of *Nuclear Physics and Cosmic Rays,* published in 1948 by the Office of Military Government for Germany, Field Information Agencies Technical (British, French and American). He has contributed articles to the *Zeitschrift für Physik* and other scientific periodicals. He belongs to the academies of science of Heidelberg, Leipzig, Göttingen, and Berlin.

Walther Bothe, who is now a widower, married Barbara Below in 1920 by whom he had several children. He has been ailing for the past year and the loss of a leg early in 1954 prevented him from attending the Nobel Prize ceremonies in Stockholm. He is a member of the Lutheran church. For recreation he enjoys music and painting.

References

Nature 174:907 N 13 '54
Newsweek 44:72+ N 15 '54
Sci N L 66:307+ N 13 '54
Time 64:70 N 15 '54
International Who's Who, 1954
Kürschners Deutscher Gelehrten Kalender, 1954
Wer ist Wer? (1955)
World Biography (1954)

BOURGUIBA, HABIB BEN ALI (bo͞or' gī-bä" hä'bēb bĕn ă-lĭ') 1904- Tunisian political leader

Address: Place aux Moutons, Tunis, Tunisia

Over 300,000 cheering Tunisians, representing every segment of the country's 3,500,000 people gathered in Tunis on June 1, 1955 to welcome home Habib Bourguiba, leader of the nationalist Neo-Destour (New Constitution) party, after more than three years in exile. His return had the blessings of his former French jailers, and Bourguiba is expected to stay and help to guide the new program of gradual home rule for Tunisia.

His release symbolized the internal autonomy granted by the agreement which Tunisia reached with France on April 22, 1955 and which was approved by the French National Assembly on July 9 by a vote of 540 to 43.

Time (May 2, 1955) called Bourguiba "the real Tunisian string-puller behind the scenes . . . an authentic political genius." His moderate counsels have helped to unify Tunisian nationalists so that the Communists have been unable to seriously infiltrate them. "We must know how to use this sovereignty in a dignified manner," he told his people at his home-coming celebration. "We must respect everyone who lives on this earth, be he French or foreigner. We must treat him as a brother as long as he respects our freedom, our personality, and our dignity."

Tunisia, a country the size of Louisiana, became a French protectorate in 1881. Full control was gradually assumed by France as French and other European settlers became the chief agriculturalists and industrialists, invested millions and paid 50 per cent of the taxes. The French colonials—150,000 in number—were the major source of conflict in the self-government drive begun in 1933 by Habib Bourguiba and the powerful Neo-Destour party, which he founded in that year.

Habib ben Ali Bourguiba, son of Ali Bourguiba, an officer in the Army of the Bey of Tunis, was born in the small fishing village of Monastir, Tunisia in 1904. His early years were spent in Tunis, where he received elementary education at a French-Moslem school and later attended a French high school. He went to Paris in 1922 and studied law and political science at the University of Paris. Upon his return to Tunisia in 1928, he was admitted to the bar.

A keen interest in politics led him to join the Destour (Constitution) party that had been organized in 1920 and had gained a series of political concessions from the French in its first years. In 1933 a group of French-educated intellectuals headed by Bourguiba, bolted the party and founded Neo-Destour, on Western-style nationalism rather than Islamic traditionalism (*Reporter*, July 7, 1953).

Described by Curt L. Heymann (Los Angeles *Times*, February 17, 1952) as a "forceful speaker whose expressions and mannerisms fascinate the masses," Bourguiba was said to have stirred the nationalism of his countrymen who joined Neo-Destour by the thousands, and gained the moral support of Tunisia's entire Moslem population. The party was outlawed by the French in 1934, and Bourguiba was arrested. He was released in 1936, and again arrested in 1938 and sent to Fort Saint Nicolos at Marseilles.

Liberated by the Germans in 1942, he made his way back to Tunis via Rome in 1943. His home-coming was climaxed by a "dramatic" appeal for "home rule," but the French were not interested. After World War II ended, Bourguiba went to Cairo to seek support of the Arab League. It was reported that he "quarreled violently" with the Grand Mufti of Jerusalem, Haj Amin el-Husseini, and accused him and other Arabs of trying to turn Tunisia into a satellite of the Middle East.

Upon his return to Tunis, Bourguiba purged the Neo-Destour party of Communists. He led his followers who were in the trade unions out of the Communist-led Confédération Générale du Travail and formed UGTT (Union Générale des Travailleurs Tunisiens), which now has 60,000 members. Assured of a large following, Bourguiba moved to Paris, where (according to the *Christian Science Monitor,* January

French Embassy Press & Inf. Div.
HABIB BEN ALI BOURGUIBA

5, 1951) he adopted a new technique. He aroused sympathy for Tunisian nationalist aspirations by his claim that he was acting in the interest of the French government "against its reactionary colonial administration." At the same time, he cautioned the Tunisians to have patience as the "real France" was sympathetic with their hopes.

U.S. News & World Report (May 9, 1952) said that a compromise was almost effected when a Tunisian, Mohammed Chenik, was named Premier in 1951. Equal membership of Tunisians and French colonials in the Cabinet was also granted, but this brought about frequent deadlocks and "froze" almost 200 ministerial decisions. However, Bourguiba continued working for Tunisian independence within the economic and cultural orbit of the French Union. He is aware of Tunisia's strategic importance in the cold war and of the significance of the North African naval and air bases constructed by the United States. In the opinion of Andrew Roth (*Nation,* February 9, 1952) Bourguiba, with his "dynamism, organizational ability and sensitivity to economic and social problems necessary to compete with the Communists," was gaining recognition.

Bourguiba flew to the United States in September 1951 and broadcast a Tunisian nationalist plea over the *Voice of America* (New York *Times,* September 14, 1951). The French government had not been consulted and was said to be "puzzled" by Bourguiba's sponsorship by the American Federation of Labor. It was learned that Irving Brown, European representative of the AFL, had arranged Bourguiba's trip to the United States. Bourguiba visited Washington, D.C., and attended the AFL convention in San Francisco before he returned to Paris.

In the meantime, Neo-Destour had confined its activities to manifestations and strikes, but before he left for Tunis, Bourguiba told *Le*

BOURGUIBA, HABIB—*Continued*

Monde (of Paris) that Tunisia would demand the negotiation of a new treaty. Before further agitation could get under way, the French sent a note to the Bey of Tunis, Sidi Mohammed el Amin Pasha, on December 15, 1951, which emphasized the rights of French citizens in Tunisia and rejected self-government.

Bourguiba demanded that an appeal be dispatched to the United Nations and the Bey complied. On January 18, 1952 Bourguiba and five of his top lieutenants were seized in their homes and taken to Tabarca, Tunisia near the Algerian border. French authorities invoked a state of siege and warned Neo-Destour that it was still under order of dissolution. A communiqué from the French Resident General, Jean de Hauteclocque, charged Bourguiba with "systematic agitation."

Removed to La Galite, an island in the Mediterranean Sea, Bourguiba was detained there and later transferred to the Île de Groix in the Bay of Biscay. In July 1955 he was brought to a château sixty-five miles south of Paris. A month later, Premier Mendès-France conferred with Bourguiba and obtained his support for a home-rule plan providing for full Tunisian control of domestic affairs and French control of foreign affairs and defense.

Mendès-France flew to Tunis on July 31 and presented the plan to the Bey of Tunis, who gave it his approval. The Bey anonunced on August 2 the appointment of Tahar ben Ammar as Premier. In September the French Premier restored the legal status of the outlawed Neo-Destour party. However, progress toward a Franco-Tunisian agreement was temporarily ended when Mendès-France's government fell on February 5, 1955.

Negotiations were resumed by French Premier Edgar Faure, who permitted Bourguiba to move to the Hôtel Continental in Paris. When the points at issue had been narrowed to two minor ones by the nominal head of the Tunisian delegation, Premier Tahar ben Ammar, and Premier Faure, an irate lobby representing French planters caused a crisis. Bourguiba had a conference with the French Premier, and later the Premiers went to work again.

On April 22, 1955 an agreement, which was regarded as a modified version of the Mendès-France plan, was finally reached. It was signed on June 3 and approved by the French National Assembly on July 9. All restrictions on Bourguiba's movements were removed and he was free to return to Tunisia.

Under the agreement the police force and court systems are to be turned over gradually to the Tunisians and the entire civil service establishment will be placed under their authority, but the 10,000 French civil servants in Tunisia will be allowed to pursue their careers there. France retains control of the Army and diplomatic service. A French general will act as Defense Minister and a French High Commissioner will replace the Resident General and will also act as Foreign Minister. France retains the exclusive privilege of providing technical and financial assistance to Tunisia, which will remain in the French currency bloc. The agreement also provides for a court of arbitration for settling differences arising out of the treaty.

The colonial French maintain that Tunisia possesses neither the resources nor the skills necessary to become a sovereign state. Burdened by an increasing birth rate and a marginal economy, Tunisia depends on a heavy influx of French capital and food. Strategically, Tunisia is an important adjunct of the defensive system of the North Atlantic Treaty Organization.

A "tumultuous" throng greeted Bourguiba upon his arrival in Tunis on June 1, 1955. For the first time since French rule was imposed, the red and white Tunisian flag flew over the entrance of ancient Carthage, near the Bey's Palace. No incidents of violence were reported for the first time in months. The elderly Bey also broke precedent and stepped from his throne to greet the "father" of Tunisian independence.

Habib ben Ali Bourguiba was married in Paris to a French girl, Mathilde Lorrain, while a student at the University of Paris. Their son, Habib Kamel, is a French citizen and lives in Paris. Bourguiba's French is said to flow with "Voltairian citations." He has been described as "handsome," "stocky" with gray hair and dark eyes, and the manners of an "astute ambassador rather than a revolutionist." Because he was stricken with tuberculosis when in his teens, his health is said to be far from robust. In a speech after he returned to Tunis, Bourguiba called upon the populace to back the new self-rule agreement—as it "marked an important milestone on the road toward complete independence" (New York *Herald Tribune*, June 2, 1955).

References

Le Monde (Paris) p 1 Ja 22 '52
Life 38:47 Je 20 '55 pors
Los Angeles Times II p5 F 17 '52
Nation 172:126+ F 9 '52
New Yorker 27:98+ F 9 '52
Sat Night 67:9+ F 23 '52 por
Time 65:30 My 2 '55 por; 65:25 My 30 '55; 65:32 Je 13 '55 por
U S News 32:39 My 9 '52

BRANCUSI, CONSTANTIN (brän'ko͞osh)
Feb. 21, 1876- Sculptor
Address: 11 Impasse Ronsin, Paris 15e, France

The "old master of modern sculpture," Constantin Brancusi has devoted a lifetime to the creation of forms that are beautiful in themselves rather than as representations of nature. In his organic abstractions of animals and birds, of the human head and figure, the Rumanian-born sculptor has sought perfection of form, contour, surface texture, and balance. "The dual range of visual and tactile perfection which Brancusi seeks in all his work," wrote A. C. Ritchie in *Sculpture of the Twentieth Century,* "combined with the mysterious, occult overtones which his forms call up, explain the extraordinary fascination of his sculpture to observers of every degree of simplicity and sophistication."

The Museum of Modern Art in New York City included Brancusi sculptures in its exhibition, Sculpture of the Twentieth Century, held during 1953, and presented a special display of his work in July 1954. The largest group of his sculptures in the United States is in the Arensberg collection, now at the Philadelphia Museum of Art. His much admired *Bird in Space* figured in a celebrated art lawsuit in 1927 and 1928, when the United States Customs authorities refused to admit the sculpture duty free, claiming it was a piece of metal and not a work of art. Although he has remained aloof from the artistic movements of his time, Brancusi has influenced a host of modern sculptors, among them such men as Amedeo Modigliani, Hans Arp, Henry Moore, and Isamu Noguchi.

Constantin Brancusi was born on February 21, 1876, at Pestisani Gorj, in the Walachia region of southern Rumania. He began his artistic education at the School of Arts and Crafts in Craiova (1894-1898), studying furniture making as well as sculpture. One of his instructors obtained for Brancusi a scholarship to the École des Beaux-Arts in Bucharest, where he received a thorough training in the academic style from 1898 to 1902 and won first prize for a standing male figure, in which every muscle was detailed with photographic exactness. The figure was acquired by the Rumanian government for the École and has been used as an anatomical model for the students at the medical school. Among Brancusi's earliest commissions were a bust of General Davila for the military hospital in Bucharest and the tomb of Pierre Stanesco for the cemetery of Borzcu.

Moving to Paris in 1904, he entered the atelier of the sculptor Antonin Mercié at the École des Beaux-Arts, and studied there until 1907. French sculptor Auguste Rodin recognized Brancusi's ability and tried to persuade him to enter his studio, but Brancusi refused. "In the shade of big trees nothing can sprout," he reportedly said. The influence of Rodin, however, was apparent in his works of this period, such as in *Boy* (1907).

As early as 1908, before the emergence of the first cubist sculpture, Brancusi gave up working from living models and began to evolve an original plastic style based on simplification of form and elimination of detail. Turning away from the realistic, Renaissance-derived tradition of the West, he looked toward Oriental, African Negro, and prehistoric Greek Cycladic sculpture for inspiration. "What is real is not the external form," he explained, "but the essence of things. Starting from this truth it is impossible for anyone to express anything essentially real by imitating exterior surface." In 1908 he started carving directly in stone: *The Kiss,* a composition of two primitive block-like figures that was called "the most abstract sculpture of its period."

His life-long preference for the primordial egg shape, first evident in the heads of the *Sleeping Muse* (1910) and *Prometheus* (1911),

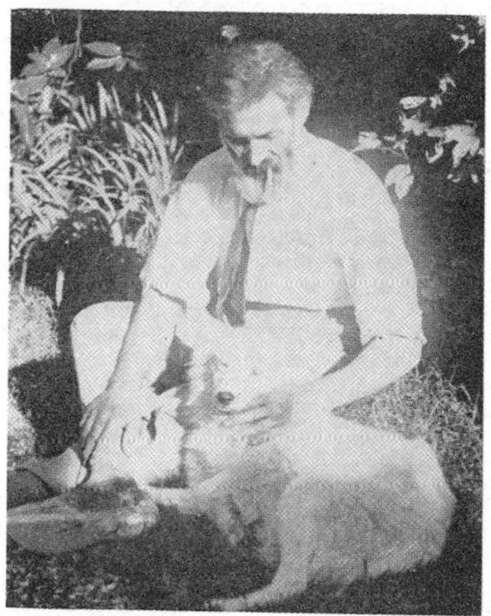

United Press

CONSTANTIN BRANCUSI

is indicated in the bronze portrait-bust of *Mlle. Pogany* (1913). Later he simplified and perfected this form in *The New Born* (1915), *Leda* (1922), *The Beginning of the World* (1924), and *Sculpture for the Blind* (1924).

In contrast to the highly polished marble and bronze surfaces of his ovoid forms, Brancusi's sculpture in wood is usually rough-hewn. The critics have related his work in this medium to African Negro sculpture, Gothic wood carvings, and Rumanian folk art. They point out that in such sculptures as *The Prodigal Son* (1914), *The Chimera* (1918), *Eve* (1920) *Adam* (1921), and *Socrates* (1923), he allowed his fantasy free reign and occasionally indulged in a satiric, grotesque humor.

Archetypal bird and animal forms occupy an important place in Brancusi's work. The first in a long series of bird forms was the *Maïastra* (the name of a mythical Rumanian bird) of 1912, and this was followed by the marble *Penguins* of 1914. His *Bird in Space,* a slender, highly polished bronze shaft that most critics consider his boldest and purest work, was completed in 1919. Further variations on the bird theme include *Bird at Rest* (1920), *Yellow Bird* (1921), *The Cock* (1924), and *Small Bird* (1929). Next to his bird forms Brancusi is best known for his *Fish*; a final version (1930) in blue-gray marble has been called his outstanding stone carving. In 1943 he executed his pearwood *Tortoise* and marble *Seal.*

In February 1927, Brancusi's *Bird in Space* created a newspaper sensation when a United States Customs appraiser ruled that it was not a work of art and was therefore dutiable. Several prominent artists and critics decided to contest this decision. The technical problem was whether the sculpture conformed to the standards of imitative representation in art prescribed by the Customs or whether it was

BRANCUSI, CONSTANTIN—*Continued*

a new form of tax evasion used to import bronze. The case was settled in Brancusi's favor in November 1928. The judge ruled that even though *Bird* bore no striking resemblance to a living object, it was a work of art "by reason of its symmetrical shape, artistic outlines, and beauty of finish" (New York *Times*, November 28, 1928).

The architectural quality of Brancusi's work has been widely praised. A large-scale version of his sculpture, *Endless Column*, rising to 118 feet, was executed in a park in the Rumanian town of Targu-Jiu. As yet unfinished is his *Bird in Space* project for a Temple of Deliverance, commissioned by the Maharaja of Indore.

Since Brancusi is a slow, painstaking worker, his production has been relatively small. He uses no preliminary models, and does all the labor himself. Believing that the art of sculpture is to call forth "the inner life" of the material he is handling, never to dictate to it, he often spends years over a single piece, patiently polishing and refining the surface.

He also devises the wooden bases and stone pedestals on which he places his work, selecting them for the qualities of color and texture that will enhance his sculptural forms. One of his innovations has been the construction of mechanical turntables, which slowly and automatically rotate the sculpture so that the observer can experience its full plastic power in motion.

Brancusi has been variously described by art critics as "the father of modern sculpture," "the most original and most important of near-abstract sculptors," and simply as "our greatest living sculptor." C. Giedon-Welcker in *Horizon* (March 1949) wrote: "His sculpture unites the radiant formal beauty of the Mediterranean with the formal wisdom and symbolism of the East." According to Lewis Mumford, almost alone among contemporary artists, Brancusi has been able to blend the organic and the mathematical, "the feeling for nature" and "the belief in formal perfection."

During his first decade in Paris, Brancusi participated in the annual exhibitions at the Salon de la Nationale (1905-1907), Salon de l'Automne (1907-1908), and the Salon des Indépendants (1910-1913). His *Princesse X* (1917), an abstract portrait in polished bronze, created such a storm of indignation at the Salon des Indépendants of 1920 that it was temporarily removed from the exhibition. He later showed work at the Salon des Tuileries of 1927 and in the Rumanian Pavilion at the International Exposition of 1937. One-man exhibitions have been held in Antwerp (1926), Moscow (1928), and other European cities.

The sculptor's work was first shown in New York at the famous Armory Show of 1913, where his *Mlle. Pogany* shared with Marcel Duchamp's *Nude Descending a Staircase* the distinction of being the two major sensations of this first exhibition of modern art in the United States. The following year Alfred Stieglitz gave Brancusi a one-man show at the Photo-Secession Gallery. Solo exhibitions were later held at the Wildenstein Galleries in February 1926 and at the Brummer Gallery in November 1926 and in November 1933. Works by Brancusi were included in the Cubism and Abstract Art (1936) and Sculpture of the Twentieth Century (1952) shows at the Museum of Modern Art.

Among the European museums in which Brancusi's work is represented are the Musée National d'Art Moderne in Paris and the Tate Gallery in London. In the United States examples of his work are included in the Museum of Modern Art and Solomon R. Guggenheim Museum in New York City; the Buffalo (New York) Fine Arts Academy; the Cleveland (Ohio) Museum of Art; and the Art Institute of Chicago in Illinois.

The sculptor, who has dark eyes and a full white beard, is a short, robust man with strong, sensitive hands. Descriptions of his personality emphasize his modesty, geniality, and uncompromising devotion to work. Once celebrated for his hospitality and cuisine, he now leads a simple, secluded life in his much-photographed studio, which is filled with large blocks of stone and trunks of trees waiting to be used. Brancusi's fondness for music developed at an early age when he mastered the Gregorian chant and constructed a violin. In recent years he has immersed himself in the writings of certain Tibetan mystics and philosophers.

References

Art N 53:24+ O '54 por
Horizon 19:193+ Mr '49
Bénézit, E. ed. Dictionnaire Critique et Documentaire des Peintres, Sculpteurs, Dessinateurs et Graveurs (1949)
Dictionnaire Biographique des Artistes Contemporains, 1910-1930
Ritchie, A. C. Sculpture of the Twentieth Century (1952)

BREECH, ERNEST R(OBERT) Feb. 24, 1897- Corporation executive

Address: b. Ford Motor Co., Dearborn, Mich.; h. W. Long Lake Rd., Bloomfield Hills, Mich.

The three-year agreement between the Ford Motor Company and the United Automobile Workers, CIO, signed on June 6, 1955, is a good thing for the workers, the company and the entire nation, in the opinion of Ernest R. Breech, chairman of the board of the Ford Motor Company. He was elected to this post on January 25, 1955, becoming the first board chairman in the company's history. "Breech is an Horatio Alger story come true," commented *Business Week*. He joined the Ford company as executive vice-president in 1946 after a twenty-one year association with General Motors Corp. and other companies. He is recognized as one of America's leading executives in the aviation and automotive fields.

At the age of thirty-seven, he became head of North American Aviation, Inc., in 1939 he was elected a corporation vice-president of General Motors and in 1942 he was chosen president of the Bendix Aviation Corporation, the company he left to join the Ford Motor Company at a salary estimated at "more than

$200,000 a year." As chairman, Breech shares basic management responsibilities with the company's president, Henry Ford 2d. In announcing Breech's election to the chairmanship, Ford credited him with playing a major role in the company's spectacular growth since 1946.

"The son of the best blacksmith in the Ozarks" (*Newsweek,* May 27, 1946), Ernest Robert Breech was born on February 24, 1897 in Lebanon, Missouri to Joseph F. E. and Martha (Atchley) Breech. "As a boy," according to the New York *Herald Tribune* (January 30, 1955), "he worked with an older brother in his father's blacksmith shop, where carriage making was a specialty." At Lebanon High School he was a good enough baseball player to earn an offer of a tryout with the St. Louis Browns' professional club.

In 1915 Breech entered Drury College at Springfield, Missouri, with the hope of becoming a lawyer. In 1917 he left college, where he had achieved a scholastic average of 93, to join the accounting department of Fairbanks, Morse and Company, a Chicago firm, at a salary of $15 a week. At night he studied accountancy at the Walton School of Commerce, Chicago, from which, by taking correspondence courses, he was able to graduate in half the usual time. Cost accountancy was especially interesting to him.

"I realized," Robert Coughlan (*Life,* February 28, 1955) reported Breech as saying, "that it was here that a business stood or fell—on cost controls. That was the nut of any business." Breech is a "quick person, who in 1920 read a book on accounting one night and the next day began setting up a new system for a Chicago manufacturer" (*Newsweek,* February 7, 1955). In 1921 he won the degree of C.P.A. from the University of Illinois, Urbana.

From 1920 until 1922 he was an auditor for Adams and Westlake. In the latter year the Illinois Manufacturers Cost Association invited him to discuss means of establishing machine-hour rates. "In the audience was the treasurer of the Yellow Cab Manufacturing Company, who hired Ernie on the spot," wrote *Newsweek* (May 27, 1946). Breech served as comptroller of the company until 1929. When Yellow Cab merged with General Motors in 1925, Breech was retained in his post, and in 1927 became a director of the Yellow Truck and Coach Manufacturing Company.

"Young Breech made a deep impression on General Motors executives," according to *Look* (April 10, 1951), "and by 1930 was general assistant treasurer of GM." In that capacity he supervised the merger of the General Aviation Corporation and North American Aviation, Inc., then a GM affiliate. In 1934, thanks to his "nervous energy and keen talent for figures," he became president and chairman of the board of North American Aviation. Three years later he was appointed a group executive at GM, and in 1939 he became vice-president in charge of the household appliance division and of aviation subsidiaries.

In February 1942, on his forty-fifth birthday, Breech resigned his GM vice-presidency to accept, wrote *Time* (March 9, 1942), "the grand-

Wide World

ERNEST R. BREECH

est birthday present of his life: the presidency of crucial Bendix Aviation Corporation," a leading manufacturer of airplane parts. "In the fast-moving aviation business," *Time* commented, "Breech is a sprinter." A year after he assumed the presidency, the company tripled its output; within two years, it had multiplied its annual gross, from $40,000,000 to one billion dollars.

"As president of Bendix Aviation Corporation, selling both to Ford and General Motors, and as top dog in a key company whose importance in defense production was vital, Ernie Breech had arrived," commented *Look* magazine (June 30, 1952). On June 30, 1946 Breech resigned from Bendix and severed his remaining connections with GM to become a director and executive vice-president of the Ford Motor Company. "Working with young Henry Ford 2d, president of Ford," *Business Week* observed (May 25, 1946), "Breech will correlate the strenuous efforts the company is making in production, engineering, development, and sales to regain the top sales position in the industry."

Since the end of World War II the Ford company had been losing an estimated $68,000,000 annually (*Fortune,* April, 1950). Upon assuming the presidency of the company, Henry Ford 2d, grandson of the founder, had introduced some order into its affairs, and inaugurated some reforms, but the task of reorganization turned out to be too massive and too complicated for a young and relatively inexperienced executive.

"Breech, it seems in retrospect," in Robert Coughlan's words, "had been training all his life for the job" that Ford offered him in 1946. Ford "had heard of Breech and knew a little about his record as a free-wheeling executive and trouble shooter at GM. Meeting him, he liked him." Later he "invited him to take management of Ford and remodel it on the GM

BREECH, ERNEST R.—*Continued*

pattern. Breech was both flattered and horrified: he had a pretty good idea of Ford's troubles. He politely turned down the offer. But he did agree to study the company. . . . Henry renewed his offer. Breech signed a ten-year contract giving him the extreme latitude he knew he needed and reported for work on July 1, 1946."

When he joined Ford, Breech stated, the company was "an awkward, misshapen giant suffering from hardening of the arteries" (New York *Times,* January 30, 1955). An initial step in the rehabilitation of the company was the working out of a method for the orderly, progressive and complete decentralization of the management. "That was an idea Ford 2d brought with him to the presidency. The professional managerial 'savvy' required to translate the concept into the elaborate organization" that ultimately evolved, came from Breech. "That, plus a knack both for picking men and for using them most effectively, was what Breech had to sell" (*Business Week,* June 13, 1953).

Another important phase of Breech's contribution to the company's regeneration was a vast development program. Between 1946 and 1953 the company spent $900,000,000 in expanding its facilities. This program "required construction of thirteen manufacturing plants across the country, sixteen parts depots or warehouses and four engineering buildings as well as the enlarging and modernizing of twenty existing plants" (New York *Times,* October 4, 1953).

By 1955 the sum had risen to $1,700,000,000—none of it borrowed, but all of it "plowed back" from the company's rising profits. As a result, Ford production and sales have increased sharply in the last few years, and, as *Newsweek* (February 7, 1955) reported, the company "accelerated from a poor third" in the automotive field, behind General Motors and Chrysler, "to strong second since hard-chinned Ernie Breech took the wheel." In announcing Breech's elevation to the first board chairmanship in the company's history, a promotion that makes him alternate chief officer, Henry Ford 2d paid him a generous tribute "for the transformation of the company, from one that was losing money to an expanding, aggressive leader in the industry" (New York *Times,* January 30, 1955).

Addressing the Harvard Business School's twenty-fifth annual national business conference on June 11, 1955, Breech stated that "knotty problems" concerning American industry were solved in the three-year pact of the Ford Motor Company with the United Automobile Workers, CIO. "It has been Ford policy for years," he declared, "to stabilize production and employment, to minimize layoffs through better planning and to use overtime pay to meet production peaks rather than hire temporary workers." He stated that his company had been working for some time on a plan of private supplementation of unemployment compensation "that would give substantial added security to our workers in ways consistent with private enterprise principles. . . . Such a plan should not shackle management's freedom to manage. . . . It should not offer unemployment benefits so great as to remove the incentive to work. The present plan meets every one of those requirements" (New York *Times,* June 12, 1955). (The key provisions of the pact are published on page 22 of the New York *Times,* June 7, 1955). The UAW-CIO (United Automobile, Aircraft and Agricultural Implement Workers) has some 1,500,000 members.

Besides the professional connections mentioned, Breech has been a director of Transcontinental and Western Air, Inc., of Pan-American Airways, and of Western Air Express. He was a member of the Anglo-American Productivity Council which functioned under the European Cooperation Administration. From 1942 until 1945 he was chairman of Detroit's Central Aircraft Council. He received in 1953 the annual Brotherhood Award given by the National Conference of Christians and Jews in recognition of "his continuing efforts toward the furtherance of understanding and friendship among those who have different religious beliefs."

Drury College, of which he is a trustee, has conferred upon him an honorary LL.D. degree. In March 1955 he was named to an eight-member panel formed "to study all phases of the impact of peaceful applications of atomic energy in the United States." Breech is a member of the Illinois Society of Certified Public Accountants and of the Society of Automotive Engineers. He is a Mason, and belongs to the Bloomfield Hills Country Club of Birmingham, Michigan, and to the Recess, Athletic, Detroit, and Economic clubs of Detroit. He married Thelma Rowden on November 11, 1917; the Breeches have two sons—Ernest Robert and William Howard. Breech is a Protestant.

A writer for the New York *Times* (October 4, 1953) noted that "Breech, for all those brain cells lined up in his head like the buttons on a calculator, knows how to get away from it all and to have fun. He can find time to fish from a rowboat as well as from his cabin cruiser on the Great Lakes. . . . He is something of a raconteur and his associates particularly delight in his use of dialects." *Business Week* described him as "small-statured, energetic, decisive in making his viewpoints known."

Breech defined the character of management in an article he contributed to *Look* (April 10, 1951) entitled "America's Secret Weapon." "Management, first of all," he wrote, "is a matter of spirit—a feeling of resourcefulness and responsibility and enthusiasm for always doing things better. Second, it is people—the millions of Americans who share in the direction of our unsurpassed production machinery. Put them together, and America's secret weapon comes out as the free-wheeling ingenuity and competitive drive of free men, constantly needled by the urge to beat others at the job of providing better things and services and more of them."

On July 11, 1955 the Ford Motor Company announced that it is making seat belts available to their dealers since the engineering staff learned in full-scale car-crash tests that less injuries result to drivers when held behind the steering wheel.

References

Bsns W p36 My 25 '46 por
Christian Sci Mon p14 Ja 29 '55 por
Fortune 41:15 Ap '50 por
Life 38:90+ F 28 '55 por
Look 15:108 Ap 10 '51 por; 17:49+ Je 30 '52 por
N Y Herald Tribune II p1 Ja 30 '55 por
N Y Times p26 My 17 '46 por; III p3 O 4 '53 por; p33+ Ja 26 '55 por
Newsweek 27:73+ My 27 '46 por
Read Digest 67:41+ Jl '55
Time 39:78 Mr 9 '42 por; 47:83+ My 27 '46 por
Who's Who in America, 1954-55
Who's Who in Commerce and Industry (1953)
World Biography (1954)

BRENTANO (DI TREMEZZO), HEINRICH VON

June 20, 1904-Foreign Minister of the Federal Republic of Germany; lawyer

Address: b. Auswärtiges Amt, Bonn, Germany; h. Ohlystrasse 58, Darmstadt, Germany

An advocate of European unity, Dr. Heinrich von Brentano, a founder and leader of the Christian Democratic Union in West Germany, served in 1952-1953 as chairman of a committee charged by the European Coal and Steel Community with framing a constitution for a projected European federation. His committee's work and the entire concept of federal union were dealt a severe blow in 1954 when France rejected the European Defense Community (EDC). However, the signing of the London and Paris agreements in October 1954 restored Dr. von Brentano's hope for a sovereign and rearmed West Germany joined with European and other nations for mutual defense and cooperation. This hope was close to realization in late December 1954 when France, by a vote of 287 to 260, accepted the pacts.

On June 6, 1955 Chancellor Konrad Adenauer resigned as Foreign Minister and designated Dr. Heinrich von Brentano as his successor in the Foreign Office.

Before entering politics in 1945, Dr. von Brentano was a lawyer in the Superior Provincial Court, Darmstadt. As leader in the Bundestag of Chancellor Konrad Adenauer's CDU, Dr. von Brentano has supported a foreign policy aimed at alliance with the Western powers. He has also worked for the unification of West and East Germany, but has opposed the methods proposed by the Soviet Union.

Heinrich von Brentano di Tremezzo was born on June 20, 1904 in Offenbach am Main, Hesse, Germany. He is the son of Otto von Brentano di Tremezzo and the former Lilla Schwerdt-Brentano. Heinrich's father, a barrister and notary, served as Hessian Minister of the Interior and of Justice and was a member of the German National Assembly and of the German Reichstag. Heinrich's brother Clemens is the German Ambassador to Italy; his brother Bernard is a poet, novelist and literary critic.

Reared in Darmstadt, Heinrich attended the Humanistisches Gymnasium there and was graduated in 1922. He then studied at the universities of Frankfort, Giessen and Munich and passed the state law examinations in 1925 and 1929. In 1930 the University of Giessen conferred on him the degree of Doctor of Law for his thesis "Rechtsstellung des Parlamentspräsidenten."

The young lawyer began his career in 1932 when admitted to the Superior Provincial Court (of Cassation), Darmstadt. He spent the years when the Nazis were in power trying civil cases there. After the German generals' July 1944 plot against Hitler failed, he was imprisoned. In 1945 he began to devote himself to politics. Dr. von Brentano became a founder of the CDU of Hesse. He served as a member of the constitutional assembly and of the Landtag (Provincial Diet) of Hesse.

After his election as president of the organization committee of the Christian Democratic Union and Christian Socialist Union (CDU/CSU), he served as deputy in the Stuttgart district council and as a member of the Parliamentary Council (Constituent Assembly) of West Germany. He was elected to the Bundestag (the lower house of the West German Parliament) in August 1949 and later became leader of the CDU/CSU group there.

In this position in the Bundestag, Dr. von Brentano has rallied support at home for Chancellor Adenauer's policies; he has also promoted them abroad as a delegate to various international assemblies. While attending a meeting of the Consultative Assembly of the Council of Europe in Strasbourg in August 1950, he said that the German people were not seeking rearmament to further national interests, but to contribute their productive capacity and man power for the defense of the European community. At that meeting he was elected a vice-president of the Consultative Assembly.

He appeared before the Special Political Committee of the United Nations in Paris on December 8, 1951 and said that "the main cause of the troubled order in Europe is Germany's division, and some way must be found to terminate it." He asked that neutral investigators be sent into both East and West Germany to find out whether conditions would permit genuinely free all-German elections.

In debates in the Bundestag in February 1952, Dr. von Brentano supported the idea of rearmament equality and the eventual creation of a high command and general staff to direct West Germany's ground and air forces in a European defense community. This German attitude caused concern and uneasiness among the Western nations, particularly the French. Uneasiness increased in April 1952 when Adenauer—then advocating a conference between France, Great Britain, the United States and the Soviet Union on the unification of Germany—declared that the European army treaty and peace contract being negotiated by West Germany and the Western allies would not be binding on a united Germany. He insisted,

Wide World
HEINRICH VON BRENTANO

however, that negotiations with the Soviet government should not be allowed to hold up the integration of Western Europe. Supporting Adenauer, Dr. von Brentano went on record in favor of four-power negotiations for all-German elections as a step toward the unification of his country.

On September 22, 1952 Dr. von Brentano was unanimously elected president of the six-nation Schuman plan committee charged with framing a constitution for a projected European federation. The committee was formed by the *Ad Hoc* Assembly of the European Coal and Steel Community whose members are France, West Germany, Italy, Belgium, the Netherlands and Luxembourg.

"The post to which Dr. Heinrich von Brentano was elected," commented a New York *Herald Tribune* editorial (September 25, 1952), "carries with it high honors and grave responsibilities. As chairman . . . the German political leader has a remarkable opportunity to affect the course of history." The editorial further described him as "the chief architect of this ambitious endeavor to unite Western Europe." The aim of Dr. von Brentano's committee was to create a political authority with supranational powers to direct and coordinate policies of the already existing heavy industry community (the European Coal and Steel Community) and the proposed defense community (EDC) of six of the Western European nations.

On March 10, 1953, in the House of Europe in Strasbourg, a constitutional convention of fifty-five European delegates completed a document called the Constitution of Europe which, if ratified by the member countries, would place them under a sovereign European political authority. Such acceptance, however, was beset with many obstacles. German delegates felt they could get ratification in their Parliament if France did not press too hard for control of the Saar.

French delegate Guy Mollet had withdrawn from the constitutional committee, pointing out that without Great Britain in the federal union, a six-power Europe would never become a third force capable of acting as a balancing power between the United States and the Soviet Union. He also expressed French fears of a German national army. In December 1953 Dr. von Brentano declared that French distrust was becoming an obstacle to the integration of West Germany with Europe and said that the main task of the two nations was to overcome that distrust.

At the four-power conference in Berlin in early 1954, Vîacheslav M. Molotov, Soviet Foreign Minister, rejected the Western plan for free all-German elections. Dr. von Brentano then spoke against Molotov's counterproposal for a provisional all-German government and an all-German referendum to choose between a peace treaty and military association with the West. He charged that Molotov had come to Berlin "not to unify Germany but to split up the Western powers."

As French acceptance of EDC became more and more doubtful during the first months of 1954, the Social Democratic opposition in the Bundestag leaned more and more toward holding further talks with the Soviet Union on the question of the unification of Germany. As CDU/CSU parliamentary leader, Dr. von Brentano opposed such talks and worked for the continuation of Adenauer's policy of ties with the West even though the policy was then considered to be on the brink of failure. When the French National Assembly defeated EDC in August, news commentators observed that four years of effort to "rearm Germany and forge a united Europe had reached a dead end."

The signing of the Final Act of London in early October 1954, however, encouraged the German leaders in their hopes for West Germany. After further negotiations were held in Paris on details of the Final Act, Adenauer agreed to the signing of the pacts of Paris under which a sovereign and rearmed West Germany would be admitted to the North Atlantic Treaty Organization and to the projected Western European Union (an expanded Brussels Treaty Organization).

Before signing the Paris pacts, French Premier Pierre Mendès-France insisted on a settlement under which the Saar would be "Europeanized" but controlled economically by France until a general German peace treaty is written. Adenauer felt it was necessary to agree to these terms. Dr. von Brentano faced serious opposition in the Bundestag on the Saar question and on other points in the Paris pacts.

Dr. von Brentano has been described by Theodore H. White in the *Reporter* as "a pink-cheeked, earnest, bespectacled pillar of Konrad Adenauer's government." He weighs 198 pounds, is about six feet tall, has blue-grey eyes and dark blond hair. Heinrich von Brentano is a member of the Roman Catholic church. He is a bachelor. Formerly he enjoyed sports, but has had no time for such recreation in recent years, turning instead to books, paintings and music in his moments of leisure.

References

N Y Herald Tribune p5 S 23 '52; p22 S 25 '52
Newsweek 45:38 Je 20 '55 por
Wer ist Wer? (1951)

BRIDGMAN, P(ERCY) W(ILLIAMS) Apr. 21, 1882- Physicist; university professor emeritus; author

Address: h. 10 Buckingham Pl., Cambridge, Mass.

For advancing man's knowledge of the behavior of matter and for his contributions as teacher and philosopher, Dr. P. W. Bridgman, recently retired professor of physics at Harvard University, has achieved world renown. His investigation into the properties of substances under very high pressures has been his lifework, earning for him the Nobel Prize in 1946 as well as other citations. His book *The Physics of High Pressure* (Macmillan, 1931) has become the standard work on the subject.

On February 15, 1955 the General Electric Company of Schenectady, New York announced that diamonds had been created synthetically. The new process, based on over twenty years of work by Bridgman, was developed by a G.E. team of five scientists. Before they began work four years ago, only Bridgman had attained pressures of more than 750,000 pounds per square inch. The team managed to hold fantastic pressures and temperatures and thus the carbon atoms of the coal dust "melt" and rearrange themselves into the crystal structure of diamonds.

Dr. Bridgman has formulated new concepts on the properties of crystals at normal pressures and on the application of thermodynamics to electrical phenomena in metals. He has sought to evolve concepts which would explain the relation of science to civilization. In a speech before the American Physical Society on January 23, 1943, he stated: "In the long run, society is a better place for every one when there is intellectual freedom and encouragement and flourishing activity in pure science" (*Science,* February 12, 1943). His philosophical approach to physical problems—"operational analysis"—is presented in the books *Dimensional Analysis* (Yale University Press, 1922) and *The Logic of Modern Physics* (Macmillan, 1927), and in other of his works.

Percy Williams Bridgman was born on April 21, 1882 in Cambridge, Massachusetts, the son of Raymond Landon and Mary Ann Maria (Williams) Bridgman. His father was a newspaper reporter and author. Young Bridgman received his early education in the public schools of Newton, Massachusetts. He recalls that a high school teacher was responsible for encouraging his scientific interests.

Wide World

P. W. BRIDGMAN

Following his graduation in 1904 from Harvard University with an A.B. degree, Bridgman remained at the university to continue his education. He received his master's degree in 1905 and his doctorate in 1908. He was a fellow for research at Harvard (1908-1910) and was appointed an instructor in physics in 1910 and an assistant professor three years later. He was advanced to the status of full professor in 1919. He won Harvard's highest scientific post in 1926, when he was appointed Hollis Professor of Mathematics and Natural Philosophy. Bridgman was named Higgins University Professor by the Harvard trustees in 1950. At the end of the 1953-1954 academic year, he retired from the faculty.

His work has been directed toward studying the behavior of liquids, solids and gases under extremely high pressures. His introduction into the field was quite by accident. "I was engaged in an optical experiment," he later wrote, "under the quite modest pressure of 1,000 pounds per square inch, where one of the problems was the designing of a packing plug for a hole. On examining the plug after it was designed, I saw . . . that it automatically became tighter as pressure increased, and thus could never leak, no matter how high the pressure, provided only that the walls of the containing vessel did not break.

"The packing at once opened an enormous field, for the highest pressure reached in previous research was about 45,000 pounds per square inch, and the limit was set by leaks, and not at all by the strength of the containing vessels. The multitude of the field opened is shown by the fact that now after nearly twenty years work, I do not feel that I have much more than begun" (*Scientific American,* July 1927).

Bridgman's results were of great interest to the world of science. The physicist said: "The most striking effect produced by high pressures

BRIDGMAN, P. W.—*Continued*

is in the change of the melting point of many substances or in the different crystalline forms which are stable under high pressure although not stable under low pressure. Ordinary ice becomes unstable at pressures greater than 29,000 pounds per square inch, and is replaced by other forms, one of which is stable under a pressure of 290,000 pounds at temperature as high as 180° F., thus producing a paradoxical substance—'hot ice'" (New York *Times*, June 19, 1930).

In order to carry on further experimentation, Bridgman developed an apparatus which would not burst under higher pressures. *Nature* (December 7, 1946) wrote: "By constructing the vessels of the steel known as 'carboloy' and by special methods of construction, including, for the highest pressures, the immersion of the pressure vessel in a fluid which is itself maintained at 30,000 atmospheres [about 441,000 pounds], he has pushed the limit up to 100,000 atmospheres." Bridgman also worked out new methods of measuring pressure during his experiments.

By the late 1940's he could state that he had been able to produce up to 6,000,000 pounds of pressure per square inch. His more recent experiments indicate that he can crush atoms. As David Dietz of the New York *World-Telegram and Sun* (May 15, 1954) wrote, "He found that when the element caesium was subjected to high pressure it contracted until a pressure of 375,000 pounds to the square inch was reached. From there on increased pressure caused no change until a pressure of 675,000 pounds was reached. Then the metal contracted another 12 per cent. The only possible explanation is that at this high pressure the atoms of the metal actually were crushed, the outer cloud of electrons collapsing."

What are the practical results of these pressure experiments? "New and unexpected phenomena have been discovered and fresh light has been thrown on phenomena already known but only imperfectly understood," wrote Niels H. de V. Heathcote in *Nobel Prize Winners in Physics, 1901-1950*. Bridgman's work has been and is being used by physicists, chemists, engineers, and geologists.

Several months before the outbreak of World War II in Europe, Bridgman announced in *Science* magazine (February 24, 1939) that he had closed his laboratories to all visitors from totalitarian countries. Explaining his action, he wrote: "A citizen of such a state is no longer a free individual, but he may be compelled to engage in any activity whatever to advance the purposes of that state. . . . Cessation of scientific intercourse with the totalitarian states serves the double purpose of making more difficult the misuse of scientific information by these states and of giving the individual opportunity to express his abhorrence of their practices."

While some scientists protested against Bridgman's action and argued for the universality of science, others defended his action. Dean Christian Gauss of Princeton University pointed out that Bridgman's work "releases immense reservoirs which can be used more easily for destructive rather than constructive purposes" (New York *Times*, February 25, 1939). In an editorial on February 24, the New York *Times* hailed Bridgman's "no admittance" sign.

After the United States had entered World War II, Bridgman's methods for strengthening the metal in cannons and other military equipment were used. On his departure for Sweden to receive the award of the Nobel Prize after the war, Bridgman called for "free circulation among scientists" in peacetime and the interchange of scientific knowledge (New York *Herald Tribune*, December 6, 1946).

Awards which the physicist has received other than the Nobel Prize include the Rumford Medal of the American Academy of Arts and Sciences (1917), the Cresson Medal of the Franklin Institute (1932), the Roozeboom Medal of the Royal Netherlands Academy of Sciences of Amsterdam (1933), and the Comstock Prize of the National Academy of Sciences (1933).

Bridgman has been hailed for his work in "that wide frontier where philosophy and physics meet in their search for ultimate reality." His contributions to journals on scientific and philosophical questions have been extensive. He wrote *The Thermodynamics of Electrical Phenomena in Metals* (Macmillan) in 1934 and *The Nature of Physical Theory* (Princeton University Press) in 1936. Two years later Macmillan published his *The Intelligent Individual and Society*, which was received as an "exhilarating and unsettling book, impressive in its brutal frankness." In 1941 he presented *The Nature of Thermodynamics* (Harvard University Press). Bridgman's *Reflections of a Physicist* (1950) and *The Nature of Some of our Physical Concepts* (1952) were published by the Philosophical Library.

Writing in the *Yale Review* (spring 1945) on "The Prospect for Intelligence," Dr. Bridgman discussed the attitude of the community toward unusual ability, in connection with the military draft. "It is easy in a democracy," he wrote "to take the position that all are of equal value and therefore all must receive equal treatment, irrespective of natural gifts. . . . A philosophy of democracy like this is blind to the very undemocratic distribution of talents by nature. . . . From the long-range point of view it is important for *everyone* that unusual ability, so long as it is accompanied by social responsibility, be cherished, encouraged, stimulated, and given any special treatment necessary to induce it to produce to capacity. . . . As technological improvement advances, as the standard of living rises, and as increasing numbers acquire a degree of leisure, there is an increasing tendency for the effective level of intellectual ideals and attainment to become that of the mass average."

Speaking at the Massachusetts Institute of Technology in March 1948, Bridgman stated: "In the face of a fact, there is only one possible course of action for the scientist, namely acceptance. . . . In the face of the fact, the scientist has a humility almost religious."

Bridgman is a fellow of the American Academy of Arts and Sciences, an honorary fellow of the Physical Society (London), a past president of the American Physical Society, and a member of numerous other organizations. In 1949 he was elected to membership in the Royal Society of London. His Greek-letter societies are Phi Beta Kappa and Sigma Xi. He has received honorary degrees from several American and foreign universities.

The physicist married Olive Ware on July 16, 1912. They have a daughter, Jane, and a son, Robert Ware. Bridgman has dark hair and heavy dark brows. He has been characterized as "mild" in manner. He wears baggy tweeds, smokes a pipe and is known as an outgoing, friendly person. He is easily disturbed by ringing telephones, but relaxes completely while "working with his Oriental poppies and delphiniums" at his summer home in New Hampshire.

References

Nature 158:825+ D 7 '46; 163:793 My 21 '49
Time 26:36 D 9 '35
American Men of Science vol. I (1955)
Heathcote, N. H. de V. Nobel Prize Winners in Physics, 1901-1950 (1953)
Who's Who in America, 1954-55

BROGLIE, LOUIS (VICTOR PIERRE RAYMOND), PRINCE DE (dē brô"glē')

Aug. 15, 1892- French physicist; university professor

Address: b. Institut Henri Poincaré, 11 rue Pierre Curie, Paris V^e^, France; h. 94 rue Perronet, Neuilly-sur-Seine, France

Much of present-day research in atomic physics has been made possible by the considerations of theoretical physics conducted by Prince Louis de Broglie, a counselor of the French High Commission on Atomic Energy and Nobel Prizewinner. Under his sponsorship, a paper warning of the dangers of further hydrogen bomb explosions was read before the Académie des Sciences of France in November 1954. The *Christian Century* (December 15, 1954) noted: "Prince Louis de Broglie, secretary of the French Académie des Sciences . . . writes in the academy's review that enough hydrogen bombs have already been exploded to create deadly dangers for the world's animal and plant life. He declares that the physical phenomena already produced outstrip the capability of scientists to calculate their ultimate efforts."

In 1923 de Broglie discovered the wave nature of the electron which gave a new and unexpected direction to research in quantum theory. For this, he was awarded the Nobel Prize in Physics in 1929. He has the distinction of being made a member of both the Académie Française and the Académie des Sciences. De Broglie's work laid the foundations on which Schrödinger, Dirac, and others constructed the new system of wave mechanics which has proved so successful in dealing with problems of atomic physics.

The son of Victor, Prince de Broglie, and of the former Pauline d'Armaillé, Louis Victor Pierre Raymond de Broglie was born on August 15, 1892 in Dieppe, France. His grandfather, Jacques Victor Albert de Broglie, was Premier and Minister of Foreign Affairs from 1873 to 1874. His great-grandfather fought in the American Revolutionary War as chief lieutenant to the Marquis de Lafayette. The de Broglie family originated in Italy and founded the French branch in Normandy before the eighteenth century. The title of Duc is held by the head of the family, while younger brothers are designated as Prince. Louis' elder brother, Maurice, who succeeded to the title upon the death of his father in 1906, is known for his researches in nuclear physics, X rays, and radioactivity.

Louis de Broglie studied at the Lycée Janson-de-Sailly and received his *baccalauréat* in history in 1909 from the Sorbonne. However, he has stated in an interview with André Gillois, which is recorded in *Que Etes Vous?* (1953): "After passing the examinations in history, I felt that I was more interested in scientific philosophy and in science. . . . I was brought to science by philosophy, by generalizations, and by the books of [Henri] Poincaré." This interest led him to obtain a *licence* in science in 1913 from the Faculty of Sciences, University of Paris. In this period he was also interested in paleography.

Mobilized in 1913, de Broglie was assigned to the radio-telegraph branch of the French Engineering Corps. During much of his period of service he worked at the wireless station of the Eiffel Tower in Paris. In 1919 he took up his studies again in the physics laboratory of his elder brother. The subsequent development of his thought was chronicled in "Vue d'ensemble sur mes travaux scientifiques," which he contributed to a commemorative volume in honor of his sixtieth birthday in 1952. In this book, *Louis de Broglie, Physicien et Penseur,* Nobel Prize winners Albert Einstein, Erwin Schrödinger, Enrico Fermi, Jean Perrin and Paul Dirac discussed various aspects of his work.

Niels H. de V. Heathcote, in *Nobel Prize Winners in Physics, 1901-1950* (1953), pointed out that until de Broglie's establishment of the wave theory, two contradictory theories were coexistent: Philipp Lenard's, asserting that ultraviolet light falling on a metal plate caused the ejection of electrons, whose energy was completely independent of the intensity of the incidental light, and Einstein's, which assumed that the incidental light transmitted its energy to the electrons in packets equal to hv, with h representing Max Planck's constant, and v, the frequency of incidental light.

Such were the puzzles which confronted physicists. This gave de Broglie the idea that "electrons . . . could not be represented as simple corpuscles, but that to them also must be attributed a periodicity. . . ."

"Thus I arrived at the following general idea," stated de Broglie, "which has guided my researches: for matter, just as much as for

Agence Diffusion Presse, Paris
PRINCE LOUIS DE BROGLIE

radiation, in particular light, we must introduce at one and the same time the corpuscle concept and the wave concept . . . it must be possible to establish a certain parallelism between the motion of a corpuscle and the propagation of the wave which is associated with it."

In this way, explained Heathcote, by attributing wavelike properties to matter, de Broglie "succeeded in representing the motion of the material particle as a combination of waves having slightly different velocities of propagation, at regular intervals . . . the waves would combine to form a wave-crest, the crest disappearing at one point to reappear an instant later at the next. The velocity of the crest—the so-called 'group velocity'—is entirely different from the velocities of the various waves which combine to form the crest. De Broglie identified this group velocity with the velocity of the material particle; the distance between successive crests is the wave length of the 'matter waves' and is known as the de Broglie wave length."

Charles Mauguin, one the four members of the doctoral jury to which de Broglie presented his doctoral thesis, "Recherches sur la théorie des quanta," at the Sorbonne in 1924, recalls the astonishment and scepticism of his colleagues upon being confronted with this revolutionary concept. In the same year de Broglie was awarded his doctorate.

The contribution made by de Broglie in establishing the universal connection between particles and waves was obtained "apparently by a process of pure reasoning from mathematical relations suggested by relativity. . . . It stimulated Schrödinger to seek for an explanation of the stationary states of atoms as a resonance phenomenon and led him to his famous wave equation, which is the accurate extension to curved orbits of de Broglie's relations for a particle on a straight course" (*Nature,* June 6, 1953).

In 1927 came the direct verification of de Broglie's ideas by Clinton J. Davisson and Lester Halbert Germer working with slow electrons, and by G. P. Thomson working with fast electrons, and a new era began in the understanding of atomic processes. "The precise relationship of the waves to the particles remains a subject of controversy; what is established is that one must carry out calculations to determine the motion of the waves and then interpret them in terms of probabilities for the particles" (*Nature,* June 6, 1953).

De Broglie gave a recapitulation of his work to date at the Congress of Solvay in 1927, for by then, it was already evident that his theory had completely transformed all considerations of atomic phenomena. World-wide attention to his discovery came in 1929, when he received the Nobel Prize in Physics. He was also awarded the Henri Poincaré Medal of the Académie des Sciences in 1929.

Much of de Broglie's time since 1926 has been devoted to teaching, at first as a lecturer at the Faculty of Sciences of the University of Paris where, in 1928, he was appointed professor of theoretical physics at the Henri Poincaré Institute. In 1943, to help make the bonds between physicists and mathematicians closer, de Broglie founded the center of studies in applied mathematics at the Henri Poincaré Institute.

"Teaching is an interesting thing," de Broglie said in his interview with André Gillois, "which goes well enough with research." During the 1930's, his research was chiefly concerned with electrons and light. From these came a new theory of the photon, which he established in a note published in the *Revue Générale des Sciences* of January 1934. "A photon," noted de Broglie, "must be constituted by two complementary corpuscles, as are the electron and the positron, the emission of a photon corresponding to the creation of a pair of these demiphotons (neutrinos)."

Since both Prince de Broglie and his brother (the former as a theoretical physicist and the latter as an experimental physicist) had profoundly influenced atomic thought prior to World War II, in 1945 they were named counselors to the French High Commission on Atomic Energy. Deeply interested in the peaceful development of atomic energy, Prince de Broglie is concerned with strengthening the bonds between science and industry.

Elected a member of the Académie des Sciences in 1933, de Broglie became its permanent secretary in 1942. On October 8, 1944, his distinction as a writer was marked by his election to the Académie Française, to which he was ceremoniously inducted by his elder brother on May 31, 1945. (Their father and grandfather had also been members of the Académie Française.)

De Broglie in 1953 was one of four foreign members elected to the Royal Society, London, England. He is a fellow of the Academy of Sciences of Sweden, Academy of Sciences and Letters of Cracow, Academy of Science of Bucharest, Academy of Science of Lima, and

Société de Physique et Histoire Naturelle in Geneva, and a member of the Bureau des Longitudes. In 1954 he was named a grand officer of the Legion of Honor.

In May 1952 de Broglie was awarded the Kalinga Prize, established by the Indian industrialist M. Patnaik and bestowed by the United Nations, in the amount of £1,000 "for the work which has most contributed to the popularization of scientific knowledge." Other honors he has received are the Albert-I[er] Grand Prize of Monaco (1932) and the Order of Leopold of Belgium. In June 1953 he received the grand prize of the Society of Engineers of France.

The Prince is the author of more than twenty books, several of which have been published in English, including: *Selected Papers on Wave Mechanics* (Blackie, 1928), *An Introduction of Wave Mechanics* (Methuen, 1930), *Matter and Light* (Allen & Unwin, 1939 and Dover, 1946), and *The Revolution in Physics; A Non-Mathematical Survey of Quanta* (Noonday Press, 1953).

It was in his capacity as permanent secretary of the Académie des Sciences that de Broglie introduced to its members one of the major studies of the effect of thermonuclear explosions on the human race. By his sponsorship, scientific circles learned of the work of Charles-Noël Martin, a researcher on the staff of the Centre National des Recherches Scientifiques. In Martin's communication read by de Broglie on November 22, 1954, and quoted by *Figaro* the following day, the issue of both immediate and future harmful effects from radioactive fall-out was raised.

For exercise, de Broglie likes walking. He enjoys "reading, reflection, or games like chess."

References

Hommes et Mondes no83 Je '53
L'Illustration 87 pt2:583 N 23 '29 por
Sci Am 142:183 Mr '30
Dictionnaire Biographique Français Contemporain (1954)
Diamant-Berger, M. Que êtes vous? (1953)
Heathcote, N. H. de V. Nobel Prize Winners in Physics, 1901-50 (1953)
Who's Who, 1955
World Biography (1954)

BROSIO, MANLIO (GIOVANNI)

(brōs'ĭō, män'lĭō) July 10, 1897- Ambassador from Italy to the United States

Address: b. c/o Embassy of Italy, 1601 Fuller St., Washington 9, D.C.; h. 2700 16th St., Washington, D.C.; Via Bertola 86, Turin, Italy

For "the top post in the Italian diplomatic service," Manlio Brosio was chosen as Ambassador to the United States in January 1955. Although not a career diplomat, he has served in similar capacities in Moscow and in London. He hopes to strengthen the bonds between Italy and America, and to continue the work of his predecessor, Alberto Tarchiani, who had served ten years as Italy's postwar Ambassador to the United States. Brosio proposes to strive for moral and, if necessary, economic support for his country.

Italy's foreign policy, as he sees it, "is in perfect harmony with the policy of the United States." "We have fully understood," he declared in his first public address in this country, "that the present stand of the United States about Formosa has no provocative intention whatever, but is a serious attempt to draw a clear-cut line in a troubled area where uncertainty could be fatal" (New York *Times*, February 16, 1955).

Manlio Giovanni Brosio was born on July 10, 1897 in Turin. His father, the late Edoardo Brosio, was a judge. His mother was Fortunata (Curadelli) Brosio. His birthplace is the second largest city in northern Italy, and a great industrial center. At the age of eighteen, Manlio enlisted in 1915 in the Alpine Corps. He served for three years during World War I as an artillery officer. Toward the end of the conflict he was captured by the Austrians and was for a brief period a prisoner of war. His government awarded him the Silver Medal and the Cross for Valor.

Like his father, young Brosio decided to make the law his career. He was graduated from the University of Turin in 1920 with the degree of Doctor of Jurisprudence. For the next twenty-two years he followed his profession in his native city. He made a reputation in the practice of corporation law. As a member of the Liberal party, he was active in politics from the start of his law career. His political mentors were the philosopher, the late Benedetto Croce, and the economist who later became President of Italy, Luigi Einaudi. One of his closest associates was Piero Gobetti, then regarded as the leading writer of the Liberal party.

Brosio served as central secretary of the Rivoluzione Liberale movement in Turin from 1922 to 1925. During this period he wrote for *La Rivoluzione Liberale*, the mouthpiece of the movement. He also contributed to legal and other specialized periodicals, such as *Foro Italiano*, and to the Turin newspaper *La Stampa*.

He withdrew from active participation in politics soon after the Fascist regime took over Italy and spent most of his time at his legal practice. He did not, however, lose sight of his political principles or sever his contacts. He was in constant touch during the entire Mussolini era with anti-Fascist groups and their leaders, especially Croce and Einaudi. During the German occupation, he was active as a member of the underground National Liberation Committee (1943-1944).

Resuming his formal political activity after the liquidation of Fascism and the end of World War II, he was general secretary of the Liberal party in 1944 and 1945. He entered the national government as a Minister without Portfolio in the (Ivanoe) Bonomi Cabinet in 1944. He became vice-president of the Council of Ministers in the (Ferruccio) Parri govern-

MANLIO BROSIO

ment (1945). Later that year he was appointed Minister of War in the Cabinet of Premier Alcide de Gasperi.

His career in the government service took him into the field of diplomacy when he was sent to Moscow as Ambassador in January 1947. His five years in that post made him the dean of the Moscow diplomatic corps. He tried to familiarize himself with every phase of Russian life and thought. He was reputed to have arisen at seven o'clock each morning to study the Russian language. At the same time he was learning English.

Instead of returning to Italy for their leave of absence in 1947, Brosio and his wife visited the United States. A tour of two and one-half months took them to most of the important cities from New York to San Francisco.

Brosio was transferred to London in 1952, to serve as Italy's Ambassador there. He and Signora Brosio established a considerable reputation for entertaining. Among their dinner guests at the Embassy was the Queen Mother Elizabeth, just before her visit to the United States in 1953. This was regarded as a social triumph, as it is not the custom of royalty to attend embassy dinners.

While in his London post, he helped toward accommodation of the rival claims of Italy and Yugoslavia with respect to the Free Territory of Trieste. Brosio, negotiating in the spring of 1952 with Great Britain and the United States, secured greater responsibility for Italy in the civil administration of Zone A of the territory. According to the Italian peace treaty of 1947, pending final settlement of the status of the territory, Yugoslavia would occupy Zone B, and the United States and Great Britain, Zone A, which included the city of Trieste. "Without yielding anything to Italian aspirations of sovereignty over Zone A," the United States and Great Britain agreed with the Italian government on May 9, 1952 to let Italians take over civil posts in that zone. This settlement followed serious rioting in Zone A in March 1952, in favor of the restoration of Trieste to Italy.

Settlement of the dispute over Trieste came on October 5, 1954, when a Memorandum of Understanding was signed by the Ambassadors to Great Britain, Manlio Brosio of Italy and Vladimir Velebit of Yugoslavia, and representatives of the U.S. and British governments. The agreement called for Italy to take over Zone A, including the city of Trieste. Yugoslavia would substitute civil administration for military occupation of Zone B, which would also include the Crevatini area of Zone A. Yugoslavia was to have free use of the port of Trieste.

Brosio married a cousin, Clotilde Brosio, on November 1, 1936. Like her husband, she is a native Piedmontese. Accompanying the Brosios when they arrived in this country aboard the Italian liner *Cristoforo Colombo* on January 31, 1955 was the Ambassador's sister, Signorina Emma Brosio. They also brought with them their two-year-old Scotch terrier, Bud.

Brosio told ship news reporters that he was giving up his favorite sport, tennis. He had found it too strenuous, he explained, for a man of fifty-eight. He indicated, however, that he still found enjoyment in swimming and mountaineering. And he added that he had every intention of keeping up his custom of reading, wherever he was stationed, to get to know the country and its people. He has been described as a "tall man with the rough-hewn face of a Roman emperor." Brosio has a reputation for perseverance, will power, and scholarliness.

Ambassador Brosio wrote a letter to the editor and publisher of *Theatre Arts*, published in the May 1955 issue, in which he stated his conviction that the Italian theatre, "which remains glorious in the field of opera, and preserves, in certain places, the traditions of the classic theatre, is now renewing itself in the dramatic field." He stated that he had had many opportunities to frequent the French, Russian and British theatres, and is an enthusiastic spectator of theatrical performances. "I have seen how the theatre alone can touch the heart of the public and arouse its interest in art, in history, and in the daily social activities by an immediate participation in the creative work of the actors. From this comes its social value and the importance of an exchange of such experiences among the different peoples of the world."

References

N Y Herald Tribune p3 N 19 '54 por; p3 F 4 '55; II p3 F 6 '55 por
N Y Times p2 O 30 '54 por; p18 Ja 31 '55; p12 F 1 '55; p9 F 16 '55
Washington (D.C.) Post p22 N 20 '54 por; p26 F 2 '55 por; p7 My 7 '55
Chi è? (1948)
Who's Who, 1955
World Biography (1948)

BROWN, HARRISON (SCOTT) Sept. 26, 1917- Geochemist; university professor; author

Address: b. c/o California Institute of Technology, Pasadena 4, Calif.; h. 250 E. Mariposa St., Altadena, Calif.

"To what extent can man subjugate selfishness to generosity, ignorance to wisdom, and hate to love?" asks geochemist Harrison Brown in his book, *The Challenge of Man's Future* (Viking, 1954). A scientist who is "thoroughly at home in the tangle of sciences that bear on man's future on earth," Professor Brown is "also at home in history and sociology and . . . is a good writer" (*Time,* March 22, 1954). In his books, articles and lectures he has frequently pointed out the position of "overwhelming responsibility" held by citizens of the United States "in this time of grave decision when our survival depends upon the victory of wisdom and knowledge over stupidity and dogma."

During World War II Brown worked on the atomic bomb at the University of Chicago and was assistant director of chemistry at the Clinton Engineer Works at Oak Ridge, Tennessee. After the war he taught chemistry at the Institute for Nuclear Studies at Chicago, and since 1951 has been professor of geochemistry at the California Institute of Technology in Pasadena. He is known for his work on the chemical composition of meteorites, the planets and the sun. In 1947 he was awarded the $1,000 prize of the American Association for the Advancement of Science, and in 1952, won the award in pure chemistry of the American Chemical Society. In April 1955 he was appointed one of six new editors-at-large of the *Saturday Review.*

Harrison Scott Brown was born in Sheridan, Wyoming on September 26, 1917, the only child of Harrison H. Brown, a livestock broker, and Agatha (Scott) Brown, a music teacher. When the boy was ten years old, his father died, and Mrs. Brown moved to San Francisco. Young Harrison reportedly "built his own chemistry lab" at Galileo High School, from which he was graduated in 1934.

While studying at the University of California in Berkeley, Brown helped to support himself by playing the piano in taverns, an experience he terms "an eye-opening extension of my education." Professor R. D. Fowler aroused the youth's interest in nuclear chemistry and after Brown's graduation with a B.S. degree in 1938, he followed Professor Fowler to the Johns Hopkins University at Baltimore, Maryland, to do graduate work in that field. Brown's research was supported in 1940 and 1941 by a Du Pont Fellowship. His doctoral dissertation was in two parts: "Thermal Diffusion Coefficient of Argon" and "Construction of a Mass Spectrometer for Isotope Analysis."

After receiving his Ph.D. degree in 1941, Brown remained at Johns Hopkins as an instructor in chemistry. He planned to devote his research time to investigating the chemical composition of the universe, but following the Japanese attack on Pearl Harbor, he went to Chicago as a research associate and during 1942

Elliott Erwitt

HARRISON BROWN

and 1943, worked on the atomic bomb at the plutonium project at the University of Chicago. "I think the biggest thrill was the first time I set eyes on plutonium through a microscope," he has said. It was "quite a day" when the first self-sustaining chain reaction in the uranium pile took place at the university's Stagg Field squash court.

From 1943 to 1946, Brown was at Oak Ridge, Tennessee, as assistant director of chemistry at the Clinton Engineer Works plutonium project. While there he contributed to the development of a flow sheet, first used at the Oak Ridge pilot plant and later put into operation at the Hanford plutonium production plant near Pasco, Washington. *Chemical and Engineering News* (April 21, 1952) wrote of Brown and his work at Oak Ridge: "His ability to grasp theory, to devise and carry out very difficult experiments employing techniques new to him, and to create new ideas, led to many key contributions which added to the development of the atomic bomb. Because of their confidential nature," his many contributions of value in the laboratory and also in the administrative scheme during this period have not been published.

After the dropping of the A-bombs at Hiroshima and Nagasaki and the end of World War II, Brown became executive vice-chairman and trustee (Dr. Albert Einstein was chairman) of the Emergency Committee of Atomic Scientists, formed to arouse the public to the new responsibilities and dangers of the atomic age. Brown made a country-wide lecture tour, giving 102 speeches in three months, in the year his book, *Must Destruction Be Our Destiny?* (Simon & Schuster, 1946), was published. Brown dedicated the book "to humanity, in the hope that it may exist longer than recent events would lead us to suppose."

(Continued next page)

BROWN, HARRISON—*Continued*

In the book he discusses the viewpoints of scientists "as citizens" concerning the social and political implications of atomic energy. J. E. Jackson in the San Francisco *Chronicle* (July 31, 1946) commented: "It is mostly a restatement, yes, but it is done with new simplicity and undeniable authority, and by a young man . . . doubly worth listening to." Thomas K. Finletter wrote in the *Saturday Review* (August 24, 1946): "The scientific facts are soberly assessed. The military implications are calmly and sensibly appraised."

Back at the University of Chicago in 1946 as assistant professor of chemistry at the Institute for Nuclear Studies, Brown resumed this interrupted research. His report, "Elements in Meteorites and the Earth's Origin," won him the annual $1,000 prize of the American Association for the Advancement of Science for the paper in 1947 making "the most notable contribution to science." Being just thirty years old, Professor Brown was the youngest man to receive the award since its establishment in 1923. He became associate professor of the Institute for Nuclear Studies at Chicago in 1948.

At the university Brown's research program was directed toward developing an understanding of the chemical relationships between the stars, planets, and meteorites; an understanding of the distribution of elements in the earth; the determination of the relative abundances of elements in the universe; and the determination of the age of the meteorites, the earth and the elements. His study of the chemical composition of 107 meteorites that had fallen on the earth during the past century supported the theory that meteorites are fragments from the cosmic explosion of a planet almost identical to the Earth in composition and similar to Mars in size (*Chemical and Engineering News,* February 2, 1948 and April 21, 1952).

He and his co-workers developed two methods, radiometric analysis and isotope dilution analysis, to help determine the presence of minute concentrations of elements in meteorites. These studies of meteorites, Brown has said, may well become the "Rosetta Stone" which will help answer questions about the history of the universe.

In addition to his scientific papers, Harrison Brown has written reviews and articles for the *Saturday Review, Nation,* and the *American Scholar.* He was a co-author of *Years of the Modern* (Longmans, 1949). Brown spoke on "The Social Responsibility of Science" on March 6, 1949 at the New York *Herald Tribune* Forum and urged his fellow scientists to "develop, wherever possible, constructive solutions to the technical problems that confront mankind: the production of food, clothing, and shelter."

In early 1950 Brown received national attention when he stated that if the U.S.S.R. had decided to make a hydrogen bomb, it was probably ahead of the United States in its program and that a hydrogen bomb's radioactivity could exterminate most if not all of the world's population. His position was supported by three world-famous physicists—Frederick Seitz, Hans Bethe, and Leo Szilard—during a University of Chicago *Round Table* radio program on February 26, 1950.

Brown moved to the California Institute of Technology as professor of geochemistry in the division of geological sciences in 1951. He received the American Chemical Society's annual award in pure chemistry in 1952. Speaking at a meeting of the ACS that year, he stated: "The chemist, the geologist, the astronomer and the physicist, working closely together, can reconstruct successfully the process by which our solar system was formed. The records have not been destroyed. We have only to learn to read them correctly and fit them into the master pattern." He edited the first of a three-volume international catalogue about meteorites, *A Bibliography on Meteorites* (University of Chicago Press), published in 1953.

On a trip to the British West Indies, Brown observed in the "tropical paradise" a miniature version of "forces identical with those that bring misery and starvation on a large scale to the greater portion of humanity." His analysis of the population-and-resources situation, when published as *The Challenge of Man's Future,* was described by *Time* as "readable and frightening." Harrison Smith wrote: "There are no wild guesses in this book, no as-yet-undreamed inventions, no escapes to other planets. It is logical, elaborately documented, and it is terrifying" (Washington *Post and Times Herald,* March 21, 1954).

Harrison Brown has gray eyes and brown hair, is five feet ten inches tall, and weighs 170 pounds. On May 25, 1938 he married Adele Scrimger; their son, Eric, was born at Oak Ridge. In October 1948 the couple was divorced. Brown married Rudd Owen on November 11, 1949. He enjoys traveling, going to the theatre, seeing ballets, reading, listening to records, and playing on the piano what has been described as a "mean barrelhouse blues." He belongs to the American Association for the Advancement of Science, the American Chemical Society, the American Physical Society, and the Geological Society of America, and is a member of Sigma Xi and Phi Beta Kappa.

In *The Challenge of Man's Future* he states his belief that "man has the power, the intelligence, and the imagination to extricate himself from the serious predicament that now confronts him . . . which necessitates an understanding of the relationships between man, his natural environment, and his technology."

References

Chem & Eng N 26:310 F 2 '48; 30:1625 Ap 21 '52
N Y Post Mag p47 Ja 28 '48 pors
Sat R 36:14 Mr 20 '54 por; 38:23 Ap 23 '55 por

American Men of Science (1955)
Who Knows—and What (1954)
Who's Who in America, 1954-55

BROWNSON, CHARLES B(RUCE) Feb. 5, 1914- United States Representative from Indiana; businessman

Address: b. House Office Bldg., Washington 25, D.C.; h. 3561 N. Pennsylvania St., Indianapolis 5, Ind.

An increasingly influential figure among the "younger Republicans" in the U.S. House of Representatives is Charles B. Brownson of the Eleventh District of Indiana. In the Eighty-third Congress he was chairman of the Government Operations Committee's subcommittee on international operations; he investigated duplication and waste, and made suggestions for greater operational economy in government. He began his third consecutive term in Congress in January 1955 and continues to serve on the Government Operations Committee.

Since 1936 Brownson has been president of an Indianapolis wholesale paint and paper business. He served with distinction in the U.S. Army during World War II, during which he was on the planning staff for the Normandy invasion. In November 1952 he was elected "by the largest Congressional majority" in the history of the Hoosier state.

Charles Bruce Brownson was born on February 5, 1914 in Jackson, Michigan. In his early childhood he moved with his parents, Charles Matthew and Helen Gray (Oxby) Brownson, to Flint, where he attended grade schools and Flint Central High School. He majored in psychology at the University of Michigan in Ann Arbor (1931-1935).

On August 1, 1935, some weeks after his graduation, he commenced at Fort Sheridan, Illinois a year of training as a second lieutenant in the U.S. Army Reserve. On completing his training, he went to Indianapolis and bought a bankrupt wallpaper and paint business. Brownson incorporated this enterprise in 1936 and has served as its president since that time.

As a first lieutenant in the Army Reserve, Brownson began five years of active military duty on February 10, 1941. He attended the Adjutants General School in 1942 and the Command and General Staff School, Fort Leavenworth, Kansas in 1943.

Assigned as executive officer to the assistant chief of staff, G-1, of the First Army, he was a member of the planning staff for the Normandy invasion. Landing in Normandy on "D Day plus one," Brownson served under General Omar N. Bradley. He was transferred to the Pacific Theater with the First Army Planning Headquarters in the Philippine Islands on August 5, 1945. Discharged on February 27, 1946, he holds the rank of lieutenant colonel in the Reserve. He has been decorated with the French Médaille de Reconnaissance as well as with the American Legion of Merit, Bronze star, and European Theater Medal with five combat stars and invasion arrowhead.

After the war Brownson returned to Indianapolis and became active in civic and veterans' groups. He organized the Republican Veterans of World War II and in 1947 became that organization's chairman for Marion county, Indiana. He was also the recipient in 1947 of a Junior Chamber of Commerce Distinguished Service Award. In 1948 he became chairman of the advisory council of the Marion County Juvenile Court.

In 1950 Brownson was a candidate for the U.S. House of Representatives and was elected on November 7, 1950 to represent the Eleventh (Marion county) District of Indiana. He was assigned to the Committee on Expenditures in the Executive Departments. Brownson did "earnest committee work" to promote efficiency and economy in government, and received the editorial praise of the New York *World-Telegram and Sun* on March 29, 1951 for "opposing a $16,000,000 pork outlay for fancy reserve corps armories." He "boldly said that Indianapolis could go without a proposed $750,000 drill hall because there weren't many reservists left to use it."

Brownson's voting record during the first session of the Eighty-second Congress (1951) shows that he favored a reduction in the Government's civil payrolls (April), prohibiting government building of defense plants (July) a $350,000,000 reduction in the Administration's economic-aid-to-Europe bill (August), and a $7.5 billion foreign assistance bill (August). He was against the draft extension-Universal-Military-Training bill (April) and reasonable profits under all price ceilings (July).

With three other Representatives, Brownson introduced an amendment on January 8, 1952 to the Administration-endorsed Universal Military Training bill. The amendment provided for compulsory military training during the last two years of high school and six to eight weeks in summer camp after graduation. On March 4 Brownson voted to shelve the UMT bill; the House vote for shelving was 236 to 162.

Other important votes cast by Brownson in 1952 were in favor of reducing Federal jobs by 10 per cent (April), a $46 billion ceiling for military spending during 1953 (April), cutting economic aid to Europe by $615,000,000 (May), ending consumer price controls on June 30, 1952 (June), terminating Federal rent controls on September 30, 1952 except in critical defense areas or where local authorities request their continuance (June) and overriding the Presidential veto of the Walter-McCarran immigration bill (June). Brownson voted against invoking the Taft-Hartley act in the steel strike (June).

Seeking and winning re-election to Congress on November 4, 1952, Brownson defeated his Democratic opponent by 51,527 votes. During the Republican-controlled Eighty-third Congress in January 1953 Brownson served on the House Government Operations Committee and the Public Works Committee. He was a member of the subcommittee on roads of the Public Works Committee and strongly supported a Federal highway program.

As chairman of the subcommittee on international operations of the Government Operations Committee in the Eighty-third Congress, Brownson opposed a housing program for American officials in Germany because it was too costly. As a result, the Bureau of the Budget in May reduced from $19,000,000 to about $7,650,000 the appropriation for this

Wide World

CHARLES B. BROWNSON

project. With other members of this subcommittee, Brownson visited Korea in October 1953 to make an appraisal of the expenditure of funds allotted for reconstruction. He was sharply critical on a radio broadcast in December of the building of a luxury hotel at Seoul (Clayton Knowles, New York *Times*, December 21, 1953).

In the first session of the Eighty-third Congress (1953), Brownson voted "yea" on the statehood for Hawaii bill (March), the quitclaim offshore oil bill (April), reducing soil conservation payments (May), private power development on the Niagara River (July), extension of the excess-profits tax (July), a $4.4 billion foreign aid appropriation (July), and admitting into the United States 217,000 refugees from Iron Curtain countries (July).

On the following measures he voted "nay" in 1953: continuing the public housing program (April), increasing funds for public power (April), maintaining the nonpartisan character of the Tariff Commission (June), and boosting funds for the Air Force (July).

At the beginning of the second session of the Eighty-third Congress (1954), the Wiley-Dondero bill came before the legislators. It provided for the creation of a St. Lawrence seaway development corporation, with authority to borrow up to $105,000,000 from the U.S. Treasury. Brownson submitted an amendment requiring that the U.S. share of the seaway be financed by private capital. On May 6 the House rejected Brownson's amendment and passed the original bill (Brownson voted against the bill).

His 1954 voting record indicates that he favored the general tax revision with dividend relief (March), a one-year extension of the Trade Agreements Act (June), the $3.3 billion foreign aid authorization (June), the flexible farm price support program (July), a combined postal rate and pay raise (July) and revision of the Atomic Energy Act of 1946 (July). Representative Brownson was re-elected to Congress in November 1954.

On January 7, 1955, shortly after the Eighty-fourth Congress convened, Brownson and other members of the international operations subcommittee in the previous Congress reported that "the grade and quality of the cotton shipped" in aid of the Spanish textile mills had been "almost invariably" below the grade specified, and that the result had been "ill will on both sides, a poor beginning for the United States defense assistance program" (Washington *Post and Times Herald*, January 8, 1955).

In 1955 Brownson voted to increase the salary of U.S. Congressmen by $10,000 (February) and to extend the reciprocal trade program to June 30, 1958 (February). He was opposed to restoring rigid farm price supports (May).

When in Indianapolis Brownson attends the Tabernacle Presbyterian Church. He is a thirty-second degree Mason and a Shriner and is a member of the Indiana Societies of Chicago and Washington, Indianapolis Press and Athletic Clubs, Optimist Club No. 1, Sigma Nu fraternity, and American Political Science Association. He is a charter member of the Ernie Pyle Post, Veterans of Foreign Wars, and was a commander of the John H. Holiday Post of the American Legion.

His wife is the former Christine Phyllis Augspurger; the Brownsons, who were married October 22, 1938, have two daughters, Nancy Gray and Judith Ann, and one son, Charles Christopher.

William H. Hessler wrote that Brownson favors foreign technical assistance programs and that he is a "free trader, in the sense that he would have the country move by stages to even greater reciprocity" and has been "worried by the fact that labor groups are . . . vying with manufacturers . . . for protectionism" (*Reporter*, December 8, 1953).

References

Reporter 9:24+ D 8 '53 por
Congressional Directory (1955)
Who's Who in America, 1954-55

BROZ, JOSIP *See* Tito

BRUCKER, WILBER M(ARION) (brŭk' ẽr) June 23, 1894- Secretary of the Army; lawyer

Address: b. c/o Department of the Army, Washington 25, D.C.; h. 4,000 Cathedral Ave., N.W., Washington 16, D.C.; 56 Vendome Rd., Grosse Pointe Farms, Mich.

The new head of the 1,100,000-man United States Army is Wilber M. Brucker, who was appointed on June 22, 1955 as Secretary of the Army by President Dwight D. Eisenhower to succeed Robert T. Stevens, who resigned. Brucker, a successful trial lawyer, had been general counsel and security chief of the Department of Defense since 1954. Brucker's nomination as Secretary was confirmed by the Senate on July 11, 1955 and he took office later that month. He was Governor of Michigan from 1931 to 1933 and has been active in Republican politics in his home state.

Wilber Marion Brucker was born in Saginaw, Michigan on June 23, 1894, the son of Ferdinand and Roberta (Hawn) Brucker. His father was a Michigan lawyer and a politician, who was Democratic Representative from Michigan to the Fifty-fifth Congress (from 1897 1899). He died when Wilber was nine years old. Wilber helped his family by selling newspapers and weeding sugar beets, and was graduated from the Saginaw high school in 1912. While there, according to *Time* (July 4, 1955), he "resolved to become an orator when [defeated] by a girl in a school debate." As a student at the University of Michigan in Ann Arbor, he was made a member of the varsity debating team. He waited on table to earn part of his expenses at the university and in 1916 he was awarded the LL.B. degree.

In that year he joined the 33d Infantry of the Michigan National Guard and went to Mexico in General John J. Pershing's expedition against Pancho Francisco Villa. After the United States joined World War I, Brucker entered the U.S. Army and rose from corporal to the rank of first lieutenant. He served in France with the 166th Infantry, 42d (Rainbow) Division, and took part in the battles of Aisne-Marne, Château-Thierry, Champagne, Saint-Mihiel, and Meuse-Argonne. He was cited by General Headquarters of the American Expeditionary Force and was awarded the Silver Star.

After his return from the war, Brucker was admitted to the Michigan bar, began a private practice in Saginaw, and became assistant prosecuting attorney in Saginaw county. In 1923 he was made prosecuting attorney of the county and four years later, assistant attorney general of Michigan. He became attorney general in 1928 and served for three years. Elected Governor of Michigan during the Depression for the 1931-1933 term, he cut his own salary by 10 per cent (to $4,500 a year). When asked how it seemed to be Governor, Brucker answered: "I feel like a Vagabond King. I handle millions (theoretically) at the office all day and then go home at night and question my wife about how she spent that last $5 I gave her" (Washington *Post and Times Herald*, June 24, 1955). He opposed state aid for jobless industrial workers and in the Democratic landslide of 1932, he lost his campaign for re-election.

He went to Detroit, where he became a member in the law firm of Clark, Klein, Brucker & Waples. He also served as director of the First Federal Savings and Loan Association of Detroit. In 1936 he was named delegate at large to the Republican National Convention from Michigan and, having won the Republican Senatorial nomination from Senator James Couzens, ran for election, but was defeated by Prentiss M. Brown. He became chairman of the Fourteenth Republican Congressional District Committee in 1944, and reported *Time*, "dutifully rang doorbells in GOP campaigns." He was chairman of the Michigan State Convention in 1948 and was a Michigan delegate and member of the platform committee at the Republican National Convention that year.

U. S. Army

WILBER M. BRUCKER

On the recommendation of Charles E. Wilson, U.S. Secretary of Defense, President Eisenhower nominated Wilber M. Brucker as general counsel of the Department of Defense on April 6, 1954. His nomination was confirmed by the Senate on April 19, 1954 and he was sworn into office on April 23, 1954. In this post he has also been in charge of the Pentagon's internal security system (Washington *Post and Times Herald*, June 23, 1955).

During hearings on the U.S. Government employee security program by a Senate Government Operations subcommittee on March 9, 1955, Brucker urged legislation to help the Department of Defense keep subversives out of defense plants and other strategic facilities. Earlier, in February 1955, he had stated that 4,000 defense plant employees had been suspended on security charges in eighteen months. Brucker also told the subcommittee that "a substantial number" of ex-Defense Department employees reported ousted as "security risks" actually had not been fired through security procedures, but were probationary workers dropped for "unsuitability."

Brucker announced a new defense plant program, effective April 4, 1955, under which a central office in the Pentagon in Washington would screen and review security cases. Before ordering suspensions, military security officials in defense plants would have to secure the office's approval. He admitted that more than a "desirable number of offhand suspensions" by such officials had taken place and stated that the central office was expected to lower the number of suspensions and to speed clearances

BRUCKER, WILBER M.—*Continued*

of defense plant workers who sometimes were suspended for as long as six months because of accusations later found to be baseless.

According to the New York *Times* (June 23, 1955), Brucker "was regarded as a supporter of Senator [Joseph R.] McCarthy [of Wisconsin] before Brucker came to Washington . . . in 1954. But in March 1955 Brucker laughed in Senator McCarthy's face and otherwise sought to ridicule him in a series of hearings on the [Major] Irving Peress case." (The Army's promotion and honorable discharge of Peress, a dentist who refused to answer questions about Communism, had touched off the Army-McCarthy dispute in 1954; further hearings were conducted in March 1955 by the Senate Permanent Subcommittee on Investigations on "who promoted Peress"; as general counsel of the Department of Defense, Brucker was involved in some of the subcommittee's meetings; for the subcommittee's final report, see the New York *Times,* July 15, 1955.)

Appearing as a witness before the subcommittee on March 19, 1955, Brucker "reared back in his chair and guffawed" when McCarthy accused President Eisenhower of creating a "conspiracy" to keep executive branch officials from talking about the Peress case. Later, when McCarthy asked military witnesses complicated questions, Brucker interrupted: "Now wait; don't answer that. There are three or four questions in that one, Senator. Split 'em up and we'll answer" (*Time,* July 4, 1955).

Testifying before the Senate Foreign Relations Committee in June 1955 on the proposed ratification by the United States of the 1949 Geneva conventions for the protection of war victims, Brucker stated that Communist China was violating international law as well as the Korean armistice by detaining U.S. fliers captured during the Korean war. He said that the 1949 conventions, to which Communist China had indicated its adherence, required repatriation of prisoners of war "without delay" after hostilities ended. Brucker urged U.S. ratification of the conventions, which are designed to modernize and in some respects broaden international law relating to war prisoners and civilians in wartime. The Senate voted unanimous approval of the conventions on July 6, 1955.

When questioned in a television interview on *Today* after his appointment as Army Secretary in June 1955 by President Eisenhower, Brucker stated that one of the big problems facing the Army is "retaining the best personnel, both officers and men, who are gradually filtering out because of present and future prospects." He asserted that "some way has to be found of handling morale and all those other little intangibles" (*Christian Science Monitor,* June 23, 1955).

He belongs to the Michigan and American bar associations and has served as chairman of the A.B.A. committee on professional ethics and grievances. He is a member of the American Legion and the Veterans of Foreign Wars, and is a past national president of the Rainbow Division Veterans. He is a Mason and an Elk, and belongs to the Delta Sigma Rho and Sigma Delta Kappa fraterniites. He received an honorary J.D. degree from the University of Detroit (1931), from Hillsdale College in Michigan (1932), and from Alma College in Michigan (1932). He is a Presbyterian.

Wilber Marion Brucker was married to Clara Hantel of Saginaw, Michigan on August 18, 1923. He has one son, Wilber Marion Brucker 2d, a lawyer. He is five feet ten inches tall and weighs 182 pounds. He enjoys playing golf and swimming in the pool at his home in Grosse Pointe Farms, Michigan. His wife has said that he "used to like to walk with his friends when they went hunting, but he would never shoot anything himself. He's too kind hearted." Mrs. Brucker has been the educational director of a School of Government in Detroit, which has about 200 members and is affiliated with the General Federation of Women's Clubs. "We have speakers on current affairs," she has said, "and put on a May Day luncheon each year to combat the Communist celebration."

The Washington *Post and Times Herald,* in an editorial on June 23, 1955, stated: "Brucker is personable and is liked by his associates as an individual. He is scholarly and cautious in his approach; yet he has created a reputation for vigor and conviction in his appearances on Capitol Hill." The Washington *Post* has reported one of Brucker's favorite stories: At a party before Brucker's appointment as Army Secretary, a Russian general asked Brucker if he had ever seen military service. "I was a corporal in the Army," Brucker answered. "Well," said the general, "don't let it give you an inferiority complex. Often there's a general's brain in a private's shoes."

References

Christian Sci Mon p6 Je 22 '55
N Y Herald Tribune II p5 Je 26 '55 por
N Y Times p17 Je 23 '55
Newsweek 46:20 Jl 4 '55 por
Time 66:17 Jl 4 '55 por
Washington (D.C.) Post p40 Je 24 '55 por
World's Work 60:75 Ap '31 por
Martindale-Hubbell Law Directory, 1952
Who's Who in America (Sup. O '54)
Who's Who in United States Politics (1952)

BRYAN, ERNEST R(OWLETT) Aug. 14, 1906-Dec. 17, 1954 President of the International Society of Christian Endeavor; editor of the *Christian Endeavor World* since 1947; former special writer for the U.S. Public Health Service; official of the World Peace Foundation (1929-36); since 1946 headed project supervision, motion picture and training films production of the U.S. Navy; author of *America Turns to Social Security* (1938). See *Current Biography* (July) 1950.

Obituary

N Y Times p84 D 19 '54

BUCK, PAUL H(ERMAN) Aug. 25, 1899- University professor; library administrator
Address: b. c/o Harvard University Library, Cambridge, Mass.; h. 9 Kirkland Pl., Cambridge, Mass.

Selected in accordance with Harvard's "tradition of scholar-librarians," Paul H. Buck in the summer of 1955 became director of the Harvard University Library and librarian of Harvard College (now the Library of the Faculty of Arts and Sciences.) He thus heads the country's oldest library (founded in 1638) and largest university library (comprising some 5,850,000 books), with research facilities that rank with those of the Library of Congress and the New York Public Library.

For almost thirty years Professor Buck has been teaching American history at Harvard and in 1938 was awarded the Pulitzer Prize for his book, *The Road to Reunion; 1865-1900.* Known also as a university administrator, he contributed to the establishment of a number of important educational programs during his years as dean of the Faculty of Arts and Sciences and as provost.

Paul Herman Buck, who was born to Henry John and Adele (Kreppelt) Buck on August 25, 1899, is a native of Columbus, Ohio. As he has said, he grew up in Columbus "around the corner from the public library." After graduating from East High School, he attended Ohio State University in Columbus for the B.A. degree, conferred in 1921. He received his M.A. degree from Ohio State in 1922, the year in which his *Evolution of the National Parks System* was published.

In further graduate study in history, undertaken at Harvard University, Buck made much use of the famed historical collection in the Widener Memorial Building. He was granted the M.A. degree from Harvard in 1924 and the Ph.D. degree in 1935. Under a Sheldon traveling fellowship he spent a year (1926-1927) studying in France and Great Britain. In 1926 he also joined the staff of Harvard as an instructor in history and was advanced to assistant professor in 1936, to associate professor in 1939 and to full professor of history in 1942.

While teaching at Harvard, Buck carried on extensive research at the university library and other libraries in the East and Southeast, which resulted in his study of Reconstruction years in the South, *The Road to Reunion; 1865-1900.* It was published in 1937 (Little) and the following year won the Pulitzer Prize for Buck as "a distinguished book on the history of the United States."

Emphasizing "the varied threads of reconciliation," political, social and cultural, *The Road to Reunion* shows how true peace developed in a relatively short time. "Within a generation after the close of the Civil War the particularistic aspirations of North and South had lost their bitter edge," Buck pointed out, "and an American nationalism existed which derived its elements indiscriminantly from both the erstwhile foes." He calls this "speedy reconciliation . . . based upon integrated

John Brook

PAUL H. BUCK

interests . . . a striking illustration of the dynamic force exerted by nationalism in the nineteenth century."

In his review of the book for *Current History* (August 1937), N. B. Cousins observed: "The care with which Professor Buck has composed *The Road to Reunion* is manifest on every page. As a scholar, he is chary of the all-conclusive statement and his first allegiance is to the facts."

Dr. Buck served as associate dean of the Harvard Faculty of Arts and Sciences from 1939 to 1942, dean from 1942 to 1945 and provost of the university and ex officio dean from 1945 to 1953. He was second only to Harvard's president James B. Conant in responsibility and during Conant's absences on government service in World War II, was called upon to carry on the policies of the university.

As dean and provost, Buck was chairman of the Harvard committee that in 1945 wrote *General Education in a Free Society,* and he had a large share in putting into effect in Harvard College its objective of preparing students for responsible citizenship. Lamont Library, an indirect result of the publication of the committee's survey, was opened in January 1949 and included conference rooms suited to new methods of teaching the humanities.

Other projects that Buck helped to establish were the Allston Burr Senior Tutors to arrange for individual or small-group tutoring in each of Harvard's seven residential houses; a new division of applied science, combining the efforts of engineers, physicists and mathematicians in training "a new kind of engineer"; and a department and laboratory of social relations to encourage cooperation among sociologists, social psychologists and social anthropologists. He aided in creating in 1949 the Russian Research Center and also supported a pro-

BUCK, PAUL H.—*Continued*

gram of international and regional studies to train students for foreign service in several special fields.

When President Conant left Harvard in early 1953 to become U.S. High Commissioner to West Germany, Buck was made chairman of a four-man committee for the Harvard Corporation which administered the university until Nathan M. Pusey took office as president in October 1953. In February of that year it was announced that Buck, as acting president, would head an official university committee of Harvard educators to study cases of faculty members implicated in Congressional loyalty or security investigations. The committee would gather opinions and statements from the professors involved and would recommend policy to the Harvard Corporation.

Buck resigned his administrative duties in late 1953 to return to teaching and research, and in 1953 his *Nature and Needs of Higher Education* was published. Announcement was made in October 1954 that he had been chosen successor to Keyes D. Metcalf as director of the Harvard University Library and librarian of Harvard College, to assume his new post in the summer of 1955. He is expected to continue to give some time to teaching history.

The Harvard Library, which began with some 400 books bequeathed by John Harvard in 1638, is one of the most complete literary and historical collections in the world. Its main library, formerly the Harvard College Library, whose principal collection of 1,990,768 volumes is in the Harry Elkins Widener Memorial Building, was transferred in 1948 on the joint recommendation of Buck and Metcalf from an independent department of the university to the Faculty of Arts and Sciences. The Houghton Library of 150,804 volumes houses Harvard's collection of rare books and manuscripts, ranging from medieval writings to contemporary works such as the Thomas Wolfe papers. The Lamont Library provides about 100,000 volumes on open shelves easily accessible to students.

Among the eighty separate libraries comprising the Harvard University Library are those of the Law School and the Graduate School of Business Administration, as well as several scientific collections. The library is affiliated with the Arnold Arboretum, Fogg Art Museum and other research institutions. Harvard also participates in the New England Deposit Library, a cooperative storage for infrequently used books, established during World War II.

Soon after the announcement of his appointment as director of Harvard's library services, Buck gave an address at a conference of the Association of Research Libraries. "I used to find the resources of the Harvard Library very helpful when attracting professors to our faculty," he said. "Our salary scale, which is rather high, was less important. . . . The most important consideration was the morale of the faculty, which involved the university's policies with regard to academic freedom and the way in which a professor is allowed to operate. Second only to this in importance was the library. In terms of cash, I estimate it was worth $3,000 a year per man. This is a consideration that should not be lost sight of by those who administer great universities" (*College and Research Libraries*, April 1955).

Dr. Buck's other educational activities include his chairmanship of the board of the Dumbarton Oaks Research Library and Collection in Washington, D.C., membership on the board of the center for advanced study in the behavioral sciences under the Ford Foundation (appointed in 1952), and trusteeship of Smith College (appointed in 1952) and of the High Altitude Observatory in Boulder, Colorado. From 1944 to 1946 he was a member of the civilian advisory committee of the U.S. Navy and from 1949 to 1953 a member of the Commission on Financing Higher Education. He served as an editor of the *Journal of Southern History* from 1941 to 1947 and has contributed to historical periodicals and to the *Dictionary of American Biography*.

He belongs to the American, Mississippi Valley and Southern historical associations, Massachusetts Historical Society, and American Agricultural Society. He is chairman of the committee on American culture of the American Council of Learned Societies. Honors conferred on Buck are chevalier of the Legion of Honor (1951), and degrees from Coe College (LL.D., 1945), Ohio State University (LL.D., 1945), Tufts College (LL.D., 1946), Harvard College (Litt.D., 1946) and Princeton University (Litt.D., 1947). His Greek-letter societies are Phi Beta Kappa and Kappa Sigma, and his clubs are Harvard Faculty, Tavern (Boston), and Harvard (Boston and New York). He married Sally Burwell Betts on December 21, 1927. Buck is an Episcopalian.

In announcing the appointment of Buck to head Harvard's libraries, President Pusey said of him: "No one is more alert to the challenge given the library by every educational advance, or more aware of the crucial part the library has played, down through history, in accumulating and disseminating knowledge. He knows the faculty and its needs for research and teaching, the students' needs for learning, and he knows the library intimately both as scholar-user and as administrator-friend."

References

Coll & Res Lib 16:209+ Ap '55 por
Library J 79:2158 N 15 '54

Directory of American Scholars (1951)
Who Knows—And What (1954)
Who's Who in America, 1954-55
Who's Who in Massachusetts, 1942-43
World Biography (1954)

BULGANIN, NIKOLAI A(LEKSANDROVICH) (bŭl-gä-nēn nē-kŏ-lä-ī' ă-lěks-än-drŏ-vēch') June 11, 1895- Premier of the U.S.S.R. Communist party official

Address: b. c/o The Kremlin, Moscow, U.S.S.R.

On February 8, 1955 the Soviet government removed Georgi M. Malenkov from the Premiership and advanced Marshall Nikolai A. Bulganin from Minister of Defense to

Premier. He headed the U.S.S.R. delegation to Geneva, Switzerland for the "Big Four" meeting "at the summit" the week of July 18, and conferred with President Dwight D. Eisenhower, Prime Minister Anthony Eden, and Premier Edgar Faure on ways of resolving the issues that for ten years have set the East against the West.

Premier Nikolai Bulganin has a reputation as a brilliant administrator who turned his hand successfully to work in the security police, industry, finance and government.

After World War II Bulganin became the chief symbol of civilian and Communist party control over the Soviet armed forces, a man depended upon to maintain military efficiency on the reduced budgets of peacetime. At the same time he has been one of the Soviet's most persistent advocates of military preparedness, constantly warning against any relaxation in the face of "threats" from the West.

Bulganin is also one of the nine members of the Presidium, or executive organ, of the Central Committee of the Communist Party of the Soviet Union, and a delegate to the Council of Nationalities of the U.S.S.R. Supreme Soviet from the City of Moscow.

Nikolai Aleksandrovich Bulganin was born in Nizhni-Novgorod (now the city of Gorky) on the Volga River east of Moscow, June 11, 1895, the son of a factory clerk. He attended secondary school, but soon left to work as a clerk and then as a textile worker.

In 1917, after the February revolution that overthrew the Czar and before the Bolshevik seizure of power in October, Bulganin joined the Bolshevik party. After the October Revolution he was assigned to the All-Russian Extraordinary Commission, the dread Cheka. From 1918 to 1922 he held responsible posts in this organization, fighting counter-revolutionaries first in his home city of Nizhni-Novgorod, and later in Turkestan and Moscow.

With the end of the Civil War period in 1922, the Communist party transferred its major effort from suppressing dissidents to rebuilding the country's economy. Bulganin was assigned by the party to responsible posts in the Supreme Council of the National Economy from 1922 to 1927. He was then appointed director of a Moscow electrical plant which he rapidly built into one of the largest and most advanced in the country. For this he was awarded the Order of Lenin. It was apparently at this time, also, that he was married—to a girl who worked in his electrical factory.

Having proved his talents in the field of industry, Bulganin then began a rapid rise in the government and the party. In January 1931 he was named chairman of the Moscow Soviet of Workers' Deputies—a position equivalent to that of mayor. In 1934 at the Seventeenth Congress of the party, he was named to the Central Committee. Briefly, in 1937, he became the chairman of the Council of Peoples Commissars of the Russian Federative Socialist Republic, and in the same year in the elections for the First Supreme Soviet of the U.S.S.R. he was named by the City of Moscow to

Sovphoto

NIKOLAI A. BULGANIN

Council of Nationalities. In 1938 he was made a vice-chairman of the Council of Peoples Commissars of the U.S.S.R. and simultaneously head of the Administration of the State Bank.

When the dangers of war began to loom over the Soviet Union, Bulganin was put in charge in 1940 of a newly created Board of Metallurgical and Chemical Industries, under the Council of Peoples Commissars, and led those industries to new heights of production in preparation for war.

In the first days of the German attack on the Soviet Union, in the summer of 1941, Bulganin was given the rank of a lieutenant general in the Soviet Army and assigned to direct work with the military. From 1941 to 1943 he was a member of the War Council of the Western Front, organizing the population of Moscow for the desperate defense of the city against the German onslaught. For his success he was awarded the military orders of Suvurov, Kutuzov and the Red Banner.

For brief periods Bulganin served as a member of the War Councils, first of the Second Baltic Front and then of the First Byelorussian Front. He was promoted from lieutenant general to colonel general on July 30, 1944, and a few days later was named the Soviet representative to the Polish Committee of National Liberation, the Soviet-sponsored "puppet" government for "liberated" Poland.

Bulganin was promoted again on November 15, 1944 to be a full Army General and a week later was named a Deputy Commissar for Defense and a member of the State Defense Committee, replacing Marshal Kliment Yefremovich Voroshilov in the "inner cabinet" that directed the war effort.

The Polish Government gave Bulganin its highest decoration in 1945. When the Soviet Government in March 1946 transformed the

BULGANIN, NIKOLAI A.—*Continued*

old commissariats into ministries, he became a Deputy Minister for General Affairs in the Ministry of Armed Forces. In the same month the Central Committee of the party elected him a member of its Organization Bureau and an alternate member of its Political Bureau.

Stalin gave up the responsibilities of Minister of the Armed Forces in March 1947, and Bulganin was chosen to succeed him. Bulganin was also named, at the same time, a deputy chairman of the Council of Ministers of the U.S.S.R. In November 1947 he was promoted to Marshal of the Soviet Union, the country's highest military rank, in recognition of "his outstanding services during the Great Patriotic War." The Central Committee of the party in February 1948 advanced him to a full member of the Political Bureau.

Bulganin relinquished the responsibilities of Minister of the Armed Forces in March 1949, but in his capacity of Deputy Chairman of the Council of Ministers apparently continued to exercise policy control. He took an active part in the 1949 and 1952 conferences in Moscow with the leaders of Communist China, and he made trips to Bulgaria and Czechoslovakia which were followed by army shakeups.

Bulganin was one of the major speakers at the Nineteenth Congress of the Communist party of the Soviet Union in October 1952, and immediately after the congress he was elected by the Central Committee to its Presidium, a body replacing the Political Bureau.

In the party reorganization that followed the death of Stalin in March 1953, the Central Committee Presidium was sharply reduced in size, but Bulganin remained as one of its members. In the government reorganization he again assumed direct control of the armed forces, as Minister of Defense. At Stalin's state funeral Bulganin was one of the pallbearers.

Klement Gottwald, the president of Czechoslovakia, was taken seriously ill at Stalin's funeral and died a few days afterward. Bulganin headed the Soviet delegation at his funeral in Prague and was again called upon to serve as a pallbearer.

In the crisis of June and July 1953, when Lavrenti Beria was arrested and the powers of the security police sharply curtailed, Bulganin led the way in winning the support of the Army commanders for the Government's move—a support without which the move could hardly have succeeded.

Bulganin was awarded the Order of the Red Star in April 1954 for his years of service in the Soviet Army. During the year he went on official missions to Warsaw and Peiping. On his return from the latter journey he inspected the defenses of Manchuria, and may also have witnessed an atomic test in Siberia.

In late November he was present at a reception in Moscow given by Soviet Foreign Minister Vîacheslav M. Molotov to delegates attending a conference of eight Eastern European Communist countries, called to consider common defense measures to counter the rearming of Western Germany. Bulganin told the delegates, "Whether you decide on a joint staff or a single command, we [the military men] welcome your determination to pay more attention to your defenses" (New York *Times,* December 1, 1954).

Called "handsome and witty" by Harrison Salisbury, the New York *Times* correspondent who spent five years in Moscow, Bulganin has the bearing of a professor or scientist, an erect figure, of more than average height, and wears a mustache and goatee, once dark blond but now white.

Former Ambassador Walter Bedell Smith described him in his memoirs as "an able administrator and executive, and a brilliant speaker." At receptions, he said, Bulganin is "distantly courteous," but foreigners dealing with him "have thought him reasonable, intelligent and able."

In many of his speeches Bulganin has accused the Western democracies of warmongering. "Imperialist forces headed by the United States," he charged in March 1954, "openly carry on a policy of preparing a new war against us and the People's Democracies."

Following the Big Four meeting in Geneva, he voiced some doubts as to President Eisenhower's proposal for the mutual inspection of military establishments of the United States and the Soviet Union (New York *Times* August 5, 1955).

Harry Schwartz, the Russian expert of the New York *Times,* calls Bulganin "the personification of the managerial revolution in Russia, the revolution which has shifted power from the ideological fanatics of Lenin's day to the current coterie of administrators, party bosses and industrial technicians." Into whatever field he delved, Schwartz noted, "his administrative brilliance more than made up for his lack of technical knowledge."

References

N Y Herald Tribune II p3 Mr 9 '47 por
N Y Times Mag p9 Ag 2 '53
Time 61:34 Mr 16 '53
U S News 34:62 Mr 13 '53
International Who's Who, 1954
World Biography (1954)

BURKE, ARLEIGH A(LBERT) Oct. 19, 1901- United States Naval officer

Address: b. Office of the Chief of Naval Operations, U.S. Navy Dept., Washington 25, D.C.; h. 4529 Hawthorne St., N.W., Washington, D.C.

Although Rear Admiral Arleigh A. Burke ranked ninety-third on the United States Navy's list of line admirals, he was nominated by President Dwight D. Eisenhower on May 25, 1955 to succeed Admiral Robert B. Carney as Chief of U.S. Naval Operations. His appointment surprised the Pentagon, the New York *Times* (May 26, 1955) reported, as it is believed that he is the first rear admiral with a subordinate command to be elevated to the high Navy post. He took office in August 1955, automatically becoming a vice-admiral.

Nicknamed "thirty-one knot Burke" by Admiral William F. Halsey in 1943, he was noted for the high speed at which he carried his destroyer squadron into twenty-two combat engagements in the Pacific battles of World War II. He holds many distinguished service awards.

His participation in the "Admirals' revolt of 1949," against emphasis on the B-36 Air Force bomber in the Armed Forces unification plan, reportedly delayed Burke's promotion to rear admiral. The appointment was finally approved by President Harry S. Truman on December 29, 1949. He was a member of the United Nations Military Armistice Commission at Kaesong, Korea during the summer of 1951.

Arleigh Albert Burke was born in Boulder, Colorado on October 19, 1901, the son of Oscar A. and Claire (Mokler) Burke. His parents were of Swedish and Pennsylvania Dutch stock (his paternal grandfather changed his name from Bjorkegren). Arleigh was the eldest of six children. They lived on a 170-acre farm far from the ocean. Young Burke attended the State Preparatory School in Boulder and the Naval Academy Preparatory School at Columbia, Missouri, before his appointment to the United States Naval Academy from the Second District of Colorado in 1919. *Time* (July 17, 1944) wrote that "his heart was in the Navy from the time he was able to walk" and that at Annapolis he had no time for athletics or "midshipmen's monkey-business."

After graduation from the Naval Academy in 1923, Ensign Burke was attached to the U.S.S. *Arizona* for five years, with duty in several divisions which included a course of instruction at the Naval Torpedo School on North Island, San Diego, California. He was transferred to the U.S.S. *Procyon,* flagship of the Fleet Base Force, in April 1928. During his year of service on the *Procyon,* he received a Letter of Commendation for the "rescue of shipwrecked and seafaring men" on December 4, 1928.

He returned to Annapolis in June 1929 for postgraduate instruction in ordnance engineering (explosives) and also studied at the Postgraduate School, University of Michigan, where he received an M.S. degree in engineering in June 1931. He continued under instruction in naval ordnance activities and joined the U.S.S. *Chester* in June 1932, as assistant gunnery and main battery officer. Two of the next five years were spent on duty in the Navy Department's explosives section at the Bureau of Ordnance in Washington. He assisted in outfitting his first destroyer, the U.S.S. *Craven,* at the Bethlehem Shipbuilding Corporation, Quincy, Massachusetts, and was the ship's executive officer from September 1937 to June 1939.

In command of the U.S.S. *Mugford,* flagship of Destroyer Division Eight, Destroyers Battle Force, in 1939, Burke trained its gunners to "razor fineness" and set a new destroyer shooting record and won the gunnery trophy in competition (*Time,* July 17, 1944). He returned to

U. S. Navy

REAR ADM. ARLEIGH A. BURKE

the Bureau of Ordnance in July 1940 and was with the inspection division of the naval gun factory at the Navy Yard in Washington, D.C., until January 1943.

He attained the rank of captain on May 1, 1943 and in September of the same year was designated commander, Destroyer Squadron 23 (two divisions) which was known as "Little Beavers" after Captain Burke dressed each ship with a new insignia—a character from Fred Harman's comic strip *Red Ryder*—called "Little Beaver." *Time* reported that on October 31, 1943, the squadron "swept around the Solomons bastion at Bougainville at thirty-one knots and shot up Jap airfields one after the other while Marines stormed ashore at Empress Augusta Bay." When a Japanese task force came, Burke led the Little Beavers task force in sinking a cruiser and four destroyers. Navy men commented that they had never seen anything like the "fury and deadly precision of the Little Beavers' attack."

When ordered to stop the Japanese from evacuating Buka Island on November 24, 1943, Captain Burke headed his ships up "The Slot" and sent a message to some American transports in his path—"Stand aside. I'm coming through at thirty-one knots." He did, and reached Buka in time to sink three Japanese transports (New York *Herald Tribune,* May 26, 1955). He became known as "King of the Cans," and the nickname "thirty-one knot Burke" was added after this feat. The Little Beavers were also credited with the destruction of a number of other ships and about thirty enemy aircraft.

Under Admiral Marc A. Mitscher, with the temporary rank of commodore, Burke was aboard the flagship *Bunker Hill* when she was severely damaged by an attack of two suicide dive bombers off Okinawa in May 1945, and he succeeded in evacuating all hands. The second

BURKE, ARLEIGH A.—*Continued*

flagship was hit by a suicide plane on May 14th, and he again arranged for transfer to a new ship. He was detached from staff duty in July 1945, and became head of the research and development division in the Bureau of Ordnance at Washington, until recalled to staff duty with the Atlantic Fleet in January 1946. Two years later, he became an assistant to the Chief of Naval Operations in the organizational research and policy division.

As head of the "Operation 23" research team, which supplied material ostensibly to facilitate the Navy's cooperation with the Army and the Air Force to comply with the terms of unification in the National Security Act, it was Captain Burke's job to brief the officers who testified before the House Armed Services Committee in 1949. The inquiry arose over the Navy's dispute with the Air Force on the merits of the B-36 intercontinental bomber, and it brought Burke into disfavor with some of the civilians in the Truman Administration. Harlan Trott (*Christian Science Monitor,* January 4, 1950) reported that Burke had not "relished" the assignment, although he believed in the Navy's case for a "strong, independent naval air arm based on big, fast, far-reaching aircraft carriers."

When the Navy Selection Board met on November 12, 1949, Captain Burke's name was put on a list with twenty-two other captains for promotion to rear admiral. There were reports that Burke's name had been stricken from the list because of his activities in support of the Navy's "revolt" (New York *Times,* December 30, 1949). The board reconvened and on December 5th, a revised list was flown to the President at Key West, Florida. All navy officers who presented their views in the controversy were promised that "no reprisals" would be made, so when the list was not returned immediately, members of Congress said that a committee would "look into the matter" if Burke's name was eliminated (Washington *Post,* December 13, 1949).

The list, which contained twenty-three names and included Captain Burke, was approved. Jim G. Lucas (New York *World-Telegram and Sun,* January 9, 1950) called it a "victory for Admiral Sherman" who "went to bat for a fellow officer." (Admiral Forrest P. Sherman had replaced Admiral Louis Denfeld as Chief of Naval Operations two months earlier.)

Captain Burke was given a "top level" assignment on January 18, 1950 as Navy secretary to the research and development board. His promotion to rear admiral was confirmed by the U.S. Senate on July 10, 1950 and in September, he became deputy chief of staff to the commander of U.S. Naval Forces in the Far East. After the successful Inchon amphibious landings, Admiral Burke expressed the opinion that the failure of the North Koreans to put up much resistance meant that they had over-extended themselves (New York *Times,* September 16, 1950).

While the Admiral was a member of the Military Armistice Commission—May to September 1951—Bert Andrews (New York *Herald Tribune,* August 19, 1951) observed that he "lightened things up" with his "grin and his blarney," which may have had a part in softening the Communists into reasonableness.

During the next two years, he was director of the strategic plans division of Naval Operations, and in November 1954 was designated Commander of the Destroyer Force of the Atlantic Fleet, at Norfolk, Virginia. His appointment as Chief of Naval Operations was confirmed by the U.S. Senate on June 7, 1955.

In addition to the Navy Cross, Distinguished Service Medal with Gold Star, Legion of Merit with Gold Star, the Silver Star Medal, Purple Heart Medal, Presidential Unit Citation Ribbon with three stars, Admiral Burke holds the Asiatic-Pacific Campaign Medal with two silver and two bronze stars, and many others which include the Presidential Unit Citation from the Republic of Korea. He is a member of the American Chemical Society, the American Institute of Chemical Engineers, and the Iota Alpha honorary fraternity for chemical engineers.

Arleigh Albert Burke was married on June 7, 1923 to Roberta Gorsuch of Washington, D.C. The admiral is of medium height and has been called "husky, precise," and "wisecracking." W. H. Lawrence (New York *Times,* May 26, 1955) described Burke as a "volatile, exuberant man" who is "popular with both enlisted men and officers."

Thoroughly wrapped up in the U.S. Navy, Burke has not developed many hobbies or sports proficiencies. But he did find time to build a house for himself—a cottage in Virginia, near the Great Falls of the Potomac and a few miles from Washington. He designed the house himself (he was influenced by Japanese architecture), bought a set of power tools from Sears, Roebuck, and put it up with some professional help (*Newsweek,* June 6, 1955). A fellow negotiator at the Panmunjom armistice negotiations with the North Koreans remarked about Burke: "He never lost his temper or turned a hair when he was talking to them" (*Time,* June 6, 1955).

References

Aviation W 62:11 My 30 '55
Christian Sci Mon p12 My 25 '55
N Y Herald Tribune p1 My 26 '55 por
N Y Times p 1+ My 26 '55 por
Newsweek 45:28 Je 6 '55 por
Time 44:55 Jl 17 '44 por; 58:21 Jl 16 '51 por; 65:25 Je 6 '55 por
Who's Who in America, 1954-55

BURNS, E(DSON) L(OUIS) M(ILLARD) June 17, 1897- United Nations official; Canadian Government official and Army officer

Address: b. c/o United Nations Truce Supervision Organization, Jerusalem, Palestine; Department of Veterans Affairs, Ottawa, Canada; h. 6 Park Rd., Ottawa 2, Canada

Major General E. L. M. Burns of Canada, known as "an exceptionally brilliant and efficient civil servant," was appointed in August

1954 by Secretary-General Dag Hammarskjöld as chief of staff of the United Nations Truce Supervision Organization in Palestine. Burns termed his new post "a ticklish one," noting that relations between Israel and Jordan were "full of tension" (New York *Times,* August 4, 1954).

In Jerusalem, his appointment was held indicative that "the Western powers are anxious over the deterioration of the Middle East situation and that more energetic action will be taken to put an end to the steadily rising tension" (Ottawa *Citizen,* August 6, 1954).

The affairs of the United Nations have concerned General Burns since 1947. He was national president of the U.N. Association in Canada in 1952-1953 and was an alternate delegate to the fourth session of the General Assembly in New York in 1949. In the Army before World War II, he helped to develop air photo survey techniques. Following distinguished service as a Canadian Army field commander during the war, Burns became director general of rehabilitation in his country's Department of Veterans Affairs in 1945. Since 1949 he has been Deputy Minister of the department and is now on leave of absence from this post.

Eedson Louis Millard Burns was born in Westmount, Quebec on June 17, 1897, the son of George Eedson and Louise (Wills) Burns. He received his education at Lower Canada College, Montreal, where he was nicknamed "Tommy," after the popular heavyweight boxing champion of the period, Tommy Burns. His friends still call him by this name.

Following service for a year with the 17th Hussars, Burns entered the Royal Military College, Kingston, Ontario in 1914 and majored in engineering and mathematics. Six months later, in 1915, he was granted a wartime commission in the Royal Canadian Engineers and sent to France, where he served with the Signals and general staff. For his action on the Somme in 1916, he won the Military Cross (British).

Between World Wars I and II, Burns held important staff appointments in Canada's peacetime Army. While an instructor in military engineering with the rank of captain, at the Royal Military College during 1926, he wrote an article entitled "Defense in Modern Warfare" (*American Mercury,* February 1926). Two years later he left his teaching post to attend Staff College, Quetta, India from 1928 to 1930. During this period he was advanced to the rank of major in the Royal Canadian Engineers and continued to write articles on the subject of war.

In "Study of War," which appeared in the *American Mercury* (October 1930), Burns attacked pedantic methods of military training. "It is a peculiar fact," he stated, "that while war is the most fascinating pursuit known to man, yet instruction in it . . . is usually made so dull that at least seven soldiers out of ten in peacetime become disgusted with their lifework and give themselves over to drink, bridge, golf or polo."

When assigned to the general staff of the geographical section in the National Defense Headquarters at Ottawa in 1930, he directed experimental work in air photo survey and developed a number of techniques using air photos for mapping purposes. During 1936-1937 he was president of the Canadian Institute of Survey and served as an associate member of the committee for survey research of the National Research Council. He was awarded the Order of the British Empire in 1939.

Nat. Film Bd. of Canada
E. L. M. BURNS

Assigned to London in 1939, he aided General H. D. G. Crerar in establishing military headquarters there for Canadian troops. He made several trips between England and Canada during the next four years while holding various senior staff appointments. In April 1941 he succeeded British Brigadier M. C. Dempsey as brigadier of the Canadian Corps general staff, in charge of all military operations of the overseas army.

He commanded the Fourth Canadian Armoured Brigade and the Second Canadian Infantry Division during their training period. "He was always a popular officer," wrote Phil Shackleton in *Saturday Night* (August 1, 1950), " . . . because his men had confidence in his proven ability and fair dealing."

In 1943 Burns was promoted to the rank of major general and early in 1944 was placed in command of the Fifth Canadian Armoured Division in Italy. The next spring he was commanding officer of the First Canadian Corps (formed within the British Eighth Army) when it broke through the German line at Liri and later through the Gothic line on the Adriatic coast, capturing Rimini. For this service, he was awarded the Distinguished Service Order of the British Empire. Near the close of World War II he was general officer in charge of the Canadian Section, 21st Army Group headquarters, in northwest Europe.

When he joined Canada's Department of Veterans Affairs in Ottawa in 1945, as director general of rehabilitation, Burns stated that he

BURNS, E. L. M.—*Continued*

was "anxious to have a crack at life outside the service" and was convinced that "the veteran himself is best qualified to help other veterans" (*Saturday Night,* August 1, 1950).

For a year he organized educational and training programs and counseling service for men discharged from military service. After he was made Assistant Deputy Minister of Veterans Affairs in 1946, his duties became chiefly administrative. In July 1950 he was named Deputy Minister of Veterans Affairs.

The General became active in the affairs of the United Nations in 1947-1948, when he was president of the Ottawa branch of the U.N. Association in Canada. In his article, "U.N. Armed Force Plan Difficult to Realize," in *Saturday Night* (December 13, 1947), Burns discussed the military staff committee's report to the Security Council in April 1947 on a proposed United Nations armed force to guarantee the security of the nations of the world. He wrote: "The arguments and disagreements of the military committee uncomfortably recall the endless and fruitless conferences on disarmament under the League of Nations. . . . The causes are the same. . . . No real political accord has preceded the military discussions."

He was an alternate delegate for Canada at the fourth session of the United Nations General Assembly in New York in 1949. In the same year he wrote two articles on aims and methods in the event of a third World War, published in *Saturday Night,* March 1 and 8, 1949. In the first, "Democracies' War Aims Must Exceed Simple Idea of Enemy's Defeat," he emphasized that without "international inspection and control of atomic energy undertakings . . . no scheme of preventing atomic warfare can be effective." And in the second, "Victory for Atlantic Pact Nations Must Be Won in the Field of Ideas," he stressed the need for "final victory" in both "economics and ideas."

Burns's participation in the activities of the U.N. Association in Canada brought him the office of national president in 1952 and 1953. On August 2, 1954 U.N. Secretary General Dag Hammarskjöld appointed Burns chief of staff of the U.N. Truce Supervision Organization in Palestine, to succeed Denmark's General Vagn Bennike, whose one-year term had expired. He took up his new duties in the Israeli sector of Jerusalem on September 2, 1954.

In a report to the Security Council of the U.N. on September 15, 1954, General Burns warned that armed raids along the Israeli-Jordanian border "if not stopped rapidly, may develop into hostilities extending like a brushfire" (New York *Times,* September 15, 1954). He also stated that Israel's boycott of the Jordan-Israel Mixed Armistice Commission, begun in March 1954, barred U.N. investigation of Israeli charges that Jordan had violated the cease-fire armistice agreement drafted on the Island of Rhodes in 1948. A few days later Burns was invited by Israel's director general of the Ministry of Foreign Affairs, Walter Eytan, to "undertake a general study of the conditions prevailing along the border" (New York *Times,* September 27, 1954).

The General was credited with a "major success" on October 4, 1954, when he revived the special committee of the Israeli-Egyptian Mixed Armistice Commission (which had been inactive for three years) as an appeals panel for decisions of the commission. The return of Israel to the Israeli-Jordanian Mixed Armistice Commission on October 20, 1954 was also attributed to his efforts. Israel then proposed to the commission that "all except three of the 1,500 complaints from both sides" be removed from its agenda (New York *Times,* October 26, 1954). Jordan countered with the demand that all or none of the complaints be dropped.

Israel opposed a method introduced by Burns to control Israeli-Jordanian hostile border incidents by placing U.N. observer patrols along border areas. The General stated that his action supported the Security Council resolution of August 11, 1949 which charged the U.N. Truce Supervision Organization "with observing and maintaining the cease-fire" (New York *Times,* September 26, 1954). He settled the controversy on December 1, 1954 in an agreement with Israeli chief of staff, Meshe Dayan, allowing Israeli officers to accompany U.N. observers on trips to border areas.

Reporting to the U.N. Security Council on October 27, 1954, Burns described a deadlock in his attempts to investigate Egypt's seizure of the Israeli freighter *Bat Galim* in the Gulf of the Suez. On November 19, 1954 the U.N. Truce Supervision Organization announced that the Mixed Israeli-Egyptian Armistice Commission had ruled that Egypt had not produced sufficient evidence that the *Bat Galim* had fired on Egyptian fishermen, and requested that Egypt "come quickly to an arrangement for the release" of the freighter (New York *Herald Tribune,* November 20, 1954).

Burns married Eleanor Phelan on December 3, 1927 and they have one daughter. He is described as having a "soldierly bearing and straight-forward manner" and as being "outwardly reserved" (*Saturday Night,* August 1, 1950). He plays "what he terms an indifferent piano . . . and he is an ardent gardener."

References

N Y Times p3 Ap 28 '41; p5 Ag 4 '54; p14 S 15 '54; p6 S 27 '54
Sat Night 65:11 Ag 1 '50; 69:3 Ag 21 '54
Canadian Who's Who, 1952-54

BURPEE, DAVID (bûr' pê) Apr. 5, 1893-
Seedsman; horticulturist

Address: b. c/o W. Atlee Burpee Co., 18th St. and Hunting Park Ave., Philadelphia 32, Pa.: h. Fordhook Farms, Doylestown, Pa.

A harbinger of spring for many American gardeners each year is the arrival of the catalogue of the W. Atlee Burpee Company, the largest mail order seed house in the world. The firm has been headed by David Burpee, the son of the founder, since 1917. Luther Burbank once wrote to David Burpee: "I consider your house the most reliable seed house in the world, and I think this would be the verdict of the public at large." Burpee's interest has been to develop seeds which would grow in any garden, rather than to experiment with seeds which only experts could grow.

"Flowers have fashions just like clothes," Burpee once said. "It is the production of these 'fashion flowers' that keeps the hybridists and plant breeders busy." He has directed the investigation which led to the development of the first ruffled sweet peas, first African-French hybrid marigolds, first marigolds with odorless foliage, first hybrid zinnias, first double hybrid nasturtiums, and the first tetraploid snapdragons. His work has increased the productivity and improved the taste of countless vegetables.

David Burpee was born in Philadelphia, Pennsylvania on April 5, 1893, the son of Washington Atlee and Blanche (Simmons) Burpee. The Burpee family is descended from Huguenot ancestors originally named Beaupré and from William Pitt, Earl of Chatham. David's father, who had begun an animal and seed selling business with a partner in 1876, started his own firm, the W. Atlee Burpee Company, in 1878. David's brother, Washington Atlee Burpee, Jr., is now vice-president and treasurer of the seed firm.

Young David attended the Blight School in Philadelphia, the Doylestown High School and the Culver Military Academy in Indiana and also traveled to Europe several times. In 1913 he studied horticulture at the College of Agriculture, Cornell University. In 1914 he became his father's assistant and the following year general manager of the company. His father died on November 26, 1915. At that time the firm had over 300 employees handling nearly 10,000 orders daily. In 1917 he became president of the W. Atlee Burpee Company.

"Father never made a mistake," David Burpee once said. "He tried his seeds to be sure they would grow, and he just blazed ahead on his merchandising ideas. Since then we have tested them and find them all to be right." The slogan which the firm still uses, "Burpee's Seeds Grow," resulted from a contest sponsored by W. Atlee Burpee in 1890.

In an interview with a correspondent of the *Christian Science Monitor* (June 21, 1947), Burpee spoke of the development of the seed-growing industry in the United States. During World War I, foreign vegetable seeds could no longer be imported and American seedsmen "expanded to the extent where they could supply the nation's entire needs," he explained. "They never went back to foreign importations."

After the war many American gardeners had more time to grow flowers and the industry began expanding. Commenting on the effect on seed firms of the depression of the early 1930's, Burpee said, "Always in previous times of depression, sales of vegetable seeds jumped ahead. . . . But in the latest depression, vegetable seeds didn't increase in sales at all—in

Kaiden-Keystone

DAVID BURPEE

fact they dropped a little—but flower seeds made a tremendous gain! My idea is that the last depression was so bad that people had to have some way to forget themselves, and they found it in flowers."

In 1937 the Burpee company employed more than 400 persons in the spring months, when over 10,000 orders were received daily. During the last three years of World War II, the company shipped more than 100,000,000 pounds of American vegetable seeds under the Lend Lease program to the other Allied nations. Burpee said that in 1947 not only was the nation self-sufficient in growing seeds, but its exports were growing rapidly. By 1955 about ten per cent of the firm's total business was in exports.

To satisfy the changing tastes of gardeners and to meet competition, the company is constantly experimenting and developing new varieties, colors, shapes and textures of flowers and vegetables. Most of the firm's work is done on its Fordhook Farms in Pennsylvania and at the Floradale Farms in California. In 1954 the company reported the development of the golden "snap" beans without fiber. The popular "Big Boy," the largest of the Burpee first generation hybrid tomatoes, has a fine flavor and often weighs over two pounds. The Burpee hybrid cantaloupe, outstanding for quality, was developed in 1955.

When David Burpee was fourteen years old, his father offered him $1,000 if he could find a seed of a yellow sweet pea; he was unsuccessful and up to the present time, no one else has found one. In 1954 the Burpee firm announced its offer of $10,000 for seeds from a white marigold. Burpee pointed out that "white is white because it is the perfect combination of all colors canceling one another out. . . ." If he had a pure white marigold, he might be able to shock it into a "bust-up," or mutation, that

BURPEE, DAVID—*Continued*
could yield many new marigold colors (Frank J. Taylor, *Saturday Evening Post,* March 21, 1951).

Burpee's new giant hybrid zinnia is the result of experiments over many decades. The flower, which had been found by the Spanish explorers in Mexico, taken to Europe and developed there, was re-introduced to the United States in the 1890's by W. Atlee Burpee. Luther Burbank developed this strain of the flower for about twenty-five years and after his death in 1926, his head gardener worked on it for a decade. Then the Burpee scientists developed it for another fifteen years and made it bigger and more colorful in order to please amateur flower growers.

But David Burpee, wanting a still more attractive zinnia, sent some seeds to the University of California, where bombardment with X rays failed to produce the "bust-up" he wanted. Then he had the zinnia plants fertilized with radioactive phosphorus. This also failed, but when colchicine was sprayed on the plants, he got the "bust-up" he desired, and such strains as the curly-petaled, the pastel-shaded and the chrysanthemum-like (the new giant Burpee hybrid) resulted. (Other methods of inducing mutations than those already mentioned are mutilation of plants, aging of seed or of pollen, and hydroponics.)

In 1937 Burpee was able to sell seeds for an "odorless" marigold through the crossing of one such plant found by his experimenters (after what was described as a "monumental smelling bee" in the marigold fields) with a marigold with odorless foliage grown from seeds sent to Burpee by a missionary in China, the Reverend Carter D. Holton. The company found, however, that most people like marigolds with some odor. The first super-double nasturtium, which had seventy-five petals, was grown by Burpee; at first its seeds and cuttings sold for ten cents a piece.

Half a million bees were hired by Burpee in 1939 to pollinate small brown-red French marigolds with the large African yellow-and-orange variety. This produced a medium-sized red-and-gold marigold, but these beautiful flowers had sterile seeds. Eventually, with the use of colchicine, he was able to double the chromosome count of the African marigold from 24 to 48. It was then a normal mate for the French variety and the resulting flowers had fertile seeds.

The way in which many of the seeds are prepared for selling was once described by Burpee. In order to obtain sweet pea seeds, the crop is first cut with a mowing machine. It is then spread on large sheets of canvas to cure in the sun for six weeks or more after which it is threshed, carefully cleaned and sacked. Then the seeds are put into hoppers and finally into a brown labeled package ready for sale from the three mail order houses (in Clinton, Iowa; Riverside, California; and Philadelphia). Some seeds must be hand-picked as they become ripe—at times (as with pansies and violas), this ripening will spread over a period of weeks or months.

Among the famous Burpee customers have been the Duchess of Windsor, the Rockefellers, Henry Ford, and Madame Chiang Kai-shek, but Burpee has described the majority of his customers as "home-owners, suburbanites and residents of small towns and rural districts, who are a very steady, conservative type of people, substantial and domestic." Burpee prepares a special Blue List catalogue for commercial growers who buy vegetables and flower seeds in very large quantities.

In selling his product, David Burpee has learned that, contrary to the usual business principle, cutting the price of seeds reduces the sales of those seeds, and that the name of a variety of a flower or vegetable is an important factor in its commercial success (a muskmelon named Hoodoo did not sell, but another with the same characteristics named "Hearts of Gold" became very popular).

The seedsman is chairman of the board of James Vick's Seeds, Inc., and a director of the Market Street National Bank in Philadelphia, Agricultural Missions, Inc., in New York, and of the Abington Memorial Hospital. He is a vice-president of the National Sweet Pea Society of Great Britain, former president of the American Seed Trade Association, honorary life president of the Canadian Society of Philadelphia, councilor of the Colonial Society and Society of New York, life member of the Société Nationale d'Horticulture of France, and member of the New England Society and the English Speaking Union of Pennsylvania.

His clubs are the Union League (a director; and a vice-president from 1933 to 1935), Poor Richard, Fourth Street, Racquet and Art Alliance in Philadelphia, the Advertising in New York, the Doylestown Country, the Huntingdon Valley Country, and the Bachelors' Barge. His fraternity is Delta Upsilon. His political affiliation is with the Republican party.

He married Lois Torrance, a horticulturist, on July 18, 1938. Their children are Jonathan and Blanche Elizabeth Burpee. David Burpee has brown eyes and dark brown hair. He is six feet tall and weighs 170 pounds. His favorite recreations are horseback riding and fox hunting. He has often been quoted as saying at dinner parties, "There is an old Chinese proverb that if you want to be happy for an hour, get drunk. If you want to be happy for a weekend, get married. If you want to be happy for a whole week, kill your pig and eat it. But if you want to be happy all your life, become a gardener." Then he adds, "and plant Burpee's seeds."

References

Life 20:53+ Ap 22 '46 por

National Cyclopædia of American Biography vol 16 (1937)

Who's Who in America, 1954-55

Who's Who in Commerce and Industry (1953)

BUTLER, JOHN Sept. 29, 1920- Choreographer; dancer
Address: 1125 6th Ave., New York 36

For his fifth season dancer John Butler has been choreographer for the New York City Opera Company. He came to this assignment from a varied background which included work in Broadway shows, nightclubs, motion pictures, dance recitals and television. A long-time member of Martha Graham's company, he now heads his own group, the John Butler Dance Theatre, which presents his own compositions. This group appeared in his two ballets *Three Promenades with the Lord* and *Davy Crockett* at the ANTA Theatre in New York during May 1955, as part of the American Dance presented by the B. de Rothschild Foundation.

He has made numerous dance arrangements for television shows, the most notable being for *Amahl and the Night Visitors* and *Adventure*. For the Opera Company he has devised many new ballets for such standard works as *Aïda* and *Carmen, La Traviata* and *Rigoletto,* also staging the American première of Béla Bartók's one-act opera, *Bluebeard's Castle.* In the last two seasons his work has also been seen at the Jacob's Pillow (Lee, Massachusetts) and New London (Connecticut) Dance Festivals.

John Neilson Butler, the son of Minnie (Neilson) Butler, a railroad sales agent, and Kent Butler, a railroad official, was born in Greenwood, Mississippi, on September 29, 1920. Educated in public schools, Butler attended Mississippi State College for a year. Preparation for his future career began with the study of ballroom, tap and exhibition dancing in Greenwood. In 1942 he moved to New York to study ballet, and taught ballroom dancing at the Donald Sawyer Dance Studios to support himself.

The following year he won a scholarship with the Dance Players, an organization headed by Eugene Loring which was then operating at New Hope, Pennsylvania. After a summer's study with Loring, Butler auditioned for Martha Graham and was accepted as a member of her company.

His first appearance in a musical show was in *Oklahoma* in 1943, in which he danced the role of Curly. In 1944 he danced in another musical, *On the Town;* the following season he appeared in a third, *Hollywood Pinafore.*

When Martha Graham's company opened for a week's engagement at the Ziegfeld Theatre in February 1947, the offering included *Appalachian Spring,* with Butler cast in the role of the Revivalist. ". . . he dances it excellently," the New York *Times* dance critic commented, although the second performance, in which *Deaths and Entrances* (a fantasia on the theme of the Brontës) was presented with Butler cast as the Poetic Beloved, brought qualified comment from the same critic, who thought Butler danced this part "admirably, but play[ed] it characterlessly."

In 1948 Butler was back on Broadway when he danced opposite Valerie Bettis in *Inside U.S.A.* In the same year Metro-Goldwyn-Mayer's *Words and Music* was released in which Butler danced with Allyn McLerie. This association resulted in the two dancers teaming up for night club work in a number of engagements including a New York appearance at the Hotel Pierre.

JOHN BUTLER

Beginning in 1947 Butler has choreographed for most of the major television shows including *The 54th Street Revue,* the *Uptown Jubilee,* the Longine Christmas and Thanksgiving shows (for which he did the dance arrangements for four successive years); the *Colgate Comedy Hour*; the *Kate Smith Show* (five shows a week for a year and a half); the *Orchid Award*; the *Ford Show*; the *Eddie Fisher Show; Omnibus* (eight productions); *Adventure* (seven productions); and *Camera Three* (six shows). For NBC Opera Theatre, Butler has choreographed dances for *Amahl and the Night Visitors, Salome, The Marriage of Figaro, The Would-be Gentleman,* and *Macbeth.*

It was Butler's choreography for the première presentation on television of *Amahl and the Night Visitors* in 1951 which led to his engagement as choreographer by the New York City Opera Company when the Gian-Carlo Menotti opus was added to the repertoire. In the fall of 1952 Butler's name first appeared on the opera company's programs as dance director. His work in staging Béla Bartók's *Bluebeard's Castle,* given its American stage première on October 2 brought mixed critical comment.

Walter Terry of the New York *Herald Tribune* hailed it as "a choreographic event of major significance . . . it represents a new departure in opera ballet. Actually, there is no ballet at all. There is instead the flow of dance, and as John Butler, the City Opera's choreographer who staged the production, has directed this flow of action, purposefulness and dramatic power result." On the other hand, Francis D.

BUTLER, JOHN—*Continued*

Perkins, music critic of the same paper, commented, "The advantages of this choreographic treatment can be open to debate."

During 1953 Butler restaged the dance arrangements he had made the previous year for *Carmen, Aïda, Amahl and the Night Visitors,* and other operas, undertaking new assignments for *La Cenerentola, Die Fledermaus, La Traviata, Love of Three Oranges,* and other productions. In summing up Butler's work, Walter Terry wrote: "Butler has brought imagination, fine craftsmanship, tastefulness, energized beauty, and, most important of all, dramatic purposefulness to almost every one of his ballet assignments" (New York *Herald Tribune,* May 3, 1953).

Butler was again seen in the Martha Graham company in the spring of 1953 at the Alvin Theatre, when he reappeared in *Deaths and Entrances.* "On this occasion," the New York *Times* critic wrote, "John Butler and Robert Cohan as the two principal men danced with utmost persuasion, characterizing admirably and playing with full dramatic clarity," and the critic for the New York *Herald Tribune,* in writing of Butler's work in the role of the Dark Beloved, commented that he was "particularly impressive in his handling of an enormously difficult assignment."

At the Jacob's Pillow Dance Festival, held annually at Lee, Massachusetts, a Butler ballet *The Masque of the Wild Man* was presented in July 1953, as well as a trio from *Amahl,* and dances from *La Cenerentola* and *Pagliacci.* In August Butler contributed to the American Dance Festival held in the Palmer Auditorium at New London, where he again presented *The Masque of the Wild Man* and also a new work, *Malocchio.*

The first ballet, set to fifteenth-century recorder music, deals with a noblewoman "bored to that point where only cruelty can stir her interest"; the second is concerned with the persecution of a girl who is presumed to have the evil eye and is based on a special score by Aldo Provenzano. "Both pieces are macabre little vignettes," Martin of the New York *Times* commented, "concerned far more with pantomime than with dancing and not sharp enough to be very effective."

A new composition entitled *The Brass World* was offered in May 1954 at the Brooklyn Academy of Music by Butler, heading his own company. In this work a brass bed is used to convey the idea of life, death, and dream. Walter Terry of the New York *Herald Tribune* was impressed with Butler's second appearance at the Jacob's Pillow Festival the following July when *Three Promenades with the Lord* was offered. Terry wrote that it was "a completely captivating creation, energized by religious fervor, suffused with warm humanity, and spiced by engaging witticisms." A second review on July 18, 1954 referred to the work as "the special high spot" of the festival.

For the spring season of the New York City Opera Company at the City Center opening March 17, 1955, Butler prepared new dance arrangements for *Don Pasquale* and *The Merry Wives of Windsor.* He also presented his own dance company at the Brooklyn Academy of Music, offering a new version of *The Brass World* (now entitled *The Haunted World*), *Three Promenades with the Lord, Frontier Ballad,* and *Adventure.*

Notable among Butler's recent presentations for TV are his choreography for *Adventure,* a program presented by the American Museum of Natural History; the latter received *Dance* magazine's fourth award for "its imaginative and experimental approach to the dance."

In an article in the dance section of the New York *Times* (September 7, 1952) Butler discussed the pros and cons of television as a dance medium. "We accept a time situation which requires us to choreograph too fast," he wrote. "A dance, a ballet, and sometimes both will have to be composed in one day, the orchestration made ready on the second, and the performance itself on the third. . . . We have accepted unhappily but tacitly the inferior standards thrust upon us . . . [yet] there are mechanical and compositional aspects of great value to the choreographer."

Butler has referred to the work at City Center as "a very pleasant hysteria, [where] people work ten times as hard [as on television] for practically no money. But they are doing something they care about very much."

Butler, who has hazel eyes and brown hair, is six feet two inches in height and weighs 170 pounds, has been described by a *World-Telegram* writer as "the handsome young choreographer who looks like a suave and refined Li'l Abner." His fraternity is Kappa Sigma. His hobby is his collection of drawings, paintings, and sculpture, which includes works by Henri Matisse, Giorgio di Chirico, Édouard Vuillard, Lyonel Feininger, Georges Braque, and Massimo Campigli.

References

N Y Times II p7 S 7 '52 por
N Y World-Telegram p33 O 1 '52
Chujoy, A. ed. Dance Encyclopedia (1949)

BUTLER, PAUL M(ULHOLLAND) June 15, 1905- Political party official; lawyer

Address: b. c/o Democratic National Committee, 1001 Connecticut Ave., N.W., Washington, D.C.; c/o Jones, Obenchain & Butler, 800-10 Odd Fellows Bldg., South Bend 1, Ind.

"In the United States it is the constitutional duty of the minority party to scrutinize, to challenge, to debate the actions of the majority. . . . If failures are ignored, because no one dares to mention them, they will never be corrected" (New York *Times,* December 11, 1954). This was stated by Paul M. Butler, who became chairman of the Democratic National Committee on January 1, 1955. By unanimous vote he succeeded Stephen A. Mitchell, who resigned to resume the practice of law. Butler, whose principal task will be to manage national campaigns, has been an active member of the bar in South Bend, Indiana since 1927 and has participated in local and state politics for over twenty years. In 1952 he became a member of the Democratic National Committee.

Paul Mulholland Butler is of Irish descent and was born in South Bend, Indiana on June 15, 1905 to Mary E. (Mulholland) and James P. Butler, a railroad mail clerk who later became a street commissioner and collector of internal revenue in South Bend. Paul was graduated from South Bend High School in 1922 and Notre Dame Preparatory School in 1923. He received the LL.B. degree from the Notre Dame University College of Law in 1927. During his last two years at the college he worked as a part-time reporter for the South Bend *Tribune*.

Admitted to the bar of Indiana in 1927, Butler began to practice law. Since 1932 he has been a partner in the South Bend law firm of Jones, Obenchain & Butler. Entering politics in 1926, Butler became a precinct worker and has been active in every election since that time. In 1938 he managed the unsuccessful campaign of George N. Beamer, who ran for the U.S. House of Representatives. Butler served as the chairman of the South Bend Young Democratic Club, chairman of the Third District of Indiana, and in 1948 he was elected a member of the Indiana state general committee. In 1939 he was attorney for the South Bend board of education.

The lawyer was elected Indiana committeeman in 1952 for a four-year term ending in May 1956. He defeated Frank Martin McHale, who had served on the committee for fifteen years. At the Democratic National Convention in 1952, Butler worked to obtain the Presidential nomination for Governor Adlai E. Stevenson of Illinois. In the following year Butler became one of eleven members of the executive committee of the Democratic National Committee.

A proposal was made by Butler in 1953 to hold a mid-term convention in order to formulate a national platform. He stated: "The Democratic party will not speak in the 1954 election with a single, clear voice if 435 candidates for Congress and thirty-three candidates for the Senate have no party platform and thereby are allowed to represent their views as being the official position of our party on vital national issues" (New York *Post,* December 12, 1954).

When Butler became a candidate in 1954 for the position of chairman of the Democratic National Committee, the *New Republic* (November 29, 1954) commented: "Butler is Mitchell's personal choice to succeed him. Chairman Mitchell argues that Butler would assure continuity in the job since he endorses Stevenson's principles and represents a successful effort to take the leadership of a state party organization away from a backward machine."

Other candidates for the post were Michael V. DiSalle, former price stabilizer, who was supported by former President Harry S. Truman; James A. Finnegan, president of Philadelphia's city council; and F. Joseph Donohue, a former commissioner of the District of Co-

Chase, Ltd.

PAUL M. BUTLER

lumbia. Butler was elected on December 4, 1954 by the Democratic National Committee. He received seventy votes, leading the other candidates by a margin of 2 to 1.

A motion was approved to declare his election unanimous. This was the first time since 1912 that the committee itself chose a chairman instead of approving the selection of a Democratic President or strong party leader.

The New York *Times* (December 5, 1954) said that Butler's election was "brought about by a coalition of Southern, Far Western, Mountain, and Midwestern states. It represented, to a degree, a desire of the less popular states to avoid domination of the Democratic party by states with big urban populations in the East and North." A few days after his election Butler visited Truman, with whom he exchanged a pledge of cooperation. Butler was installed in his new office on January 1, 1955 at a salary of $25,000 a year.

The Democratic National Committee was created at the Democratic convention of 1848 when a motion proposing a central committee with a member from each state was adopted. When the Republican party was organized in 1854, a central Republican committee was formed. Today there are 108 members in the Democratic National Committee, one committeewoman and one committeeman from each state in the Union and each U.S. territory.

On December 5, 1954 Butler stated: "The responsibility is with the President to see that the nation is united and there is ever-increasing evidence of his lack of capacity to do it" (*Times,* December 6, 1954). Eisenhower answered this charge on December 8 by saying that Butler, as a politician, "looking in the glass, sees only the reflection of doubt and fear and the kind of confusion he often tries to create" (New York *Times,* December 9, 1954).

(Continued next page)

BUTLER, PAUL M.—*Continued*

In a speech at Washington and Lee University in Lexington, Virginia, Butler remarked that the Democrats are "understandably annoyed . . . at the many professions of attentiveness to the principle [of bipartisanship] and the regularity with which it is ignored by the Eisenhower administration" (New York *Times,* February 24, 1955).

Addressing a Jefferson-Jackson Day dinner, Paul Butler charged: "Once again the special interests occupy the plush chairs of influence in a Republican administration . . . they are grasping hungrily for control of atomic power." Later Butler commented that the proposal to reduce income taxes by twenty dollars a year was "soundly conceived" so far as the fiscal policy of the government is concerned. "The Democrats will fasten on the President personally the responsibility for its defeat if it is defeated" (New York *Times,* March 8, 1955). This proposal was passed in the House by a vote of 210 to 205 but rejected in the Senate by 50 to 44 votes during the first session of the Eighty-fourth Congress.

After Butler stated in early March that Mrs. Dwight D. Eisenhower's health may influence the President against seeking a second term, he was severely criticized by Republican leaders for bringing the health of the first lady into the political arena. In defending himself, Butler stated: "All I referred to, in answer to questions by the press, were published reports . . . that Mrs. Eisenhower has not been in robust health, that her strength has been taxed by her official duties, and that her mother does not want her to live in the White House another four years" (New York *Times,* March 11, 1955).

Butler is a member of St. Joseph county, Indiana, and American bar associations, a director of the South Bend Community Chest, and a member of the South Bend Association of Commerce and the American Red Cross. He has served as president of the local Chamber of Commerce, Notre Dame Club of St. Joseph Valley, and Catholic Charities of South Bend, and Grand Knight of the Knights of Columbus. Butler has been a guest lecturer on politics at various universities in the Midwest.

Anne S. Briscoe and Paul M. Butler were married on September 24, 1934. Their five children are Maureen Anne, Paul M., Jr., Karen Anne, Kevin J., and Brian. Butler has gray hair and is of medium height and slender build. He attends St. Joseph's Roman Catholic Church. For relaxation he enjoys watching Notre Dame football games. He calls himself a "Wilsonian Democrat." The *Christian Science Monitor* (December 6, 1954) described Butler as fitting the "Mitchell pattern . . . of . . . loyalty to the party, eagerness to work, and a studious approach to his task."

"Politicians have an honorable role in our society," Butler has said. "They are the natural peacemakers of our people. Their supreme task is to compose great domestic crises and prevent society from tearing itself apart" (New York *Post,* December 12, 1954).

References

N Y Herald Tribune p 1+ D 5 '54 por; II p3 D 12 '54 por
N Y Post p2M D 12 '54 pors
N Y Times p 1+ D 5 '54
Martindale-Hubbell Law Directory, 1952
Who's Who in America, 1954-55

BYRD, HARRY F(LOOD) June 10, 1887- United States Senator from Virginia; farmer; publisher

Address: b. Senate Office Bldg., Washington 25, D.C.; h. "Rosemont," Berryville, Va.; The Shoreham, Washington, D.C.

NOTE: This biography supersedes the article which appeared in *Current Biography* in 1942.

Known as "Mr. Economy" and the "watchdog of the treasury," Harry F. Byrd of Virginia, a member of the United States Senate since 1933, has been battling for many years against deficit spending and for the "pay-as-you-go" principle in fiscal affairs. Long a member of the Senate Finance Committee, he is today its chairman, and since 1941 has also served continuously as chairman of the Joint Committee on Reduction of Nonessential Federal Expenditures. Prior to his 1926-1930 term as Governor of Virginia, Byrd had served for ten years in the state Senate.

Harry Flood Byrd was born on June 10, 1887 in Martinsburg, West Virginia to Eleanor Bolling (Flood) and Richard Evelyn Byrd, a lawyer and later speaker of the Virginia House of Delegates. He is a direct descendant of William Byrd, who came to Virginia from

Wide World

HARRY F. BYRD

England in 1674. His mother's brothers, Henry D. Flood and Joel West Flood, served as United States Congressmen from Virginia. Harry F. Byrd's younger brothers are Admiral Richard Evelyn Byrd, the explorer, and Thomas Bolling Byrd.

When Harry was a young child, the family moved to Winchester, Virginia, where Byrd's father established the Winchester *Star.* At the age of sixteen Harry, who was a student at the Shenandoah Valley Academy, left to assume management of the newspaper, which was then in poor financial condition. Under his direction it soon became solvent. When he was twenty, he established, and from 1907 to 1910 managed, a newspaper in Martinsburg, West Virginia.

Since 1906 Byrd has been an apple grower, having started by leasing orchards. Today his chain of Shenandoah Valley orchards (in which his brother Tom is a partner) is one of the largest in the world. In 1923 he acquired the Harrisonburg (Virginia) *News-Record* and still acts as the publisher of that newspaper.

Entering Virginia politics as the protégé of Henry D. Flood and U.S. Representative (later Senator) Carter Glass, Byrd served as a state senator from 1915 to 1925. As a member of the Commonwealth Senate, he led a successful fight in 1923 "against a $50,000,000 bond issue for roads, and thus became identified with the 'pay-as-you-go' principle which has been the guiding star of his fiscal and political philosophy ever since" (Virginius Dabney in the *Saturday Evening Post,* January 7, 1950). He also served as state fuel commissioner during 1918 and 1919.

In 1925 he was elected Governor of Virginia for a four-year term. During his administration the legislature of Virginia passed in 1928 the first "antilynching" law enacted by a Southern state. The *U.S. News & World Report* (January 14, 1955) noted that Byrd "found the state with a deficit, [and] left it with a surplus."

At the Democratic National Convention of 1932, when Franklin D. Roosevelt received the nomination for the office of the President of the United States, Byrd was a "favorite son" candidate, and received twenty-five votes before his name was withdrawn.

Byrd's efforts in helping to manage the national Democratic party treasury during the 1932 campaign were so effective that Franklin D. Roosevelt "decided that he simply must have that man Byrd in the Senate" (Gerald W. Johnson in *Life,* August 7, 1944). When Virginia's senior Senator Claude A. Swanson resigned to become Secretary of the Navy, Governor John G. Pollard appointed Byrd on March 4, 1933 to fill Swanson's Senatorial seat. In November 1934 he was elected to a full six-year term. Roosevelt's insistence on bringing Byrd to Washington has been called "one of the most amusing ironies of recent American politics," because Byrd was to emerge as "an early critic of the . . . New Deal" (*Saturday Evening Post,* January 7, 1950).

Between 1933 and 1940, when he was re-elected without opposition to a second full term in the Senate, Byrd opposed a number of measures urged by Roosevelt such as the National Recovery Act and the agricultural aid program. In October 1941 he was named chairman of the Rules Committee and of the new Joint Committee on Reduction of Nonessential Federal Expenditures and has remained in the latter post during his entire career in the Senate under both Democratic and Republican control.

In an article in the *Reader's Digest* (November 1941) Byrd assailed Roosevelt's defense program as a "failure" and recommended the banning of all strikes in defense industries and a complete reorganization of "administration defense machinery." At the Democratic National Convention of 1944 Byrd was a candidate for the Democratic nomination and received eighty-nine votes.

In the first session of the Seventy-ninth Congress (1945) Senator Byrd opposed the confirmation of Henry A. Wallace as Secretary of Commerce (March), a $250,000 appropriation for the Fair Employment Practice Committee (June) and easing the excess profits tax (July). He voted for extending the Trade Agreements Act to 1948 (June), the Bretton Woods Agreement bill (July) and ratification of the United Nations Charter (July).

During the 1946 session Byrd voted "yea" in regard to the Case strike control bill (May), making labor unions legally responsible for breach of contract (May) and subjecting labor activities to the provisions of the antiracketeering law (May). He voted "nay" on the following issues: raising the minimum wage (April) and a $3.7 billion loan to Great Britain (May).

When Senator Byrd sought nomination for a third full Senate term in 1946, he was confronted with his first opposition in the Virginia Democratic primaries in twenty-four years. However, he was able to defeat his labor-endorsed adversary, Martin A. Hutchinson, by 140,000 to 81,000 votes. He was re-elected in the general election of November 5, 1946.

In the following session (1947) he voted for banning portal-to-portal pay suits (March), limiting the Presidency to two terms (March) and overriding the Presidential veto of the Taft-Hartley bill (June). In foreign affairs he cast his vote against the Greek-Turkish aid bill (April).

The Senator was appointed in 1947 to assist the Hoover Commission on Organization of the Executive Branch of the Government. During the 1948 session Byrd was against the European Recovery Program (Marshall Plan) in March. He opposed a motion providing that no Federal funds should be disbursed in any state for the support of any sectarian school (March), the Federal aid to education bill (May), and admitting 200,000 displaced persons (May). He favored overriding the Presidential veto on exempting the railroads from antitrust laws (June).

On December 8, 1949 Byrd proposed that the fiscal 1951 budget be held to $36 billion to avert "national insolvency," and suggested discharging about 250,000 of the Government's 1,000,000 civilian employees. His 1949 roll call votes indicate that he favored school aid for low income states only (May) and the North Atlan-

BYRD, HARRY F.—*Continued*

tic Security Pact (July). However, he was one of twenty-one Senators who were for a reservation denying any pledge to give military supplies, including the atom bomb, to NATO nations (July). He was against forbidding segregation in public housing (April), using Economic Cooperation Administration funds to absorb farm surpluses (August), the foreign military aid bill (September), and extending 90 per cent farm price supports indefinitely (October).

Senator Byrd in 1950 was recorded against a $45,000,000 appropriation for the Point IV program (May) and a $100,000,000 loan to Spain (August). He was in favor of overriding the President's veto of the Communist control bill (September). In the 1951 session he cast affirmative votes to forbid the sending of further troops to Europe without the consent of Congress (April) and to prohibit assistance to any country allowing shipments of arms or ammunition to the Soviet bloc (August).

In the 1952 session he endorsed the offshore oil bill (April), abolition of the Reconstruction Finance Corporation (April), extension of the Defense Production Act (June), overriding the Presidential veto of the Walter-McCarran immigation bill (June), and the fair trade bill (July). The Senate adopted by a vote of 49 to 30 on June 10, 1952 a proposal by Byrd requesting the President to use the national-emergency provisions of the Taft-Hartley act to halt the strike of the United Steelworkers of America. The House joined the request by a vote of 288 to 164 on June 26.

Running for a fourth full Senate term in 1952, Byrd defeated Colonel Francis Pickens Miller in the Democratic primary election of his state. He was re-elected at the general election on November 4. The *U.S. News & World Report* (August 14, 1953) commented that the Democratic party, headed in Virginia by Byrd "is one that politicians marvel at. . . . Fundamentally, the strength of the Byrd organization . . . rests on the poll tax. . . . The total vote, consequently, is usually very light by comparison with the state's voting potential . . . a situation on which organizations grow strong."

During the Presidential campaign of 1952, *Time* (October 27, 1952) reported that while Byrd "did not, in so many words, ask anyone to vote for Eisenhower," he did declare that he would not "endorse the national Democratic platform or the [Adlai E.] Stevenson-[John J.] Sparkman ticket." Virginia's twelve electoral votes went to General Eisenhower.

Significant votes cast by the Senator in the first session of the Eighty-third Congress (1953) were against pressuring France to free Indochina (July) and against admitting 209,000 more refugees from Iron Curtain countries (July). In the second session (1954) Byrd was opposed to the St. Lawrence seaway bill (January), the Alaska-Hawaii statehood bill (April), and additional funds for the Tennessee Valley Authority (May). He favored the Bricker amendment restricting the President's treaty-making powers (February) and permitting the Atomic Energy Commission to engage in commercial power production (July). He cast his vote for the resolution censuring Senator Joseph R. McCarthy of Wisconsin for his conduct toward the Senate and the (Arthur V.) Watkins committee (December).

The 1955 roll call indicates that Byrd opposed increasing the salaries of Congressmen (February), a $20 tax cut to families with incomes of not more than $5,000, plus a $10 tax cut for each dependent other than husband or wife (March), the Administration's highway bill (May) and the Administration's foreign aid program (June). Byrd favored confirming the appointment of John Marshall Harlan to the U.S. Supreme Court (March) and extending the reciprocal trade program for three years (May). Presently he is serving on the Senate Armed Services Committee as well as on the Finance Committee.

The New York *Herald Tribune* (January 17, 1955) reported that Byrd stated on January 16 that he would fight to end economic aid except for a "reasonable amount" of Point IV assistance (then distributed by the Foreign Operations Administration). In regard to the bill continuing the national debt limit at $281,000,000,000 for another year (which was passed by Congress and signed by the President in June 1955), Byrd stated that the bill was "necessary to maintain the fiscal integrity of the United States Government." He said that without the extra borrowing authority, the Government would not have enough cash to pay its bills (New York *Times*, July 1, 1955).

Addressing the Chamber of Commerce of the United States on May 4, 1955, Senator Byrd stated: "It can be said for . . . the first 124 years in the life of our republic we were on a pay-as-you-go basis. I think it can be accurately said that we laid the foundation for our strength today as the greatest nation in the world. . . . Today the direct debt of the Federal Government is 280 billion dollars. Our debt is equivalent to . . . everything of tangible value in the United States. . . . If we add to this Federal debt the debts of the states and localities, we have an amount in excess of $300 billion in direct public obligations. . . ." (*U.S. News & World Report,* May 13, 1955).

Harry F. Byrd and Anne Douglas Beverley were married on October 7, 1913. Their sons are Harry Flood, Jr. (a Virginia state senator), Beverley, and Richard Evelyn Byrd. Their daughter, Westwood, died in 1952.

He keeps his stocky figure in trim through regular exercise such as hunting, swimming, and long walks. He is a Mason, Elk, and Moose, and his religious affiliation is with the Protestant Episcopal church. On February 23, 1953 Byrd received, with Senator Robert A. Taft of Ohio, the American Good Government Society's citation for "independence of mind, courage of conviction, and fidelity to public duty." He was awarded an honorary LL.D. degree by the College of William and Mary in 1926, and he is an honorary member of Phi Beta Kappa.

In the New York *Times* on April 10, 1953, Arthur Krock commented on the "rare combination of integrity, ability, courage" and "specialized knowledge of complex subjects" which have "given Senator Byrd a unique place in the Senate and made him its strongest force on many great and controversial occasions."

References (see also magazine and newspaper indexes)

U S News 39:56+ Jl 8 '55 por

Biographical Directory of the American Congress, 1774-1949 (1950)
Congressional Directory (1955)
International Who's Who, 1954
National Cyclopædia of American Biography, Current Volume E (1937-38)
Who's Who in America, 1954-55
Who's Who in United States Politics (1952)
World Biography (1954)

CAFÉ FILHO, JOÃO (FERNANDES CAMPOS)

CAFÉ FILHO, JOÃO (FERNANDES CAMPOS) (kȧ″ fä′ fē′lyōō zhwouN) Feb. 3, 1899- President of Brazil

Address: Presidential Palace, Rio de Janeiro, Brazil

The man who has inherited the responsibility of guiding Brazil through its most critical period in modern times is João Café Filho, who assumed the office of President following the suicide of President Getúlio Vargas on August 24, 1954. Faced with riots and a serious economic crisis, President Café Filho moved fast to avert revolution. Communist agitators were rounded up and jailed and before he was sworn into office on September 3, he formed a new cabinet composed of experts. He hoped by these actions to inspire confidence in his country's stability. Brazil, a federation of twenty-one states, is the largest country in South America, with a population of about 57,000,000.

Continuing a practice he began while Vice-President (he was elected in 1950 for a five-year term on a coalition ticket), Café Filho still opens his door to the public one day each week. Any resident of Brazil who wants to talk to the President goes to the Palacio Cattette, writes his name and address in a book, and waits his turn. When his name comes up, a Presidential aide summons him to the palace by telegram. Many of the visitors are favor-seekers; many are old and poor. The President denies those who ask his help in bypassing civil-service examinations or circumventing existing laws (*Time,* November 8, 1954).

At the age of nineteen, João Café Filho became an editor in Natal, his native city. In the ten years that followed he started other newspapers and was forced to move from each because of his militant political editorials. He took an active part in the 1930 revolt that first brought Vargas to power, and was elected in 1934 and again in 1945 to the Federal Chamber of Deputies. He was not always in agreement with Vargas and was once forced to take refuge in Argentina. During the 1950 Presidential campaign, he was a leader of the Social Progressive party. Vargas headed the Labor party. As Vice-President, he did not participate in policymaking in the Vargas Administration.

Of Indian-Portuguese ancestry, João Fernandes Campos Café Filho was born on February 3, 1899 in Natal, State of Rio Grande do Norte, the son of João Fernandes and Florencia Campos Café. His father was a civil servant. (*Filho* means *junior,* and the English version of the name João Café Filho is John Coffee, Junior.) João's early education was in a Protestant mission school in Natal. Later he attended Natal's public high school but did not graduate.

On his first job as editor of the Natal *Gazeta* in 1918, he waged a campaign against the state government and the paper was closed. He founded *O Jornal do Norte* and continued to fight for reforms in government and gained a reputation as a "political oppositionist." The paper was suppressed in 1926, and Café Filho fled to the state of Pernambuco and founded *Gazeta do Bezerros* and served as secretary to the mayor of Bezerros. By 1928 he was editor of *A Noite,* an opposition paper in Recife, and spent seventy days in jail for his attacks on the state government (New York *Herald Tribune,* August 25, 1954). He moved to Rio de Janeiro in 1929 and secured an editorial post with *A Manho.*

When the Liberal Alliance was organized in 1930, headed by Getúlio Vargas and João Pessôa, Café Filho returned north to Paraiba, and reopened *O Jornal do Norte* as the organ of the new reform movement. Early in October 1930 forces of the Vargas revolution deposed the state government and Café Filho led an armed group to Natal. The *Brazilian Bulletin* (September 1, 1954) stated that he became Natal's chief of police and immediately freed all political prisoners. The New York *Times* reported of this period that Café Filho was later arrested and charged with plotting against the government, but in 1932 he was again chief of police and was badly wounded in an attempt to assassinate him.

Two years later he was elected to the Federal Chamber of Deputies from Rio Grande do Norte and served until President Vargas dissolved Congress on November 10, 1937. In disagreement with Vargas' policies, Café Filho was forced to take refuge at the Argentine Embassy and was later permitted to go to that country. He wrote anti-Vargas articles in the Argentine press, was interned for several months and in 1938 returned to Brazil. He worked for a bus company in Rio de Janeiro for the ensuing seven years.

He was again elected to the Chamber of Deputies from his home state in 1945 and became floor leader for the Social Progressive party and served on many important committees. Eurico Gasper Dutra was then President and Café Filho attracted attention by his investigations of government agencies.

The Social Progressive party nominated him for Vice-President in 1950 and withdrew its Presidential nominee in return for Vargas' support of Café Filho. "Thus," *Time* (September 13, 1954) said, "Café Filho was swept into office in an administration with which he had little sympathy." He presided over the Senate, but had no part in the functions of the admin-

Wide World

JOÃO CAFÉ FILHO

istration. He made numerous attempts to facilitate relations between the President and the press, and much of his time was spent visiting countries in South America and Europe. *France Illustration* (September 22, 1951) showed the Brazilian Vice-President receiving the Cross of the Legion of Honor from President Vincent Auriol. A plan to visit the United States in October 1954 was canceled after the death of President Vargas.

Criticism of the Vargas Administration developed over a long period. The *Christian Science Monitor* (August 30, 1954) stated that although the Communist party had been outlawed in 1947, the Vargas Labor party and the Communists obviously had a working agreement. *Newsweek* (October 18, 1954) reported that the arbitrary high price for coffee cut the sales of Brazil's chief export crop and wrecked the country's foreign exchange.

U.S. News & World Report (September 3, 1954) recorded that Vargas sponsored a law that prohibited foreigners from engaging in the exploration and production of oil. The cost of Brazil's oil purchases went to more than $200,000,000 a year. When prices skyrocketed, the President decreed wage increases up to 300 per cent, a rise which caused employers to discharge thousands of workers. New industries which flourished in the large cities attracted so many farmers that food shortages and housing problems resulted and transportation and power had not kept pace with the country's needs.

In the midst of these difficulties, according to *Life* (September 6, 1954) "an assassin's bullet intended for an anti-Vargas editor, killed an air force major." The *Atlantic Monthly* (November 1954) said that Benjie Vargas, the President's brother, was implicated. Anti-Vargas mobs rioted in the streets and demanded the President's resignation. It was reported that Air Force and Army generals called on Vargas and requested him to relinquish the Presidency. Vice-President Café Filho was aroused at dawn on the morning of August 24 and was told that Vargas had agreed to take a leave of absence and to turn over the government to him. A few hours later, Getúlio Vargas shot himself. As news of his suicide spread, hatred was transferred to Vargas' enemies. Communists seized the advantage and led demonstrations against anti-Vargas newspapers and the United States Embassy (*Newsweek,* September 6, 1954).

Café Filho took over his new duties without ceremony and expedited every means at his command to restore order, while armed troops held Rio de Janeiro like "a city at war." A hundred Communist leaders were arrested and by the end of the week the situation was under control.

A twenty-four hour general strike set for September 2 to demonstrate the strength of labor forces aligned against the new government proved to be "a fiasco." The New York *Times* (September 3, 1954) reported that only a third of São Paulo's workers responded and Rio de Janeiro unions withdrew in advance.

Meanwhile President Café Filho named a coalition cabinet, pending the results of the October 3 Congressional elections. *Time* (September 6, 1954) praised his selection of Raul Fernandes—"an old friend of the United States"—as Foreign Minister and Eugênio Gudin—"a highly esteemed, deflation-minded Rio economics professor"—as Finance Minister.

President Café Filho cannot be a candidate in the next Presidential election (October 1955) because of a law enacted in 1946 which prohibits a President from succeeding himself. Although he took no part in the 1954 Congressional election, the results of the election held on October 3, which were not known until late in the month, disclosed that the Labor party backed by left-wing politicians was defeated in most of the states.

Austerity was the keynote of a radio speech made by the President in mid-September when he informed the people of the $250,000,000 deficit in the 1955 budget. Shortly after that, the new Finance Minister visited the United States and obtained a loan of $160,000,000 from the Federal Reserve Bank of New York, with a pledge that Brazil would not touch its gold reserve until the loan was repaid (*Business Week,* October 16, 1954).

The New York *Times* (October 21, 1954) reported that coffee—still a serious factor in the country's financial crisis—had caused President Café Filho to declare that if United States importers continued with their "virtual boycott" of Brazilian coffee, restrictions must be placed on American imports. The dollar exchange which averaged $40,000,000 a month before July 1954 had shrunk to $14,000,000 a month. The oil shortage posed a still more acute problem. Although the new President favored the participation of foreign capital, it was doubted, according to the *Christian Science Monitor,* that modification of the "Petrobras" law could be made in the near future. A new tax bill and a wage adjustment bill had better chances of improving conditions.

Speaking at the Conference of American Ministers of Finance held in Rio de Janeiro on November 22, 1954, President Café Filho urged the delegates of the twenty-one American nations to see to it that posterity did not judge their efforts at economic cooperation as "too little and too late." He recalled that the idea of a customs union and even a single currency for all the American countries had been discussed for more than a century. He suggested that a "daring formula" might well be within the scope of the conference (New York *Times*, November 23, 1954)

João Café Filho was married on September 17, 1933 to Jandira Fernandes Oliveira. Their son, Eduardo Antonio, was born in 1943. The family did not move from their three-bedroom apartment to the Presidential palace for some weeks after Café Filho took office. He is said to have simple tastes, enjoys swimming with his son and watching soccer games. He also likes to read and to relax with his collection of stuffed Amazonian animals and birds, and to putter in the kitchen making coffee. He is of medium build, has black hair and brown eyes and the reputation of being one of the best dressed men in the country. He is the first Protestant to be President of Brazil.

One of his first acts on assuming the Presidency was to dismiss the Vargas bodyguards. When asked who his chief guard would be, he answered: "My wife."

References

Brazilian Bul 256:3 S 1 '54 por
Christian Sci Mon p7 Ag 26 '54 por
N Y Herald Tribune p7 Ag 26 '54
N Y Times p4 Ag 25 '54; p4 Ag 28 '54 por
Newsweek 44:34+ S 6 '54 por
Time 64:38 S 13 '54 pors; 64:40 N 8 '54 por; 64:44+ D 6 '54 pors
U S News 37:12 S 3 '54 por
Washington (D.C.) Post p4 Ag 25 '54

CALLENDER, JOHN HANCOCK Jan. 18, 1908- Architect

Address: b. 33 W. 42d St., New York 36; h. 242 W. 11th St., New York 14

A national authority on single family houses, John Hancock Callender is chairman of the committee on housing of the New York Chapter of the American Institute of Architects. For over twenty years he has been engaged in housing research, and since 1945 has been active as a designer of "custom-built" homes for individual clients and as a consultant to various private and federal housing agencies.

He is the author of *Before You Buy a House* (Crown, 1953), which is based on material prepared by him for the Southwest Research Institute of San Antonio, Texas and the Architectural League of New York. The book contains an evaluation chart to be used when considering the purchase of a house, and lists 134 points to check. "Any family, no matter what its size, needs, or taste, can buy a house more intelligently after reading this," commented the Chicago *Sunday Tribune*. Callender taught architecture at Pratt Institute in Brooklyn, New York during 1954 and at Columbia University in New York from 1952 to 1953. He completed in June 1955 a year's research at Princeton University School of Architecture on stainless steel curtain walls, at the request of the American Iron and Steel Institute.

John Hancock Callender was born on January 18, 1908, in Kansas City, Missouri, the son of Alonzo Lee Callender and the former Lola Hancock. His father was in the wholesale millinery business. He has one sister, Marjorie Weaver. His ancestors were early settlers in Missouri, having "followed Daniel Boone from Kentucky." John was reared in his native city and attended Westport High School. His principal extracurricular activity was debating. He worked after school in local architects' offices, in a bank, and as a delivery boy. During summer vacations, he sold tickets in the railroad station.

Before he was graduated from high school in 1924, John had decided he wanted to become an architect. He competed for a four-year scholarship to Yale University, winning second place and choice as alternate. He applied for and received a small scholarship for his first year at Yale. The second year, the winner of the original four-year scholarship left college because of illness, and Callender, as alternate, received this assistance for the next three years. In addition, he worked as a waiter and bus boy and tutored during the summers.

In his junior year at Yale, Callender left college for six months to work full-time as tutor to the children of an American sugar planter in the Dominican Republic. Upon his return to college, he continued to take courses in architecture, while majoring in English, as there was no undergraduate major in his field. He won a prize for an essay in American literature, was elected to Phi Beta Kappa, and was awarded the A.B. degree by Yale in 1928.

Callender studied at the School of Architecture of Yale University for two years. In 1931 he took a position in housing research with the John B. Pierce Foundation, New York City, where he remained until 1943. "My work," he has explained, "consisted of devising new methods of architectural construction, and of studying materials with the idea of producing low-cost housing by technical means rather than by government subsidy or by playing with interest rates." He was concerned especially with prefabrication.

As research secretary of the National Committee on Prisons and Prison Labor, Callender wrote in 1931 that "the architect should approach the problem of designing a prison exactly as he would approach that of any other building" (*Architectural Forum*, September 1931).

He discussed designs for schools in the United States in the *Architectural Forum* (De-

Kay Simmon

JOHN HANCOCK CALLENDER

cember 1933) and termed 80 per cent of all rural schools and 60 per cent of all urban elementary schools "completely antiquated."

Callender undertook formal study in the School of Architecture at New York University in 1935, and received his B. Arch. degree in 1939. During World War II, between 1943 and 1945, he served with the Army Engineers, Manhattan District, employed on the atomic bomb project at Columbia University. His work involved supervision of laboratory remodelings and additions.

Beginning private practice in New York City in 1945, Callender designed houses for "fairly well-to-do" individual clients. He served as consultant to the National Housing Agency on the Veterans Emergency Housing Program during 1946 and 1947. This program was an effort to promote "an industrialized or factory method of mass production of houses, largely by prefabrication."

As a consultant, Callender advised the Quality House Institute program from 1947 to 1953, which he described as "a promotion idea to get speculative builders to build better houses of good quality costing a little more money, instead of producing houses of poor quality in order to cut prices." Sponsored from 1947 to 1949 by the Revere Copper & Brass, Inc., and from 1949 to 1953 by the Southwest Research Institute, San Antonio, Texas, the institute also tried to convince merchant builders that to employ architects was the first way to improve buildings. "I believe," Callender says, "that the institute program made a perceptible impression on speculative builders, and that they are now building better single family houses for sale to the public."

As a consultant to the U.S. Government's Housing and Home Finance Agency on Demountable Defense Housing in 1952, Callender made several trips to Washington, D.C., to review the agency's plans and to advise that more standard dwellings (rather than the temporary structures put up during World War II) be constructed in the event of another emergency.

The architect was moderator of the panel meeting of the Architectural League of New York in November 1953, which discussed "legal obscurantism" in public housing and the need for "neighborhood conservation" (New York *Times,* November 27, 1953). In his post as chairman of the committee on housing of the New York chapter of the American Institute of Architects, Callender is aiding in a study of what can be done to stem the deterioration of New York City areas.

Callender is the author of a number of articles and book reviews. He prepared Building Types Study Number 181 on "Apartment Houses" and Number 186 on "Houses," which appeared in the December 1951 and May 1952 issues, respectively, of *Architectural Record.* His pamphlet entitled *Introduction to Studies of Family Planning* (John B. Pierce Foundation, 1944) is the report of a research study on how to improve building materials and methods of construction in order to reduce the cost of housing. Photographs of his architectural work have appeared in such magazines as *Architectural Forum, House & Garden, Life,* and *McCall's.*

Commenting on Callender's book *Before You Buy a House,* the reviewer for the *Christian Science Monitor* (July 10, 1953) observed that the author "has not included one traditional type of home in the 100 or so pages of home patterns and floor plans," but stated that the book "provides the reader with a basic understanding of what his future house should contain without promising to convert the amateur into an expert."

Among the factors which Callender discussed, to aid prospective house buyers, is orientation, "a new word for a very old fact—one that man has understood and applied since the Stone Age when he discovered that a cave, protected from the cold winds and where the sun could shine in at the entrance, made a comfortable home." He suggests that architects can assist in designing houses so that the principal rooms will be exposed to the sun in the winter and to the prevailing breeze in the summer. He also discusses the greatly increased use of large picture windows and glass walls from floor to floor. "But nobody wants to live in a fishbowl," he wrote. "If you have the glass heavily curtained in order to protect your privacy, then you lose all of the advantage of having it. Privacy, like orientation, is frequently neglected by builders." He pointed out that residential streets are deliberately curved in order to cut down the speed of traffic and to discourage through traffic from using them.

Callender married Mary Carnwath in 1933, and they have one daughter, Janet. He is five feet ten inches tall, weighs 165 pounds, and has brown eyes and gray hair. His "hobby" is an old house in Chestnut Hill, Connecticut, which he says "takes all" his time "to keep up with."

Reference

Christian Sci Mon p11 Jl 10 '53

CALLERY, MARY June 19, 1903- Sculptor

Address: b. c/o Curt Valentin Gallery, 32 E. 57th St., New York 22; h. The Barn, RFD 2, Huntington, Long Island, N.Y.

Some of the attenuated sculptures of Mary Callery have been compared to Yogi contortionists seated in a languid, limber position. One critic has characterized her work as "a ballet in bronze," as her figures balance and weave their rhythmic patterns in space. Among the favorite subjects of her linear sculpture are acrobats and dancers. With bodies "as slim as spaghetti and as flexible as Indian rubber men," they defy the rules of human proportion "with graceful nonchalance" as they "pyramid in acrobatic exuberance." Her sculptures, whose keynote is "excessive slimness," wrote art critic Henry McBride, "fit in with the architectural simplicities that have come upon the whole modernistic world."

Miss Callery received her first training at the Art Students League in New York. In 1930 she moved to Paris, where her acquaintance with Pablo Picasso and other leading modern artists strongly influenced her work. Her sculpture is represented in a number of public and private collections, and she has recently executed several important commissions for public buildings. Her one-man show at the Curt Valentin Gallery in New York from March 15 to April 9, 1955 was the fifth to be held there since her first one in 1944.

Born in New York City on June 19, 1903, Mary Callery is the daughter of James Dawson and Julia (Welch) Callery. Her father began his career in his father's leather manufacturing business. At the time of his death in 1932, he was president of the Diamond National Bank and chairman of the board of the Pittsburgh Railways Company. His daughter showed her first interest in sculpture at the age of twelve, when she modelled a bear cub out of clay. She grew up in Pittsburgh, returning to New York to attend Miss Spence's School, from which she was graduated in 1921.

Thereafter, for four years, Miss Callery took the sculpture course given by Edward McCartan at the Art Students League in New York. In 1930 she went to Paris and spent two years in the atelier of the Russian-French sculptor, Jacques Loutchansky. She worked in a somewhat classical style, influenced perhaps by Aristide Maillol.

Remaining in Paris for the next eight years, she slowly developed her personal sculptural style under the influence of her friendship with the painters Pablo Picasso and Amédée Ozenfant, the sculptor Henri Laurens, and the art critic Christian Zervos. Of Picasso, she has said: "The more one saw, the greater he became. I find myself even now often repeating the things I became aware of through him. He was always so generous to aspiring artists." According to C. C. Cunningham (Wadsworth Atheneum *Bulletin*), "aspects of her work show Picasso's influence," but it is from the "mechanical forms of Fernand Léger that Callery's style seems to have been derived."

Blackstone Studios

MARY CALLERY

During her stay in Paris, Miss Callery's sculpture was accepted at the Salon des Tuileries. When World War II broke out in 1939, she served as an ambulance driver for the American Hospital at Neuilly. She returned to the United States after the fall of France in 1940.

Miss Callery's first show, consisting of seventeen sculptures, executed after her return from Paris, opened at the Buchholz Gallery in October 1944. In *Art Digest* Margaret Breuning commented on the sculptor's "highly personal ideology of design. . . . She has succeeded in conveying a fresh imaginative quality." The reviewer for *Architectural Forum* praised the "forthright and vigorous character" of her work. The exhibit was dominated by a nine-foot-long *Reclining Figure,* which one critic placed "well up in the ranks of significant modern sculpture."

In April 1947 Miss Callery's second exhibition was held at the Buchholz Gallery. "Whereas before she used her spidery bronze forms to bound space and hold it in as part of her composition," wrote Aline B. Louchheim (*Art News*), "now she . . . has pulled the . . . figures into an even further elongation, subtly thickening or thinning them to catch a light or cast a shadow. Thus they maintain the swift rhythm of linear art, but they move *within* space." The most ambitious piece in the show was the open frieze *Amity* (1947), a linked procession of five figures that Miss Louchheim described as "among the most successful of contemporary out-of-doors sculptures."

In March 1950 Miss Callery's work of 1948 and 1949 was shown at the Buchholz Gallery. Praising the new sculpture as "by far the best that she has done to date," the New York *Times* reviewer found the progress of "the highly original style" she had evolved "perfectly consistent," but he added that it was "a limited

CALLERY, MARY—*Continued*

style, happier in small scale than in large." Judith Kaye Reed wrote in *Art Digest* (April 1, 1950): "A modern who can pare substance down to slender, pencil-like forms without substituting sterile symbols for the fluid grace of living matter, Miss Callery works with unfailing taste and sensibility." Among the works singled out for special comment were *Pyramid*; the "stick" figures of *Equilbrist,* fashioned out of iron rail; *Woman in Space,* suspended from a slab of heavy glass; and *Standing Woman* and *Mural Composition.* in which Miss Callery collaborated with Léger, who provided painted panel backgrounds for the sculptor's plaster figures.

Miss Callery's fourth solo appearance in New York was held at the Curt Valentin (formerly Buchholz) Gallery in October-November 1952. Fairfield Porter (*Art News,* November 1952) considered Miss Callery a sculptor with a graphic talent: "The gesture counts most. . . . This gesture is not necessarily the gesture of caricature, though it may be, as in the bronzes of the dog, Piet . . . a gesture that . . . characterizes the way [her simplified figures] relate to the space around them."

Included among the twenty-two works in the show were *The Young Diana,* commissioned for an architect's home in Texas; a symbolic bronze plaque of *Orpheus; Seated Figure,* a monumental bronze girl; and *Perhaps,* a linear composition of three figures balancing on the lengthened arms of a fourth figure. Her sculptures command top prices—from $400 to $3,000.

The most recent showing of Miss Callery's sculpture took place at the Valentin Gallery in March-April 1955. "The new Callerys seem to me a considerable advance over her earlier work," commented Robert M. Coates (*New Yorker,* March 26, 1955). "The work is much tighter in design than heretofore, and . . . she has introduced more modelling, while the new emphasis on compact design has saved her from those awkward moments in the older pieces. . . . There is also, I think, a much better feeling for sculptural rhythm and balance."

In the opinion of Martica Sawin (*Art Digest*), the exhibition was "a richly varied show of fresh, unrepetitive work." Highpoints of the show were two pieces conceived architecturally, for public buildings: *Three Birds in Flight,* a twelve-foot sculpture in aluminum, now suspended in the glass entrance space of the Alcoa Building in Pittsburgh; and *The Fables,* taken from La Fontaine, a frieze-like sculpture to be installed as a grille on the façade of Public School No. 34 on East Twelfth Street in New York City.

At each of her New York exhibitions, Miss Callery has included a few portrait busts executed in a more traditional, realistic style. Among these are heads of J. B. Neumann, Benjamin Fairless, and Wallace K. Harrison. Regarding this aspect of her work, Miss Callery has observed: "It is a different fascination to work from real life. The work done without a model helps unendingly when one is face to face with nature. All the things one has found poor when working alone suddenly become clear when one has the opportunity again to work from actuality. . . . The change from nature to one's own imagination and vice versa is continually enriching."

Outside New York, Miss Callery has had one-man shows at the Arts Club of Chicago, in January 1946, and at the Margaret Brown Gallery in Boston, in March 1951. She has participated in the Whitney Museum's sculpture annuals, the American Sculpture show at the Metropolitan Museum in 1951, and the Sculpture of the 20th Century exhibition at the Museum of Modern Art in 1953. Her sculpture was exhibited in Paris with a one-man show at the Galerie Mai in October 1949, and this was followed by a second solo exhibition at the Galerie Cahiers d'Art late in 1954.

Works by Miss Callery are represented in the permanent collections of the Museum of Modern Art, Addison Gallery of American Art (Andover, Massachusetts), Wadsworth Atheneum (Hartford, Connecticut), Toledo Museum, and the San Francisco Museum of Art. Among the private collections that contain examples of her sculpture are those of Sturges Ingersoll, Nelson Rockefeller, the late Joseph Pulitzer, Jr., Mrs. John D. Rockefeller III, Mrs. David Levy, Mrs. Max Ascoli, and Mr. and Mrs. Burton Tremaine.

Miss Callery is a member of Artists Equity Association and the Association of Women Artists. In 1923, she was married to Frederic René Coudert, Jr., a lawyer, and later a member of the 80th to 84th Congresses from the 17th New York District. They had one child, Caroline Callery Coudert Bard. This marriage ended in divorce. On May 11, 1934, Miss Callery married Carlo Frua de Angeli, of Milan. They were divorced in 1936. The artist, who stands five feet eight inches tall and weighs 148 pounds, has gray eyes and blond hair. Her political party is the Democratic. Her hobby is gardening. She owns an outstanding collection of the works of Picasso and Léger.

In the notes for the catalogue of her 1955 exhibition, Miss Callery has stated: "What should a sculpture be? Above all it must be plastic. But to be a work of art, to me, it must have its emotional life. One must like the thing, be attracted to it, or even be repulsed. It must work on you. Only then does it become living. . . . I would like the spectator to have a special pleasure in each object I make, a fresh vision."

References

Life 33:143 N 17 '52 por

Who's Who in American Art (1953)

CAMPNEY, RALPH OSBORNE June 6, 1894- Canadian Minister of Defense

Address: b. Ministry of Defense, Ottawa, Ontario, Canada; h. 265 Daly Ave., Ottawa, Ontario, Canada; 4629 W. 2d Ave., Vancouver, British Columbia, Canada

As Canadian Minister of Defense, Ralph Osborne Campney, Queen's Counsel and Member of Parliament, directs his country's defense commitments to the North Atlantic Treaty Organization (NATO) as well as Canada's policies of mutual aid with the United States and Great Britain. He was named to this post in July 1954 by Prime Minister Louis S. St. Laurent. The Vancouver *News-Herald,* while admittedly taking pride in its own citizen, noted that "it shared with the rest of the nation the confidence that he will measure up in every way to the demands of his high office."

Campney was trained in history, economics, and the law, and he has shown himself to be a skillful director of several large business corporations. A member of Parliament since 1949, Campney worked closely with the former Minister of Defense, the Honorable Brooke Claxton, as parliamentary assistant and as associate minister. Campney was also solicitor general of Canada from 1952 to 1954.

Ralph Osborne Campney was born on June 6, 1894, on a farm near Picton, Ontario, the son of Frank and Mary Emily (Cronk) Campney. He studied at the rural school and at Picton Collegiate, where he won medals for his oratorical ability and for rapid calculation. Following his graduation in 1910, young Campney taught school for several years.

He enrolled at Queen's University, Kingston, Ontario in 1914 as a student of medicine, but his academic training was interrupted by World War I. Campney enlisted as a private with the No. 5 Stationary Hospital (Queen's), and served at a base hospital in Egypt during the Dardanelles campaign, and in France during the Battle of the Somme. Switching to the infantry in 1917, after two years with the medical corps, Campney, commissioned an officer, was stationed with the 19th Canadian Infantry Battalion, fighting in France and Belgium. Wounded at Passchendaele, he was sent back to England for convalescence, but soon joined the Royal Flying Corps, with which he served until the Armistice.

Upon his return from the service in 1919, he studied history and political science at Queen's University, and was graduated two years later with the B.A. degree. He was awarded the Gowan prize and scholarship in political science and the Lochhead scholarship in colonial history. In his senior year, he was elected president of the Alma Mater Society and chairman of the athletic board, and earned a letter for collegiate debate.

He subsequently studied law at Osgoode Hall, Toronto, where he accumulated more scholastic honors, but also incurred the displeasure of the faculty for founding the Gladstone Club, the first political organization on the campus.

Called to the Ontario bar in 1924, he was appointed secretary to the Canadian delegation to the League of Nations, where he served under Dr. Oscar Douglas Skelton. He returned from Geneva to act as political secretary to the Canadian Prime Minister, W. L. Mackenzie King. From 1926 to 1929 he was private secretary to the Honorable James Malcolm, Minister of Trade and Commerce.

Deciding to return to private law practice, Campney became a member of the bar in Vancouver, British Columbia, in 1929, and a member of the firm, Campney, Owen, Murphy & Owen.

Monte Everett

RALPH OSBORNE CAMPNEY

He interrupted his private practice in 1936 to accept the first chairmanship of the National Harbors Board. A. O. Tate, Canadian journalist, has commented: "Since he had had no active association with port affairs and sea transportation, his appointment puzzled shipping men. But Ralph Campney succeeded in his aim of unifying and coordinating the administration of Canada's salt water ports which had been, up to then, entrusted to local commissions" (Toronto *Star Weekly,* November 20, 1954). The *Liberal Spokesman,* in the August 1954 issue, praised his work in setting up the harbor administration "as a model of non-political organization." Campney resigned in 1940, after having successfully completed the reorganization.

Standing for his first political contest in the by-election of 1948, Campney was defeated. The next year, he was successful in his bid to represent Vancouver Center in the Dominion House of Commons. He has been serving as a member of the Canadian Parliament since that time, having been re-elected in 1953.

His first assignment was as chairman of the Parliamentary committee dealing with the unification of the armed services, provided for in the National Defense Act of 1950, which he helped to draft. He was appointed parliamentary assistant to the Minister of Defense, the Honorable Brooke Claxton, in January 1951, serving in that capacity until his selection as solicitor general of Canada in October 1952.

Campney was named associate minister of national defense in February 1953, holding the legal and defense posts together. He resigned the solicitor generalship in January 1954, and succeeded Claxton as Minister of Defense in July of the same year. His appointment was acclaimed by the public and the press, for the new Minister had shown his ability to handle administrative detail as well as astuteness in formulating policy. As the director of the

CAMPNEY, RALPH OSBORNE—*Cont.*
Defense Department, Campney has been responsible for the administration of a two billion dollar budget, acknowledged to be Canada's biggest single business.

Self-assurance and certainty mark Campney's approach to his job. The Toronto *Star Weekly* (November 20, 1954) has explained: "Campney believes he can get more work done with less physical and mental wear and tear than men of a different temperament—and the Minister's generally even temper is no doubt a reason for his vigorous health and administrative ability. He also has enough steam and stamina to 'hit the hustings' for a grueling political campaign. If he hasn't an evening engagement, he will take home with him a few files to which he can devote a couple of hours of study and contemplation. They usually are knotty problems requiring that sort of attention. Next day, when decisions are needed, they are based on thoughtful consideration rather than snap judgment."

Campney attended the annual review meeting of the NATO Council of Ministers in December 1954. At this conference, Canada discussed participation in security and defense activities. Although the policy decisions at NATO have been made in favor of the further development of thermonuclear weapons, and Great Britain and the United States have disclosed that they are expanding their supply of atomic artillery, Campney and top Canadian military leaders have not completely followed suit. Instead, the government has announced a program to expand the facilities of the Petawawa Military Camp and the erection of the Gagetown Military Camp in New Brunswick, Canada.

This policy has aroused some Parliamentary opposition. The Ottawa *Letter* (December 18, 1954), criticizing these activities, has written: "Surely a government with any faith in the soundness of [the] conclusion that the next war would be fought with atomic weapons would call a summary halt to the construction of such establishments and conserve the funds for intelligent preparations for atomic warfare." However, in June 1955, Canada signed a pact with the United States to exchange "atomic information for mutual defense purposes" (New York *Times,* June 16, 1955).

This pact was drawn up under the provision of the U.S. Atomic Energy Law that permits the exchange of restricted atomic information for the development of defense plans and the training of personnel in the use of and defense against atomic weapons.

Defense Minister Campney figured in the Canadian military dispute involving Air Vice Marshal John L. Plant. When the Marshal suggested that the Canadian Army should be abolished, so that money and manpower could be concentrated on the Air Force, Campney ordered his demotion and transfer. Believing that Plant's remarks were made in jest, he nevertheless insisted that they were "highly inappropriate coming from a service officer" (New York *Times,* June 7, 1955). Campney declared that he was preparing a body of rules for government officials to follow in their public addresses.

G. V. Ferguson, editor of the Montreal *Star,* writing for the Washington *Post and Times Herald* (June 12, 1955), commented: "Nothing more sharply points up the differences between the United States and Canadian systems of government than this incident. In Canada, we adhere strictly to the theory that civil servants (including admirals, generals and air marshals) shall be seen and not heard."

The Minister's enjoyment of flying has made him a keen advocate of air research and development. He has served as president of the Air Force Officers' Association of Vancouver, and as chairman of the British Columbia Committee of the Air Cadet League of Canada, as well as a director of this last organization. He is a member of the university council and the board of trustees of Queen's University, his alma mater. Campney belongs to the Royal Ottawa Golf Club, the Rideau Club in Ottawa, and the Vancouver Club in his home city. He was appointed Dominion King's Counsel in 1940.

Mrs. Campney is the former Vera Wilhelmina Farnsworth, to whom he was married on November 25, 1925. They have a son, Alan, a graduate of Queen's University (Bachelor of Commerce degree, 1951) and the University of British Columbia (LL.B. degree). Campney spends his leisure hours fishing, gardening or reading. Much of his reading is about the American Civil War, which he has studied closely, and Abraham Lincoln. Some of Campwhile some of his wife's forbears defended the Confederacy.

Ralph Campney is five feet ten inches tall, weighs 220 pounds, and has blue eyes and brown hair. He is jovial and hearty in manner, which makes people like him immediately. He believes that it may be time to re-examine the entire Canadian defense organization in order to get the most for each taxpayer's dollar. Whatever his plans, the country stands solidly behind him, for as the *Liberal Spokesman* (August 1954) has written, "he is a man who has a record for making good his promises."

References

Can Bsns 24:64 Ja '51
Sat Night p4 Je 25 '55
Toronto Star Weekly p11 N 20 '54 por
Vancouver News-Herald p4 Jl 3 '54

Canadian Who's Who, 1949-51
International Who's Who, 1954
Who's Who in Canada, 1953-54

CARNEGIE, DALE Nov. 24, 1888- Author; lecturer

Address: b. c/o Carnegie Institute for Effective Speaking and Human Relations, 22 W. 55th St., New York 19; h. 27 Wendover Rd., Forest Hills, N.Y.

Bulletin: Dale Carnegie died on November 1, 1955.

(Continued next page)

DALE CARNEGIE

"Believe that you will succeed, and you will," a maxim from *How To Win Friends and Influence People* by Dale Carnegie, author and lecturer, and "Learn to love, respect and enjoy other people," an axiom from *How To Help Your Husband Get Ahead* by Dorothy Carnegie were used to launch the 1955 spring sessions of the Dale and Dorothy Carnegie Courses for Women.

A pioneer in public speaking and personality development, Dale Carnegie is best known for his book *How To Win Friends and Influence People,* of which over 1,300,000 copies have been sold by Simon & Schuster. It has been translated into thirty-five languages. He has written several other books including *How To Stop Worrying and Start Living,* a best seller in 1948, and also operates the Carnegie Institute for Effective Speaking and Human Relations. His wife is vice-president of the Dale and Dorothy Carnegie Courses for Women, which they organized in 1950. Carnegie's courses have "saved many a tongue-tied Caspar Milquetoast from the tortures of fear" noted *Collier's* (January 15, 1949). Carnegie discovered "the magic combination of great names and simple truths," observed Margaret Case Harriman (*Saturday Evening Post,* August 14, 1937).

Dale Carnegie was born in Maryville, Missouri on November 24, 1888, the second son of James William and Amanda Elizabeth (Harbison) Carnegie. The family lived on a farm close to a river that overflowed every spring, ruined the crops and kept them in poverty. Mrs. Carnegie, a devout Methodist, wanted her two sons Cliff and Dale to become missionaries. The family moved to Warrensburg, Missouri where Dale liked to recite at local festivities and, encouraged by Nicholas M. Souder, a schoolteacher who boarded wih the family, he joined the high school debating team. He lost every debate until he attended a Chautauqua lecture and, impressed with the personal testimony of a speaker, copied the style.

After he entered the State Teachers' College at Warrensburg, Missouri in 1904, his ambition to become a Chautauqua lecturer led him to practice recitations on the horse that he rode to and from college. He left there in 1908 and his first job was with the International Correspondence School as a salesman in Alliance, Nebraska. He sold only one course, gave up the job, and went to Omaha to sell for Armour & Company. By 1911 he had saved $500 and he started East to take a course in public speaking. A train acquaintance convinced him that he should try acting.

In New York he enrolled in the American Academy of Dramatic Arts. Among his classmates were Guthrie McClintic and Howard Lindsay. He realized that the theatre was not his forte after he had played the part of Dr. Hartley in a road show of *Polly and the Circus.* Returning to New York, he applied to the Young Men's Christian Association on 125th Street for a job teaching public speaking and was hired. He took a course at the Columbia University School of Journalism in 1913, and a short-story writing course at New York University in 1914. Adolph E. Meyer (*American Mercury,* July 1943) wrote that the professor of the NYU course predicted that Carnegie would do "big things." He was soon selling essays to *World Outlook, American Magazine, Illustrated World, Pictorial Review, Rotarian,* and *Scholastic,* while continuing his teaching at the Y.M.C.A.

When his income had increased to $500 a month, he rented an office in Times Square, scheduled new courses, hired substitute instructors for his widely scattered classes, and wrote pamphlets to standardize his methods. His name had been spelled Carnegey—although his father had claimed distant kinship with Andrew Carnegie, the millionaire—until 1916, when about to give a lecture at Carnegie Hall, Dale changed it to Carnegie.

During World War I he spent a year and a half at Camp Upton, New York. After his discharge, Lowell Thomas offered him a job as business manager for his "With Allenby in Palestine and Lawrence in Arabia" lecture tour. The lectures were such a "sensation" that Carnegie was engaged to present a second string tour simultaneously, throughout the United States and Canada in 1921 and 1922.

Carnegie was married in 1921 to a French Countess. They traveled abroad for several years, then established a home in Forest Hills. The marriage ended in 1931.

After his travels, Carnegie had reassembled his classes and collected his pamphlets in a book called *Public Speaking; A Practical Course for Business Men* (Association Press, 1926). It became a standard text for public speaking courses and was reissued as *Public Speaking and Influencing Men in Business* in 1931. *Lincoln The Unknown* (Century, 1932) was his second book.

Mindful of the success of his first book, he collected data for new pamphlets, hired research workers to find information about well-

Hal Phyfe

DOROTHY CARNEGIE

known men, selected the most prominent, and toured the country for personal interviews. *Little Known Facts about Well Known People* (Greenberg, 1934) resulted, and was the basis for a radio show on WOR. The program was so popular that *Five Minute Biographies* (Greenberg, 1937)—the actual radio sketches—became his fourth book.

Dale Carnegie's *How To Win Friends and Influence People* became an overnight best seller. Margaret Case Harriman (*Saturday Evening Post,* August 14, 1937) wrote that within six months, he had made $125,000 and was in demand for lectures, radio shows and magazine articles. A column of "capsule preachments" was syndicated in seventy-one daily newspapers. Carnegie re-organized his courses as the Carnegie Institute for Effective Speaking and Human Relations, appointed class directors from his alumni, and selected and trained area managers who conduct over 300 classes throughout the United States, and in Canada, Europe and South America.

Of the book, James Thurber (*Saturday Review of Literature,* January 30, 1937) wrote that the "disingenuities in his set of rules" and case histories stood out "like ghosts at a banquet." The New York *Times* (February 14, 1937) commented: "By all means let us follow the sensible advice so cheerfully offered. . . . Improvement in tact and imagination may indeed make us more efficient and agreeable." As of November 1954, 1,300,000 copies of the book have been sold, according to its publishers, Simon & Schuster.

Another best seller was Carnegie's *How To Stop Worrying and Start Living* (Simon & Schuster, 1948). Thomas Lask (New York *Times,* June 20, 1948) wrote that Carnegie's "latest blueprint for a social Garden of Eden" was "so choked with formula, exhortation and case history" that no reader would be "entirely unrewarded." *Time* (June 14, 1948) commented that he had interviewed everybody from General Omar N. Bradley to Dorothy Dix and that the "assault on worry" was composed of "worry-warts' case histories." The *Reader's Digest* ran several condensed chapters of the book in 1948 and 1949.

CARNEGIE, DOROTHY (REEDER PRICE) Nov. 3, 1912- Instructor; author

Address: b. c/o Carnegie Courses for Women, 22 W. 55th St., New York 19; h. 27 Wendover Rd., Forest Hills, N.Y.

Dorothy Reeder Price, who was to become Dale Carnegie's second wife, was born in Tulsa, Oklahoma, on November 3, 1912, the daughter of Henry Maston and Victoria (Robertson) Price. After a year at the University of Oklahoma, she married one of her fellow students and did not return to college. Her daughter, Rosemary Vanderpool, was born two years later. The marriage terminated in divorce after a few years and Dorothy found a job as a stenographer.

Dorothy's mother took a Dale Carnegie course and advised her to do so. When Carnegie visited Tulsa to lecture, a mutual friend introduced them. Dorothy told Carnegie that it was her ambition to live in New York, but she never expected to realize the ambition. After he had returned to New York, he offered her a job as his secretary. She accepted the job and ten months later, on November 5, 1944, they were married. Mrs. Carnegie takes a great interest in her husband's work and helped him to organize specialized courses for women.

Following her husband's methods, Mrs. Carnegie collected "how-to" case histories and incorporated them in *How To Help Your Husband Get Ahead in his Social and Business Life* (Greystone, 1953). In a review of the book, F. D. Heron (Chicago Sunday *Tribune,* October 4, 1953) wrote that the author had prescribed a pattern for wives to get along with their husbands, and "help them win friends and influence people." A condensation of the book appeared in *Coronet,* January 1954.

In her article, "How to Help Your Husband Succeed" in *Better Homes & Gardens,* April 1955, Mrs. Carnegie wrote: "Many students in my courses seem to operate on AC current when their husbands perk along on DC." She recommended that women be enthusiastic, and encourage their husbands to be enthusiastic, and to work together as a team. "Share his interests and ideals," she advised, and if he wants to switch his career in mid-stream because he is unhappy or ill-suited in his present job, help him to strike out for himself. "Try some intelligent listening. Be a sounding board or a wailing wall," she suggested.

Mrs. Carnegie frequently accompanies her husband on his lecture tours. She also conducts classes at the school in New York, has appeared as guest on many radio and television programs, and is writing a book on the premise that women should "grow up, rather than grow old." The family live in a large, comfortable house in Forest Hills with their daughter Donna Dale Carnegie, born December 11, 1951.

Mrs. Carnegie's daughter by her first marriage, Rosemary Vanderpool (Mrs. J. O. Crom), attends the University of Wyoming.

Carnegie has been described as an affable man, with a "well-turned sense of humor" and the ability to generate enthusiasm. He has gray hair and gray eyes. Mrs. Carnegie is five feet nine inches tall, and slender, with reddish-brown hair and green eyes. Carnegie enjoys puttering in the garden and walking through the countryside. Mrs. Carnegie's hobbies are fencing and ballet-dancing. Both enjoy reading Shakespeare and are members of the Shakespeare Club of New York. Mrs. Carnegie also belongs to the Fencers Club in New York and the Women's Club of Forest Hills. It has been said that her favorite maxim is: "A woman's sense of humor expresses itself to best advantage when she laughs at her husband's jokes." And that his favorite is "Cooperate with the inevitable."

References (see also magazine and newspaper indexes)

Am Mercury 57:40+ Jl '43
Colliers 123:26+ Ja 15 '49 por
Newsweek 46:70+ Ag 8 '55 por
Sat Eve Post 210:12+ Ag 14 '37 por
Who's Who in America, 1954-55
World Biography (1954)

CARNEGIE, MRS. DALE *See* Carnegie, Dale

CARROLL, JOHN Aug. 14, 1892- Artist; art instructor

Address: b. c/o Art Students League of New York, 215 W. 57th St., New York 19; 152 W. 57th St., New York 19; h. East Chatham, N.Y.

The favorite subjects of artist John Carroll are "delicate gazelle-eyed girls who look as if they were made out of whipped cream and moonlight." Even when he paints portraits of real people he is influenced by his favorite model, his wife, "Pinky," whose ethereal beauty seems to dominate much of his work. In the art world this penchant for "wan madonnas" is regarded as a paradox, for Carroll himself has been described as "a gargantuan man built like a pugilist" who is very fond of outdoor sports and raising cattle. His portraits and landscapes hang in most of America's leading art museums. In April 1954 he was awarded the $1,500 first prize in the Benjamin Altman competition at the National Academy of Design, New York City, for his painting, *Mother and Child,* and in the same year the Metropolitan Museum of Art purchased his *Spring Bonnet.*

It is Carroll's theory that art should be dreamy and imaginative in contrast with the school of realists exemplified by the paintings of Thomas Hart Benton, John Steuart Curry and Grant Wood. He prefers to paint an inviting picture of his subject, whether it be a woman, a hunt meeting, a prize fight, or a landscape. "If I wanted to paint a picnic scene," he says, "instead of showing a picnic site littered with tin cans and bottles and rubbish, I would paint something that would make the spectator want to go on a picnic" (*Time,* August 24, 1942).

Peter A. Juley & Son

JOHN CARROLL

John Carroll was born on August 14, 1892 on an Atchison, Topeka, & Santa Fe Railroad train that happened to be passing through Wichita, Kansas. His ancestors came from Maryland. His father, Hur Carroll, was born in West Virginia, but moved with his wife, the former Veda Peck, to California in 1892, where he established a branch of the Cudahy Packing Company. Young John was brought up on a ranch.

After demonstrating obvious drawing talent since the age of five and after attending public schools, he studied at the Mark Hopkins Art Academy in San Francisco. He attended the University of California for two years (1913-1915) as an engineering student. At California he was a fullback on the football team and punched cattle on the side.

On seeing the painting of Frank Duveneck at the San Francisco Fair in 1915, he left the university to study painting under Duveneck in Cincinnati, Ohio. He enlisted in the U.S. Navy in World War I, joining "to fight, not to paint" (he considered the World War II system of arming artists with brushes only so they could "paint the war" was utter nonsense), and was mustered out as an ensign in 1918.

After the war he spent some time in Macon, Georgia, painting the inmates of an insane asylum and this unusual experience possibly inspired the ethereal and "other world" quality of his later work. He became one of the early members of the Woodstock artists colony in New York. He supported himself by making picture frames for fellow artists, designing stained glass windows for Tiffany's in New York, and copying the old masters on commission in the Metropolitan Museum of Art.

(Continued next page)

CARROLL, JOHN—*Continued*

His first Manhattan showing was in 1922 at the Daniel Gallery. His first serious recognition came when he won the purchase prize of Philadelphia's Pennsylvania Academy of the Fine Arts, which financed a trip to Europe. He received the first prize at the Pan-American exhibition in Los Angeles in 1925 and in 1926 he was appointed professor of painting at the Art Students League in New York City. He returned to Europe for one year in 1927 on a Guggenheim Fellowship. His portraits of diaphanous women, exhibited at the Rehn Gallery in 1928, attracted attention and in 1930 he left the Art Students League to become head of the painting department of the Detroit Society of Arts and Crafts where, "lavishly paid by patrons Edsel Ford and Alvan Macauley, he began to teach a worshipful flock of younger artists" (*Time,* August 24, 1942).

His portraits bring prices up to $3,000 and a great deal of comment—not all of it favorable. Some artists claim that the prehensile fingers of his ethereal ladies are so long as to suggest a fourth joint. One critic prescribed for Carroll's languorous women a diet of liver and orange juice.

These attacks are almost completely ignored by his subjects, by art juries, curators, viewers, and Carroll himself. The ladies whose portraits he paints usually emerge as a composite of themselves and Mrs. Carroll, the former Georgia ("Pinky") Finckel, an art student, whom Carroll met in Woodstock, New York and whom he married in 1936. Mrs. Carroll's portrait *Artist's Wife,* is displayed at the Art Museum of the New Britain (Connecticut) Institute. "She is barely five feet tall," wrote Ernest W. Watson (*American Artist,* January 1951), "and cannot weigh over ninety pounds. . . . She has been the determining factor in Carroll's work. 'Even when she is not the sitter,' as Harry Salpeter once commented, 'her image guides the intellect and brush of the artist.'"

His work is represented in such museums as the Detroit Institute of Arts, the Whitney Museum of American Art (New York City), the Omaha (Nebraska) Joslyn Art Museum, the Addison Gallery of American Art (Andover, Massachusetts), the Toledo (Ohio) Museum of Art, the Honolulu (Hawaii) Academy of Arts, and the Newark (New Jersey) Museum. He received the Altman Prize in 1948 at the National Academy of Design for his *Clare Luce as Camille* and again in 1954 for his *Mother and Child*; the Norman Waite Harris Silver Medal of the Art Institute of Chicago (1927); the Gold Medal of the Detroit Institute of Arts (1935), and an award from the Scarab Club (1936).

Carroll returned to the Art Students League as professor of painting in 1944 and has taught there ever since. He maintains a West Fifty-seventh Street studio and commutes from his 300-acre farm at East Chatham, New York. He is a cooperating artist in Portraits, Inc. Carroll believes that "imagination is the finest characteristic of the American people"; the figures in his paintings cater to that imagination. He aims "to produce pictures which move the observer to an emotional reaction that contributes to his delight in living" (*Newsweek,* August 30, 1943).

During World War II, as his contribution to the war effort, Carroll raised beef. He still enjoys pitching hay, rounding up the cattle, and shingling a roof. His friends say that he ably plays swing music on the concertina. "Good art," he once said, "is seldom inspired by current events or political ideas. A painter's job is to idealize his subjects." Fox hunting is his favorite recreation, and he keeps a pack of fox hounds on his farm.

According to Ernest W. Watson in *American Artist* (January 1951), "Carroll's brush, although caressing with a thistledown touch in part, also registers great vigor in bold lines and sweeping strokes with a large, full brush. Indeed, watching the artist at work one is impressed by the verve of his attack. . . . It is as though, having achieved the delicacy of face and figure, he is impatient to pick up his big brushes again and finish off the canvas quickly."

References

Am Artist 15:28+ Ja '51 por
Life 8:118 My 13 '40 por
Newsweek 22:90 Ag 30 '43
Time 40:51 Ag 24 '42
Who's Who in America, 1950-51
Who's Who in American Art (1953)

CASE, CLIFFORD P(HILIP) Apr. 16, 1904- United States Senator from New Jersey; lawyer

Address: b. Senate Office Bldg., Washington 25, D.C.; h. 345 Elm Ave., Rahway, N.J.

"If the needs of this country are not met by middle-of-the-road progressivism, the problems won't be met, and the time will come when only extremist solutions are possible," said Clifford P. Case, United States Senator from New Jersey, who was confirmed in this post on December 14, 1954 after a recount of the votes of the November 2, 1954 election, the closest Senatorial race in the history of the state. Case, a Republican, defeated Democratic Congressman Charles R. Howell by 3,507 votes. Senator Case occupies the seat left vacant by Robert C. Hendrickson, who is now Ambassador to New Zealand.

As Representative to Congress from the Sixth Congressional District of New Jersey, from January 1945 to August 1953, Case was known as an advocate of civil rights legislation and the bipartisan foreign policy. After resigning from the House, he served as president and director of the Fund for the Republic. Case, who was a member of a New York law firm from 1939 to 1953, is a strong supporter of President Dwight D. Eisenhower and was active in the movement to nominate Eisenhower as the Presidential candidate of the Republican party in 1952.

Clifford Philip Case was born in Franklin Park, New Jersey on April 16, 1904, the oldest of the six children of Clifford Philip and

Jeannette (Benedict) Case. His paternal ancestors were natives of New Jersey for about six generations, and an uncle, Clarence Edwards Case, was formerly chief justice of the state Supreme Court. His father was minister of the Dutch Reformed Church in Franklin Park, and later moved to a pastorate in Poughkeepsie, New York.

Young Case grew up in Poughkeepsie and was graduated from Poughkeepsie High School in 1921. Politics and current events were frequently discussed in his home. His father died when he was sixteen, and Clifford helped to pay for his tuition at Rutgers University in New Brunswick, New Jersey by accepting part-time jobs and playing the pipe organ in church on Sundays. He was on the lacrosse team, a member of the glee club, and was elected to Phi Beta Kappa.

After receiving the B.A. degree from Rutgers in 1925, Case attended Columbia University School of Law, earning the LL.B. degree in 1928. In the same year he was admitted to the New York bar and obtained a position with the law firm of Simpson, Thacher & Bartlett in New York City. He was a member of this firm from 1939 to 1953.

Entering politics in 1937, Case was elected to the Rahway (New Jersey) common council, on which he served from 1938 to 1942. For the next two years he was a member of the House of Assembly (the lower chamber of New Jersey's Legislature). On November 7, 1944 he was elected to the Seventy-ninth Congress of the United States from the Sixth District (Union county) of New Jersey. He was reelected four times by wide margins. In 1952 he received the support of the Americans for Democratic Action, Congress of Industrial Organizations, and American Federation of Labor, and he polled 20,000 more votes than any other candidate ever received in that district and ran 10,000 votes ahead of Eisenhower's majority.

In the Seventy-ninth Congress, Case served on the committees on war claims, claims, and civil service. He was assigned to the Judiciary Committee in the Eightieth Congress and continued as a member of that committee during his service in the House.

The Congressman's voting record regarding labor issues indicates that he opposed the strike control bill (February 1946), supported the banning of portal-to-portal pay suits (February 1947), favored overriding the veto of the Taft-Hartley bill (June 1947), and was against the amendment to the defense production bill requesting the President to invoke the Taft-Hartley act in the 1952 labor dispute in the steel industry (June 1952).

In regard to national security, Congressman Case opposed establishing a permanent Un-American Activities Committee (January 1945), supported the Communist control bill which he had helped to draft (May 1948), favored a bill to give Congress access to secret files of certain government agencies (May 1948), supported the security bill (March 1950), and favored overriding the veto of the Communist control bill (September 1950).

Wide World

CLIFFORD P. CASE

Voting on civil rights measures, Case favored an anti-poll tax measure (June 1945), a proposal to prevent segregation or discrimination in the Women's Reserve of the Coast Guard (April 1948), and the creation of a Fair Employment Practices Commission to prohibit discrimination in employment (February 1950).

On other domestic issues the Representative voted "nay" on a resolution to submit to the states a constitutional amendment for the House to participate in ratification of treaties (May 1945); "yea" on the bill to extend price controls to June 30, 1946 (June 1945) and on a $5.9 billion tax cut (October 1945). He also approved overriding the veto of the tidelands oil bill (August 1946), overriding the veto of a bill to exclude newspaper and magazine vendors from coverage under the Social Security Act (April 1948), and a long-range housing bill (June 1949).

Other roll call votes show he was against a bill prohibiting the Federal government from regulating certain independent natural gas producers (March 1950), against the Lodge-Gossett constitutional amendment to alter the method of electing the President (July 1950), for a conference report to extend the Federal old age and survivors insurance system (August 1950).

Case supported a bill increasing Social Security benefits (June 1952), a compromise wage-price-rent control bill (June 1952); opposed overriding the veto on the McCarran-Walter immigration bill (June 1952), the off-shore oil bill relinquishing to the states coastal lands previously claimed by the Federal government (April 1953). He voted for the bill to extend the excess profits tax (July 1953).

Among votes cast by Case on defense measures were those favoring the manpower draft bill (February 1945), drafting nurses into the armed forces (March 1945), a combination draft-Universal Military Training bill (April

CASE, CLIFFORD P.—*Continued*

1951), and an amendment to the defense appropriations bill to limit to forty-six billion dollars the amount to be spent by the military in 1953 (April 1952).

A supporter of the bipartisan foreign policy, Case voted in favor of: extending the Trade Agreements Act to 1948 (May 1945), a second appropriation of $1,350 million for the United Nations Relief and Rehabilitation Administration (December 1945), the European cooperation bill (March 1948), economic aid to Korea and Formosa (February 1950), the foreign economic assistance bill (March 1950), the aid to India bill (June 1951), the mutual security bill (June 1952), and a $4.4 billion foreign aid appropriation (July 1953).

A bill to make lynching a Federal crime was introduced by Congressman Case in 1947. It would make local communities liable for civil damages of $2,000 to $10,000 for a lynch victim or his survivors. Seeking to remove allegedly discriminatory features of the Displaced Persons Act of 1948, Case introduced a bill in July 1948 to permit entry of immigrants according to proportions of national groups in European refugee camps and to eliminate the requirement that 30 per cent of the displaced persons admitted be agricultural workers.

On February 6, 1953 Case announced his candidacy for Governor of New Jersey. However, he withdrew from the gubernatorial race before the primary election because of the "lack of necessary funds."

On August 14, 1953 Case resigned from Congress to accept the $40,000-a-year presidency of the Fund for the Republic. The fund was established to "support activities directed toward the elimination of restrictions on freedom of thought, inquiry and expression in the United States, and the development of policies and procedures best adapted to protect those rights in the face of persistent international tension." This project was granted $15,000,000 by the Ford Foundation.

Case resigned from the presidency of the Fund for the Republic in March 1954 to become the Republican candidate for U.S. Senator from New Jersey. He was nominated without opposition and was supported by President Eisenhower. Opposition during his campaign came from the CIO and AFL, then supporting Charles R. Howell, a Democrat, and a faction of the Republican party which called itself the Committee for a Stronger Republican Party. An attempt by some of Case's opponents to stage a write-in campaign for former Congressman Fred A. Hartley, Jr. collapsed in September.

During the course of the campaign Case traveled about 35,000 miles. He criticized the investigative methods of Joseph R. McCarthy (Wisconsin Senator) and said he would vote, if elected, against seating McCarthy on any committee with investigative functions (Earl Mazo, New York *Herald Tribune,* December 19, 1954).

On November 2, 1954 Case defeated Howell by a margin of 3,369 votes. A recount was called and on December 14 Case was confirmed as Senator by 3,507 votes. After taking office in January 1955, Senator Case served on the Republican Committee on Committees and moved that Senator McCarthy be removed from the Government Operations Committee. Case's motion was ruled out of order by Senator John W. Bricker, chairman of the committee. Soon thereafter, Case said that "to pursue the matter further at this time would not be fruitful" (New York *Herald Tribune,* January 12, 1955). In the Eighty-fourth Congress Case serves on the committees on the District of Columbia and on the post office and civil service.

Together with Senators Irving M. Ives (of New York) and Ralph E. Flanders (of Vermont), Case introduced a bill in January 1955 providing for Federal and state subsidies for voluntary prepaid health and medical care programs operating at a loss and authorizing an increase of $25,000,000 to stimulate construction of health service centers, on a matching Federal-state basis, for out-patient use.

On January 18, 1955 Case co-sponsored a bill with Senators Ives and Leverett Saltonstall (of Massachusetts) to alter the Immigration and Nationality Act of 1952 by eliminating the authority given to consuls to grant or deny visas with virtually no standards for guidance, and the discrimination against naturalized citizens, and establishing the 1950 instead of the 1920 census figures as the basis for determining immigration quotas.

The Senator received the *Liberty* magazine award in 1951 and the 1953 medal of merit of the New Jersey department of the Jewish War Veterans. He is on the board of the New Jersey Society for Crippled Children and Adults, the board of foreign missions of the Reformed Church in America, and he serves on the board of trustees of Rutgers University. Other organizations in which he holds membership are the American, New York state, and New York county bar associations, and the Association of the Bar of the City of New York. He is an Elk and a member of Delta Upsilon. His clubs are the Downtown Association (New York) and Metropolitan (Washington, D.C.).

Ruth Miriam Smith and Clifford P. Case were married on July 13, 1928; their children are Mary Jane (Mrs. William M. Weaver), Ann and Clifford Philip, 3d. The Senator is five feet eleven inches tall, weighs about 150 pounds, has reddish-brown hair, and a boyish smile. Damon Stetson (New York *Times,* October 29, 1954) called the Senator "a sensitive and intense person." Case enjoys tennis, piano playing, reading, and listening to classical records. His nickname is "Buddy." The Cases' home in Rahway is a restored Victorian house.

References

N Y Herald Tribune p5 Ap 17 '54; II p3 O 10 '54 por; p83 O 21 '54
N Y Times p21 O 28 '54; p16 Ja 4 '55
N Y World-Telegram p29 Ag 25 '54 por
Biographical Directory of the American Congress, 1774-1949 (1950)
Who's Who in America, 1954-55

CASSIDY, CLAUDIA Music, ballet and drama critic

Address: b. c/o Chicago Tribune, Tribune Tower, Chicago, Ill.; h. 191 E. Walton Pl., Chicago, Ill.

For over thirteen years readers of the Chicago *Tribune* have been reading and arguing about Claudia Cassidy's lively and caustic daily column, "On the Aisle." Some have even called her reviews "vitriolic" and "sulphuric," but she herself maintains that she is simply a critic "who hates mediocrity." As music, ballet and drama critic, she reports on Chicago's theatrical and concert fare, and, for the past four summers, has covered European operas, plays and festivals. These were published in her book, *Europe—on the Aisle* (Random House, 1954). Previous to joining the staff of the Chicago *Tribune* in 1942 she had written music and drama reviews for the Chicago *Journal of Commerce* (1925-1941).

"A brilliant phrasemaker, Miss Cassidy has the ability to make people continue to read her no matter what they think of her notions and opinions," commented Richard B. Gehman in *Theatre Arts*, July 1951. "She has developed a style wholly her own. It is clear, forceful writing, a beautifully versatile vehicle for her opinions."

Claudia Cassidy was born in the early 1900's in Shawneetown, Illinois, just across the Ohio River from Kentucky. Her father was George Peter Cassidy and her mother, Olive (Grattan) Cassidy. She remembers the showboats on the Ohio River, and with them began her interest in the theatre. Her girlhood was spent in Chicago.

Miss Cassidy attended the University of Illinois in Urbana, where she majored in drama and journalism. She studied music with private teachers. After receiving her bachelor's degree, she obtained a job as secretary on the Chicago *Journal of Commerce* in 1925. Glenn Griswold, her employer, knowing of her ambition to be a journalist, on occasion allowed her to write an editorial. She recalls writing on the "coal crisis" and also being sent to Florida to report on a bond issue.

One night she was asked to fill in for Paul Martin, the music and drama critic, who was ill. "To my lasting surprise," she has recalled, "by the happy accident of being handy . . . I was given the job" (*Editor & Publisher*, March 10, 1951). During the ensuing years she was the drama and music authority on the *Journal of Commerce*, and became known as the most astute music critic in Chicago.

In late 1941 she went to Marshall Field's new Chicago *Daily Sun*, to organize the theatre and music department there and to write the criticisms. But she left less than a year later to become music and drama critic for the Chicago *Tribune*, published by Colonel Robert R. McCormick.

Having lived in Chicago during what is often called its "golden age," the 1920's, Miss Cassidy remembers its fine opera company and theatres, where plays were put together with the same professional care and attention usually given to

CLAUDIA CASSIDY

Broadway productions. In succeeding years, when writers and artists moved to New York, Miss Cassidy remained in Chicago and fought to maintain the high standards in which she believes. Today the revived theatre and opera groups in Chicago are grateful to her; she has helped young and creative groups such as the Playwrights (repertory) Theatre Club and the Lyric (opera) Theatre to gain a foothold.

One of the Cassidy campaigns has been against slipshod or jaded road companies being sent to Chicago with Broadway plays. "Until New York satiates, Chicago starves," was her comment on the Chicago theatre situation in 1948. "In the main," she wrote, "Chicago's theatre consists of New York hits in various stages of repair, brought to us either in duplicate or with what remains of the original company at the end of the New York run and perhaps a tour, and bedraggled little turkeys arriving from the environs of Hollywood, presumably by way of the sewage system" (New York *Times*, August 15, 1948). Trips to New York enable her to compare the Chicago company with the original Broadway performance.

During Miss Cassidy's campaign to remove a conductor of the Chicago Symphony Orchestra, the *Tribune* received 200 complaining letters in a week. According to *Time* (February 5, 1951), she offered to resign, but Colonel McCormick thought that 200 letters to a music department revealed an astonishing number of readers.

Covering three different fields, Claudia Cassidy makes it a matter of personal pride to know her subjects. Over 500 musical and drama reference books line the shelves of her office, and most of them look worn by regular use. According to *Theatre Arts* (July 1951), Miss Cassidy is one of the five most perceptive, informed and scholarly critics in American journalism.

(Continued next page)

CASSIDY, CLAUDIA—*Continued*

She has been called a perfectionist; others maintain that her long tenure and increasing power in the realm of opinion have given her a sense of infallibility. She has tried, she says, to be a good reporter first, and a critic, second, and to communicate to her readers, by the use of "exact words," her impressions. Actors who have received adverse comment in her column are convinced that she can determine the fate of any show venturing into Chicago, but the evidence shows that a number of plays have flourished at the box office despite her unfavorable criticism.

Occasionally, she has praised the work of an unknown playwright and has urged her readers to go to the theatre to see a "promising play," as when she praised Tennessee Williams' *The Glass Menagerie*, which opened in Chicago on December 26, 1944, and cited for particular approval the actress Laurette Taylor, who was making her comeback. The play's impact in Chicago (where it played for thirteen weeks) became too significant to be called a tryout, and in the published book, credit is given to "the Civic Theatre, Chicago, Illinois" where it was "first produced."

The critic is inclined toward plays of originality and freshness. "Sometimes shows that shoot at the moon and fail are more interesting than those that aim at mediocrity and score a bull's-eye," she stated (New York *Times*, August 15, 1948).

Since 1950 the columnist has toured Europe every summer with her husband, covering places and interviewing people as well as reviewing all the important music festivals and theatrical offerings. Her book, *Europe—on the Aisle* (Random House, 1954), is a compilation of these European adventures. The *Saturday Review* (July 3, 1954) commented that "she does nice things with descriptions . . . it is all of interest and frequently reveals something of a soul that belies her reputation for being the Lizzie Borden of the Midwest culture circuit . . . for lowering the axe on American theatrical endeavor." Her report of the season in Chicago appears in the annual edition of the *The Best Plays* (originally edited by Burns Mantle; now edited by Louis Kronenberger).

Miss Cassidy keeps up an active correspondence with personalities in the drama, music, and dance fields, as well as meeting the deadlines on her daily column. The cluttered living room of her small apartment, filled to the ceiling with piled records, looks more like a music shop than a residence (*Theatre Arts*, July 1951).

On June 16, 1929 Miss Cassidy was married to William John Crawford, a Chicago businessman. The journalist is red-haired, somewhat resembles her friend, Tallulah Bankhead, and speaks quietly with a pleasant voice. She remains serene in the midst of the controversies she ignites. She is a good cook and a hearty eater. Her religion is Roman Catholic.

An enthusiastic traveler, Miss Cassidy wrote in *Europe—on the Aisle* that she is a bad bargainer because she does not like to see artists underpaid in any currency. "Next to Italy, which is my second home," she wrote, "I think I could love Spain best of all . . . we crossed twenty borders and met courtesy in all languages."

Her advice concerning the job of writing criticism, is: "Stay out of the quagmires of jargon and the deadly rut of routine. Search for informed opinion, not prejudice. Take to each new experience the fresh, undivided attention it has a right to expect if it has any claim to attention at all." Her own concept of a critic's job runs counter to that of playwright Maxwell Anderson's that a critic is "judge, jury and firing squad." Her fellow first-nighters of the press regard her as a "good critic" (*Editor & Publisher*, March 10, 1951).

References

Ed & Pub 84:28 Mr 10 '51 por
Theatre Arts 35:14+ Jl '51
Time 40:38 S 28 '42 por; 57:42 F 5 '51
Who's Who in America, 1954-55
Who's Who in Chicago and Illinois (1950)

CASTILLO ARMAS, CARLOS (käs-tē' yō) Nov. 4, 1914- President of Guatemala

Address: b. Palacio Nacional, Guatemala City, Guatemala; h. Casa Presidencial, Guatemala City, Guatemala

A plebiscite held in Guatemala on October 10, 1954 approved Carlos Castillo Armas as constitutional President by an almost unanimous vote. He was sworn in on November 6, for a five-year term by the Constituent Assembly, whose sixty-six members had been elected the previous month. The new government replaced the regime of President Jacobo Arbenz, who resigned on June 27, 1954, the tenth day of the anti-Communist revolt led by Colonel Castillo Armas.

A graduate of Escuela Politécnica, Guatemala's military academy, Colonel Castillo Armas was commandant of the school under President Arévalo. He supported the opposition against the election of Arbenz in 1950 and according to *Newsweek* (June 28, 1954) was jailed and escaped a year later to exile in Honduras. Soon after the U.S. Central Intelligence Agency exposed the Czech shipment of munitions to Guatemala, Castillo Armas emerged from obscurity as leader of the Army of Liberation and on June 17, 1954 moved into Guatemalan territory.

The revolt continued until peace talks were arranged in San Salvador. The colonel agreed to become a member of a five-man junta on July 2 and two months later was named President by the Cabinet. His first responsibility was to purge his country of Communists.

Carlos Castillo Armas was born in Santa Lucia Cotzumalguapa, Escuintla, Guatemala on November 4, 1914, the son of Raimundo and Josefina (Armas) Castillo Pivarel. He attended school in the village of La Democracia, Escuintla, and later the Escuela Normal in Guatemala, and in January 1933 entered Escuela Politécnica. He was a classmate of Jacobo Arbenz and one of the honor students of the graduating class of 1936. He remained at the school as an instructor until 1944 and then joined other young officers in the revolt that drove dictator General Jorge Ubico and his successor, General Federico Ponce, into exile.

After Juan José Arévalo became President in 1945 Major Castillo Armas was sent to the U.S. Army Command and General Staff School at Fort Leavenworth, Kansas for two years. Before he returned to Guatemala, he visited West Point. In the rank of lieutenant colonel, he served as commandant of Escuela Politécnica for two years and then became chief of the fourth military district.

There was political rivalry in the Arévalo Cabinet between Colonel Francisco Arano, chief of the armed forces and Colonel Jacobo Arbenz, Defense Minister. After Arano's death in July 1949, Arbenz was nominated President. As reported by *Newsweek* (June 28, 1954), Colonel Castillo Armas, who had favored Arano, headed a "desperate and unsuccessful revolt" five days before Arbenz was elected in 1950. Castillo Armas was badly wounded and arrested. The following summer he tunneled his way out of prison and sought refuge in the Colombian Embassy and was later given safe conduct out of the country. For three years he lived in Tegucigalpa, Honduras and quietly collected arms, money and men for the "liberation" of Guatemala.

Richard and Gladys Harkness wrote in the *Saturday Evening Post* (October 30, 1954) that the U.S. Central Intelligence Agency had learned that the Swedish freighter *Alfhem* carried a $10,000,000 cargo which included 1,900 tons of munitions from Czechoslovakia listed as optical-laboratory equipment and destined for Guatemala. CIA director, Allen Dulles, placed this disclosure before the National Security Council and on May 17, Secretary of State John Foster Dulles publicized the danger of Guatemala's crushing neighbor countries in an attempt to get control of the Panama Canal. The Defense Department flew military supplies to Honduras and Nicaragua, and Castillo Armas, the Harkness story said, "obtained sufficient guns and munitions to equip each man in a force of anti-Communist refugees with a burp gun, a pistol and a machete."

"A ghost radio station inside Guatemala, and another just over the border," (*Newsweek,* June 28, 1954) was "bombarded with anti-Communist exhortations." The "Red-tinged" government swept aside all constitutional guarantees and arrested hundreds of anti-Communists. *Time* reported that Castillo Armas radioed the Guatemalan people—"I shall be with you very soon." Esquipulas, Chiquimula and Puerto Barrios were entered on June 17, and gasoline tanks at the Pacific port of San José were bombed.

According to the New York *Times* (June 22, 1954) Castillo Armas had set up a provisional government inside Guatemala and called for the surrender of President Arbenz and his "Communist-supported regime." The regular Army, estimated at 6,000, did little fighting. Castillo Armas was said to have from 2,000 to 3,000 men.

Wide World

COL. CARLOS CASTILLO ARMAS

After an all-day conference with top Army leaders on June 27, Arbenz yielded and turned over the government to Colonel Carlos Enrique Diaz, chief of the armed forces. A three-man junta formed by Diaz lasted twenty-four hours. Castillo Armas, convinced that Diaz was a "front" for Arbenz, bombed Guatemala City's Fort Matamoras. Diaz sent for U.S. Ambassador John E. Peurifoy, who had earlier been asked whether the United States would recognize a junta headed by Diaz. Milton Bracker (New York *Times Magazine,* July 11, 1954) wrote that Colonel Elfigo Monzón and two other colonels ousted Diaz at the point of machine guns.

A new three-man junta was set up, headed by Monzón, and a cease-fire was agreed upon. The next day Castillo Armas and Monzón flew to San Salvador for peace talks. Twelve hours later there was a deadlock over which colonel should take top power. After the arrival of Peurifoy, who had arranged for the talks, a peace pact was signed on July 2, with Monzón as head of a five-man junta. The instability of the arrangement was made clear, according to *Newsweek* (July 19, 1954), when "cheering *guatematecos*" hailed Castillo Armas as the "conquering hero."

Six days later two of the members resigned and Castillo Armas was named provisional President. Colonel Monzón and Major Enrique T. Olvia remained. A test of strength came on August first, after a day-long revolt, started by cadets and supported by units of the regular Army at Aurora Air Base, protesting the continuance of the "Liberation" Army. The New York *Times* (August 8, 1954) estimated that a crowd of 40,000 assembled in front of the National Palace and cheered Castillo Armas and

CASTILLO ARMAS, CARLOS—*Continued*

hooted the Army. The next day he moved from the rented house where he had been living to Casa Presidencial.

The resignation of Monzón and Olvia on September 1, left Castillo Armas in control and he was formally named President by the Cabinet. The retirement of the two Army officers was made as "an open gesture of solidarity," the *Christian Science Monitor* (September 2, 1954) quoted Castillo Armas, and added that the two men would remain in the new government. It had been apparent that except for anti-Communist measures, most of Castillo Armas' attention had been absorbed by a "behind-the-scenes battle for power."

Time (July 26, 1954) reported that 3,500 suspected Communists had been arrested and all leftist parties dissolved. New judges were appointed for all judicial posts and government personnel overhauled. About 900 refugees, Arbenz among them, had taken shelter in nine foreign embassies.

The new government expropriated the assets of eighty-nine former officials, including Arbenz, as "legitimate indemnity for damages, thefts and other harmful acts to public funds" (New York *Times,* September 8, 1954). Under international rules governing political asylum, the refugees could not be apprehended by Guatemalan authorities; therefore, safe conduct was granted. Arbenz, with seventeen others, flew to Mexico on September 9.

In Washington, D.C., the House Subcommittee on Communist Aggression in Latin America heard testimony, early in October, wire-recorded by President Castillo Armas, who spoke in English, on "how Moscow-directed Communists emerged with power and influence under the regime of . . . Jacobo Arbenz" (*Time,* October 11, 1954). It was the first recorded testimony ever taken by a committee of Congress from a foreign chief of state.

The decree which deprived illiterates of the vote (72 per cent of the population), issued by the junta government in July, was lifted for one day on October 10 to permit an oral "si" or "no" answer to the question of whether President Castillo Armas was approved. *Newsweek* (October 25, 1954) stated that 99 per cent approved. Sixty-six deputies were elected the same day to serve without pay in the Constituent Assembly. When sworn into office by the Assembly on November 6, the President pledged to maintain the principle of Presidential succession. His term will expire on March 15, 1960.

With a public debt estimated at $50,000,000, the President decreed emergency taxes to raise $6,200,000 in revenue. The United States offered $6,425,000 in economic and technical aid, with a portion of that amount in the form of a loan. The sum of $1,425,000 was allotted for work on the Inter-American Highway. Private capital has been encouraged to invest in Guatemala's economic development. The Arbenz agrarian law was revoked and cases of expropriated landowners reviewed under a temporary statute. The United Fruit Company, the largest landowner, after the case was reviewed, proposed a new operating contract (New York *Times,* November 11, 1954).

This contract, now in effect, gives Armas' government 30 per cent of the company's yearly profits in Guatemala, retroactive to January 1, 1954. United Fruit agreed to drop its $15,000,000 claim for land that was seized by the Arbenz government. Unifruitco turns over 100,000 acres in the Tiquisata area of the west coast (*Business Week,* January 1, 1955).

President Carlos Castillo Armas is married to Odilia Palomo. Their religion is Roman Catholic. *Newsweek* describes him as "a tall, thin professional soldier, soft-spoken and ascetic-looking." He has black hair and brown eyes. At the opening session of the Assembly on October 29, 1954, the President said: "My policy will keep Guatemala equally distant from every extremist ideology. It will be inspired in a healthy nationalism which does not reject cooperation with other nations."

References

El Imparcial (Guatemala City) p 1 Jl 3 '54 pors
N Y Times p2 Je 19 '54 por
N Y World-Telegram p7 Jl 3 '54 por
Newsweek 43:47 Je 28 '54
Time 63:38 Je 28 '54 por

CASTILLO NÁJERA, FRANCISCO Nov. 25, 1886-Dec. 20, 1954 Former Mexican diplomat and physician; Ambassador to United States (1935-45); represented Mexico on the U.N. Security Council (1946); had a major role in negotiating trade agreements with U.S. and settling agrarian and oil claims of Americans. See *Current Biography* (May) 1946.

Obituary

N Y Times p23 D 22 '54

CENERAZZO, WALTER W. 1912- (sĕn-ĕr-ä'zô) Labor union official

Address: b. c/o American Watch Workers Union, 479 Moody St., Waltham, Mass.

The "mainspring of the American Watch Workers Union" is its president, Walter W. Cenerazzo, head of an independent labor organization of some 8,000 members. Cenerazzo once summarized his career in these words: "I joined a union in my teens. . . . I started with the Typographical Union, the oldest and strongest citadel of American union democracy. . . . I have worked as a union printer in the composing rooms of 200 newspapers from Massachusetts to California; I have organized the unorganized as a representative of the American Federation of Labor; and the American Watch Workers Union has done me the honor of making me its president."

In January 1949, Cenerazzo was honored by the United States Junior Chamber of Commerce as one of "the nation's ten outstanding young men of 1948" in recognition of his championship of "cooperative capitalism." He has been active in recent years in efforts to restrict the importation of Swiss watches. "Although trained as a labor organizer," Charles W. Moore wrote in *Timing a Century; History of the Waltham Watch Company* (1945), "Cenerazzo is predominantly an administrator and economist."

Walter W. Cenerazzo was born in Somerville, Massachusetts, near Boston, in 1912. After working as a printer, he began his career as an organizer in 1937, working for the blacksmith and candy workers' unions of the AFL. The following year he organized the Gloucester Seafood Workers' Union in Massachusetts, and later became its business agent.

In 1941 he organized the employees of the Waltham Watch Company for the AFL's International Jewelry Workers' Union. However, "because of dissatisfaction with what he termed the organizing laxity of the national union," according to *Fortune* (January 1947), he dissolved the Waltham local of the International Jewelry Workers' Union, AFL, on October 28, 1943, and founded the Waltham Watch Workers Union, an independent union. From Waltham he went on to organize the workers at the Elgin National Watch Company, and from there to the Hamilton Watch Company, where his union won a bargaining election decisively in May 1944.

In an article in *Reader's Digest* (November 1944) he wrote: "My experiences (as a union member, organizer and official) convince me that the American labor movement, in order to survive, must be democratic; and that it can be made democratic, as a whole, only by new broad national action. If that action is not taken by labor, it will be taken by law."

At a labor-management conference held in Washington in November 1945, Cenerazzo announced tentative plans for the formation of a third national federation of labor unions unaffiliated with either the AFL or CIO. Such a federation, he indicated, would be dedicated to union democracy and labor-management cooperation. "Let us demand," he asserted, "that every one of our affiliates practice the fundamentals of union democracy and that they recognize the rights of management in collective bargaining. Let us work out a program dedicated to free enterprise, barring from memberships all those following the Communist party's philosophy" (New York *World-Telegram*, November 15, 1945). In February 1947, he applied, in behalf of his union, for an AFL charter, but the application was rejected at a tempestuous meeting.

An advocate of closer cooperation between management and labor, Cenerazzo, in an article entitled "How to Lick Class Struggle," wrote: "In my opinion any person who is a company man and is opposed to unions is a class-struggler; and any person who is a union man and is opposed to the company is a class-struggler. We in America must be both company-minded and union-minded. Our objectives must be identical. The prosperity of the company must be the paramount issue in our minds. For, when there are no profits, corporate enterprise starts to drown and employment is lost for management and the employees" (*Reader's Digest,* September 1949).

Wide World

WALTER W. CENERAZZO

On January 14, 1949 the United States Junior Chamber of Commerce announced its selections of "the nation's ten outstanding young men of 1948." Among the winners, who were chosen by a panel of judges which included General Dwight D. Eisenhower, was Cenerazzo, who was cited "for his 'cooperative capitalism' program and advocacy of what he terms democracy in labor union organization" (New York *Times,* January 15, 1949).

Cenerazzo's third major professional concern, in addition to union democracy and "cooperative capitalism," has been what he considers the threat of the Swiss watch industry to American watchmakers, and indirectly, to national security. Beginning in 1943, "in vehement agitations before Congressional committees," he fought the cause of the American jeweled-watch manufacturers "in their fight for quotas and higher tariffs on Swiss watches."

Testifying before the Senate Finance Committee in February 1949, he requested that a special commission be created to study the possibility of Congressional protection for the American watchmaking industry in the interest of national defense. He emphasized the essential defense role that American watchmakers played in the production of precision-timing instruments (New York *Times*, February 20, 1949).

Commenting on Cenerazzo's position, Sylvia F. Porter of the New York *Post* (April 7, 1949) wrote: "At the first sign of normal competition, the old isolationist pressure goes on for 'protecting' the home boys." George E. Sokolsky, on the other hand, remarked in the New York *Sun* (April 11, 1949): "I find nothing notable to contest in Mr. Cenerazzo's conten-

CENERAZZO, WALTER W.—*Continued*

tions. . . . The United States cannot afford to lose a precision industry. Although it would be nice to make the Swiss rich, it would make more sense to protect American production."

During a tour of Switzerland in August 1949, Cenerazzo conceded that Swiss watchworkers enjoyed a relatively high standard of living, but added that their wages were considerably lower than those of their American counterparts. The New York *Times* (August 24, 1949) quoted him as saying: "We have no desire to stop Swiss watch imports into the United States. At no time have we ever tried to restrict Swiss watch imports to over one-half of the American market. Our problem is that the Swiss watch importer takes your product and brings it into the United States at a cost, with duty and transport paid, of $4.40 less than we can produce them for in the United States."

When the 100-year-old Waltham Watch Company closed in February 1950, Cenerazzo charged that the "dumping" of Swiss watches on the American market was responsible for the decline of the domestic industry. He pointed out that employment in the American jeweled-watch industry had shrunk by more than 3,100 workers in fourteen months. Within the months that followed, he strongly urged the Reconstruction Finance Corporation to grant additional funds to the Waltham company to enable it "to process and sell its inventory of watches in order to get money for further operations." After being in bankruptcy for the third time in its history, the company was reorganized in 1951.

In testimony submitted to the U.S. Tariff Commission in February 1954, Cenerazzo advocated the imposition of higher duties on Swiss watches and watch movements, and warned that unless this were done, the resulting loss of domestic skill in the manufacture of timing devices would imperil the national defense.

An insight into his economic views may be gained from an address he delivered at the International Students Center of Harvard University on January 8, 1950. "The United States program for reciprocal trade," he told his audience, "does not and will not help either the American worker or foreign workers. All it does is make the importer richer at the expense of both the American worker and the foreign worker. For this reason I have advocated for some time a twofold program in the field of foreign trade, which, in my opinion, if carried out, would create a middle class of people with purchasing power in every country in this world.

"I believe the United States should lead the way by creating a Board of Foreign Trade. . . . In the distribution of Point IV money the second part of my program would come into play, for I would allow no nation to participate in obtaining any of this money unless they first adopt in the constitution of their country a bill of rights comparable to ours and establish a separation of the powers between the executive, legislative and judicial branches so that dictators could no longer function or gain a foothold in the future." In September 1953 Cenerazzo was appointed to a special commission to study Congressional and judicial salaries.

The question of increasing the tariff on Swiss watches was resolved in July 1954 by President Eisenhower on recommendation of the U.S. Tariff Commission. The tariff was raised up to 50 per cent on imports of watch movements of seventeen jewels or less. President Rodolphe Rubattel (see *C.B.,* 1954) of Switzerland protested to the President as did the Watchmakers of Switzerland.

According to the Swiss watch manufacturers, the increased tariff has had a damaging effect on the amount of trade done between the United States and Switzerland. Former transactions between the countries had resulted in a favorable balance of trade for America worth five hundred million dollars (see advertisements of the Watchmakers of Switzerland in the New York *Times,* May 4, and July 18, 1955).

The labor leader was described in *Fortune* (April 1949) as "the Terrible Turk of the American Watch Workers Union." As Charles W. Moore sees him, Cenerazzo "has the zeal of a prophet but the patience essential to a successful negotiator."

References

Fortune 35:198 Ja '47 por
PM p13+ Ja 5 '47
Read Digest 45:56+ N '44; 55:81 S '49
Moore, C. W. Timing a Century (1945)

CHAPMAN, HELEN LOUISE BUSCH

See Chapman, Mrs. Theodore S.

CHAPMAN, MRS. THEODORE S. Apr. 20, 1904- Women's organization official

Address: b. c/o General Federation of Women's Clubs, 1734 N St., N.W., Washington 6, D.C.; h. Homeridge Farm, Jerseyville, Ill.

Clubwomen throughout the United States headed by Mrs. Theodore S. Chapman, president of the General Federation of Women's Clubs, worked during 1954 to force objectionable crime and horror books off the newsstands in many states. Among other projects being directed by Mrs. Chapman is an international contest of local achievement, designed to help overseas communities to make civic improvements. The prizes, provided by a Sears-Roebuck Foundation grant of $100,000, will be awarded at the G.F.W.C.'s convention to be held in Kansas City, Missouri in May 1956.

During a press conference in Washington, D.C. on July 6, 1954, Mrs. Chapman explained that the federation favors a stronger United Nations and opposes admission of Red China. "I feel sure," she stated, "that the majority of our members [in the United States] recognize . . . that we don't have to have a third World War to show us we can't go it alone."

Mrs. Chapman, a former high school and college teacher, heads the largest international organization of women which has 5,000,000 members in the United States and 6,000,000 in over forty other countries. Before her election as president in June 1954 for a two-year term, succeeding Mrs. Oscar A. Ahlgren, she served the G.F.W.C. in various executive posts for seven years.

Helen Louise Busch was born on April 20, 1904 in Coldwater, Michigan, one of four daughters of Jeannette (Morrison) and Francis X. Busch, a lawyer. She completed her high school education at Martin College, Pulaski, Tennessee in 1922. After attending Blackburn College, Carlinville, Illinois, she entered the University of Wisconsin in Madison, where she majored in history, joined the Alpha Gamma Delta sorority, and earned her A.B. degree in 1926.

Miss Busch first became active in club work in 1928 in Chicago, where from 1933 to 1938 she taught history and economics in Chicago high schools. She took postgraduate studies at the University of Chicago, prepared a thesis on Stephen A. Douglas, and in 1936 received the M.A. degree. For one year (1938-1939) she taught in Monticello College, Illinois.

Following her marriage on June 28, 1939 to Theodore S. Chapman, a lawyer, farmer and banker, she moved to Homeridge Farm, Jerseyville, Illinois, where she continued her club interests. After her husband's death, she supervised the operation of her 270-acre farm with the aid of a manager.

Mrs. Chapman became president of the Illinois Federation of Women's Clubs in 1945 and served until 1947. For the next three years she was education chairman and among her recommendations were a $3,000 minimum salary for public school teachers, improved standards for teacher-training and certification, and revision of school curriculums.

Elected second vice-president of the G.F.W.C. in 1950, Mrs. Chapman served in this post for two years. The federation was among the sponsors of Operation Wings of Freedom, which on August 13, 1951, sent 2,000 balloons carrying 2,000,000 copies of a message of encouragement to the people of Czechoslovakia. The organization received the American Design Award of 1951, presented by Lord & Taylor, for its help in strengthening the democratic system.

During 1952 and 1953, while Mrs. Chapman served as first vice-president, the G.F.W.C. withdrew its support of Federal aid to education, sought a review by Congress of the Immigration and Nationality Act of 1952, opposed budget cuts in the U.S. Department of Health, Education and Welfare, and requested the Federal Communications Commission to maintain TV channels for educational purposes.

As an official of the G.F.W.C. and an experienced farm operator, Mrs. Chapman was selected, with three other clubwomen, to investigate the reasons for the sharp increases in the price of Brazilian coffee in the winter of 1953-1954. As guests of the Brazilian Coffee Institute in February 1954, the four women inspected frost-burned coffee plantations, and came away convinced that high labor costs, increased world consumption, crop-damaging frosts, and "the normal operation of the law of supply and demand" had caused prices in the U.S. to spiral. She disagreed sharply with the Federal Trade Commission's contention that speculation and irregularities in the coffee market had caused the high prices.

MRS. THEODORE S. CHAPMAN

The federation at its sixty-third annual convention in Denver elected Mrs. Chapman its president. She took office on June 3, 1954. Stating that her two-year administration would devote special attention to juvenile delinquency which has its basis in the inadequate home, she urged clubwomen to teach the young by example.

"Instead of the atomic age, let us call our time 'the age of responsibility,'" she said, "and determine to solve our problems ourselves and not leave them for the proverbial 'George' or the United States government. We must look at our times with purpose and confidence instead of fear" (*Christian Science Monitor,* June 7, 1954). She also expressed a desire for greater international cooperation of G.F.W.C.'s members throughout the world. "The foreign policy of a free nation is based upon public opinion, and we of the General Federation have great influence upon the development of that opinion," she stated (New York *Times,* June 5, 1954).

President Eisenhower in a message to the delegates at the convention praised the federation for more than half a century of service to the nation. The organization adopted resolutions asking for gradual reduction of trade barriers between nations, urging Congress to help states provide for safety and beautification of highways, and calling for a revision of the U.S. Civil Service to provide for a strong, nonpartisan career service founded on loyalty to country. It also asked its member clubs to aid in the recruitment of student nurses and to study the nation's mental health problem.

Mrs. Chapman attended a three-day conference in Washington, D.C. on juvenile delinquency the last week in June 1954, sponsored by the U.S. Department of Health, Education and Welfare. She announced the organization

CHAPMAN, MRS. THEODORE S.—*Cont.*

of a "youth conservation" division in a new department of community affairs in the federation. "It will be our effort . . . to bring about a revival of secure, responsible, God-loving homes in America," she said (Washington *Post,* June 30, 1954).

Aroused by the need to eliminate crime and horror comic books, members of the more than 16,000 clubs in the United States swung into action and, as a result, during 1954 local ordinances were passed, existing laws were enforced, and the objectionable comic books were forced off the newsstands in many states. In Ohio the federation set up "book swap" booths, manned by librarians, offering one free book (from among 200 juvenile books) to each child in exchange for ten horror comic books. Mrs. Chapman gave assurances that the drive would continue in 1955 "to get bad comics off the newsstands, away from children, and out of the home."

The federation president on August 2, 1954 presented to the National Park Service of the U.S. Department of Interior a check for $209,583, raised by member clubs in the United States, District of Columbia, Alaska, and Puerto Rico, to restore the first floor of Independence Hall in Philadelphia, Pennsylvania. The G.F.W.C. in September 1954 began a "get-out-the-vote" campaign to secure the election of men of "integrity" in the nation (New York *Times,* September 12, 1954).

The federation began a drive in February 1955 to raise $3,000,000 for construction of a 500-foot cross and inter-denominational center atop Bald Knob Mountain in Shawnee National Forest, Illinois.

The clubwoman was on the citizens advisory council of the U.S. Senate Post Office Committee, Board of Public Welfare Commissioners of Illinois, and board of the Dwight Reformatory for Women in Illinois. She is now a member of the advisory committee of the Illinois Youth Commission correctional services and a trustee of Monticello College, Blackburn College and the Trail Rangers of America (Boys' School-Home), Grafton, Illinois.

Among her organization memberships are the American Association of University Women, Daughters of the American Revolution, P.E.O., Chicago woman's board of the Salvation Army, American Association for the United Nations, and Chautauqua Woman's Club, New York. She is a Republican and a Presbyterian. She has blue eyes and brown hair, weighs 150 pounds, and is five feet four inches tall. Her hobbies include swimming, gardening, and playing the piano and solovox.

References

Christian Sci Mon p7 Je 7 '54
N Y Herald Tribune II p1 Je 6 '54; p12 Ag 3 '54
N Y Times p29 Jl 7 '54
Newsweek 43:59 Mr 1 '54
Time 63:33 Mr 1 '54
Washington (D. C.) Post p30 Je 14 '54 por; p42 Je 30 '54
Who's Who in America, 1954-55

CHASE, HARRY WOODBURN Apr. 11, 1883-Apr. 20, 1955 Educator; chancellor of New York University (1933-1951); president of University of North Carolina (1919-1930); president of the University of Illinois (1930-1933); among major developments at New York University during his chancellorship were the NYU-Bellevue Medical Center, the Washington Square Law Center and the Alumni gymnasium of the University Heights campus; known as a firm believer in academic freedom and broader educational opportunities; member of the board of directors of Metropolitan Opera Association, trustee Town Hall, and New York Public Library. See *Current Biography* (June) 1948.

Obituary

N Y Times p29 Ap 21 '55

CHASE, JOSEPH CUMMINGS May 5, 1878- Artist; writer

Address: 2228 E. Woodstock Pl., Milwaukee 2, Wis.

That a portrait should bear the likeness of the sitter is the credo of Joseph Cummings Chase, America's dean of portrait painters. He explains this statement further by saying that, although a likeness is part of the "unwritten contract," it is still more "a personal contract that the painter makes with *himself* that in addition he will furnish his sitter a composition so good in design that following generations will take pleasure in the portrait even though they have not seen the sitter in the flesh" (*American Artist,* May 1954).

Chase's art career covers a span of over fifty years, beginning in 1904 with his winning of the Grunwaldt poster competition in Paris and still flourishing today in his studio in Milwaukee, Wisconsin, where he moved from his National Arts Club studio in New York in 1954. As the U.S. Army's official portrait painter in both world wars, he recorded on canvas 142 officers of the AEF including General John J. Pershing and his staff; also many "doughboys" who had been cited for heroism in World War I, and several officers of the Allies including Marshal Ferdinand Foch. These 142 oil portraits are in the permanent collection of the National Museum at the Smithsonian Institution in Washington, D.C.; he also painted portraits of thirty-one generals who commanded the U.S. Army and those of the general staff and ten Congressional Medal of Honor winners in World War II.

He is emeritus professor of art at Hunter College, New York, and is the author of seven books including *Soldiers All, An Artist Talks About Color, My Friends Look Good To Me* (1933) and *My Friends Look Better Than Ever* (1950). In his long career he has recorded on canvas many hundreds of notable Americans of the twentieth century, including five Presidents of the United States, ambassadors, educators, actors, and industrialists, in addition to military leaders.

Joseph Cummings Chase is a "down-Easter," born in Kents Hill, Maine on May 5, 1878 to Alden Fitzroy and Louisa (Allen) Chase. He is a descendant of Aquilla Chase and his wife, first settlers in Newburyport, Massachusetts in 1639. "Not relishing the blue laws," said Chase, "my ancestor soon left and traveled by oxcart to Woodstock, Maine." Joseph attended the local schools and prepared for an art career at Pratt Institute, New York, the Pennsylvania Academy of Fine Arts in Philadelphia and at the Académie Julien in Paris, where he was a pupil of Jean Paul Laurens.

Moving to New York he "covered" prize fights, famous trials, political conventions and meetings at the Waldorf for three metropolitan dailies, did magazine and book illustrations and sketched many famous personalities. His work became known and as early as 1910 he turned his talent and energy to portrait painting and was sought by men and women in the theatrical and musical worlds, in business and government. He had a studio atop the Hotel Chelsea for thirty-seven years, and in 1944 moved to a studio apartment at the National Arts Club on Gramercy Park "so as to be next door to his favorite club, The Players."

As head of the art department of Hunter College of the City of New York, Chase influenced many art students and art teachers. During this period he wrote *Decorative Design* (1915) and *Drawing Made Easy* (1919).

In *The Romance of an Art Career* (J. H. Sears, 1928) Chase wrote, "I am very much alive to the design element of the picture, the relationship of the masses to each other, the relationship of one color to another. . . . It may have likeness, but without art design, it will prove to be a picture unpleasant to live with." This book was based, in part, on a series of articles appearing in the *Saturday Evening Post* in 1927.

Another helpful book for art students was *An Artist Talks About Color* (Wiley, 1930). Palettes of leading artists of the day were shown. Chase's own palette for portraits consists of rose madder, Chinese vermilion, cadmium organe, lemon yellow (or cadmium yellow light), yellow ochre, ultramarine blue (or cobalt blue), emeraude green (or Talens green) burnt umber and zinc white.

One of the most productive periods of Chase's career occurred during World War I when General John J. Pershing cabled for a portrait painter to illustrate the historical record, and the U.S. Government's Art Committee headed by Charles Dana Gibson commissioned him as AEF portrait painter. He painted 142 portraits of generals and war heroes, covering the fronts by automobile. He used five cars; four of them were demolished with him inside. Two chauffeurs were killed.

All of these paintings were used in the Fifth Liberty Loan Drive and were displayed in so many shop windows on Fifth Avenue that it was dubbed "Chase Avenue."

Through reproductions and text Chase tells the story of these war days in his book *Soldiers All* (1920) prefaced by a letter from a colonel in the historical branch of the War Department in which he concludes, "More than any American artist, Joseph Cummings Chase has succeeded in preserving the likenesses of the foremost officers and men of the AEF—a task that was made possible by the personal interest of General Pershing."

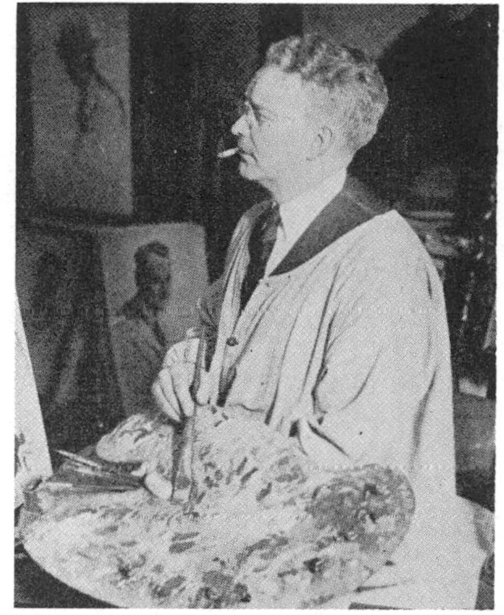

JOSEPH CUMMINGS CHASE

All his busy life Chase has been asked that question, "How long does it take to do a portrait?" He gave the answer in a recent article in the *American Artist* (May 1954), "The number of sittings varies with the sitter and other conditions. I used to plan upon two or three sittings of three hours each. With a direct attack three or four sittings are likely to be enough, but no one likes to promise. I prefer seven or eight hours for the first sitting." This vividly contrasts the conditions under which he painted in World War I when the average time allowed was only two hours and the studio was "sometimes a fine chateau, sometimes a dugout, sometimes a shack in the devastated area, sometimes a castle on the Moselle or on the Rhine. The painting was done at any hour of the day or night as circumstances permitted, and by any light that was available—even the light of a candle."

During World War II, when Chase was again commissioned to paint portraits of U.S. generals, he did not go to the battle fronts, but thirty-two top-ranking generals and ten GI's who won the Congressional Medal of Honor visited him in his studio at the National Arts Club or in Washington, D.C. "In two respects," Chase told Ed Wallace (New York *World-Telegram,* June 7, 1948), "I found all generals alike. First of all, they are prompt, and every general told me he had the finest wife in the world."

The generals whose portraits were painted by Chase included the four generals of the Army, George C. Marshall, Henry H. Arnold, Douglas MacArthur, Dwight D. Eisenhower, and the combat generals Omar N. Bradley,

CHASE, JOSEPH CUMMINGS—*Cont.*

Mark W. Clark, J. Lawton Collins, George S. Patton, Jonathan M. Wainwright, and twenty-two others; also ten Congressional Medal of Honor soldiers selected from the list of 289, one-half of whom were killed in action.

When General Eisenhower was looking at Chase's portrait of Sergeant Joseph E. Schaefer, a Medal of Honor winner, he commented: "You know, I pinned a lot of medals on little fellows like that who did more than anybody else to win that war."

The five Presidents of the United States whose faces Chase recorded on canvas were Theodore Roosevelt, Woodrow Wilson, Warren G. Harding, Franklin Delano Roosevelt and Dwight D. Eisenhower. Among those whose portraits he has painted are Charles Coburn, Dorothy Stickney, Kathleen Norris, Gladys Swarthout, Helen Wills, Jascha Heifetz, Owen D. Young, John D. Rockefeller, Jr., and Sir Cedric Hardwicke.

Many a theatrical star's portrait has been painted by him in a dressing room backstage or first sketched in a seat out front. Loved and admired by the stage folk, he was acclaimed by them at an exhibition of 153 of his portraits of stage personalities at the Los Angeles Museum in 1943.

That Chase loves to paint is felt by all who come in contact with him. As a person understanding human nature he asks his sitter to work with him. He invites the family in while the portrait is being painted and encourages them to make suggestions (*American Artist,* May 1954).

Chase has never lost the zest for his work or for people. "For the portrait painter every moment is a crucial moment," he said, "and his nerves tingle with the necessity of snatching the mood and the changing expression of his sitter. . . . Every sitter presents a new problem. There is no formula for procedure. Beginning a portrait is always a new attack."

His book *My Friends Look Better Than Ever* (Longmans, 1950) is a second volume of anecdotes and reminiscences, a sequel to *My Friends Look Good To Me* (Sears, 1933).

H. I. Brock commented (New York *Times,* January 21, 1951), "Some anecdotes are familiar and cherished by the group of elders who are sharers in Joe's memories. . . . Yet there are many that are new and enrich the store. And all are interwoven with tributes of admiration, affection and understanding."

In 1945 he married Cora E. Binzel, a professor at Cornell University. They now reside in Milwaukee, Wisconsin. He is a member of The Players, Dutch Treat Club, Eastern Arts Association, College Art Association, National Arts Club, and American Artists Professional League. Chase is five feet seven inches in height, weighs 170 pounds, has "blue-gray" eyes and "blond-white" hair. He says that he usually votes Republican and his religious affiliation is "any and all churches."

The new canvas on the easel looks "just as frightening" to Chase as it did fifty years ago. An artist friend asked him, "Joe, does it get easier?" to which Chase replied, "Always it gets harder," and both artists agreed that if they could be satisfied with what they used to do, it might get easy, but they "keep on demanding more of ourselves."

References

Am Artist 18:44+ My '54
N Y Times p13 Ag 19 '47
N Y World-Telegram Je 7 '48
Who's Who in America, 1954-55
Who's Who in American Art (1953)
Who's Who in New York, 1952
World Biography (1954)

CHIDLAW, BENJAMIN W(ILEY) Dec. 18, 1900- United States Air Force officer

Address: c/o Department of Defense, Washington 25, D.C.

When the Continental Air Defense Command was created on September 1, 1954, General Benjamin W. Chidlaw was assigned by Secretary of Defense Charles E. Wilson as its commander in chief. The new command which is charged with providing the air defense of the United States includes Army, Navy, Marine Corps, and National Guard units as well as those of the Air Force.

A specialist in aeronautical engineering, Chidlaw supervised the design and construction of the first American jet aircraft during World War II. In that period he also participated in directing campaigns in southern France and Italy. In 1951 he was appointed to head the Air Defense Command, which was designated one of the three "major commands" by the Air Force Organization Act of 1951.

In June 1955 General Chidlaw retired, after thirty-three years of active duty. General Earle Partridge (see *C.B.* 1955) was named his successor.

Born to William Matson and Margaret May (Johnson) Chidlaw on December 18, 1900, Benjamin Wiley Chidlaw is a native of Cleves, Ohio. After being graduated from Woodward High School in Cincinnati, Benjamin worked as a railroad yardman. He was appointed to the U.S. Military Academy at West Point and received the B.S. degree and was commissioned a second lieutenant in the Air Service in 1922.

Lieutenant Chidlaw was sent to Brooks Field, Texas for primary flight training and then to the Air Corps Advanced Flying School at Kelly Field, Texas, from which he was graduated in 1924. He remained at Kelly Field for a while as a flying instructor before proceeding to Clark Field in the Philippine Islands to join the 3d Pursuit Squadron. In October 1926 Chidlaw returned to Brooks Field. He became a first lieutenant in 1927 and in the following year was made assistant staging commander and final check pilot. The officer attended the Air Corps Engineering School at Wright Field, Ohio and was graduated in 1931. For the next five years, Lieutenant Chidlaw remained at

Wright Field as project officer of the training and transport aircraft branch of the Air Corps Matériel Division.

"During his early flying days," stated the New York *Times* (August 9, 1954), "he experimented with and was instrumental in the development of the turbo-supercharger, the mechanism that opened the upper sky to pilots, and the retractable landing gear." He also "helped develop the first controllable-pitch propeller" and in the 1930's "worked on a four-engine bomber" which was the forerunner of the B-17 Flying Fortress.

In 1935 Chidlaw was promoted to the rank of captain. He was graduated from the Air Corps Tactical School at Maxwell Field, Alabama in 1936 and from the Command and General Staff School at Fort Leavenworth, Kansas one year latter. Transferred to Langley Field, Virginia, he joined the 2d Bombardment Group and later became assistant chief of staff for matériel at General Headquarters, Langley Field.

Captain Chidlaw was assigned to the supply division of the office of the Chief of the Air Corps in March 1939. He was later transferred to the matériel division as chief of the experimental engineering branch and was promoted to the rank of major (permanent) in July 1940, lieutenant colonel (temporary) in September 1941, and brigadier general (temporary) in 1942.

According to the New York *Times* (August 9, 1954), early in World War II General Henry H. ("Hap") Arnold, commanding general of the Army Air Forces, asked Chidlaw what he knew about the design and construction of jet airplanes. Chidlaw replied that he did not know much about it. "Well, you'd better find out," Arnold said and placed Chidlaw in charge of building a jet airplane within a year.

The first American jet plane, a kerosene-burning Bell fighter was in the air within thirteen months, although its existence was kept secret until a joint American-British announcement was made in January 1944. Chidlaw was one of the first pilots of the jet-propelled plane. For his part in its development, the officer was awarded the Legion of Merit.

As chief of the matériel division in the office of the Assistant Chief of Air Staff for matériel, maintenance and distribution, Chidlaw represented the U.S. Army Air Forces on several RAF-AAF joint technical meetings. In April 1944 Chidlaw was assigned to the Mediterranean theater as Deputy Commander of the 12th Tactical Air Command. He helped plan and direct the air attack which made possible the break-through of American ground forces at Cassino in Italy. After participating in the invasion of southern France, he "organized and commanded the 22d Tactical Air Command which supported the Fifth Army's drive up the Italian peninsula." Allied Army Headquarters at Rome announced early in October 1944 that Chidlaw had "assumed command of the United States 12th Air Force Fighter Command."

U. S. Air Force

GEN. BENJAMIN W. CHIDLAW

In April 1945 Chidlaw became a major general (temporary) and commander of the Mediterranean Allied Tactical Air Forces, composed of the American 12th Air Force, the British Desert Air Force and associated service elements. General Arnold, who was in Italy at that time, told of having seen Chidlaw's fliers and the Fifth Army "in action together" and said both were "magnificent." Chidlaw is credited with having flown nineteen combat missions before the end of the war.

For his service during World War II, the general was awarded the Distinguished Service Medal, Air Medal and Bronze Star Medal. His foreign honors are the French Legion of Honor and Croix de Guerre with Palm, Brazilian Order of the Southern Cross and Aeronautical Medal of Merit, and Polish Cross of Valor. He was made a Commander of the Order of the British Empire.

Upon the surrender of the German forces in the Mediterranean, the general was appointed deputy commanding general for operations of the Air Technical Service Command (later redesignated Air Matériel Command) at Wright Field. Chidlaw, who was promoted to lieutenant general (temporary) on October 1, 1947, was named by President Harry S. Truman on August 17, 1949 as commanding general of the Air Matériel Command.

Transferred to Ent Air Force Base, Colorado Springs, Colorado, Chidlaw became commanding general of the Air Defense Command beginning July 28, 1951 and a "four star" general (temporary) on October 29. The Air Defense Command is specifically "charged with intercepting an enemy attack through radar detection and dispatch of fighter craft" (New York *Times,* January 29, 1952). It has "operational control" over the Army Antiaircraft Command.

(Continued next page)

CHIDLAW, BENJAMIN W.—*Continued*

When "Operation Skywatch," covering 6,000 posts in twenty-seven states and using Civilian Air Defense "spotters" was undertaken on July 14, 1952, the results were only "half effective," because there were only about 150,000 volunteers instead of a needed 500,000. Afterward, General Chidlaw pointed out that since "radar, like television, operated on a line-of-sight principle," there were many areas with "no detection capabilities" because of the earth's curvature. "Unless there is an adequate corps of civilian watchers on the ground," he warned, "aircraft can fly undetected through these areas."

In conjunction with Air Vice-Marshal A. L. James of the Royal Canadian Air Command, the American general directed "Exercise Signpost," a training maneuver which took place at the end of July 1952. Military personnel and civilian volunteers participated and about 2,000 planes were used in connection with simulated attacks on New York, Washington and other cities.

On January 1, 1953 it was announced that "hundreds of U.S. Air Force men" were already "moving into Canada to man radar stations . . . built . . . to cover the routes Russian bombers would use if they were to attack American cities" (New York *Herald Tribune,* January 3, 1953).

A radical change occurred in the thinking of Air Force policy makers who had emphasized long-range bombing potential after sixty Soviet T-39 jet bombers had flown in perfect formation over Moscow. The Soviet T-39's and T-37's are able to fly 600 miles per hour and are believed to be capable of reaching any target in the United States. It was known also that the U.S.S.R. had about 1,200 TU-4 heavy bombers stationed at new bases in the Arctic (*Time,* December 20, 1954).

The Department of Defense, accordingly, created in August the Continental Air Defense Command, a "setup similar to a war theater command," which would "give the Air Force direct control of Army and Navy detection, warning and defense units" including "the Army's growing system of 'Nike' antiaircraft missiles" (John D. Morris in the New York *Times,* August 4, 1954). General Chidlaw was named to the new command, with headquarters at Ent Air Base in Colorado Springs, where he was also to continue as head of the Air Defense Command, which he had built up to "about 2,000 jet fighter interceptors on round-the-clock alert" (New York *Times,* August 9, 1954).

The Air Force disclosed on August 11, 1954 that a large number of "radar warning platforms" and "helicopter landing fields" are to be constructed at sea. These will be "an adaptation of the so-called 'Texas Towers' on which numerous successful oil well rigs have been constructed."

General Chidlaw and his associates, however, had no illusions that these would provide 100 per cent protection. Elie Abel (New York *Times,* November 21, 1954) said that the general has "little patience with officers who underestimate Soviet progress in weapons technology." The "guiding precept" at Continental Air Defense Headquarters, this writer stated, was that even "an air defense system 90 per cent effective in blunting a thermonuclear attack on the United States might not be good enough to guarantee national survival."

If the enemy was willing "to risk 500 planes" with hydrogen bombs, "fifty might get through to their targets." Thus "the important question . . . is not how high a percentage of enemy planes can be shot down but how much destruction compressed in a brief period the country can stand and still keep going."

The New York *Times* (August 9, 1954) described General Chidlaw as "a quiet man" whose "military bearing . . . makes him look even bigger than his six-foot-quarter-inch, 190-pound frame". The general is gray-haired and wears horn-rimmed glasses. His Air Force ratings are "command pilot" and "combat observer." He is credited with "the knack of getting others to get things done." For recreation he enjoys squash and golf; he plays in the middle 70's. The general is a member of the Quiet Birdmen. Benjamin W. Chidlaw married his boyhood sweetheart, Lillian Marie Braun, on May 1, 1923. The couple has one son, Ben Evan.

References

Gen Army 2:10+ Ap '54 por
N Y Times p7 O 6 '44 por; p6 Ag 18 '49 por; p8 Ag 9 '54
Time 64:15+ D 20 '54 por

International World Who's Who (1949)
Who's Who in America, 1954-55

CHILDS, RICHARD S(PENCER) May 24, 1882- Business executive; organization official

Address: b. c/o National Municipal League, 47 E. 68th St., New York 21; h. 149 E. 73d St., New York 21

Known as the "father" of the city-manager plan of municipal government, and also of the short ballot principle, Richard S. Childs has combined the career of business executive with that of civic reformer and publicist. He has been, successively, general manager of the Bon Ami Company, an associate of A. E. Chew in the export business, an officer of the American Cyanamid Company, and the executive vice-president of the Lederle Laboratories. He was chairman of the Citizens Union from 1943 to 1950. He is the author of *Short-Ballot Principles* (Houghton Mifflin, 1911), and *Civic Victories* (Harper, 1952). In 1954 Childs was the recipient of the La Guardia Memorial Association Award. For many years he has been chairman of the executive committee of the National Municipal League. He is a well-known figure in New York City, "but he is also known throughout the nation for his influence on better municipal government."

Childs' city administration plan, now known as the council-manager plan, is "the fastest growing form of local government in the United States today," wrote Bernard Cutler (New York *Herald Tribune*, February 23, 1952). "It has been widely praised as the most workable way of running a city by both political scientists and voters in the communities where it has been tried." According to estimates made in 1955 by the National Municipal League, 1,269 communities and counties have adopted the plan, 40 per cent of American cities have come under it, and 25,000,000 people are governed by it.

Richard Spencer Childs, the son of William Hamlin and Nellie (Spencer) Childs, was born on May 24, 1882 in Manchester, Connecticut. William Childs, in partnership with his cousin, founded the Bon Ami Company, and made a fortune of $5,000,000. When Richard was ten the family moved to Brooklyn, New York, where the boy received his early education, and was graduated in 1900 from the Polytechnic Preparatory School. He went on to Yale University, and was graduated in 1904 with the A.B. degree.

Having a predilection for both business and writing, Childs first took employment with the Erickson Advertising Agency. At the outset of his business career his work as a publicist also began. Upon graduation he cast his first vote and was, in his own words, "mortified" to learn that he had to ballot for nineteen candidates, only four of whom he had ever heard of before. He was astonished by the fact that his father knew no more than he did in this matter.

"I decided then that the trouble with our municipal governments was not the voters' apathy," he has said. "The trouble was that the ballot was too long." From an office adjoining that of the advertising agency and with a staff of two, Childs began to advocate a form of ballot which would not "disfranchise" voters by confronting them with candidates for a multiplicity of petty offices. Making use of experience gained from advertising work, Childs began a campaign of pamphleteering, circulating an essay he had written embodying his ideas.

"He had been out of college only four years when he published an article in the *Outlook* called 'The Short Ballot,'" the New York *Times* commented in an editorial on December 11, 1954. "This was the beginning of a mission that he pursued with a gift of zeal and a talent for clarity of argument that have not dwindled to this moment." Among the outstanding citizens of the day who gave immediate support to Childs' program were Theodore Roosevelt and Charles Evans Hughes. The Short Ballot Organization, with Woodrow Wilson as president and Childs as secretary, came into existence in 1910. A year later, Childs' book, *Short-Ballot Principles*, was published.

At about this time he read an editorial in which the writer argued that the commission form of municipal government, then coming to the fore, was just like a business corporation. "I sputtered that it was not like a business corporation at all," Childs has said, "for if it

Pach Bros.

RICHARD S. CHILDS

were, there would be a manager under the board of directors, instead of having the board members each undertaking the management of a separate department."

Shortly after this, Childs had occasion to order the drafting of a bill which would make the commission plan available by local referendum to upstate New York cities. The office of city manager was drafted into the bill at Childs' instigation. However, the idea was rejected. Soon after, Childs read that the Board of Trade of Lockport, New York had appointed a committee to look into the commission plan. He wrote to them saying that they might have the bill, already prepared, to introduce as their own in the 1911 legislature. They accepted, and Childs then offered to write a pamphlet in support of the plan, which he would have printed and mailed at his own expense, over the signature of the Lockport Board of Trade. This also was accepted, and the promotion of the city-manager form of municipal government was under way.

The Lockport charter was not approved by the Legislature, but the widespread publicity given to the manager plan led to its adoption by the town of Sumter, South Carolina in 1912. Again, Childs offered to carry the expense of a publicity campaign anonymously, which he did. In 1913, Dayton, Ohio became the first sizable American city to engage a city manager. "After that," Childs has said, "the sweep of the council-manager plan across the country couldn't be stopped. It was all accomplished in the brief period between 1910, when I concocted the plan and planted it in Lockport, to 1914, when City Manager Henry M. Waite in Dayton began startling the country by the progressiveness of his administration."

Childs entered his family business in 1911, becoming general manager of the Bon Ami Company. Except for time off as a dollar-a-

CHILDS, RICHARD S.—*Continued*

year man for the War Department in 1918, he was general manager until 1920. He became associated in 1921 with A. E. Chew in the export business, being assistant to the president from 1928 to 1935. In 1929 he became a director of the American Cyanamid Company, and from 1944 to 1947 a member of the general staff. He served as executive vice-president of its subsidiary, the Lederle Laboratories from 1935 until his retirement in 1944.

Throughout the active years of his business career, Childs continued his work for the short ballot and the council-manager plan as well as engaging in numerous other civic-reform activities. According to Frederick Woltman of the New York *World-Telegram and Sun* (January 8, 1955), Childs "headed up at one time or another just about every civic organization of note in the city." Among the numerous positions he has filled are: president (1928-1940) of the City Club; chairman of the Citizens Union; vice-president of the American Political Science Association; and chairman of the board of the Institute of Public Administration.

For more than thirty years Childs has served continuously on the council of the National Municipal League; from 1927 to 1931 he was its president and has since been chairman of its executive committee. Since his retirement, Childs is a full-time volunteer worker for the league. In his second book, *Civic Victories,* (Harper, 1952), Childs explains the objectives of the organization. In general, it aims "to carry toward complete coverage the council-manager plan of municipal and county government . . . simplify the internal organizations, as well as tasks ([curtail] opportunities for mischief) of political party managements . . . get rid of obscure elective offices everywhere and bring the few elective offices that remain into the comparative safety of focused public scrutiny."

Commenting on this book, W. D. Ogdon wrote in the New York *Times* (January 11, 1953) that its "breadth defies brief summary and so does its usefulness. It is practical politics. It should be meat and drink for the college student, the citizen who wants to know how to go about improving his home town, the state legislator who thinks there may be a better way of doing things, but who wants tested ideas." H. S. Buttenheim wrote in the *Annals of the American Academy of Political and Social Science* (September 1953): "Here is a book that will be an inspiration to many a young man and woman looking forward to a career in civic or public service; and it will help to give courage and guidance to citizens' organizations . . . that have not yet modernized their election and administrative machinery." E. W. Weidner stated in the *American Political Science Review* (June 1953), "While the argument pursued is not always consistent. . ., *Civic Victories* remains an important and worth-while volume. It is the best statement of local reform politics to date."

The 1,269 communities and counties which have now adopted the council-manager plan of government vary in size, ranging from Teterboro, New Jersey, with a population of twenty-eight, to Cincinnati with its 504,000 population. Maine, with a hundred and eleven, leads all other states in the number of council-manager communities. California is second with ninety-six.

Richard Childs married Grace P. Hatch of Chicago on June 15, 1912. Three daughters were born to them, one now deceased. Childs belongs to Phi Gamma Delta fraternity and the Yale and City clubs. He is a Presbyterian and a Republican. He is five feet ten inches tall, weighs 165 pounds, and has blue eyes. Among his hobbies are golf and yachting. In announcing that Childs would receive the La Guardia Memorial Association Award in December 1954, Newbold Morris, chairman of the association, said: "Mr. Childs' extraordinary record of devoted public service establishes him as an outstanding figure in the long, uphill fight for better municipal government" (New York *Times*, December 11, 1954).

References

N Y Herald Tribune p10 F 28 '52
N Y Times p12 D 11 '54
N Y World-Telegram p3 Ja 8 '55 por

Childs, R. C. Civic Victories (1952)
Who's Who in America, 1952-53

CHURCHILL, SARAH Oct. 7, 1914- Actress

Address: b. c/o National Broadcasting Company, 30 Rockefeller Plaza, New York 20

Principally occupied between 1952 and 1954 as mistress of ceremonies and actress on the Sunday afternoon television program *Hallmark Hall of Fame,* the British actress Sarah Churchill has given notable performances in the roles of Florence Nightingale, Joan of Arc and Anne Bradstreet, and as Ophelia opposite Maurice Evans in *Hamlet* and as the Queen in *Richard II.* She acted the leading role in John Cecil Holm's Broadway play *Gramercy Ghost* in 1951, and in Philip Barry's play *The Philadelphia Story* on tour in 1949. She also had the lead in *Soldier's Bride* on March 20, 1955, on the Hallmark program on the NBC-TV network.

Miss Churchill played in the Metro-Goldwyn-Mayer film *Royal Wedding* (1951) and had previously appeared in three British and two Italian pictures and in numerous stage productions in London and the provinces. She served for four years in the Women's Auxiliary Air Force and was aide to her father, Sir Winston Churchill, at the Teheran, Cairo and Yalta conferences.

Sarah Churchill was born in Admiralty House, London, England on October 7, 1914, the third of four children of Sir Winston Leonard Spencer Churchill and Lady Clementine Ogilvy (Hozier) Churchill. Her grandmother was the American heiress Jennie Jerome, whose father, Leonard K. Jerome, was a Wall Street financier and part-owner of the New York *Times* during the editorship of Henry Jarvis Raymond in the 1850's. Her grandfather was Lord Randolph Churchill. Her brother, Major

Randolph Churchill, and her sister, Diana, who is Mrs. Duncan Sandys, are her elders. Her sister, Mary, who is Mrs. Christopher Soames, is younger.

At the time of Sarah Churchill's birth, her father was First Lord of the Admiralty (1911-1915) in Herbert Asquith's Cabinet. Her childhood and girlhood were divided between homes in London and the Churchill country estate at Westerham in Kent, and between periods of attendance first at the Notting Hill High School for Girls in London and North Foreland Lodge at the seaside in Broadstairs.

With the consent of her mother and her father (who nicknamed her "Mule" because of her obstinacy), Sarah "went to a sort of semi-school in Paris" for eighteen months, then a professional school in London for two years. "We did all kinds of dancing—ballet, tap, and folk dances," she has said. "We worked five hours a day, and there wasn't a bone in my body that didn't ache at night" (*Scholastic*).

Early in 1936 Sarah Churchill sought an audition with the London producer Charles B. Cochran, then casting for a new revue. She introduced herself as Sarah Smith, but was recognized by Cochran, who agreed to engage her if she could obtain the consent of her parents. Her father had no objection, providing that "Miss Smith" would not be unduly exploited. Cochran obliged by having all the girls in his chorus wear identical red wigs, making it difficult for audiences to identify the red-haired "Smith" girl as Churchill's daughter. The revue in which she made her stage debut was *Follow the Sun*, which opened at the Adelphi Theatre in London on February 4, 1936. Miss Churchill also understudied one of the principals, the American actress, Claire Luce.

Another American (naturalized) in the company of *Follow the Sun* was the actor Vic Oliver (born Viktor Samek in Vienna), whom Miss Churchill married on December 24, 1936 at the Municipal Building in New York City. She made her first New York appearance at Loew's State Theatre as a $100-a-week dancer in Oliver's own vaudeville revue *Follow the Stars*. After two years in London cabaret shows and in vaudeville Miss Churchill decided to become a dramatic actress, and acted in repertory and experimental theatre for about three years.

She appeared in over thirty different roles, including Lucrezia in *Mandragola* (at Ashley Dukes's little Mercury Theatre in London in December 1939), Hypatia Tarleton in Shaw's *Misalliance* (at the Embassy, London in January 1940) and Ann in a revival of Sutton Vane's *Outward Bound* at the New Theatre, London in August 1940. In her husband's revue *Plays and Music*, she performed the balcony scene from *Romeo and Juliet* and played the same scene opposite Leslie Howard in a British Broadcasting Corporation radio performance. The Prime Minister's actress-daughter (Winston Churchill had succeeded Neville Chamberlain as Premier about one year earlier) was seen in the title role of J. M. Barrie's *Mary Rose* (as revived at the suburban "Q"

SARAH CHURCHILL

Theatre at Kew Bridge near London in July 1941). She made her first film, *He Found a Star*, in 1940.

Enlisting for World War II service in the Women's Auxiliary Air Force in October 1941, Miss Churchill specialized in photo and map interpretation. She also attended the Teheran and Cairo conferences of late 1943 and the Yalta Conference of February 1945 as her father's official Air Force aide.

Demobilized on November 30, 1945, Miss Churchill joined a repertory theatre at Henley-on-Thames and was seen in *Squaring the Triangle*. She played her first dramatic "lead," on tour in England as the persecuted Mrs. Manningham in a revival of Patrick Hamilton's *Gas Light*, known in the United States as *Angel Street*. Her effective performance in the British film *Spring Meeting* led to an American film offer, but after a visit to Hollywood she declined it. Her first postwar picture, filmed in Italy in the fall of 1946, was the Vicandro film *When in Rome* followed by the Universalia film *Daniele Cortis*, released in 1947. This led to a British film contract with Alexander Korda and she appeared in *All Over the Town*, her first picture to be released in the United States. A New York *Times* reviewer described her performance as a reporter on a rural newspaper as "alert and pleasantly poised." In May 1948 Miss Churchill was seen at the Garrick Theatre in London as Henrietta in a revival of Rudolf Besier's *The Barretts of Wimpole Street*. She appeared at the "Q" Theatre as Rowena Weatherby in a "try-out" of Roland Pertwee's play *The House on the Sand* on April 21, 1949.

Her picture was on the cover of *Life* on May 23, 1949, and an appearance on the Tex McCrary and Jinx Falkenburg show led to her being offered the role of Tracy Lord opposite Jeffrey Lynn in a revival of Philip Barry's *The Philadelphia Story* for a Theatre Guild tour.

CHURCHILL, SARAH—*Continued*

The play opened at the McCarter Theatre in Princeton, New Jersey on June 27, 1949. Her sixteen-week tour of the summer playhouses ended at Atlanta, Georgia early in October.

Miss Churchill, who had been divorced from Vic Oliver in 1945, was married to the British photographer Antony Beauchamp (pronounced "beecham") at Sea Island, Georgia on October 18, 1949. In November she began a transcontinental tour in *The Philadelphia Story* which wound up in California in the following spring. Under contract to Metro-Goldwyn-Mayer, she then supported Fred Astaire and Jane Powell in the musical *Royal Wedding.* Reviewing this film for the New York *World-Telegram and Sun* on March 9, 1951, Alton Cook paid tribute to Miss Churchill's "winsome dignity and charm" in the role of an English chorus girl, and predicted that "she would be an amusing comedienne if a witty role ever came her way."

On April 26, 1951 Miss Churchill made her first appearance on the New York legitimate stage, being seen at the Morosco Theatre as Nancy Willard in John Cecil Holm's play *Gramercy Ghost.* "Miss Churchill gives an adroit and mettlesome performance in a genuine comic style," was the comment of Brooks Atkinson in the New York *Times.*

She made her television debut on October 7, 1951, when Hall Brothers, Inc., manufacturers of "Hallmark" greeting cards, sponsored over CBS-TV the first of the fifteen-minute Sunday afternoon programmes entitled *Hallmark Presents Sarah Churchill.* "It emerged as one of those intimate little 'guest-interview' shows," stated *Variety,* which noted that "on hand as . . . initial guest was Mrs. Eleanor Roosevelt." Sharman Douglas and Samuel Goldwyn were among subsequent guests in the series, which lasted until the end of the year.

The sponsors then decided to transfer their popular *Hallmark Playhouse* from radio to television and Miss Churchill was engaged as "hostess" or mistress of ceremonies for the new series, *Hallmark Hall of Fame.* Although the program made a rather inauspicious beginning on NBC-TV on Sunday, January 6, 1952, with *Dr. Serocold,* the quality of the plays soon greatly improved. *Variety* characterized as a "fine job" Miss Churchill's portrayal of Florence Nightingale on February 3. When Miss Churchill appeared as Anne Bradstreet, the New York *World-Telegram and Sun* television critic Harriet Van Horne was able to report on "a fine moving play . . . altogether a worthy vehicle" for the Churchill personality and talent. "She's a thorough professional, the Prime Minister's daughter," Miss Van Horne wrote. "Her competence is of the quiet kind. She never overplays her scenes. And she speaks and moves with the sure grace that comes of theatre training."

Television history was made on April 26, 1953, when the *Hall of Fame* presented, after three weeks of rehearsal and an expenditure of $180,000, a two-hour TV performance of *Hamlet,* with Maurice Evans as the Prince of Denmark. Miss Churchill was "surprisingly effective" as Ophelia (*Time*) and "managed some touching effects" in the mad scene (John Beaufort in the *Christian Science Monitor*). In the second *Hall of Fame* two-hour Shakespearean presentation *Richard II,* on January 24, 1954, Miss Churchill played the Queen to the Richard of Maurice Evans and was praised for a "very distinguished performance" (John Crosby in the New York *Herald Tribune*).

"Sarah looks as little like John Bull as anyone I know," stated Bob Willett in an article appearing in the Canadian weekly *Saturday Night.* "Standing five feet five inches, she has a graceful, well-proportioned figure, . . . inquisitive green eyes and a patrician profile. Her classic features are said to resemble those of her paternal grandmother." She has (Kate Cameron has remarked) the "same slender, long frame" as Lady Churchill, while the shade of her russet or auburn hair is very close to that of her famous father in his young manhood. "She enjoys traveling," wrote Mary Braggiotti in the New York *Post,* "and is glad to be in a profession that often demands it. . . . She also likes to dance; to read biography, poetry and current books; and to play tennis." Her greatest taste delight is eating avocado pears, and she enjoys cooking and "the sandwich life" in America.

She believes that television audiences show a real appreciation for serious drama. Her fan mail has been heaviest after productions like *Hamlet,* and much comes from high school students. "I suppose the stage is my first love," Miss Churchill admits, "but I do think TV is good for Shakespeare. The listener can hear all the words . . . in the close-up treatment of TV" (*Scholastic*).

References

Cue 18:15 S 3 '49 por; 20:15+ Ap 21 '51
Life 26:77-8+ My 23 '49 pors
N Y Herald Tribune p23 My 16 '50 por; V p3 My 28 '50 por
N Y Times p6 Mr 29 '45; p24 O 18 '49 por; II p5 Jl 2 '50
Saturday Night 69:13+ F 6 '54
Scholastic 63:6 D 9 '53 por
TV Guide 4:20 D 7 '51 por
Time 45:72 Ap 9 '45
Who's Who in the Theatre (1952)
Winchester's Screen Encyclopedia (1948)

CISLER, WALKER (LEE) Oct. 8, 1897-

Utilities executive

Address: b. c/o Detroit Edison Co., 2,000 2d Ave., Detroit 26, Mich.; h. 1,071 Devonshire Rd., Grosse Pointe Park, Mich.

The president and director of the Detroit Edison Company, one of the largest power companies in the United States, is Walker Cisler, who has been described as "an executive's executive of the highest level." Cisler joined the company in 1943 in a technical capacity, became an executive vice-president in 1948, and was promoted to his present posts in 1951. For nineteen years earlier he had been associated with the Public Service Electric & Gas Company of New Jersey. The Detroit Edison Company and subsidiaries reported gross revenues for the fiscal year ending May 31, 1955 as $204,808,923, compared with $193,277,657 in 1954.

Cisler has been a consultant to the U.S. Army, the Department of State, the Atomic Energy Commission, and the National Security Resources Board, and to the Mexican government. He has also been chief consultant on electric power to the Economic Cooperation Administration, Mutual Security Administration, and Foreign Operations Administration. In recent years he has been particularly interested in the peaceful possibilities of atomic energy and is the president of the Atomic Industrial Forum, the Fund for Peaceful Atomic Development, and the Atomic Power Development Associates. The latter group authorized a budget of $3,815,000 for 1955 "for research and development toward finding economically practical means of using nuclear fuels in generating electric power" (New York *Times,* February 2, 1955) and is planning to build a 100,000-kilowatt nuclear power plant, at a cost of $45,000,000, to be ready in 1958.

The son of Louis H. and Sara S. (Walker) Cisler, Walker Lee Cisler was born on October 8, 1897 in Marietta, Ohio, and spent his early years near West Chester, Pennsylvania. He was graduated from Cornell University in Ithaca, New York, where he played football and ran track, and earned keys from two honor societies, Tau Beta Pi and Phi Kappa Phi.

He received an M.E. degree in 1922, and went to work as a cadet engineer for the Public Service Electric & Gas Company of Newark, New Jersey. He rose steadily during his association with the company, becoming a test engineer in 1924, assistant chief engineer in 1926, planning and installation engineer in 1930, general superintendent of generation in 1935, assistant general manager of the electrical department in 1936, and assistant chief engineer of that department in 1938.

According to *Fortune* (March 1952), Cisler seemed to be in 1941 "one of those many competent engineers who make a career of working in a utility, where seniority counts heavily in promotion and most employees have a sense of security as their chief reward. The very fact that Cisler was loaned in mid-1941 to a pre-Pearl Harbor defense agency . . . indicates that his superiors considered him slightly expendable."

In the months preceding U.S. entry into World War II, however, and during the war as well, Cisler demonstrated uncommon executive talent. As head of what came to be the equipment production branch of the Office of War Utilities, War Production Board, from September 1941 until October 1943, he helped to mobilize electric power for national defense by inducing manufacturers of electrical equipment to integrate their production schedules with the needs of the defense program. Within two years he had solved the major problems of his assignment, and accepted an offer to become chief engineer of power plants for the Detroit Edison Company.

Detroit Edison Co.
WALKER CISLER

Before he could begin his new job, however, Secretary of War Henry L. Stimson "asked him to join the Army and rebuild power plants right behind the Allied armies in North Africa, Sicily, and Italy. That he did. . ." Subsequently, with the rank of colonel and as chief of the public utilities section of SHAEF (Supreme Headquarters, Allied Expeditionary Forces), on the staff of General Dwight D. Eisenhower, he worked on the rehabilitation of other European power systems.

The "most dramatic" of his achievements in this connection, as *Business Week* (December 1, 1951) phrased it, was his work in Paris. Having learned from underground sources that when the Germans moved out of the city there would be no fuel for power, he devised a plan for relaying power over a badly damaged transmission line from hydro installations in southern France held by resistance troops. "He organized fast-moving repair teams. Then he had Air Force planes fly reconnaissance over the line to find out where it was damaged. Whenever a section of the line fell into Allied hands, a team would move in and fix it. The first Allied troops arrived in Paris toward the end of August 1944. By September 6 Cisler's power was flowing into the city."

Until December 1945 Cisler served in Europe and then he returned to the Detroit Edison Company, where he was chief engineer of power plants until 1947. The next year he became an executive vice-president. He was made chairman of Edison Electric Institute's electric power survey committee. Meanwhile, he served as a member of the public utilities panel that prepared the electric power program developed under the Marshall Plan.

As chief power expert of the ECA, he investigated the program of power rehabilitation in nine European countries, including Greece, in 1949. He was executive secretary of the

CISLER, WALKER—*Continued*

AEC Industrial Advisory Group in 1947 and 1948. In September 1951 he was chosen a director of the Detroit company, and in December, succeeded James W. Parker as president of the firm.

"Seldom, if ever before," remarked *Electrical World* (December 10, 1951), "has an electric utility replaced a president so well known in the industry with another of equal prominence." Cisler faced formidable problems of administration growing out of the company's postwar development. "Cisler must now reorganize the management," *Business Week* (December 1, 1951) reported, "create more middle-level managers, and delegate authority to them." He also presided over a four-year $237,000,000 expansion program, designed to increase the company's capacity more than 50 per cent—to 2,500,000 kilowatts, which is its capacity in 1955 (*Business Week,* March 19, 1955).

Cisler has become absorbed in the problems of the use of atomic energy for peaceful purposes, and has become one of the leading spokesmen for various interested groups. In 1953 he endorsed a National Security Resources Board recommendation that the Atomic Energy Act of 1946 be amended to allow wider industrial development of atomic power, and announced that his firm, in conjunction with the Dow Chemical Company, would use private funds to build a power reactor if legislation permitted. A few months later he suggested specific revisions of existing legislation for that purpose. The revised Atomic Energy Act (1954) provided, among other things, for encouraging private business to participate in developing industrial uses for atomic energy.

In September 1953 Cisler became a co-founder and president of the Atomic Industrial Forum, Inc., a non-profit association for those interested in the peace-time development of atomic energy by all phases of industry; the forum in July 1955 had a membership of 320 organizations and over 1,000 individuals. When President Dwight D. Eisenhower proposed in December 1953 the formation of an international atomic energy pool to be administered for peaceful purposes under the United Nations, Cisler vigorously supported the plan. He reported the following month that atomic energy represented a power potential twenty-three times greater than the present generating capacity of the country. The Atomic Industrial Forum, after collaborating with the AEC, brought out in May 1955 a comprehensive forecast on the future of private atomic energy in the United States (See the *Christian Science Monitor,* May 16, 1955 and *Time,* May 23, 1955).

In December 1954, with an initial grant of $150,000 from the Ford Foundation, the Fund for Peaceful Atomic Development, Inc., was created to "bring together foreign and American scientists, industrialists, and other individuals, serve as an information clearinghouse, and provide scholarships and training in the field of atomic energy." Cisler was chosen president of the new organization. In Cisler's own words, the fund "seeks to put to work all of the private resources available in this country and abroad so as to improve the welfare of men and women throughout the world and raise their living standards by means of atomic energy." Cisler also heads Atomic Power Development Associates, a body which comprises thirty-three electric utility, manufacturing, engineering and research companies.

Besides the connections already cited, Cisler is a director of a number of business firms, including the Holley Carburetor Company, the Detroit Bank, the Burroughs Corporation, and the Fruehauf Trailer Company. Honors conferred upon him include the American Bronze Star, the French Legion of Honor and Cross of War with Palm, the Order of the British Empire, the Netherlands Order of Orange Nassau, the Belgian Order of Leopold, and the Greek Royal Order of the Phoenix.

He is a fellow of the American Institute of Electrical Engineers and of the American Society of Mechanical Engineers (he is chairman of the ASME nuclear energy application committee), and chairman of the Michigan committee of the Newcomen Society in North America. He is also a trustee of Cornell University and of the Cranbrook Institute of Science in Bloomfield Hills, Michigan, and a member of the University of Detroit Lay Advisory Board. His clubs are the Country and Athletic of Detroit, the Metropolitan of Washington, D.C., and the Engineers' of New York.

The utilities executive married Gertrude Demuth Rippe on July 28, 1939; the Cislers have two adopted children—Richard Rippe and Jane Rippe. He is "a man who hates to waste time," *Fortune* remarked of Cisler, "he is the new businessman, one of the administrators of the new American capitalism."

References

Bsns W p72+ D 1 '51 por
Elec World 131:6 D 10 '51 por
Fortune 45:122+ Mr '52 por
N Y Herald Tribune p80 O 21 '54 por
N Y World-Telegram p17 Je 7 '52 por
Time 59:92+ Mr 10 '52 por
Who's Who in America, 1954-55
Who's Who in Commerce and Industry (1953)
Who's Who in Engineering, 1954

CLARK, PAUL F(OSTER) Nov. 19, 1892- Insurance executive

Address: b. John Hancock Mutual Life Insurance Co., 200 Berkeley St., Boston 17, Mass.; h. 485 Warren St., Brookline 46, Mass.

During his entire business career Paul F. Clark has been associated with the John Hancock Mutual Life Insurance Company, of which he was elected president in 1944, after serving for six years as vice-president. As general agent in the Boston area from 1921 to 1938, Clark led the entire company in the sale of life insurance. He has taken an active interest in the training of insurance agents, in recruiting women to sell insurance, and in the promotion of ethical standards for the profession.

The ninety-three-year-old John Hancock company set new records in total life insurance and assets during 1954, Clark announced in his annual report, made public February 15, 1955. Total insurance, he said, covered 9,300,000 individual policy owners, amounting to $15,832,-000,000, an increase of 8 per cent over the previous year. More than $1,000,000 in benefits were paid out every working day. The first "650" electronic "brain" calculator of the International Business Machines Corporation was delivered to the John Hancock company in December 1954 to be used in its extensive mortgage-accounting work.

Paul Foster Clark is a descendant of colonists from England and a relative of George Rogers Clark, the American Revolutionary frontier leader. Paul was born on November 19, 1892 in Dayton, Ohio, one of the four children of Joseph Dayton Clark, a lawyer and judge, and Lulu Helen (Foster) Clark. While attending Staunton Military Academy in Virginia, Paul worked at various jobs during the summers. After his graduation in 1911, he attended Denison University in Granville, Ohio for one year.

Clark then attended the Wharton School of Finance and Commerce, University of Pennsylvania, where he studied under Dr. S. S. Huebner, an authority on life insurance. At the school Clark was a member of the football squad, a director of the Wharton Association, and a member of Phi Delta Theta and Beta Gamma Sigma. During vacations he worked as a salesman for the Aluminum Cooking Utensil Company. Upon graduation in 1915, with a B.S. degree, he joined the insurance agency headed by his uncle Ernest J. Clark, general agent of John Hancock in Maryland and the District of Columbia.

Immediately putting into practice Huebner's theory that the great need was for a policy to protect home mortgages, Clark read lists of new mortgages each day and then called on each new home owner to urge him to purchase a policy that would pay the mortgage in the event of his death. This field of insurance selling was relatively unexplored in 1915. Clark did not hold with the "fear-of-death" technique for selling insurance. Instead, he emphasized the business prudence aspects of insurance purchasing. Within three months of joining the Baltimore office he had written $52,000 worth of insurance, a large portion of it being mortgage insurance. By 1920 Clark was selling more than $1,000,000 worth of insurance a year. During World War I he served in the U.S. Army as a lieutenant in the procurement section of the Ordinance Department.

He was invited by John Hancock in 1921 to become its general agent in Boston. Six years after taking over the Boston agency, Clark's concern was producing $20,000,000 worth of ordinary life insurance. During the seventeen years that he headed this agency, the firm was the largest agency in the company and the leader in selling life insurance. Seventy-five full-time agents were attached to Clark's firm, one-third of whom were women.

PAUL F. CLARK

Elected vice-president of John Hancock in October 1938, Clark was placed in charge of 186 district agencies which write a major share of the company's ordinary life insurance policies. He also directed the activities of the department handling group insurance. In February 1941 Clark was elected a member of the board of directors, and in December of 1944 he was named to the top executive post, succeeding Guy W. Cox.

The organization over which Clark presides has been in existence since April 21, 1862, when it became the first company in the state to be organized along the reform principles of the Massachusetts Nonforfeiture Law of 1860. Within five years of its founding, the company had $10,000,000 in life insurance on its books. In 1955 it has almost sixteen billion dollars of life insurance in force.

Like other insurance companies, the John Hancock makes some of its most important decisions when it invests the money of its policyholders. A *Fortune* article (April 1948) describes Clark as a "resourceful, forceful, well-poised person who would make a tough, quick-witted competitor in any man's business." When he is investing the company's money, however, he is conservative, regarding his company "strictly as a fiduciary or trustee, and not . . . as an entrepreneur." In April 1947 Clark, who had been considering an investment for John Hancock in a housing project in Los Angeles, decided against the investment on the grounds that Los Angeles was going through a real-estate inflation and had higher building costs than other areas in the country (*Time*, April 14, 1947).

During World War II, John Hancock's employees sold over $68,000,000 worth of war bonds. The company opened Hancock Village, a housing development of 800 homes for war

CLARK, PAUL F.—*Continued*

veterans in 1947, and two years later John Hancock's new home office in Boston was completed.

For its advertising campaign which is "built around perceptive, sensitive re-creations of the lives and ideals of great figures from American history," the John Hancock company was the first choice in 1953 of the *Saturday Review*'s First Annual Advertising Awards committee and the fourth choice in 1954 of the Second Annual Advertising Awards committee. The *Saturday Review* based its selections in part on advertising which "enlarged the reader's knowledge of our American social, cultural, or economic institutions."

Since 1927, when the American College of Life Underwriters was organized, Clark has been a trustee. Clark was chairman of the National Association of Life Underwriters in 1928-1929 and organized the association's Million Dollar Round Table to give those agents who had sold $1,000,000 worth of insurance annually an opportunity to be more closely associated. Clark was president of the American Society of Chartered Life Underwriters from 1934 to 1935 and is a director of the Life Insurance Association of America.

At the 1953 convention of the Institute of Life Insurance which elected Clark its chairman, it was announced that heart disease in all its forms, the nation's greatest killer, will cost life insurance companies $1 billion in death claims in 1953 and that "research in this field was made the first undertaking of the insurance medical research fund financed by life insurance companies" (New York *Times,* December 11, 1953). (The John Hancock company has participated in the fund since 1945.)

Paul F. Clark is a director of the First National Bank of Boston, Armour & Company, Seaboard Air Line Railroad Company, Boston Insurance Company, Freedoms Foundation, and Boston Young Men's Christian Association (member, international committee, Y.M.C.A.); a member of the board of commissioners of sinking funds of City of Boston, advisory board of the Massachusetts Investors Trust, Massachusetts Investors Second Fund, Massachusetts Investors Growth Stock Fund, Inc., committee on government expenditures of U.S. Chamber of Commerce, industrial advisory committee to the Secretary of the Treasury, and Committee to Visit the School of Public Health of Harvard University, Harvard Medical School and the School of Dental Medicine; and a trustee of the Committee for Economic Development, Protein Foundation of Harvard University, Suffolk Savings Bank, Boston Municipal Research Bureau, Baptist Home, New England Baptist Hospital, New England Deaconess Hospital, Garland School of Homemaking, Boston University, and Northeastern University; and an alumni trustee of the University of Pennsylvania.

The John Newton Russell Memorial Award for outstanding service to the institution of life insurance was presented to Clark in 1945. He received the honorary LL.D. degree from the University of Pennsylvania in 1947 and an alumni citation from Denison University in 1949. He is a fellow of the American Academy of Arts and Sciences and a member of the Newcomen Society of England.

His clubs are the Country (Brookline), Balk Peak Colony (Melvin Village, New Hampshire), Algonquin, Chicago, Commercial-Merchants (Boston) Yeamans Hall (Charleston, South Carolina), Varsity (Philadelphia), Harvard (Boston), and University of Pennsylvania Clubs of New England. He is a 32d degree Mason and a member of the Society of the Sons of the Revolution.

Anne Quast and Paul F. Clark were married on February 19, 1917. They have a daughter, Jean Quast (Clark) Boas. Their son, Paul F. Clark, Jr., died in action in 1944 while serving with the U.S. Army. Clark is a Republican and an Episcopalian. He is five feet eleven inches tall, weighs 190 pounds, and has blue eyes and gray hair. For hobbies Clark enjoys the Scottish sport of curling, golf, travel, collecting Currier prints, and reading. He has a reputation for hard work and only recently reduced his work week to six and a half days. Clark advises young people who are beginning their careers: "You must have a sense of obligation to your talents. . . . You must have character enough to create a plan and then the patience to adhere to the plan" (Boston *Post,* July 17, 1953).

References

Boston Post F 17 '47; Jl 17 '53
Eastern Underwriter p3+ D 15 '44 por
Weekly Underwriter D 12 '53 por
Who's Who in America, 1954-55
Who's Who in Commerce and Industry (1953)
Who's Who in Insurance (1955)
World Biography (1954)

CLAYTON, P(HILIP THOMAS) B(YARD), REV. Dec. 12, 1885- British clergyman; social service leader

Address: All Hallows Porch Room, Byward St., London E.C. 3, England

One of the "most senior" of the chaplains to Her Majesty Queen Elizabeth II is the Reverend P. B. Clayton, who was a chaplain to three previous British monarchs. He is best known as the "founder-padre" of Toc H, the interdenominational world-wide organization for Christian service, chartered in 1922. Today it includes some 2,000 groups in sixty-four countries. Toc H is the outgrowth of Talbot House, a rest and recreation center established in Belgium for servicemen on their way to and from the battlefront near Flanders during World War I.

Clayton has been the vicar for the past thirty-three years of the Guild Church of Toc H, the City of London's historic All Hallows. He has written several books, and lectured and traveled widely in Africa, Asia and North America, encouraging young people to set up practical projects for the betterment of social conditions. He was decorated with the Military Cross for his ministrations to the wounded in World War I, and saw duty as a chaplain to Britain's tanker fleet and Merchant Navy during World War II.

Born in Queensland, Australia, on December 12, 1885, Philip Thomas Byard Clayton was the youngest of the three sons of Reginald Byard Buchanan and Isabel (Sheppard) Clayton. His father had migrated to northern Australia for reasons of health, but returned to London when his youngest boy was only one year old. Successful in business, the elder Clayton eventually retired to Beaulieu in Hampshire, where he became a Justice of the Peace.

Young Clayton attended the Colet Court and St. Paul's Schools, Hammersmith, London before following his brothers to Oxford University in 1906 with a Squire Scholarship at Exeter College. He received his B.A. degree with a "first class" in theology in 1909, having by that time resolved to follow the calling of his grandfather, the Reverend Samuel Clayton, vicar of Farnborough in Hampshire.

After studying for one year under Dr. Armitage Robinson, then Dean of Westminster, Clayton was ordained deacon of the Church of England in 1910. In that year his monograph, *Encaustic Mediaeval Tiles*, was published. This study brought him election as a fellow of the Society of Antiquarians in 1913.

Upon his ordination to the diaconate, Clayton became one of the eighteen curates assisting the Reverend Cyril Garbett (now Archbishop of York), vicar of the Church of St. Mary's Kingston at Portsea, Hampshire. His work was with the naval personnel at Portsmouth Naval Base. "[They] gave to him a loyalty and devotion which continued in many cases throughout their lives."

Father Clayton, who was ordained a priest of the Church of England and awarded the M.A. degree by Oxford University in 1912, described his experiences in Portsea in *The Work of a Great Parish* (1912). The late Gilbert Keith Chesterton's character of the rotund and beaming priest-detective in *The Innocence of Father Brown* was said to have been suggested by young "Tubby" Clayton.

Early in World War I Father Clayton was chaplain to the 16th General Hospital. As Brigade Chaplain to the 6th Division he was assigned to assist Senior Chaplain Neville Talbot in establishing at Poperinghe, Belgium, a place where men could worship and relax from the strain of battle. This center (which was named Talbot House in memory of Gilbert Talbot, who had been killed in the first German liquid fire attack) was opened on December 15, 1915.

Clayton placed above the door of Talbot House the motto "All Rank Abandon Ye Who Enter Here." An upper room, formerly a hayloft, became "the most beautiful place of worship on the western front," and here some 100,000 officers and men of all faiths prayed or meditated. The story of this "soldiers' club" has been told in Father Clayton's *Tales of Talbot House in Poperinghe and Ypres* (Chatto and Windus, 1919; revised edition, 1925).

British Inf. Services

REV. P. B. CLAYTON

During 1919 he was "tutor of service" to the Ordination Test School established as a training center for chaplains. He went to London in 1920 to establish a rest center and hostel at 23 Queens Gate Place named "Toc H, Mark I." ("Toc H" is the British signal code for Talbot House.) The second and third hostels, Mark II and Mark III, were opened in 1921. Clayton visited Canada and the United States in 1922 to raise funds for these projects. In August the Archbishop of Canterbury named Clayton vicar of All Hallows, Barking-by-the-Tower. This historic church, founded in 675 A.D., is located near the Tower of London. It soon became known as "the Guild Church of Toc H."

On December 14, 1922 King George V signed for Toc H a "Royal Charter of Incorporation," and the Prince of Wales, who was interested in the original Talbot House, became its first patron. This charter specified as among the objectives "to promote among all people a wide human interest in the lives and needs of their fellows," and "to mitigate by habit of mind and word and deed the evils of class consciousness" (*Official Year-Book of the Church of England*).

Subsequent tours by Clayton of the British Empire, the United States, South America and the Near East resulted by 1928 in the extension of Toc H throughout the English-speaking world and capturing the imagination of youth by its call to service and sacrifice. As each new branch was formed it was entrusted with a "Lamp of Maintenance, first lighted by the patron and relighted with simple ceremony at every meeting in remembrance of the 'Elder Brethren' and in rededication to the task they left unfinished—building a 'new Jerusalem'" (*Encyclopedia Britannica*).

As Vicar of All Hallows, Clayton first planned and launched in 1926 the Tower Hill Improvement Scheme outlined in *The Pageant*

CLAYTON, P. B., REV.—*Continued*

of *Tower Hill* (Longmans, 1933). Two chapters were written by Clayton and the chronicle of the Tower by the historian B. R. Leftwich. Clayton's Kiplingesque book *Plain Tales from Flanders* (Longmans) appeared in 1929 and was followed in 1932 by *Earthquake Love* (Geoffrey Bles), a collection of articles which had appeared in *The Times* (of London) and other newspapers and serials.

In 1932 he was appointed to the Royal Ecclesiastical Household as one of the many Chaplains to King George V; and in the 1933 New Year's Honours List Clayton was named a Companion of Honour.

Largely as a result of Clayton's efforts, Tower Beach was made available in 1934 as a play area for children. He also was active in the British Leprosy Relief Movement, to which Toc H gave active support. Clayton, who had been named honorary chaplain to the Port of London Authority in 1924, became in addition the senior chaplain to the Anglo-Iranian Oil Company in 1929.

When World War II began, Father Clayton was rejected as too old for military service, but was assigned by the Archbishop of Canterbury in October 1939, to administer a Toc H chapter at Scapa Flow dedicated to the "care of sailors, soldiers, airmen, fishermen and the crews of trawlers, drifters and minesweepers" (Gault MacGowan, New York *Sun*, June 13, 1940). In December 1941 he was appointed a chaplain of the Anglo-Saxon Tanker Fleet and sailed on a number of voyages. He ended his World War II service in 1944 as a chaplain of the Merchant Navy in the Indian Ocean and the Mediterranean.

Interviewed by Cecelia Ager in *PM* (June 8, 1942) Clayton predicted that the United States would have to "rise to its full height of leading a world. That's a terrific destiny," he said. "It can be like a load on the hearts of men, or like a bugle call—whichever way you take it."

On the morning of December 9, 1940 a German bomb struck the Church of All Hallows; the east wall was demolished, and fires gutted the edifice. At the invitation of a number of friends in America, Clayton lectured in the United States and Canada during 1947 and raised funds for both Toc H and All Hallows. A group was organized in 1948 as the Winant Volunteers (named in memory of U.S. Ambassador John G. Winant) consisting of young American men and women pledged to go each summer at their own expense to the London slums to aid children. A similar Canadian unit, the Osler Volunteers (named in memory of Sir William Osler), was formed.

Early in 1953, after revisiting Australia and New Zealand, Father Clayton was again in the United States to seek support for Toc H and the rebuilding of All Hallows Church. "Partial restoration has been accomplished," he said, "but $350,000 is still needed." *Newsweek* (March 16, 1953) observed that "All Hallows Barking's roof is now of American steel, its bells are from Canada, the copper for its spire plus fine woods and lead are [contributed] from Australia, New Zealand and Tasmania." The late Queen Mary had started the fund for the restoration of the organ, on which Albert Schweitzer is said to have made his recordings of Bach compositions.

Father Clayton participated in her Majesty's coronation procession in June 1953. His visit to the United States that year coincided with the publication by the Oxford University Press of *The Impudent Dreamer*, his biography by the Reverend Melville Harcourt, rector of St. Ann's Episcopal Church in Brooklyn, New York. (This book was published in England by Hodder and Stoughton under the title *Tubby Clayton.*)

Among the 2,000 Toc H groups established in sixty-four countries are several in South Africa where tuberculosis hospitals have been built to aid the natives. In Britain, noted *Newsweek* (March 16, 1953), "Toc H'ers visit prisons. In Australia they sponsor a Young Farmers League." The 1954-1955 *Official Year-Book of the Church of England* records that in the United Kingdom the organization has "some 1,500 branches and twenty-three residential houses . . . for young men."

It has been said of Clayton that "his hobby is the work he has at heart." He keeps near at hand "a constellation of old briars, a cairn [terrier] named 'Chippie,' and a range of teapots brewing a flow of tannin at all hours." He is a member of the Royal Automobile Club. Canon Harcourt has summed up his friend as an "old-fashioned man" who "believes that dreams come true." Physically, he has been described as about five feet tall and squarely built. Since boyhood he has been affectionately known by the nickname of "Tubby."

References

Newsweek 9:59 Mr 30 '42
Washington (D.C.) Post p15 Mr 16 '53
Kelly's Handbook to the Titled, Landed and Official Classes (1951)
Who's Who (1954)

CLEMENT, FRANK G(OAD) June 2, 1920- Governor of Tennessee; lawyer
Address: b. State Capitol, Nashville, Tenn.; h. Dickson, Tenn.

When a large majority of the Tennessee electorate in 1952 chose Frank G. Clement as Governor at the age of thirty-two, he became the youngest Governor in the United States. He was re-elected in November 1954 for a four-year term. He adheres to the "liberal" wing of the Democratic party, and he is known for his "modern-dress revival of the William Jennings Bryan type of oratory" (*Harper's*, March 1955). Some of his party's leaders are heralding Clement "as the Democrats' answer to Richard Nixon."

To critics who called him too young during his gubernatorial campaigns, he replied: "If that's the only fault you can find, you'd better vote for me. I can outgrow that, but my opponents can't outgrow their faults" (*Harper's*, March 1955). Before his election to the governorship he was successively a special agent for the Federal Bureau of Investigation, a commissioned officer in the U.S. Army, general counsel for the Tennessee Railroad and Public Utilities Commission, and a practicing attorney.

Frank Goad Clement was born in Dickson, Tennessee, on June 2, 1920, the son of Robert Samuel and Maybelle (Goad) Clement. His father was an attorney, and the family was active politically. At the age of ten, while attending local schools, he decided to become Governor, and said to a schoolmate moving to another town: "Don't forget to work for me there when I run for governor" (*American Magazine,* October 1953). At fourteen he was tutored in public speaking by an aunt who operated the Shipp School of Expression in his native town.

Young Clement attended Cumberland University in Lebanon, Tennessee in 1939. In 1940 he entered the law school at Vanderbilt University in Nashville, Tennessee. He obtained the highest marks in the state bar examination in 1941 and was awarded the LL.B. degree in 1942.

In employing him as a special agent at the age of twenty-two, in Chicago in 1942, the FBI waived its minimum age requirement of twenty-three. He resigned in 1943 to enlist as a private in the U.S. Army. After attending officer candidate school, he was commissioned a second lieutenant. He was later promoted to first lieutenant and served at several Army posts in the United States.

After receiving his military discharge in 1946, Clement was appointed general counsel for the state Railroad and Public Utilities Commission by Governor James Nance McCord, whose campaign he had aided. He demonstrated outstanding skill as "a champion of the people" in rate case fights (*Saturday Evening Post,* January 29, 1955). His success brought him offers from other states. Georgia employed him at $100 a day for twenty-six days to prepare a rate case which he won against a utility company.

Active in veterans' and political organizations, he made frequent speeches and from 1946 to 1948 was state chairman of the Young Democrats Club. His activities in the American Legion brought him the post of state commander for Tennessee in 1948.

Two Tennesseans, Leslie Hart of the Nashville *Banner* and G. Edward Friar, a Knoxville lawyer, recommended in 1950 that Clement aim for the governorship. He set up his own law firm in Nashville. For a short time during the Korean war, Clement returned to Army service and was stationed at Camp Gordon, Georgia.

To promote Clement's gubernatorial campaign, the financial support of Robert Crichton, a Nashville businessman, and the political support of Edward H. Crump, Democratic politician of Shelby county, Tennessee, were obtained. In the primary, in August 1952, he defeated Governor Gordon Browning, who was seeking re-election. Clement promised, if elected, to carry on the state's affairs in a goldfish bowl. He was elected Governor on November 4, 1952, winning the largest popular vote in the state's history.

Wide World

FRANK G. CLEMENT

When Governor Clement signed a bill raising trucking limits from 42,000 to 55,980 pounds, the press and his political foes charged him with sacrificing Tennessee's "aging, crumbling" highways to the trucking industry. Clement declared the accusations "unfair, untruthful and bitter," and claimed that he had "maintained his independence and refused to be intimidated" (*Newsweek,* March 16, 1953).

The Tennessee state legislature in March 1953 agreed in "a stormy session" to float a $5,000,000 bond issue to fulfill Clement's campaign promise to provide all public school children with free textbooks (*Newsweek,* March 30, 1953), but this program was called inadequate by some teachers and parents. The Governor secured from his legislature authorization in 1953 to appoint a commission on educational television. The Tennessee legislature made "one of the largest increases in state aid" to public schools during 1955, appropriating about $20,000,000 more a year for the next two years than provided in the last two years (New York *Times,* May 22, 1955).

Despite vigorous opposition and the loss of his former supporters, Crichton, Crump and Friar (as described in the *Saturday Evening Post* article "The Things They Say About the Governor!" by Harold H. Martin, January 29, 1955), Clement won re-election with a plurality of 286,000 in 1954 over his opponent, former Governor Gordon Browning. His inauguration on January 18, 1955, was for a four-year term, following an amendment to the Tennessee constitution increasing the governor's term of office from two to four years, but prohibiting re-election.

Clement is chairman of the Commission on Mental Health Training and Research of the Southern Regional Education Board. As the result of a study directed by him and Dr. Nicholas Hobbs of George Peabody College,

CLEMENT, FRANK G.—*Continued*

Nashville, the Southern Governors Conference in Boca Raton, Florida, in November 1954, approved a program to pool resources for regional mental health centers, financed by an $8,000-a-year contribution from each state.

Governor Clement has vigorously opposed the Dixon-Yates contract as a plan "to feed private power into the Tennessee Valley Authority public power system" (New York *Times*, February 27, 1955). Clement's views are recorded in the *Reporter* (December 8, 1953) in an article entitled, "Don't Let TVA Be Wrecked, Mr. President!" Clement is the head of a state legislative committee to develop a public power policy for Tennessee.

So far, wrote Wilma Dykeman in *Harper's* (March 1955), Clement's attitude on the question of the Supreme Court ruling on segregation has been "noncommittal. While resorting to none of the extremist threats of some of the deep-South Governors, he has made no open affirmation in favor of the decision either." Commenting on the Court's ruling on May 31, 1955, which gave local Federal judges complete discretion in bringing about racially integrated public schools, Governor Clement stated that "Tennessee shall continue to send all our children of whatever race, creed or color to good public schools" (New York *Times*, June 1, 1955). Tennessee has a constitutional provision that prohibits Negroes and whites from attending public schools together.

While giving the principal address at the Kiwanis International Convention in New York City, Clement declared "Asia is pretty much lost," and "the United States is being isolated" (New York *Times*, June 23, 1953). On domestic issues, he has opposed Ezra Taft Benson's farm program, and has called the Small Business Administration ineffective.

In May 1955 he headed the Governors' committee on the distribution of the antipolio vaccine perfected by Dr. Jonas E. Salk, which met with Mrs. Oveta Culp Hobby, Secretary of the Department of Health, Education and Welfare. At a Governors' conference, which was held in Washington, D.C., Clement arranged for a photograph of himself and the next three youngest Governors, Orville L. Freeman of Minnesota (age thirty-seven), George M. Leader of Pennsylvania (age thirty-seven) and John F. Simms, Jr. of New Mexico (age thirty-nine). Asked by Governor W. Averell Harriman of New York the reason for the group photograph, Clement replied: "This is the 'I-Want-To-Be-President Club'—and I'm the manager!" (Washington *Post and Times Herald*, May 12, 1955).

As reported by Drew Pearson in the Washington *Post and Times Herald* (May 12, 1955), Governor Clement emerged from the Governors' Conference "with his political stock boosted. He impressed the other Governors with his articulate, outspoken manner."

The Governor is described as a political evangelist, who intermingles Biblical themes with campaign speeches (*Harper's*, March 1955). He is often in a church pulpit on Sundays as a lay preacher. He has praised the work of Teenagers for Christ, headed by Don E. Johnson in Memphis, which he regards as one answer to juvenile delinquency. "They should be given our prayers and assistance," declared Clement (*Christian Science Monitor*, May 21, 1955).

The United States Junior Chamber of Commerce named Clement one of the "ten outstanding men of 1953." Former President Harry S. Truman said: "Tennessee has had many great governors in its history, but they have one now that can measure up to any of them" (New York *Times*, April 25, 1955). The Governor is a thirty-second degree Mason, and a member of Sigma Alpha Epsilon and Phi Delta Phi fraternities. His church affiliation is Methodist.

He married Lucille LaVerne Christianson on January 6, 1940. Their children are Robert Nelson, Frank Goad and James Gary. Clement is a six footer, "handsome, friendly," with "an uncanny ability to remember names and faces" (*American Magazine*, October 1953).

References:

Am Mag 156:51 O '53
Harper 210:48+ Mr '55
Newsweek 41:43 Mr 16 '53; 41:85 Mr 30 '53
Sat Eve Post 227:22+ Ja 29 '55 pors
Who's Who in America, 1954-55
Who's Who in United States Politics (1952)

CLEMENTS, EARLE C. Oct. 22, 1896- United States Senator from Kentucky; former Governor of Kentucky; farmer

Address: b. Senate Office Bldg., Washington 25, D.C.; h. Morganfield, Ky.

Described as "an immensely skilled politician whose talent for unobtrusive behind-the-stage carpentry makes him an effective instrument of government," Senator Earle C. Clements, Democrat of Kentucky, became in July 1955 acting majority leader of the upper house of Congress after Senator Lyndon B. Johnson of Texas had become ill. Previously Clements was assistant leader or Democratic "whip" in the Senate, where he has served since 1950. He has been politically classified as a "moderate" Democrat and his greatest contribution is considered to be that he presents to the Southern Democratic leaders in the Senate, the problems and claims of other members of the Democratic party with varying points of view.

He received his initial experience in Congress as Representative of the Second Kentucky District from 1945 to 1947, and from December 1947 until the time he entered the U.S. Senate, he was Governor of Kentucky. He is at present a member of the Senate Committee on Appropriations and of the Committee on Agriculture and Forestry.

Earle C. Clements was born in Morganfield, Union county, Kentucky on October 22, 1896. He attended public schools and the University of Kentucky at Lexington. In World War I he enlisted in the U.S. Army as a private in 1917, and was discharged with the rank of captain in the infantry. For a while after the war he coached football at Morganfield High School. His business interests are farming and stockbreeding.

In 1922 Clements began his career in public office as sheriff of Union county, Kentucky. He completed two terms in this post, and in 1926 became clerk of the county. Here he served until 1934, when he became county judge. He held this office for eight years and then was elected to the state Senate of Kentucky in November 1941. After serving in his state legislature from 1942 to 1944, and as the Senate's majority leader in 1944, he was elected Representative from the Second Kentucky District to the U.S. Seventy-ninth Congress in November 1944. Two years later, he was re-elected to the Eightieth Congress.

During his career in the House Clements served on the Committee on Agriculture and on the Committee on Post Office and Civil Service, to which he was appointed in 1945, and 1947, respectively. He introduced a bill to help stabilize the price of fire-cured and dark-air cured tobacco. This bill was amended, passed both the House and Senate, and was enacted in July 1945.

In the first session of the Seventy-ninth Congress, Clements favored the extension of the Lend-Lease act (March), the passage of the Bretton Woods Agreement bill (June), the extension of the Emergency Price Control and Stabilization acts of 1942 (June), and continued participation of the United States in the work of the United Nations Relief and Rehabilitation Administration (December). During the following session (1946), he voted "yea" on providing additional funds for housing units for families of servicemen and veterans (March), and on extension of the Selective Training and Service Act of 1940 (April).

On the House floor in the first session of the Eightieth Congress (1947) Clements spoke in support of the John E. Rankin amendment to increase the funds for the Rural Electrification Administration. In speaking about the Tennessee Valley Authority program, he told the House on June 11, 1947: "I consider this constructive program of regional development one of the outstanding contributions and accomplishments of the great Roosevelt Administration."

During 1947 Clement was recorded as "not voting" on either the recommittal or passage of the rent control bill (May), and on the bill to reduce the income tax rates, passed over President Harry S. Truman's veto (July). He voted against the Labor-Management Relations (Taft-Hartley) bill of 1947 (June). Clements resigned his Congressional post, following his election on November 4, 1947, as Governor of Kentucky for a four-year term, with a plurality of approximately 125,000 votes over his Republican opponent, Eldon S. Dummit, state attorney general.

Inaugurated as Governor of Kentucky on December 9, 1947, Clements succeeded Republican Governor Simeon Willis. He had the endorsement of both the CIO and AFL unions and the support of a Democratic-controlled state legislature. Under his administration, the Kentucky gasoline tax was increased two cents

Wide World

EARLE C. CLEMENTS

to help finance an extensive rural road improvement program. In addition, he enlarged the state education budget by $10,000,000, and secured an amendment of the Day Law to permit hospitals to accept Negroes for post-graduate training in nursing, medicine, and surgery.

During his campaign speeches as Democratic candidate for the U.S. Senate from Kentucky in 1950, Clements said he would work "for a continuing progressive program of Federal aid to education, conservation extension services, road building and public health" (New York *Times*, November 1, 1950). His candidacy against Republican former circuit court judge Charles Dawson was supported by what the New York *Times* called "one of the most efficient political organizations" in Kentucky's history. Republicans complained to the U.S. Senate subcommittee on elections and privileges that more than $360,000 was allegedly spent on this campaign (New York *Times*, November 9, 1950). Clements won easily over his opponent on November 7, 1950.

Resigning as Governor, Clements was sworn in on November 27, 1950 as a member of the U.S. Senate and completed the unexpired term of Alben W. Barkley. He began his six-year term in January 1951, with the Eighty-second Congress. Described as a "Senate type," who "lives for the Senate," he was immediately accepted as a member of the "inner club," or "ultimate power," in this body, stated William S. White in the New York *Times* (November 7, 1954). He became chairman of the Senate Democratic campaign committee in the spring of 1952, and that year strongly supported Adlai E. Stevenson as Democratic Presidential candidate.

Senator Clements was named Democratic "whip" of the Senate in January 1953, and in that role "gained the confidence of most of his party colleagues" (New York *Times*, May 31,

CLEMENTS, EARLE C.—*Continued*
1954). A member of the Democratic National Committee, in the reorganization of Congress in 1953 he was given a key position as liaison man between this committee and the Senate Democrats.

In the first session of the Eighty-second Congress (1951), Clements favored passage of the Defense Production bill (June), an amendment increasing payments provided by the Social Security Act (July), and control of exports to Iron Curtain countries (August). He did not vote on the Reciprocal Trade Agreements Act amendment (May), and opposed a resolution advising the President to secure Congressional approval before sending more than four divisions of ground troops to Europe under the North Atlantic Security Pact (April).

Proposals which Senator Clements supported in the second session of the Eighty-second Congress (1952) included recommitting the bill for Alaska statehood (February), overriding the President's veto of the immigration bill (June), and ratification of the protocol to include Germany in the North Atlantic Treaty Organization (July). The next year, during the first session of the Eighty-third Congress, he reversed his stand on Alaskan statehood, after visiting the territory as a member of the Senate Committee on the Interior, declaring on September 21, 1953 he would support the bill in 1954 if it were considered by Congress together with Hawaii's statehood claims.

The Senator's voting record during 1953 shows he opposed the Hendrickson and Case amendment to the tidelands bill to allow United States jurisdiction over the outer continental shelf (June). He voted "yea" on the McClellan amendment to the Mutual Security Act to accept foreign currency for surplus commodities (July), and on the constitutional amendment to provide equal rights for men and women (July).

In the following session (1954), with two other Senators, he drew up a joint bill to allow the U.S. Department of Agriculture to distribute surplus food in unemployment distress areas. In the Democratic-controlled Eighty-fourth Congress (1955), Clements declared he was "freely and willingly" supporting the Senate's authorization for President Eisenhower to defend Formosa, if necessary, by taking war action (New York *Times,* January 29, 1955). Clements and Senator Everett M. Dirksen of Illinois toured the Far East in June 1955 to make an on-the-spot inspection of the U.S. foreign aid program.

As acting majority leader of the Senate in March 1955, during a brief illness of the majority leader, Lyndon B. Johnson of Texas, Clements claimed the Senate Democrats would push "as vigorously as possible" and make a party fight for the $20-a-person income tax cut (New York *Times,* March 2, 1955). He became acting floor leader again on July 5, 1955 for the rest of the first session of the Eighty-fourth Congress, when Senator Johnson again became ill.

The Senator is married to the former Sara Blue and has one daughter, Elizabeth Hughes. He is stocky, wears glasses, and has a genial expression. He enjoys eating hominy grits and sausage for breakfast. Commenting on the Eisenhower Administration's legislative program for the Eighty-fourth Congress, Clements said: "I am glad to see him (the President) embracing so many things that the Democrats have so long stood for. . ." (New York *Times,* January 8, 1955).

References

N Y Herald Tribune p2 Ja 3 '53
N Y Times p21 N 6 '47; p4 N 5 '48; p19 My 31 '54; p12 Jl 11 '55 por
N Y Times Mag p6 Ja 2 '55
Biographical Directory of the American Congress, 1774-1949 (1950)
Congressional Directory (1955)
Who's Who in America, 1954-55
World Biography (1954)

COFFIN, HENRY SLOANE, REV. DR Jan. 5, 1877-Nov. 25, 1954 Clergyman; author, educator; born in New York City; graduated from Yale University (1897); ordained a Presbyterian minister (1900); pastor of Bedford Park Church, New York (1900-1905) and of Madison Avenue Church (1905-1926); associate professor of theology (1904-1926) at Union Theological Seminary and its president (1926-1945); was elected moderator of General Assembly of Presbyterian Church of U.S.A. (1943); author of many books including *Religion Yesterday and Today* (1940); noted as a liberal in theological and social thinking, and as an eloquent preacher. See *Current Biography* (Apr.) 1944.

Obituary

N Y Times p29 N 26 '54

COLLIER, CONSTANCE Jan. 22, 1880-Apr. 25, 1955 Actress; dramatic coach; acted on the London stage in Sir Herbert Beerbohm Tree's company; portrayed leading roles in plays by Shakespeare, Shaw, Somerset Maugham and Arthur Pinero; appeared with John and Lionel Barrymore in a New York production of *Peter Ibbetson* and on tour; also in *Dinner at Eight;* received in 1954 "distinguished service to Shakespeare award" for training and guidance given to actors in interpreting Shakespearean roles. See *Current Biography* (July) 1954.

Obituary

N Y Times p29 Ap 26 '55

COLLINS, SEABORN P. Nov. 2, 1912- Veterans organization official; businessman

Address: b. c/o American Legion National Hdqrs., 700 N. Pennsylvania St., Indianapolis 6, Ind.; 886 N. Main St., Las Cruces, N. Mex.

By unanimous vote at the Washington, D.C. convention on September 2, 1954, Seaborn P. Collins was chosen national commander of the American Legion for 1954-55. Collins, a World War II Air Corps flyer, uses his own plane in traveling around the country to visit the Legion's departments and posts. At home, in Las Cruces, New Mexico, he has business interests in real estate, insurance, contracting, and lumber.

The American Legion, the world's largest veterans organization, directs its efforts chiefly toward strengthening national security and obtaining passage of laws to benefit veterans. Collins, as its head, has "a powerful position," the *U.S. News & World Report* (September 10, 1954) points out. "It is a job that has launched some of its holders on political careers." In October 1955 J. Addington Wagner was elected to succeed Collins.

Born on November 2, 1912, Seaborn P. Collins was the oldest of three children (two boys and a girl) of the Reverend Seaborn P. Collins, a Presbyterian minister, and Rosa E. (Hipp) Collins, a teacher of Latin and Greek. His native town, Mabelle, Texas, is now a part of Abilene. During his high school years there he worked at several strenuous jobs, such as laying pipe in the oil fields. "I was young but big and strong for my age," he recalls, "so I was able to do it" (*American Legion Magazine*, November 1954).

Operating a café enabled Collins to pay college expenses for himself and his brother and sister. He was graduated with a B.S. degree in 1932 from Daniel Baker College in Brownwood, Texas (now incorporated into Howard Payne College). For the next four years he was employed by the U.S. Department of Agriculture, in an agency that was one of the predecessors of the present Farmers Home Administration.

Collins then became farm and ranch manager of the C.C. Slaughter estate in Texas. With thousands of acres spread over several counties, the property has been described as a "far-reaching domain of oil wells, mesquite, cattle and cotton." During the course of his three years on the estate he purchased an adjoining 3,900-acre ranch, which he operated at the same time. He also learned to fly and bought a Piper Cub plane so that he could more quickly handle business matters in scattered sections of the estate.

Soon after the Japanese attack on Pearl Harbor, Collins tried to enter military service but was barred because of an eye disability. He served for about a year in a civilian capacity as flight instructor for both the Army and Navy, in Fort Sill, Oklahoma and in Jacksonville, Texas.

Having obtained a waiver of his disability, he enlisted in the Air Corps in January 1943, received flight training until November 1944, and was commissioned a flight officer. As an Air Transport Command pilot, he ferried C-17 planes from the United States to the South Pacific and then for about a year flew "the Hump" in the China-Burma-India theater.

When he was discharged in December 1945, he returned to Las Cruces, New Mexico, where he had moved just before the war. He decided to become a realtor after a month's experience in the real-estate office of his father-in-law,

SEABORN P. COLLINS

George R. Quesenberry, who left Collins in charge while he took a vacation. During that period Collins' negotiation of a sale of a farm earned him $1,500 in commissions.

For a time he sold real estate in association with his father-in-law, but this partnership was dissolved when Collins started project developments to help relieve the housing shortage among the town's 15,000 inhabitants. Between 1949 and mid-1954 he built about 500 homes, most of them in the under-$10,000 bracket, and by the end of that period was ready to build about 300 more. Collins' home building enterprise is called Southwestern Builders, Inc. He is the president of this company as well as of a real-estate and insurance agency and of companies dealing in building materials, road construction, and investment and finance.

Collins joined the Joe Quesenberry Post No. 10 of the American Legion in Las Cruces in January 1946. The following year he became commander of his post, and then after a term (1948-1949) as area commander he was elected department commander of New Mexico for 1949-1950, the first World War II veteran to hold that office. He served for four years in a number of positions on the department level: chairman of national security, vice-chairman of the legislative committee, member of the finance committee, and director of the New Mexico Boys State. From 1947 to 1949 he was also a member of the department's membership committee.

On the national level he was a member of the Legion's housing committee (1948-1949), vice-chairman of military affairs committee (1952-1953) and chairman of the national security commission (1953-1954). He is a member of Voiture 1346, Forty and Eight.

Elected at the Legion's thirty-sixth annual convention, meeting in Washington, D.C., Collins on September 2, 1954 succeeded Arthur

COLLINS, SEABORN P.—*Continued*

J. Connell of Middletown, Connecticut as national commander. In his acceptance speech he called attention to the Legion's fight against Communist infiltration and subversion in the United States. "The American Legion," he said, "is the object of bitter Communist hatred, and in a sense this hatred is a measure of our success" (New York *Herald Tribune*, September 3, 1954).

The next day at a press conference Collins pledged his efforts to carry out a convention resolution giving top priority on the Legion's legislative program to the establishment of Universal Military Training. He said he would "go down the line" for the convention's other resolution, some of which called for stepped-up defense measures and serious consideration of a diplomatic break between the United States and the Soviet Union.

In keeping with the practice of Legion national commanders to undertake one particular project for which they will be known in the organization's history, Collins announced that he would start a drive for membership. He hopes to increase the Legion's 2,800,000 members to 3,000,000. In visiting as many as possible of the Legion's 17,200 posts in the United States, he pilots his own plane, a new Riley Twin.

One of Collins' early important speeches as commander was made in Los Angeles on September 22 at the American Federation of Labor convention. He urged that the United States, with other free nations, fix a "point of no return" for Communist aggression. "We must determine a line which the Communists must not cross," he explained. "And we must serve notice that if they do cross it, then the consequence will be immediate and total military retaliation against Russia itself" (New York *Times*, September 23, 1954).

On a visit to the White House on December 9, 1954 Collins told President Eisenhower that the Legion would support any move by the Administration to secure the release of the group of U.S. airmen held by Communist China. A few days later Collins appeared on the television program *Youth Wants to Know*, of which the American Legion is one of the producers. He said that as a last resort, after peaceful measures had failed, he would favor an economic blockade of Red China to force the release of the imprisoned flyers.

Collins has often spoken on the subject of peaceful coexistence between Communist nations and the democracies. In a February 1955 address in Brooklyn, New York, he expressed his view that conditions in the world today are not favorable to coexistence. Referring to the U.S.S.R., he stated that there was "no such thing as peaceful coexistence with a nation that has sworn to destroy us" (New York *Times*, February 6, 1955).

A leading participant in Las Cruces community affairs, Collins has been chairman of the city planning board and of the Dona Ana County Hospital board and president of the Mesilla Valley Chamber of Commerce. He is chairman of the Fourth Army Advisory Committee, a liaison group between Las Cruces civilians and military officials at White Sands Proving Grounds. He has also served as adviser to a committee to remove the New Mexico educational system from political control.

Among the organizations in which he is interested are the National Association of Home Builders, Boy Scouts, Girl Scouts, American Red Cross, March of Dimes Fund of the National Foundation for Infantile Paralysis, and Lions. In November 1954 Howard Payne College awarded him a Man of the Year plaque. Collins' political party is the Democratic. A Presbyterian, he is chairman of the board of trustees of Las Cruces' First Presbyterian Church.

Collins married Lelia Jane Quesenberry on July 7, 1938; they have a son, Rex, and a daughter, Kay. The Legionnaire is six feet three inches tall and weighs 210 pounds. "He's easy-going and informal," as pictured in the *American Legion Magazine*, "till he gets down to business." Collins has said that "UMT is the only fair and effective way of providing the manpower to insure America's safety. . . ."

References

Am Legion Mag 57:18 N '54 por
N Y Times p11 S 4 '54
U S News 37:16 S 10 '54

CONNER, NADINE Feb. 20, 1913- Singer

Address: b. c/o Metropolitan Opera Association, Inc., 147 W. 39th St., New York 18; h. Compton, Calif.

Wearing a pair of her mother's shoes—silver sandals with Louis XV heels—Nadine Conner made her debut at the Metropolitan Opera House singing the role of Pamina in Mozart's *The Magic Flute*. In the thirteen years since her debut the California-born soprano, who was completely trained in the United States for her musical career, has often worn the same pair of shoes, both for "good luck and her comfort." Known for her versatility in operatic roles (she has sung such parts as Gretel, Rosina, Susanna, Zerlina, Mimi, Marguerite, Lauretta, Gilda and Violetta), she added the fifteenth role to her repertory on November 27, 1953 when she sang the part of Mélisande in Debussy's *Pelléas and Mélisande*. Her first role in the 1954-55 season was that of Susanna in Mozart's *The Marriage of Figaro* on December 9, 1954.

Miss Conner has long been an enthusiastic advocate of operas sung in English. She was given the role of Mimi in the English-language version of Puccini's *La Bohème* at the Metropolitan Opera House during the season of 1952-53. She was heard by a nation-wide audience in the first televised production of the opera which she had sung on many occasions in Italian. Designer of all her own clothes and costumes, Miss Conner was recently voted best-dressed woman in the opera world by the Fashion Institute. She has also been heard on television and radio, and in concert halls and in motion pictures.

Nadine Conner was born in Compton, California on February 20, 1913, and lived on her grandfather's farm not far from Los Angeles. She was descended from colonial (English) stock.

Her great grandmother (Mary White) is believed to have been the first white child to travel by sailing ship from New York to California by way of Cape Horn. Her great-grandfather, who drove an ox-team to join the 1849 gold rush, went into the gold fields and disappeared.

Miss Conner's parents, who had been stage troupers, founded what they called The Literary Society, in which their children acted and sang. Miss Conner is the youngest of seven children, having three brothers and three sisters, all of whom are talented singers. Her mother played the piano and her father the violin, doing a program that ranged from Shakespeare to Gilbert and Sullivan.

Nadine Conner began piano lessons at an early age, but, being a bashful child, she was told that it was doubtful that she could appear in public. She studied dramatics at the Compton High School for four years, and sang alto in the glee club. She began studying voice privately with an experienced dramatic tenor from Mexico named Amado Fernandez. Miss Conner relates: "I was trained as a dramatic soprano; it wasn't until later, when I tried out my voice in big halls, that I found it wasn't large enough, so I decided to concentrate on lyric qualities" (*Musical America,* December 15, 1953). Upon finishing high school she was given a scholarship in music at the University of Southern California, there winning the Euterpe Opera Scholarship.

Her first chance professionally came as the result of a radio program opening the current season of the Hollywood Bowl. After she had sung, with other university students, the radio station offered her a contract, and she became staff vocalist on station KHJ, Los Angeles, while still a university student. There her singing was so well received that before long she was appearing with such stars as Bing Crosby and with Sigmund Romberg, and on shows like the Cresta Blanca and the Coca-Cola hour, the last one being her first starring show.

During her seven years in radio, Miss Conner sang commercials, boogie-woogie, coloratura and contralto songs, as well as co-starring with Nelson Eddy on the Vicks program and performing on the *Show Boat* hour. She also took part in an Hawaiian trio.

When the Los Angeles Opera company was founded by Albert Coates in connection with the WPA in 1939, Nadine joined it, and for the next two years gained practical experience in singing, stage movement and dramatics, while performing, in English, the roles of Marguerite in *Faust* and Violetta in *La Traviata.* The singer looks back on these years as the best she ever had from the point of view of experience.

It was while singing with the Los Angeles Opera that she was noticed by Earl Lewis, treasurer of the Metropolitan Opera Association. Lewis recommended her to the conductor Bruno Walter, who suggested that she go to New York and audition for the Metropolitan Opera itself. Miss Conner, who has never lost an audition, was heard by Edward Johnson, then director of the Metropolitan, and was signed to a contract. Under Bruno Walter's baton she appeared on December 22, 1941 in the role of Pamina, in Mozart's *The Magic Flute.* The New York *Herald Tribune* critic, Francis D. Perkins, commented: ". . . she played and sang the role with remarkable poise and a confidence that seemed natural, rather than assumed for the occasion . . . the singer . . . also was able to interpret the character with an appealing and appropriate sense of youth and wistfulness."

Bender

NADINE CONNER

Her next appearance was as Micaela in *Carmen,* followed by Sophia in *Der Rosenkavalier.* She sang her first full-length role as Marguerite in Gounod's *Faust* on December 19, 1944. Her performance was generally praised, although some fault was found with the lack of power in her voice, her notes being described rather as "warm and sweet."

Miss Conner sang the role of Lauretta in *Gianni Schicchi,* by Puccini, on February 11, 1944, and achieved success with the English version of Humperdinck's *Hansel and Gretel,* which was produced at the Metropolitan on December 27, 1946. The New York *Sun* found: "Nadine Conner, as Gretel, and Risë Stevens, as Hansel . . . made up the best brother-and-sister act to be heard at the Metropolitan in recent times." She has no real favorites among her roles since they are all sympathetic characters that thrill the audience.

Until the 1950 season Miss Conner had missed only one opera performance. In 1950 Roberta Peters, her understudy, first substituted for her as Zerlina in *Don Giovanni.* On several occasions since that time Miss Peters

CONNER, NADINE—*Continued*

has substituted for Miss Conner when she was indisposed, notably on January 29, 1954 in the role of Susanna in Mozart's *Le Nozze di Figaro.*

In her fifteenth role at the Metropolitan she sang the part of Mélisande in November 1953. Although others in the cast were also singing that opera for the first time, the music critic of the New York *Times* (November 28, 1953) thought the production "the best that we have seen this season."

Aside from appearing at the "Met," Nadine Conner was seen in the Twentieth-Century-Fox World Artists motion picture *Of Men and Music,* released in November 1950, in which she sang operatic duets with Jan Peerce. She makes frequent concert tours and is a well-known recording star, her record of *Hansel and Gretel* in the Columbia Masterworks album being widely appreciated by opera record lovers.

Miss Conner is five feet three inches tall, has russet hair and blue-green eyes. She weighs 115 pounds. She married Dr. Laurance Heacock, the doctor who treated her for appendicitis, in 1939. They have adopted two children, Sue Lynn and Loren David. Besides designing her clothes, Miss Conner enjoys knitting, gardening, and taking pack trips into the Sierra mountains with her husband, where she likes to fish in the mountain streams. On evenings when she is singing at the "Met" she eats "an enormous dinner" at five o'clock. Unassuming and friendly, she is popular with her associates at the "Met," and has been known to devote time to helping a fellow singer control a bad case of jitters.

"If it ever threatened my domestic happiness, I would quit the opera and concert stage," said Miss Conner. "When we were married I was willing to settle down to housekeeping, but my husband wanted me to continue." Six months of each year, as Mrs. Heacock, she lives at Compton, California.

References

Hobbies 53:55 O '48
Mus Am 72:15 D 15 '52; 73:10+ D 15 '53 pors
N Y Daily Mirror p12 D 26 '46
N Y Herald Tribune p15 D 23 '41
N Y Post p18 N 22 '41
N Y Times p12 N 28 '53
Opera N 6:3 N 24 '41

COON, CARLETON S(TEVENS) June 23, 1904- Anthropologist; archaeologist; university professor; author

Address: b. c/o University Museum, University of Pennsylvania, Philadelphia, Pa.; h. Beaumont Lane, Devon, Pa.

In a speech at the Book and Author Luncheon in Washington, D.C. on January 19, 1955, anthropologist Carleton S. Coon, author of *The Story of Man* (Knopf, 1954), said that mankind is entering a new kingdom—atomic science—and consequently will get smarter. He pointed out that every time an organism goes through a change it gains intelligence, as when birds got wings and flew, and when man's ancestors, the monkeys, came out of the jungle onto the plains. Dr. Coon's book, which has been called "the first anthropological account of human history which is both readable and authoritative," traces the history of man 50,000 years from the Ice Age to the present, offering some unorthodox views and upsetting some prevalent theories as to man's origins.

Since 1948 Dr. Coon has been curator of ethnology at the University Museum, Philadelphia, Pennsylvania, and professor of anthropology at the University of Pennsylvania. From 1927 until 1948 he taught archaeology and anthropology at Harvard University, except for a period during World War II when he served in the U.S. Department of State and as a major in the U.S. Army. He is the author of over a dozen books which deal with his field work in the Middle East, the Balkans and North Africa. Among his important discoveries were the remains of a 50,000-year-old primitive Neanderthal man in North Africa in 1939 and three skeletons of presumably 75,000-year-old human beings located in Hotu Cave in northern Iran in 1951. During 1954 he excavated Kara-Kamar in northern Afghanistan and in 1955, he excavated two caves in the Arabia Deserta in Syria. He has appeared as a regular panelist on the Columbia Broadcasting System television program, *What in the World?*, which won the Peabody Award in 1952.

Carleton Stevens Coon was born on June 23, 1904 in Wakefield, Massachusetts, the son of John Lewis and Bessie (Carleton) Coon. He was graduated from Phillips Academy, Andover, Massachusetts, in 1921 and received his A.B. degree (*magna cum laude*) from Harvard University in 1925 and was elected to Phi Beta Kappa. "Carl" was influenced by Professor Earnest Albert Hooton to make anthropology his career. In 1928 he received the A.M. and Ph.D. degrees from Harvard. From 1927 until 1948 he taught anthropology at Harvard, rising from instructor to professor in 1946, with leave for service with the U.S. Government from 1942 to 1945.

He worked as special assistant to the U.S. Department of State during 1942 and 1943, and was a major in the U.S. Army from 1943 to 1945. Since 1948 he has headed the general ethnology section of the University of Pennsylvania, has taught anthropology and has conducted many expeditions under the auspices of the University Museum, which was founded in Philadelphia in 1889. It is concerned with the study of man, particularly as exemplified by the remains of ancient civilizations. Its activities comprise field research in archaeology and ethnology conducted through its expeditions to all parts of the world. Dr. Coon installed a Hall of Man at the University Museum which shows the links in the chain of man's development.

During 1949 Dr. Coon headed an expedition to northern Iran, near the Russian border. In Belt Cave he found more than 31,000 artifacts showing the beginnings of agriculture including sickles whose edges were coated with chemicals from cut grain (*Pathfinder,* May 16, 1951).

Some of the objects were "dated" at about 6,050 B.C. by measuring the radioactive carbon they contained. This method of Carbon-14 dating to determine the age of ancient objects was inaugurated by Dr. Willard F. Libby (see *C.B.*, 1954) at the University of Chicago. Specimens from Belt Cave, consisting of charred bone, were among the first that Dr. Libby studied. From the thousands of animal bones dug up it appears, according to Dr. Coon, that the goat was the earliest animal to be domesticated, followed closely by the sheep, and that the pig and ox came later (*Archaeology*, Summer 1951).

Returning to Iran in 1951, Dr. Coon and his colleague, Louis Dupree, excavated Hotu Cave (so called because when a visitor shouts "Ho!" it echoes "Tu!"). The immensely thick deposits showed almost continuous occupation, "a complete and unbroken cultural sequence through the Iron Age, Bronze (or Copper) Age, and Neolithic or New Stone Age. Below the latter was a layer of fallen rock, debris from a collapse of the cave ceiling some time before 10,000 B.C. Below this fallen rock were layers of sands and gravels dating from the last glacial period. At a depth of thirty-nine feet, in a deposit of hard-packed gravel, there appeared the fossilized bones of human beings" (*Archaeology*, Summer 1951).

Photographs and descriptions of these "geologically ancient skeletons" (two women and one man) appeared in *Life* (May 21, 1951) and in archaeological and anthropological journals including the *Bulletin of the Philadelphia Anthropological Society* (May 1951) and the *Proceedings of the American Philosophical Society* (June 20, 1952). Dr. Coon concluded from the Iranian cave skeletons that a true Homo sapiens may prove to have been much older than subhuman types, which had been found elsewhere, such as the 50,000-year-old Neanderthal man. "We have proven," he said, "that men of human type existed contemporaneously with more primitive forms elsewhere. . . . Here we are on the main line of evolution" (*Time*, May 7, 1951). This view is held by some other scholars.

Dr. Coon wrote in *The Story of Man*: "The skeletons . . . cover in all probability the same period [at the end of the Ice Age], though we are not yet certain about the age of all of them. They represent tall, lanky people with strong chins and narrow noses, though all were by no means alike. . . . These people had much in common with present-day Nordics."

As discussed by John J. O'Neill (New York *Herald Tribune*, July 20, 1952), "instead of a genetically pure human race supposed to have existed in ancient days and from which the present variegated inhabitants of the earth descended, these well-preserved skeletons . . . clinch the demonstration that thousands of years ago man had as mixed a genetical composition as he has today, and that small inbred groups can show wide variations."

Among Dr. Coon's books, some of which are used as college textbooks, are: *Tribes of the Rif* (Peabody Museum, 1931); *Flesh of the Wild Ox* (Morrow, 1932); *Measuring Ethiopia*

CARLETON S. COON

and Flight into Arabia (Little, 1935); *Races of Europe* (Macmillan, 1939, 1954); *Principles of Anthropology*, written in collaboration with Eliot D. Chapple (Holt, 1942; J. Cape, 1948, 1953); *Races*, written with other authors (Thomas, 1950); and *Cave Explorations in Iran, 1949* (University of Pennsylvania Museum, 1951).

His book, *Caravan: The Story of the Middle East* (Holt, 1951) received favorable reviews. The New York *Times* (November 25, 1951) reviewer wrote: "A distinguished anthropologist draws on field experience stretching back nearly three decades for fascinating accounts of villagers, townsmen, mountaineers, herdsmen, men of the desert—and how they live. Honest borrowings from other scholars give his book the sparkling contrasts of good mosaic work."

In *The Story of Man*, Dr. Coon reveals the immense new knowledge of the distant past which scientists have garnered since World War II: "It cannot be said that man is descended from apes," he wrote, "but rather that apes are descended from ground-living primates that almost became men." He explained why men are rulers of the earth. The apes became specialized. One type of ape stayed in the forest and developed powerful arms for tree to tree swinging. Others tried the grasslands and developed powerful jaws and teeth, the better to capture and kill land-roaming animals. Other primates "remained unspecialized in everything except those features that prepare them for human living" and became the ancestors of men. "As we know from history of extinct reptiles and mammals," Coon wrote, "lack of specialization is the key to survival past all kinds of changes of climate and terrain and to success in competition with other animals."

Dr. Coon belongs to the American Anthropological Association, American Association of Physical Anthropologists, and the American

COON, CARLETON S.—*Continued*
Academy of Arts and Sciences. He is a member of Sigma Xi. His clubs are the Cosmos (Washington, D.C.) and Franklin Inn (Philadelphia). Among Dr. Coon's honors are the Legion of Merit (1945) and the Viking Medal in Physical Anthropology (1952). He is also a Membre D'Honneur of the Association de la Libération Française du 8 Novembre, 1942. He has been a panel member on the Peabody Award-winning television program *What in the World?* between 1952 and 1955 when not away on expeditions. He is called "Cannon-ball Coon" by his associates.

In 1926 Dr. Coon married Mary Goodale, by whom he had two sons, Carleton S. and Charles Adams. This marriage was terminated. In 1945 he married Lisa Dougherty Geddes, who draws the maps for many of his books. He is a member of the Congregational church. Dr. Coon speaks ten languages, including the obscure tongues of desert tribes.

References

Sat R Lit 34:25 D 8 '51 por
Time 57:46 My 7 '51 por
Directory of American Scholars (1951)
Who's Who in America, 1954-55

COOPER, (LEON) JERE July 20, 1893-
United States Representative from Tennessee; lawyer

Address: b. House Office Bldg., Washington 25, D.C.; h. Dyersburg, Tenn.

With the organizing of the Eighty-fourth Congress of the United States in January 1955, the chairmanship of the powerful House of Representatives Ways and Means Committee was assigned to a Tennessee Democrat, Jere Cooper, who had been a member of the committee since 1932. He succeeded Daniel A. Reed (Republican) in the chairmanship. Cooper's record has been summed up by the New York *Times* as one of "fairly consistent support for New and Fair Deal measures."

A proponent of the Hull Reciprocal Trade Agreements Act, Chairman Cooper authored the first piece of major legislation to be filed in the Eighty-fourth Congress, a bill to extend the trade agreements and to increase the President's power to regulate tariffs. Representative Cooper, who was first elected to Congress in 1928, is one of the senior members of the House in length of service.

A native and resident of western Tennessee, Leon Jere Cooper was born July 20, 1893 on a farm in Dyer County; he was the eldest of the five children of the late Joseph W. and Viola May (Hill) Cooper. His parents moved to the county seat, Dyersburg, where the elder Cooper obtained employment in the cotton-oil mill of which he later became superintendent. For a long time, however, the family circumstances were straitened. "I worked from the time I was twelve years old," Cooper said (as quoted by Sidney Shalett in the *Saturday Evening Post*, January 8, 1955. "I never had a stitch of clothes bought for me by anyone but my own self from that time on."

Jobs as a grocery delivery boy and clerk and as an apprentice butcher helped support him during his years at the high school in Dyersburg, where he was "a diligent scholar and a model of deportment" and where he became manager of the school baseball and football teams. From Martha Hamilton, a local teacher of elocution, Jere Cooper received private lessons which were paid for out of the savings of his mother, who also provided her son with a full-length mirror for rehearsing speaking gestures. In a regional oratorical contest he won a medal awarded by the United Daughters of the Confederacy.

Deciding on the law as a profession, he enrolled at Cumberland University, Lebanon, Tennessee. This institution, of which the late Secretary of State Cordell Hull was also an alumnus, was in actuality a law school rather than a university, and at that time required only one year of attendance to qualify for a degree. To meet expenses, Cooper borrowed money and earned extra money by pressing his fellow students' white flannel trousers.

After receiving his LL.B. degree from Cumberland in 1914, Cooper was admitted to the Tennessee bar at the age of twenty-two, and began the practice of law in Ewell Weakley's Dyersburg office. When the United States entered World War I, in 1917, he enlisted in the Second Infantry Regiment of the Tennessee National Guard.

Commissioned a first lieutenant, he was transferred with his unit to Company K of the 119th Infantry, Thirtieth Division, of the U.S. Army, in which he served for the balance of the war, participating in a number of important engagements on the French and Belgian fronts. Promoted to captain in July 1918, Cooper served as regimental adjutant until his discharge on April 2, 1919.

Cooper resumed his law practice in Dyersburg, where he organized the local post of the American Legion. He was made state commander in 1921 and became a member of the Legion's national executive committee one year later. He was elected to the Dyersburg City Council and appointed to the school board and to the office of city attorney, which he held for eight years, beginning in 1920.

His first notable activity in politics came in 1924, when he managed the successful campaign of General Lawrence D. Tyson for a seat in the U.S. Senate. When former Judge Finis J. Garrett, Representative of the Ninth Tennessee District in Congress, resigned in 1928, Cooper became a candidate for his vacated seat. Victorious over four rivals in the Democratic primaries, Cooper went on to win over his Republican opponent by 16,967 votes in the election of November 6, 1928.

He represented the Ninth District in the Seventy-first through the Eighty-second Congresses. With the reapportionment of seats as the result of the 1950 census, Cooper became in the Eighty-third and Eighty-fourth Congresses the representative of the new Eighth District.

Seated in the Republican-controlled Seventy-ninth Congress in March, 1929, the freshman Representative from Tennessee was assigned first to the Flood Control Committee (he represented a district threatened by overflow of the Mississippi and its tributaries). He was subsequently assigned to the elections and veterans affairs committees.

When a Democratic vacancy occurred on the Ways and Means Committee in 1932, Cooper was chosen over many senior members for the post. Since that time the Tennessee legislator has been assigned continuously to this committee, which is responsible for the formulation of all Federal taxation and revenue-raising legislation.

Representative Cooper in general supported Administration legislation in the early New Deal era, but was at that time opposed to the Tennessee Valley Authority. When the House Interstate Commerce Committee heard testimony in March 1935 on the Rayburn-Wheeler holding bill opposed by the power companies, he charged that the TVA was "distributing propaganda among schools" (New York *Times*). With his assignment to the Ways and Means Committee, Cooper had begun studying to improve his knowledge of taxes and of parliamentary procedures. In March 1939 he was named by Ways and Means Committee Chairman Robert L. Doughton of North Carolina to be chairman of a subcommittee to handle all tax legislation.

"From 1940 on," Sidney Shalett has observed, "[Cooper] was called on more and more by Democratic Speaker Sam Rayburn to preside over House sessions on controversial matters and to function as a Democratic trouble shooter." *Time* (May 3, 1943) referred to Cooper as the "committee's best tax brain" and credited him with doing the "pulling and hauling" which enabled the Ways and Means Committee to produce a generally acceptable "pay-as-you-go" income tax measure.

"My philosophy on taxes is very simple," Cooper explained. "I believe the Sixteenth Amendment to the Constitution means just what it says, which, in effect, is that Congress shall have authority to levy and collect taxes on income from whatever source derived. . . . I think everyone should pay a fair share to the support of the Government" (*Saturday Evening Post*, January 8, 1955).

When he was named vice-chairman of a special committee in 1945 to inquire into the responsibility for the Pearl Harbor disaster, *Newsweek* referred to Cooper as "another party wheelhorse whose slow, verbose questioning of witnesses often resembles a filibuster." This "quiet, shy man of extreme caution," who has been nicknamed "Sphinx" by reporters (New York *Times*), is popular in his district. Although his renomination has usually encountered little opposition, he was challenged in the primaries in 1946 by a young war veteran named Lyle Cherry, and in 1950 he came within 1,600 votes of losing to Robert A. Everett, who made flood control his principal issue.

In contrast with his earlier stand, Cooper in recent Congresses has opposed efforts to curtail the T.V.A. He has voted consistently for renewal of the reciprocal trade agreements initiated by former Secretary of State Cordell Hull, and has voted with regularity against the

Wide World

JERE COOPER

recurrent anti-poll-tax and fair employment practices bills. In the Republican-dominated Eightieth Congress he favored the overriding of President Truman's veto of the Taft-Hartley law and in the Eighty-first Congress voted passage of the subversive activities control bill in the face of Presidential objections. Cooper supported the tidelands oil bill in 1948 and again in 1950, and, although representing a largely agricultural district, has been critical of the Brannan farm plan.

With the return of Congress to Democratic control in January 1949, Robert Doughton resumed the chairmanship of the Ways and Means Committee he had vacated two years earlier; but by October of that year the *U.S. News & World Report* observed that the elderly North Carolinian had "really . . . lost control of the Committee" to Cooper, who was "inclined more to the New Deal side of tax issues."

Since Doughton was not a candidate for re-election in 1952, Cooper would, as the ranking Democrat, have become chairman of the Ways and Means Committee if his party had retained its majority in the House. However, with the Republican control of the Eighty-third Congress, the chairmanship was taken over by Daniel A. Reed of New York (a long-time advocate of reduced federal expenditures and taxation). A majority of the new committee recommended in June 1953 the bill to renew the reciprocal trade agreements (contingent on the inclusion of a rider increasing membership in the Tariff Commission from six to seven). Cooper led a vigorous but fruitless fight in the House against this provision.

He was one of the committee members reporting favorably on an extension of the excess profits tax. When the G.O.P. claimed credit for tax reductions scheduled for 1954, he accused the Republicans of "laying down a psychological smoke screen," maintaining that

COOPER, JERE—*Continued*

coming cuts had been voted two years earlier by the previous Democratic-controlled Congress (New York *Times*, September 27, 1953).

On August 10, 1953 Cooper was appointed to President Eisenhower's new seventeen-member bi-partisan Commission on Foreign Economic Policy. In an address to the Mid-south World Trade Institute in September, he warned that we must move "swiftly to liberalize . . . trade policies and to seek reduction of trade barriers throughout the free world generally to ease the dollar gap." Cooper made his first television appearance on March 16, 1954 as one of three leading Democrats (the others were House Floor Leader Sam Rayburn and Senator Walter George) assembled to answer a plea by President Eisenhower for passage of the tax bill then pending. "We Democrats," stated Cooper, "propose to change this tax program by eliminating the provision which will give a special advantage, worth hundreds of millions of dollars, to . . . those fortunate enough to own corporation stock."

Cooper's voting record in the Eighty-third Congress shows that he favored the St. Lawrence Seaway project, social security expansion, and flexible as opposed to rigid farm price supports. He opposed statehood for Hawaii and relaxation of the immigration laws to admit 217,000 refugees from Communism.

In January 1955, when the Democratic-controlled Eighty-fourth Congress convened, Cooper became chairman of the House Ways and Means Committee and also of the Democratic Committee on Committees, a post carrying "much influence in choosing Democrats to sit on other committees" (New York *Times*, January 5, 1955). On January 24 the Joint Committee on Internal Revenue Taxation chose him as chairman.

Early in the first session of the Eighty-fourth Congress Cooper moved to implement President Eisenhower's recommendations for a liberalized trade policy by sponsoring an Administration bill which would extend the Reciprocal Trade Agreements Act for another three years and would increase the President's authority to lower tariffs. This recommendation, and a similar measure introduced by a Republican member of the Ways and Means Committee, Robert W. Kean of New Jersey, were drafted under the supervision of Clarence B. Randall, chairman of the President's Commission on Foreign Policy. Hearings on the Cooper bill, "H.R.1," were scheduled to begin on January 17.

The Congressman has been variously characterized as "shrewd," "courtly," and "the loneliest man in Washington." His marriage to Mary Lucille Rankley, who came to Dyersburg from Kentucky to teach history in the high school, took place on December 30, 1930. Mrs. Cooper died of pneumonia on October 2, 1935, leaving one son, Jere Cooper, Jr., who died in his sixteenth year. Cooper's colleagues say he "lives, eats and breathes" the House, and Sidney Shalett notes that "the few dinners and balls he goes to are almost entirely connected with official Congressional functions or with the Tennessee State Society." His "favorite athletic fete is the annual baseball game between House Democrats and Republicans, which he attends as a spectator." He is a Mason, Knight Templar, Shriner, Maccabee and Moose; his fraternity is Kappa Sigma. A Presbyterian in faith, Jere Cooper has been for twenty years an elder of a church in which he was once the Sunday School superintendent.

References

Biographical Directory of the American Congress, 1774-1949 (1950)
Congressional Directory (1954)
Who's Who in America, 1954-55

CORBETT, JIM 1875-Apr. 19, 1955 Big-game hunter; author; born of British ancestry in India where he early became interested in the jungle; worked for over twenty years for a railroad company in India; from 1920 to 1936 spent much time in Tanganyika, Africa, where he hunted and tracked big game; supervised growing of coffee and maize on his plantation on slopes of Mount Kilimanjaro; his most famous book, about killer tigers in India, was *Man-Eaters of Kumaon* (1946), translated into many languages. See *Current Biography* (May) 1946.

Obituary

N Y Times p29 Ap 21 '55

COTTRELL, (IDA) DOROTHY (WILKINSON) July 16, 1902- Author

Address: b. c/o William Morrow & Co., Inc., 425 4th Ave., New York 16; h. Pioneer House, Tennessee Rd., Homestead, Fla.

Reprinted from the *Wilson Library Bulletin* Sept. 1955

Dorothy Cottrell's novels are set in far-away lands of adventure and enchantment which she knows intimately through her own background and travels. The fact that since childhood she has been chair-fast—a victim of polio—has never dampened her enthusiasm for travel and adventure nor her zest for living. She regards herself not as one who miraculously overcame almost insuperable difficulties, but as one who has been able simply to come to terms with the realities of a major disability and to build a constructive life around her physical limitations. "Certainly I would like to be able to walk," she writes, "but if the good fairy of the old stories offered me the one gift, the ability to walk would not be the thing I would ask for. More years with my husband than I may normally expect, the ability to write better—a dozen things—would come before it."

Ida Dorothy Wilkinson was born in New South Wales, Australia, July 16, 1902, to Walter Barwon and Ida C. Wilkinson. After the attack of polio when she was six years old, she spent some time on a ranch belonging to her uncle in Queensland where at the age of ten she was a crack shot with a rifle and an expert "dingo howler." (The dingo is a wild dog, an enemy of sheep, an imitation of whose disagreeable howl is used by hunters to lure him out into the open.) She gave up shooting dingoes at the age of twelve in order to pursue the study of art. Although she made progress at the Royal Academy in Sydney, she abandoned this pursuit after a few years to devote herself to writing.

On May 21, 1922, the young writer married Walter MacKenzie Cottrell. Mrs. Cottrell's first novel, *The Singing Gold,* a story of outdoor life in Queensland, was serialized in the *Ladies' Home Journal* in 1928. She sent it in hoping to realize $100 on it and was surprised to receive a check for $5,000. The book was published by Houghton, Mifflin, Boston (1929) and was reprinted twice within a month of publication. *Earth Battle* (in America *Tharlane*), a romance about ranch life in Australia, was published in 1930. Two famous animal stories followed: *Winks, His Book* (Houghton, 1932) about a little dog and *Wilderness Orphan* (Angus, 1936) about "Chut," a pet kangaroo. *Wilderness Orphan* was made into a movie.

Critical appraisal of Mrs. Cottrell's work has been generally favorable. Of her story *Wilderness Orphan* the American naturalist Donald Culross Peattie remarked in the *Saturday Review of Literature:* "Not to have a kangaroo for a friend and pet is almost more than I can stand after reading Mrs. Cottrell's book." The New York *Times* found that the author "wrote with sympathy, in prose of unusual quality with a touch of sentimentality where her human characters are concerned, but the animals are treated on their own terms. There is evocative magic in her calling up of the atmosphere of the Australian country. . . . In regional literature, as well as in studies of nature, she has won a place of her own." In his summation of her work in *20 Australian Novelists* (1947) Colin A. Roderick felt that her "Chut," the kangaroo, fell short of Jack London's *Call of the Wild* by its assumption in the animal of motives which coexist with complex human powers.

Concerning *The Silent Reefs* (Morrow, 1953), a mystery-adventure story with a Caribbean setting, critics were more or less agreed that while the characterization was of the all-good versus all-bad school so common to magazine fiction, the atmosphere, plotting, and writing were praiseworthy and rewarding. "Mrs. Cottrell's quaint, old-fashioned formality of writing is attractive," V. P. Hass commented in the Chicago *Tribune,* and he summed up the book as "an adventure yarn out of the top drawer." Rex Lardner described it in the New York *Times* as "a fascinating study of intrigue and integrity in a colorful setting."

Mrs. Cottrell advises that she would have written more if she and her husband were not so thoroughly imbued with wanderlust. As they are both boating enthusiasts, and as her disability has not curbed her adventuresome spirit, she willingly abandons her typewriter to board any vessel which will sustain her wheelchair. Indeed, she once attempted to negotiate a rowboat on the Miami River in spite of her doctor's specific warning that she should not do it. She might have succeeded notwithstanding the doctor's warning had not a sea cow loomed up out of the water next to the bow. The sight of this 1500-pound aquatic creature so unnerved her that she fell overboard, sustaining a serious injury. "I broke my back, spending four years flat on same," she said. It was not until the end of 1945 that she was able to take up writing again.

DOROTHY COTTRELL

The Cottrells now divide their time between Florida, where they have a farm, and the smaller islands of the West Indies. As she has said, they prefer the little islands "that still grow Elizabethan flowers and whose people use words that ceased to be part of normal English three centuries ago." In an article in the *Saturday Evening Post,* "How to Wear a Wheelchair" (June 10, 1950), she concludes: "To wear your wheelchair or your disability successfully . . . always remember . . . the fact that it is better to be lame in the foot than the head."

References

Sat Eve Post 219:10 My 24 '47 por; 222:44+ Je 10 '50 pors

Roderick, C. A. ed. 20 Australian Novelists (1947)

Who's Who in Australia, 1950

COUVE DE MURVILLE, (JACQUES) MAURICE (kōōv dẽ mūr-vĭl') Jan. 24, 1907-
French Ambassador to the United States

Address: b. c/o The French Embassy, 2535 Belmont Rd., N.W., Washington, D.C.; h. 2221 Kalorama Rd., N.W., Washington, D.C.; 44, rue du Bac, Paris 7ᵉ, France

When Henri Bonnet announced his retirement as French Ambassador to the United States in late 1954, Maurice Couve de Murville, "one of France's youngest and most brilliant diplomats," was appointed to succeed him. Couve de Murville is well known to American officials, since he has often dealt with them in the course

French Embassy Press & Inf. Division

MAURICE COUVE DE MURVILLE

of his visits to the United States and during his service as a French deputy to many of the "Big Four" foreign ministers' conferences since the end of World War II. In 1955, on his arrival in the United States to take up his ambassadorial duties, he stated that the need for solidarity between the United States and France was becoming "more complete and more necessary."

Originally a career official in the Ministry of Finance, Maurice Couve de Murville entered diplomacy following his escape from Vichy France in 1943 to join the provisional French government under General Charles de Gaulle in North Africa. His most recent posts have been those of Ambassador to Egypt and French representative to the North Atlantic Treaty Organization. He is an officer in the French Legion of Honor.

Jacques Maurice Couve de Murville, the son of Edouard and Hermine (Caesar) Couve de Murville, was born in Reims on January 24, 1907. Until shortly before the French revolution, the Couve de Murville family had lived on Mauritius, an island near Madagascar. From then until the present, the family has been established in France. Maurice's father was a well-known judge. After finishing his secondary schooling, young Maurice received his doctorate in law, his licentiate in literature from the Sorbonne, and a diploma in history from the École des Sciences Politiques.

He passed the examinations and became an inspector of finance in 1930. Seven years later he was promoted to assistant director in the Ministry of Finance and then in 1938 an associate director of foreign finance, in which capacity, reported *PM* (March 28, 1943), "he was chief French architect of the Anglo-French currency pooling agreement of December 1939." In 1940 Couve de Murville became director of external finance of the Ministry of Finance. Following the armistice of 1940 and the establishment of the Vichy government, he remained at his post. Eventually, because of his "republican sentiments," he was dismissed by the Vichy administration and deprived of his French citizenship.

For some time he was obliged to remain in France, until he found a way through Spain in 1943 to North Africa, where he offered his services to the Free French government. Late in March 1943 he was appointed civilian secretary-general of the North African command, to succeed Jean-Marie-Joseph Bergeret as "official alter ego in civil matters" to General Henri Honoré Giraud, civil and military commander in chief of French North Africa.

In June of that year, Couve de Murville became finance commissioner of the French Committee of National Liberation in Algiers and was able to announce that "the public loan has succeeded beyond almost all hopes, and one of the most important successes of our war financial policy has been the development in our territories, under present circumstances, of a real market for public loans." He was succeeded in this post by Pierre Mendès-France in November 1943.

Early in 1944, as French member of the Allied Advisory Council on Italian Affairs, Couve de Murville negotiated with Italian Foreign Minister Alcide de Gasperi on French recognition of the Italian government of Dr. Ivanoe Bonomi. Since he had pursued the major part of these negotiations, Couve de Murville in 1945 was named Ambassador to Italy by the provisional French government.

The explanation of French policy concerning Germany also came within Couve de Murville's province. In 1945 he headed a group of experts who went to London for this purpose and in November 1945 he was sent to Washington, D.C. to present to the U.S. State Department the French plan for the internationalization of the Ruhr basin and for the separate administration of the Rhineland. The New York *Post* later reported that he "returned from Washington with clear impressions that the U.S. would not discuss sympathetically the French thesis unless France first showed its willingness to cooperate" on the establishment of a central administration for Germany.

After his appointment as director-general of political affairs in the Ministry of Foreign Affairs in 1945 and as Deputy Foreign Minister, Couve de Murville attended numerous international conferences. During the summer of 1946 he was present at the Paris peace conference and in the fall, at the Foreign Ministers' Council meeting in New York, where he substituted for Georges Bidault. This was held simultaneously with the meeting of the United Nations General Assembly, which Couve de Murville attended as a member of the French delegation under Alexandre Parodi.

In an interview with the press late in 1946, Couve de Murville summarized France's policy toward Germany, advocating its federation under a decentralized government, the internationalization of the Ruhr, and the restoration of the German economy. At the same time he expressed doubt that Germany could be built into a democratic state without a long period of education to that end.

When the preliminary negotiations toward a peace treaty for Germany and Austria got under way in London early in 1947, Couve de Murville was sent as France's deputy. At this time, the French government abandoned its demand for the political separation of the Ruhr and the Rhineland from the rest of Germany, but announced that it still favored a decentralized type of government for Germany. Official nominations to the French delegation to the Foreign Ministers' Council in 1947 again made Bidault its chairman, and Couve de Murville one of the delegates.

Until 1950 Maurice Couve de Murville served as deputy to the Foreign Minister at all of the sessions of the council, thus participating in September 1948 at the Paris "Big Four" meeting, where he attacked the Soviet proposal—similar to one previously advanced by the U.S. Secretary of State James F. Byrnes—to place Italian colonies under U.N. trusteeship. The French view on this plan, stated Couve de Murville, was that it would place too great an administrative burden on the young organization. In another discussion on the disposal of Italy's former colonies, he advocated restoration of the Somaliland to Italy as "a well-deserved tribute to the successful efforts that country has already made to wipe out the traces of the recent past and to resume its democratic traditions."

The decision on the colonies was left to the U.N. General Assembly, which in 1949 voted for Libya to become independent by January 1, 1952 and for Italian Somaliland to be placed under Italian administration for ten years (within the U.N. trusteeship system) before gaining independence. Couve de Murville told the assembly that France abstained from the voting because, among other reasons, it did not think that either colony would be ready for independence at the time set. In 1950 the assembly voted for a federation of Eritrea and Ethiopia under the crown of Haile Selassie, Ethiopian emperor.

The Deputy Foreign Minister attended the conference which established NATO in 1949 and in the following year was alternate representative to the fifth General Assembly meeting. Appointed French Ambassador to Egypt in 1950, the diplomat filled that post for four years, during which time Egypt underwent a "bloodless" revolution, overthrew the monarchy, and became a republic.

Couve de Murville was recalled to Paris in September 1954 to replace Hervé Alphand as French representative to NATO. He had held this post only a short time when it was announced that he had been chosen to succeed Henri Bonnet as Ambassador to the United States. "His long acquaintance with the German problem and his many former contacts with United States officials," wrote Lansing Warren of the New York *Times* (November 4, 1954), "have especially fitted Couve de Murville to replace the present Ambassador, who has reached retirement age." On January 31, 1955 Couve de Murville presented his credentials to President Eisenhower.

Writing about the "instability" of the French governmental system after the fall of Pierre Mendès-France's Cabinet, the New York *Times* (February 16, 1955) noted that in Couve de Murville's judgment, "the present system represents another 'ancien régime' which is yielding to another 'revolution' staged by the younger generation that is giving France new vitality."

Married on November 10, 1932 to Jacqueline Schweisguth, Maurice Couve de Murville is the father of Juliette (Madame Patrice Vieljeux), Dorothée, and Béatrice. He is of Protestant faith. He has been described as "tall, lean and handsome"; he smokes a pipe. Card-playing is his indoor amusement, and riding and golf occupy him outdoors. He also enjoys reading the classics. His great enthusiasm, reports the New York *Times*, "is for the city of Paris. When he is not there, he longs ardently to return, and his hobbies do not alleviate the longing, say those who know him."

References

Le Monde S 16 '54
PM p8 N 5 '46
N Y Times p7 N 13 '46 por; p4 N 4 '54 por; p4 Ja 28 '55 por
Washington (D.C.) Post p3B N 14 '54 por
Dictionnaire Biographique Français Contemporain (1954)
Who's Who in France (Paris), 1953-54
World Biography (1954)

COYNE, JAMES E(LLIOTT) July 17, 1910- Governor of the Bank of Canada; lawyer

Address: b. c/o Bank of Canada, 234 Wellington St., Ottawa, Ontario, Canada; h. 738 Eastbourne, Ottawa, Ontario, Canada

After serving for five years as deputy governor of the Bank of Canada, James E. Coyne became its second governor on January 1, 1955, succeeding Graham F. Towers. In line with his reputation for "tackling large and complicated problems," Coyne, as head of the government's central bank, is helping with a reassessment that Canada is undertaking with a view toward stimulating its economy and reducing unemployment (*Christian Science Monitor*, March 14, 1955).

Coyne, who was a Rhodes scholar, practiced law for a few years until he became more interested in economics and joined the research staff of the Bank of Canada in 1938. During World War II, he was secretary of the Foreign Exchange Control Board for about a year and a half, financial attaché at the Canadian Embassy in Washington, D.C., and a member of the Royal Canadian Air Force. He returned to the Bank of Canada late in 1944 and became executive assistant to the governors.

James Elliott Coyne was born in Winnipeg, Manitoba, Canada on July 17, 1910, the elder son of James Bowes and Edna Margaret

Capital Press Service

JAMES. E. COYNE

(Elliott) Coyne. His father, an attorney, became Justice of the Manitoba Court of Appeals in 1946. James Elliott, his brother John and sister, Mary Margaret, attended public schools in Winnipeg. The boys went on to the University of Manitoba in Winnipeg (James received his B.A. degree in 1931) and both won Rhodes scholarships. James entered Oxford University in England and received his B.C.L. degree in 1934. His brother John later established a law practice in Ottawa.

James entered his father's law firm on his return to Winnipeg and was admitted to the Manitoba bar. When the late J. E. Ralston, chief counsel for the Turgeon Royal Commission, needed a junior counsel during his survey of the grain trade in 1937, young James E. Coyne was chosen. While traveling with the commission, he met Graham F. Towers, governor of the Bank of Canada (see *C.B.*, February 1952), who was on a tour of the prairies to examine the finances of the western provinces. Coyne had discovered that his study of the economics of wheat production was more interesting to him than the practice of law, and accepted, in 1938, Towers' offer to become a member of the central bank's research staff.

One of his first assignments with the bank was a comparative study on financial problems that affected the federal states. Later he was one of a group entrusted with the establishment of the Central Mortgage Bank, an institution designed for debt adjustment in Western Canada. The Mortgage bank was dissolved before it got under way early in 1939, because of the possibility of war in Europe, and the same group of bank officials was assigned to plan the control of foreign exchange. Coyne was secretary of Canada's Foreign Exchange Control Board from September 1939 to early in 1941.

He was loaned to the Department of Finance in March 1941 for service as financial attaché to the Canadian Embassy in Washington, D.C. The Ottawa *Citizen* (November 19, 1954) wrote that Coyne, while in Washington before the United States had entered World War II, handled "one of the toughest jobs of the war—the problem of how to buy supplies so desperately needed from a strictly neutral country."

When Coyne returned to Canada in December 1941 he helped to organize the over-all price ceilings of the War-time Prices and Trade Board as assistant to chairman Donald Gordon (see *C.B.*, October 1950), and served as deputy chairman in 1942. In November 1942 he enlisted in the Royal Canadian Air Force and trained as a pilot, only to discover that age limitations prevented his entering the overseas service. He was thirty-four when he went back to the Bank of Canada in 1944 as executive assistant to the governors.

Coyne's legal training, his knowledge of economics, and the fact that he was a "hard worker"—often devoting evenings and weekends to complete special projects—determined his appointment as deputy governor of the bank when Donald Gordon resigned to become president of Canadian National Railways, in December 1949, according to *Saturday Night* (December 13, 1949.) As deputy governor, Coyne's responsibilities included the direction of the bank's "operations in the government securities market, and the bank's activities in connection with the savings bond campaigns" (Montreal *Star,* November 15, 1954.)

The Bank of Canada began its operations on March 11, 1935, and until the retirement of Graham F. Towers at the end of 1954, had but one governor. The appointment of Coyne to the governorship on November 18, 1954 was later approved by the Cabinet. He assumed his new duties on January 1, 1955 at a reputed salary of $50,000 a year, said to be the highest paid government banking official in Canada.

According to the Bank of Canada Act (1934), the central banking institution's duties are to regulate credit and currency "in the best interests of the economic life of the nation," and to mitigate "fluctuations in the general level of production, trade, prices, and employment, so far as may be possible within the scope of monetary action." The federal government's banker and chief adviser on economic and fiscal matters, the Bank of Canada issues its securities and has assumed control of bank note issue and management of the national debt.

Within several months after Coyne became governor, the Bank of Canada had reduced the interest rate from two to one and a half per cent. This brought the Canadian dollar close to parity with the American dollar (New York *Herald Tribune,* February 27, 1955). Bruce Hutchison, writing in the *Christian Science Monitor,* March 14, 1955, noted that Canadian exporters had long complained that the Canadian dollar, at a substantial premium over the American dollar, was a barrier to the nation's exports and encouraged imports. The government, acting through the central bank to reduce the value of the Canadian dollar, had attempted to stimulate circulation of money internally, to create a slight inflation, and to satisfy Canadian industry.

Unemployment figures estimated at nearly seven per cent of a growing labor force and the federal government's budgetary deficit were other factors that caused the economic reassessment. Coyne indicated that neither he nor other Canadian experts were disturbed about the deficit, and stated that "under conditions of less than full employment a deficit is almost automatic if there has been a previous balance" (*Christian Science Monitor*, March 14, 1955).

James Elliott Coyne, familiarly known as "Jim," is a bachelor. Meg McLaughlin (*Saturday Night*, December 13, 1949) described him as a quiet man with a "definite charm . . . tall . . . good-looking . . . with a ruddy complexion . . . and . . . a resemblance to Gary Cooper," and an air of being "relaxed and intent at the same time."

His apartment in Ottawa is lined with pictures and books. For recreation, he is said to enjoy reading and discussing his favorite topics — economics, history and politics — with friends. He has a reputation as a good cook of the "eggs, steak and cans variety." During the summer, he likes to swim and play golf. He is a member of the Canadian Institute of International Affairs and a director of the Industrial Development Bank and of the Central Mortgage & Housing Corporation.

References

Montreal Star p 1+ N 15 '54
Ottawa Citizen N 19 '49 por
Sat Night D 13 '49 por; 70:3 D 18 '54 por
Who's Who in America, 1954-55

CULLEN, HUGH ROY July 3, 1881-

Businessman; philanthropist

Address: b. 1710 City National Bank Bldg., Houston 2, Texas; h. 1620 River Oaks Blvd., Houston 6, Texas

Texas oil millionaire Hugh Roy Cullen has given away approximately 93 per cent of his fortune (which is estimated at $250,000,000). Known as "the king of the Texas wildcatters," he is one of the pioneers in the oil business who discovered millions of barrels of oil in Harris and Ford Bend counties, including areas which geologists and big companies had abandoned. His generosity has made the University of Houston the fastest growing university in the United States.

Other recipients of Cullen donations have been the Girl Scouts, Houston College for Negroes, Y.M.C.A., Y.W.C.A., Texas Medical Center in Houston, several Houston hospitals, Baylor School of Medicine in Houston, Gonzales Warm Springs Hospital for Infantile Paralysis, the Houston Symphony Orchestra, and Houston art museum. He established the Cullen Foundation in 1947 to aid educational, medical and charitable institutions. It receives the income of 18,511 acres of oil-bearing lands, estimated to be worth $160,000,000.

Cullen has readily admitted that it is easier for him to give away $1,000,000 now than it was $5 in his youth. "My wife and I are that selfish we wish to see our money spent during our lifetime," he has said, "so that we may derive great pleasure from it." The oilman is an ardent champion of individual rights and has taken an active interest in political campaigns throughout the United States. In Texas he is regarded as a friend of labor.

Descended from English and Scottish colonists, Hugh Roy Cullen was born on July 3, 1881 in Denton county, Texas to Cicero and Louise (Beck) Cullen. His grandfather, Ezekiel Cullen, who fought with the Texas Raiders, was a member of the legislature of Texas and a founder of the Texas public school system. Hugh Roy, who grew up in San Antonio, had one brother and five half brothers and sisters. Shortly after the birth of his younger brother, Dick, his mother and father separated. Hugh Roy was introduced to the writings of Charles Dickens, Washington Irving, James Fenimore Cooper, and Sir Walter Scott by his mother.

At the age of twelve, Hugh Roy left public school and went to work in a factory in San Antonio, sacking candy at $3 a week. Each week he gave his mother his entire salary. He devoted his evenings to serious reading and to the study of maps and charts. Several years later he worked in the office of Ralli Brothers at Schulenburg, one of the largest cotton buying firms in the world. When he was eighteen he obtained a position with W. B. Clarkson as a cotton buyer.

Shortly after his marriage to Lillie Cranz on December 29, 1903, Cullen established himself as an independent cotton buyer and he began to ship cotton all over the world. His reputation for honesty and reliability soon earned him $250,000 of credit with only his word as collateral. He acquired a seat on the Houston Cotton Exchange and also became a real-estate operator. He helped to arouse public sentiment in Houston for a $3,000,000 bond issue to finance the construction of municipal wharves along the Ship Canal (which was completed in 1914) to handle incoming ocean vessels.

Traveling throughout Texas during 1917, Cullen leased land for oil prospecting and learned the wildcatter's tool—"creekology," the "down-to-earth clues, such as the course of rivers and creek-beds and dry streams, which he patched together with geological data until the formations of the earth far below seemed to spread out like a map in his mind" (*Hugh Roy Cullen*, his biography published in 1954).

Later he and J. M. West founded the South Texas Petroleum Company with $10,000 of working capital. Cullen's first profitable discovery was at Pierce Junction. Here the well yielded 2,500 barrels of oil a day, but went dry in two years. After three "heartbreaking years" at Damon's Mound, Cullen returned to Pierce Junction and discovered another well, almost as good as the first.

For three decades geologists and oil experts had failed in their attempts to draw oil from the rich Humble field because of the "heaving or Jackson shale." Cullen developed a special

HUGH ROY CULLEN

method of washing iron pipe with water instead of mud and forcing it beyond the shale with the result that his well at Humble brought 5,000 barrels a day. His next discovery was in 1927 at Blue Ridge, where five productive wells were drilled. A group of Wall Street investors offered to establish a corporation with Cullen as president and sell securities to the public. Bonds would be issued up to $60,000,000, of which half would be turned over to Cullen and West. Cullen refused saying: "If the company didn't turn out to be a success, I wouldn't have any right to the $15,000,000—I'd have to use my portion to pay back the bondholders."

In July 1930 Cullen's persistence and "uncanny prescience" was rewarded by the discovery of a $100,000,000 oil field at Rabb's Ridge. Cullen and West sold their interests in the Rabb's Ridge well for $20,000,000 and then abrogated their partnership. In 1932 Cullen formed the Quintana Petroleum Corporation, which is now run by himself, three sons-in-law and a grandson. The corporation discovered oil on the Tom O'Connor ranch in southeast Texas. The reserves in these wells are estimated at 500,000,000 barrels.

For his "originality of thought, daring and vision in the development of methods of drilling deep wells" Cullen received the Doctor of Science degree from the University of Pittsburgh in 1936.

In the midst of his fabulous prosperity, Cullen's only son, Roy Gustave, was fatally injured in 1936, when an unstable derrick toppled. Cullen gave $260,000 to erect the Roy Gustave Cullen Memorial Building at the University of Houston. Since that time Cullen has donated to the university over $26,500,000, which has enabled it to develop from a single wooden building on the San Jacinto High School campus to nine colleges, over forty-five new buildings and 250 acres. Its $300,000 television station provides free lessons in languages, psychology, Shakespearean drama, and piano playing. Cullen's first contribution to the university was contingent upon a policy of offering higher education to children of families with modest incomes.

During the economic depression of the 1930's, Cullen became interested in politics and "fired a broadside of telegrams" on members of Congress. He organized the Texas Regulars to oppose supporters of Franklin D. Roosevelt within the Texas Democratic party.

In the 1952 Presidential campaign Cullen actively supported General Dwight D. Eisenhower. Theodore H. White wrote that Cullen contributed money to thirty-four election campaigns in twenty-three states; twenty-two of his choices were winners. White stated that Cullen "has been credited with a share in the defeat of former Senators Scott Lucas of Illinois, Frank Graham of North Carolina, and Claude Pepper of Florida" (*Reporter,* May 25, 1954).

Cullen wants to prevent "bureaucratic involvements" of government in industry. However, he stated: "I am not opposed to proper regulation. There are those in all industry who need regulation. But it should be regulation of a free enterprise, in which politics should play no part."

He believes in a partnership of labor and management. In Norway and Sweden he observed employees, as stockholders, participate with managers in formulating policies. In writing to Thomas E. Dewey in 1944 he said: "The social revolution taking place in this country cannot be stopped until labor assumes a financial as well as moral responsibility. The only way this can be brought about is for labor to 'sit on the same side of the table' with capital." Organized labor in Texas has recognized him for many years as a staunch supporter of fair labor practices, and he was made an honorary member of the Musicians' Protective Association, American Federation of Labor.

Described as a tall, stocky man, slightly stooped, with twinkling gray eyes and a good crop of shaggy gray hair that was once black, Hugh Roy Cullen has the weather-beaten appearance of a man who has worked for a great part of his life outdoors. His white "witch elk" boots are his trademark in the oil fields. He and his wife live in a white mansion surrounded by famous camellia and azalea gardens. His four daughters are Lillie Cranz (Mrs. Paul Portanova), Agnes Louise (Mrs. Isaac Arnold), Margaret Ruth (Mrs. Douglas Marshall), and Wilhelmina Daisy (Mrs. Corbin J. Robertson).

Among honors conferred on Cullen are the Distinguished Service Award of the Mid-Continent Oil & Gas Association, Good Citizenship Medal of the Texas Society of the Sons of the American Revolution, National Citizenship Award of the Veterans of Foreign Wars, and the Horatio Alger Award of the American Schools and Colleges Association. He is a member of the Sons of the Republic of Texas, Huguenot Society and Academy of Political Science and an honorary member of the American Hospital Association. On September 22, 1951 Governor Allan Shivers announced a state-wide "Cullen Day" for Mr. and Mrs. Cullen's "excellent record of Christian stewardship." His clubs are the Houston Country, Bayou, River Oaks Country, and Houston in Houston, and the Southern Society in New York. He holds the honorary LL.D. degree from Baylor University (1945) and the University of Houston (1947).

Commenting on the biography by Edward W. Kilman and Theon Wright, *Hugh Roy Cullen: a Story of American Opportunity* (Prentice-Hall, 1954), the New York *Times* reviewer wrote: "The authors have no axe to grind . . . a warm, simply told tale of a he-man American who has known extreme sorrow and has experienced whatever joys come with making a billion dollars and giving most of it away."

The "king of the wildcatters" once remarked: "As long as I am an American, I intend to use my God-given right to fight for the things I believe made America strong, and to defend my country against the foreign 'isms' and the European and Asiatic political systems that I believe will make us weak, and ultimately destroy us" (*U.S. News & World Report,* February 11, 1955).

References

Christian Sci Mon p9+ My 7 '47 por
N Y Times p17 Mr 29 '47 por
Newsweek 31:20 F 9 '48 por
Time 49:29 Ap 7 '48 por
U S News 38:68+ F 11 '55 por
Kilman, E. W. and Wright, T. Hugh Roy Cullen (1954)
National Cyclopædia of American Biography Current Volume G (1946)
Who's Who in America, 1954-55

DALEY, RICHARD J(OSEPH) May 15, 1902- Mayor of Chicago

Address: b. City Hall, Chicago 2, Ill.; h. 3536 S. Lowe Ave., Chicago 9, Ill.

The mayor of America's second largest city, Chicago, and a leading figure in the Cook county Democratic party for twenty years, is Richard J. Daley. Elected on April 5, 1955 for a four-year term, he defeated two "reform" candidates, Republican Robert E. Merriam and incumbent Mayor Martin H. Kennelly, a Democrat. National attention was focused on the campaign and Daley received the support of former Governor Adlai E. Stevenson of Illinois, Democratic Presidential candidate in 1952, and senior Senator Paul H. Douglas of Illinois. Both the Democratic and Republican National Conventions were held in Chicago in 1952, and the Democratic party has announced that its 1956 Convention will also be held there.

Daley had served in the Illinois General Assembly (state legislature) from 1936 to 1946, as deputy comptroller of Cook county, and as director of the state department of finance when Stevenson was Governor. He had been serving as Cook county clerk and chairman of the county's Democratic party at the time of his election as mayor.

Richard Joseph Daley, of Irish descent, was born on the west side of Chicago, in the neighborhood of the stockyards, on May 15, 1902, the only child of Michael and Lillian (Dunn) Daley. As a youngster Dick sold newspapers at the corner of 35th and Halsted Streets, and upon graduating from DeLaSalle High School, went to work in the stockyards during the day, while he attended classes at De Paul University at night. He obtained both his college and law school education at De Paul, graduating with the LL.B. degree in 1933. In the same year he was admitted to the bar and became a practicing attorney. He later served as private secretary to four Cook county treasurers.

His first bid for public office took the form of a write-in campaign when the Democratic candidate for state representative from the ninth district died just before the primary. The campaign was a success and Daley was a member in the Illinois House of Representatives from 1936 to 1938. Elected to the state Senate in 1938, he served for two four-year terms. He was minority leader of the Senate from 1941 to 1946.

While in the legislature, Daley was an active exponent of public welfare measures. He fought to exempt food from the sales tax and worked for passage of a law to make Cook county tax assessments more equitable. He also supported the state grants to municipalities for housing developments. His only political defeat was for the post of Cook county sheriff in 1946.

After being appointed deputy comptroller of Cook county in 1946, Daley served in that post until 1949, when Governor Adlai E. Stevenson appointed him director of the Illinois department of finance. As Stevenson's legislative consultant as well, Daley helped to guide Stevenson's programs through the General Assembly. When the county clerk, Michael J. Flynn, died early in 1950, Daley was appointed to fill the vacancy. He was elected to a full term in the fall of 1950, and re-elected in 1954. He resigned that office after his election as mayor.

As county clerk, Daley supervised the microfilming of records. He also installed an International Business Machines system which made statistics concerning the citizens of Cook county readily available. (The population of Chicago had grown from 2,185,283 in 1910 to 3,620,962 in 1950.) Chicago was incorporated as a city in 1837, and was largely destroyed in the great fire of 1871. Today it is the largest meat-packing center in the world, one of the major grain centers, and is noted for its Merchandise Mart, the second largest office building in the world, exceeded only by the Pentagon in Washington, D.C. Its Natural History Museum ranks among the world's foremost museums, its Art Institute of Chicago wields much influence in the field of art, and its University of Chicago is noted for its faculty of outstanding scholars.

When Colonel Jacob M. Arvey retired in 1953 from the Cook county chairmanship of the Democratic party, Daley succeeded him. One of his innovations was to give the voters a choice in county judicial elections. Previously the practice had been for the two parties to

Wide World
RICHARD J. DALEY

agree on identical slates of candidates for the Superior and Circuit courts. Daley announced that the Democrats were abandoning the coalition system and running their own slate of candidates. "I have implicit confidence in the ability of the people to make the right decisions in all elections including judicial elections," said Daley at the time.

Daley's name was entered in the Democratic primary, held on February 22, 1955, and opposing him were Martin H. Kennelly, the incumbent mayor, and Benjamin S. Adamowski. As a businessman Kennelly had made a fortune in the storage and trucking business, and had been drafted in 1947 by the Democratic party as a nonprofessional "reform" candidate. He had been Chicago's mayor for two terms and was popular with businessmen and the press.

Time (April 16, 1951) observed that "Kennelly had tidied up the civil service and improved the police department a bit, but Chicago's crawling slums were as bad as ever, and crime was still a big problem. His own reputation for honesty was widely respected, but graft still bit deep into the city's pockets, and Kennelly did little to control the politics-ridden city council." Kennelly received 234,775 votes and Daley 364,839 votes in the primary election.

After Kennelly lost the primary, three of Chicago's four newspapers transferred their support to his Republican opponent, Robert E. Merriam, former alderman and the son of the late Professor Charles E. Merriam of the University of Chicago (who had twice been a candidate for Chicago's mayor). The younger Merriam had been an active Democrat until the fall of 1954 when he renounced Chicago party leaders as "machine-run." The Republicans took him over as their candidate for mayor, but the conservatives in the Republican party could remember that he had supported Stevenson for the Presidency of the United States in 1952.

During the campaign Daley's supporters argued that Merriam was "immature." The Republican contention was that Daley, because of his long political affiliations, would be beholden to an organization which had its seamy side. Both candidates promised a streamlined city council, a cleanup in the police force, improved public schools, better transportation and increased civil service. Mayor Kennelly also entered the race, and it is believed that he reduced Daley's majority.

While Daley's personal integrity was not questioned, even by his political opponents, his linkage with city politics and the so-called "machine" became a vital issue in the 1955 campaign. The election was reported in the press throughout the nation. Only one Chicago newspaper, the *American*, belatedly supported him.

Of the city's 1,946,477 registered voters, 1,289,121 voted, and Daley defeated Merriam by a vote of 708,660 to 581,461. Chicago has been Democratic since 1931, and the Democrats have lost only two mayoralty elections in the last sixty-seven years.

Summarizing the election issues, Godfrey Sperling, Jr., (*Christian Science Monitor*, March 26, 1955) wrote: "In the minds of a large segment of the public the battle is not Merriam vs. Daley. It is Merriam vs. the machine. Exaggerated or not, it is this viewpoint which lends the dramatic proportions to a fight which has become a temporary focal point of American politics."

The *U.S. News & World Report* for May 27, 1955, printed an extensive study of Chicago politics, and included an interview with Mayor Daley. When he was asked "What do you regard as your biggest opportunity, your biggest task, that you can accomplish in [your] four years?" Daley replied, "First . . . restore, rebuild and revitalize the spirit of Chicago which did so much to build this city. Our forefathers who came here had great courage and great imagination and boldness. . . . My big task will be to dedicate myself to restoring that kind of thinking about the city."

Daley is a member of the American, Illinois State and Chicago bar associations. He married Eleanor Guilfoyle in 1936, and the couple have seven children, Patricia, Mary, Eleanor, Richard, Michael, John, and William.

Popular at ward meetings, Daley is a dynamic speaker who presents his ideas energetically rather than with intellectual finesse. His close associates admire his intelligence, and note that he has a temper, which was revealed during television programs when newspapermen asked him insinuating questions. (Most political leaders avoid showing hostility to reporters during campaigns.) He is short and stocky. His religion is Roman Catholic.

Mayor Daley has "a friendly, but unaffected, directness of manner which seems to characterize every phase of his busy life," wrote Alan Whitney in the North Side (Chicago)

DALEY, RICHARD J.—*Continued*

Sunday *Star* (September 24, 1950). "Dick Daley impressed us as a man who, in a unique degree, has become well educated and has achieved leadership without losing contact with the people."

References

Christian Sci Mon p9 Mr 26 '55 por; p 1 Ap 6 '55 por
Life 38:52+ F 21 '55 pors
N Y World-Telegram p5 Ap 6 '55 por
Newsweek 45:18+ Ja 3 '55 por
North Side (Chicago) Sunday Star S 24 '50; O 11 '53 por
Time 65:22+ Mr 7 '55 por; 65:27 Ap 18 '55 por
U S News 38:81 Mr 4 '55 por; 38:16, 35 Ap 15 '55; 38:46+ My 27 '55 por

DARRELL, R(OBERT) D(ONALDSON)

(dăr' ĕl) Dec. 13, 1903- High-fidelity critic; editor; discographer

Address: Balmoral, The Vly, Stone Ridge, N.Y.

Rudolph de Harak

R. D. DARRELL

An expert in electronically recorded music, R. D. Darrell has been called the "Bach of high fidelity." His pioneer work, *Gramophone Shop Encyclopedia of Recorded Music* (Gramophone Shop, 1936), instituted discography and made him nationally known. He has been editor and writer for a number of leading periodicals in the field of recorded music, and in 1952 was discographic consultant to the music division of the New York City Public Library. His book, *Good Listening* (Knopf, 1953), appeared in 1955 in the New American Library reprint "Mentor" series in a revised edition. Currently, Darrell writes a semi-technical column, "Highs and Lows," for the *Saturday Review,* and an audio and music book review column "Listener's Bookshelf," for *High Fidelity.*

Robert Donaldson Darrell was born in Newton, Massachusetts on December 13, 1903, the son of Ernest Willis and Elizabeth (Donaldson) Darrell. He has one sister, Josephine. His paternal ancestry is English, and his mother, who was born in Nova Scotia, is of Scotch-Irish descent. The elder Darrell, a native of Boston, Massachusetts, played the trombone and contrabass as a semi-professional musician.

Young Robert attended the local public schools in Newton, Massachusetts, and was editor of the Newton High School *Review.* After his graduation from high school in 1922, he went to Harvard College for a few months, on a Cobb scholarship. Then he left in 1923 to enter the New England Conservatory of Music in Boston. Here he engaged in "quasi-independent studies" for three years. His major was composition, under Warren Story Smith, and five songs which he wrote, won the conservatory's prize for music composition in 1925. In the same year he attended the Concord Summer School of Music.

"Failure to win a prize with a large orchestral composition at the New England Conservatory of Music in 1926," Darrell has said, led to his free-lance writing career. At that time, he was given an opportunity "to do a few . . . reviews" for Warren Storey Smith of the Boston *Post.* Following this, came a chance meeting with Richard G. Appel, a staff member of the music division of the Boston Public Library, which resulted in Darrell's participation in the formation in 1926 of the first American record magazine, *Phonograph Monthly Review.* He reviewed records for four years and became its editor and publisher in 1930.

His next step was writing reviews for *Music Lovers' Guide,* which brought him to New York City in 1932. He joined the staff of the Gramophone Shop in 1934 as record researcher and consultant. From 1937 to 1939 he edited the *Gramophone Shop Supplement.* The publication in 1936 of his *Gramophone Shop Encyclopedia of Recorded Music,* the initial compilation of its kind, brought him nationwide recognition.

A reviewer for the New York *Times* (July 26, 1936) wrote: "This encyclopedia of recorded [classical] music is a real encyclopedia, far removed from the mere catalogue. . . . Under each composer's name is a careful critical résumé, and these well-written paragraphs are exceedingly interesting." In *Current History* (November 1936), the book critic described Darrell's encyclopedia as "the most ambitious and most comprehensive work on the subject yet published."

In 1939 Darrell became editor of the *Steinway Review of Permanent Music* (now the *Review of Recorded Music*). He enlisted in the U.S. Signal Corps Reserve in August 1942 and was honorably discharged on February 23, 1943. In that year, his book, *Highroad to Musical Enjoyment,* was published by the RCA Victor Company. He took postgraduate study at the Radio Television Institute in New York City, electing the electronic technician's course.

DARRELL, R. D.—*Continued*

From 1943 to 1946 Darrell served as senior writer and then supervising editor, for the instruction book department of Hazeltine Electronics Corporation, Little Neck, New York. His interest in electronics and high-fidelity sound equipment increased, and he prepared for the company an unsigned series of Army-Navy electronic gear instruction books. Then he returned to what had become the syndicated *Review of Recorded Music*, as its editor from 1947 to 1950.

In 1951 he compiled *Schirmer's Guide to Books on Music and Musicians* (Schirmer), which Ennis Davis (*Music Journal*, October 1952) called "an invitation to reading." Davis added that "to the serious researcher on a musicological mission the Darrell volume will perhaps have limited value. Darrell has blithely tossed away many important works with the notation that they are out of print." Roland Gelatt wrote in the *Saturday Review of Literature* (July 28, 1951): "If Mr. Darrell had not banished the foreign-language books to the appendix . . . I could pronounce his compendium without fault."

During 1952 Darrell was "classical" record reviewer for *Down Beat* magazine and he also began writing his column "Highs and Lows" for the *Saturday Review*. Referring to "the great 'high-fidelity' movement" in his *Saturday Review* column (August 29, 1953), he called for more specialized tastes—for "close-up, wide-range undiffused sound." Discussing "Chromium-Plated Vulgarity" in the *Saturday Review* (December 25, 1954), he called it a Herculean work to clear "a path through the tangled underbrush of tastelessness which is springing up in No Man's Land where the boundaries of engineering, esthetics, and commercialism overlap in the contemporary world of sound recording and reproduction."

He described " 'presence' and reverberation" as "two notable virtues of high-fidelity recording and reproduction," and "realistic recreation of percussive thunders and glitters" as another. "But," he wrote, "like all artistic virtues, these easily become boring or objectionable when they are carried to excess, when they concentrate excessive attention on themselves, or when they are musically out of place."

The Electronic Music Synthesizer, designed by Dr. Harry F. Olson to "coax musical sounds out of vacuum tubes," was termed by Darrell, a "fabulously complex" invention, and an "exciting harbinger of an impending *deus ex machina* for an ever-nearing cybernetic musical age" (*Saturday Review*, April 30, 1955). On the same date in his column, he advised that the Tape-of-the-Month Club, which every month provides its members with preview tape samples of recordings, offers "obvious advantages to any tape fan anxious to build up a miscellaneous pre-recorded library as cheaply and easily as possible."

In the field of discs, Darrell wrote that "all but the most insatiable of 'hi-fi' fanatics have begun to gag over 'demonstration' releases of high-decibel spicing and scanty musical or educative substance" (*Saturday Review*, April 30, 1955). "The danger, if not the sheer impossibility," he asserted, is defining high fidelity in any way that excludes "esthetic values and human experimental needs."

His book, *Good Listening* (Knopf, 1953), was described by Virginia Kirkus (August 15, 1953), as "a valuable little handbook for the majority of today's record collectors." The *Saturday Review* (October 31, 1953) described it as "entertaining" and stated that "the author's own predilections . . . emerge pretty clearly and without dogmatism." Darrell has written articles for *Hound and Horn, Musical Mercury, Sewanee Review, Victor Record Review* and *Electronics*, as well as papers for the Institute of Radio Engineers, Audio Engineering Society and Music Library Association.

A John Simon Guggenheim Fellowship was awarded to him in 1939. Ennis Davis described him in *Music Journal* (October 1952): "Darrell talks, thinks and acts with the same zest and drive that show up in his writing and editing." He is a charter member of the Audio Engineering Society, and an associate member of the Institute of Radio Engineers and the Acoustical Society of America. His other organization memberships include the Radio Club of America and the Ulster County Historical Society. He is a Democrat.

On September 30, 1930 Darrell married Emma Cartright Bourne, an artist. They were divorced in 1936. He has hazel eyes and "ex-red" white hair. He is five feet seven inches tall and weighs 120 pounds. His recreation includes reading, "particularly history and psychology," and walking. "What bothers me most," he avers, "is the too frequent perversion of great music itself when virtuoso interpreters and engineers run wild in the quest of distinctly 'different' and 'sensational' presentations of familiar materials" in recordings (*Saturday Review*, December 25, 1954).

Reference

Mus J p14+ O '52 por

DAVIS, BENJAMIN O(LIVER), JR. Dec. 18, 1912- United States Air Force officer

Address: b. c/o United States Air Force, The Pentagon, Washington, D.C.

On October 27, 1954 President Dwight D. Eisenhower designated as the first Negro general in the history of the United States Air Force Benjamin O. Davis, Jr., a West Point graduate and World War II combat pilot. The son of the first Negro general in the U.S. Army, Davis was director of operations and training of the Far East Air Forces, stationed in Tokyo. In June 1955 he was named vice-commander of the Thirteenth Air Force, now based at Clark Field in the Philippines. He is also commander of the newly created Air Task Force based on Taipei, Formosa. During World War II, as commander of the 332nd Fighter Group, he flew sixty combat missions, and was repeatedly decorated for bravery in action.

Benjamin Oliver Davis, Jr., was born in Washington, D.C., on December 18, 1912, the only son of Benjamin Oliver and Elnora (Dickerson) Davis. He has two sisters—Olive Elnora (Mrs. George W. Streator) and Elnora Dickerson (Mrs. James A. McLendon). His father, who entered the U.S. Army during the Spanish-American War, achieved the rank of brigadier general in October 1940. During World War II the elder Davis served successively as commanding general of the 4th Cavalry Brigade, special adviser and coordinator to the commander of the European Theater of Operations, and assistant to the inspector general. He retired from active duty in 1948.

Young Davis' mother died when he was five, and for the next two years he lived with his grandmother. He received his elementary education in the public schools of Washington, D.C. At the age of eight he was taken to Alabama, where his father had been assigned to teach military science at Tuskegee Institute. Four years later the family moved to Cleveland, Ohio, where Davis attended Central High School and was president of his class. He was graduated in 1929, Ben Richardson wrote in *Great American Negroes* (1945), "with one of the highest scholastic averages of the entire student body of the city."

From 1929 until 1930 Davis attended Western Reserve University in Cleveland, Ohio. Then, for the next two years, he studied at the University of Chicago, majoring in mathematics and hoping eventually to become an instructor in the subject. However, in 1932 he was recommended for an appointment to the United States Military Academy at West Point. Having little hope that he would gain admittance, or, if he achieved so much, that he would succeed at "The Point," from which no Negro had been graduated in fifty years, he failed the first time he took the entrance examinations. His initial failure, however, provided him with the incentive he had previously lacked, and after applying himself assiduously to his preparatory studies, he succeeded on his second attempt and thus became a "plebe," or first-year man.

His stay at West Point included a form of hazing known as "the silent treatment." Throughout his first year, none of Davis' fellow cadets ever spoke to him, or answered when he addressed them. He endured these slights with such impressive fortitude, however, that at a ceremony marking the end of the year his classmates cheered him vociferously.

Arna Bontemps wrote in *We Have Tomorrow* (1945), "Ben Davis, Jr., had stood the most severe test any boy had stood at West Point in at least fifty years, and he had passed it to the satisfaction of the whole class of his fellows. The wall of silence fell down like the walls of Jericho, and was never raised again." Davis was graduated with the rank of second lieutenant on June 12, 1936.

The first year after winning his commission he served as a company officer of the 24th Infantry at Fort Benning, Georgia. Then he attended the Infantry School on that post, and was graduated in 1938, when he became an instructor in military science and tactics at Tuskegee Institute, an assignment that lasted until 1941. During this tour at Tuskegee he was promoted to first lieutenant (June 12, 1939) and to captain (September 9, 1940). From February 1941 until May of that year he had "the pleasant assignment," in Richardson's phrase, of being aide-de-camp to his father at Fort Riley, Kansas.

U. S. Air Force

BRIG. GEN. BENJAMIN O. DAVIS, JR.

Beginning flight training in May 1941, he was graduated with the first Negro air cadets from the Advanced Army Flying School in March 1942 and, after being transferred to the Air Corps the following May, was placed in command of the 99th Fighter Squadron at Tuskegee. Meanwhile, on March 1, 1942, he had been promoted to major and lieutenant colonel. The next year he went overseas with the 99th, and served as commanding officer of its fighter unit in the North African, Sicilian and Italian campaigns.

Following his return to the United States on October 5, 1943, he assumed command of the all-Negro 332nd Fighter Group at Selfridge Field, Michigan, and directed group training until January 1944, when he took the unit overseas and into combat as part of the 12th Fighter Command of the Mediterranean Allied Air Forces under General Ira C. Eaker. Equipped with the P-39 and the P-47, his unit "strafed enemy shipping and did low-level skip-bombing at Cassino, Anzio and other points in Italy."

On May 29, 1944, he was promoted to the rank of full colonel. "It was a happy moment for both father and son in September 1944," wrote Bontemps, "when Brigadier General Benjamin O. Davis, Sr. (see *C.B.*, 1942), proudly pinned the Distinguished Flying Cross on the breast of Colonel Benjamin O. Davis, Jr., before members of the 332nd Fighter Group in Italy." The group was later assigned to the 15th Air Force, and by February 1945 it

DAVIS, BENJAMIN O., JR.—*Continued*
had completed 200 missions with the 15th "and had served as escort to heavy bombers without losing a single bomber to enemy fighters."

On April 16, 1945, according to a report in *PM* (June 27, 1945), Davis "led a strafing attack on railway targets in Austria, remaining in the danger area for an hour to destroy locomotives and rolling stock. The action won him the Silver Star for gallantry—the first time it has been awarded to a Negro fighter pilot in the Army."

On June 21, 1945 Davis was placed by General Eaker in command of the 477th Composite (bomber and fighter) group at Godman Field, Kentucky, and about a month later he became field commander. The New York *Times* (June 25, 1945) remarked editorially that Davis' appointment marked "another first for the precedent-breaking Davises, father and son," pointing out that the younger Davis was "the first [Negro] to hold such an important command in the Army Air Corps. It is officers like the Davises," the editorial continued, "who have done much to break down prejudice within the Army officers' corps."

Assuming command of the Lockbourne Army Air Base in March 1946, Davis was charged with responsibility "for activities of the 55th Fighter Wing, the 82nd Troop Carrier Squadron, Army Air Force Reserves, Army Air Corps communications facilities, U.S. Air Force Weather Detachment, the 449th Signal Battalion, and the 332nd Fighter Wing." He retained this command until 1949.

Entering the Air War College at Maxwell Air Force Base, Alabama. in August 1949, Davis was graduated the following June. He then became a staff planning officer in the plans division of the office of the deputy chief of staff for operations at Air Force Headquarters, Washington, D.C., until January 1951, when he was named chief of the fighter branch in that office. In July 1953 he entered the Advanced Jet Fighter Gunnery School at Nellis Air Force Base, Las Vegas, Nevada. Joining the Far East Air Forces that November, he assumed command of the 51st Fighter-Interceptor Wing of the Fifth Air Force. A half year later he was named director of operations and training of the Far East Air Forces.

In February 1954 *United States News & World Report* stated: "Benjamin O. Davis, Jr., now is being looked over by a Pentagon selection board for promotion that will make him the first Negro general in the U.S. Air Force. Colonel Davis has already headed the fighter operations branch of the Air Force, moved from that job last [year] into the kind of post often held by a brigadier general—command of the 51st Fighter-Interceptor Wing in Korea." On October 27, 1954 the contemplated promotion became a reality when President Eisenhower elevated Davis to the rank of brigadier general.

Reorganization of the Air Force in the Pacific area, which brought General Davis to Taipei, Formosa in June 1955, resulted in five airports being prepared there for American operations. This makes it possible for U.S. Air Force commanders to bring in planes from the Philippines, Japan or Okinawa. Under this reorganization the Thirteenth Air Force has switched from the jurisdiction of the U.S. Far East Air Forces to that of the Pacific Air Command, under the over-all supervision of Admiral Felix B. Stump (see *C.B.*, 1953), chief of the Pacific Fleet.

In addition to the Distinguished Flying Cross and the Silver Star, Davis has been awarded the Air Medal, with four Oak Leak Clusters, the Legion of Merit Award, and the French Croix de Guerre with Palm. He accepted a Presidential Unit Citation granted the 332nd Fighter Group for a hazardous mission over Berlin during World War II. He is rated a senior pilot. The Army officer married Agatha Scott, of New Haven, in 1936. He is six feet two inches tall.

References

U.S. News 36:8 F 26 '54 por
Washington (D.C.) Post p12 O 28 '54 por
Bontemps, A. We Have Tomorrow (1945)
Martin, F. ed. Our Great Americans (1953)
Richardson, B. Great American Negroes (1945)
Who's Who in Colored America (1950)

DAVIS, EDWARD W(ILSON) May 8, 1888- Metallurgical engineer
Address: b. c/o Reserve Mining Co., Silver Bay, Minn.

Through the ingenuity and persistence of Professor Edward W. Davis, "the father of taconite," a new billion-dollar industry has emerged in Minnesota, which has far-reaching implications for national defense. Aroused over the possibility of the depletion of the rich iron ore deposits on the Mesabi Range in Minnesota, he spent more than thirty-five years developing a commercially feasible process for extracting iron ore from a rock called taconite. (It is believed that the word "taconite" is derived from the Indian *tachkanick*, which means forest wilderness.)

The Reserve Mining Company begins in the fall of 1955 its new taconite plant, the E. W. Davis Works, which makes use of Davis' method, at Silver Bay, Minnesota. Early in 1957 the Erie Mining Company will begin producing iron ore from taconite, and the Oliver Mining division of the United States Steel Corporation is expanding its two experimental taconite plants. Within twenty years the taconite industry is expected to represent an investment of 1.5 billion, and to ship annually from Minnesota 30,000,000 tons of taconite, approximately one-third of the nation's ore requirements at present production.

On June 15, 1955, after thirty-nine years of service on its faculty, Davis retired from the University of Minnesota in Minneapolis. He joined the university's mines experiment station in 1913, became its superintendent in 1925 and its director in 1939. In 1952 he resigned the director's post to devote his efforts to the commercial development of taconite, but retained his professorship. Dr. James L. Morrill, president of the university, praised Davis for having "had the energy to carry forward, sometimes in the face of crushing discouragement, the patient and persistent endeavor that all fundamental research involves. He has had the perseverance of a crusader" (Two Harbors [Minnesota] *Chronicle & Times,* July 16, 1953).

The son of Walter Clarance and Della Mendenhall (Wilson) Davis, Edward Wilson Davis was born in Cambridge City, Indiana on May 8, 1888. After receiving the B.S. degree from Purdue University, Lafayette, Indiana in 1911, he spent a year as a testing engineer with the Westinghouse Electric and Manufacturing Company, and later worked for the General Electric Company. He became an instructor at the University of Minnesota's School of Mines in 1913, and taught there for two years. From 1915 until 1918 he was employed as a testing engineer by the Mesabi Iron Company of Duluth, Minnesota. He returned to the University of Minnesota in 1918 (he received an E.E. degree from Purdue that year) and remained there until his retirement from academic life thirty-seven years later. Appointed superintendent of the university's mines experiment station in 1925, he became its director in 1939 and served in that capacity until 1952.

While still a young man Davis became concerned over the possibility of depleting iron ore deposits on the Mesabi Range, and warned that it would eventually be necessary to extract iron from the iron-bearing rock surrounding the rich ore deposits. To this end he urged the development of a process to beneficiate the lean rock and the adoption of a state tax structure that would promote such a development by taxing the finished product rather than the ore in the ground, thus inviting private investment. "For years," as a writer for *Steel* (January 24, 1955) noted, "his cause was a lost one."

Hartzell Spence later confirmed Davis' fears of exhausting Mesabi ore reserves. He wrote in *Nation's Business* (August 1954): "The economy and security of the United States are pegged to steel. Steel in turn has been 75 per cent dependent on the fabulous iron riches of the Mesabi Range in Minnesota and adjacent deposits along Lake Superior. When war and postwar requirements wolfed 100,000,000 tons of ore a year, the depletion of U.S. resources ceased to be merely a future anxiety."

An important event in Davis's career was his meeting in 1913 with John G. Williams, a regent of the University of Minnesota, who owned large tracts of taconite lands, and sought a use for them. "He asked Professor Davis to experiment. . . . Taconite is a rock—technically an iron-bearing chert or shale, one of the hardest substances known to man. . . . [It] is about 25 per cent pure magnetic-iron particles, if they can be sprung from their natural prison. The entire eastern third of the Mesabi Range is overlaid with it to a depth of 175 to 300 feet. . . . The professor went to work on un-co-operative taconite, to achieve magnetic separation of the good iron from

Univ. of Minnesota
EDWARD W. DAVIS

finely-ground rock. By 1915 he had perfected the magnetic separator which is the crux of today's billion-dollar industry" *Nation's Business* (August 1954).

However, the tax problem and a number of technical difficulties remained unsolved. In 1941 the Legislature of Minnesota finally passed a law which placed a tax on processed taconite, but exempted from tax the value of holdings in the ground and capital invested in taconite production. Two years later Davis demonstrated his process, including his newly designed "pelletizer" to representatives of thirteen companies, proving that production of pig iron from taconite was economically practicable. On May 28, 1948 the Minneapolis *Star* reported that "for the first time in history" finished pig iron had been produced "from the rock called taconite" at the University of Minnesota's mines experiment station. The following day the New York *Times* announced: "Using new processes invented by Prof. E. W. Davis . . . and other methods . . . low grade ores can now be prepared for use in any blast furnace at a cost of only about $2 per ton."

The Reserve Mining Company constructed a vast taconite processing plant, costing more than $180,000,000, at Silver Bay, Minnesota and named it the E. W. Davis Works. "Started four years ago," Thomas E. Mullaney wrote in the New York *Times* (June 12, 1955), "this huge development on Lake Superior's verdant north shore will begin pouring out this fall marble-size pellets of concentrated iron ore at the rate of 4,000,000 tons a year. They will move down the lakes to the blast furnaces of the Republic Steel Corporation and Armco Steel Corporation, joint owners of this trail-blazing enterprise." The Erie Mining Company, U.S. Steel Corporation and Bethlehem Steel Company have also formed extensive development plans based on Davis's research. Mul-

DAVIS, EDWARD W.—*Continued*

laney pointed out that "the nation is assured of a great new industry that will represent an investment of more than $1.5 billion by 1975—an ace in the hole for America's security and expanding economy."

Although the birth of the taconite industry is widely credited to Davis' almost singlehanded persistence, he has said that no one man could have worked out the processes involved; that there are scores of individuals, including his associates at the mines experiment station in Minnesota, people in the iron ore, steel and equipment-manufacturing industries, who should share the credit. Davis' method has been applied commercially to jasper rock in Humboldt, Michigan and to magnetites at Mineville, New York.

From his new home in Silver Bay, Minnesota, Davis, who will be a metallurgical consultant of the E. W. Davis Works, will be able "to watch from his front window ore trains arriving from Babbitt, Minnesota and taconite boats steaming off into Lake Superior" (Leonard Inskip in the Minneapolis *Sunday Tribune*, May 22, 1955).

Davis is a member of the American Mining Congress, American Institute of Mining and Metallurgical Engineers, American Association for the Advancement of Science, and Eastern States Blast Furnace and Coke Oven Association. His fraternity is Phi Kappa Sigma. Purdue University conferred the honorary E.D. degree upon him in June 1955. Following his retirement from the University of Minnesota on June 15, 1955 he was made a professor emeritus. He holds about fifteen patents on ore dressing machinery and similar devices. Davis served with the War Production Board in 1944. He is a Republican and a Mason. His clubs are the Minneapolis Engineers and the Campus. On June 4, 1914 he married the former Jessie Mary Campbell; the Davises have three children, Jane, Martha and Ruth. The engineer has been described as tall and wiry and is called "Bud" by his friends.

According to *Nation's Business*, "Professor Davis is a vigorous dynamo who can paddle twenty-two miles across a Canadian lake to his summer cottage." He has many new plans and is particularly interested in Minnesota's peat bogs. The processing of taconite requires huge quantities of electricity, and he sees Minnesota's 7,000,000,000 tons of peat as a source of cheap fuel. He takes a lively interest in hunting, fishing, and golf.

"The future of northern Minnesota depends on what people can do with rocks like [taconite]. . . ," Professor Davis has said, alluding to unexploited fields of manganese, titanium, copper and nickel in Minnesota. "These deposits, like taconite, are of low-grade ores which await development of new mining and processing techniques and tremendous investment of capital" (Minneapolis *Sunday Tribune*, May 22, 1955).

References

Minneapolis Sunday Tribune My 22 '55
American Men of Science (1955)
Who's Who in Engineering, 1954

DAVIS, JOHN W(ILLIAM) Apr. 13, 1873-Mar. 24, 1955 International and corporation lawyer; Solicitor General of the United States and Ambassador to Great Britain during Woodrow Wilson's Presidency; Democratic nominee for President in 1924, being defeated by Calvin Coolidge; a leading authority on constitutional law and champion of states' rights; argued successfully in 1952 before the U.S. Supreme Court that President Harry S. Truman had exceeded his constitutional rights in seizing private property (steel mills); made 140 appearances before the Supreme Court—more than any other attorney in American history. See *Current Biography* (Mar.) 1953.

Obituary

N Y Times p1+ Mr 25 '55

DAVIS, ROY H(ENRY) June 15, 1885-Industrialist

Address: b. c/o Atlas Steels, Ltd., Welland, Ontario, Canada; h. "The Silo," Fonthill, Ontario, Canada

The president of Atlas Steels, Ltd., the leading Canadian producer of tool and specialty steels and the largest company of its kind in the British Commonwealth, is Roy H. Davis. He established the firm in 1928 when, with the aid of United States capital, he purchased a small plant, Canadian Atlas Steels, Ltd. In celebrating its twenty-fifth anniversary in 1952 the company attributed much of its steady advancement to the direction of its president. Davis had a background of experience with such specialty steel companies as Firth Sterling Steel Company of McKeesport (Pennsylvania) and Crucible Steel Company of America, with each of which he had held managerial posts.

Roy Henry Davis was born June 15, 1885 in Amity, Oregon, the son of Z. A. Davis and Amelia (Morton) Davis. He received his early education at the schools of Eugene, Oregon and then attended the University of Oregon. An appointment as midshipman took him to the United States Naval Academy at Annapolis, Maryland from which he was graduated in 1909. There followed four years of service in which he did special ordnance work and served with the Atlantic Fleet on the U.S.S. *Kansas* and the U.S.S. *Arkansas*.

While Davis was at Annapolis, his imagination was stirred by visits to steel mills, as related in the article "Vulcan's Apprentice" in *Saturday Night*. On resigning from the Navy he secured a position in 1913 with the U.S. Coal and Coke Company in Gary, West Virginia as a mechanical and electrical engineer, and continued in the employ of this subsidiary of the U.S. Steel Corporation until 1915. In that year he joined the staff of the Washington Steel and Ordnance Company, a New York firm, and remained with it for two years.

He then, at the age of thirty-two, left it to become general manager of the Firth Sterling Company of McKeesport, Pennsylvania, a tool steel manufactory. This plant, under his management, was one of the first in the Pittsburgh district to introduce the eight-hour day in the steel industry. In 1923, offered the management of one of the plants of Crucible Steel Company of America, well-known manufacturers of tool and specialty steels, Davis accepted and was put in charge of its Park Works at Pittsburgh.

In 1928 Davis saw the opportunity offered by Canadian Atlas Steels, Ltd, an American firm making tool and other specialty steels in a small plant at Welland, Ontario. Located in the industrialized Niagara area, the plant site was central, close to rail and water transport, to the power of Niagara Falls, and to the labor supply. Business trips for Crucible Steel had acquainted Davis with the area and with Canadian economic conditions, and he began to raise capital and open negotiations to purchase the firm.

"Canada impressed me," Davis has said. "It became an inspiration to me because of the great opportunity which future development offered. I could visualize industrial growth in steel along the pattern evolved in the Pittsburgh area." His vision and his reputation in the steel industry procured him financial backing in the United States.

The story is told that a prospective backer who asked to see the plant was persuaded to invest by Davis' telling him, "You don't want to see the plant, it's nothing much but some old machinery and old buildings. I'm asking you to invest in your belief in me and what I can make of that plant." In June 1928 negotiations were completed and Davis became president of the new company, Atlas Steels, Ltd.

Davis moved to Canada, became a naturalized Canadian citizen in 1935, and took charge of the development of the plant's production of tool and specialty steels. His experience lay in the manufacture of mining and hollow drill steels, tool, special machinery, magnet, valve and other specialty steels. To put the small plant on an efficient production basis, expansion of facilities was immediately undertaken. In the course of the first five months buildings were rearranged, production lines straightened, an overhead crane, electric furnaces and new heating equipment were installed, and provision was made for operating hammers with compressed air.

Emphasis was put on turning out products of high quality, and a policy of keeping abreast of new developments in machinery and processes was adopted, together with the practice of plowing back profits. For several years financing as well as production and sales received the president's attention.

In June 1952 Atlas Steels, Ltd, celebrated its twenty-fifth year of production. From a small plant with a payroll of thirty-five and a net profit of $3,517 its first year, it had been developed into a concern with installations stretching for one mile along the Welland Canal, a payroll of over two thousand at full production, and a net profit of upward of $2,500,000 in its anniversary year. It had become the major producer of tool and specialty steels in Canada, with branches or agencies in fifty-eight countries. Despite world depression

Karsh, Ottawa

ROY H. DAVIS

in its early years, the firm had advanced steadily, installing its first melting furnace in 1930-1931—thereafter it could melt its own metal rather than buy steel billets—starting metallurgical and chemical laboratories in 1932, increasing manpower to over 100.

In the post-depression years plant and equipment expansion, organization of its own sales force and establishment of branches with warehouses in Montreal, Toronto, Hamilton, and Winnipeg enabled Atlas to meet Canadian demand in special steels and to enter the export market. The years of World War II brought government-aided expansion to 700 per cent of pre-war size, with more than 90 per cent of production going directly into war work in the form of gun barrels, breech blocks, and shell steel.

In the post-war years Atlas entered the manufacture of stainless steel in sheet and strip forms with the installation of Canada's first mill for the making of hot rolled sheets (1950-1951) and its first mill for hot and cold strips (1951-1954). (The company had formerly produced stainless steel in billet, rod, bar and wire forms.) Another first for the company is the installation of machinery for the continuous casting of steel, a process previously applied in North America only to nonferrous metals. Atlas Steel, Ltd., announced in November 1954 that this machinery had started full-scale production.

The new mills and the $1,400,000 continuous caster are part of Atlas' $12,000,000 stainless steel production line. Since the company's capacity now exceeds Canadian demand, Atlas has begun a campaign to increase the market for stainless steel, in part by providing information on the uses of the product.

For its 1949 annual report Atlas Steels was awarded the Silver Oscar of Industry by the *Financial World,* and the presentation was made

DAVIS, ROY H.—*Continued*

to president Davis at the annual *Financial World* awards dinner in New York. In tribute to the importance and high quality of his steelworkers Davis commissioned world-renowned photographer, Yousuf Karsh, to make a series of portraits in action of the men who operate the machines at Atlas. The series was displayed in the chief cities of the world.

The industrialist is a director of the Toronto General Trusts Corporation, the Port Weller Dry Docks (St. Catharines, Ontario), and is a member of the board of governors of Hamilton (Ontario) College and of the advisory council of the Export Credits Insurance Corporation.

By his marriage in 1911 to Marion Marlin of Pittsburgh he has three daughters and one son, Richard; the latter is manager of personnel and public relations at Atlas Steels, Ltd., and is a member of its board of directors. Roy H. Davis is six feet one inch tall, and weighs 170 pounds.

Golfing, hunting, riding and fishing are his recreations; his clubs are the Toronto and the National (both in Toronto), the Vancouver (Vancouver, British Columbia), the Welland (Welland, Ontario), and the Lookout Point Country (Fonthill, Ontario).

References

Bsns W p162+ N 6 '54 por
Sat Night 65:33 Ja 31 '50; 68:25 Mr 7 '53
Canadian Who's Who, 1952-54
Directory of Directors, 1951

DEAKIN, ARTHUR Nov. 11, 1890-May 1, 1955 British labor leader; began work at the age of thirteen in a South Wales steel mill; a labor organizer since eighteen; succeeded Ernest Bevin as general secretary of the Transport and General Worker's Union (Britain's largest union) in March 1946; headed World Federation of Trade Unions in 1948, but withdrew after deciding that Communists controlled it; appeared three times on Royal honor lists "for services to trade union movement." See *Current Biography* (Jan.) 1948.

Obituary

N Y Times p21 My 2 '55

DÉAT, MARCEL Mar. 7, 1894-Jan. 5, 1955 French politician; journalist; pro-Nazi Minister of Labor in France's Vichy government during World War II; known as an anti-Semite, anticlericalist, and an Anglophobe; first elected to French Parliament in 1926; was leader of French defeatists before World War II; edited Paris newspaper *L'Oeuvre;* condemned to death in absentia in 1945 in France for collaboration with Germans. See *Current Biography* (Jan.) 1942.

Obituary

N Y Herald Tribune p18 Ap 1 '55

DE BROGLIE, LOUIS, PRINCE *See* Broglie, Louis (Victor Pierre Raymond), Prince de

DE GIVENCHY, HUBERT *See* Givenchy, Hubert (James Taffin) de

DEHLER, THOMAS (dā-lẽr) Dec. 14, 1897- Member of the Bundestag; lawyer

Address: b. Bundeshaus, Bonn, Germany; h. St. Getreustrasse 35, Bamberg, Germany

The leader of Germany's Free Democratic party, the second largest in Chancellor Konrad Adenauer's coalition government, is Dr. Thomas Dehler, who served as Minister of Justice in the first Cabinet of the Federal Republic of Germany. An "old-fashioned liberal" and a "stormy petrel" in politics, Dr. Dehler led the movement within the government coalition against acceptance of the Saar agreement in 1955. Several times he brought his party close to the breaking point with the Chancellor, but he effected last-minute reconciliations in the interest of unity.

Thomas Dehler was born on December 14, 1897, in Lichtenfels, Germany. His parents belonged to well-established butcher and brewery families. The boy attended the Gymnasium in Bamberg until 1914, when World War I interrupted his education. Entering the army, he rose to the rank of officer in the field artillery. After the war he studied law and political science at the universities of Freiburg, Würzburg and Munich. He was a member of the board of directors of the student republican organization and a founder of the antifascist *Reichsadler*. This was later incorporated into the *Reichsbanner Schwarz-Rot-Gold*, an association of republican ex-servicemen cofounded by Dehler in 1924.

Seeking to stem the rising tide of Nazism in the 1920's, the student helped to defend the plant of the Social Democratic newspaper in Munich when it was raided by Nazis. He received his doctorate in law and in political science, passed his bar examinations in 1923, and began the practice of law in Munich. Two years later he married Irma Franck, the daughter of a Jewish art dealer in that city. Some time afterward, the couple settled in Bamberg, where Dr. Dehler continued his practice of law.

With the dissolution of the *Reichsbanner Schwarz-Rot-Gold* in 1933, Dr. Dehler became a member of the German Democratic party; when this became illegal, he worked with underground opposition groups. In 1938 the Gestapo arrested him for having defended "troublesome" enemies of Nazism "too enthusiastically" in the law courts. Dr. Dehler was imprisoned. According to an account by G. Eilers in *Die Weltwoche* (September 3, 1954), one of Dr. Dehler's friends who had influence with Heinrich Himmler vouched for the good conduct of the lawyer, and Dehler was released from prison.

After World War II broke out in 1939, he took part in the Polish campaign as a sergeant-major and fought in the French campaign. Because of his underground activities, he was imprisoned in the Rositz concentration camp in 1944, but was released when he became dangerously ill.

At the end of the war, American authorities in Germany appointed Dr. Dehler chief administrator of the district of Bamberg. Subsequently he served as general public prosecutor in Bamberg at the Court of Appeals, where he pushed through almost single-handed the denazification proceedings in Bavaria. He resigned from this post in protest against the appointment to a Bavarian ministership of Alfred Loritz, a politically controversial figure. Dehler later became a district judge. After the Free Democratic party (FDP) was founded, Dr. Dehler took over in 1946 the presidency of the Bavarian district. From 1947 to 1949 he was a member of the Bavarian Landtag (provincial diet). He participated in the Constituent Assembly at Bonn in 1948, was elected to the Bundestag (the lower house of the West German Parliament) in August 1949, and was appointed Minister of Justice in the Cabinet formed by Konrad Adenauer, who became Chancellor and later, in 1951, Foreign Minister.

As Minister of Justice, Dehler did away with many of the legal inconsistencies that had developed during the postwar split-up of the *Reich*. He introduced some measures to provide a foundation for the functioning of a supreme court. He introduced new social legislation, providing for reforms in the rights of families, equal rights for women, and broad improvements in the penal code. His speech before the Bundestag opposing the reintroduction of capital punishment made him famous throughout Germany.

In the struggle over treaties to rearm West Germany and restore its sovereignty, Dr. Dehler has played the role of a "provocative and stinging gadfly" in the Chancellor's Cabinet. In January 1950 he was reported to have declared that Germany's responsibility for World War I had been no greater than France's; that "Hitler was a product of the Versailles treaty and of France's own despondency"; and that France in seeking economic annexation of the Saar was operating on the myth of German aggression, when in fact "there has been no German aggression since Frederick II." This speech called forth a demand for a retraction by the French High Commissioner for Germany, André François-Poncet. Adenauer apologized for his Minister of Justice and declared that Dehler's speech had been distorted by the press.

In December 1951 Dr. Dehler absolved the German people and especially German generals, "even Goering," of desiring World War II, saying it was Hitler's fault and his alone. On behalf of all major parties in the Bundestag, he had earlier appealed to the Allies, in November 1950, to cease extraditing Germans for war crime trials in other countries and to lighten the sentences of war criminals awaiting execution. The death sentence, he said, was in conflict with the abolition of capital punishment under the new German constitution. Resentful of the loss of German territory, Dr. Dehler declared in November 1952: "The time must come again when Prussia in a reconstituted German *Reich* once again fulfills its duty of maintaining Western culture in central Europe" (New York *Times,* November 22, 1952).

Bundesbildstelle, Bonn
THOMAS DEHLER

Dr. Dehler was not reappointed as Minister of Justice after the 1953 elections, but became floor leader of his party in October 1953. At that time the Free Democrats joined the opposition Social Democrats in condemning the government's plans for settling the French-German Saar dispute by "Europeanizing" the area. The party leaders said, "The Saar is German and must remain German" (New York *Herald Tribune,* October 29, 1953).

They thereby jeopardized Adenauer's foreign policy, which had ratification of the European Defense Community (EDC) treaty as its aim, since France would not ratify this treaty until the Saar problem was settled to its own satisfaction. On March 6, 1954, Dehler was elected chairman of the FDP, replacing Vice Chancellor Franz Blücher, who had withdrawn after holding the post since 1948. The party, which held forty-eight seats in the Bundestag compared to 244 held by Adenauer's Christian Democrats, declared its intention of developing into a "third force" between the Christian Democrats and the Social Democratic opposition.

As it became increasingly clear in the first half of 1954 that France would reject the EDC, Adenauer's efforts to keep West Germany firmly allied with Western Europe met increasing opposition at home, particularly from the FDP, the Socialists, and from businessmen who wanted eastern trade outlets. "Is it not necessary," Dr. Dehler asked in the spring of 1954, "to enter into conversations with the rulers in Moscow and Peiping?" Adenauer called such talk "appeasement," but Dehler contended that "direct diplomatic relations between West Germany and the Soviet Union are absolutely necessary" (*Time,* June 21, 1954).

(Continued next page)

DEHLER, THOMAS—*Continued*

After EDC had been defeated in August 1954, Dehler accused Adenauer of meddling in French politics and of sending a representative to Paris to lobby for the downfall of the French Premier, Pierre Mendès-France. A caucus of Free Democrats recommended Adenauer's withdrawal as foreign minister. On October 23, 1954 Adenauer agreed to the signing of the Paris agreements, under which a sovereign and rearmed West Germany would be admitted to the North Atlantic Treaty Organization (NATO) and to the projected Western European Union (WEU—an expanded Brussels Treaty Organization). Mendès-France, as a condition of his signing these accords, insisted that the Saar territory be "Europeanized," but controlled economically by France until a German peace treaty could be written. Adenauer felt it necessary to agree to these conditions. His action was immediately condemned by Dr. Dehler, who charged that the Chancellor had departed from the principles for a Saar settlement laid down by the coalition parties and that he had failed to inform his Cabinet before signing the accord.

During the stormy election campaigns in Hesse and Bavaria in November 1954, Dehler warned that if the Bundestag approved the Saar agreement in its present form, his party would be faced with the problem of withdrawing from the coalition. When the election returns were in, Adenauer had gained four seats in the Bundesrat (the upper house of the German Parliament). He was thus assured of the two-thirds majority needed to ratify the Paris accords. *Time* reported that Dr. Thomas Dehler, "the chastened leader" of the right-wing Free Democrats, "hastened to reassure newsmen that he and the Chancellor had no differences."

During the Bundestag debates on the Paris treaties in February 1955, Dr. Dehler again assailed the Saar accord as a "tawdry sell-out to France." He protested that the false idea had gotten around that Adenauer is the "paladin" of German democracy and that all other Germans are "just a heap of nationalists" (New York *Herald Tribune,* February 28, 1955). The Bundestag passed the Paris agreements on February 27, 1955. It accepted provisional settlement for the Saar as a semi-autonomous territory under the WEU, but economically linked to France—this arrangement is subject to approval by the Saarlanders and will remain in force until a final peace treaty for both West and East Germany is signed. The Bundesrat also approved the measures, and after they were ratified by the other participating nations, the Federal Republic of Germany became a sovereign state on May 5, 1955.

"The strong, fearless, upright, manly attitude shown throughout his stormy life," wrote G. Eilers, "stamps Dehler as one of the most outstanding personalities in the political life of the Federal Republic of Germany." At the invitation of the U.S. State Department, Dehler visited the United States in April and May 1954 to study its government administration and judicial systems.

The German politician works hard, often devoting his week ends to his job. According to his wife, "he looks upon politics as a duty." A devoted family man, Dr. Dehler considers family life the first social test of a politician. "Always look at the wife who stands behind a man, and then you will know what you can expect from him," he said. His slim, dark-haired wife is a highly-educated woman, interested in art and literature. Their daughter Elisabeth is now married.

Dr. Thomas Dehler considers himself "the defender of the bastions of the true democracy against the menacing dangers." He lives simply, drives a Volkswagen, and has as his favorite pet a little brown dachshund.

References

Die Weltwoche S 3 '54 por
N Y Times p17 D 16 '51
International Who's Who, 1954
Wer ist Wer? (1955)

DE KOONING, WILLEM (de kōn'ing)
Apr. 24, 1904- Artist

Address: b. c/o Sidney Janis Gallery, 15 E. 57th St., New York 22

The powerful abstractions and controversial paintings of women by Willem de Kooning have earned him recognition as "one of the most respected older artists of the so-called abstract-expressionist group, which has made such a vital contribution to American painting over the past decade."

After years of comparative obscurity, de Kooning came to prominence following his first one-man show in 1948 in New York. He was awarded first prize in 1951 at the Art Institute of Chicago's annual survey of American painting. In 1954 he was selected by the Museum of Modern Art as one of the two painters to represent the United States at the 27th Biennale International Art Exhibition in Venice, Italy.

Willem de Kooning was born in Rotterdam, Holland, on April 24, 1904, the son of Leendert and Cornelia (Nobel) de Kooning. His father was a beer bottler, who ran a "pub." When Willem was twelve years old, he left school and became an apprentice to Jan and Jaap Gidding, who headed a large firm of commercial painters and decorators. It was Jaap Gidding who first took him to Rotterdam's Academie voor Beeldende Kunsten en Technische Wetenschappen, where he attended evening classes for eight years. In 1924 he was graduated from the academy as a certified artist and craftsman.

In an interview with Martha Bourdrez (Knickerbocker, May 1950), de Kooning stated: "Bernard Romein had a terrific influence on my life. He was like a rebel and through him I got to know the work of Frank Lloyd Wright, Piet Mondriaan, and Walt Whitman." About 1920 he was introduced to the de Stijl group of Dutch abstract artists formed by Theo van Doesburg and Mondriaan.

At the age of twenty-one, in 1926, de Kooning sailed for the United States. On his arrival, he reportedly knew only one word of English:

"Yes." But he was immediately enthusiastic about New York's skyscrapers and "the way people worked." While making his living as a housepainter and as a free-lance commercial artist, he visited art galleries on his lunch hours and painted on Sundays.

He began painting in an abstract style about 1934, and he soon made friends with a group of New York abstract artists including Stuart Davis and Arshile Gorky (with whom he shared a studio). After 1935 de Kooning joined the WPA Federal Art Project for a year. In 1939 he executed the stylized, semi-abstract mural, *Medicine,* for the outer wall of the Hall of Pharmacy at the New York World's Fair.

When his *Portrait of a Man* (1941) was exhibited in a group show at McMillen, Inc., in January 15, 1942, an *Art Digest* critic wrote: "A strange painter is Willem de Kooning who does anatomical men with one visible eye, but whose work reveals a rather interesting feeling for paint surfaces and color." Among the works of this period that de Kooning has since exhibited are *The Glazier* and *Young Tumbler* (both 1935), *Seated Woman* (1937), *Two Men* (1938), *Seated Figure* (1939), and *Man and Boy* (c. 1942).

The first one-man show of de Kooning's work in New York was held at the Egan Gallery in April 1948. It consisted of ten abstractions, mostly in black and white, of which Renée Arb wrote in *Art News,* "Technique is lavish and versatile; draftsmanship elegant and concise." In the opinion of Clement Greenberg (*Nation,* April 24, 1948), the show immediately established de Kooning as "one of the four or five most important painters in the country."

At the 25th Venice Biennale in June 1950, de Kooning was one of six artists representing the United States. The director of the Museum of Modern Art's collections, Alfred H. Barr, Jr., who chose de Kooning, Jackson Pollock, and Arshile Gorky as the three leaders of abstract expressionism in the United States, introduced de Kooning as follows: "Influenced by the late Cézanne and by Gorky, his dense, compact style controls forms which seem to struggle against strong surface tension." Among de Kooning's better known abstractions are *The Marshes* (1947), *The Mail Box* (1948), *Asheville* (1949), and *The Attic* (1949).

His second one-man show took place at the Egan Gallery in April 1951. Observing that this show represented "a notable advance" in clarity of concept and content over de Kooning's earlier work, the New York *Times* (April 15, 1951) reviewer wrote: "He arrives at stimulating solutions while remaining within the field of 'pure' painting." It was announced in October 1951 that de Kooning's *Excavation* had been unanimously awarded the $2,000 Logan Medal and purchase prize at the Art Institute of Chicago's 60th annual survey of American painting. In her report on the show for the New York *Times* (October 28, 1951), Aline B. Louchheim commented favorably on "the forcefulness and energy of the action in the picture and the tensions between the paint surfaces" and the "radiant beauty which glows out."

Courtesy, Sidney Janis Gallery
WILLEM DE KOONING

A one-man exhibition of de Kooning's work at the Sidney Janis Gallery in March 1953 was considered by the critics to mark a new phase in his development. Abandoning complete abstraction, he returned to a more figurative style in six large oil paintings and a group of pastel sketches, all of which were variations on the image of a seated woman—a theme that had preoccupied him since 1950. These figures of the woman, with their "ox eyes, . . . pointy teeth, and vaguely voracious little smiles," were called "monuments of confusion" by Otis Gage (*Art Digest,* April 15, 1953).

To James Fitzsimmons (*Arts & Architecture,* May 1953), the exhibition seemed "the most controversial that New York has had in several years." He believed that at least two paintings, *The Woman, I* and *The Woman, III* were "probably great. Great in their horror, as the Isenheim Altarpiece, Goya's *Disasters of War,* certain images of Kali, and Picasso's *Guernica* are great." *Woman, I* was described in the Museum of Modern Art's 25th Anniversary Catalogue as "one of the most admired by young artists" and by several critics as "the most deeply disturbing."

In the spring of 1954 the Museum of Modern Art purchased the privately-owned American Pavilion at the Venice Biennale Exhibition and announced that the works of two painters—Willem de Kooning and the social realist Ben Shahn (See *Current Biography,* December 1954)—had been selected to represent contemporary creative effort in the United States at the 27th Biennale show, which opened in June. Twenty-seven of de Kooning's paintings and drawings were displayed in the pavilion. According to *Time* (June 28, 1954), de Kooning's women were "certainly the most violent and perhaps the most powerful paintings in the entire Biennale."

(Continued next page)

DE KOONING, WILLEM—*Continued*

Although de Kooning works rapidly, his output is comparatively small, because he often concentrates on a single picture for months at a time. He makes a continuous series of drawings which are cut apart, reversed, exchanged, and taped onto the canvas in varying positions to study the possibilities of change. He then frequently paints on these paper overlays to test differences of color and drawing. He employs many unconventional methods of applying the paint to the canvas.

In an article for *Magazine of Art* (October 1950), Louis Finkelstein described de Kooning's work as "the younger man's revolt against the hegemony of Picasso and the School of Paris —not in the way of a narrow provincialism, but in terms of new needs and meanings for modern vision." Thomas B. Hess believes that one of de Kooning's major contributions has been his ability to "give pulse and motion to the unrecognizable, to endow the abstract form with tragedy or laughter, and on its own terms. . . ."

A retrospective exhibition of de Kooning's works was held at the School of the Boston Museum of Fine Arts in 1953 and was later shown at the Workshop Art Center in Washington, D.C. De Kooning has participated in such group exhibitions as the Virginia Museum of Fine Arts Biennial (1950); the "Abstract Art in America" survey at the Museum of Modern Art (1951); and the "Young American Painters" show at the Solomon R. Guggenheim Museum (1954). His paintings are included in the collections of the Museum of Modern Art, St. Louis Museum, and Art Institute of Chicago, as well as in the private collections of Nelson Rockefeller, Mrs. John D. Rockefeller, 3d, Duncan Phillips, Helena Rubinstein, and others.

James Thrall Soby in the *Saturday Review* (February 5, 1955) stated that the market for twentieth-century American art continues to rise, and lists de Kooning among the prominent "abstract and/or expressionist artists" whose "best canvases fetch as much as $3,000 apiece."

The painter served on the faculty of Black Mountain College in North Carolina in 1948, and taught at the Yale School of Fine Arts from 1950 to 1951. He was married on December 7, 1943 to Elaine Marie Fried, who writes criticism for *Art News* and is also a painter. De Kooning has been described as "a handsome man . . . with grayish hair, light blue-brown eyes, and a sensitive mouth."

Of his work, he has said: "Painting isn't just the visual thing that reaches your retina, it's what is behind it. I'm not interested in 'abstracting' or taking things out or reducing painting to design, form, line, and color. I paint this way because I can keep putting more and more things in—drama, anger, pain, love, a figure, a horse, my ideas about space. Through your eyes it again becomes an emotion or an idea. It doesn't matter if it's different from mine as long as it comes from the painting which has its own integrity and intensity."

References

Art N 52:30 Mr '53
Knickerbocker My '50 por
Mag Art 41:54 F '48
Time 57:63 Ap 30 '51 por
Hess, T. B. Abstract Painting: Background and American Phase (1951)
Ritchie, A. C. Abstract Painting and Sculpture in America (1951)
Who's Who in America, 1954-55

DE LOS ANGELES, VICTORIA *See* Angeles, Victoria de los

DENIEL, ENRIQUE, CARDINAL PLA Y *See* Pla y Deniel, E. Cardinal

DER HAROOTIAN, KOREN (dĕr hă-rōō'tē-äN kŏr'ĕn) Apr. 2, 1909- Sculptor

Address: R.F.D. 9-W, Castle Rd., Orangeburg, N.Y.

The emotions of man, his eternal battle against evil, and the sense of turmoil in an age of wars and revolutions are given symbolical expression when transfixed in wood or stone by the chisel of the Armenian-born American sculptor, Koren Der Harootian. Originally a painter, he turned to sculpture while a resident in Jamaica, the British West Indies, where he carved heroic figures in lignum vitae, eucalyptus and other hard woods. His work often deals with allegorical and Biblical themes.

In 1954 he received a $1,000 grant from the National Institute of Arts and Letters in New York. The sculptor is represented in private and museum collections in the United States and Great Britain. The Metropolitan Museum of Art in New York City has his *Prometheus and the Vulture* in its permanent collection.

For his sculpture *Descent from the Cross,* described by Howard Devree in the New York *Times* as a "highly reverent but unconventional" work, Der Harootian received the George D. Widener Memorial gold medal at the annual art exhibition of the Pennsylvania Academy of the Fine Arts in 1954. Walter E. Baum of the Philadelphia *Bulletin* was of the opinion that the "Der Harootian figure is carved with much of the interpretive zeal that characterized the work of the old sculptors of Christian eras when symbolism meant so much to the church."

The fifth of the seven children of Haroutun and Nevart (Mouradian) Der Haroutunian, Khoren Der Haroutunian (who became known as Koren Der Harootian) was born on April 2, 1909 in Ashodavan, near Kharput in Armenia (Ashodavan, then under the rule of the Ottoman Empire, is now part of modern Turkey). Koren had two brothers, Bedros and Haigaz, and four sisters, Marian, Rose, Isqouhi, and Zemruth. His father was a priest of the Armenian Orthodox Church and the schoolmaster in the small town until his death in the Turkish massacres of 1915. After the rest of the family had taken refuge in the mountains, Koren became separated from them, was captured by the Turks, and was made to work as a shepherd.

A year later his brother Bedros found him and led him across the Russian border to rejoin his family. After a short while the mother and her children were obliged, because of the Russian Revolution of 1917, to go to Constantinople (now Istanbul) Turkey. Since Koren's health had been severely impaired, he had to spend almost a year in a hospital there and underwent several operations.

The family eventually went to the United States and in 1921 settled in Worcester, Massachusetts, where Koren attended grammar school and the North High School, from which he was graduated in 1928. To Miss Anna McAuliffe, a high school art instructor, he credits his ambition to make art his career. He attended the classes of Victor Humann and other teachers at the Worcester Art Museum school and financed his purchases of art materials by selling newspapers.

By means of a grant for art study from his high school, the youth was able to spend two summers—1928 and 1929—painting at Provincetown and Gloucester, Massachusetts. Upon receiving the St. Wulstan scholarship of $250 in 1930, the young painter went to New York. There his water colors came to the attention of the late art dealer Caz Delbos, who happened to see the young man standing outside his gallery in the rain and invited him to come in. From this chance encounter came Der Harootian's first one-man show, held at the Delbos Galleries in 1930.

Upon the invitation of a friend, Der Harootian decided to visit Jamaica. His trip was made possible by the sale of twelve of his water colors at $60 apiece. The drawings and paintings he did there of the landscape and people came to the attention of Sir Hugh Walpole, the novelist, who discerned their inherent sculptural form and suggested to the painter that he begin to work in three dimensions. (The writer described one of Der Harootian's water colors in his novel *The Inquisitor.*)

Some of Der Harootian's early paintings of Jamaica were shown in 1931 at the museum there, and others were exhibited in New York by Delbos that year. Edward Alden Jewell, then the New York *Times* art critic, found Der Harootian's work "vividly alive, splendid alike in drawing and in color, quite worthy of being compared with the work in this medium by masters like Winslow Homer and [John Singer] Sargent." In the fall of 1931 Francis Henry Taylor, then director of the Worcester Art Museum, presented a Der Harootian one-man show, from which the water color *Patience* was bought for the museum's permanent collection.

By the time Der Harootian held another show in Jamaica in 1938, he had sold enough paintings to finance a trip to England and had completed five mahogany sculptures. After his arrival in London, he worked on his paintings and sculptures in a studio in Soho. Examples of his work were shown at the Zwemmer Gallery in its 1938 Christmas show, at Goupil's 1938 and 1939 salons, and at the Leicester Galleries' 1939 summer exhibition, to which he contributed the sculptures *Bird and Fish* (in lignum vitae) and *Creation* (in mahogany). Another mahogany piece, *Hermaphrodite,* was included in a 1938 show which toured the British Isles. In Jamaica the availability of native woods had led Der Harootian to use that medium, but in London he worked on his first stone pieces, which included animal studies based on sketches he had drawn at the London Zoo.

Paul Bogosian

KOREN DER HAROOTIAN

After he had returned to Jamaica in 1940, Der Harootian concentrated primarily on sculpture; his themes often reflected an intense concern with contemporary conflict. *Suffering Mankind, Dying Warrior,* and *Fallen Grenade Thrower* date from this period. When Der Harootian went back to the United States in 1944 he brought these sculptures which were shown at the Kraushaar Galleries in the fall of 1945.

A change in concept was evident in Der Harootian's work of the succeeding period, when the predominance of a mystical element became evident. Some of the pieces which revealed this new trend in Der Harootian's work were shown at the Whitney Museum of American Art and the Pennsylvania Academy exhibitions in 1946 and 1947, at the Art Institute of Chicago, and at the Sculptors Guild, Inc., in 1948.

With the increasing monumentality of his work, Der Harootian in the fall of 1948 obtained the use of the open air space north of Washington Square in New York where the Sculptors Guild had just held its showing, and exhibited fifty-two of his sculptures there (these included *Thinker, Orpheus and Euryd-*

DER HAROOTIAN, KOREN—*Continued*

ice, and *David and Goliath*). The New York *Herald Tribune* found the show "a ripe and ringing testimonial to accomplishment from both physical and esthetic viewpoints. . . . These exhibits . . . are equipped with strength and meaning sufficient to give pause to the most casual observer" (September 19, 1948).

At the 1949 Whitney exhibit, Der Harootian's *Sea bird and Fish* was considered "quite the most striking design in the entire show" by the New York *Herald Tribune* critic. *Time* observed of his sculptures: "The fact that they seemed far less abstract than they were in actuality was a measure of the sculptor's power to create illusions without slavish copying."

Time (May 30, 1949) characterized Der Harootian's *Rebellious Slave* as one of the "best of the relatively representational items" at the Fairmount Park Art Association's Third International Exhibition of Sculpture, held at the Philadelphia Museum of Art in May 1949. Der Harootian, as well as José de Creeft, Jacques Lipchitz, Jacob Epstein and others, were commissioned to execute pieces to complete the Ellen Phillips Samuel Memorial which is located on the bank of the Schuylkill River in Philadelphia; Der Harootian will be represented by an eight-and-a-half-foot figure which will be entitled *Inventor.*

The sculptor began work on the symbolic piece in 1950 after he moved from New York City to a Rockland county studio, where he was able to carve the monumental figure out of doors. At the 1950 Sculptors Guild annual exhibit, his *Job*, "wondrously and affectionately tooled in Vermont black marble," was singled out by Belle Krasne (*Art Digest*, April 1, 1950) as "the show's religious triumph." The May 1950 exhibition of the Society of Audubon Artists at the National Academy of Design in New York found Der Harootian the recipient of the $100 prize for his *Pillar of Salt.* During February and March 1950 he had his first one-man show in Philadelphia at the Art Alliance; the Philadelphia *Inquirer* spoke of the "impressiveness" of certain pieces shown.

In conjunction with the painter Vaclav Vytlacil, Der Harootian exhibited at the studio of the Rockland Foundation at West Nyack, New York in the summer of 1953. His contributions included *Leda and the Swan* and *Crowned with Thorns.* On exhibition at the American Academy of Arts and Letters in New York in the spring of 1954 were six sculptures by Der Harootian. On May 26 he was awarded the $1,000 annual grant in sculpture by the National Institute of Arts and Letters. The citation accompanying the grant said it was "in recognition of a distinguished artist whose sculptures in stone and wood reveal strong spiritual and emotional depth." *Jonah* was especially noted by the art critics. During that spring, Der Harootian also contributed his "massively rhythmic reclining mother and child," *Birth of Davit of Sassoun* (based on an Armenian legend), to the Whitney annual exhibition.

Other awards received by Der Harootian for his sculpture are the first prize (1944) of the Springfield (Massachusetts) Art League, the gold medal (1948) and first prize (1950) of the Society of Audubon Artists, and an honorable mention (1950) from the Architectural League of New York.

A critical study of Der Harootian's work by Ralph M. Pearson in *The Modern Renaissance in American Art* (1954) quotes the sculptor as saying: "Sculpture is a combination of the physical, the intellectual and the spiritual. I think of stone and wood in terms of their own growth—as something living and fluid.... Only when the intellect dominates the emotions will the two work together for spiritual quality."

While a resident in England, Der Harootian on May 13, 1939 married Hermine Ohanesyan, an artist, singer and writer. At one time, the sculptor was devoted to sports—running, swimming, wrestling, and boxing; now he prefers to study literature and music. He belongs to the Armenian Orthodox Church, and is a member of the Sculptors Guild, the Society of Audubon Artists, and the Rockland Foundation. He is about five feet four inches tall, weighs 125 pounds, and has black hair and brown eyes. *Time* quotes him as calling sculpture "a beautiful profession" which he would not change "for anything in the world." He works directly in wood or stone; he once explained this, saying: "If I make a sketch or clay model first, I find that my best has gone into it. I prefer to work the stone direct."

References

Am Artist 10:22+ N '46
Worcester (Massachusetts) Sunday Telegram p3+ Jl 10 '49 por
Pearson, R. M. The Modern Renaissance in American Art (1954)
Who's Who in American Art, 1953
World Biography (1954)

DE SAPIO, CARMINE G(ERARD) Dec. 10, 1908- Secretary of State of New York; Democratic National Committee member; New York County Democratic Committee chairman; leader of Tammany Hall

Address: b. c/o Tammany Headquarters, 331 Madison Ave., New York 17; Democratic State Committee, Hotel Biltmore, New York 17; New York Department of State, 270 Broadway, New York 7; h. 37 Washington Sq. W., New York 11

Described as "the miracle man of practical politics," Carmine G. De Sapio, as leader of the New York County Democratic organization (known as Tammany Hall), supported the successful candidacies of Robert F. Wagner for Mayor of the City of New York in 1953, and of W. Averell Harriman for Governor of New York State in 1954. In recognition of his growing political importance, De Sapio was elected Democratic National Committeeman from New York State in February 1954. Another honor came to him in December 1954 when Governor Harriman named him Secretary of State of New York. The reform program which he started when he assumed leadership of Tammany in 1949, and his approach to politics can be summed up by his often repeated phrase, "good government is good politics" (*Life,* June 6, 1955).

Carmine Gerard De Sapio, the elder of the two sons of Gerard and Marietta De Sapio, was born on December 10, 1908 on the lower West side of Manhattan, where his parents still live. His mother was born in America, and his father came to New York from Italy when he was a boy. Until 1926, when a strike put them out of business, the elder De Sapios ran a horse-drawn trucking firm; Carmine helped out in the business each day after attending St. Alphonsus Parochial School.

While he was still attending high school, De Sapio became interested in politics and joined the Huron Democratic Club located in the First Assembly District, West, where he was always on hand to run errands, help someone in trouble or find lodging for a dispossessed family. De Sapio wanted to be a lawyer, but after attending Fordham Preparatory School, St. John's College of Fordham University and Brooklyn Law School, he was forced to give up studying because of an attack of rheumatic fever, which resulted in an eye inflammation that still requires him to wear tinted glasses.

He soon became the youngest precinct captain in New York City. In 1935 Daniel E. Finn, Jr., leader of the First Assembly District, West, got him a job as secretary to City Court Justice Vincent S. Lippe at $3,500 a year. This job lasted for two years, after which Finn obtained for De Sapio the position of secretary, for several months, to Judge Louis Valente. In the summer of 1938 Finn, who had become sheriff of New York, made De Sapio his deputy sheriff.

With the encouragement of a small dissident group, De Sapio decided in 1939 to run for district leader against Finn, whose family had controlled the area for over fifty years. By this time De Sapio had become important in the Tamawa Club. The results of the primary, held in September, were indecisive, but a run-off in October gave De Sapio the victory. However, Tammany Hall leaders refused to seat him on the executive committee. (Various reasons are advanced for this and for De Sapio's rapid advance in the Hall in "Carmine G. De Sapio: The Smile on the Face of the Tiger" by Richard L. Heilbroner, *Harper's Magazine,* July 1954; in "The Tiger Who Looks Like a Banker," *Saturday Evening Post,* April 23, 1955, by Joseph and Stewart Alsop; and in "New Territory for a New-Style Boss" by Cameron Hawley, *Life,* June 6, 1955.)

Although De Sapio became secretary to General Sessions Judge John J. Freschi at $5,750 a year in January 1940, he left several weeks later because he felt the job was a "peace offering" to get him to drop his fight for the district leadership (New York *World-Telegram and Sun,* January 24, 1955). He worked in his family's real-estate business, organized by

Wide World

CARMINE G. DE SAPIO

his parents after having to sell the trucking firm. De Sapio was finally seated as district leader in 1943.

After supporting Frank Sampson, who became leader of Tammany Hall, De Sapio was recommended by the county committee for Democratic commissioner on the New York City Board of Elections and was elected by the New York City Council in 1946. De Sapio and his faction later succeeded in ousting Sampson and replaced him with Hugo Rogers.

In July 1949 De Sapio became the first American of Italian descent ever to be elected leader of Tammany Hall. (For a history of Tammany Hall—the Society of St. Tammany —and its relation to politics and the New York County Democratic Committee since its organization after the American Revolution see the *Encyclopædia Britannica.*)

In De Sapio's first important elections, those of November 1950, he is credited with engineering the coalition with the Republicans and Liberals that unseated Representative Vito Marcantonio in the U.S. Congress. For the mayoralty post in New York City, however, De Sapio backed Ferdinand Pecora instead of Vincent R. Impellitteri, who won on an independent ticket. In 1950 De Sapio was almost defeated in the Hall for another term as commissioner of elections, and later, petitions were circulated against him as Tammany leader.

Following testimony of underworld figures in March 1951 before the U.S. Senate Special Committee to Investigate Organized Crime in Interstate Commerce (headed by Senator Estes Kefauver of Tennessee) that they knew De Sapio, the Tammany leader denied the allegation that Frank Costello was the "real boss" of the Hall. He pointed out that it was inevitable for him to meet men of the under-

DE SAPIO, CARMINE G.—*Continued*

world, but he emphasized: "The main thing is that they have never influenced me" (New York *Post*, January 28, 1955).

Soon after he became leader, De Sapio took steps to change the reputation of Tammany Hall to that of a modern political organization, "geared to the times and interested in 'political service.'" De Sapio named the first Puerto Rican district leader, Anthony Mendez, and backed Hulan Jack, Manhattan's first Negro borough president. The Tammany Hall leader also helped to get Judge Harold A. Stevens on the Court of General Sessions, highest judicial post held by a Negro in New York State at that time (in 1955 Harriman appointed Stevens a State Supreme Court Justice; he is the first Negro in New York's history to hold that position). Under De Sapio's leadership, four young "liberals"—among them a former official of the League of Women Voters—have been elected district leaders and seated on the executive committee. De Sapio who has lectured on politics at New York University, Manhattan College, and Fordham University, is the first Tammany leader to be so honored.

When the 1953 mayoralty election came up, De Sapio and Edward J. Flynn, Bronx County Democratic party leader, were the only two county leaders to support Robert F. Wagner (see *C.B.*, 1954). De Sapio took a postcard poll of 41,000 registered Democrats who voted four-to-one against Impellitteri for mayoral candidate. A month before Wagner won the September primary, Flynn died and De Sapio became his political heir. On November 3, 1953 Wagner won the election for Mayor of the City of New York by a plurality of 360,078 over his Republican opponent, Harold Riegelman.

In May 1955 the New York County Democratic Committee adopted a series of by-laws, advocated by De Sapio for several years, dealing with election reforms. The new by-laws are designed to transfer power from party leaders to rank and file members by providing for the direct election of district leaders by enrolled voters; abolishing the extra "synthetic" vote given certain members of the executive committee; placing the election of women co-leaders in each district on an independent basis; and defining district boundaries before the primaries (New York *Times*, May 24, 1955). Other steps taken by De Sapio to reform Tammany are: reduction of the number of county committeemen from an unwieldy 11,762 to 3,471 in 1953 (prior to the state law's deadline); the establishment of rent-control clinics; support of permanent personal registration; and a twenty-six-point program pledging support of legislation cleaning up waterfront conditions disclosed by the State Crime Commission.

In February 1954 the Democratic State Committee elected De Sapio a Democratic National Committeeman to succeed Edward J. Flynn. His position as a major power in Democratic politics was "unquestionably established" when W. Averell Harriman, the man De Sapio backed for Governor of New York State, was elected in November 1954. Franklin D. Roosevelt, Jr., had strong upstate support for the Democratic gubernatorial nomination, but De Sapio, after taking a state-wide preference poll of 150,000 registered Democrats, decided that Harriman had more "experience as an administrator."

Soon after Harriman was elected, De Sapio resigned his $12,000-a-year job as commissioner of elections to accept Harriman's appointment as Secretary of State at a salary of $17,000 a year, plus a tax-free $3,000 expense allowance. The New York County Democratic Committee elected De Sapio as county chairman on December 14, 1954, a position distinct from the one he holds as county leader.

Because New York State has ninety-six delegate votes at national party conventions, De Sapio is expected to have a vital role in choosing the Democratic presidential ticket in 1956. Adlai E. Stevenson, Democratic presidential candidate in 1952, said, "If it were my ambition to seek the Democratic presidential nomination next year, I would welcome the support of Carmine De Sapio and Tammany Hall" (New York *Times*, May 18, 1955). When pressed for his position on the 1956 Democratic nominee several months later, De Sapio stated: "I'm confident that the delegation from New York will prefer Averell Harriman as its designee for the nomination for President" (New York *Times*, July 3, 1955).

Carmine Gerard De Sapio was married to Theresa Natale in 1937. They have one daughter, Geraldine. "He is six feet one inch [tall], weighs 195 pounds, has dark wavy hair, gray at the temples, and is smartly but conservatively dressed," wrote the New York *World-Telegram and Sun* (January 26, 1955). He has an insurance business, organized in his name, in which he is largely inactive.

In March 1955 the Israel Bond Organization honored him with its distinguished leadership award. He is a member of the Elks, Knights of Columbus, the Grand Street Boys Association, and the National Democratic Club. De Sapio starts seeing people in his apartment at 8 A.M. and often works until one o'clock the next morning.

De Sapio has said, "You're living in the past if you think you can still force the public to swallow any candidate you nominate. . . . We have to offer the public what it wants—a slate of reputable officials who will give them good government—and after they're in office we'll follow through to see that the people get what we promised them" (*Life*, June 6, 1955).

References

Harper 209:23+ Jl '54
Life 38:157+ Je 6 '55 pors
N Y Post p4+ Ja 24-31 '55 pors
N Y Sunday Mirror p39 Mr 14 '54 por
N Y World-Telegram p15 Ja 24 '55 por; p15 Ja 25 '55; p25 Ja 26 '55
Sat Eve Post 227:17+ Ap 23 '55 pors
Time 65:14+ D 27 '54 por
Washington (D.C.) Post p25 D 3 '54 por; p10M O 31 '54

DEVINY, JOHN J(OSEPH) June 19, 1882-Feb. 10, 1955 Printer; began with U.S. government as apprentice printer and became assistant director of the Bureau of Engraving and Printing (1924-26) and Public Printer in charge of the Government Printing Office (1948-1953); was an original staff member of the Federal Social Security program and assistant director of Bureau of Old Age and Survivors Insurance; served as international treasurer and president of the International Association of Printing House Craftsmen. See *Current Biography* (Sept.) 1948.

Obituary

N Y Times p23 F 11 '55

DE WOHL, LOUIS Jan 24, 1903- Author
Address: b. c/o Curtis Brown, Ltd., 347 Madison Ave., New York 17; h. Hotel Ascot, Lavaterstrasse 15, Zurich, Switzerland

Reprinted from the *Wilson Library Bulletin* Dec. 1955

LOUIS DE WOHL

On May 10, 1948, Louis de Wohl, who had just published a novel based on the life of Julian the Apostate, had an audience with Pope Pius XII. The writer asked His Holiness to suggest the central figure for his next novel. "After a moment's reflection," the Pope suggested St. Thomas Aquinas. In March 1950 de Wohl made a special pilgrimage to Rome to place the resultant book, *The Quiet Light,* (Lippincott) in the hands of its august sponsor. It was selected by the Gallery of Living Catholic Authors as the best book of Catholic fiction for the year 1950, and was followed by three more novels based on the lives of great saints of the Church.

Ludwig von Wohl-Musciny was born in Berlin, Germany, January 24, 1903, the son of Lajos Wohl, Knight of Musciny, an officer in a crack Hungarian cavalry regiment, also a judge and mine-owner, and Baroness Victoria H. J. (von Dreifus) Wohl. At five the boy had taught himself to read by studying names and inscriptions on shops, and to write in block letters; until he was eleven he was educated at home by private tutors. From 1914 to 1920 he attended the Royal Prinz Heinrichs-Gymnasium in Berlin. The family lost its money when Louis was seventeen. After dabbling awhile in dress designing and acting as publicity man for UFA, the biggest German film company, he set to work in earnest to write fiction.

Beginning with *Der grosse Kampf (The Big Fight),* published by K. F. Koehler in Leipzig in 1925, de Wohl wrote "good yarns with lots of action." Sixteen of them were made into motion pictures. (In 1955 he was at work on his fifty-fourth book, of which nine have been published in the United States.) His travels were extensive, through Turkey, Egypt, Syria, Tripolitania, Algiers, Tunisia, India and Ceylon. His special interest was the study of comparative religion in these countries. Disapproving of the moral disintegration he saw in Hitler's Germany, de Wohl left that country in 1935. Taking passage to England, he soon learned English by systematic study of children's books for ages six to eight, then ten to twelve. Two years later he wrote an autobiography, *I Follow My Stars* (Harrap, 1937), in English. Though naturalization was suspended in Great Britain during World War II, de Wohl succeeded in becoming a captain in the British Army, where he created his own "psychological research bureau" in the Division of Psychological Warfare.

In 1947 de Wohl published his first novel in the United States, *The Living Wood.* The *Catholic World* said of this story of Helena, mother of Constantine, the first Christian emperor, that reading it was "like unfolding a richly illuminated manuscript." Writing in the *Saturday Review of Literature,* in a review of *Throne of the World* (Lippincott, 1949), a novel about Attila the Hun, Nathaniel Rothman stated that de Wohl had "many qualities beyond a facile romanticism. He wields, for one thing, a very capable scholarship that gives backbone to his work." Myles Green in the New York *Times,* however, objected to the "heavy, intrigue-ridden love interest," and *Commonweal* found the novel generally overwritten.

The *Catholic World* said of *The Quiet Light* that though it "sheds little insight into either Thomas or Thomism, it makes agreeably active reading." "A fluent and picturesque tale," commented the English *Spectator. The Restless Flame* (1951) was based on the life of St Augustine. "Setting and character interact to give us an unusually interesting historical novel," said the Chicago *Sunday Tribune,* but the New York *Times* thought it "woodenly written, clogged with turgid drama, foggy dialectics, undigested philosophy." St. Ignatius Loyola is the hero of *The Golden Thread* (Lippincott, 1952), which the Springfield *Republican* described as "entertaining and enjoyable, but utterly lacking in either depths of conception or moving mysticism." Of *Set All Afire* (1953), a fictionized

DE WOHL, LOUIS—*Continued*

biography of St. Francis Xavier, the New York *Times* wrote: "Xavier's generosity speaks to every age and seldom so clearly and compellingly as in this book." *The Second Conquest* (Lippincott, 1954), which was science fiction with a religious content, bewildered the critics. "H. H. Holmes" (Anthony Boucher), in the New York *Herald Tribune,* called it "a misbegotten hybrid," and Virginia Kirkus observed that the book would surprise readers, "who have found this author's fictionized biographies of early Church fathers worthwhile in scholarship and research." *The Spear* (Lippincott, 1955), a story of early Christianity, was well received by the reviewers. The New York *Times* called it "a moving portrayal of life . . . during the time of Tiberius," and the New York *Herald Tribune* wrote: "De Wohl's imagination is tempered by a broad knowledge of the times of which he writes, and his taste, in terms of his legitimate intention as an historical novelist, is reliably good."

De Wohl came to the United States in 1949 and has lived in New York and in California. He now lives in Switzerland. He married Ruth Lorch in 1953. A Roman Catholic and an active worker in the Church, he was made Knight Commander of the Order of the Holy Sepulchre of Jerusalem in 1954. De Wohl is fair in complexion, with blond-gray hair and hazel eyes; he is six feet tall and weighs 300 pounds.

Reference

Hoehn, M. A. ed. Catholic Authors (1952)

DEXHEIMER, W(ILBUR) A(PP) Apr. 20, 1901- United States Government official; engineer

Address: b. c/o Bureau of Reclamation, U.S. Department of the Interior, Washington 25, D.C.; h. 3636 16th St. N.W., Washington 10, D.C.

A political unknown, but a widely respected engineer, W. A. Dexheimer was appointed commissioner of the Bureau of Reclamation of the U.S. Department of Interior on July 13, 1953. He had been an associate engineer on the Hoover Dam project, had built airstrips in the Far East during World War II, and helped to solve construction problems in Australia, Formosa and Mexico since the war. At the time of his appointment by President Dwight D. Eisenhower, he was assistant to the chief of the construction engineering division of the bureau in Denver, Colorado. His name was submitted to the President by Secretary of Interior Douglas McKay.

Dexheimer's speeches since his appointment have carried much weight as coming from a consulting engineer who has also had over twenty-five years of experience in the reclamation bureau. "For quite a while the [reclamation] engineers haven't had much to do with policy and decisions but now we are going to run the Reclamation Bureau," he said (Denver *Post,* August 16, 1953). He has predicted that irrigation facilities for five million new acres of land would be built in the next five years and power facilities would grow by a million kilowatt hours of hydroelectric power from reclamation projects (*Rocky Mountain News,* December 5, 1953).

Wilbur App Dexheimer was born on April 20, 1901 in Denver, Colorado, the son of William J. and Emma (App) Dexheimer. He was graduated from North Denver High School in 1920 and attended the University of Denver from October 1921 to June 1922. He received a Bachelor of Science degree in civil engineering from the Colorado Agricultural and Mechanical College in 1926, and was president of his class in his junior and senior years. He was employed by the Denver and Rio Grande Western Railroad as clerk and safety engineer and in 1926, while still in college, was assistant city engineer of Fort Collins, Colorado.

During 1927 and 1928 he was location engineer for the Union Oil Company of California. Joining the Bureau of Reclamation in 1928, he became chief of a survey party, which located canals, tunnels, and structures in Ellenberg, Washington. He worked on the Yakima project and later in the Cle Elum project in Washington, on the Salt River project in Arizona, and on construction in Nevada.

For two years, 1936 to 1938, he worked on the Bartlett Dam, another important structure in the southwestern United States, and described it in *World's Highest Multiple Arch Dam* (1938). In 1938 Dexheimer was transferred to California as chief inspector on the Shasta Dam Project. He directed the work of nearly 400 bureau engineers at the site and was responsible for the location, construction compliance with specifications, and contractor payments for work on the dam and power plant, key structure of the Control Valley Project, and the second largest dam ever built by the Bureau of Reclamation.

Dexheimer entered the Army Corps of Engineers in 1942 as a captain. He became staff engineer for General Joseph W. ("Vinegar Joe") Stilwell in the China-Burma-India theater of war, supervised all engineering and construction work, and carried out liason with the British General Staff and the Chinese government.

Upon receiving his discharge, in the rank of lieutenant colonel, Dexheimer went to China as assistant chief engineer for the Morrison-Knudsen International Company and for a year acted as consulting engineer for the government of the Republic of China at Shanghai. He made studies of railroads, ports, highways and reported to the Chinese government on the feasibility of construction and repair.

After the Morrison-Knudsen assignment was completed in 1947, he rejoined the Bureau of Reclamation and was assigned to the Denver staff office of the commissioner as assistant to the chief construction engineer. During the following five years he had administration of construction projects costing over $200,000,000 each year.

He was called as consultant by the Appropriations Committee of the House of Representatives in 1950. He was consulted three times, in 1950, 1952, and 1953, by the Australian government regarding construction problems. His work on Australia's largest hydroelectric project was published in 1952. With another top bureau engineer, A. B. Reed, he took a third trip to the "down under" country, to make final adjustments in plans for two irrigation tunnels and a dam, part of Australia's Snowy Mountain hydroelectric project, the plans for the tunnel and dam having been drawn up in Dexheimer's office in Denver. Before returning home in March, Dexheimer flew to Formosa, where he directed a bureau team inspecting a proposed dam and power plant for the Chinese Nationalist government. He also served as a consulting engineer on hydroelectric projects for the city of Seattle.

According to press reports, he had a ready answer when called by Ralph Tudor, Under Secretary of the Interior, and asked if he would accept the post of commissioner. It was, "No." A second call from Tudor, whom Dexheimer had known during his army service, and persuasive arguments from other friends, finally made him decide that it was his duty to accept if offered the position (Denver *Post,* July 16, 1953).

Fifteen minutes after the White House announced his appointment on July 13, Dexheimer took the oath of office. At a press conference the following day he said he thought the bureau's budget could be trimmed further and still perform its public functions. Both McKay and Dexheimer indicated they intended to cut public information and other activities of the bureau outside the engineering field (*Christian Science Monitor,* July 24, 1953). Returning to Denver, Dexheimer "made it plain the Interior Department won't do anything that can be done by private business" (*Rocky Mountain News,* July 16, 1953).

The Associated Press on August 16 quoted Commissioner Dexheimer as saying that a "pet idea" of his for years had been that natural resources should not be tampered with "until we've had the benefit of the best thinking to try to be sure a planned development will not hamper or prevent greater benefits from the ultimate development."

"We hope now to do a more businesslike job," he said. "We will try to get Congress to appreciate that we need planning money in advance so that we can prepare more realistic reports on the feasibility of projects to back up appropriation requests." He outlined a future for the bureau in which local and private interests would bear a much greater share of the responsibility for reclamation and power development.

On September 20, 1953 the Denver *Post,* in front page headlines, quoted Dexheimer as saying that a national water policy was the bureau's "greatest need." On December 5, at a meeting in Fort Collins of the Chi Epsilon civil engineering society, he said that the bureau would continue the search for new water and that developing new sources of irrigation water was the primary aim of the bureau.

W. A. DEXHEIMER

In a speech prepared in October for the Reclamation Association, the commissioner put himself on record for a reclamation program based on local responsibility just as the Department of the Interior has declared it is the duty of local communities to meet their power needs. "We will be glad to assist, of course, but the major responsibility, the initiative, is yours, for you are the people who know best what you want and why you want it. Rather than have the bureau act as salesman we ask you to be the salesmen both locally and in Congress" (Denver *Post,* October 14, 1953).

Dexheimer was decorated for his war service with the Bronze Star. He is one of the four American citizens to receive the Chinese Order of the White Cloud. He is a member of Alpha Tau Omega, Scabbard and Blade, Pi Delta Epsilon, the A.F. and A.M., the American Society of Civil Engineers, and the Aviation Country Club.

Dexheimer met his wife, Johnnie Hadnot, in 1936 when he was working on a dam project near Phoenix, Arizona. She was a registered nurse in charge of the hospital at the project site. They were married on July 1, 1938, and have one son, Stephen Michael.

An active person, at school Dexheimer was fond of boxing, wrestling, and tennis; he now names as favorite recreations golf, swimming, and fishing. He is five feet eight inches tall, weighs 165 pounds, and has blue eyes and gray hair.

In 1950 the Dexheimers built a brick ranch house in Lakewood, following his own design. It is placed on a rise from which they can overlook Denver and have an unrestricted view of

DEXHEIMER, W. A.—*Continued*

the snowcapped mountain range. Leaving this home was one reason for his wife's original reluctance about going to Washington, said Dexheimer, adding, "But she's always gone along with whatever seems best for me to do."

References

Christian Sci Mon p2 Jl 24 '53
Denver Post p19 Ja 29 '53; Mr 2 '53; p2 Jl 16 '53; Roundup Section p5 Ag 16 '53; O 14 '53
Eng N Record p21 Jl 16 '53; p22 Ag 27 '53
N Y Times p15 Jl 14 '53
Rocky Mountain News p5 Jl 16 '53; D 6 '53
Time 62:10 Jl 27 '53 por
Who's Who in America, 1954-55
Who's Who in Engineering, 1954

DHEBAR, U(CHHARANGRAI) N(AVALSHANKER) (tā-bär') Sept. 21, 1905-
Indian political leader

Address: b. 7 Jantar Rd., New Delhi, India

The President of the Indian National Congress is U.N. Dhebar, who was selected for this post by Prime Minister Jawaharlal Nehru in November 1954. His subsequent program of discipline and austerity and a policy of progressive socialism (adopted at the sixtieth annual session of the Congress, India's most powerful political party, in January 1955) resulted in a landslide victory for the Congress in the Andhra state election in March (*Christian Science Monitor,* March 15, 1955) and the defeat of the Communist party which had previously held great influence.

Dhebar, who is familiarly known as "Dhebarbhai" (Brother Dhebar), gave up his career as a lawyer in 1936 to join the movement of Mohandas Gandhi, and he is credited with being the chief architect of the Indian state of Saurashtra. He was the secretary of the Kathiawar Political Conference during its struggle for the freedom of 222 princely states and their union in the new state. In 1948 Dhebar became chief minister of Saurashtra and retained the post until he was named Congress president. Under his administration, Saurashtra built more schools, hospitals and railway facilities per capita than any other state and consolidated land reforms more effectively.

Uchharangrai Navalshanker Dhebar was born in Gangajala, a hamlet near Jamnagar in what is now the state of Saurashtra on September 21, 1905, the fifth of eight children born to Navalshanker Vrajlal and Ujambai Dhebar. His parents were average middle-class Nagar Brahmins. His father was for many years on the staff of a newspaper in Rajkot. Uchharangrai attended Taluka elementary school in Rajkot, and later, the Tutorial High School, Gowalia Tank, in Bombay. After his mother died, he returned to Rajkot and was graduated from Saurashtra High School in 1922. His father sent him to St. Xavier's College in Bombay, but Dhebar had to leave in 1923 and take a job because of his father's illness.

For four and a half years, Dhebar was employed as a clerk in the office of a solicitor in Bombay. He studied law privately and passed the Bombay high court pleaders' examination with high distinction in Hindu law in 1928. In the following year he began to practice in Rajkot in the court of the Western India States Agency and won the respect of his colleagues and judges as well as litigants.

The writings of Leo Tolstoy influenced him to work for the emancipation of India's underfed peasants. He discussed a program of constructive work in the rural areas with Mohandas Gandhi, who advised him to work in the area of the Kathiawar peninsula on the west coast of India. The Mahatma gave Dhebar his blessing.

During Gandhi week in 1936, Dhebar publicly announced his retirement from the legal profession in order to join India's struggle for freedom. Before he could begin his reform program, a famine in neighboring villages drew him into relief work. He attended his first Congress session in December 1936, at Faizpur, where he received Sardar Vallabhbhai Patel's support for his plans in Kathiawar.

In Rajkot, after Dhebar had organized a union among the workers in a cotton mill, the Dewan of Rajkot ordered the deportation of fourteen members of the union's executive committee. The order was cancelled after Dhebar announced that the union would "fight to the finish."

According to the *Amrita Bazar Patrika* (January 21, 1955) politics in the states of Kathiawar had been suspended for some years by princely order. To secure the needed reforms, Dhebar revived the Kathiawar Political Conference in 1937 and was elected secretary. People who had been "crushed under exploitation and repression" were enthusiastic and the conference was so successful that it remained in force and Dhebar continued as secretary until 1948.

On the advice of Sardar Patel, Dhebar called a meeting of the Rajkot people's assembly in 1938, and a resolution demanding the establishment of a responsible government in Rajkot within thirty days was passed. The time expired and Dhebar, in response, led the Rajkot *satyagraha* (nonviolent civil resistance movement). Gandhi fasted during February 1939 in cooperation with the *satyagraha,* and Dhebar was imprisoned for five months. The Marquess of Linlithgow, then Viceroy of India, intervened, and the outcome was considered a victory for Dhebar.

Gandhi selected Dhebar to conduct an individual *satyagraha* at Viramgam in 1941, but before much headway was made, Dhebar was imprisoned for six months. He joined the "quit India movement" in 1942 and with three other leaders was arrested. They served three and a half years and devoted their time to a study of economic and political problems.

While Dhebar was incarcerated, the Princes of Kathiawar enforced the "attachment scheme," a merger of small states and estates with neighboring larger states. After Dhebar's release from prison, the Kathiawar Political Conference denounced the "attachment scheme" and demanded the formation of the state of Saurashtra with transfer of power to the people.

The partition of the Indian Empire into the Dominions of India and Pakistan (within the British Commonwealth of Nations) on August 15, 1947 brought quick changes in the Kathiawar peninsula. The Nawab of Junagarh (then a state in Kathiawar) favored union with Pakistan, but the majority of the people opposed this. Under Dhebar's guidance, a provincial government was formed and the Nawab was compelled to escape to Pakistan. The state was surrendered to the government of India on November 9, 1947.

The Kathiawar Princes revised their attitude and on January 17, 1948 signed a Covenant for the formation of the union of the states of Kathiawar. His Highness Jam Saheb was chosen Rajpramukh (head of state). Dhebar and Jam Saheb agreed that Gandhi should be invited to inaugurate the Union, and together went to see him in New Delhi.

Dhebar was one of the last persons to talk with Gandhi before his assassination on January 30, 1948. The tragedy increased his determination to build the new state according to Gandhian principles. The inaugural address was made on February 15, 1948 by Sardar Patel when the state came into being as the Union of Saurashtra. The state is composed of 222 former princely states, includes the major portion of the Kathiawar peninsula, and has a population of over 4,000,000.

In the election which followed, the Congress won forty-one of forty-five seats in Saurashtra's constituent assembly and Dhebar became chief minister. Saurashtra accepted the constitution of India which came into force on January 26, 1950 and which established India as a sovereign independent republic (within the Commonwealth), consisting of a union of twenty-seven states and other territories.

Negotiations were held between the landowners of Saurashtra and the Dhebar administration and an agreement was reached whereby landowners would be allowed to retain a maximum of 120 acres of land for personal cultivation. This was followed in 1951 by legislation, which enabled the tenants to become the undisputed occupants of the land.

When violations of the new laws occurred, Dhebar attempted to deal with them by nonviolent methods. However, he invoked the Preventive Detention Act and the lawbreakers were taken into custody, when the nonviolent techniques failed. When news of this action reached Parliament, Prime Minister Nehru defended Saurashtra's chief minister and called Dhebar "one of the humblest and quietest of men in India."

Other reforms included new schools and hospitals, the removal of "untouchability," and improvement in the status of women. Dhebar

Press Inf. Bureau Government of India

U. N. DHEBAR

wanted to resign in 1953, but the people prevailed upon him to continue as chief minister. However, after the executive working committee of the Indian National Congress elected Dhebar as president of the Congress in late 1954, he resigned as Saurashira's chief minister.

In January 1955 at its sixtieth annual session the Congress adopted a policy of progressive socialism which calls for government control of resources, the trades, and industries. This new policy together with a reshuffle in the New Delhi Cabinet and a new Congress president had a noticeable effect on the peasants of Andhra. Dhebar campaigned in the state, and his "verbal lashings" at power-hungry elements appealed to his audiences. The election returns in March gave the Congress party an overwhelming majority. The *Christian Science Monitor* (March 14, 1955) noted that the Congress has been forced, by its "race to keep ahead of Communist China . . . to attempt, through democratic methods, what the Indian Communists promise to do through violence and revolution."

Prime Minister Nehru stated on April 3, 1955 that India did not intend to move toward widespread nationalization, but would be interested in nationalizing only where the prevailing industrial set up was impeding progress. He added that India had benefited by foreign capital and was still interested in attracting it—on India's own terms (New York *Times,* April 4, 1955).

Dhebar, whom Gandhi called a "true and brave reformer," was married to Srimati Manuben Dhebar. She died in 1944 while Dhebar was in prison. Dhebar has one son. He occupies two simple rooms in New Delhi near his office and subsists on maize, bread and buttermilk. He spins the yarn for his white, spotless attire. He has never been abroad and is little

DHEBAR, U. N.—*Continued*

known outside of India. Reporters have described him as good-humored and industrious. He is of medium height and thin, has a small mustache, and wears spectacles. It has been said that his greatest assets are integrity, simplicity and a missionary zeal.

References

Amrita Bazar Patrika (Calcutta) Ja 21 '55
Hindu (Madras) Ja 17 '55
Time 64:34 N 22 '54

DICKEY, JOHN SLOAN Nov. 4, 1907-

College president; lawyer

Address: b. c/o Dartmouth College, Hanover, N.H.; h. Tuck Drive, Hanover, N.H.

Dedicated to the development of "public-mindedness" among students, John Sloan Dickey, president of Dartmouth College, is nationally known as the originator of Dartmouth's "Great Issues" course, the purpose of which is to "relate a liberal arts education to the responsibilities of adult living." The college's endowment and assets during Dickey's administration have increased by over $12,000,000. Dickey, a lawyer by training and profession, served for seven years in the United States Department of State prior to his inauguration in November 1945 as Dartmouth's twelfth president. He is an authority on world trade and international relations and is a trustee of several educational foundations.

JOHN SLOAN DICKEY

"Liberal arts," Dickey has said, "describes a study of subjects pertinent to the kind of life a man lives in contrast with the way he makes his living. . . . At Dartmouth we not only create a desire for thought, we give a man experience in thinking" (*Saturday Evening Post*, September 13, 1952).

Born in Lock Haven, Pennsylvania on November 4, 1907, John Sloan Dickey is the son of Gretchen (Sloan) and John W. Dickey, a manufacturer. After attending school in Lock Haven, John entered Dartmouth College, where he was a Rufus Choate scholar and worked part time. He was elected to Phi Beta Kappa and received the A.B. degree in 1929 with highest honors in history.

Entering Harvard Law School, Cambridge, Massachusetts, Dickey studied under Francis Bowes Sayre, then director of the Harvard Institute of Criminal Law. Dickey also worked part time at the Massachusetts department of correction.

Awarded the LL.B. degree at Harvard and admitted to the Massachusetts bar in 1932, Dickey began private practice with the Boston law firm of Gaston, Snow, Saltonstall & Hunt (later Gaston, Snow, Hunt, Rice & Boyd). When Francis Bowes Sayre became commissioner of the Massachusetts department of correction, Dickey joined his staff as an assistant. In the following year, after Sayre was appointed Assistant Secretary of State, Dickey took a leave of absence from his law firm to go to Washington as Sayre's assistant and also as assistant to the legal adviser of the Department of State.

Returning to his Boston law firm in 1936, Dickey became a partner in 1940. During this period, he was also active in Dartmouth affairs. He served for five years as assistant agent for his class, and from 1936 to 1940 was an officer of the Dartmouth Alumni Association of Boston.

Again he took a leave of absence from his law firm to return to Washington in 1940 as special assistant to Secretary of State Cordell Hull. In that year he became special assistant to Nelson A. Rockefeller, coordinator of Inter-American Affairs. Dickey was named acting chief of the division of world trade intelligence in July 1941 and in 1943 was appointed special consultant to Secretary Hull on matters relating to the Trade Agreements Act.

When the Office of Public Affairs was established within the State Department in 1944, Dickey became its director responsible for the informational and cultural exchange aspects of foreign relations. He also lectured on American foreign policy at the School of Advanced International Studies. At the United Nations Conference on International Organization in 1945, he served as public liaison officer for the U.S. delegation.

After Archibald MacLeish resigned in 1945 as Assistant Secretary of State for Public and Cultural Relations, Dickey was named to the post. He held this position until late in 1945 when he was appointed the twelfth president of Dartmouth, succeeding Ernest Martin Hopkins, who resigned after a twenty-nine-year tenure of office. Dickey was inaugurated on November 1, 1945, becoming one of the youngest college presidents in the country at that time.

Chartered by King George III in 1769 "for the education and instruction of the youth of Indian tribes . . . and also of English youth and any others," Dartmouth College opened in a single log hut at Hanover, New Hampshire in the following year, with a faculty consisting of the first president, the Reverend Eleazar Wheelock, and one assisting faculty member. The general curriculum has "always remained within the tradition of the liberal arts," and the college's official statement of purpose affirms the expectation that "students and graduates will have strength of character and convictions consistent with the ideals of free men."

Addressing the Dartmouth Alumni Association of New York on April 11, 1946, President Dickey promised that under his administration Dartmouth would continue to "emphasize the liberal arts curriculum" and would develop "public-mindedness." In an address to the same group a year later, he stated that he would "oppose the injection of prejudice by national fraternities into the operation of local chapters at the college." (On March 25, 1954, the student body voted to end fraternity discrimination because of race, religion or nationality.)

Dickey contributed an article, "Our Treaty Procedure Versus Our Foreign Policies" (*Foreign Affairs,* April 1947), in which he said that "our procedures for the democratic review and execution of international engagements" are in "an unholy mess," and indicated that Article II, Section 2 of the Constitution (requiring two-thirds vote of the Senate for the authorization or review of treaties) is "the heart of the trouble." Prior joint Congressional-Executive authorization, Dickey wrote, "gives the legislative branch an opportunity for taking a positive initiative in foreign policy formulation (rather than mere review) . . . [and] is a far broader base for public understanding and popular support of a public policy than two-thirds action in the Senate alone." At the U.N. Trade and Employment Conference held in Havana, Cuba in 1947, he served as an adviser to the U.S. delegation.

President Dickey's innovation, the "Great Issues" course, added to the curriculum in October 1947, was made possible by a three-year grant of $75,000 from the Carnegie Corporation. This course, which all seniors are required to take, has as its assignments readings in the New York *Herald Tribune,* the New York *Times,* other newspapers, periodicals, and government documents. Its lectures and discussions "present issues confronting the public-minded man who is concerned with the building of a sound economic order, the maintenance of a just peace, and the search for values which will enable our culture to survive."

Under Dickey's guidance a new department of Russian civilization has been instituted. A northern studies program was developed after Vilhjalmur Stefansson presented to Dartmouth in 1951 a gift of his collection of 35,000 volumes, 18,000 pamphlets, manuscripts and other matter relating to the polar regions. During the 1951-1952 academic year Army and Air Force units were added to the existing Navy ROTC unit at Hanover, and the George H. Howard cash awards were established for faculty members who "have made notable contributions to the improvement of undergraduate instruction." In addition, the William Jewett Tucker Foundation was established and the position of dean of the Tucker Foundation was created to further the moral and spiritual work of the College.

In October 1952 Dickey announced that Dartmouth had received an anonymous gift of $1,000,000 which would go toward providing twenty scholarships annually to "outstanding youths throughout the country" and are to be known as the Daniel Webster National Scholarships in honor of this famous member of Dartmouth's class of 1801.

A financial report, issued in October 1953 by Dartmouth, disclosed that during President Dickey's administration the assets of the institution had increased to more than $42,000,000. The student body (all men) at Dartmouth in 1954 consisted of 2,857 members and there were 309 teachers.

Mrs. Dickey is the former Christina Margaret Gillespie. The Dickeys, who were married on November 26, 1932, have two daughters, Sylvia Alexander and Christina Louise, and one son, John Sloan, Jr. Dr. Dickey's religious affiliation is with the Presbyterian Church. He belongs to Theta Chi fraternity. He received the honorary LL.D. degree from Tufts College (1945), Brown University (1946), Middlebury College (1946), Amherst College (1947), University of New Hampshire (1953), and Columbia University (1954).

He has served on the Presidential Committee on Civil Rights and the U.S. panel of experts studying the disarmament problem. He is a trustee of the World Peace Foundation, Committee for Economic Development, Brookings Institution, Rockefeller Foundation, and Wellesley College. He is a member of the Ford Foundation board of overseas training and research and a public representative of the board of governors, New York Stock Exchange.

He has been described in *Newsweek* as "a tall, slender, unassuming man . . . whose casual friendliness frequently masks an immense knowledge of foreign affairs." As a lawyer by training, "he chooses words carefully, he coins phrases, he gives a thorough answer to a big question" (John G. Mearns in the New York *Herald Tribune,* November 18, 1951).

References

N Y Herald Tribune p21 Ag 30 '45 por
N Y Times p14 Ag 30 '45 por; p32 N 1 '54
Sat Eve Post 225:28+ S 13 '52 por
National Cyclopædia of American Biography current vol G, 1943-46
Who's Who in America, 1954-55
Who's Who in American Education, 1951-52
World Biography (1954)

DIEM, NGO DINH *See* Ngo-dinh-Diem

DOBBS, MATTIWILDA July 11, 1925-
Singer
Address: c/o S. Hurok, 711 5th Ave., New York 22

Fresh from triumphs at London's Royal Opera House and Milan's La Scala, American-born coloratura soprano Mattiwilda Dobbs made her debut at New York's Town Hall on March 8, 1954. The young Negro singer sang the role of Zerbinetta in Richard Strauss' miniature opera, *Ariadne auf Naxos*, presented by Thomas Scherman's Little Orchestra Society, and the audience and critics gave her a rousing ovation. "She immediately proved herself to be one of the gifted bravura singers now before the public," reported Olin Downes (New York *Times*, March 9, 1954). "Miss

Iris, Paris

MATTIWILDA DOBBS

Dobbs has more than an exceptional virtuosity in song. She has temperament and charm . . . and [is] a coloratura of exceptional range."

She first came to prominence in the musical world when she won the International Music Competition in Geneva, Switzerland in October 1950. After making her professional debut in Paris she became the first Negro to sing a principal role at La Scala in Milan, Italy. She has sung leading operatic roles at the Edinburgh, Glyndebourne and Holland festivals, and, in 1954, before Queen Elizabeth II at London's Royal Opera House at a gala performance of Rimski-Korsakov's *Le Coq d'Or* in honor of King Gustaf VI and Queen Louise of Sweden, at which she was decorated with the Order of the North Star.

Making her second appearance on the stage of Town Hall on January 23, 1955, Miss Dobbs was greeted by a capacity audience to hear her first concert recital. During the summer of 1955 she made her first round-the-world tour which included thirty-five concerts in Australia and appearances in such cities as Singapore and Bangkok. She returns to the United States in October to make her American operatic debut with the San Francisco Opera Company. She has recorded complete performances of *The Pearl Fishers* and *Zaide*, and Angel Records has recently released two solo LP records of selections from her concert and operatic repertoire.

Mattiwilda Dobbs was born in Atlanta, Georgia on July 11, 1925, the fifth of six daughters of John Wesley Dobbs, a railroad mail clerk. Her father had worked his way through three years of college, and with the aid of his wife, by much self-sacrifice, managed to give all of his daughters a college education. Mattiwilda, next to the youngest, was very shy. At the age of eight she had rehearsed a little duet with her younger sister, June; when June became sick, Mattiwilda, terribly frightened, quaveringly sang the song alone.

At the age of seven she began to study the piano and had become a proficient pianist by the time she was fifteen. She began to discover her voice, but, timid still, sang only for her family. She was persuaded to join the choir of the First Congregational Church, and, on entering Spelman College in Atlanta, she began voice lessons with Naomi Maise and Willis James.

Her father, deciding that the best musical instruction must be given her, took her to New York after she had been graduated in 1946 as valedictorian of her class with the B.A. degree.

In New York, Mme. Lotte Leonard was her teacher for four years (1946-1950). She studied Spanish at Teachers College, Columbia University, and received her M.A. degree. In 1947 she was a soloist in the University of Mexico's festival of music and drama, and in the same year she won a Marian Anderson scholarship.

During 1948 she was granted two scholarships to study opera at the Mannes Music School (now the College of Music) in New York, and at the Berkshire Music Center, Lenox, Massachusetts. She went to Paris in 1950 for two years' study with Pierre Bernac, on a $3,000 John Hay Whitney Opportunity Fellowship. In October 1950 she competed against hundreds of singers from four continents in the International Music Competition held at Geneva, Switzerland. The night before the finals in the competition Miss Dobbs had sprained her ankle severely, but took nothing to assuage the pain for fear it would interfere with her singing. After winning the first prize, she sang in Paris where she was heard by S. Hurok and signed under his management.

Beginning her professional career with orchestral appearances in European capitals, Miss Dobbs gave recitals in France, Sweden, Holland and Luxembourg during the 1951-1952 season. During the Holland festival in 1952 she sang a leading role in Igor Stravinsky's *The Nightingale*. She appeared at La Scala Opera House in Milan, Italy as Elvira in Rossini's *L'Italiana in Algeri* on March 4, 1953. Later that month she sang the role of the Queen of the Night in Mozart's *The Magic Flute* at the opera house in Genoa. A tour of Scandinavian capitals was an outstanding success.

She sang at the Glyndebourne Opera Festival in England in June 1953, appearing as Zerbinetta in Richard Strauss' *Ariadne auf Naxos.* This resulted in her being engaged to sing three parts at the Royal Opera House, Covent Garden, London during the 1953-1954 season. She sang the Queen in *Le Coq d'Or,* Gilda in *Rigoletto,* and the Forest Bird in *Siegfried.*

The young singer made her New York debut on March 8, 1954 at Town Hall with Thomas Scherman's Little Orchestra. "A beautiful Negro girl, [gifted] with a gorgeous coloratura voice, stopped the show at Town Hall last night," reported music critic Louis Biancolli (New York *World-Telegram and Sun,* March 9), "a richly gifted Southern girl who had been garnering glory in Europe and has now returned to add her own country to her list of conquests."

Miss Dobbs' performance at Covent Garden in July 1954 was an intermingling of drama and tragedy. The Royal Opera Company sent for her to appear in *Le Coq d'Or,* as it was to be a performance attended by British and Swedish royalty. Miss Dobbs, who had been scheduled that same night to sing at the Glyndebourne Opera Festival, rushed to London to rehearse for what was to be the high point in her musical career. Four days before the performance her husband, Luis Rodriguez, a Spanish journalist and radio script writer, died. They had been married only a year. Miss Dobbs, upholding the tradition that the show must go on, sang the leading feminine role of the Queen of Shemakhan. As the final curtain fell, Miss Dobbs was summoned to the Royal Box and was decorated by King Gustaf VI with his country's Order of the North Star.

During the 1954 fall season at Covent Garden Miss Dobbs added the role of Olympia in *The Tales of Hoffmann* to her repertoire. She also sang in concerts in Paris, Belgium, Holland and London, and returned to the United States to sing again in New York at Town Hall, on January 23, 1955. The New York *Times* reported the next day that "the total impression was of an event in which a charming young woman displayed a light, beautiful voice, which was ever so agile and always fresh, clear and ravishing in its tonal purity. . . . She sang two sets of French art songs and two groups of German lieder; the Werner Egk *Variations* formed her chief display piece, and here her skill as a coloratura singer was exhibited most brilliantly. Not only could she negotiate all its intricate difficulties with accuracy and élan, but every note of it was pretty."

"There is more technical work to be done before Miss Dobbs can realize her amazing potentials," commented *Musical Courier* (February 15, 1955), "but these seem limitless. Enunciation was frequently faulty; however, an innate sense of style and proportion was in evidence, and a gift for stage and interpretation helped the artist greatly in pleasing presentations of her numbers."

Irving Kolodin, commenting on her Town Hall concert in the *Saturday Review* (February 5, 1955), praised her ability to "sing any sequence of high, fast-moving notes with dazzling purity of sound and persuasive ease," but suggested that "if Miss Dobbs is to have more than a short, spectacular success and a swift decline, she should look to the building of her middle and low voice, acquire a more subtle command of languages, and, in a word, put a solid foundation under her artistic penthouse."

In March 1955 she sang again with the Little Orchestra Society in Town Hall and then she embarked on a tour of the Caribbean and Central America, a tour of Western Europe, and a three-months series of concerts in Australia and the Far East. On her earlier concert tour, which included the West Coast, Albert Goldberg of the Los Angeles *Times* commented: "She is a new star of the first magnitude. A voice of often miraculous beauty . . . fascinating ease and uncanny accuracy."

The young soprano makes her headquarters in an apartment in Madrid, Spain, but still considers Atlanta her home.

References

Mlle 40:63 Ja '55 por
Newsweek 44:54 Jl 12 '54 por
Time 61:54+ Mr 16 '53 por
Grove, G. Dictionary of Music and Musicians (Blom, E., ed.) (1955)

DOUGHTON, ROBERT L(EE) Nov. 7, 1863-Sept. 30, 1954 Former member of the House of Representatives; merchant, farmer, stock raiser and state Senator in North Carolina before his election to the House of Representatives on the Democratic ticket in 1911; chairman of the House Ways and Means Committee in every Congress from 1933 to 1952 except the Eightieth; author of the first social security law and many tax bills for the New Deal and Fair Deal; after retirement in 1952 served as national Democratic committeeman for North Carolina. See *Current Biography,* (July) 1942.

Obituary

N Y Times p17 O 2 '54

DOWNES, OLIN Jan. 27, 1886—Aug. 22, 1955 Music critic of New York *Times* for thirty-two years; began his career at age of twenty as critic on Boston *Post* where he worked for eighteen years; was a popular lecturer at Chautauqua, Berkshire Festival, Brooklyn Academy of Music and Boston and Harvard Universities; commentator for Sunday broadcasts of New York Philharmonic-Symphony Orchestra; his published works include *The Lure of Music, Symphonic Masterpieces;* edited *Songs of Russia* and, with Elie Siegmeister, *A Treasury of American Song;* on board of American National Theatre and Academy. See *Current Biography* (Mar.) 1943.

Obituary

N Y Times p23 Ag 23 '55

DREYFUS, CAMILLE (EDOUARD) Nov. 11, 1878- Chemist; business executive
Address: b. c/o Celanese Corporation of America, 180 Madison Ave., New York 16; h. Hotel Pierre, 5th Ave. & E. 61st St., New York 21

Fortisan and Arnel are the names of new products added to the long list of man-made materials manufactured by the Celanese Corporation of America, of which Dr. Camille Dreyfus is the founder and now chairman of the board. Cellulose acetate fiber was perfected by Dreyfus and his brother Henry in their laboratories in Switzerland before World War I, and they were the first to manufacture it commercially.

Under the leadership of Camille Dreyfus as president of the Celanese Corporation of America from 1925 to 1945, the firm expanded from its original plant in Cumberland, Maryland to include about ten factories. It is a leading domestic producer of cellulose acetate fiber and a variety of cellulose acetate fabrics suitable for use in home decoration and for both civilian and military wearing apparel. Celanese also produces plastics and many commercial chemicals.

CAMILLE DREYFUS

One of the six children of Henrietta (Wahl) and Abraham Dreyfus, Camille Edouard Dreyfus was born in Basel, Switzerland on November 11, 1878. His father was a banker. Young Dreyfus attended the University of Basel and left that institution in 1902 with the M.A. and Ph.D. degrees and continued his studies at the Sorbonne in Paris until 1906. After working in Basel to gain experience, in 1910 he and Dr. Henry Dreyfus (who died in 1944) established their own chemical laboratory in the same city.

They began the manufacture of cellulose acetate, the first noninflammable type of celluloid; half of their production went into motion picture film, the other half into the manufacture of toilet articles. Meanwhile the brothers continued their research in an attempt to make a fiber from cellulose acetate and eventually succeeded, but before the new material could be marketed commercially, World War I intervened.

A solution of cellulose acetate was used for military purposes. At that time airplane wings were wooden frameworks covered with silk and thus likely to catch fire when hit by incendiary tracer bullets; noninflammable cellulose acetate "dope" spread over airplane wings and fuselage greatly reduced this danger. To ensure the availability of this material, in 1914 Great Britain invited Dreyfus to come to that country, and a large plant for the production of cellulose acetate was constructed outside of London.

When the United States entered the war, Dreyfus was asked by Secretary of War Newton Diehl Baker to establish a plant in the United States. The American Cellulose and Chemical Manufacturing Company was incorporated in 1918 with Dreyfus as president and construction was begun on a factory at Cumberland, Maryland. Before it was completed, the war had ended and the military market had disappeared.

Dreyfus spent the next six years in perfecting his cellulose acetate fiber and methods for producing it. In December 1924 the first "Celanese," as the yarn was named, was manufactured by the Cumberland plant. The name of the corporation was changed to the Celanese Corporation of America the following year with Dreyfus retaining the presidency. The firm of J. P. Morgan and Company, Incorporated, was associated with the corporation in 1926 as underwriter of a stock issue.

The Celanese Corporation, which had shown a profit for every year of production since 1925, had its first really big year in 1939. The following year exceeded even that in volume; the company had at this time grown more than 700 per cent since 1929. A new plant was built near Pearisburg, Virginia, and the labor force was increased by 2,000, bringing the total number of employees up to 12,000. Dreyfus held 223 patents in the United States in 1940, most of them concerned with the production of cellulose acetate.

In 1932 the company began experiments to produce acetic acid, which it had formerly purchased from chemical companies, from natural gas. After examining Celanese's plans for chemical production, the U.S. War Production Board decided that Celanese should participate in the wartime chemical program and authorized the construction of a plant in Bishop, Texas.

The building was not completed until the war's end, and the factory was then converted to the production of chemicals for use by Celanese and for sale to other companies. In addition to acetic acid and acetic anhydride, chemicals important in the production of cellulose acetate, the plant makes formaldehyde, methanol, propyl alcohol, and trioxane (a fuel for heating Army rations in the field).

Celanese Mexicana, S. A., a Mexican affiliate of the Celanese Corporation of America, was formed in 1944 with Dreyfus as president. On August 23, 1945 Dreyfus was elected chairman of the board of Celanese Corporation of America and was succeeded by Harold Blancke as president. The change was made to increase the active managerial staff. Dreyfus continues as the executive head of the company.

British Columbia granted the Celanese Corporation Forest Management Licence No. 1 in 1948, which gave the company the right to obtain lumber from a forest area over 200 miles long in perpetuity on a sustained yield basis (only the number of trees replaceable by natural growth could be cut). A pulp mill to supply the raw material (wood pulp) for cellulose acetate was built at Prince Rupert, B.C. in 1951.

Responding to objections by the Celanese Corporation, the Federal Trade Commission ruled in 1951 that Celanese fiber should be called "acetate." This reversed a 1937 ruling which designated both acetate and viscose as "rayon." Although acetate and viscose are both produced from the same materials their characteristics and uses vary. Acetate dries quickly, drapes gracefully and can be permanently pleated.

The Celanese Corporation also produces woven and knitted fabrics. It introduced warp-knit rayon to the United States and is its largest manufacturer. It is the third largest producer of viscose in the country, following American Viscose Corporation and E. I. du Pont de Nemours & Company, and its biggest producer of acetate. With the end of World War II it also began the manufacture of plastics including plastic film for package purposes, and Fortisan, a fiber of exceptional strength which can be used in place of silk in parachutes and for other military purposes.

Early in 1953 Celanese profits showed a decline, which was attributed to the "evils of scare buying and accumulation of inventories arising at the beginning of the Korean war" (New York *Times,* March 10, 1953).

The sales of its chemical products continued to increase despite severe competition and the impact of lower dollar returns per unit of product (New York *Times,* March 9, 1955).

In October 1954 the Celanese Corporation announced a new synthetic fiber, Arnel, which is completely washable, nonshrinkable, fast drying, blends well with other fibers and is inexpensive. Pleats stay in even when the fabric is put in a washing machine and "tumble dried" at high heat. Its technical name is cellulose triacetate. Another material which its research chemists are using is polyester resin, combined with glass fibers, which has high promise of many uses in the industry. Celanese purchased the Marco Chemicals of Linden, New Jersey in 1953 where such resins are manufactured.

It was announced in March 1955 that Celanese had begun semicommercial production of Celluflex CEF which gives unique fire retardant properties to such substances as cellulose acetate, ethyl cellulose, nitrocellulose, butadiene-acrylonitrile, and rubber chloride.

Dreyfus serves as chairman of the board for the American Cellulose and Chemical Manufacturing Company, Ltd., Celanese Lanese Corporation, Celanese Pan-American Company, Inc., Celluloid Corporation, New London Fabrics Corporation, Pabin Corporation, and Williamsport Textile Corporation. He is the managing director of the British Celanese, Ltd.

Among the organizations of which Dreyfus is a member are the American Chemical Society and American Association for the Advancement of Science. He is a trustee of the Pestalozzi Foundation and a director of the Bibliotheca Helvetica, Inc. He is a Chevalier in the French Legion of Honor and in 1940 he received the Modern Pioneer Award of the National Association of Manufacturers. His clubs are the Quaker Ridge Golf (Mamaroneck, New York), Manhattan, Chemists (New York), and Royal Automobile (London). He is a member of Congregation Emanu-el. On September 18, 1931 Dreyfus married Jean Tennyson, a singer.

References

Chem & Ind 47:520 N '40
Fortune 37:84 My '48 por
N Y Times II p 1 Jl 1 '41
Who's Who in America, 1954-55
Who's Who in Commerce and Industry (1953)

DUNNOCK, MILDRED Jan. 25, (?)- Actress; teacher

Address: b. c/o The Playwrights' Company, 1545 Broadway, New York 36; h. 26 E. 81st St., New York 28

Despite a creditable number of appearances in successful Broadway plays and Hollywood pictures, Mildred Dunnock still considers herself more of a school teacher than an actress, since her teaching has been "continuous" over two decades. Drama critics and audiences have come to expect from her consistently excellent performances as in her role of Big Mama in Tennessee Williams' Pulitzer Prize-winning play, *Cat on a Hot Tin Roof,* which opened on Broadway on March 24, 1955. Among her most notable stage characterizations have been that of Linda Loman in Arthur Miller's *Death of a Salesman* and as Lavinia Hubbard in Lillian Hellman's *Another Part of the Forest.*

Television audiences have seen her on major network shows, notably in *Studio One, Kraft Television Theatre,* and *Philco Playhouse* productions. Her motion picture appearances were in *The Corn Is Green* and *Death of a Salesman.* Her teaching career began in Baltimore, Maryland at the Friends School there, and she has continued it over the years at the Friends School, Brooklyn, New York; at the Masters School, Dobbs Ferry, New York; at Milton Academy in Milton, Massachusetts, and at the Brearley School in Manhattan. In September 1954 she began teaching classes in oral interpretation of literature and drama at Barnard College in New York, where she has the rank of associate in English.

(Continued next page)

Marcus Blechman

MILDRED DUNNOCK

Mildred Dunnock was born in Baltimore, Maryland, the daughter of Walter Dunnock, president of the Dumari Textile Company, who is now retired, and Florence (Saynook) Dunnock. She received her early education at Public School 59 in Baltimore, and then at Western High School. She attended Goucher College, Baltimore, and received her A.B. degree, having majored in English. She was "burned by a footlight fire," she admits, when she played leading men in college productions. She wanted to set out for New York and a stage career, but her father objected, and she accepted his dictum and took a teaching position at the Friends School in Baltimore. In her spare time she acted with the Vagabond Players and also with the Johns Hopkins University players. With the latter group she played opposite John Van Druten in one of his plays, *The Return Half*.

Moving to New York, she taught school and studied at Columbia University for her M.A. degree, and took part in several plays produced by the Morningside Players. One of these plays, *Life Begins,* was later produced on Broadway by Joseph Santley, who invited Miss Dunnock to appear in the role of Miss Pinty, a nurse. The play, a hospital drama by Mary Macdougal Axelson, opened at the Selwyn Theatre on March 28, 1932, but lasted only eight performances.

Miss Dunnock taught English at the Friends School in Brooklyn, and later at the Spence School in Manhattan. She was general understudy for the women's roles in Franz Werfel's spectacle, *The Eternal Road,* staged by Max Reinhardt, at the Manhattan Opera House. The play opened on January 7, 1937, and ran for 153 performances. Miss Dunnock coached some of the cast in speech, having been recommended by Rosamond Pinchot.

Her next Broadway appearance was in the role of Agnes Riddle in Lulu Vollmer's play, *The Hill Between,* which opened at the Little Theatre on March 11, 1938 and ran for eleven performances. Gertrude Macy of the Guthrie McClintic office recommended her for a role in Katharine Cornell's expensive 1938 failure, *Herod and Mariamne,* which closed in Pittsburgh. She appeared in summer stock as Prossy in George Bernard Shaw's *Candida,* which starred Laurette Taylor.

Miss Dunnock acted the leading role of a Welshwoman in a play, *The Comedy of Good and Evil* by Richard Hughes presented on April 7, 1938 at the West 20th Street Theatre by the Playroom Club; the play was brought to Broadway as *Miss Minnie,* starring Josephine Hull, and Miss Dunnock's performance was seen by producer-director Herman Shumlin. He asked her to try out for the role of Birdie in Lillian Hellman's *The Little Foxes,* but her marriage and the birth of her daughter in 1939 prevented her from appearing in the play. However, the next season, she visited Shumlin and asked if she could read for the role of the fluttery Welsh schoolteacher, Miss Ronberry, in Emlyn Williams' play, *The Corn Is Green,* which starred Ethel Barrymore. Shumlin gave Miss Dunnock the part, and the play opened at the National Theatre on November 26, 1940, and ran for 477 performances. When Warner Brothers made the film version of *The Corn Is Green,* with Bette Davis in the starring role, Miss Dunnock repeated her stage portrayal.

At the Brearley School she taught English and elocution, and among her pupils were the daughters of actor Fredric March, composer Irving Berlin and composer Richard Rodgers.

While playing in *The Corn Is Green* Miss Dunnock maintained her teaching schedule, from 8:30 A.M. to 4:35 P.M. except on two matinee days. At noon she went home to be with her young daughter, Mary Melinda (Linda) Urmy. "People don't think you can act if you're a schoolteacher," she told Peter Kihss (New York *World-Telegram,* March 25, 1941), "but teaching is something I intend to keep up. . . . The arrangement is only possible because I have such an understanding headmistress. It's a good thing, too, my husband likes the theatre." She told Helen Ormsbee (New York *Herald Tribune*, March 6, 1949): "I could apply only for parts in early fall productions that would be rehearsing before school opened, and I always had to have permission from the school. If the play toured a few weeks before coming to New York I got a substitute to teach my classes."

Following appearances in several plays which had brief runs, she played in Philip Barry's fantasy *Foolish Notion,* starring Tallulah Bankhead and Donald Cook, which opened at the Martin Beck Theatre on March 14, 1945 and ran for 103 performances. "Mildred Dunnock shines as an actress rival of Sophie, giving as good as she receives in an encounter with polite savagery," wrote E. C. Sherburne in the *Christian Science Monitor* (March 14, 1945).

Her next stage role was as Madame Tsai, the Chinese mother in *Lute Song,* which had been adapted from the Chinese by Sidney Howard and Will Irwin, and which starred Mary Martin. It played 142 performances at the Plymouth Theatre, after opening on February 6, 1946. The play, based on the original *Pi-Pa-Ki,* by Kao-Tong-Kia, has for centuries occupied somewhat the same position on the Chinese stage as *Hamlet* in the English theatre. Miss Dunnock's performance was described as "excellent" by Howard Barnes (New York *Herald Tribune,* February 7, 1946).

Her next Broadway role was as the half-crazed Lavinia, mother of the vicious Hubbard brood in Lillian Hellman's *Another Part of the Forest,* which opened on November 20, 1946 at the Fulton Theatre. William Hawkins wrote in the New York *World-Telegram* (November 21, 1946): "Mildred Dunnock does a magnificent job of sustaining the role of the semi-hysterical Lavinia." The play ran for 182 performances.

In Rose Franken's play *The Hallams,* which opened on March 4, 1948 at the Booth Theatre, Miss Dunnock played the unpleasant Etta Hallam, and her characterization was praised, but the play closed after twelve performances. In the role of Williams, a faithful theatre maid, Miss Dunnock "gave a capital performance" in Ruth Gordon's "valentine" to the theatre world of the 1890's, but this play, *The Leading Lady,* closed a week after its opening on October 18, 1948.

Her longest Broadway engagement was for 742 performances in Arthur Miller's *Death of a Salesman* which opened at the Morosco Theatre on February 10, 1949, and which won the Pulitzer Prize, the New York Drama Critics Circle award, and several other awards. "Mildred Dunnock gives the performance of her career," wrote Brooks Atkinson (New York *Times,* February 11, 1949) "as the wife and mother—plain of speech but indomitable in spirit." She played the same role opposite Frederic March in the Stanley Kramer Company motion picture production, presented by Columbia Pictures in December 1951. "As the long-suffering wife," commented Bosley Crowther (New York *Times,* December 21, 1951), "Mildred Dunnock is simply superb, as she was on the stage [in her] portrayal of a woman who bears the agony of seeing her sons and husband turn out failures."

Under José Quintero's direction, Miss Dunnock appeared in Jane Bowles's play, *In the Summer House,* which starred Judith Anderson and opened on December 29, 1953 at the Playhouse Theatre. It drew "mixed" reviews, but the critics were unanimous in acclaiming Miss Anderson and Miss Dunnock. "Miss Dunnock is superb . . . she plays the more crucial scenes with unerring insight. It is beautiful work," commented Brooks Atkinson (New York *Times,* December 30, 1953). "She does her finest job of acting," wrote William Hawkins (New York *World-Telegram and Sun,* December 30, 1953), "as the widow and weakling who becomes quite grand over a bottle. It is honest, fleet and subtle performing." The play closed after fifty-five performances.

Although Miss Dunnock has often played the roles of pathetic, or timorous ladies, she broke away from type in her current role of Big Mama in *Cat on a Hot Tin Roof,* at the Morosco Theatre. Walter Kerr wrote in the New York *Herald Tribune* (March 25, 1955): "Mildred Dunnock is startingly fine in an unfamiliar sort of role: the brash, gravel-voiced outspoken matron."

She has been active in the American National Theatre and Academy (ANTA) productions, appearing for two weeks in 1950 and 1951 in *Peer Gynt,* Paul Green's adaptation of the Henrik Ibsen play, produced by Cheryl Crawford. She also appeared in *The Wild Duck* at the City Center, playing the role of Gina. She is a member of the Actors' Studio.

Besides *The Corn is Green* and *Death of a Salesman* Miss Dunnock's work before the Hollywood cameras has included the role of a lady doctor in *The Girl in White, I Want You,* and in 1952 the Warner Brothers remake of *The Jazz Singer,* starring Danny Thomas, in which she played the Orthodox Jewish mother. When 20th Century-Fox Film Corporation made a film, *Kiss of Death,* photographed on the streets of New York, Miss Dunnock played the role of a woman in a wheel chair.

Miss Dunnock has made frequent appearances on such television shows as *The Web, Suspense, Omnibus* and *Inner Sanctum.* One of her widely acclaimed performances was on the *Kraft Television Theatre* when she played on May 13, 1954, with Carmen Mathews, in Greer Johnson's *The Worried Songbirds.* Another outstanding performance was with Betty Field in *Hide and Seek* on the Philco Playhouse on February 7, 1954.

Offstage, with the drab wigs removed, Miss Dunnock has "dark waving hair, an extremely attractive, animated face and large dark eyes" (William Hawkins, New York *World-Telegram,* April 2, 1947). She is five feet six inches tall. For relaxation she likes to do needle point. She is fond of old houses and china. Miss Dunnock is married to Keith Urmy, who is in the banking business. Their sixteen-year-old daughter, Linda, attends Milton Academy. They have an apartment in Manhattan and a country home in Pound Ridge in Westchester County, New York.

References

N Y Herald Tribune p4 VI Ap 6 '41; p3 V Mr 6 '49 por
N Y World-Telegram p30 Ap 2 '47 por
Theatre Arts 33:31 Je '49 por
Vogue 125:43+ Je '55 pors

EINSTEIN, ALBERT Mar. 14, 1879-Apr. 18, 1955 Physicist; mathematician; humanitarian; the twentieth century's greatest scientist; won Nobel Prize in physics (1921); his Special Theory of Relativity (1905) and its equation $E=Mc^2$ formed the keystone in the modern concept of the atom; he escaped from Hitler regime in Germany; became U.S. citizen, 1940; although an ardent pacifist, he wrote to President Franklin D. Roosevelt on August 2, 1939 informing him of the possibilities of

EINSTEIN, ALBERT—*Continued*

nuclear warfare; this warning launched America's $2 billion atomic bomb project; in 1953 he announced his Unified Field Theory and renounced the quantum theory (the latter still held by most physicists); author of many books on physics; also on Hitlerism; Zionism; philosophy; and autobiographies. See *Current Biography* (May) 1953.

Obituary

N Y Times p 1+ Ap 19 '55 pors

ELIZABETH II, QUEEN OF GREAT BRITAIN Apr. 21, 1926-

Address: Buckingham Palace, London, S.W. 1, England

NOTE: This biography supersedes the article which appeared in *Current Biography* in 1944.

The Head of the British Commonwealth of Nations, Her Majesty Queen Elizabeth II, acceded to her throne on February 6, 1952 following the death of her father, King George VI, and was crowned on June 2, 1953. Her full title in the United Kingdom and Dependent Territories is Elizabeth II, by the Grace of God, of the United Kingdom of Great Britain and Northern Ireland and of her Other Realms and Territories, Queen, Head of the Commonwealth, Defender of the Faith.

Her Majesty is the sixth woman to occupy the English throne in her own right, her predecessors having been Mary I, Elizabeth I, Mary II, Anne, and Victoria. The Consort of Queen Elizabeth II is His Royal Highness Prince Philip, Duke of Edinburgh; their son, Prince Charles, born in 1948, is the Heir Apparent.

The daughter of Prince Albert Frederick Arthur George, then 13th Duke of York and later King George VI, and the former Lady Elizabeth Angela Marguerite Bowes-Lyon (youngest daughter of the 14th Earl of Strathmore and Kinghorne), Princess Elizabeth was born on April 21, 1926 at 17 Bruton Street in London.

When christened in Buckingham Palace, she was given the names Elizabeth (for her mother), Alexandra (for her great-grandmother, the Consort of King Edward VII, "the Peacemaker"), and Mary for her grandmother, the Consort of George V). At that time it seemed unlikely that the little girl would ever occupy the throne, for her father's older brother, the Prince of Wales (later Edward VIII and now Duke of Windsor) was the Heir Apparent.

Princess Elizabeth, whose nickname was "Lilibet," and her younger sister, Princess Margaret Rose (see *Current Biography,* November 1953), were closely guarded during their early childhood spent at the Duke of York's town house at 145 Piccadilly Circus and at the Royal Lodge in the Great Park of Windsor Castle. Elizabeth's mother taught her to read and introduced her to such juvenile classics as the Beatrix Potter animal stories. Princess Elizabeth began her intense interest in horses at the age of four, when her grandfather, King George V, presented her with a Shetland pony.

In October 1933 the young Princesses were placed under the tutelage of Marion Crawford ("Crawfie"). From a special governess, Madame de Bellaigne, Elizabeth learned to speak French fluently; she also took piano and singing lessons. She enjoyed reading American comic strips, especially *Mutt and Jeff* and *Li'l Abner,* and was fond of A. A. Milne's books. At the age of thirteen, Elizabeth studied constitutional history privately with Henry Marten of Eton College.

The future of Princess Elizabeth was altered by the death of her grandfather, King George V, on January 20, 1936 and by the abdication from the throne of his heir, Edward VIII, in December, which brought her father to the throne as King George VI on December 11, 1936. Through her father's accession Princess Elizabeth became "Heir Presumptive" to the throne; the title of "Heir Apparent" was withheld in favor of a possible male heir.

Following the outbreak of World War II, the Princesses lived for five years at Royal Lodge on the grounds of Windsor Castle in Berkshire, while the King and Queen spent most of their time in London. Elizabeth's voice, which is clear and precise, was first heard by the public on October 13, 1940, when she delivered a three-minute radio message to the children of the Empire. In 1943 the Princess, who is an excellent pianist, accepted the presidency of the Royal College of Music.

King George VI named his elder daughter an honorary colonel of the Grenadier Guards on her sixteenth birthday and on the same day at a regimental review she made her official debut. So far as the Crown was concerned, Elizabeth "came of age" on her eighteenth birthday (April 21, 1944); from that time on she could rule without a Regent in the event of her accession to the throne. By revision of the Regency Act of 1937 (which King George requested of Parliament in 1943), she also became a member of the Council of State, which acts for the monarch during his absences from the country. When the King made a secret visit to Italy in July 1944, his daughter signed acts of Parliament in his name.

Princess Elizabeth had long wished to join one of the wartime services, but was unable to obtain her father's consent until March 5, 1945, when she became a subaltern of the Auxiliary Territorial Service and passed a difficult course in motor transport maintenance and driving.

In January 1947 she set sail with her parents and sister for a good-will visit to the Union of South Africa and other areas in Africa. It was during this, her first trip outside the British Isles, that Princess Elizabeth became twenty-one years of age. "I declare before you all," she stated on a radio broadcast from Cape Town to the entire Empire, "that my whole life, whether it be long or short, shall be devoted to your service and the service of the great imperial family to which we all belong."

On July 10, 1947 the King and Queen announced the betrothal of their "dearly beloved daughter the Princess Elizabeth to Lieutenant

Philip Mountbatten, R.N., son of the late Prince Andrew of Greece and Princess Andrew, to which union the King has gladly given his consent." The marriage ceremony was observed in Westminster Abbey on November 20.

His Majesty the day before had approved that the dignity of a dukedom be conferred upon the bridegroom by the "title of Baron Greenwich . . . Earl of Merioneth and Duke of Edinburgh." The King also authorized the "use of the prefix His Royal Highness" by Philip (See Duke of Edinburgh, *Current Biography*, October 1947). The Duke and Duchess of Edinburgh were installed as members of the Most Noble Order of the Garter in April 1948, and in the following month they represented the British Crown on a four-day official visit to Paris.

On November 14, 1948, His Royal Highness Prince Charles Philip Arthur George (who is now Duke of Cornwall and Heir Apparent) was born. Their second child, Princess Anne Elizabeth Alice Louise, was born August 15, 1950. Prior to the birth of their daughter, Anne Princess Elizabeth and the Duke of Edinburgh had paid official visits to Athens and to Rome and the Vatican. In October and November 1951 they made a tour of Canada and a brief visit to Washington, D. C., where they were entertained at the White House by President and Mrs. Harry S. Truman.

On January 31, 1952 the Princess and the Duke of Edinburgh embarked on what was to have been a tour of Africa, Ceylon, Australia and New Zealand. They were near Nairobi, capital of Kenya Colony, when on February 6, 1952 they received the news of the death that day of King George VI, and of Elizabeth's accession to the throne.

Elizabeth was formally proclaimed Queen on February 8, 1952, following her immediate return to London. Her titles are styled in seven different ways. Six ways describe the relationship to the Crown of six members (Australia, Canada, Ceylon, United Kingdom, New Zealand, and Union of South Africa) of the Commonwealth.

Each of the six countries passed acts enabling it to have a title for the Queen recognizing her as its monarch and acknowledging the British monarchy as the symbol of unity of the Commonwealth. Pakistan and India, the other members of the Commonwealth, do not recognize the Queen as their monarch, but accept her as Head of the Commonwealth (*Statesman's Year-Book*, 1954).

The Queen decreed on April 9, 1952 that "she and her children and their descendants be styled and known as the House and Family of Windsor," but that the Duke of Edinburgh, who ranks as "first gentleman of the realms," is to retain the surname of Mountbatten. The Coronation of Queen Elizabeth II took place on June 2, 1953. (Her Majesty receives an annuity of approximately $171,000 plus expenses; Prince Philip receives about $118,000.)

Soon after the Coronation the Queen and her Consort proposed to begin again in November 1953 the Commonwealth tour which had been cut short by the death of King George VI. This brought up the matter of the Regency Act of 1937, which "makes provisions for the functions of the Crown to be performed in the absence or incapacity of the monarch" and which named the next adult in succession as regent and entrusted authority, in the absence of the sovereign, to the Council of State, consisting of "the sovereign's Consort and the four adults next in succession" to the throne (New York *Times*, July 23, 1953).

Portrait by Dorothy Wilding

ELIZABETH II, QUEEN OF GREAT BRITAIN

On November 4, 1953 Elizabeth II asked Parliament to change the Regency Act and accordingly it was amended on November 19 and now specifically designates the Duke of Edinburgh as regent presumptive for his son, and also includes the Queen Mother in the Council of State. The projected trip began as scheduled and the royal couple traveled about 50,000 miles in a tour of fourteen countries which ended in May 1954.

Honorary degrees which the Queen has received include the Bachelor of Music degree from the University of London (1946), the D.C.L. degree from Oxford University (1948), Doctor of Music degree from the University of Wales (1949), and the LL.D. degree from Edinburgh University (1951). Several J. Arthur Rank films have been made which record important events in Elizabeth's reign, including *A Queen is Crowned* (1953), *A Queen's World Tour* (1954) and *Royal Symphony* (1954); also numerous 16mm. films (see *Educational Film Guide*, 1953-1955).

Queen Elizabeth has a petite figure, about five feet four inches tall. Her eyes are blue, her naturally wavy hair is brown, and she smiles with genuine gaiety.

She is greatly interested in the royal stables and rarely misses a racing event and is an amateur photographer. Her Majesty is credited

ELIZABETH II—*Continued*

with a keen sense of humor. The Queen's "grace, confidence and natural consideration for others have seldom been equaled in English history" (*McCall's*, April 1953).

Selected References (see also magazine and newspaper indexes)

Christian Sci Mon p3 O 25 '47 por
The Times (London) p9 F 7 '52 por
Bocca, G. Elizabeth and Philip (1953)
Burke's Peerage, Baronetage and Knightage (1953)
Clay, C. Long Live the Queen (1953)
Crawford, M. Elizabeth the Queen (1952); Happy and Glorious! (1953); Little Princesses (1950)
Dimbleby, R. Elizabeth Our Queen (1953)
Johnston, L. Elizabeth Enters (1953)
Morrah, D. Princess Elizabeth, Duchess of Edinburgh (1947)
Nickolls, L. A. Reign of Elizabeth II (1952)
Peacock, I.C.L.H. Her Majesty Queen Elizabeth II (1954)
Sheridan, L. Queen and Her Children (1953)
Winn, G. H. Young Queen (1953)

EMERY DEWITT (MCKINLEY) Dec. 12, 1897-July 22, 1955 Founder (1937) of National Small Business Men's Association to give "little man" of business an opportunity to voice his opinion in national affairs; served as president for seventeen years; president and treasurer of Monroe Letterhead Corporation of Akron, Ohio (1929-1950); in 1941 became a partner in DeWitt Emery and Associates, a public relations and management counsel firm. See *Current Biography* (Oct.) 1946.

Obituary

N Y Times p8 Jl 23 '55

EMRICH, DUNCAN (BLACK MACDONALD) (ĕm'rĭk) Apr. 11, 1908- Folklore specialist; author

Address: b. c/o Folklore Section, Library of Congress, Washington 25, D.C.; h. 1517 30th St., N.W., Washington 7, D.C.

Delving into America's history for regional folk songs and other folklore material and preserving them for posterity has been part of the work of Duncan Emrich, chief of the Folklore Section of the Library of Congress since 1946. In recent years he has often been before the public—as the author of several books on the folklore of the American West (one of the latest is *The Cowboy's Own Brand Book*, Crowell, 1954).

Between October 1953 and June 1954 he was a regular weekly participant on *Weekend*, a two-hour NBC Sunday radio program. Emrich was formerly an instructor in English at Columbia University and an assistant professor of English at the University of Denver in Colorado.

Duncan Black Macdonald Emrich was born on April 11, 1908 in Mardin, Turkey, the son of Richard Stanley Merrill and Jeannette (Wallace) Emrich. His parents were at that time United States missionaries in Turkey. His brother is the Right Reverend Richard Stanley Merrill Emrich, Jr., Bishop of the Episcopal Church of the Diocese of Michigan. Prior to World War I, the Emrich family returned to the United States. Duncan's father died before the family went back to Turkey in 1920, where Mrs. Emrich served with the Near East Relief.

Duncan Emrich took his college preparatory courses at Phillips Academy in Andover, Massachusetts, from which he was graduated in 1926. He then entered Brown University in Providence, Rhode Island and while majoring in English, he won the Hicks prize and the Preston Gurney literary prize. He became a member of the Zeta Psi fraternity and the Owl Club. Duncan spent his summer vacations in the West: he worked on a cattle ranch in Arizona and helped build roads in Yosemite National Park. After receiving his A.B. degree in 1932 from Brown, Emrich went to Columbia University, where he earned an M.A. degree in English in 1933.

He next traveled to Spain, where he studied at the University of Madrid. In 1934 he was awarded the degree of Doctor en Letras. His major interests at Madrid were Spanish and Arabic literature. Returning to America, he enrolled at Harvard University and worked in the field of comparative literature. He was named Shattuck scholar and was also an Austin fellow. In 1937 he was awarded a Ph.D. degree, for which he had offered the thesis "Studies in the Legend of Avicenna."

While in Europe he also did graduate work at the Sorbonne in Paris, the universities of Aix-en-Provence and Nancy (France), and the University of Cologne (Germany). In 1937 Emrich accepted a position at Columbia University as an instructor in English. He retained this post until 1940 when he transferred to the University of Denver with the rank of assistant professor of English. He edited *Who Shot Maggie in the Freckle and Other Ballads of Virginia City, Nevada* (1940) and *Casey Jones, and Other Ballads of the Mining West* (W. H. Kistler, 1942).

Joining the U.S. Army in January 1943, he attended the Command and General Staff School at Fort Leavenworth, Kansas. Commissioned a first lieutenant, he was assigned to Military Intelligence. He later served with the rank of major as the official American historian in the secretary of the General Staff's office, Supreme Headquarters, Allied Expeditionary Force (SHAEF). He helped prepare General Dwight D. Eisenhower's "Report on Operations in Northwest Europe." Emrich discusses this important three-page document in an article written for the New York *Times Magazine* (May 5, 1946). Before Emrich left the army in August 1945, he was awarded the Croix de Guerre by the French government.

Duncan Emrich was appointed in 1945 to the position of chief of the Archive of the American Folk Song Section of the Library of Congress. He succeeded Alan Lomax, the noted folk ballad collector. In 1946 the responsibilities of the Folk Song Section were taken over by the Folklore Section of the Library and Emrich was named chief of the enlarged section.

Folklore, according to the *Encyclopedia Americana,* is the "science which embraces all that relates to ancient observations and customs, to the notions, beliefs, traditions, superstitions, and prejudices of common people." Folklore, as an organized study, began in the United States in 1888 when the American Folklore Society was instituted at Cambridge, Massachusetts to collect the folklore remains in this country; for example, old English folklore, Negro folklore in the South, Indian tribal lore, French-Canadian lore, and Mexican lore. The study of folklore is "of great assistance to the ethnologist, the sociologist, and the historian, as well as to the student of comparative mythology and of the science of religion."

One of the main functions of the Folklore Section is to collect and preserve all types of American folk music. The library now possesses phonograph recordings (on tape, wire, discs, and cylinders) amounting to more than 60,000 titles of folk music. These were made in a wide variety of localities. In the recording laboratory (a unit made possible by a grant from the Carnegie Corporation of New York), the library has the facilities for the duplication of folk songs for wide distribution, for the preservation of important musical events, and for the recording of literary material.

The section has also done much work in the collecting of other folklore material. In 1947, according to the annual report of the Librarian of Congress, Luther H. Evans, Emrich's effort was "to perfect widespread cooperative collecting arrangements with collectors in the field and with other institutions." During 1947 Emrich traveled widely in the West and because of these trips, a number of universities established collecting centers and projects.

The Folklore Section also operates on an international level. In 1948 Emrich attended two international conferences—the International Folk Song Commission in London and the International Commission on Folk Arts and Folklore in Paris—with the purpose of arranging for exchange of materials. His mission was successful and the library now has exchange and gift agreements with many foreign folklore institutions, such as the Scottish Folklore Institute and the Irish Folklore Commission.

Luther H. Evans stated in his annual report of 1950 that through the library's "encouragement of state archives of folklore, and independent collecting by scholars throughout the United States, the general preservation of American folklore has become an accepted matter and thus a great body of traditional culture has been preserved. It is possible to say, in 1950, that the pioneering phase of field collecting and establishment of archives has come to a close, and that in the future, emphasis should be directed to coordinated efforts, to the elimination of duplication, to the strong encouragement for scholars and others to use—in fairly exhaustive studies—the materials already gathered."

The Library of Congress
DUNCAN EMRICH

Emrich has not confined his folklore interests to the duties directly connected with the Library of Congress. He has written articles on folklore for such publications as the *Southern Folklore Quarterly* and the *Western Folklore Quarterly.* He is also the author of several popular books on folklore. *It's an Old Wild West Custom* (Vanguard, 1949) deals with the people, customs, songs, ideals, and religion of the West. In a preface Emrich states that it is "not a book of history, of social custom, or of folklore. It has something of each, but not enough to be considered a volume on those subjects." *Comstock Bonanza* (Vanguard, 1950) is an anthology of the works of such old-time Western writers as J. Ross Browne, Dan de Quille and Bret Harte. Lucius Beebe, writing in the *Saturday Review of Literature* (December 2, 1950), called it "excellent and valuable . . . a source book of Nevada letters." *The Cowboy's Own Brand Book* is devoted to making clear the meaning of the more than 500,000 distinctive brands used on cattle.

Another of his recent activities was appearing on NBC's radio program, *Weekend,* which was patterned after a Sunday newspaper and consisted of a series of short-time segments or "pages." Emrich's part on this show was to relate early American customs, superstitions and folklore tales and to encourage listeners to send in information on folklore and regional folk songs. He received a large response from all over the United States.

He was named a Guggenheim fellow in 1949 and was a lecturer under the Fulbright program at the Italian universities of Rome, Naples and Palermo in 1952 and 1953. He is a fellow of the National Council of Religious

EMRICH, DUNCAN—*Continued*

Higher Education, a member of the board of governors of the Middle East Institute in Washington, D.C. and of the executive council of the American Folklore Society, and a vice-president of the International Commission on Folk Arts and Folklore.

Emrich married Marion Vallat on February 20, 1940. Mrs. Emrich shares her husband's enthusiasm for collecting folk art and crafts and for traveling. Emrich is five feet ten inches tall and weighs 160 pounds. He has brown eyes and brown hair. He is a Democrat and an Episcopalian.

References

Directory of American Scholars (1951)
Who Knows—and What (1954)
Who's Who in America, 1954-55

ENDERS, JOHN F(RANKLIN) Feb. 10, 1897- Bacteriologist; university professor

Address: b. c/o Harvard Medical School, Boston, Mass.; Children's Hospital, 300 Longwood Ave., Boston 15, Mass.; h. 64 Colbourne Crescent, Brookline, Mass.

ROBBINS, FREDERICK C(HAPMAN) Aug. 25, 1916- Bacteriologist; university professor

Address: b. c/o Western Reserve School of Medicine, Cleveland, Ohio; Cleveland City Hospital, Cleveland, Ohio

WELLER, THOMAS H(UCKLE) June 15, 1915- Bacteriologist; university professor

Address: b. c/o Harvard University School of Public Health, Boston, Mass.; Children's Hospital, 300 Longwood Ave., Boston, Mass.

Wide World
JOHN F. ENDERS

Man's conquest of disease by immunization passed another milestone when it was announced on April 12, 1955 that an antipoliomyelitis vaccine had proved approximately 80 per cent effective. The vaccine was made possible by the basic researches of Dr. John F. Enders, Dr. Frederick C. Robbins, and Dr. Thomas H. Weller, who discovered the "ability of poliomyelitis virus to grow in cultures of different tissues," for which they received the 1954 Nobel Prize in medicine and physiology on December 10, 1954. Dr. Jonas E. Salk (See *Current Biography,* May 1954) developed the antipolio vaccine from polio viruses cultured by the Enders-Robbins-Weller technique. Dr. Salk said: "Dr. John Enders pitched a very long forward pass and I happened to be in the right spot to receive it."

Medical authorities recognize that the results of the work by the Enders "team" in tissue culture techniques have significance far beyond the problem of polio. Other virus diseases such as the common cold, measles, pneumonia, and even, perhaps, cancer may be eventually brought under control through vaccines developed as a result of their discovery.

John Franklin Enders, the senior member of the "team," was born on February 10, 1897 in West Hartford, Connecticut, the son of John Ostrom Enders and Harriet Golden (Whitmore) Enders. His brother, Ostrom, is a banking executive. Enders served as an ensign, and later lieutenant, j.g., in the United States Naval Reserve Flying Corps from 1917 to 1920.

He received the A.B. degree from Yale University in 1920, and from Harvard University the M.A. degree in 1922 and the Ph.D. degree in 1930. Enders served as an assistant in the Harvard Medical School's department of bacteriology and immunology (1929-1930), an instructor (1930-1935), assistant professor (1935-1942), and associate professor since 1942.

During World War II Dr. Enders was a civilian consultant on epidemic diseases to the Secretary of War from 1942 to 1946; between 1945 and 1949 he was associated with the Civilian Commission on Virus and Rickettsial Disease, U. S. Army. It has been in his capacity as chief of the research department of infectious disease, Children's Hospital, Boston, that his Nobel Prize-winning work in virus research was accomplished. He is also a consultant to the Research and Development Board, which is under the direction of the U. S. Secretary of Defense.

As an associate of Hans Zinsser, Enders helped to develop a method of producing antityphus vaccine and collaborated with Zinsser and LeRoy D. Fothergill on the book, *Immunity; Principles and Application in Medicine and Public Health* (Macmillan, 1939). Enders also participated in the published symposium on *Virus and Rickettsial Diseases* (Harvard University Press, 1940). He has written innumerable papers for scientific and medical periodicals and is editor of the *Journal of Immunology.*

Dr. Enders is a member of the Society of American Bacteriologists, American Association of Immunologists (of which he was president in 1952), American Public Health Association, National Academy of Sciences, American

Association for the Advancement of Science, Harvey Society, Sigma Xi, Alpha Omega Alpha (honorary), and is a fellow of the American Academy of Arts and Sciences. His clubs are the Harvard in Boston and the Brookline Country. In 1954 he received an Albert and Mary Lasker Foundation Award from the American Public Health Association.

His marriage to Sarah Frances Bennett took place on September 17, 1927. They had two children, John Ostrom, 2d, and Sarah. His first wife is deceased. On May 12, 1951 Dr. Enders married Mrs. Carolyn Keane and has a stepson, William Edmund Keane.

Frederick Chapman Robbins, the youngest of the trio, was born on August 25, 1916, in Auburn, Alabama to Christine F. (Chapman) and Dr. William Jacob Robbins. His father, a noted mycologist and director of the New York Botanical Garden, is internationally known for his discoveries in plant life. His mother, a member of Phi Beta Kappa from Wellesley College, was also involved in botanical research prior to her marriage. Dr. Robbins is the oldest of three brothers. The youngest, Daniel, is a research engineer; the second, William, is doing research in rheumatic fever.

Frederick grew up in Columbia, Missouri, where his father was at that time professor of botany at the University of Missouri. He attended that institution and played polo and won ribbons as a horseman. Robbins received the B.A. degree in 1936 and the B.S. degree in 1938. His M.D. degree (1940) was earned at Harvard Medical School.

During World War II Robbins served in the Army Medical Corps and worked on the isolation of the Rickettsia of Q fever (Queensland fever or quadrilateral fever). Rickettsiae are parasitic microorganisms which are responsible for Rocky Mountain spotted fever and some types of typhus, among other diseases.

After the war Robbins was assistant resident from 1946 to 1947 and resident in 1948 at Children's Hospital in Boston. In 1948 he became a National Research fellow in virus diseases working with Enders and Weller. Until 1952 he was also associate professor of pediatrics at Harvard University Medical School. He is now professor of pediatrics at Western Reserve University School of Medicine in Cleveland and chief of the pediatrics and contagious diseases department of Cleveland City Hospital.

In 1948 he married Alice Havemeyer Northrop, who was a researcher before her marriage. As a result of Dr. Robbins' Nobel award, their daughter, Christine, became both the daughter and granddaughter of Nobel laureates. Her maternal grandfather, Dr. John H. Northrop, was co-winner of the 1946 Nobel Prize in chemistry. Dr. Robbins and Dr. Weller also shared the Mead Johnson Award in 1953 for contributions to pediatric research.

Thomas Huckle Weller was born in Ann Arbor, Michigan on June 15, 1915 to Elsie (Huckle) and Dr. Carl Vernon Weller, chairman of the pathology department, University of Michigan. He received the B.S. degree in 1936 and the M.S. degree in 1937, both from the University of Michigan. At Harvard University Medical School he was a classmate of Robbins and received the M.D. degree in 1940. In 1938 he won a fellowship of the international health division of the Rockefeller Foundation. He interned in pathology and bacteriology in 1941 and in medicine in 1942.

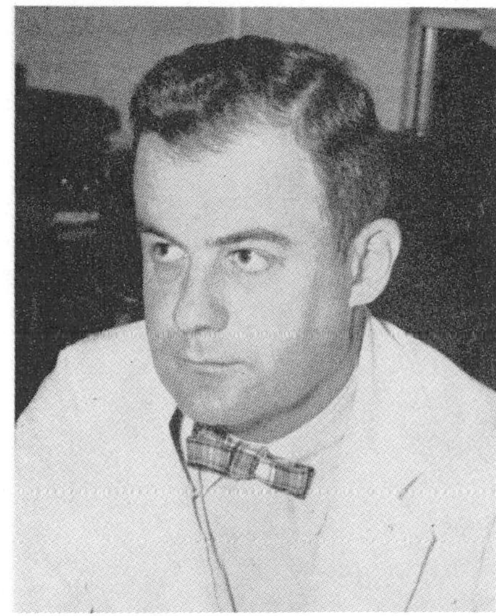

Wide World

DR. FREDERICK C. ROBBINS

Weller was the chief of the parasitology, bacteriology and virus sections of the U. S. Army's Antilles Department Laboratory in San Juan, Puerto Rico during World War II. He has been working with Dr. Enders since 1946. Weller was a research fellow in pediatrics at Children's Hospital during 1947 and 1948 and was certified as a pediatrician in 1948. He is now Richard Pearson Strong professor of tropical public health at the Harvard School of Public Health and assistant director of the research division of infectious diseases at Children's Hospital in Boston. Weller has been area consultant in tropical diseases for the Veterans' Administration since 1949. In addition to his work on the polio virus, he has isolated and propagated the causative agent of chicken pox and of shingles.

Dr. Weller is married to the former Kathleen R. Fahey and has four children. He holds memberships in the American Medical Association, American Society of Parasitologists, American Society of Tropical Medicine, and American Public Health Association.

Contributors to the National Foundation for Infantile Paralysis' "March of Dimes" will be gratified to learn that almost 3,000,000 of their dimes were expended to finance the work in viruses performed by John F. Enders and his associates. Beginning in 1946 the "team" of researchers concentrated their efforts on the problem of "culturing" the virus responsible for polio.

The polio virus, magnified 77,000 times by the electron microscope, resembles a ping-pong ball. One million of them, side by side, would

Wide world

DR. THOMAS H. WELLER

make a line not even one inch long. In some way they grow and reproduce, causing progressive decay in the tissues which they attack. Prior to the Enders-Robbins-Weller discovery, it had been believed that the polio virus would grow only in nerve tissues of humans and a few species of live monkeys. Experimentation was very expensive because each monkey cost $30 to $40 and died in the process of testing. Moreover, the vaccine which was sought could not be derived from extracts of virus-carrying monkey nerve tissue because something in the tissue itself, which could not be refined out, proved more virulent than the polio itself.

The Enders-Robbins-Weller research "team" reported on January 28, 1949 in *Science*: "It would seem that multiplication of the Lansing strain of poliomyelitis virus . . . has occurred . . . in cells not of nervous origin." In subsequent experiments they demonstrated that the other two strains of polio virus (Brunhilde and Leon) could also be grown in tissue cultures.

Their technique is known as the roller tube method. It gives the virus the food and air, without which it could not live. Bits of monkey kidney tissue are distributed on the wall of the test tube. The nutrient, which is a solution of sixty-six chemicals, is added. The tube is then placed in a revolving drum in a horizontal position. The air surrounding the drum is kept at constant temperature and humidity. The rotation of the drum alternately covers the tissue with nutrient and exposes it to the air in the culture tube. Under these conditions the culture thrives. The tissue is then inoculated with polio virus, and the virus multiplies on the tissue and destroys it within five days.

An immediate result of this research was to provide scientists with a means of "seeing" the virus in an ordinary microscope and studying its degenerative action on the tissue cells. This phenomenon gave physicians a means of diagnosing suspected polio cases within one week. Previous positive diagnosis was possible only through the use of a monkey injected with a sample derived from the patient. One month later, the monkey either would or would not develop polio symptoms.

Basil O'Connor, the president of the National Foundation for Infantile Paralysis, in presenting in New York the American Medical Association's 1953 Passano Foundation Award of $5,000 to Dr. Enders, stated: "Dr. Enders has brought almost to an end the era of plodding; control of infantile paralysis may be very much closer than we would have dared to anticipate. . . ."

On March 28, 1953 in the *Journal of the American Medical Association,* Dr. Jonas E. Salk announced that he had used the Enders-Robbins-Weller technique for growing polio virus in cultures of non-nervous tissues and had developed (under a research grant from the National Foundation for Infantile Paralysis at the University of Pittsburgh) a safe vaccine to immunize against all three types of crippling poliomyelitis. On April 12, 1955 the world learned of the successful results of the vaccine mass tests of American school children during 1954. (See biographies of Dr. Herman E. Hilleboe and Dr. Henry W. Kumm, *Current Biography,* June 1955).

When notified of the Nobel Prize, Dr. Enders said: "I am so happy that the three of us who have worked together have shared this honor. . . . In a way it is symbolic, because no discovery in the scientific world is due to the efforts of any one man, but always results from the work of many people."

References

N Y Herald Tribune p2 O 22 '54 pors
N Y Times p 1+ O 22 '54 pors; p21 Ap 13 '55 por; p56 Ap 17 '55
N Y World-Telegram Mag p14+ N 27 '54

American Men of Science (1949)
Directory of Medical Specialists (1951)
Rockefeller Foundation Directory of Fellowship Awards, 1917-50
Who's Who in America, 1954-55

ERVIN, SAMUEL J(AMES), JR.

ERVIN, SAMUEL J(AMES), JR. Sept. 27, 1896- United States Senator from North Carolina; lawyer

Address: b. Senate Office Bldg., Washington 25, D.C.; h. Morganton, N.C.

An interim appointee from North Carolina in the United States Senate, Judge Samuel J. Ervin, Jr., occupied the seat of the late Clyde R. Hoey during part of the second session of the Eighty-third Congress. Appointed June 5, 1954 to serve until the fall election, he was elected on November 2 to fill out the balance of Senator Hoey's term expiring January 1957.

Ervin was a member of the Senate's select committee to study censure charges relating to Senator Joseph R. McCarthy of Wisconsin. He was a signatory of the report of this committee which recommended censure of McCarthy on a number of counts. The Senate's vote in early December 1954 to condemn McCarthy sustained in a large part the select committee's report.

During the first session of the Eighty-fourth Congress Ervin was a member of the permanent subcommittee on investigations (of the Senate Committee on Government Operations) which heard testimony on bribes and payoffs. He stated that the Pentagon should bar from further contracts any firm which had paid graft to Government employees (New York *Times*, June 5, 1955).

In 1946 Ervin had served for some months in the House of Representatives; previously he had been a member of three North Carolina legislatures, and a County and Superior Court judge. He was appointed an associate justice of the North Carolina Supreme Court in 1948.

Samuel James Ervin, Jr., is a native and lifelong resident of Morganton, Burke County, North Carolina. He was born on September 27, 1896, one of six children of Samuel James and Laura Theresa (Powe) Ervin. Sam attended the public schools of Morganton. He then studied at the University of North Carolina and received his A.B. degree at Chapel Hill in 1917.

Being of military age, Samuel enlisted for World War I service; as a private in the 28th infantry regiment of the First Division he participated in the Cantigny engagement (the first American battle of the war) and later fought through the Aisne-Marne offensive. In the course of eighteen months on the French front, Sam Ervin was twice wounded and twice cited for gallantry; he was decorated with the Purple Heart with one Oak Leaf Cluster, the Silver Star, the Distinguished Service Cross, the United Daughters of the Confederacy's Cross of Military Service, and the French Fourrargère.

Although admitted to the North Carolina bar in 1919, Ervin did not practice law for another three years. Instead, he enrolled at the Harvard University Law School, receiving his LL.B. degree in 1922. Politically active as a Democrat almost as soon as he had set up law practice, Ervin represented Burke County in the North Carolina General Assembly at the sessions of 1923 and 1925. In 1930 he began seven years on the North Carolina State Democratic executive committee, and in 1931 again represented Burke County in the General Assembly.

On conclusion of the 1931 session Ervin served for six years as a judge of the Burke County Criminal Court. In 1937 Governor Clyde R. Hoey appointed him to the judgeship in the North Carolina Superior Court which he retained until 1943, when he resigned to resume private law practice at Morganton. Ervin, who was licensed to practice before the Interstate Commerce Commission, the Tax Court of the United States and the United States Supreme Court, was a member of the North Carolina State Board of Law Examiners for the two years beginning 1944.

Wide World

SAMUEL J. ERVIN, JR.

Ervin's brother, Joseph, who had been practicing law in Charlotte since 1925, was elected in 1944 to represent the Tenth North Carolina District in the Seventy-ninth Congress. A victim of osteomyelitis and, presumably, despairing of any relief from this disease, he took his own life on December 25, 1945 (*obituary*, New York *Times*, December 26, 1945). As the result of a special election held January 22, 1946 to fill the legislative vacancy, Samuel Ervin, who was unopposed, went to Washington to serve out his brother's unexpired term.

Seated in the Seventy-ninth Congress, Ervin was assigned to the House of Representatives Post Office and Post Roads Committee. He voted in the 1946 session for the Case strike control bill (February), for a guarantee of reasonable profits under O.P.A. (April), and for the British loan (July), but against exemption of teen-agers from the draft (May). Declining nomination for re-election in November 1946, he resumed law practice at Morganton until February 3, 1948, when Governor Gregg Cherry appointed him an associate justice of the North Carolina Supreme Court. From 1947 to 1949 he held the chairmanship of the Commission for the Improvement of the Administration of Justice in North Carolina.

The senior U.S. Senator from North Carolina, former Governor Clyde R. Hoey, had been re-elected in 1950 for the term ending January 1957. He died in Washington on May 21, 1954 and on June 5 Governor William B. Umstead of North Carolina named Judge Ervin to occupy the vacated seat until the November election. Sworn in as a Senator six days later, Judge Ervin was assigned to the District of Columbia Committee and to the Senate Government Operations Committee. The latter committee was headed by Senator Joseph R. McCarthy of Wisconsin, who was under attack for alleged abuse of witnesses called before a special subcommittee on Communist infiltration and for holding "one man" hearings.

On July 30 Senator Ralph E. Flanders of Vermont, introduced to the Senate a resolution condemning the junior Senator from Wisconsin. After several days of debate and after the term censured had been substituted for condemned, the Senate on August 2 voted to set up a six-member select committee to study censure charges. Ervin voted in favor of such a committee and also endorsed an amendment requiring a list of specific charges. Membership of the select committee was announced by Vice-President Richard Nixon on August 5. Republican Senator Arthur V. Watkins of Utah was named chairman and Ervin became one of five other members.

"When I was trying to find some excuse to make to my own conscience for escaping service on that committee," Ervin later explained to the full Senate (reported in the New York *Times,* November 16), "I made the statement that I ought not to serve. . . . But after I had considered the question and conferred with four of the most experienced and respected members of the minority in the Senate, I came to the conclusion that the members of the committee should be selected by the Senate, rather than by pro-McCarthyites or anti-McCarthyites."

In its report released on September 27, the select committee unanimously recommended that McCarthy be "censured" on some of the six counts considered. The Senate met on November 8 in its first "extended session" in 178 years of existence, for the specific purpose of acting on the Watkins report. The next day (November 9) Senator McCarthy released the text of a scheduled speech in which he asserted that the Communist party had "extended its tentacles" into the Senate to make the committee studying the censure charges its "unwitting handmaiden" (New York *Times,* November 17, 1954).

On November 15 Ervin made his first major speech on the McCarthy issue on the Senate floor. "He began softly, sprinkling his speech with tarheel stories," reported the New York *Times.* Then he went on to criticize McCarthy for fleeing "to his customary refuge—his claim that he is the symbol of resistance to Communist subversion, and that any Senator who fails to make obeisance to him is doing 'the work of the Communist party.' As a result of Senator McCarthy's activities . . . this monstrous idea has found lodging in the minds of millions of loyal and thoughtful Americans: that Senators are intimidated by Senator McCarthy's threats of libel and slander...." (New York *Times,* November 16, 1954).

On December 1 the Senate voted 67 to 20 in favor of the committee's first censure count: to condemn McCarthy for his alleged contemptuous conduct toward a Senate subcommittee investigating his financial affairs in 1951 and 1952. The following day by a vote of 67-22 it passed a final resolution in which it condemned McCarthy for "failure to cooperate" with the subcommittee at that time and for his conduct toward the Senate and Watkins committee during the censure proceedings. Like all the Democrats who were present during the voting, Senator Ervin supported the censure resolutions.

Senator Ervin's voting record in the Eighty-third Congress showed him differing from his fellow North-Carolinian, Senator Alton A. Lennon, in favoring appropriations for nineteen Army divisions instead of seventeen (June 17), and being paired against extension of the reciprocal trade act for three years instead of one (June 24). He opposed raising unemployment benefits (July 13), reduction of foreign aid by five million dollars (August 3), and the principle of flexible rather than rigid farm price supports (August 9).

According to the New York *Times,* he was criticized by "several newspapers in his home state . . . because he sided with the Eisenhower Administration in opposing public power features of the atomic energy bill," although (July 26) he voted against cloture to cut short Senator Wayne Morse's "filibuster" against the bill.

At the time of Ervin's appointment to the Senate, Governor Umstead had promised to recommend the former judge to the Democratic State Committee as the party's nominee for the final two years of the late Senator Hoey's term; he was duly nominated, and elected on November 2 on the Democratic ticket.

As a member of the Eighty-fourth Congress (1955), the Senator voted to increase Congressional salaries from $15,000 to $22,500 (February), extend the reciprocal trade agreements program (May), override the Presidential veto of a postal pay increase (May), and to maintain the Marine Corps' strength at 215,000 men (June). He was recorded against confirming the appointment of John Marshall Harlan to the U.S. Supreme Court (March) and against the Administration's highway bill (May).

Senator Ervin is an elder of the Presbyterian Church, a thirty-second degree Mason, and a junior Knight of Pythias. He belongs to the American and North Carolina bar associations, the North Carolina Bar Association of the Interstate Commerce Commission, the American Judicature Society and the Phi Delta Phi fraternity. He is also a member of the Sigma Upsilon literary fraternity.

He has been a trustee of the University of North Carolina and of North Carolina's Davidson College. His service organizations include the American Legion, Veterans of Foreign Wars, Disabled American Veterans, the Society of the First Division, and the Army and Navy Legion of Valor. Other organizations of which Ervin is a member are the North Carolina Literary and Historical Association, the Southern Historical Association and the Society of Mayflower Descendants in the State of North Carolina. He is a director of the First National Bank of Morganton and a member of the Morganton Chamber of Commerce. The Senator's club is the Kiwanis.

Samuel James Ervin, Jr., and Margaret Bruce Bell of Concord, North Carolina were married June 18, 1924. They have one son, Samuel James 3d, and two daughters, Margaret Leslie and Laura Powe. "Ervin, who reminds some of the late Chief Justice Fred M. Vinson," a writer in the Washington *Post and Times Herald* has commented, "is an easy-talking, quick-smiling man. . . . He prefers to be known as Sam, rather than the more formal Samuel." Elsewhere his "fondness for fishing for crappie and bass" has been noted.

"I believe in clinging to the tried and true landmarks of the past," Senator Ervin said, "but I am willing to test the soundness of new issues" (New York *Times,* August 6, 1954).

References

N Y Herald Tribune p24 Je 6 '54; p5 Ag 6 '54
N Y Times p38 Je 6 '54 por; p6 Ag 6 '54
American Bar (1947)
Congressional Directory (1955)
Who's Who in America, 1954-55
Who's Who in the South and Southwest (1954)

HELEN EUSTIS

EUSTIS, HELEN (WHITE) Dec. 31, 1916- Author

Address: b. c/o Doubleday and Co., 575 Madison Ave., New York 22; h. 508 E. 87th St., New York 28

Reprinted from the *Wilson Library Bulletin* February 1955

The first novel by Helen Eustis was the memorable and blood-curdling psycho-thriller *The Horizontal Man* (1946). Her second novel was an equally memorable idyll of young boyhood, *The Fool Killer* (1954). Two novels more different in spirit, tempo, and style than these can scarcely be imagined. But they share in common one thing at least—their author's sure-fire gift of readability. Versatility—and not mere virtuosity—is Miss Eustis' trademark. Her aim, she told an interviewer in 1954, was to do a series of books—a mystery and a boy's book (these now done), and a gothic romance ("the governess sort of thing"), a Western, and "one about a dreadful female." All this she regards as practical education in the novelist's art. "The idea was not just to see whether I could do it, but as education. I decided I had to find out how to write a novel."

A descendant of Scotch, English, and Irish ancestors, Helen White Eustis was born in Cincinnati, Ohio on December 31, 1916 to Harold Claypoole Eustis, a stockbroker and later a department store executive, and Bessie Mitchell (Langdon) Eustis. She was an only child, and her mother died when she was very young. Her father remarried, however, providing her with "a ready-made family" of two stepsisters and a stepbrother. As a child, Miss Eustis recalls, "I found company and refuge in books." and when her father's new marriage brought her into a new situation, she says, "I believe I turned to writing as a means of reasserting my own importance."

At Hillsdale School in Cincinnati, Helen Eustis was encouraged in her writing ambitions by her English teacher, and she edited the school magazine. At Smith College, from which she received her B.A. degree in 1938 with a major in art ("with the vague idea of becoming a commercial artist"), she was further encouraged by the award of a gold medal for a novel she wrote at college (never published). After graduation she went to New York and studied psychology at Columbia University.

She held two brief jobs writing advertising copy, but marriage and the birth of a son ruled out for her a full-time career. She soon began writing for the magazines. Her short stories first appeared in *Accent, Chimera,* and *Story* in 1941 and 1942. By 1944 she was represented in *Best American Short Stories,* and since that time her stories have been published in the *New Yorker, Mademoiselle, Harper's Bazaar, Cosmopolitan, Saturday Evening Post,* and other periodicals. She has also written nonfiction for these magazines, what she calls "pseudo-psychological articles on family relations"—on marriage, raising babies, growing old, a variety of "how to" articles ("How to Enjoy a Split Personality," "How to Get Anything You Want").

Miss Eustis' ambitious plans for writing a series of books began with a mystery, and her first published novel was the now-classic thriller, *The Horizontal Man* (Harper, 1946), an expert and sophisticated murder story set in a New England women's college, which won the Mystery Writers of America's "Edgar" as the best first mystery of 1946. "It is a tribute to Miss Eustis' talent," H. R. Hays wrote in the New York *Times* (March 31, 1946), "that

EUSTIS, HELEN—*Continued*

she is able to weld together the various elements in her novel and maintain an excellent tension. She has written a splendid first book—and one hopes she will not succumb to a formula, as so many have done, but will continue to experiment and develop."

Since then Miss Eustis has shown no sign of succumbing to any formula. Her next book, *The Captains and the Kings Depart* (Harper, 1949), was a collection of her short stories. To these she carried over none of the stereotypes of the murder mystery genre—only the sharp and narrow focus of the unimpassioned observer. Nona Balakian commented in the New York *Times* (September 25, 1949): "Whether she is writing fantasy or melodrama, satire or love story, her manner is that of an urbane writer, interested in those hidden facets of relationships which are the actual source of dramatic action. . . ."

The Fool Killer (Doubleday, 1954) was the long-planned boy's book, and by the time Miss Eustis was ready to write it, she had an eager audience in the person of her twelve-year-old son. "You couldn't say I wrote it for him, but we did share it," she said. As she wrote, she read it to him, and when it had his approval, she knew that she was on the right track. The book is narrated by twelve-year-old George Mellish, an orphan living somewhere in the Middle West just after the Civil War. George is not a bad boy but as he happily admits, "Nobody has ever accused me of being outright good." He runs away from his guardians, meets an assortment of strange and colorful characters—among them a living embodiment of the legendary Fool Killer who went about chopping up fools—and ultimately finds love, tenderness, and a home.

Reviewers found the book a poignant and haunting novel—a "completely adult story about an appealing child forced to learn difficult truths about the nature of good and evil," wrote Joanna Spencer in the New York *Herald Tribune Book Review* (February 7, 1954), and Hal Borland in the New York *Times* of the same date, described it as "a story of high drama, and she underplays it deliberately, with superb effect."

Miss Eustis lives in New York City with her son, Adam Eustis Fisher, by her first marriage to Alfred Young Fisher, a professor of English. Her second husband was Martin Harris, a magazine photographer. She is now divorced.

A firm believer in the theory that a writer learns by reading, she reads, she says, "like a vacuum cleaner." She also enjoys cooking and traveling. She is an Episcopalian. She has brown hair and brown eyes, is five feet eight inches tall, and weighs 145 pounds.

References

N Y Herald Tribune Bk R p2 Mr 14 '54 por
N Y Times Bk R p14 F 28 '54 por
Who's Who in America (Sup. Ap '49)

EVANS, BERGEN (BALDWIN) Sept. 19, 1904- Author; university professor

Address: b. c/o Alfred A. Knopf, Inc., 501 Madison Ave., New York 22; h. 2313 Bur Oak Rd., Northfield, Ill.

Reprinted from the *Wilson Library Bulletin* May 1955

A tripartite career—in academic life, writing, and television—is managed with a blend of scholarship, wit, and urbanity by Bergen Evans, professor of English (now on leave from Northwestern University), author of *The Spoor of Spooks* (Knopf, 1954) and *The Natural History of Nonsense* (Knopf, 1946), and moderator of the TV word quiz *Down You Go.* His books debunking long-cherished fallacies are, although serious in purpose and carefully documented, highly diverting in style. His literate television manner and evocative question-and-lecture technique are a refreshing change from the banalities of many masters of ceremonies.

The questions on the CBS-TV program, *The $64,000 Question,* sponsored by Revlon, were prepared by a staff of ten, headed by Bergen Evans. The program achieved top-listener rating during the summer of 1955.

Bergen Baldwin Evans was born in Franklin, Ohio, September 19, 1904, one of six children. His father, Rice Kemper Evans, was a doctor, in the family tradition: "All the men in our family were doctors in Franklin—four generations of them. My great-great-grandfather was a doctor, owned the drugstore *and* the marble yard (i.e., tombstones). He couldn't lose." His mother, Louise (Cass) Evans, contributed stories and poems to magazines. When Bergen was four, his father gave up medicine, entered the consular service, and was assigned to Sheffield, England. The Evans family lived near Sheffield, at Totley, on the Derbyshire Moors, a place he recalls as being (in 1909) "more rural and backward than anything conceivable in the modern world." In 1915 the children were sent back to Franklin. There he attended high school, working nights and Saturdays (beginning at thirteen) in a paper mill.

At fifteen he entered Miami University in Oxford, Ohio, as an English major. He studied and worked waiting on table, editing the annual, drawing newspaper cartoons—and received his B.A. degree in 1924. He was a member of Phi Beta Kappa and the winner of a prize in moral philosophy. Choosing an academic career, he went on to graduate work at Harvard University (M.A., 1925); went back to Miami to teach for three years; studied as a Rhodes Scholar (1928-1931) at Oxford University (B.Litt., 1930); and then returned once more to Harvard (Ph.D., 1932). The subject of his theses at Oxford and Harvard was Samuel Johnson as a biographer. In 1932 he became an instructor at Northwestern University; he has remained there ever since and is now a full professor.

As a specialist in the field of English literature he collaborated with psychiatrist G. J. Mohr in writing *The Psychiatry of Robert*

Burton (Columbia University Press, 1944), an evaluation of *The Anatomy of Melancholy* showing how close the seventeenth century writer came to modern psychological insight into emotional disorders. His first book to attract popular attention was *The Natural History of Nonsense* (1946), a merciless but entertaining attack upon all sorts of vulgar errors, which he had been collecting for his own amusement since 1934. Utilizing the skill he had been developing since his first experience in writing—"lampooning my fellow students and teachers from the second grade on"—he exploded such Sunday supplement myths as the existence of children adopted by wolves and the graying of hair overnight. In a *New Republic* review on October 7, 1946 A.V.A. Van Duym commented that he "punctures, deflates and ridicules with a zest and wit that make his book wholly delightful." *The Spoor of Spooks and Other Nonsense* (1954) added a further round of ammunition to what has been called his "arsenal for skeptics." Here the popular delusions exposed to the light of rational investigation included, among others, talking horses, dowsing, and the activities of supermen. John Lardner, writing in the New York *Times* November 7, 1954, found "considerably more than a learned and witty parlor ikon-buster" in those passages which concentrate on "sustained, eloquent social criticism."

The Evans bibliography is a varied one. He has edited and written introductions to a collection of essays, editions of *Tristram Shandy* and Boswell's *Johnson,* and an H. Allen Smith anthology. He has also contributed more than fifty articles to *Harper's, Atlantic Monthly, Reader's Digest, Esquire,* and other magazines. At present he is collaborating with his sister on "a sort of dictionary of contemporary English and American usage—Fowler for a larger audience and brought somewhat more up to date." He has been on leave from Northwestern for the past two years in order to complete this work.

If his antisuperstition crusade appeals only to the more sophisticated, his *Down You Go* program reaches a wide audience on many levels. But the same wry humor, the same surprising twists of language are evident. The panel, trying to guess a familiar phrase or slogan, is often stumped by the clues he devises—clues such as "the best way to get rid of old blades" (answer: swords into plowshares).

On August 5, 1939 Bergen Evans married Jean Whinery (an occasional *Down You Go* panelist). He has two young sons, and lives near Chicago in Northfield, Illinois. He has brown hair and brown eyes; he weighs 160 pounds and is five feet eight inches tall. He has lectured extensively in the Middle West and travels a great deal (but wishes he didn't have to). His favorite literary work is *King Lear.* Avoiding nonvocational activities "like the pestilence," he lists his recreations: "None.

BERGEN EVANS

I loathe sports and hobbies." His TV appearances—he has been a moderator on four shows and a panel member on another—are modestly attributed to "sheer good luck."

References

Newsweek 42:87 Jl 20 '53 por
Sat R 37:13 N 13 '54 por
Who's Who in America, 1954-55

FADIMAN, CLIFTON (PAUL) May 15, 1904- Radio and television master of ceremonies; literary critic

Address: b. 217 E. 61st St., New York 21

NOTE: This biography supersedes the article which appeared in *Current Biography* in 1941.

Essayist and literary critic Clifton Fadiman is the panel leader and master of ceremonies of the National Broadcasting Company's radio program, *Conversation,* and also is moderator of the television panel show, *The Name's the Same* on the American Broadcasting Company network. He is well remembered as the affable moderator of the radio quiz program, *Information, Please!* throughout its decade of popularity (1938-1948) during which listeners tried to "stump the experts." His experience in the publishing world has included seven years as general editor of the publishing firm, Simon & Schuster (1929-1935), and ten years as the book reviewer on the *New Yorker* (1933-1943).

Since 1944 he has been a member of the board of judges of the Book-of-the-Month Club and since 1951 the contributor of monthly essays to *Holiday* magazine. He edited two anthologies, *I Believe* (1939) and *Reading I've Liked* (1941) and wrote introductions to new editions of works by Tolstoy, Ambrose Bierce, Herman Melville, Henry James, Charles Dick-

ABC-TV

CLIFTON FADIMAN

ens, and other authors. His book, *Party of One,* is a collection of his own essays, which became the August 1955 alternate Book-of-the-Month Club selection.

Clifton Paul Fadiman was born in Brooklyn, New York on May 15, 1904, the second of three sons of Isidore Michael and Grace Elizabeth Fadiman. His father was a pharmacist who had emigrated from Russia and his mother, a nurse. When "Kip" was only five years old his elder brother Edwin taught him to recite geographical data and to become an omnivorous reader. He attended Brooklyn Boys High School and worked as a soda-jerker in his father's drug store. During his high school days he assisted his elder brother, a Pulitzer scholar at Columbia University, in operating a newspaper, the Forest Hills (Long Island) *Reporter.*

After completing high school "Kip" was still too young for college, and worked for two years as an office boy for a steamship line and later an insurance clerk before following his brother to Columbia University. In 1923 he lectured on French symbolist poetry for the People's Institute; by 1924 he was contributing book reviews to the *Nation* and articles to other national periodicals. Also in his undergraduate days, he managed a book store in New York City's Pennsylvania Station; peddled rare books; made from the German what is still a standard translation of Nietzsche's *Ecce Homo;* and edited the student magazine *Morningside.*

To the celebrated "honors course" conducted at Columbia by the late John Erskine, Fadiman later ascribed his mastery of the "art" of serious reading. "For two years," he wrote in the prologue to his anthology *Reading I've Liked* (Simon & Schuster, 1941) "we read and talked about one great book a week . . . it was by far the most valuable course I took at college." After being graduated from Columbia in 1925 with a Phi Beta Kappa Key in addition to his A.B. degree, Fadiman taught high school English at the Ethical Culture School in New York City for the next two years. He also continued his lecturing for the People's Institute.

He collaborated with William A. Drake on the English translation of Franz Werfel's *The Man who Conquered Death* (Simon & Schuster, 1927), and in that year became the firm's manuscript reader and assistant editor. He urged the partners, Richard Simon and M. Lincoln Schuster, to build up their general literature and fiction lists, and his own first "best-seller hunch" was Ethelreda Lewis's *Trader Horn,* which had been rejected by four other publishers. Over 170,000 copies were sold under the "Essandess" (S & S) imprint. In 1929 Fadiman was made general editor of Simon & Schuster, and in the next six years examined over 25,000 manuscripts and interviewed some 2,000 authors. He was responsible for the firm's acceptance of Hans Fallada's *Little Man, What Now?,* Josephine Johnson's Pulitzer Prize novel *Now in November,* and Ernest Dimnet's *The Art of Thinking.*

As a book reviewer for the *Nation, Stage,* and *Harper's Bazaar,* Fadiman acquired a reputation for urbanity, "a man who wore his mantle of erudition with a debonair flourish." In his ten years (beginning in 1933) as book editor of the *New Yorker* he remained unswervingly impatient with what he regarded as pretentiousness, mistiness, mountebankry, or torturing of the English language. "I look for clarity above all in what I read," he wrote. Thus he gave high praise to Sinclair Lewis, but did not join the admirers of Charles Morgan, Gertrude Stein, and William Faulkner.

Shortly after giving up his editorship at Simon & Schuster in 1935, he became interested in the Limited Editions Club, for whose edition of *The Voice of the City and Other Stories* by "O. Henry" he provided an introduction. (He wrote a critical essay in 1943 as the introduction to Edith Wharton's *Ethan Frome*). In addition, Fadiman became one of the four editors of the Readers Club, engaged in republishing distinguished books which had been neglected on their first appearance.

When Dan Golenpaul started his *Information, Please!* radio program on May 17, 1938 as an NBC sustaining program, Fadiman was its moderator; and six months later, with a permanent "panel" consisting of Franklin P. Adams, John Kieran, Oscar Levant, and "Kip," it attained sponsored status. (The original sponsor was Canada Dry; later it was Lucky Strike cigarettes). Listeners submitted questions, and, if any were able to "stump the experts," they were given sets of the *Encyclopaedia Britannica* as a reward. The program was quickly listed as "one of the five best on the air," and in 1940 it was awarded the first *Saturday Review of Literature* plaque for "distinguished service to American literature." By 1942 the program was estimated to have some 9,000,000 listeners weekly.

The introduction and biographical notes to *I Believe,* a collection of credos by eminent contemporaries, were written by Fadiman in 1939 and he edited for the same firm, Simon & Schuster, his anthology, *Reading I've Liked,* in 1941. (The 64-page "informal prologue" headed "My Life Is an Open Book" contains much autobiographical matter as well as a statement of Fadiman's critical canons).

In 1942 Fadiman supplied the introduction to the Modern Library edition of Tolstoy's *War and Peace,* and in May of that year contributed to the *Atlantic* an article entitled "The Ghost of Napoleon?" pointing out parallels to the career of Hitler which he had detected while rereading Tolstoy. In October, 1943 he contributed to the same periodical an essay on Herman Melville which later formed the introduction to a handsome edition of *Moby Dick* published by the Heritage Press. At the end of 1943 Fadiman resigned from the *New Yorker,* and in March of the following year he became a member of the editorial board of the Book-of-the-Month Club, a position he retains today.

Continuing his radio activities, he moderated another radio show, *Keep 'Em Rolling* in addition to *Information, Please!* He also operated, with his brothers Edwin and William, "a flourishing radio talent agency, Fadiman Associates, Ltd." (*Time,* September 27, 1943).

During World War II Fadiman was a member of the Writers War Board. In 1945 he edited a selection of *The Short Stories of Henry James* for inclusion in the Modern Library; he wrote the introduction to *The Collected Works of Ambrose Bierce,* (Citadel Press, 1947) and in 1949 he contributed to Simon & Schuster's edition of *The Pickwick Papers.*

In a panel discussion at the Columbia Faculty House on May 3, 1947 Fadiman created something of a stir in academic circles by advocating a compulsory curriculum for all students and the abolition of organized college sports. After the withdrawal of *Information, Please!* from the air in 1948, Fadiman lectured extensively.

In November 1951 Fadiman began writing a monthly essay in *Holiday* under the title, *Party of One.* A number of these, together with earlier writings, comprise the contents of *Party of One* (World Publishing Company, 1955), the first book to carry Fadiman's name as author rather than editor or compiler. In the New York *Herald Tribune,* Lewis Gannett observed that Fadiman "claims enthusiasm and clarity as his own virtues, and he is right.... He can be slick but he can also be wise." Orville Prescott (in the New York *Times*) noted that while the selections "range from the trivial to the highly significant," two qualities were outstanding. One was "enthusiasm" and the other the author's "stubborn refusal to be intimidated by literary fashions and the opinions of others." He wrote the introduction to *Thirty Years,* a collection of John P. Marquand's shorter works (Little Brown, 1954).

Television began to occupy part of his time in 1952, as the "emcee" of the Columbia Broadcasting System's program *This Is Show Business.* In July 1954 he helped as moderator, to launch the CBS-TV "panel quiz" program *What's in a Word?* On June 27, 1954 another Fadiman program, *Conversation,* had moved to a Saturday night "spot" on NBC radio after an ineffective debut on television. The radio version of *Conversation* (which is devoted to informal talks by Fadiman and Columbia professor Jacques Barzun with one or more guests) proved successful. Jack Gould noted in the New York *Times* (January 30, 1955), that "in the television version several rules were violated. The conversation was supposed to flow on cue, which it never can." For radio presentation, however, "the show is recorded, so that the dull 'small talk' at the outset can be edited out."

Among *Conversation's* guests in the spring of 1955 was Margaret Truman who conversed on etiquette. On June 12, 1955 Fadiman became a "communicator" for the NBC summer weekend radio program, *Monitor;* and on June 28 he took over as master of ceremonies of the ABC TV Tuesday evening panel show, *The Name's the Same.*

By his marriage in 1927 to Pauline Elizabeth Rush (who was for nine years the editor of *Child Study Quarterly*), "Kip" Fadiman has one son, Jonathan Rush. The couple were divorced in 1949, and in 1950 Fadiman married Mrs. Annalee Jacoby, widow of Melville Jacoby, and co-author with Theodore White of *Thunder out of China.* Fadiman has been described as "big, blond," and "personable." He enjoys tennis, cycling, and collecting wines.

In the July 1955 *Holiday* Fadiman discussed some of the things he has learned after a year of his radio program, *Conversation,* and "the audience response to this eccentric attempt to revive a moribund and even somewhat discredited art." He concluded that the program will never be "big-league" stuff, but that it has a special quality of intimacy and of naturalness which appeals to a sizeable number of listeners who "like to escape, not into some infantile dream-universe, but into the larger world of general ideas."

Celebrated as a master of the "atrocious" pun, Fadiman told Lewis Nichols (in an interview for the New York *Times Book Review,* April 24, 1955) that he wants to write a book which shall be "a sort of last word on the pun." His *The American Treasury* is to be published by Harper's in November 1955.

References

N Y Herald Tribune Bk R p2 Ap 24 '55 por
N Y Times Bk R p28 Ap 24 '55 por
Scholastic 40:17+ F 16 '42 por
Wilson Lib Bul 16:284 D '41 por
Kunitz, S. J., and Haycraft, H. eds. Twentieth Century Authors (1942)
Motion Picture and Television Almanac, 1955
Who's Who in America, 1954-55
World Biography (1954)

FARMER, GUY (OTTO) Sept. 13, 1912- United States Government official; lawyer

Address: h. 4123 Harrison St., N.W., Washington 15, D.C.

In its umpire role of interpreting the law when either labor or management complains of unfair practices, the National Labor Relations Board, according to chairman Guy Farmer, is a "controversial agency," largely because it administers a "controversial law." Farmer likens the National Labor Relations Act to a tree, of which the 1935 Wagner act is the trunk and the 1947 Taft-Hartley act the branches. Since some unions would chop off the branches and some employers chop away the trunk, the five-man N.L.R.B., which must care for the entire tree, frequently finds itself "menaced by the axes of the rival woodsmen."

The first appointee of a Republican Administration in the eighteen-year history of the N.L.R.B., Farmer took office in July 1953 to serve out the remainder of the term of Paul M. Herzog, who resigned. The term expired on August 27, 1955 at which time Farmer resigned and returned to private law practice.

GUY FARMER

Farmer has specialized as a management adviser on labor law. He has favored a policy of decentralization in the work of the board, believing that "Uncle Sam's long arm has reached out to assert itself over too many labor-management situations which ought to be resolved closer to their origin."

Guy Otto Farmer was born to Harbert and Kate (Bell) Farmer at Foster Falls, Wythe County, Virginia on September 13, 1912 and was brought up at Maybury, near Elkhorn in West Virginia's McDowell County. His father was a coal miner. Guy attended the local high school and on graduation in 1930 entered West Virginia University at Morgantown, where he majored in government. Having received his A.B. degree in 1934, Farmer enrolled at the West Virginia University Law School, was granted his LL.B. degree in 1936 and in the same year was admitted to the West Virginia bar. He has a Phi Beta Kappa key and is a member of the Phi Alpha Delta legal fraternity and the Order of the Coif.

While a law student he applied for a Rhodes scholarship, which was awarded him on December 16, 1935. The scholarship, which carried a stipend of £400 a year for two years, enabled him to study in England at Oxford University from the fall of 1936 to the summer of 1938. He was not a candidate for a degree.

On his return to the United States, Guy Farmer joined the Washington, D.C. office of the National Labor Relations Board in 1938 as a $2,600-a-year attorney. He subsequently headed the N.L.R.B. legal staff at both Minneapolis and Los Angeles prior to 1943, when he was made an associate general counsel at the Board's Washington headquarters. According to a Washington *Post* editorial, Farmer especially impressed colleagues with his "practice of examining facts closely and shaping his conclusions in accord with the circumstances of each case."

Farmer resigned from government service in 1945 to begin private practice as an associate in the main office of Steptoe & Johnson, a leading District of Columbia law firm which maintained branches at Clarksburg and Charleston, West Virginia. The senior partner in the firm was Louis A. Johnson, later Secretary of Defense in the Cabinet of President Truman.

Admitted to the District of Columbia bar in 1946, Farmer became a specialist in labor law, working largely in management counseling and sometimes handling cases for his clients before the N.L.R.B. In representing management clients he "kept the respect of labor unions by scrupulously fair courtroom performances" (*Time*). From 1948 to 1949 Farmer lectured on labor law at West Virginia University. He became a partner in Steptoe & Johnson on January 1, 1949.

In January 1953 the National Labor Relations Board was composed of five appointees of outgoing President Harry S. Truman, with Paul M. Herzog as chairman. The occurrence of three vacancies during the year made possible the gradual creation of a "new" Board in which the majority were members chosen by President Dwight D. Eisenhower. The first change in personnel came with the resignation of Herzog and the nomination of Farmer to serve until the expiration of the five-year term on August 27, 1955. The Board maintains about twenty regional offices in addition to its headquarters in Washington and in 1953 employed 1,390 persons.

At his swearing-in as chairman of the N.L.R.B. on July 13, 1953, Farmer expressed his belief that "collective bargaining" constituted "one of the main cornerstones of our free democratic society." He stressed that he was undertaking his present work "not as a partisan of management or of labor" and that he intended at all times to give the Taft-Hartley law "an honest and impartial interpretation and an even-handed application."

He had earlier indicated the likelihood of future changes in the attitude of the Board when he commented on the argument by "some Taft-Hartley proponents" that "the board misconstrued the intent of Congress" in certain decisions rendered between 1947 and 1953. Farmer stated unequivocally that these so-called "landmark" decisions "ought to be fully reexamined by the board whenever cases with the same problems come up" (New York *Times*, July 13, 1953).

The first important N.L.R.B. decision taken after Guy Farmer's confirmation as chairman was handed down on July 25, when it was ruled that "a concern could not refuse to bargain with a newly certified union solely because the firm had a long term contract with another union." Farmer, who was often at odds with the Truman holdover members of his Board, dissented with majority opinions four successive times during the latter part of August. His fourth dissent was on what the United Press described as "the key issue of authorization cards."

As the N.L.R.B. changed from a Democratic-appointed to a Republican-appointed majority, it was occasionally charged with following an anti-labor policy. The American Federation of Labor in August 1954 cited a number of decisions to illustrate this "trend." These included permitting employers to question individual workers about union sympathies, and reversing the Bonwit Teller ruling which held that an employer who made a non-coercive speech on company time be required to provide time and premises for the union to make a speech in reply.

Among the decisions of the Board, under Farmer's chairmanship, that are regarded as having "gone in organized labor's direction" are requiring an employer to furnish payroll data to the union for collective bargaining (July 1954) and permitting unions to discuss stock-purchase plans as "fringe" benefits at the bargaining table (October 1954).

Generally less controversial than labor practice cases are those involving questions of union representation. In December 1953 and again in May 1954 the Board held elections among the longshoremen of the Port of New York to determine whether the International Longshoreman's Association or the AFL would be the recognized union. The ILA won.

Business Week (November 6, 1954) noted, "The most important arena of continuing conflict between Republican and Democratic labor policy experts is the National Labor Relations Board." It further observed that "one of the biggest points of disagreement" among its members is "federal-versus-state control over labor affairs of small business."

Farmer has long favored a withdrawal of the N.L.R.B. from local disputes, arguing that Congress intended the board to "regulate cases having substantial impact on interstate commerce." In June 1954 the Board laid down a series of rulings to cut its jurisdiction over local labor-management relationships which do not affect national economy. Later in the year, when declining jurisdiction over certain cases, the two other Eisenhower appointees, Philip Ray Rodgers and Albert C. Beeson, voted in agreement with Farmer. The Democratic member, Abe Murdock, strongly opposed the new jurisdictional rules, and Ivar Peterson, a political independent, found fault with the Board's "arbitrary and categorical" manner in restricting its jurisdiction.

Farmer is a member of the West Virginia State, District of Columbia, and American bar associations. He is a Protestant in faith. Farmer is married and the father of three children, Guy, Jr., Katherine and Mark. With a height of five feet eight and a half inches, he weighs about 150 pounds; he has brown eyes and gray hair. The Washington *Post* has described him as "personable and easy in manner" with "a faculty for getting things done."

References

N Y Herald Tribune II p 1 Jl 19 '53 por
N Y Times p13 Jl 14 '53 por
Time 62:10 Jl 27 '53
U.S. News 35:88+ Jl 17 '53 por
Washington (D.C.) Post p8 Jl 8 '53; p22 Jl 10 '53
American Bar (1947)
Who's Who in America, 1954-55

FARRAR, MRS. JOHN (CHIPMAN) *See* Farrar, Margaret (Petherbridge)

FARRAR, MARGARET (PETHERBRIDGE) (fär'ẽr) Mar. 23, 1897- Crossword puzzle editor

Address: b. c/o The New York Times, 229 W. 43d St., New York 36; h. 16 E. 96th St., New York 28

Daily commuters, housewives, students, and other eager and constant "doers" of crossword puzzles have reason to be grateful to Margaret Farrar, editor of these puzzles for the New York *Times* since 1942. She has been called the "world's supreme authority on crosswords." She began editing them for the New York *World* in 1920 and in 1924 collaborated with two others to produce the first *Cross Word Puzzle Book,* published by Simon & Schuster, which touched off a "world-wide craze." In 1955 she edited the seventy-fifth book in the series.

Margaret Petherbridge was born in New York City on March 23, 1897, a daughter of Henry Wade and Margaret Elizabeth (Furey) Petherbridge. Her father was an executive with the National Licorice Company in Brooklyn, New York and her brother Henry is now associated with the firm. She has a sister, Mrs. Elizabeth P. Lamson. After her graduation from Berkeley Institute in Brooklyn in 1916, she went to Smith College in Northampton, Massachusetts, where she majored in history.

New York Times

MARGARET FARRAR

She sang in the glee club, was a song leader, and for three years was elected captain of the basketball team.

After receiving her B.A. degree in 1919, she was employed by the National City Bank of New York to do "filing and figuring." After a year she left to take a secretarial course and went to the New York *World* as secretary to the Sunday editor, John O'Hara Cosgrave. "In the Sunday room of the *World*," she recalled, "was my real education and here someone handed me my first crossworld puzzle, together with the job of shepherding them into the Sunday magazine each week—a job no one else wanted."

"The big event in the crossworld puzzle field," she wrote, "was the publication of the first book of them in April 1924 by Simon and Schuster—their first publication that rocketed into a world-wide craze." She edited this book with F. Gregory Hartswick and Prosper Buranelli, two *World* men who had occasionally helped her to pick out the Sunday puzzles. After her marriage to John Chipman Farrar, a publisher and author, on May 28, 1926, she continued editing these Simon & Schuster puzzle books, which appeared at the rate of about two a year.

Newspapers throughout the country began publishing puzzles after 1924. "And no paper has ever been able to drop it," stated Max Schuster recently. "The crossword is as much a journalistic fixture as the weather report." The longest "hold-out" was the New York *Times*. Finally, Mrs. Farrar has written, "the New York *Times Sunday Magazine* started a puzzle page in February 1942 under my editorship. In September 1950 the daily *Times* introduced a crossword puzzle on its book page. It begins to look as if the crossword puzzle were here to stay!"

Although she has constructed many puzzles, she has stated that she does not "construct all those appearing in the New York *Times* and in the books—merely edit the work of other very clever constructors." Those whose puzzles have been published include a sea captain, a jeweler, a honeymooning couple, an Army sergeant, a schoolboy, a schoolteacher, a businessman, a Brooklyn letter carrier, an advertising executive, and occasionally persons in state prisons. One of the early crosswords of the *Times Sunday Magazine* section, that of June 14, 1942, was constructed by Arthur Hays Sulzberger, publisher, and Charles Merz, editor of the newspaper.

A crossword puzzle is usually constructed by beginning backwards. A word list is first composed—words of the same number of letters are grouped under the same list. Then the words are placed, more or less haphazardly, into the squares, usually in the corners first so that black squares may be fitted around them to form a pattern. Once the longer words are placed, the shorter ones are fitted in. When the diagram is complete, the constructor then begins to make his definitions. Those for the Sunday newspaper are harder than those for the daily editions.

When editing a puzzle someone has submitted, Mrs. Farrar works out the puzzle herself. If it interests her, if it is not too easy, she accepts it. In the final editing, she checks it again for errors and makes sure that words and definitions are not being repeated from one puzzle to the next. Trade names are not used; neither are the names of diseases when they can be avoided. Short words have to be used in crosswords, but Mrs. Farrar tries to avoid the clichés anf if one has to be used, gives an uncustomary definition for it.

"Mistakes? There are enough to prove I'm human," Mrs. Farrar has said. "During the war we had the Russians taking an important objective two weeks before they really got there—I suppose they're still marvelling about the prophetic insight of *Times* reporters and the queer places they hide their news." Occasionally typographical errors occur, she has said, but mainly in vertical words which "the human eye seems to be less qualified to contend with."

Mrs. Farrar is credited with being responsible for the change from dull definitions to more spirited, humorous, and current ones. The kinds of definitions and the way of numbering them started with Mrs. Farrar. The trend at present is toward using current events in the definitions and titles of movies, books, and plays. Topical puzzles are also one of her innovations —puzzles which center on one theme, such as Christmas foods, different foreign countries, animals, occupations, cities, authors or sports.

Crossword puzzles had been appearing in the *World* since December 1913 and had been started there by a man named Edward Wynne. More than 350 had appeared when Margaret Petherbridge joined the newspaper. She and Prosper Buranelli, in an article for *Collier's* magazine (January 31, 1925), explained what they thought it was which made people so eager to do crosswords: "the fascination of words common to an articulate race; self-education; and time-killing."

"From the most ancient times," they continued, "men have been mystically beguiled with words and with tricks that can be done with words. Magic, prophecy, and religion enter here. . . . There were supposed to be mysterious relations between words that could be joined in some construction. A magical relation was thought to exist between the words in a word square. And word squares were used as cabalistic decorations and as amulets for thousands of years."

Word squares are mentioned among the ancient Greeks and Romans, wrote Mrs. Farrar, "as devices used by sorcerers in the working of their magic. The mystical Jewish cabalists of the early Christian era gave their attention to word forms. . . . The ancient Hindus, neglectful of nothing mysterious and recondite, knew how to build words into forms with double readings. . . ."

Mrs. Farrar has also edited puzzle books for four series of Pocket Books and several books of puzzles reprinted from the New York *Times*. She has done editorial work in the juvenile field, in cook books, and in mystery stories for Farrar & Rinehart and for Farrar, Straus & Cudahy of which her husband is president. In the 1920's and 1930's her articles appeared in several national magazines; her article "Move as if Driven" (New York *Times Magazine*, February 2, 1947) tells how to solve diagramless puzzles.

In Eugene Tachlis' article on crossword puzzles in *Collier's* (March 4, 1955), he wrote that Mrs. Farrar's biggest problem is to cut down on short words and clichés. She likes to tie in words with current events.

Her activities have also included being a member of the Children's Book Committee of the Child Study Association (1935-1942) and of various committees for the Lincoln School, Scarborough School and Smith College. During World War II she did publicity work for the Red Cross and the War Council in Ossining, New York.

The Farrars are the parents of three children: John Curtis, Alison (Mrs. George M. Wilson), and Janice (Mrs. Peter Weeks). Mrs. Farrar has light blue eyes and brown hair. She is five feet five inches tall and weighs 128 pounds. She belongs to the Episcopal Church and her political affiliation is with the Republican party.

For recreation she enjoys swimming, walking, reading, and "a modicum" of television. "After thirty-five years of crossword puzzle work," she has written, "I find ever-increasing interest and enjoyment in it, and am excited by the beauty and infinity of words. One of the pleasantest aspects is the knowledge that a lot of people have a lot of fun with the puzzles."

References

Colliers 135:50+ Mr 4 '55 por
Pub W 165:1734+ Ap 17 '54 por

FARRINGTON, MRS. JOSEPH R(IDER)

See Farrington, Elizabeth Pruett

FARRINGTON, (MARY) ELIZABETH PRUETT

May 30, 1898- United States Delegate from Hawaii

Address: b. House Office Bldg., Washington, D.C.; h. 82 Kalorama Circle, N.W., Washington, D.C.; 3180 Pacific Heights Rd., Honolulu T. H.

The Delegate for the citizens of the Territory of Hawaii to the United States Congress is Mrs. Elizabeth Pruett Farrington, who on July 31, 1954 was chosen in a special election to complete the term of her husband, Joseph R. Farrington, who died during his sixth term as Delegate. In the regular November election of 1954 she was chosen for a full two-year term. She was the fourteenth woman elected to the Eighty-third Congress and is the first woman to represent the Territory of Hawaii. For many years active in political affairs, Mrs. Farrington served as president of the National Federation of Women's Republican Clubs from 1949 to 1953.

The Territory of Hawaii, which consists of twenty islands, nine of which are inhabitable, was annexed by the United States Government on August 12, 1898 when the transfer of sovereignty took place. The Territorial government was established on June 14, 1900. The Hawaiian Islands have desired to achieve the status of statehood for many years. In 1950 a constitution was drafted and later ratified by the people of Hawaii. The Territorial legislature sent a special delegation of legislators and citizens to Washington in May 1954 to implement the drive for statehood.

Continuing her husband's efforts in Congress to secure statehood for Hawaii, Mrs. Farrington, soon after her election, began to work for passage of the bill then before Congress. After Congress failed to enact this proposal in the Eighty-third Congress, Mrs. Farrington introduced a new Hawaiian statehood bill in January 1955.

Mary Elizabeth Pruett was born in Tokyo on May 30, 1898 to Robert Lee and Josephine (Baugh) Pruett, who were American missionaries. Miss Pruett's early experiences in the Far East stimulated her interest in world affairs. This interest was continued when she came to the United States to study at the Ward-Belmont Junior College, Nashville, Tennessee and later at the University of Wisconsin in Madison, where she majored in journalism.

She received her B.A. degree in 1918 and then began a career as a Washington correspondent for several Wisconsin, Michigan, and Iowa newspapers. On May 17, 1920, she was married to Joseph R. Farrington (See *Current Biography*, May, 1948), at that time a newspaper reporter. Farrington's father had served as Governor of the Territory of Hawaii and was general manager and publisher of the Honolulu *Star-Bulletin*. When, in 1934, her husband succeeded his father as general manager of the family newspaper, Mrs. Farrington began an active interest in civic, social, and

Glogan Studio
ELIZABETH PRUETT FARRINGTON

Americanization work in Hawaii, serving as president of the Junior League of Honolulu and of the Honolulu Hospital Social Service Association. The rehabilitation work following the Pearl Harbor attack of 1941 also absorbed Mrs. Farrington's energies.

In 1942, after serving for eight years in the Territorial Senate, Joseph R. Farrington, a Republican, was elected Delegate to the U.S. Congress. On their return to the nation's capital, Mrs. Farrington joined the League of Republican Women in the District of Columbia and the 78th Club, composed of wives of the new members in Congress. Her husband continued to represent Hawaii until his death, and Mrs. Farrington during this period became increasingly prominent in Republican projects. From 1947 to 1949 she was the president of the District League of Republican Women and chairman for public relations for the National Federation of Women's Republican Clubs. On January 1, 1949 she became president of the National Federation of Women's Republican Clubs and was re-elected in 1950 for the term ending in January 1953. (The organization is now known as the National Federation of Republican Women.)

The organization which Mrs. Farrington headed for four years had at the time of her presidency approximately 500,000 members. The purposes of the federation are to encourage an informed electorate, to build good will for the Republican party, and to participate in local community programs. In order to further these aims, Mrs. Farrington initiated a school of politics in 1950, at which precinct workers were briefed on national issues, the history of American political parties, Republican party aims, and political techniques. Mrs. Farrington said at the time that the sessions were "the businesslike approach to a sales technique with which we intend to carry our Republican party to the greatest political victory in its history" (*Christian Science Monitor*, May 2, 1950).

Another idea developed during Mrs. Farrington's presidency took the form of a pamphlet, *Know Your Precinct*, written by Mrs. Olga Paul Irvine, which guided Republican workers in their local community activities. Mrs. Farrington also initiated a survey program of each community in order to inform party workers of such local questions as housing needs, church membership, and special community projects. She urged the invitation of all women, regardless of party affiliation, to club meetings. During the 1952 Presidential campaign, Mrs. Farrington was an active party worker.

Joseph R. Farrington died on June 19, 1954 in the middle of his fight to secure the enactment of Hawaiian statehood in the Eighty-third Congress. His wife was selected by a vote of 43,247 to 19,590 in a special election to complete his unexpired term (which ended on December 31, 1954), defeating Delbert Metzger, a Democrat. She took office on August 4 and immediately began to work for Hawaiian statehood.

Mrs. Farrington visited President Eisenhower and important members of the House in order to seek their support. In spite of the fact that the campaign platforms of both parties had urged statehood for Hawaii, a bill embodying this proposal died in the House Rules Committee during the Eighty-third Congress after it had been passed in both Houses (in the Senate it had been incorporated in a proposal also granting statehood to Alaska). To those critics of the bill who feared loss of Federal control of strategic defense areas in Alaska, Mrs. Farrington has suggested that northern Alaska be made a military reservation.

Although Hawaii, in the 1954 elections, chose its first Democratic legislature in its fifty-four-year history, Mrs. Farrington in her bid for re-election won over the Democratic opponent, John A. Burns, by 818 votes out of 139,000. A territorial Delegate is a nonvoting member of the House of Representatives. The office, however, carries with it the right to offer legislation, to speak at Congressional sessions, and to serve on committees. Presently, Mrs. Farrington serves on the Agriculture Committee, Armed Services Committee, and Interior and Insular Affairs Committee.

One of Mrs. Farrington's first acts in the Eighty-fourth Congress was to submit a new statehood bill for Hawaii. On April 19, in answer to charges that communism is such a menace in Hawaii that it should be denied statehood, Mrs. Farrington stated that the charges are "extravagant, undocumented, and unsupported," and that communism "has never been rampant" in Hawaii, and the subversive element there is "definitely on the wane" (Washington *Post and Times Herald*, April 20, 1955).

Mrs. Farrington has two adopted children, Beverly (Mrs. Hugh F. Richardson) and John. While serving as president of the National Federation of Women's Republican Clubs she gained a reputation for being a "dynamic" leader, with a "humor . . . which has endeared her . . . to her fellow clubwomen."

References

Ind Woman 34:22 Ja '55
N Y Herald Tribune X p40 O 30 '49 por
U S News 37:8 Ag 20 '54 por
Washington (D.C.) Post p3S Ap 9 '50
Congressional Directory (1955)
Who's Who in America, 1954-55

FATEMI, HOSSEIN 1918-Nov. 10, 1954 Former Iranian Government official; helped establish National Front party and took a leading part in furthering nationalization of the oil industry; publisher and editor of National Front newspaper; Minister of Foreign Affairs (1952-53) in cabinet of former Premier Mohammed Mossadegh; was convicted of charges of rebellion against the monarchy and executed. See *Current Biography* (May) 1953.

Obituary

N Y Times p5 N 11 '54

FATH, JACQUES Sept. 6, 1912-Nov. 13, 1954 Fashion designer; one of the "big three" of Parisian *haute couture;* studied bookkeeping at the Commercial Institute, Vincennes; opened his first salon in 1937; served in the French Army in World War II as a gunner, and won the Croix de Guerre with Palm and Legion of Honor; established himself as a leader of fashion in postwar Paris by an extensive publicity campaign; held first showing in New York in March 1949 with his wife as model; his collections have been characterized as "wearable glamour" and have proved especially popular in the United States, Canada, and Latin America; his firm in Paris employs more than 600 persons. See *Current Biography* (Apr.) 1951.

Obituary

N Y Times p89 N 14 '54

FEININGER, LYONEL (CHARLES ADRIAN) (fī'nĭng-ẽr) July 17, 1871- Artist

Address: 235 E. 22d St., New York 10

"Bach has been my master in painting," declared artist Lyonel Feininger, a musician by early training, and a composer of organ fugues, whose mature paintings have been constructed with the precision of compositions by Bach.

During half a century he has received many tributes for his abstractions of skyscrapers, sailing ships and locomotives. Feininger, an American by birth and citizenship and European by long residence abroad, exhibited his first works in Berlin in 1904. Between 1919 and 1933 he taught art at the Bauhaus school in Germany. Since 1939, when his paintings were included in the "Nineteen Living Americans" exhibition at the Museum of Modern Art in New York, he has been represented in major museums in the United States.

One of the earliest American artists to practice cubism, Feininger "long ago profited from its lessons. . . . Feininger's genius is to produce this fusion . . . between nature and art. . . . Traversing without faltering the tight-rope between naturalism and abstraction . . . his work has a marvellous quality" (*Studio,* August 1954).

In his 1954 exhibition at the Curt Valentin Gallery, he won acclaim for both his water colors and his oils which seem "almost artless in their simplicity." Feininger has said, "What I want is to capture some of the cosmic wonders." Critics and public concur that he succeeds in communicating his ideas by his "dramatic and lyrical use of light" (*Brooklyn Museum Bulletin,* Summer 1954).

When Lyonel Charles Adrian Feininger was born on July 17, 1871 in New York City at 85 St. Mark's Place, his father was playing a Beethoven quartet in the next room (*Life,* November 12, 1951). His father, Frederick William Feininger, and mother, the former Elizabeth Cecilia Lutz, were professional musicians. The predominantly musical atmosphere of the Feininger household was a major influence on Lyonel and his sisters. Two other childhood impressions also were fixed in his memory—the ships in New York's East and North rivers, and the countryside near Sharon, Connecticut, where he often stayed with friends while his parents were on tour.

During his boyhood he began to draw, chiefly locomotives, and later he built a number of ship models. His musical instruction was begun in 1880 by his father (a German immigrant and veteran of the Civil War), with the result that by the time he was twelve years old, Lyonel was playing the violin in public concerts. He also became known as a champion bicyclist.

At the age of seventeen he went to Germany for further musical studies, but he soon found that he was more interested in art. After studying for a time at the Kunstgewerbeschule in Hamburg, he enrolled in 1891 at the Academy of Art in Berlin in order to be with his mother, who had separated from his father. In 1892 he spent six months studying at the Colarossi Academy in Paris.

Upon returning to Berlin, Feininger began to acquire a reputation throughout Europe for his work as a political cartoonist, caricaturist, and illustrator. His work appeared in *Karikatur, Ulk,* and *Lustige Blätter,* with which he was associated from 1895 to 1900. He resumed his studies in Paris in 1906 and contributed to *L'Assiette au Beurre, Le Témoin,* and other French publications. In 1907 he was signed to a contract by the Chicago (Sunday) ***Tribune*** to produce two comic strips, "The Kin-Der-Kids" and "Wee Willie Winkie's World," in which

Kosti Ruohomaa from Black Star
LYONEL FEININGER

critics have discerned the emergence of the whimsical fantasy and refined line which characterize his later work.

Feininger, whose work had been exhibited at the Glaspalast in Berlin in 1904, decided in 1907 to devote himself entirely to painting, inspired by, but not subservient to, the cubist work he had seen in Paris. His paintings were exhibited at the Berlin Secession show in 1910, and he was invited to join the *Blauer Reiter* (Blue Riders) group for the 1913 Berlin show, at which his pictures were hung in conjunction with those of Franz Marc, Wassily Kandinsky, and Paul Klee (the Swiss painter who became a close friend).

Although classified as an enemy alien by the German government after the United States entered World War I in 1917, Feininger remained in Berlin, working quietly on his paintings, developing the locomotive and ship and architectural themes characteristic of his brush. With the establishment of the Bauhaus school in Weimar in 1919, he received an invitation from architect Walter Gropius to become an instructor there. Feininger was in charge of the graphic arts workshop and the printing press of the school, and of the publication of its annual, the *Bauhaus Graphik.* When the new building was completed in Dessau in 1926, he became artist-in-residence. An ardent yachtsman, Feininger spent most of his summers sailing on the Baltic, a region often portrayed in his work (such as *Zirchow V,* now in the permanent collection of the Brooklyn Museum). He won the Dusseldorf prize in Germany in 1928, and in 1931 he was honored by a major retrospective show in the National Gallery at Berlin.

When the National Socialists came to power in Germany, the Bauhaus school was closed, Feininger's paintings were removed from the Moritzburg Museum at Halle, and the artist found himself in disfavor as a "decadent bourgeois." Feininger, although not Jewish, and aloof from politics, decided to return to the United States. He taught for two summers at Mills College in Oakland, California. He established his home in New York City and in 1938 painted the outdoor murals for the marine transportation and the masterpieces of art buildings at the New York World's Fair.

Ruth Lawrence, commenting on his work in a University of Minnesota catalogue accompanying an 1938 exhibition of his work there, found similarities between his work and that of John Marin, with Feininger's distinguished by its freedom and radiance: "He is able to call forth visions of unlimited horizons."

A retrospective exhibit of Feininger's painting since 1909 held jointly at the Buchholz and Willard galleries in New York in early 1941 allowed Carlyle Burrows of the New York *Herald Tribune* to choose what seemed to him the "high marks" of the painter's career, "the geometrically designed *Marine* of 1927 and the *Last Voyage,* a schooner subject with rainbow sea." That year Feininger received the first prize at the Corcoran Gallery Biennial in Washington, D.C., for his *Gabendorf II.* In 1942 he won an award at the Los Angeles Museum of Art. During 1943 three exhibitions by Feininger were held at the Willard, Nierendorf, and Buchholz galleries. In March of that year Feininger received the $2,500 third prize for *The Church* in the Metropolitan Museum of Art show.

A survey of paintings done by Feininger from 1940 to 1943 was collected by Curt Valentin for a Buchholz show in February 1944. With Marsden Hartley, Feininger was honored by an immense retrospective show at the Museum of Modern Art in October and November 1944. Emily Genauer of the New York *World-Telegram* felt that "the sense of largeness, which is one of Feininger's great gifts," was lost in his later paintings, and preferred the monochromatic, prismlike compositions of his earlier canvases. To the *Art News* critic, on the other hand, the "continuity and progression" of Feininger's development was most evident, "so that image follows image as sounds follow each other in music." The monograph for the exhibit contains a biographical note by Alfred H. Barr, Jr., and a critical one by Alois Schardt. During the summer of 1945 Feininger taught at Black Mountain College in North Carolina.

Feininger's 1946 show at the Buchholz and Willard galleries was described by Howard Devree of the New York *Times* as "one of the outstanding one-man shows of the season." Commenting on the introduction of human figures in the painter's customarily abstract canvases, Devree said, "A note of fantasy has been added to his sketchily suggestive manner."

Feininger's accomplishment over sixty years of production in his chosen art was the subject of a joint retrospective exhibition at the Buchholz and Schaeffer galleries in the spring of 1950. Stuart Preston of the New York *Times* (April 16, 1950) identified a schism in the painter's output, between the early canvases, with their "Latin matter-of-factness" and the later work in "the German tradition of mystical realism" marked by "subjective, quasi-philosophical overtones."

In honor of Feininger's eightieth birthday, a large show was held at the Curt Valentin Gallery in March 1952, when his "architectonic method of building up a composition" was remarked upon by Dorothy Adlow of the *Christian Science Monitor* (March 29, 1952). The painter himself told *Time's* reporter, "a boat moving in the atmosphere sets up stresses and movements in the air. That is what I visualize, and the pattern and organization of those stresses."

Both oils and water colors by Feininger were shown at the Curt Valentin Gallery in April 1954, the water colors particularly impressing the New York *Herald Tribune* reviewer with their "cobwebby style . . . which quietly and vaguely reasserts its charm." Critic Emily Genauer referred to Feininger's "chords of color," and pointed out that his pictures are composed "like organ fugues. There is contrapuntal arrangement of planes, to correspond with musical polyphony."

Throughout the United States, it is possible to view Feininger's work in the collections of such institutions as the Baltimore Museum of Art, Boston Museum of Fine Arts, Metropolitan Museum of Art, Whitney Museum of American Art, Art Institute of Chicago, Detroit Institute of Arts, Minneapolis Institute of Arts, and the Addison Gallery of American Art in Andover, Massachusetts. In addition to galleries in Germany, his work is in the Tate Gallery, London and the Musée du Jeu de Paume, Paris.

Lyonel Feininger was married to Julia Lilienfeld on September 25, 1905. Aline Louchheim of the New York *Times* (March 23, 1952) described the painter at eighty: "He is a tall, spare, dignified man with a long ovid head and beautifully transparent white skin that stretches over high cheek bones. The gauntness of his face, the gentle expression of his blue eyes, and the quiet grace of his hands reinforce his likeness to one of the figures on the west portal at Chartres [Cathedral]."

Although he has devoted his major energies to painting, Feininger composed a number of organ fugues between 1921 and 1926, which were "very well received" by German music critics, according to Alfred V. Frankenstein. The tradition of music in the Feininger family is continued by the painter's youngest son, Laurence, a Catholic priest and musicologist. Andreas, the eldest son, is a photographer, whose work is frequently seen in *Life* magazine; Lux, the middle son, a painter of ships and locomotives, teaches art at Harvard University.

References

Art Digest 28:8+ My 1 '54 por
Art Q 14 no 1:19+ '51
Chicago Art Inst Bul 42:65+ S '48
Mag Art 31:278+ My '38
Time 59:74 Ap 7 '52

Contemporary Painting in Europe (1939)
Who's Who in America, 1954-55
Who's Who in American Art (1953)

FEISAL II, KING OF IRAQ (fī'säl) May 2, 1935-

Address: Qasr al-Zuhur, Baghdad, Iraq

The reputed site of the Garden of Eden and the area on which were built the ancient kingdoms ruled by Hammurabi and Nebuchadnezzar II are included in the modern kingdom of Iraq, ruled by Feisal II, who was proclaimed King at the age of three and took the royal oath on his eighteenth birthday, May 2, 1953. Feisal is a descendant of the Abbasid caliphs, the dynasty which ruled Baghdad from about A.D. 750 to 1258.

Iraq is the world's sixth biggest oil-producing nation. The oil wells are operated on a fifty-fifty profit-sharing agreement, and Iraq's revenues from oil were estimated at $150,000,000 for 1954. According to *Newsweek* (February 28, 1955) 70 per cent of Iraq's share is earmarked to finance the development of the country, whose population exceeds 5,000,000. In world politics, Iraq became an important link in Middle Eastern affairs as the first Arab nation to join a mutual defense pact with the West. The pact was ratified by Turkey and Iraq on February 26, 1955 and six weeks later by special agreements with Great Britain and Pakistan.

Feisal, whose full name is Feisal ibn Ghazi ibn Feisal el Hashim, was born on May 2, 1935 in Qasr al-Zuhur (Palace of Roses), Baghdad, the only son of King Ghazi and Queen Aliyah and the grandson of Feisal I, the first King of Iraq. Queen Aliyah was the daughter of King Ali of the Hejaz (now included in Saudi Arabia)—the eldest brother of King Feisal I—who settled in Iraq after he lost his throne. Another brother, Abdullah I, was the first King of Transjordan (now the Hashemite Kingdom of Jordan), and the youngest brother, the Emir Zaid, served as Iraq's Ambassador to England.

The four brothers were the sons of Sherif Hussein of Mecca, who became King of the Hejaz and who was of the thirty-eighth generation of the Hashemite family descended from the Prophet Mohammed. The Hashemite family, from which the Abbasid caliphs sprung, belonged to the Koreish, the most distinguished of the Hejaz tribes, who were custodians of the Holy Kaaba at Mecca until Mecca was taken over by Saudi Arabia in 1926.

Before Feisal had reached his fourth birthday, his father was killed in a motor accident on April 4, 1939, and Feisal succeeded him. Parliament appointed the Emir Abdul Ilah, son of King Ali and brother of Queen Aliyah, Regent and Heir to the throne.

Formal education for the little King began when an English governess was appointed in 1940. Later he was tutored in Arabic, art, physics, chemistry, and history of the Arabic world. In the fall of 1943, King Feisal was sent to the Royal Bilat, the official palace of the Court, where a tutor conducted classes for five or six other Iraqi boys of the same age, in order to establish a routine and provide companionship for the young King. Among his favorite childhood toys were a General Grant tank with wheel chains forged out of gold and

FEISAL II, KING OF IRAQ

a miniature Hurricane fighter. On May 2nd, his eighth birthday, he made his debut on the air, broadcasting in English over the British Broadcasting Corporation, and sent his "good wishes to Britons and Americans" (New York *Times*, May 3, 1943). In May 1946, King Feisal paid his first visit to England.

He entered Sandroyd Preparatory School near Salisbury, England in the fall of 1947 and the Iraqi Embassy in Kensington Palace Gardens became his official residence. After two years, he continued his education at Harrow, where his father had also attended the famous preparatory school. His studies included Islamic law and Arabic history and customs. Young Feisal developed a keen interest in sports while at Harrow and was the author of a book on judo entitled *How To Defend Yourself.* It was published in Arabic, when the King was sixteen, and became a manual for Iraq's Army and a "best seller in Baghdad." He remained at Harrow until June 1952 and was awarded the General Certificate of Education. Upon his return to Baghdad, he was given a tremendous ovation.

Accompanied by the Regent, Emir Abdul Ilah, King Feisal II toured the United States for five weeks in the summer of 1952. His itinerary included Brooklyn's Ebbets Field for a Giant-Dodger game; a visit to Washington, D.C., as guest of President and Mrs. Harry S. Truman; Fort Knox, Kentucky; Muscle Shoals in Alabama; the Hoover Dam; and automobile factories in Detroit, Michigan. He told reporters that he was "particularly interested in studying American irrigation projects" on the West Coast. Mayor Vincent R. Impellitteri of New York presented him with the city's Medal of Honor.

Celebrations on Accession Day, May 2, 1953, began with a display of fireworks on the west bank of the Tigris River at dawn. The King wore a field marshal's uniform, with a white tunic that glittered with medals and gold braid and a plumed white helmet, and was driven in his carriage through cheering crowds to the Parliament building, where he took the royal oath.

In a short speech which followed, he paid solemn tribute to the late Queen Mother Aliyah, who had died in December 1950, and to the Prince Regent Abdul Ilah, whose guidance had been a "source of inspiration and confidence."

At the ceremonies tribal sheiks from the provinces wore sashes and tasseled turbans, and the Arab delegates were adorned in golden-hemmed robes and the traditional headdress, the white kaffiyeh, with black or gold cord. There were delegations from over thirty countries.

On the same day, King Feisal's cousin King Hussein, a schoolmate at Harrow and the grandson of the late King Abdullah, was enthroned as King of Jordan. The New York *Times* (May 3, 1953) reported that simultaneous accessions of the two Hashemite Kings meant that "neither had seniority in the exercise of royal prerogatives."

Under the 1924-1925 constitution, Iraq is a hereditary monarchy with a bicameral Parliament. The Senate is named by the King for a term of eight years; the 138-member Chamber of Deputies is elected popularly for four years. Executive power is vested in a Council of Ministers, headed by the Prime Minister, who is chosen by the monarch.

A land with oil reserves estimated at 10,500,-000,000 barrels, Iraq has recently begun a five-year plan to develop other areas of her economy with revenues from oil. To combat the flooded Baghdad area, with parched deserts beyond the inundated area, construction has been started on three diversion dams, and four other dams have been planned. An irrigation system to reclaim 1,000,000 acres of desert land is included in the program. *Newsweek* (February 28, 1955) noted that Iraq's aim is to remake itself as a "constructive answer to Communism in one of the world's most strategic areas."

Preliminary exploration has indicated that Iraq also has rich deposits of sulphur, limestone, bitumen, and glass sand. French, West German, American, British, Italian, Belgian and Swiss companies are investing in Iraq.

The defense pact, signed by Turkey, Iraq, Great Britain and Pakistan in 1955, was regarded by the Western Powers as a step toward a Middle East security system against Communist aggression. Iraq's participation in the alliance was negotiated by Premier Nuri as-Said (see *C.B.,* June 1955) with the approval of the young King.

King Feisal II is five feet four inches tall, slender, and has dark wavy hair and large black eyes. He speaks fluent English with a British accent. His collections of paintings and antiques are said to show excellent taste, and he has done considerable painting himself. (His paintings were included in an Anglo-Arabic exhibition in London.) He collects stamps and enjoys boxing, skiing and jazz. The King is very popular with his people, who appreciate his sense of responsibility. "It is my duty," he once said, "to act for the whole community . . . the monarch is the first servant of the community."

Feisal II has been the recipient of the Order of Al Hashimi, Order of Feisal I, Order of Al Rafidain, Order of Al Nahdha, Order of Al Istiqlal, Order of Hussein I (of Jordan), American Military Merit award, Order of Cedar (Lebanon), Order of Solomon (Ethiopia), Military Merit award (Spain) and Lion of the Netherlands.

References

N Y Times p1+ Ag 13 '52 por; p1+ My 2 '53 por
Time 56:66 Jl 30 '51 por
International Who's Who, 1954
Middle East—Who's Who in the Middle East, 1955
New Century Cyclopedia of Names (1954)
World Biography (1954)

FERGUSSON, ERNA Jan. 10, 1888- Author

Address: b. c/o Alfred A. Knopf, 501 Madison Ave., New York 22; h. Albuquerque, N.M.

Reprinted from the *Wilson Library Bulletin* June '55

Some travel books treat people in any country—except the writer's—as odd and freakish; others treat people as dissimilar only in their customs and language. Erna Fergusson writes the second type. There are at least two reasons for this: her heredity and her early environment. Her father, Harvey Butler Fergusson, was an Alabaman of English Tory and French Huguenot ancestry; the parents of her mother (the former Clara Mary Huning) were of German descent and had traveled across the plains to New Mexico with a wagon train.

This background with its European standards, Southern traditions, and the whole overlaid with the western frontier speech, a lot of Spanish and a dash of Indian, all served to relieve her of many of the prejudices and intolerances that hamper so many people. "Even though I speak no foreign language perfectly, one never sounds like gibberish to me; I also realize that there are many religions—I always had good friends who were Catholics, Jews, Quakers, and assorted Protestants. And dark skins neither frighten nor disgust me. All this in my unconscious has doubtless helped me to make friends in the countries I have written about." She is the sister of Harvey Fergusson, the novelist, and Francis Fergusson, the critic. Most of her books have been published by Knopf; her latest is *Mexico Revisited* (1955).

Erna Fergusson was born in Albuquerque, New Mexico and in 1930 with an M.A. from tending the Girl's Collegiate School in Los Angeles, California, she was graduated in 1912 with an A.B. degree from the University of New Mexico and in 1930 with an M.A. from Columbia University in New York City. Later, she received an honorary degree, Litt.D., from the University of New Mexico.

Elliott Erwitt

ERNA FERGUSSON

After her graduation, Erna Fergusson taught for several years in the Albuquerque public schools, grade and high school. Since then, for many years, she has lectured in a variety of places such as the University of New Mexico summer school, the University of Nebraska, and to groups of librarians. One thing that has been very influential in her life and writing has been the fact that since 1936 she has been a speaker in Mexico, in Guatemala, and around South America for the seminars of the Committee on Cultural Relations with Latin America, whose guiding spirit is Hubert Herring. She has also served on Dr. Herring's faculty at the summer school of Claremont University in California.

Miss Fergusson began her writing career on the Albuquerque *Herald*, and did some articles for the *Century Magazine* and other magazines. Since then she has become famous for her colorful, sympathetic studies of many peoples. Her first book, *Dancing Gods* (1931) is the result of her work as the first woman dude wrangler who took tourists to see Indian dances. Of this book the *New Republic* (November 25, 1931) wrote, *"Dancing Gods* is at once an excellent guidebook and a valuable piece of reporting." *Fiesta in Mexico*, written in 1934 on a trip into the most remote parts of Mexico, is described by Ruth Benedict in *Books* as "a book for all those who enjoy the color and movement of folk life."

She recorded in *Guatemala* (1937) her impressions of that country, especially of the Indians. Katherine Woods says of this book in the New York *Times* (February 28, 1937), "Miss Fergusson has approached her subject with peculiar objectivity, enriched by keen alertness, warm sympathy, natural scholarship, and genuine insight." Of her *Venezuela* (Knopf, 1939) Ernest Gruening, in the *Saturday Review*

FERGUSSON, ERNA—*Continued*

of Literature (January 14, 1939), wrote, "She has produced a travel book which is well above the average and provided an introduction to those who want to know about one of our nearer neighbors."

In 1940, Erna Fergusson's interest was centered in the manners and customs of *Our Southwest*, and then in 1942 she described the life and customs of Hawaii in *Our Hawaii*. The *New Yorker* (March 7, 1942) praised the book as "colorful, lavish, expertly written."

Chile (1943 was hailed in the *Annals of the American Academy* (May, 1943) by W. R. Crawford as "the best book on the country in our language." Of *Cuba* (1946) the *Weekly Book Review's*, B. D. Wolfe wrote on November 24, 1946, "It would not have been presumptous or inappropriate of Miss Fergusson to have named this book *The Intelligent Traveler's Guide to Cuba*."

A change of pace in 1948 produced *Murder & Mystery in New Mexico* (Armitage Editions), nine true stories of murder mysteries in New Mexico, which J. H. Jackson praised in the *San Francisco Chronicle* (November 9, 1948): "This collection belongs among the books of any connoisseur of true crime, and also on the shelves of all who collect in the byways of Americana." And Miss Fergusson's book, *New Mexico* (1951), was as well reviewed as her others had been. "This is a solid, splendid book," *Library Journal* (December 15, 1951).

This blue-eyed, gray-haired writer (she is five feet eight inches tall and weighs 150 pounds) has for twenty years combined her work and her recreation, for she loves to travel by motor "practically anywhere" and she "likes dealing with Indians and with Spanish speaking peoples." Her political affiliation is Democratic; her only club membership is with the Women Geographers; and her permanent home is in Albuquerque, New Mexico.

Reference

Who's Who in America, 1954-55

FERMI, ENRICO Sept. 29, 1901-Nov. 28, 1954 Physicist; "father" and "architect" of the atomic bomb; born in Italy and educated in Europe; taught at universities of Florence (1924-26) and Rome (1927-38); awarded Nobel Prize for physics (1938); came to United States where he became professor at Columbia University (1939) and University of Chicago (1945); his early experiments in artificial radioactivity, using slow neutrons, led directly to discovery of uranium fission; leader of group which designed and put into operation first atomic reactor in 1942; worked on A-bomb at Los Alamos; also known for the Fermi-Dirac statistics and perfection of a theory of beta ray emission in radioactivity; received special award of $25,000 from U.S. Atomic Energy Commission (1954) for work on atomic bomb. See *Current Biography* (Oct.) 1945.

Obituary

N Y Times p 1+ N 29 '54

FERMOR, PATRICK (MICHAEL) LEIGH Feb. 11, 1915- Author

Address: b. c/o John Murray, Ltd., 50 Albemarle St., London W. 1, England

Reprinted from the *Wilson Library Bulletin* December 1955

The Anglo-Irish author Patrick Leigh Fermor has been compared with Lawrence of Arabia for his gift of language and his audacity. His books on travel and his novels set in exotic locales have an immediacy and authenticity which his own life might lead us to expect. Although his parents had intended a military career for him, he preferred to see the world first as a civilian and wandering scholar. Later when he joined the Irish Guards during World War II, his venturesome spirit led him to undertake dangerous missions while a Commando in the resistance movement in Greece and Crete. After the war he began to write. "At his best," commented the *Manchester Guardian*, "he writes a lively and suggestive prose, with a disarming wit and a use of metaphor which is often brilliant."

Patrick Michael Leigh Fermor was born on February 11, 1915, the son of the late Sir Lewis Leigh Fermor and Eileen (Ambler) Leigh Fermor. His father was a Fellow of the Royal Society and distinguished by the Order of the British Empire. Young Patrick Michael was educated at King's School, Canterbury, and spent the prewar years on tours through the Continent and the Near East, traveling extensively in the Greek archipelago. His experiences fostered his lasting interest in the history of language and in the traditional life of remote areas.

Upon the outbreak of World War II, he enlisted in the Irish Guards and became liaison officer to the Greek Headquarters in Albania. He fought in the battles of Greece and Crete, and after the fall of Crete, he returned there to organize the resistance movement and to command guerrilla operations on the island between 1942 and 1944.

It was during the two and a half years he spent on the island disguised as a shepherd that he led a perilous expedition, the objective of which was to capture and deliver to the British authorities in Cairo a Nazi officer, Major General Karl Kreipe, who commanded the 22,000 German troops on Crete. An account of the exploit is to be found in a book written by Major W. Stanley Moss, *Ill Met By Moonlight* (1950). Major Moss was associated with Leigh Fermor in the action. They hid out during the day with friendly villagers. Leigh Fermor passed the time reading *Alice in Wonderland* and *The Oxford Book of Verse* while listening to the clump of hobnailed boots of German soldiers.

Working on an island completely occupied by enemy troops, Leigh Fermor and Moss, at the head of a handful of Cretan guerrillas, abducted the General, using his own car to escape through Herakleion, the capital city—which was, of course, swarming with Nazi troops—and started on a search for a radio operator who could reach Cairo and arrange for their escape from the island. There were only three such on the entire

PATRICK LEIGH FERMOR

island. The first one could not send their message because his transmitter was out of order. Since the entire Nazi force was by this time combing the island for them, Major Moss and Leigh Fermor dispatched two runners with messages for the other two radiomen and took to the hills with their prisoner.

After three weeks of dodging the search parties with the help of the guerrillas, they finally received a message giving a rendezvous point on the coast. Slipping between two large encampments of the enemy, they reached the boat and made good their escape to Cairo. The General, who is now a bond salesman in Germany, is grateful to them for his capture as the two other Nazi generals on Crete were subsequently executed by the Greek authorities as war criminals.

Major Leigh Fermor completed his war service in North Germany as a team commander in the Special Allied Airborne Reconnaissance Force. After the war, he spent a year as deputy director of the British Institute in Athens before resuming his travels which took him to the Caribbean area during 1947 and 1948.

His first book, *The Traveller's Tree* (1950) won the Heinemann Foundation Prize for literature in that year and the Kemsley Prize in 1951. The book, describing Fermor's journeys through the Caribbean Islands, was published in the United States by Harper. It was followed in 1953 by *A Time To Keep Silence* and *The Violins of Saint-Jacques* in 1954. Fermor has also contributed to various magazines including the *Atlantic, Holiday* and *Reader's Digest.*

The London Sunday *Times* found *The Traveller's Tree* the work "of a born writer," noting that Fermor "is the ideal traveller, inquisitive, humorous, interested in everything." The New York *Herald Tribune* reviewer remarked that he covered his material in a "literate and polished style," while the *Christian Science Monitor* praised the "verve and enthusiasm" with which he addressed himself to his subject.

Reactions to *The Violins of Saint-Jacques,* a tale of an island in the Antilles, were somewhat mixed. The London *Times Literary Supplement* noted that while it is "excellent as a nostalgic account of a graceful, colorful, feudal way of life, . . .it remains a tale of travel rather than a novel." The *New Statesman and Nation* praised the author's "fine visual imagination," but found in the story "little more than a splendid spectacle." The *Manchester Guardian,* however, called the book "a perfectly successful small masterpiece."

Fermor is an honorary citizen of Herakleion, Crete, in recognition of his exploits there during the war. He also holds the Distinguished Service Order (1944) and the Order of the British Empire (1943). He is a fellow of the Royal Geographical Society and of the Royal Society of Literature. His clubs are the Traveller's, Pratt's and the Special Forces in London and the Cercle Huysmans in Paris. His chief recreation is travelling.

References

Newsweek 38:100 N 5 '51 por
Read Digest 63:121+ S '53
Who's Who, 1955

FERNANDEL, May 8, 1903- Actor

Address: b. 15 ave. Trudaine, Paris 9ᵉ France; h. Villa Les Milleroses, route des Trois-Lucs, Marseilles, France

"The face of Fernandel is as . . . unforgettable as the Eiffel Tower," observed *Life,* "it has helped to make him his country's greatest comic attraction." The French actor's latest film, *The Sheep Has Five Legs,* opened at the Fine Arts Theatre in New York City on August 9, 1955 to much acclaim. "Britain may have its Alec Guinness, but France still has Fernandel to match against him in any sort of contest of comic talent," observed Bosley Crowther (New York *Times,* August 10, 1955), while Alton Cook in the New York *World-Telegram and Sun* commented, "Fernandel [who plays six roles] . . . ranges through idiocy, brutality, glee and astute charm. . . . There is no duplication in the roles except that they are all very funny."

Americans became familiar with Fernandel's "owlish, toothy, flexible face" not only in imported motion pictures but also in photographer Philippe Halsman's book, *The Frenchman* (Simon & Schuster, 1949), which contained twenty-four pictures of the French comedian as he answered in pantomime Halsman's questions. The book sold over 100,000 copies.

Since 1930 Fernandel has appeared in over 110 films, becoming best known in the United States for his tragicomic roles such as Felipe in *The Well Digger's Daughter* (1946) and the country priest in *The Little World of Don Camillo* (1953). This role proved so popular that Fernandel has made three other films about the character of the hot-tempered padre.

Sam Levin, Paris

FERNANDEL

His 1954 films included *The Red Inn, The French Touch,* and *Public Enemy No. 1* (their English titles). The film star has made many song recordings and radio appearances.

Fernand Joseph Désiré Contandin was born of Provençal stock on May 8, 1903, in Marseilles, France, to Denis Charles, a bookkeeper, and Désirée (Bedouin) Contandin. Fernand, who at the time was "all teeth," made his debut at the age of five in a melodrama at the Théâtre Chave. He attended school during the day, and in the evening, with his father and brother he appeared in many of the music halls of Marseilles, and later Fernand entertained at weddings and parties.

When his father was mobilized during World War I, Fernand left school and worked successively in a bank, a soap factory, an importing business, a rug firm and again in a bank. Meanwhile he continued to perform wherever and whenever he could. By the time he was seventeen his voice had become "deep, colorful, flexible, agreeably resonant," wrote Carlo Rim in his biography, *Fernandel* (1952).

While working at the Banque Populaire Provençale, Fernand became friends with Jean Manse, a bank clerk who later became Fernand's chief song writer, and with Jean's sister, Henriette, (whom he later married). In December 1922 when the Eldorado theatre in Nice offered Fernandel a contract, the young man quickly decided to give up banking. Until 1922 he had always used his father's stage name: Marc Sined. In Nice for the first time he appeared as Fernandel, a name given him by Henriette's mother who always called him Henriette's Fernand or "Fernand d'elle". The name was propitious; his performance in Nice led to several other engagements.

Upon completion of compulsory military training, Fernandel returned to Marseilles and worked in a soap factory to support his wife and their first child, Josette. In the evening he accepted music hall engagements. When a Parisian performer at the Paramount Théâtre in Marseilles failed to please the audience, Fernandel was asked to substitute. His performance won him a contract on the Paramount vaudeville circuit and he traveled throughout France and North Africa (later on the Pathé circuit); everywhere audiences responded immediately to his humor.

The film director Marc Allégret offered him a role in a talking film, *Le Banc et Le Noir* by Sacha Guitry, starring Jules Raimu (see *C.B.*, 1946 obit). Film critic Paul Reboux wrote: "Fernandel—remember this name; it will become famous!" From 1931 to 1933 Fernandel appeared in twenty-five movies. He starred in shows at the Empire and European theatres in Paris. He then played a triumphant season in 1933 in Marseilles in the play *Oh, que Combine!*

Although critics praised his acting, they commented sharply on the mediocre films in which Fernandel wasted his talents. His luck turned in 1934 when Marcel Pagnol signed him for the part of Saturnin, a country bumpkin, in *Angèle.* After this success he was starred in several other movies including *Les Bleus de la Marine*, followed by Jean Manse's operetta, *Ignace*, which had successful performances in both Marseilles and Paris and was made into a film by Pierre Colombier in 1937. Between films he performed at the Porte Saint-Martin theatre in Paris in *Le Rosier de Madame Husson* an operetta which had a triumphant success.

Among the films Fernandel made in 1936 under Christian Jaque's direction were *Un de la Légion* and *Josette*, in which Fernandel's ten-year-old daughter played the title role. In *Les Rois du Sport* he was co-starred with Raimu, but "the two great comedians somehow nullified each other's effect," commented Carlo Rim. More successful were two films directed by Pagnol in 1937: *Regain*, in which Fernandel portrayed Gédémus, a country buffoon, and *Le Schpountz*, in which he played Irénée, a village simpleton. By 1938 Fernandel's picture was seen in magazines, shop windows and bars and in advertisements for hair lotion, shaving cream and tooth-paste. He continued to appear in four or five films each year.

Mobilized into the French army, Fernandel served for a time with the Fifteenth Division of Supply and then with the Theatre of the Army. Demobilized in 1940, he appeared in a series of films: notably *La Fille du Puisatier,* produced by Pagnol, which again combined the talents of Raimu and Fernandel, this time with great success. Raimu played the part of Pascal, the well-digger, and Fernandel was Felipe, his assistant. The American version, *The Well Digger's Daughter*, opened in New York City on September 30, 1946. "Fernandel plays with zest, matching Raimu's acting," commented the *Christian Science Monitor* reviewer. "He puts fun and warmth into the role of the rejected suitor." He personally directed the film *Simplet* in 1940 which found favor with audiences of children.

During the occupation of Nazi troops in Marseille and Paris, Fernandel had to limit his movie-making and theatre work. When he appeared on the stage of the A.B.C. music hall in Paris in 1945 he was forbidden by the Nazis to sing his military songs. His brother-in-law, Jean Manse wrote lyrics in 1946 for another operetta for Fernandel, *Les Chasseurs d'images*, which opened at the Théâtre du Châtelet. His films that year were *Pétrus, Coeur du Coq, Escale au soleil;* in 1947 he appeared in *Emile l'Africain*; in 1948 he was in *Si ça Peut Vous Faire Plaisir* and *L'Armoire Volante*. He made his first tour of the United States and Canada in 1948 but his performance in Town Hall in New York City met with a "mixed" reception by the critics who found it "too Gallic" for American audiences.

Cast in his first serious stage role in 1949, he appeared in *Tu n'as sauvé la vie* by Sacha Guitry. Despite adverse reviews the play ran for 200 performances and was made into a film in 1950. Fernandel played a highly dramatic role in the film *Meurtres* (1950). *L'Auberge Rouge*, produced in 1951 was "saved by Fernandel's acting," according to Louis Chauvet of *Figaro*. That same year he appeared in *The Little World of Don Camillo*, released in the United States in 1953. Critics on both sides of the Atlantic hailed his portrayal of the country priest as one of Fernandel's "truest, most moving and most amusing creations."

Coiffeur pour Dames, the adventures of a sheep-shearer turned hair-dresser, was produced in 1952, as was *Le Retour de Don Camillo*. In 1953 Fernandel and an entire French film company journeyed to New York to make *L'Ennemi Public No. 1*. In this, the comedian played the part of a near-sighted American sporting-goods demonstrator who innocently becomes mistaken for a notorious gangster. During its production, *Life* (October 6, 1953) ran a series of pictures of Fernandel personifying a gallery of American types with the same droll humor he had already brought to French and Italian types. *L'Auberge Rouge*, shown in the United States in 1954 as *The Red Inn*, brought Fernandel praise from American film critics. *Coiffeur pour Dames* as *The French Touch* was also seen in New York in 1954. "The coiffeur is played with great flair by Fernandel" wrote William K. Zinsser in the New York *Herald Tribune* (September 2, 1954).

Other Fernandel films in 1953 were *Carnaval, Mam'zelle Nitouche, Le Mouton a Cinq Pattes* (*The Sheep Has Five Legs*, English title, 1955) and a second sequel to *Don Camillo*. During 1954 he worked on *Le Printemps, l'automne et l'amour*. In an interview with Robert Chazel of the *Journal de Paris* on November 26, 1954, Fernandel announced that he plans to make only two films a year in the future.

The French actor is a Chevalier of the Légion d'Honneur, an Officer of the Académie, and has been awarded the Palmes Académiques. When on vacation from making films, he lives in Les Milleroses, the large home he had built near Marseilles for his wife, the former Henriette Manse, and their four children: Josette, Janine, Franck and Gerard. (The happiest day of his life, he said, was when his son Franck was born.) He also enjoys fishing at Carri-le-Rouet where he has a summer home and likes to cook his own catch. His favorite sports are bowling, bicycling and horseback riding. He collects rare editions of Molière, and enjoys modern murder mysteries.

Commenting on Fernandel's nimble skill in playing six roles, a father and five sons, in *The Sheep Has Five Legs* Bosley Crowther called the farce "probably the cleverest and most hilarious French comedy we've seen since the war" (New York *Times*, August 10, 1955). William K. Zinsser observed in the New York *Herald Tribune* on the same date, "Fernandel is a joy throughout! . . . He is one of the most versatile comic actors of the day."

References

Crapouillot 8:75 '50 por
Barlatier, P. Mémoires de Fernandel (1938)
Dictionnaire Biographique Français Contemporain, 1954
Rim, C. Fernandel (1952)
Who's Who in France (Paris), 1953-54

FEYNMAN, R(ICHARD) P(HILLIPS)

(fīn'măn) May 11, 1918- College professor; physicist

Address: b. California Institute of Technology, Pasadena, Calif.; h. 844 Alameda St., Altadena, Calif.

The Albert Einstein Award of 1954 was presented to Dr. R. P. Feynman, who has contributed some of the most important work developed during the past decade in quantum electrodynamics. He devised the "Feynman diagram" and propounded a mathematical explanation for the behavior of liquid helium. While still in his twenties, Feynman was a group leader of the Los Alamos (New Mexico) project for the development of the atomic bomb. He held an associate professorship at Cornell University and is now a professor at the California Institute of Technology in Pasadena.

Richard Phillips Feynman was born on May 11, 1918 in New York City to Melville Arthur and Lucille (Phillips) Feynman, and was reared in Far Rockaway, New York. He has a younger sister. His father was sales manager in a company which manufactured uniforms. The younger Feynman was influenced by his father, who was deeply interested in the natural sciences.

After he was graduated from Far Rockaway High School in 1935, Feynman continued his education at Massachusetts Institute of Technology in Cambridge, Massachusetts, where he received the B.S. degree in 1939. He completed his graduate work as Proctor fellow at Princeton University in New Jersey, receiving the Ph.D. degree in 1942. His thesis was entitled "The Principle of Least Action in Quantum Mechanics."

His postgraduate work led to his assignment on the atomic bomb project at Los Alamos, New Mexico, where he was a group leader from 1942 to 1945. Appointed an associate professor of theoretical physics at Cornell University in Ithaca, New York, Dr. Feynman

R. P. FEYNMAN

remained there until 1950, when he moved to his present post as a full professor at the California Institute of Technology.

Articles detailing Professor Feynman's contributions to quantum mechanics have appeared in the *Physical Review* and other professional journals. He constructed a quantum theory of electricity and magnetism, which resolved the inaccuracies of earlier theories of quantum electrodynamics dealing with the interaction of atoms with radiation fields. He also propounded the Feynman diagram, a means for accounting for possible particle transformation.

More recently, Dr. Feynman has been investigating the properties of liquid helium. Helium can be turned into liquid only at 452 degrees below zero Fahrenheit and solidified at that temperature under 375 pounds per square inch pressure.

Before Feynman worked on liquid helium it had been studied by other scientists. Liquid helium manifests characteristics of a "superfluid" in that it flows freely through microscopically thin tubes through which ordinary fluids have to be forced. Although liquid helium acts as if it has no viscosity, it does have thickness, because a whirling paddle will slow down in the fluid. Moreover, in flowing from one container to another through a tube, the liquid loses heat. Another property of the fluid is its ability to creep up and down the walls of a container in defiance of gravity.

Several years ago two physicists, Dr. L. Tisza, an American, and Dr. Lev Landau, a Russian, tried to explain the behavior of liquid helium in a manner that was not principally mathematical. Dr. Landau said that at very cold temperatures the liquid helium could handle energy in only one way, with bundles, which he called "phonons." Phonons must be regarded as waves of energy. The lower the temperature the fewer the phonons, the less the energy.

Thus some of the helium's behavior is explained. The liquid helium can flow through a long thin tube because the individual helium atoms do not jiggle—they have no energy. The phonons are too large to get inside the tube; they remain behind among the other atoms, tending to heat them. In regard to creeping up the sides of the jar, it was explained that liquid helium can stick to the walls of the container like any liquid. Being cold, it does not evaporate and it forms a thin plate between itself and the glass wall.

Continuing the work of Landau, Tisza and others, Feynman demonstrated mathematically that the phonon explanation is essentially correct; his contribution obeys all the laws of atomic physics. In addition, he showed mathematically that the helium atoms between three degrees and seven degrees above absolute zero can hold energy by moving in collections shaped like smoke rings called "rotons."

The mathematics that Feynman used is called "quantum mechanics," a technique that has been used to explain every atomic phenomenon that occurs outside the atomic core, the nucleus. Until Feynman devised his theory, liquid helium had resisted such description.

In January 1954 Dr. Feynman participated in a conference at the University of Rochester in New York, where many of the nation's distinguished physicists (such as Dr. J. Robert Oppenheimer, Dr. Hans A. Bethe, and Dr. Edward Teller) joined in an attempt to formulate a unified theory of atomic structure to include the many new subatomic particles, mesons, neutrinos and others, which the last twenty years of research have brought to light. Many participants left the conference with the feeling that the problem of the theory of the atom would not be solved for a long time.

A conference to which he was invited, but did not attend, was one held in Moscow under the auspices of the Soviet Academy of Sciences early in 1955. No "classified" subject matter appeared on the agenda of the conference. Dr. Feynman was interested in going because it would have given him an opportunity to meet Landau and to discuss recent advances in the field with him. Feynman also felt that the conference would "have been valuable on both sides" (New York *Times,* April 7, 1955).

After receiving the invitation, Dr. Feynman wrote to the U.S. Department of State and to the U.S. Atomic Energy Commission in January requesting their advice. He waited almost two months for a reply and then wrote to Georgi N. Zaroubin, U.S.S.R. Ambassador to the United States, and advised him that he would like to attend the conference, but he could not afford the cost of the trip. He received a prompt reply from the Soviet Embassy informing him that the Soviet government would pay his traveling expenses.

On the basis of this offer, Dr. Feynman accepted the invitation. In early March he received a letter from the general manager of the Atomic Energy Commission, Major General Kenneth D. Nichols, who strongly recommended that he not take the "unwarranted risk" of going to Moscow. In the story appearing in the New York *Times,* April 7, 1955, Dr. Feynman is quoted as agreeing that there were "several reasons why it may have been unwise for me to go." He pointed out that in view of his work on the atomic bomb during World War II, and his consultation with the U.S. Army in 1954 on a highly classified project, the Government's decision was understandable.

It was announced on March 13, 1954, on the eve of the seventy-fifth birthday of Dr. Albert Einstein, that the Einstein Award of 1954 was won by Dr. Feynman. The award, established by Admiral Lewis L. Strauss (chairman of the U.S. Atomic Energy Commission) on March 14, 1949 in memory of his parents, is granted triennially and includes a gold medal and $15,000. It is the highest honor, next to the Nobel Prize, to which a physicist may aspire. The previous Einstein Award (1951) was shared by Dr. Julian Schwinger and Dr. Kurt Gödel.

On June 29, 1942 Feynman was married to Arline H. Greenbaum, who died in June 1945. His second wife is Mary Louise Bell, whom he married on June 28, 1952. The scientist is five feet eleven inches tall and weighs 160 pounds; he has brown eyes and hair. Professor Feynman belongs to the American Physical Society, American Association for the Advancement of Science, and National Academy of Sciences. His fraternity is Pi Lambda Phi.

References

N Y Times p8 Mr 11 '54 por
Nature 173:524 Mr 20 '54
American Men of Science (1955)
Who's Who in America, 1954-55

FIELD, HENRY Dec. 15, 1902- Anthropologist

Address: b. 3551 Main Hwy., Coconut Grove 33, Fla.

"But how do you know where to dig?" This question has frequently been asked of Henry Field, one of the world's foremost explorer-anthropologists. In his autobiography *The Track of Man* (Doubleday, 1953), he answers some of the questions of laymen and describes how he selects a place to dig, how he excavates a centuries-old skeleton, how he transports his findings, and how he sets them up in a museum. Dr. Field was curator of physical anthropology at the Field Museum of Natural History, Chicago (now the Chicago Natural History Museum) from 1931 to 1941. More than 20,000,000 visitors have seen the two exhibition halls, the Races of Mankind and Prehistoric Man, which he set up in 1933 and which include the famous bronze sculptures by Malvina Hoffman.

His autobiography relates, in layman's language, much of what he has learned in a lifetime of search on four continents for information about the origins, migrations, and racial affiliations of prehistoric man. He is the author of a five-volume survey, *The Anthropology of Iraq* (1940-1953), and of over 300 technical articles on ancient and modern man. In 1950 he became a research fellow at the Peabody Museum, Harvard University, which published his *Contributions to the Anthropology of the Caucasus* in 1953.

Henry Field was born in Chicago, Illinois on December 15, 1902, a grandnephew of the American merchant and philanthropist, Marshall Field. He was taken as a youngster to England to live. His mother, divorced, had married Captain Algernon Burnaby, owner of the ancient Baggrave estate in Leicestershire. Asked what he wanted for his twelfth birthday, Henry requested a day's work from his stepfather's two best laborers, because he wanted to excavate a Saxon village on the estate. This was his first "dig," and here he uncovered his first archaeological objects.

His mother took him to Rome in 1915 for a visit to his step-grandfather, Thomas Nelson Page, United States Ambassador to Italy. There, under the guidance of the American sculptor, Moses Ezekiel, Henry toured the ancient ruins—the Forum, Coliseum, and Baths of Caracalla. The Queen of Italy presented Henry with several precious objects found in a royal tomb at Ostia. These treasures, together with his prized Saxon village finds, constitute the only archaeological items in his possession today. His many other finds are lodged in museums.

His interest in early man continued while he was at Eton College, England, from which he was graduated in 1921. He entered New College, Oxford, where L. H. Dudley Buxton, professor of anthropology, exerted a strong influence on him. It was during his college days, too, that his granduncle Barbour Lathrop, world traveler, took a hand in forwarding his ambitions. Lathrop, a great believer in the educational advantages of travel, encouraged Henry to spend less time on "book learning" and to start "digging."

Stimulated by Dr. Buxton's lectures, Henry yearned to join an expedition and make discoveries of his own. The opening of Tutankhamen's tomb in 1922 was making headlines. Pamphlets from Chicago told of the Field Museum and Oxford University joint expedition, which was excavating in the Middle East at Kish. Field's interest began to center on the ancient city. In November 1925, after he had been awarded his B.A. degree by Oxford, he received a letter from his Uncle Barbour, who bolstered his travel advice with a check for $1,000. Field took this opportunity to go to Kish, instead of spending his Christmas vacation at home.

Accompanying Henry Field on the journey was his revered professor, Dr. Buxton. They traveled by way of Egypt, the Valley of the Kings, where, in the dimly lit shaft cut into the hillside, Henry had one of his wishes granted—to see the golden coffin which had held the mummy of King Tutankhamen. They traveled to Jerusalem and then walked to Bethlehem. Going on to Baghdad, they finally

HENRY FIELD

came to Kish. Field looked with awe on this spot, once a focal point between Asia, Africa, and Europe, and vowed to dedicate himself to the search for the answers to the anthropological problems of the Near and Middle East, particularly those relating to the origins and migrations of prehistoric man.

Many generations ago, Kish had been a bustling city, verdant, close by the Euphrates River. Now, it was a desert, and during many a hot desert hour, Field was to hear the workmen's Arabic chant, "May the scorpion sting the pickman" (a wishful hope which would relieve them from work) while he was alert for their shout "Adham" (Arabic for Adam, meaning "man"), the signal that bones had been found, or "Maktub," that a stone tablet with inscriptions had been excavated.

During this first sojourn at Kish, Field and Buxton uncovered the first complete Babylonian skeleton found in that region. His study of the ancient dwellers of Mesopotamia had now really begun. As he watched the workers toiling in the trench one day, the thought came to Field: if it were possible to bring to life these skeletons of 5,000 years ago and dress them in today's Arab clothing, would they look the same? How could it be proved?

With that question, Field had determined his life's work. By correlating physical anthropology with an anthropogeographical study of Iraq and the adjoining areas, including work in the Caucasus, Iran, Saudi Arabia, and all the surrounding Southwestern Asia, he might possibly, in twenty-five years, have the answer.

From that day on, Henry Field became an anthropogeographer. His interest was not only in the land and its peoples, but also in the natural history of the areas he visited. From his expeditions, besides bones and skeletons and precious artifacts, he brought back plant, animal, and insect specimens.

After his return to Oxford for further study, young Field had another opportunity for doing interesting field work. Upon the invitation of the Abbé Henri Breuil, one of the world's leading authorities on cave art, he went to Spain where he saw caves whose walls show some of the earliest prehistoric art. In 1926 he received a diploma in anthropology from Oxford. He followed this with a summer course at the University of Heidelberg in Germany and an exhaustive tour of European museums.

In the fall of 1926 he joined the Field Museum in Chicago as assistant curator of physical anthropology. There he was soon given the opportunity to realize another dream, that of portraying the story of man in two adjoining exhibition halls, one dealing with prehistoric men of the Stone Age, the other with all the races of mankind. Field traveled the equivalent of four times around the world in search of background information, to take photographs, and to assemble prehistoric collections. In 1930 he received the M.A. degree from Oxford University and the following year, became curator of physical anthropology at the Field Museum.

Describing the Hall of Races of Mankind (Chauncey Keep Memorial Hall) at the Field Museum of Natural History, Dr. Field wrote in *Science* (August 18, 1933): "The hall contains 87 life-size bronze sculptures (30 full-length figures, heads and busts) representing typical members of the more important divisions of the human race. In presenting this... to the public in June 1933, the museum has departed boldly from all precedence for anthropological exhibits. Malvina Hoffman, an American sculptor of international repute, spent five years studying, photographing and modeling... under the close supervision of eminent scientists." The Hall of Prehistoric Man has large dioramas ranging from the Chellean to the lake dwellers of Switzerland, about 250,000 to about 5,000 B.C.

Following the opening of the two halls, Dr. Field resumed his field work as leader of the Field Museum expedition to Iraq, Iran, and the Caucasus. In 1937 he received the D.Sc. degree from Oxford. World War II interrupted his foreign travels, and in 1941 he went to Washington, D.C. to do special research on the Near East for the U.S. government. When reports reached Washington that there was serious unrest in Trinidad, a vital link in the bauxite shipping chain, Field was sent there by President Franklin D. Roosevelt to report on the situation on that British West Indies island.

He came back with more than the report. His talks with merchant seamen survivors of Allied ships which had been torpedoed by Nazi submarines suggested to him the development of a shark repellent which is now standard equipment in lifeboats. Dr. Field worked on improving rescue equipment and also on providing waterproof Bibles, hymnals, popular songbooks, and other items for seamen and aviators who might be compelled to be in open boats or rafts for prolonged periods of time.

After the war he went as a member of the United States mission to Moscow and Leningrad for the 220th anniversary celebration of the Academy of Sciences of the Soviet Union. He then engaged in anthropological research in Tepoztlán, Mexico. He was invited to join the University of California's expedition to Africa in 1947; his book, *Contributions to the Anthropology of the Faiyum, Sinai, Sudan, Kenya*, was published by the university's press in 1952.

In his article "Sinai Sheds New Light on the Bible" (*National Geographic Magazine*, December 1948) Field described the African expedition. His job was "to measure and describe in detail every Bedouin willing to submit to the calipers, compile all available tribal data, and search for surface Stone Age sites." He found some tools which proved the existence of ancient man in the northern area beyond the Suez Canal and almost as far eastward as the Palestine border. These included hand axes "tentatively estimated to be 100,000 years old." He found some inscriptions hammered into the rocks of Wadi Feiran, Sinai some fifteen centuries ago which, Dr. Field relates, were an ancient version of "Kilroy Was Here." Most of the Nabataean inscriptions say, "I, son of ———, passed this way." In 1950 Field led the Peabody Museum-Harvard University expedition to the Persian Gulf areas and Saudi Arabia.

Harry L. Shapiro, reviewing *The Track of Man* in the *Saturday Review* (November 7, 1953), wrote: "The author . . . has somehow failed to extract the broader commentary that might have engaged the general reader. This is all the more to be regretted since the book is an interesting one." On the other hand, Dr. Roy Chapman Andrews (New York *Times*, October 25, 1953) commented: "Field has a gift for painting vivid word pictures and imparting his enthusiasm to the reader. Essentially this is a scientific autobiography. . . . Yet in every page is the feeling of a man with a deeply serious purpose in life and an almost religious dedication to an idea."

Dr. Field has blue eyes and gray hair. He is five feet eleven inches tall and weighs 195 pounds. He was married on February 5, 1953 to Julie Rand Allen, director of the Crandon Park Zoo in Miami, Florida. He has one daughter, Marianna, by a former marriage to Mrs. Placidia White Knowlton. He is a Democrat and an Episcopalian. He belongs to numerous scientific organizations throughout the world and is a member of the Explorers Club in New York. For recreation he enjoys playing golf.

References

American Men of Science (1949)
Field, H. The Track of Man; Adventures of an Anthropologist (1953)
Who's Who in America, 1954-55

FILHO, JOÃO CAFÉ *See* Café Filho, João (Fernandes Campos)

FLECK, JACK Nov. 8, 1922- Professional golfer

Address: 917 Iowa St., Davenport, Ia.

In the 55th National Open Golf Championship held during June 1955 an unknown player, Jack Fleck, tied Ben Hogan, four-time winner of the tournament, and in the play-off won the championship by three strokes on the difficult Olympic Club course in San Francisco. Fleck carded a one-under-par 69 score on the last round before a crowd of over 70,000, taking the title from the 1954 Open Champion, Ed Furgol.

The young professional golfer, who had never before won a major tournament, was a guest at the White House on July 11 along with other sports celebrities at which President Dwight D. Eisenhower launched a program to get more young Americans interested in athletics to improve physical standards and to help curb juvenile delinquency.

John Fleck was born on November 8, 1922 in Bettendorf, Iowa, one of the five children of Louis Fleck. His father lost his truck farm in the late 1920's, and Jack worked on a daily paper route to help out financially. Jack recalls that when the Western Open was held in Davenport (a city five miles from Bettendorf) in 1936, he "snuck in with some other kids, but they chased us. But I saw enough to like what I saw."

At the age of fifteen he started to caddy at the Davenport Country Club and was allowed to play each Monday, caddy's day. On the other days he played sand-lot golf. He stroked an 89 in his first caddy championship, using borrowed clubs.

In Davenport High School he was top man on the golf team and immediately after graduation he turned professional. Discontent with the factory jobs into which his father had urged him, he took a job in Des Moines as an assistant pro, a club cleaner actually. He enlisted in the Navy in 1942, and was on the Utah beach head in Normany on D-Day.

After he was released from service in 1945, he received appointment to the two municipal golf shops at Duck Creek and Credit Island golf courses in Davenport. In 1950 he married and was able to continue his golf playing through his wife's encouragement and aid (she managed the golf shops while he was on tour).

Entering local tournaments, he was among the prize winners at one held in Grand Rapids, Michigan in 1949 and at Miami, Florida in 1951. In the National Open he failed to qualify for the last thirty-six holes in 1950, and in 1953, he finished fifty-second. He won the Waterloo (Iowa) open in 1953, the Rochester (Minnesota) open in 1954, and finished eighth place in the 1954 Celebrities tournament in Washington, D.C. Prior to winning the National Open, Fleck had won $2,700 for his play during 1955 on the tournament circuit.

Qualifying for the National Open tournament held in San Francisco in June 1955, Fleck knew that Ben Hogan was favored to win (despite the veteran's limp due to an old injury). Sam Snead, Gene Littler, and Ed Furgol were also mentioned as possible winners.

Wide World

JACK FLECK

The Olympic Club's lake-side course was changed for the tournament to make it more difficult for the experts.

By the fourth round the difficult course had conquered most of the players. Hogan finished his fourth round with a score of 70, his lowest round in the tournament. Fleck was still out on the fairway when Gene Sarazen and Joe Dey of the U.S. Golf Association were congratulating Hogan on a record fifth National Open triumph.

Going into the final round, Fleck had taken a five because of a poor approach on the fourteenth hole and had been overlooked by the gallery. On the fifteenth, he shot an iron to within four feet of the pin and took one birdie. All he could hope for on the 603-yard sixteenth hole was par five, and he got it. The seventeenth had a curving fairway and a hidden green. Playing conservatively, he again took par.

For the eighteenth he needed a birdie for a three-under-par score of 67 that would tie Hogan's total. Fleck's drive went into the rough. With his wedge he lifted the ball high into the sharply sloping green to within seven feet of the pin. He stroked the critical shot into the cup for a birdie and a tie.

On Sunday, June 19, the play-off was held. Hogan dropped a stroke on the par-four fifth hole. After hooking his second shot into the bunker on the sixth, Fleck recovered to within twenty-five feet of the pin, then sank an amazing shot for par. On the short eighth, both players were on the green in one. Hogan then sank a fifty-foot putt and Fleck coolly sank his eight footer.

On the ninth hole Fleck sank a twenty-five foot putt for a birdie three and was two strokes up on Hogan. Another long putt of eighteen feet on the tenth gave Fleck his third straight birdie. He was leading the veteran by three strokes. Hogan took a stroke from Fleck on the eleventh hole only to give it back on the twelfth. He then cut Fleck down on the fourteenth and seventeenth holes to a lead of a single stroke.

On the final hole Hogan drove into the foot-high rough which all but obscured the ball. He used one stroke to uncover it. A second stroke moved it three feet, and a third brought it to the fairway. Hogan stroked a fine twenty-five foot putt, but took six for the hole. Fleck using a spoon to drive off the eighteenth tee, was easily on in two, and babied his two putts to the cup for a par four, and one under par total, scoring a 69 to Hogan's 72.

Although Hogan had played consistent golf throughout the tournament with only a few strokes over par, Fleck had scored under par twice. Al Laney of the New York *Herald Tribune* (June 20, 1955) called his putting "astounding," and *Time* magazine (June 27, 1955) noted that Fleck had a "fluid swing." Fleck's putting average was 27½ per round, as against a par of 36.

His award for first place was $6,000, and requests for personal appearances, exhibition dates and endorsements immediately began to add to this sum (about $35,000 is the usual sum an Open Champion can make). President Eisenhower, who was in San Francisco at the time, congratulated Fleck. The golfer's home town gave him a new car and a parade.

His wife, the former Lynn Burnsdale of Chicago, also plays golf. They have a four-year-old son, Craig Carroll. Fleck is six feet one inch tall and weighs 164 pounds. He has wavy dark brown hair and green eyes. "He does not smoke or drink spirits, so he won't endorse cigarettes or whiskey; he does drink an occasional glass of beer" (*New Yorker*, July 9, 1955). He hopes to continue his duties at the local courses in Davenport. In a transcription to Lawrence Robinson for a series of articles in the New York *World-Telegram and Sun* (June 27-July 2, 1955), Fleck stated, "I want to be a playing champion and prove that I'm no flash in the pan." In the P.G.A. tournament at Northville, Michigan on July 23 he was defeated in the third round by Tommy Bolt.

References

New Yorker 31:15+ Jl 9 '55
Sports Illus 26:19+ Je 27 '55 por

FLEMING, SIR ALEXANDER Aug. 6, 1881-Mar. 11, 1955 British bacteriologist; professor emeritus University of London; awarded Nobel Prize in Medicine in 1945 (with Dr. Ernst Boris Chain and Sir Howard Florey) for discovery of penicillin ("the miracle drug") and its use for the cure of infections; taught at St. Mary's Hospital Medical School and conducted some of his research in its Wright-Fleming Institute of which he was formerly director; also furnished original description of lysozyme; his research work on immunology, general bacteriology, chemotherapy, and human blood are also well known; knighted in 1944. See *Current Biography* (Apr.) 1944.

Obituary

N Y Times p19 Mr 12 '55

FOSS, JOE *See* Foss, Joseph Jacob

FOSS, JOSEPH JACOB Apr. 17, 1915- Governor of South Dakota; aviator

Address: b. State Capitol, Pierre, S.D.; h. Governor's Mansion, Pierre, S.D.

Joe Foss, a Marine hero of World War II, winner of the Congressional Medal of Honor, and the first ace to destroy as many enemy planes as Captain Eddie Rickenbacker did in World War I, was inaugurated Governor of South Dakota on January 4, 1955. In his inaugural address Foss advocated a constitutional convention to revise the basic laws of his state, a long-range building program for educational institutions, and the creation of a state disaster fund to meet blizzard and drought emergencies without Federal assistance.

Joseph Jacob Foss was born on a farm near Sioux Falls, South Dakota, on April 17, 1915, to Frank Ole and Mary Esther (Lacey) Foss. He is of Norwegian and Scotch-Irish descent. At the age of twelve Joe saw Charles A. Lindbergh soon after his solo flight to Paris, and airplanes and flying then became Joe's principal interest. (While Foss was serving with the U.S. Marines in the Pacific, Lindbergh was assigned to his Marine outfit as civilian technical expert, and Foss became acquainted with his boyhood hero.)

When Joe was a senior at Washington High School in Sioux Falls, his father was accidentally killed and for the following three years Joe ran the farm. After graduating in 1936 he attended Sioux Falls College and Augustana College, in Sioux Falls, and earned his B.A. degree in business administration from the University of South Dakota in Vermillion in June 1940. At the university his athletic interests were boxing and football, and he played the saxophone in the band. He also waited on tables and worked during the summers on his family's farm or at a local packing plant.

During World War II Foss joined the U.S. Marine Corps and was sent to officers' training school at Pensacola, Florida and was commissioned a second lieutenant. His unit was assigned to the Pacific theater and there became known as "Joe's Flying Circus." Of the seventy-two planes which the unit was credited with having shot down, Foss destroyed twenty-six.

The Denver *Post*, April 15, 1951, gives the following account of his hazards: "Joe ran into a lot of bullets. They ripped his plane to shreds and forced him into at least three dead-stick landings, one of them in the sea off the Japa-

Miller Studio

JOSEPH JACOB FOSS

nese-occupied island of Malaita in the Solomon group." However, Foss's worst experience was with an obsolete Japanese biplane.

"Joe made a pass at the crate, which was barely moving, and was forced to slip under it to avoid a collision with its tail. But the biplane tipped too, and the Jap rear gunner sprayed Foss. Foss finally shot the [plane] down, but before he did, a bullet tore through the head of his fighter [plane] and across his right temple. His engine came unstuck and he tried a water landing, and that's where he almost got it. He forgot to unbuckle the leg strap of his parachute and went under with the plane. He finally got loose just in time."

Foss was awarded the Bronze Star, Silver Star, and Purple Heart, and on May 18, 1943 he received the Congressional Medal of Honor from President Franklin D. Roosevelt at the White House. He was discharged in 1945 with the rank of major.

After the war, Foss refused many offers from big business, because, he has said: "I didn't want to be a dancing bear" (*Time*, January 10, 1955). He returned to Sioux Falls and lived with his family in a converted barracks. With Duane L. (Duke) Corning, an old friend, he built a marginal one-plane venture into a paying business, the Joe Foss Flying Service, with thirty-five airplanes and ten employees, and offering instruction and chartered flights. In March 1953 this business was destroyed by fire and Corning and Foss established the Foss Motor Company, Packard car dealers, in Sioux Falls. The company is no longer under Foss's active management although he is still its president.

Foss organized the South Dakota Air National Guard and commanded the 175th Flight Squadron of the guard. During the Korean conflict, he served with the U.S. Air Force as

FOSS, JOSEPH JACOB—*Continued*

a colonel directing training. He now holds the rank of brigadier general in the guard and the U.S. Air Force Reserve.

Entering politics, Foss was elected overwhelmingly to the state House of Representatives in 1948 from Minnehaha county, and served two regular terms and one special session. In 1950, he was one of five candidates who ran in the Republican gubernatorial primary, which was won by Sigurd Anderson, who subsequently served as Governor of South Dakota for two terms. Four years later Foss won the Republican nomination and in the November election was elected by 57 per cent of the voters.

On January 4, 1955 Foss became South Dakota's twentieth Governor. More than 4,500 people crowded into the capital to attend Governor Foss's reception; this included many wartime friends. In his inaugural address the Governor approved of a Korean veterans bonus (passed by the legislature on February 26, 1955, giving 50 cents a day for those who served in the United States and 65 cents for duty abroad), pledged support to the effort to make the state penitentiary a model institution, and recommended studies for various state departments aimed toward increasing efficiency.

"Our state laws," Foss also stated, "should recognize Indians as first-class citizens. . . . [However] their rehabilitation is a Federal obligation. The treaties which guaranteed certain benefits to the Sioux tribes of South Dakota were made with the Federal Government. . . . The state should take whatever steps are necessary to assure that the Federal Government fulfills its obligations. . . ." (*Daily Capital Journal,* January 4, 1955).

Climbing aboard a bucket loader, Foss, who is a strong advocate of attracting new industries to his state, broke ground on June 24, 1955 for a $2,500,000 uranium processing mill in Edgemont, South Dakota. The plant will be constructed by the Mines Development Company of Golden, Colorado and will process 200 tons of uranium ore a day.

Another advantage for the state was seen in August 1955 when Missouri River waters began running over the new Gavins Point Dam, a rolled-earth structure extending 8,700 feet across the Missouri River on the Nebraska-South Dakota border; its three 33,333-kilowatt generators have the capacity to produce 100,000 kilowatts of electricity. Gavins Point Dam is one of several main stem dams, which will, upon completion, comprise an integrated system of reservoirs for flood control, improved navigation, power facilities and irrigation along the nation's longest river. The Missouri River control program was authorized by Congress in 1944 and is being constructed by Federal agencies in cooperation with ten state governments, including that of South Dakota.

Joe Foss was married to June Esther Shakstad, on August 9, 1942. They have three children, Cheryl June, Mary Jo, and Joseph Frank. Foss is a cigar-chewing six-footer, weighing 180 pounds, with curly black hair and brown eyes. He is his own pilot in his travels as Governor. For relaxation he enjoys hunting and fishing. His church is the Methodist.

The Governor is an Elk, Shriner, American Legionnaire, and a member of the Kiwanis, Veterans of Foreign Wars, on the National Board for Crippled Children and Adults, vice-chairman of the aeronautical committee of the American Legion, a member of the American Battle Monuments Commission, and chairman of the 1954 Easter Seal Campaign. He also founded a family camp for handicapped children and their parents. Hall Bartlett, independent film producer, announced on August 4, 1955 that he had obtained permission to dramatize the story of "Smoky Joe."

References

Argus-Leader (Sioux Falls, South Dakota) p8B Ja 2 '55; p3 Ja 4 '55

Daily Capital Journal (Pierre, South Dakota) p6 Ja 5 '55

Denver (Colorado) Post p40 F 13 '49; Ap 15 '51

N Y Times p55 N 14 '55

Rocky Mountain News (Denver) Mr 11 '51

Time 65:13 Ja 10 '55 por

Who's Who in America (Sup. O '54)

Who's Who in United States Politics (1952)

FREDERIKA (LOUISE), CONSORT OF PAUL I, KING OF THE HELLENES

Apr. 18, 1917-

Address: h. Royal Palace, Athens, Greece; Tatoi, Greece

"We must put ourselves at the disposal of the people," Queen Frederika, Consort of Paul I, King of the Hellenes, has said. "We are not to be served, but to serve." Through her encouragement of the Greek people during World War II and the Communist war, her help in the rehabilitation of the country, her work for Greek children, and her ability in making friends throughout the world, the German-born Queen has served Greece in many ways.

Since her husband took the oath as King in 1947, it has been one of Queen Frederika's duties to help him to maintain but not overstep the power given to the monarch in the "crowned republic" of Greece. The King and Queen enjoy a great personal popularity among their subjects and have been described as "democratic, anti-stodgy, fun-loving but also hard-working" rulers (*Scholastic,* November 18, 1953).

During an official visit to the United States in the fall of 1953, the Royal Couple visited President and Mrs. Dwight D. Eisenhower at the White House and then toured the country; everywhere the King and Queen were well liked and much admired by the Americans. The purpose of the trip, according to a speech given by King Paul at a state dinner in Washington,

D.C., was to "give thanks for American civil and military aid to Greece" in the war against the Communists and in rebuilding the country.

Frederika Louise Thyra Victoria Margarita Sophia Olga Cecilia Isabella Christa, Princess of Hanover, Princess of Great Britain and Ireland, Duchess of Brunswick-Lüneburg was born on April 18, 1917 in the Castle of Blankenburg, Germany. She is the third of five children and the only daughter of the Duke and Duchess of Brunswick-Lüneburg. Her father, Ernst Augustus, was the great-grandson of the first King of Hanover, uncle of Queen Victoria of Great Britain. "Have you ever thought," Frederika once asked Winston Churchill, "that my father would now be King of England if your Queen Victoria had died before ascending the throne?" Her mother, Victoria Louise, was the daughter of Kaiser Wilhelm II of Germany, Queen Victoria's grandson; Frederika is therefore a great-great granddaughter of Queen Victoria.

Within a year after her birth, Frederika moved with her family to Gmunden, Austria, where she grew up. She shared most of her brothers' games and preferred their toy soldiers to her own dolls. She was first educated by her mother and an English governess and was considered "a bright, alert, gay and affectionate tomboy."

Max Eastman once asked her how she had felt as a little girl about being a princess; Queen Frederika replied: "I felt troubled. I used to debate the question with myself very seriously. 'What right have you to be on top without going through the struggle to get there?' It disturbed me for a long time and do you know what finally quieted my mind? It was reading Plato. You remember, he divided all the citizens into different groups: the workers, the soldiers and the leaders. Each had his own function, and the leaders, in order to perform theirs, had to be trained for it from childhood. . . . I quieted my uneasiness about my own hereditary position by deciding to use it as Plato's leaders did" (*Reader's Digest*, September 1949).

When she was seventeen years old, she was sent to the North Foreland Lodge Girls' School, near Broadstairs, Kent, in England. There she was at the top of her class for five terms. After two years at the school, she went to a girls' agricultural school in Obernkirchen, Germany where she took courses in home and farm economy. Later she attended a school in Florence, Italy; there the girls (many of whom were American) made their own beds and called each other by their first names. The Princess came to be called "Freddy" and even "Fried Egg."

While at school in Florence, Frederika visited her relatives, Princess Helen of Romania and Princess Irene of Greece, sisters of George II, then King of the Hellenes. There she often saw the King's brother, Crown Prince Paul, heir to the Greek throne. After he left Florence, he corresponded with the Princess for about a year. The engagement of Prince

Royal Greek Embassy Inf. Service

QUEEN FREDERIKA

Paul and Princess Frederika (first cousins once removed) was announced at Gmunden in 1937.

The proposed marriage was approved by the royal families concerned, the Hohenzollerns, the Hanovers, the Glücksburgs (who rule Greece) and the Windsors, and on January 9, 1938, the Greek heir apparent and the German Princess were married by the Archbishop of Athens in the Greek Orthodox Church; forty bishops and fifty-five princes and princesses attended.

"I was born a full-blooded barbarian," Frederika once said, "and I came to Greece to be civilized." After her marriage, she began learning the language of her new country, and was received into the Greek Orthodox Church. She and the Crown Prince lived in a small villa at Psychico outside Athens, where their first child, Princess Sophia, was born on November 2, 1938. The present heir to the Greek throne, Prince Constantine, was born there on June 2, 1940.

After Italy attacked Greece in October 1940, Crown Prince Paul became a member of the Greek General Staff, and Princess Frederika headed a drive which gathered woolen clothing valued at $528,576 for the under-equipped Greek Army. She appeared in hospitals and at the front. The army stopped the attack of Mussolini's soldiers and pushed them back into Albanian territory, but when Hitler sent the German Army into Greece, the country was overrun. The Royal Family went first to Crete, then to Egypt, and finally settled in South Africa. There Princess Irene, the godchild of Jan Christiaan Smuts, was born on May 11, 1942 to Princess Frederika and Crown Prince Paul.

(Continued next page)

FREDERIKA, QUEEN—*Continued*

During the four years that the family remained in South Africa, Princess Frederika organized the Crown Princess' Relief Fund, which had branches all over the Western world. The $2,000,000 which the fund collected was used for the immediate relief of the populace after the liberation of Greece in October 1944. The Royal Family returned to their country two years later, after King George II had been recalled to the throne by a plebiscite held in September 1946; they found Greece devastated by World War II and under attack by Communist guerrilla forces.

King George II died on April 1, 1947 and Prince Paul succeeded him as King of the Hellenes; Frederika became Queen. The efforts of the Royal Couple toward ending the war with the Communists and toward strengthening the solidarity of the Greek people and their government were strenuous. In addition to helping in various welfare projects, the Queen traveled with the King all over Greece; they went to the battle fronts in jeeps, crossed mountains on the backs of mules, slept on dirt floors, and ate with the peasants.

One of the Queen's visits to the war fronts particularly endeared her to the people of Greece. When King Paul was sick in bed with typhoid fever in January 1948, the Queen took his place in reviewing the troops at Ioannina. She asked to go also to Kónitsa, where there was fierce fighting between the Greek and Communist forces, but the Greek Commanding General refused. Finally, after the town fell to the Greeks, the General yielded; the Queen was the first civilian to enter the town. The tired soldiers recognized her and cheered. The Queen responded, saying: "My husband is sick and I belong at his bedside, but I think he must love you more than he does me, for he sent me to be with you in his place."

The Communists were finally defeated in Greece in 1949 and the Queen began coordinating the work of all Greek philanthropic organizations to aid in the rehabilitation of her country. The Queen's Fund (which developed from the Crown Princess' Relief Fund) now supports the children's agricultural centers (which give village children technical training and improve their social and living standards), fourteen colonies for orphaned children (an outgrowth of fifty-two emergency colonies founded in July 1947 for children fleeing from the Communists), five children's nurseries, and a home for infants. Queen Frederika often visits these homes and takes an active interest in the children.

The fund gives money for equipping children's hospitals and for helping the Y.W.C.A. The workers in Greece work one Sunday each year and contribute their wages for that day to the Queen's Fund. The Queen once teased her husband: "The workmen often go on strike against you, but for me, they even work on Sundays." She is an honorary president of the Greek Girl Guides Association, and heads the annual "Woolens for Soldiers" drive.

The Greek Royal Couple frequently make state visits. In June 1952 the Queen accompanied her husband on a trip to Turkey at the invitation of the President, Celâl Bayar. She attended the funeral of Queen Mary of Great Britain in March 1953, and in the fall of that year, visited the United States with her husband. They entertained Tito, President of Yugoslavia, in June 1954. The King and Queen in the summer of 1954 had as their guests nearly ninety of their royal relatives on Greece's new liner *Agamemnon* during a cruise through the Greek islands.

"Of course, we are national symbols," Queen Frederika once said of herself and her husband, "but that doesn't mean we must be figureheads." According to William Atwood (*Life*, November 20, 1950), she has tried to influence the selection of prime ministers in Greece. "All that she and Paul have done so far," Atwood wrote, "is indication enough of what a tragedy it would be to Greece if the Queen did not realize that despite all her enormous personal popularity the Greeks, like most peoples today, will not stand for royalty which does not know its place." In late 1953, *Time* commented: "The Royal Couple's unfailing charm and devoted example are still a major factor in the relative contentment of Greece today."

According to Fleur Cowles (*Look*, November 2, 1954), the Queen worries about the problems her children face as royal students and once told them: "You are royal. You'll have less fun than others but you've been chosen—perhaps by God—so be *proud* of it." Crown Prince Constantine attends a school near Athens where boys from "all walks of life" go, and where, in addition to following regular studies, they build their own play fields and have a small garden. The King and Queen plan for him to go to military school and also to work in the mines, fields and factories in order to learn about the Greek people and their problems. The two princesses attend a school in Germany.

"Education in this country is prehistoric," the Queen said once. "The children are crammed with lessons they don't remember. . . . My idea is to start a new modern Greek school, which would run on quite a new system. The present teachers would continue to give book lessons—that is all they know how to give. But there would be new teachers to teach the children how to be decent human beings. They would instill in them a personal responsibility to the community. In our country, freedom has come to be considered as a piece of personal property of the citizen, rather than as a personal responsibility. An ideal democracy is one in which every person carries his share of the burden" (*Look*, October 20, 1953).

Vernon Pizer (*Independent Woman*, October 1952) wrote that the Queen's "sparkling blue eyes, her short brown curls, her dimples, her lissome figure, make her easily one of the most attractive of the royal personalities living today." Queen Frederika speaks English well and uses many American slang expressions which King Paul refers to as the "Queen's English." In her spare time she likes to read or listen to classical music.

The palace in Athens is run with a staff of sixteen members; the Queen is attended by four ladies in waiting. She often "takes over the big kitchen herself to prepare with her own hands the kind of party meal children love" (*Independent Woman*). The children keep their pet dogs, donkeys and ponies at the palace outside Athens in Tatoi. The members of the family usually spend the summer on the island of Petalii where they can enjoy fishing, swimming and sailing.

References

Ind Woman 31:290+ O '52 pors
Life 29:137+ N 20 '50 por
McCall's 81:40+ O '53 por
Read Digest 55:124+ S '49 por
Time 62:35+ O 26 '53

FREEHAFER, EDWARD G(EIER) Feb. 11, 1909- Librarian

Address: b. c/o New York Public Library, 5th Ave. & 42d St., New York 18; h. 205 Carol Ave., Pelham, N.Y.

The world's largest public library system, the New York Public Library, with its renowned reference department and eighty branches in Manhattan, the Bronx and Richmond, is headed by Edward G. Freehafer, the sixth and youngest director in the library's history. Except for a short period at Brown University Library, Freehafer has spent his entire career at the New York Public Library and held among other positions those of chief of personnel and chief of the reference department before being appointed director in December 1954.

More than 1,000,000 readers a year go to the library's central building, famous for its stone lions guarding its Fifth Avenue entrance, in search of "information, inspiration, education, and recreation," as Freehafer has expressed it (New York *World-Telegram and Sun*, February 5, 1955).

Edward Geier Freehafer was born in Reading, Pennsylvania on February 11, 1909, the only child of Edward Franklin Freehafer, a furniture dealer, and Martha Frances (Weitzel) Freehafer. Completing his courses at the Reading High School for Boys in 1926, he entered Brown University in Providence, Rhode Island. With philosophy his major subject and music one of his main extrascholastic interests, he became a member of the Philosophy Club, the University Orchestra, and the University Glee Club. He also belonged to Kappa Sigma fraternity.

During his senior year at Brown, Freehafer became interested in library service and after receiving his B.A. degree in 1930, he worked as a volunteer in the Reading public library. "I wanted to see if I liked the idea of working with books and bringing books together with people," he later told Muriel Fischer of the New York *World-Telegram and Sun* (February 5, 1955). He went to New York to study at the Columbia University School of Library Service, worked in 1931 and 1932 as a student assistant at the university's School of Business library, and was granted his B.S. degree in 1932. Soon afterward he joined the staff of the New York Public Library as an assistant on a summer replacement basis.

The New York Public Library ranks with the Library of Congress and Harvard University Library as one of the three largest in the United States. The consolidation in 1895 of the Lenox Library, the Astor Library and the Tilden Trust formed the basis for the reference department, which is supported by private funds and which has been compared in excellence with the British Museum in London and the Bibliothèque Nationale in Paris. Eighty miles of shelves and stacks are needed to house the department's 3,500,000 books in the library's central building.

The library's eighty branches in Manhattan, the Bronx and Richmond are maintained by the City of New York. (In January 1955 the city's budget director, Abraham D. Beame, suggested a consolidation of the public libraries of New York, Brooklyn and Queens; this proposal was expected to be discussed further later in the year.) The total number of bound volumes and pamphlets owned by the library is about 6,000,000 and it subscribes to 18,137 periodicals. Its circulation figure for the year ending June 1953 was 10,316,580 books.

In 1948 the Central Reference Collection made its first public drive for funds, and since that time individuals, organizations and corporations have contributed approximately $2,000,000 which supplements the endowment funds of the library.

Operating its own printing plant, the library publishes six periodicals and numerous literary research papers. Its permanent exhibitions include the history and development of printing and a collection of United States postage stamps (1850-1926). Among its recent special exhibitions were those on Hans Christian Andersen, Italian political posters, flying, and German book illustration. In the spring of 1955 the library had a major exhibition on baseball, the first of its kind in thirty years. The library also presents recorded daily concerts of less often heard music, held in Bryant Park (next to the library) in warm weather, exhibits of paintings, and motion pictures in its various branches.

Freehafer's first job was "pushing buttons at the delivery desk" in the main reading room at the central building. He served as reference assistant in the main reading room and economics division (with brief experience at the main information desk) from 1932 to 1936, when he became general assistant in the director's office. From 1941 to 1944 he was chief of the American history and genealogy division and from 1942 to 1944 acting chief of the acquisition division.

For fifteen months in 1944 and 1945 Freehafer held the post of assistant librarian of Brown University Library. "I felt a nostalgia for Brown," he said in an interview for the *New Yorker* (January 29, 1955), "and I

Blackstone Studios

EDWARD G. FREEHAFER

thought it might be refreshing to become acquainted with another library's problems. Well, I discovered that Brown had problems similar to those [of the New York Public Library], though on a smaller scale—space, money, and the need for preserving material printed on poor paper."

Freehafer returned to the New York Public Library in 1945 as executive assistant. Two years later, when he was made chief of the newly formed personnel office, he organized a system-wide personnel unit. (The library has over 2,000 employees.) Previously his experience had been in the privately financed reference department. As personnel chief for seven years, he had the opportunity to handle administrative problems in both the central reference department and in the branch libraries supported by public funds.

On January 1, 1954 Freehafer became chief of the reference department, in succession to Paul North Rice. He saw as "the major areas of activity [in this post] the wider development of services to the public and attention to the large problem of procedures for further extending the book collection of over 3,500,000 volumes" (*Bulletin of the New York Public Library*, November 1953).

About a month after beginning his new assignment, Freehafer was called upon to take up the added duties of acting director of the library during the illness of the director, Ralph A. Beals. Beals died on October 14, 1954, and on December 8 Freehafer was appointed to succeed him as director. Morris Hadley, president of the library, quoted the trustees as being confident that they "had picked the best man for the most challenging library post in the world."

Among the problems facing Freehafer was the replacement of the defective fifty-year-old electric system in the stacks. As progressive sections of the shelves were blacked out, boys had the problem of manipulating readers' call slips, a pencil, a flashlight and armloads of books. This was solved by a gift of miners' head lamps from Olin Industries, New Haven, Connecticut. The new electric system cost $77,000.

The library's foremost difficulty, Freehafer explained in an enumeration of current problems, is financial: "Costs have risen out of proportion to income from endowment." The second problem he described as "the need for space to house constantly growing research collections," and added, "the appeal for more community branch libraries is constant." The third problem is "to preserve vast quantities of material now disintegrating because of the poor paper often used for printing during the late nineteenth and early twentieth centuries." Books published before 1860, Freehafer pointed out, have a high rag content and are in less danger of falling apart than more recent books.

The library's 1955 drive for $400,000 was successful, surpassing the goal by $29,178, donated by individuals, firms and foundations.

Since 1951 Freehafer has been a member of the examining committee for public librarians' certificates of the University of the State of New York. He belongs to the Bibliographical Society of America, American Library Association, New York Library Association, New York Library Club and the Grolier Club. He is also a member of Rotary International and the Men's Club of Pelham, New York.

Freehafer and his wife, the former E. Isabel Houck, who was a schoolteacher before her marriage on July 7, 1934, have a fifteen-year-old son, John Geier Freehafer. The librarian is five feet eleven and a half inches tall, weighs 180 pounds and has blue eyes and light-brown hair. He serves as an auxiliary policeman in Pelham and is an elder of the Huguenot Memorial (Presbyterian) Church of that village.

His research in the field of New England history has produced "A Nantucket Ghost Walks Again—Over the Teacups" (*Bulletin of the New York Public Library,* October 1940) and "A Downeaster Aboard Ship, 1843-45" (*Books at Brown*, published by Friends of the Library of Brown University). Two of his hobbies are restoring early American furniture and collecting books in the Pennsylvania Dutch dialect. He is also a bass violist.

While not a "bookworm," Freehafer has said, "I admire, love and respect books and did quite a lot of reading in my youth. But I'm interested in other things as well, even sports" (New York *World-Telegram and Sun*, February 5, 1955). He enjoys playing tennis and watching baseball.

References

Bul of N Y Public Lib 57:567 N '53
Cue 24:13 F 12 '53 por
Library J 80:57 Ja 1 '55
N Y World-Telegram Mag p3 F 5 '55 por
New Yorker 30:16 Ja 29 '55
Pub W 166:2402 D 25 '54
Who's Who in Library Service (1955)

FULBRIGHT, J(AMES) WILLIAM Apr. 9, 1905- United States Senator from Arkansas
Address: b. 259 Senate Office Bldg., Washington 25, D.C.; h. Fayetteville, Ark.

NOTE: This biography supersedes the article which appeared in *Current Biography* in 1943.

The chairman of the Banking and Currency Committee of the U.S. Senate, which opened "a friendly study" of the stock market during March 1955, is the junior Senator from Arkansas, J. William Fulbright. The Senator, a Democrat, is now serving his second term in the upper house of Congress. His earlier political experience consisted of one term as a U.S. Representative, from 1943 to 1945. He has also been an attorney for the U.S. Government, a business man, and a university president, a Rhodes scholar, and has been awarded ten honorary degrees.

Fulbright's name is associated with the Fulbright resolution of 1943, which precipitated the organization of the United Nations, and the Fulbright Act of 1946, which established a program for American scholars to study abroad and foreign students to attend American universities.

Wide World

J. WILLIAM FULBRIGHT

James William Fulbright was born on April 9, 1905 in Sumner, Missouri, the son of Jay and Roberta (Waugh) Fulbright. His father, a farmer, moved his family to Fayetteville, Arkansas in 1906, and there became highly successful. When he died he left his widow and six children interests in a lumber business, farm properties, banks, real estate, a newspaper, and other enterprises. Fulbright's mother assumed the direction of these projects and published the *Northwest Arkansas Times* of Fayetteville.

Young Fulbright attended the University of Arkansas at Fayetteville where he was a member of the football team and senior class president. Following his graduation with the A.B. degree in 1925, he won a Rhodes scholarship to Oxford University in Oxford, England where he achieved honors in history and political science. He also was captain of the Pembroke College team at Oxford and played soccer. He received the B.A. degree in 1928 and the M.A. degree three years later, and an honorary fellowship.

Returning to the United States, he entered the Law School of George Washington University in Washington, D.C., where he received the LL.B. degree with distinction in 1934. He was admitted to the bar of the District of Columbia in 1934 and became an attorney for the Department of Justice. The following year he was an instructor in law at George Washington University, and later joined the law faculty of the University of Arkansas and directed several of his family's businesses. From 1939 to 1941 he served as president of the university. (Accounts of his "dismissal" or "resignation" appear in the *American Magazine,* June 1951 and the *Nation,* February 20, 1954.)

In 1942 Fulbright became a candidate for a seat in the U.S. House of Representatives and was elected from the Third District of Arkansas on November 3. After being sworn in as a member of the House, Fulbright introduced a brief resolution in June 1943 favoring the creation of an international organization dedicated to preserving peace, and to participation by the United States therein. Fulbright stated: "I believe that our recent experiences and the history of government over the centuries, which is largely the chronicle of man's efforts to achieve freedom by the control of arbitrary force, indicate that only by the collective action of a dominant group can security be attained."

The House of Representatives adopted the Fulbright Resolution on September 21, 1943 by a vote of 360 to 29. On November 5, the Senate passed the (Tom) Connally (Democrat of Texas) Resolution, which is similar to the Fulbright declaration, by a vote of 85 to 5.

As a delegate to an international conference on education held in London in 1944, Fulbright proposed a four-point program visualizing the reconstruction of essential educational facilities. The conference adopted his proposals and recommended the establishment of an organization to work for their realization. Its report was the basis for what later became the U.N. Economic and Social Council.

That summer Fulbright became a candidate for the U.S. Senate. He was elected on November 7, 1944, defeating the incumbent, Mrs. Hattie W. Caraway, and Governor Homer M. Adkins. Shortly after taking his Senate seat, he again submitted a brief resolution, "the first to be offered in favor of world freedom of the press" (*Public Men in and out of Office,* 1946).

After the United Nations charter was drafted in 1945, Fulbright expressed disappointment with several features in its structure. One was the concept of national sovereignty. Another was the veto power (*New Republic,* August 6, 1945). Generally, however, he supported the U.N. "It's disappointing," he told Jerome

FULBRIGHT, J. WILLIAM—*Continued*

Beatty, "but what's the alternative—back to tooth and claw? We must keep on trying to make it work" (*American Magazine,* June 1951).

During his first term as a Senator, Fulbright was assigned to the Committees on Banking and Currency, Education and Labor, Public Buildings and Grounds, and Immigration. In the first session of the Seventy-ninth Congress (1945), he voted for an extension of the Trade Agreements Act (June), the United Nations Charter (July) and the U.N. participation bill (December). He voted against an appropriation for the Fair Employment Practice Committee (June) and a reduction in the excess profits tax (July).

In December 1945 an act, providing that credits acquired by the United States through the sale of surplus property abroad be used for the exchange of students and professors to promote international understanding, was introduced by Fulbright. The bill, which is now known as the Fulbright Act, was signed by President Harry S. Truman on August 1, 1946. It grants travel expenses, tuition and maintenance to American scholars for graduate study and research. It also provides traveling expenses for foreign students at American colleges and universities. (A description of the Fulbright Act is in *Collier's Encyclopedia,* 1950-1951).

Fulbright voted affirmatively in the second session of the Seventy-ninth Congress (1946) on the British loan (May), the Case strike control bill (May), and a constitutional amendment granting equality of rights under the law without regard to sex (July). He opposed cloture for an F.E.P.C. filibuster (February) and state title to offshore oil lands (July). In 1947 he voted for the Greek-Turkish aid bill (April) and to override the Presidential veto of the Taft-Hartley bill (June). He opposed the two-term limit for the Presidency (March), the use of private injunctions in jurisdictional strikes (May), limiting foreign relief to $200,-000,000 (May), and granting exemption from antitrust suits to railroads (June).

The Senate roll call indicates that in 1948 Fulbright voted for the tax reduction bill (March), for the Federal aid to education bill (April), to increase the soil conservation fund (May), and to admit 200,000 (as against 100,000) displaced persons (May). He opposed cutting the European Recovery Program appropriation (March).

In January 1949 Fulbright became a member of the Senate Foreign Relations Committee. During the 1949 session he favored a coalition revision of the Taft-Hartley law (June), the North Atlantic Security Pact (July), the foreign military aid bill (September), and the indefinite extension of 90 per cent farm price supports (October). He voted against the prohibition of segregation in public housing (April), and a 50 per cent reduction in European arms aid (September). The next year he supported an appropriation of $45,000,000 for the Point IV Program (May) and a loan of $100,000,000 to Spain (August).

When Fulbright ran for a second term in 1950, he was unopposed. In February 1951, after an investigation by a subcommittee (of the Senate Banking and Currency Committee) which Fulbright headed, he issued a report charging that political pressure and personal favoritism influenced the granting of Reconstruction Finance Corporation loans. Fulbright's conduct of public hearings was praised. He "proved an adroit questioner," *U.S. News & World Report* (March 4, 1955) commented. "With his disarming smile and soft voice, he would reduce a complicated situation to a few simple and devastating questions." On the Senate floor he warned: "Democracy is more likely to be destroyed by the perversion of, or abandonment of, its true moral principles than by armed attack from Russia" (*Time,* April 9, 1951).

In the first session of the Eighty-second Congress (1951), he voted for the draft extension and universal military training bill (March), a bill to reduce Government civilian payrolls by 10 per cent (June), and a tax increase of $5,500,000,000 (September). He opposed bills prohibiting the sending of additional troops to Europe without Congressional consent (April), authorizing rent increases up to 37 per cent (June), and placing an absolute ban on Allied trade with the Soviet bloc (August).

In the second session (1952) he approved the granting of power to the President to seize steel plants (June), use of the Taft-Hartley law in the steel strike (June), and overriding of the President's veto of the McCarran-Walter immigration bill (June). On these measures he voted negatively: a bill to abolish the RFC (April) and a bill to end wage and price controls on June 30, 1952 (May).

The following year (1953) Fulbright voted to confirm Charles E. Bohlen as envoy to the U.S.S.R. (March), to return Senator Wayne Morse (of Oregon) to his former committee posts (May), and to admit 209,000 Iron Curtain refugees (July). He voted against the offshore oil bill (May) and a penalty against nations trading with the Communist bloc (July).

In the second session of the Eighty-third Congress (1954) he voted to liberalize Congressional pensions (February), to build 140,000 public housing units (June), to revise the Atomic Energy Act (July), and to make membership in the Communist party a crime (August). He voted against the St. Lawrence seaway bill (January), the Bricker treaty amendment (February), and statehood for Hawaii and Alaska (April).

On February 2, 1954 Fulbright cast the sole vote in opposition to granting an appropriation of $214,000 to the permanent subcommittee on investigations (of the Senate Government Operations Committee), then headed by Senator Joseph R. McCarthy (Republican of Wisconsin). On July 31, in response to protests that the resolution submitted by Senator Ralph E. Flanders (Republican of Vermont) calling for the censure of McCarthy was not specific enough to support such action, Fulbright offered an amendment listing six specific charges.

On March 3, 1955 the Senate Banking and Currency Committee, under Fulbright's chairmanship, began three weeks of hearings on the rise in stock market prices between September 1953 and January 1955. After these hearings the Federal Reserve Board on April 22 raised margin (down payment) requirements in the stock market from 60 to 70 per cent, in an effort to restrain speculation. The order applied only to future purchases of stock. In July the committee opened hearings on a bill introduced by Fulbright to bring under the regulation of the Securities and Exchange Commission all issues traded on the unlisted or over-the-counter market. The bill excludes securities of those companies with less than $5,000,000 in assets, or with fewer than 500 security holders. Thus, some 1,500 additional companies would have to file with the SEC, regular financial statements, annual reports, proxy information and reports on inside trading. (This bill is now pending).

The roll call for 1955 indicates that the Senator favored increasing Congressional salaries (February), a $20 income tax cut (March), and overriding the Presidential veto of the postal pay bill (May). He was recorded against the Administration's highway bill (May). In June he opposed limiting public housing to 70,000 units, the atoms-for-peace ship, and supported maintaining the Marines at their present strength of about 215,000 men. Aside from his chairmanship of the Banking and Currency Committee, Fulbright is presently serving on the Senate Foreign Relations Committee.

Senator Fulbright is a member of Sigma Chi, Phi Delta Phi, Phi Beta Kappa, the Order of the Coif, and the Rotary Club of Fayetteville. He married the former Elizabeth Kremer Williams on June 15, 1932; the Fulbrights have two daughters, Elizabeth Williams and Roberta Waugh Fulbright. His religious affiliation is with the Disciples of Christ Church.

Jerome Beatty described him in these words: "He is nearly six feet tall, lithe, gentle, quiet, modest, and moves with the relaxation of a trained athlete. . . . He accomplishes effortlessly an enormous amount of work. . . . Week-end golf and long walks keep him in good physical condition."

References

Am Mag 151:26+ Je '51 por
Colliers 115:14+ F 10 '45 por
N Y Times Mag p 17+ Mr 6 '55 por
Nation 178:146+ F 20 '54
Biographical Directory of the American Congress, 1774-1949 (1950)
International Who's Who, 1954
National Cyclopædia of American Biography Current Vol. G. (1943-46)
Salter, J. T., ed. Public Men In and Out of Office (1946)
Who's Who in America, 1954-55
World Biography (1954)

FUNK, WILFRED (JOHN) Mar. 20, 1883- Writer; editor; publisher

Address: b. 270 Park Ave., New York 17; h. 16 Erwin Park Rd., Montclair, N.J.

Evidence that thousands of people are interested in acquiring a larger vocabulary may be seen in the wide sale of books by Dr. Wilfred Funk, lexicographer and publisher. For a decade he has contributed to the *Reader's Digest* the popular feature, "It Pays to Increase Your Word Power," which tests the reader's linguistic knowledge. His book, *30 Days to a More Powerful Vocabulary,* prepared in collaboration with Norman Lewis, first published in 1942 (latest reprint, 1954), has sold more than 1,400,000 copies.

Books of similar purpose by Funk include *The Way to Vocabulary Power and Culture* (1946) which is now in its tenth printing, *Word Origins and Their Romantic Stories* (1950) and *Six Weeks to Words of Power* (1953). A "master of the champagne touch," Funk knows how to bring excitement to authoritative material based on conscientious research. Readers testify to the entertaining value as well as the usefulness of his books which "give a better understanding of language, inculcate a love for words, and help to improve one's speaking and writing." Funk has been fascinated by the way in which words take on new meanings, how the language shifts, changes and grows.

For fifteen years (1925-1940) Funk was president of the publishing firm of Funk & Wagnalls. He established a publishing house under his own name in 1940 and has since devoted his attention to writing books nearer the tradition of his father, who had been founder and editor in chief of Funk & Wagnalls Standard Dictionary Series. He has written several collections of light verse. He was on the editorial staff of the *Literary Digest* for many years and later became the owner of several magazines, including *Your Life.*

The name of Funk was already a distinguished one in the field of publishing when Wilfred John Funk was born on March 20, 1883 in Brooklyn, New York, the son of Isaac Kaufman and Helen Gertrude (Thompson) Funk. His father in 1876 had founded a publishing firm which two years later was reorganized as Funk & Wagnalls. Among the widely read publications of this company have been the *Homiletic Review,* the *Literary Digest,* Emily Post's blue book of etiquette, the Standard Dictionary Series and a number of encyclopedias.

In his high school years at Adelphi Academy in Brooklyn, New York, and at Choate School in Wallingford, Connecticut and St. Paul's, Concord, New Hampshire, Wilfred Funk found football and debating his most enjoyable extra-scholastic activities. From childhood he had wanted to be a writer and publisher, and while studying in Princeton University he majored in English, edited a literary magazine and was class poet. He also belonged to Dial Lodge and played on the golf team.

(Continued next page)

WILFRED FUNK

Leaving Princeton in 1909 with a Litt.B. degree, he entered his father's publishing company, where he was given a variety of assignments, including directing the work of the educational department and preparing advertising copy. He is said to have been one of the most skillful mail-order letter writers of the day. When his father died in 1912, Funk became secretary of Funk & Wagnalls. Two years later he was advanced to vice-president and in 1925 began his fifteen years in the office of president.

Some years earlier Funk had joined the staff of the *Literary Digest* and while sharing the editorial responsibilities he wrote many poems for its pages, as well as for other nationally circulated magazines like *Good Housekeeping*. These verses, with additions, were later collected and published in several volumes. The humorous and satirical *Manhattans, Bronxes and Queens,* a 1931 publication of Robert M. McBride & Company, was written to show "one side of Manhattan—the light, sophisticated, supposedly smart and—somewhat—amusing."

Two other books of Funk's poetry published by McBride are *Light Lines and Dears* (1932) and *It Might be Verse* (1938). *Love, Life and Laughter* (1942, E. P. Dutton & Company) is a complete collection of his poems. "Quite good journalism this. Nothing more" was the comment of the *Saturday Review of Literature* (January 21, 1933) on *Light Lines and Dears.* Other critics admired Funk's quick changes of pace and mood and compared him, to advantage, with English poet Austin Dobson as an author of light verse.

So You Think It's New (Funk & Wagnalls, 1937) was Wilfred Funk's first volume of prose. It cited historical facts to show that ancient civilizations were familiar with many of the practices and devices generally thought to belong only to contemporary culture. "If Mr. Funk stretches a parallel now and then," observed the New York *Herald Tribune* reviewer (November 14, 1937), "it will hardly disturb those who tackle this volume either for information or for merriment."

His second book of prose, *When the Merry-Go-Round Breaks Down*! (Funk & Wagnalls, 1938) is a collection of excerpts from the press for the years during which the United States suffered its major depressions. Each of the half dozen economic crises from 1836 to 1937 was considered "the worst depression in the history of the world."

For a short time during this period of creative output in poetry and prose, Funk was editor in chief of *Literary Digest* (1936-37). After that magazine was purchased by the *Review of Reviews,* he established the Kingsway Press, of which he is president and director. He is also president and director of Yourself Publications, Your Health Publications and Publications Management; co-owner and vice-president of *Success Today* and *Marriage*; and owner and editorial director of *Your Life, Your Health, Your Personality* and *Woman's Life.* The best known of these publications, *Your Life* (founded in 1937), offers "articles by experts on your financial success, your charm, your children, your health, your love-life, your personality, your happiness. 'Easy to take,' but addressed to the 'live-minded reader'" (*Periodical Handbook,* 1954).

While continuing his interest in the Kingsway Press, Funk resigned from the presidency of Funk & Wagnalls in April 1940 and announced his intention of founding a new publishing house, Wilfred Funk, Inc., in New York, to issue both fiction and nonfiction books. The first volume under Funk's authorship produced by this firm was *If You Drink* (1940), an informative discussion of the effects of alcohol upon the human body and a plea for moderation in drinking. Harry Hansen of the New York *World-Telegram* (September 17, 1940) described it as a "temperance tract" and a "chatty book." The light touch that Funk gives to all his writing was noted by the Springfield *Republican* reviewer (November 4, 1940), "If one never drank a drop he would still get a lot of enjoyment from reading this book."

With the publication in 1942 of *30 Days to a More Powerful Vocabulary,* Funk made a strong claim for a recognized place in the field of word study, which has been generally associated with his family name. This practical guide in vocabulary building, prepared in collaboration with Norman Lewis, has sold nearly 1,500,000 copies.

Notably illustrative of Funk's skill in combining meticulous scholarship with entertaining factual exposition is his *Word Origins and Their Romantic Stories* (1950). Instead of listing his 3,000 words in the usual alphabetical order, he organized his material into about a dozen categories to cover such groupings as "Romance behind business terms," "Word stories of your garden," and "Political terms and their origins." The result of extensive research by Funk and much re-checking by linguistic scientists, the book was praised in the Springfield *Republican* (May 7, 1950) as an aid in "the quest for new values in language."

"We are accustomed to think of our miscellaneous and polyglot speech as the 'English' language," wrote Funk, "yet it is doubtful whether more than one word in fifty in our vocabulary actually originated in that little patch of island we call England."

Dr. Funk (he owes his title to an honorary Litt. D. degree conferred by Oglethorpe University in 1932) has been a member since the spring of 1946 of the board of trustees of the public library in Montclair, New Jersey, where he has made his home for many years. He belongs to the Author's League, Players, Banshees, National Press Club (Washington, D.C.), Linguistic Society of America, Society of Illustrators, Artists and Writers, Circus Saints and Sinners, Baker Street Irregulars, and Montclair Golf Club. His clubs in Southampton, Long Island, where he has a summer residence, are the National Golf, Meadow, Southampton and Southampton Yacht.

He was married on July 29, 1915 to Eleanor McNeal (Hawkins). They have three children: Peter Van Keuren, Eleanor Joan and Sally McNeal. Another son, Wilfred John Funk, Jr., was killed in action during World War II. The author-publisher has green eyes and gray-brown hair, and stands five feet nine inches tall, with a weight of 156 pounds. His church is the Episcopal. He votes as an independent Democrat.

The world of words is a fascinating one to Funk. "I wish that the reader might be encouraged to walk among words as I do," he wrote in the preface of one of his books, "like Alice in Wonderland, amazed at the marvels they hold."

References

N Y Times p21 Ap 12 '40 por
Pub W 137:1587+ Ap 20 '40 por; 149: 3032 Je 8 '46
Who's Who in America, 1954-55
Who's Who in New York, 1952
World Biography (1954)

GARBO, GRETA Sept. 18, 1905- Actress
Address: c/o Metro-Goldwyn-Mayer Studios, 10202 W. Washington Blvd., Culver City, Calif.

Fourteen years after her retirement from motion pictures, Greta Garbo in 1955 remains the favorite actress of millions of fans in many countries. "[She] is still rated by many as Hollywood's most beautiful, glamorous and outstanding star," Nathaniel Benchley observed in a *Collier's* article, "and her activities, no matter how trivial, are considered legitimate news by the European and American press." A full-length biography, *Garbo,* written by John Bainbridge, was published by Doubleday in March 1955.

During her sixteen-year association with Metro-Goldwyn-Mayer, she starred in some twenty-four motion pictures. A revival in February 1955 of *Camille,* produced in 1936, has shown, as Ed Sullivan expressed it, that "Garbo's box office appeal apparently is indestructible." At the Trans-Lux Normandie theatre in New York it played to a capacity audience, grossing more than $19,700 in its first week. *Ninotchka,* a 1939 comedy, is another of the Garbo pictures successfully re-released since her last film, *Two-Faced Woman,* was made in 1941.

Born Greta Lovisa Gustafsson on September 18, 1905 in Stockholm, Sweden, Greta Garbo is the daughter of Karl and Anna Gustafsson. She had an older sister, Alva, and a brother, Sven. She grew up in a somewhat shabby section of the city and in childhood enjoyed winter sports like sledding and skating. From the age of seven she attended the Catherine Elementary School, and soon after graduating at fourteen, she was confirmed in the Swedish State Church.

Her father died the year she finished school and Greta found it necessary to go to work. While making plans to become an actress, she was employed as a latherer in a barbershop, as a clerk in Bergstrom's department store, and as a model. A chance meeting at the store with actor-director Erik Petschler led to her first motion picture role, that of a bathing beauty in a 1922 comedy, *Peter the Tramp.*

With Petschler's help she was admitted to Stockholm's Royal Dramatic Theatre School, where she studied for two seasons (1922-1924). In 1923 she was introduced to Mauritz Stiller, the foremost director in the Swedish film industry. He gave Miss Gustafsson the name Greta Garbo, cast her in *The Story of Gösta Berling,* and became a strong influence during her training as an actress. He accompanied his protégée to Berlin in 1925, where she played in a film directed by G. W. Pabst which was later seen in the United States under the title *Streets of Sorrow.*

When Stiller was offered a three-year contract in 1925 with Metro-Goldwyn-Mayer, he insisted that the studio also give a contract to Greta Garbo, whom he described as "an actress who will be the greatest in the world" (*Life,* January 17, 1955). They arrived in New York in July 1925 and in Hollywood two months later, with Garbo under a MGM contract for $400 weekly.

Garbo's first American picture was *The Torrent* (1926), in which she appeared opposite Ricardo Cortez as a Spanish peasant girl who became an opera star. Its success led MGM to cast her in a similar type of movie, *The Temptress.* Stiller was chosen to direct the film, but was withdrawn from that assignment after a few days. Before returning in 1928 to Sweden, where he died soon afterward, he continued to help guide her career.

The Flesh and the Devil, based on Hermann Sudermann's novel *The Undying Past* and directed by Clarence Brown, was released in early 1927 and at once proved to be a tremendous box office hit. Garbo in the role of the

Wide World

GRETA GARBO

seductress Felicitas was "undeniably alluring," as one critic remarked. Her association with John Gilbert, who had the male lead, became both off and on the screen one of Hollywood's most highly publicized romances.

Following the release of *The Flesh and the Devil,* Garbo, whose weekly salary in 1927 had risen to $750, negotiated a new contract with MGM whereby she would eventually receive $5,000 a week. (By the mid-1930's she was reportedly earning from $250,000 to $300,000 a picture.) Among her movies seen in 1929 were *Wild Orchids* and *The Single Standard,* both co-starring Nils Asther; *The Divine Woman,* based on the life of Sarah Bernhardt; and *A Woman of Affairs.* One of her last silent films, *The Kiss,* was made soon after her return in 1929 from a visit to Stockholm.

The screen adaptation of Eugene O'Neill's *Anna Christie* (1930), Garbo's first sound picture, was widely advertised by MGM with the slogan "Garbo Talks." In a review for the New York *Herald Tribune* (March 15, 1930), Richard Watts, Jr., described the star's voice "as a deep, husky, throaty contralto that possesses every bit of that fabulous, poetic glamour that has made her the outstanding performer of the motion picture."

In the early 1930's moviegoers saw her in *Romance* (1930), with Clark Gable in *Susan Lennox—Her Fall and Rise* (1931), with Robert Montgomery in *Inspiration* (1931), with Ramon Novarro in *Mata Hari* (1932), as the famous dancer and spy, and with Melvyn Douglas in Luigi Pirandello's *As You Desire Me.* She played one of the main characters, Grusinskaya, in Vicki Baum's *Grand Hotel,* which won the award of the Academy of Motion Picture Arts and Sciences as the best picture of 1932.

After finishing her work in *Grand Hotel,* Garbo made another visit to Sweden, where she spent some time collecting information about Queen Christina and her reign, for Hollywood writers to use in preparing a script. Her reportedly long-standing ambition to play the part of the Swedish Queen was realized in 1933. At Garbo's request, John Gilbert was given the leading male role in *Queen Christina.* One press notice stated that as Christina she reached "the height of her dramatic genius." A New York *Herald Tribune* reviewer noted, "For breath-taking beauty, the final close-up of Miss Garbo in *Queen Christina* has generally been accepted as the high point of recent cinema achievement."

MGM's presentation of Somerset Maugham's *The Painted Veil,* with Garbo and George Brent, was released in 1934. The following year, appearing with Fredric March and Freddie Bartholomew, she had the title role in *Anna Karenina,* for which she won the New York Film Critics Award. *Love,* a 1927 version of Tolstoy's tragic novel, had been one of the very popular Garbo-Gilbert films. Richard Watts, Jr., thought "the present version definitely its superior in every way." The New York *Times* critic Andre Sennwald found *Anna Karenina* to be "a dignified and effective drama which becomes significant because of that tragic, lonely and glamorous blend which is the Garbo personality."

She also won the New York Film Critics Award for her work in *Camille,* a 1936 screen production of the drama and novel of Alexandre Dumas fils, which presented Garbo as Marguerite Gautier and Robert Taylor as Armand Duval. Howard Barnes of the New York *Herald Tribune* spoke of "the sheer magic of her acting" and of her "magnificent and unforgettable performance." Her next role was Marie Walewska in *Conquest* (1937), with Charles Boyer as Napoleon.

Under the direction of Ernst Lubitsch, Garbo in 1939 played her first comedy part, the title role in *Ninotchka,* a gay satire on Bolshevism. "The great actress reveals a command of comic inflection which fully matches the emotional depths or tragic power of her earlier triumphs," Howard Barnes commented. "It is a joyous, subtly shaded and utterly enchanting portrayal. . . ." When *Ninotchka* was revived in 1947, it was enthusiastically received in the United States. The next year it had record-breaking runs in Italy, where at the request of the U.S. State Department, MGM sent thirty-five prints for showing during an electioneering period.

Two-Faced Woman (1941), Garbo's second comedy, has been called her only unsuccessful picture. Upon its release in November 1941, it was given a "C or Condemned" classification by the National Legion of Decency. MGM then made several changes to remove objectionable features, but the critics found little to praise in the movie. "Miss Garbo's current attempt to trip the light fantastic," a New York *Times* reviewer wrote, "is one of the awkward exhibitions of the season."

Garbo, at thirty-six, withdrew from the field of entertainment. Some Hollywood observers attributed her retirement to the unfavorable notices given her last picture. Others pointed out that World War II had brought about the loss of the European market, which accounted for half the profits from her pictures. Since 1941 there have been many reports and rumors of her return to the screen. In 1949 she went to Italy under contract to producer Walter Wanger to be filmed in Balzac's *La Duchesse de Langeais*. After some delay, this project was given up.

Frequent revivals of her pictures, especially at the Museum of Modern Art Film Library in New York, have made her work known to the new generation of moviegoers. In 1950 *Daily Variety* published the results of a poll in which men and women who have been in the film industry for more than twenty-five years named Garbo as the best actress of the half century. George Cukor, who directed *Camille* and *Two-Faced Woman*, once said, "She can walk across a set and give every other actress in the world a lesson in grace and poise."

It was reported in 1952 that she had refused an offer of $18,000 to do a television version of *Anna Karenina*. The success of the revival of *Camille* in 1955 gave rise to many rumors about the possibility of Garbo pictures soon being seen on TV.

Off screen, both before and since her retirement, Garbo has been a legendary figure, the subject of many fabulous, often contradictory, reports. This is due partly to early publicity stories from Hollywood which created an image of the star as a "mysterious stranger." Garbo herself, less outgoing in personality than an actress is expected to be, has been reluctant to face newsmen and offer accurate information about her activities. "It is a paradox," noted a New York *Herald Tribune* writer (July 1, 1951), "that by dodging publicity she has become one of the most publicized women of the world."

During an infrequent press interview, on her arrival from Sweden in 1946, she told newsmen, "I haven't been elusive. Being in the newspapers is awfully silly to me. Anyone who does a job properly has a right to privacy. You'd think the same if you were in the same boat" (New York *Times*, September 4, 1946). She became a United States citizen in 1951 and in recent years has lived most of the time in New York City, sometimes using the pseudonym Harriet Brown.

"No woman lives who would not change her face for Garbo's," photographer Antony Beauchamp believes. Considered one of the world's most beautiful women, she has purple-blue eyes and brown hair, is five feet seven inches tall and weighs about 127 pounds. She wears little make-up and favors tailored clothes. Her facial expressions, mannerisms and hair styles have been copied by many of her fans and by a large number of other actresses.

References

Colliers 129:13+ Mr 1 '52 pors
Life 38:84+ Ja 10; 38:76+ Ja 17; 38:113+ Ja 24 '55 pors
N Y Times Mag p4+ Ja 14 '40 pors
Bainbridge, J. Garbo (1955)
Laing, E. E. Greta Garbo; the Story of a Specialist (1946)
Motion Picture and Television Almanac, 1953-54
Who's Who in America, 1954-55
World Biography (1948)

GARY, RAYMOND Jan. 21, 1908- Governor of Oklahoma

Address: Executive Mansion, Oklahoma City, Okla.

Elected to office by the largest majority of any Oklahoma governor since 1938, Democrat Raymond Gary began his four-year administration on January 10, 1955 with strong public backing for a program which had as one of its main provisions immediate consideration of a state constitutional amendment to prepare the way for ending segregation in public schools. Gary had previously served for fourteen years in the state Senate, where he was known as "a serious student of government" (New York *Times,* November 14, 1954).

Governor Gary, in answer to a highly critical *Saturday Evening Post* article on April 30, 1955, entitled "Oklahoma is in a Mess," by his predecessor, Governor Johnston Murray, stoutly defended his state in "I Say Oklahoma's O.K.!" which appeared in the *Saturday Evening Post* (July 9, 1955). "This is a young and vigorous state—from 'tepees to towers' in less than fifty years of statehood," he emphasized. "We have muscles we haven't used yet." After discussing Oklahoma's advancements in industry, agriculture, and social welfare, he concluded, "Many of our problems are mere growing pains, for we have not yet even approached our full potential." Oklahoma, comprising an area of 69,919 square miles in the Southwest, had a population in 1950 of 2,233,351 inhabitants. (The 1954 census shows an increase of some 24,000.) Efforts are being made, Gary said, to bring in new industries to balance agriculture and the state has embarked on "the most ambitious highway program in its history."

Raymond Gary, who has said that he is part Cherokee Indian, was born on January 21, 1908 on a farm in Marshall County, Oklahoma. Before making government and politics his career, he taught school and served as county superintendent. This experience later proved valuable to him in writing school legislation in the Oklahoma Senate, of which he became a member in 1940.

As chairman of the Senate's appropriations committee for three sessions, Gary also had an important role in planning the state's financial program. In his article for the *Saturday Evening Post* he referred to his fourteen years as a state senator and wrote in defense of his colleagues, "I have served with many of our

Wide World

RAYMOND GARY

present legislators, and know them well. They are not all great statesmen, but neither are they crooks or clowns. . . . I know the great majority are hard-working, conscientious public servants, sometimes little appreciated for the service they give the state."

Gary was holding the title of president pro tempore of the Senate when he became the Democratic candidate for Governor in 1954. In the November election he defeated his Republican opponent, Reuben Sparks, by more than 106,000 votes. Soon after his victory he stated that one of the most important problems of his administration would be revision of Oklahoma laws to conform to the U.S. Supreme Court decision outlawing segregation in public schools.

Since the banning of segregation would necessitate a change in the financial structure for maintaining public schools, Gary explained, the legislature would have to submit a constitutional amendment at a special election. Such an amendment was submitted on April 5, 1955 and was decisively approved by Oklahoma voters. "The amendment's passage was a big victory for Governor Raymond Gary," the New York *Times* (April 6, 1955) noted, "who had practically staked the reputation of his administration by putting all of his support behind the proposal."

Further progress was made toward ending segregation the following June when the Oklahoma state Board of Regents for higher education voted to admit Negroes to all state colleges and universities. Previously, undergraduate Negro students had been required to attend Langston University, a segregated school, although for several years graduate schools in state universities had been open to Negroes.

Another constitutional amendment that Gary has urged is that the state legislature prevent road-user funds from being diverted to other departments. In a pre-inauguration statement he spoke of his belief that during his administration he would have $220,000,000 available for a highway program. He later declared, "In the next four years we will build a minimum of 2,500 miles of new state highways, plus several hundred bridges, adding approximately 25 per cent to our present mileage—without increasing taxes or floating bonds" (*Saturday Evening Post,* July 9, 1955). Among the road development projects being considered by the state legislature, as reported in the New York *Times* (May 15, 1955), were an extension of the Turner Turnpike to link Tulsa, Oklahoma with Joplin, Missouri, and a new toll road from the turnpike to the Texas border.

Speaking at the Governors Conference held in Chicago in August 1955, Gary recommended that the Governors ask the Federal Government to turn gasoline taxes back to the states for highway purposes, and to underwrite bonds for toll-road construction up to 25 per cent of their value (New York *Times,* August 11, 1955).

Governor Gary was among the witnesses who testified in behalf of independent oil producers in mid-March 1955 in Washington, D.C. before the Senate Finance Committee, which was conducting hearings on the Administration foreign trade bill. While he indicated approval of the general principles of the reciprocal trade agreements extension bill, he urged the adoption of an amendment limiting foreign oil imports to 10 per cent of domestic consumption. Calling attention to an increase of 156.25 per cent in unemployment in Oklahoma's oil industry during 1954 and a decrease of 16,021,000 barrels in oil production, he said that "cheap foreign oil produced by cheap foreign labor threatens the entire domestic industry (New York *Times,* March 16, 1955).

Oil, along with natural gas, is one of Oklahoma's most important sources of income. Since the sinking of the first oil wells in 1901, six years before Oklahoma was admitted to the Union, oil has greatly influenced the economy of the plains state and has led to the growth of large cities like Tulsa and Oklahoma City. Gary is not in agreement with Oklahoma's strict policy of oil conservation. "I have argued for a raise in the oil 'allowable' to keep Oklahoma's share in the market," he has explained. "While we have [conserved] our oil, increasing our daily output only 10 per cent since 1935, Texas' production has tripled, Kansas' has doubled, New Mexico's has almost quadrupled and Louisiana's has quintupled" (*Saturday Evening Post,* July 9, 1955).

One of the nation's foremost winter wheat producing states, Oklahoma ranked third in 1953 with 70,776,000 bushels. Other important crops are rye, corn, cotton and sorghum. Cycles of insufficient rainfall, especially in the panhandle area, periodically threaten the state's agricultural production and have made Oklahoma part of the so-called "Dust Bowl" of the Southwest. According to *Business Week* (June 18, 1955), although the drought of the past five years—"in terms of its dryness and its winds—may be just as bad as those of the 1930s, its effects have been nowhere near so severe."

Irrigation has done much to improve the condition of Oklahoma farmers, but Gary, as *Business Week* reported, recently pointed out that the water table in his state's Texas County dropped three feet in the past year. "We will have to learn water conservation, too," he said, and announced that he would urge the legislature to overhaul the water and soil conservation laws.

Gary, having promised the voters during his gubernatorial campaign that there would be no rise in taxes, is proud that he is one of a small number of Governors in the United States who did not ask their legislatures for a major tax increase in 1955. He discussed in the *Saturday Evening Post* his attitude toward Oklahoma's practice of operating on a "pay-as-you-go" basis: "The legislature cannot appropriate more money than the average annual expenditures of the previous three years. This makes us tighten our belts sometimes, but it also keeps our feet on the ground in an era when the Federal debt continues to soar and many a state also is going deep into the red."

A prosperous businessman, Governor Gary operates a company which distributes wholesale and retail petroleum products in Texas and Oklahoma. He also has agricultural interests. He is married and lives on a 420-acre farm in Marshall county.

Reference

N Y Times p58 N 14 '54

GEORGE, WALTER F(RANKLIN) Jan. 29, 1878- United States Senator from Georgia; former judge

Address: b. Senate Office Bldg., Washington 25, D.C.; h. Vienna, Ga.; The Mayflower, Washington 6, D.C.

NOTE: This biography supersedes the article which appeared in *Current Biography* in 1943.

In length of continuous service now the senior member of the U.S. Senate, Democrat Walter F. George of Georgia was first elected to the upper chamber of the Federal legislature in November 1922. Thus began an uninterrupted service of over thirty-two years in which he has distinguished himself on many important committees. As the chairman of the Foreign Relations Committee in the Eighty-fourth Congress convened in January 1955, he wields much influence with both Democrats and Republicans and has been called "the king-pin of the bipartisan foreign policy." He is leading the movement in the Senate for a negotiated cease-fire with the Chinese Communists.

As president pro tempore of the Senate, George is third in line of succession to the Presidency. He presides over the Senate in the absence of Vice-President Richard M. Nixon. His speech in the Senate in January 1955 favoring the Formosa resolution is regarded as "a showpiece of bipartisanship." His proposal for a Big Four conference, made on a television program in March, made headlines around the world and sent "the White House and State Department (and apparently the Kremlin) into a furious reappraisal of the subject" (*Collier's*, May 13, 1955). (Such a conference "at the summit" was held in Geneva, Switzerland in July 1955.)

Over the years Senator George has been an advocate of reciprocal trade, Lend-Lease, United Nations, good-neighbor policy and the North Atlantic Treaty. "In the cold war George has endorsed Greek-Turkish aid, the Truman Doctrine and the Marshall Plan, and supported President Truman's decision to oppose the Communists in Korea. . . . On the Far East his outlook follows the Democratic, rather than right-wing Republican philosophy. He opposed U.S. intervention in Indochina and a naval blockade of the Chinese coast" (*Collier's*, May 13, 1955).

Walter Franklin George was born on January 29, 1878 near Preston, Georgia. He was the elder of the two children born to Robert Theodric and Sarah (Stapleton) George, who were respectively of Welsh and English ancestry. His father was a tenant farmer near Preston in southwestern Georgia. Walter began his education in a country grade school in Webster county and completed his secondary schooling at Houston Institute near Cordele in nearby Crisp county.

His early ambition was to practice dentistry, but his success at the age of fifteen as a substitute speaker at a Masonic meeting turned his thoughts to the legal profession. As an undergraduate at Mercer University, a Baptist institution at Macon, he won medals for extempore speaking in four successive years. At Atlanta in his twentieth year he gained the southern intercollegiate oratorical championship with an address on the U.S. Constitution.

Having taken his B.S. degree at Mercer in 1900 and his B.L. in 1901, George began law practice in Vienna (the Dooly county seat, not far from Cordele, and his legal place of residence ever since). Within five years he had "cornered so much practice that some lawyers . . . [asked] him to run for city solicitor, in the hope that these duties would keep him so busy that more cases would fall to them" (Rufus Jarman in the *Saturday Evening Post*, May 19, 1945). The young lawyer waged instead a successful campaign for solicitor general (a post he held from 1907 to 1912) for the Cordele Judiciary Circuit.

George became judge of the Superior Court of the Cordele Circuit in 1912 and a judge of Georgia's Court of Appeals in January 1917. In October 1917 he was appointed to a vacancy on the Supreme Court of Georgia and was subsequently twice elected to regular terms on this bench.

Having resigned from his state's Supreme Court early in 1922, George resumed private practice for a brief period. When Georgia's U.S. Senator Thomas E. Watson died later in the year, George became a candidate for Watson's unexpired term. He was elected by

Wide World

WALTER F. GEORGE

a landslide vote on November 7, 1922 and took his seat in the Senate on November 22. George was elected to a full Senate term in 1926 and was re-elected in 1932, 1938, 1944, and 1950.

In his Senate career he has been a member of twelve committees and chairman of five. He was assigned to the Finance Committee in 1926 and two years later to the Foreign Relations Committee.

At the Democratic National Convention of 1928 he received 52½ votes as a "favorite son" candidate for the Presidential nomination. He defended the right of "the Wets . . . to oppose the Eighteenth Amendment and the Volstead Act" (although he was himself a teetotaler) and he campaigned in behalf of his party's nominee, Governor Alfred E. Smith of New York.

Although a "states-righter" as well as a conservative, who opposed the nomination of Franklin D. Roosevelt in 1932, George subsequently voted for much New Deal legislation including the Agricultural Adjustment Act, the Tennessee Valley Authority Act and the National Industrial Recovery Act (1933); the Securities Exchange Act (1934); and the Social Security Act (1935). He voted against the anti-lynching bill (1935), the Guffey coal bill (1936), and the wage-hour bill (1938).

Spearheading the Senate opposition to President Roosevelt's Supreme Court enlargement bill in 1937, George made a nation-wide radio address against the measure. Although Roosevelt endorsed Georgia's New Dealer Lawrence Camp for Senator in 1938, George won two-thirds of the state's counties in the November balloting.

George was given the chairmanship of the Senate Foreign Relations Committee in November 1940. He shared with Senator Alben W. Barkley of Kentucky the leadership of the successful fight for passage of the Lend-Lease Act (1941).

George also favored the Hull reciprocal trade agreements. In August 1941 he resigned the Foreign Relations Committee chairmanship to accept that of the Senate Finance Committee.

He kept a watchful eye on Treasury requests and military expenses. He assailed the OPA as a threat to free enterprise and was regarded as largely responsible for the adoption in 1943 of the compromise "pay-as-you-go" income tax measure substituted for the (Beardsley) Ruml Plan. He favored a wartime Federal sales tax. In April 1945 George sponsored the act which provided for social security payments to servicemen.

In January 1946 George opposed a Truman Administration fair employment practices bill and defended the right to filibuster. In general in the Seventy-ninth Congress he "provided with others the hard core of most of the opposition to the Fair Deal" (*U.S. News*, April 15, 1949).

When the G.O.P. organized the Eightieth Congress in January 1947 he yielded the Finance Committee chairmanship to Republican Eugene D. Millikan of Colorado. George continued to urge that taxes be kept down as far as was consistent with the national safety. With the return of the Democrats to the control of Congress in January 1949, George resumed the Finance Committee chairmanship.

In Senate roll calls he voted against forbidding segregation in public housing (April 1949) and against federal aid for the needy disabled (June 1950). He supported a $100,000,000 loan for the Franco government in Spain (August 1950) and did not favor an absolute ban on Allied trade with the Soviet bloc nations (August 1951) or a liberal substitute for the immigration bill (May 1952).

In July 1952 George made the speech which placed the Presidential candidacy of his junior colleague, Senator Richard B. Russell, before the Democratic National Convention. When the Republicans gained control of Congress in the 1952 elections George gave up his chairmanship to Millikan but continued to serve on the Finance Committee as well as on the Foreign Relations Committee.

When the so-called "Bricker amendment" to limit the President's treaty-making powers came before the Senate in February 1954, George offered a compromise proposal stipulating that "an international agreement other than a treaty shall become effective as an internal law of the United States only by an Act of Congress." The substitute did not have sufficient support to be sent by Congress to the states for consideration. Also in February George introduced a bill to increase personal exemption for income tax payers; although the George bill was not adopted, it had the effect of prodding the majority Republicans to "increase their own tax relief program" (*Newsweek,* March 1, 1954).

Significant ballots cast by Senator George in the Eighty-third Congress were in favor of the tidelands oil bill (May 1953) and against "pressuring" France in the Indochina crisis (July 1953). In the second session he voted for commercial power production by the Atomic

Energy Commission (July 1954), against substituting flexible for rigid farm price supports (August 1954), and in favor of making membership in the Communist party a crime (August 1954).

When the Democrats began organization of the Eighty-fourth Congress in January 1955, Senator George was elected president pro tempore of the Senate. George did not claim the chairmanship of the Finance Committee, but accepted instead that of the Foreign Relations Committee.

At the end of November 1954 George had announced full agreement with the Eisenhower Administration in opposing the demand of Senator William F. Knowland of California for a blockade to "pressure" Communist China to release eleven American airmen held on espionage charges. (These airmen were released in August 1955.) George was formally consulted on the text of the proposed treaty with Nationalist China which guarantees protection by the United States of Formosa and the Pescadores (the defense pact was signed on December 2, 1954, and ratified by the Senate on February 9, 1955 by a vote of 64 to 6).

Early in 1955 George called on the Senate to support President Eisenhower by passing the Formosa resolution and thus show the world that America was united in the crisis. "What is the alternative?" George asked. "The President chose a courageous course," he said, "a course which would be taken only by a prudent, patient man who knows the pitfalls of the course and knows the horrors of war." (The Formosa resolution was passed by the Senate by a vote of 85 to 3, on January 28. It gave President Eisenhower emergency authorization to use U.S. armed forces to protect Formosa and the Pescadores Islands.)

On the *Meet the Press* program of March 20, Senator George advocated the calling of an early Big Four meeting (of the heads of state of the United States, Great Britain, U.S.S.R., and France) to consider means to avert a third world war. The Administration indicated support of this proposal, with reservations. George has frequent consultations on foreign-policy problems with Secretary of State John Foster Dulles. He led the SEATO pact and Paris agreements to approval in the Senate.

In the Eighty-fourth Congress Senator George voted in favor of an increase in Congressional salaries, and against the Administration tax bill substitute giving a tax cut to families with incomes under $5,000 a year (February 1955). He introduced a major amendment to H.R. 1 to protect the U.S. textile industry against "undue competition from Japan." The George amendment sharply restricts the tariff-setting powers of the President.

In a speech on foreign policy on April 24 before the American Society of Newspaper Editors, George said that the United States ought to be willing to talk with representatives of the Chinese People's Republic as a "first step" in an effort to find a solution to problems in the Far East. Asked about representation from Nationalist China at such a meeting, George replied: "Of course, if we were going to dispose of any of their contentions or rights, they would have to be represented directly or indirectly" (New York *Times*, April 26, 1955). On April 29 he clarified this view by saying that Chiang Kai-shek's interest could be represented by "any agreed representative," such as a neutral nation.

The Senator is serving on the John Marshall Bicentennial Month Commission, the Joint Committee on Internal Revenue Taxation, and the Joint Committee on Reduction of Nonessential Federal Expenditures. His present term in the Senate will expire in January 1957.

For relaxation he watches television and reads mystery stories. *Time* (April 25, 1955) related that when he shaves in the morning, "sometimes . . . a parakeet named Bobbie perche[s] atop his head." George's voice has been described as "low-pitched, of ante-bellum sweetness" except when in "awesome crescendo in Senate debate."

He avoids formal social occasions as much as possible, and at their small Washington apartment, or their home in Vienna, he likes to do the cooking for his wife. He married Lucy Heard on July 9, 1903. She is known to her friends as "Miz Lucy." They had two sons, Heard Franklin, the elder, and Marcus, the younger. Marcus, a lieutenant in the U.S. Navy, was killed in air combat during World War II. Senator George holds honorary LL.D. degrees from Mercer, Columbia, and Brown universities and Union College. The Mercer Law School was renamed in 1947 the Walter F. George School of Law.

Selected References (see also newspaper and periodical indexes)

Colliers 135:32+ My 13 '55 pors
Fortune 45:85+ F '52 por
Life 36:112 Ap 19 '54 por
N Y Times VI p6 Ja 2 '49 por; VI p12+ Mr 13 '55 pors
Sat Eve Post 217:22+ My 19 '45 pors
Time 65:22+ Ap 25 '55 pors
U S News 36:60+ Mr 5 '54 pors; 38:12 Ja 7 '55 por
Biographical Directory of the American Congress, 1774-1949 (1950)
Congressional Directory (1955)
National Cyclopædia of American Biography, Current Volume F, 1939-42
Who's Who in America, 1954-55
World Biography (1954)

GIBSON, HUGH (SIMONS) Aug. 16, 1883-Dec. 12, 1954 U.S. diplomat; author; thirty years a Foreign Service officer; former Minister to Poland, Switzerland, Belgium, Luxembourg; Ambassador to Brazil; associated with Herbert Hoover in international relief work during World War I; was director of the Provisional Intergovernmental Committee for European Migration (1951 until his death) See *Current Biography* (Jan.) 1953.

Obituary

N Y Times p 1+ D 13 '54

GIVENCHY, HUBERT (JAMES TAFFIN) DE Feb. 21, 1927- Fashion designer
Address: b. 8 rue Alfred de Vigny, Paris 8ᵉ, France; h. 4 rue Fabert, Paris 7ᵉ, France

Since his "phenomenal" debut in Paris *couture* in February 1952 at the age of twenty-five, Hubert de Givenchy has continued to receive international recognition for his dress designs. Before opening his own fashion house "on a shoestring," he worked for eight years in the dressmaking establishments of Fath, Piguet, Lelong and Schiaparelli. His first collection, capturing the "spirit of youth," was executed with such flawless technique, workmanship and delicate detail, that he won immediate acceptance among leading buyers from New York, where his separate skirts and tops have proved exceptionally popular. Fashion reviewers have frequently praised the unusual embroidered and printed materials used in his collections. In 1954 he helped to launch the tubular evening dress. In New York his designs have been seen in Fifth Avenue stores and on television.

HUBERT DE GIVENCHY

Hubert James Taffin de Givenchy, the son of Béatrice (Badin) and Lucien Taffin de Givenchy, was born on February 21, 1927, in Beauvais, where his mother's family had lived for generations. His father was an administrator; his brother Claude is an assistant director of Air France in Washington, D.C. Hubert's maternal grandfather was a pupil of Jean Baptiste Camille Corot and an administrator of the Beauvais and Gobelin tapestry industries. From earliest childhood the boy grew up in an atmosphere of art and decorative design.

After attending the Beaux-Arts school in Paris, Hubert studied law, but his love of designing drew him to the *haute couture*. He showed some sketches for dress designs to Jacques Fath, who quickly recognized his talent and took the seventeen-year-old boy into his shop as an apprentice-designer. (De Givenchy has said that Fath and Carmel Snow, editor of *Harper's Bazaar*, influenced him greatly in his choice of a career.) Two years later de Givenchy moved to the house of Piguet. When Christian Dior left the establishment of Lucien Lelong, de Givenchy stepped into his place. In 1949 he joined the design staff of Mme. Elsa Schiaparelli, remaining with her for three years. He quickly established a reputation in her *boutique* on the Place Vendôme with his designs for blouses, cardigan dresses, and interchangeable "separates" which especially appealed to American clients.

In February 1952 Hubert de Givenchy opened his own *maison de couture* in fashionable Parc Monceau, at 8 rue Alfred de Vigny, formerly the residence of the chocolate magnate, Émile Justin Menier. "The time hardly seemed propitious for anyone to be opening a new house—least of all for a youngster without too much money," commented *Life* on March 3, 1952. Four fashion-design establishments including Piguet and Molyneux had been forced out of business the previous year, while sales in other houses had dropped.

Operating "on a shoestring," Hubert de Givenchy and his model, Bettina Graziani, who had resigned her position as top fashion model in Paris to join the new enterprise, prepared for their first show. By working with a small staff in cramped quarters, the designer was able to reduce his prices one-third. Bettina handled the publicity, made contacts with important U.S. fashion editors, and posed for pictures. The first show proved "as smoothly elegant as the most experienced houses in Paris could put on," even though Bettina had to help set up chairs, press clothes in the dressing room, model them, and then come out to sell them.

After the spring fashion shows, *Life* reported that "the two most talked-of designers were the old master, Dior, and a brash newcomer, Hubert de Givenchy." Not his lower prices but his designs brought him "the biggest salon ovation heard in five years and sales of 7,000,000 francs ($20,000) the first day, spectacular for a new small house." The designs he showed were youthful and fresh, featuring separate skirts and tops and original accessories, such as a paper-lantern-pleated babushka, "Garbo" hats and a big-sleeved "Bettina Blouse" of washable shirting which at once had an enormous popularity. His high-styled coats and sumptuous ball gowns proved de Givenchy could compete with seasoned masters of fashion design.

As a result of his immediate international recognition, the young designer was invited with a group of Paris *couturiers* to show eight of his gowns at the "April in Paris" pageant at the Waldorf-Astoria Hotel in New York. For this occasion he created six new gowns, two of them costing 1,000,000 francs ($2,800). Their lavish embroideries were done by workers of the houses of Lesage and Rébé.

Hubert de Givenchy explained his philosophy of dress in an interview with Virginia Pope (New York *Times*, April 21, 1952). He believes costumes should be so constructed that a woman can easily transform them by changing parts to suit her mood and needs. For this reason he makes an extravagant evening gown two piece, so that if the woman does not wish to wear the décolleté top, she can substitute a simple jersey bodice. This gives the client "the pleasure of feeling herself a bit of a creator of her own style."

His succeeding collections continued to attract wide attention, and he soon opened a *boutique* at the entrance to his showroom. Here he has interpreted his idea of "separates" in simple, young clothes adapted to modern life and designed on a "very personal note." He has shown jeweled headbands with matching pendant earrings to set off evening dresses; shawls which "give grace to women"; bits of fur that add charm to many costumes; tiny tambourine hats over black chiffon head-scarves for after-dark dresses.

His collection in February 1954 was described as "exciting, young and beautifully styled, with impeccable tailoring foremost." Utilizing both the princess silhouette and the tailored sheath with hip-draped belt, he placed emphasis on clever decorative touches. Silk prints and embroideries were particularly outstanding in his afternoon and dinner dresses.

When the fashion world was debating the flat silhouette of Dior in August 1954, de Givenchy continued to be "inspired by the young figure with its tender curves." His dresses were "100 per cent feminine" with billowing skirts below shaped bodices. Rosette Hargrove reported in the New York *World-Telegram and Sun* that the collection was "the most colorful yet in the annals of the *haute couture.*" It showed violets, ochre, rosewood, rose reds, lichen greens, hydrangea and flag blues in soft dressmaker suits designed for younger women with straight roomy coats in darker shades to be worn over the suits.

From the start, de Givenchy's designs have been popular in the United States. He has visited New York twice yearly to fulfill his numerous contracts with American houses. In September 1954 his suits were selected by Andrew Goodman of Bergdorf Goodman, New York for a special show of foreign fashions; at Henri Bendel's his white satin evening sheath with mink interlaced around the shoulders was part of the store's "top-drawer" collection. Gowns from his workroom were also worn in the fashion show of *couturier* models sponsored by the Celanese Corporation of America at the opening night of the Metropolitan Opera House in October 1954, and were seen on television.

At the third anniversary of the House of de Givenchy in February 1955, Bettina appeared in an organdie version of the blouse that had made fashion history in cotton shirting. De Givenchy's youthful design was stripped of all frills and emphasized line. His sports clothes featured sweater effects; his coats were sometimes sleeveless and collarless. High funnel necklines were shown on suits and ensembles. His basic technique was best illustrated in draped satin evening sheaths, a style he has done much to popularize.

Hubert de Givenchy designs all the models shown in his collections and likes to work alone. His fabrics are unusual in design, color and texture. He has made gowns of iridescent ivory satin; dresses of organdies, linens and cottons embroidered with fruits, vegetables, bamboos, fish and oysters. His satins have been printed with exquisite designs from Louis XV wood paneling. One white organdie dinner gown had Louis XV monkeys climbing over it and was worn with a pistache stole. His silk prints "bring freshness and diversity to an area that is too often overloaded with banality and fashion clichés," noted a writer for *American Fabrics* (summer 1953) who added that Fath and Dior include many of de Givenchy's prints in their collections.

The tallest as well as the youngest of the leading Paris designers, Hubert de Givenchy is six feet six inches in height and weighs 210 pounds. He has black hair and blue eyes. His religion is Protestant; his political affiliation, Liberal. Skiing, tennis, swimming and horseback riding are his favorite sports. He is almost as much interested in interior decoration as in his work and dreams of building a house in the country according to plans that he has drawn. He likes to browse in antique shops and has a rare collection of jeweled fish, topaz, and other gems.

References

Life 32:61+ Mr 3 '52 por
N Y Times p18 Ap 21 '52 por

GLEASON, JACKIE Feb. 26, 1916- Comedian; musician; television producer

Address: b. Park Sheraton Hotel, 7th Ave. and 56th St., New York 19

Often called "Mr. Saturday Night" because of the popularity of his hour-long Saturday evening entertainment on the Columbia Broadcasting System television network, the comedian Jackie Gleason first entered the television field in the autumn of 1949 and headed the *Jackie Gleason Show* from September 1952 to June 1955. Earlier in his career he had played in four Broadway musical shows after an apprenticeship in carnival and cabaret work.

Following what was described as "the biggest financial deal in TV history," Gleason began his appearance in the fall of 1955 in a new half-hour Saturday night filmed television program, *The Honeymooners,* under the sponsorship of the General Motors Corporation on the Columbia Broadcasting System. This is being filmed by a new DuMont process called "Electronicam." In addition to his television show he has conducted the "Jackie Gleason Orchestra" in six albums of recorded mood music for Capitol Records. Among these is the well-known *Music for Lovers Only.*

Herbert John Gleason, the younger son of Herbert and Mae (Kelly) Gleason, was born on February 26, 1916 in Brooklyn, New York. He was reared and educated in Brooklyn, where on graduation from Public Grade School 73 in January 1931 he also briefly attended both the

JACKIE GLEASON

Bushwick and the John Adams High Schools. His brother died when Jackie was three; when he was eight his father, an insurance clerk, disappeared. From that time on until her death in 1932, Mrs. Gleason supported herself and Jackie by working in the change booth of a subway station.

Jackie early displayed a quick wit and a sense of humor in school theatricals and at church social events and won first prize in an amateur night contest at the local Halsey Theatre. At the age of sixteen he was engaged as master of ceremonies at Brooklyn's Folly Theatre; later he worked as a barker, in a carnival and as master of ceremonies in Pennsylvania and New Jersey resorts, and toured with carnival shows on the Eastern seaboard.

Beginning in 1935 Jackie was engaged at Newark's (New Jersey) Miami Club for nearly three years as assistant "emcee" and "bouncer" and for a while supplemented an income of about $75 a week by disc jockeying for radio station WAAT in Newark. Two years of steady cabaret work at Club 18 and Leon and Eddie's in New York City began in 1938. Jackie's debut in Broadway musical comedy was made late in May 1940 in the short-lived Shubert production *Keep Off the Grass.*

While entertaining at Club 18, the comedian was seen by the motion picture producer Jack Warner and a one-year Hollywood contract resulted. Gleason was given small comedy or melodrama parts in *Navy Blues* (1941), *All Through the Night* (1942) and *Larceny, Inc.* (1942). For Twentieth Century Fox he appeared in the musical *Springtime in the Rockies* (1942) and *Orchestra Wives* (1942).

On returning to New York, the comedian began with a short-lived appearance in November 1943 in *Artists and Models,* which led to his engagement in the musical, *Follow the Girls* at the New Century in New York on April 8, 1944. Lewis Nichols, reviewer for the New York *Times,* had thought Jackie "pretty funny" in *Artists and Models,* and liked him even better in *Follow the Girls.* He described Jackie as "rotund, with a fat man's beaming face," and predicted that "some day when he gets the words" he would be wonderful instead of just very good.

A scene in which Gleason (who already weighed 250 pounds and who cherished his *avoirdupois* because he could "get away with more as a fat man") was disguised as a WAVE was a factor in the success of this far from exceptional musical comedy, which ran for 882 performances. While in *Follow the Girls* Gleason replaced Bob Crosby on the NBC-Old Gold Sunday night radio show. By 1946 the comedian was collecting $1,000 a week for appearances at Billy Rose's Diamond Horseshoe; and two years later he acquired the services of his present business manager, George ("Bullets") Durgom. At the Broadhurst in New York for six months beginning January 13, 1949 Gleason appeared in the musical show *Along Fifth Avenue* with comedienne Nancy Walker.

Gleason's remarkable advance in television began in the autumn of 1949 when he appeared for twenty-six weeks in the TV version of the *Life of Riley* radio series. He came East, and was immediately engaged for the DuMont *Cavalcade of Stars* video show. "He began," H. I. Phillips has commented, "with little more than the brassy routine of the typical video comic," and was "no bargain in the American home until he scored with *The Honeymooners,"* a "tenement sketch out of O. Henry and George Ade," in which he appeared as Ralph Kramden, a bus driver. Audrey Meadows in the role of the young wife, and Art Carney through his characterization of a sewer worker with generally disastrous good intentions, "are the answer to a showman's prayer."

Other characterizations by Gleason, included the Poor Soul, Joe the Bartender, and the broadly delineated society playboy, Reggie Van Gleason, 3d. During his two years with *Cavalcade of Stars,* Jackie's "popularity rating" rose from 9 to 28 despite what Leo Rosten described in *Look* as the "fearsome competition of televised prize fights," and in September 1951 he headed NBC-TV's Sunday evening *Colgate Comedy Hour,* while continuing Friday night appearances on the DuMont show.

In September 1952 Jackie began a Saturday night hour-long CBS television program, the *Jackie Gleason Show,* at a contract calling for $300,000 a year to cover his entire production unit and a personal salary of $10,000 a week. The Marilyn Taylor dancers, and precision dancing effects directed by June Taylor supplemented previously proven Jackie Gleason entertainment ingredients, with the result that the show soon exceeded in popularity rival programs on other networks.

In December 1952 Gleason received the *TV Guide* citation as "best comedian" of the year. "Today," observed Leo Rosten (*Look,* June 15, 1954), "he is known as Mr. Saturday Night. No one in television ever rose so fast so soon."

The comedian offers his own explanation of what makes each of his characterizations "tick." "All my characters are psychologically constructed," Gleason has said. "Each is consistent. . . . I give each character a saving grace, a touch of sympathy."

Although he does not read music Gleason has composed the melodies of several numbers including "Lover's Rhapsody," "White House Serenade" and "Melancholy Serenade" (the "signature" of his show) and is credited with the score of the "original symphony in ballet" entitled *Tawny*, which was a feature of the *Jackie Gleason Show* of May 31, 1953, and of which June Taylor was the choreographer. Jack Gould in the New York *Times* called *Tawny* "a poem for eye and ear, a simply superb example of inspired television artistry."

In May 1953 Jackie made his debut as a dramatic actor in the CBS-TV Studio One production of *The Laugh Maker,* and in December 1954 gave a "taut and convincing portrait of an unscrupulous politician . . . in a play by Carey Wilbur called *Short Cut*" (*Time,* December 20, 1954). On February 3, 1955 he appeared as Aubrey Piper in a CBS-TV adaptation of George Kelly's comedy, *The Show-Off.*

Since early in his television career the comedian's affairs have been handled by a corporation, Jackie Gleason Enterprises, and during 1954 this corporation "grossed $4,000,000 from the sale of record albums, music scores, clothing designs and . . . television appearances" (John Molleson in the New York *Herald Tribune*). On December 20, 1954 it became known that the corporation had just entered into what Marie Torre of the New York *World-Telegram and Sun* has called "the biggest financial deal in TV history."

The contract provides that the Buick division of the General Motors Corporation sponsor a half-hour show on CBS-TV Saturday night which will offer thirty-nine weekly film recordings by Gleason of *The Honeymooners* during the height of the "season," with thirteen of these films being repeated in the summer. The contract calls for payment to Gleason of $7,000,000 for the entire production over a two-year period, and a further $4,000,000 for a third year, assuming that the option is renewed. Gleason's GM-sponsored half-hour TV show began on October 1, 1955.

Jackie Gleason and the former dancer Genevieve Halford were married in Newark, New Jersey on September 20, 1936 and have two daughters, Linda and Geraldine. The Gleasons separated in 1941, were reconciled in 1948, and parted again in 1951; in June 1954 Mrs. Gleason was granted a permanent legal separation and financial settlement.

He is six feet tall, with nearly black hair and blue eyes, and, when he chooses to use it, "a bucket of Irish charm," notes Michael Drury in *Collier's.* His religion is Roman Catholic. "His voice is as rough and powerful as a steel cable but he can spin it out to the finest silk." Leo Rosten says he "looks like a king-sized leprechaun" and that he "weighs anywhere from 185 to 285 pounds—depending on the moon, the tides and his diet." Gleason does much nocturnal reading and has become much interested in the J. B. Rhine theories of extrasensory perception.

References

Colliers 128:18+ Ag 25 '51 pors; 135:34+ Mr 18 '55 pors; 135:36+ Ap 1 '55 pors
Coronet 34:61+ My '53 pors
Life 33:87+ S 29 '52 pors; 38:23+ Ja 24 '55 pors
N Y Times II p 11 My 20 '51
New Yorker 30:30+ S 11 '54
Newsweek 40:66+ O 6 '52 por; 43:72 Mr 1 '54 por
Time 65:52 Ja 3 '55
Motion Picture and Television Almanac, 1955
World Biography (1954)

GOBEL, GEORGE (LESLIE) May 20, 1920- Television comedian

Address: b. c/o National Broadcasting Co., 30 Rockefeller Plaza, New York 20; Gomalco Enterprises, Hollywood, Calif; h. Sherman Oaks, Calif.

The winner of the Peabody, Sylvania and "Emmy" (the "Oscar" of television) awards for the outstanding comedian of 1954 was George Gobel, whose comic style has been compared with that of Will Rogers, Robert Benchley and Charles Butterworth. His program has been broadcast since October 2, 1954 over NBC-TV on three Saturday nights a month. Television audiences have been familiar with his dry wit and story-telling technique since 1952, as he has made guest appearances on many programs. In the words of *Variety* (May 12, 1954), Gobel is "something of a mimic, very much of an actor, a passable guitarist and a comic songster."

The *George Gobel Show* is called by radio-television critic, John Crosby, "one of the brightest things to come along this season, the most original and the most consistent" (New York *Herald Tribune,* November 7, 1954).

Chosen by producer David O. Selznick as the only "live" comic for TV's two-hour *Diamond Jubilee of Light* show on October 24, 1954 (commemorating the seventy-fifth anniversary of Edison's invention of the incandescent lamp), Gobel satirized the electronic calculator in a monologue called "altogether superb foolishness" by the New York *Times* (October 25, 1954) television critic, Jack Gould.

George Leslie Gobel was born in Chicago, Illinois, on May 20, 1920, the only child of Herman and Lillian Gobel, both native Chicagoans. His mother was a former piano teacher. George assisted his father, the owner of a grocery store, and "distinguished himself doing imitations of the customers" (*American Weekly,* December 5, 1954). He attended public schools in Chicago and was graduated from Roosevelt High School. He learned to play the guitar while in grammar school, and on Sundays he sang in the boys' choir at Saint

GEORGE GOBEL

Stephen's Episcopal Church. At the age of twelve, he sang a solo with this choir on radio station WLS, which resulted in a contract to appear on the Chicago station in NBC's *National Barn Dance* program.

When his voice changed, he was unable to continue singing soprano to the accompaniment of his guitar for about $75 a week in NBC's barn dance show and other programs initiated in Chicago. He therefore took small dramatic and "soap opera" parts. During his minor role in the *Tom Mix Show,* he acted the "side" of the boy who said: "I'll hold your horse for you, Tom."

After completing high school, Gobel sang on radio stations in Chattanooga, Tennessee, and in St. Louis, Missouri. In his spare time he learned to fly airplanes and in 1943 enlisted in the U.S. Army Air Force, became a pilot, and then a flight instructor. He spent most of his off-duty hours developing comedy routines to entertain his fellow fliers, who provided a frank and critical audience and responded especially to his "deadpan" delivery.

Upon his discharge from the service in 1945, Gobel held the rank of first lieutenant. He decided to enter the entertainment field, rather than pursue an aviation career. "I broke into the club date market in the Chicago area," he recalled. "I realize how fortunate I have been to test, build and shape comedy material before hundreds of different types of audiences, presented under all types of working conditions."

Gobel developed "his style and his self-confidence at a nice, leisurely pace," declares his first booking agent and present partner in Gomalco Productions, David O'Malley (*TV Guide,* December 4, 1954). After seven years of playing in night clubs, hotel rooms and convention halls, Gobel was telecast by Columbia Broadcasting System on about thirty occasions as a guest with the Garry Moore program in 1952.

The next year he appeared on many of NBC-TV's leading shows, including seven weeks in the Hoagy Carmichael program on *Saturday Night Revue,* which brought him immediate popularity with video audiences. He also was telecast on the *Colgate Comedy Hour,* the *Spike Jones Show* and *Who Said That?*

When Gobel submitted his own script for his first guest appearance on the *Saturday Night Revue,* the director complained that it contained no jokes. "But jokes are not George's forte," wrote Hal Humphrey (New York *World-Telegram and Sun,* August 1, 1953). "He deals in dry humor." Gobel says of his own style, "I didn't think about it until other people started describing it. . . . I guess it's offbeat, casual" (*Time,* November 22, 1954).

NBC producer Joe Bigelow, who brought Gobel on television after seeing his act at the Statler Hotel, Los Angeles, explained that it was "a night-club routine that could go on television intact and remain within TV's purity code" (*Newsweek,* October 18, 1954). The comedian's charm, a staff writer of *TV Guide* (December 4, 1954) pointed out, "lies in his ability to look short and inconspicuous, talk in a quiet monotone and exhibit no energy whatsoever."

For more than a year, while under a five-year contract with NBC-TV, Gobel waited for his employer to decide upon a suitable format "that his comfortable, subtly shaded humor would fit into," and permit him to star in a program of his own (*Newsweek,* October 18, 1954). He moved to California with his family, collected his checks, continued to make guest appearances on the network at intervals, and added to his income with night club fees.

He tried "to arrive at the magic formula" NBC wanted in a format, and early in 1954 worked with one of Jack Benny's previous writers (Washington *Post,* January 24, 1954). "Maybe it's because I sometimes use a guitar, and sing a little, they think of that homespun or bucolic nonsense," he said. ". . . I'm really a city boy at heart."

When Gobel introduced his own NBC-TV show on October 2, 1954, "he was the hit of the new season" (*TV Guide*, December 4, 1954). Promising nothing, he said: "This show might just keep you from getting sullen." Then he went "from monologue to sketch to song to commercial and back to monologue again so smoothly that televiewers forgot to unplug their attention during commercials," wrote a *Newsweek* commentator (October 18, 1954).

Discussing the premiere of Gobel's television show, *Variety*'s (October 6, 1954) critic noted that the comedian "had a quite funny, quite smooth and distinctly professional kickoff." The reviewer for the New York *Times* (October 4, 1954) wrote that Gobel "has the enormous advantage of being a relatively new face, but even so his low pressure and offbeat humorous approach is often good fun in itself. He knows the art of relaxation and ambles all over the studio casually dropping his dry quips as he goes."

Gobel has four writers assisting him in providing material for his program—Hal Kanter, Jack Douglas, James Allerdice and Harry Winkler. He has promised not to have "a permanent cast, a regular opening and closing, or any set situations" for his show, but "a format without a format" (*Newsweek,* October 18, 1954). His programs often include his "TV guest wife," or his "guest" brother-in-law.

The television critics were unanimous in praising Gobel's monologue on the *Diamond Jubilee of Light* show on October 24, 1954. R. L. Shayon of *Saturday Review* (December 4, 1954), wrote that "the most-remembered moment" of the *Jubilee* was ". . . Gobel's hilarious, impious, average-man's monologue ribbing the electronic lightning-speed calculator." John Crosby, in the New York *Herald Tribune* (October 27, 1954) thought it "just about the funniest monologue I've heard since Robert Benchley's 'Treasurer's Report.'"

On March 7, 1945 it was announced that Gobel had won the 1954 "Emmy" award of the Television Academy of Arts and Sciences and on April 10, he won the George Foster Peabody television award.

He is making his movie debut in a remake of the picture *The Lady Eve,* playing opposite Mitzi Gaynor; the film will be entitled *The Birds and the Bees.*

Gobel, whose income was recently said to be approaching $7,500 a week, is described by Lloyd Shearer as "mild-mannered, friendly, intelligent, unpretentious, family-loving, open-minded—and modest . . ." (Washington *Post and Times Herald,* November 28, 1954). The comedian himself says: "But I'm a born worrier . . . on Sunday I start worrying about next week's show."

He married Alice Humecki, his high school sweetheart, in December 1942. They have three children: Gregg, Georgia and Leslie. Gobel is five feet five and one-half inches tall, weighs 127 pounds, and has blond crew-cut hair. He enjoys playing golf, and he is an ardent baseball fan. According to *Cue* (November 6, 1954), the television star's one-line comment on the *Diamond Jubilee of Light* program in praise of Edison, "if it weren't for electricity, we'd all be watching television by candlelight," will become "one of the gems of the decade."

Gobel wrote an article for *Collier's* (May 13, 1955) on the subject of child guidance. "Being a successful parent isn't easy," he wrote. "It requires nerves of steel, the patience of a saint . . . and a strong right hand (or left hand, as the case may be)."

References

Am W p13 D 5 '54 por
Life 37:69+ D 27 '54 por
N Y Times Mag p17 N 7 '54 por
Newsweek 44:65 O 18 '54; 44:44+ D 27 '54 por
Time 64:52 N 22 '54 por
TV Guide 2:9 D 4 '54 por

GOLD, HERBERT Mar. 9, 1924 Author; university professor

Address: b. c/o Wayne University, Detroit 1, Mich.; h. 3046 Clements, Detroit, Mich.

Reprinted from the *Wilson Library Bulletin* Feb. 1955

A veteran, a college teacher, recipient of two literary fellowships, author of two novels—one stream-of-consciousness, one on a race problem—Herbert Gold, now thirty-one, fits the pattern of a modern young writer as described by Malcolm Cowley in his *The Literary Situation.* Gold has also contributed to a variety of periodicals, including the *New Yorker, Harper's Bazaar, Mademoiselle, Collier's, Yale Review, American Mercury, Atlantic, Antioch Review, Furioso, Discovery, Partisan Review, Avon Modern Writing,* and *Botteghe Oscure.* His stories have been reprinted in *O. Henry Prize Stories* (1954). He is under contract to the Atlantic Monthly Press to write a novel to be called "The Man Who Was Not With It."

Herbert Gold was born in Cleveland, Ohio, March 9, 1924, the eldest of the four sons of Samuel S. Gold and Frieda (Frankel) Gold. When he was in grade school, a teacher, Ruth Collins, told him that he would be a writer, and this impressed the boy so much that "I had to spend years learning to undo my eleven-year-old notion of what good writing is." After graduating in 1942 from the Lakewood, Ohio, High School, where he wrote for the school paper and went in for swimming and tennis (which he still enjoys), he went to New York City. At Columbia University, young Gold wrote for student publications, both literary and humorous, and worked as a writer and switchboard operator. From 1943 to 1946 he was in the United States Army (Intelligence), but he obtained his B.A. in humanities in 1946.

At the University of Paris (the Sorbonne), Gold continued his philosophical studies on a Fulbright Fellowship. He was a lecturer in philosophy and literature at Western Reserve University, Cleveland, from 1951 to 1953. Experience as night manager of a hotel in 1951 proved useful when Gold was conjuring up Harry Bowers' Green Glade Hotel for his second novel, *The Prospect Before Us,* (World Publishing Company, 1954). The previous year, Gold had spent in Haiti, writing and living on an Inter-American Cultural Relations grant.

In *Birth of a Hero* (Viking, 1951), Gold's first novel, he traced the emotional progress of Reuben Flair, a middle-class, educated family man of forty-five, who has hitherto led an unquestioningly routine existence. James Kelly in the New York *Times* (September 16, 1951) termed its style "rich and rolling, with intoned rhythms and phrasing," but said that its construction was muddled. The San Francisco *Chronicle* (September 30, 1951) likewise praised Gold's "vigorous, figurative use of words," noted "many obscurities and the lack of a stirring plot," but summed it up as "an artistic job." In the *Saturday Review of Literature* (September 8, 1951) Harrison Smith observed that Gold "has something to say in his first

HERBERT GOLD

novel that is worth listening to in these days when most of our serious fiction is cluttered with the tag ends of psychoanalysis and drowned in a morbid interest in sexual aberrations and misanthropy."

Virginia Kirkus termed Gold's next novel, *The Prospect Before Us*, "distasteful" and warned public libraries to "be particularly careful" when considering its purchase. James Kelly in the New York *Times* (February 14, 1954), called the novel "a cerebral performance with a tangle of long, long thoughts, most of them entertainingly presented in colorful, runaway language. A high fidelity ear and eye are at work here." "Despite its shabby, melodramatic plot line," said *Time* (February 22, 1954), "the novel is alive with the nervous tempo of big-city sounds and smells." In *The New Leader* for March 1, 1954, Granville Hicks devoted his department "Living With Books," to "Three New Novels about Negroes Which Transcend the Old Formulas." Although Gold "uses the Negro problem as his point of departure," he "goes far beyond it in a subtle and meaningful study of human relationships," wrote Hicks. "One of the important elements in Gold's success is his mastery of a colloquial style. The dialogue is so perfect that it seems artless, and when it serves his purpose, he uses the same style in his narrative."

In April 1948, he married Edith Zubrin, a former professional model. In June of the same year he was awarded his M.A., his thesis being "Truth in Literature and Philosophy." The Golds have two daughters: Ann, five, and Judith, three.

Herbert Gold stands five feet eleven inches tall, is black-haired and brown-eyed, and weighs 155 pounds. His favorite authors include Homer, Shakespeare, Balzac, Dostoevsky, and Joyce. He is now a member of the department of English at Wayne University, Detroit, Michigan, a post he assumed in 1954. Among his sports, the author includes ice skating, and as recreation, "raising my children."

GOLDEN, JOHN June 27, 1874-June 17, 1955 Producer; playwright; composer; actor; considered dean of Broadway producers and patriarch of New York show business; produced over 150 plays and musicals, such as *Lightnin', The First Year, Seventh Heaven, Three Wise Fools, Claudia, Susan and God,* and *The Male Animal;* wrote *Hip Hip Hooray* and other plays; composed songs "Poor Butterfly" and "Goodbye Girls, I'm Through"; helped launch program for giving free theatre tickets to soldiers; supported New York City Center; was a founder of ASCAP and a shepherd of The Lambs. See *Current Biography* (March) 1944.

Obituary

N Y Times p17 Je 18 '55

GOLDWATER, BARRY M(ORRIS) Jan. 1, 1909- United States Senator from Arizona

Address: b. Senate Office Bldg., Washington, D.C.; h. Phoenix, Ariz.

Elected from the traditionally Democratic state of Arizona on November 4, 1952, United States Senator Barry M. Goldwater, a Republican, is at present serving as chairman of his party's Senatorial Campaign Committee. A department store executive, Goldwater had held only one other elective office, that of a city councilman of Phoenix, Arizona, before his election to the Senate. He is a member of the Senate Banking and Currency Committee and the Labor and Public Welfare Committee and has also served on the Joint Committee on the Economic Report and the Corregidor-Bataan Memorial Commission.

During World War II Goldwater was an instructor in fighter gunnery. His overseas service was with the Air Transport Command. Today he is the only qualified jet pilot in the Senate.

Barry Morris Goldwater was born in Phoenix, Arizona on January 1, 1909 to Baron and Josephine (Williams) Goldwater. One of his uncles was mayor of Prescott, Arizona for twenty-six years and was a delegate to the Arizona constitutional convention. Barry attended Staunton Military Academy in Virginia. In 1928 he was a student at the University of Arizona in Tucson and was elected to the Sigma Chi fraternity. He left college in 1929 to enter his family's department store business, Goldwater's, Inc. A year later he was commissioned a second lieutenant in the Arizona National Guard.

In 1937, the year in which he became president of Goldwater's, Inc., Goldwater was the recipient of a U.S. Junior Chamber of Commerce award. A devotee of the outdoors, Goldwater made four expeditions on the Colorado River. In the 1930's he was one of the first white men to navigate successfully the Colorado

River rapids in the Grand Canyon. In 1940 he wrote *Journey Down the River of Canyons* and *Arizona Portraits.* His book *An Odyssey of the Green and Colorado Rivers; the Intimate Journal of Three Boats and Nine People on a Trip Down Two Rivers* appeared in 1941.

Transferred to the U.S. Army Air Forces in 1941, Goldwater served in World War II as an instructor in the Air Transport Command in the Far East. On release from active duty in November 1945 he held the rank of lieutenant colonel. He rejoined the Arizona National Guard as a colonel, after organizing its air arm as its chief of staff for seven years. Colonel Goldwater is now an officer of the Air Reserve and flies regularly. After the war he returned to his position as president of Goldwater's Inc.

A director of the Association on American Indian Affairs and an authority on the Indian tribes of Arizona, Goldwater served on the advisory committee on Indian affairs of the U.S. Department of the Interior from 1948 to 1950. In 1949 he was elected to the Phoenix city council and was named the city's "man of the year." Goldwater was re-elected to the city council in 1951. During the gubernatorial race in 1950, Goldwater managed the successful campaign of Howard Pyle, who was opposed by Ana Frohmiller, a Democrat.

The Arizona Republican organization selected Goldwater in 1952 to oppose the state's junior Senator, Ernest W. McFarland, for re-election to a third term. McFarland was the Democratic majority leader of the Senate in the Eighty-second Congress. In the November polling Goldwater defeated McFarland by 132,263 votes to 125,358. The Republican Presidential candidate, General Eisenhower, carried the state by 150,032 votes to 109,428 for Governor Adlai E. Stevenson of Illinois, the Democratic standard bearer.

The new junior Senator from Arizona took his seat in the Eighty-third Congress in January 1953 for the term ending in January 1959. (He resigned from the presidency of Goldwater's, Inc., and is now chairman of the board.) On March 15, 1953 the Senator said that the Taft-Hartley law had failed to rout Communists from the labor movement, and he sponsored a bill to give the Subversive Activities Control Board the responsibility for deciding whether a union was Communist-dominated and to void the rights and privileges of a union found to be unpurged.

An amendment to the foreign aid bill was introduced by Goldwater in July 1953. It provided that no funds would be made available to France until that country had given "satisfactory assurances" of her intention to "free" Viet-Nam, Cambodia and Laos. This proposal was rejected by the Senate by a vote of 64 to 17.

During his first year (1953) in the Senate, Goldwater was recorded in favor of confirming Albert M. Cole as housing administrator (March), the offshore oil bill (May), an across-the-board cut in appropriations (May), summary firing powers for Cabinet officers (June), using foreign aid to reduce farm surpluses

Wide World

BARRY M. GOLDWATER

(July), decreasing the foreign aid ceiling by one billion dollars (July), a provision (to a Constitutional amendment assuring equality under the law to men and women) which would sustain benefits already granted to women by law (July), selling government-owned rubber plants (July), admitting 209,000 refugees from Iron Curtain countries (July), and penalizing nations trading with Communist China (July).

The Senator voted against confirming Charles E. Bohlen as Ambassador to the U.S.S.R. (March), an amendment providing that Federal revenues from oil leasing be used as grants to education (June), increasing soil conservation payments (June), profits tax relief for small business (July), and $400,000,000 more for jet bombers (July).

Early in May 1954, when revision of the Taft-Hartley act was debated, Goldwater submitted an amendment which, if adopted, would in effect "turn over control of labor management disputes to the several states except with respect to 'national emergency' disputes" (*Christian Science Monitor,* May 5, 1954).

It would require unions to have the support of 95 per cent of the employees in a plant, instead of a simple majority, in order to claim exclusive bargaining rights. Goldwater's proposal was supported by the Administration. The states, Goldwater is believed to have said, "should be allowed even to outlaw collective bargaining if they so wished" (*Christian Science Monitor,* May 5, 1954).

Goldwater was one of twenty-two Senators who voted on December 2, 1954 against the "censure" of Senator Joseph R. McCarthy of Wisconsin for his conduct toward the Senate and the (Arthur V.) Watkins sub-committee during the censure proceedings. He stated: "I feel the Republican administration has conducted a vigorous fight against communism and that Senator McCarthy has been a leader in that fight" (*World-Telegram and Sun,* December 7, 1954). He later said that it was "improper" for Senator McCarthy to charge that the censure move had stopped the McCarthy committee from investigating Communists.

In 1954 Senator Goldwater voted "yea" in regard to the authorization of the St. Lawrence seaway (January), a Constitutional amendment limiting the treating-making powers of the President (February), reducing the home appliance tax (March), a Constitutional amendment fixing the membership of the U.S. Supreme Court permanently at nine justices (May), authorizing the construction of 140,000 public housing units (June), the tax revision bill (July), the atomic energy bill (July), a proposal to cut $500,000,000 from the foreign aid bill (August), and the farm bill (August).

He voted "nay" on the following proposals: an amendment maintaining 90 per cent farm price supports (April), an amendment increasing the lending authority of the Rural Electrification Administration by $35,000,000 (June), an amendment adding $10,000,000 to the school lunch program (June), and an amendment substituting a three-year trade act for the Administration's one-year extension bill (June).

He also opposed an amendment to the tax revision bill increasing the income tax exemption by $100 a year (June), an amendment to remove special depreciation provisions for business from the tax revision bill (July), the foreign aid bill (August) and an amendment making Communist party membership a crime (August).

In January 1955 Senator Goldwater was named to succeed Senator Everett M. Dirksen of Illinois as chairman of the Republican Senatorial Campaign Committee. He later said that the odds are "heavily stacked" against the party's effort to regain control of the Senate in 1956 (New York *Times*, February 21, 1955). (Approximately one-third of the seats in the Senate will be contested in 1956.)

Goldwater's voting record in the first session of the Eighty-fourth Congress (1955) indicates that he approved a resolution authorizing the President to take action, if necessary, in defense of Formosa (January), a measure to increase Congressional salaries from $15,000 to $22,500 a year (February), and the confirmation of John Marshall Harlan as an Associate Justice of the U.S. Supreme Court (March).

He voted against a proposal to give a twenty-dollar tax cut to families with incomes of not more than $5,000 a year plus a ten-dollar tax cut for each dependent other than husband or wife (March).

In a letter to the *Reporter* (April 7, 1955) Senator Goldwater took issue with Senator Richard L. Neuberger in regard to Federal development of power dams. He wrote: "The approach of the public-power advocate is the approach of the person interested in getting the Federal government into the operation of all American business, and these people generally forget that the Constitution says nothing about the Federal Government being in business."

Margaret Johnson and Barry M. Goldwater were married on September 22, 1934. Their children are Joanne, Barry, Jr., Michael, and Margaret. The Senator is an Episcopalian. He is a Mason, Shriner, Elk, and a member of the Eastern Star, Alianza, Veterans of Foreign Wars, American Legion, Wings, Woodmen of the World, and Royal Photographic Society. Goldwater is also a director of the American Institute of Foreign Trade, Heard Museum, Museum of Northern Arizona, and St. Joseph's Hospital. His hobbies are aviation, photography and deep-sea fishing. The Department of the Interior announced on November 27, 1954 that the Senator had "discovered a big natural bridge" in Grand Canyon National Park.

In the U.S. Senate on April 28 Goldwater discussed "Airpower as our National Strategy." He did not suggest abolishing surface military forces, but urged: "We must use air weapons for national survival . . . accept the influence of powerful air forces upon international behavior (Vital Speeches, May 15, 1955).

References

N Y Times p16 N 6 '52
Newsweek 44:23 Mr 7 '55 por
Washington (D.C.) Post p26 Ja 20 '53 por
Congressional Directory (1954)
Who's Who in America, 1954-55
World Biography (1954)

GORDON, DOROTHY Radio and television moderator; author

Address: b. c/o The New York Times Youth Forums, 229 W. 43d St., New York 36

For those adults who persist in thinking that America's teenagers are chiefly concerned with riding hot-rods, hunting celebrities' autographs, and playing juke boxes, Dorothy Gordon offers, through her New York *Times* Youth Forums, an eye-opening rebuttal. Students of more than 800 schools in New York, Connecticut, New Jersey, Vermont and other states have participated in her weekly panel discussions of important national and international issues. The forums, which began in a lecture hall in 1943, and have been heard on radio since 1945, and over the Du Mont television network since October 3, 1953, are dramatic testimony to the growing sense of responsibility among today's young people. Her program won the George Peabody Radio Award in 1951.

Mrs. Gordon, who started her career as a singer of folk songs for children, is a veteran of hundreds of children's broadcasts, including the first radio program for children over WEAF in 1924. She directed the music programs on Columbia Broadcasting System's *American School of the Air,* produced the very popular *Children's Corner* and *Yesterday's Children* on CBS, NBC and Mutual networks, directed children's radio programs for the Office of War Information (OWI) and wrote scripts for the U.S. State Department during World War II.

She is the author of seven books for children: *Sing It Yourself* (1928), *Around the World in Song* (1930), *Dorothy Gordon's*

Treasure Bag of Game Songs (1939), and *You and Democracy* (1951), published by E. P. Dutton; *Come to France* (1939) and *Knowing the Netherlands* (1940), published by the American Book Company; and *All Children Listen* (1942), published by George W. Stewart.

After moderating the *Times* Youth Forums for nearly twelve years, Mrs. Gordon can still say, "Aren't the children amazing?" She is convinced that children today "feel that they are very close to what is happening in the world, and whatever happens is going to affect them, and that they are going to take their places as leaders, and not only as leaders because everyone cannot be a leader, but as participants in the right to preserve democracy."

In a speech before the U.S. Chamber of Commerce in April 1954 Mrs. Gordon urged that American high schools give instruction in communism as a *comparative* form of government, *not* taught by communists, but by competent instructors in political science. "The young people beg for this," she said. "They claim that only in that way will they learn what is the threat of communism. I agree with them, and that we must trust our teachers to give this course, having faith that students will reject Marxism and will accept democracy as the best form of government evolved by free men. I have faith in our youth."

Dorothy Gordon was born Dorothy Lerner in Odessa, Russia to Leo and Rose (Schwarz) Lerner. Her parents were both American-born. Because her father was an international lawyer associated with the diplomatic service, the family traveled a great deal, particularly in the Balkan countries. Before Dorothy was ten her mother had taken her to many music festivals held in small villages. "As far back as I can remember," Mrs. Gordon recalled, "I was fascinated by the colorful costumes and the dances and the songs. My youthful mind absorbed all these things and I found that I was singing the songs in the various languages just as easily as I would in English." (She knows seven languages and can sing songs of fourteen different countries in their original tongue.)

Although she attended various schools abroad for brief periods she also received instruction from private tutors. When her parents discovered that Dorothy had a voice that should be trained, she studied in Italy with Gabriel Sibella, with Roberto Moranzoni (who later became conductor of the Metropolitan Opera House), and with Gabriel Gills. She returned to the United States and was graduated from Hunter College with the A.B. degree. In Europe, she took graduate courses at the Sorbonne, University of Paris. She gave several concerts which included groups of folk songs.

Following her marriage to Bernard Gordon, a prominent New York lawyer, she devoted her time to bringing up her two sons, Frank and Lincoln. She believes that they really influenced her to begin her career, for she soon discovered there was practically nothing available in the entertainment field for children in New York City. "This was before radio," she pointed out. "This surprised me because as a child in the European countries, I never had any difficulty finding things to go to. I remember the pantomimes in England during the Christmas holidays, and the puppet shows and special concerts for children. I used to sing a great deal to my children, and Lincoln said to me one time, 'Why don't you sing to other children, too?' I asked 'What shall I sing, what do you think other children would like?' And that started it."

New York Times

DOROTHY GORDON

After the first concert at the Princess Theatre (which proved an outstanding success), Mrs. Gordon, wearing the costumes of various countries, gave many concerts for children between 1923 and 1929 throughout the United States and Canada. She made her first radio appearance on Station WEAF on April 7, 1924, during 1924 and 1925 sang folk songs over Station WJZ, and in 1929 produced and broadcast programs for children for the British Broadcasting Corporation in London. She returned to America in 1931 and until 1933 was director of music programs on the Columbia Broadcasting System's *American School of the Air*.

She met Sir James Barrie and asked permission to present *Peter Pan* over the radio. He was reluctant, but Mrs. Gordon pointed out that it would be on the CBS *American School of the Air* program, which went into schools throughout the United States, and that millions of children would hear it. "I remember saying, 'If you believe in fairies, you must use the magic of radio to have *Peter Pan* reach out to many more children.' Then he turned to Harold Child, British drama critic (who had introduced me to Barrie), and remarked, 'You know, I say, Dorothy Gordon is the Peter Pan of America. She will *never* grow old.'" So Peter Pan made his debut on the radio on Mrs. Gordon's program in 1931.

(Continued next page)

GORDON, DOROTHY—*Continued*

In 1933 she persuaded A. A. Milne to allow her to sing his *Winnie the Pooh* songs and tell his stories over the radio, and in 1935 she obtained permission from Rudyard Kipling to broadcast his *Just So* stories. Mrs. Gordon wrote the scripts for these dramatizations and often played some of the roles.

In 1940 Mrs. Gordon conducted over NBC's Blue network one of her most popular programs, *Yesterday's Children*. Many famous men and women appeared on the program and told why a particular book had been their favorite. President Franklin D. Roosevelt's was *Swiss Family Robinson;* Mrs. Roosevelt's was *The Little Lame Prince;* Mayor Fiorello La Guardia's was *Black Beauty;* Helen Hayes' choice was *Alice in Wonderland* and *Helen's Babies;* Eddie Cantor's was *David Copperfield;* Governor Herbert Lehman's favorites were the books of Horatio Alger; Fanny Hurst's was *Uncle Tom's Cabin;* Mrs. Gordon's own favorite was *Little Women*.

In organizing the first youth forum, held on April 3, 1943 at Times Hall, 240 West 44th Street, in New York City, Mrs. Gordon visited public, private and parochial schools in the New York area, talked with the teachers, and arranged to have the children choose their own representatives to attend. Eight students, from different economic and racial backgrounds, were selected for the panel.

The invited audience was largely adults, representing various women's groups, educational associations and psychologists. "I lost my voice the day before the first forum," Mrs. Gordon recalled, "but recovered it in time to introduce the children. I asked 'If Hitler had lost his voice, would there have been a war?' A little boy not over ten or eleven, immediately answered: 'Of course there would have been a war!' He went right into political conditions in Europe, it was the most amazing thing. Then the ideas flew back and forth among the youngsters, and it had a wonderful effect upon the adult audience. Afterwards some of them said to me, 'Why, to listen to these young people talk, we have hope for the world!'" This forum, and subsequent ones, were broadcast over Station WMCA. The British Broadcasting Corporation asked Mrs. Gordon to do a transatlantic panel, with students in England and in America discussing the war and what it meant to them. The program, recorded by telephone and cable, was very successful.

In the fall of 1943 Mrs. Arthur Hays Sulzberger, wife of the publisher of the New York *Times,* who had heard Mrs. Gordon's programs and knew her as a panel-member of several discussions on child education, asked her to join the staff of the *Times* and to moderate the Youth Forums on a regular schedule. These were held in Times Hall between 1943 and 1945, and were occasionally broadcast over Station WMCA. When the *Times* bought Station WQXR the Forums went on the air as a regular weekly series. At that time, the children who participated were from the ages of nine to eleven. "We gave them some pretty difficult questions to discuss," Mrs. Gordon recalls.

Later, an advisory board, after studying recordings of the programs, suggested that groups of older children be used. The Forums now have about one program each month in which college students participate, and three programs in which high school pupils discuss current issues. All the programs are recorded, and study outlines are supplied to individuals and schools following each radio and television program.

Mrs. Gordon was invited to institute similar youth forums in many cities throughout the country. People discovered that to conduct a forum informally, and to elicit spontaneous discussion, is a specialized technique. When asked just what this technique consists of, Mrs. Gordon told a *Current Biography* writer, "I never realized that I had this ability, but I really think that I have developed it because it is an outgrowth of the many years of entertaining young people, being with them, liking them, trying to understand their point of view."

She emphasized that "the most important thing is to be well-informed, on *both* sides of the topic. As a moderator, you cannot be subjective, you have to be completely objective. This requires a great deal of reading. I try to read from six to eight newspapers each day. Fortunately, I have a photographic mind and can read very quickly. By reading different papers I can tell what paper a student has been reading by the things he is saying. To keep things going in the discussion, so there are no lulls, is something like being a conductor of an orchestra. While each player uses his own instrument, it's a part of the whole thing, and the conductor has to keep it together."

Among recent topics discussed by panels of six young people on the Youth Forums have been: "How Can We Keep Free Asia Free?" on October 3, 1954, led by Prince Wan Waithayakon, Permanent Representative to the United Nations from Thailand; "Is Co-existence with Russia Possible?" with Harrison Salisbury, New York *Times* correspondent, formerly in Moscow, as guest, on November 7; "Do We Understand the Meaning of Free Enterprise?" led by Clement D. Johnston, president of the Chamber of Commerce of the United States.

Mrs. Gordon is five feet two inches tall, weighs 134 pounds, has blue eyes and gray hair. In politics she is an independent. Her hobby is oil painting, which she enjoys doing at her summer home on Lake Sunapee, New Hampshire. She is the proud grandmother of seven grandchildren. Her son, Frank, is a New York lawyer and her son, Lincoln, is an executive of the Foreign Operations Administration (FOA).

In 1950 she was named "The New York State Mother of the Year"; in 1951 she received *McCall's* radio broadcasting award; in 1954 she was given the Columbia Scholastic Press Gold Key Award. Her Youth Forum won the coveted George Foster Peabody award. On March 3, 1953 she received a certificate of honor from Town Hall Club of New York "as a builder of good citizens and champion of the free exchange of ideas."

She is firmly convinced that "we cannot keep our youth in a vacuum on world affairs. 'Children should be seen and not heard' is a slogan of the past. 'The world's problems are our problems, too,' today's children declare. Issues are examined and probed, with a curious far-seeing evaluation. They want to talk and discuss and *think*. So give the youth a platform," she urges, "but see that the platform is used thoughtfully, and under adult guidance. When we encourage a flow of ideas between young people of varying backgrounds, and encourage them to think about the world and humanity, we are planting the seeds of democracy."

References

Audio-Visual N 19:3 por O '53
N Y Times II p13 S 27 '53 por

GORMAN, HERBERT SHERMAN Jan. 1, 1893-Oct. 28, 1954 Author; self-educated; was a reporter for Springfield (Mass.) *Republican* (1915); a member of editorial staff of Springfield *Union* (1916-18), New York *Sun* (1918-21), New York *Evening Post* (1921-23), New York *Times* (1923-27), New York *Herald Tribune* (1927-28); during 1920's and 1930's was a leading book critic of the New York *Times*; was an intimate friend of James Joyce and wrote *James Joyce; His First Forty Years* (1924) and *James Joyce* (1939); included among his books are *The Wine of San Lorenzo* (1945), *The Cry of Dolores* (1947), and *The Breast of the Dove* (1950). See *Current Biography* (Mar.) 1940.

Obituary

N Y Times p21 O 29 '54

GRAHAM, WINSTON 1909- Author

Address: b. c/o Doubleday & Co., Inc., 575 Madison Ave., New York 22; h. Treberran, Perranporth, Cornwall, England

Reprinted from the *Wilson Library Bulletin* Nov. 1955

The county of Cornwall, England, a familiar setting in opera, ballet and literature, has attracted the interest and talent of the British author, Winston Graham. He first moved to this coastal countryside from Manchester at the impressionable age of seventeen. Some twenty years later he began writing a series of historical novels about eighteenth century Cornwall, *Demelza* (Ward, Lock, 1946; Doubleday, 1953), *The Renegade* (Doubleday, 1951), *Venture Once More* (Doubleday, 1954), and *The Last Gamble* (Doubleday, 1955), which follow the fortunes of Ross Poldark and his wife Demelza, a miner's daughter.

The lists of the Doubleday Dollar Book Club have included several of Graham's books: *Cordelia* (1950), *Night without Stars* (1950), and *Fortune is a Woman* (1953). *Demelza* was a selection of the Book League of America in 1953.

WINSTON GRAHAM

Descended from Lancashire stock, Winston Mawdsley Graham was born in 1909 in Manchester, England to Albert Henry and Anne (Mawdsley) Graham. His maternal great-grandfather, Thomas Mawdsley, worked with the 7th Earl of Shaftesbury and others on the factory legislation of the 1840's and 1850's.

A delicate boy, Winston left school at the age of sixteen and continued his education with a tutor. He began writing novels at the age of twenty-one, and, he has said, "owes a great deal in the early stages" to his mother, who, by then a widow, supported him and enabled him to "devote his whole time to writing when the achievement was hardly enough in itself to justify it." Graham's early novels were destroyed when the firm which published them was "blitzed" in 1941. ("I would not wish to resurrect any of them," he commented recently.)

For five years during World War II Graham served in the Coastguard Service. He resumed writing with *The Merciless Ladies* (Ward, Lock, 1944), which was purchased for filming. However, this was prevented by the recession which occurred in the British film industry at that time; his books *Take My Life* (Ward, Lock, 1947) and *Night without Stars* were later produced by the J. Arthur Rank organization.

Night without Stars, a suspense novel whose hero is a partially blind English lawyer, was called by James Kelly "credibly motivated and compelling as to character and place" (New York *Times,* September 3, 1950). The background of *Cordelia,* a novel of a young woman and her domineering father-in-law in Manchester in the 1860's, was "its most distinctive element" according to W. K. Rugg (*Christian Science Monitor,* January 26, 1950). Virginia Kirkus called it "a substantial and rather soberly romantic story."

(Continued next page)

GRAHAM, WINSTON—*Continued*

Riley Hughes (*Catholic World,* March 1952) commented that the chief merit of *The Renegade* "lies in its circumstantial historical background, with its fund of information about the trades and manners of eighteenth century Cornwall, rather than in the slight love story." *Demelza,* another of the Poldark series, "is more than a collection of romances. . . . It offers realistic and somber descriptions of Cornish farmers, fisherman and miners pushed to the verge of revolution by unjust laws" (W. A. S. Dollard in the New York *Times,* March 8, 1953).

The reviewer in the *Saturday Review* (March 12, 1955) observed that Graham in *The Last Gamble* "engineers the adventures of the Poldarks in a manner that hangs on to the reader's interest." Whitney Betts (New York *Times,* May 9, 1954) wrote that *Venture Once More* "is a leisurely novel which transports the reader to its milieu and makes its characters one's friends." Other books by Graham include *The Forgotten Story* (Ward, Lock, 1945 and 1949), *Take My Life* (Ward, Lock, 1947), *Jeremy Poldark* (Ward, Lock, 1950 and 1953) and *Warleggan* (Ward, Lock, 1953).

Francis Iles observed in the London *Sunday Times* that *The Little Walls* (1955) was "a quite remarkable achievement" and Francis Grierson in the London *Daily Mail* commented: "An absorbing story, a brilliant study in psychology, and an acidly witty characterization of believable people." Lenore Glen Offord in the San Francisco *Chronicle* described Graham's *Fortune is a Woman* (1953; a Doubleday Dollar Book Club choice, 1954), a suspense novel of fraud in the art world, "an extremely good, readable, exciting story."

Among his favorite authors are W. Somerset Maugham, John P. Marquand, John Galsworthy, and Graham Greene. Aside from reading Graham enjoys, traveling, lawn tennis, swimming, and rose-growing. With Mrs. Graham, who was Jean Mary Williamson before their marriage in 1939, he spent two months in the United States in 1950, and later visited the West Indies. The Grahams have a son, Andrew Winston Mawdsley Graham, and a daughter, Anne Rosamund Mawdsley Graham. The writer has blue eyes, dark brown hair, stands six feet and weighs 170 pounds. He is a Liberal-Conservative and a member of the Church of England. His clubs are the Savile, Brook Street and Mayfair.

Reference

Author's & Writer's Who's Who (1948-49)

GRAZIANI, RODOLFO Aug. 11, 1882-Jan. 11, 1955 Italian military leader; conquered Ethiopia and became its Viceroy; led Italian troops in North Africa in World War II; later was Mussolini's minister of defense; after war, was sentenced to prison for collaboration with the Nazis; freed by government amnesty in 1950 and thereafter was active in supporting neo-Fascists in Italy; remained a hero to most of the Italian people. See *Current Biography* (Apr.) 1941.

Obituary

N Y Times p27 Ja 12 '55

GREBE, JOHN J(OSEF) (grĕ'bê) Feb. 1, 1900- Physical chemist; inventor

Address: b. c/o Dow Chemical Co., Midland, Mich.; h. 5 Chippewa River Rd., Midland, Mich.

Prior to the Atomic Energy Act of 1954, a few business firms had conducted research in the field of nuclear physics; among them was the Dow Chemical Company which, in 1953, appointed Dr. John Josef Grebe to the position of director of nuclear research and development. Grebe is devoting his efforts to the peaceful uses of atomic power. He was formerly the Dow company's research counselor (1950-1953) and director of its physical research laboratory (1924-1948). He has been chief advisor to the U.S. Army Chemical Corps since 1949.

A noted industrial scientist, Grebe has made contributions to the field of science, which include "outstanding achievement in the plastics industry" as well as electronic and chemical analysis and inventions. He is credited with having made possible the wartime production of styrene for synthetic GR-S rubber and for discovering a great many new uses for this plastic. He holds more than forty patents in the fields of power generation, electrochemistry, air conditioning, and synthesis of organic compounds.

The son of Carl and Gertrude (Erbes) Grebe, John Josef Grebe was born in Uerzig, Rhineland, Germany, on February 1, 1900. Fourteen years later the Grebes arrived in the United States, settling in Cleveland, Ohio. In 1918 John was graduated, valedictorian, from the East Technical High School of Cleveland. He became an American citizen in 1921.

An honor student in college, Grebe received his B.S. degree from the Case School of Applied Science (now Case Institute of Technology), also in Cleveland, in 1924, and was elected to Sigma Xi. He remained at the Case School to obtain his master's degree (1927), and, in 1935, his alma mater presented him with the honorary D.Sc. degree. His choice of his particular field of endeavor, Grebe has asserted, was influenced by Thomas A. Edison and Dr. Dayton C. Miller, then a professor of physics at Case.

Beginning his career with the Dow Chemical Company on July 1, 1924, Grebe was director of its physical research laboratory until 1948. In this capacity, his work was concerned with research on electrochemical analysis and control, heat transfer fluids, electrolysis of fused salts, thermal power cycles, and the chemical treatment of oil wells.

In 1946 Grebe was "loaned out" to the U.S. Government at its Oak Ridge, Tennessee reservation, where, he has said, he spent nine months "for training and work on the application of nuclear energy to the industrial operations of this country." In the same year he was a civilian observer at the Bikini bomb tests.

Returning to Dow Chemical Company, Grebe was research assistant to the president from 1948 to 1950, research counselor from 1950 to 1953 and director of nuclear research and development since 1953. In 1952 he was a consultant on research organization for the U.S. Air Force at Wright-Patterson Air Force Base, Dayton, Ohio.

The scientist has made valuable contributions to the commercial process of recovering magnesium from sea water. Today, Dow, "with increased production facilities for magnesium, is anxious to promote the metal's use in consumer goods" (*Business Week*, January 22, 1955). These consumer goods include table tops and strong, lightweight luggage (one new product is called Ultralite and is manufactured by Shwayder Brothers, makers of Samsonite luggage, of magnesium covered with vinyl plastics).

Prior to World War II Grebe was looking for an improved electronic insulating material. Since pure polymerized hydrocarbons are well suited for this purpose, his research led him to styrene. Grebe did much of the major research work in the United States on the production and polymerization of styrene. Polymerized styrene is a thermoplastic, a rigid plastic with unusual optical and electrical qualities. It can be produced in a wide range of colors, and is in great demand at the present time. Another plastic developed by Grebe is butadiene, used in producing a number of chemical products and certain plastics, as well as synthetic rubber. He also helped to develop Saran, a synthetic plastic.

Among his inventions is a compact unit for doing housework—a power plant in the home that can wash the dishes, wash, dry and iron clothes, freeze food, and provide all bathroom facilities. The entire unit weighs about 3,500 pounds, a little bigger than an automobile. The unit could be installed in the home or added on and is composed of magnesium, plastics and glass.

As early as 1943 Dr. Grebe warned the nation that it was depending too much upon mechanical inventions, and therefore made itself more vulnerable to destruction. He said, "Let me shock you by advocating a new research in the direction of much older and more common tools, the shovel, the ax, the saw, and the bow and arrow." It was a good idea, he thought, to get ". . . close to life without machine tools and transported vital materials" (*Newsweek*, December 6, 1943).

In early 1955 Dow announced that it was setting up a new subsidiary, Nederlandsche Dow Maatschappij, to produce chemicals at Rotterdam, the Netherlands. The subsidiary will import some raw materials from Dow's U.S. plants and will manufacture and sell in the Netherlands and world markets a full line of Dow polystyrenes, glycols, and magnesium alloys (*Business Week*, January 29, 1955).

JOHN J. GREBE

The inventor is a director of the Ewing Development Company and vice-president and director of Dowell, Incorporated, a subsidiary of the Dow Chemical Company. He is a fellow of the American Association for the Advancement of Science, American Institute of Chemists, and Society of Chemical Industry. He maintains membership in the American Chemical Society, American Institute of Chemical Engineers, American Physical Society, and others. His clubs are the Kiwanis, Midland Country, and Saginaw Valley Torch in Midland. Articles written by Grebe have appeared in a number of engineering publications and scientific journals.

On March 2, 1929 Grebe married Hazel Amanda Holmes. They have five children, Ruth Elaine, Joanne Hazel, John Holmes, Carolyn Louise, and James Carl. The scientist is over five feet ten inches tall, weighs 180 pounds. His eyes are hazel colored, his hair brown. One of his greatest interests is vocational guidance for the youth of the nation. Grebe is especially fond of travel. He is a Lutheran.

For his work in the development of the sun screen he received the Certificate of Merit from the Franklin Institute of Philadelphia in 1942; he was awarded the Chemical Industry Medal of the Society of Chemical Industry in 1943 in recognition of his contributions toward the solution of problems pertaining to the automatic control of chemical reactions; and he received the John Wesley Hyatt Award in 1947 for his discoveries regarding styrene.

References

Mod Plastics 24:109 My '47
N Y Times p36 Ap 24 '47; p40 Je 25 '53
American Men of Science (1955)
Who's Who in America, 1954-55

GREGG, MILTON F(OWLER) Apr. 10, 1892- Canadian Minister of Labour

Address: c/o Department of Labour, Parliament Bldgs., Ottawa, Ontario, Canada; h. Thorn Cottage, Fredericton, New Brunswick, Canada

It is the conviction of Canada's Minister of Labour, Milton F. Gregg, that opportunities for economic improvement must be made available for every member of the community as well as for industrial enterprise. Gregg, who succeeded the late minister, Humphrey Mitchell, on August 7, 1950, believes that his government can contribute toward greater economic opportunity by providing education, training, and job-counselling and placement services. During his administration a women's bureau has been established and the Fair Employment Practices Act, the Old Age Assistance Act, and the Old Age Security Act have been passed by the Canadian Parliament. He had previously been Minister of Veterans Affairs and Minister of Fisheries. He became a Privy Councillor and representative for the constituency of York-Sunbury, New Brunswick to the House of Commons in 1947.

National Film Bd.

MILTON F. GREGG

Known as the "father" of officer training in the Canadian Army, Gregg, who attained the rank of brigadier during World War II, was in command of Canada's training centers for officers in England and North America. Upon his retirement from the Army he became president of the University of New Brunswick, serving in that office until 1947. He was awarded the Military Cross and the Victoria Cross for conspicuous bravery in World War I.

Of United Empire Loyalist stock, Milton Fowler Gregg was born on a New Brunswick, Canada farm in Mountain Dale, on April 10, 1892, the son of George Lord and Eliza Celia (Myles) Gregg. His family background was Conservative politically. After attending the local public schools, he enrolled at the provincial Normal School in Fredericton, New Brunswick. In this city, he became a public school teacher in 1910 and taught for two years. He also served as a private with the Princess Louise 8th Hussars, Sussex, New Brunswick, and later qualified as a cadet instructor.

Resuming his academic studies, Gregg entered Acadia University in Wolfville, Nova Scotia. When World War I broke out, he interrupted his education to enlist in the Army. He was sent overseas with the first Canadian contingent in 1915 as a member of the Black Watch Regiment. After being wounded in the battle of Festubert (France) in May of that year, he was posted to the Imperial Officers' Training Corps. He served as a second lieutenant with the King's Own Royal, Lancashire Regiment, then was transferred to a command in the Royal Canadian Regiment.

While leading a trench raid in June 1917, Gregg was again wounded and won the Military Cross for "conspicuous gallantry" (*Labour Gazette,* September 1950). A bar was added to his Military Cross for his courage in repelling an enemy attack in August 1918 at Arras, France, during which he was wounded again. In the following month he was engaged in battles which won him the Victoria Cross "for most conspicuous bravery" in penetrating the Hindenburg Line at Cambrai, France, single-handed. Demobilized from the Army in April 1919, he left the service with the rank of adjutant.

Deciding to enter government service, he became a member of the Soldier's Civil Re-Establishment, where he helped war veterans to become adjusted to civilian life. He continued in the Non-Permanent Active Militia (NPAM), and was a major in the 16th Infantry Brigade. During the early 1920's, he was attached to the Soldier Settlement Board. Then he left the civil service to engage in his own business in New Brunswick. Meanwhile, he kept a close contact with the Canadian Legion and served with the New Brunswick Rangers. Acadia University awarded him an honorary M.A. degree in 1920.

When the post of sergeant-at-arms became vacant at the House of Commons in Ottawa, Gregg was appointed to that office (1934) which he held for five years. At the same time he served as honorary Dominion treasurer of the Canadian Legion, and commanded a company in the Governor General's Foot Guards.

At the outbreak of World War II, Gregg offered his services to the Canadian Army and in December went overseas as second in command of the Royal Canadian Regiment. He took a course with the British commandos, and in February 1940 was assigned to the West Nova Scotia Regiment in England as a commanding officer with the rank of lieutenant colonel. In April 1941 he was given command of the Canadian Officers' Training Unit in England.

In March 1942 Gregg received a promotion to the rank of colonel and returned to Canada to command the Officers' Training Corps at Brockville, Ontario, where his country decided to centralize its officer training. Early in 1943, he again went overseas to study modern infantry training, and in September of that year was assigned the rank of brigadier and put in command of the Canadian School of Infantry at Vernon, British Columbia; he remained there until the end of the war. According to *Saturday Night* (October 4, 1947), Gregg "played a major role in building the big Canadian Army," and at Brockville "turned out most of the young leaders of the Army." For his services he was awarded the Order of Commander of the British Empire.

After his retirement from the Army, Gregg became president of the University of New Brunswick in Fredericton. During his administration, he made the university better known among high school students, and "was able to enthuse the staff and students in the same way in which he inspired officer-cadets and their instructors" (*Saturday Night,* October 4, 1947). In 1947 he was appointed Minister of Fisheries and a Privy Councillor.

Entering politics as a Parliamentary candidate for the constituency of York-Sunbury, New Brunswick, Gregg won a seat in the by-election of October 20, 1947, to which he was re-elected in the general election of June 1949, and again in 1953. On January 19, 1948 he also became Minister of Veterans Affairs, and was reappointed on November 15, 1948 in the Cabinet of Louis S. St. Laurent. Two years later, on August 7, 1950, he received his present appointment.

As Minister of Labour, Gregg places emphasis on greater productivity, improved labor-management relations, collective bargaining "as far as possible with a minimum of reliance on outside assistance," and prevention of inflation (*Labour Gazette,* October 1954). He told the Canadian Congress at Labour at its tenth anniversary convention in Winnipeg, Manitoba in September 1950: "We have got past believing that poverty can be eliminated . . . by Act of Parliament. . . . The great social projects of our time have to be made economically possible through the productivity of our people" (*Labour Gazette,* November 1950). He advised the Trades and Labour Congress, meeting in Halifax, Nova Scotia, in September 1951, that ". . . the threat of inflation is second only to the threat of war" (*Labour Gazette,* November 1951).

Gregg has called the Old Age Assistance and Old Age Security Acts, effective January 1952, "one of the best old age security programs in the world" (*Labour Gazette,* November 1951). He stated in September 1954 that "unemployment insurance has been of considerable help in maintaining the wage earner's purchasing power" (*Labour Gazette,* October 1954). With respect to the rehabilitation of the disabled, he declared that ". . . money is not *spent* on rehabilitation, but *invested*" (*Labour Gazette,* June 1953).

The Minister of Labour was called in consultation with Prime Minister St. Laurent in August 1954 to deal with the threatened strike of about 145,000 railway workers. The strike was settled by "compulsory arbitration" (*Saturday Night,* January 8, 1955). After unemployment began reaching about 14 per cent of Canada's labor force in the summer of 1954, Gregg declared it "would not be solved by waving a magic wand over the country."

In a three-day Parliamentary debate in February 1955 on unemployment, Gregg answered criticism of the Opposition. He admitted that in January there were 570,000 workers registered at the 200 National Employment Offices across Canada. But, he pointed out, of these 59,610 were re-employed during January, and 450,400 were receiving regular and supplementary unemployment benefits (*Saturday Night,* March 19, 1955). However, labor unions are insistent that payments to the unemployed are inadequate. By June 1955 the number of unemployed had fallen to an estimated 157,000, the lowest point since November 1953.

On the international front, the Minister of Labour approves technical assistance programs and other forms of aid that will increase productivity in countries needing industrial development. He claims that if Canada is to fulfil her part under the United Nations' Charter and NATO, she will have to divert some of her production and wealth into channels that "will exert unnatural pressures" on her economic structure (*Labour Gazette,* September Supplement 1950).

The King's Jubilee Medal was awarded to Gregg in 1935 and the Coronation Medal in 1937. He received an honorary D.C.L. degree from Acadia University in 1944, and holds honorary LL.D. degrees from the University of New Brunswick and the University of Dalhousie, Nova Scotia.

On August 25, 1919 Gregg married Amy Dorothy Alward. They have a daughter, Eleanor Jean (Mrs. Alexander Grant). The Minister is described as "an energetic and persuasive person who invariably throws everything he has into the task in hand" (*Saturday Night,* October 4, 1947). For recreation, he enjoys hunting and fishing. His church affiliation is Baptist.

He has called for "a solid body of protective legislation—for both workers and employers", including minimum wage legislation, workmen's compensation, unemployment insurance, factory inspection, and the protection of health and safety of workers (*Labour Gazette,* July 1953). Gregg believes that Canada "is following a liberal monetary policy and has undertaken legislative changes which will broaden the flow of mortgage funds for home building."

References

Labour Gazette 50:1307+ S '50
N Y Times p8 Ag 8 '50
Sat Night p 10+ O 4 '47
Canadian Who's Who, 1952-54
Who's Who, 1955
Who's Who in Canada, 1953-54

GRIFFITHS, MARTHA W(RIGHT) Jan. 29, 1912- United States Representative from Michigan; lawyer

Address: b. House Office Bldg., Washington, D.C.; h. 12080 Montrose Ave., Detroit, Mich.

Winning a seat in the United States House of Representatives on the Democratic ticket, Martha W. Griffiths was elected to Congress from Michigan's Seventeenth District on November 2, 1954. In 1953 she became the first woman judge of Recorder's Court, Detroit, Michigan. An experienced lawmaker as well as lawyer, she served as representative to the Michigan Legislature from Wayne county, First District, from 1949 to 1952. Her efforts are aimed, she says, at "making Democracy a living force."

Tenschert

MARTHA W. GRIFFITHS

Martha Wright was born in Pierce City, Missouri, on January 29, 1912, the daughter of Charles Elbridge, a letter carrier, and Nell (Sullinger) Wright. Her ancestors were both English and French. She has one brother, Edward. After attending the local public schools, she graduated in 1930 from Pierce City High School, where she had been a member of the debating society.

Miss Wright next entered the University of Missouri at Columbia, and particularly enjoyed the political science classes. She participated in discussions on the subject with a fellow student, Hicks G. Griffiths, whom she married after completing college. The University of Missouri awarded her the A.B. degree in 1934. She then went with her husband to study law at the University of Michigan, Ann Arbor, Michigan, from which she received the LL.B. degree in 1940. She was on the editorial staff of the *Michigan Law Review.*

Admitted to the Michigan bar in 1941, Mrs. Griffiths joined the legal department of the American Automobile Insurance Company. After the United States entered World War II, she took a post as a contract negotiator in the Detroit district for the Army Ordnance, where she worked until April 1946. Then she opened her own office for the practice of law.

Her husband joined her in business within a few months, after completing his service with the Office of Price Administration. The next year, in 1947, a former college classmate, G. Mennen Williams, now Governor of Michigan, became a partner, and the firm was renamed Griffiths, Williams & Griffiths. Mrs. Griffiths was called "a good trial lawyer" by Detroit Judge W. McKay Skillman, writing in the *Detroit Lawyer* (January 1954).

After deciding to enter state politics, she ran in the primary election for a seat in the Michigan House of Representatives in 1946 but was defeated; she ran again two years later and was elected. In 1949 she was a member of the interim committee of this legislature, set up to codify the public utility laws. During her legislative office, she also served on the House judiciary and conservation committees. On November 7, 1950 she was re-elected to the House for a second two-year term.

As a state legislator, she sponsored amendments liberalizing the unemployment compensation act, and also supported the enriched flour bill providing for flour processors to restore the vitamins and minerals lost in milling. In recognition of her legislative efforts and understanding of public questions, she was acclaimed in 1951 as one of Michigan's ten best legislators, by the Capitol Press Corps.

Although she won over three rivals in the 1952 Democratic primary election for representative from Michigan's Seventeenth District to the U.S. Congress, Mrs. Griffiths lost the race in the general election by a slim margin to Charles G. Oakman. In her campaign, she attracted nation-wide publicity by touring her district in a housetrailer and meeting as many citizens as possible in their own neighborhood or in front of their homes. During these informal visits with the voters, she served them fruit juice, coffee and cookies, and talked with approximately 40,000 persons.

Mrs. Griffiths was appointed on April 1, 1953, by Governor G. Mennen Williams of Michigan, a recorder and judge of Recorder's Court, Detroit, the first woman to receive such an appointment. A few months later, on November 2, she was elected a judge to this court for a short term expiring December 31, 1953. While in this post, she exclaimed: ". . . sometimes as I sit on the bench and find it my duty to pass sentence on my fellow man, I wish that I could have been a judge before I was a legislator" (*Detroit Lawyer*, January 1954). She added: ". . . It is at least an unusual experience to assist for four years in making the laws of this state, and then sit as a judge of people charged with breaking those laws."

In court she held monthly meetings with her nine colleagues, consulted psychiatrists and probation officers prior to felony sentences, and, as a court recorder, was a member of the City Elections Commission. Of her service, her colleague, Judge W. McKay Skillman, writes: "Judge Griffiths wasn't the easiest judge on the Recorder's Court bench. Lawyers and defendants found her possessed of a keen sense of justice, a good analytical mind, and the courage to act for the good of the community" (*Detroit Lawyer,* January 1954). She passed judgment on more than 24,000 persons, and conducted 430 criminal examinations, including a long and difficult teamsters' conspiracy case.

During her second campaign for a seat in the U.S. Congress as Representative from Michigan's Seventeenth District, conducted in 1954, Martha W. Griffiths again employed the housetrailer methods of her 1952 appeal to voters. She won the Detroit seat in Congress from her Republican opponent, Charles G. Oakman, on November 2, 1954, and became the first woman to be sent to Congress from this District. She told William C. Tremblay in an interview for the Detroit *News* (November 3, 1954): "I owe my election to all the girls who went out and rang doorbells and invited housewives to meet me."

In the first session of the Eighty-fourth Congress (1955), Martha Griffiths was appointed to the House Committees on Banking and Currency, and on Government Operations. During this session, she introduced bills to increase the pay of employees in the field service of the Post Office Department (January), to promote development of public library service in rural areas (January), to arrange for the distribution of certain surplus food commodities to needy persons by means of a food-stamp plan (February), and to amend the Housing Act of 1937 to provide housing for elderly people with low incomes (February).

The Congresswoman protested on the floor of the House on March 29 against the sale to magazines of public information that is denied to reporters on the ground of national security. She stated that ". . . it is repugnant to the American tradition for a Government official to use information, to which we are all entitled, for private gain" (*Congressional Record*).

On January 25, 1955 she voted "yea" on the bill authorizing the President to use the U.S. armed forces to defend Formosa, and told the House: "Under such circumstances a positive vote of the Congress serves as a warning to the world that we stand as one to protect ourselves at all times anywhere in the world" (*Congressional Record*).

Mrs. Griffiths' record in the first session of the Eighty-fourth Congress also shows her voting in favor of extending the Universal Military Training and Service Act (February), increasing salaries of Congress and judiciary members (February), and opposing dropping the $20 income tax cut and the Eisenhower Highway program.

She won a commendation by the Detroit City Council in 1953, and was named one of twelve "women of achievement" in that city by the Detroit *Free Press,* for her accomplishments as a judge in the Recorder's Court. She is a member and legal advisor to the Michigan Business and Professional Women's Clubs. Other organizations of which she is a member include the Eastern Star, Michigan Humane Society, Michigan and Detroit bar associations, and Detroit Historical Society. In 1947 and 1948 she was a member of the Michigan Democratic State Central Committee. Her church affiliation is Presbyterian. She has brown hair and eyes, and greatly enjoys reading.

References

Detroit Lawyer p5+ Ja '54
Detroit News p22 N 3 '54
Detroit Times p19 N 1 '54
Ind Woman 34:22 Ja '55
Congressional Record (1955)
Michigan Official Directory and Legislative Manual, 1951

GRONCHI, GIOVANNI (grŏń'kē) Sept. 10, 1887- President of Italy

Address: b. Quirinal Palace, Rome, Italy

The third President of the Republic of Italy is Giovanni Gronchi, leader of the left-wing faction of the Christian Democratic party, who was elected on April 29, 1955 to succeed Luigi Einaudi. His victory was achieved with the support of left-wing parties and in spite of opposition from certain leaders within his own party. He is expected to take a more active part in government affairs than the ceremonial position to which other Italian Presidents have adhered, according to C. L. Sulzberger (New York *Times,* July 6, 1955).

Since the age of fifteen Gronchi was a leader in the Christian Democratic movement. He was elected to Parliament and served briefly in Benito Mussolini's government but because of his opposition to Il Duce, he was obliged to retire from politics. For twenty years he devoted himself to commerce and industry, and during World War II was active in the underground and later served on the National Liberation Front. He was Minister for Industry and Commerce in several postwar governments and participated in the trade union movement. For seven years he was Speaker of the Chamber of Deputies.

In his initial speech as President, Gronchi stated: "The standard of living of a great many families remains very low, and the inert or insufficiently utilized labor potential is still too great." He recommended "the elimination of unemployment as the first problem to be resolved in order of urgency" (*Current History,* August 1955).

Giovanni Gronchi was born in Pontedera in the province of Pisa, Italy on September 10, 1887, the son of Sperandio and Maria (Giacomelli) Gronchi. He went to work at an early age and later earned his way through the University of Pisa, from which he was graduated with degrees in letters and in law. As a youth he became one of the leaders of the Christian Democratic movement founded in 1902 by Romolo Murri, a priest, with whom Don Luigi Sturzo collaborated. This movement sought political autonomy for Catholics and improvement of conditions of the Christian trade union organizations. In World War I

Wide World

GIOVANNI GRONCHI

Gronchi fought as a volunteer and earned a medal for valor. In 1919, under Sturzo's leadership, he helped to found the Populari (Popular party), predecessor of the Christian Democratic party.

Elected to Parliament in 1919, Gronchi became a member of the Parliamentary Group. He was active in trade unions and was appointed head of the Confederation of Christian Workers in 1919. In 1922 he became undersecretary for Industry and Commerce in Mussolini's government, holding this office until a meeting of anti-Fascist leaders was held in Turin in August 1923, which resolved upon a policy of noncollaboration with Mussolini. As a member of the Opposition in Parliament, Gronchi was one of the leaders of the Aventine movement. When the King refused to hear the Opposition's motion against the Fascist party. Gronchi was forced to retire by parliamentary mandate. He then turned to commercial interests in Milan.

In World War II Gronchi established contact with underground groups and rapidly became one of the leaders in the political and military struggle in Italy. With Alcide de Gasperi, he represented the Christian Democratic party on the central committee of the National Liberation Front. He was Minister for Industry, Commerce and Labor during the first two Ivanoe Bonomi governments (June 18, 1944-June 19, 1945), and the Ferruccio Parri government (June 21-December 8, 1945). In the first de Gasperi government, formed in December 1945, Gronchi was Minister of Commerce.

After Italy voted to become a republic on June 2, 1946, Gronchi was elected to the Constituent Assembly and later became president of its Parliamentary Group, holding this office until the dissolution of the Assembly. On the labor front, he served as president of the Committee for Trade Union Agreements and was responsible for Christian Trade Union policies up to the time when these organizations became independent of the Italian General Confederation of Labor.

Elected Speaker of the Chamber of Deputies on May 8, 1948, Gronchi emphasized in his opening address the need for fundamental reforms to incorporate the working classes into the Italian government and called for the preservation of peace, maintaining that Italy should be "the point of union, not the line of demarcation" (New York *Times,* May 9, 1948). Later, he criticized the government's internal policy as being under pressure from reactionary capitalist and land-owning groups.

Between 1951 and 1954 Gronchi supported the idea that "fellow-traveling" Socialist Pietro Nenni and his followers could be lured away from their working alliance with the Communists (New York *Herald Tribune,* October 24, 1954). On this platform, he several times aspired to the Premiership, but was opposed by his own party and President Luigi Einaudi. Gronchi was criticized for his lenient treatment of Communist "shock-troop" tactics in the Chamber of Deputies. He was reappointed Speaker on July 25, 1952, and re-elected deputy in 1953. He helped to steer the North Atlantic Treaty Alliance and the Western European Union treaties through the Chamber of Deputies in the face of strong opposition.

On April 29, 1955 Gronchi was elected President of delegates from regional councils to succeed Luigi Einaudi, a Liberal Catholic who ran for re-election. The Christian Democratic party led by Premier Mario Scelba and Amintore Fanfani, party secretary-general, had supported Cesare Merzagora, President of the Senate and an Independent. Gronchi had received strong support from Communists and left-wing Socialists and from former Premier Giuseppe Pella, a Christian Democrat. After the third ballot, when Gronchi's strength had become evident, Scelba tried to persuade him to withdraw. Upon Gronchi's refusal, Scelba and Fanfani reluctantly gave him their support. Gronchi was elected on the fourth ballot by the overwhelming vote of 658 out of a possible 833. Gronchi's election received approval from all sections of the press, and the Vatican found it desirable to have a militant Catholic at the head of the Italian state. However, Gronchi immediately stressed his independency of both right and left, refuting the charge that he was a neutralist and against NATO.

According to *Time* (May 9, 1955), "Gronchi's victory was a humiliating defeat for Scelba's shaky four-party coalition of the center; it was an open defiance of Fanfani's personal leadership of the big Christian Democratic party, which has firmly guided Italy into the anti-Communist front since the war." An editorial in the New York *Times* (May 20, 1955), observed that Gronchi's inaugural speech "showed an intention to seek to influence the orientation of Italian politics from the Center toward the Left." But Leo J. Wollemborg, writing for the Washington *Post and Times Herald* (May 8, 1955), found that "Nothing seems farther from his mind and character than to assume the role of a partisan President."

As President, Gronchi serves a seven-year term at a salary of $20,000 a year. Although his office is largely ceremonial, his power to designate a new Premier entails great responsibility. Upon taking his oath of office on May 11, 1955, he called for greater power for the "working masses and the middle classes" in running the country. He expressed his belief that the extreme left-wing parties should be admitted into the government. To admit them peacefully, he said, was a "fundamental interest of Italian democracy." He also praised the people of America for their aid to postwar Italian reconstruction.

On May 12 President Gronchi refused to accept a formal offer of resignation from Premier Scelba and his Centrist coalition government, pending the outcome of regional parliamentary elections in Sicily on June 5. Scelba on May 18 warned against the "stupidity and error" of a "flirtation with Nenni's fellow-traveling Socialists" and said the Christian Democratic party had reason to be proud of its achievements in the eight years since Communists were ousted from the government.

Alarm was expressed in Italy at the unfavorable American reaction to Gronchi's election. However, this was to some extent dispelled when on May 23 an agreement was signed providing for $50,000,000 worth of U.S. cotton, wheat and tobacco to be sent to Italy. At the signing ceremony, Scelba and Mrs. Clare Booth Luce, U.S. Ambassador to Italy, stressed the friendship and collaboration between their two nations. Of significance also was Gronchi's appointment of Mario Luciolli, pro-Western Minister of the Italian Embassy in Washington, as his foreign affairs adviser (New York *Times,* May 21, 1955).

Mario Scelba was forced to resign as Italy's Premier on June 21, 1955 after the Republican party (one of the four parties composing the coalition of Scelba's government) refused to concur in a recent Cabinet reshuffle and after a bitter factional disagreement within his own party. Gronchi, on June 26, formally charged Antonio Segni, a Christian Democrat, with the task of forming a new government. Segni presented his Cabinet on July 6; it is similar in policy and personnel to that of Scelba.

The President of Italy has been described as having gray-blond hair and blue eyes. He is married and has two children who share his hobby of collecting model trains. Described as proud, stubborn, a brilliant orator and a militant Catholic, Gronchi has been called "one of the ablest and most ambitious figures in Italian politics." "His superior skill and tact" as Speaker of the Chamber of Deputies and his "independence from party machines have earned him the respect and potential support of many disparate groups in Parliament," wrote Wollemborg, who further characterized Gronchi as a "steadfast champion of the democratic form of government."

References

Time 65:30 My 9 '55 por
Washington (D.C.) Post p3E My 8 '55
Chi è? (1948)
World Biography (1954)

GROUÈS, HENRI ANTOINE *See* Pierre, Abbé

GUEDEN, HILDE Sept. 15, 1923- Singer

Address: b. c/o Metropolitan Opera Association, 149 W. 39th St., New York 18; Hurok Attractions, 711 5th Ave., New York 22

Making her Metropolitan Opera debut as Gilda in *Rigoletto* on November 15, 1951, the Viennese soprano Hilde Gueden, "blonde, beautiful and glorious-voiced," has been singing "alluringly and fetchingly" in such varied roles as Rosalinda in the Johann Strauss operetta *Fledermaus,* as Zerlina in Mozart's *Don Giovanni,* Musetta in Puccini's *La Bohème,* Micaela in Bizet's *Carmen* and Anne Trulove in Stravinsky's *The Rake's Progress.* She portrayed Zdenka in Richard Strauss's opera *Arabella,* on February 11, 1955. "Miss Gueden has a most attractive, clear, and ringing voice," commented Paul Henry Lang, the New York *Herald Tribune*'s new critic, "with which she can do anything she wishes—and that's just what she did."

Under the management of impresario S. Hurok, she appears in concert, on television, and radio. She records for London FFRR records. Of her latest album, *Rigoletto,* John Briggs in the New York *Times* (February 20, 1955) commented: "Miss Gueden's Gilda is delightfully expressive, agreeable in tonal quality. . . ."

Hilde Gueden was born in Vienna on September 15, 1923 of Austrian, Italian and Hungarian ancestry. Her father, Fritz Geiringer, and her mother, Frida Brammer, were both musicians. Her mother attended the Vienna State Academy of Drama at the same time as Elizabeth Bergner. Her father was a member of a well-known Italian-Austrian industrial banking family. Her musical education began at the age of seven when she took piano lessons, and she started her vocal studies at fourteen. When just sixteen, she accepted a role in the production of *Goodbye, Goodbye* by Robert Stolz, composer of a number of popular operettas.

At that time Miss Gueden had no particular desire for a stage career, but was encouraged by her mother and soon became an operetta favorite. During the run of *Goodbye, Goodbye,* she began serious preparation for her career as a singer. She studied dramatics at the Max Reinhardt School and ballet at the Vienna State Opera. She also learned to speak French, English and Italian fluently. She appeared with the Danish tenor, Max Hansen, in the operetta *Hearts in the Snow.* This was her last appearance on the Vienna stage until after World War II.

With the coming of Hitler and the Nazi occupation, Miss Gueden, whose mother was of Jewish extraction, found it difficult to pursue her career, and managed to make her way to Switzerland. Robert Denzler, director of the Zurich Opera House, engaged her to sing Cherubino in *Le Nozze di Figaro* in 1939, and

HILDE GUEDEN

she proved so popular with audiences that she sang during the next two years major lyric and coloratura parts. Owing to the persecution of her mother and sister under the Nazi regime in Austria, she returned to Vienna.

In 1941 Miss Gueden went to Munich, Germany where she made her debut at the Staatsoper as Zerlina in *Don Giovanni* in a performance conducted by Clemens Krauss. The composer, Richard Strauss, was in the audience while she was singing in *Così Fan Tutte,* and met the young soprano backstage after the opera. He urged her to learn the role of Sophie in his *Rosenkavalier.* She has since made this role "particularly her own" commented *Time* (January 14, 1952). After Strauss heard her in the part, he gave her his photograph inscribed: "To my Sophie Gueden."

In Italy in August 1942 she sang for the directors of the Teatro Reale at Rome. Engaged as a leading singer, she made her debut in December of that year in *Rosenkavalier* under the baton of Tullio Serafin. She sang at the Maggio Fiorintino in Florence and for a time lived quietly in Venice. After the war she was invited to appear at the Salzburg Festival in Austria, where she has been a regular artist since 1946, singing a wide variety of roles.

In 1947 the young soprano became a regular member of the Vienna State Opera and in the same year she was added to the roster of La Scala in Milan, Italy. As a tribute to her successes, she was appointed *Kammersängerin* of the Vienna Staatsoper in 1950, one of the youngest singers to be accorded such recognition.

Rudolf Bing, now manager of the Metropolitan Opera House in New York, first heard Miss Gueden when she was singing in Paris while touring with the Vienna State Opera in 1947. The next season he invited her to sing Zerlina in *Don Giovanni* at the Edinburgh Festival; she also sang at England's Glyndebourne Opera Festival. Since 1951 she has divided her time between her Austrian and Italian operatic engagements and her seasons at the "Met," where she made her debut on November 15, 1951 singing Gilda in *Rigoletto.* "Vivacious and hard-working," Miss Gueden has "measured up right to the last eighth note," commented *Time,* January 14, 1952, "in every role she has tackled since."

She has developed an enormous repertoire in several different languages, and has also proved a capable recitalist for the concert stage. Unusual roles do not faze her, whether it be in Kurt Weill's *Mahaggany,* Boris Blacher's *Romeo and Juliet,* Benjamin Britten's *The Rape of Lucretia,* Paul Hindemith's *Mathis der Maler.* She can also "give out with an American pop tune in the best Broadway tradition."

She sang the leading soprano role of Anne Trulove in Igor Stravinsky's *The Rake's Progress* at its American premiere on February 14, 1953, which was broadcast over Station WABC from the "Met" stage. "Musical beauty Miss Gueden gave us to the full," commented Virgil Thomson (New York *Herald Tribune,* February 22, 1953), "for this she was ideally cast. But the words seemed quite beyond her present powers of English enunciation."

Her characterizations have been described as "appealing," and sung with "musicianship and understanding," and her vocal technique "admirable." The critics united in acclaiming her portrayal of Eurydice in Gluck's *Orfeo ed Euridice* at the "Met" on February 24, 1955.

Shortly after her debut at the Metropolitan Opera in 1951 Miss Gueden was married to L. Lacey Herman. She told a reporter for *Pictorial Review* (May 11, 1952) that she had her heart set on coming to America. Since her arrival here she has considerably changed her hair style and make-up. "Gone is her former long hair, her thinly plucked eyebrows, her false eyelashes, her thin, Continental-style lipstick pattern." She looks, now, more like an American girl. Her only worry is to keep from catching cold, because she has to sing on an average of twice a week all season.

Miss Gueden's repertoire is large, for she learns quickly, she says, and since she can play the piano, she can study without an accompanist. She is as self-possessed on the operatic stage as she is during press interviews. "I'm not a nervous performer," she says, "at least not after the first few minutes."

When she begins to learn a new part she "lets it ripen" for about ten performances, and then takes a new look at it, histrionically as well as vocally. "One must never stop studying" she said (New York *Times,* December 2, 1951). William Hawkins described her in the New York *World-Telegram and Sun* (February 13, 1953) as having "a remarkable voice, the figure of a show girl, a lovely bright face and the indefinable quality known as charm."

References

N Y Times II p7 D 2 '51
N Y World-Telegram p18 F 13 '53

GUGGENHEIM, MRS. HARRY F(RANK) *See* Patterson, Alicia

GUPTILL, ARTHUR L(EIGHTON) (gŭp'tĭl) Mar. 19, 1891- Publisher; author; editor

Address: b. c/o Watson-Guptill Publications, Inc., 24 W. 40th St., New York 18; h. 37 Brownley Dr., Stamford, Conn.

The founder and co-editor of the magazine *American Artist* (which has the world's largest art magazine circulation) is Arthur L. Guptill. He has had vast experience as an art publisher as well as a teacher of commercial and fine art, advertising, architecture and interior decoration. He is president of the Watson-Guptill Publications, specialists in art books, and he is also the author of a series of art books for amateurs and professionals which have had extensive sale and are written in a "'down to earth' style that has become a Guptill trademark" (*Design,* February 1949). He founded the Amateur Artists Association of America, Inc., in 1951.

ARTHUR L. GUPTILL

Arthur Leighton Guptill was born on March 19, 1891, in Gorham, Maine, the son of Edward William and Nellie Ann (Stewart) Guptill. His New England forebears include a maternal grandfather who was a leading lumberman, merchant and packer of canned goods, and a paternal grandfather who—in addition to being a merchant and lumberman—was a superintendent of schools in Maine, a collector of customs and a member of the state legislature. Arthur's father was in the insurance and real estate business in Portland, Maine.

While attending public schools in Gorham, Arthur enjoyed sketching pictures, although he received no formal art instruction. He learned lettering from a local sign painter. In high school he painted scenery and made posters for theatricals; other extracurricular interests included playing the violin and athletics. Encouragement to study art came from one of his school teachers and from a friend, William P. F. Robie, the son of a Maine governor. This friend introduced him to an art teacher, Alfred E. Moore, of Portland, Maine, who taught him privately for several years.

After graduating from high school in 1909, Guptill took a special course at Gorham Normal School. He was interested in architecture, engineering and manual training, as well as in drawing and painting. Later, at Pratt Institute in Brooklyn, he majored in architecture. To help finance his education, he worked summers as a hotel clerk at Peaks Island House, Maine and did drafting and commercial art work.

Guptill was a part-time teacher at Pratt from 1912, after his graduation, until 1937, except for occasional short leaves. From 1914 to 1916 he took postgraduate study in architecture at the Massachusetts Institute of Technology, winning five medals and the Class of 1904 Prize in architectural design. He became a registered architect in New York in 1916 and free-lanced in advertising, commercial art, and designing of buildings, ornamental detail and furniture. He has said, "I really got ahead because I was lazy. . . . I didn't have the patience to spend the long, tedious hours that a draftsman must keep over his drawing board" (*Portland Sunday Telegram and Sunday Press Herald,* November 17, 1940).

With George E. Bearse of Portland (now deceased), Guptill in 1919 established the firm of Bearse and Guptill, Architectural Designers and Illustrators, which continued in operation in New York until 1925. Meanwhile, the free-lance artist turned a considerable amount of his attention to the advertising field, developing an art and advertising service that produced design and copy for catalogues, books, booklets and other printed matter.

During 1924 Guptill traveled and studied in Europe and that summer was a member of the faculty of the European School of Art Appreciation. Two years previously he had brought out his book, *Sketching and Rendering in Pencil* (Pencil Points Press, 1922), which first expressed his interest in amateur artists and originally appeared serially in the magazine *Pencil Points* (now *Progressive Architecture*). In the summer of 1925 he taught at the Chicago School of Applied Art.

A building slump in the depression of the 1930's markedly decreased Guptill's free-lance business in architectural design. For the next seven years he served as part-time art director at Reinhold Publishing Corporation and simultaneously managed his own advertising art studio. He furnished promotional material for artist's supplies, telling how to use the product and giving examples of the finished work. In his instructional advertising he often used contests, question and answer departments, or short sketches of famous artists. From 1934 to 1937

GUPTILL, ARTHUR L.—*Continued*
he conducted "Guptill's Corner" in *Pencil Points,* a department emphasizing architectural sketching and rendering.

In collaboration with Ralph W. Reinhold and Ernest W. Watson, Guptill founded the Watson-Guptill Publications, Inc., in 1937 and established the magazine *Art Instruction,* which became *American Artist* in 1940. He was co-editor of the magazine and the writer of such columns as "The Amateur Page" and "The Amateur Artist." He served as the executive vice-president of the company until 1951, when he was made president.

During the summers of 1937, 1938 and 1939 Guptill taught art at the Boothbay Studios, Boothbay Harbor, Maine. Two years later he accepted the post of art director of the magazine *Gourmet,* which he held until 1953. For several years he was also assistant treasurer of Gourmet, Inc., publishers of the magazine.

Guptill began what he considers his most important work in 1951, when he founded and became president of the Amateur Artists Association of America, Inc., a nonprofit membership organization chartered in the state of New York. New chapters of the AAAA are being formed at the rate of about fifty a year throughout the United States. A National Amateur Art Festival held for nine days in New York City in May 1953 brought members from the entire country, who entered their oils, watercolors and black-and-whites in the festival competition.

Guptill is currently designing and conducting a home study course, carried on by mail, for the amateur artist in drawing and painting Within a month of its inception in February 1954, it brought more than 1,000 responses. "I feel I am fundamentally a teacher," he says "and that this work with amateurs is the greatest opportunity to teach there is."

Recognized as an authority on drawing methods and teaching of techniques, he based his *Drawing with Pen and Ink* (Reinhold, 1928) on his experiences as an instructor at Pratt Institute and on his work as an illustrator. The New York *Herald Tribune* (February 24, 1929) described the book as "the most comprehensive manual on black-and-white art that has yet been published in America."

Emphasizing the techniques of different media, Guptill prepared his book *Freehand Drawing Self-taught* (Harper, 1933) for junior high and high schools, and for first-year courses in art institutes and colleges. He included a portfolio of sketches in pencil, charcoal and wash and line by European and American artists.

School Arts Magazine (June 1936) appraised Guptill's *Color in Sketching and Rendering* (Reinhold, 1935) as "undoubtedly the most exhaustive volume on architectural sketching and rendering ever published." In *Pen Drawing* (Watson-Guptill, 1937) Guptill explains with simple text and illustration the fundamentals of this art. His concept of it is enlarged in his article "Recent Trends in Pen Drawing" (*American Artist,* December 1941), where he points out that "pen drawing, together with pen-like brush drawing, is so individual that it not only shows a great variety of treatment at any given period, but is subject to more rapid and conspicuous changes in style than are other media."

In *Norman Rockwell, Illustrator* (Watson-Guptill, 1946), Guptill included miniature reproductions of 240 covers that the artist made from 1916 to 1946 for the *Saturday Evening Post,* together with information about his methods and his personal life.

Pencil Drawing Step-by-Step (Reinhold, 1949) replaced Guptill's 1922 publication and standard work, *Sketching and Rendering in Pencil,* "anticipating the needs of the beginner and the skilled artist alike" (*School Arts,* December 1949). His *Oil Painting Step-by-Step* (Watson-Guptill, 1953) was a reprint of articles published in *American Artist* (1951), and his forthcoming *Water Color Painting Step-by-Step* will comprise material he presented in "Guptill's Corner" how-to-do-it column on watercolor painting. Guptill advised in an article in *American Artist* (April 1952) that "watercolors are especially convenient for use in quick sketching—for direct work from nature . . . this calls for a high degree of competence." Among the books that he has edited and designed is *Lumiprinting* by Joseph Di Gemma (1942).

Arthur L. Guptill married another artist, Ethel Marguerite Weir, on August 4, 1914. They have a son, Arthur Leighton, Jr. Guptill is a Republican and a Congregationalist, and he belongs to the American Institute of Architects, the Art Directors Club and the Pratt Architectural Club. He has blue eyes and light brown hair, stands five feet nine and one-half inches tall, and weighs 175 pounds. His hobbies include photography, carpentry and craftwork, gardening and reading. "Art is both my vocation and my avocation," he states.

References

Leaders in Education (1948)
Who's Who Among North American Authors (1939)
Who's Who in America, 1954-55
Who's Who in American Art (1953)
Who's Who in the East (1953)

GYÖRGYI, ALBERT (VON NAGYRAPOLT) SZENT- *See* Szent-Györgyi, Albert (von Nagyrapolt)

HALEY, ANDREW G(ALLAGHER)
Nov. 19, 1904- Lawyer; astronautical society official

Address: b. Haley, Doty & Wollenberg, 1735 De Salles St., Washington 6, D.C.; b. c/o American Rocket Society, Inc., 500 Fifth Ave., New York 36; h. 3815 Huntington St., Washington 15, D.C.

As vice-president of the International Astronautical Federation and a director and former president of the American Rocket Society, Andrew G. Haley has been one of the chief advocates of the feasibility of unmanned space satellites. His unorthodox viewpoint was vindicated with the announcement, on July 29, 1955, at an extraordinary news conference at the White House, that the United States plans to launch the first man-made, earth-circling satellite into space between 1957 and 1958.

Haley has had a curious combination of careers in two such seemingly disparate professions as the law and the science of rocket propulsion. Beginning his legal practice in the fields of radio and hydroelectric power, he was counsel for the Federal Communications Commission, and has practiced before the courts of the District of Columbia and the state of Washington and before the Supreme Court of the United States. During the 1930's he became interested in rockets and space travel; this initial enthusiasm developed into a dedicated devotion to the science of astronautics in subsequent years.

Andrew Gallagher Haley was born in Tacoma, Washington on November 19, 1904 to Christopher Joseph and Kathleen Rose (Gallagher) Haley. When he was sixteen Andrew became a journalist on the staff of the Tacoma *News-Tribune,* holding this position from 1920 to 1923. He studied law at Georgetown University in Washington, D.C., earning the LL.B. degree in 1928 and in the same year he was admitted to the bar of the District of Columbia. In 1934 he received the B.A. degree from George Washington University in Washington, D.C. In 1929 he returned to the state of Washington, was admitted to the Washington bar, and conducted a private law practice in Tacoma from 1929 to 1933. From 1933 to 1939 he was counsel for the Federal Radio Commission and the FCC. He returned to private practice in 1939.

His interest in rocket propulsion was stimulated by the clients whom he represented before the Board of Immigrations Appeal. These included leading scientists who were driven from Europe in the 1930's by the Nazis and were seeking refuge in the United States. Haley's interest in the plight of these persecuted intellectuals soon grew beyond the limits of his official legal capacity, and he began to establish personal relationships among them. An especially important influence was the friendship he developed with Dr. Theodore von Kármán (see *C.B.,* May 1955), the world renowned aerodynamicist, when the lawyer was helping von Kármán's sister to enter the United States after fleeing from Nazi Germany.

Haley's first official position in the rocket development movement was as a founder, with von Kármán and others, of the Aerojet Engineering Corporation of Azusa, California, a commercial enterprise that pioneered in key projects in jet and rocket propulsion during World War II. Haley served as president and managing director of Aerojet from 1942 to 1945. During the war he was also a lecturer at the First Jet Propulsion School in 1943, an institute organized under military orders, and on the staff of the Judge Advocate, U.S. Army Air Forces in 1942, with the rank of major.

Tenschert

ANDREW G. HALEY

Simultaneously with his participation in the rocket movement, Haley still carried on a career in the field of jurisprudence. In 1948 he became a partner in the firm of Haley, Doty & Schellenberg (now Haley, Doty & Wollenberg), dealing with administrative, radio and television law. This practice engages much of his energies today. He also was legal adviser to the International Telecommunications Conference of eighty-seven nations, which met in Atlantic City, New Jersey in 1947; and the Fourth InterAmerican Radio Conference held at Washington, D.C. in 1949. He was industry adviser to the Third North American Regional Broadcasting Conference at Montreal, Canada in 1949 and in Washington, D.C., and Havana, Cuba in 1950.

Since the end of World War II Haley's pursuits have more and more closely been involved with astronautics. He served as an adviser on aircraft to the U.S. Senate Special Committee to investigate the National Defense Program from 1945 to 1946, and wrote a special report for that committee urging Congress to accelerate the rocket research and development program. He has been vice-president of the International Astronautical Federation since 1951.

In the American Rocket Society Haley was a director of the organization from 1951-1952 and was elected vice-president in 1953. He served as president in 1954 and is now a member of the board of directors.

The American Rocket Society was organized in 1930 as the American Interplanetary Society by a group whose principal occupation was writing science fiction. Eventually, however, influenced by the work of Dr. Robert H. Goddard, an American scientist who is considered the founder of modern rocketry, active experimentation on rockets was begun. Currently, there are more than 4,500 members and sub-

HALEY, ANDREW G.—*Continued*

scribers. Its headquarters are at 500 Fifth Avenue, New York City. It publishes a monthly publication, *Jet Propulsion.*

As chairman of the committee on space flight Haley was responsible for enlightening the public about the reality of the developments in the field of rockets and for educating the Government about the military implications and potentialities of these inventions. He described some of the difficulties of heading the American Rocket Society in the *New Yorker* (December 11, 1954). "My problem is disabusing people of the idea that this is all Buck Rogers stuff. The great new prime mover is the rocket power plant. I've been telling [Congressman] Joe Martin and [Senator] Stu [W. Stuart] Symington that."

Recently Haley has differed with those scientists who have supported the thesis that the United States should attempt to erect an artificial satellite that would rotate about the earth and carry scientific and military equipment operated by *human beings* on the satellite. Haley attacked this scheme as impractical, stating that the satellite would be an easy target for earth-launched rockets. Another point in Haley's argument is that much of the scientific data that would be obtained from a manned satellite would be made available just as easily by an unmanned space vehicle.

In an interview with Roland Sawyer (*Christian Science Monitor,* March 11, 1955), Haley stated that an artificial, unmanned satellite could be built within two years at a cost of approximately $20,000,000 and stationed about 250 miles outside the earth's gravitational pull. Asked what we would learn from this space rocket, Haley replied: "Why, we're going to find out what some of the planets, the moon, Mars and Jupiter are really like. We don't know if the moon is covered with volcanic ash, no one knows how deep, solid lava, or what. When we get our satellite on station it may tell us."

According to Haley, the next point of interplanetary colonization will be the moon. Once this is accomplished, the asteroids will be accessible to conquest by spacemen. In an article appearing in the Camden (New Jersey) *Post* (January 3, 1955), he stated, "I believe these small bodies will play an immense part in the conquest of space. Here we have natural power plants waiting to take human beings on trips of distances scarcely imaginable. . . ." However, he continued, "a state of national emergency still exists, the real peace is yet unknown to mankind. Our . . . first duty is to aid in the work of successfully defending our country and free people everywhere."

The plan to launch an unmanned satellite was announced by President Eisenhower on July 29, 1955, and will be built about the size of a basketball and will be blasted by rockets into an orbit around the earth sometime between July 1957 and December 1958. It will circle the earth at an altitude of between 200 and 300 miles and at a speed of 18,000 miles an hour. "Three rockets" (as explained by Richard Witkin in the New York *Times,* July 30, 1955) "will be mounted nose to tail. The rear, or bottom rocket would be fired for initial take-off. The middle one would provide a second accelerating shot when the first had spent itself and fallen away. The top rocket would provide a final kick when the second had exhausted its fuel and dropped off. The satellite would remain in its orbit around the earth for days or weeks, with its speed neutralizing the effect of gravity. Eventually, as it slowed down and encountered some drag, gravity would gradually take over . . . air friction would heat it until it finally disintegrated like a meteor."

The attorney is a member of the Institute of Aeronautical Sciences, Society of Motion Picture and Television Engineers, Radio Pioneers, American Television Society, and many foreign astronautical associations. He is also a fellow of the British Interplanetary Society and Sociedad Argentina Interplanetaria. Haley holds memberships in the Bar Association of the District of Columbia, Federal Communications Bar Association, Delta Theta Phi fraternity, and National Press Club.

On December 1, 1934 Haley married Delphine de la Croix. They have two children, Delphine de la Croix Haley and Andrew Gallagher Haley, Jr. Haley has blue eyes and dark hair. The collecting of antiques is Haley's chief recreational pursuit. He is presently busy writing a book about rockets and space travel while seated at an eighteenth century desk which once belonged to the British author Horace Walpole.

References

New Yorker 30:32+ D 11 '54
Empire Law List, 1954-55
Martindale-Hubbell Law Directory, 1955
Who's Who in America, 1954-55
World Biography (1954)

HALL, FRED(ERICK LEE) July 24, 1916-
Governor of Kansas; lawyer

Address: b. State House, Topeka, Kan.; h. 2205 Hart St., Dodge City, Kan.

A self-described "progressive moderate," Republican Fred Hall was elected to a two-year term as Governor of Kansas in November 1954 with little support from the Republican party's regular organization. His earlier break with the party during his two terms as Lieutenant Governor (1950-1954) had won him a reputation as a Republican of independent spirit.

A few months after taking office in January 1955, Governor Hall received considerable attention in the national press by vetoing a "right-to-work" bill, which would have made compulsory union membership unlawful. His action was regarded as reversing a country-wide trend in state legislatures to ban union-shop contracts. Objecting to the efforts of some proponents of the bill to turn farmers against labor, Hall said, "America is essentially a classless country. Those who would put one group of people against another to make it otherwise, are doing their country a great disservice" (*Time*, April 11, 1955).

Frederick Lee Hall was born to Fred L. and Etta (Brewer) Hall in Dodge City, Kansas on July 24, 1916. He studied at the University of Southern California in Los Angeles, which awarded him the A.B. degree in 1938 and the LL.B. degree in 1941. During 1938 he was a member of the International Inter-collegiate Debating Team, which traveled in the United States and Europe.

After his law school graduation he became an attorney for the Douglas Aircraft Company, Incorporated, in Long Beach, California. In 1942 he joined the staff of the War Production Board as assistant executive director of the combined productions and resources board and served in that capacity until 1944. During the following year he was associated with the law firm of Lillard, Eidson, Lewis & Porter in Topeka, Kansas, and after being admitted to the Kansas bar in 1946 was employed as an attorney for Ford County until 1948. Hall set up his own law practice in Dodge City in 1949.

Since his college days Hall had been active in the Republican party, having served as chairman of the Young Republicans at the University of Southern California in 1938 and of Ford County in 1946 and 1947. He was a delegate to the Midwest Young Republicans Council Meeting in 1948 and the following year to the Young Republicans National Convention. In 1949 he was a member also of the Young Republicans constitutional revision committee.

A candidate on the Republican ticket for Lieutenant Governor of Kansas, Hall was elected to that office in 1950. Almost immediately, according to the New York *Times* (August 7, 1952), he "tangled" with the administration of Governor Edward F. Arn. "The Governor sought to have the Senate strip him of his powers as president of the state Senate where he exercised potent influence on state legislation through the appointment of committees." A split in the party was avoided when Hall agreed to share his power with the president pro tempore of the Senate.

When Hall sought the nomination to a second term as Lieutenant Governor, he was opposed in the Republican primary on August 5, 1952 by state senator Wayne W. Ryan, who had the support of Governor Arn. Winning over Ryan by more than 11,000 votes, Hall soon afterward announced that he would be a candidate for the governorship in the 1954 election.

In his campaign for the gubernatorial nomination in early 1954, he made government reform the chief issue of his platform: "Let's clean up Topeka as President Eisenhower has cleaned up Washington." His opponent in the Republican primary election was former state senator George Templar, who had the backing of out-going Governor Arn and the regular party organization, as well as most of the leading newspapers in Kansas. Hall's victory in

Wide World

FRED HALL

the August primary was regarded by Murray J. Gart of the *Christian Science Monitor* (August 10, 1954) as a triumph for "a young and vigorous element" of the state's Republican party.

Defeating Democrat George Docking by a substantial majority on November 2, 1954, Hall became one of the youngest Governors ever elected in Kansas. The principal challenge of his administration, the Governor-elect said, would be to start a long-range program to mitigate damage caused by floods and droughts. Kansas, the country's leading winter wheat-producing state (providing about one-fifth of the nation's supply), suffered a severe flood in 1951 and a severe drought in 1954, when more than 5,600,000 acres in southwestern Kansas were turned into a "dust bowl" by wind erosion. On May 25, 1955 the town of Udall, Kansas was virtually demolished by a tornado resulting in eighty deaths. In answer to a plea by Governor Hall, President Eisenhower declared Kansas' tornado-ravished sections a "major disaster" area and authorized "such funds as are necessary to supplement state and local efforts."

In his inaugural address on January 10, 1955 Hall alluded to his estrangement with the Kansas Republican party organization by stating that "never before in our state has a Governor owed so little to so few and so much to so many" (*New Republic*, April 18, 1955).

One of the recommendations made by Hall in his message to the Kansas Legislature in January called for strengthening the laws regulating the sale and distribution of crime and horror comic books in the state. This is a subject of much interest to Hall, who in 1948 was a member of an American Bar Association committee which studied the problem of crime comics. "As a lawyer," he has said (*Christian Science Monitor*, March 29, 1955), "I do not

HALL, FRED—*Continued*

believe that reasonable regulation [by both Federal and state governments] would in any way affect freedom of the press."

Hall's veto of the "right-to-work" bill passed by the legislature in March, drew praise from U.S. Secretary of Labor James P. Mitchell, who expressed his view that the Governor "demonstrated commendable courage and devotion to the best principles on which our country was founded. He has done a service to the working people and employers of Kansas. They would have been deprived by this legislation of the right to enter into collective-bargaining agreements providing for union security" (*Christian Science Monitor*, April 4, 1955).

When his veto was sustained in the legislature, Hall issued a statement declaring, "The Republican party never has been, is not now and cannot be an antilabor party any more than it can be an antifarm or antibusiness party. We certainly should not try to make it so in Kansas." With Democratic support, Hall was able to get a number of his measures approved in the legislature in the spring of 1955, including his high school aid proposal, a small-loan bill, and a labor-management bill which outlawed jurisdictional strikes and secondary boycotts and permitted "all-union" agreements approved by secret vote of a majority of employees.

Another bill signed by Hall in April 1955 abolished the thirty-eight-year-old Kansas Board of Review, a censorship agency which had the function of banning motion pictures that it considered unsuitable for public entertainment. Eric A. Johnston, president of the Motion Picture Association of America, hailed the Governor's action: "Every believer in freedom of expression will rejoice that Kansas has repealed its ancient censorship law" (New York *Times*, April 8, 1955).

When the U.S. Supreme Court opened hearings on April 11, 1955 on plans for enforcement of its May 17, 1954 judgment against racial segregation in public schools, attorneys for Kansas told the court that their school system had put desegregation into effect and a formal court order that segregation be ended was unnecessary.

As part of his program to make the Kansas prison system more modern and effective and to free it entirely from partisan politics, Governor Hall in July 1955 appointed a six-member advisory committee on penal and correctional institutions to study conditions in the state. Noting that Hall has been interested in introducing a "more human touch" in government social services, Henry M. Christman of the *Christian Science Monitor* (July 14, 1955), quoted the Governor as observing, "It is not only more humane to do the very best we can to treat and rehabilitate prisoners, but this is good government."

Hall is a member of the District of Columbia, California and Kansas bar associations and has served as national chairman of the legislative drafting committee of the American Bar Association. Among other organizations to which he belongs are the Elks, Lions, Chamber of Commerce, and Western Kansas Development Association. He has performed military service in the Kansas State Guard. His fraternities are Phi Alpha Delta and Phi Kappa Tau. He is a Methodist and a trustee of the Methodist Hospital Association.

The Governor and his wife, the former Leadell Schneider, whom he married on April 25, 1942, have two children, Frederick Lee, 3d and John Tracy. Hall is blond-haired and stocky in build, and "an orator of the old school who can sway audiences."

References

Christian Sci Mon p5 Ag 10 '54
N Y Times p62 N 28 '54
New Republic 132:7 Ap 18 '55
Who's Who in the Midwest (1954)
Who's Who in United States Politics (1950)

HALPERT, EDITH GREGOR Apr. 1900-
Art dealer; collector

Address: b. c/o The Downtown Gallery, 32 E. 51st St., New York 22; h. 32 E. 51st St., New York 22

An art enterprise known to most American artists and one respected by a wide circle of art critics is The Downtown Gallery, established in 1926 in modest quarters in New York City's downtown section and in 1955 occupying an entire building in the heart of mid-town Manhattan. The guiding spirit and director of the gallery is Edith Gregor Halpert, a pioneer in the introduction and commercial sponsorship of contemporary American art.

While continuing to exhibit and sell the works of such noted artists as Jack Levine, William Zorach, Ben Shahn, and Yasuo Kuniyoshi (who had been with the gallery for many years), Mrs. Halpert since 1951 has also sponsored a new group of still unknown young American artists, most of them considered extreme abstractionists. She has also devoted considerable time to the collection and sale of American folk art much of which has been bought by important museums and private collectors. In September 1954 she exhibited at the Associated American Artists Galleries in New York sixteen weather vanes made from old molds which she discovered in a new England junk yard.

Edith Gregor Fivoosiovitch, born in Odessa, Russia in April 1900, came to the United States in May 1906. Her parents were Gregor and Frances (Lucom) Fivoosiovitch; her sister is the present Mrs. Michael Watter of Philadelphia, Pennsylvania. Her family settled in New York City, where she spent her formative years. While still attending Wadleigh High School, in 1914, she began to study art at the National Academy of Design. The next year (1915) she worked under Leon Kroll and Ivan Olinsky, and later Frederic A. Bridgman, who was associated with the Art Students League.

During summer vacations she worked successively in the foreign office of R. H. Macy & Company and in the advertising department of Bloomingdale's store. In 1917 she became full-time assistant to the advertising manager of Stern's department store where she wrote copy and did sketches for advertisements.

She shifted her career to business management when, in 1918, she became a "systematizer" for the Cohen Goldman firm and handled special records and organizational work. In 1920 she became an employee of the investment bankers, S.W. Straus & Company. During the five years she was with this firm she became personnel manager, head of the correspondence department, and systematizer. In the summer of 1925 she was invited by the Galeries Lilloises to reorganize its department store in Lille, France. This task successfully completed, she returned to the United States to begin the project of running a gallery for contemporary American artists.

In the 1920's few modern American artists were being exhibited and very little of their work was being sold. Mrs. Halpert recognized the talent of such artists as Ben Shahn, Yasuo Kuniyoshi, Jack Levine, William Zorach, Charles Sheeler, Jacob Lawrence, and Stuart Davis. Only Zorach and Davis were known, but even they were not selling their work because of their "unorthodox" approach, stated *Life* (March 17, 1952).

Married to an artist, Samuel Halpert, since 1918, and fully aware of the economic difficulties and frustrations of contemporary artists, she began in 1926 to exhibit their paintings and sculptures in three small rooms at 113 West 13th Street, in Manhattan's Greenwich Village. The exhibition rooms were given the name of The Downtown Gallery, a name which was continued even after Mrs. Halpert had moved her operations uptown (in 1940 the gallery became located at 43 East 51st Street; five years later it was transferred to 32 East 51st Street, its present site).

Some of the artists who first joined Mrs. Halpert in her endeavors have since become prominent American painters, whose works may command as much as $6,500 a piece; and contemporary art is no longer unappreciated or considered unorthodox. In reviewing the achievements of The Downtown Gallery, *Art Digest* (October 15, 1945) stressed the influence Mrs. Halpert has had in directing the paths of American art and declared that her choice of artists and works were "convincing testimony to the good taste, artistic sensitivity, and executive skill" of the director. "Few have equaled," the article concluded, "her success along pioneering paths."

While the gallery was still getting established, Mrs. Halpert began selling the pictures, weather vanes, old family portraits, still-lifes on velvet, and other pieces of Americana that she had discovered on her frequent trips in New England, Pennsylvania and New York. She would buy objects for small sums, clean and restore them, and often sell them for many times what she had paid for them.

This aspect of her activities became so successful that in 1929 she added a new wing to her exhibition quarters—the American Folk Art Gallery. "These things," she explained in *Time* (September 1, 1947), "are not cute a bit and they're not quaint either. They're art. The one quality they all share is design, you see, and that's what contemporary artists emphasize, too. Our modern painters have learned a lot from these folk· artists." Among the American "old masters" whose works she exhibited were William M. Harnett and Edward Hicks.

EDITH GREGOR HALPERT

In 1951 Mrs. Halpert reorganized the ground-floor room in her exhibition building so that young and relatively unknown artists could be introduced to the public. The gallery guaranteed to purchase a specified number of paintings each year and to pay all the costs of presentation and promotion. In return, the artists gave the gallery a four-year option to purchase any of their pictures, on an annually rising scale. Buying at a comparatively low price, the gallery can then sell at a low price to a new group of first art purchasers. Previously, with their regular artists, Mrs. Halpert reported in *Art Digest* (December 15, 1951), the gallery offered "a permanent sponsorship, with no expense to the artist whatever, other than the 33⅓ per cent commission when a sale is effected."

At her gallery she has given special exhibitions of artists from U.S. cities other than New York, in order to "keep regional artists working at home," where they can develop their own styles, and yet to make them "known on a national scale." In 1947 she brought the work of Boston artists to New York and in 1954, the work of Chicago painters.

In her article, "Is Reviewing Responsible?" in *Art Digest*, April 15, 1954, Mrs. Halpert stated that museum attendance has grown tenfold in the past decade, with almost an equal increase in sales. "In contrast to this," she wrote, "the number of art pages in newspapers and art publications has decreased shockingly." She deplored the recent custom of send-

HALPERT, EDITH GREGOR—*Continued*
ing novices to view exhibitions of the work of well-known artists, and suggested that the trainees be sent to see and criticize new painters.

In addition to her work with The Downtown Gallery, Mrs. Halpert has organized a number of other exhibits. In the summer of 1930, for instance, she organized the first municipal art exhibition for Atlantic City, New Jersey. The same year she organized the *"Thirty-Three Moderns"* exhibition for the Grand Central Galleries in New York City. In 1934 she was in charge of the first municipal art exhibition, sponsored by Mayor Fiorello H. La Guardia of New York. She organized the exhibition and allocation program for the WPA Art Project in the summer of 1936.

Mrs. John D. Rockefeller, Jr., bought a "comprehensive cross-section" of Mrs. Halpert's Americana collection for the reconstructed colonial town of Williamsburg, Virginia. Mrs. Halpert also helped with the new museum at Shelburne, New Hampshire. She is the author of articles which have appeared in such publications as *House & Garden, Antiques, Art in America,* and *Seventeen.* Her wide knowledge of American art has brought her to the radio microphone and the lecture platform.

She was described by *Newsweek* as a "white-haired, comely, scrappy little woman who believes in American art and loves to go to bat for it." She has blue eyes, is five feet, two inches tall, and weighs 128 pounds. Mrs. Halpert, a widow since 1930, has living quarters in her 51st Street gallery. She enjoys gardening, traveling, reading, looking at art, and meeting people.

Charm (June 1955) lists her contributions to American art as "first, encouraging artists to follow through in their own way, giving them backing and understanding—but *never* direction; second: introducing new collectors, as well as old, to American art and encouraging them to grow with it; and third: placing each of her artists in forty or more museums."

References

Art Digest 18:14 F 15 '44; 20:10 O 15 '45
Art N 44:26 O 15 '45
Charm p108+ Je '55 por
Life 32:87+ Mr 17 '52 por
Newsweek 29:97 My 5 '47 por
Time 50:58 S 1 '47

HALPERT, MRS. SAMUEL *See* Halpert, Edith Gregor

HAMPDEN, WALTER (DOUGHERTY) June 30, 1879-June 11, 1955 Actor of Shakespearean and romantic roles; played in *Cyrano de Bergerac* over 1000 times; portrayed Hamlet, Cardinal Richelieu, Macbeth, Shylock, Othello, Petruchio, Henry V, Richard III, and the Admirable Crichton; began movie career in 1939 with *The Hunchback of Notre Dame*; played the "aging actor" in *All About Eve* (1950); among his last films were *The Silver Chalice* and *Sabrina* (1954); was host on the Mutual network's radio series *Great Scenes from Great Plays* (1948) and also played Cyrano; made television debut in 1949 as Macbeth and his last Broadway appearance as Deputy-Governor Danforth in Arthur Miller's *The Crucible*; resigned his presidency of The Players on October 8, 1954. See *Current Biography* (May) 1953.

Obituary

N Y Times p86 Je 12 '55

HANNIKAINEN, TAUNO (HEIKKI) (hän″nĭ-kī′nĕn tou′nō) Feb. 26, 1896- Finnish conductor; cellist

Address: b. c/o Helsinki City Symphony Orchestra, Katariinankatu 1, Helsinki, Finland; h. Raisiontie 11,C,27, Helsinki, Finland

Finland's outstanding conductor, Tauno Hannikainen, was appointed to the most attractive post in his profession in his native land in 1941, but ten years elapsed before he was able to take his baton to lead the Helsinki City Symphony Orchestra. During that decade he enhanced a reputation already established in Europe by appearing as guest conductor throughout the United States, as regular conductor of the Duluth Symphony Orchestra, and as assistant conductor of the Chicago Symphony Orchestra under Artur Rodzinski. Since his return to Helsinki, he has continued to interpret with unique authority the compositions of his great fellow countryman, Jean Sibelius.

Tauno Heikki Hannikainen was born on February 26, 1896, at Jyväskylä, in south central Finland, the son of Pekka Juhani and Laura Alfhild (Nikander) Hannikainen. His family had long been associated with music; his mother was the daughter of a cantor and before her marriage had been a music teacher and singer; his father was a music teacher, violinist, composer, and editor of the first music journal in Finland. Three of Tauno's four brothers became professional musicians: Arvo, a violinist and concertmaster of the Helsinki orchestra; Väinö, a harpist in the same orchestra; and Ilmari, a composer, pianist, and professor at the Sibelius Academy in Helsinki.

Tauno attended the lyceum of his native Jyväskylä until he was eighteen. From 1914 to 1917, he was a student at Helsinki University and at the Helsinki Conservatory (Sibelius Academy), where he studied piano, organ, and especially cello. His career, like many others, was to some extent disturbed by the era of war and revolution from which Finland emerged as an independent state; for his part in the struggle Hannikainen was awarded the Civil War Medal.

During these years, he was a cellist in the Helsinki City Symphony Orchestra, and with his brothers Ilmari and Arvo, toured Europe as the Trio Hannikainen. He was chosen as assistant to the conductor of the Finnish Opera Association, Oskar Merikanto, and succeeded him as regular conductor in 1922. Meanwhile he continued his musical education. He studied conducting in Berlin, Milan, Vienna, and Paris, and added to his skill at the cello under the guidance of André Hekking and Pablo Casals in Paris.

In 1927 Hannikainen left the Helsinki Finnish Opera to accept his first position as conductor of an orchestra, the Turku Symphony. He remained at Turku for twelve years, and achieved a solid reputation throughout Finland and much of Europe as a result of his appearance as guest conductor with the orchestras of Helsinki, Stockholm, Berlin, Leipzig, Warsaw, and Riga.

Scandinavian organizations in the United States planned a tercentenary celebration in 1938 in honor of the landing of Swedish and Finnish colonists in America, and the Finnish government chose Hannikainen to conduct a special concert for the festival. His first appearance with a major United States orchestra was as guest conductor during the summer of 1938 of the Boston Symphony.

An interesting side light to this visit is told by Philip Binham, who reports that Hannikainen, unable to speak English, learned and delivered a 28-minute speech in that language on the subject of "Sibelius at Home" before a women's club in Boston, only to retire in some confusion when an unexpected question period followed the linguistic tour de force (*Finlandia Pictorial,* November 1953).

He returned to Finland with contracts to appear as guest conductor for the orchestras of Boston, London, Paris, and Warsaw. His European commitments were invalidated by the outbreak of World War II in 1939, but he appeared in a series of five concerts with the Boston Symphony Orchestra early in 1940. The first of these, held on February 2 in Symphony Hall, included three of Sibelius' works, one of which, "Lemminkäinen's Homeward Journey," received its Boston première. In New York City he conducted the orchestra in the Symphony No. 1 of Sibelius before a cheering Carnegie Hall audience.

By this time the "winter war" between Finland and the Soviet Union was nearing its close. Tauno Hannikainen and his wife, the operatic soprano Anne Arvida Niskanen, whom he had married on June 21, 1933, devoted themselves tirelessly to concertizing on behalf of Finnish, British, and Norwegian relief organizations, and gave many recitals in the United States. Hannikainen also appeared as guest conductor in many cities throughout the United States and Canada. While he was thus establishing an enduring reputation in the Dominion and America, his name was being considered for the conductorship of the Helsinki City Symphony Orchestra.

This orchestra was the result of a merger in 1914 of the Philharmonic Society of Helsinki, founded by Robert Kajanus in 1882, and the Helsinki Symphony, founded by Georg Schneevoigt in 1912. Kajanus was its conductor until his death in 1933, followed by Schneevoigt, who retired in 1939. While guest conductors filled the vacancy, a lively competition for the position, described by Paul Sjoblom

Oscar & Associates, Inc.

TAUNO HANNIKAINEN

(New York *Times,* April 13, 1941) as "singularly attractive . . . on several counts," resolved itself to a choice between Toivo Haapanen and the absent Hannikainen.

The music council of the Helsinki city administration came to a tie vote, whereupon the issue was left to the administration as a whole. Hannikainen's victory, according to Sjoblom, was partly due to his success in the United States, where he remained for the duration of World War II.

When the Duluth (Minnesota) Symphony Orchestra's conductor, Paul Lemay, joined the U.S. Air Force in 1942, Hannikainen was chosen as his successor. The orchestra, founded in 1932 by a group of volunteers, had retained much of its amateur enthusiasm under the baton of Lemay, who developed its musical qualities to a professional level with the help of an appreciative community.

Hannikainen required even more discipline. DeWitt John has written (*Christian Science Monitor,* September 21, 1946): "Schooled in the more formal traditions of Europe, he insisted on strictly businesslike rehearsals and hard work." As a result, according to John, "the Duluth organization has won an enviable place in the constellation of American symphony orchestras." Its members are workingmen, housewives, and businessmen.

In July 1946 Hannikainen was guest conductor of the Chicago Symphony Orchestra at the Ravinia Park festival. He later conducted several concerts with that orchestra over the radio and at Orchestra Hall, and on February 24, 1947, he was chosen to become assistant conductor of the Chicago Symphony, effective in October. Subsequently Hannikainen became associate director, and conducted eighty-five concerts during the 1949-1950 season.

(Continued next page)

HANNIKAINEN, TAUNO—*Continued*

In the spring of 1951 Hannikainen's appointment as musical director and conductor of the Helsinki City Symphony Orchestra was renewed, and he returned to his native land where he is known as an authoritative interpreter of the works of Sibelius. The Sibelius festivals, such as the birthday concert at Royal Festival Hall in London in 1952, have offered Hannikainen his most auspicious opportunities for conducting the composer's works. The mid-June Sibelius Festival at Helsinki, with Hannikainen and guest conductors, has become an annual Finnish musical institution. At the 1954 festival the Helsinki City Symphony Orchestra performed at four of the eight concerts, and Hannikainen shared the honors with Sir Thomas Beecham.

The Finnish conductor has been especially interested in working with young musicians. When he took over the Duluth Symphony, a vigorous Junior Symphony of high school performers was already functioning, and Hannikainen rehearsed the young musicians and conducted their spring concerts. While assisting Rodzinski with the Chicago Symphony, Hannikainen conducted the Youth Orchestra of Greater Chicago. In Helsinki he organized a youth orchestra, which gave a concert in May 1954.

His own interpretations have been characterized (in the Riga, Latvia, *Briva Zome*) as youthfully exuberant. A critic in the New York *Times* found his performance compounded of "complete poise and control, the balancing of all elements, power held long in reserve for shattering climaxes, and reigning over all, a sovereign nobility."

When asked by Philip Binham to list the important attributes of a conductor, he replied: "He must be born to conduct, he must study, he must work—and he must have an orchestra!"

The musician has blue eyes and brown, or perhaps "sandy," hair. He weighs 160 pounds and is five feet ten inches tall. An adopted son, Eero Ylermi Hannikainen, a chemical engineer, lives in Whittier, California. Tauno Hannikainen is a Lutheran. He received an honorary doctorate of music from the American Conservatory of Music (Chicago) in 1950, and the Finnish government's Commander of the Order of the Finnish Lion decoration in 1953. The conductor's memory is exceptional. He remembers scores by sound and sight, recalling the parts for every instrument.

Hannikainen belongs to the Musicians Club of America, International Music Association (London), National Association of Opera, and the Tavern Club (Chicago). He also is a member of the Chicago Federation of Musicians, an honorary citizen of Boys Town, Nebraska, and an honorary member of the International Mark Twain Society of St. Louis, Missouri.

References

Thompson, O. (ed.) International Cyclopedia of Music and Musicians (1949)
Who's Who in America, 1954-55
World Biography (1948)

HARLAN, JOHN MARSHALL May 20, 1899- Associate Justice of the Supreme Court of the United States

Address: United States Supreme Court Bldg., 1 First St., N.E., Washington, D.C.; h. 1677 31st St., N.W., Washington, D.C.

The United States Senate on March 16, 1955 confirmed by a vote of 71 to 11 the nomination of John Marshall Harlan of New York as Associate Justice of the U.S. Supreme Court to succeed the late Robert H. Jackson. Harlan served as a judge of the U.S. Court of Appeals for the Second Circuit from March 1954 until he was sworn in as Associate Justice on March 28. He was the chief counsel of the New York State Crime Commission from 1951 to 1953, special assistant attorney general of New York state from 1928 to 1930, and assistant to the U.S. Attorney for the Southern District of New York from 1925 to 1927. He served as a Colonel in the Army Air Forces during World War II. Until his designation to the bench, Harlan was a member of the New York law firm of Root, Ballantine, Harlan, Bushby & Palmer.

Justice Harlan is the grandson and namesake of the Associate Justice of the U.S. Supreme Court who served from 1877 to 1911 and who was the sole dissenter in the case of *Plessy v. Ferguson* in 1896, which established the "separate but equal" doctrine in matters of racial segregation. He is a direct descendant of George Harlan, a Quaker from Durham, England who came to America in 1687 and became Governor of Delaware in 1695. Harlan's great-grandfather James Harlan was a U.S. Congressman from Kentucky from 1835 to 1839.

John Marshall Harlan was born in Chicago on May 20, 1899 to John Maynard and Elizabeth Palmer (Flagg) Harlan. His father was an attorney and a city alderman in Chicago, twice a nominee for the mayoralty of Chicago, and an independent candidate for the governorship of Illinois.

Young Harlan received his early education at the Appleby School in Oakville, Ontario, Canada and the Lake Placid School in New York. In 1916 he entered Princeton University, where he was a member of the editorial staff of the *Daily Princetonian* and president of his class for three years. He received the A.B. degree with honors in 1920. During 1917 and 1918 he was a member of the Students' Army Training Corps, and in 1919 he was a seaman, second class, at the Great Lakes Naval Training Station.

A Rhodes scholar at Balliol College, Oxford University in England, Harlan received the B.A. degree in jurisprudence in 1923. After his return to the United States he entered New York Law School and joined the law firm of Root, Clark, Howland, Buckner & Ballantine on September 21, 1923. He received the LL.B. degree from New York Law School in 1924 and was admitted to the New York bar in 1925.

Resigning temporarily from his position with the law firm, Harlan served as chief of the prohibition division in the office of Emory R. Buckner, U.S. Attorney for the Southern District, New York. He helped to prosecute the late Earl Carroll, theatrical producer, in May 1926 for perjury for which Carroll served his sentence.

By appointment of Governor Alfred E. Smith, Harlan served as special assistant attorney general of New York state from 1928 to 1930. He investigated the sewer scandals of Queens county which involved overpayment by the city of about $10,000,000 for sewers and pipe and helped to prosecute the late Maurice Connolly, former Queens borough president, in October 1928 for conspiracy to defraud the city. Connolly, who was represented by Max Steuer, served his sentence.

After returning to the practice of law, Harlan was made a member in 1932 of the firm when it became known as Root, Ballantine, Harlan, Bushby & Palmer. Harlan was defense counsel for the administrator of the $5,000,000 estate of Georgiana G. R. Wendel in 1936. In this case he helped to expose a group of conspirators in Germany, of the same name, who tried unsuccessfully to claim one of their kin as the illegitimate daughter of the deceased and hence a legal heir.

From April to October 1940 Harlan and Emory R. Buckner represented the New York Board of Higher Education in its final attempt to retain Bertrand Russell on the faculty of the College of the City of New York. The case was dropped on October 21, 1940.

In the summer of 1940 Harlan took a businessmen's training course in Plattsburg, New York. He became a civilian consultant to the U.S. War Department in 1942. Later he served with the U.S. Army Air Forces in England as chief of operations, analysis section, of the Eighth Bomber Command. Following service as commanding lieutenant colonel in the Army Air Forces, he was promoted in February 1944 to colonel of the air division, U.S. Group Control Council for Germany. He was discharged in March 1945. For his efforts in World War II, he was decorated with the Legion of Merit, French Croix de Guerre, and Belgian Croix de Guerre. Harlan was admitted to the bar of the U.S. Supreme Court in 1945 and to the District of Columbia bar in 1947.

Appointed chief counsel of the newly created five-man New York State Crime Commission on March 31, 1951, Harlan served without salary until 1953. He helped to investigate the water-front rackets in New York City and gambling activities in Staten Island, Long Island and upstate New York.

Harlan was one of four attorneys defending Pierre Samuel du Pont, Irénée du Pont, Christiana Securities Company, and Delaware Realty and Investment Corporation from November 1952 to December 1953 in the government's antitrust suit against members of the du Pont family and six defendant corporations including E. I. du Pont de Nemours Company, General Motors Corporation, and United States Rubber Company. In this case, which was brought in the U.S. District Court in Chicago, the Government charged the defendants with violation of the Sherman and Clayton acts.

Pointing out that "the size of the du Pont interests has remained the basic target," Harlan emphasized that "bigness is not yet an antitrust

Wide World
JUSTICE JOHN MARSHALL HARLAN

violation, and it will be a 'sorry day' if it ever becomes one" (New York *Times,* November 20, 1952). He said the "guts of the law suit" were the trade relations between the three large companies.

On December 3, 1954 the case was dismissed. The court held that "du Pont did not invest in General Motors with the purpose of restricting that company's freedom to purchase in accordance with its own best interests . . . concerted action does not necessarily constitute conspiracy. . . . It does so only if the object of the action is to restrain trade or commerce. The court finds none of the actions taken in concert had as their objective, or necessary consequence, the imposition of any limitation upon the free flow of trade or commerce" (New York *Times,* December 4, 1954).

Another important antitrust suit in which Harlan served as counsel for the defense in 1952 was the case of the *United States v. Imperial Chemical Industries, Ltd.,* et al., tried in May of that year in the U.S. District Court for Southern New York wherein it was held that compulsory licensing of patents may not be required by the Government in the absence of legislative authority.

President Eisenhower nominated John Marshall Harlan as judge of the U.S. Court of Appeals for the Second District, which includes New York, Vermont and Connecticut, in January 1954, to succeed Augustus N. Hand. After being confirmed by the Senate on February 9, 1954, Harlan was sworn in on March 4, 1954 and at that time resigned from Root, Ballantine, Harlan, Bushby & Palmer (which then became Root, Ballantine, Bushby & Palmer).

While on the bench of the Federal Court of Appeals, Harlan heard the case of the *Air Line Pilots Association, International,* et al. *v. Civil Aeronautics Board,* in July 1954, and

HARLAN, JOHN MARSHALL—*Cont.*
held that ". . . increasing maximum duty aloft from eight to ten hours" on the type of non-stop-transcontinental flights concerned "would have no adverse effect on safety" (*Federal Reporter,* Volume 215). He maintained that the "power" of the board to make the special air regulation in question was "not open to any real doubt."

In October 1954 Harlan heard the case of the *United States of America, appellee, v. Elizabeth Gurley Flynn,* et al., defendants appealing judgments of conviction for "conspiring to violate the Smith act by willfully advocating and teaching the duty and necessity of overthrowing the Government of the United States by force and violence." The jurist upheld Judge Edward Jordan Dimock's decision in the U.S. District Court for Southern New York. He said: "It is clear from the record that Judge Dimock spared no pains to insure that the defendants should have a fair and impartial trial" (*Records of Court of Appeals for Second Circuit,* October 1953-November 5, 1954). The U.S. Supreme Court refused to review this conviction on January 10, 1955.

President Eisenhower nominated Harlan on November 9, 1954 to fill the Supreme Court's vacancy caused by the death of Associate Justice Robert H. Jackson on October 9. The New York *Herald Tribune* (November 10, 1954) noted: "President Eisenhower, as in his selection of Chief Justice [Earl] Warren, has chosen with . . . profound realization that the Supreme Court's wisdom and stature depend above all on the character of its members."

The Supreme Court on November 22, 1954 postponed arguments which had been scheduled for December 6 on how and when to end public school segregation because of the vacancy on the court. The tribunal unanimously had held in two separate rulings on May 17, 1954 that public school segregation is unconstitutional. This decision overruled the "separate but equal" doctrine laid down in the *Plessy v. Ferguson* case of 1896 as it pertains to public education.

After the Eighty-third Congress failed to act on Harlan's nomination, Eisenhower resubmitted the nomination to the Eighty-fourth Congress on January 10, 1955. An editorial in the New York *Times* (February 25, 1955) asserted that one of the reasons the Senate has taken so long a time to approve Harlan's nomination is that "the longer confirmation can be delayed, the longer the Supreme Court's decrees implementing the antisegregation decision can be delayed, because argument on this vital matter will not be heard until there is a full court."

During hearings of the Senate Judiciary Committee in February 1955 which concerned his nomination, Harlan stated that "while we must ally ourselves with the other free nations, any such arrangements must be made with a due regard for the Constitution and the laws of the United States" (New York *Herald Tribune,* February 26, 1955). Harlan was confirmed by the Senate on March 16 and he took the constitutional and judicial oaths on March 28. He is the eighty-ninth man to sit on the high bench since the Federal judiciary was established in 1789. The New York *Times* (March 18, 1955) commented editorially: "We can count on Judge Harlan to display . . . statesmanship, knowledge of law and a sense of justice."

After Harlan took office, the Supreme Court heard arguments from April 11 through April 14, 1955 on the question of the decrees it should issue in order to carry out its decisions on segregation.

In three decisions of the Court on May 23, which cleared witnesses of contempt in Congressional hearings, Harlan concurred in the Quinn case but dissented in the Emspak and Bart cases (New York *Times,* May 24, 1955).

The jurist is a member of the American and New York bar associations, New York County Lawyers Association, and Association of the Bar of the City of New York. He has served as president of the Havens Relief Fund, as a director of the Legal Aid Society and a trustee of the United States Trust Company. His clubs include the Century Association, Downtown Association, University, Fairfield County Hunt in Connecticut, and Ivy in Princeton, New Jersey.

Ethel Andrews and John Marshall Harlan were married on November 10, 1928. They have a daughter, Evangeline (Mrs. Wellington A. Newcomb). Harlan is an honorary fellow of the Metropolitan Museum of Art. He is a Republican and a Presbyterian. He enjoys biographical and historical books, music, golfing, fishing and gardening. Harlan is six feet one inch tall, weighs 185 pounds, and has gray hair.

In June 1954 Harlan stated at the annual commencement assembly of the Brooklyn Law School: "We must be vigilant not alone against those who seek to destroy or weaken us from without; we must also be alert to resist the irresponsible and superficial utterances of those false prophets among us who preach that our free institutions and processes are inadequate to protect us from the schemings of those who would undermine from within" (New York *Times,* June 1, 1954). He was awarded the degree of Doctor of Laws by Princeton University in June 1955.

References

Christian Sci Mon p2 Ja 15 '54; p3 N 10 '54 por
N Y Herald Tribune p6 Ap 1 '51 por; p18 Ap 2 '51; p1+ N 9 '54; II p3 N 14 '54
N Y Post p2M N 14 '54 pors
N Y Times p18 N 9 '54
N Y World-Telegram p1 N 8 '54; p4 N 9 '54 por
New Yorker 30:40+ D 4 '54
Time 64:18 N 22 '54 por

Martindale-Hubbell Law Directory, 1954
Who's Who in America, 1954-55
Who's Who in New York, 1952
World Biography (1954)

HAROOTIAN, KOREN DER *See* Der Harootian, K.

HARRIS, WALTER (EDWARD) Jan. 14, 1904- Canadian Minister of Finance; lawyer
Address: b. c/o Ministry of Finance, Ottawa, Ontario, Canada; h. Markdale, Ontario, Canada

Since Walter Harris became Canada's Minister of Finance on July 1, 1954 he has been in the public eye as a vigorous opponent of the proposed Trans-Canada pipeline, as an advocate of income tax cuts, and as a possible successor to Prime Minister Louis St. Laurent, should the latter decide to retire. Harris succeeded Douglas Abbott as Minister of Finance after serving more than four years as Minister of Citizenship and Immigration. He has been described as "the new star rising in the Liberal skies" of Canada, and although he is not too well known by the general public, he is highly regarded by leaders of the Liberal party.

For a brief period in 1952 he was Acting Secretary of State for External Affairs, and since 1940 has been a Member of Parliament. *Newsweek* (July 19, 1954) observed: "His cautious conservatism makes him unpopular with left-wing Liberals. And when opposition Conservatives complain of the government's 'contempt of Parliament' they are usually thinking of Harris and his skill in political strategy and tactics."

Walter Edward Harris was born in Kimberley, near Markdale, Ontario, on January 14, 1904, the son of Melvin and Helen (Carruthers) Harris. His place of birth and his ancestry led Prime Minister St. Laurent to say later that Harris "typifies and exemplifies the solid qualities of the Canadians of rural Protestant Ontario of sturdy English and Scottish stock" (*Newsweek*). Brought up in a modest home, with an older brother and sister, Harris enjoyed what he calls a "comfortable and commonplace" boyhood (*Maclean's Magazine,* August 15, 1954). When Walter was five years old, the family moved from the farm to Toronto, where his father became a carpenter. Walter attended the Humberside Collegiate School—history was his favorite subject and football his extracurricular activity.

When he finished his secondary schooling in 1921, Harris started working for a Toronto law firm as an articled clerk, and studying law part time at Osgoode Hall Law School. In 1926 he was admitted to the bar and set up a law practice of his own in Toronto. The first year brought him less than $1,000, and the next four averaged little more. He decided in 1931 to establish a practice near his birthplace, in Markdale, Ontario.

His first opportunity to indulge his political ambitions, harbored in high school and spurred by hearing a political speech of Mackenzie King in Toronto in 1921, came while he was a law student, when he served as secretary of the Ward Six Liberal Association in Toronto. In the early 1930's, he was made secretary of the provincial, then of the federal Liberal Association of Grey Bruce, Ontario.

His effort in 1935 to win the Liberal nomination from Grey Bruce to the House of Commons was defeated by seven votes. Four years

Capital Press Service
WALTER HARRIS

later he ran again and won the Liberal nomination. In the 1940 general election he defeated Miss Agnes MacPhail, a Progressive, by a majority of 1,400 votes.

At the outbreak of World War II in 1939, Harris had joined the local Grey and Simcoe Foresters regiment. It was called to active duty in June 1940, six weeks after he had started attending Parliament. The politician "tackled the army as he tackles everything else—with a studious determination," wrote Michael Barkway in *Saturday Night* (July 5, 1952). Harris read books on strategy and in 1942 was in England with a group of Canadian officers receiving training and staff courses. His commanding officer called him his best officer and declared that Harris would have been promoted "further and faster" if he had not been a Member of Parliament (*Maclean's*).

Returning to Canada in January 1943, Walter Harris made his maiden speech in the House of Commons and urged his country's acceptance of immigration as a necessary postwar policy. The following summer he was a squadron commander with Canada's Third Armored Tank Brigade overseas and acted as personal assistant to the administrating officer. He was put in command of a tank squadron with the Canadian Sixth Armored Regiment in June 1944 and about a month later he was wounded in the right foot while in action in Normandy. He was released from war service with the rank of major.

Back in Canada in 1945, Harris retained his parliamentary seat in that year's general election (as he did also in the elections of 1949 and 1953) and began his rapid rise to his present position. He displayed his skill in diplomacy in the House of Commons in late 1945, when he was named chairman of a committee chosen to select from about 3,000 entries a design for the Canadian national flag. It was his

HARRIS, WALTER—*Continued*

task to bring the committee "subtly" to choosing the design preferred by Prime Minister Mackenzie King, which he succeeded in doing. The Prime Minister rewarded him with an assignment as a parliamentary delegate to the United Nations General Assembly in New York.

After he came back to Canada from attending the U.N. meeting, Harris was appointed on October 30, 1947 by Mackenzie King as parliamentary assistant to Louis St. Laurent, then Secretary of State for External Affairs. That year Harris was also made vice-chairman of the parliamentary committee on seat redistribution. He helped to settle legal details relating to the new form of government Newfoundland would assume. St. Laurent placed increasing confidence in Harris' political judgment, and on succeeding Mackenzie King as Prime Minister, made Harris his parliamentary assistant on November 15, 1948.

Harris became a member of the Cabinet on January 18, 1950, when he was sworn in as Minister of Citizenship and Immigration. In his new post he was regarded as "no pushover for sob stories, but as a man . . . willing to interpret the regulations with compassion and a sense of humor" (*Maclean's*).

Criticism of Walter Harris' immigration policy also came from the Canadian director of the United Steelworkers of America, C. H. Millard, who called it "silly, absurd, discriminatory and ineffective on several counts" (*Maclean's*). More than 600,000 of Canada's million postwar immigrants entered during Harris' period in office.

As Acting Secretary of State for External Affairs in 1952, Harris advised the House of Commons of a twenty-year lease to the United States of about 7,000 acres of the Royal Canadian Air Force base at Goose Bay, Labrador, in the North Atlantic and Arctic air routes. He called this station "in effect a joint defense installation" (London *Times*, December 18, 1952).

He rapidly acquired a reputation of being "the most knowledgeable minister in the House" in parliamentary procedure. He found that "the best way of learning what goes on" in government is to attend meetings of the Cabinet's Treasury Board, which supervises departmental expenditures. While leader of the House of Commons during 1953-1954, he demonstrated his ability for smoothing out differences of opinion. Opposition members found him "hard but fair" (*Maclean's*).

After his appointment as Minister of Finance in 1954, Harris presided, in the absence of Lester B. Pearson, Secretary of State for External Affairs, at the fourth annual meeting of the Economic Consultative Committee of the Colombo Plan at Ottawa in October 1954, when Japan, Thailand and the Philippines were admitted as full members. He was appointed by Prime Minister St. Laurent as a member of a Cabinet committee to recommend legislation permitting the government to aid the advancement of the arts in Canada. Early in November 1954 Harris gave his approval to an amalgamation agreement between Canada's Dominion Bank and the Bank of Toronto.

Harris was one of three Canadian Cabinet ministers sent to Washington, D.C. in January 1955 to ask for U.S. cooperation in accepting certain international limitations on subsidized farm product exports, as a means of advancing the Geneva negotiations for revising the General Agreement on Tariffs and Trade (GATT).

In February 1955 it was reported that Harris did not support a proposal for the Canadian government to underwrite $275,000,000 in bonds to help finance a 2,200-mile east-west natural gas pipeline, which would be built by Trans-Canada Pipe Lines, Ltd. The proposal, in this form, was rejected by the Cabinet, but a later revision is still being considered.

When presenting his annual report and budget to the Parliament in April 1955, Harris declared a deficit for the fiscal year 1954-1955 of $148,300,000, credited mostly to a falling off of Canada's postwar boom that year. To stimulate production and reduce unemployment, the Canadian government decided to cut taxes and to increase the national debt (by an estimated $160,000,000). Harris proposed lowering indirect and direct personal and corporate income taxes. Large taxpayers would pay about 3 per cent less in taxes, the majority of taxpayers, 12 per cent, and corporations, 2 per cent. Excise taxes were also cut. Harris estimated that it would be possible to reduce government spending by $95,000,000 in 1955-1956 over the previous fiscal year.

The Minister of Finance has described himself as "an advanced Liberal." His clubs include the Rideau (Ottawa) and the Ontario (Toronto), and his religious affiliation is Baptist. He is a Mason (Past Master). He neither smokes nor drinks and is said to be a man who "isn't afraid to say 'I don't know.' "

Walter Harris married Grace Elma Morrison in 1933. Their children are Robert Walter, Elma Fern and Margaret Helen. He is nearly six feet tall, weighs about 200 pounds, and has brown eyes and dark hair. He enjoys reading at home or going on a family picnic. Although he works a six-day, and often a seven-day week, he says: "What I'm doing now is what I've wanted to do all my life. I like it all."

References

Bsns W p178+ Ap 16 '55 por
Macleans Mag 57:7+ Ag 15 '54 por
Newsweek 44:44 Jl 19 '54 por
Sat Night 67:19 Jl 5 '52
Who's Who in Canada, 1953-54

HARRISON, EARL G(RANT) April 27, 1899-July 28, 1955 Former U.S. Government official; lawyer; U.S. Commissioner of Immigration and Naturalization (1942-1944); was dean of the University of Pennsylvania Law School (1945-1948); appointed in 1940 as U.S. representative on the Inter-Governmental Committee on Refugees; Director of the Carnegie

Endowment for International Peace; second senior partner in law firm of Schnader, Harrison, Segal & Lewis. See *Current Biography* (Aug.) 1943.

Obituary

N Y Times p17 Jl 30 '55

HARTMAN, GRACE 1907-Aug. 8, 1955 Dancer; comedienne; with her former husband, Paul Hartman, she appeared in Broadway revues, musicals, and supper clubs as "satirists of the dance"; acclaimed for their performances in *Red, Hot and Blue* (1936), *Angel in the Wings* (1947) and *Tickets, Please!* (1950); after the dance couple separated she appeared on television shows as a comedienne. See *Current Biography* (Nov.) 1942.

Obituary

N Y Times p25 Ag 9 '55

HASS, HANS Jan. 23, 1919- Zoologist; undersea explorer

Address: b. c/o Rand McNally & Co., Box 7600, Chicago 80, Ill.; Doubleday & Co., 575 Madison Ave., New York 22; h. Vaduz, Liechtenstein

One of a steadily growing number of men and women who have made the undersea world their career, Hans Hass, Viennese zoologist, has explored the waters of five continents. He has studied—often at harrowingly close range—the activities and habits of such deep-sea inhabitants as sharks, barracuda, and giant manta rays. His equipment for underwater research includes simply watertight goggles, swimming "fins," a spear, occasionally a diving helmet (although he finds that this restricts his mobility), and a watertight camera.

The record of his explorations is available in three books—*Diving to Adventure* (Doubleday, 1951), *Manta: Under the Red Sea with Spear and Camera* (Rand McNally, 1953), and *Men and Sharks* (Doubleday, 1954)—and in a documentary motion picture, *Under the Red Sea*, which won a prize in the 1951 Venice Film Festival. More technical and scholarly studies by Hass have appeared in German periodicals, and for a number of years he has lectured in many countries on his explorations.

He sees infinite possibilities of future development of the resources of the sea. He writes in *Men and Sharks:* "The oceans lie infinitely far-flung and infinitely mysterious: their exploitation is perhaps the greatest economic undertaking that still awaits execution."

Hans Hass was born in Vienna on January 23, 1919, and learned to swim as a child in the Old Danube (a branch of the Danube River), near his parents' weekend house. On summer vacations, while his father, a lawyer, was detained on business in Vienna, he went with his mother to Juan-les-Pins on the French Riviera. Here he met the American author Guy Gilpatric, a spear-fishing enthusiast. Gilpatric in-

HANS HASS

troduced young Hass to the pleasures and perils of the sport and recommended the proper equipment—goggles and a harpoon.

In 1936 Hass went to England as an exchange student. He also studied in Paris, but he did his formal academic work at the Vienna Technological Academy, the University of Vienna, and later at the University of Berlin. He had matriculated in law, but fascinated as he was by science since his boyhood, when he had first studied a drop of water under a friend's microscope, it was inevitable that he should combine this interest with his enthusiasm for undersea life. He therefore turned from law to zoology.

Although his interest in the sea was scientific, it was also deeply personal. He writes in *Diving to Adventure:* "Fish are not nearly so dull and tiresome as most people think. On the contrary, their natures are as varied and as colorful as their shapes. Many of them have pronounced traits of character that positively challenge comparison with human beings."

With the proceeds of a sale of an article on his deep-sea adventures off the Riviera, Hass bought a camera, protected by a watertight case, so that he might record his next trip with photographs. He also bought (and was the first to introduce in Vienna) a pair of swimming "fins." Although he prefers to do his underwater work unencumbered by diving apparatus and has reached a depth of seventy-five feet without special equipment, Hass has used a diving helmet, with which he experimented in his student days and reached a depth of 125 feet.

In 1938 Hass led his first underseas diving and photographing expedition. With a group of college friends he chartered a cutter and conducted his party on a tour of the waters off the coast of Yugoslavia. Here Hass met and killed his first shark. The incidents of this trip supplied him with ample material for a popular lecture series and with the proceeds from this, in 1939, Hass prepared his next expedition—to the West Indies.

His plans for this trip were complicated by the growing political tension in Europe—the annexation of Austria by Germany and the threat of war. Hass and his party succeeded in reaching Curaçao, however, and in the Caribbean they collected numerous specimens for study. Also in the Caribbean Hass made the discovery that man has nothing to fear from sharks. "If I wanted to photograph a shark," he writes in *Diving to Adventure,* "I pretended to flee as conspicuously as possible, thus awakening the instinct in every beast of prey to chase what tries to escape. And I actually succeeded thus in luring sharks after me. When I saw that they were close enough, I would suddenly spin and swim toward them with camera . . . ready. And before the creatures had recovered from their surprise and turned away in disgust, I already had their image on film."

By lectures and articles, and the sale of his pictures, Hass was able to buy his own yacht, the *Sea Devil* (later confiscated as spoils of war), and to finance an expedition to Greece in 1942.

This expedition was planned as both a scientific field trip and as a motion picture venture. Hass was already acquainted with the difficulties of photographing sharks. He saw a group of fishermen who were illegally blasting schools of fish with dynamite. He observed that sharks were drawn by the vibrations of the explosion to the scene, where they knew there would be food, and soon Hass was using dynamite to lure them within camera range.

The photographs and specimens which Hass collected from this expedition narrowly escaped destruction after he had gone from Greece to Italy, where he was "the last and only guest" at the famous Zoologic Station at Naples. As the fighting came nearer the station, he prepared to leave. The railway car in which he stored his materials for the trip to Germany exploded in an air raid only minutes after he had managed to retrieve them. Hass took them to Berlin, where he completed his work for the doctorate in zoology at the Friedrich-Wilhelms-Universität.

When the war ended, Hass found himself without funds or equipment for a large-scale expedition. He resolved therefore to go to Africa to explore the Red Sea waters by himself. In Port Sudan, with the cooperation of British officials, he was able to get a boat and explore the coral reefs of the Red Sea. Once again Hass had numerous encounters with sharks, but the most dramatic of his adventures was with the giant manta rays, which he photographed at close range.

Four months after his return Hass was able to finance a second expedition to the area. On this trip he filmed the motion picture *Under the Red Sea,* which won an international first prize at the 1951 Venice Film Festival. Among the most interesting parts of the film were a scene showing the reaction of the fish to the "Blue Danube" waltz music (relayed to the bottom of the sea through a hydrophone) and the series of shots of the giant rays—scenes which Otis L. Guernsey, Jr., described in the New York *Herald Tribune* (November 30, 1952) as "about as cinematic as you can get without strangling the audience as it holds its breath."

To date, three books by Hass have appeared in English translation, all of them illustrated with his photographs. The first of the books was *Diving to Adventure,* recounting his early underseas experiences and his expedition to the Caribbean. *Manta: Under the Red Sea with Spear and Camera* was an account of his first Red Sea expedition, and *Men and Sharks* described his expedition to Greece. The reviewers have found his books lively and informative, although several have objected to the digressions on his companions on these expeditions and to his tendency at times to "overdramatize" his adventures (W. B. Hayward in the New York *Times,* October 28, 1951).

Hass has found a deeper satisfaction than the mere thrill of adventure in his explorations. As he discovered the beauties of underwater life, he used the harpoon less and the camera more frequently. He describes the shark as "the most beautiful of all living animals," and he writes affectionately of almost all the undersea creatures except the moray eel and the graceful but savage barracuda.

In 1950 Hass married Lotte Berl. He has a son by an earlier marriage. His wife is an undersea explorer herself and accompanied Hass on the second Red Sea expedition. She appears in the film *Under the Red Sea.* In 1952 they traveled to Australia to study the waters of the Great Barrier Reef, and in 1953, on their 120-foot yacht *Xarifa,* they led an expedition to South American waters. When not deep under water, they live high up in the Alps in Liechtenstein, where they enjoy skiing.

References

Christian Sci Mon p3 My 16 '50; p6 N 9 '50

N Y World-Telegram p6 N 22 '52

Hass, H., Diving to Adventure (1951); Manta; Under the Red Sea with Spear and Camera (1953); Men and Sharks (1954)

HATCHER, HARLAN (HENTHORNE)

Sept. 9, 1898- University president; author

Address: b. The President's Office, University of Michigan, Ann Arbor, Mich.; h. 815 S. University Ave., Ann Arbor, Mich.

Since becoming president of the University of Michigan at Ann Arbor, Michigan in 1951, Dr. Harlan Hatcher has been expanding the university's physical plant for the use of its nearly 20,000 students. He has headed the successful campaign for $6,000,000 needed to complete the Michigan Memorial Phoenix Project which includes a nuclear reactor and research facilities for exploring the peaceful uses of atomic energy.

A well-known educator, Hatcher had previously been associated with Ohio State University in Columbus as a student, instructor, professor, dean and vice-president. He has written numerous books, both fiction and nonfiction, particularly concerning the cultural history of Ohio and the Great Lakes region.

Discussing the purpose of a liberal education and the responsibilities of American educational institutions, Dr. Hatcher said recently, "The future of America will be strong if we continue, as we will, to advance our mastery over the physical world and our ingenious manipulations of its power. The future of America will be wiser if we weigh and consider the journey over which we have come to this point, and become better informed as a people about the successes and the failures of mankind in [our] wayward attempts to live on this earth."

Harlan Henthorne Hatcher was born in Ironton, Ohio, a town on the banks of the Ohio River, on September 9, 1898, the son of Robert Elison and Linda (Lesley) Hatcher. His family soon moved to Kentucky, where Harlan's father taught school. He prepared for college at the Morehead Normal School in Kentucky and from October 1 to December 21, 1918 served in the United States Army as a private.

After his return from the Army, Hatcher entered Ohio State University where he was elected to Phi Beta Kappa and received the A.B. degree in 1922. He earned the M.A. degree in English in 1923, and the Ph.D. degree in English in 1927. His thesis, "The Versification of Robert Browning," was published in 1928 by the Ohio State University Press. He also did postgraduate work at the University of Chicago in 1925, and in 1928 he traveled in Italy, France and England to study various aspects of Renaissance literature.

Beginning his career as an instructor in English at Ohio State University in 1922, Hatcher continued in this position until 1928, when he was made an assistant professor. He became a full professor in 1932. Speaking before the Modern Language Association of America to teachers of literature, he stated: "It is the permanent glory of letters to reveal the nature and the wonder of life itself, and it is the chief distinction of our profession to tend and to nurture the flame."

During World War II, from 1942 to 1944, Hatcher served as a lieutenant in the U.S. Naval Reserve and was stationed at Chapel Hill, North Carolina. He retired to inactive duty on May 7, 1944. He was appointed in that year as dean of the College of Arts and Sciences at Ohio State University and in 1948 assumed the duties of vice-president. While at the university, Hatcher wrote: "It is a good, but not a quiet life; there is nothing 'cloistered' about a modern state university with [more than] 15,000 students! In fact, I periodically escape from the rush of the university into the peace and contemplative quiet of New York."

On May 21, 1951 the Board of Regents of the University of Michigan announced that Dr. Hatcher had been chosen the eighth president,

HARLAN HATCHER

to succeed Dr. Alexander Ruthven. At his inauguration on November 27, Hatcher stated: "The university can and does and will render its greatest service to the state by being strong in its central mission—to teach and add to knowledge and to make this knowledge [available] to all."

The University of Michigan, founded by a group of public-spirited men in 1817 now numbers nearly 20,000 students. It receives annually fixed appropriations from the state, and the university's Board of Regents, elected directly by the people of the state of Michigan, has entire control of the affairs of the university. Its lands comprise 18,500 acres, of which about 974 are in or near Ann Arbor. Instruction is carried out by fifteen schools and colleges, including those for the study of law, medicine, social work, business administration, library science, and natural resources. The university has museums of art, archaeology, paleontology, anthropology, and zoology, and supports a symphony orchestra, a concert band, and several choirs.

Plans for the building of the North Campus were announced by President Hatcher in the fall of 1951, and since that time several buildings have been completed. During his administration the university's physical plant has also been expanded by the completion of two new buildings in the hospital area, by a three-unit classroom addition to one of the lecture buildings, and by a swimming pool building.

In 1953 President Hatcher announced completion of the Michigan Memorial-Phoenix Project campaign for $6,500,000 to build a nuclear reactor to be used in nonmilitary research. The Ford Motor Company Fund contributed $1,000,000 for this purpose. Several scores of research projects, in medicine, botany, bacteriology, engineering, physics and chemistry, have been started.

(Continued next page)

HATCHER, HARLAN—*Continued*

Various other developments which have taken place at the university since Hatcher became president have included reorganization of the nursing curriculum so that all students in this field now earn a bachelor's degree, and the establishment of a summer institute in the Near East to assist in training experts for work in that area. The university's work in educational television has also been expanded so that it now operates its own television station on which lectures, demonstrations, dramas and documentaries are presented.

It was at the University of Michigan that the evaluation of the mass field trials of the (Dr. Jonas E.) Salk anti-polio vaccine was made; on April 12, 1955 it was announced at the university that the vaccine was effective and would be used nationally.

Hearings were held in Michigan in 1954 by the Un-American Activities Committee of the U.S. House of Representatives, at which two faculty members of the University of Michigan refused on constitutional grounds to answer questions about their political affiliations and beliefs. A subsequent hearing was held by President Hatcher and his faculty advisory committee, at which the two professors "did not convince . . ." [Hatcher] that they were "sufficiently opposed ideologically to the Communist party" (*Nation*, November 6, 1954) and they were asked to resign. Another faculty member who had invoked the Fifth Amendment before the House Committee, indicated "strong disagreement with the Communist party" and was allowed to maintain his connection with the university (New York *Times*, August 27, 1954).

Dr. Hatcher has written three novels: *Tunnel Hill* (Bobbs-Merrill, 1931), *Patterns of Wolfpen* (Bobbs-Merrill, 1934), and *Central Standard Time* (Farrar & Rinehart, 1937). Of the latter novel the New York *Times* observed: "*Central Standard Time* is a well-intentioned and fairly clever novel, with some nice touches of satire, but it is too glib and stereotyped to cut very deeply and it adds very little to what one can deduce from the front page news." On the other hand the reviewer for the *Boston Transcript* commented: "Professor Hatcher's writing is mature and thoughtful" (*Book Review Digest*, 1937). His *Creating the Modern American Novel* (Farrar & Rinehart, 1935) is a study of the development of American fiction from 1900 to the mid-1930's. For Harcourt Brace & Company, Hatcher edited in 1941 *Modern American Dramas, Modern British Dramas,* and *Modern Continental Dramas*, and in 1948, a new, shorter edition of the three books entitled *Modern Dramas.* A new edition of *Modern American Dramas* appeared in 1949. Hatcher edited in 1953 *A Modern Repertory*, a collection of plays published by Harcourt Brace.

The educator has long been interested in the history and development of the Great Lakes region, especially his native state of Ohio. His books include: *The Buckeye Country; A Pageant of Ohio* (Kinsey, 1940; revised edition, Putnam, 1947); *The Great Lakes* (Oxford, 1944); *Lake Erie* (Bobbs-Merrill, 1945); *The Western Reserve; The Story of New Connecticut in Ohio* (Bobbs-Merrill, 1949); *A Century of Iron and Men* (Bobbs-Merrill, 1950); and with Frank Durham, *Giant from the Wilderness; The Story of a City* [*Cleveland, Ohio*] *and its Industries* (World, 1955).

He contributed to *The History of the State of Ohio*, volume VI, edited by C. F. Wittke and published by the Ohio State Archaeological and Historical Society in 1944 and wrote the foreword to *Johnny Appleseed, A Voice in the Wilderness; The Story of the Pioneer John Chapman* (Swedenborg Press, 1945). His articles have appeared in such periodicals as the *Saturday Review, PMLA* (Publication of the Modern Language Association of America), *English Journal, College English,* and *Educational Method.* His article "Colleges for Citizens" appeared in the April 4, 1953, issue of the *Saturday Review.*

Hatcher's various interests in education and writing have also led him to serve as state director in Ohio of the Federal Writers' Project from 1937 to 1939; as editor of the *Ohio Guide* (Oxford, 1940); as book editor of the Columbus (Ohio) *Citizen* (from 1938 to 1944); and as an adviser to *College English* (from 1938 to 1948).

He holds seven honorary degrees: from his alma mater, the University of Michigan, as well as five other colleges and universities. The Ohio Governor's Award was presented to him in 1949 for his contribution to the advancement of the state's prestige. He also was awarded the Ohioana Grand Medal in 1950. He is a Commander in the Netherlands Order of the Orange Nassau.

Dr. Hatcher holds memberships in the Modern Language Association of America, the American Association of University Professors, National Council of Teachers of English, the Great Lakes Historical Society, and the American Historical Society. He became a trustee of the Ohio State Archaeological and Historical Society in 1947 and is a director of the Ann Arbor Bank. His clubs include the Faculty, Crichton, Torch, Players, Kit-Kat, and University Golf. He is a Democrat.

Harlan Henthorne Hatcher married Frank Wilson Colfax on December 29, 1922. She is deceased. On April 3, 1942 he married Anne Gregory Vance of New Haven, Connecticut and has two children, Robert Leslie and Anne Linda. For recreation he enjoys playing golf and tennis, and traveling. Wednesday afternoon tea for the university students has become a tradition at President Hatcher's residence.

In a speech on American cultural maturity, Hatcher pointed out that American writers are just beginning to look toward their own heritage and customs for subject matter. "The material for American writers has hardly been touched," he concluded. "It lies about us on every hand ready for the writer with imagination to see it, feel it, and interpret it. The environment of a great state university is the proper place to foster a healthy American culture and to train artists to draw strength from it and in turn to make their contribution to it."

References

N Y Times p33 My 22 '51 por
Newsweek 37:86 My 28 '51
Directory of American Scholars (1951)
International Who's Who, 1954
Leaders in Education (1948)
Kunitz, S. J., and Haycraft, H. eds. Twentieth Century Authors (1942)
Who's Who in America, 1954-55
Who's Who in the Midwest (1955)
World Biography (1954)

HATOYAMA, ICHIRO (hŏt-o-yä-mä ē-chē-rō) Jan. 1, 1883- Premier of Japan

Address: b. 1 Nagatacho 2-chome, Chiyoda-ku, Tokyo; h. 10 of 7, Otowa-cho 7-chome, Koishikawa, Tokyo

The first Japanese political leader to campaign by radio and television, Premier Ichiro Hatoyama received more votes in the national election held in Japan on February 27, 1955 than any Japanese Diet candidate in history and was re-elected as Premier in the lower house of the Diet (Parliament) on March 18. Hatoyama was selected as "caretaker" Premier in the Diet on December 9, 1954, after Premier Shigeru Yoshida withdrew before a coalition of Socialists and conservatives could approve a motion of non-confidence in his regime.

The Hatoyama government faces the task of fulfilling election promises by creating a more independent national policy and by establishing increased economic strength through seeking continued support of the United States and at the same time expansion of trade with the Communist world (New York *Times,* March 8, 1955.) Japan, growing in population at the rate of 1,000,000 persons a year, with a total land area smaller than California, and with its empire gone, can neither feed all its people nor provide enough raw materials for its industries (*Time,* March 14, 1955).

In March 1955 Hatoyama discussed trade policies with Foreign Operations Administrator Harold E. Stassen, who, during his visit to Japan, proposed that as an alternative to trade with Communist countries, Japan should concentrate on Southeast Asia. The New York *Herald Tribune* (March 10, 1955) reported that a memorandum asking the United States to support a multilateral aid program for Southeast Asia was presented to Stassen.

Ichiro Hatoyama was born in Tokyo on January 1, 1883, the elder son of Kazuo and Haruko (Matsumoto) Hatoyama. His father was a Yale graduate and a lawyer and was at the time head of Waseda University and speaker of the lower house of the Japanese Diet. His mother founded the Kyoritsu Women's University and was well known as a writer on cultural subjects and homemaking. Ichiro's parents planned for him to be a politician. A second son, Hideo, was also destined for public life and has been a member of the Japanese Diet.

Ichiro Hatoyama studied law at the Tokyo Imperial University and was graduated in 1907. He practiced law for about a year and was then elected as assemblyman in the Tokyo Municipal Assembly and later named chairman of the assembly. He entered national politics in 1915 and won a seat in the lower house of the Diet. The "powerful" Seiyukai political party made him chief party secretary and he was re-elected to the Diet for successive terms.

During the Premiership (1927-1929) of Baron Gi-ichi Tanaka, Hatoyama was chief cabinet secretary. He was Minister of Education in Premier Ki Inukai's Cabinet (1931-1932) and was reappointed to this position in Premier Makoto Saito's Cabinet in 1932. Hatoyama visited Europe in 1937 and upon his return, he wrote *Sekai no Kawo* (The Face of the World).

According to *U.S. News & World Report* (December 17, 1954), the book praised the dictators of Europe and became a best seller in Japan in 1938. Hatoyama failed to win the presidency of the Seiyukai, which position usually led to the Premiership, because Japan's generals and admirals disapproved of his foreign style of living, Western clothes and "democratic" ideas. His 1942 political campaign brochure that commended Premier Hideki Tojo, also failed to impress the militarists. Nevertheless, Hatoyama was one of the few not favored by Tojo who were elected to the Diet in 1942.

During most of World War II, Hatoyama remained at his country home in Karuizawa. He emerged after Japan's surrender and organized the Liberal party, of which he became president. He told Darrel Berrigan (New York *Post,* December 27, 1945) that his was a "center party—just to the right of the Socialists," but outlined conservative plans which he would carry out as Premier. General Douglas MacArthur's directive of January 4, 1946 (ordering the Japanese government to remove from office all "active exponents" of military government and bar them from the elections) had not included Hatoyama, but on April 4, 1946 the Tokyo Foreign Correspondents' Club focused attention on Hatoyama's 1938 book and on the 1942 brochure.

Hatoyama won his seat in the Diet in the April 10 election and was expected to become Premier. Acting Premier Baron Kijuro Shidehara advised him to form a Cabinet and asked Emperor Hirohito to nominate him as Premier. On May 4, 1946 a directive by General MacArthur forbade Hatoyama to take his seat in the Diet or to hold government office. Lindesay Parrott (New York *Times,* May 5, 1946) commented that Russian and Chinese delegates of the Inter-Allied Council had "severe objections to Hatoyama's possible Premiership." Among the charges against him were "shared responsibility" in the 1927 Tanaka Cabinet's amendment of the Peace Preservation Law and the suppression of free speech which followed, and the "mass arrest of teachers" while he was Minister of Education.

(Continued next page)

Wide World

ICHIRO HATOYAMA

Shigeru Yoshida took over the Premiership and the reins of the Liberal party while Hatoyama filed a formal appeal. He asserted that the evidence against him was "either false as to facts, or falsely interpreted" (Burton Crane, New York *Times,* November 1, 1947).

After the new Japanese Constitution came into effect on May 3, 1947 and after two Premiers filled short terms, Yoshida was re-installed as Premier. Hatoyama suffered a paralytic stroke that affected his left side. After his vindication in mid-1951, he made plans to return to political life. Mac R. Johnson (New York *Herald Tribune,* December 31, 1951) reported that Yoshida was unwilling to give up the Premiership as agreed.

A new election was held after the San Francisco Peace Treaty became effective in 1952, and Hatoyama was elected to the Diet. The New York *Times* (October 25, 1952) reported that according to an "uneasy truce" arrangement he would support Yoshida as Premier. The Diet was dissolved in March 1953 after a non-confidence vote. Hatoyama formed a splinter party of dissident Liberals, but Yoshida was re-installed as Premier in May 1953.

The next upset came in 1954 after Premier Yoshida had visited the United States. According to *Newsweek* (November 22, 1954) he failed to bring back "substantial promises of U.S. aid." Japan was said to be close to bankruptcy in international finances. Hatoyama withdrew from the Liberal party and with his followers and the Progressives, founded the Democratic party. A few hours before a non-confidence vote could topple the government—on December 7, 1954—Premier Yoshida resigned.

Two days later, Hatoyama was named Premier with the guarantee given to the Socialists that the Diet would be dissolved and a national election held within three months. He formed a new Cabinet with Mamoru Shigemitsu as Deputy Premier and Foreign Minister. The latter had signed Japan's surrender to the Allied powers and later served a seven-year prison term as a war criminal, but has stated that he has "no grudge" against those who had condemned him (New York *Times,* December 11, 1954.)

Determined that his regime would extend beyond the "caretaker" period, Premier Hatoyama campaigned vigorously on radio and television before the elections, to be held in February. He promised that Japan would not alter its close ties with the United States, but talked about the possibilities of further trade with Red China and of ending the state of war with the Soviet Union (which had not signed the San Francisco Peace Treaty). Despite his physical handicap, he made at "rice roots" level a whirlwind tour which Dorothy Brandon (New York *Herald Tribune,* February 17, 1955) described as "reminiscent of American politics."

The February 27 election was considered "a smashing success" for Hatoyama, who received 149,541 votes. His party won 185 seats in the House of Representatives in the Diet. The platform measures for "normalized" relations with the Communist world and for increased independence from foreign countries were said to be largely responsible. *Time* (March 14, 1955) pointed out that his party lacked the two-thirds majority necessary for changes in the Constitution, notably the "no-war" clause. Hatoyama has stated that Japan should rearm to "protect the peace" and thus wants to change the 'pacifist clause' in the Constitution.

In the House of Representatives Hatoyama was re-elected as Premier by a vote of 254 to 160, but his candidates for speaker and vice-speaker were defeated by a coalition of the Liberal and Socialist parties. This was regarded as an indication that Hatoyama has only a "tenuous hold at best on the reins of power" (William J. Jorden, New York *Times*, March 19, 1955). In Hatoyama's new Cabinet, Shigemitsu continued as Foreign Minister.

After Hatoyama became Premier, Moscow was quick to offer to discuss "practical measures" to restore relations, and the Japanese leader announced his willingness to negotiate. According to the New York *World-Telegram and Sun* (March 14, 1955) the return of the Habomai and Kurile islands which "Russia took home from Yalta" would be requested.

As part of his program for easing tensions in Asia and placing Japan in a new relationship with her Asian neighbors, Hatoyama has promised to seek a friendly settlement of disputes with South Korea largely over property claims and fishing rights. The Premier also said that the Japanese hope "that their reluctance to spend more for arms shall not prejudice the United States in granting economic and military assistance" (New York *Times*, March 20, 1955).

Hatoyama is pressing his government's "recognition of 'two Chinas,' the Communist and the Nationalist governments" as a "keystone of Japanese foreign policy in Asia," according to Robert Trumbull of the New York *Times*

(March 26, 1955). By this policy Hatoyama hopes that Japan can establish peaceful political and economic ties with all its neighbors.

Ichiro Hatoyama was married in 1907 to Kaoru, eldest daughter of Sakae Terada. They have one son, Iichiro, and four daughters, Yudyko, Reiko, Keiko, and Nobuko. The Hatoyama's have seven grandchildren. Their son is a graduate of the Tokyo Imperial University law school and is employed in the Ministry of Finance. His wife—Yasuko—is the daughter of Shojiro Ishibashi, wealthy rubber manufacturer and one of Hatoyama's chief backers.

The Premier's wife is president of Kyoritsu Women's University, which his mother founded. The family have inherited wealth and live in Tokyo in a large mansion, furnished in Western style. Hatoyama wears Western clothes and before his illness was a golf enthusiast. He still plays go, a game similar to chess. He enjoys music and art and has a garden noted for its many varieties of roses.

Premier Hatoyama has gray hair and brown eyes and is of medium build. He is said to have a jovial, mild-mannered but courtly air. One or two of his aids usually accompany him and he carries a gnarled black cane. He is a Christian—a Baptist—and a Master Mason.

References

N Y Times p4 D 10 '54
Time 65:34+ Mr 14 '55 pors
Who's Who in Japan, 1941-42

HAUSER, (BENGAMIN) GAYELORD

1895(?)- Nutritionist

Address: b. c/o Farrar, Straus and Cudahy, Inc., 101 5th Ave., New York 3

Gayelord Hauser has lectured on food since 1923 and has written the best sellers *Look Younger, Live Longer* (1950) and *Be Happier, Be Healthier* (1952). He conducted a daily syndicated newspaper column in 1951 and a television program during 1952 in which he added sun therapy to his earlier theories of body-building.

To compile his book, *Gayelord Hauser's New Guide to Intelligent Reducing*, published by Farrar, Straus and Young in January 1955, the nutritionist visited universities, research centers and commercial laboratories in Europe, South America and the United States to collect new information about food. With "characteristic Hauser exuberance" he emphasizes that eating can be fun, and dieting need not be onerous.

His ideas on food have attracted a wide following in motion picture, theatrical and society circles as well as with the general public despite the fact that some of his claims for his diets have been criticized by the medical fraternity. His ten-day diet and twenty-eight-day diet, contained in *Look Younger, Live Longer*, were published in *Cosmopolitan* magazine and have been distributed by the Literary Guild and translated into twelve languages.

Bengamin Gayelord Hauser is the name legally adopted in 1923 by Helmut Eugene Benjamin Gellert Hauser, a native of Tübingen in Württemberg, and the eleventh of the thirteen children of a Lutheran schoolmaster. He was sixteen years old when in 1911 he came to the United States from Germany to join an elder brother, Otto Robert, the pastor of a church in Milwaukee, Wisconsin. The boy contracted tuberculosis of the hip and underwent a series of operations, but his case was adjudged hopeless. Noel F. Busch, writing in the *Saturday Evening Post*, August 11, 1951 (with the benefit of access to Hauser's uncompleted memoirs), ascribed the beginning of his eventual recovery to the naturopath Dr. Benedict Lust, who "recommended long warm baths, clay packs and herb teas," during which treatment Hauser also "tried another therapeutic oddity called naprapathy, an offshoot of osteopathy." In 1922 Doctor Lust also recommended that Hauser try *Nahrungswissenschaft* (food science), "then burgeoning in Switzerland." Hauser visited relatives living near Basel, where "a monk named Brother Maier put him on a diet of salads, fruit juices, vegetable broths and herbs," and "after a few weeks his hip abscess closed for good."

Deciding to learn more about "the power of food," Hauser visited Vienna, where he "absorbed . . . eagerly" the caloric theory taught by Pirquet, and later went to Zurich where "Dr. Bircher-Benner and his two sons with their ideas on sunlit foods were teaching people how to eat their way back to health" (*Diet Does It*). Another goal in his "food pilgrimage" was Dresden, where he met the food chemist Dr. Ragnar Berg, and in Copenhagen he visited Dr. Mikkel Hindhede, whose "favorite maxim" was "undereat rather than overeat."

Although he is not a doctor of medicine, Hauser has (states a release by his publishers) received degrees from the University Philotechnique of Brussels and from the International Faculty of Sciences in London. At one time he studied at the Chicago College of Naprapathy and acquired the right to use the letters "N.D."

On returning to Chicago and obtaining a court order changing his name to Bengamin Gayelord Hauser, he began in 1923 "to dispense his newly acquired food lore from a small office at 116 Michigan Boulevard" (*Saturday Evening Post*, August 11, 1951). He addressed groups in Midwestern cities, urging a dietetic regimen in which five Vitamin B-containing "wonder foods"—brewers' yeast, powdered skim milk, yogurt, wheat germ and blackstrap molasses—were specified for daily use.

In the late 1920's Hauser became a partner in the Milwaukee firm, Modern Food Products, Inc., which specialized in an herb laxative "Swiss Kriss," and later included "Hauser broth." (The *Journal of the American Medical Association*, April 17, 1937, and *Hygeia*, February 1938, give details about the Federal Trade Commission's investigation into the claims for the firm's products.)

GAYELORD HAUSER

Moving to California in 1927, he quickly built up a following in the Hollywood film colony, including Adele Astaire (who later, as Lady Cavendish, introduced him to notables in London and Paris.)

Hauser's manual *Harmonized Food Selection, With the Famous Hauser Body-Building System* was published in New York by Tempo Books in 1930 and was followed by *Food Science and Health, With the Famous Hauser Eliminative Feeding System* (1931), *Types and Temperaments, a Key to Foods* (1931), *Child Feeding, Written for Mothers* (1932), *Dictionary of Foods,* in collaboration with Dr. Ragnar Berg (1932), *Keener Vision Without Glasses* (1932), *Better Eyes Without Glasses* (1938), *Here's How to be Healthy* (1934) and *Eat and Grow Beautiful* (1936).

In the course of the next ten years Hauser interested many celebrities in following his diets. These included Lady Mendl (the former actress Elsie de Wolfe), Paulette Goddard, Marlene Dietrich, Greta Garbo, Gloria Swanson, Queen Alexandra of Yugoslavia, Baron Philippe de Rothschild, Herman Baruch, the Duchess of Windsor, and many others.

In a demonstration at the St. Regis Hotel in New York in February 1942, he delivered (stated *Time*) "the kind of message that makes M.D.'s shudder." (For a description of the Hauser showmanship see the *New Yorker,* July 1, 1950.) The nutritionist's vogue gained additional impetus with the appearance of his *Diet Does It* (Coward-McCann, 1944) and the popularity of *The Gayelord Hauser Cook Book.*

Of *Look Younger, Live Longer* (published by Farrar Straus and Company and the Literary Guild in February 1950), Morrison Wood wrote in the Chicago *Sunday Tribune* that it offered "sane and sound advice that should make the mature years of life a healthier and happier time." At first the book was not widely reviewed, yet it immediately took and held first place on the national nonfiction best seller lists and by the end of 1953 it had sold over 500,000 copies in the "trade" edition alone, and had been translated into twelve languages. The French edition carried an introduction by the Duchess of Windsor. The book was condensed in *Reader's Digest* and *Omnibook* and serialized in the Hearst newspapers.

Already the editor of his own magazine, *Diet Digest,* Hauser began his syndicated daily column for King Features in March 1951. The Doughnut Corporation of America placed on the market in 1952 the new "Gayelord Hauser Bread" and Hauser made a series of television broadcasts under the sponsorship of a frozen orange juice company.

A revised edition of *Diet Does It* was issued in 1952. *Be Happier, Be Healthier* (Farrar, 1952) has as its theme "that from the sun, air, earth and water, the green things we depend upon extract all that is good, all that is required, for health." It advocates the taking of sun baths to "transmit as yet unknown but important vitamins to our internal bodies," as well as sitz baths for "relaxing hydrotherapy" (*Time,* November 17, 1952).

Gayelord Hauser's New Guide to Intelligent Reducing; How to Reduce and Stay Reduced for Life advances his theory that the "hungerstat" is the craving for the right food, the "appestat" is the acquired appetite for "overcooked vegetables, devitalized bread, soft drinks and oversweet desserts." Hauser discusses psychiatric and psychosomatic reasons for obesity. He describes a new licorice drink from France and a new sweetner made from Jerusalem artichokes as valuable sources of minerals. Hauser advises obese people to have a mid-morning bracer and a mid-afternoon lift and a cocktail of fruit or vegetable juice to curb their hunger and to insure against overeating at meals.

Hauser has homes in New York City, California, Sicily and his native Black Forest which he has shared with Frey Brown, his business manager since 1924. "Good clothes are one of the two luxuries, outside of wonder foods, to which Hauser is addicted," Noel F. Busch wrote (*Saturday Evening Post*). The other is high powered automobiles. Hauser's chief hobby is his collection of porcelain and ceramic dishes in the shape of vegetables and fruits. His canine companion is a Sealyham terrier. In *Look Younger, Live Longer* "big-boned" Gayelord Hauser gave his height as six feet three inches and his weight as 215 pounds. The *New Yorker* has described Hauser as "slim and immaculate."

Concerning the collecting of antiques Hauser said, "There are not enough years in a lifetime to collect all the beautiful things available. Collecting is stimulating to the mind and invigorating to the soul" (*Hobbies,* April 1948).

References

New Yorker 26:18+ Jl 1 '50
Newsweek 23:97+ Mr 13 '44
Sat Eve Post 224:30+ Ag 11 '51 por
Time 39:58 F 16 '42; 60:63 N 17 '52

HAYDEN, MELISSA Apr. 25, 1928- Ballerina

Address: b. c/o New York City Ballet, 130 W. 56th St., New York 19

Much critical acclaim has been bestowed upon the young ballerina, Melissa Hayden, whose work for the past several seasons has been largely with the New York City Ballet. John Martin in the New York *Times* wrote: "A more powerful dramatic dancer or a more technically superb one it would be hard to find" (November 30, 1950) and in the same year, Walter Terry in the New York *Herald Tribune* asserted, "Melissa Hayden was perfection itself . . . a bravura performance which I seriously doubt could be equalled by any other soloist of the ballet."

Her work was seen by motion picture audiences in the dance sequences of the Charles Chaplin film *Limelight* in 1952, and in various *pas de deux* with André Eglevsky on television. She was a prima ballerina with Ballet Theatre on tour during 1953, and after a year's absence returned to the New York City Ballet, where she danced the principal role in Jerome Robbins' *The Cage* on February 16 and George Balanchine's *Pas de Trois* (II) on March 6, 1955, in which she "accomplished her airborne actions and fast footwork with fine dash" (Walter Terry, March 7, 1955).

Melissa Hayden, whose real name is Mildred Herman, was born in Toronto, Canada on April 25, 1928, the daughter of Russian-born Jacob and Kate Herman. She attended Landsowne Street elementary school. At the age of thirteen she began her ballet training at the Boris Volkoff Ballet School, where she remained four years. While still at the school, she worked as a bookkeeper and part-time secretary and attended dance classes at night. Anatole Chujoy, editor of *The Dance Encyclopedia*, chanced to see Melissa in the ballet class and encouraged her to become a professional ballet dancer. Melissa took his advice and went to New York City in 1945.

She became a member of the *corps de ballet* at Radio City, where she was under the direction of the ballet mistress, Florence Rogge, a fellow Canadian. She lived in an inexpensive rooming house with other girls from the company and returned once a month to Toronto to visit her parents and renew her visa. She continued to perfect her technique and attended classes at the School of American Ballet and the Vilzak-Shollar.

The choreographer, Michael Kidd, seeing Miss Hayden dance, recommended her to Lucia Chase, director of Ballet Theatre, who offered her a place in the company's *corps de ballet.* Within nine months she was elevated to the rank of soloist. She remained with Ballet Theatre for two and a half years, appearing both in the United States and in Europe.

Miss Hayden left the company to accept an engagement with the Ballet Alicia Alonso on a tour of South America. While in Buenos Aires, she received a letter from a friend, the ballet dancer Nicholas Magallanes, a member of the New York City Ballet under the artistic direction of George Balanchine, asking if she

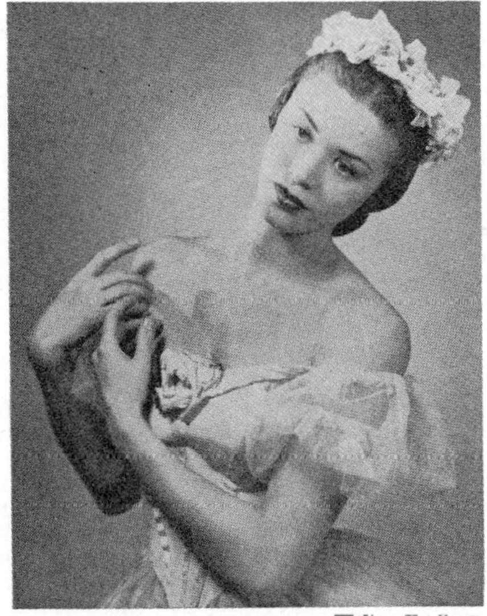

Walter E. Owen

MELISSA HAYDEN

would be interested in working in the company in which he was engaged. Melissa wrote that she would be interested, and when Balanchine cabled a return ticket to her, the young dancer entered a new phase of her career.

It was in her work with the New York City Ballet that Miss Hayden rose swiftly to the top rank of ballerinas. In December 1950, the dance critic, John Martin, wrote that within a year she had turned "what was always an impressive talent into what can only be recognized as an incipient greatness."

In February 1950 Miss Hayden had appeared at City Center in the première of a ballet *The Duel* by William Dollar, "a tragic melodrama in dance set in the days of the Crusades. A Christian warrior falls in love with a Saracen girl. While masked, they meet in combat. Not until after her mask flies off does he recognize his victim" (*Life*, May 12, 1952). Reviewing the première at City Center, John Martin commented: "It is danced magnificently by Melissa Hayden, who brings a tremendous dramatic strength onto the stage with her, as well as a technique that is lithe, powerful and supremely controlled. It is no less than an inspired performance" (New York *Times*, February 25, 1950).

The young ballerina won further honors the same spring with her work in *Illuminations*, a ballet by Frederick Ashton of the Sadler's Wells Ballet, based on a group of poems by Rimbaud set to music by Benjamin Britten, with scenery and costumes by Cecil Beaton.

During the summer of 1950 the New York City Ballet was seen in London. Miss Hayden recalled that on the last night the company danced at Covent Garden, "the gallery took up a collection and presented everyone in the group with flowers. It is something one just doesn't expect . . . or ever hope to experience again" (*Theatre Arts* magazine, February 1952). Upon the company's return to New York, the

HAYDEN, MELISSA—*Continued*

first presentation of the season included *The Duel* and Melissa Hayden won fresh accolades. "It is a truly magnificent piece of work and the little ballet belongs to her completely" (New York *Times*, November 30, 1950).

In December of the same year she appeared in Jerome Robbins' ballet, *The Age of Anxiety*. On this occasion Martin commented: "There is a mature, dramatic grasp of the role. . . . Here is truly danced emotion. There is no question that Miss Hayden dominates the work" (New York *Times*, December 4, 1950).

In the fall season of 1951 a new ballet, *The Miraculous Mandarin*, was presented, the choreography, following Lengyel's scenario, composed by Todd Bolender to music of Bartók. "As the girl, Melissa Hayden gave a highly keyed, melodramatic enactment. . . . At moments she seemed to be overdoing the act, but elsewhere was highly effective" (*Herald Tribune*, September 7, 1951). The *Times* critic wrote: "Miss Hayden's performance is sheer black magic," and Douglas Watt in the *New Yorker* commented that Miss Hayden was "savagely effective."

Following a five-month tour of Europe, the City Ballet opened its 1952 fall season with Frederick Ashton's *Picnic at Tintagel* on the bill, Miss Hayden taking the principal feminine role, previously filled by Diana Adams. Walter Terry stated: "One could have wished, I think, for a trifle more lyricism" (New York *Herald Tribune*, November 5, 1952).

A few nights later she appeared in *The Cage*. "To follow Miss [Nora] Kaye in a role created especially for her highly individual and dramatic gifts is quite a large order," John Martin commented, "and it cannot be said that Miss Hayden altogether filled it. . . . [Her] generally nervous quality largely defeats the choreographer's purpose."

When she appeared in the title role of Balanchine's choreography of Stravinsky's *Firebird*, Martin wrote, "A stunning performance it proved to be. Technically, of course, Miss Hayden is able to do virtually anything she elects to do, and she brought the full force of her taut, nervous energy into play. . . . Miss Hayden has never given a more magnificent account of herself." Other ballets and pieces in which Miss Hayden was seen in the 1952-1953 season were *Symphony in C*, *Valse-Fantaisie*, *Kaleidoscope*, *The Five Gifts*, and *Caracole*.

Signed for the dance sequence in Charles Chaplin's film *Limelight* (released in November 1952), Melissa Hayden doubled for Claire Bloom and danced *Death of a Harlequin* with André Eglevsky as her partner.

"Something new in the way of traveling ballet units" was announced in the New York *Times* (February 22, 1953), the first "Ballet Quintet," its personnel to consist of Maria Tallchief, Melissa Hayden, Patricia Wilde, André Eglevsky, "and probably Michael Maule," all stars of the City Ballet, taking to the road for a short tour between "seasons" at the City Center. In April Miss Hayden left the New York City Ballet, after an association of three and a half years, to rejoin Ballet Theatre; her first appearance on her return was during the four-week "coronation season" in London, opening July 10. During that summer she danced at the twelfth Jacob's Pillow Dance Festival, conducted by Ted Shawn at Lee, Massachusetts, appearing with Michael Maule, the duo offering a suite from *Swan Lake* and the grand *pas de deux* from *Don Quixote*.

Following its London season, the Ballet Theatre company made an extended tour of Europe and gave one performance at the Metropolitan Opera House on December 28, 1953, before departing on a transcontinental tour. Miss Hayden appeared in *The Combat*, a somewhat modified version of *The Duel*, with new costumes and setting. The company returned to the Metropolitan Opera on May 12, 1954, where Miss Hayden danced in Robbins' *Interplay* and in Antony Tudor's *Gala Performance*.

She rejoined the New York City Ballet company in February 1955, after a year's retirement. She performed a principal role "with great sensitivity" in the George Balanchine ballet *Ivesiana* (set to music by the late Charles Ives) in March, and was acclaimed for her dancing in *Pas de Trois* (II). The New York City Ballet closed its four-week season in which $175,000 was paid by the public for tickets, and reported a small surplus.

Miss Hayden was married to Donald Hugh Coleman, Jr., in February 1954; they have an infant son, Stuart Hayden Coleman. She is dark-haired with blue eyes, five feet five inches in height, and weighs 110 pounds. She is still a Canadian citizen, now in this country under a permanent resident status. She won the *Mademoiselle* Merit Award in 1952.

References

Dance Mag 27:36 Ja '53
Theatre Arts 36:13 F '52 por
Chujoy, A. The New York City Ballet (1953)

HAYS, ARTHUR GARFIELD Dec. 12, 1881-Dec. 14, 1954 Lawyer; made millions representing Wall Street brokers, bankers, corporations, theatrical celebrities; his reputation was world-wide for championing civil liberties; assisted in the defense of Sacco and Vanzetti, the Scottsboro Negroes, John Thomas Scopes, Tom Mooney; author *Democracy Works* and other books; was general counsel to the American Civil Liberties Union (1912 until his death). See *Current Biography* (Sept.) 1942.

Obituary

N Y Times p31 D 15 '54

HEARST, WILLIAM RANDOLPH, JR. Jan. 27, 1908- Journalist; publisher

Address: b. 959 8th Ave., New York 19; h. 810 5th Ave., New York 21

When William Randolph Hearst, Jr., was elected by Hearst Consolidated Publications, Inc., in February 1955 as editor in chief of the Hearst newspapers, he took over a post that had remained vacant since the death of his father in 1951. The vast and influential publishing empire which the elder Hearst had founded and controlled, comprised at that time eighteen newspapers and eleven magazines. During the first six months of 1955 the Hearst newspapers, which now have a combined daily circulation of over 5,000,000 and a combined Sunday circulation of over 7,000,000, gained 10.7% in advertising linage, more than in any similar period in their history.

For almost twenty years Hearst, Jr., has been publisher of the New York *Journal-American*, the largest afternoon paper of the Hearst chain. Other well-known Hearst publications are the widely circulated *Good Housekeeping* magazine and the *American Weekly*, a magazine supplement read by some 10,000,000 readers.

Early in 1955 Hearst was the subject of headlines in many newspapers when his visit to the Soviet Union coincided with important changes in top government positions. His reports of interviews with Communist party secretary Nikita S. Khrushchev and newly appointed Premier Marshal Nikolai A. Bulganin were widely read by the American and British public which was speculating on the effect of these changes on Allied-Soviet relationships. The publisher visited Israel in June and interviewed Defense Minister David Ben-Gurion on the Israeli-Arab problem.

The second of five sons of William Randolph and Millicent Veronica (Wilson) Hearst, William Randolph Hearst, Jr., was born in New York City on January 27, 1908. His brothers are John, George, David and Randolph Apperson. The famed newspaper chain may be said to have been started by his grandfather, George Hearst, a wealthy silver miner of the West and later U.S. Senator from California who, presumably for political reasons, bought the San Francisco *Examiner* in 1880.

The Senator's son, William Randolph Hearst, took over the proprietorship of the paper in 1887 and in less than twenty years acquired five more newspapers to form the nucleus of a publishing domain that at one period included as many as thirty-one newspapers in various parts of the country. The editorial policies of these papers led Kenneth Stewart and John Tebbel to comment on Hearst in *Makers of Modern Journalism* (1952): ". . . it is entirely safe to say that no more controversial figure ever existed in the [journalism] business."

At an early age William Randolph Hearst, Jr., showed an interest in newspaper work, and during his vacations from a military academy in San Rafael, California, he worked as a "fly boy" in the press room of his father's New York *Mirror*. In 1925 he entered the University of California, where he became a member of Phi Delta Theta fraternity. After two years he left school to begin a career in journalism.

Young Hearst in 1928 joined the staff of the New York *American*, one of the first papers founded by his father. Beginning as a police station cub reporter, he soon became assistant to the city editor. In 1936 he was made publisher of the *American*, which after a merger the following year was named the *Journal-American*.

Wide World
WILLIAM RANDOLPH HEARST, JR.

This merger was part of a large-scale consolidation of Hearst newspapers and properties which had reached their peak during the 1920's. (One estimate of the elder Hearst's wealth in his most prosperous years is $150,000,000). A series of financial crises during the depression of the 1930's forced a policy of retrenchment. It began in 1937 under a regency of which William Randolph Hearst, Jr., was a member, and reduced the newspaper properties by almost 40 per cent. Some of the magazines and radio stations controlled by Hearst were also sold. During World War II increased advertising raised the operating revenue of the newspaper chain substantially.

From 1943 to 1945 Hearst, Jr., was in Europe as a World War II correspondent. "The chief himself [his father] edited his copy," according to *Time* (August 27, 1951), "wired him to stop writing about bombing raids until he flew in one (Bill did)." At the end of the war, in 1945, Hearst, Jr., was made publisher of two Sunday supplements, *Puck—The Comic Weekly* and the *American Weekly*. The latter, founded by his father in 1896, has some 10,000,000 readers. He continued as publisher of the New York *Journal-American*, which in 1954 had a daily circulation of 660,246 and a Sunday circulation of 866,233.

Shortly after the death of William Randolph Hearst on August 14, 1951, *Business Week* presented an inventory showing that "the empire publishes eighteen daily and/or Sunday newspapers, plus four Sunday magazine-comic supplements. It publishes nine monthly magazines, three of which have British editions. It operates the largest newspaper feature syndicate—King Features—and the International

HEARST, WILLIAM R., JR.—*Continued*

News Service, a major wire news service, plus International News Photos, a major picture service." Among its other companies are newsprint and paper making services, radio and television stations.

Among the Hearst corporation's magazines are *Good Housekeeping* (circulation 3,442,781), *Cosmopolitan* (1,170,292), *House Beautiful* (622,477), and *Harper's Bazaar* (351,363).

The Hearst "family trust", established by Hearst, Sr. in his will, is operated by trustees including his five sons and eight executives of Hearst enterprises. The estate's latest appraisal valuation (according to a report in the New York *Times*, May 29, 1955) is $56,712,045. The family trust controls 30,000 shares of Class A stock in the Hearst Corporation, valued at $2,400,000, the only shares whose owners have voting rights. The Hearst "effects", ranging from his antique and art collections to pine and fir on the late publisher's estate in California "valued at over $20,000,000" are being sold by the Hearst family (New York *Times*, July 25, 1955).

For Hearst's sons and other executives some of the difficulties in operating the "big, diverse and troublesome" publishing empire, as *Business Week* (September 22, 1951) described it, were removed when former motion picture actress Marion Davies (beneficiary of Hearst, Sr.'s will), agreed after his death to relinquish "all rights she may have to act as voting executive for the stock of the Hearst Corporation" (New York *Herald Tribune*, October 31, 1951).

Meanwhile, on August 30, 1951, Hearst, Jr., had been named president of Hearst Consolidated Publications, while his brother Randolph Apperson Hearst was elected chief executive of the Hearst Publishing Company, of which Hearst, Jr., was vice-president. He has also been director of Hearst Enterprises, Inc., and vice-president and director of the Hearst Corporation and Hearst Radio, Inc.

After his father's death Hearst, Jr., headed a seventeen-man editorial committee set up to guide the policies of the newspapers, and on February 26, 1955 he was elected by directors of Hearst Consolidated Publications to succeed his father as editor in chief of the Hearst papers. These now include the New York *Journal-American;* New York *Mirror;* Chicago *American;* Detroit *Times;* Pittsburgh *Sun-Telegraph;* Albany *Times-Union;* Boston *Record-American;* Boston *Advertiser;* Baltimore *News-Post;* Baltimore *American;* Milwaukee *Sentinel;* San Antonio *Light;* Los Angeles *Examiner;* Los Angeles *Herald-Express;* San Francisco *Examiner;* San Francisco *Call-Bulletin,* and Seattle *Post-Intelligencer.*

In late 1951 he announced his intention of doing away with "the oldish elements that have crept into operations" of the newspapers, (*Time*, December 31, 1951). Besides making a number of changes in top personnel, he called for more local news stories and more objective reporting. Among the old-time editorial policies that were abandoned, according to *Time,* was the long-standing Hearst campaign against vivisection.

To boost the circulation of the *American Weekly* and meet growing competition from other Sunday magazine sections, Hearst hired a magazine specialist, Ernest V. Heyn, who stressed articles on home making, hobbies, health, arts and sciences. In the May 4, 1952 issue of that supplement Hearst pointed out, "We have modernized and dramatized the covers, the features, the illustrations, the art work, the type, the very lettering in which the name of the magazine is printed." He also announced that henceforth the *American Weekly* would be printed on giant roto presses in plants in New York, Chicago and San Francisco. (Circulation in 1953 was 9,577,815 readers).

Accompanied by *Journal-American* columnist Frank Conniff and J. Kingsbury Smith, European manager of the International News Service, Hearst made a visit to Moscow in January-February 1955 to observe at first-hand daily life in the Soviet Union capital. "It is a strictly journalistic trip," he explained. "Every reporter should get as close as possible to the source of news on a big story, and I applied for a Russian visa with that purpose in mind." Hearst reported his observations in a series of eight articles, widely distributed by International News Service, which covered such subjects as the attitude of the Soviet people toward America and toward U.S. atomic might, living conditions in the U.S.S.R., religion, and the "burdensome life" of women in Soviet society.

One of the high government and political officials whom he interviewed was Marshal Georgi K. Zhukov (on February 7), shortly afterward to become Defense Minister. Telling Hearst of his war-time friendship with President Dwight D. Eisenhower, Zhukov also said that it was his "dream" to visit the United States some day. On his return home, Hearst called on President Eisenhower and told him that the U.S. "policy of strength without provocation—keeping our guard up—was paying off" in the U.S.S.R. (New York *Times,* February 20, 1955).

When interviewed by a CBS commentator, Larry Lesueur, on the *Longines Chronoscope* television program, February 28, 1955, Hearst stated that although conditions in Leningrad and Moscow were better than he had been led to expect, living standards were much lower than in Paris and other European cities even in the poorest sections. He also said that he experienced no anti-Americanism, no hostile attitudes while in Russia. He came away with the impression that Khrushchev was the "strong man" in the Kremlin today.

On the same day Hearst expressed similar views in an address before a "jam-packed" National Press Club luncheon in Washington, D.C. "While in Moscow," he added, "I gained the impression that Communism was moving ahead in many fields which the present Western strategy overlooks or considers minor. The arms race is not the only event in which they are competing with us. They have taken sports and culture—they call it—and the impressionable years of youth and transformed them into arenas of the cold war." He urged that the United States answer the Soviet challenge in the area of cultural achievement.

Hearst, Jr., belongs to the American War Correspondents Association, and his clubs are the New York Athletic, F Street and National Press (Washington, D.C.), and Burning Tree (Baltimore, Maryland). He is an Episcopalian. On July 29, 1948 he married Austine McDonnell, author of a society gossip column and former wife of Hearst columnist Igor (Cholly Knickerbocker) Cassini. Their children are William Randolph 3d and John Augustine Clinton. Hearst's two previous marriages were terminated by divorce.

The publisher is six feet one inch tall and bears a close resemblance to his father. During the years before World War II he used to fly his own plane and was interested in aviation as a hobby. His sports include swimming, tennis, and hunting.

On June 18, 1955 President Eisenhower named Hearst to serve on his Committee for Traffic Safety.

References

Bsns W p 110+ S 22 '51 por
Newsweek 41:81 My 25 '53
Time 58:50+ Ag 27 '51 por

America's Young Men, 1938-39
Business Executives of America (1950)
Coblentz, E. D. ed. William Randolph Hearst (1952)
Who's Who in America, 1954-55
Who's Who in Commerce and Industry (1953)
World Biography (1954)

HEDTOFT, HANS (CHRISTIAN) Apr. 21, 1903-Jan. 29, 1955 Prime Minister of Denmark; leader of Socialist party there for last fifteen years; active in resistance against Nazi occupation in World War II; member of Rigsdag (Parliament) since 1935; as Prime Minister (1947-50, 1953-55) advocated strong national defense and supported NATO. See *Current Biography* (Mar.) 1949.

Obituary

N Y Times p85 Ja 30 '55

HEINLEIN, ROBERT A(NSON) (hīn' līn) July 7, 1907- Author; engineer

Address: h. 1776 Mesa Ave., Broadmoor, Colorado Springs, Colo.

About two years before the first nuclear chain reaction took place and five years before the first atomic bomb exploded, Robert A. Heinlein wrote a story published in *Astounding Science Fiction* magazine called "Blowups Happen," about engineers working on an uranium bomb. Using only the information available to him in 1940, he was able to give an accurate portrayal of the technological and human problems which would confront the real-life scientists several years later. It has been predictions such as this, backed by an all-around knowledge of scientific facts, and experience as a mechanical engineer, that have done much to make Heinlein one of the leading science-fiction writers.

Heinlein's output includes more than one hundred magazine stories, twenty books, numerous radio and television scripts, two feature motion pictures, and many engineering reports. His stories have appeared in the *Saturday Evening Post, Collier's, Blue Book, Argosy,* and *Town and Country.* The movie *Destination Moon* (Eagle-Lion, 1950), for which he wrote the scenario, was based on his book *Rocket Ship Galileo* (Scribner, 1947). Among his other books are *The Green Hills of Earth* (Shasta, 1951), *Rolling Stones* (Scribner, 1952), *Assignment in Eternity* (Fantasy, 1953), *Revolt in 2100* (Shasta, 1953) and *Star Beast* (Scribner, 1954).

The principle by which Heinlein writes may be shown in his own definition of science fiction. It is, he says, "speculative fiction in which the author takes as his first postulate the real world as we know it, including all established facts and natural laws." Then, by using "tight" reasoning, the possibilities of the real world are unfolded. Adherence to this doctrine has won wide acclaim for Heinlein.

An example of his scientific procedure is his keeping of a chart on which he marks an accurate history for the centuries to come, up to 2600 A.D. Each one of his stories is given a specific place in future time. The events in the lives of his characters are carefully recorded and their significance to the progress of mankind explained.

Born in Butler, Missouri on July 7, 1907, Robert Anson Heinlein is one of the seven children of Rex Ivar and Bam (Lyle) Heinlein. Of Irish, German and French extraction, the family traces its beginnings in America back to 1750. Young Robert was graduated from Central High School, Kansas City, Missouri in 1924, and soon thereafter he won an appointment to the U.S. Naval Academy, Annapolis, Maryland, where he majored in naval science. While studying there he won the title of Navy champion with the dueling sword. Following his graduation from the academy in 1929, he was assigned as a line officer with the U.S. Fleet, where he served until 1934. In that year he was retired for a physical disability which, he says, eventually led to writing as a career. Once out of the Navy, Heinlein entered the University of California, Los Angeles, to take postgraduate work, specializing in mathematics and physics. Because of ill health, he left the university without completing his studies.

He wrote his first story in 1939 and continued writing until the attack on Pearl Harbor. He served during the war as a mechanical engineer at the Naval Air Material Center at Philadelphia. After the war he resumed his writing of science fiction.

"Heinlein's worlds are real; his people are real," Mark Reinsberg has written in the introduction to Heinlein's *The Green Hills of Earth.* "Entirely aside from prophecy, there

J. M. Egbert

ROBERT A. HEINLEIN

are two positive characteristics of Heinlein's work that stand out. . . . One is verisimilitude," and the other is "his underlying conception of men, and Man." "This conception is neither grandiose nor tragic," he says. It is as if "Heinlein had acquired a comprehensive view of the universe by ranging far and wide to examine the various forms of organic striving (life) in one nebula after another, and after a very careful consideration (and with great reservations) had returned to Earth to back the human species with all his money in the cosmic competition."

Reviewing his book, *Between Planets* (Scribner, 1951), F. C. Smith in the New York *Times* (November 11, 1951) wrote, ". . . you can almost catch yourself thinking you may as well take the next bus down to the space port." Such a feeling of immediacy, although the reader is projected into the future, is further exemplified in *Rolling Stones,* a humorous book for young readers. Here a family travels to the asteroids in a second-hand spaceship.

As have other writers in the field, Robert A. Heinlein has tried to bring science fiction out of the comic book category. "Speculative fiction," he explains, "is usually thought of as pure fantasy and classed with the comic books, but I try to follow the Jules Verne-H. G. Wells tradition of careful and conservative extrapolation of known scientific fact—that is, I believe my own pipe dreams." To distinguish between good and bad science fiction, it is necessary, he points out, to "know something of the science yourself or enlist competent advisers."

Since 1947 he has had one book published each year by Charles Scribner's Sons, among them *Red Planet* (1949) and *Farmer in the Sky* (1950). Other publishers of his books are Fantasy Press, Shasta Publishers, Doubleday (including *Waldo, and Magic, Inc.,* 1950) and Gnome Press (*Sixth Column,* 1949). There have been about twenty foreign editions.

Reviews of most of his work have been favorable. H. H. Holmes, in the New York *Herald Tribune,* wrote of *The Puppet Masters* (Doubleday, 1951): "Even such a tired theme becomes freshly exciting in Heinlein's hands. The taut, melodramatic plotting, the skillful indirect exposition, the careful thinking through of details make for a nuclear-reactor-propelled thriller with a deeper conviction of reality than the average spy or detective story." Basil Davenport's review in the New York *Times* noted: "In this book he has done the difficult job of creating a race whose thinking is really alien to our own. . . . By any standards, this is first-rate entertainment with likable characters, excitement and plenty of hard-boiled humor."

Starman Jones (Scribner, 1953) is a science fiction book for young readers. Reviewer Holmes commented, "His nominally 'juvenile' novels . . . are regularly more satisfying than most adult science fiction—even, at their best, topping much adult Heinlein—and *Starman Jones* is probably the best yet."

Commenting on the novelette, *The Man Who Sold the Moon* (Shasta, 1950), Basil Davenport in the New York *Times* (January 7, 1951) wrote that the story presents a "splendid mixture of idealism and hornswoggling," and that "this is straight science-fiction somewhere near the best."

In an article entitled "Life in 2000 A.D." (*Galaxy,* February 1952), Heinlein has shown that he has no fear in making forecasts of the great things to come in the life of man. "Space travel," he wrote, "we will have not fifty years from now, but much sooner. It's breathing down our necks." He predicted that the housing shortage will be eliminated in fifteen years and that new technology will make every existing house obsolete. Cancer, the common cold, and tooth decay will be conquered. Mankind will not destroy itself and, by the end of the century some of us will have visited all parts of the solar system. Travel will be fast and inexpensive: a thousand miles an hour for one cent a mile.

Heinlein conceded that there are some things we will not get. For example, we will not be able to travel through time or faster than the speed of light. We will not control telepathy or "radio" transmission of matter. Laboratory creations of life and scientific proof of personal survival after death we will never know. There will be no lasting peace.

Robert Heinlein has brown eyes, brown hair, weighs 172 pounds and stands six feet tall. He is a member of the Democratic party and attends the Methodist Church. He holds membership in the American Association for the Advancement of Science, Author's League of America, American Society of Mechanical Engineers, American Rocket Society, and United States Figure Skating Association. His hobbies are astronomy, semantics, figure skating, cats, fiscal theory, politics, civil liberties, talking, and traveling. He is an expert rifleman and can fire the pistol with great accuracy, using either his right or left hand.

He was married in 1948 to Virginia Gerstenfeld, at that time a lieutenant in the WAVES and a test engineer and chemist. Since the war they have lived in Colorado, with occasional stays in California.

Heinlein is a man, wrote Mark Reinsberg, "who has given to the imaginative future a daily life . . . entertaining and even . . . unexpected. . . . But not since old Father Wells himself has anyone laid down a framework of the future as persuasive as Robert Heinlein's, and many readers have now come to regard it as definitive. . . . He is fascinated by the possibilities of tomorrow and he's doing what he can, in his writing, to influence the vote." Robert Heinlein is dedicated to the future of the human race and has done "a remarkable job in opening men's eyes to the wonderful possibilities of things to come."

Reference

Reinsberg, M. Preface to The Green Hills of Earth by Heinlein, R.A. (1950)

HENDL, WALTER Jan. 12, 1917- Conductor

Address: b. 3409 Oak Lawn Ave., Dallas 19, Tex.; h. 5030 Park Lane, Dallas, Tex.

Now in his fifth season as conductor of the Dallas (Texas) Symphony Orchestra, Walter Hendl is the product of American rather than European musical traditions. Between 1945 and 1949 he was assistant conductor of the New York Philharmonic Symphony Orchestra and taught at the Juilliard School of Music from 1947 to 1950. He has also conducted concerts in European and South American capitals.

Since 1953 Hendl conducted the Chautauqua (New York) Symphony Orchestra, giving twenty-four concerts in July and August to which audiences of over 175,000 were attracted. In May and June 1955 Hendl and Thor Johnson conducted the Symphony of the Air (the former NBC Symphony) in its tour of the Far East.

As a program planner, Hendl has given special attention to American composers. "For the aid and encouragement of American musicians," he was awarded the 1953 Alice M. Ditson Award of $1,000 by Columbia University. He believes that "jazz and show music contain examples which . . . can only be called good music . . . and will find a permanent place in our musical culture."

Walter Hendl was born in West New York, New Jersey on January 12, 1917 to William and Ella (Kittel) Hendl. As a boy he took piano lessons but it was not until his fifteenth year, when he began to attend concerts in New York, that he considered music as a career. Then he began to study the piano seriously with the well-known teacher Clarence Adler. At the age of eighteen he won the New Jersey State Music Contest sponsored by the Griffith Foundation.

WALTER HENDL

In 1938 he was awarded a piano scholarship with David Saperton at the Curtis Institute of Music in Philadelphia and in 1939 a conducting scholarship with Fritz Reiner. Hendl later told Carter Harman (New York *Times*, March 27, 1949) that after a month Reiner suggested that he abandon conducting and return to the piano. He had just been told to give up the piano and try conducting. He asked Reiner for another chance. "He gave me the chance," Hendl recalled. "I learned every note of the next assignment—it was *Till Eulenspiegel*—by heart. At the end of the course two years later he had to admit that in a decade I might become a respectable conductor."

At the same time that Hendl was studying with Reiner, he was teaching music at Sarah Lawrence College, Bronxville, New York. In the summers of 1941 and 1942 he received a scholarship to study at the Berkshire Music Center under Serge Koussevitzky. He also appeared at the Berkshire Music Festival near Lenox, Massachusetts as student conductor and pianist. Between the years 1942 and 1945 he was an administrative sergeant in the Army Air Force Ferry Command stationed in Delaware. While there, he organized a band known as the "Jive Bombers." Following a spinal injury he spent several months in an Army hospital in great pain. When he was most discouraged, Mrs. Francis McFarland, a civilian defense volunteer officeworker, asked him to play for the veterans at Halloran Hospital (Staten Island). He agreed unenthusiastically. Before he knew it, Hendl was enjoying life again.

Learning that the authors of the forthcoming Broadway show *Dark of the Moon* were looking for a composer, Hendl, who had never composed before, set to work and submitted a sample piece. He was immediately signed up as both composer and conductor. Hendl continued to play weekly for the patients of Halloran

HENDL, WALTER—*Continued*

Hospital for a year after his discharge. During the run of *Dark of the Moon* Fritz Reiner attended a performance and was so pleased with his former student that he invited Hendl to conduct Reiner's orchestra, the Pittsburgh Symphony. He also conducted a few concerts of the Boston "Pops" Orchestra. Another activity was organizing and directing a series of lecture-discussions on American music in Town Hall, New York.

When the post of assistant conductor of the New York Philharmonic Symphony fell vacant in 1945, Hendl was chosen by conductor Artur Rodzinski and began his duties there on November 20. Two weeks later, Dr. Rodzinski became ill. On December 8th Hendl was told that he would have to conduct the concert that evening. "I sort of swallowed twice and blinked a few times," he told a New York *Herald Tribune* reporter. ". . . we went on rehearsing—the men were wonderful about it." He spent the afternoon going over the scores with Dr. Rodzinski.

The New York *Times* critic Noel Straus reported on December 9 that Hendl had "directed the lengthy and exacting program in a serious, intelligent and creditable manner." Robert Bagar of the New York *World-Telegram* wrote that "his fine and musicianly performance in a difficult program not only brought an emotional thrill to a capacity audience but stamped him a batonist to be reckoned with."

The young musician's next triumph came on January 3, 1946, when he made his debut as piano soloist in George Gershwin's *Piano Concerto in F* with the Philharmonic Symphony. Olin Downes of the New York *Times* found this performance the "best . . . we have heard. He made the most of the lyrical ideas by his musicianship and beauty of tone, and he showed that the music was to be sung on the keyboard in its melodic aspects, and not merely pounded and whirled." Critics of the New York *Post,* New York *Sun, PM* and *Musical America* joined in the praise.

During 1947 Hendl conducted his first "Pop" Concert at Carnegie Hall, and some of the Lewisohn Stadium concerts. He also conducted several children's concerts, at the first of which he played his own composition, *Little Brass Band.* The New York *Times* reported that he was "the surprise of the day, becoming, in addition to a serious musician, a persuasive and charming speaker." The New York *Herald Tribune* described Hendl's music as "eminently charming, well orchestrated and containing some fine solo writing."

In addition to conducting the Philharmonic Symphony Orchestra frequently and playing much contemporary American music, Hendl became an instructor and conductor at the Juilliard School of Music (New York) in 1947. He conducted the Juilliard Summer Symphony, designed to give young orchestral musicians additional practice and training. In December 1948 the New York *Times* found that Hendl's "conducting showed the benefits of increased experience . . . verve and authority."

At the age of thirty-two, in 1949, Walter Hendl became the youngest permanent conductor of a major American symphony orchestra. His success with the Dallas Symphony Orchestra was instantaneous and he was immediately offered a contract for three more years. During the 1951-1952 season the subscription series was completely sold out. One of Hendl's accomplishments was arranging a musical *rapprochement* between Dallas and its rival, Fort Worth. Fort Worth now has regular concerts by the Dallas Symphony. Under his direction the Dallas Symphony brought good music to large audiences by playing in a local movie theatre. With the orchestra he has made extensive tours and has invited such celebrated artists as Gregor Piatigorsky, Vladimir Horowitz, Artur Rubinstein and Kirsten Flagstad to appear with them.

In the summers of 1949 and 1950 he conducted numerous concerts in South America sponsored by Braniff Airways and made an extensive musical survey in eight countries, interviewing young composers and performers.

He spent part of the summer of 1951 in Europe making recordings of compositions by Virgil Thomson and Aaron Copland for the American Recording Society (sponsored by the Alice M. Ditson Fund of Columbia University). He also conducted concerts in Vienna and Paris. He returned to Europe in the summer of 1952 to make additional records for the series, raising his total to nineteen compositions and making him the conductor who had recorded the most major American works. The summer of 1953 was his first as the musical director of the Chautauqua (New York) Festival. After an absence of five years from the podium of the New York Philharmonic Symphony he returned in February 1955 to conduct the orchestra in a concert which was the occasion for the world première of Heitor Villa-Lobos' Second Concerto for violincello and orchestra.

Among his own compositions are *Concerto for Toys and Orchestra, Loneliness, A Village Where They Ring No Bells.* Hendl has said that "the twentieth-century musician cannot be a specialist. He must become what the classical musicians were: capable of tackling any musical job that turns up" (New York *Times,* March 27, 1949).

The blond, blue-eyed, tall (six feet two inches), slim musician married Mary Newbold Williams, a former actress, in 1945. They have a young daughter, Susan. Hendl belongs to the American Federation of Musicians, Phi Mu Alpha and the Variety Club of Texas. His favorite games are table tennis and gin rummy; he also likes to swim and play tennis. He enjoys reading and one of his favorite authors is Sholem Asch.

References

Mus Am 66:24 Ja 10 '46; 66:12 N 25 '46
N Y Times p46 D 9 '45; II p7 Mr 27 '49; II p6 Ag 6 '50; p11 S 23 '50
Time 54:32 D 26 '49 por
Who is Who in Music (1951)
Who's Who in America, 1954-55

HESBURGH, THEODORE M(ARTIN), REV. May 25, 1917- University president

Address: b. University of Notre Dame, Notre Dame, Indiana

REV. THEODORE M. HESBURGH

One of the largest and oldest Catholic institutions of higher education in the United States is the University of Notre Dame whose president is Father Theodore M. Hesburgh, C.S.C., S.T.D. Executive vice-president since 1949, he succeeded Father John J. Cavanaugh to the presidency in 1952.

The new president, only thirty-five years old when he began his six-year term of office, heads an institution which has a student body of approximately 5,000, an alumni numbering around 20,000 and a faculty of 472 priests and laymen, the latter including both Protestants and Jews as well as Roman Catholics.

Hesburgh's book, *God and the World of Man* has been called "one of the best religious texts for college students" (*Ave Maria*, March, 1950).

Theodore Martin Hesburgh was born in Syracuse, New York on May 25, 1917, the son of Theodore Bernard and Anne Marie (Murphy) Hesburgh. He attended Holy Rosary Grade School and Holy Rosary High School from which he was graduated in 1934. Young Hesburgh then entered the University of Notre Dame near South Bend, Indiana and the Congregation of the Holy Cross. He made his confession of faith in the congregation on August 16, 1936 and without remaining to complete his course went to Rome, Italy to prepare at Gregorian University for the baccalaureate degree in philosophy, conferred on him in 1940.

Hesburgh was still abroad when Cardinal Eugenio Pacelli was elected Supreme Pontiff, taking the name of Pope Pius XII, and sent home for publication in the August 10, 1940 issue of *Ave Maria* (a periodical for the Catholic laity published at Notre Dame) a vivid description of the crowds waiting outside the Sistine Chapel.

For three years beginning in the summer of 1940 Hesburgh was an advanced theological student at Holy Cross College at Washington, D.C. After the United States entered World War II, he became an auxiliary chaplain in the Army at Fort Myer, Virginia. Ordained to the priesthood at the University of Notre Dame on June 24, 1943, Father Hesburgh served as chaplain of the National Training School for Boys at Washington for about a year.

A postgraduate student at Catholic University in Washington, he was awarded the degree of Doctor of Sacred Theology there in 1945, sity in Washington, he was awarded the degree having offered "The Relation of the Sacramental Characters of Baptism and Confirmation to the Lay Apostolate" as his thesis. This dissertation was published under that title in 1946 by the Catholic University of America Press and was also published by the Ave Maria Press in the same year as *The Theology of Catholic Action.*

James K. Sawyer stressed that it established "the fact of the lay apostolate, how it came to be re-emphasized in modern papal documents." He quoted Father Hesburgh's statement that "in many cases the Christian layman is the sole point of contact between the saving message of Christ and the secularized world," commenting that the author "searches the sources not for Catholic Action as an organization but for its activity" (*Ave Maria*, August 24, 1946).

Father Hesburgh returned to the University of Notre Dame to become chaplain of the Veterans Club in 1945 and then chaplain of the married veterans at the university. Later he became an assistant professor of religion and the head of the department of religion. The priest was promoted to executive vice-president of the institution in 1949.

He is credited with a major role in establishing the committee of international cultural relations of the Association of American Colleges which was launched in 1949 with partial financial support from the Rockefeller Foundation; the program of Latin-American studies jointly undertaken by the College of Arts and Letters and College of Commerce; and the general program of liberal education inaugurated by the College of Arts and Letters in 1950.

When Father Cavanaugh completed his presidential term (the term is limited to six years by canon law because the university is owned and controlled by the U.S. Province of the Congregation of the Holy Cross, and its president is also the religious superior of the Notre Dame community), it was announced on June 27, 1952 that Father Hesburgh would be his successor.

The University of Notre Dame was established in 1842 by Father Edward Frederick Sorin and six brothers of the Congregation of the Holy Cross who had come to the United States to establish a college.

The institution began its instruction in a log building in 1843, on what is now a 1,700 acre campus comprising fifty buildings. From the original College of Arts and Letters it has

HESBURGH, REV. THEODORE M. *—Continued*

grown to include schools of science, law, engineering, commerce, a graduate summer school, the first medieval institute in America, a research center for the U.S. Air Force, and a department of audio-visual education.

In his first semester as president Father Hesburgh released on January 3, 1953 a "ten-point program" relating to the televising of intercollegiate football games. (The National Collegiate Athletic Association, of which Notre Dame is a member, had for the past two years pursued a policy of limiting television to only one game on a national hook-up on any Saturday in the belief that unrestricted televising would discourage attendance at games between smaller colleges. Notre Dame, whose football teams have been famous since the days of Coach Knute Rockne, was opposed to "controlled television.")

After emphasizing that "both football and television can be good elements in American life" and that "television can promote greater public interest in the educational institutions of which the teams are just one dramatic aspect," the Notre Dame program asserted that "there is one normal restriction that should operate in the selection of what games should be on television, namely public interest in the game."

The University of Notre Dame introduced in the fall of 1954 a new liberal arts curriculum, which constitutes the first major curriculum change in the university's College of Arts and Letters in more than thirty years. In June 1955 Hesburgh was named to a second three-year term as president of Notre Dame.

The university president is a member of the committee on educational television of the National Catholic Education Association, committee of college self studies of the Ford Foundation Fund for the Advancement of Education, Ford Motor Scholarship Board, planning committee of the Association for Higher Education's National Conference on Higher Education, Catholic Theological Society of America, and National Conference on Family Life. He has brown eyes and black hair. He is five feet ten inches tall and weighs 175 pounds.

"There is reason for new hope in the very fact that all of us, Protestants, Catholics, Jews, have recognized a needed strength in working together as God-loving and God-fearing Americans, standing united against those who deny God," Hesburgh said at the first National Conference on Spiritual Foundations of American Democracy, held in Washington, D.C. on November 9, 1954.

Speaking at the Association of American Colleges conference in January 1955 he called for "unity of knowledge" in liberal education instead of "piling course on diverse course" (New York *Times*, January 16, 1955).

References

N Y Times p17 Je 28 '52

American Catholic Who's Who, 1954-55
Who's Who in America, 1954-55
World Biography (1954)

HILDEBRAND, JOEL H(ENRY) Nov. 16, 1881- Chemist; organization official

Address: b. c/o University of California, Berkeley 7, Calif.; h. 500 Coventry Rd., Berkeley 7, Calif.

When Dr. Joel H. Hildebrand, professor emeritus of chemistry at the University of California, was awarded the Willard Gibbs Medal, one of the highest awards in his field, on September 25, 1953, he was described as a "world-renowned teacher of chemistry, formulator of wise educational policy, important and far-seeing military and government adviser in both World War I and II." On December 13, 1953 he was elected president for the year 1955 of the American Chemical Society, the largest scientific organization in the world, representing nearly 70,000 scientists. He succeeded Dr. Harry L. Fisher to this office for a one-year term. Dr. Hildebrand's research has been chiefly in the fields of solubility of liquids, gases and non-electrolytes. He is as highly regarded among educators for his methods of teaching science as he is among scientists for his theoretical contributions.

Speaking at the meeting of the American Association for the Advancement of Science in Berkeley, California on December 28, 1954, Dr. Hildebrand said: "Joe Doe should be set straight on the impossibility of long keeping secret any discoveries in basic science. . . . Nature can reply to questions asked in Russian just as easily as to those asked in English. . . . We had better abandon the notion that any secret suffices to give security, and go instead for security by achievement and continual progress" (New York *Times*, December 29, 1954).

Joel Henry Hildebrand was born in Camden, New Jersey on November 16, 1881, to Howard Ovid Hildebrand and Sarah Regina (Swartz) Hildebrand, and was reared in Camden and in Wayne, Pennsylvania. His father was in the life insurance business. He attended high school in Wayne, where he played football and edited the school paper. He also manifested so much talent in chemistry that he was given the run of the school's laboratory facilities for experimentation.

One of his first successful experiments there enabled him to disprove a classification scheme of the chemical elements which had been advanced by the American chemist, Josiah Cooke (1827-1894). In his own words, this experiment gave Hildebrand "confidence in the experimental method and a disrespect for authority," attitudes which have continued to guide him in his educational philosophy.

After graduating from high school, he continued his education at the University of Pennsylvania, winning the entrance prize in mathematics in 1898. His collegiate career was distinguished by his election to the honorary scholastic fraternity Phi Beta Kappa and to Sigma Xi, honorary fraternity for science research. He was on the varsity rowing crew and freshman football team and was awarded the honor for varsity athlete with the highest academic standing. He was also president of his graduating class. He received his B.S. degree in chemistry and physics in 1903 and the Ph.D. degree in chemistry in 1906. After a year's study abroad he returned to instruct in physical chemistry at his alma mater where he remained until 1913.

His European studies were in Berlin University under the eminent German physical chemist and 1920 Nobel Prize winner, Walther Nernst (1864-1941) who was doing considerable work in solubility and electrolysis. During his tenure as instructor at the University of Pennsylvania, Hildebrand continued his own researches, and in 1913 he published his widely known and still much respected paper, "Some Applications of the Hydrogen Electrode in Analysis, Research, and Teaching," in the *Journal of the American Chemical Society*. The hydrogen electrode is one of the electrodes in an apparatus used in the determination of hydrogen ion concentration (ph). Hildebrand's extensive work with this apparatus has caused the electrode to be nicknamed the "Hildebrand electrode."

The publication of this paper attracted the attention of the National Bureau of Standards and of the University of California, both of which invited Dr. Hildebrand to join them. He chose the University of California which gave him the opportunity of more extensive research under Dr. G. N. Lewis (American chemist, 1875-1946), and where, as assistant professor of chemistry, he developed his new approach to the teaching of science. He believed that the routine "demonstration" experiments common to most science lecture and laboratory sessions were mere verifications of memorized facts or principles, and were insufficiently stimulating to college students. He set up his experiments in such a way as to encourage them to reflect on the phenomena involved and think their way through to logical conclusions based upon the data observed. Not only has he practiced this method with success himself, but he has also trained others to emulate his practice elsewhere and has incorporated his ideas in a textbook of chemistry which is widely used in American colleges.

By 1916 Dr. Hildebrand had begun publishing papers in the fields of solubility and the structure of liquids, which have been the principal, although by no means the exclusive, concerns of his subsequent research. Taking as his problem the question of just what causes different substances to dissolve to varying degrees or not at all in one or another solvent, he has elaborated a theory of the (physical) interaction of the dissolved substance with the solvent on the basis of the cohesive forces of the molecules of each, and has suggested that the solubility of a given substance in a given solute is related to their similarity in respect to these cohesive forces. The cohesive force is called internal pressure and its value may be derived from data on the energy of vaporization of a liquid or from an analysis of the molecular arrangements of a solid. He has demonstrated that solubility in a given solvent diminishes as the internal pressures of solutes increases.

JOEL H. HILDEBRAND

While his conclusions in the problem of solubility are generally applicable, Dr. Hildebrand's emphasis has been on the solubility of non-electrolytes, compounds which do not appear to dissociate into electrically charged components (ions) in solution. In his work on the nature of liquids, Dr. Hildebrand has been able, through the study of the scattering of X rays passed through them (in a manner similar to that which has led to the discovery of the crystal lattice structure of solids), to draw conclusions as to their specific structure which may be mathematically expressed.

A noteworthy corollary to his investigation of gases was his suggestion to the U.S. Bureau of Mines during the late 1930's that a mixture of helium and oxygen be used in place of plain air for divers and caisson workers to prevent caisson disease (the "bends"), a practice which has been adopted by the U.S. Navy and has permitted deeper and safer descents under water. Among other interests of Dr. Hildebrand have been emulsions, compounds of fluorine, and vapor pressures to which the "Hildebrand Rule" has reference.

He placed his scientific knowledge at the disposal of the nation during the two World Wars. In World War I he advanced from captain to lieutenant colonel, serving as director of the Chemical Warfare Service laboratory in France and as commandant of the Experimental Field and Officers' Gas Defense School, and receiving the Distinguished Service Medal. In World War II he was a consultant to the Quartermaster General and to the War Production Board, and he was a member of the Chemical Referee Board of Production Research and Development. He served abroad in 1943-1944 as scientific liaison officer for the Office of Scientific Research and Development attached to the American Embassy in London.

(Continued next page)

HILDEBRAND, JOEL H.—*Continued*

In recent years Dr. Hildebrand has been dean of men, dean of the College of Letters and Sciences and dean of chemistry at the University of California. It was during his tenure in the last post in 1950 that a dispute over the proposed loyalty oath for teachers took place. Hildebrand was an outspoken leader in opposition to the oath, a non-Communist declaration, not because of any sympathy with Communists, but because he felt, along with other prominent members of the faculty, that the oath, by being required of teachers alone, was discriminatory with regard to that particular group and added nothing to the oath of allegiance already signed by all university employees.

The matter was brought to the California State Supreme Court which two years later decided unanimously in favor of the faculty. In public statements made since the dispute, Dr. Hildebrand has been as definite in his criticism of teachers who tend to tolerate subversion in the interest of academic freedom as he has been in his opposition to "self-appointed watchdogs of patriotism now abroad in the land who irresponsibly pin red labels on anyone whom they wish to destroy." It is his belief that insofar as the teaching profession is concerned, the responsibility for the problem of Communists in the field is best left to the members of the profession who can differentiate between what is subversive and what is merely the healthy exercise of independent thinking (New York *Times*, September 19, 1952).

Among Dr. Hildebrand's many honors are the William H. Nichols medal (1939) for his work on the solubility of non-electrolytes, the King's Medal for Service in the cause of Freedom (1948) for his work in England in World War II, and the first Scientific Apparatus Makers Award (1952) in recognition of his many past contributions to chemical education. He is an honorary Fellow of the Royal Society of Edinburgh, honorary life-member of the Faraday Society, a fellow of the American Physical Society, a member of the American Association for the Advancement of Science.

He is the author of *Principles of Chemistry* (Macmillan, latest edition 1952), *Solubility of Non-Electrolytes* (American Chemical Society, monograph series, 1950), co-author of *Reference Book of Inorganic Chemistry* (Macmillan, 1947), co-author of *Ski Mountaineering* (University of California Press), co-author with his daughter, Louise, of *Camp Catering* (Stephen Daye Press), and over 160 papers on scientific subjects. He has been associate editor of the *Journal of the American Chemical Society* and of the *Journal of Physical Chemistry.*

Actively interested in athletics, Dr. Hildebrand is an enthusiastic mountain-climber and skier, and has been president of the Sierra Club, a group interested in mountaineering and conservation. His proficiency at skiing led to his being chosen to manage the U.S. Olympic Skiing team in 1936.

Dr. Hildebrand married Emily J. Alexander on December 17, 1908. Their four children, three boys and a girl, are all in the professions. The scientist is five feet nine inches tall, weighs 155 pounds, and has blue eyes and white hair. He enjoys the music of Bach, is a skillful photographer and a composer of limericks. His motto is "Whatever is worth doing at all is worth doing well."

References

Chem & Eng N 27:1429 My 16 '49; 30:1293 Mr 31 '52
N Y Herald Tribune p21 D 14 '53
N Y Times p31 Ap 16 '50; p17 S 19 '52; p7 S 26 '53
Sci Am 160:277 My '39
American Men of Science (1949)
Who's Who in America, 1954-55

HILL, WILLIAM S(ILAS) Jan. 20, 1886- United States Representative from Colorado

Address: b. 1327 House Office Bldg., Washington 25, D.C.; h. 122 Jackson Ave., Fort Collins, Colo.

Re-elected to the United States House of Representatives on November 2, 1954, William S. Hill, a Republican, began his eighth term as Congressman from Colorado's Second District. In the Eighty-third Congress he was chairman of the Select Committee to Conduct a Study and Investigation of the Problems of Small Business. Hill has favored government supports to farmers and since 1945 has been a member of the Agriculture Committee. He headed a subcommittee studying the Federal crop insurance program in 1947 and the agriculture livestock subcommittee in 1953. Before going to Washington, Hill served as a member of Colorado's legislature and as a teacher and school superintendent.

William Silas Hill was born on a farm near Corning, Kansas on January 20, 1886 to Squire C. and Mary Francis (Longley) Hill. He attended college in Chillicothe, Missouri and the Kansas State Normal School at Emporia. From 1905 to 1919 Hill taught in rural schools in Kansas and Colorado, where he acquired a homestead. For several years he took courses at the Colorado State College of Agriculture and received a degree in science. He served for one year as superintendent of the Cache la Poudre Consolidated School of Larimer county, Colorado.

In 1919 Hill began a four-year association with the Colorado Agricultural and Mechanical College in Fort Collins as an agriculturalist, specializing in work with 4-H Clubs. He was the secretary of the Colorado State Farm Bureau in 1923. Four years later he became owner and manager of the Standard Mercantile Company of Fort Collins and continued in this work until 1953.

Entering politics in 1924, Hill was elected to Colorado's General Assembly and re-elected in 1926. In 1939 he served as secretary to the late Ralph L. Carr, then Governor of Colorado.

The next year Hill was elected on the Republican ticket to the U.S. Congress from Colorado's Second District, which is largely agricultural. He has been re-elected to each of the subsequent Congresses. Most recently he was elected to the Eighty-fourth Congress on November 2, 1954 when he defeated Lacy Wilkinson, a Democrat, by a margin of 15,000 out of 137,000 votes in an area where 70 per cent of the voters were registered Republicans.

Representative Hill was assigned to the House committees on irrigation and reclamation, Indian affairs and labor in 1941. During his first years in Congress he voted against extending the term of service of draftees (1941) and the Lend-Lease bill (1941). He favored the War Labor Disputes Act (1943) and U.S. membership in the United Nations Relief and Rehabilitation Administration. In 1945 the Congressman became a member of the Agriculture Committee.

During the first session of the Seventy-ninth Congress (1945) Hill favored establishing a permanent Committee on Un-American Activities (January), continuing the subsidy programs of the Reconstruction Finance Corporation (May), and an anti-poll tax bill (June). He voted against the employment-production bill proposing the creation of a council of economic advisers to the President (December). In regard to foreign policy he voted against an extension of the Trade Agreements Act (May) and in favor of pledging a second appropriation of $1,350 million for UNRRA (December).

In the following session (1946) Hill's voting record indicates support of the Case strike control bill (February), reasonable profits under OPA ceilings (April), an extension of price control for nine months (April), draft exemption for boys of teen age and fathers (May), and overriding the OPA bill veto (June). He was recorded against a $400,000,000 appropriation to subsidize production of scarce building materials (May) and against a $3,750 million loan to Britain (July).

A bill introduced by Hill on February 28, 1947 proposed to continue the wool price support program from April 15 to December 31, 1948, at a level not less than that in effect in 1946, and proposed to give authority to the Secretary of Agriculture to set import quotas on raw foreign wools. On April 8, 1947 Representative Hill was named to head a subcommittee of the House Committee on Agriculture charged with studying operations of the Federal crop insurance program.

In 1947 he favored, in roll calls in the House, limiting the Presidency to two terms (February), banning portal-to-portal pay suits (February), the Greek-Turkish aid bill (May), and overriding the veto of the Taft-Hartley bill (June). He voted "nay" on the rent control extension bill (May).

Hill cast his vote in 1948 for the individual income tax reduction bill (February), a six billion dollar foreign aid bill (April), overriding the veto of a bill to exclude newspaper and magazine vendors from coverage under the Social Security Act (April), the subversive activities control bill (May), an extension of the Trade Agreements Act to June 30, 1949 (May), a $4,000,000 appropriation to begin work on a new steam plant for the Tennessee Valley Authority (May), the displaced persons bill (June), and overriding a veto on a bill which would permit railroads to enter into rate agreements without becoming liable to prosecution under the antitrust laws (June).

Wide World
WILLIAM S. HILL

In the first session of the Eighty-first Congress (1949) votes cast by Hill included approval of repealing Federal taxes on margarine (April), striking out the public housing section of the long-range housing bill (June), exempting independent gas producers from regulatory powers exercised by the Federal Power Commission (August), and reducing European arms aid by 50 per cent (August). He opposed extending the long-range housing bill (June).

During the second session (1950) the Representative favored eliminating loans for housing cooperatives from the 1950 housing act (March), two billion dollars more for farm price supports (June), and overriding the veto of a bill granting increases in pay to World War II veterans in the postal field service (June).

Congressman Hill in 1951 voted for the combination draft-UMT bill (April) and for banning the use of the quota system for livestock slaughtering (July), and prohibiting control of commodity margins. He was opposed to the $7.5 billion mutual security aid bill (August). In the following year he supported a ceiling on military spending of forty-six billion dollars (April), a reduction in economic aid to Europe of $615,000,000 (May), ending price controls on all consumer goods on June 30, 1952, terminating Federal rent controls on September 30, 1952 except in critical defense areas or where local governmental authorities request

HILL, WILLIAM S.—*Continued*

the continuance of the Federal rent control system (June), overriding the veto of the (Francis E.) Walter-(Patrick A.) McCarran immigration bill (June), and maintaining 90 per cent farm price supports (July).

The roll call of the first session of the Eighty-third Congress (1953) indicates that Hill favored the statehood for Hawaii bill (March), the offshore oil bill relinquishing to the states coastal lands previously claimed by the Federal government (April), extension of the excess profits tax (July), the $4.4 billion foreign aid appropriation (July), and admitting 217,000 refugees from Iron Curtain countries (July). He opposed reduction in soil conservation payments (May) and keeping the nonpartisan Tariff Commission (June).

As chairman of the agriculture livestock subcommittee, Representative Hill presented a four-point emergency program to the House Agriculture Committee on February 20, 1953. In order to bolster declining cattle prices, the report recommended increased Federal buying of meat for the school lunch program, strengthening of existing credit sources to stabilize the cattle market, expanded military procurement of beef until a 120-day supply for the armed services is stockpiled, and the use of import controls on beef. It cited sales of New Zealand beef in the United States as a factor that "can have a disastrous effect on the market," even though the quantity is "relatively insignificant" (New York *Times,* February 21, 1953).

While Hill was chairman of the Select Committee to Conduct a Study and Investigation of the Problems of Small Business, hearings were held in Denver in April 1953 on the mining situation. Hill said that metal mines are closing under the impact of falling prices.

When the bill making wiretap evidence admissible in court was called to a vote, Hill supported it and opposed an amendment to it prohibiting interception of messages without the approval of a Federal judge (April, 1954). In the 1954 roll call he also voted for Social Security expansion (June), the sliding-scale farm support program (July), a bill amending the Atomic Energy Act of 1946 (July), and a bill providing immunity for witnesses before Congressional committees and grand juries (August). He voted against a raise in the personal income tax exemption from $600 to $700 (March) and also an amendment to the anti-Communist bill making it a felony to be a Communist (August).

Addressing the Independent Grocers' Alliance, Hill stated on August 9, 1954 that "today we face huge crop surpluses. But our rate of population growth is beginning to catch up with our total agricultural productive area. Only the increasing efficiency of our food marketing system has delayed the full impact of our population growth during the last ten years" (New York *Herald Tribune,* August 10, 1954). He also said that in the next decade we will need 5,000 new supermarkets which will require an investment of $500,000,000.

In the first session of the Eighty-fourth Congress Hill favored an extension of the Trade Agreements Act (February), shelving a measure granting statehood to Hawaii and Alaska (May), raising the minimum wage to $1 an hour (July), and the Administration's highway program (July). He was opposed to increasing the salaries of Congressmen (February), an 8.3 per cent (as opposed to a 7.6 per cent) postal pay raise (April), and to restoring rigid farm price supports (May).

On March 25, 1907 William S. Hill and Sarah Rachel Trower were married; they have two children, Alden Trower Hill, an attorney, and Marjorie Anita (Mrs. Louis E. Hunter). The Congressman is a Rotarian, an Elk, and a member of the International Order of Odd Fellows and the Fort Collins Chamber of Commerce. He is a Presbyterian. In 1947 the Colorado Agricultural and Mechanical College conferred on him an honorary doctor of science degree.

References

Biographical Directory of the American Congress, 1774-1949 (1950)
Congressional Directory (1954)
Who's Who in America, 1954-55
Who's Who in United States Politics (1952)

HILLEBOE, HERMAN E(RTRESVAAG)
Jan. 8, 1906- Physician; public health official
Address: b. c/o New York State Department of Health, Albany 1, N.Y.; h. 25 Pinedale Ave., Delmar, N.Y.

In recognition of Dr. Herman E. Hilleboe's achievements in the field of tuberculosis prevention, and his present work as Commissioner of Public Health in the New York State Department of Health, the American Public Health Association voted him president-elect for 1953-1954, and he took office in October 1954 for a one-year term. Dr. Hilleboe has been Commissioner of Health since 1947 when Republican Governor Thomas E. Dewey appointed him. On December 10, 1954 Democratic governor-elect W. Averell Harriman reappointed him to this post.

During 1954 Dr. Hilleboe was active in promoting the mass field tests of Dr. Jonas Salk's anti-polio vaccine in the public schools of New York State. (For details, see Dr. Salk's biography, *Current Biography,* May, 1954). Dr. Hilleboe announced on February 9, 1955 that school children would be treated with the Salk vaccine this year if approved by the U.S. National Institutes of Health. It was announced on April 12 that the Salk vaccine had proved 80 to 90 per cent effective against paralysis by any type of polio virus. (See Dr. Henry W. Kumm's sketch, in this volume.)

Following the announcement, Dr. Hilleboe stated that 725,000 children between five and fourteen years of age would be vaccinated in New York State in 1955. It was later decided to reduce the shots from three to two, thus increasing the number of children immunized to 1,100,000.

Dr. Hilleboe is credited with initiating and promoting a practical method of "mass-screening" for possible tuberculosis, with the result that nearly 9,000,000 individuals have been examined and the chest X-rays showed that some 60,000 had tuberculosis.

Herman Ertresvaag Hilleboe was born in Westhope, North Dakota on January 8, 1906, the son of Peter S. and Inga (Jacobson) Hilleboe. He attended elementary schools in Park River, North Dakota and Minneapolis, Minnesota. Following his graduation from Lafayette High School in Red Lake Falls, Minnesota in 1923, he entered the University of Minnesota, where he received his Bachelor of Science degree in 1927 and his Bachelor of Medicine degree in 1929. In June of 1929 he was licensed to practice medicine in the state of Minnesota.

Dr. Hilleboe began his medical career as a rural general practitioner in Swanville, Minnesota, but left his practice after a year to serve an internship at the University of Minnesota Hospitals in Minneapolis. In December of 1931 he received his M.D. degree from the university. Following his internship he started graduate training in pediatrics on a Rockefeller Foundation fellowship. From January 1933 until July 1934 he was resident physician and teaching assistant in pediatrics at the University of Minnesota Hospitals.

In the fall of 1934 Dr. Hilleboe left the University of Minnesota for further training, this time to earn his degree of Master of Public Health at the Johns Hopkins School of Hygiene and Public Health. He completed his graduate work in 1935 and was certified as a medical specialist by the American Board of Preventive Medicine and Public Health. Combining his experience in pediatrics and public health, he worked from 1935 to 1939 as chief of the tuberculosis and crippled children's programs of Minnesota in the division of social welfare.

In June 1939 Dr. Hilleboe was commissioned as a senior assistant surgeon in the U.S. Public Health Service, which in the fall of that year sent him to the Scandinavian countries, England, Germany, and France to make special studies on tuberculosis. Joint research studies in international tuberculosis control were started at this time in cooperation with the State Serum Institute at Copenhagen, and have been continued in Denmark and the United States.

During World War II Dr. Hilleboe, who was called to active duty in the U.S. Public Health Service in January 1942, carried on tuberculosis control work among industrial employees throughout the United States, and from November 1942 until the end of the war he had additional duties as chief tuberculosis control officer for the Coast Guard. In July 1944 he was appointed as the first chief of the newly created division of tuberculosis control of the Public Health Service. After two years in this position he was promoted to the rank of assistant surgeon general and was made associate chief of the Bureau of State Services. In this capacity he supervised the divisions of hospital survey and construction and tuberculosis control.

DR. HERMAN E. HILLEBOE

According to Dr. Leonard A. Scheele, present Surgeon General of the Public Health Service, Dr. Hilleboe deserves credit for the Public Health Service's tuberculosis screening program which operated on a nation-wide scale until 1954. Dr. Hilleboe initiated the "whole development of a feasible method of mass-screening a population for tuberculosis through the use of small inexpensive film," said Dr. Scheele in an interview with the New York *Times* on February 28, 1954. In the seven years that the program was under the direction of the Public Health Service nearly 9,000,000 people were X-rayed, 60,000 of whom were found to have tuberculosis.

Dr. Hilleboe's appointment to his present position as head of New York State's Health Department came early in 1947 when Governor Thomas E. Dewey requested the Public Health Service to grant Dr. Hilleboe leave of absence to serve in that post. He took office on July 1, 1947, succeeding Dr. Edward S. Godfrey, who retired.

As Commissioner of Health Dr. Hilleboe is concerned with the care of chronic diseases, a practical mental health and hygiene program, rehabilitation facilities, new hospital construction, and the problem of distribution of general medical care. In his official capacity he acts as chairman of the Interdepartmental Health Council, chairman of the Joint Hospital Survey and Planning Commission, a member of the Youth Commission, and a member of the Public Health Council of New York State. Aside from performing these duties as New York State Commissioner of Health, he also serves as a member of both the cancer advisory committee to the National Cancer Institute and the advisory committee to the chronic disease and

HILLEBOE, HERMAN E.—*Continued*

tuberculosis division of the Public Health Service. He is chairman of the federal-state relations committee of the Association of State and Territorial Health Officers, and is on a three-man committee for that association, which cooperated with the National Foundation for Infantile Paralysis in selecting the areas of the United States in which Dr. Jonas Salk's experimental anti-polio vaccine was tested during 1954.

In twenty counties of New York State (outside New York City) 94,156 children in the first, second and third grades received the Salk vaccine during 1954. An equal number received the placebo, which contained all the same ingredients except for the basic one that fights polio. "In New York State," declared Dr. Hilleboe, "our use of the vaccine appears to have reduced the number of polio cases by 75 per cent. This is really a remarkable result" (New York *Times,* April 13, 1955).

In 1949 he served as American representative on the expert committee on tuberculosis of the World Health Organization, and in February 1951 he was appointed a member of the expert advisory panel on tuberculosis of the World Health Organization. Dr. Hilleboe's other advisory posts are with the Rockefeller Foundation as a member of the board of consultants for medicine and public health, and with the Milbank Memorial Fund as a member of the technical board.

Speaking at the annual conference of state and territorial health officers held in Washington, D.C. in December 1954, Commissioner Hilleboe asserted: "Because the use of radiation in industry and in the community is gaining so rapidly a special problem faces the health officer who wishes to prepare now to meet what may well become one of our most significant environmental health problems of the future" (New York *Times,* December 9, 1954).

On January 18, 1955 Dr. Hilleboe announced that the State Public Health Council has revised the sanitary code for the atomic age and had approved regulations designed to protect the public against radiation from X-rays, radioisotopes and other radioactive materials. The new chapter of the code was the result of more than a year's study of the dangers associated with handling radioactive substances and equipment, and becomes effective on July 1 throughout New York State except in New York City, which is revising its own code.

On March 3, 1955 Dr. Hilleboe issued a letter to chiefs of medical staffs in all hospitals in upstate New York urging that routine administration of oxygen to prematurely born babies be discontinued, since blindness can be caused if such infants are exposed to high concentrations of oxygen during the first ten days of birth. The disease, he said, is called retrolental fibroplasia and has been on the increase during the past twelve years (New York *Times,* March 4, 1955).

Dr. Hilleboe also finds time for an active career in teaching and writing. He is professor of public health and preventive medicine at Albany Medical College, associate professor at Columbia University School of Public Health, and visiting lecturer at Harvard University School of Public Health, Johns Hopkins School of Public Health, and University of Michigan School of Public Health. Since 1931 he has written over 150 articles mostly dealing with the subjects of public health and tuberculosis. His articles have appeared in such journals as *Health News, New York State Journal of Medicine, Public Health Nursing, American Journal of Public Health, American Review of Tuberculosis, Modern Hospital,* and the *Journal of the American Medical Association.* He is coauthor, with Dr. Russell H. Morgan, of the book *Mass Radiography of the Chest* (Year Book Publishers, 1945).

Professional societies to which Dr. Hilleboe belongs include: Albany County Medical Society, American College of Chest Physicians, American Epidemiological Society, American Statistical Society, American Association for the Advancement of Science, National Tuberculosis Association, and Theta Kappa Psi medical fraternity. He serves on the executive committee and the governing council of the American Public Health Association, was president-elect of the association in 1953-1954, and is president in 1955. He is an alternate delegate of the house of delegates in the Medical Society of the State of New York.

Dr. Hilleboe holds an honorary Dr. Sci. degree from the University of Rochester, and in 1951 he was presented with the outstanding achievement award of the University of Minnesota. Dr. Hilleboe's clubs include the Cosmos Club in Washington, D.C., the Fort Orange Club of Albany, and the Albany Country Club. He is a Lutheran.

On September 28, 1929 Hilleboe married Alida Claire Champeau of Red Lake Falls, Minnesota. Their children are Joyce-Elaine, Theresa-Ann, and Herman E., Jr. Dr. Hilleboe stands five feet ten and a half inches tall, has blue eyes, brown hair, and weighs 190 pounds.

References

N Y Herald Tribune p15 N 17 '53
N Y Times p24 Je 29 '47 por; p20 Jl 3 '47; p71 F 8 '54
American Men of Science (1949)
Who's Who in America, 1954-55
World Biography (1954)

HILTON, JAMES Sept. 9, 1900-Dec. 20, 1954 British author; best known for *Good-bye, Mr. Chips* and *Lost Horizon,* whose imaginary locale, Shangri-La, became a part of the language; also wrote screen scenarios, the most famous was his adaptation of Jan Struther's *Mrs. Miniver*; the last of his fourteen novels was *Time and Time Again* (1953). See *Current Biography* (Sept.) 1942.

Obituary

N Y Times p23 D 22 '54

HOLIFIELD, CHET (CHESTER EARL) (hŏl'ĭ-fēld) Dec. 3, 1903- U.S. Representative from California; businessman

Address: b. House Office Bldg., Washington 25, D.C.; 5172 Whittier Blvd., Los Angeles, Calif.; h. 2606 Cameron Mills Rd., Alexandria, Va.; 433 S. Montebello Blvd., Montebello, Calif.

An eyewitness of atomic and hydrogen test bomb explosions and a long-time member of the Joint Committee on Atomic Energy, U.S. Representative Chet Holifield believes that letting the people know the "ugly effects" of the bombs is the only way to bring about a realistic civil defense program. "Suppression of the facts is not only an insane policy of self-deception," he said in a speech in early 1955, "but it is a threat to national survival."

For the past twenty-five years Holifield has operated his own manufacturing concern in the men's clothing trade. Since 1943 he has represented California's Nineteenth District and he has become widely regarded as a liberal Democrat and one of the leading public power advocates in Congress. He was involved in a number of political controversies in 1955 among them his frequent dissents on reports presented to Congress by Herbert Hoover's Commission on Organization of the Executive Branch of the Government (of which Holifield is a member), his sharp criticism of the Atomic Energy Commission contract for 600,000 kilowatts with Dixon-Yates (a public utility combine), and of President Eisenhower's proposal to build a $35,000,000 atomic-powered merchant vessel as a floating goodwill emblem. Holifield was a member of the United States delegation at the United Nations Atoms for Peace conference held in Geneva, Switzerland in August 1955.

Chester Earl Holifield was born to Ercie Vira and Bessie Lee (O'Brady) Holifield in Mayfield, Graves County, Kentucky on December 3, 1903. When he was very young, the Holifield family moved to Springfield, Arkansas, where Chet attended public schools. His mother died during his boyhood.

Leaving high school before graduation, Holifield went to Montebello, California in 1920. He found work in a tailor shop and later, with his father, established his own business in the manufacturing and selling of men's apparel.

The depression of the 1930's and introduction of the New Deal turned Holifield's attention to politics. From 1934 to 1938 he was chairman of the Los Angeles County Democratic Central Committee for the Fifty-first District and from 1938 to 1940 chairman of the California State Central Committee for the Twelfth Congressional District. He served as delegate to the Democratic National Convention in 1940, 1944, 1948 and 1952.

"He managed a successful campaign for Jerry Voorhis," Oliver Pilat wrote in a New York *Post* "closeup" (April 23, 1948), "and when the Voorhis district was split up to allow for increased California population, he was elected to Congress in his own right." In the political victory in November 1942 which sent

Wide World

CHET HOLIFIELD

Holifield to the Seventy-eighth Congress, he received 34,722 votes to his opponent's 20,033. He has been re-elected to each succeeding Congress, and in 1946 when he won both Republican and Democratic nominations—a situation possible under California's cross-filing laws—he polled 50,000 votes as compared with 1,000 votes for his rival. In the 1948 campaign he was invited to file in Henry Wallace's third party primary, but refused.

During his first year (1943) in Congress Holifield approved continuation of the lend-lease program, and spoke in Congress against anti-labor legislation. His experience in merchandising made him especially interested in prices and rationing, and he opposed the freezing of prices without regard to increased production costs and the freezing of wages without regard to increased food costs.

In an appeal to the President in 1945 to revise the Government's rigid wage policy, Holifield led a group of Congressmen who prepared a petition "to restore the original authority of the War Labor Board to approve or direct such wage adjustments as may be necessary and which will not substantially affect the cost of living" (New York *Times*, July 21, 1945). As a member of the House Military Affairs Committee he dissented in October 1945 from that committee's approval of a bill which he believed discriminated against labor unions by imposing penalties on workers but not on employers for contract violation.

Holifield voted "yea" in May 1945 to extension of the trade agreements act to 1948 and "nay" in December to exempt railroads from antitrust laws. In 1946 he opposed the Case strike control bill (February) and draft extension (April), and supported the President's strike control bill (May) and a $400,000,000 housing subsidy program (May). In the Eightieth Congress, opening in 1947, he was against

HOLIFIELD, CHET—*Continued*

a two-term limit for the Presidency (February), the rent control extension bill (May) and the Greek-Turkish aid bill (May). He voted in 1948 to reject the Republican tax reduction bill (February) and favored repeal of Federal taxes on oleomargarine (April), the tidelands oil bill (April) and the displaced persons bill (June).

An outspoken opponent of the House Committee on Un-American Activities, Holifield voted in January 1945 against giving that committee a permanent status and in May 1948 against the Mundt-Nixon Communist control bill approved by the committee. On a number of occasions in 1947 and 1948 he defended Dr. Edward U. Condon, director of the National Bureau of Standards, against attacks made by the committee. In June 1947 he spoke in behalf of Hollywood's motion picture personnel against the committee's charges of immorality and Communist affiliation.

One of the proposals that Holifield made in Congress in 1949 (June) was for an investigation to find out why the U.S. policy against cartels in Germany was being "subverted." He was much occupied during the Eighty-first Congress as chairman of a House expenditures subcommittee which dealt with programs recommended by the Commission on Organization of the Executive Branch of the Government (the first Hoover commission).

On measures before the House concerning foreign aid Holifield in recent years has supported Marshall Plan extension (April 1949) and the Korea-Formosa economic assistance bill (February 1950). He opposed a $350,000,000 cut in economic aid to Europe and approved a $7.5 billion foreign assistance bill (August 1951); he was in favor of $4.4 billion foreign aid appropriations (July 1953).

Domestic legislative proposals which he supported were the long-range housing bill (June 1949), voluntary-compliance Fair Employment Practices Commission (February 1950), draft-extension Universal Military Training bill (April 1951), statehood for Hawaii (March 1953), retention of nonpartisan tariff commission (June 1953) and admission of 217,000 refugees from Communism (July 1953). During 1954 he approved a bill to make wiretap evidence admissible in certain types of cases (April). He also voted for social security expansion (June), and an increase in unemployment compensation benefits (July).

He was in favor of a $2 billion increase in farm price supports in June 1950 but against retention of 90 per cent of parity farm price supports in June 1952. He also opposed a $600,000,000 cut in Federal spending (May 1950), a cut in Tennessee Valley Authority appropriations (March 1952), the use of the Taft-Hartley act to end the steel strike (June 1952) and a cut in soil conservation payments (May 1953).

For many years Holifield has been a member of the Joint Committee on Atomic Energy and in 1946 was a member of a special evaluation commission on the atomic bomb tests at Bikini atoll. He has given much of his attention to problems of civilian defense and in early 1950 introduced a measure for the creation of a commission to study the possibility of establishing an alternate seat of government as a precautionary measure in the event of an atomic attack on Washington.

After witnessing the hydrogen bomb test in the Marshall Islands on March 1, 1954 as an official observer, Holifield repeatedly urged on radio and television programs and in Congress that the President inform the public of the facts concerning the bomb. He advocated that actual demonstrations be arranged for unrestricted public observation. In June 1955 while participating in a discussion on the National Broadcasting Company's *American Forum of the Air,* he stressed the importance of raising the Civil Defense Administration to Cabinet level.

Through his membership on the Joint Atomic Energy Committee Holifield has become a key figure in the public-vs.-private power controversy. He urged caution in June 1953 in accepting proposed changes in the atomic energy act which would allow private industry to build reactors for electrical power. He has also been a strong critic of the controversial Dixon-Yates contract providing for construction of a steam plant by a private power group which would sell power to the Atomic Energy Commission. The project called for building a steam-generating plant at West Memphis, Arkansas to supply power across the Mississippi River to the Tennessee Valley Authority's Memphis, Tennessee installations.

When the Democrats regained control of Congress in January 1955, he was one of ten committee members who signed a resolution asking the AEC to cancel the contract. In February he suggested that all members of the AEC resign because of dissension over the contract and other issues. (The Dixon-Yates contract was cancelled on July 11, 1955 by President Eisenhower after the city of Memphis (Tennessee) decided to construct its own power plant.)

As a member of the Committee on Government Operations and chairman of its subcommittee on executive and legislative reorganization during the Eighty-first and Eighty-second Congresses, Holifield may be regarded as a specialist in government administration. He was chosen to serve as one of twelve commissioners on the Commission on Organization of the Executive Branch of the Government (the second Hoover commission) set up at the direction of the Eighty-third Congress in 1953 to study and make recommendations on government practices. The commission expired by law on June 30, 1955.

"The most voluble dissenter among commission members," observed W. H. Lawrence in the New York *Times* (May 22, 1955), "has been Representative Chet Holifield." Holifield frequently filed disagreements with the commission's reports on Government personnel and civil service, Federal lending services, and legal services and procedures.

In his dissent on the report on Federal health and medical services, he stated in February 1955 that he was opposed to curtailment of medical and hospital facilities "in the face of impending civilian defense needs." He charged in May that the task force report on water resources and power was biased in favor of private power, and in June he expressed his opinion that the report on foreign aid "intrudes in the area of foreign policy by making restrictive recommendations which could hamper the Executive, antagonize our allies and thwart our objectives." (Washington *Post and Times Herald,* June 6, 1955).

In February 1955 Holifield voted for the foreign trade agreements bill without restriction of Presidential powers and for the bill raising the salaries of Congressmen and Federal judges. He was one of eight Democratic Representatives who in March opposed the bill to extend corporation and excise taxes at present levels for another year. In July he joined with Senator Clinton P. Anderson, Democrat of New Mexico, in introducing an amendment to the Atomic Energy Act of 1954 to curb what they charged is "one-man rule" of the AEC, and to give each member of the commission, including the chairman, "equal responsibility" (New York *Times,* July 23, 1955).

Holifield has been secretary of the Caneer Company, Inc., since 1936. He is a member of the Chamber of Commerce, the East Los Angeles Forum Club, the Lions International of Montebello and the Moose.

He and his wife, the former Vernice Caneer, were married when they were eighteen years old and have four daughters, Lois Anita (Mrs. William Mulholland), Betty Lee (Mrs. Robert H. Feldmann), Willa Mae (Mrs. Donald Lee Douglas), and Jo Ann (Mrs. Donald Williams). A fifth daughter is deceased. California's Congressman has blue eyes and blond hair, is five feet nine inches tall and weighs about 200 pounds. He belongs to the Church of Christ, in which he and his father served for some years as lay preachers.

References

N Y Post p57 Ap 23 '48 por
Congressional Directory (1955)
Who's Who in America, 1954-55
Who's Who in United States Politics (1952)

HOLLISTER, JOHN B(AKER)

(hŏl'ĭs-tẽr) Nov. 7, 1890- United States Government official; lawyer

Address: b. Department of State, Washington 25, D.C.; h. 1831 Keys Crescent, Cincinnati, Ohio

The responsibility for reorganizing the United States foreign economic aid program from a year-to-year operation into an integral part of a long-range international policy belongs to John B. Hollister, a Republican, who became director on July 1, 1955 of the new International Cooperation Administration. At that time this agency superseded the Foreign Operations Administration (FOA) which had been headed by Harold E. Stassen who became special assistant to President Eisenhower on disarmament, a newly created Cabinet post. As administrator, Hollister supervises the nonmilitary aspects of foreign aid, which includes technical assistance on some 2,000 projects in fifty-five countries.

For the past seven years Hollister has been the senior partner of the Cincinnati law firm of Taft, Stettinius & Hollister. Among other posts he has held are executive director of the Commission on Organization of the Executive Branch of the Government, chairman of the mission to the Netherlands for the United Nations Relief and Rehabilitation Administration (UNRRA) after World War II, a member of the U.S. House of Representatives (1931-1936), and with the American Relief Administration in Poland and Lithuania after the First World War.

John Baker Hollister was born in Cincinnati, Ohio on November 7, 1890 to Alice (Keys) and Howard Clark Hollister, a judge of the U.S. District Court for the Southern District of Ohio. He is a descendant of John Hollister, who came from England to America in 1642. John attended public schools in Cincinnati and later St. Paul's School in Concord, New Hampshire. Entering Yale University in 1907, he was graduated with the A.B. degree in 1911. For a year he studied at the University of Munich in Germany before entering Harvard Law School. Young Hollister received the LL.B. degree from Harvard in 1915 and was admitted to the bar of Ohio in that year. He began his career as a law clerk in the office of Worthington, Strong & Stettinius in Cincinnati. In 1919 the firm became Worthington, Strong, Stettinius & Hollister.

During World War I he taught at the Heavy Artillery School, Fort Monroe, Georgia. Later Hollister was a captain of the 46th Artillery, Coast Artillery Corps in France. In 1919 he served with the American Relief Administration, headed by Herbert Hoover, in Poland and Lithuania. Returning to Cincinnati he organized, with Robert A. Taft and John L. Stettinius, the law firm of Taft, Stettinius & Hollister and became its senior partner in 1948.

Entering politics, Hollister became a candidate for membership in the U.S. House of Representatives in 1931 to fill the vacancy left by the death of Nicholas Longworth. Lemuel F. Parton (New York *Sun*, December 5, 1942) recalls that during the campaign, when politicians were "sidestepping the prohibition issue," Hollister frankly stated that he had taken a postgraduate course in drinking at Heidelberg, and that it was one of his happier memories. He was elected from Ohio's First District in November 1931.

In his first session in Congress Hollister voted to repeal the Eighteenth Amendment of the Constitution (December, 1932) and against overriding the Democratic tariff bill veto (May, 1932). Re-elected to the Seventy-third and Seventy-fourth Congresses, Hollister (according to the New York *Times*, May 5, 1955) contended "long and heatedly for a balanced bud-

Department of State

JOHN B. HOLLISTER

get" while New Deal demands for emergency appropriations mounted. He saw in the Roosevelt Administration a "steady encroachment on American liberties." In his last term, he was ranking Republican member of the House Banking and Currency Committee.

During the first session of the Seventy-third Congress (1933) he was opposed to the following measures: the administration farm relief bill (March), the national industrial recovery bill (May), the Muscle Shoals conference report (May), and exempting public plants from the power tax (June).

His voting record for 1934 indicates that he favored reduction of the letter rate to 2 cents (February), overriding the independent offices veto (March) and rejecting the 10 per cent supertax on incomes (May). He was against the gold reserve bill (January), emergency air mail bill (February), reciprocal tariff bill (March), stock exchange-control bill (May) and an unemployment census (June).

In 1935 Hollister voted against the social security bill (April), the Eccles banking bill (May), overriding the Presidential veto of the bonus bill (May), the Guffey-Snyder coal bill (August), and the holding company death sentence compromise (August). He supported the ship subsidy bill (June).

During his last session in Congress in 1936 Hollister voted for a compromise neutrality resolution (February), the dairy protection amendment (February), to exempt Reconstruction Finance Corporation bank stock from taxation (March), and to return control of relief to the states (May). He opposed the soil conservation bill (February), as well as the Administration tax bill (April), and the Frazier-Lemke mortgage inflation bill (May).

As a delegate to the Republican National Convention in 1940, Hollister captained the Taft-for-President forces and strongly opposed Wendell L. Willkie (*Time*, December 7, 1942), but later campaigned for Willkie, the Republican Presidential candidate, and became a director of the Associated Willkie Clubs of America. Hollister served in 1945 as chairman of the mission to the Netherlands for UNRRA.

Former President Herbert Hoover selected Hollister in 1953 to be executive director of the Commission on Reorganization of the Executive Branch of the Government. The work, which included a study of the operations of the FOA, was completed on June 30, 1955. In its report the Hoover commission recommended that foreign aid be continued, but stated that at least $360,000,000 a year could be saved by improved administration of the program. It recommended curtailment and reorganization of technical aid which had "over-expanded" beyond its original "modest" concept.

On April 30, 1955 President Eisenhower appointed Hollister to head the new International Cooperation Administration, which was to succeed the FOA on July 1, 1955. The Hollister designation, *Business Week* (May 7, 1955) noted, was regarded as a compromise because the appointee has the confidence of conservative Republicans. *Time* (May 16, 1955) observed that the appointment might overcome Congressional resistance to foreign spending, and added that to many the Hollister nomination was not "in harmony" with his predecessors, former foreign aid administrators Paul G. Hoffman, W. Averell Harriman and Stassen.

Hollister answered this speculation by saying that he "would not have accepted the job if he had any thought of wrecking the program" (New York *Herald Tribune*, June 26, 1955). On May 6 Hollister stated "I am convinced that both the best prospects of peace, and the requirements of our own security, make it imperative that the United States continue" foreign aid (New York *Herald Tribune*, May 7, 1955). The U.S. Senate confirmed Hollister as ICA's head on June 19, 1955.

The International Cooperation Administration is a semiautonomous agency within the Department of State. As its head Hollister is in charge of all economic phases of the U.S. foreign aid program, including technical assistance. Thus, Hollister's assignment is to administer the economic parts of a $2.7 billion foreign aid bill passed by Congress in July 1955. The Department of Defense supervises the military phases of the measure.

Now a part of ICA, the foreign technical assistance or Point IV program was authorized by the Foreign Economic Assistance Act of 1950 in order to further the political stability and economic and social progress of peoples living in underdeveloped areas by participating with individual countries in technical cooperation projects. (For further details see Jonathan B. Bingham, *C.B.*, 1954.) It was known officially as the Technical Cooperation Administration and was transferred from the Department of State to the Mutual Security Agency on June 1, 1953, and then to the Foreign Operations Administration later in 1953. By

1955 TCA had about 2,000 projects in over fifty-five countries and overseas territories. The number of American technicians abroad had increased from 1,506 in 1953 to 1,928 in March 1955.

On May 5, 1955 the Washington *Post & Times Herald* noted that one of Hollister's chief tasks will be to "convince the people of Asia that this country has a genuine concern for their welfare beyond treaties and guns. . . . The real rivalry in Asia is between China and India; and the way to resist China's magnetism is to strengthen the independent governments, including India. That will require . . . technical help and modest capital expenditures tailored to individual needs—to assist the development of resources."

On August 15, 1917 Hollister was married to Ellen West Rollins. Their children are Anne Montgomery (Mrs. J. J. Stevenson, Jr.), Alice Keys (Mrs. Clarkson Beard), and John Baker, Jr. John B. Hollister, Sr., was a member of the Cincinnati Board of Education (1920-1929) and on the board of governors, American National Red Cross. He is a director of the New York Life Insurance Company, Pennsylvania Railroad, Standard Brands, Incorporated, and other firms.

The attorney is a member of the American, Ohio and Cincinnati bar associations and a trustee of the Colored Industrial School of Cincinnati, Cincinnati Art Museum and other civic organizations. His fraternity is the Psi Upsilon and his clubs are the Yale (New York), Racquet (Philadelphia), Bohemian (San Francisco), and Metropolitan (Washington), among others. Hollister is a Presbyterian.

References

N Y Herald Tribune II p5 Je 26 '55 por
N Y Sun p16 D 5 '42
N Y Times p14 My 5 '55
Time 65:27 My 16 '55 por

Biographical Directory of the American Congress, 1774-1949 (1950)
Who's Who in America, 1954-55
World Biography (1954)

HOOPER, C(LAUDE) E(RNEST) May 31, 1898-Dec. 15, 1954 Statistician; originator of the Hooper "coincidental" method of radio surveys obtained by telephone interviews to determine what programs radio owners listen to; entertainers' contracts judged on their "Hooperating." See *Current Biography* (Apr.) 1947.

Obituary

N Y Times p38 D 16 '54

HORDER, THOMAS J(EEVES) HORDER, 1ST BARON Jan. 7, 1871-Aug. 13, 1955 Physician to Queen Elizabeth II, George VI and Edward VIII of Great Britain; chairman, Shelter Hygiene Committee of Ministry of Home Security and Ministry of Health; worked for U.N. Food and Agricultural Organization; opponent of National Health Service; specialized in cancer and diseases of heart and stomach; author of *Essentials of Medical Diagnosis* (1929) among other books; created baron in 1933. See *Current Biography* (July) 1944.

Obituary

N Y Times p80 Ag 14 '55

HORNER, H(ORACE) MANSFIELD Sept. 12, 1903- Aircraft corporation executive
Address: b. United Aircraft Corp., 400 Main St., East Hartford 8, Conn.; h. 105 Bloomfield Ave., Hartford, Conn.

The United Aircraft Corporation, whose president is H. Mansfield Horner, was awarded $1,061,400,000 in defense contracts from July 1953 (when the Korean conflict ended) to December 1954) and thus, according to the U.S. Department of Defense, led all other American firms in the volume of military orders received in this period (New York *Times*, May 24, 1955). The corporation is composed of the Pratt & Whitney Aircraft division, which produces aircraft engines; the Sikorsky division, which manufactures helicopters; and the Hamilton Standard division, which produces propellers. In 1926 Horner joined the Pratt & Whitney Aircraft Company and in 1943 became president of United Aircraft. The com pany's jet engine, the J-57, was used in the winning planes in the Collier Trophy Awards of 1952 and 1954.

Horace Mansfield Horner was born in New Haven, Connecticut on September 12, 1903, the son of Leonard S. and Julia Stuyvesant (Barry) Horner. He attended Phillips Academy in Andover, Massachusetts and received his B.S. degree from the Sheffield Scientific School of Yale University in 1926. Summers spent on his grandfather's farm in Virginia rounded out his education, he has said, and introduced him to the joys of the swimming hole and the thrills of exercising hunters, as well as to plowing with a horse and harrowing with a tractor.

While Horner was still an undergraduate at Yale, he went to see a friend of his father's about a job. The friend, Frederick B. Rentschler, founder and now chairman of United Aircraft, gave him the job, but warned him that there "wasn't much opportunity" in it. Young Horner started, after graduation, as "outside stock chaser and messenger" for the one-year-old Pratt & Whitney Aircraft Company, which at that time employed fewer than 100 men, but had faith in a new airplane engine.

The faith was not misplaced, and the engine, the air-cooled Wasp, brought the United States to the lead in air power almost overnight. When the Navy ordered 200 Wasp engines, Horner was placed in charge of locating and evaluating 200 subcontractors. They were found and the engines were delivered. The Wasp proved itself so superior to liquid-cooled engines that the Navy converted almost entirely to them, and the Army's orders were not far behind. The Wasps, the Hornets, and the Wright

Pratt & Whitney Aircraft
H. MANSFIELD HORNER

Whirlwind (also produced by Rentschler), engines which changed the picture for aviation, ushered in a new era.

These were the engines used by Charles A. Lindbergh on his record-breaking transcontinental flight, by Howard Hughes for a transcontinental record, by Wiley Post for his flight around the world. These were the engines in James H. (Jimmy) Doolittle's racers, in Pan American's Martin flying boats that made the first transoceanic commercial flights, in the Navy's new carrier-based fighters, and in the plane that won the world's altitude record for the United States (*Time,* May 28, 1951).

The Pratt & Whitney Aircraft Company, meanwhile, became the Pratt & Whitney Aircraft division of United Aircraft Corporation. Horner, who had been appointed assistant treasurer in 1927, advanced through the positions of assistant secretary, assistant sales manager (in 1934), and assistant general manager (1938) to that of general manager in 1940. He became vice-president for manufacturing and a director of United Aircraft Corporation in 1942. Forty-year-old Horner was the youngest of the three men who have held the post when he was elected president of United Aircraft in 1943.

During World War II United Aircraft expanded its own facilities considerably, but Rentschler and Horner also used the licensee plan to produce the engines. Other manufacturers were licensed to produce Wasp engines, with no profit or royalty rights accruing to United. The results were that United supplied about 50 per cent of U.S. military aircraft engine power during the war; its Hamilton Standard division made about 75 per cent of all U.S. military aircraft propellers; its Chance Vought division (since 1954 a separate corporation) was an important builder of Navy shipboard fighters; and its Sikorsky division produced all of the helicopters used during the emergency period.

After the war, Horner and United Aircraft had a new problem to face. While all of their energies had been going into maintaining U.S. air supremacy with piston engines, Germany and Great Britain had been pioneering with a new type of engine—the jet. The United States was not even in the running in the new field.

In 1945 United began to occupy itself seriously with the jet. During the following year United founded a jet-research laboratory at a cost of $12,000,000. The next year the U.S. rights to the Rolls-Royce Nene jet engine were purchased, and United concentrated on studying jets.

Engineers at United discovered that the gas turbine engine costs more in time and money in actual initial designing, but that the design lends itself better to theory and analysis than that of the piston engine, and that the gas turbine engine is generally easier to build and assemble than the piston engine. Despite the great forces built up within the jet, the rotating principle of its action causes less fatigue to its parts than does the up-and-down action of the piston engine.

The parts themselves are, on the whole, less intricately shaped and therefore easier to machine and finish in the gas turbine. Materials, on the other hand, are a large problem. Forgings and castings are still needed, as they are in the piston engine, but the jet also calls for a great amount of difficult sheet metal work. High temperatures in the gas turbine mean new alloys, capable of resisting oxidation and retaining their strength at these temperatures.

In addition, there are problems of thermodynamics and aerodynamics raised by the jets and of lubrication. Although friction is not such a menace in the jet, the heat produced tends to disintegrate and force out of the engine regular lubricants. There is also the elementary but very expensive problem of more and different tools and machines to make the new parts. In 1947, the 19XB axial-flow engine was built with 5,250 tools. An estimated 20,000 tools were necessary for the axial-flow J-57, the engine that carried the F-100 Super Sabre along at 755 miles an hour in 1953.

As Horner explained to the Dallas, Texas chapter of the Society for the Advancement of Management on May 13, 1953: "The jet engine pushes the airplane forward by emitting a high-speed, small-diameter stream of gas. The turboprop engine is of the same general design except its turbine power is mostly used to drive a propeller, which, in turn, pushes a large-diameter stream of air rearward at a much lower velocity. Now it is a fundamental law of nature that moving the large mass of air slower is more efficient than moving the small mass faster." In 1954 United was experimenting with turboprop engines, but is still using the turbojet J-57 engine, from the latest reports. (For details of the turboprop and turbojet engines see *Time,* July 4, 1955.)

Igor Sikorsky, (see *C.B.,* 1940) engineering manager of the Sikorsky aircraft division of United announced in January 1954 that the XHR2S was the largest helicopter ever put into regular production and predicted that it would be powered by gas turbine engines when it is produced for commercial uses. The helicopter, which can carry twenty-six battle-equipped men and three jeeps, was developed for the U.S. Marine Corps by United (New York *Herald Tribune,* January 19, 1954).

The Sikorsky division of the United Aircraft Corporation assigned ten helicopters to aid in rescue work during the floods in the New England and Middle Atlantic states on August 18 and 19, 1955. The Sikorsky helicopters rescued more than 450 persons.

The airplane, Horner has said, "has an unbelievable potential. It is transportation unlimited. To realize that potential, we must have courage, we must utilize every skill and all our ingenuity to teach ourselves how to design and manufacture our products so that they are better and certainly not much more expensive" (Address before the New England Council, November 20, 1953).

Horner has been a member of advisory committees to the Harvard Graduate School of Business Administration, the National Advisory Committee for Aeronautics and the Munitions Board of the U.S. Department of Defense, and a member of the committee on national defense of the U.S. Chamber of Commerce. He is a former chairman of the Aircraft Manufacturers Council, East Coast and of the Aircraft Industries Association; and a former member of the Aircraft Industries Association's executive committee. He received the honorary Doctor of Engineering degree from Rensselaer Polytechnic Institute in 1948. The Southern New England Telephone Company elected him a director in June 1954.

Horner, called "Jack" by his friends, has graying hair, weighs 185 pounds, and is six feet tall. He was married on June 25, 1926 to Lela Thomas Shumate. They have two children, Leonard M. and Lela Burwell Horner. He enjoys salmon fishing and duck hunting.

References

Fortune 43:16+ Mr '51 por
Time 57:93 My 28 '51 por
Who's Who in America, 1954-55
World Biography (1954)

HULL, CORDELL Oct. 2, 1871-July 23, 1955 former Secretary of State; "father" of the United Nations; won the Nobel Peace Prize in 1945; carried out the foreign policy of the United States for nearly twelve years (1933-1944) under President Franklin D. Roosevelt; founder of the Reciprocal Trade Program (1934); except for two years as Democratic National Chairman, he was a member of the U.S. Congress, either as Representative or Senator, from 1907 until called into the Cabinet in 1933; as early as 1936 he foresaw the war that was coming in the rise of the Axis dictatorships; he issued repeated warnings that Japan would strike and when envoys were sent on December 7, 1941 he spoke scathingly of Japanese perfidy at Pearl Harbor; ardently believed that unhampered trade dovetailed with peace; that high tariffs and trade barriers led to war; a key figure in laying the groundwork for the United Nations (1945); developed the "good neighbor" policy toward Latin America; author *Memoirs* (1950). See *Current Biography* (Aug.) 1940.

Obituary

N Y Times p1+ Jl 24 '55 pors

HURLEY, ROY T. June 3, 1896- Industrialist

Address: b. c/o Curtiss-Wright Corp., Wood-Ridge, N.J.

As president and chairman of the Curtiss-Wright Corporation, Roy T. Hurley is one of the leading spokesmen in the United States for a Government policy favoring the expansion of the aircraft industry as an essential arm of defense. Through his company's intensive development of turboprop-jet engine production, he is also given a large share of the credit for America's expansion in jet engine manufacture. His company, according to an announcement of the U.S. Air Force, is one of the several now working to build an atomic-powered airplane. The firm has fourteen divisions and subsidiaries in New Jersey, New York, Ohio, and Holland.

Since becoming head of the company in 1949, Hurley has acted first, to divest it of marginal operations, such as certain experimental activities and the production of air frames; second, to concentrate the company's efforts in the production of aircraft engines and propellers; and third, to develop diversified interests in such fields as electronics and plastics. In 1949 the company was showing a net loss of $1,909,309, annual sales were $128,578,227, and the backlog of unfilled orders was $132,700,000. By 1954 the company had a net income of $19,377,279 for the year, sales of $475,084,435, and a backlog of unfilled orders of $750,000,000 (New York *Times,* March 14, 1955).

Roy T. Hurley was born in New York City on June 3, 1896, the son of Edward and Phoebe (King) Hurley. He was educated in that city's public schools. In 1916 he went to work as an aircraft engine mechanic for the B. F. Sturtevant Company at Hyde Park, part of Boston, Massachusetts. The next year he became an inspector of airplanes and engines in the New York district office of the U.S. Army.

From 1921 to 1927 Hurley was chief engineer of the B. G. Aircraft Spark Plug Company of New York City, and then vice-president and general manager of the Moto-Meter Gauge and Equipment Company of Long Island from 1927 to 1931. He was with the Hurley-Townsend Company of New York, manufacturers of aviation spark plugs, from 1932 to 1935. When that company was acquired by the Bendix Aviation Corporation of Detroit, Michigan, he became a staff executive on production matters.

(Continued next page)

ROY T. HURLEY

Bendix lent Hurley to the War Department for a year and a half during World War II. During that time he served as a production adviser to various generals in Army Ordnance. In September 1944 Hurley was elected a vice-president in charge of manufacturing at the Bendix Aviation Corporation and assigned to prepare for the conversion to production of peacetime goods. Hurley left Bendix in 1948 to join the Ford Motor Company of Dearborn, Michigan, as director of manufacturing engineering. For Ford he directed the establishment of a manufacturing engineering system for motor car production. Also during 1948 he served with the Eberstadt Task Committee of the Hoover Commission and as a consultant to Major General F. M. Hopkins, Jr. at the Wright-Patterson Air Force Base in Dayton, Ohio.

Hurley was elected president and director of the Curtiss-Wright Corporation on August 8, 1949. By then he had acquired a reputation as an expert in low-cost industrial production. He was chosen as president during a management reorganization of the company being directed by Paul Shields, a Wall Street investment banker.

In line with the new policies of the company, Hurley announced in October 1950 that the firm was discontinuing air-frame manufacturing and would concentrate on engine and propeller manufacturing in New Jersey. A few days later it was announced that Curtiss-Wright had concluded a seven-year renewable agreement with Armstrong Siddeley Motors, Ltd., of England for an exchange of designs.

This agreement was hailed as one of the most important postwar developments in aviation (New York *Times,* October 6, 1950), because it means that British jet engine designs, far ahead of those of the United States at that time, could be joined with U.S. industrial production methods, far ahead of those of the British. In return for the right to manufacture British jet engines—the Sapphire turbo-jet, and the Python, Mamba and Double Mamba turbo-props—the Curtiss-Wright Corporation gave Armstrong Siddeley several million dollars and the right to produce the new Curtiss propellers.

In January 1951 Hurley announced that his company was forming a new electronics division, for the consolidation of the company's activities in that field, in a new plant at Carlstadt, New Jersey. With the purchase of this plant, Curtiss-Wright also acquired a plastics business, and this was transferred to a new subsidiary, the Columbia Protektosite Company.

In the next month Hurley announced the development of an extrusion process of making aircraft propellers—pressing them from blocks of molten metal, rather than manufacturing them from parts welded together. A metals processing division was set up at a plant purchased in Buffalo, New York, and a large extrusion press installed there.

He went to England in mid-June 1951 together with Lieutenant General K. B. Wolfe, deputy chief of staff of the U.S. Air Force for matériel. Great Britain at that time was trying to get 400 Sabre jet fighters from the United States to replace her obsolete fighter planes. The United States, however, was reluctant to relinquish that large a share of its jet-engine output. General Wolfe and Hurley proposed a compromise solution—the United States would supply Britain with 500 Sabre jet air frames and 3,800 machine tools, with which the British could produce enough of their own Rolls Royce-Avon jet engines to complete the planes.

The Curtiss-Wright Corporation was named by the U.S. Senate's Select Committee on Small Business in the summer of 1951 as one of ten companies that had received 40 per cent of the dollar volume of defense contracts awarded since the Korean conflict began. Hurley said that although his company then had more than $1,000,000,000 in government contracts for engines and propellers, more than 60 per cent of its production was let out to subcontractors in twenty states, with many of them employing fewer than 500 persons.

After Hurley was named chairman as well as president of Curtiss-Wright in late 1951 (succeeding Paul Shields, who resigned), he announced that his company had made a careful study of the aircraft procurement policies of the U.S. Government, and had presented a program which it felt would reduce costs and at the same time lead to a stronger aircraft industry. The Government, he contended, must enable aircraft manufacturers to plan five to eight years in advance rather than from year to year for their expansion programs. He also urged that the Government allow the industry to make greater profits, through accelerated amortization, so that it would be financially prepared to meet the expansion required for a strong defense industry (New York *Times,* February 7, 1952).

In June 1952 Hurley was awarded the annual airpower trophy by the New Jersey Wing of the Air Force Association. The following month the board of the Curtiss-Wright Corporation presented him with a plaque and a sailboat for his achievements in industry. Roswell L. Gilpatric, Under Secretary of the Air Force, sent a greeting on the latter occasion saying he "knew no one who had done more for aviation and the mobilization program." In August 1952 Hurley was one of the major speakers at an air preparedness symposium at the sixth annual convention of the Air Force Association in Detroit.

One of the reasons for the tribute to Hurley at this time was that the American aircraft industry, thanks to the engines produced by Curtiss-Wright, had won back the lead in air transport. Foreign and domestic airlines, once strongly tempted to turn to British Comets and other all-jet craft, were now ordering the Lockheed Super Constellations and Douglas DC-7's powered by Wright-made turboprop engines.

In September 1952 Hurley announced that his company had a new entrant in the race to power the air transports of the future—a turbo-compound engine, a conventional piston engine with three exhaust-driven turbines to increase its power. This engine, he said, was "expected to dwarf in power any aircraft engine yet made public" and could easily drive a commercial transport at a speed of 450 miles an hour four times as far as a jet-powered transport without refueling. The company set up an automatic assembly line to manufacture this type of engine.

The division of Curtiss-Wright known as Curtiss-Wright Europa N. V. of Amsterdam was established in 1953 to provide parts and service for the company's engines in use by fighter planes of the North Atlantic Treaty Organization (NATO) countries. During 1954 the company took another major step in diversification with the purchase of licenses to manufacture a number of Swiss and German electronics and supersonic devices.

In his annual report for 1954, Hurley stated that greater efficiencies in the company's engine division had saved the U.S. Air Force $28,000,000 in that year. Curtiss-Wright engines are used in Martin's B-57 night intruder bombers, in Lockheed's F-104 fighter, and in many other military planes.

Through the years Hurley continued his demands for U.S. Government policies more favorable to the growth and war-preparedness of the aircraft industry. In May 1954, at the Aircraft Trade Show in New York City, he was presented with a plaque for "his patriotic efforts to create a stronger aircraft industry in the interest of national defense, air commerce and a free world."

New products shown by Curtiss-Wright in New York in 1955 include a mobile camera for closed-circuit industrial television, heat resistant plastics, and a black light for police, which allows observation in the dark without the knowledge of the persons under surveillance.

Hurley was married on October 3, 1953, to Esther Sarchian, his administrative assistant at the Curtiss-Wright main office in Wood-Ridge, N.J. He has two daughters, Nancy Ann and Patricia Ann, by his previous marriage to Ruth Applebee, whom he married on June 3, 1917. He is a member of the American Ordnance Association and the Society of Automotive Engineers. His clubs include the Wings and the Rockefeller Center Luncheon in New York; and the Athletic and Recess in Detroit.

References

N Y Times p26 S 15 '44; p33 Ag 1 '49
Who's Who in America, 1954-55
World Biography (1954)

HUSSEIN I, KING OF HASHEMITE JORDAN (hōō-sīn') Nov. 14, 1935-

Address: Royal Palace Za'Afaran, Amman, Jordan

The Hashemite Kingdom of Jordan contains the Biblical lands of Moab, Gilead and Edom and holy places of the Christian religion, including the old city of Jerusalem and the town of Bethlehem. Today, King Hussein I is the constitutional ruler. Proclaimed King at the age of sixteen, after his father King Talal was deposed because of ill-health, Hussein was enthroned on May 2, 1953.

With a population of about 1,400,000 in a land area of 34,750 square miles, Jordan's strategic importance stems from its location at the eastern approaches to the Suez Canal and the narrow land bridge between Asia and Africa. For more than a year, Jordan has been involved in an internal dispute over a closer alliance with Iraq. The New York *Times* (May 1, 1955) reported that Great Britain and Turkey were encouraged by Jordan's refusal to join the proposed Egyptian-Saudi Arabian-Syrian alliance (designed as a counterweight to the Turkish-British-Iraqi-Pakistani security pact) and commented that King Hussein was known for his pro-British sympathies. The uneasy truce between Jordan and Israel has frequently been disturbed by border clashes.

According to the Moslem calendar, which began when Mohammed fled from Mecca, Hussein ibn Talal ibn Abdullah el Hashim's birth date is May 2, 1935. By the Western calendar it is November 14, 1935. He was the first child born to the Emir Talal and the Hashemite Sherifa (Princess) Zaïn. The event took place in Amman, the ancient Hellenistic city of Philadelphia. Two younger sons and a daughter were born to the Emir Talal and the Sherifa Zaïn.

A direct descendant of the prophet Mohammed, Hussein's great-grandfather, the Sherif Hussein of Mecca, was King of the Hejaz and played a prominent role in the Arab revolt that freed the territories now known as Syria, Iraq and Jordan from Turkish domination at the end of World War I. His grandfather, Abdullah I, was the Emir of Transjordan from 1923 to 1946 and became King of Transjordan

Wide World

HUSSEIN I, KING OF HASHEMITE JORDAN

after the country became an independent kingdom in 1946. (In 1949 Transjordan adopted the name of Hashemite Kingdom of Jordan.)

Prince Hussein attended the British missionary kindergarten in Amman, the Moslem College of Amman, and Victoria College in Alexandria, Egypt. According to the New York *Times* (August 12, 1952) young Hussein was a favorite of King Abdullah. The young Prince was with Abdullah, when the latter was assassinated on July 20, 1951 in Jerusalem by an anti-Western fanatic.

There was some opposition to Crown Prince Talal's accession to the throne; he was in Switzerland "receiving medical treatment" (New York *Times,* August 12, 1952). However, he took the royal oath on September 6, 1951, and his younger brother, Prince Naif, acted as Regent for two months, and was replaced by a three-man Crown Council. Hussein was made Crown Prince and a few days after his father was enthroned was sent to Harrow in England for his senior-year studies.

Acting on the testimony of doctors, who confirmed that King Talal was mentally ill, the Jordanian Parliament removed Talal from the throne on August 11, 1952 and proclaimed Crown Prince Hussein as the King. The three-man Crown Council was continued as a Regency Council. In the fall of 1952 King Hussein flew to London to attend the Sandhurst Royal Military College for a special course. Queen Elizabeth II of Great Britain invested Hussein on April 4, 1953 as a Knight Grand Cross of the Royal Victorian Order.

As May 2, 1953 was King Hussein's eighteenth birthday by the Moslem calendar and the eighteenth birthday by the Western calendar of his cousin King Feisal II of Iraq, the two Kings were enthroned on the same day. *Newsweek* (May 11, 1953) said that Jordan's third King, dressed in the blue and gold uniform of an Arab Legion officer, took the royal oath before an enthusiastic crowd in the Parliament building. Armored cars, jeeps and mounted lancers of the Arab Legion escorted the King in a spectacular parade. Salutes of 101 guns were fired in Amman and in old Jerusalem.

Jordan was taken from Turkey by the British in World War I and was separated from the Palestine mandate in 1920. Britain recognized Jordan's independence, subject to the mandate, in 1923. After cooperating fully with the British during World War II, Jordan was recognized as completely independent and the mandate was abolished on March 22, 1946. A constitutional monarch, the King rules with the aid of a Cabinet responsible to Parliament, which is popularly elected. The country is poor; *Time* (May 11, 1953) noted that Jordan is "three-fifths desert, with no oil, no industrial raw materials, tortuous roads and one inaccessible port. . . ." Britain gives Jordan an annual defense subsidy of £3,000,000.

After the village of Kibya was attacked by Israeli forces in October 1953, the King visited the frontier settlement and presented the Mayor with the equivalent of $1,400 as a personal contribution toward rebuilding the village. A later raid on a Jordan village near Bethlehem in March 1954 by armed Israelis caused King Hussein to call an emergency meeting of the Cabinet. He then hurried to the scene accompanied by General John Bagot Glubb, British commander of the Arab Legion.

After a United States mission, headed by Eric A. Johnston, proposed cooperative use of the water of the Jordan Valley by Jordan, Syria and Israel, the Premier of Jordan, Fawzi el Mulki, stated: "Jordan is fully prepared to continue bearing economic hardship rather than participate in any project leading to cooperation with Israel. . . ." (New York *Times,* November 15, 1953).

The New York *Times* (April 19, 1954) said that King Hussein had appealed to the American people to "let love and faith be more articulate" concerning the 900,000 Palestine Arab refugees, who settled in Jordan in tents and grottos after the establishment of the state of Israel in 1948. Following another raid in September 1954 near Jerusalem, the King said that unless Israel ended its "aggressions," Jordan would be "compelled to reconsider" her attitude toward the truce, arranged between the two countries in April 1949.

Israeli and Jordanian representatives reached an agreement on May 10, 1955 at the U.N. Mixed Armistice Commission Headquarters in Jerusalem to accord prisoner-of-war treatment to soldiers or policemen captured during border clashes.

Another problem confronting the King is the proposed federation of Jordan and Iraq, an idea which had been supported by Abdullah. Several Cabinet members favor such a federation because it would increase Jordan's strength against Israel and because they feel that the rich oil deposits of Iraq would benefit the struggling Jordan economy, which "currently must depend on annual British subsidies" (*Christian Science Monitor,* March 2, 1954).

An opposing faction, led by the Queen Mother, fears that a Jordanian-Iraqi union would make Jordan a province of Iraq and King Hussein would be reduced to the role of viceroy to his cousin in Baghdad. To combat the movement, Queen Zaïn arranged a meeting between her son and King Saud of Saudi Arabia. (The Hashemites are traditional opponents of Saud's family.) It was reported that King Saud gave Hussein money to strengthen Jordan's national guard, which is not under British command.

In December 1954 Hussein visited London to negotiate changes in the March 15, 1948 treaty with Great Britain. By provision of the treaty, Great Britain is committed to aid Jordan, if an outside force should declare war upon her. In return, the British are permitted to maintain two air bases in Jordan, which are now equipped with jet aircraft. Final decision in regard to altering the treaty is pending further discussion.

On February 27, 1955, the engagement of King Hussein to his distant cousin, the Sherifa Dina Abdel Hamid was announced. Their great-great-grandfather was Sherif Aun of Mecca. The Princess, a member of the Hashemite family, received a master's degree from Girton College, Cambridge University and later taught English literature at Cairo University in Cairo, Egypt.

The marriage ceremony took place on April 19, 1955, and in accordance with Islamic tradition, the bride was in another room. The marriage contract was signed by King Hussein and the bride's father, Sherif Abdel Hamid el-Aoun, in the Royal Palace Za'Afaran. Only male members of the Hashemite family were present, which included the King and Crown Prince of Iraq, and Hussein's brother, Crown Prince Mohammed of Jordan.

King Hussein is of medium height and has dark eyes, a small mustache and a gracious manner. He is a pilot and enjoys skiing, boxing, reading, American movies, fencing, horseback riding and Italian spaghetti. His English is fluent and he speaks some French. Visitors are said to be impressed with his "self-confidence and deep earnestness."

References

Los Angeles Times p22 My 2 '54 por
N Y Times p1 Ag 12 '52 por; p15 Ap 20 '55 por
N Y World-Telegram p13 Ag 16 '52 por; II p1 My 3 '53 por
Newsweek 40:38 Ag 25 '52 por
International Who's Who, 1954
Middle East—Who's Who in the Middle East, 1955
New Century Cyclopedia of Names (1954)
World Biography (1954)

JARMAN, SANDERFORD Nov. 24, 1884-Oct. 15, 1954 United States Army officer; was graduated from U.S. Military Academy (1908); served in World War I with the 29th Division; built up defenses of Panama Canal (1939-41); commanded East coast anti-aircraft defenses, and troops in Central Pacific during World War II; received Distinguished Service Medal. See *Current Biography,* (Sept.) 1942.

Obituary

N Y Times p87 O 17 '54

JOHNSON, ARNOLD M(ILTON) Jan. 11, 1907- Business and baseball club executive

Address: b. c/o Automatic Canteen Company of America, 1430 Merchandise Mart, Chicago 54, Ill.; h. 1500 Lake Shore Drive, Chicago 10, Ill.

With a group of associates Arnold M. Johnson, the "amiably firm business tycoon," purchased the Philadelphia American League Baseball Club in November 1954, and transferred the team to Kansas City, Missouri, to become the present Kansas City Athletics. Johnson was associated with the City National Bank and Trust of Chicago for twenty years beginning in 1932, becoming a vice-president in 1945. Since 1953 he has been vice-chairman of the Automatic Canteen Company of America, the country's leading candy and refreshment vending machine enterprise.

Of Swedish ancestry on both sides, Arnold Milton Johnson was born on January 11, 1907 in Chicago, Illinois, where his father, Carl William Johnson, was in the building construction business and later became the owner of several laundry plants. (His mother was Alma Magnuson before her marriage.) He has one elder brother, Earl, who is now the treasurer of the Kansas City Athletics, Inc.

The Johnsons were not poor, but as a boy Arnold earned his own pocket money by organizing a squad of boys to distribute advertising matter, and by undertaking an after-school newspaper delivery route. He cheered for the Chicago White Sox at Comiskey Park, and he played first base on sandlot ball teams.

At Chicago's Hyde Park High School, from which he was graduated in 1924, he played a little basketball, but was better remembered as a book-lover and student. He studied business administration at the University of Chicago and was elected to the Kappa Sigma fraternity and the presidency of the student council.

Having received the Ph.B. degree from the University of Chicago in 1928, Arnold Johnson had the choice of half a dozen openings in business; he chose to enter the employ of Lamson Brothers, a Chicago stock and grain brokerage establishment, at only $75 a month. In 1929, again to extend his experience as an accountant, he transferred to the Chicago office of the New York brokerage firm of Merrill and Lynch (now Merrill Lynch, Pierce, Fenner & Beane). He took courses in business law and subsequently joined another bond firm as the organizer of a statistical department.

Johnson's first long-term connection began late in 1932, when the Central Republic Bank and Trust Company, established in Chicago by Charles G. Dawes, former Vice President of the United States, was refinanced to form

Maurice Seymour
ARNOLD M. JOHNSON

the present City National Bank and Trust Company. Dawes made Johnson a minor officer in the new bank. "General Dawes," Johnson recalled, "was one of the greatest men I knew. . . . I tried to learn from him, as we all did" (Kansas City *Star,* November 14, 1954).

In 1938, when Johnson had been with the City National for about six years, he became the secretary of a bondholders committee which studied the problems of the Northwestern Terra Cotta Corporation, a Chicago concern. This company had current liabilities of not less than $1,500,000 and assets of only $50,000; Johnson, however, had faith enough in terra cotta as an industrial necessity to invest some of his own money in the distressed enterprise and to prevail on others to supply the balance of necessary refinancing. Elected to a directorship (his first in any company), he instituted personnel changes, and was largely responsible for keeping the company on a modestly solvent basis until World War II, when its products came into governmental demand. (He is now chairman of the board.)

Taking leave of absence from the City National Bank in 1942 to join the United States Navy for World War II service, Johnson was commissioned a lieutenant senior grade. He trained as a gunnery officer but later was reclassified as a navigator and assigned the command of an amphibious boat group in the Pacific Theater. He participated as beachmaster in seven island landings and narrowly escaped death at Luzon in the Philippines in January 1945, when he was chief of staff and operations officer of the U.S.S. *Callaway;* he was "ordered ashore" just before a Japanese suicide plane attacked the ship, killing the officer who had replaced him on the bridge. For his World War II services Johnson was awarded the Bronze Star and the Legion of Merit and was honorably discharged in 1946 with the rank of lieutenant commander. He was named vice president of the City National Bank in 1945.

In Chicago in the post-war years he became a director of the Infant Welfare Society and treasurer of the Sister Kenny Foundation of Illinois, and was active in Community Fund and Boy Scout drives. He extended his business interests by purchasing stock in various firms dealing with the City National Bank, including the Denver Terra Cotta Company, the Blakely Oswald Printing Company of Chicago, the Batavia (Illinois) Body Company, the Dayton (Ohio) Western Tablet and Stationery Company, and the New York publishing firm of Henry Holt & Company. (He is today the chairman of the board in the first two, and a director of the others).

After General Dawes died in 1951 Johnson resigned from the bank and became associated with the Automatic Canteen Company of America, established in 1929 by Nathaniel and Louis Leverone of Chicago to dispense candy bars, chewing gum and other items through vending machines. (This company, was described by the Federal Trade Commission in 1948 as "one of the largest outlets for candy and confectionery in the United States").

Near the end of 1951, the elder Leverone brother, Louis, was considering disposing of his holdings, and Johnson persuaded "Chicago attorney J. Arthur Friedlund to assemble an investing group which put up $1,500,000 to buy out Louis," (Arthur Mann in the *Saturday Evening Post,* April 9, 1955). Johnson, thus became vice-chairman of the Automatic Canteen Company of America. He has been given major credit for negotiating the merger in 1953 between Automatic Canteen and a competitor, the Rowe Corporation, thereby almost doubling Automatic's sales volume.

The company grossed $70,000,000 in 1953 and by the spring of 1955 was described as "in the $100,000,000 a year class" (Arthur Mann). Today the company's "canteens" sell, in addition to chewing gum and confectionery, "a variety of things, from fruit juices and coffee to soups, sandwiches, pies and pastry" (Kansas City *Star,* November 14, 1954).

Johnson's first connection with organized baseball came through a complicated real estate transaction as described in the *Saturday Evening Post* (April 9, 1955). The owners of the New York American League ("Yankees") Baseball Club, who also owned Yankee Stadium in New York City, and minor league "farms" with their real estate including the Triple A Kansas City "Blues," decided that there would be certain tax advantages if they sold their real estate (but not the clubs) at the same time receiving from the purchasers long-term leases to the baseball parks and stadium. (Transactions of this nature have been fairly frequent in recent years.) Johnson was brought into the transaction by business associates who also had business connections with the owners of the Yankees, and in December 1953 a special New

York corporation headed by Johnson purchased both the Yankee Stadium and the Kansas City "Blues" ball park for $6,500,000.

Johnson's corporation then sold the property occupied by the Yankee Stadium to the Knights of Columbus, who leased the land back to the corporation, which in turn leased the stadium to the "Yankees." The transaction did not, however, cover the "Blues" Stadium in Kansas City, which remained the property of Johnson and his associates.

The idea of bringing Kansas City back into the major leagues—the western Missouri metropolis had briefly held a National League franchise in 1886—is said to have originated with Ernie Mehl, sports editor of the Kansas City *Star,* in March, 1953. In May 1954, Johnson paid an inspection visit to Kansas City. "When I was looking over the property there, Ernie Mehl . . . suggested that while I was at it why didn't I get a major league franchise and move it to Kansas City? Sounded good to me" (*Christian Science Monitor,* October 13, 1955).

The Philadelphia Athletics of the American League, owned by octogenarian Connie Mack and his sons Roy and Earle, were known to be heavily in debt; Johnson organized a syndicate (including Nathaniel Leverone, Johnson himself, and his brother Earl) for the purchase of the club and in August 1954 had $4,000,000 ready for this purpose. The voters of Kansas City approved a $2,775,000 bond issue to enable the municipality to purchase the "Blues" Stadium for $650,000, to double deck the park to provide a seating capacity of upwards of 30,000, and to make other improvements necessary to meet major league requirements. (The stadium was leased back to Johnson for five years, with renewal options).

The Johnson group made a formal offer for the purchase of the Athletics as early as August 3, and on November 8, 1954, after rejecting the offer of a rival group pledged to keep the Athletics in Philadelphia, the American League club owners finally voted to authorize the sale of the Philadelphia club and its Connie Mack Stadium to the Johnson associates for approximately $3,500,000 and to approve transfer of the franchise to Kansas City.

Subsequently the Connie Mack Stadium was sold to the Philadelphia National League Club for $1,675,000. "Actually the remaining investment of myself and my associates in the Kansas City Athletics after the sale of the Philadelphia Stadium," Johnson informed *Current Biography,* "was almost $2,000,000, without taking into account needed working capital for the baseball operation."

With the chartering of Kansas City Athletics, Inc., as a Missouri corporation, Nathaniel Leverone became chairman of the board, Arnold Johnson the president, and Earl W. Johnson the treasurer. (Connie Mack was given the title of honorary chairman of the board, while Roy Mack was named a vice-president). Arnold Johnson was under no illusions as to the quality of the team he had brought to Kansas City; it had finished in last place in the American League in 1954, had no adequate farm system, and possessed few dispensable good players for trading purposes. "We are going to get a ball club," Johnson nevertheless promised. "It can't be done quickly. Our goals are the first division in three years and a pennant contender in five. . . . We are ready to spend $1,000,000 in the next three years. I know material is scarce. But there are some good players in the minors who can be bought."

In November 1954 Louis Boudreau, former manager of the Boston Red Sox, was engaged for two years as manager of the Athletics; and to build up the farm system, working agreements were arranged with five minor league clubs. In the season which began on April 12, 1955 with a victory by the Athletics over the Detroit Tigers at the rebuilt Kansas City Municipal Stadium, the Athletics soon were drawing regular crowds of 20,000 to their home games. By mid-July the team was sixth out of eight in the league standings.

Arnold Johnson likes to travel; he has been around the world and has made five trips to Europe. Hunting and fishing are now his favorite outdoor recreations; his hobbies include the collecting of clocks and Oriental art. He is a member of the Chicago Athletic Association and the Saddle and Cycle, Post and Paddock, and South Side Swedish Clubs in Chicago, the Fin 'n' Feather Club of Dundee, Illinois; the Kansas City Club; and the Everglades and Bat and Tennis Clubs in Palm Beach, Florida. He is a Republican and a Presbyterian. His wife is the former Carmen Coye Burr of San Francisco; they were married on October 6, 1945.

Wendy Alexis, their daughter, was born in 1948 and Jeffrey Burr, their son, in 1950. Johnson stands at six feet one and a half inches and is around 190 pounds in weight; his eyes are blue and his hair blond. He has been described as "personable, square-shouldered," and as the possessor of "a contagious good humor."

References

Christian Sci Mon p 11 O 13 '54
Kansas City (Mo.) Star D p 1+ N 14 '54 por
Look 19:71+ Mr 22 '55 por
N Y World-Telegram p34 O 13 '54
Sat Eve Post 227:25+ Ap 9 '55 por
Poor's Register of Directors and Executives (1955)
Who's Who in Commerce and Industry (1953)

JOHNSON, NELSON T(RUSLER) Apr. 3, 1887-Dec. 3, 1954 Former U.S. Ambassador to China and Australia; Assistant Secretary of State; secretary general of the Far Eastern Commission to work out postwar problems, which post he resigned in 1950. See *Current Biography* (Jan.-Feb.) 1940.

Obituary

N Y Times p17 D 4 '54

JOHNSON, U(RAL) ALEXIS Oct. 17, 1908- United States Ambassador to Czechoslovakia

Address: b. United States Embassy, Prague, Czechoslovakia; h. 2019 Rosemount Ave., Washington 10, D.C.; Glendale, Calif.

For nearly twenty years a "career officer" in the United States foreign service, U. Alexis Johnson attained one of the top diplomatic posts in November 1953, when he was sworn into office as United States Ambassador to Czechoslovakia. He was named to this office after about two years as deputy assistant Secretary of State for Far Eastern Affairs, during which time he worked (in the words of President Dwight D. Eisenhower) "unceasingly on the Korean armistice and . . . made a unique contribution toward bringing it about."

U. ALEXIS JOHNSON

In July 1955 he was assigned by the Department of State to represent the United States in talks on repatriation at Geneva, Switzerland with Wang Ping-nan, Communist China's Ambassador to Poland, to seek the release of eleven American airmen and some forty American civilians being held by the People's Republic of China. On July 31. 1955, the airmen were officially released and were flown to Hong Kong the next day. The American civilians have not all been freed.

Earlier in his career, Ambassador Johnson had been attached to embassies or consulates at Tokyo, Seoul, Tientsin, Mukden, Rio de Janeiro and Yokohama, and was interned by the Japanese in Manchuria during 1942. Between October 1949 and November 1951, Johnson was successively deputy director and director of the State Department's Office of Northeast Asian Affairs, and in September 1951 was an adviser to the U.S. delegation to the Japanese Peace Treaty Conference in San Francisco, California. In April 1954 he was placed on leave of absence from his post at Prague, Czechoslovakia, to become what the New York *Times* called "virtual chief of staff" of the American delegation to the Geneva Far Eastern Conference, and towards the end of the Conference served as acting chief of the delegation.

The only son of the late Carl Theodore Johnson and the former Ellen Irene Forsse, Ural Alexis Johnson was born on October 17, 1908 in Falun, Kansas. His father's parents emigrated from Sweden to the United States in 1865 and those of his mother in 1842. The elder Johnson was the cashier of the Falun State Bank, and it was in Falun that Alexis and his sister Rella Forsse (now Mrs. Gerald Warner) received their early schooling.

At the end of the boy's freshman year at the Falun Rural High School in 1923, the family moved to Glendale, California, where Johnson's father was occupied first as assistant cashier of the Hollywood National Bank, Hollywood, California, and later as cashier of the American National Bank in Glendale. Alexis attended the Glendale Union High School, completing in 1927 a secondary education which had been interrupted by one year of illness. His extracurricular activities included debating, as well as the school newspaper and year book.

Entering Occidental College in Los Angeles, he majored in economics (and worked in a bank on a part-time basis to meet his expenses). He became a member of the debating team and was elected to the Tau Kappa Alpha debate and oratory fraternity and to the social fraternity Psi Delta Chi. By the time of his graduation with the A.B. degree in 1931, Johnson had determined on a consular and diplomatic career.

Throughout the academic year 1931-1932 he was a student at the Georgetown School of Foreign Service in the District of Columbia. "In 1932 I took and passed examinations for the Foreign Service," Johnson has informed *Current Biography*. "However, because of the economy measures then put into effect in the Government, no appointments were made until 1935. Between 1932 and my appointment in 1935, I held a number of temporary jobs with various private firms in Washington, eventually obtaining a permanent job with 'Call Carl, Inc.,' a large garage chain where I was office manager."

Finally appointed to the U.S. Foreign Service as of October 1935, Johnson was assigned to the American Embassy at Tokyo, Japan, where in the following month he began two years of duty as an attaché and "language officer for Japanese language study." Johnson was reassigned in December 1937, to Korea (then a part of the Japanese Empire) and served as U.S. vice-consul at Seoul (then Keijo) until the end of June 1939, when he was ordered to Tientsin, China, for temporary duty as vice-consul.

Back in Seoul by the following November, Johnson remained there until the beginning of July 1940, when he assumed the duties of U.S. vice-consul at Mukden in Japanese-dominated Manchukuo (Manchuria). After the Pearl

Harbor attack of December 7, 1941, vice-consul Johnson was interned at Mukden and remained in Japanese hands until July 1942, when he was one of the diplomatic personnel exchanged under the auspices of neutral Portugal.

After his return to the United States, Johnson was assigned to Rio de Janeiro, Brazil, as vice-consul and later, second secretary; he commenced his duties there in December, 1942.

By the early summer of 1944 United States forces were securely established on many Pacific islands; reoccupation of the Philippines was being planned; and B-29's were ready for their first bombing raids on the Japanese homeland. Vice-consul Johnson, in view of his experience in the Orient, was recalled from Brazil and assigned by the State Department to the U.S. Army Civil Affairs Training School established at the University of Chicago for training military government officers for occupation of Japan.

Appointed as consul at Manila, Johnson entered the Philippines capital immediately after the surrender of the city to the Americans, and from March to August, 1945, worked (he tells us) "with the military authorities . . . in the processing, screening and transportation from the Philippines of American and other Allied prisoners of war and internees liberated from the Japanese."

Detailed by the State Department to General Douglas MacArthur's headquarters in Japan for similar duty, Consul Johnson in August 1945 "traveled throughout Japan . . . prior to the entry into Japan of any Allied forces except in the immediate Yokohama-Tokyo area."

After a brief return to Seoul, where he had been detailed to "advise and assist" General John R. Hodge's XXIV Corps Headquarters "on military government problems" in Korea, Johnson was assigned by the Department of State in October 1945 to open an office in Yokohama to perform all consular functions for all of Japan and Okinawa.

On July 26, 1946 he was decorated with the Medal of Freedom for "meritorious service . . . in the Philippine Islands and Japan from March 15, 1945 to March 2, 1946." The official citation made specific mention of the "outstanding competence" he displayed in "the solution of repatriation and other complex problems" at both Manila and Tokyo. "In addition," the citation continued, "he aided materially in the formulation of policies and the resolution of legal problems. . . ."

Promoted to consul general in June 1947, Johnson remained at Yokohama until the summer of 1949, when he was recalled to Washington to become deputy director of the State Department's Office of Northeast Asian Affairs, the agency within the Bureau of Far Eastern Affairs, which executes responsibility for the general conduct of foreign relations with the countries of the Far East. Johnson became director of this office in February 1951.

He served as an adviser to the U.S. delegation to the Japanese Peace Treaty Conference at San Francisco, California, in September 1951 and on November 30, 1951 he was named as Deputy Assistant Secretary of State for Far Eastern Affairs; and as such he served during the next two years under three Assistant Secretaries: Dean Rusk, John Allison, and Walter Robertson.

In 1952 Johnson was again in the Far East in connection with negotiations for the truce in Korea, of which he was later to be described as "one of the architects" (*Associated Press*). His service in this respect was recognized by President Dwight D. Eisenhower in a letter dated July 27, 1953.

Johnson's views on the origins, problems, ideology and future of "Maoism" may be found in the paper entitled "China's Role in the Communist Movement in Asia" which is included in the symposium *The Threat of Soviet Imperialism,* edited by C. Grove Haines (Johns Hopkins Press, 1954).

When the Eisenhower Administration took office in January 1953, Johnson (as a State Department "career officer") retained his Deputy Assistant Secretary's post under the new Secretary of State, John Foster Dulles, and even "made speeches defending the Acheson policy on the Far East" (*U.S. News & World Report,* December 18, 1953). As a class one Foreign Service officer since June 20, 1951, he was "in line" for an embassy; and on November 10, 1953 he was nominated to be United States Ambassador to Czechoslovakia in succession to George Wadsworth, who was transferred to Saudi Arabia and Yemen.

Johnson was praised by Dulles "for his work on the Korean truce negotiations" when sworn in at Washington on November 20. Ambassador Johnson presented his credentials to the Communist President of Czechoslovakia, Antonín Zápotocký, on December 31, 1953, and shortly thereafter "succeeded in negotiating the release" on February 4, 1954 "of John Hvasta, an American citizen imprisoned by the Czechs, who escaped from prison and after a long period of hiding sought asylum in the American embassy at Prague."

Ambassador Johnson was named by Secretary Dulles to be a titular adviser to the U.S. delegation to the Far Eastern Conference meeting in Geneva, Switzerland beginning April 26, 1954; and for this purpose he was placed on leave of absence from Prague. The conference "failed to solve the Korean problem" (New York *Times,* July 10, 1954) but it was considered that some progress was achieved in improving the prospects of prisoners in Communist Chinese hands, and on the basis of information supplied by Johnson, an advance was made towards bargaining for the repatriation of nationals detained by both sides.

When at the beginning of the ninth week (June 21) the conference took up immediate consideration of the military situation in Indo-China, and both Secretary Dulles and Under-Secretary of State Walter Bedell Smith withdrew, Ambassador Johnson, who was characterized by the former as a "competent and senior diplomatic official" (New York *Times,* July 9, 1954), became the acting chief of the United States delegation.

Johnson and Patricia Ann Tillman were married March 21, 1932 and are the parents of two girls and two boys: Judith Ann Johnson was born in Washington, D.C. in 1934;

JOHNSON, U. ALEXIS—*Continued*

Stephen Tillman Johnson in Tokyo, Japan, in 1936; William Theodore Johnson in Seoul, Korea, in 1938; and Jennifer Ellen Johnson in Rio de Janeiro, Brazil, in 1943.

He belongs to the Foundry Methodist Church in Washington, D.C., and is a member of the Asiatic Society of Japan. He has blue eyes and brown hair and stands at an even six feet, weighing 190 pounds. Mountain climbing is his favorite outdoor recreation.

References

N Y Herald Tribune II p5 Jl 31 '55
N Y Times p6 Jl 27 '55
N Y World-Telegram p5 Jl 30 '55
Who's Who in America, 1954-55
World Diplomatic Directory, 1951

JOHNSTON, CLEM(ENT) D(IXON)

Nov. 7, 1895- Organization official; business executive; farmer

Address: b. c/o Chamber of Commerce of the United States, Washington 6, D.C.; h. "Bluehills," R.F.D. #1, Roanoke, Va.

As spokesman for some 1,100,000 businessmen represented by the Chamber of Commerce of the United States, Clem D. Johnston has often voiced that organization's opposition to wage, price and rent controls and too much government interference in national economy. In a January 1955 talk at the National Press Club in Washington, D.C., he spoke of competitive capitalism as "the most revolutionary force in the world," but one that is now being stifled by "an increasing blanket of controls and restraints" (*Christian Science Monitor,* January 29, 1955).

Before becoming president in April 1954, Johnston had been active in the national Chamber of Commerce for twenty-two years, including two terms as director and five terms as vice-president. For more than a decade he has been acting as a non-paid consultant to various Federal departments and agencies, among them the Reconstruction Finance Corporation, Office of Price Administration, U.S. Navy, and Office of Civil Defense Planning. He describes himself as "a typical businessman, and in no sense of the word a 'big business' man." His experience as a wholesale grocer, warehouse operator and cattle farmer in Roanoke, Virginia convinces him that "tough competition" produces more goods and services for more people.

Johnston's one-year term as president ended in May 1955 at which time he became chairman of the board of the U.S. Chamber of Commerce, and A. Boyd Campbell succeeded him to the presidency.

Clement Dixon Johnston was born in Crestwood, Kentucky on November 7, 1895, the son of Clement Browne and Lulu Gullat (Johnston) Johnston. He has one brother and a sister. His father operated a grocery business in nearby Louisville. Clem, as he prefers to be called, attended local schools, graduating in 1913 from Louisville Male High School.

Completing his college courses in three years at Centre College in Danville, Kentucky, he received his B.S. degree in 1916. During his college years he was captain of the track and football teams, student representative in the athletic council, and business manager of the school paper and annual magazine. Of his athletic ability, he says: "Maybe I wasn't an all-American but I was durable. I had to be. I was the only center on the squad" (*Nation's Business,* June 1954).

Six months after Johnston had entered Harvard University Medical School in 1916, he was commissioned in the U.S. Army as a second lieutenant in the Twenty-second Infantry and later rose to the rank of captain of the Thirty-third Infantry, stationed in the Panama Canal Zone.

His father's death in 1919 made Johnston change his plans for an Army career and return to Louisville to become sales manager of the family grocery firm, Johnston Brothers Company. (He maintained his Army connection as a reserve officer until World War II.) In 1926 he sold his wholesale grocery concern in Louisville and moved to Roanoke, Virginia to convert his father-in-law's grocery firm into the Roanoke Public Warehouse. He was proprietor of this merchandise warehousing venture until 1952. Re-entering the wholesale grocery business in 1935, he was made president of the Williamson (West Virginia) Grocery Company and later of the Bristol (Virginia) Grocery Company.

Within the next few years he became an officer of nine wholesale grocery companies in Virginia and West Virginia. He is currently director of six, including Abingdon Grocery Company and Mullens Grocery Company. Among other concerns of which he is a director are Sublette Feed & Supply Company, Southern Investment Company, and Walker Machine and Foundry Corporation.

Johnston, who had been elected to the Roanoke Chamber of Commerce in 1931, began his work for the U.S. Chamber of Commerce the following year when he was named to the organization's resolutions committee. He became a director in 1934 and vice-president for the Southeastern division in 1937. He advised the U.S. Senate Banking and Currency Committee in 1941 that the Chamber of Commerce majority objected to the House and Administration price control bills because they would "create a great new bureaucracy" (New York *Times,* December 13, 1941).

When the United States entered World War II, Johnston, in the rank of lieutenant colonel, was called to active duty and served in 1942 and 1943 at the Pentagon in Washington, D.C. as chief of the warehousing section, Army Ordnance Field Service. (During 1941 he had been warehouse consultant to the U.S. Office of Defense Transportation). Besides checking on warehousing requirements, he helped to recruit trained men for the department. He was assigned to China in 1944 as ordnance supply officer and staff quartermaster, "Z" forces under General Joseph W. Stilwell.

Just before the end of the war, he was recalled to the United States to establish surplus property centers in the nation. In 1944-1945 he was consultant on warehousing to the Reconstruction Finance Corporation, and in 1945-1946 was employment chairman of the warehouse industry advisory committee of the Office of Price Administration. He then left for the Far Pacific to set up a supply system for the U.S. Navy in approximately 300 islands previously administered by the Japanese.

In 1948 he became deputy director of the Office of Civil Defense Planning, under Secretary of Defense James V. Forrestal. In this post, Johnston recommended aid to Europe on an "industry-to-industry" basis through the Economic Cooperation Administration, instead of by a "government-to-government" approach (New York *Times,* June 12, 1948). He stated that the success of the European Recovery Program "lies in working directly with individual industries."

While a member of the House Appropriations Committee advisory staff in 1953, Johnston took part in a check on military and warehouse expenditures which reduced by $5 billion the 1954 military budget. He received an appointment in 1953 as chairman of the highways task force of the Federal Commission on Intergovernmental Relations, previously headed by Clarence Manion, and also became head of a national federation named Project Adequate Roads. On May 4, 1954 he told delegates of the Highway Transportation Congress that the country's annual economic losses because of insufficient highways were at least $3 billion. He has been a member of the public advisory board for the Foreign Operations Administration since July 1954.

Continuing his activities in the U.S. Chamber of Commerce, meanwhile, Johnston was chairman of the committee on international, political and social problems from 1947 to 1949 and became head of the policy committee in 1952. He stated at the National Marketing Conference in Detroit on March 1, 1950 that "at least $100 million a week of risk capital was required if American business were to keep on an even keel," and more was necessary if it "were to expand" (New York *Times,* March 2, 1950). He added that Government loans, guarantees and subsidies weakened the free enterprise system and delayed the "day of reckoning."

Johnston was elected president of the U.S. Chamber of Commerce on April 28, 1954, succeeding Richard L. Bowditch. In his first speech in this new post, he said "a climate of full, free competition—with fitting rewards for outstanding achievement" were necessary for a "fuller, vastly better" national life (*Christian Science Monitor,* April 29, 1954).

At the annual meeting of the chamber held in May 1955 the delegates endorsed a national sales tax, a U.N. review conference to reappraise the U.N. Charter, and the principle that industrial use of atomic energy should be "fully opened to competitive private enterprise." They opposed the plan for issuing bonds to finance the Federal Government's part of the Eisenhower highway program.

CLEM D. JOHNSTON

An honorary LL.D. degree from Centre College was awarded Johnston in 1951. He is a member of Omicron Delta Kappa society of Virginia Polytechnic Institute, elected in 1953, and of Beta Theta Pi fraternity. His clubs include the Shenandoah (Roanoke) and the Roanoke Country. Johnston is a former president of the American Warehousemen's Association and a former district governor of Rotary International. His church affiliation is Methodist.

Curious to learn about people and places, in 1927 Johnston embarked on a round-the-world cruise; and in 1929 he toured Africa, the Balkan countries in 1937 and Alaska in 1950. Discussing his globe-trotting, he has said: "I've learned that mental processes are pretty much the same everywhere, regardless of color, culture or religion" (*Nation's Business,* June 1954).

Johnston married Alice Jane Huff on January 31, 1922; she died on October 15, 1945. His second wife is the former Lutie Walcott Douthat, whom he married on July 21, 1950. Johnston is six feet two and a half inches tall, weighs 190 pounds, and has brown eyes and brown hair. He collects first editions, likes to fish, and enjoys activities on his 450-acre beef cattle farm, "Bluehills." Johnston, reported *Newsweek* (May 10, 1954), calls himself "an Eisenhower Democrat."

References

N Y Times p32 S 1 '38; p15 D 13 '41; p23 Je 12 '48; p39 Mr 2 '50; p19 Ag 29 '53; p20 D 21 '54
Nations Bsns 42:38, 41 Je '54
Newsweek 43:77 My 10 '54

American Men in Government (1949)
Who's Who in America, 1954-55
World Biography (1954)

JOHNSTON, ERIC A(LLEN) Dec. 21, 1896- Association official; businessman
Address: b. c/o Motion Picture Association of America, Inc., 1600 Eye St., N.W., Washington 6, D.C.; h. 2615 31st St., Washington, D.C.

NOTE: This biography supersedes the article which appeared in *Current Biography* in 1943.

As president of the Motion Picture Association of America since 1945, Eric A. Johnston travels extensively abroad, and as chairman of the U.S. Government's International Development Advisory Board, he explores opportunities for putting American private capital to work in many countries. In addition to these activities he has advanced the Jordan River development plan and other programs designed to conciliate differences in the Near East. His skill in conciliating viewpoints has brought him numerous Government assignments under Presidents Dwight D. Eisenhower, Harry S. Truman and Franklin D. Roosevelt.

Wide World

ERIC A. JOHNSTON

Although educated as a lawyer, Johnston has devoted his career largely to business, carrying his business principles into Government service and expounding them in hundreds of speeches and magazine articles. As president of the Chamber of Commerce of the United States for four terms (1942-1946), the youngest man ever to hold that office, Johnston enhanced the prestige of the chamber by interpreting American industry to the public. His services to the U.S. Government won him the Medal of Merit in 1947 and the post of Administrator of the Economic Stabilization Agency in 1951. The motion picture industry gave him a new contract in 1954 which runs to October 15, 1961 at a reported annual salary of over $100,000.

As chief administrator of the movie code of morals, Johnston answered recent criticism and denied that there is any "laxity" in the code. "We are doing an excellent job in bringing good family type entertainment to the screen," he stated, and pointed out that no one picture has too much violence, but "it is the accumulated effect of pictures dealing with violence" (New York *Herald Tribune,* May 21, 1955).

An articulate spokesman for free enterprise, Johnston is convinced that the fundamental answer to why Americans enjoy world industrial and commercial leadership "is that our economy is sparked by competition and we thrive on expanding markets. In most other societies, the economy is restricted, production is rigged, prices are fixed and markets are captive" (*Vital Speeches,* October 15, 1951).

Eric Allen Johnston was born in Washington, D.C., on December 21, 1896 to Bertram Allen, a pharmacist, and Ida F. (Ballinger) Johnston. His father died soon after the family moved to Spokane, Washington, and Eric sold newspapers to help out while attending primary school. He worked as a longshoreman and law librarian while a student at the University of Washington in Seattle, where he took his LL.B. degree in 1917.

After being graduated, he served four years in the U.S. Marine Corps. He sustained a severe head injury while serving as a member of the U.S. legation guard in Peking (now Peiping), China and was invalided out of the service in 1922, having attained the rank of captain.

Returning to Spokane, Johnston sold vacuum cleaners from door to door. He was so successful that in 1923, he and a friend bought the business and renamed it the Brown-Johnston Company, which is now one of the largest distributors of household appliances in the Northwest and of which Johnston is presently a director. About a decade after forming the Brown-Johnston Company, Johnston organized the Columbia Electrical and Manufacturing Company which became a leading manufacturer of electrical appliances in the Northwest. Johnston now is its chairman of the board. Named a trustee in 1933 of the Washington Brick & Lime Company, Johnston paid off the company's $260,000 indebtedness within ten years and increased minimum wages from 37 to over 70 cents an hour.

Elected president of the U.S. Chamber of Commerce of the United States in 1942, he startled its anti-New Deal conservative members by visiting the White House. President Roosevelt, who had set aside five minutes for his visitor, talked with him for nearly twenty minutes. Later, Johnston arranged White House conferences of representatives of labor and management and was influential in bringing about labor's no-strike pledge of World War II. Labor had "a reserved liking" for him because he had urged liberal employment policies. One-quarter of the net profits, before taxes and dividends, of his own companies are distributed among the workers in a profit-sharing plan (*U.S. News & World Report,* February 2, 1951).

Although Johnston approved many phases of the New Deal in principle, he objected to "efforts to legislate by administrative decree, a tendency to excessive centralization of Government and emphasis on what he considered defeatist ideas" (*U.S. News & World Report*, February 2, 1951).

His ability as a conciliator at the White House was awarded by posts in three Administrations, the Roosevelt, the Truman and the Eisenhower. He served on the advisory board of the Office of Economic Stabilization, Committee for Economic Development, management-labor policy committee of the War Manpower Commission, Committee for Drafting Federal Employees, War Mobilization and Reconversion Committee, advisory committee of the Economic Cooperation Administration (1948), advisory board of the Mutual Security Agency, and as personal representative of President Eisenhower on a mission to relieve tensions in the Near East.

The philosophy expressed in Johnston's speeches and articles, are typified in an article in the *Reader's Digest*, February, 1943, in which he wrote: "I am for capitalism, and most all labor leaders I know are really just as much for it as I am. . . . They know that either private business or Government bureaucracy must save the country when the war is over; and they prefer private business."

On the other hand, in the New York *Times Magazine* (January 25, 1953), he gave business this warning: "In the Nineteen Twenties business was on top of the heap. It was cut down by the voters for abuse of its power. Then labor got into the saddle in the Thirties and repeated the mistakes that business had made earlier. So the voters cut labor down to size for the same reason. . . . The American people will always smack down any group that tries to use political power to gain special privileges at the expense of the whole society."

"Capitalism went under in Europe," he wrote in *Fortune* (February, 1949), "not because capitalism as a system failed, but because the European businessmen failed capitalism. . . . The great challenge—the great opportunity—before the American businessman today is to find new ways to diffuse the benefits of capitalism among more people. I am not talking about sharing the wealth. I am talking about creating new wealth to share."

In President Truman's Point IV program he saw an opportunity to diffuse these benefits. "As a businessman," he declared, in accepting the chairmanship of the International Development Advisory Board, "I regard it as a prudent investment. It gives a hand to those who are willing to use their own. It gives a hand in two ways: by sharing our techniques, our genius for production and our store of knowledge; by making it possible for private American capital to make investments or to enter into working partnerships with local capital on an equitable basis" (*Department of State Bulletin*, February 4, 1952).

"It was the clear intent of the Act for International Development," he told a group of economists, "that the enormous potential of American investment capital should become an instrument of foreign policy. The idea of public action and private enterprise pulling in harness literally permeates the law" (*Department of State Bulletin*, May 12, 1952).

The difficulties of doing business abroad are discussed by Johnston in an article in *Collier's* (March 18, 1955) entitled "The Dollar is a Fighting Word." Describing how American distributors recovered proceeds of film rentals in Sweden, he wrote: "We canvassed American-Swedish trade and learned that an American steel company wanted a steady supply of high grade Swedish ore, but couldn't get a long-term lease on two ships to haul it. . . . The movie companies used their frozen kronor to pay [a Swedish shipyard] for building the ships. The ships were turned over to a shipping line, which contracted to haul ore for the steel company on a ten-year lease—payable, naturally, in dollars. The movie companies collect 10 per cent of this operating fee until they get back the cost of the ships—then they become the property of the shipping line."

Johnston was instrumental in 1954 in getting together industrialists and bankers representing $1 billion in "risk" capital for continuing study of investment possibilities in atomic energy projects.

The office of the Motion Picture Association of America in Washington, D.C., is now Johnston's principal base of operations. He succeeded Will H. Hays (see *C.B.*, 1943) as director of this trade organization on September 9, 1945. The association acts as a self-regulating, policy-making organization for the movie industry and has as members almost all Hollywood producers. Foreign showings of American movies bring in about 43 per cent of the industry's gross revenue. Johnston has stated that export of American films has "two great by-products—it helps to create a market for other American goods and it conveys American ideas and ideals."

In an article "How the Movies Get Their Money Out of Europe" by Ben Pearse (*Saturday Evening Post*, November 27, 1954), Johnston described some of the functions of the Motion Picture Export Association, of which he is the head. This association handles the foreign financial affairs of the ten largest movie producers. "We hope the day will come," said Johnston, "when restrictions on trade and currencies are at a minimum. But we can't hold our breath until the day arrives. We are just trying to get along in the world as it is." Accepting commodities from dollar-short countries provides the motion picture industry with such barterable items as tankers, wood pulp, whiskey, beef and tulip bulbs. American producers also make films on location in countries where currency has been accumulated in payment for rental of Hollywood-made films.

Among the problems handled by Johnston for the motion picture business is censorship. The industry's production code comes up for public scrutiny and criticism from time to time, and during 1955 was criticized severely by James Francis Cardinal McIntyre (see *C.B.*, 1953), Archbishop of Los Angeles, and the Rev. Thomas F. Little, executive secretary of

JOHNSTON, ERIC A.—*Continued*

the National League of Decency. Johnston answered his critics on May 20, defending the production code as a "form of restraint."

He stated that "if our movies were half as bad as some people complain there would be censorship laws in all states and cities. . . . The goal of producers is to make pictures reasonably accepted by reasonable people" (New York *Post*, May 22, 1955). He said it was evident that there was "an accumulation of violence in pictures" and that "next year's films will be less concerned with brutality" (New York *Herald Tribune*, May 21, 1955).

Other phases of the MPAA are the community service department, title registration bureau, foreign and theatre and television service departments. Johnston has stated that he favors subscription television. He has been successful in obtaining agreements with both foreign governments and distributors under which the major film companies have received sizable remittances on their "frozen" motion picture earnings abroad (New York *Times*, September 22, 1954).

Johnston has honorary degrees from many colleges and universities, including Whitworth College in Spokane (1943), of which he is a trustee. Johnston is tall, lean and fit. He never worries and is at home with all sorts of people. He spent eight weeks in Russia in 1944 at Moscow's invitation and had a three-hour talk with Stalin. In his only venture into politics, he was defeated in an attempt to be elected to the U.S. Senate as a Republican from the state of Washington in 1940.

He married Ina Harriet Hughes on October 22, 1922. The Johnstons have two daughters, Harriet Ballinger (Mrs. William Carlin Fix) and Elizabeth Hughes (Mrs. Herbert Butler). Johnston is an Episcopalian and a Republican. He is the author of *We're All In It* (Dutton, 1948).

"It is on the front of social ideas and political concepts," Johnston has stated, "that the real contest with communism must be fought and won. . . . That is why I want to see skilled and friendly Americans, as many as we can send, go into the underdeveloped countries on specific missions of helpfulness" (*Department of State Bulletin*, October 6, 1952).

References

Newsweek 44:77+ O 18 '54
Scholastic 49:13 O 28 '46
Time 57:18 Ja 29 '51 por
U S News 30:28+ F 2 '51 por; 31:26+ Jl 13 '51
Bell, L. Eric Johnston *In* Forbes, B. C. ed. America's Fifty Foremost Business Leaders (1948)
Business Executives of America (1950)
Fitzhugh, H. L., and Fitzhugh, P. K. Concise Biographical Dictionary of Famous Men and Women (1949)
National Cyclopædia of American Biography Current Vol H (1952)
Who's Who in America, 1954-55
Who's Who in Commerce and Industry (1953)
World Biography (1954)

JOHNSTONE, MARGARET BLAIR, REV. Feb. 9, 1913- Minister; author; lecturer

Address: b. c/o Union Congregational Church, Groton, Mass.; h. Main St., Groton, Mass.

"Hold on. Don't run. One step more." These seven words are the personal credo of the Reverend Mrs. Margaret Blair Johnstone, Congregational minister, writer, lecturer, and marital counselor. One of her principal themes is "religion at work in life," and she declares she was not "called" but "driven" by God into the ministry (New York *Times Book Review*, June 27, 1954).

Since October 1950 Mrs. Johnstone has been pastor of the Union Parish, which includes the congregations of the Union Congregational Church (Groton, Massachusetts) and the Christian Union Church (West Groton). Previously she had developed an experimental church program which is now known as the Essex Parish in New York State, and had served as minister of Chicago's Addison Street Congregational Church. She is the author of the book, *Create Your Own Tomorrow* (Doubleday, 1950), and her autobiography, *When God Says "No": Faith's Starting Point* (Simon and Schuster, 1954).

Margaret Blair was born in Detroit, Michigan on February 9, 1913, the daughter of Williams Tubbs and Margaret (Rhoads) Blair. Her father had been a Methodist clergyman in Wyoming Conference, Pennsylvania, and her mother, a schoolteacher. She has a brother, Williams T., who is a minister in West Palm Beach, Florida. Her parents taught her the three steps in her personal credo that have led her to a successful adjustment to life and to a career as a minister of the gospel.

She attended Western High School in Detroit. After her father died, her mother took the family to Redford, a suburb of Detroit, where Margaret was graduated from Redford High School in 1929. She was active in forensic, swimming, and Y.W.C.A. groups, and worked after school in a music store. When she was fourteen years old, she preached her first sermon in the local Calvary Methodist Church. "From the first I loved to make speeches," she wrote in her autobiography.

Offered a tuition scholarship to Albion College, Michigan, Margaret entered in 1929, and majored in sociology and psychology. During her first year, she earned her expenses for board and room by waiting on table, typing theses, and working as college reporter on the town newspaper. In her sophomore year, she prepared and served breakfast for the college dormitory, and thus gained her living expenses in full. She took part in debating and Y.W.C.A. activities, and received the Albion College Baldwin Oratorical Prize.

Influenced by her mother's wish that she become a teacher, she prepared for this profession, but when she received her A.B. degree in 1933 during the depression, she found no teaching position available. Upon the suggestion of the college dean, she decided to prepare for social work, and studied at the Chicago Theological Seminary. She earned both her resident and tuition expenses there, and held a field work post at the Chicago Commons settlement house.

Her major course subjects were religion and mental health, and religion and the arts. The former was taught by Dr. Anton Boisen, one of the four persons she states influenced the choice of her lifework. The others were Dr. Arthur C. McGiffert of the seminary, Dr. Fred Eastman, and the Reverend John A. Yeoman. She received the B.D. degree from the seminary in 1937; her thesis was entitled "The Life of Henry George."

Miss Blair served as a student minister of Addison Street Congregational Church in Chicago from October 1934 until May 1937, and helped to increase the membership, finances, and activities of the deteriorated parish. Before she had a single course in the procedures, she conducted funerals, married couples, and baptized babies. After considerable debate, in May 1935, the Chicago Congregational Advisory Board granted Miss Blair, its only woman applicant, a license to preach.

Ordained a minister of the Congregational Church on May 28, 1937, she accepted a call as minister of the Addison Street Congregational Church. In defending herself as a candidate for ordination, she had said: "My ministry, as I see it, is to identify myself with those who, though they have lost faith, *will* find new life in the process of rediscovery. To me faith is life's growing edge."

During her ten-year association with the Addison Street church, the size of the congregation increased from eighty-one members to 200, and the parish became self-supporting. Miss Blair's success brought her invitations to speak in various churches. Her marriage to Joseph Franklin Johnstone and the birth of two children did not interrupt her professional career.

For a brief period in the summer of 1944, Mrs. Johnstone became discouraged and considered leaving the ministry. That fall, however, encouraged by her husband, she decided to accept an offer from the New York Congregational Christian Conference to develop an experimental church program in Wadhams, New York. Beginning her services in April 1945, she built up a unified parish (now called the Essex Parish) among the villages of Wadhams, Whallonsburg, Essex and Willsboro.

The Reverend Robert Howland joined her in administering to this parish, which covers an area of 150 square miles, has four churches, and includes 500 families representing Congregational, Methodist, Presbyterian, and Baptist denominations. In 1950, she reported that the annual parish budget had increased from about $3,000 in 1945 to $12,000.

Concurrently with her work in the Essex Parish, the young minister began writing articles for magazines (*Coronet, Collier's, Look,* etc.). Her subjects included religion and morals, marriage and family problems, social ethics, and personality integration. During the summer of 1950, she signed a professional lecture contract. She now uses her thirty days of

REV. MARGARET BLAIR JOHNSTONE

annual vacation for lecturing throughout the country. One of her popular lectures is "How to Live on 24 Hours a Day."

An illness of several months, in 1950, interrupted her parish work, but brought her a new dimension of understanding. In her autobiography she tells how she progressed from faith that "consisted of what I knew" to the belief that "faith is what you go on when you don't know." In June 1949 she had led a seminar on methods for reviving rural churches, held by the International Council at Wellesley College in Massachusetts, and had been invited by Albert Buckner Coe, superintendent of the Massachusetts Congregational Conference, to be a candidate for a church in his state.

In May 1950 the Reverend Mrs. Johnstone accepted a call to become the minister of the Union Parish which has a membership of about 450 persons in Groton and West Groton, Massachusetts. Selected after twenty-nine men candidates had been rejected, she was installed on October 29, 1950.

Her ministry emphasizes counseling people, and she considers her premarital counseling important. "Just as her articles get 'terrific reader-response,' so does her premarital and postmarital counseling," wrote Barbara A. Browne (Lowell *Sun,* September 10, 1950). Of the hundreds of couples who have taken her counseling course, and the vow she requires that they will keep in touch with her at least once every five years after their marriage, only three, she stated in her autobiography, have not remained married.

In her article entitled "How to Live With a Woman" (*Collier's,* July 11, 1953), the woman minister gave her basic rule for making a marriage "practically invulnerable": "Establish an us-against-the-world feeling, and never lose it." Discussing "Sex Education for Parents" (*Coronet,* April 1951), she claims that "what

JOHNSTONE, M. B., REV.—*Continued*

we need most in sex education, both as parents and children, are not facts of life, but facts for living."

Of her autobiography, *When God Says "No": Faith's Starting Point,* Margaret Parsons wrote: "It is a fast-moving narrative, with a sense of humor which makes the most of every incident having a touch of the ridiculous. . . [The author] shows herself as still growing, changing, testing, accepting, and rejecting in her spiritual life" (Worcester *Telegram,* April 11, 1954).

Dr. Ben Bradford commented on the book in a review for the New York *Times* (June 27, 1954), "Moralizing in theme but never 'preachy' in tone, this book will help any person seeking a firmer faith in these troublesome times."

She married Joseph Franklin Johnstone, an advertising salesman, on April 10, 1939. Their children are Joan Margaret and Joseph Blair. She is five feet ten inches tall, weighs 150 pounds, has brown eyes and brown hair. She is an independent voter. Among her hobbies are antiques, music, "reading, of course," and knitting.

Reverend Mrs. Johnstone is described as a "forceful preacher" (Worcester *Telegram*). Asked if men attend the church of a woman minister, she replied: "They certainly do" (Boston *Traveler,* October 25, 1950). She feels that "faith is not a collection of beliefs, but the boiled-down essence of experiences. That essence is like maple syrup. If it is the real thing it never comes cheaply or without hard work."

References

Boston Traveler O 25 '50
Lowell Sun p36 S 10 '50 por
Worcester Evening Gazette p7 N 11 '50

JONES, SIR HAROLD SPENCER Mar. 29, 1890- British astronomer

Address: Royal Greenwich Observatory, Herstmonceux Castle, Sussex, England

The director of the Royal Greenwich Observatory of England and the Astronomer Royal is Sir Harold Spencer Jones, who is the tenth in a span of 280 years to hold the title. The Observatory, now in process of removal from its location on the Thames River, a short distance from London, to a site at Herstmonceux Castle, Sussex, was established at Greenwich in 1675 by King Charles II "for the finding out of the longitude of places for perfecting navigation and astronomy." Since 1884 the observatory is the place upon which the world's zero of longitude is reckoned (known as the Greenwich meridian), on which is based a world time system, Greenwich Mean Time.

Sir Harold Spencer Jones who was appointed in 1933 as Astronomer Royal, devoted ten years of calculation and computation to a new estimate (made public in 1941) of the sun's distance from the earth. He is the author of the books *General Astronomy, Worlds Without End,* and *Life in Other Worlds.*

The eldest son of the late H. C. Jones, an accountant, Harold Spencer Jones was born March 29, 1890 in Kensington, a residential borough of London. He completed his secondary education at Latymer Upper School in Hammersmith and then won a scholarship to Jesus College, Cambridge, where he distinguished himself in "Geometrical and Physical Optics, Electricity and Magnetism, Astronomy and Celestial Media" (London *Times,* December 23, 1932).

Having received his B.A. degree in 1911, Spencer Jones continued his studies at Cambridge University, winning many scholastic prizes in natural science. In 1912 he was also awarded a B.Sc. degree by London University.

When the chief assistant to the Astronomer Royal, Sir Frank Dyson, resigned in 1913, Jones was appointed to the vacant position. During World War I he served at the Woolwich Arsenal as assistant director of inspection of optical instruments for the wartime Ministry of Munitions. Also in 1914 Jones received his M.A. degree from Cambridge, was elected to a fellowship at Jesus College, and began the first of nine years as editor of *The Observatory.*

Resuming his duties at the Greenwich Observatory in 1918, he worked chiefly on problems of variations of latitude, stellar photometry, the measurement of star distances and the preparation of magnetic charts for the Admiralty. In 1922 his *General Astronomy* (Arnold and Company) was published. This work is still a standard textbook, a third edition having been issued in 1951.

For ten years beginning in 1923 Jones was His Majesty's Astronomer in South Africa at the Cape of Good Hope, where he began a program which has since determined the distance of more than 1,200 stars in the southern hemisphere and the measurement of their proper-motions. In this work, and in the compilation of the orbits of double stars, Jones collaborated with the Yale University Observatory in Johannesburg. In 1925, when the star Nova Pictoris made its appearance, he worked in association with the Union of South Africa's Johannesburg Observatory, participating in discoveries about the way in which a star is born. He received a Sc.D. degree in 1925 from Cambridge University. At the time the International Astronomical Union convened in 1928 at Leyden in the Netherlands, he was named to head its Solar Parallax Commission.

The minor planet Eros was due to make its closest approach to the earth in 1931, and the belief was held that on the basis of measurements made of its distance from the earth's center at that time it would be possible to make a more accurate computation of the sun's distance from the earth than had ever been feasible before. Several nations and twenty-five observatories were asked to carry out this work between October 1930 and May 1931. Some 2,847 photographic plates were used, the most significant results being achieved with the two photographic telescopes at the Cape of Good Hope Observatory.

Although ten more years of computation and calculation were to pass before the new estimate of the sun's distance from the earth was made public, the importance of the work of the Solar Parallax Commission was recognized by the scientific world. Dr. Jones was made a fellow of the Royal Society in 1930. When consideration was given to finding a successor to the Astronomer Royal, Sir Frank Dyson (who was due to retire on February 28, 1933) the choice fell on Dr. Jones. The King's sanction of his appointment to this £2,500-a-year post was announced on December 22, 1932. (The appointment is made by the Prime Minister, and the Astronomer Royal is an employee of the Admiralty.)

Meanwhile (1935), he had completed his second book, *Worlds Without End* (published in Great Britain by English Universities Press and in the United States by Macmillan Company, and later revised for a third edition issued in 1948), which describes in terms comprehensible by the layman not only the relationship of the earth, its moon, and the other planets in our solar system, but that of our solar system to other universes.

Great Britain's telephone service is operated by the Post Office, which in 1936 instituted the first "talking clock" controlled by a signal each hour from the Royal Observatory. (For his Halley Lecture delivered at Oxford University on June 5, 1939, Dr. Jones chose "The Earth as a Clock" as his subject.) Some time before World War II, the first of the crystal quartz clocks, which have superseded the old pendulum clocks, had been installed at Greenwich under the Astronomer General's direction; and during the war an Air Almanac was instituted to assist airmen in air navigation, a companion service to the Nautical Almanac, originally produced by the Royal Observatory.

Life on Other Planets, Jones's third book, was published in 1940 (in Britain by English Universities Press and in the United States by Macmillan Company) and is in 1955 in a third revised edition. This work, which combines a description of the solar universe with a study of the chemical and other conditions necessary for the maintenance of living organisms, demonstrates the possibility of some kind of life (although probably not intelligent human life) on Mars, and the likelihood that life will develop on Venus in future eons.

Reviewing it in *Nature,* Sir James Jeans called it "a model of what such a book should be, popular and scientific." Sir Arthur Eddington, in *The Spectator,* found that "many interesting lines of astronomical inquiry are brought together in this book," which "shows science, not so much in a conquering phase, as hard pressed to make a little progress against formidable obstacles."

"The goal for which astronomers have so long been seeking has at last been reached." So wrote Dr. Jones in the first number of the professional quarterly *Endeavour* (January 1942) regarding the conclusions of the Solar Parallax Commission first released towards the end of the preceding year. The new estimate—

British Inf. Services
SIR HAROLD SPENCER JONES

which has not yet been superseded—of the distance of the sun from the earth is 93,005,000 miles, with a margin of error of 9,000 miles. (The previous estimate was 92,900,000 miles.) As a result of his ten years of calculation "the most exact value of the moon's mass was also determined" (*Encyclopedia Americana*).

Dr. Jones became Sir Harold Spencer Jones in June 1943. The year before, he had contributed the chapter on planets to *Science Looks Ahead* (Oxford University Press), compiled by A. M. Low. His brief historical survey, *The Royal Observatory* (Longmans), written for the Science in Britain Series, was published in London in 1943 and New York in 1944. His popularly written *Picture of the Universe* was a 1947 publication in the Raven Books series. He is the author of the chapters "Structure of the Universe" in Herbert Dingle's *Century of Science* (Roy Publishers) and "Astronomy" in A. E. Heath's *Scientific Thought in the Twentieth Century* (Watts), both published in the United States in 1951.

Air pollution through London smoke, together with growing impairment of night observation because of neon signs, caused the Admiralty to purchase Herstmonceux Castle in Sussex as a new site for the Royal Observatory. (The castle, which dates back to 1440, stands in 370 acres of grounds and is about sixty-six miles from London.) Prior to World War II the magnetic department had been moved from Greenwich to Leith Hill in Surrey, and in 1948 removal of the main observatory to Herstmonceux (expected to be completed in 1956) was begun. It is here that "the great telescope, memorial to Sir Isaac Newton, with a reflecting mirror of ninety-eight inches diameter" is being installed. The name Royal Greenwich Observatory has been retained. The Greenwich meridian remains the world's zero of longitude, with Greenwich Mean Time being now "figured one minute and twenty seconds away from the meridian."

During a lecture tour of the United States in the winter of 1948-1949, the Astronomer Royal announced that the atomic clock developed by the Bureau of Standards in Washington "would probably be substituted for the time-keeping apparatus" at the Royal Observatory. A room at Herstmonceux was subsequently set aside for the atomic clock, which is governed by vibration of ammonia molecules, and, in the view of Sir Harold, "seems to be an almost absolute measure of time."

Addressing the Royal Institution at London on May 23, 1952, the Astronomer Royal gave what (in the words of John Hillaby of the New York *Times*) "amounted to official approval" of the "new theory of creation for all universal matter" which had been put forward four years earlier by the Cambridge astrophysicists Thomas Gould and Herman Bondi. In the course of his address Sir Harold "explained how cosmic matter (atomic or subatomic hydrogen) could be created out of the energy of the universe." The author of articles advocating the adoption of a new universal calendar as well as the twenty-four-hour clock as the standard timepiece, Sir Harold in December 1953 spoke at the Hayden Planetarium in New York on the topic "Is There a Need for Calendar Revision?" He strongly endorsed the proposals of the World Calendar Association. It was announced that Sir Harold will be succeeded by Richard V. Woolley on January 1, 1956, when he retires as the director of the Royal Greenwich Observatory and as the Astronomer Royal.

Among the organizations and institutions in which Sir Harold has held executive positions are the Royal Astronomical Society, British Astronomical Association, Horological Institute, and Institute of Navigation, National College of Horology and Instrument Technology. He is an honorary member of the American Astronomical Society, the United States National Academy of Science, the American Academy of Arts and Sciences, and the Royal Swedish Academy, the Royal Danish Academy, and the Royal Belgian Academy. He has won many medals. The universities of Copenhagen and Brussels are among several that have granted him honorary degrees. His clubs are the Athenæum and United Service.

Jones married Gladys Mary Owers on May 18, 1918. They have two sons, David Henry Spencer (born 1923) and John (born 1933). Sir Harold and Lady Jones now occupy quarters in Herstmonceux. "It's not one of those grim castles," he explains. "The rooms are light and airy. It's the earliest large brick building—rose-pink brick—in England."

References

Illus Lond N 215:377 S 10 '49 por
N Y Herald Tribune p 1 D 7 '53 por
Nature 152:665+ D 4 '43
Burke's Peerage, Baronetage, and Knightage (1953)
Who's Who, 1954
World Biography (1954)

JONES, ROBERT EDMOND Dec. 12, 1887-Nov. 26, 1954 Theatrical designer; credited with starting the "new stagecraft" in 1915 which superseded the realistic settings in David Belasco's productions; noted for his scenic designs for Eugene O'Neill's plays; also designed settings and costumes for ballet and opera; wrote *The Dramatic Imagination* (1941). See *Current Biography* (Nov.) 1946.

Obituary

N Y Times p13 N 27 '54

JORDAN, W(ILBUR) K(ITCHENER) Jan. 15, 1902- College president; historian

Address: b. c/o Radcliffe College, 10 Garden St., Cambridge 38, Mass.; h. 76 Brattle St., Cambridge 38, Mass.

"One of the great cultural revolutions of our time has been the transfer from men to women of the responsibility for our cultural values," said W. K. Jordan, president of Radcliffe College. "This is an enormous responsibility, and I have faith in women." As head of the college, which in 1954 celebrated its seventy-fifth anniversary, Jordan has helped in the development of the "joint instruction" system now existing between the women's educational institution and Harvard University.

Before succeeding Ada L. Comstock in the presidency in 1943, Jordan was with the University of Chicago as professor of history and as general editor of the university's press. From 1937 to 1940 he was professor of history at Scripps and Claremont colleges in California and previously had taught at Harvard University. In addition to performing administrative duties at Cambridge, Jordan holds a position on the Harvard staff as professor of history.

Wilbur Kitchener Jordan was born in Lynnville, Indiana on January 15, 1902, the son of William and Emma (Shepard) Jordan. He spent his early years in Indiana and attended Oakland City College there. He majored in history and was awarded the B.A. degree in 1923. The next year he had a position as instructor in history at the University of Missouri, where he stayed until 1925. He then entered Harvard University, majored in history, and was granted an M.A. degree in 1926. From then to 1931, when he received his Ph.D. degree from Harvard, he spent much of his time in research abroad, in 1929 holding the Harvard Sterling traveling fellowship. On the completion of his graduate studies, he became an instructor in history and tutor in history, government, and economics at Harvard. In 1934 he also began a period as tutor in history at Radcliffe College. He remained in Cambridge until 1937 when he accepted the position of professor of history at Scripps and Claremont colleges, California. After three years in California he moved to the University of Chicago, first as associate professor and later as both full professor of history and general editor of the University of Chicago Press.

The university press with which Jordan was associated is the second oldest in the United States—it was organized in 1891. Publishing approximately 100 books a year, it serves principally as a means of printing the discoveries and teachings of the Chicago faculty. In addition, it publishes textbooks and the syllabus used in the general introductory courses taken by all students. A small number of non-technical volumes are published each year in economics and in social and political subjects for distribution to the general public.

In 1943 Jordan left Chicago and became president of Radcliffe College. He again joined the Harvard faculty and since 1946 has been a professor of history there. Radcliffe College, which has an enrollment of some 1,000 undergraduate and graduate students and which occupies sixteen acres in the Harvard Square section of Cambridge, had its origin as the Society for the Collegiate Instruction of Women, founded in 1879 to educate women in subjects similar to those taught at Harvard. In 1894 the school received its present name (in honor of Ann Radcliffe, Lady Mowlson), as well as the privilege of awarding degrees, provided that such degrees received the approval of Harvard executives.

Until 1943, when Jordan became president, students at Radcliffe received all instruction in quarters separate from Harvard students. Although the college had its own faculty, many courses were given by Harvard professors and in most cases these courses were duplicates of ones given the Harvard students. As a wartime measure it was suggested that such duplication could be avoided by permitting the upper-class women students to attend classes in the Harvard buildings, with Radcliffe turning over a major portion of its tuition fees to Harvard. Now the privilege of attending Harvard classrooms has been extended to women in all but a few courses. Labeled "joint instruction" by the cooperating administrations, this practice has had the effect of establishing a coeducational system at Harvard, although in extracurricular activities the institutions are separate.

In his inauguration speech President Jordan spoke of the destruction of honest scholarship under Fascism and emphasized the duty of scholars to guard their intellectual integrity; he also pointed out the effect of war on the recognition of the abilities of women, who now expect no favors or need make no apologies as they participate "fully and fruitfully in the ordinary activities of the world about them."

In 1951 at a forum on the subject of the responsibilities of women in the national emergency, he stated that he did not favor a draft of women at that time and urged the increased use of educated women in professional, administrative, and scholarly programs, where they could be employed to better advantage than in "riveting." Jordan was among the twenty-five prominent residents of Massachusetts who in January 1951 sent a letter to President Truman

Peter Rossiter

W. K. JORDAN

advocating immediate formation of an Atlantic Union, a free federation of democracies to meet the critical international situation.

Jordan's scholarly work has been in the field of English history. His most significant contribution has been a four-volume work, *The Development of Religious Toleration in England,* published between 1932 and 1940. Of the first volume, which covered the period from the Reformation to the death of Queen Elizabeth I, Harold Laski wrote in the *New Statesman and Nation:* "With this book, a new scholar of the highest promise enters the field of historical studies."

In the second volume, Jordan treated the period from the accession of James I to the convention of the Long Parliament (1603-1640); in the third volume, the period from the convention of the Long Parliament to the Restoration (1640-1660); and in the fourth, he dealt with the "attainment of the theory and accommodations in thought and institutions, 1640-1660." Well received by English and American critics, the work was praised for the "picturesqueness" of the writing and the richness and interest of the subject matter. The London *Times Literary Supplement* commented that the fourth volume "is characterized, as its predecessors have been, by great erudition, minute research, and the magisterial authority of its conclusions. . . . Not only the massive erudition, but the lucid marshaling of so much evidence compels admiration."

In *Men of Substance* (1942), Jordan examined the religious, political, and social thinking of two English revolutionists, Henry Parker and Henry Robinson, during the period from 1642 to 1660. While agreeing with other reviewers on the scholarly merits of the work, R. M. Krapp in *American Historical Review* thought the presentation "verbose, repetitious,

JORDAN, W. K.—*Continued*

and muddy" and Harold Laski in the *New Statesman and Nation* found that the book suffered from too many facts.

President Jordan is a fellow of the Royal Historical Society of England and a member of the American Academy of Arts and Sciences, the American Historical Association, and the historical societies of Vermont, Massachusetts and Cambridge. He serves on the advisory council of the Folger Shakespeare Library in Washington, D.C., on the board of trustees of the Emma Willard School (Troy, New York) and of the Protein Foundation, on the advisory board of the Longy School of Music (Cambridge), and as a member of the corporation of the Winsor School, Boston. He belongs to the Old South Association of Boston.

He is an honorary member of the Harvard chapter of Phi Beta Kappa and was in 1943 the recipient of a Guggenheim fellowship. The following year he received an honorary L.H.D. degree from Bates College (Lewiston, Maine). His church is the Episcopal. He married Frances Ruml on April 13, 1929. She was the dean of Radcliffe College from 1934 to 1939.

References

N Y Times p14 Ag 20 '43 por
Directory of American Scholars (1951)
Leaders in Education (1948)
Who's Who in America, 1954-55
World Biography (1954)

JULIANA, QUEEN OF THE NETHERLANDS Apr. 30, 1909-

Address: Soestdijk Palace, Baarn, the Netherlands

NOTE: This biography supersedes the article which appeared in *Current Biography* in 1944.

The reign of Queen Juliana, sovereign of the royal house of Orange, has been notable for the Netherlands' vigorous support of international cooperative efforts such as the Marshall Plan, NATO, the Benelux union, and projects for a European army. She has ruled Holland's more than 10,000,000 inhabitants since the abdication of her mother, Queen Wilhelmina, on September 4, 1948 after half a century on the throne.

A constitutional and hereditary monarch, the Dutch Queen may be said to *possess* but not to *exercise* power; she possesses "the right to be consulted, the right to encourage, the right to warn"; in practice, the political decisions are those of the Cabinet and Parliament. The friendly, informal manner of Queen Juliana has won many friends for her country, especially in the United States which she has visited on several occasions.

The early years of Juliana's reign comprised the difficult postwar period of rehabilitation and adjustment following the tyrannical Nazi occupation. Granting independence to Indonesia in 1949 cost the Netherlands most of her empire in the East Indies. The devastating floods of February 1953, which inundated a large area of the lowlands and caused damage estimated at $200,000,000, also threatened the economic recovery of Holland (the name popularly applied to the entire Netherlands empire).

Nevertheless, under Juliana's rule, the Netherlands has changed from a debtor to a creditor nation, producing by 1953 about 50 per cent more goods than it had before the war. The income from its oil refineries in Curaçao and Aruba in the Antilles (West Indies), which are among the largest in the world, from its agricultural and dairy products, and its traditional Dutch industry and thrift have all contributed to its economic stability.

Juliana was born on April 30, 1909, in the Royal Palace at The Hague, province of South Holland. Her parents were the twenty-eight-year-old Queen Wilhelmina and Prince Henry (Wladimir Albert Ernst) of the Netherlands, Duke of Mecklenburg-Schwerin. A salute of fifty-one guns heralded the arrival of the Princess; it was a joyous event as the royal pair had waited eight years for a child. It meant that another woman would rule Holland; Wilhelmina had begun her reign in 1890, in her early years under the guidance of her mother, Princess Emma, as regent.

The new Princess was baptized Juliana Louise Emma Marie Wilhelmina, Princess of Orange-Nassau, Duchess of Mecklenburg, each name honoring a distinguished relative: Juliana, the mother of William the Silent, founder of the Dutch Republic in the sixteenth century and of the dynasty of Orange-Nassau; Louise de Coligny, William the Silent's fourth wife; Queen Emma, Wilhelmina's popular mother; the Grand Duchess Marie of Mecklenburg, Juliana's paternal grandmother; and Queen Wilhelmina herself.

The first years of the life of Juliaantje (little Juliana), as the Dutch people called her, were not greatly different from those of any other child. Pictures of the period show her in the sandbox, riding a pony or playing with dolls at Het Loo, a palace originally built as a hunting lodge. Later, during World War I, The Royal Family lived mostly in Huis Ten Bosch (House in the Woods) near The Hague.

Princess Juliana was privately tutored with a few other girls in a class led by Miss B. Cohen Stuart, who followed the methods of Jan Ligthart, then Holland's most progressive educator. She learned to skate, to ride a horse and a bicycle, and to speak French, German and English. She also studied Latin and Greek, history, geography, constitutional law, economics, mathematics and physics.

On April 30, 1927, when she was eighteen, Princess Juliana came of age, according to the Netherlands Constitution. She was then given her own income, household staff and home, the Kneuterdijk Palace at The Hague. She became a member of the Dutch Reformed Church and a member of the State Council, the Queen's highest advisory body. From then on she always accompanied the Queen in the "golden coach" on the third Tuesday in September for the annual opening of Parliament.

In September 1927 Juliana entered the University of Leiden, founded in 1575 by William the Silent. She enrolled as a regular student under the name of Julia van Bueren and studied Dutch literature, Indonesian law, international law, ethnology and history. After two and a half years she was awarded an honorary degree in literature and philosophy.

During the economic depression of the 1930's Juliana formed a National Crisis Committee to help alleviate distress. Her work during the next five years as honorary chairman of this group was, as one biographer put it, "a course in knowledge of life as it is." In 1934 she became president of the Netherlands Red Cross, after the death of her father, who had headed that organization for many years.

On September 8, 1936 her engagement to the German Prince Bernhard of Lippe-Biesterfeld was announced. Bernhard (Leopold Frederic Everhard Jules Curt Charles Godfrey Pierre) had taken his law degree in Berlin in 1935 and then, having joined the staff of I. G. Farben, worked in the Berlin, Paris and Amsterdam offices of the German dye trust.

The two young people (the Princess was twenty-seven and the Prince, twenty-five) are said to have met and fallen in love while attending the 1936 Olympic winter games in Garmisch-Partenkirchen (Germany). Because of the unpopularity of Nazism in the Netherlands, careful investigation was made of the political ideas of Prince Bernhard.

Following the approval of Queen Wilhelmina and the government, the couple were married at a simple Calvinist ceremony in the old Groote Kerk in The Hague on January 7, 1937. They moved into Soestdijk Palace the following April; the modernized old white mansion, a wedding gift from Queen Wilhelmina and the Dutch people, continues to be their home.

On January 31, 1938 their daughter, Princess Beatrix (now heiress-apparent), was born. A second daughter, Princess Irene, was born on August 5, 1939. On May 10, 1940 German troops invaded Holland, thereby violating its neutrality. During the occupation the country suffered heavily. Nearly all of its Jewish population (some 112,000) were exterminated. Prince Bernhard joined with Dutch troops still resisting the Nazi invaders. Later in the year (1940) Queen Wilhelmina appointed him chief liaison officer between the Dutch and British armed forces. Dutch forces fought alongside the Allies against Germany and Japan.

Princess Juliana and her two children left The Hague on May 12, 1940, going first to London as the guest of Lord Bledisloe. Then in June the Princess accepted an invitation from her aunt, Princess Alice, wife of Canada's Governor-General, the Earl of Athlone, to come to the Dominion. The trip was made in secrecy on the Dutch cruiser *Sumatra*. On Juliana's arrival in Canada she addressed the people over the radio. "Do not give me your pity," she told them. "Pity is for the weak and our terrible fate has made us stronger than ever before." During the war years the family lived in Ottawa, where Juliana's third child, Princess Margriet, was born on January 19, 1943.

Netherlands Inf. Service

JULIANA,
QUEEN OF THE NETHERLANDS

In exile Juliana was active in war charities and made several trips to the United States, spending the 1942 and 1944 summers in New England. Her visit in November 1943 to Surinam (Dutch Guiana) made her the first member of the house of Orange ever to go to that Netherlands colony in northeastern South America.

Back in Holland after the war, Juliana continued her social welfare activities, working for the relief of the thousands of destitute. One of her concerns was the plight of Europe's displaced persons. On two occasions she wrote to President Harry S. Truman appealing for a new approach to the refugee problem. The whole royal family, reunited, returned to Soestdijk. Here, on February 18, 1947, Princess Maria Christine was born. The older daughters were sent to Kees Boeke's Workshop, a progressive school in the vicinity.

Well trained by her mother to assume the responsibilities of royalty, the Crown Princess acted many times as secretary to Queen Wilhelmina and in October 1947 was designated as regent, to reign for several months while the Queen rested. After fifty years of rule, Wilhelmina abdicated in favor of Juliana, who was inaugurated as Queen of the Netherlands in a solemn service in the fifteenth-century Nieuwe Kerk in Amsterdam on September 6, 1948. (According to the tradition, Dutch rulers are enthroned, but not crowned, since the crown belongs to the Republic.)

Before taking the oath on the Constitution Juliana said: "I have been called to a task so heavy that no one who has the least notion of it would desire it, and at the same time so splendid that I can only say, 'Who am I that

JULIANA, QUEEN—*Continued*
I should be allowed to perform it?'" (*World*, May 1954).

Throughout World War II when the Dutch East Indies was occupied by the Japanese, nationalists were active, and in August 1945 they established the Republic of Indonesia, which claimed rule over Java, Madura and Sumatra. Dutch opposition led to warfare which continued until 1947 even after the Dutch recognition of the republic by the Cheribon agreement. Finally, after a conference at The Hague, mediated by the United Nations, Indonesia became a sovereign country on December 27, 1949.

The Queen presided at the ceremony at which the 300-year-old sovereignty of the Dutch East Indies was transferred to the United States of Indonesia, comprising the republic of Indonesia and fifteen Dutch-supported states. (Federation gave way to a unified republic in August 1950, headed by President Soekarno, linked to the Netherlands "only through a union under the Dutch crown." This union ended in August 1954. Indonesia no longer legally recognizes the sovereignty of Queen Juliana, but Dutch economic interests are safeguarded by the new agreement.) The end of the Dutch East Indian empire has raised many new problems: the Netherlands has had to absorb an influx of hundreds of thousands of returning Dutch settlers and many Eurasians.

The Netherlands is governed by a coalition Cabinet representing the Catholic People's Party and the Labor Party, and is headed by Prime Minister-President Willem Drees. The following powers, conditioned by the operation of ministerial responsibility, as expressed by the requirement of a ministerial counter-signature, are vested in the Crown by the Netherlands Constitution: authority to enforce the laws, including authority to make regulations; command of the armed forces; power of appointment and removal; conduct of foreign relations; power of initiative in legislation (shared with the Legislature); power to approve or disapprove bills; power of summoning, adjourning, proroguing, and dissolving the Legislature and the power of pardon.

On November 8, 1953 Queen Juliana stood on a new dike to help her people celebrate the final damming-out of the North Sea waters that had brought the disastrous flood of February of that year which had cost the lives of over 2,000 people. The Queen took an active part in rescue work. "She arrived in the striken provinces on the first day, traveling by boat, plane and helicopter, in boots, an old coat, a kerchief around her head" (*World*, May 1954).

Since becoming Queen, Juliana has paid official visits to France, Great Britain, Luxembourg, and the United States. During her twenty-one-day tour of the United States in April and May of 1952, the Queen, who writes her own speeches and speaks English fluently, addressed a joint session of Congress and made a number of speeches in various parts of the country.

The late Anne O'Hare McCormick in the New York *Times* commented that her speeches had a flavor of their own and that they were "fresh, unconventional and personal—not ready-made diplomatic addresses, not speeches from the Throne, but the utterances of an unpretentious woman of good sense and great goodwill who comes here to share her thoughts with people she knows well." Another writer for the *Times* observed, "Her speaking voice has a hushed, sincere quality that borders on the dramatic" (Daniel L. Schorr, New York *Times Magazine*, March 30, 1952).

In an address at Columbia University in New York City, where Juliana received an honorary LL.D. degree in April 1952, she discussed the basic aims and achievements of education. Other American honorary degrees awarded to Juliana are from Hope College in Holland (Michigan), Mount Holyoke College, Princeton University, and Central College in Pella (Iowa), a center of Dutch immigration. The Netherlanders' Queen has also been honored in Great Britain, recently during a visit in May 1954 when she was honored by London's historic Worshipful Company of Carpenters.

Queen Juliana was the patron in late 1954 of the first major show of Dutch paintings held in the United States since 1909. The international loan exhibition, "Dutch Painting, The Golden Age," was made up of nearly a hundred paintings by such masters as Hals, Rembrandt, Steen and Vermeer borrowed from collections in the United States and Europe. After the New York showing at the Metropolitan Museum of Art from October 30 through December 19, 1954, the exhibition was scheduled to be seen at the Toledo (Ohio) Museum of Art and the Art Gallery of Toronto (Canada).

Known for her dislike of pomp and elaborate ceremony, Queen Juliana, in one of the earliest acts of her reign, abolished the curtsy as an outmoded expression of respect. She also broke with royal tradition by not naming her four children after relatives. Her household at Soestdijk is informal; Juliana plans the family meals and spends as much time as she can with her children. "To a Queen," she has been quoted as saying, "her duties as a mother are as important as they are to any other Dutch woman."

The Queen has light brown hair, blue eyes, and is five feet eight inches tall. She plays the violin and is fond of music, the theater, and sports, particularly skating and skiing. She has a good sense of humor and simple tastes.

References

Christian Sci Mon p9 Mr 31 '52 por
N Y Herald Tribune p28 Ap 15 '49 por; II p 1 Ap 6 '52 por
N Y Times Mag p12 Mr 30 '52 pors
N Y World-Telegram p27 Ap 2 '52 por
Pathfinder 59:22 Ap 9 '52 pors
Scholastic 60:6 Ap 16 '52 por
This Week p12 Mr 23 '52 pors
Who's Who in America, 1954-55
World Biography (1954)

KAGANOVICH, LAZAR M(OISEYEVICH) (kŭ-gŭ-nô'vyĭch lȧ zŭr-y') Nov. 22, 1893- Soviet government and Communist party official

Address: Council of Ministers, Moscow, U.S.S.R.

NOTE: This biography supersedes the article which appeared in *Current Biography* in 1942.

Sovphoto

LAZAR M. KAGANOVICH

As one of the five first deputy chairmen of the U.S.S.R. Council of Ministers, Lazar M. Kaganovich has far-reaching powers in the fields of transport and labor policy—and "he has demonstrated . . . his virtuosity as perhaps the finest administrator in Moscow." "His record of success on difficult missions gives him a special prestige," wrote W. W. Rostow (*The Dynamics of Soviet Society,* 1953).

Since 1918 Kaganovich has been a member of the All-Russian Central Executive Committee and has consistently been re-elected to this body and its successor, the U.S.S.R. Supreme Soviet. He was in charge of the construction of the famous Moscow subway and was influential in the rise to power of both Nikita S. Khrushchev and Nikolai A. Bulganin—respectively the heads of the present Communist party and the Soviet government. In 1934 Kaganovich was elected chairman of the party's Control Commission and directed the beginning of the 1934-1939 purges of the party ranks. He was "one of the top men" during this period, according to *Fortune* (September 1946).

Lazar Moiseyevich Kaganovich was born on on November 22, 1893 in the village of Kabany (now called Kaganovitch) in Kiev, of a poor Jewish family. He went to work at the age of fourteen in Kiev shoe factories, and became a skilled tanner. In 1911, when he was eighteen years old, he joined the Bolsheviks and became active in organizing party and trade union groups, leading strikes, and carrying on propaganda against the Czar's government.

In 1915 he was arrested and sent back to his native village. But he soon left, and under assumed names carried on party and union work in Kiev, Ekaterinoslav (now Dnepropetrovsk), Melitopol, and Yuzovka (now Stalino). Soon after the February revolution of 1917, which overthrew the Czar, Kaganovich went into the army and became the leader of the Bolshevik organization among the troops at Saratov.

The Provisional Government arrested Kaganovich, and after his escape he became the leader of the Bolshevik organization in Gomel. In the Bolshevik revolution of October 1917, he led the Gomel uprising. Kaganovich, as head of the Gomel organization, played a crucial role at this critical moment by convincing the Mogilev forces of the Provisional Government not to march to Petrograd to suppress the Bolsheviks and so Alexander Kerensky's Provisional Government was forced to flee.

As reported by Walter Duranty in *Stalin & Co.* (1949), "In the next two years, Kaganovich helped to organize the Red Army, without taking much personal part in the Civil War. He did, it seems, raise a rebellion of railroadmen and other workmen behind the lines of General Mamontov in the province of Voronezh. At that time [Klementii] Voroshilov was attacking Mamontov with an army from the front."

The Central Committee reassigned Kaganovich in September 1920, to Tashkent in Central Asia where, working under Joseph Stalin and Voroshilov, he played a major role in establishing Soviet power in Turkestan. Thus at the age of twenty-seven Kaganovich became one of the leading Bolshevik administrators as a member of the Council of Commissars of the new Turkestan Republic and finally the Mayor of Tashkent. (Later the Turkestan Republic was divided among the newly created Soviet Socialist Republics of Kazakh, Kirgiz, Tadzhik, Turkmen and Uzbek.)

In the latter part of 1920 War Commissar Leon Trotsky sought to dragoon and militarize the trade unions, but was opposed by Stalin. Kaganovich supported Stalin's view, and a short time later he was brought back to Moscow to work in the All-Russian Central Executive Committee (to which he had been elected in 1918), under Viacheslav M. Molotov in charge of the placement of party personnel.

Kaganovich was elected a member of the Central Committee of the Communist party in 1924 and served as one of this committee's secretaries in 1924 and 1925. He was assigned as general secretary of the Ukrainian Communist party from 1925 to 1928 and tried to pacify and rebuild that war-ravaged area. At the same time he pushed through the party's program of industrialization and collectivization. One of his chief lieutenants was Krushchev. In 1928 he moved back to Moscow to hold the post of secretary of the Central Committee of the Communist party of the Soviet Union. In that year the party was in the midst

KAGANOVICH, LAZAR M.—*Continued*
of a dispute over the role of the trade unions led by Mikhail Tomski. Kaganovich was elected to the presidium of the All-Union Council of Trade Unions (Michael T. Florinsky, *Towards an Understanding of the U.S.S.R.,* 1951).

Two years later, in 1930, Kaganovich was made a full member of the Political Bureau (Politburo, now known as the party Presidium). This organ is the inner executive committee or controlling body of the Russian Communist party and is the top policy and decision-making body in the party hierarchy. He has been re-elected consistently since then. In April 1930 he replaced Molotov as the first secretary of the Moscow region party organization.

Continuing to hold this post until March 1935, he directed an almost complete reorganization and reconstruction of the capital area and its economy. Again, as in the Ukraine, one of his chief assistants was Khrushchev. And he placed Bulganin in charge of the Moscow city government. One of his major accomplishments at this time was directing the construction of the famed Moscow subway.

After being placed in charge of the Central Committee's agriculture department in 1933, he made repeated trips throughout the Soviet Union to oversee the work of collectivization and grain collection. He directed the organization of party sections in machine tractor stations and collective farms, and in one year brought order out of chaos in the farm program. For his successful development of agriculture in the Moscow region, and changing the area from a consumption to a production basis, Kaganovich was awarded the Order of Lenin in 1933.

Another problem to which Kaganovich was assigned was that of transport. While production in other fields had soared, the railroads were unable to keep up and the economy was threatened with paralysis. To try to straighten this out, Kaganovich was named Commissar of Railways in 1935. Under his regime investment was poured into the railroads, the primary form of transport in the Soviet Union. In one year alone (1935) the railroads took a fifth of all the iron and steel produced within the country. For his success in reorganizing transport Kaganovich was given the Red Banner of Labor.

Kaganovich moved over to the post of People's Commissar of Heavy Industry in 1937, but in April 1938, after dividing heavy industry up between a number of commissariats, he returned to the post of People's Commissar of Transport. In August 1938 he was named assistant chairman of the Council of People's Commissars of the U.S.S.R. as well. In January 1939 Kaganovich took over as People's Commissar of the Fuel Industry, which he divided as he had the heavy industry commissariat, and continued until 1941 as People's Commissar of the Oil Industry.

During part of World War II (1942-43) Kaganovich was a member of the State Defense Committee, the super-cabinet that directed the national defense effort. He relinquished the post of People's Commissar of Transport in April 1942, became vice-chairman of the Committee for Coordination of all Transport. From December 1944 until 1946 Kaganovich was again vice-chairman of the Council of People's Commissars, and in 1946 he took over as Minister of the Construction Materials Industry, which was of crucial importance in the postwar reconstruction of Russia.

After the worst drought in fifty years had ruined the 1946 harvest in the Ukraine and touched off widespread misery and discontent, Kaganovich was rushed to the area to replace Krushchev as party secretary there. By the end of the next year the harvest was excellent, industry was back in production and reconstruction was well on the way. Khrushchev resumed his post and Kaganovich returned to Moscow as a deputy chairman of the Council of Ministers in 1947.

At the 1952 congress of the party held in October, Kaganovich was named to the Commission to Revise the Party Program. In the reorganization of the government after the death of Stalin on March 5, 1953, he was made a first deputy chairman of the Council of Ministers, in general charge of transport. Early in 1955 he assumed an additional position—chairman of the State Committee on Labor and Wages. In this post the "Iron Commissioner of yore," as Paul Wohl of the *Christian Science Monitor* (June 9, 1955) called him, is to "wield the broom as chairman of a committee which is to control all ministries and administrations and improve their work."

On Kaganovich's sixtieth birthday in 1953 he was again awarded the Order of Lenin. Besides his native village in the Ukraine, there is a city near Moscow, two villages in the Russian republic and one each in the Kirgiz and Tadzhik republics named for him.

His only trip outside the Soviet Union was to Prague in May 1955, for the anniversary of the liberation of that city from the Nazis. His brother, Mikhail, however, visited the United States in 1937 when he was a Deputy Commissar of Heavy Industry in charge of aviation. Kaganovich also has a sister named Rosa, who reportedly became Stalin's third wife. Kaganovich married a party worker in the trade unions, and there have been unconfirmed reports that his son Mikhail was married to Stalin's daughter Svetlana (New York *Times,* March 6, 1953).

General Walter Bedell Smith, former U.S. Ambassador to the U.S.S.R., has called Kaganovich "the best administrator in the Soviet Union," and Walter Duranty, a former New York *Times* correspondent in Moscow, says he has a "broad Rabelaisian humor." His speeches; some observers report, sparkle with humor and abound in human interest.

Time (June 6, 1955) wrote about him: "Kaganovich—one of the few original Bolsheviks to survive the purges, worked his passage across the Stalinist years by performing a score of . . . jobs for the old dictator. During the early collectivizations he forcibly put down peasant uprisings against the regime and punished whole areas by seizing foodstuffs and creating artificial famines. . . . He [is now] regarded as the chief advocate of the current collective leadership."

References

Bsns W p22+ My 15 '48
Fortune 34:228 S '46
Life 11:19 Jl 14 '41
N Y Times Mag p13 Ja 10 '54
Time 61:34 Mr 16 '53
U S News 34:62 Mr 13 '53
Duranty, W. Stalin & Co. (1949)
International Who's Who, 1954
Rostow, W. W. The Dynamics of Soviet Society (1953)
World Biography (1954)

KAPITZA, PETER L(EONIDOVICH)

(kȧ'pyĭ-tsŭ pyô'tẽr) June 26, 1894- Soviet physicist

Address: b. Institute for Physical Problems of the Academy of Sciences, Kalujskoe shosse 32, Moscow, U.S.S.R.

The nuclear physicist who first liquefied helium is Peter Kapitza, a Russian, whose experiments with high magnetic fields, low temperatures in studies of electrical properties of matter and the liquefaction of gases have won him international renown. There has been much speculation among scientists and journalists as to his whereabouts in the Soviet Union during recent years, and as to his contribution to working out the physical problems of the structure of the atom and producing the hydrogen bomb. It was announced on April 15, 1955 in the newspaper *Vechernaya Moskva* (*Evening Moscow*) and reported in the New York *Times* (July 30, 1955) that the U.S.S.R. had placed him on a committee in charge of building an earth-satellite.

Impetus to the Russian project was given by the announcement that the United States Government on July 29, 1955 would take the first major step toward interplanetary flight—the launching of an unmanned earth satellite in space, scheduled for 1957 or 1958. Thus the two countries now appear to be in a race for the glory of being the first to complete this objective.

Kapitza was assistant director of magnetic research at the Cavendish Laboratory, Cambridge University, England from 1924 to 1932 and a fellow at Trinity College from 1925 to 1934. While on a visit to Russia in 1934 he was detained by the Soviet government (whether willingly or unwillingly cannot be determined), and became director of a new Institute for Physical Problems of the Academy of Sciences, in Moscow. In 1945 he reportedly headed an expedition studying cosmic rays near Lake Karagel in the Armenian Soviet Socialist Republic, and in November of that year announced the discovery that protons were knocked from lead by cosmic rays.

Peter Leonidovich Kapitza was born in Kronshtadt, Russia on June 26, 1894 (old style calendar), son of Olga (Stebnitsckiy) and General Leonid Kapitza, who served in the Czarist corps of engineers. He attended secondary school at Kronshtadt and during the revolution was a student at the Petrograd Polytechnical Institute.

After his graduation in 1919 he remained at the institute as a member of the faculty of engineering until 1921, when he went to England to study at Cambridge University under Sir Ernest Rutherford, who won the Nobel Prize in chemistry in 1908 and was created the 1st Baron of Rutherford in 1921.

At Cambridge, Kapitza began his researches into the generation and precise measurement of very intense magnetic fields. Academic honors came rapidly; in 1923 he was named to the Clerk Maxwell fellowship at Cambridge, the following year he was named assistant director of magnetic research at the Cavendish Laboratory, and in 1925 he was named a fellow of Trinity College. One of Kapitza's colleagues at the laboratory was (Sir) John Cockcroft (see *C.B.*, 1948), who later became director of Great Britain's Atomic Energy Research Establishment at Harwell.

In the course of his researches Kapitza invented a new method for liquefying gases, and succeeded in producing liquid helium (which condenses at only a few degrees above absolute zero) with much less difficulty by his improved technique. His method, which is widely used in the U.S.S.R. to produce large volumes of liquid gas for research and industry, is based on the principle of adiabatic expansion, that is, the super-cooled gas is suddenly allowed to expand, as it approaches the condensation point, without further temperature change, the expansion completing the liquefying process. The practical success of this method is a tribute to Kapitza's engineering and mechanical skill as well as his mastery of the theory involved, for the principle was well-known.

Kapitza devised apparatus with which to obtain magnetic fields six to eight times greater than ever before. For studying the reactions of metals in these intense fields it was necessary to have the lowest possible temperature, to cut molecular action to a minimum.

The reports on Kapitza's experiments published in professional journals won him a high scientific reputation, and in 1929 he was elected a fellow of the British Royal Society and a corresponding member of the Academy of Sciences of the U.S.S.R. He was named to the Messel research professorship of the Royal Society, which offered Cambridge University a grant to build a special laboratory for Kapitza (New York *Times*, December 2, 1930).

This new laboratory, named for Ludwig Mond, was opened at Cambridge University on February 3, 1933. However, Kapitza was able to use it for only a short time. In the summer of 1934 he went to Russia, as he had done in previous years, to deliver lectures and also to attend a scientific conference. A few days before he was to return to England the Soviet government informed him that he must remain in Moscow.

Sovphoto

PETER L. KAPITZA

Lord Rutherford made a strong appeal for the release of Kapitza. "While no one disputes that the Soviet authorities have a legal claim upon Professor Kapitza's services," he wrote (*The Times* of London, April 29, 1935), "their sudden action in commandeering them without any previous warning has profoundly disturbed the university and the scientific world." This and other appeals were fruitless, and by the fall of 1935 Cambridge University accepted the offer of the Soviet government to buy the equipment of the Mond Laboratory at cost—$50,000. It was transported to Moscow and set up at the Institute for Physical Problems, which had been established for Kapitza's research.

Although compelled to remain in the Soviet Union, he was not isolated. Kapitza, who lived in a small, British-style cottage built near his laboratory and was allowed to wear British tweeds which he loves, was visited by Cockcroft and other former colleagues at Cambridge. At the same time he continued to publish reports of his nonmilitary work abroad.

At the Institute for Physical Problems Kapitza continued his work on the problem of the liquefaction of gases and by 1938 he had perfected a simple turbine device, no larger than a match box and weighing about half a pound, which could produce between fifty-five and sixty-five pounds of liquid air an hour at a fraction of the cost of previous processes.

This device was of tremendous industrial importance, and Kapitza obtained a patent on it in the United States (New York *Times,* May 3, 1942). It revolutionized the Soviet steel industry. By substituting oxygen (distilled from liquid air) for air in blast furnaces, steel output could be increased five or six times while costs were reduced by 25 to 30 per cent.

Many honors were conferred upon Kapitza and his associates. For development of the gas liquefaction device they were awarded in 1938 a bonus of 25,000 rubles by the U.S.S.R. Academy of Sciences, and the next year Kapitza was elected a full member of the academy. In 1941 he was awarded a Stalin Prize of 100,000 rubles, and in 1942 the Faraday Medal of the Council of Electrical Engineers of England.

In 1943 he was awarded another Stalin Prize and the Order of Lenin. In the following year the American Franklin Institute of Philadelphia honored him with its Franklin Medal for "remarkable contributions to experimental physics." In 1945 he was made a Hero of Socialist Labor and in 1946 a member of the National Academy of Sciences of the United States. He accepted the diploma of the Royal Danish Academy in 1946 (New York *Times,* July 9, 1946).

Scientists of the Western world, who had presumed that Kapitza had been detained in Russia against his will were surprised to find him, when they saw him in June 1945 at the 220th anniversary of the Russian Academy of Sciences "a convinced Communist" (reported by Marquis W. Childs, New York *Post,* November 16, 1945).

Some observers believe he was the key man in the research that led in August 1953 to the explosion of the first Soviet hydrogen bomb (New York *Times,* August 20, 1953). In 1955 it was announced that Kapitza was a member of a committee formed to launch an earth-satellite in space.

He is a member of the Soviet Interdepartmental Commission for the Coordination of Scientific Research Work on Inter-Planetary Communication.

Kapitza has two sons, and has been married twice. His first wife, Nadezhda Tschernosvitova, died. He later married Anna Krylova, the daughter of the Soviet mathematician A. N. Krylov. His British colleagues recall how Kapitza appeared "bitterly anti-Communist; his father had been a Czarist aristocrat, and his young wife and child had perished in the famine that followed the Bolshevik revolution."

Richard E. Lauterbach, a news service correspondent who visited the scientist at his Moscow laboratory in the summer of 1946 described Kapitza (*Science Illustrated,* March 1948) as "a pleasant, well-fed, square-faced man of medium height with big, baby-blue eyes and light brown hair which swirls uncombed over his wide, unwrinkled forehead." He enjoys playing chess.

References

Chem & Eng N 24:759+ Mr 25 '46
Look 18:24 Jl 13 '54
Nature 149:241 F 28 '42
Newsweek 43:46+ Mr 1 '54
Sci Illus 3:24+ Mr '48
Science 99:367+ My 5 '44

International Who's Who, 1954
Who's Who, 1955
World Biography (1954)

KÁRMÁN, THEODORE VON *See* von Kármán, Theodore

KASNER, EDWARD Apr. 2, 1878-Jan. 7, 1955 Mathematician; taught at Columbia University for fifty years; believed in making mathematics interesting and wrote several books to that end, including *Mathematics and the Imagination*; invented word "googol" (representing the number one followed by 100 zeros); known for work in conformal geometry and geometry of divergent series. See *Current Biography* (Nov.) 1943.

Obituary

N Y Times p13 Ja 8 '55

KAUR, RAJKUMARI AMRIT Feb. 2, 1889- Indian Cabinet Minister; social worker
Address: b. Ministry of Health, New Delhi, India; h. 2 Willingdon Crescent, New Delhi, India; "Manorville" Summer Hill, Simla West, India

As a guest of the Rockefeller Foundation, Rajkumari (Princess) Amrit Kaur, India's Minister of Health and only woman Cabinet member, made her first visit to the United States in October 1954. The Princess studied new trends in medical education for use in postgraduate courses at the All-India Institute of Medical Science in New Delhi, India. Canada and Puerto Rico were included in her tour and she spoke before many groups on India's health problems.

Princess Amrit was one of the founders of the All-India Women's Conference, and in 1930 joined the secretarial staff of Mohandas Gandhi. For sixteen years she worked with him in the struggle for India's independence. She was elected to Parliament as a member of India's Congress party, and became Minister of Health in 1947.

During the ensuing period, she has instituted many health, education and welfare reforms, notably the national malaria-control and child-welfare programs. She was the first woman to serve on the advisory board of education for the government of India. As India's chief delegate, Princess Amrit attended five sessions of the World Health Organization assembly and was president of the assembly in 1950. She has written many articles on social reforms.

The only daughter of Raja Sir Harnam Singh and Rani Lady Harnam Singh, Rajkumari Amrit Kaur was born on February 2, 1889 in Kapurthala Palace in Lucknow, India. The family were the rulers of Kapurthala. Her father was created hereditary Raja in 1907, and was decorated for public service in 1922 by the British government. Early recollections of the Princess were of the customary "pomp and ceremony" of the period.

With her six brothers she went to England; they were placed under the guardianship of an English vicar who reared them in simple austere fashion. Princess Amrit attended the Sherborne School for Girls in Dorsetshire and London and later studied at Oxford University.

Life in England gave the Princess an awareness of her own country's problems and she returned to India determined to interest others in social reforms. With her mother, Princess Amrit worked to alleviate the hardships of peasants in nearby areas. During World War I, the Princess became a nurse and worked in several hospitals. She met Gandhi in 1919 and believed in his ideals, but was not able to participate actively in public life until after her father's death in May 1930.

Convinced that women in government could solve many problems that affected women and children, Princess Amrit helped to establish the All-India Women's Conference in 1927, and wrote articles appealing to the educated women of the country. Of this period, she wrote in a pamphlet called *To Women* (1935) that since a high percentage of the women of India were illiterate, her earlier writings met with little success, except to make her realize that she must work with Gandhi.

In 1930 she became Gandhi's secretary. Interviewed by Marquis W. Childs (Washington *Post*, October 31, 1950) in New Delhi, the Princess said that she had accompanied Gandhi to one of India's poorest villages and they had done the work of the "untouchables" such as sweeping the streets. Gandhi had considered "complete abnegation and sacrifice" necessary to set an example of simple living as part of the process of education..

During her sixteen years of active work with Gandhi, Princess Amrit served on the board of trustees of the All-India Spinners' Association and the Hindustani Talimi Sangh, which assisted peasants in handicrafts and helped to establish the Lady Irwin College for Domestic Science in New Delhi. On behalf of several women's organizations, she spoke on woman's place in the new Constitution before Lord Lothian's Franchise Committee in 1932, and repeated her comments the following year before the Joint Select Committee of the British Parliament.

She was elected president of the All-India Women's Conference in 1938, and in the same year became the first woman member of the advisory board of education for the government of India. During the "Quit India movement" (Gandhi's nonviolence demonstration to free India), which attracted world-wide attention in 1942, the Princess was arrested with other leaders and spent nearly three years in prison.

Soon after her release in 1945, Princess Amrit went to London as deputy leader of the Indian delegation to the United Nations Educational, Scientific and Cultural Organization, and the following year, attended the Paris session of UNESCO in the same capacity. She was elected to the provisional Parliament of India in 1947. (The provisional Constitution permitted literate women to vote and hold office. Universal suffrage was not granted until January 26, 1950.)

When Nehru assumed the Premiership on August 15, 1947, he appointed Princess Amrit as Health Minister. After India became a Republic, another election was held in January 1952 and the Princess was elected to the House

Information Service of India

RAJKUMARI AMRIT KAUR

of the People (lower house of Parliament) from Himachal Pradesh, a backward mountain area, and was reappointed as Health Minister. She was also Minister of Communications in 1951 and 1952.

After Gandhi's assassination on January 30, 1948, Princess Amrit continued to speak of him as a "living presence" and to be guided by his philosophy. She headed the Indian delegation to the annual meetings in Rome and Geneva of the WHO for four consecutive years (1948-1951) and again in 1953, and was president of the assembly in 1950. The Indian Council of Child Welfare and a maternal health project were started in 1949, as the result of her knowledge of such activities in other countries. Her report of the WHO assembly held in Geneva in May 1950 appeared in the *United Nations Bulletin* (June 15, 1950) and told of the adoption of a four-year international plan to combat communicable diseases, malaria and tuberculosis. (Malaria, alone, killed 1,000,000 out of 100,000,000 cases annually in India, prior to 1949.)

Medical colleges have increased from seventeen to thirty-five and two nursing schools were established under Princess Amrit's public health program.

Speaking before the United Nations, as reported in the New York *Times* (October 30, 1954), the Princess cited the progress made in the antimalaria campaign as "one of the triumphs of international cooperation." The United Nations had allocated $667,000 for DDT to spray homes and swamps and equipment valued at $850,000 for a DDT plant in India. The United States had also donated DDT. In the fight against tuberculosis, the U.N. had contributed over $1,000,000. Within a period of five years the maternal and infant mortality rate had declined, and life expectancy in India had risen from twenty-seven to thirty-two years.

While in Ottawa, Canada, the Princess, according to *Saturday Night* (November 20, 1954), spoke to several groups and credited the Rockefeller and Ford Foundations and the Colombo Plan with lending invaluable support to India's health program. She said that plans to produce penicillin were going forward and would extend to other antibiotics. In her article "Real Hope For the Tens Of Millions" *United Nations* (December 1954) Princess Amrit related that food production in the Himalayan Terai, once a malarial swamp, had increased by 30 per cent. In three tuberculosis-control centers—New Delhi, Travancore and Patna—14,000,000 people had been inoculated against that disease.

In an interview with the Health Minister after she returned to New Delhi, Homer Bigart in the New York *Herald Tribune* (March 24, 1955) wrote that the Princess estimated that by 1961, the nation-wide spraying campaign would have caused such a sharp drop in malaria that the Ministry could begin a campaign against typhoid and dysentery. On May 6, 1955 the (Jonas E.) Salk anti-polio vaccine formula was presented to the Princess by the U.S. Ambassador to India, John Sherman Cooper. She said that India would immediately undertake the manufacture of the anti-polio vaccine.

Princess Amrit Kaur usually wears a colorful native costume. She has been described as a small woman with gray hair, dark eyes and a dynamic personality. Following the custom of all unmarried girls and women of the princely house of Kapurthala, she uses the name Kaur. Her brother, Raja Maharaj Singh, inherited their father's title. He was a delegate to the United Nations in 1946 and 1947 and Governor of Bombay from 1948 to 1952. The Princess is a devout Christian and a strict vegetarian. She is fond of children and flowers and likes Western music and drama. She is president of the Delhi Music Society.

Outside of her work, her keenest interest is in sports. As a girl, she was a tennis champion, and is now president of the All-India Lawn Tennis Association and the National Sports Club of India and chairman of the Rajkumari Sports Coaching Committee which she founded.

Among welfare agencies in which she holds office are the Indian Red Cross Society, International Red Cross, League of Red Cross Societies, Tuberculosis Association in India and St. John's Ambulance Brigade. She was president of the All-India Conference of Social Work in 1948 and 1949. The princess has said that she found joy in the pioneer work of building India after its independence and added: "I believe whole-heartedly in . . . Gandhi's creed of truth and nonviolence as the only way for world peace and prosperity."

References

Ind Woman 27:282+ O '48 por
N Y Times p13 O 30 '54 por
Indian and Pakistan Year Book and Who's Who, 1948
International Who's Who, 1954
World Biography (1954)

KAZANTZAKIS, NIKOS (kä-zän-tzä'kĭs nē'kōs) Dec. 2, 1885- Greek author; playwright

Address: b. c/o Simon & Schuster, Inc., 630 5th Ave., New York 20; h. Villa Manolitz, Antibes, France

The author of more than thirty books of drama, prose, poetry, and philosophy, Nikos Kazantzakis is widely regarded as a distinguished man of letters. Most of his work has been translated from the Greek into other languages, and two of his novels have been published in the United States. Of his book *Zorba the Greek,* the December 21, 1953 issue of *Time* noted that it was "the richest, most exuberant novel of the year." Thomas Mann wrote that the novel *The Greek Passion* "is without doubt a work of high artistic order, formed by a tender and firm hand, and built up with strong dynamic power" (*Saturday Review,* January 23, 1954).

NIKOS KAZANTZAKIS

Kazantzakis served as director general in the Greek Ministry of Public Welfare after World War I and as Minister of State in 1945. At the invitation of the British Council, he visited England at two different periods to study the intellectual life of the people, and the French government invited him to study the intellectual life of postwar France. He has also been director of the bureau of translation of the classics, United Nations Educational, Scientific, and Cultural Organization.

Born in Candia, Crete on December 2, 1885, Nikos Kazantzakis is the son of Michael and Maria (Christodoulzki) Kazantzakis. His early years were spent on the island of Crete, which furnished the background for some of his later literary work. He attended the University of Athens, was graduated in 1906 and remained at the university to study law.

After he received a Doctor of Laws degree, he went to France where he studied philosophy with Henri Bergson. He also studied literature and art for four years in Germany and Italy. When Kazantzakis returned to Greece, he devoted his time to writing. His first published book was a novel, *The Serpent and the Lily.* The University of Athens awarded him literary prizes for his dramas *The Dawn Glows* and *The Foreman.*

After the first World War, in 1919, Kazantzakis accepted the post of director general in the Ministry of Public Welfare. At that time thousands of Greeks were stranded and in grave danger of starvation in the Caucasus and Southern Russia after a series of civil wars. As head of a rescue mission, Kazantzakis arranged for first-aid measures, food, clothing, medical supplies and transportation. About 150,000 Greeks were returned to Greece with the assistance of the mission. He resigned in 1927 when the work of the mission was accomplished to resume his literary activities.

With the aim of helping people of different nationalities to understand each other, Kazantzakis made several journeys to countries in Europe, Asia and Africa and wrote a series of travel publications on Spain, Russia, China, and Japan. The British Council invited him to survey the customs of the people of Britain and he spent seven months in England. His booklet, *England,* was the result of this visit. Before World War II, he lived on the island of Aegina, devoting himself to literary and philosophical work.

His books on philosophy, *Nietzsche and the Philosophy of Law, Bergson,* and *Asceticism,* have been used as textbooks in several European universities. Some of his plays and novels written in metrical form were transposed into narrative form when translated from the Greek into other European languages.

His work was interrupted in 1945 during the political strife in Greece when he accepted the appointment as Minister of State in the (Themistocles) Sophoulis Cabinet. Kazantzakis had hoped to be of service in adjusting the difficulties that had arisen between the political parties. He resigned when his efforts failed. On the anniversary of Greek independence, March 25, 1946, his historical play, *Kapodistrias,* was produced by the National Theatre in Athens.

Another invitation to visit England was extended by the British Council to Kazantzakis in 1946. He returned and spent four months among intellectual circles, and wrote on the intellectual life of postwar Britain. The French government urged him to visit Paris to study the intellectual life of France. Before Kazantzakis could begin this survey, he was appointed director of the bureau of translations of the classics for UNESCO. This covered all nations and all periods. He held this post during 1947 and 1948. He was elected president of the

Greek Writers' Society in 1950, and in 1952 he was a leading candidate for the Nobel Prize in Literature.

The Odyssey, his Homeric epic in 33,333 lines of seventeen syllables each, was translated into English prose by Kimon Friar for *New Directions in Prose & Poetry # 13* (New Directions, 1951). The epic as composed by Kazantzakis was three times the length of Homer's *Odyssey* and began where Homer ends. "Voyage with Charon," from his epic, translated by Kimon Friar, appeared in *Poetry* magazine (June 1951). Other selections from *The Odyssey,* "The Bed," "The Oar," and "The King of the Bulls," were published in *New World Writing #2* (New American Library, 1952). A series of classics which Kazantzakis translated into modern Greek verse included Homer's *Odyssey* and *Iliad,* Goethe's *Faust* and Dante's *Divine Comedy.*

Zorba the Greek, a novel, was published in London (Lehmann, 1952) and was his first novel published in the United States (Simon & Schuster, 1953). Zorba is an old Greek workman, who is a philosopher and hedonist. He goes to Crete to be in charge of the workmen in a mine. In Crete he accomplishes fantastic feats of physical prowess and tells erotic stories of his adventures. The London *Times Literary Supplement* (October 3, 1952) reported that the book was for those whose tastes run to "banquets, rather than utility snacks." *Time* (April 20, 1953) said that Zorba was every man who cast "a larger shadow on the world" than the world cast upon him. Richard Winston (New York *Herald Tribune,* April 19, 1953) commented that the novel was written with a "gay good humor and a striking originality."

A second novel, *The Greek Passion* (Simon & Schuster, 1953), published in the United States, relates the story of the Turkish town of Lycovrissi, where the Greek Orthodox priests and elders "found it easy, a year ahead of time, to fill most of the parts in their Passion play... the chosen actors never gave their Passion play. Instead, along with the townsfolk of Lycovrissi, they lived it. . . . Kazantzakis shows how the suffering and crucifixion of Christ in Roman Judea might be re-enacted in a modern setting. . . ." (*Time,* January 11, 1954). Harrison Smith (*Saturday Review,* January 23, 1954) called it a "strange and wild story" whose forty or more characters "come vividly to life." *The Greek Passion* was also translated into Norwegian, Swedish and German. The German edition of a later novel *Die Letzte Versuchung* (The Last Temptation) was placed on the Roman Catholic index of "forbidden books" (New York *Times,* April 29, 1954).

Elèni Samios and Kazantzakis were married in 1945. They are living in France and Kazantzakis is continuing his study of French intellectual life. Travel and reading are his favorite forms of recreation. Kazantzakis has gray hair and black eyes and is of medium build. He has no political affiliations and has described himself as "free" in matters of religion.

Reference

Laughlin, J. ed. New Directions in Prose & Poetry # 13 (1951)

KEENAN, JOSEPH B(ERRY) Jan. 11, 1888-Dec. 8, 1954 Former U.S. Government official; lawyer; was assistant to the U.S. Attorney General in prosecuting "Machine Gun" Kelly and other racketeers; headed the Justice Department's criminal division and wrote the Lindbergh kidnapping law; chief prosecutor, International Military Tribunal before which Japanese Premier Hideki Tojo and twenty-seven Japanese militarists were charged with "crimes against humanity." See *Current Biography* (Sept.) 1946.

Obituary

N Y Times p33 D 9 '54

KELLY, E(VERETT) LOWELL Nov. 15, 1905- University professor; psychologist; association official

Address: b. c/o American Psychological Association, 1333 16th St., N.W., Washington 6, D.C.; University of Michigan, Ann Arbor, Mich.; h. 1115 Woodlawn Ave., Ann Arbor, Mich.

A specialist in clinical psychology who is known for his work in personality measurement, personnel selection, and training techniques, Dr. E. Lowell Kelly became president of the American Psychological Association in September 1954 for one year. (His successor is Dr. Theodore M. Newcomb.) Dr. Kelly is professor of psychology and director of the bureau of psychological services at the University of Michigan in Ann Arbor. He has been a consultant to the United States Office of Naval Research, the Institute of Mental Health of the United States Public Health Service, and the Selective Service System. At present he is a consultant to the Veterans' Administration.

Dr. Kelly has attempted to apply the techniques of clinical psychology in recruiting, selecting and training personnel, with the goal of meeting national needs in peace and war. For his wartime service with the Navy, Kelly received the Secretary of the Navy's Letter of Commendation with ribbon in 1945.

Everett Lowell Kelly was born in Kokomo, Indiana on November 15, 1905, one of the four children of Maude E. (Vickery) and Alva Elmont Kelly, a farmer. Young Kelly was graduated in 1923 from a local high school, where his extracurricular interests had been dramatics and basketball. Continuing his studies at Purdue University in Lafayette, Indiana, he majored in science and mathematics. His interest in the application of mathematics to psychology was stimulated at Purdue by Professor H. H. Remmers. Kelly was a member of the Amateur Radio Club, a part-time operator at the university radio station WBAA, and an associate member of Sigma Xi during his senior year.

After receiving his B.S. degree from Purdue in 1926, Kelly began his career in Taiban, New Mexico as a principal and high school teacher. In 1927 he became research assistant at the

Colorado State College of Education (Greeley) for two years, receiving his M.A. degree in psychology in 1928. The *Journal of Educational Psychology* published in March 1927 "An Empirical Study of the Validity of the Spearman-Brown Formula as Applied to the Purdue Rating Scale," based on work done by Kelly in collaboration with H. H. Remmers and N. W. Shock.

Appointed a research assistant at Stanford University in Palo Alto, California, Kelly worked with Professor Lewis Madison Terman. Kelly has written that Professors Terman and Walter Richard Miles, then of Stanford, were important in influencing him in the choice of his lifework. In 1930 Kelly received his Ph.D. degree in psychology from Stanford University. His doctor's thesis, "An Experimental Attempt to Produce Artificial Chromæsthesia by the Technique of the Conditioned Response," appeared in the *Journal of Experimental Psychology* (June 1934). In 1930 he accepted an assistant professorship of psychology at the University of Hawaii; he became an associate professor and director of admissions in the following year.

By means of a Social Science Research Council fellowship awarded in 1932, Kelly studied in Europe at universities in Berlin and Vienna. He returned to the United States in 1933 and was appointed an assistant professor at the University of Connecticut in Storrs. He became an associate professor and head of the psychology department in 1937.

Returning to Purdue University in 1938, Kelly served as an associate professor of psychology and director of the Psychological Clinic. During his four years there, he pursued the study of personality, attempting to isolate and measure traits and to devise accurate rating scales. He developed tests for the prediction of marital compatability and determined some factors for success in marriage. The psychologist at this time directed a project for improving techniques in basic flight instruction for the Civil Aeronautics Administration. In this work Kelly was concerned with adapting standard procedures of educational psychology rather than conducting experimental work.

In 1942 Kelly was called to active duty in the U.S. Navy. He was commissioned a lieutenant and served with the Bureau of Aeronautics, Bureau of Medicine and Surgery, and on the staff of Naval air training. Among the problems with which he was concerned were recording of flight instructions, selection and training of flight instructors, measurement of achievement, preparation of instructional materials, and the use of counseling techniques. He issued *U.S. Navy Patter,* which standardized vocabularies among naval flight instructors.

After attaining the rank of Commander in 1946, Dr. Kelly accepted a professorship in psychology at the University of Michigan. In 1949 he also became the director of the university's bureau of psychological services. From 1946 to 1951 he served as consultant to the Office of Naval Research; in 1946-1947 he was chief psychologist for the Veterans' Administration in Columbus, Ohio; and since 1946 he has been consultant to the U.S. Veterans' Administration.

Univ. of Michigan

E. LOWELL KELLY

In the spring of 1946 the Veterans' Administration completed plans for training large numbers of clinical psychologists in the graduate departments of psychology of many universities. The University of Michigan, in conjunction with this program, accepted the assignment of predicting differential success in training and in clinical competence of the students and evaluating techniques in selecting students.

In commenting on the study, Hans Jurgen Eysenck, in the chapter "Personality" in *Annual Review of Psychology, 1950-1952,* said: "Ultimately a solution to problems in the field of personality depends more on advances in methodology than on almost any other developments. The most impressive experiment under this heading is the Michigan study. . . . The organismic versus analytic approach may have become appreciably nearer solution through work such as that of Kelly and his assistants. . . ."

As consultant to the Selective Service System, a post he held from 1948 to 1953, Dr. Kelly was a member of a committee which attempted to clarify the seeming conflict between the need for training professionals and the military need for man power and recommended the draft deferment of students of particular ability. Kelly has stated: ". . . facts concerning differences in human ability must be allowed for if we are not to squander one of our most precious national resources. We doubt that a nation can afford to have certain young men spend two years in military service if the same nation is likely to need them even more a few years later as high level specialists in either a military or civilian organization" (*Science News Letter,* December 30, 1950).

(Continued next page)

KELLY, E. LOWELL—*Continued*

While Dr. Kelly was serving on the council of representatives, the governing body of the American Psychological Association, the council voted unanimously in September 1950 that the claims by La Fayette Ronald Hubbard, author of *Dianetics: The Modern Science of Mental Health; A Handbook of Dianetic Therapy* (1950), "are not supported by empirical evidence of the sort required for the establishment of scientific generalizations. In the public interest, the association . . . recommends to its members that the use of the techniques peculiar to Dianetics be limited to scientific investigations designed to test the validity of its claims" (New York *Times,* September 9, 1950).

Under the American Psychological Association's system of selecting its president a year in advance, the election of Dr. Kelly as its president for 1954-1955, to succeed Dr. O. Hobart Mowrer, was announced on August 29, 1953. Kelly had already served on several of the association's committees. He is also a past president of the Michigan Psychological Association (1948-1949) and is a fellow of the American Association for the Advancement of Science.

On December 25, 1938 he married Lillian Isaacs. They have two daughters, Patricia Ann and Pamela Jane, and a son, Paul Alan. Kelly is a trustee of the Huron Valley Amateur Radio Association and president of the Ann Arbor Cooperative Society, Inc. He is a Unitarian and a Democrat. Professor Kelly has hazel eyes and gray hair, is over five feet nine inches tall and weighs 175 pounds. Reading biography and flying model airplanes are among his favorite recreations.

References

N Y Times p19 S 8 '50; p52 Ag 30 '53
Time 41:39 Ap 26 '43
Leaders in Education (1948)
Who's Who in America, 1954-55
Who's Who in American Education, 1951-52

KELLY, GRACE (PATRICIA) Nov. 12, 1929- Actress

Address: b. c/o Metro-Goldwyn-Mayer Studios, 10202 W. Washington Blvd., Culver City, Calif.

The best motion picture actress of 1954, as selected by the New York Film Critics, is Grace Kelly, who, according to *Life* magazine, "has suddenly become the most valuable acting property in the movies." A member of the well-known Kelly family of Philadelphia and the daughter of a millionaire, Grace Kelly has in rapid succession appeared in a number of "prestige" films playing opposite such established stars as Gary Cooper, Clark Gable, Bing Crosby, and Ray Milland.

She was voted the best actress by the Academy of Motion Picture Arts and Sciences for 1954, winning the "Oscar" for her role in *The Country Girl.*

Under contract to Metro-Goldwyn-Mayer, she has been borrowed by other studios at a reported price of $50,000 a picture. The Hollywood columnist, Louella O. Parsons, says of her, ". . . in all the years I have been covering motion pictures, I have never known a new actress to be so much in demand." The motion picture director, Alfred Hitchcock, described Miss Kelly as "one of those people who fit into any leading-lady part."

Born in Philadelphia, Pennsylvania on November 12, 1929, Grace Patricia Kelly, one of the four children and second daughter of John Brendan and Margaret (Majer) Kelly, is a member of a family who has made news in business, politics, sports, and the theatre. Her father, a former Olympic oarsman and at one time, like his wife, a teacher of physical culture, is now a wealthy contractor. Reportedly beginning with a loan of $7,000 in 1919, he has built up a construction business estimated to be worth $18,000,000. He was formerly a Democratic City Committee Chairman and ran for the office of mayor in Philadelphia in 1935. As vice-president of the Fairmount Park Commission he sponsored the municipally operated playhouse in Philadelphia, for which he was honored at a luncheon given by the Actors Equity Association and the Association of Theatrical Agents and Managers in 1954.

Grace Kelly is the niece of George Kelly, Pulitzer Prize-winning playwright, author of *Craig's Wife,* and also of Walter C. Kelly, who was the well-known "Virginia Judge" of vaudeville. Her brother Jack won the Diamond Sculls at Henley, England in 1947, and again in 1949, thus fulfilling an ambition once held by his father, who had found himself disqualified from competing in the Henley regatta because he had done manual labor (bricklaying). Grace has two sisters, Margaret, an artist, and Lizanne, a college student.

The Ravenhill convent school and later the Stevens School, both in Germantown, Pennsylvania, provided Grace Kelly's education. She then attended the American Academy of Dramatic Arts in New York, where she studied for two years. During this period she worked as a photographer's model and earned enough in her second year to pay for her own tuition; she also obtained a number of acting engagements on television.

Summer stock gave her further theatrical experience; she appeared at the Bucks County Playhouse, the playhouse in Fairmount Park, and at Elitch Gardens in Denver, Colorado. Her debut on Broadway came in 1949 with the presentation of August Strindberg's play, *The Father,* starring Raymond Massey. The play ran for two months.

Hollywood now engaged her services and she was next seen (1951) in a bit part in the Twentieth Century-Fox film, *Fourteen Hours,* starring Paul Douglas. In 1952 she came to the fore with her portrayal of the Quaker wife in *High Noon,* playing opposite Gary Cooper. The film, directed by Fred Zinnemann and produced by Stanley Kramer, a United Artists release, was highly praised by the critics. Cooper's role was the major one in the picture;

Bosley Crowther in the New York *Times* picked out Grace Kelly as "among the best" in the supporting cast.

Following her appearance in *High Noon,* Miss Kelly was signed to a seven-year contract by MGM. She returned briefly to Broadway, however, appearing in the play *To Be Continued,* which opened in April 1952, but was shortly withdrawn.

Her next assignment in pictures placed Miss Kelly in a featured role. This was in *Mogambo,* released in the fall of 1953. An MGM offering, filmed in Africa under the direction of John Ford, it starred Clark Gable and Ava Gardner. Again Miss Kelly was cast in the role of a wife, this time an English one. "Miss Kelly gets the most chance at footage because of her position in the romantic triangle," the *Variety* critic commented. She received an Academy Award nomination for her role as a supporting actress and also the *Look* award for her work in the picture.

Warner Brothers borrowed the young actress for the film *Dial M for Murder,* directed by Alfred Hitchcock and released in the spring of 1954, in which Miss Kelly shared starring honors with Ray Milland. *Time* magazine observed, "As the intended victim, Grace Kelly is not required to do much more than look beautiful and vulnerable, and she accomplishes both with patrician distinction." Bosley Crowther wrote that she did "a nice job of acting the wife's bewilderment, terror and grief."

Paramount next borrowed Miss Kelly from MGM, to present her in *Rear Window,* opposite James Stewart and again under Hitchcock's direction. The film was released in August 1954. *Time* said that she played "the career girl with a subtle junior-executive swagger"; the New York *Herald Tribune* critic, Otis L. Guernsey, Jr., wrote: "As for Miss Kelly, she has never looked more lovable, and that is saying a great deal." Alton Cook in the New York *World-Telegram and Sun* commented on "the sad, earnest sweetness" with which she played her part.

The Country Girl, a screen version of Clifford Odets' play, was presented in December 1954 by Paramount and starred Bing Crosby and Grace Kelly, under the direction of George Seaton. "In the role of the wife who has tasted the last dregs of undiluted bitterness and humiliation, Grace Kelly is almost haggard in spite of her prettiness," Otis L. Guernsey, Jr., wrote. Alton Cook found that she "rises to the stoutest demand of her career so far. She has a complex character, with many of its details essential all the way but only implied until the finish. . . . She manages with assurance and vigor." She won the 1954 "Oscar" for her performance.

In MGM's *Green Fire* (1954) Miss Kelly, playing a Brazilian coffee plantation owner, was "as beautiful and as stubborn as finely tempered steel," according to Otis L. Guernsey, Jr. Archer Winsten (New York *Post*) commented that in the film, "nothing happens that adds to the laurels of Stewart Granger, Grace Kelly or Paul Douglas. They've all done better when better opportunities were offered."

GRACE KELLY

A faithful movie adaptation of James A. Michener's novel, *The Bridges at Toko-ri* with William Holden and Miss Kelly was released in January 1955. It portrays the contribution of Navy fliers in the Korean conflict.

In the judgment of *Life* magazine, the basis of Miss Kelly's success "is her combination of freshness, ladylike virtue, and underlying sex appeal." Van Johnson refers to her as the "thoroughbred type." Bing Crosby commented, "She has a good mind, a sense of humor, is considerate of those around her. She worked her head off to get the performance the director wanted from her."

Miss Kelly is about five feet six inches tall and weighs around 115 pounds. She has been described as having "corn-colored hair and cool blue eyes." She has an apartment in Hollywood and one in New York. For recreation she enjoys painting and sketching, and knitting. She says of herself, "I've had the breaks, and if I don't hit, it'll be my fault."

References

Life 32:142 My 5 '52 pors; 36:117+ Ap 26 '54 por
N Y World-Telegram p18 N 11 '54
Sat Eve Post 227:28+ O 30 '54 pors
Time 63:102 My 24 '54 por; 65:46+ Ja 31 '55 pors

KELLY, NANCY Mar. 25, 1921- Actress
Address: b. c/o Jane Broder, 40 E. 49th St., New York 17

After years of work in the theatre, motion pictures and radio, beginning in early childhood, actress Nancy Kelly achieved wide recognition for "the finest performance of her career" in *The Bad Seed,* Maxwell Anderson's hit play of

Talbot

NANCY KELLY

the 1954-1955 Broadway season. She received the American Theatre Wing's Antoinette Perry ("Tony") Award in March 1955.

As a child she appeared in over fifty Hollywood films, and in leading roles since 1938 in such pictures as *Stanley and Livingstone, Jesse James,* and *To the Shores of Tripoli.* Broadway critics first began to notice her when she portrayed the role of Blossom in Rachel Crothers' play *Susan and God* in 1937. She is remembered for her poignant performance as Marion Castle in *The Big Knife* in 1949 and as Emily Crane in *Season in the Sun* in 1950.

Nancy Kelly was born in Lowell, Massachusetts on March 25, 1921 to John A. Kelly and Ann Mary (Walsh) Kelly. She was the oldest of four children; her brothers are John A. Kelly, Jr., and Clement; her sister is Carole Elizabeth Kelly. Her father was a theatre ticket broker in New York City, where the family moved shortly after Nancy was born. Her mother was a model for the artist James Montgomery Flagg and later for the John Robert Powers model agency.

At the age of one year Nancy made her professional debut in a Flagg magazine illustration. She was regularly employed as a child model and was named America's Most Healthy Child at the age of five by a group of professional photographers. Nancy was educated at the Immaculate Conception Academy in New York City, St. Lawrence Academy, Long Island, and the Bentley School for Girls, where she participated in dramatic productions.

Her interest in acting came early and was inspired, Miss Kelly has said, by her mother. "Mother would tell bedtime stories," and then "we would act them out together," she has related (New York *Times,* November 27, 1938). Nancy Kelly began her screen career at an early age and by the time she was eight years old she had appeared in approximately fifty pictures. She "retired" from motion pictures after completing *Girl on the Barge* (1929).

Returning to New York, Miss Kelly made her first appearance on Broadway in A. A. Milne's *Give Me Yesterday,* which opened on March 4, 1931 and starred Louis Calhern and Sylvia Field. In the play Nancy Kelly, Jane Wyatt and Peter Donald, Jr., enacted the imaginative life of three small children.

A new channel for her acting talent was opened in 1934 when, at the age of thirteen, she began to appear in numerous roles on the radio. Programs on which she was heard included *Forty-Five Minutes from Hollywood, Renfrew of the Mounted, Cavalcade of America, The Wizard of Oz, Gangbusters, Myrt and Marge, Aunt Jenny's Real Life Stories,* and *The Shadow.* She participated regularly in *The March of Time* program for which she did imitations of famous personalities.

A notable achievement was scored by Miss Kelly in 1937 when she played the role of the bespectacled adolescent Blossom with braces on her teeth and loneliness in her heart in Rachel Crothers' comedy *Susan and God.* The play opened on October 7, 1937 at the Plymouth Theatre and starred Gertrude Lawrence.

In his review of the play, Brooks Atkinson referred to Miss Kelly's performance as one of "poignant simplicity and unstudied charm" (New York *Times,* October 8, 1937). Critic Joseph Wood Krutch wrote: "I am not sure that the most amusing portrait is not really that of the daughter [played by Nancy Kelly]" (*Nation,* October 23, 1937).

Success on Broadway led to an invitation from Hollywood and the girl who had left the film capital in 1929 returned in 1938 as a leading lady. She appeared in *Submarine Patrol* (1938), *Stanley and Livingstone* (1939), *Jesse James* (1939), *Tail Spin* (1939), *He Married His Wife* (1940), *A Very Young Lady* (1941), *Friendly Enemies* (1942), and *To the Shores of Tripoli* (1942). The *Motion Picture Herald-Fame* Poll for 1942 included Nancy Kelly as one of the "Stars of Tomorrow."

Other pictures in which she played include *Tornado* (1943), *Women in Bondage* (1944), *Gambler's Choice* (1944), *Show Business* with Eddie Cantor (1944), and *Double Exposure* (1944). In a 1951 interview Nancy Kelly reflected about these years: "I wish young actors wouldn't feel compelled to rush off to Hollywood as soon as they make good. They don't give themselves a chance to learn their trade honestly by scuttling the stage and scurrying West" (*Pictorial Review,* September 23, 1951).

On December 23, 1942 Miss Kelly appeared on Broadway in Terence Rattigan's *Flare Path,* a play which had been a hit in London, with Arthur Margetson and Alec Guinness, but it closed on January 2, 1943. Returning to Hollywood, Miss Kelly was seen in the motion pictures *Song of the Sarong* (1945), *Murder in the Music Hall* (1946), and *The Woman Who Came Back* (1946). Of her acting in the latter, Archer Winsten (New York *Post,* March 14, 1946) noted: "Nancy Kelly gives a much better performance than in the days when she was a well-advertised young star. . . ." The actress also was active in theatre productions on the West Coast.

A bitter play about Hollywood life brought Nancy Kelly back to New York to be featured in Clifford Odets' *The Big Knife* as Marion Castle, the wife of movie star Charlie Castle, played by John Garfield. Although the reviews were "mixed," the play, which opened on February 24, 1949, ran for 108 performances. The critical appraisal of Miss Kelly's work was favorable. "A beautiful performance," Brooks Atkinson commented, "the part of the wife is complex . . . and Nancy Kelly plays it with a kind of wistful beauty and authenticity" (New York *Times,* February 25, 1949).

Her first co-starring role in New York came in 1950 opposite Richard Whorf in Wolcott Gibbs's *Season in the Sun,* which opened on September 28, 1950 and played for 367 performances. Miss Kelly enacted the role of the wife of a disillusioned magazine writer who tries to become a novelist. William Hawkins wrote that the play is "a sophisticated uproar," and Nancy Kelly "wins your complete sympathy and holds it. The wife she plays is graceful and deserving of deep affection" (New York *World-Telegram and Sun,* September 29, 1950).

In the following season Nancy Kelly was starred in A. B. Shiffrin's *Twilight Walk* as a free-lance magazine writer with an interest in criminal psychology. Despite her personal success, the play, which opened on September 24, 1951, closed after eight performances. "Nancy Kelly, who can be relied on to pay playwrights the rare compliment of trying to figure out what goes on in their addled heads, did her best for this one" (*New Yorker,* October 6, 1951).

The years of hard work came to fruition when Nancy Kelly was starred in the part of Christine Penmark in Maxwell Anderson's play based on William March's novel *The Bad Seed,* which opened at the Forty-sixth Street Theatre on December 8, 1954.

The reviews of Miss Kelly's acting were glowing. Walter F. Kerr wrote: "Though Miss Kelly has done attractive work on Broadway before she has never really prepared us for the brilliance of the present portrait. The role is an almost unbearable, certainly an unrelieved, series of interlocking crises: the woman is simultaneously discovering that her daughter [played by Patty McCormack] is a criminal and that it is she herself who has passed on the taint" (New York *Herald Tribune,* December 19, 1954).

Brooks Atkinson observed: She "never forgets that she is not playing a figure in a melodrama, but a human character tortured beyond human endurance" (New York *Times,* December 19, 1954).

"Extraordinary skill and restraint" characterize her playing, commented Wolcott Gibbs, and hers is "a remarkable exhibition of passion under firm and intelligent control" (*New Yorker,* December 18, 1954). An Antoinette Perry Award of the American Theatre Wing was bestowed on Nancy Kelly on March 27, 1955 as the best actress of the season for her performance in *The Bad Seed.* After its twentieth week, the play was moved to the Coronet Theatre.

Miss Kelly was first married to the actor Edmund O'Brien; her second marriage was to Fred Jackman, Jr., a cameraman. On November 25, 1955 she was married to Warren Caro, executive director of the Theatre Guild.

She has medium brown hair, blue eyes and is slender. When living on the West Coast her favorite recreation is horseback riding. "All of us should realize," she has said, "that when we are successful we should thank our lucky stars" (*Pictorial Review,* September 23, 1951).

References

N Y Post pM5 Ag 12 '51 por
N Y Sunday News II p4 F 18 '51 por
N Y World-Telegram Ap 11 '49
Pictorial R p12 O 29 '50 por
Theatre Arts 39:28+ Ap '55 pors

Motion Picture and Television Almanac, 1953-54

KING FEISAL OF IRAQ *See* Feisal II, King of Iraq

KING HUSSEIN OF JORDAN *See* Hussein I, King of Hashemite Jordan

KITT, EARTHA Jan. 26, 1928- Actress; singer

Address: b. c/o Virginia Wicks, 548 E. 87th St., New York 28

"Nobody who goes to see *Mrs. Patterson* will doubt that Eartha Kitt is destined to be one of the major figures of our theatre," William Hawkins (New York *World-Telegram and Sun*) wrote in his review of the play which opened at the National Theatre on December 1, 1954, starring the actress-singer in her first dramatic role on Broadway. Variously described as "impressively feline," "salty," "earthy," "sultry," "incendiary," "sloe-eyed," with a "haunting voice," Eartha Kitt rose from abject poverty to become a famous night club singer, and has now demonstrated her talent as a dramatic actress.

Steps to stardom began for Eartha at the age of sixteen with a Katherine Dunham scholarship, followed by a five-year tour with the Dunham troupe. She made her night club debut at Carroll's in Paris and was soon the "rage of Paris," London and other cities. Orson Welles chose her as Helen of Troy for his European production of *Faust.*

Miss Kitt's fame "snowballed" during the two-year run of the revue *New Faces of 1952,* on Broadway and on tour. Her songs, recorded by RCA Victor, have made her a national jukebox favorite and led to appearances as guest artist on popular television shows.

Born January 26, 1928 in the back-country town of North, South Carolina, Eartha Kitt grew up in extreme poverty. Her father, William Kitt, a share-cropper, had his first good

EARTHA KITT

harvest in years and his daughter was named Eartha to "thank the earth." He disappeared soon afterward and two years later was reported dead. Her mother, Anna Mae (Riley) Kitt, tried to continue the little farm, but there was nothing left when she died. Eartha, then six, and her little sister, Anna Pearl, drifted from neighbor to neighbor, half-starved and beaten occasionally. She picked cotton in exchange for food and shelter until her mother's sister, Mamie Lue Riley, who lived in New York, sent for her when she was eight years old. She arrived in Harlem wearing the only clothes she owned.

There was little money and Eartha, left alone most of the time while her aunt worked as a domestic, created a world of fantasy dominated by her fondness for singing and dancing. They lived in a Puerto Rican-Italian section and Eartha picked up the languages of her playmates. She won prizes at public school for her interpretative dancing and sang in the Salem Methodist Church choir. She was enthusiastic about sports—played baseball and became a champion pole vaulter. At fourteen, she left school and worked in a Brooklyn factory sewing army uniforms. Whatever money she could save paid for piano lessons. Soon after her sixteenth birthday, a friend arranged an audition with Katherine Dunham which resulted in a dance training scholarship.

Miss Dunham selected Eartha for the troupe which toured the United States, Mexico and South America; and when it was discovered that the girl could sing, she was taught Haitian, African and Cuban songs and soon became the vocalist for the group. In Hollywood, during 1947, the troupe danced in a brief sequence in *Casbah.* In the spring of 1948 Eartha appeared with the Dunham group at the Prince of Wales Theatre in London, before an audience that included members of the Royal Family. The troupe also toured Paris and other European cities and Eartha was given more solo roles.

When the troupe returned to the United States, Eartha decided to stay in Paris. *Cue* (November 27, 1954) described how she found a room in a small hotel along the Seine and a singing job at Carroll's, one of the smart night clubs where she was an instantaneous success. The French called her "the rage of Paris." She was greeted with equal acclaim at Churchill's in London, and at the Kervansaray in İstanbul, where "her dazzling gowns and the multilingual virtuosity of her singing" impressed Continental night club habitués.

Early in 1951 her aunt Mamie died and Eartha flew to New York for the funeral. On returning to Paris she was asked by Orson Welles to play Helen of Troy in *Faust.* She had only two days to learn the part, but on opening night her performance drew high praise from the critics. Later, the play was shortened to concert form for a brief tour through Germany and Belgium. In an interview with Ted Poston (New York *Post,* January 30, 1955), Miss Kitt said: "I learned so much from Orson Welles—just by keeping my mouth shut and listening. He gave me my first chance at a legitimate stage role." The Parisian newspaper *France-Soir* gave her second place in its annual award for "the greatest acting achievement of the year" (1951) for her performance as Helen of Troy.

After *Faust* closed, Eartha starred in two French films and was preparing for a third when Monte Proser of La Vie En Rose invited her to sing at his New York night club. Her debut was not a success. However, at Max Gordon's Village Vanguard in 1952 she established her "first solid American success, twenty-five weeks to capacity business" singing "C'est Si Bon" (Robert Wahls, New York *Sunday News,* January 30, 1955) and sophisticated European songs.

Producer Leonard Sillman saw her and gave her a part in his revue *New Faces of 1952,* which opened on May 16, 1952. Brooks Atkinson (New York *Times,* May 25, 1952) praised her "combustible singing" of the song "Monotonous" which described "the boredom of a worldly lady surfeited with luxury." For almost the entire run of *New Faces,* Eartha sang at the after-theatre show at the Blue Angel night club where she broke the all-time attendance record.

RCA Victor recognized her as a stylist and made the "Eartha Kitt Album" and the Turkish folk song single "Uska Dara." "C'est Si Bon," "I Want to be Evil" and "Santa Baby" were also jukebox favorites. When Twentieth-Century Fox Film Corporation produced *New Faces* in CinemaScope, Eartha sang several new songs especially composed for her.

While in Hollywood Miss Kitt sang at Mocambo (November 10, 1953) and surpassed a thirteen-year attendance record. She gave a "command performance" for the King and Queen of Greece on November 13. After the tour of *New Faces* Eartha began to prepare for the leading role in *Mrs. Patterson* for which producer Leonard Sillman had chosen her. She appeared on several television programs including the *Colgate Comedy Hour, Your Show of Shows,* and *Toast of the Town.* Edward R. Murrow's *Person to Person* program showed Eartha at home in her Riverside Drive penthouse on September 11, 1954.

From $350 a week at the Village Vanguard early in 1952 Eartha Kitt's night club earnings had increased to $10,000 weekly when she appeared at El Rancho in Las Vegas in April 1954. *Variety* praised her calypso "Somebody Bad Stole de Wedding Bell." She returned to La Vie En Rose in June and this time was hailed as "one of the season's triumphs."

The play *Mrs. Patterson,* by Charles Sebree and Greer Johnson, might well have been written about Eartha's early life, but was not. Walter F. Kerr (New York *Herald Tribune,* December 2, 1954) called her "an enchanting gamin" in her portrayal of Teddy Hicks, the fifteen-year-old daughter of a Kentucky laundress who built a dream life around the white people whom she envied. The songs interpolated into the drama were written especially for Eartha. The play closed on February 26, 1955 after 101 performances. In an interview (New York *Times,* December 6, 1954), Eartha said that in preparing for the part she had studied the actions of her pet cats "Tex" and "Finnegan" because "cats respond very much the same way as children."

The actress is five feet two inches tall and weighs 105 pounds. Her hair, a reddish brown, is dyed black and her eyes—dark brown—have been described as signals for lightning changes in mood. People who have worked with her have commented on her capacity for hard work and painstaking precision. She speaks six languages fluently. She likes sports and plays tennis and golf when possible. A "conservative Democrat," she is interested in politics, but takes no active part. Her religion is Protestant. A "voracious reader," she reads about four books a week. She is writing her autobiography. She smiles off reported romances, and is very humble about her rise from "Cinderella" to the "rage of Broadway and Paris." Her RCA Victor records sell over 600,000 each. Her latest is "The Heel," released in February 1955.

When Miss Kitt made a $10,000 contribution to the North Side Center Home for Orphans in New York, she told an official of the organization that the dream of her life was to meet Albert Einstein. The official arranged it. As the seventy-five-year-old physicist received her in his Princeton home, he said, "My dear, you are so young." Over teacups, as reported in *Newsweek* (January 31, 1955), they talked. When she asked a question about reincarnation, Dr. Einstein did not know the English word, so she spoke in German. Later she said: "He was warm and affectionate. I didn't feel like an idiot, as I thought I would."

References

Colliers 133:93+ Je 11 '54 pors
Miami Herald p23E Ja 23 '55
N Y World-Telegram p25 Jl 9 '52 por
San Francisco Chronicle Mag p16 D 6 '53 por

KLEIST, PAUL LUDWIG (EWALD) VON Aug. 8, 1881-Nov. (?) 1954 Former German Army officer; was lieutenant of hussars and regimental commander during World War II; commanded forces that invaded Holland, Belgium and northern France; occupied Belgrade, Yugoslavia and captured Kiev and Rostov, U.S.S.R. (1941); was captured by U.S. troops (1945); considered a master of blitzkrieg; sentenced to fifteen years by a court in Yugoslavia (1948); turned over to U.S.S.R. and died in prison there. See *Current Biography* (July) 1943.

Obituary

N Y Times p17 N 6 '54

KNIGHT, FRANCES G(LADYS) July 22, 1905- United States Government official

Address: b. 1717 H St., N.W., Washington, D.C.; h. 2940 Edgevale Terrace, N.W., Washington 8, D.C.

In the fiscal year ending June 30, 1955 the U.S. Passport Office issued or renewed passports to over 480,000 Americans as compared with some 180,000 in 1946. The processing of passports should be "streamlined, mechanized, and speeded up," in the opinion of Miss Frances G. Knight, new head of the Passport Office, to keep pace with this increased demand by the travel-minded American public. Miss Knight, a public relations expert and a U.S. Government employee for all but two years since 1934, succeeded Mrs. Ruth B. Shipley to this office on May 1, 1955.

Miss Knight joined the State Department in 1949 as a radio information specialist for the *Voice of America* division of the Office of International Information. From April 1953 until assuming her present post, she was assistant deputy administrator in the Bureau of Security and Consular Affairs under which the Passport Office is administered.

The only child of an English father and a Czechoslovakian mother, Frances Gladys Knight was born at Newport, Rhode Island, on July 22, 1905. (Her father, the late Frederick Knight, died in England in 1950; her mother is the former Fanni Smolik.) As a child Frances lived in New York City, Paris, Prague and the principality of Monaco. She attended Hunter High School in New York City and the École pour Jeunes Filles at Monte Carlo in Monaco. She received the A.B. degree in journalism from New York University in 1926 and took graduate courses at Columbia University.

Miss Knight was on the editorial staff of a religious publication from 1925 until 1934, when she became a division chief with the National Recovery Administration.

Beginning in 1936 she was employed by the Works Progress Administration for three years as deputy director of information. She then was public relations consultant to the White House conference on children. From 1941 to 1942 she held the post of special assistant to the head of the National Defense Advisory

Department of State

FRANCES G. KNIGHT

Commission. From 1942 until the end of World War II Miss Knight was with the Office of Civilian Defense as director of public advice and counsel.

Engaged in 1946 by the American Retail Federation, a commercial association with headquarters in Washington, D.C., Miss Knight was director of public information. In 1948 she was made a special consultant to the chairman of the House of Representatives Appropriations Committee, and in October 1949, she was appointed a radio information specialist with the Office of International Information, Department of State. Fluent in the French, German and Czech languages, Miss Knight was closely associated with the *Voice of America* broadcasts.

In 1952 Miss Knight became assistant deputy administrator of the State Department's Bureau of Security and Consular Affairs. This bureau is charged with directing the security program of the State Department and the Foreign Service, providing technical direction for the consular program of the Foreign Service, and directing activities related to the control of international traffic in arms. The Administrator of the bureau is also the Administrator of the Refugee Relief Program. Operating under the bureau is the Passport Office, then directed by Mrs. Ruth B. Shipley (see *C.B.*, 1947). Thus Miss Knight became associated with the Passport Office and in cooperation with Mrs. Shipley—conducted a survey of passport activities.

The Department of State announced on March 31, 1955 the retirement of Mrs. Shipley and Miss Knight's appointment as her successor. (Miss Knight was Ruth B. Shipley's personal choice.)

Before World War I passports and visas were required in few countries, but after 1914 they became an almost universal necessity for traveling abroad. In his article entitled "Is Passport 'Political Document?'" (Washington *Post and Times Herald*, June 12, 1955), Murrey Marder wrote: "In various phrasing" the State Department has "stated through the years that a passport is a 'political document' and its use is a 'privilege' controlled by the Government as a part of its conduct of foreign affairs." Under the Internal Security Act of 1950 passports are specifically to be denied to "persons who are members of groups found to be 'Communist-action' or 'Communist-front.'"

From her predecessor Miss Knight inherited a number of controversial applications including that of Professor Owen Lattimore (the authority on Far Eastern affairs against whom the U.S. Government dropped its perjury case later in June 1955), whose request for a passport to enable him to fill lecture and conference engagements in Europe had been held up since March 12. On May 20, 1955 Miss Knight authorized the issuance of a passport to Lattimore, winning the editorial praise of the Washington *Post and Times Herald* (May 22, 1955) for having thus "inaugurated her administration with a decision that reflects high credit on her judgment and sense of fairness."

Another case was that of Max Schachtman of the Independent Socialist League, who had been denied a passport for three and half years on the ground that the Independent Socialist League was one of the allegedly subversive organizations on the U.S. Attorney General's list. Schachtman brought a suit against the State Department in a Federal district court. When the court ruled for the defendant, the plaintiff took his case to the U.S. Court of Appeals of the District of Columbia.

On June 23, 1955 the court ruled unanimously that the State Department did not have "exclusive control" of passport issuance and could not deny a passport without "due process of law." All citizens have a "natural right" to travel abroad and membership in an organization the Attorney General had listed as subversive was not a valid cause for abrogating this right. This decision is susceptible of reversal by the U.S. Supreme Court.

Shortly afterwards, the Passport Office announced on July 6 that a passport would be issued to Dr. Martin D. Kamen, a radiobiologist, who had been denied a passport for eight years. On June 6 Dr. Otto Nathan, executor of the late Dr. Albert Einstein's estate, was granted a passport by court order.

It was made public on July 7 that passports would be issued to the sociologist, Dr. Clark Howell Foreman, director of the Emergency Civil Liberties Committee of New York, and to Willard Z. Park, head of the American Ethiopian Corporation. Both had formerly been denied passports and had taken their cases to the courts. At the same time it was made known that a "limited" passport would be issued to Joseph Clark, foreign editor of the Communist *Daily Worker* to permit him to attend the Big Four Conference at Geneva in July.

On July 23 it was announced that former Judge William C. Clark, whose wish to visit

Berlin had been opposed by U.S. Ambassador James Bryant Conant, would be granted an "unrestricted" passport for Germany.

The Passport Office occupied the Winder Building near the White House. The building was built in 1848 and provides antiquated facilities which have handicapped the operations of Miss Knight's staff. It was announced in early August by the General Services Administration, the Government's housekeeping agency, that about 65,000 square feet in a modern, air-conditioned office building will be available for the Passport Office in the near future. (In September Miss Knight and her staff moved into these new quarters.)

Miss Knight feels it is necessary to reorganize her agency. "When people planned months ahead to go overseas," she told Bess Furman of the New York *Times* (July 3, 1955), "they didn't mind waiting three weeks for a passport. Today London and Paris are an overnight hop." "The war scare," she pointed out, "has subsided, and Americans are on a colossal traveling spree. Tourist and family rates are very attractive"; credit travel is helping to interest people of modest income; there are more retired people who want to travel, and pensions and social security are making travel possible (New York *Times*, July 11, 1955).

Frances Knight has blonde hair and blue eyes; her height is five feet five inches. Her church is Presbyterian. She has visited all of the states of the Union, the territory of Hawaii, and thirty-four foreign countries and is an associate member of the Foreign Service Association. On September 15, 1935 she became the wife of Wayne William Parrish, a publisher.

References

N Y Herald Tribune p4 Ap 2 '55 por
U S News 38:16 Ap 8 '55
Department of State Biographic Register (1954)
Who's Who in Commerce and Industry (1947)

KNIGHT, GOODWIN (JESS) Dec. 9, 1896- Governor of California; lawyer

Address: b. The Capitol, Sacramento, Calif.; h. Executive Mansion, Sacramento, Calif.

In the election of November 1954 the incumbent candidate on the Republican ticket, Governor Goodwin Knight of California, won a four-year term as chief executive of the nation's second most populous state. The previous year as lieutenant governor he had succeeded to the governorship to fill the unexpired term of Earl Warren, who had been appointed Chief Justice of the United States Supreme Court.

Knight, a lawyer and former judge, operated a successful gold mine for more than a decade. He has long been a favorite of the "conservative" wing of California's Republican party. Described as a back-thumping, hand-shaking type of political figure, he is a skillful electioneer who campaigns by visiting all parts of the state, making frequent speeches and meeting as many voters as possible.

A descendant of early Western settlers, Goodwin Jess Knight was born in Provo, Utah on December 9, 1896 to Jesse J. Knight, a lawyer and mining engineer, and Lillie Jane (Milner) Knight. Both parents were natives of Provo. His mother was the daughter of English-born John B. Milner, who served for fifty years on the Utah bench. When Goodwin was eight years old, his family moved to Los Angeles, where he attended public schools. In his teens he wrote *Good's Budget of Boys' Stories* (1910). During his junior year at Manual Arts High School he was president of the student body.

Before entering Stanford University he worked for a year in the lead and zinc mines of southern Nevada and also was employed as a reporter on the Los Angeles *News* (no longer published). He left Stanford before graduation to serve for a year (1918-1919) during World War I with the U.S. Navy as an apprentice seaman aboard a coastal submarine chaser in both Pacific and Atlantic waters. He then returned to the university to complete his studies.

During his senior year he was manager of the yearbook, *Quad*, and for three years was a staff member of the *Stanford Illustrated Review*. Other out-of-classroom interests were debating and football. He was graduated from Stanford with the B.A. degree in 1919, won the competitive $2,000 Telluride Scholarship, and spent the year 1919-1920 studying at Cornell University in Ithaca, New York.

As a young man, Knight was a political follower of Hiram W. Johnson. In 1920 he worked in the Johnson-for-President campaign headquarters in New York City and during the 1924 Presidential contest campaigned for Johnson in Los Angeles County.

Admitted to the California bar on March 28, 1921, he engaged in private law practice in Los Angeles until 1925 when he began a ten-year partnership with Thomas Reynolds. At his father's suggestion he invested part of his earnings in Los Angeles real estate, and in 1932 he bought a gold mine, the Elephant-Eagle Mines, in the Mojave Desert in California. Two years later when the Federal government raised the price of gold, operation of the mine began to show a profit. As reported by Stanley P. Isaacs in the *Nation* (May 29, 1954), during the first nine years Knight took $2,000,000 from the mines.

One of his earliest important political appearances was at the 1934 Republican State Convention, where he made the keynote speech against the campaign of Democratic candidate Upton Sinclair for the California governorship. Knight supported the candidacy of Frank Finley Merriam, who soon after he became governor appointed Knight a judge of the Superior Court of Los Angeles County. Knight was then elected to the bench in 1936 and re-elected in 1942.

Wide World

GOODWIN KNIGHT

During his eleven years (1935-46) on the bench, Knight was frequently in the news because of the prominence of the people involved in some of the cases that he handled, such as the Mary Astor child-custody case in 1936. "His opinions," commented *Fortnight* (November 18, 1946), "have followed the steadiest lines of judicial reasoning." Ernest Havemann (*Life*, March 29, 1954) noted that in 7,000 cases his decisions were overruled by higher courts only fourteen times.

With the backing of Governor Earl Warren, Knight in 1946 ran for the office of lieutenant governor on the Republican ticket and was elected on November 5 by a majority of 330,000 votes. Since Warren was defeated in November 1948 for the Vice-Presidency on a ticket with Governor Thomas E. Dewey of New York as the Republican Presidential candidate, Knight remained in the post of lieutenant governor. The San Francisco *Chronicle* (October 4, 1953) quoted him as remarking at that time, "Some people say I'm a bitter man and desperately disappointed because I did not become California's governor. Well, they're right!"

In the 1950 primary election when Knight was again a contender for the office of lieutenant governor, he won both the Republican and Democratic nominations. (California's system of cross filing makes it possible for rival candidates to bid for the nomination of each other's party.) As lieutenant governor, Knight had the duty of presiding over the Senate and achieved an intimate working relationship with the legislature. He was also required to serve as acting governor when Governor Warren was out of the state. During a radio speech in 1953 he estimated that in the aggregate he had been acting governor for the equivalent of more than a year.

Knight, who was considered close to the right wing of the Republican party and had the support of the conservatives opposing Warren's "progressivism," made it clear that he did not agree with the governor on issues of social philosophy. He was unwilling to endorse Warren's proposal for pre-paid health insurance and objected to the fair-employment practices act advocated by Warren. The lieutenant governor, a member of the board of regents of the University of California, also differed with Warren by siding with the university regents who wanted teachers to take a special loyalty oath. (Many prominent faculty members thought the oath discriminatory. The matter was brought to the California State Supreme Court which decided in favor of the faculty.)

Soon after Governor Warren made known his intention not to seek a fourth term, Knight in September 1953 announced his candidacy for governor in the 1954 election. His objective, he stated, was "to conduct a business-like administration with emphasis on reduced spending . . . the cost of government can be cut without jeopardizing services essential to the people" (New York *Times*, September 20, 1953). At the end of the month, however, on September 30, President Dwight D. Eisenhower announced the appointment of Governor Warren as Chief Justice of the United States Supreme Court. Automatically succeeding Warren, Knight took his oath of office on October 5, 1953 to become the thirty-first governor of California.

The new governor was already very well known to the people of California because of the many speeches he had made in all parts of the state in the course of his seven years as lieutenant governor. According to Havemann's article in *Life*, during his first fifty-nine days as governor, Knight made eighty-four speeches, later reducing his average to nearly a speech a day. In a radio report to the people soon after he had taken office he spoke of the needs of the state's growing population and pledged support of the freeway and highway program, building of adequate rapid transit systems in metropolitan areas, and development of water resources.

Another program that Knight discussed at this time concerned ridding the atmosphere of smog. Later in his tenure, in October 1954, he attempted to deal directly with the problem by asking five Southern California oil refineries to shut down indefinitely in order to test the effect on the smog conditions that had troubled the Los Angeles area for about three weeks. He also announced that he was allocating $100,000 for the study of the health aspects of smog.

Soon after becoming governor, Knight succeeded in having the state legislature increase weekly maximum unemployment insurance payments from $25 to $30. This action, popular with labor, won him the endorsement of the AFL in the June 8, 1954 primary election. His opponent on the Democratic ticket, Richard Graves, a public administration expert and former "Warren Republican," had the backing of the CIO. Knight easily won the Republican nomination, but failed in his efforts to gain the gubernatorial nomination of both major parties, as Warren had done in 1946. His pluralities established new records for volume of votes in California's primary elections for governor.

One of the issues in the campaign for the fall election concerned expenditure of more than $65,000,000 that had accrued to the state since 1947 from offshore oil royalties. Under present law 70 per cent of this sum is allocated to development of beaches and parks, with 30 per cent being given over to the general fund. Governor Knight expressed the opinion that $45,000,000 was too large a sum to spend at one time on beaches and parks and indicated that in 1955 he would ask the legislature to increase the amount of money allowed to the general fund from this source. His Democratic opponent described the proposal as "part of a frantic effort to balance an unbalanced state budget . . . one more evidence of an unsound, stopgap financing" (New York *Times*, September 19, 1954).

At the polls on November 2, 1954, Knight defeated Graves by about 500,000 votes, a figure that indicates support from a sizeable number of independent voters and registered Democrats, as well as from Republicans. Gladwin Hill of the New York *Times* (November 7, 1954) observed, "Governor Knight's haste in calling attention—through morning-after telegrams to news organizations—to his wide margin of victory revived speculation that he had Presidential aspirations."

Other public offices held by Knight have been the chairmanship of the Interstate Cooperation Commission and membership on the Toll Bridge Authority, Lands Commission, Council of State Governments, and the Disaster Council. He is a member of the law firm of Knight, Gitelson, Ashton and Hagenbaugh, and belongs to the American and the California state bar associations. He holds membership also in the American Legion, Veterans of Foreign Wars, and the Alpha Delta Phi, Phi Alpha Delta (law), Sigma Delta Chi (journalism) and Delta Sigma Rho (debating) societies. In Sacramento his clubs are Sutter, University and Del Paso Country; in Los Angeles, the Press and Jonathan. He is also a member of the Pasadena Athletic Club, a 32d degree Mason, Shriner, Eagle, Odd Fellow, Knight of Pythias and Elk. An Episcopalian, he serves as vestryman of his church.

By his marriage to Arvilla Pearl Cooley on September 9, 1925, Knight is the father of two daughters, Marilyn (Mrs. Robert A. Eaton) and Carolyn. In October 1952 Mrs. Knight died. On August 2, 1954 Knight was married to Virginia Carlson, widow of a World War II air force bombardier.

California's broad-shouldered governor is five feet ten inches tall and weighs 185 pounds. "Between his own quick and friendly wit and the joke file he carries in the back of his head, he can be very amusing indeed," Havemann of *Life* has written. "Goodie" Knight, as his friends call him, is also pictured as informal, affable and energetic. "I have no other interests, no other task except politics," the *Nation* quotes Knight as having said about his work. "I've freed myself of all worries. . . . I'm just trying to do my best in one field—politics."

References

Christian Sci Mon p4 O 16 '53
Life 36:117+ Mr 29 '54 pors
Los Angeles Times p2+ O 1 '53 por
Nation 178:461+ My 29 '54
San Francisco Chronicle Mag p4 O 4 '53 por; p3 O 31 '54 por
Who's Who in America, 1954-55
Who's Who in United States Politics (1950)

KNIGHT, RUTH ADAMS (YINGLING)

Oct. 5, 1898- Author

Address: b. Doubleday and Co., 575 Madison Ave., New York 22; h. Heartwell Hill, Woodbury, Conn.

Reprinted from the *Wilson Library Bulletin* Mar. 1955

Ruth Adams Knight's profession has always been that of a writer, of books, short stories, newspaper articles, and radio scripts. Miss Knight is now embarking on a writing career in a new medium—that of television. "I am confident," she says earnestly, "that much of the good literature of the future may be produced for this medium. To condemn TV because of the poor quality of some programs is as illogical as to condemn all books because the cheap and the vulgar as well as the inspiring and the profound may appear between hard covers."

Ruth Knight was born Ruth Adams Yingling on October 5, 1898, a few blocks from the fort in Defiance, Ohio. Her father (John Carson Yingling), of Dutch ancestry, was the son of a famous circuit-riding Methodist preacher. Her mother (the former Lucy Celeste Adams Shead), a descendant of Jacob Adams, forebear of both John and Samuel, had taught a "select" school before her marriage.

Almost as soon as she learned to read, Ruth Knight began to write. She won prizes for essays during her school years in Toledo. She also found time for an active social life—dancing, swimming, skating, and serving as a sorority officer.

While studying at Toledo University, Miss Knight did special features for the Toledo *Times*. Eventually, she was offered a job on the staff.

By her early twenties, Ruth Knight was not only an established reporter but she had been made drama editor of the expanded Sunday section, and ran a daily theater and movie column, as well as the literary and book review section. In 1930, she moved to New York, although for a time she continued to edit the book section, while she went on with her writing. To this she added scripts for that new medium—radio. After an apprenticeship, she began to write for the networks, scripts for such sponsored shows as *Cavalcade of America*,

RUTH ADAMS KNIGHT

Dr. Christian, Death Valley Days, and *Show Boat,* among many, including her own program, *Brave Tomorrow.* The *Christian Science Monitor* designated her documentaries and dramatic scripts as among the most distinguished on the air. By 1940, Miss Knight was a top radio writer.

Suddenly she realized she had neglected her first love, fiction. She had done a number of nonfiction books—*Stand by for the Ladies!* (Coward-McCann, 1939), the first vocational book on radio for women; also *Lady Editor* (Dutton, 1941), in collaboration with M. Shuler, and *Opera Cavalcade* (1938), the story of the Metropolitan. Now she began to write fiction in earnest, and her short stories appeared in *Collier's, Cosmopolitan, McCall's,* and *Redbook.* The *American Mercury* published "What a Darling Little Boy!" and it was included in a volume of the *O. Henry Memorial Award Prize Stories of 1944.* She wrote with Jean Hersholt, star of the radio program *Dr. Christian,* a novel, *Dr. Christian's Office* (Random House, 1944).

The books for teenagers, for which she is best known, began at this time. *Valiant Comrades* (Doubleday, 1943), a story of dogs of war, was well received by dog lovers, adult and juvenile, and was followed by *Brave Companions* (Doubleday, 1945), the story of a blind soldier and a Seeing Eye dog. A third dog book, *Luck of the Irish* (Doubleday, 1951), was also praised.

By far the most significant and certainly the most challenging of Miss Knight's books are those which deal with the vital problems of today's young people. *It Might Be You* (Doubleday, 1949), the first in this group, is a collection of eight stories dealing with intolerance through the ages.

Day After Tomorrow (Doubleday, 1952) tells in fiction form the way in which Communism tries to penetrate our high schools. *Top of the Mountain* (Doubleday, 1953) was the first book in which Miss Knight endeavored to promote international understanding among young people. In it, an American boy gains a new view of the world and, with the aid of his Swiss friend, finds himself.

Adult fiction also occupied Miss Knight, and two novels, both of which had magazine publication prior to book form, were published—*Women Must Weep* (Hale, 1941) and *Fare by My Side* (Morrow, 1948). She experienced two thrilling trips across the St. Bernard Pass in winter. All this provided background material for two books on a general list, with special interest for teenagers—*Halfway to Heaven* (McGraw-Hill, 1952), the story of the St. Bernard dog, and *The Land Beyond* (McGraw-Hill, 1954), a story of the Children's Crusade. The German, Italian, and French editions of *Halfway to Heaven* were published in 1955. *The Land Beyond* is the story of a lad who went on that tragic crusade with his "tiger dog" Regis, descendant of the dogs brought back to Europe from the Orient by the first Crusaders.

Miss Knight's marriage to Raymond Knight ended in divorce. She is a slender, pretty woman, with the trim figure of a girl. Her son (John Adams Knight) and daughter (now Mrs. Elizabeth Lou Knight Bixby) each have two children who are her "dearest friends." Miss Knight's interests are as varied as her work. Her warmth of personality and personal charm are as frequently felt at theatrical "first nights" as in her Connecticut farmhouse, Heartwell Hill. She travels extensively, has made numerous trips to the West Coast. She enjoys the desert and owns a small place near 29 Palms, California. But her heritage is New England and her roots are there.

References

Scholastic 61:42-T S 24 '52 por
Who's Who in the East (1953)

KNOLL, HANS G(EORGE) (nōl) May 8, 1914- Furniture and textile manufacturer

Address: b. c/o Knoll Associates, Inc., 575 Madison Ave., New York 22; h. 29 Sutton Pl. S., New York 22

Bulletin: Hans G. Knoll died on October 8, 1955.

During the past decade Hans G. Knoll, president of Knoll Associates, Inc. and Knoll Textiles, Inc., has demonstrated that modern designs in furniture and textiles and modern interiors for hotel rooms, offices, and college dormitories can meet the changing needs of contemporary living and at the same time result in a profitable business operation. Knoll has a large internationally-known staff of furniture and textile designers and operates several factories in the United States and Europe where chairs, sofas, chests, beds, desks, and fabrics are manufactured. The Knoll group "represents the collaboration of architect, designer,

HANS G. KNOLL

research engineer, and manufacturer at a high level of creative productivity . . . in solving design problems and in applying new scientific techniques to furniture making."

Knoll Associates has planned and executed such projects as the offices of the Carnegie Endowment for International Peace in New York City; the student union building of Ohio State University in Columbus; the offices of the Federal Reserve Bank in Detroit, Michigan; the complete furnishings of Bando Hotel in Seoul, Korea and of the Center for the Advanced Study in Behavioral Sciences in Palo Alto, California; the redecorating of the United States Embassies at Havana, Stockholm and Copenhagen; and the art gallery at Yale University. In the late 1930's, when most furniture manufacturers considered modern designs a hazardous investment, Knoll began to expand his operations until the Knoll name on a product is now, according to *Life* magazine, "almost as familiar as names like Tiffany or Hattie Carnegie."

Hans George Knoll was born in Stuttgart, Germany on May 8, 1914, the son of Walther C. and Maria (Vollmoeller) Knoll. The manufacture of furniture, particularly contemporary innovations, has been a family occupation for several generations. His father is in the furniture manufacturing business and his brother has also worked in that field.

Young Knoll was raised in Switzerland and England and received his education from various private institutions on the Continent. He had a thorough training in all phases of design and was familiar with the operations of furniture manufacturing. From 1933 to 1935 he worked with the Jantzen Knitting Mills in Brentford, England. His first independent work was as president of Plan, Ltd., a small interior design firm in England, from 1935 to 1937. He came to the United States in 1938 and in the following year established the Hans Knoll Furniture Company in New York City. Later Knoll Associates came into existence.

"It was my whole idea to develop new products working with well-known designers," Knoll has said, "and to encourage their particular talents." He also determined that he would produce nothing but modern furniture and fabrics, even if such a decision were to prove a financial loss. At that time, most American furniture manufacturers produced relatively few modern pieces and depended on the more traditional pieces to offset any losses they might have to take on the sale of the unconventional articles. Soon Knoll Associates was distributing over $3,000,000 worth of completely modern furniture and textiles a year.

During World War II, when materials for furniture and decorative fabrics were difficult to procure, the firm's designers used wood and metal scraps to create stools and chairs; they turned to tweeds when the more usual textiles had high military priority; they converted Army-rejected parachute belting into webbing for lightweight chairs; and, in order to save on scarce lumber, they designed slanting drawer fronts which did not require handles. In this way new materials and new techniques contributed to the creation of modern designs and original methods of production.

In 1953 the textile and furniture operations of the company were divided into two parts: Knoll Textiles now handles fabrics and Knoll Associates is responsible for furniture and interior planning. Knoll International, Ltd., a related company, issues licenses to international manufacturers who produce Knoll furniture and textiles outside the United States.

Many of the leading designers in America and Europe are associated with Knoll. These include Italian-born artist Harry Bertoia, whose wire chairs are a frequent sales item; George Nakashima, who has designed a modern version of the traditional Windsor-type chair; the sculptor Isamu Noguchi, who has contributed a number of designs to the Knoll workshops; the architect Eero Saarinen, whose molded reinforced plastic chairs are best sellers; color specialist and fabric designer Eszter Haraszty; and architect Ludwig Mies van der Rohe, whose leather and metal chairs and sofas are among the most popular items in the Knoll collection.

These artists sell their designs to Knoll who manufactures and distributes the articles and pays royalties to the creators on each sale. He owns several factories in Pennsylvania and in Europe where the furniture and textiles are made, many by hand. He has showrooms in New York, Chicago, Detroit, Dallas, Washington, D.C., Miami, and Boston; and in several European cities (Paris, Brussels, Stuttgart, Stockholm and Zurich); in Cuba, and in Toronto, Canada. Numerous retail stores also carry Knoll furniture and fabrics.

The planning unit of Knoll Associates designs and executes interiors for offices, such as those for executives of the Aluminum Company of America in Pittsburgh and the Columbia Broadcasting System, Inc. in New York; for auditoriums; museums (in 1953 Knoll Associates designed a room for the Dallas Museum

KNOLL, HANS G.—*Continued*

of Fine Arts); and retail stores. The Knoll display rooms and New York offices feature photomurals, sliding panels, low, soundproof partitions, a reflecting pool, and especially designed desks. The firm's use of colors—"hot violent shades" of pink, violet, fuchsia, yellow, and peacock blue—has been praised by many newspaper and magazine writers.

Recent projects include a tourist court whose rooms have open closets and ample luggage racks instead of chests of drawers; a 600-room women's dormitory and an administration building for the University of Michigan in Ann Arbor.

Among the other projects which the Knoll planning unit has done for educational institutions are the study and lounge areas of the Virginia Museum of Fine Arts in Richmond and the student union building at Southern Methodist University in Dallas, Texas. It did the complete installation of the executive offices of the New York, New Haven and Hartford Railroad Company in New Haven, Connecticut and work for the hospitals and offices of the U.S. Veterans Administration throughout the country.

Knoll's wife, Florence (Schust) Knoll, whom he married in 1944, is an American-trained architect and designer who has contributed furniture and textile designs to the catalogue of Knoll Associates. She joined the staff in 1943 as director of the planning unit and since her marriage, has continued to direct that section of the firm. The Knolls live in an apartment overlooking the East River which is reflected in a large mirror over the living-room fireplace. They travel widely and on these trips they combine visits to museums and artists' studios with business engagements. Knoll is six feet tall, weighs 160 pounds, and has blond hair and blue eyes. He is a member of the River Club of New York and the Arts Club of Chicago. He became a United States citizen in 1947.

References

Christian Sci Mon p6 Ja 25 '50 por
Who's Who in America, 1954-55

KOONING, WILLEM DE *See* de Kooning, Willem

KOTELAWALA, SIR JOHN (LIONEL) (kō'tĕl-à-wäl"à) 1897- Prime Minister of Ceylon

Address: Colombo, Ceylon

One of the most articulate critics of communism at the April 1955 meeting of leaders of twenty-nine Asian and African nations in Bandung, Indonesia, was Ceylon's Prime Minister Sir John Kotelawala, who assailed Red colonialism in both Europe and Asia. Sir John was in a large part responsible for this historic conference because it was through his initiative that the five Asian sponsor nations of the meeting—the Colombo Powers—were first called together the preceding year, in his country's capital city, to discuss problems of common interest.

He is a founder and the present leader of Ceylon's United National party. Ceylon, a former British Crown Colony and since 1948 a Dominion in the British Commonwealth of Nations, is a small island of strategic importance, lying at the southern tip of India. Tea and rubber are its principal exports. Kotelawala, with a record of more than twenty years in the legislature, became Prime Minister of Ceylon in 1953. He has since then also held the posts of Minister of Defense, Minister of External Affairs, and Minister of Transport and Works.

John Lionel Kotelawala was born in 1897 into a wealthy Buddhist family of Ceylon. He was educated at Royal College in Colombo and at Christ's College, Cambridge University, in England, where he studied agriculture. He was captain of the cricket team at Royal College and while in England played cricket for the Indian Gymkhana Club.

When he returned to Ceylon in 1920, Kotelawala, who owns plumbago mines and coconut groves, gave his attention to the management of his estates. He joined the Ceylon Light Infantry as a commissioned officer, rose to commanding officer and retired in 1939 in the rank of colonel.

Under the Donoughmore constitution, which went into effect in 1931, the colony of Ceylon achieved a measure of self-government through a State Council, most of the members of which were elective. Kotelawala, representing Kurunegala in this first State Council, served briefly in 1933 as Acting Minister of Agriculture and Lands. After his uncontested re-election to the State Council in 1936, he was appointed Minister of Communications and Works.

A notable accomplishment in this office was his inauguration of the Aberdeen-Laksapana Hydro-Electric project, Ceylon's biggest power project. He was also largely responsible for the introduction of civil aviation into the country, for the establishment of Air Ceylon, Ltd. (the island's first airline to provide regional and international services), and the building of a modern airport at Ratmalana, near Colombo.

As a member during World War II of Ceylon's War Council, set up to coordinate military activities with civil administration, Kotelawala was mainly concerned with the Essential Services Labour Corps, which guaranteed the availability of a labor force in the event of any emergency that might impede the war effort. At the end of the war he was chairman of the Post-War Problems Committee.

He remained a member of the State Council until 1947 when that legislature was replaced, under the Soulbury constitution, by a Parliament with a House of Representatives and a Senate. The Ceylon Independence Act was approved by King George VI on December 10, 1947, and on February 8, 1948 Ceylon became a Dominion within the British Commonwealth.

The 1947 election brought Kotelawala a seat in the House of Representatives, which has ninety-five elected members and six members named by the Governor General of Ceylon. He

Department of Information, Ceylon

SIR JOHN KOTELAWALA

was also chosen leader of the House of Representatives. Since 1948 the dominant political party in Ceylon has been the United National party, of which Kotelawala was a founding member and one of the first vice-presidents.

In the Cabinet of Ceylon's first Prime Minister, Don Stephen Senanayake, Kotelawala held the position of Minister of Transport and Works. Through his initiative the Colombo Port Development Project was begun in 1950—an undertaking designed to modernize the port of Colombo. Sir John (he was created Knight of the British Empire by King George VI in 1948) first visited the United States in May 1950, en route to Montreal, Canada for the International Civil Aviation Conference.

Upon the death of the elder Senanayake in March 1952, his son Dudley Senanayake, a cousin of Kotelawala, became Prime Minister. Kotelawala, who retained his seat in the 1952 Parliamentary election, continued to function as Minister of Transport and Works until October 12, 1953 when he was called upon to replace the retiring young Senanayake and form a new Cabinet. Prime Minister Kotelawala also holds the portfolios of Defense, External Affairs, and Transport and Works.

After taking office, the Prime Minister said, "I must make it quite clear that I shall have no truck with those who believe in revolutionary methods in politics and it will be one of my foremost duties to stamp out Communism in this country" (New York *Times*, October 16, 1953). One measure undertaken by his government was to increase the penalty for political subversion.

As noted in the Western press, however, Kotelawala did not attempt to modify a trade agreement concluded with Communist China the previous year whereby Ceylon sells rubber to China at a price higher than that of the world market and buys rice from China under world market prices. Since rubber is a war material, the United States, under the Battle Act, refused to grant economic aid to Ceylon. Kotelawala explained his government's position in December 1953 when he rejected an offer for a good-will mission from Red China: "We sell you rubber, you sell us rice. Ceylon has no other friendship or dealing with Communist China. Nor does she want it" (New York *Herald Tribune,* December 14, 1953).

Sir John was chairman of a conference of Prime Ministers of five South Asian nations India, Pakistan, Burma, Ceylon and Indonesia —which met at Colombo in late April and early May 1954, at the suggestion of the Ceylon Prime Minister. The significance of the conference (Neal Stanford in the *Christian Science Monitor* (December 10, 1954), was that "it set up an association of Asian powers in an area of power vacuum."

Among the results of the meeting was a resolution regarding the Indochina war, which was placed before the Geneva conference of world powers then deliberating for cessation of hostilities in Indochina. Kotelawala noted in July that the eventual terms of the Indochina cease-fire were in general agreement with the recommendations set forth at the Colombo conference. (Although Ceylon had a more or less neutral position during the war in Indochina, Sir John had permitted U.S. planes carrying French paratroopers to Dienbienphu to land at Ceylon's Katunayake airport.)

In April 1955 the five Colombo Powers sponsored a meeting of twenty-nine nations of Asia and Africa representing over 1,300,000,000 people including Communist China, at Bandung, Indonesia. Sir John, in a speech which "shocked" the conference and received much favorable comment in the Western press, posed the question: "If we are united in our opposition to colonialism, should it not be our duty to declare our opposition to Soviet colonialism as much as to Western imperialism?" He further asked how non-Communist countries can "regard coexistence as anything but a snare and a delusion until such time as the Cominform is dissolved" (*Time,* May 2, 1955).

The speech was reportedly disconcerting not only to Red China's Premier Chou En-lai, but also to India's Prime Minister Jawaharlal Nehru, a staunch neutralist and advocate of coexistence. At Bandung Sir John also presented his views on the Formosa crisis, including the proposals that Generalissimo Chiang Kai-shek retire "gracefully" and that a plebiscite be held after a five-year trusteeship.

The Bandung conference issued as one of its resolutions a request that membership in the United Nations be made universal. In June 1955 Kotelawala, who protested that Ceylon had been kept out of the U.N. because of the "cold war" between Communist and anti-Communist nations, asked that Asian and African U.N. members be called upon to sponsor a demand for membership for Cambodia, Ceylon, Japan, Jordan, Laos, Libya and Nepal.

While making a world tour in November and December 1954 Sir John paid a good-will visit to the United States. While discussing Ceylon's refusal to join the American-initiated Southeast Asia Treaty Organization (SEATO), he said in New York: "What SEATO failed to take into account is the fact that the defense of Asia must first be an economic defense. The military aspect is secondary" (*Christian Science Monitor,* December 2, 1954).

American aid to Ceylon, Sir John further stated, might make it possible for his country to cancel its rubber trade agreement with Red China. He suggested that economic assistance might be a subject of his conversations with President Dwight D. Eisenhower. But, he added, "I do not come here with cap in hand" (New York *Herald Tribune,* December 2, 1954).

The government of Ceylon has received requests from United States and British commercial companies for permission to exploit the country's deposits of ilmenite, a mineral used in the production of atomic energy. Registered Ceylonese corporations were given permission to develop this mineral. The World Bank has sent advisors to help the Ceylon government establish a finance corporation, and has promised foreign exchange loans and the services of technicians to aid in developing small-scale industries.

Ceylon is one of the "recipient" countries participating in the Colombo Plan (not to be confused with the Colombo Powers) which was set up at a meeting of Commonwealth Foreign Ministers in Colombo in January 1950 to improve living standards in South and Southeast Asia. The United States and several other nations, including some members of the British Commonwealth, are "donor" or "supplying" countries for this $8 billion economic development project. Kotelawala's government announced in April 1955 that in expectation of aid from the United States under this project, it had planned a large-scale economic program of agricultural and industrial expansion.

For years the relationship between Ceylon and India has been troubled by the question of the status of some 1,000,000 residents of Indian origin now living in Ceylon, which has a total population of about 8,000,000 in an area of 25,330 square miles (about the size of the state of West Virginia). In October 1954 Kotelawala and Nehru issued a joint statement agreeing within the next two years to register the Indians in Ceylon as either Ceylonese or Indian nationals. The two leaders, however, failed to reach agreement on all phases of the problem.

In recognition of his share in the contribution made by the Colombo Powers to attainment of peace in Indo-China, Kotelawala received from the President of France the Order of the Legion of Honor. He was later awarded the Grand Cross of the Legion of Honor (France), the Great Cross of the Service Order (Germany), and the Grand Cross of the Order of Merit (Italy). He was admitted as a member of Her Majesty's Most Honorable Privy Council in April 1954.

Sir John has insisted upon equality of all religious groups in Ceylon as an official policy of his government. In his speeches he often refers to tenets of his own faith, Buddhism. He is married and has a daughter. Polo, tennis and riding are his recreations, and his clubs are the Orient and Sinhalese Sports. He is noted for his lavish hospitality and at his estate at Kandawala offers elephant rides as entertainment for his guests.

References

Christian Sci Mon p4 F 20 '54; p16B D 10 '54
N Y Times p16 O 13 '53
Who's Who, 1955

KRESS, SAMUEL H(ENRY) July 23, 1863- Merchant; philanthropist

Address: b. 114 5th Ave., New York 11; h. 1020 5th Ave., New York 28

Bulletin: Samuel H. Kress died on September 22, 1955.

Founder of one of America's earliest chain stores, Samuel H. Kress is now chairman of the board of the corporation which owns 264 five, ten and twenty-five cent novelty stores bearing his name. Since the early 1920's he has devoted much of his great wealth to the purchase of over 2,000 art masterpieces, most notably medieval and Renaissance Italian painting and sculpture. In 1929 he established the Samuel H. Kress Foundation to acquire additional works of art for eventual donation to museums throughout the United States, and to provide monetary grants to medical institutions and organizations.

Over forty museums have received paintings and sculpture from the foundation, the greatest beneficiary being the National Gallery of Art in Washington, D.C., of which Kress is president and a trustee. In 1955 David E. Finley, director of the National Gallery, announced that more than 150 paintings and sculptures had been added to its extensive Samuel H. Kress collection. The new additions would be "placed on permanent display on March 17, 1956, commemorating the fifteenth anniversary of the National Gallery." They include works by Titian, Tintoretto, Veronese, Watteau, and Zurbarán, and the *Small Crucifixion* by the early sixteenth-century German artist Matthias Grünewald, whose paintings are very rare.

Samuel Henry Kress is directly descended from a German settler who came to Northampton county, Pennsylvania, from Hesse-Nassau in 1752 and later fought in the American Revolution with the county militia. The eldest of the five children (four sons and a daughter) of John Franklin and Margaret Dodson (Connor) Kress, he was born on July 23, 1863 at Cherryville, Pennsylvania. His father operated a drugstore and in 1880, moved to Centralia, Pennsylvania, to become the business manager of a colliery.

Sam Kress, who attended grade and high schools at Slatington, Pennsylvania, a town near Cherryville, earned extra money peddling papers and working in local stone quarries (*Life,* November 16, 1953). He qualified for a teacher's license at the age of seventeen, and from 1880 to 1887, was occupied as a schoolmaster. His salary is said to have been $25 a month, but in seven years he had saved enough money to buy a small stationery and novelty store at Nanticoke, Pennsylvania.

In 1890 he acquired a wholesale stationery and toy business at Wilkes-Barre, Pennsylvania. Much impressed by Frank Winfield Woolworth's success in Pennsylvania, Sam Kress resolved to carry the idea of five and ten cent stores to another part of the country; in 1896 he opened in Memphis, Tennessee the S. H. Kress and Company five, ten and twenty-five cent store. "From the beginning," *Life* wrote (November 16, 1953), "the store was mobbed and within nine months had taken in more than $31,000."

Kress then established stores in ten other southern cities, and by 1900 he had disposed of his Pennsylvania retail and wholesale businesses and had moved to New York City to establish a permanent headquarters for his five, ten and twenty-five cent store chain. Seven years later (1907), when S. H. Kress and Company became a corporation with Samuel H. Kress as president, there were already fifty-one Kress stores doing a collective business of about $3,000,000 a year.

Business monopolized the interest and energy of Sam Kress during the first two decades of the twentieth century. "The person who got Kress started on a collector's career," *Life* has stated, "was Mrs. de Lora Kilvert, the cultured and beautiful ex-wife of an American illustrator. About 1920 Mrs. Kilvert, determined 'to get Sam interested in beautiful things,' began to lead him on a round of art galleries."

On a visit to Italy in 1921 Kress met the Florentine art dealer Count Alessandro Contini-Bonacossi, who "launched him on a . . . purchase program of Italian art," which assumed "full scale" proportions, particularly after 1924, when Kress yielded the presidency of S. H. Kress and Company to a younger brother, Claude, and became the chairman of the board.

"True to his mass-merchandise training," *Life* continued, "Kress generally bought art in big lots, and because of this passion for wholesale buying ended up with a sizable number of second and third-rate paintings. But he also obtained many prizes." Dealers reportedly found him a knowledgeable bargainer, not only for paintings and sculpture, but for medieval and Renaissance velvets and brocades, of which he was also a collector.

The millionaire had already passed his sixty-fifth birthday when in 1929 he incorporated the Samuel H. Kress Foundation "to promote the moral, physical and mental welfare of the human race." An early research grant was to the Georgia Warm Springs Foundation (of which Kress is today a trustee), and from the Kress collection loans or donations of painting and sculpture were made to small municipal or university museums, the only qualification being that such museums be located in states served by the Kress stores. In the first ten years of the Kress Foundation, some seventy-five works of art were lent or given to museums in San

Wide World

SAMUEL H. KRESS

Antonio, Texas; Charlotte, North Carolina; Montgomery, Alabama; Wichita, Kansas; Seattle, Washington; Memphis, Tennessee; Phoenix, Arizona; and Savannah and Macon, Georgia.

During another visit to Italy in 1929, Kress undertook to finance the restoration of the Gonzaga Palace at Mantua and historic landmarks at Spoleto, Ravenna and elsewhere, in recognition of which he was subsequently decorated with the Grand Cross of the Order of the Crown of Italy.

In the 1930's Kress was a client of the art dealer Joseph Duveen (created a Baron in 1933), who negotiated one of the most widely publicized of the Kress art purchases, that of Duccio di Buoninsegna's *Calling of St. Peter and St. Andrew* from the Clarence Hungerford Mackay Collection, in August 1935. Duveen's ablest restorer of masterpieces, Stephen S. Pichetto, became the art adviser whose judgment Kress trusted the most.

Kress presented to New York City's Metropolitan Museum of Art Luca di Tommè's *Madonna and Child,* a noteworthy specimen of the rare fourteenth century Siena school of painting. In December 1936 he was elected to the Metropolitan's board of trustees. Two more paintings were presented by the Kress Foundation to the Metropolitan in January 1938. Also in 1938 Kress purchased (through Duveen) the celebrated *Adoration of the Shepherds* by Giorgione. This masterpiece of Italian painting, now in the National Gallery at Washington, D.C., was displayed in a window of the Kress store on Fifth Avenue in New York City during the Christmas shopping season of 1938.

The National Gallery of Art was created as a bureau of the Smithsonian Institution by joint resolution of Congress approved on March 24, 1937 and is the outgrowth of be-

KRESS, SAMUEL H.—*Continued*

quests by millionaire Andrew William Mellon, Secretary of the U.S. Treasury (1921 to 1932), who provided funds for the erection of a $15,000,000 building as well as donated his own collection of paintings and sculpture to supply the "nucleus" of a permanent art exhibition in the nation's capital. Mellon had expressed the hope that his bequest would "attract other gifts from other citizens who may in the future decide to contribute works of art of the highest quality," and this hope was to be fulfilled by Joseph E. Widener, Chester Dale and others, but most notably and extensively by Samuel H. Kress.

In July 1939 Kress wrote to President Franklin D. Roosevelt offering the National Gallery the gift of 375 paintings and eighteen pieces of sculpture, mainly Italian, and said to have been valued by Duveen at more than $25,000,000. Included in the original Kress gift were the Duccio and Giorgione paintings already mentioned, and a *Madonna and Child* by Giotto, another by Fra Lippo Lippi, Titian's *Lady with a Mirror,* and works by Bellini, Pinturicchio, Ghirlandajo, Mantegna, and Fra Angelico. Kress personally made the formal presentation of these works at the dedication of the National Gallery on March 17, 1941.

David E. Finley (see *C.B.,* 1951), the director of the National Gallery, announced in July 1944 the receipt, from the Kress Foundation and Samuel H. Kress, of a group of nine French paintings of the eighteenth century, including Watteau's *Italian Comedians,* two *Allegories* by Boucher, and three pictures by Fragonard. In October 1944 Kress and the Kress Foundation gave the National Gallery seventy-one additional Italian paintings (including a Raphael) and twenty-six pieces of sculpture, one of which was Verrocchio's bust of Lorenzo the Magnificent.

In February 1945 Samuel H. Kress had the honor and satisfaction of being elected president of the National Gallery of Art. Later in 1945 he suffered a paralytic stroke which has left him bedridden. His eyesight began to fail. Distribution of the Kress Foundation's resources, both in funds and works of art, was placed in the hands of Rush H. Kress, one of the founder's younger brothers.

A grant for research and experimentation was made by the Kress Foundation to the American Heart Association in 1948, and to the New York University-Bellevue Medical Center a gift described as "in excess of $8,000,000" was donated by the Foundation in January 1949. The Memorial Center for Cancer and Allied Diseases in New York City was given a betatron unit by the Kress Foundation in 1952, and a year later, the National Practical Nurse Education Association received a Kress grant of $30,000 for its recruiting program. In December 1953 the New York University-Bellevue Medical Center received $1,268,941 for construction of a medical science building.

Since its establishment in 1929 the Kress Foundation has acquired some 2,000 works of art, valued well over $75,000,000. In order to "place" the entire collection by 1960, Rush H. Kress stepped up the distribution program; thus by 1950 the William Rockhill Nelson Gallery of Art at Kansas City, Missouri had received from the foundation twenty-two early Italian paintings and six sculptures, while in 1951 the National Gallery was able to celebrate its tenth anniversary with the unveiling of a fourth gift from the Kress Foundation consisting of numerous additional paintings, including *Adoration of the Magi* by Fra Angelico and Fra Lippo Lippi, Gozzoli's *Dance of Salome,* and works by Dürer, Titian, Tiepolo, Ingres and Poussin.

Also in 1951 the University of Arizona's museum in Tucson received from Kress a group of twenty-five paintings, including Francesco Guardi's *Church of Santa Maria della Salute.* Tintoretto's *Allegory of Vigilance* was one of thirty works presented in 1952 to the Birmingham (Alabama) Museum of Art; and in the same year important Kress gifts were made to museums in Portland, Oregon, and Seattle, Washington. The Honolulu (Hawaii) Academy of Arts now houses Luca Signorelli's *Madonna and Child with Saints,* as well as thirty-two other Italian paintings presented by Kress. One of the largest Kress donations was to the Houston (Texas) Museum of Fine Arts, which in 1953 received thirty-seven Italian and Spanish paintings valued at $1,000,000.

The Isaac Delgado Museum of Art at New Orleans, Louisiana, during 1953 unveiled thirty-one paintings, gifts of Kress, including Tiepolo's *Portrait of a Boy Holding a Book.* In February 1955 the M. H. de Young Memorial Museum in San Francisco, California received forty-four paintings (including a "magnificent" St. Francis by El Greco) from the Kress Foundation.

To commemorate the fifteenth anniversary of the National Gallery of Art on March 17, 1956, more than 150 paintings and sculptures added to the Samuel H. Kress collection will go on permanent display.

The Kress stores totaled 264 in number in the United States and territories in July 1955; net earnings of the chain during 1953 were $9,026,-294. Kress is a Mason, and a member of the Sons of the American Revolution and the Loyal Legion of the United States. He belongs to the Lutheran Church and is a Republican. His paintings and sculptures, which he calls "my children," appear to be the bachelor merchant's sole hobby.

References

Life 35:148+ N 16 '53 pors
New Yorker 27:40+ N 3 '51
Newsweek 44:82+ D 6 '54
Time 34:30 Jl 24 '39 por

Behrman, S. N. Duveen (1952)
Business Executives of America (1950)
National Cyclopædia of American Biography Current Volume G (1946)
Who's Who in America, 1954-55
Who's Who in Commerce and Industry (1953)
World Biography (1954)

KRISTIANSEN, MRS. ERLING *See* Selinko, Annemarie

KRUPP (VON BOHLEN UND HALBACH), ALFRED (FELIX ALWYN) (kro͞op fŏn bō'lĕn o͞ont häl'bäk äl'frāt) Aug. 13, 1907- German industrialist

Address: b. c/o Fried. Krupp, Altendorfer Strasse 103, Essen, West Germany; h. Werden, West Germany

The Krupp works, which produced munitions used by German armies in the Franco-Prussian War, World War I, and World War II and which is now helping West Germany in its rapid economic recovery, is owned by Alfred Krupp. He succeeded his father in 1943 as head of the firm, which at present is producing ships, locomotives, Diesel trucks, tools, machinery, and home fixtures.

According to an agreement with the Allies, Krupp has promised to manufacture only goods for peacetime use and to sell his coal, iron, and steel holdings. His total fortune has been estimated to be worth about $140,000,000. The firm, which reportedly lost four-fifths of its property through bombing, dismantling, and deconcentration, is expanding its international operations in Asia, Europe, and South America. In 1954 its executives reported the firm's first profits since 1945.

Alfred Felix Alwyn Krupp von Bohlen und Halbach was born in the Villa Hügel, the Krupp home near Essen, Germany, on August 13, 1907. His father, Gustav Georg Friedrich Marie von Bohlen und Halbach, had married Bertha Krupp, heiress to the Krupp works, on October 15, 1906 and on the following day, had been given the legal right by Kaiser Wilhelm II to add the name Krupp to his own surname. Soon thereafter he took the controlling seat on the board of directors of the Krupp firm.

On his father's side, young Alfred is descended from the American General William Henry Charles Bohlen, who fought in the War between the States, and is a distant relative of Charles E. Bohlen, U.S. Ambassador to the Soviet Union. Alfred had five brothers and two sisters; one brother died in infancy, two others died during World War II, and one sister is deceased. The remaining brothers are Berthold and Harald, the latter was a prisoner of war in Russia until October 1955.

The Krupp works was founded about 1810 by Friedrich Krupp. His son, the first Alfred Krupp—the "Cannon King"—expanded the firm, developed the process of making cast steel, and began the manufacture of ordnance, railroad tracks and switches. His breech-loading rifle and other armaments were used by the Prussian soldiers during the Franco-Prussian War. After his death in 1887, his son Friedrich Alfred became head of the works and added the manufacture of machinery. In the latter part of the nineteenth century the Krupp firm began providing social benefits—housing, hospital care, pensions—for their workers.

Wide World

ALFRED KRUPP

At Friedrich Alfred's death in 1902, when the firm had about 40,000 workers, his daughter Bertha became the owner. She held 159,996 of the 160,000 shares issued by the limited company. For her the "Big Bertha" guns of World War I were named. After the war, the Krupp works was forbidden to manufacture most armaments; from 1918, when the company employed about 170,000 workers, the total personnel decreased to 40,000 in 1933 just before Hitler came to power. By 1935 there were 90,000 Krupp workers.

Alfred attended the Real-Gymnasium in Essen-Bredeney and passed the examinations in 1925. He became associated with the firm that year, learning about its basic processes by working in the numerous factories. Later he studied at the Technische Hochschule in Aachen and in 1934 received his engineer's diploma. He worked in the Dresden Bank in Berlin for a year and then assumed certain administrative duties with the Krupp firm. In 1936 he became a deputy board member and two years later, a full board member.

In 1938 he also became a member of the Nazi party and during World War II he served with the rank of colonel in the Nazi flying corps. In 1943 Adolf Hitler, by the "Lex Krupp," made the Krupp family a dynasty whereby Krupps would hereditarily always be head of the firm. Alfred Krupp became chairman of the board; at that time the factories covered a total of five square miles and employed 160,000 people (including slave laborers). Some observers have noted that the Krupp works "almost single-handedly kept Adolf Hitler's huge war machine rolling."

When U.S. troops found Gustav Krupp in 1945, he was unable to stand trial because of sickness (he died in 1950), and so the Allied powers brought charges against his son and other Krupp directors for "planning, preparing,

KRUPP, ALFRED—*Continued*

initiating and waging aggressive war." However, evidences of acting in violation of the Versailles Treaty, bringing Adolf Hitler to power, and supporting his military campaigns, were found in Nuremberg to apply only to the elder Krupp (for information concerning Gustav Krupp see Louis P. Lochner, *Tycoons and Tyrant,* 1954). Charges against Alfred Krupp and the other directors on this count were dismissed by the court for "lack of prima facie evidence" in the spring of 1948.

Later that year Alfred Krupp and ten other former Krupp officials were tried and convicted before a U.S. military tribunal for the "deportation, exploitation and abuse of slave labor"; six of the defendants, including Alfred Krupp, were convicted of "plunder and spoliation"—of using the war to enlarge and extend their industrial empire by looting industries in occupied countries (George W. Herald, *United Nations World,* April 1953).

The prosecution contended that Alfred Krupp "not only accepted, but actively sought to employ concentration camp inmates and, for that purpose, built factories near the camps of Markstädt and Auschwitz" (George W. Herald). The use of 520 women from eastern European countries under terrible living conditions in Essen caused the death of many of them. The firm used a total of about 75,000 foreign workers and 25,000 prisoners of war in their factories.

During his trial, Krupp stated: "As a member of the fifth generation which produced steel, the fourth generation which forged weapons, I should like to add one thing. Never in my parents' home . . . did I hear one word or experience one act which welcomed or promoted any war at any place or at any time." Alfred Krupp was sentenced to the confiscation of all his property and to twelve years in prison on July 31, 1948.

On January 30, 1951 U.S. High Commissioner for Germany, John J. McCloy commuted Krupp's sentence to the time he had already been in prison (about six years) and restored to him his full property rights. "Of the many acts of clemency decided upon by McCloy, that affecting Krupp has made the greatest stir," commented Drew Middleton (New York *Times Magazine,* February 18, 1951). When Krupp left Landsberg prison in 1951 he said: "I hope it will never be necessary to produce arms again."

Under the program for decartelizing German industry, the Allies planned to divest the firm of its basic steel and coal mining properties. In March 1953 Krupp signed a special agreement with the Western powers: he pledged to sell all his coal, steel and iron assets before 1960 and never to reinvest his money in such commodities. These assets were transferred to two holding corporations, which will sell the shares to the public over the next several years. The proceeds, estimated to be about $25,000,000 to $30,000,000, will go to Krupp. He promised to produce only peaceful products and the Allies agreed to lift their controls on the other branches of his industrial empire. The West German government "refused to recognize the legal validity of these agreements with the Allies" (George W. Herald).

The post-war rebirth of the Krupp business interests is symptomatic of the whole rapid economic growth of West Germany after the war. In its drive for exports and overseas industrial assets, the firm not only sells goods, but provides long-term financing and investment partnerships and the services of Krupp engineers to other firms. As of late 1954, the firm had contracts for the construction of steel and cement plants in India; a steel mill in Pakistan; nickel, fertilizer and power plants in Greece; smelting plants in Spain and Greece; harbor installations in Basra, Iraq, Bangkok, Thailand, and Chile; plants for processing vegetable oils in the Sudan, Pakistan, and Iran. Local companies represent the Krupp interests throughout the world and on large foreign projects, Krupp engineers direct the operations, but the workers are natives (*Business Week,* September 26, 1953).

The Krupp factories in Germany are concentrated in two fields: 1) transportation—locomotives, ships, trucks, and all types of railroad equipment; 2) steel processing and industrial and agricultural equipment—from nuts and bolts to construction of complete steel mills and mining installations.

Active management of the firm is in the hands of experts. There is a general director, a head of organization and administration, and a chief of exports. The whole firm is composed of individual companies which are usually run by two men, one an engineer and the other a business expert. On most matters the boards of the individual companies have complete autonomy. The total turnover for the year 1954 was close to $238,000,000.

With the Western world's growing realization of the need for rearmament and with West Germany often taking away the markets of the other West European nations and Great Britain, some industrialists are beginning to wish that the Krupp firm would manufacture arms. "The sooner Krupp pitches in to do its share in the rearming, the better," said one British official. "I certainly don't like to see them capturing all the civilian export markets while the rest of us struggle to produce arms for the common defense" (*Time,* September 15, 1952).

Under the Paris treaties granting Germany its sovereignity and the right to rearm, the German government has agreed not to allow the manufacture of atomic weapons, but it can develop nuclear energy for civilian uses. The present plans of Krupp and other firms are dependent on the Paris agreements which entered into force on May 5, 1955.

Alfred Krupp married Mrs. Vera Knauer, a German-born American naturalized citizen, on May 19, 1952 in Berchtesgaden. He has one child by his previous marriage. He lives in a seven-room house in Werden and also spends much of his time on a family estate near Salzburg, Austria. He has been described as a "lean, tall, somewhat hunched and preoccupied man."

He used to collect art and go hunting, skiing and sailing. Now his favorite recreation is photography.

References

Colliers 132:48+ O 30 '53 por
N Y Times Mag p10+ F 18 '51 por
Newsweek 43:31 Ja 4 '54
Read Digest 67:159 S '55
U N World 7:44+ Ap '53 por
Wer ist Wer? (1955)
Wilmowsky, T. von Warum wurde Krupp verurteilt? (1950)

KUMM, (HERMAN) HENRY W(ILLIAM) (ko͞om) Feb. 26, 1901- Epidemiologist; physician; organization official

Address: b. c/o National Foundation for Infantile Paralysis, 120 Broadway, New York 5; h. 1700 York Ave., New York 28; Chocorua, N.H.

A recognized authority on preventive medicine, Dr. Henry W. Kumm, was appointed in September 1953 director of research of the National Foundation for Infantile Paralysis. During 1954 this foundation conducted mass field tests of Dr. Jonas E. Salk's newly developed anti-polio vaccine on nearly 440,000 school children. Before joining the staff of the foundation in 1951, Dr. Kumm had been associated for twenty-three years with the Rockefeller Foundation for Medical Research and had worked in the United States, Europe, Africa and South America on problems relating to the study and control of malaria and yellow fever.

After the foundation announced on April 12, 1955 that the Salk vaccine had proved 80 per cent "effective, safe and potent," Dr. Kumm stated: "More needs to be learned, however, about the duration of effectiveness of the Salk vaccine as well as better schedules for its administration, and improved manufacturing procedures. Research should also continue on simple diagnostic techniques, potential prophylactic and therapeutic drugs, and on improved methods of patient care for those persons who have already become paralyzed."

Herman Henry William Kumm was born in Wiesbaden, Germany, on February 26, 1901 to Herman Karl William and Lucy Evangeline (Guinness) Kumm. The boy, his sister (now deceased) and two brothers, were reared and educated in England, Switzerland and the United States. Through his father, who traveled extensively in Africa as a geographer, explorer and missionary secretary of the Sudan United Mission, he developed an early interest in tropical medicine.

In November 1915 Henry Kumm came to the United States. He completed his precollege training at the Summit (New Jersey) High School, where he played center on the football team in his senior year. Graduating in 1918 he entered Haverford College in Pennsylvania and received his B.S. degree in 1921, having fulfilled in three years the requirements of a four-year course. While pursuing his major studies in biology and chemistry, he held a Haverford College scholarship (1918-19), played football, served as class treasurer in his sophomore year and was elected to Phi Beta Kappa in his junior year. He earned part of his expenses by waiting on tables in the college dining room and working at odd jobs during summer vacations.

For his postgraduate courses Kumm attended the Johns Hopkins University in Baltimore, Maryland, taking his M.D. degree in 1925. He interned for a year (1925-26) at the Peking Union Medical College Hospital in China and then spent some time during 1927 as a student at the Malaria Training Station of the Rockefeller Foundation in Edenton, North Carolina. The following year he earned his doctorate in public health at the Johns Hopkins University with the thesis *The Geographical Distribution of the Malaria Carrying Mosquitoes*, published by the *American Journal of Hygiene* (monograph series 10). Earlier, through his studies at the London School of Hygiene and Tropical Medicine in England, he had been awarded a diploma in tropical medicine and hygiene (1927) and had won the Duncan Medal and the Lalcaca Medal.

Having become a member of the staff of the international health division of the Rockefeller Foundation in June 1928, Dr. Kumm went to Lagos, Nigeria with other specialists of the foundation's West Africa yellow fever commission. When he left this post in January 1930, he was sent to Bahia and Pernambuco in Brazil to work on control of yellow fever.

In his next undertaking for the Rockefeller Foundation he was stationed during 1934-35 in Kingston, Jamaica as a member of the commission to study the transmission of yaws (a contagious skin disease). He returned to Brazil in 1935-36 to investigate jungle yellow fever in Pará.

Beginning in 1937, after a year's study of immunity to malaria, conducted at the Rockefeller Institute for Medical Research in New York City, Dr. Kumm represented the foundation in a number of projects dealing with the survey and control of tropical diseases. He spent three years (1937-40) in San José, Costa Rica and one year (1941-42) in San Salvador, El Salvador engaged in problems concerned with malaria control. His work on yellow fever and its control took him to Panama in 1942 and to Bogotá, Colombia in 1943. He was assigned to carry out inquiries into the epidemiology of jungle yellow fever as director from 1945 to 1950 of the yellow fever laboratory in Rio de Janiero, Brazil.

For almost a year (June 1944 to March 1945) Dr. Kumm was stationed in Rome, Italy as a consultant to the Surgeon General of the United States Army. Assigned to the section of the public health subcommission of the Allied Control Commission which was responsible for checking malaria, he directed field studies of the use of DDT against malaria mosquitoes.

(Continued next page)

DR. HENRY W. KUMM

On study leave from the Rockefeller Foundation, Kumm spent the year 1950-51 at The Johns Hopkins School of Hygiene and Public Health, where he was an instructor in the department of epidemiology. On July 9, 1951 he became associated with the National Foundation for Infantile Paralysis as assistant director of research and on September 1, 1953, Basil O'Connor, president of the foundation, announced the appointment of Dr. Kumm as director of research to succeed Dr. Harry M. Weaver, who resigned.

The National Foundation for Infantile Paralysis is a voluntary, non-profit organization established in 1938 for the prevention, treatment and cure of poliomyelitis. "Polio: New Weapons and New Hope," an article in the New York *Times* (May 31, 1953), stated that through public donations made to its March of Dimes fund, the foundation has raised some $150,000,000 during the past fifteen years, the greater part of which has been spent in the care and rehabilitation of victims of polio and in the training of medical personnel.

In the field of polio research, which more directly concerns the responsibilities of Dr. Kumm's office, the foundation has given about $20,000,000 to sponsor projects in nearly forty medical schools, hospitals and research laboratories in the United States. During the summers of 1951 and 1952 it helped to conduct the field tests of gamma globulin and in 1954 financed a mass trial of an anti-polio vaccine developed by Dr. Jonas E. Salk (see *Current Biography*, May, 1954) with funds from the March of Dimes. The amount spent for the vaccine research and tests was $965,950. The successful results of the mass experiment were announced on April 12, 1955, the tenth anniversary of the death of President Franklin Delano Roosevelt, who had been stricken with polio at the age of thirty-nine and who had established the foundation in 1938.

The first local chapter of the National Foundation was formed in 1939 in Coshocton, Ohio. There are now 3,100 local chapters covering every county in the United States. Since 1938 over $203,600,000 has been spent for hospitalization, braces and appliances, nursing and physical therapy services for 294,000 patients.

The National Foundation for Infantile Paralysis announced on April 14 that the 9,000,000 children to be immunized at its expense during 1955 with the Salk anti-polio vaccine would get three instead of two shots. The reason for the change is the recent finding by Dr. Jonas E. Salk, originator of the vaccine, that the third, or "booster" shot, should be given no sooner than seven months after the first two "conditioning" shots. This includes those children who received the placebo or "dummy" shots in the mass tests during 1954.

During his many years of research in various parts of the world, Dr. Kumm has contributed some fifty scientific papers on tropical medicine and poliomyelitis to professional journals. Among his articles in the *American Journal of Tropical Medicine* are a report, with M. B. Waddell as co-author, entitled "Haemagogus Capricornii Lutz as Laboratory Vector of Yellow Fever" (March 1948) and a series of studies on the dispersion of forest mosquitoes in Brazil, made with O. R. Causey and H. W. Laemmert (May 1948 and March 1950). For the September 1950 issue of the same publication he collaborated with Laemmert on two papers concerning yellow fever, one of which dealt with the geographical distribution of the disease among the primates of Brazil. Another report of his findings, "Seasonal Variations in Rainfall; Prevalence of Haemagogus and Incidence of Jungle Yellow Fever in Brazil and Colombia," was published in *Transactions of the Royal Society for Tropical Medicine and Hygiene*, May 1950.

He is the author also of *The Geographic Distribution of the Yellow Fever Vectors* (1931), monograph number 12 of the *American Journal of Hygiene*, and of the chapter on the arthropod borne virus encephalitides in the seventh edition of Milton Joseph Rosenau's *Preventive Medicine and Hygiene* (1951). Two of Kumm's articles on polio, both dealing with recent progress made in the knowledge of that disease, appear in *Medicina Revista Mexicana* (March 10, 1952, published in Mexico) and *Boletín de la Oficina Sanitaria Panamericana* (June 1952, published in Washington, D.C.).

Dr. Kumm became a naturalized citizen of the United States in 1945. He is a member of the Manhattan post of the Ground Observer Corps of the Air Force. He became a diplomate in 1949 of the Specialty Board of Preventive Medicine and Public Health, and is affiliated with several professional organizations: the American Medical Association, Medical Society of the County of New York, Medical Society of the State of New York, American Public Health Association, Royal Society of Tropical Medicine and Hygiene and American Association for the Advancement of Science; member of the National Malaria Society and American Society of Tropical Medicine. In 1951 he received from the President of Brazil the Order of the Southern Cross.

Dr. Kumm was married on June 15, 1928 to Annie Joyce Beale. They have three children, William Howard, Joceline Anne and Frederick Guinness Kumm. He belongs to the Episcopal Church and gives his political preference as "Republican or independent." His height is five feet nine inches and his weight is 200 pounds. He has blue eyes and gray hair. He enjoys working in the woods around his New Hampshire home. His membership during 1949-50 in the Rio de Janiero Theatre Guild (president in 1949) indicates another of his recreational interests.

References

N Y Herald Tribune p13 S 2 '53
N Y Times p13 S 2 '53
Directory of Medical Specialists (1953)

LAMBERT, W(ILLIAM) V(INCENT)

Sept. 13, 1897- Geneticist; university administrator

Address: b. College of Agriculture, University of Nebraska, Lincoln, Neb.; h. 3845 Apple St., Lincoln, Neb.

Wide World

W. V. LAMBERT

Esteemed by fellow scientists for his thirty years of achievement in the field of animal genetics, Dr. W. V. Lambert of the University of Nebraska came into public prominence in the summer of 1955, when he headed an American agricultural mission to the Soviet Union. Prior to his appointment in 1948 as dean and research director of the University of Nebraska's College of Agriculture, he had served as administrator of the U.S. Agricultural Research Administration and on the faculty of Iowa State College of Agricultural and Mechanic Arts.

Dean Lambert, on his return from a five-week tour of the Soviet Union, said that Russian agriculture on the whole was far behind America's. "There is too much hand labor and not enough individual incentive," he said. "Our agricultural machinery is way ahead of theirs, but the Soviets are putting more emphasis on agriculture because their population [is] increasing about 3,000,000 a year."

William Vincent Lambert was born on September 13, 1897 in Stella, Nebraska. His father was George W. Lambert, his mother, the former Addie Kiester. As an undergraduate at the University of Nebraska in Lincoln, he was a member of the Reserve Officers Training Corps in 1918. He was graduated with the B.S. degree in agriculture in 1921, and received the M.S. degree from the Kansas State College of Agriculture and Applied Science at Manhattan, Kansas in 1923, and in that year the University of Nebraska published in its Zoological Laboratory Studies, the report by Lambert, W. S. Rice and H. C. A. Walker entitled "Food and Parthogenetic Reproduction as Related to the Constitutional Vigor of Hydatina Senta."

Deciding on a career in animal and poultry research, he moved to Ames, Iowa to become an instructor at the Iowa State College of Agricultural and Mechanic Arts. A Rosenberg scholarship for the year 1929-1930 made possible further studies at the University of California in Berkeley, and the acquisition there of the Ph.D. degree in genetics in 1931. He returned to Iowa State College and was an assistant professor until 1936.

For four years beginning in 1936 Dr. Lambert served at Washington, D.C. in the U.S. Department of Agriculture's bureau of animal industry as senior animal husbandman in charge of genetic investigations. Established in 1884, this bureau deals with the prevention, control, and eradication of animal diseases, conducts research on the production of livestock and their products, performs inspection duties, and otherwise seeks to protect and develop the livestock, meat, poultry and related industries.

After five years (1940-1945) as associate director of Purdue University's agricultural experiment station at Lafayette, Indiana, Dr. Lambert returned to the U.S. Department of Agriculture as assistant research administrator and in 1946 became administrator of the Department's Agricultural Research Administration. He was a member of the U.S. delegation to the United Nations Food and Agriculture Organization conferences at Copenhagen, Denmark in 1946 and Geneva, Switzerland in 1947, and in the latter year was appointed to the board of alternates of the President's scientific research board. In 1946 W. V. Lambert was given the responsibility of coordinating all research activities of the Department of Agriculture, other than economic research (see his article "The Administration of Federal Research," *Science,* February 20, 1948.)

From 1946 to 1948 he was a member of the United States-Mexican Agricultural Commission which endeavored to suppress an outbreak of foot-and-mouth disease among Mexican live-

LAMBERT, W. V.—*Continued*

stock. Dr. Lambert left the Federal service in the fall of 1948 to take over his present position as dean of the University of Nebraska's College of Agriculture and director of the Agricultural Experiment Station. In this post he has supervised the work of six experimental stations located in different sections of Nebraska, as well as the college's agricultural extension service. Dr. Lambert was a member of the British Government's scientific mission to the African colonies in 1949, and of the FAO's scientific mission to Iraq in 1952.

Issuance of an invitation to the Soviet Union to send an agricultural delegation to the United States was first suggested in February, 1955 by Lauren K. Soth, the editorial page editor of the Des Moines (Iowa) *Register*, after Nikita S. Khrushchev, First Secretary of the Communist party of the U.S.S.R., had admonished Soviet farmers "to imitate the corn-hog cycle as practiced in Iowa and other parts of the United States" (New York *Times*, July 16, 1955). "Moscow jumped at the offer" and President Eisenhower "soon endorsed the idea of exchanging visits" (*Time*, August 1, 1955).

A twelve-member Soviet delegation was named to visit this country in July and August, and the U.S. Department of Agriculture announced the names of the twelve-man American delegation to travel to the U.S.S.R. The members of the American group (which, unlike the Russian mission, was to be "unofficial" and "privately financed") were Dr. Lambert as the leader, Professor D. Gale Johnson of the University of Chicago, Dean William E. Reed, a Negro, of the Agricultural and Technical College of North Carolina in Greensboro, Lauren K. Soth, J. M. Kleiner, a farm products distributor, and a group of farmers from Iowa, Washington, Ohio and Arizona.

Prior to their departure Dr. Lambert told newsmen of the delegation's "hope to plant the seeds of goodwill and international understanding" and its intention "to keep an open mind, as well as keeping its eyes open and its ears unplugged" (Washington *Post and Times Herald*, July 13, 1955). When the group arrived by plane in Moscow on July 15 it was found that its movements were to be confined to an itinerary agreed upon by the U.S. Embassy and Soviet officials.

The delegation traveled some 10,000 miles, visiting agricultural institutes, plant-breeding stations, tractor plants, collective, and state farms in the Ukraine, Northern Caucasus, Central Asia, Western Siberia and elsewhere, but efforts to talk with Soviet farm workers were not encouraged and were further handicapped by the fact that all the members of the delegation except Russian-born Kleiner were forced to converse through an interpreter. They were accompanied by Soviet officials and Horace J. Davis, U.S. agricultural attaché in Moscow.

Returning to Moscow on August 20, the Americans conferred with high U.S.S.R. agricultural officials and submitted a fourteen-point program of criticism and recommendation which, to the surprise of many, was published in detail in the Moscow newspapers. Wastage of labor and machinery on the state and collective farms, expansion of corn production in unsuitable areas, and lack of inducement to peasant farmers to increase production, were among the criticisms. The U.S. experts also suggested that grain sorghums should be substituted in many areas too dry for corn. (An article by Lambert containing his impressions of Soviet agriculture was published in *Life*, September 18, 1955.)

The returning American delegates agreed that, although Russian farmers in general possessed only the "bare necessities," they were relatively content since (in the words of Ferris Owen) "each year they think they are having it better than ever before" (New York *Herald Tribune*, August 22, 1955). The delegates were guests of the National Press Club in Washington, D.C. "The Russians are making progress," Dr. Lambert asserted. "Don't overlook that." Interviewed on the *Meet the Press* radio and television programs on August 28, Dr. Lambert said that he had seen no sign of "any immediate food crisis in Russia." Nevertheless, he did not believe the Soviet Union had the food reserves to wage war now.

To a question by Lawrence Spivak as to the wisdom of exchanges, "particularly on scientific knowledge and on machinery," with "someone who just a day or two ago was conducting a cold war against us," Dr. Lambert replied that it seemed to him that "somehow or other we should begin to try to break down this international barrier that has existed," and that he had "the feeling that working with a nation has some of the same characteristics as working with an individual." At the same time Lambert felt that "a delegation is not the way to get next to the people." He admitted that the Russian delegation had "gained more than we gained, but we . . . got a fairly good opportunity [to see their] . . . scientific institutes [and] experiment stations."

In a syndicated article in the Washington *Post and Times Herald* (August 29), Dr. Lambert wrote at length about a large scale Soviet attempt to convert the virgin lands of western Siberia and northern Kazakhstan into a national granary. The predominantly silt loam soil was good, he thought, but there was danger that these lands would become a dust bowl unless better provision was made to check the Siberian winds.

"Russia is doing research on some of these subjects already," wrote Dean Lambert in *Life*. "There are 1,000 agricultural experiment stations and the scientists in them are well paid. . . Research publications should be freely exchanged between nations."

Dr. Lambert is a fellow of the American Academy of Arts and Sciences, and a member of the American Society of Zoologists, Poultry Science Association, Genetics Society of America, and American Genetics Association. He is a past secretary-treasurer of the American Society for Animal Production, and on the board of the Midwest Research Institute and the Farm Foundation at Chicago. His fraternities are the Phi Kappa Phi and the Sigma Xi.

He married Esther Posson September 15, 1923 and they have two daughters, Marilyn and Anne. Lambert's articles and papers have appeared in scientific journals and in the Department of Agriculture's *Yearbook* and circulars.

References

American Men of Science (1949)
Who Knows—and What (1954)
Who's Who in America, 1954-55
World Biography (1954)

LAPP, RALPH E(UGENE) Aug. 24, 1917-
Physicist; author

Address: b. Nuclear Science Service, 2500 Wisconsin Ave., Washington 7, D.C.; Bulletin of the Atomic Scientists, Educational Foundation for Nuclear Science, Inc., 5734 University Ave., Chicago 37, Ill.; h. 4201 Massachusetts Ave., Washington 16, D.C.

A physicist who has been a persistent proponent of more effective civil defense techniques against atomic and hydrogen bomb attacks is Dr. Ralph E. Lapp. In his books, *The New Force* and *Must We Hide?*, and in his lectures, magazine articles, and television appearances, he has brought to the attention of the American public the urgent need for more adequate defense. "The problem is a great one, but it is not *hopelessly* great," he contends, and recommends emergency shelters, preferably below the surface of the earth, as the fundamental rule for survival and protection from radioactive fall-out.

Dr. Lapp, who now heads the Nuclear Science Service, and is a consultant to industry, had previously been an assistant director of the Argonne National Laboratory, scientific adviser to the War Department General Staff, and head of the Nuclear Physics Branch of the Office of Naval Research. In 1946 and 1947 he was deputy executive director of the Atomic Energy Commission's Joint Research and Development Board. He is currently a special editor of the *Bulletin of the Atomic Scientists.*

On September 20,1955 Dr. Lapp stated that America's stockpile of atomic weapons is so big that it now amounts to "several tons of T.N.T. for every inhabitant of our planet." He urged President Eisenhower to disclose the size of this stockpile as a "potent force for peace" (New York *Times,* September 21, 1955).

Ralph Eugene Lapp was born in Buffalo, New York on August 24, 1917, the son of Henry R. and Lucy E. (Grammel) Lapp. He attended Canisius College in his home town and then studied at the University of Chicago where he was a Henry Strong Foundation fellow, and an instructor during his first postgraduate year. He received the B.S. degree in 1940 and the Ph.D. degree in 1946, specializing in the study of cosmic rays, showers, and bursts. He was active in the university project led by Dr. Marcel Schein who organized a cosmic ray expedition in 1943 to Mt. Evans, Colorado to study high-altitude shower phenomena. With Dr. Schein, he contributed one of many papers on the subject to the *Physical Review.*

Wide World
RALPH E. LAPP

Meanwhile, on December 2, 1942, the first nuclear chain reaction known to man had been produced at the pseudonymous "Metallurgical Laboratory" at the University of Chicago, with the aid of Enrico Fermi, Leo Szilard, Arthur Holly Compton and other scientists. Dr. Lapp was pursuing his "own nonsecret research, studying cosmic rays with equipment housed in the press box above Stagg Field." "One day," he wrote in his book *The New Force*, "while lugging down a Geiger counter I . . . soon found myself inside the stands [at Stagg Field] amid other white-jacketed men." His presence was not challenged by the guards, apparently because of his apparel and equipment, until he was ready to leave. "Shortly after the hubbub died down I 'officially' joined the project" and from 1943 to 1945, he was associate physicist and assistant laboratory director at the Metallurgical Laboratory (nucleus of the Manhattan Project).

The United States created its first Atomic Energy Commission (AEC) under the [Brien] McMahon act of August 1946. Among the commission's functions was the support of major research in the physical and natural sciences at four research centers. At one of these, the Argonne National Laboratory in Chicago, Dr. Lapp became assistant director. He was assigned as well to the AEC military liaison committee to consult with the three armed services on military applications of atomic energy. The U.S. Navy tested the effects of A-bombs in 1946 at Bikini, 2,000 miles southwest of Hawaii.

At this time, Lapp wrote, "I was still . . . trying to make up my mind whether to stick in the field of pure science or to go astray from it." He decided that "a junket to the South Pacific might help me make up my mind so . . . I . . . organized a group of thirty scientists to participate in the Bikini tests" (*The New*

LAPP, RALPH E.—*Continued*

Force). Dr. Lapp was "technically in charge of a small gunboat" laden with measuring and observation equipment.

After the Bikini tests Lapp moved out of the sphere of pure science and into the applied one of civil defense with which he is now so closely identified. He spent two years as scientific advisor to the War Department General Staff and deputy executive director of Dr. Vannevar Bush's research and development board of the AEC; and, in 1949, as nuclear physics head of the U.S. Navy's Office of Naval Research. During this period, Dr. Lapp began what was to become a concentrated written and spoken campaign on three issues: 1) civil defense against atomic attack; 2) education of civilians on atomic matters; and 3) an enlightened security administration.

In 1949 nationally circulated magazines carried articles by Dr. Lapp, such as the *Reader's Digest* (July 1949) "New Facts About the Atom Bomb" and *Newsweek's* "Young Man With a Bomb Plan" (April 25, 1949). The *U.S. News & World Report* interviewed him in April, September, and October 1949, attracting considerable comment in the nation's press.

David Lawrence in the New York *Sun* (September 27 and October 12, 1949) described Lapp as "the one scientist who seems to have specialized on defense aspects of the atomic bomb" and "one who sees no military purpose in improving the destructiveness of the A-bomb." In another column Lawrence quoted Lapp's belief that Russia also had the bomb and could produce about 100 atomic bombs if she could obtain sufficient uranium.

The United States, in Dr. Lapp's opinion was "woefully unprepared" (*Christian Science Monitor* October 1949), and he scored the futility of linking military security with number of bombs (New York *Times*, October 4, 1949). Speaking at the University of Puerto Rico in November, the physicist stressed industrial decentralization and limited building height as urban defense measures. The possibility of atomic war, he said, "argues for throwing our last ounce of effort into the United Nations as an instrument for world peace."

At this time Dr. Lapp also released his first popular book, *Must We Hide?* (Addison-Wesley Press, 1949), in which he tried "not only to report the facts in an unemotional manner, but . . . also . . . to draw logical conclusions from them" (Foreword). The book, while condemning the vulnerability to atomic attack of vertically populated American cities like New York, showed that protection against thermal radiation was "easily accomplished." People in subways or cellars, for instance, or protected by a thickness of six feet of earth would be safe, he emphasized.

Leaving Government service in 1950, he became consultant physicist to the Nuclear Science Service in the nation's capitol. With many other eminent scientists, including Dr. Hans Bethe, he was interviewed by *Life* (February 27, 1950) about the decision to make the H-bomb. Lapp warned that "we must be prepared to lose 10-15 million people in the first day of the superblitz."

Articles by Dr. Lapp have included a series in the *Scientific American* (June 1950); in the *Saturday Evening Post* (April 14, April 21 and September 29, 1951) in collaboration with Stewart Alsop, which clarify atomic science and civil defense for the general reader; in *Collier's* (February 16 and July 5, 1952); in the *Washington Post and Times Herald* (August 16, 1953); and in *Newsweek* (July 23, 1951) in which he introduced his diagram of "Target Town," a typical urban set-up which he wanted built to demonstrate A-bomb defense techniques to civil defense workers.

In the September 1953 issue of the *Bulletin of the Atomic Scientists* Dr. Lapp, as special editor, reported on an interview with Val Peterson, Federal Civil Defense Administrator in which they discussed Project East River. He edited the September 1954 issue of the *Bulletin,* which was chiefly concerned with the security case of Dr. J. Robert Oppenheimer, and in October he prodded the Federal Government for not putting into effect Operation Candor, a series of national information programs on atomic problems.

The national press took particular note of Dr. Lapp's *Bulletin* articles (November 1954 and February 1955) about radioactive fall-out. His "conservative estimate" was that "the explosion of fifty super-bombs could blanket the entire northeastern United States in a serious lethal radioactive fog."

The AEC issued its first official report on February 15, 1955 on the radioactive contamination produced by the thermo-nuclear detonation at Bikini on March 1, 1954 (which had affected the crew of the Japanese fishing vessel *Fortunate Dragon*).

Discussing the hazards, both external and internal, from fission products in his article, "Radioactive Fall-out III," in the *Bulletin of the Atomic Scientists* (June 1955), Dr. Lapp wrote that from his calculations he had deduced that concentrated radioactivity could remain lethal for a long period of time, could keep people underground like moles, and the effect of radioactive strontium ingested by farm animals or absorbed by food crops could be injurious and lingering.

Testifying before a Senate Armed Services Civil Defense Subcommittee headed by Senator Estes Kefauver (Democrat, of Tennessee), Dr. Lapp urged a combination evacuation and shelter program—planned emigrations to designated shelter areas eight to ten miles outside a city's limits. (Washington *Post and Times Herald,* May 1, 1955).

Asked to comment on the lifting of secrecy from many atomic projects at the First International Conference on the Peaceful Uses of Atomic Energy (held at Geneva, Switzerland in August 1955), Dr. Lapp said on the Columbia Broadcasting System radio on August 16, that scientists had learned that they had approached the same problems in different directions, but got "the same solutions." He also thought that "cross-fertilizing" of ideas was the best result of the conference, and that such inspiration would set off "a chain reaction in the field of knowledge."

Dr. Lapp collaborated with H. L. Andrews on the book, *Nuclear Radiation Physics* (Prentice-Hall, 1948) which was reissued in 1954. Among his other books are *Must We Hide?* (Addison-Wesley Press, 1949) and *The New Force* (Harper, 1953). He is a member of Phi Beta Kappa, Sigma XI, American Institute of Physics, Institution of Radio Engineers, Physical Society, and American Association for the Advancement of Science.

"Mine was a very modest role in the atomic energy picture. . .", Dr. Lapp wrote in his book *The New Force* (p 5), "It was my good fortune to be in on many big events in atomic energy among outstanding men. . ."

He is tall, and has light brown hair and brown eyes. He likes to climb mountains and collect seashells. He also enjoys bicycling.

The issues of bomb protection "must be faced squarely," he believes, "and must be met with ingenuity and perseverance. We must resolutely face the future with the conviction that an informed America will be an unconquerable nation."

References

Colliers 129:11 F 16 '52 por
Newsweek 33:56 Ap 25 '49
Sat R 36:13 F 21 '53
U S News 27:30+ O 7 '49 por
American Men of Science (1955)
Who's Who in America (Sup. D '54)

LE GALLIENNE, EVA (lĕ găl'yĕn) Jan. 11, 1899- Actress; author; director

Address: h. Weston, Conn.

NOTE: This biography supersedes the article which appeared in *Current Biography* in 1942.

After four decades as an actress and thirty years as a manager and director, Eva Le Gallienne still retains her enthusiasm for the theatre and its power "to spread beauty out into life." Her devotion to the idea of classical repertory theatres is undiminished by the years. From 1926 to 1932 she directed the Civic Repertory Theatre in New York City, offering thirty-four plays at popular prices. In 1946 she founded, with Margaret Webster and Cheryl Crawford, the American Repertory Theatre.

During the past decade Miss Le Gallienne has been occupied with radio productions, appearances at the New York City Center and on tour in *The Corn Is Green*. She recently toured in a Theatre Guild repertoire production *An Evening With Will Shakespeare*, has made recordings of *Romeo and Juliet* on Long-Playing discs, and has completed her autobiography, *With a Quiet Heart* (Viking, 1953) twenty years after her first autobiography, *At 33* (Longman's).

On February 3, 1955 at the Holiday Theatre, New York, Miss Le Gallienne had a starring role in John Cecil Holm's play *The Southwest Corner*, based on Mildred Walker's novel of the same name. She made her film debut in Twentieth Century-Fox's film biography of Edwin Booth, *Prince of Players*. She also staged the Shakespearean scenes and was technical adviser of the picture, which was released in January 1955.

Eva Le Gallienne was born in London, England on January 11, 1899 to the English poet, Richard Le Gallienne, and his second wife, Julie Norregaard, a Danish journalist. Brought up with her half-sister, Hesper, by their "Nanny" (Susan Stenning), Eva spent her early years in a Georgian manorhouse at St. John's Wood, London. After her parents separated, Eva's mother supported her by running a millinery shop in Paris under the name of Mme. Fedora, and Eva attended a French convent school. She recalls a happy childhood spent playing in the Luxembourg Gardens.

Each year she spent Christmas in Copenhagen, where she learned Danish folksongs from her grandmother. She studied at the Collège Sévigné in Paris and attended plays, operas and ballets. When she saw Sarah Bernhardt in *Le Prince Charmant,* Eva was so impressed that she wrote in her book *At 33,* "From that moment on, the Theatre . . . became to me the all-important aim; all my experiences, my reading, my studies from then on were focussed toward one ultimate goal."

Her summers were spent in England, where Eva and Hesper wrote poems, drew and painted, started a little magazine *The Arrow,* and gave scenes from plays, with some of Nanny's relatives comprising their faithful audience. Later, at the Chiddingfold Manor, taken over by the actor William Faversham and his family, Eva met many actors and writers including Constance Collier, who became her lifelong friend and taught her how to read Shakespearean verse.

After an unhappy interlude at a conventional English boarding school, Eva had an opportunity, in 1914, to take the role of a page in the production of Maurice Maeterlinck's *Monna Vanna,* starring Constance Collier. The outbreak of World War I prevented realization of her plans to return to Paris, so Eva was sent to Tree's Academy in London (now the Royal Academy of Dramatic Art). Here she learned fencing, dancing, voice production, elocution and played Juliet in *Romeo and Juliet.* While working after her dramatic classes as a volunteer in the soup kitchens set up for soldiers, she acquired a knowledge of cockney which stood her in good stead when she tried out for the part of the cockney slavey, Elizabeth, in *The Laughter of Fools,* directed by Frank Curzon, at the Prince of Wales Theatre. The drama critics acclaimed the sixteen-year-old actress as a "brilliant new comedienne."

Eva turned down an offer to go on tour and decided to visit America. She and her mother crossed on the American steamer *St. Louis* and during the two weeks' voyage renewed acquaintance with the popular American actress Elsie Janis. While Eva searched for work on Broadway, she and her mother stayed with the William Favershams at their home at Mattituck, Long Island, where she met theatre celebrities. But even with these contacts, Eva had difficulty

EVA LE GALLIENNE

getting a stage part because she was "too English in type for the American stage."

Eventually, Harrison Grey Fiske (husband of the famous actress Minnie Maddern Fiske) engaged Eva to play in *Mrs. Boltay's Daughters* (at fifty dollars a week) and she made her American debut as Rose, a colored maid (she was coached by Merle Maddern) so that her British accent was toned down. The play had a short run, and once more Eva "made the rounds" and each day brought the usual disappointments. "My great solace," Miss Le Gallienne recalled, "was to slip into the Public Library between visits to various offices; I was in the midst of a veritable orgy of reading. I had discovered Walt Whitman, and, even more important, I had at last discovered Ibsen."

She succeeded in obtaining a Cockney role in a play by Austin Strong in which Lewis Stone was starred, but the play closed after two weeks. Her next role was as an Irish ingénue in *The Melody of Youth,* by Brandon Tynan, directed by George Tyler and starring Lily Cahill, which ran for over four months. Eva earned seventy-five dollars a week.

Her first leading part was as Patricia Molloy in *Mr. Lazarus* by Harvey O'Higgins and Harriet Ford. She recalls that it played to enthusiastic audiences in Washington, D.C. and in Chicago, "all through one of the hottest summers on record." When it opened in New York, in spite of splendid notices, it closed after a five weeks' run. Her next play was *Mile-a-Minute Kendall* by Owen Davis. Producer Oliver Morosco fired her because she had no "pep," no "punch." "What a salutary blow it was to me, after all," she wrote later. "Every bit of conceit was knocked clean out of me!"

After playing in *Mr. Lazarus* on a West Coast tour, and then with Richard Bennett in *The Cinderella Man* at the Alcazar Stock Theatre in San Francisco, Miss Le Gallienne returned to New York and played a bit part in William Faversham's all-star revival of *Lord and Lady Algy,* produced by Winthrop Ames. She next appeared with Ethel Barrymore as an ingénue in *The Off Chance* at the Empire Theatre, and later on tour.

"It is impossible to overestimate the advantage to young players of working at the side of the great ones of their profession," Miss Le Gallienne has observed. "The two seasons I spent with Miss Barrymore were of immense importance to the development of my work." At the end of the tour Miss Le Gallienne's mother returned to London and Eva moved from an apartment on Seventeenth Street into the Hotel Algonquin so as to be near the theatres. She learned Russian from Ray Davidson Rosenbaum (sister of sculptor Jo Davidson), who ran the Russian Inn on Thirty-seventh Street, where actors ate many of their meals on credit.

Miss Le Gallienne would occasionally get a job as a "super" in a movie for ten dollars a day. She was a French dancing partner with Elsie Janis in her first "Gang Show," at the George M. Cohan Theatre. She next played in *Tilly of Bloomsbury* by Ian Hay Beith, but when the play opened at Poli's Theatre in Washington, D.C., Eva fell ill with influenza and had to withdraw from the cast.

She scored her first big success in 1920 as Elsie Dover in *Not So Long Ago,* written by Arthur Richman and starring Sydney Blackmer. Eva received her first really important notice in the *Boston Evening Transcript* from H. T. Parker. "It was important to me," she recalls, "because it did not just indiscriminately laud me to the skies. It showed me that Mr. Parker had watched my work carefully for several years."

The play was an immediate success in New York, and Miss Le Gallienne signed a three-year contract with the Shuberts. She and Mary Kennedy, another actress in *Not So Long Ago,* grew restless in the long-run show and organized a group to present plays for the added experience on their free afternoons. When someone wanted to commercialize their workshop idea and to put on public performances, Eva, "bitterly disappointed and hurt," withdrew from the project.

The Theatre Guild selected Eva Le Gallienne to play the role of Julie in Ferenc Molnár's play *Liliom,* opposite Joseph Schildkraut, and it ran through the summer of 1921 and the following winter, and then on tour. Altogether, she acted the part 948 times. On a trip to Europe she visited Molnár in Budapest and saw the amusement park which was *Liliom*'s real locale. Miss Le Gallienne's next big role was as Alexandra in Molnár's *The Swan,* produced by Gilbert Miller. In her spare time during the long run of this play, she directed Gerhart Hauptmann's *Hanneles Himmelfahrt.*

In the summer of 1924 she acted in *The Master Builder* at Jasper Deeters' Theatre, Rose Valley, Pennsylvania. After a road tour in *The Swan* she went to Paris and produced Mercedes de Acosta's *Jehanne d'Arc.* About this time she saw Eleonora Duse act, and later they became good friends. She records her reaction to Duse in *Cosi Sia*: "At the first sound of Duse's voice, at the first glimpse of her face, tears came into my eyes; tears of wonder, tears of exaltation; for the first time in this world I felt I was looking upon perfect beauty."

On Miss Le Gallienne's return from Paris she put on two special performances under her own management of *The Master Builder* and *John Gabriel Borkman* at the Booth Theatre at 10:30 A.M. at a $1.50 top price. On both occasions the house was completely sold out. This encouraged Miss Le Gallienne to plan for a repertory theatre. She took her company on tour in the two Ibsen plays and then rented an old theatre on Fourteenth Street in New York, just west of Sixth Avenue.

On October 25, 1926 the Civic Repertory Theatre opened with Jacinto Benavente's *Saturday Night.* During the years (1926 to 1932) of her management, the group presented 1,581 performances, and among the thirty-four plays were Anton Chekov's *The Three Sisters, The Cherry Orchard, The Sea Gull;* Henrik Ibsen's *The Master Builder* and *John Gabriel Borkman;* J. M. Barrie's *Peter Pan* (which had 129 performances in the six seasons) and Lewis Carroll's *Alice in Wonderland* (127 performances were given). Gregorio Martínez Sierra's *The Cradle Song* had 164 performances.

During the economic depression Miss Le Gallienne found that several of her financial backers were "literally unable to help." "Our intake at the box office had climbed to an amazingly high average," she said, "but we still needed a subsidy of at least $75,000 a year to continue our [popular price] policy and to sustain, as well, our free school [for young actors]." She moved the play *Alice in Wonderland* "uptown" to the New Amsterdam Theatre. "It seemed strange and horrible after six years of repertory to play in the same play performance after performance," she said.

After she closed the Civic Repertory Theatre on December 10, 1932, Miss Le Gallienne was absent from the Broadway scene until 1934 because of an accident on her farm in Connecticut in which her hands were badly burned. She returned to play in *L'Aiglon* with Ethel Barrymore, and in 1935 was awarded the Town Hall Club's medal of honor. In 1936 she played in the Theatre Guild's *Prelude to Exile,* in 1938 in *Madame Capet* and with Elsie Janis in *Frank Fay's Music Hall.* She directed a series of revivals of Theatre Guild shows on tour.

One of her most successful roles in 1942 was that of Lettie in *Uncle Harry,* opposite Joseph Schildkraut, a play by Thomas Job which ran for over a year in New York and for six months on the road. During this period her mother died. In 1943 Miss Le Gallienne presented *The Cherry Orchard,* aided by Margaret Webster, produced by Mrs. Carly Wharton. She played the title role in Thomas Job's adaptation of Zola's novel *Therese Raquin,* which opened on October 9, 1945.

In the fall of 1946 her dream of another repertory theatre was realized, with the opening of the American Repertory Theatre's production of *Henry VIII.* This time she had the aid of Margaret Webster and Cheryl Crawford. "I was happily engrossed in the luxury of playing three such wonderful and contrasting parts as Queen Catherine in *Henry VIII,* the Comtesse in *What Every Woman Knows,* and Ella Rentheim in *John Gabriel Borkman,*" she recalls in her autobiography, *With a Quiet Heart,* but added, ". . . the critics in the case of the ART saw fit to damn us with faint praise. . . ." Although *Androcles and the Lion* and *Alice in Wonderland* (with Bambi Linn) met with great success at the International Theatre, Miss Le Gallienne soon saw that the repertory system would have to be abandoned because of the cost of productions of less popular plays.

Since 1948 she has made each year a successful tour of the United States giving scenes from Shakespeare. In 1949 she wrote her first "juvenile," *Flossie and Bossie: A Moral Tale* (Harper & Brothers), based on her observations of two little Bantam hens in her barnyard in Connecticut. Concerning the future of repertory theatre, which gives young people an opportunity to get acting experience without the tremendous handicaps of the commercial theatre, she sees hope in Lawrence Langner's new project, an "American Stratford" in Stratford, Connecticut for Shakespearean productions. Also, she believes that young actors should have the courage and initiative to start theatres of their own.

Miss Le Gallienne was co-starred with Mary Astor at the Royale Theatre on January 13, 1954 in *The Starcross Story,* by Diana Morgan, produced by John C. Wilson. It closed in New York after one night's performance (despite the fact that the play had three favorable reviews).

Her characterization of an aged Vermonter in *The Southwest Corner* by John Cecil Holm, received Brooks Atkinson's praise in the New York *Times* (February 4, 1955): "Miss Le Gallienne plays with great sympathy and insight. The unspoken part of the story is told in illuminating acting." The play closed after thirty-six performances.

She is a co-founder of "Theatre Masterworks" programs which she and Margaret Webster and Maurice Evans are recording to form a library of plays for schools, libraries and universities. She has also translated seven of Ibsen's plays, and has completed the prefaces to *Hedda Gabler* and *The Master Builder* (published in England in 1954 by Faber). These translations are done from the actor's point of view rather than the scholar's or critic's.

The actress received honorary degrees from Tufts College (1927), Smith (1930), Russell Sage (1930), Brown University (1933), Mount Holyoke (1937). She was awarded the gold medal of the Society of Arts and Sciences and the Pictorial Review Annual Achievement Award ($5,000) in 1926.

When not on tour she lives at her farm in Weston with her companion, Marion Evensen. She has learned to weave and to paint. In the

LE GALLIENNE, EVA—*Continued*

summer of 1951 Miss Le Gallienne had a radio program over NBC for sixteen weeks in which she selected and directed her favorite plays. She personally received over 2,000 letters and thousands more were directed to the station expressing appreciation of the program.

Selected References (see also references listed in 1942 biographical sketch)

N Y Times Book R p23 My 3 '53 por
N Y World-Telegram p9 Ja 9 '54; p15 Ag 20 '53
Blum, D. C. Great Stars of the American Stage (1952)
Le Gallienne, E. At 33 (1934); With a Quiet Heart (1953)
Who's Who in America, 1954-55
Who's Who in the Theatre (1953)

LÉGER, FERNAND Feb.(?) 1881-Aug. 17, 1955 French artist; exponent of the "mechanized human figure" and abstract art; first exhibited his pictures with the Independents in Paris in 1910; joined the Cubists in revolt against representational art; lived in the United States (1940-1945), during which period he painted *The Divers, The Acrobats, The Cyclists;* returned to France and painted social subjects; noted for his ability to find lyric beauty in industrial machinery; exhibited frequently at the Museum of Modern Art in New York; painted two giant abstract murals for the United Nations General Assembly auditorium (1952); won the $4,000 grand international prize (1955) of the third biennial Modern Art Exposition in São Paulo, Brazil, for his work, *The Builders.* See *Current Biography* (Jan.) 1943.

Obituary

N Y Times p23 Ag 18 '55

LEHMAN, HERBERT H(ENRY) (lē'-măn) Mar. 28, 1878- United States Senator from New York; civic leader; former banker

Address: b. Senate Office Bldg., Washington 25, D.C.; 41 E. 57th St., New York 22; h. 820 Park Ave., New York 21

NOTE: This biography supersedes the article which appeared in *Current Biography* in 1943.

On March 28, 1955, on the occasion of his seventy-seventh birthday, Senator Herbert H. Lehman of New York was honored by his colleagues in the U.S. Senate. Majority leader Lyndon B. Johnson paid tribute to him on the Senate floor: "Few men in our history," he asserted, "have had such a distinguished and brilliant career" (New York *Herald Tribune,* March 29, 1955). After nearly thirty years working in business, largely with Lehman Brothers, a family investment banking firm, Lehman began his political career in 1928 when he was elected lieutenant governor of New York under Franklin D. Roosevelt.

During his ten-year tenure as Governor of the State of New York (1933-1942), in which he was four times elected by large pluralities on the Democratic ticket, Lehman promoted much legislation to prevent social and religious discrimination, averted strikes, introduced labor reform, old-age security and other measures implementing the Federal New Deal program. Upon taking office he had inherited a deficit of over $100,000,000; he converted this into a surplus of more than $75,000,000. He resigned the governorship to become director-general of UNNRA (United Nations Relief and Rehabilitation Administration) from 1943 to 1946. Since his election to the U.S. Senate in 1949 he has served variously on the committees for Interior and Insular Affairs, Labor and Public Welfare, and Banking and Currency.

Born in New York City on March 28, 1878 to Mayer and Babette (Newgass) Lehman, Herbert Henry Lehman was the youngest of eight children. His father, a German immigrant, had settled in Montgomery, Alabama, where he became engaged in the cotton business. Later he moved to New York, where the family's investment banking firm of Lehman Brothers was established, and became a co-founder of the New York Cotton Exchange. Young Herbert received his preparatory education at Dr. Sach's Collegiate Institute and then attended Williams College in Williamstown, Massachusetts, from which he received the B.A. degree in 1899.

After graduation he entered welfare work at the Henry Street Settlement in New York City and started in business with the J. Spencer Turner Company, a textile manufacturing firm located in Brooklyn. He began at a salary of $5 a week; by 1906 he had become vice-president and treasurer of the company. In 1908 he left to become a partner in his family's banking business.

At the outbreak of World War I in 1914 he became associated with the Joint Distribution Committee and directed the collection and disbursement of $75,000,000 for the relief of Jewish war sufferers in Europe and Palestine. Later he became a civilian assistant to Franklin D. Roosevelt, then Assistant Secretary of the U.S. Navy. In August 1917 Lehman was commissioned a captain in the Army; by April 1919 he had been promoted to the rank of colonel. He aided General George W. Goethals in supervising the purchase, storage and distribution of matériel for the American Expeditionary Force. After the war he was appointed a special assistant to Newton D. Baker, Secretary of War, and served as a member of the Contract Adjustment and War Department Claims boards. In 1919 he received the Distinguished Service Medal.

Lehman then resumed his duties with Lehman Brothers. From 1924 to 1927, while serving on a mediation committee in the garment industry, he helped to adjust numerous labor disputes. In 1926 he was named chairman of a citizens' committee on finances for New York City and of the campaign committee for Alfred E. Smith's election as Governor of New York. Two years later Lehman withdrew from business and embarked on a political career.

He was chairman of the Democratic National Committee's finance committee for the Presidential campaign of 1928 and was elected lieutenant governor of New York by a plurality of 14,000. He was re-elected in 1930 and worked for the rehabilitation of the state hospitals for the insane and the establishment of a new system of parole of criminals.

When Roosevelt was a candiate for the Presidency in 1932, Lehman ran for the governorship. In the 1934 and 1936 elections he was returned as governor. Although he was a consistent supporter of the New Deal, he demonstrated his independence in 1937 by his opposition to Roosevelt's plan to reconstitute the Supreme Court. In 1938 he ran for New York's first four-year gubernatorial term and won an unprecedented fourth term by a plurality of 64,394 votes over Thomas E. Dewey.

In December 1942, at Roosevelt's request, he resigned his office to become head of the newly created Office of Foreign Relief and Rehabilitation Operations (OFRRO). Lehman defined the aim of the agency in these words, as quoted by Robert M. Bartlett in *They Work for Tomorrow* (1943): "Our enemy is fighting to enslave mankind; we are fighting to make men free. We must feed and clothe and find shelter for the millions whose lives have been disrupted by the war." Lehman plunged into his duties with characteristic vigor: he made speeches, wrote articles, and took his first plane trip for the cause.

In November 1943 plans for joint United Nations relief activity, which Lehman had begun to formulate, were realized when over forty countries formed the United Nations Relief and Rehabilitation Administration. Lehman was chosen as director-general. "UNRRA will concern itself," Lehman wrote in the New York *Times Magazine* (January 30, 1944), "with insuring the provision of those goods and services which are needed for immediate relief after the military period. [However] . . . even in the earliest shipments some parts will consist of rehabilitation supplies; for it is intended from the very start to initiate the program of rehabilitation which alone can result in a speedy ending of the need for relief."

Repeatedly and urgently, he labored to arouse public interest in the agency's work and the government's support of its vast obligations. On March 12, 1946, offering failing health as his reason, he submitted his resignation. In his final report to the UNRRA Council, he recommended the formation of an international food control board and warned that unless the International Bank for Reconstruction and Development was fully prepared to assume relief responsibilities when UNRRA ended, the United Nations would lose all that they had gained in military victory. The United States, Italy, Czechoslovakia, and China decorated him for his work with UNRRA. After being defeated in the November 1946 election as a candidate for the U.S. Senate from New York by Republican Irving M. Ives, he served for the next three years on numerous private boards and commissions. In 1948 he was named a member of the advisory board of the Economic Cooperation Administration.

Wide World

HERBERT H. LEHMAN

On November 8, 1949 Lehman won a special election over John Foster Dulles (Republican), to complete the term of Senator Robert F. Wagner (Democrat), who had resigned. The Senator-elect from New York, *United States News & World Report* (November 18, 1949) declared, "brings into Congress a ready vote and voice for nearly, but not quite all, of President Truman's 'Fair Deal' policies." He opposed the Brannan agricultural plan and Truman's compulsory health insurance program, but on all other matters voted with the Administration. Hartley E. Howe, in summarizing Lehman's first year in the Senate in the *Nation* (October 28, 1950), wrote that he "plunged headlong into debate and the introduction of legislation."

In the course of his campaign for the 1950 elections he enunciated the principles which guided him in voting: "To increase in every way our preparedness, strength and security at home; to do the same for our allies abroad; to cooperate with the United Nations to discourage communistic or other totalitarian aggression; to maintain a sound domestic economy and control inflation; to insure an equitable sharing of the profits of national enterprise and the burdens of national sacrifice; to maintain at home an orderly government dedicated to the welfare of the people and the protection of their liberties; and to keep before himself and the people as 'a guiding light the ultimate goal of a world at peace'" (New York *Times*, October 3, 1950). On November 8 he was re-elected to the Senate, defeating Joseph R. Hanley of New York to his first full term, which expires in January 1957.

In the first session of the Eighty-second Congress (1951), he voted for the Universal Military Training bill, for the resolution on sending troops to Europe, and for Government operation of defense plants. He opposed an

LEHMAN, HERBERT H.—*Continued*

absolute ban of Allied trade with the Soviet bloc nations, a $500,000,000 cut in economic aid to Europe, and a tax increase of $5,500,000,000. In 1952 he voted against using the Taft-Hartley act in the steel strike.

A long-time advocate of a liberal immigration policy, Lehman strongly opposed the McCarran-Walter Immigration and Nationality Act of 1952, denouncing it as discriminatory. In 1952 he joined with Senator Hubert Humphrey, Jr., Democrat of Minnesota, in attempting to liberalize the bill, but their efforts met with defeat. When President Harry S. Truman vetoed the McCarran-Walter bill, Lehman applauded him for keeping faith with "the fundamental traditions of America." However, Congress overrode the President's veto and the bill became law. Lehman has continued to seek to liberalize the act.

In the first session of the Eighty-third Congress, Lehman voted to confirm Charles E. Bohlen as U.S. Ambassador to the Soviet Union and to grant tax relief to small business. He cast negative votes on the offshore oil bill granting title to the states, on granting summary firing powers to Cabinet officers, and on applying pressure to France to free Indochina. In June 1954 he joined with Senator Ralph E. Flanders (Republican of Vermont) in an effort to strip Senator Joseph R. McCarthy (Republican of Wisconsin) of his committee chairmanships, and the following month advocated censure of McCarthy by the Senate.

Lehman voted in 1954 in favor of the St. Lawrence seaway bill, appropriating increased funds for the Tennessee Valley Authority, extending the Reciprocal Trade Agreements Act for three years instead of one, raising the personal income tax exemption, authorizing commercial power production by the Atomic Energy Commission, and making Communist party membership a crime. He opposed the Bricker amendment limiting the treaty-making powers of the President and a $500,000,000 reduction in foreign aid.

He was among the few Senators who opposed the joint resolution of January 1955 granting the President discretionary powers to use American forces in the defense of Formosa and the Pescadores, and favored enjoining the President not to defend Quemoy and Matsu islands. He opposed the mutual defense treaty between the United States and Nationalist China.

For more than half a century Lehman has been active in philanthropic circles and has taken a particular interest in child welfare institutions, hospitals, and trade schools. He is a trustee of the Institute for Advanced Study in Princeton, New Jersey and the Henry Street Settlement; and a director of the National Council of the Boy Scouts of America, the American Association for the United Nations and the National Conference of Christians and Jews. He has received honorary degrees from numerous educational institutions and awards from the Sidney Hillman Foundation and the Four Freedoms Foundation. He belongs to various social clubs in New York City, Albany, and Washington, D.C.

He married Edith Louise Altschul of San Francisco on April 28, 1910; the Lehmans had three children: Peter Gerald (who was killed in World War II), John Robert, and Hilda Jane (Mrs. Eugene Paul). The late Harold L. Ickes wrote that Senator Lehman has shown "industry, imagination and real courage. When a measure is proposed to promote the public welfare or protect our cherished form of government, he will fight for it, even if he is on the losing side. He has convictions and the courage of them."

Upon the occasion of his seventy-fifth birthday, the New York *Times* observed that Lehman has had three careers, one in business, another in philanthropy, and a third in government, and added: "To all that he has done he has brought a keen intelligence, a humane spirit, and an urgent sense of responsibility."

Speaking at Carnegie Hall, New York on June 1, 1955 at the close of the American Jewish Tercentenary ceremonies, Senator Lehman urged the development of "inspired leadership" to guarantee peace and social justice. "I sense a kind of twilight," he declared, "a heavy murkiness settling around us. Ideas and ideals have lost their clear shape . . . the burning fire of positive conviction is no longer evident." He recommended formulation of a program of action based on equal rights and basic security for all, maximum distribution of the benefits of prosperity and tolerance for dissident viewpoints (New York *Times,* June 2, 1955).

References (See also references listed in 1943 biographical sketch)

Nation 171:381 O 28 '50
U S News 21:71 S 13 '46; 27:37+ N 18 '49
Bartlett, R. M. They Work for Tomorrow (1943)
Congressional Directory (1955)
International Who's Who, 1954
National Cyclopædia of American Biography Current Volume E (1937-38)
Who's Who in America, 1954-55
Who's Who in World Jewry (1955)

LEIGH-FERMOR, PATRICK (MICHAEL) *See* Fermor, Patrick Leigh

LELONG, LUCIEN Oct. 11, 1889- Fashion designer; perfumer

Address: b. 6 Place Vendôme, Paris 1ᵉ, France; 1 rue Garnier Neuilly, Paris, France; h. "Domaine de Courbois," Anglet, Basses-Pyrénées, France

For nearly thirty years the "first gentleman of fashion" in Paris was Lucien Lelong, designer and perfume and lipstick manufacturer. From 1919 until 1949, he presented a series of collections that made fashion history. During World War II, when he was in charge of regulating the French fashion industry, Lelong frustrated German attempts to transplant the *haute couture* to Berlin. Following the war he was instrumental in re-establishing trade relations between the United States and France in the important field of fashions. Forced by ill health to close his *maison de couture* at the height of its post-war success in 1948, Lelong has nevertheless continued to head his world-wide perfume business and remains an important figure in the luxury trade of France. Three current fashion leaders—Christian Dior, Pierre Balmain and Hubert de Givenchy—worked for him before opening their own houses of fashion.

Lucien Lelong was born in Paris on October 11, 1889, the son of Arthur and Valentine (Lambelet) Lelong. His father owned a textiles shop and expected his son to carry on the business. The boy was trained for a commercial career, attending the Hautes Etudes Commerciales in Paris from 1911 to 1913. In his father's shop, Lucien learned about the "eccentricities and behavior of different dressmaking fabrics." To promote sales, he decided to become a couturier and in 1914 at the age of twenty-four, prepared his first collection of gowns for presentation. Two days before the scheduled opening, he was called to fight for France.

The young man fought in the army throughout the war and was awarded the Croix de Guerre. Toward the end of hostilities, he was wounded by a shell and was hospitalized for nearly a year. In 1919, after demobilization, he found himself without funds, but managed to borrow $2,500 from a friend and opened a *maison de couture* on the Place de la Madeleine. His designs won almost immediate favor and Lelong took his place among such fashion leaders as Lanvin, Patou, Worth and Chanel.

Believing perfume to be an essential part of a woman's dress, the designer in 1924 established the Société des Parfums Lucien Lelong. His first perfume was a light, dry scent called *"N"*, said to have been named for his second wife, the Princesse Nathalie Paley. The bottles for his fragrances have been widely copied. Most unusual is the bottle for *Indiscret*, inspired by a dropped handkerchief, and most sumptuous the one for *Orgueil*, the "pride" of the establishment.

Lelong soon became "unofficial dictator of the world's female fashions." In 1937 he was elected president of the Chambre Syndicale de la Couture Parisienne. After the capitulation of France in World War II, he was placed in charge of restrictions in production and materials for the fashion industry. He made it a point of brooking "no interference with individual creative liberty, which is the life and *raison d'etre* of the Paris couture." He encouraged designers to "show faith in themselves" and "accomplish prodigies" in spite of restrictions (New York *Times*, January 19, 1941).

Throughout the war, Lelong fought against German edicts to hamper the fashion industry. "We had to keep on," he said later, "so that when the war was over we would be all ready to go again." In his concern to keep as many people employed as possible, he urged the great fashion houses to continue showing collections even though there was no profit in it during the war. In 1943 when General Joseph Goebbels ordered the fashion houses closed and the transfer of the industry's best workers to Berlin,

LUCIEN LELONG

Lelong objected, saying: "You can take our workers to Germany, but you can't make them produce art."

Two gifted designers—Pierre Balmain and Christian Dior—joined Lelong's staff in 1941 and perfected their techniques in his establishment. In Cecil Beaton's *The Glass of Fashion*, Dior acknowledged Lelong's masterful understanding of fabrics, saying he learned how the same idea and the dress could be a success or a failure depending upon the material used. Balmain left Lelong to open his own fashion house in 1945, Dior in 1946, and Hubert de Givenchy in 1949. Each now owns his own fashion establishment.

As soon as France was liberated and the Germans had departed from Paris, "the *haute couture* breathed a sigh of relief and went to work." Many tributes were paid to Lelong for his work during the occupation. *This Week Magazine* (July 14, 1946) wrote that under Lelong's able guidance French designers had been able to "maintain a front during a ghastly period. Credit is due to Lelong for holding them together and in many cases outwitting the Germans in order to do so."

In May 1945, Lucien Lelong was a member of a mission sent to the United States by the French Ministry's Office of Art and Creation to investigate conditions for re-establishing trade. To the question of American, versus French fashion creation, Lelong diplomatically replied: "There is no conflict . . . all countries must have their own creators of fashion." He pointed out that the French needed the revenues obtained from the luxury item trade to pay for critically needed food, raw materials and equipment being purchased by France from the United States.

In December 1945, Lelong was re-elected president of the Chambre Syndicale de la Couture Parisienne. Since he had already served in this position for eight years, he requested

LELONG, LUCIEN—*Continued*

that he be released from the heavy duties to which he had devoted most of his time. Members of the association persuaded him to become honorary president, a position he still holds in 1955. He also continued to serve on the board of directors.

The first post-war showings of Paris fashions were held in the fall of 1945. Noteworthy features of Lelong's collection were the "Restoration bosom" and low neckline in evening and daytime dresses, and the hour-glass or "mermaid" figure.

To help launch French fashions in America, Lelong returned in April 1946 for the opening of the *Théâtre de la Mode*, a fashion show of 200 miniature manikins dressed in the newest Parisian fashions. The designer paid special tribute to the "working girls who put their hearts into the creation of the clothes and accessories in which the dolls are dressed and made their greatest effort because they knew that they were coming to New York." Lelong also affirmed his belief in "the happy alliance of French and American designers" and that he looked forward confidently to "the exchange of ideas that will be possible between all countries in the future."

In August 1946, *PM* reported that Lelong had opened the fall fashion campaign with pastel shades of pink, champagne, nile green, banana yellow and soft beige. According to the Associated Press, "Lelong wants women to be feminine, show their shoulders and the perfect line of their hips and legs." Judy Barden of the New York *Sun* found the collection "odd" with an "endless repetition of designs" dipping back into the 1910-14 period with hobble skirts predominating. Rosette Hargrove of the New York *World-Telegram* considered the collection a "hopeful forerunner" of the return to normal living and feminine luxury and noted its resemblance to the Irene Castle era.

Although Judy Barden had found Lelong's autumn collection "disappointing", she praised his February 1947 show: "Lucien Lelong is back in his old intriguing form, but more so. His clothes are delightful, particularly his tailored suits and coats. In August 1947, she reported: "Lucien Lelong's . . . collection is thrilling, colorful and exaggerated, but always wearable." Dresses were pencil-slim, pleated, tiered or draped, and many had harem hemlines. His suits featured wasp waists, cutaway fronts and square shoulders. "Evening dresses were ravishing. They were nearly all strapless with full skirts and embroidered or draped bodices and natural waistlines."

After guiding French couture through the difficult war and post-war years Lelong in 1948 became seriously ill. His doctor ordered him to stop working. He closed his *maison de couture*, turning down many attractive offers from would-be purchasers. Lelong decided that if he could not guide the destiny of his fashion house, he did not want his name used by anyone else. However, he continued to remain at the head of his perfume business, limiting his creative activity to designing new fragrances and new luxurious containers for his products. In 1955 his perfumes are sold throughout the world. The current list of perfumes includes: *Indiscret, "N", Passionnément, Orage, Sirocco, Orgueil, Parfum "7", Elle-Elle,* and *Mon Image.*

Lelong holds the Croix de Guerre and was decorated a Knight of the Legion of Honor in 1926. His religion is Roman Catholic. By his first marriage to Nelle Audey in 1919, he had a daughter, Nicole. His second marriage, to Princesse Nathalie Paley, ended in divorce in 1935. In 1954 he was married to Madame Dancovici. They spend much of their time near Biarritz where he has recently purchased an eighteenth-century house which he is remodeling and refurnishing.

The designer has been described as a straightforward, business-like person, and rather short, with a handsome weathered face. He has blue eyes and brown hair. His hobbies are collecting rare china from Ming to Kien Long (fifteenth to eighteenth centuries) and Russian glassware from Elizabeth I to Catherine II (seventeenth and eighteenth centuries). In 1928 he purchased the special collection of the Tsars. During the years he was designing dresses, he had a studio in Montparnasse where he created sculpture. His favorite sports are horseback riding and golf.

As quoted in the New York *Sun*, (May 28, 1946) Lelong believes that "a woman should experiment until she finds the perfume that's meant for her and then wear only that until it becomes part of her identity." According to *PM* (May 19, 1946) Lelong believes "the only time a woman should change her perfume is when she is using some other perfumer's product and changes to mine."

References

N Y Sun p30 My 9 '46 por
N Y Times IV p2 N 10 '40 por
PM p18 My 26 '46
Who's Who in America, 1954-55
Who's Who in Commerce and Industry (1953)

LEMNITZER, LYMAN L. (lĕm'nĕt-sẽr) Aug 29, 1899- United States Army officer

Address: b. c/o Headquarters, Far East Command and United Nations Command, c/o Postmaster, San Francisco, Calif.; h. 3286 Worthington, N.W., Washington, D.C.

The top U.S. military post in the "potentially explosive" Far East is held by General Lyman L. Lemnitzer, who was named to succeed General Maxwell D. Taylor as Commander in Chief of the Far East Command and Commander in Chief of the United Nations Command in June 1955. Lemnitzer's dual command includes an area where the precariousness of the Korean truce presents the possibility that operations of U.S. troops might change from police duty to military action if they should be called upon to carry out the American "no force" doctrine. This is a policy that the United States seeks to apply to both the South Koreans and the Communists.

Lemnitzer became a qualified Army parachutist at the age of fifty-one and later commanded an infantry division in the Korean war. He had been one of the original planners of the Mutual Defense Assistance Program after World War II and directed foreign arms aid in the Department of Defense. His European-African-Middle East Ribbon of World War II includes six battle stars.

Lyman L. Lemnitzer, a native of Honesdale, Pennsylvania, was born to William L. and Hannah (Blockberger) Lemnitzer on August 29, 1899. He has a brother, Ernest, who is a businessman. He attended the U.S. Military Academy at West Point, New York, was graduated with the B.S. degree in June 1920, and the next month received his commission as a second lieutenant of Coast Artillery.

Following a year of study at the Coast Artillery School at Fort Monroe, Virginia, Lemnitzer was assigned to the Coast Defenses of Narragansett Bay at Fort Adams, Rhode Island. In January 1924 he entered upon a two-year period of duty with the 59th Coast Artillery at Fort Mills, Corregidor, Philippine Islands, to which he later returned, in 1931, for service with the 92d and 60th Coast Artillery.

Meanwhile, after being stationed briefly in 1926 at Fort Adams, he began a series of assignments in teaching and studying: at West Point as instructor from 1926 to 1930 and again in 1934-1935, at the Coast Artillery School as a student in 1930-1931 and as an instructor from 1936 to 1939, and at the Command and General Staff School at Fort Leavenworth, Kansas as a student in 1935-1936. He entered the Army War College, Washington, D.C., in September 1939 and upon graduation the following June was sent to Fort Moultrie, South Carolina as a battalion commander and plans and training officer with the 70th Coast Artillery. In November 1940 he was transferred to Camp Stewart, Georgia in the post of executive officer and plans and training officer of the 38th Coast Artillery Brigade.

Lemnitzer's next assignment, in May 1941, was to the war plans division of the War Department General Staff in Washington, D.C., and a month later he became assistant to the operations and training officer of the Army General Headquarters. Transferred to Headquarters Army Ground Forces in March 1942, following the entry of the United States into World War II, he served for several months as assistant chief of staff, plans division.

Having risen gradually through the ranks, Lemnitzer was promoted to brigadier general in 1942 and was given command of the 34th Antiaircraft Brigade. General Dwight D. Eisenhower made him assistant chief of staff at Allied Forces Headquarters in London, where plans were being made for the invasion of North Africa. In October 1942, preparatory to the Allied landing the following month, Lemnitzer accompanied General Mark W. Clark on a secret submarine mission to North Africa to negotiate with French army officers. He was afterward assigned briefly to Clark's Fifth Army as deputy chief of staff.

During the Tunisian campaign, in February 1943, Lemnitzer reassumed command of the 34th Antiaircraft Brigade and then was as-

U. S. Army

GEN. LYMAN L. LEMNITZER

signed to General George S. Patton's Seventh Army to command the 34th brigade in the landing phase of the Sicilian campaign. Other important assignments in Italy included commanding general of the U.S. contingent of the Fifteenth Army Group (July 1943), deputy chief of staff to the Supreme Allied Commander, Mediterranean (December 1944) and chief of staff to the Supreme Allied Commander and the Commanding General, Mediterranean (August 1945).

He had a prominent part in the negotiations which led to Italy's capitulation to the Allies in September 1943 and in discussions with representatives of the German High Command in Switzerland which resulted in the surrender of German armies in Italy and southern Austria in May 1945.

When Lemnitzer returned to the United States in late 1945, he became the Army member of the strategic survey committee of the Joint Chiefs of Staff in Washington, D.C. and held that post from November 1945 until being appointed deputy commandant of the National War College in August 1947. Chosen to head the U.S. delegation to the military committee of the Western powers in London during the summer of 1948, he was active from its early planning stages in the program of U.S. arms aid to postwar Western European military collaboration against possible Communist aggression.

In October 1949 Lemnitzer was relieved of his duties at the National War College to assume the position of special assistant on foreign military assistance in the Office of the Secretary of Defense, the following month he was appointed director of the newly formed Office of Military Assistance to coordinate arms aid to the Atlantic Pact nations. He was the military member of the Foreign Assistance Coordination Committee, which had as its func-

LEMNITZER, LYMAN L.—*Continued*

tion the integration of U.S. political economic and military policies in Western Europe.

"His is the enormous coordinating task of seeing that literally hundreds of sections, branches and agencies of the Defense Department send the right weapon to the right country under conditions which assure its use to best advantage" in the master North Atlantic Treaty defense plan, Clarke Newlon wrote in an article on the Mutual Defense Assistance Program for *Colliers* (July 12, 1950). "The general believes heart and soul that the nations of Western Europe can be helped to become collectively so strong that they can protect their own integrity and borders," Newlon continued.

In March 1950 U.S. arms aid, then planned to cost $1 billion and to include tanks, motor vehicles, artillery and smaller arms, started arriving in Western Europe. Lemnitzer disclosed in June that by the end of the month some 152,000 tons of weapons would reach Europe. Testifying shortly afterward before the House Appropriations Committee, which was considering requests for additional foreign military aid funds, he made it clear that equipment would be sent only to nations that had sufficient organized manpower to utilize it effectively.

In keeping with the Army policy of rotating its officers between staff and command assignments, Lemnitzer left his Pentagon post in November 1950, to take the basic airborne course at Fort Benning, Georgia. After being rated a qualified parachutist on December 22, 1950, he was assigned command of the 11th Airborne Division at Fort Campbell, Kentucky. He was transferred to the Far East Command in November 1951 and subsequently commanded the 7th Infantry Division in the fighting in Korea against North Korean and Chinese Communist forces.

With his promotion to the rank of lieutenant general in August 1952, Lemnitzer became deputy chief of staff for plans and research at Army Headquarters in Washington, D.C. In October of the following year he spoke at the annual meeting of the National Association of Radio and Television News Editors on the need for maintaining troop strength in Korea. He called attention to the possibility that hostilities might be resumed and declared, "Among the lessons which Korea has emphasized was that the only way to stop ground forces is with ground forces" (New York *Times,* October 27, 1953).

Lemnitzer was given the rank of full general on March 25, 1955 and was named to succeed General Maxwell D. Taylor as the commanding general of the Army Forces in the Far East and the Eighth Army. When Taylor was appointed Army Chief of Staff in June 1955, Lemnitzer replaced him as Commander in Chief of the Far East Command and Commander in Chief of the United Nations Command.

The two-year-old Korean truce was threatened in the summer of 1955 by the demand of South Korean President Syngman Rhee that the Communists give up all territory south of the 38th parallel. Later in August Rhee objected to the presence of Polish and Czech members of the Neutral Nations Supervisory Commission. Violent demonstrations on the part of South Koreans accompanied his charges that these Communist members of the truce inspection teams were guilty of espionage and his order that they leave the country.

In mid-August General Lemnitzer flew to Korea from his Tokyo headquarters for a four-day conference with Rhee in which he made clear the U.S. position that under the terms of the armistice the United Nations Command was obligated to guard all members of the supervisory commission against the use of force. Rhee subsequently issued a no-violence edict.

The Legion of Merit was awarded to Lemnitzer for his part in the secret submarine mission to North Africa during World War II. Other honors conferred are the Oak Leaf Cluster to the Legion of Merit and the Distinguished Service Medal. He received the Silver Star for gallantry in action at Mundung-ni, Korea in February 1952.

His foreign decorations include Companion of the Bath (British), Commander of the British Empire, Cavalier of the Great Cross-Royal Crown of Italy, Medalha de Guerre (Brazil), Gold Medal of Merit with Swords (Poland), Legion af Honor and Croix de Guerre with Palm (France), Royal Order of the White Eagle (Yugoslavia), and Medal of Merit (Czechoslovakia).

Lemnitzer married Katherine Mead Tryon on November 6, 1923. Their children are Lois Katherine and First Lieutenant William Lyman. His son is a graduate of West Point, class of 1951. General Lemnitzer has brown eyes and dark brown hair, is just under six feet in height and weighs about 180 pounds. He was brought up a Lutheran.

The General's hobbies are golf and fishing. On July 4, 1955 he caught from Yugawa brook at Nikko the largest rainbow trout (27 inches) ever recorded by a member of the U.S. Security Forces in Japan. The trout exceeded the 25½ inch record established in 1952 by General Mark W. Clark who was the FEC/UNC Commander at the time.

References

Gen Army 1:15+ N '53
N Y Times p2 My 29 '50 por; p32 O 21 '50
U S News 38:18 My 27 '55
Washington (D.C.) Post p2 O 21 '50
Who's Who in America, 1954-55

LENTAIGNE, WALTER D(AVID) A(LEXANDER) July 15, 1899-June 24, 1955 Retired British Army officer; during World War II succeeded General Orde Wingate as commander of the Chindit raiders in Burma; began his Army career as a second lieutenant in a Gurkha regiment when he was eighteen years old and rose to rank of major general; retired in May 1955 from service as last British commandant of the Defense Services Staff College in Wellington, India. See *Current Biography* (July) 1944.

Obituary

N Y Times p76 Je 26 '55

LEOPOLD, ALICE K(OLLER) May 9, 1909- United States Government official

Address: b. c/o Women's Bureau, Department of Labor, Washington 25, D.C.; h. Kellogg Hill Rd., Weston, Conn.

Serving America's more than 19,000,000 working women, Mrs. Alice K. Leopold has been director of the Women's Bureau of the U.S. Department of Labor since December 1953. In September 1954 she was also given the title by Secretary of Labor James P. Mitchell of assistant in charge of women's affairs. All the bureaus, offices and programs of the department will henceforth be used for the benefit of men and women workers equally. Mrs. Leopold, who has been active in politics in the state of Connecticut, believes that many women who were formerly "armchair citizens" are now participating in civic and political life, and taking their share of responsibility in their communities.

She represented the town of Weston in the state legislature (General Assembly) in 1949 and in 1950 was elected Connecticut's secretary of state. In state governmental and political activity Mrs. Leopold showed special interest in labor relations and labor legislation, introducing into the Assembly minimum-wage and equal-pay bills.

Alice Koller Leopold is a native of Scranton, Pennsylvania, born to Edmund Leonard and Lenora (Edwards) Koller on May 9, 1909. As a student of social science at Goucher College, she visited Baltimore penal and welfare institutions. "Until then," reported the New York *Times*, January 10, 1954, "people used to say of her, 'Alice always has her nose in a book.' Once she stepped among the sick and the troubled, however, it woke her up to the world outside of books, she says."

Miss Koller's second major subject in college was English literature, in which, upon receiving her B.A. degree from Goucher in 1927, she was offered a graduate scholarship at the University of Chicago. Preferring to work with people, she took a job with Hutzler Brothers department store in Baltimore. Through a training course there she learned to be a marker, wrapper and salesgirl and then advanced from assistant buyer in women's sportswear to personnel director. Later, from 1930 to 1937, she was employed as personnel director for B. Altman and Company in New York City.

Miss Koller was married to Joseph Leopold on May 22, 1931, and some years later she left the department store business to rear her family. As the mother of two boys, she grew interested in the activities of the Parent-Teachers Association in Weston, Connecticut and she served for a time as its president. "Mrs. Leopold soon observed that, political connections achieved the biggest results in influencing school progress," a Washington *Post* (November 24, 1953) writer pointed out. "So she became a member, then vice-chairman [beginning in 1942] of the town committee."

Participating also in the work of the League of Women Voters, she wrote a pamphlet for

Republican National Com.

ALICE K. LEOPOLD

that organization entitled "Don't Be an Armchair Citizen." For a number of years she was state chairman of the committee on economic welfare of the Connecticut League of Women Voters and a member of its state board. Four Connecticut governors appointed her to state committees and commissions dealing with public housing, labor relations and education.

In 1949 she was the choice of both Republicans and Democrats of Weston for a seat in the Connecticut General Assembly, the first woman to represent that district. Mrs. Leopold, who has been a member for the public on a number of state minimum-wage boards, introduced into the legislature a bill providing for a minimum wage of seventy-five cents an hour. When the bill was passed in the next session of the Assembly, Connecticut became the first state to adopt the seventy-five-cent rate. She also authored a bill requiring that women be given equal pay for equal work, a measure which was made law in October 1949.

One of four women candidates, Mrs. Leopold was elected in 1950 as secretary of state, a post that by tradition in Connecticut is usually filled by a woman. During her term in office and under her supervision a revision of the state election laws, the first since 1860, was presented to the General Assembly in 1953 and voted upon favorably. She held also the positions of commissioner of elections for Connecticut and co-chairman of the committee of elections of the National Association of Secretaries of State. Mrs. Leopold was the first woman in the history of her state to serve as acting governor. Her opportunity to occupy that post for a day or two came when three higher-ranking officials happened to be away from Connecticut at the same time.

In state politics Mrs. Leopold has been a delegate to the last three Connecticut Republican conventions. During the 1952 national

LEOPOLD, ALICE K.—*Continued*
election contest she was one of the women policy makers of the campaign of General Dwight D. Eisenhower and a member of the group that conferred with the Republican candidate at his campaign headquarters in Denver.

Mrs. Leopold's first appointment under the Eisenhower Administration was as a member of the Inter-Governmental Relations Commission. She serves also as secretary and project chairman of the commission, which in September 1953 began its task of planning future sharing of authority between Federal and state governments. Speaking at one time of the attitude of the twenty-five members toward this undertaking, she said, ". . . there is in their mind firm conviction that the commission has one of the most important jobs ever given to a group in our history" (New York *Times,* February 20, 1954).

Before the expiration of her four-year term Mrs. Leopold relinquished her post as Connecticut secretary of state to become director of the Women's Bureau of the United States Department of Labor, an appointment made by President Eisenhower in November 1953. Sworn into office on December 11 of that year, she assumed a number of duties not previously assigned to the head of the Women's Bureau. She is special adviser to the Secretary of Labor on policy matters concerning standards of employment of women and she is chairman of the Secretary's advisory committee on womenpower. Formerly this chairmanship was assumed by the Secretary himself.

In succeeding Frieda S. Miller to the $10,330-a-year position, Mrs. Leopold became the third director in the thirty-three-year history of the Women's Bureau. The function of the bureau is to serve America's 19,000,000 working women in all occupations. It publishes practical information on trades and professions and provides advice on career possibilities; cooperates with state agencies to help establish laws on wages and hours of work and to set up standards for women's employment; and carries on several projects in the international field. One of the first to offer congratulations at Mrs. Leopold's swearing-in ceremony was Miss Mary Anderson, who was the bureau's first director and who had served it for twenty-four years.

One of the director's first tasks in her new office was to call a conference on January 27, 1954 of 125 representatives of national women's organizations, the first meeting of its kind sponsored by the Women's Bureau since 1948. At smaller conferences with representatives of women's groups Mrs. Leopold discussed matters relating to the proposed Equal Rights Amendment. She expressed her own views on protective legislation for women in a speech in February before the District of Columbia League of Republican Women: "I don't happen to be one of those who believe women want equality. Equity seems to me, as a worker for legislation which protects and frees women, a much more important point of view" (Washington *Post,* February 18, 1954).

With the initiation of a new Labor Department program to better the status of women workers, Mrs. Leopold on September 28, 1954 was named assistant to the Secretary of Labor in charge of women's affairs. She would continue to serve as director of the Women's Bureau, Secretary James P. Mitchell announced, and at the same time direct a reorganization project which would enable all the divisions and offices of the Labor Department to be used to benefit women. "In general," the Secretary explained, "she will formulate policies to promote the welfare of wage-earning women, improve their working conditions, increase their efficiency and advance their opportunities for profitable employment" (New York *Herald Tribune,* September 30, 1954).

Mrs. Leopold visited Europe in early October 1954 as chairman of a group assigned to make a study for the Foreign Operations Administration of women's economic problems and their effect on family life.

In several public statements Mrs. Leopold has urged increased political activity on the part of women. "I sometimes get weary of our attitude of too great humility," she has said, "too little awareness of our title to share freely in the privileges and prerequisites once we are fully shouldering our responsibilities" (*Christian Science Monitor,* April 8, 1954). "I think the right to vote and hold public office is a basic factor in gaining self-confidence," she told delegates to the national convention of American Women in Radio and Television. "There is a place in every woman's life to combine her career with an interest in political affairs" (New York *Times,* April 24, 1954).

Speaking later in the month at a meeting of the District of Columbia Chapter of the American Society of Women Accountants, she said, "When we have more women taking an active part in politics, we'll have better people running for office because we'll elect more of our sex" (Washington *Post and Times Herald,* April 28, 1954).

For some years, beginning in 1946, Mrs. Leopold was a designer and manufacturer of toys, known as My Town Toys. She is the founder of the Industrial Relations Club of Fairfield County, a trustee of the Eastern States Exposition (1953) and of Goucher College, and a director of the Fairfield division of the National Foundation for Infantile Paralysis and of the Westport-Weston chapter of the American Red Cross.

Other organizations to which she belongs are the National Order of Women Legislators, Fairfield County Republican Women's Association, Northfield Grange, Weston Visiting Nurses Association, Daughters of the American Revolution, and Alpha Gamma Delta society. Her club memberships include the National Federation of Business and Professional Women's Club, Connecticut Council of Republican Women's Club, and Westport Women's Club. She attends the Lyons Plains Episcopal Church.

The Bridgeport *Sunday Herald* chose Mrs. Leopold as Connecticut's Woman of the Year for 1951. Recently the American Association of University Women named her one of New England's seven most outstanding women.

Mrs. Leopold's husband is a vice-president of Sullivan, Stauffer, Colwell and Bayles, a New York advertising firm. At the time of her appointment to the Federal post, one of her sons, Robert, was a student at Dartmouth College and her other son, John, was a student at Westport High School.

As pictured in the press, Mrs. Leopold has a "quick mind, a capacity for hard work, a commanding and attractive appearance . . . a vibrant personality, an artistic bent . . ." (New York *Times,* January 10, 1954). "She has a musical speaking voice, full of vitality," observed Josephine Riley of the *Christian Science Monitor* (April 22, 1954), "a mobile, expressive face; and a drive that bodes well for the working women whose cause she has espoused so confidently."

References

Christian Sci Mon p17 D 12 '53 por; p10 Ap 22 '54 por
Ind Woman 33:3 Ja '54 por
N Y Herald Tribune II p 1 Ja 24 '54 por
N Y Times p46 N 20 '53; p8 N 21 '53; p54 Ja 10 '54
Washington (D.C.) Post p43 N 24 '53 por
Who's Who in America, 1954-55

LEWIS, (JOSEPH) ANTHONY Mar 27, 1927- Journalist

Address: b. c/o New York Times, 229 W. 43d St., New York 36; h. 3233 Gunston Rd., Alexandria, Va.

Few writers have observed the whole question of security investigation as closely as Anthony Lewis, winner of the 1955 Pulitzer Prize for national reporting. The twenty-eight-year old reporter for the Washington (D.C.) *Daily News,* and now on the news staff of the New York *Times,* received the award for his series of articles in 1954 on the case of Abraham Chasanow, a civilian employee of the U.S. Navy who had been discharged as a "security risk". Lewis proved that the charges were groundless and Chasanow was reinstated.

The American Newspaper Guild also conferred on Lewis the Heywood Broun Award in 1955.

In presenting the award, the judges declared: "The job Mr. Lewis did here is newspaper work at its very best: The fate of the whole people can be bound up in the case of one citizen, and the skill and devotion which go into the examination of one citizen's case have a lasting and vital meaning for everyone. . . Lewis has spoken for all of us, and has left the entire country in his debt."

From 1948 to 1952 Lewis was a member of the staff of the News of the Week in Review section of the New York *Times.* He worked briefly for the Democratic National Committee during the 1952 presidential campaign. From December 1952 until 1955 he was employed as a general assignment reporter by the Washington *Daily News.* In September 1955 he returned to the New York *Times* New York news staff and later became a member of its Washington, D.C. bureau.

Walter Bennett

ANTHONY LEWIS

A native of New York City, Joseph Anthony Lewis was born on March 27, 1927 to Kassel Lewis, a textile executive, and Sylvia (Surut) Lewis. He has a sister, Nancy Lewis Shalit. "Tony" received his early education at New York's Horace Mann School, where he was president of the student organization and editor of the school's weekly publication. After graduation in 1944, he entered Harvard College, selecting English as his major subject. He joined the Signet Society, a literary group, and pursued his interest in journalism by working on the *Harvard Crimson,* the undergraduate daily, of which he became executive editor and finally managing editor.

For a period of about three months during World War II he served as a seaman third class in a radar technician program conducted by the Navy; he was discharged because of an eye ailment. During the summer of 1946 he worked as a copy boy for the *Times;* the following summer he spent travelling in Europe. He was graduated from Harvard University with honors in 1948.

From June 25, 1948 until August 1, 1952 Lewis wrote for the News of the Week in Review section of the New York *Times.* (On May 1, 1949 he published an article in the New York *Times Magazine* on his alma mater: "Harvard Goes Coed—But Incognito"). One day, according to a report in *Time* (May 16, 1955), "Sunday editor Lester Markel called him in, suggested that he go out and get some reporting experience. Tony Lewis went home and told his wife, 'I've been fired,' then started looking for a reporting job."

Immediately after terminating his connection with the New York *Times,* Lewis went to work for the Democratic National Committee.

LEWIS, ANTHONY—*Continued*

Until November 4, 1952 he was occupied in preparing political, social and economic summaries of the areas in which Adlai Stevenson was scheduled to speak, and in suggesting speech topics for the Democratic presidential candidate.

In December 1952, Lewis was engaged by the tabloid Washington *Daily News,* a link in the Scripps-Howard chain, and, according to *Time,* "he quickly made a mark as a byline reporter." A general assignment reporter, he wrote, among other things, crime stories and humorous features. (In May 1954 the Newspaper Guild of Washington cited Lewis in its Page One Awards for a humorous feature on algae eaters). "In a short time," according to the New York *World-Telegram and Sun,* "he was turning up stories in the Pentagon, attending presidential press conferences and interviewing politicians."

The young reporter also covered the hearings of the Senate subcommittee headed by Senator Joseph McCarthy in 1953 and became particularly interested in matters affecting internal security. "One of Mr. Lewis' jobs for the [Washington *Daily*] *News* during the last congressional election campaign," according to the New York *World-Telegram and Sun,* "was to keep a box score on the actual number of persons fired by the government, as security risks, and the number which appeared in political speeches. Frequently the two did not bear much resemblance to each other."

In the course of his explorations Lewis began checking the records of Federal employees who had been dismissed as security risks, and came upon the case of Abraham Chasanow, a civilian employee in the Navy's Hydrographic Office, who had been suspended in July 1953 as a loyalty risk after more than twenty years' service, then cleared, and finally discharged. "Chasanow wasn't a 'big name.' His firing had no political significance, in the narrow sense. He was lost in a shuffle of suspicion and red tape, and now also had lost his job."

Lewis investigated the case thoroughly and discovered that the charges against Chasanow were groundless, motivated solely by malicious gossip. He reported his finding in a series in the *News,* and in an additional article, "Victim of Nameless Accusers," in the *Reporter* (March 2, 1954) a fortnightly magazine. The articles persuaded the U.S. Government to reconsider the case and ultimately to reinstate Chasanow. Joseph Fanelli, Chasanow's lawyer, gave full credit to Lewis for the vindication of his client.

In November 1954 Lewis contributed another article in the *Reporter* considering the issue "how our Government can protect itself against disloyal and otherwise unreliable employees while at the same time protecting against injustice citizens who work for that Government and many private citizens who are now being affected by security regulations." His article reflected, Lewis stated, the views of many Washington lawyers concerned with the problem of reconciling national security and individual rights.

To remedy inequities in the existing program Lewis suggested, among other measures, the establishment of a division of personnel security within the Department of Justice to handle all reports on the security fitness of Federal personnel; the guarantee of a right to a hearing for accused personnel; the grant of subpoena powers to hearing boards; and the establishment of a national review board. He concluded that "whatever changes the Executive Branch or the Legislative or the Judicial may make, our eventual reliance must be placed on a return to what John Lord O'Brian calls one basis of our justice, the American sense of fair play."

In his article, "Security: Interim Reports" (*Reporter,* September 8, 1955), Lewis reviewed two books, *Case Studies in Personnel Security* by Adam Yarmolinsky and *The Draftee and Internal Security* by Rowland Watts. Lewis warned against "any complacency that has arisen about the state of our security programs," pointed out that "a security proceeding is a damaging process, however it ends," and gave examples of persons cleared of the charges being unable to find employment.

The American Newspaper Guild announced in February 1955 that its annual Heywood Broun Award of $500 and a citation honoring "outstanding journalistic achievement" had been won by Lewis for his Chasanow articles.

The judges—Bruce Catton, Pulitzer Prize-winning historian and editor of *American Heritage,* Edwin A. Lahey, national correspondent for the Chicago *Daily News,* and John W. Vandercook, radio news analyst—chose Lewis over more than seventy entrants. Their joint announcement read in part: "It seemed to the judges that Mr. Lewis's work was completely in the spirit of Heywood Broun (founder and first president of the Guild)—a case in which a newspaperman set out to rectify an injustice that had been done to one lone individual, in the process of which he not only relieved the individual of a grievous wrong, but also kept the people of the United States from committing an injustice against itself."

In May 1955 James B. Reston, chief of the Washington bureau of the New York *Times,* invited Lewis to discuss with him a job on that newspaper. As he sat in the newspaper's New York office "discussing the final details of a job," in *Time*'s words, "over the wire-service teletypes came an impressive but needless commendation. Lewis's Chasanow series had just won the Pulitzer Prize for the best 'national reporting of the year'."

Lewis married the former Linda Joan Rannells, a schoolteacher, on July 8, 1951; they have a daughter, Eliza, born on June 9, 1954. Lewis' religion is Jewish; he is a Democrat. The reporter is five feet ten inches tall and weighs 165 pounds; he has brown hair and brown eyes. His hobbies are gardening and collecting classical phonograph records.

References

N Y Times p28 My 3 '55
N Y World-Telegram p6 My 3 '55 por
Time 65:50 My 16 '55 por

LINDFORS, (ELSA) VIVECA (TORSTENSDOTTER) Dec. 29, 1920- Actress
Address: b. c/o Music Corporation of America, 598 Madison Ave., New York 22

On December 29, 1954 the drama *Anastasia,* adapted by Guy Bolton from a French original by Marcelle Maurette, opened at the Lyceum Theatre in New York City. The date happened to be the birthday of the Swedish actress Viveca Lindfors, who wondered if "it might be an omen." The play, in which she is co-starred with Eugenie Leontovich, has proved to be her most successful role on Broadway. Her acting won the plaudits of audiences and critics who admired the skillful way in which "she changes from a mumbling and hungry waif to a beauty of truly regal presence" (John Chapman, *Sunday News,* January 16, 1955) in the role of Anastasia, youngest daughter of the last Czar of Russia, Nicholas II.

Like Greta Garbo, Ingrid Bergman, and other well-known Swedish actresses, Miss Lindfors is a graduate of Sweden's Royal Dramatic Theatre School. She appeared for two years at the Stockholm Royal Dramatic Theatre in modern and classical plays and in eighteen European films before Warner Brothers brought her to Hollywood in April 1946. She made five pictures for that studio and has since free-lanced. For her performance in the Swiss picture *Four in a Jeep,* Miss Lindfors won the 1951 International Film Award.

Her first Broadway appearance was in John Van Druten's play *I've Got Sixpence,* in December 1952. She toured with the Theatre Guild production of *An Evening with Will Shakespeare* during 1953 and played in John Van Druten's *Bell, Book and Candle* on the "straw-hat circuit." She appeared in London in J. B. Priestley's play, *The White Countess,* and returned to Hollywood in 1954 to act in *Moonfleet* for Metro-Goldwyn-Mayer and the Paramount picture *Run for Cover.*

Elsa Viveca Torstensdotter Lindfors was born in Stockholm, Sweden on December 29, 1920, the second daughter of Torsten and Karin (Dymling) Lindfors. There was no theatre background in the family. Her father, a former army officer, who had become a book publisher, sent his two daughters to the Lyceum School for girls in Stockholm. When Viveca was fourteen she was given a leading role in a school play *Ann Sofi Hedvig.* A prominent Swedish actor declared that she had great talent, and she began to take diction and dramatic lessons.

At seventeen, she graduated from the Lyceum School and her father expected her to learn the publishing business. When she told him that she wanted to be an actress, he advised her to compete for admission to the Royal Dramatic Theatre School. Approximately 1,500 young people applied to the school (a state-operated institution) in 1937. Miss Lindfors was among the 150 selected for the three-day tests. The Boston *Sun-Post* magazine section (September 21, 1947) said that she gave a monologue by Sigrid Undset the first day, and—one of seventy the following day—did a scene from a Strindberg play. On the last day—among the final twenty—she did a Molière scene, and was one of eight selected.

VIVECA LINDFORS

During her third year studying there, Miss Lindfors was in the honor group and received a small income from the school, the equivalent of twenty-five dollars a month, which she supplemented by earnings from acting with stock companies. She graduated in 1940 and was appointed to the Royal Theatre—also sponsored by the Swedish government—and for two years appeared in classical and modern plays.

While with the Royal Theatre, she had a walk-on part with five lines in a film called *The Crazy Family.* It was shown for only a day, but brought Miss Lindfors offers from other studios. She was starred in *If I Should Marry the Minister,* and the film—released in 1941—was such a success that the actress was in great demand. Her role in the film *Appassionata,* three years later, attracted international attention. After making *Interlude* in 1945, she arranged a contract with Warner Brothers through a talent scout, Kay Brown, then connected with the Leland Howard Agency, and went to Hollywood in April 1946.

According to the New York *Herald Tribune* (August 2, 1948), Miss Lindfors rented a ranch house in Tarzana, had her furniture shipped from Sweden, combined it with Mexican plates and modern prints and prepared to live in Hollywood. Her first picture, *Night Unto Night,* was not released until June 1949 when it received bad notices. *To the Victor* and two other melodramas attracted little attention. On her next picture, *Adventures of Don Juan,* with Errol Flynn, Eileen Creelman of the New York *Sun* (December 24, 1948) commented that the Swedish star as Queen of Spain provided well-played dramatic scenes in "strong contrast to the rollicking mood" of the picture. Miss Lindfors felt that she had been miscast in all

LINDFORS, VIVECA—*Continued*

of the American films except the first one, and told Miss Creelman in an earlier interview (December 13, 1948) that she was "impatient" to return to the stage.

When her contract with Warner Brothers terminated, Miss Lindfors decided to free-lance and spend part of her time in Europe. She was starred in the Swedish film *The Saga of Singoalla* during the summer of 1949. Of *No Sad Songs for Me,* with Margaret Sullavan (Columbia Pictures), made before she went to Stockholm, Alton Cook wrote in the *World-Telegram and Sun* (April 28, 1950): "For the first time Viveca Lindfors, as the intruding girl friend, is allowed to show the full force of the smoldering passion that made Hollywood import the actress from Sweden."

Later West Coast productions included *Dark City, Flying Missile, Journey Into Light, The Raiders* and *No Time for Flowers.* For her performance in the multilingual Swiss film *Four in a Jeep,* premiered in Zurich, Miss Lindfors received the 1951 "Best Actress of the Year" International Film Award, Europe's equivalent to Hollywood's "Oscar."

Offered a role in John Van Druten's *I've Got Sixpence* in September 1952, Miss Lindfors learned the part before she reached New York for rehearsals. The play opened on December 2, 1952 and closed twenty-two days later. "Miss Lindfors is a lithe and lovely girl with an engagingly boyish stance who struggles mightily with some second-act melodramatics," commented Walter Kerr (New York *Herald Tribune,* December 3, 1952).

Miss Lindfors was back in New York early in February 1953; she had an apartment in the east nineties and a part in the Dorothy Monet play *The Wrestling and the Fall.* The play did not reach Broadway and Miss Lindfors went on tour for the Theatre Guild in *An Evening with Will Shakespeare.* An eight-week tour followed on the summer circuit with Barry Sullivan in John Van Druten's *Bell, Book and Candle.* She returned to Hollywood in 1954 to make the MGM picture *Moonfleet* with Stewart Granger and Paramount's *Run For Cover* with James Cagney.

When *Anastasia* opened on December 29, 1954 it seemed assured that Miss Lindfors would stay in New York for a while. The play, based on the possible survival of the Czar's youngest daughter after the Bolshevik executions of the Romanovs in 1918, was highly praised by Brooks Atkinson, New York *Times* (December 30, 1954). He referred to a scene in the second act where the Dowager Empress (Eugenie Leontovich) finally recognizes Anastasia as her granddaughter, as "two pieces of acting that came out of the theatre's treasure chest." Wolcott Gibbs (*New Yorker,* January 10, 1955) commented that Viveca Lindfors as the harried Princess Anastasia accomplished the "transition from rags to glory with admirable style." Miss Lindfors remained in the play until September 19 when Dolly Haas took over her role.

The outstanding scene from *Anastasia* was re-enacted for television audiences on *Toast of the Town* (Columbia Broadcasting System) on January 23, 1955. Part of the royalties from the play and the subsequent motion picture about Anastasia will be given to the woman living in poverty near Stuttgart, Germany who has long claimed to be the czar's daughter (details of her story are recorded in *Life,* February 14, 1955).

When Miss Lindfors came to the United States in 1946, she was married to a prominent Stockholm lawyer, Folke Rogard. Their two children, Jan, born in 1943 and Lena, born in 1944, were brought to Hollywood in January 1947 and have remained with their mother. Early in 1949, Miss Lindfors obtained a divorce from Rogard. On August 10, 1949—in Paris—she married Donald Siegel, a Hollywood director who subsequently directed *No Time For Flowers,* in which Miss Lindfors starred. A son, Christopher, was born to them in September 1952 in Los Angeles. The Siegels were divorced on April 29, 1953. The actress married the Hungarian-born novelist and dramatist, George Tabori, author of *Flight Into Egypt* and *The Emperor's Clothes,* in July 1954.

Miss Lindfors is five feet six inches tall and slender. She has chestnut-brown hair and deep-blue eyes. Off-stage, she usually wears casual clothes and no make-up. She enjoys skiing and swimming. Her favorite actress is Greta Garbo. She likes "frantic" New York. She became an American citizen on April 27, 1951, in Los Angeles. She speaks English with a slight accent and also speaks French and German.

Her ambition, she once told William Hawkins (New York *World-Telegram and Sun*) was to have a large theatre, where "we could have low prices and put on plays everyone is interested in, and do them with drapes, or very simply."

References

Cue 17:12 D 18 '48 por
Boston Sun-Post Mag p4 S 21 '47 por
Life 26:76 F 14 '49 por
N Y Post Mag p2 Ap 18 '48 pors
N Y Sunday News II p7 D 28 '52 por
N Y World-Telegram p30 D 13 '52; p23 Ja 7 '55
Motion Picture and Television Almanac, 1953-54

LIPPINCOTT, JOSEPH WHARTON

Feb. 28, 1887- Publisher; author

Address: b. c/o J. B. Lippincott Co., E. Washington Sq., Philadelphia 5, Pa.; h. "Oak Hill," Bethayres, Pa.

Representing the third generation of his family to head the publishing house of J. B. Lippincott Company, Joseph Wharton Lippincott is now chairman of the board, having served as president from 1927 to 1948. He is also a naturalist and author of many books about animals in wide use in schools. Two of these, *Wilderness Champion* (1944) and *The Wahoo Bobcat* (1950), have been selections of the Junior Literary Guild and also appear in the American Wildlife Series, published by Lippincott.

The J. B. Lippincott Company developed from the union of two old firms. The first was a bookstore opened in Philadelphia by Jacob Johnson in 1792; by 1850 it was doing business as Grigg, Elliot & Company. The other was a book business in Philadelphia for whom Joshua Ballinger Lippincott became an employee in 1827. Within nine years, Lippincott, at the age of eighteen, acquired ownership of the firm which was then publishing religious books. In 1850 Lippincott took over the firm of Grigg, Elliot & Company and established the firm of Lippincott, Grambo & Company, which did an annual business of over $1,500,000. The business was incorporated as J. B. Lippincott Company in 1885. It now publishes school and college textbooks, medical and pharmaceutical books, fiction, juveniles, history books and belles-lettres.

Joseph Wharton Lippincott was born in Philadelphia, Pennsylvania on February 28, 1887 to J. Bertram and Joanna (Wharton) Lippincott. He is a direct descendant of two Englishmen who settled in America in the seventeenth century, Thomas Wharton and Richard Lippincott. His paternal grandfather was Joseph Wharton, the industrialist, a founder of Swarthmore College. Wharton's gifts also enabled the establishment of the Wharton School of Finance and Commerce of the University of Pennsylvania.

At an early age Joseph was meeting famous writers in his home, many of whom contributed to *Lippincott's Monthly Magazine* (established in 1868 and discontinued in 1914). He attended the Episcopal Academy of Philadelphia, was one of the editors of the school magazine, and was graduated in 1904. He then entered the Wharton School of Finance and Commerce. He was captain of the gun team, a member of the Friars' Senior Society, and of Zeta Psi. He was graduated in 1908 with the B.S. degree and won the Terry Prize for the highest class average. He spent the summer of 1908 abroad with his grandfather, Joseph Wharton, and Andrew Carnegie and gained from Carnegie his enthusiasm for libraries.

Beginning his career with the family's firm as an office boy in 1908, he had the task of dusting books in the shipping department. He became vice-president in 1915. During World War I he served in the United States Naval Reserve. Lippincott remained in the office of vice-president until 1927 when he became president. He has served as chairman of the board since 1948. Under Lippincott's leadership the company was merged with Carrick and Evans of New York and Frederick A. Stokes of Philadelphia in 1941.

The company's best sellers while Lippincott served as president included *Kitty Foyle* (1939) by Christopher Morley, *My Friend Flicka* (1941) by Mary O'Hara, *We Took to the Woods* (1942) by Louise Dickinson Rich, *The White Tower* (1945) by James Ramsey Ullman, and *The Egg and I* (1945) by Betty MacDonald.

Since *Bun, A Wild Rabbit* (Penn, 1918) Lippincott's first book, was published, it has

Fabian Bachrach

JOSEPH WHARTON LIPPINCOTT

been followed by over a dozen others including *Red Ben, The Fox of Oak Ridge* (Penn, 1919), *Gray Squirrel* (Penn, 1921), *Persimmon Jim, The 'Possum* (Penn, 1924), *Long Horn, Leader of the Deer* (Penn, 1928), *The Wolf King* (Penn, 1933), *The Red Roan Pony* (Penn, 1934), and *Chisel-Tooth, The Beaver* (Penn, 1936). His *Wilderness Champion; The Story of a Great Hound* (Lippincott, 1944) was a selection of the Junior Literary Guild and sold over 25,000 copies.

The Phantom Deer (Lippincott, 1954) is a story of the "No Name" tiny deer, a rapidly vanishing species that live on the Florida Keys. Lippincott tells the story of their struggle to survive extinction by hunters. "The book gives an accurate and memorable account of the life of these exquisite animals," wrote Henry B. Lent in the New York *Times Book Review* (December 19, 1954). "A well-knit story, one of Lippincott's best," commented Virginia Kirkus in her July 1, 1954 *Bulletin*. "Out of these elements the author has fashioned a fine tense story of pursuit and escape, and a powerful plea for wild-life conservation," commented the Chicago *Sunday Tribune* (November 14, 1954).

Lippincott is chairman of the board of libraries of the University of Pennsylvania and a director of the Free Library of Philadelphia. He founded and each year presents the Joseph W. Lippincott Award under the auspices of the American Library Association. The prize consists of $500 and a formal certificate and is awarded for outstanding achievement in the field of librarianship. On July 17, 1950 Lippincott presented the annual award to H. W. Wilson for rendering "a great service to librarians and through them to the public" (*Wilson Library Bulletin*, September 1950).

A sports enthusiast, Lippincott has organized big game hunting expeditions in Alaska, Can-

LIPPINCOTT, JOSEPH W.—*Continued*

ada, Mexico, Bavaria, and Austria. He has hunted and fished all over the United States and has collected animals for museums; three of the trophy heads which he secured are on the lists of the largest on record. Lippincott has played polo, raced yachts, managed horse and dog shows, and won ribbons in the ring and on the turf. He has lectured with his own motion pictures and appeared on radio programs.

Lippincott served as president of the National Association of Book Publishers (a precursor of the American Book Publishers Council, Inc.) and as a director on the Council on Books in Wartime, Inc. He is on the board of business education of the University of Pennsylvania. Other organizations with which he is associated include the Philadelphia Academy of Music, Moore Institute of Art, Science and Industry, Aquarium Society of Philadelphia, Zoological Society of Philadelphia, Franklin Institute, and Academy of Natural Sciences. He has been master of the Oak Hill Beagles and master of the Fox Hounds Association of the Huntington Valley Hunt. Among his clubs are the Explorers, Philadelphia, Racket, Brook, Publishers' Lunch, and Downtown.

The publisher was married to the former Elizabeth Schuyler Mills, who died on November 20, 1943. Their children are Joseph W. Lippincott, Jr., who was elected to the board of the J. B. Lippincott Company in 1940 and now serves as executive vice-president, M. Roosevelt Schuyler Lippincott and Elizabeth Schuyler Lippincott (Mrs. E. Harry Wilkes). On September 20, 1945 he married Mrs. Virginia Jones Mathieson. His stepchildren are Mrs. Mary O'Neill and Miss Joan Mathieson.

He has been described as a man of quiet and retiring manner. He is six feet tall and weighs 165 pounds. His eyes and hair are gray-brown in color. He makes his winter home in Nokomis, Florida. In religion he is a member of the Society of Friends and in politics is a Republican.

References

Pub W 124:1857+ N 25 '33; 147:2000+ My 19 '45 por
Who's Who in America, 1954-55
World Biography (1954)

LIVINGSTON, HOMER J. Aug. 30, 1903-

Banker; organization official

Address: b. First National Bank of Chicago, 38 S. Dearborn St., Chicago, Ill.; h. 619 Keystone Ave., River Forest, Ill.

"America's banks play a significant role in every segment of the nation's life," declared Homer J. Livingston, president of the First National Bank of Chicago. "Banks safeguard the deposits of over 68,000,000 savers. They extend loans to the smallest crossroads grocery store and the greatest metropolitan industrial plant. . . . Looking ahead, it is clear that bankers shall have, in the next five to ten years, vastly enlarged demands for credit . . . to help raise even higher America's standard of living. The increase in population indicates that the American economy has great potentials for growth in the years ahead."

Livingston has advanced rapidly to the forefront of the financial world. He became one of the youngest men ever to head a major banking institution in the United States when he was made president of the First National Bank of Chicago at the age of forty-six. Further honor was bestowed upon him in October 1954 when he was elected the president of the American Bankers Association for a one-year term.

Homer J. Livingston was born on the west side of Chicago on August 30, 1903, the son of John C. and Evelyn (Lewis) Livingston. He received his early scholastic training in the public schools of Chicago, where he attended the Grant Grammar School and the Crane High School. He was given religious instruction at Chicago's Church of the Epiphany. Since his family was not wealthy, young Livingston held several jobs during summer vacations. One of these positions was as a delivery boy in a firm for which he had to drive a horse and wagon; while at another he made parts for doorstops in a Chicago machine shop and was paid $10 a week for a ten-hour day, six days a week. Entering Crane High School in 1917, Livingston followed a general academic program and played on the school basketball team, as well as on the Y.M.C.A. team.

Livingston's career in many ways exemplifies the American Horatio Alger story of the self-made man. After his graduation from high school in 1920, he took a job in the finance department of the post office so that he could attend the John Marshall Law School at night. During this period Livingston was keenly interested in politics and at one time served as precinct captain in Chicago's 18th Ward for the Republican party.

Perhaps the most decisive event in Livingston's career took place while he was still in law school. It was the custom of the First National Bank of Chicago to hire each year one of the top members of the John Marshall senior class to work in its legal department. Livingston had made such a favorable impression upon the dean of the law school that when the bank called in 1922, asking for the leading senior, the dean replied that the best man was in the second year. Livingston was interviewed by Edward Eagle Brown, then in the bank's law department and now chairman of the board at First National, who hired him on a temporary basis.

Years of hard work and intense study followed in which Livingston not only worked toward completing his law degree at John Marshall, but gained a knowledge of banking and finance as well. He received an LL.B. degree from John Marshall Law School in 1924 and was admitted to practice at the Illinois bar in the following year. At the bank he advanced from his legal clerk's position to become an assistant attorney in 1930 and an attorney in 1934. He was elected counsel in 1944 and was given a vice-presidency in the following year. The First National appointed him a director of its board in 1948, and two years later, he was elected president of the bank.

During the years in which he has been associated with the American Banking Association, Livingston has held various positions. He has been a member of the committee on Federal legislation and was chairman of the subcommittee on bankruptcy from 1940 to 1950. He became a member of the credit policy commission in 1949. He served on the legislative committee and council of administration of the Illinois Bankers Association in 1944-1945. He was elected vice-president of the A.B.A. in 1953 and president in October 1954, succeeding Everett D. Reese (see *C.B.*, March '54), at the 80th annual convention held in Atlantic City. Livingston was succeeded by Fred F. Florence at the A.B.A. convention in September 1955.

As president of the A.B.A., Livingston has traveled to every part of the nation to address various state banking organizations and many other financial groups. In these speeches he has pointed out the role played by credit and bankers in the conquest of the American frontier and the later development of the country into a vast industrial empire. From a total of $325,000,000 in loans held by banks in 1834, the amount of credit has expanded to over eighty billion dollars today. As Livingston stated in an address before the Seventh National Credit Conference on December 16, 1954, "Step by step with the growth of the country, bank credit has expanded to discharge its vital role in our economy."

He believes that bankers will have an important function in the future development of the American economy. Livingston envisages a period of population growth of nearly 2,500,000 persons each year, and believes that this growth will be reflected in a large increase in bank credit for homes, schools, hospitals, churches, and public utilities. "Another highly important factor which assures our progress in the years ahead," he said, "is the desire of Americans to change and to improve their economic well-being."

Citing many statistics to indicate this growth, Livingston stated, as an example, that during the next six years, it will be necessary to complete one new school classroom every ten minutes, every day and every night. "It is estimated," he said, "that during the next ten years, the consumption of electricity will increase 100 per cent. . . . Home installations, such as refrigerators, washing machines, air-conditioners, and many appliances still on the drawing boards, will average an estimated $5,000 per home, compared to the $1,300 average household investment today."

Besides alerting bankers to the key role that will be played by loans in future expansion of the American economy, Livingston, as president of the A.B.A., is engaged in the task of discovering new and better ways of carrying on banking and in transmitting his findings to the country's fiscal institutions. To that end, he has initiated a study of banking policies and practices based on the opinions of the various national and state supervisory and regulatory banking bodies. Although still not complete, the preliminary findings have already proved valuable in pointing up some of the weak and strong phases of current banking procedures.

Maurice Seymour

HOMER J. LIVINGSTON

In his address delivered at commencement exercises of Washington and Jefferson College, Washington, Pennsylvania on June 7, 1952, Livingston stated that America's material wealth is great, and her economic progress has been unequaled in history. "Of the automobiles in the world, 40,000,000, or 76 per cent, are in this country. Four out of five families now own life insurance. Over 40,000,000 homes have radios and nearly 20,000,000 have television. We have more home owners than any other nation. About 15,000,000 Americans own shares of stock. . . But America has also made significant gains in her cultural and religious life: There are [7,500] [public] libraries, with over 110,000,000 volumes. Today more than 50 per cent of all young people finish high school compared with only 6 per cent fifty years ago, and 10 per cent finish college compared to only 2 per cent in 1900. . . Today we have the largest church membership in relation to population in the history of the nation. Science, industry, research are the great doors to the new frontiers of national expansion." (*Vital Speeches*, September 1, 1952).

Homer Livingston holds many important posts in the business world. He is chairman of the executive committee and chairman of the stock trustees of the Chicago, Indianapolis & Louisville Railroad; a director of the Continental Casualty Company and the Continental Assurance Company; president of the National Safe Deposit Company; and a director of Sears, Roebuck and Company.

Long active in Chicago civic affairs, Livingston is a trustee of the University of Chicago and a treasurer and trustee of the Art Institute of Chicago. He is also a director and treasurer of the Chicago Boys Club; commissioner of the Chicago Medical Center; and trustee of the Chicago Child Care Society and of the Farm Foundation.

(Continued next page)

LIVINGSTON, HOMER J.—*Continued*

Livingston belongs to the Oak Park Country Club in River Forest, a suburb of Chicago. Other clubs in which he holds membership are the Commercial Club, the Chicago Club, the Union League, the Mid-Day Club, the Law Club, the Legal Club, and the Chicago Golf Club. In 1952 he was awarded an honorary LL.D. degree from Washington and Jefferson College in Washington, Pennsylvania.

The banker married Helen Henderson, an employe of the First National Bank of Chicago, on September 29, 1928. Their son, Homer J. Livingston, Jr., is now a student at Princeton University. Livingston is over six feet two inches tall, and has dark hair and a ruddy complexion. Golf and fishing are his principal forms of recreation. With his family he spends his vacations in one of the northern states or in Canada fishing for wall-eyed pike and lake trout.

Reference

Who's Who in America, 1954-55

LIVINGSTON, M(ILTON) STANLEY

May 25, 1905- Physicist; professor

Address: b. c/o Massachusetts Institute of Technology, Cambridge 39, Mass.; h. 11 Stella Rd., Belmont, Mass.

"It is a paradox of physics that the largest and most powerful apparatus is required to study that smallest of physical entities, the atomic nucleus," wrote Dr. M. Stanley Livingston, now professor of physics at Massachusetts Institute of Technology, when he described the "atom-smashing" device called the cyclotron. This earliest of several "magnetic resonance accelerators" was invented by Dr. E. O. Lawrence (Nobel Prize winner in physics, 1939), with whom Dr. Livingston worked on the design and construction details.

M. STANLEY LIVINGSTON

Since then Livingston has built other cyclotrons and has directed the work at the Brookhaven National Laboratory, Upton, Long Island, New York, on the design of its cosmotron (the most powerful in existence, operating at three billion volts). He has also aided with the theoretical development and designing of the "strong-focusing" synchrotron now under construction at Brookhaven.

Livingston is chairman of the executive committee of the Federation of American Scientists, a group of 1500 engineers and scientists interested in the "interactions of science and society." The organization indicated its disapproval of the decision in the recent J. Robert Oppenheimer case and some of its members called on President Dwight D. Eisenhower in July 1954 to ask that a special board be organized for studying the U.S. government's security program.

In a December 1954 statement, the federation declared that "the nation is paying too high a price in terms of forfeited accomplishments" because of the government's current "negative" way of suspecting scientists of loyalty, but it "welcomed" evidence that the security program was now being reviewed by the government.

Milton Stanley Livingston, one of the four children of Milton McWhorter and Sarah Jane (Ten Eyck) Livingston, was born in Brodhead, Wisconsin on May 25, 1905. He was reared in Pomona, California. His mother died in 1917. Dr. Livingston's stepmother, who bore his father five more sons, is still living in Pomona. His father was a minister, schoolteacher, and rancher.

Young Livingston attended Pomona High School and then Bonita High School in La Verne, California and was graduated from the latter in 1921. He enrolled in Pomona College, Claremont, California, where he was influenced by Professor Roland R. Tileson, who interested him in physical research after he had begun as a chemistry student. Livingston worked for his board during college terms and earned money for other expenses by working during the summers. He was on the scholastic honor roll and became a member of the gymnastics team. He was granted an A.B. degree in 1926.

Pursuing a career of research and advanced study, Livingston attended Dartmouth College, Hanover, New Hampshire and received his M.A. degree in physics in 1928. He stayed there as an instructor in physics from 1928 to 1929. He then went to the University of California in Berkeley and after working under the supervision of Dr. E. O. Lawrence, received the Ph.D. degree in 1931. His doctoral thesis, suggested by Lawrence, was entitled "The Production of High Voltage Particles without the Use of High Energy."

The thesis concerned the cyclotron which Lawrence had first described publicly in September 1930 at a meeting of the National Academy of Sciences. Livingston continued to work with Lawrence on the design and construction of the apparatus, which is used for bombarding nuclei of atoms to produce transmutations and artificial radioactivity. Articles by the two scientists on their work appeared in the *Physical Review* (April 1, 1932 and May 1, 1934).

In 1934 Livingston transferred to Cornell University as an instructor and later was made an assistant professor. While at Cornell, he and Professor Hans A. Bethe wrote a "famous" article on nuclear physics ("Nuclear Dynamics, Experimental") which filled the entire July 1937 issue of *Reviews of Modern Physics*. This and two other articles Bethe had written for the periodical have been used as textbooks.

Livingston experienced further successes in designing and constructing cyclotrons for both Cornell University and MIT to which he transferred in 1938 as an assistant professor. He is now a full professor. His articles describing later work with the cyclotron appeared in the January and February 1944 issues of the *Journal of Applied Physics*.

Between 1944 and 1945 Livingston worked as a civilian scientist for the Office of Scientific Research and Development and the Navy Department's Office of Field Service. At the Brookhaven National Laboratory between 1947 and 1948, Livingston was chairman of the Accelerator Project in charge of the design of the cosmotron. An article by Livingston, J. P. Blewett, G. K. Green and L. J. Haworth in the *Review of Scientific Instruments* (January 1950) described this design. The cosmotron helped make obsolete the accepted picture of the atom and its parts.

With Dr. Ernest D Courant and Dr. Hartland S. Snyder, Livingston developed the theoretical basis for a "strong-focusing" synchrotron in 1952. They wrote an article, describing this method of improving the apparatus design, for the *Physical Review* (December 1, 1952). The new magnetic focusing technique employs two magnetic fields successively for accelerating the subatomic particles and allows the development of accelerators up to 30 billion electron volts. An equally powerful apparatus built according to previous cyclotron or cosmotron designs would never have been economically or materially practicable—the iron requirements for the magnet alone would have closely approximated the tonnage of four "giant" battleships. (A similar "strong-focusing" technique had been developed by Nicholas C. Christofilos, but had not been known to scientists.)

It is hoped that the use of the new proton-synchrotron will illuminate the secrets of subatomic physics and assist scientists in learning about the basic structure of the atoms. The latest accelerator is now being built for an approximate cost of $20,000,000 by the Atomic Energy Commission at the Brookhaven National Laboratory. It will be over 700 feet in diameter when it is completed in five or six years.

In addition to his numerous articles in scientific periodicals, Livingston has written a book, *High Energy Accelerators* (Interscience Publishers, 1954). He is a member of Sigma Xi and a fellow of the American Physical Society.

He married Lois Robinson on August 7, 1930. By this marriage, which was terminated by divorce in 1949, he has two children, Diane and Stephen Ten Eyck. On June 7, 1952 he married Margaret Hughes, a former executive secretary at Harvard University. Livingston has gray eyes and brown hair; he is five feet ten inches tall and weighs 170 pounds. He is a Republican. For relaxation he enjoys reading, sailing, and making furniture.

References

N Y Times p 1 + S 14 '52
American Men of Science (1949)
Who Knows And What (1954)
Who's Who in America, 1954-55

LJUNGBERG, ERNST CARL (ROBERT)

July 17, 1897- Organization official

Address: b. c/o International Civil Aviation Organization, International Aviation Bldg., Montreal, Canada; h. 175 Chester Ave., Montreal 16, Canada

The Secretary General of the International Civil Aviation Organization is the Swedish aviation expert, Ernst Carl Ljungberg, whose five-year term in office expires in 1957. A specialized agency of the United Nations, ICAO was created in 1947 to promote the development of air transport and techniques of air navigation. After military training and a career as an officer in the engineering corps and on the general staff in Sweden, Ljungberg held a series of government administrative posts and since 1945 has served as director general and president of the Royal Board of Civil Aviation, central authority of civil aviation in Sweden. He has been honored with decorations by Sweden, Denmark and Finland.

Ernst Carl Robert Ljungberg was born July 17, 1897 in Östersund, Sweden, to Over-Lieutenant Carl Ljungberg and Hildur (Boheman) Ljungberg. Entering upon a military career as an ensign at the age of twenty in 1917, he proceeded to the Royal Academy of Artillery and Engineering in 1919, attaining the rank of under-lieutenant in 1920 and shortly thereafter that of lieutenant. During the period 1920-1922 he pursued advanced studies at the academy and became a lecturer there.

An officer of the Signal and Engineers Corps, Ljungberg became a captain on the General Staff in 1930 and was with the communications division of the General Staff until 1936. In 1931 he served as aide-de-camp to his Royal Highness the Crown Prince of Sweden. From 1931 to 1934 he was a member of the ship classification commission, and from 1932 until 1936 he served on the waterways board and national commission for economic defense preparedness. In 1936 he ended his active army career and entered the reserve, in which he attained the rank of major in 1940.

Ljungberg in 1936 was appointed division chief of the department of railways and aeronautics of the Board of Roads and Waterways, a post he held until 1945 when he was named director general and president of the Royal Board of Civil Aviation. The latter agency is a

Organization de l'Aviation Civile Internationale

ERNST CARL LJUNGBERG

central authority directing all aspects—economic, technical and administrative—of civil aviation in Sweden. It administers civil aerodromes through the local authorities, and it provides air traffic safety services.

Ljungberg's duties called upon him to act as head of Swedish delegations during the negotiation of bilateral air transport agreements and to participate in commissions for the inspection of Swedish air routes, aviation installations and facilities at home and abroad. He therefore became familiar with airport outlay and the administration of air traffic control in Belgium, Canada, Denmark, Finland, France, Italy, the Netherlands, Norway, Spain, Switzerland, the United Kingdom and the United States. Ljungberg has been a member of the board of the Swedish Institute of Aeronautical Research since 1940 and of the Council of Meteorology and Hydrography since 1946.

On November 15, 1951 it was announced that Ljungberg had been named to the post of Secretary General of the International Civil Aviation Organization to succeed Dr. Albert Roper, who was retiring. ICAO resulted from the conference on international civil aviation held in Chicago in November-December 1944. That conference, attended by representatives of fifty-two allied and neutral states, produced the Convention on International Civil Aviation, one of the provisos of which was the establishment of a permanent administrative agency which would come into existence thirty days after twenty-six nations had ratified the Convention and had deposited their ratifications with the State Department of the United States.

ICAO was set up on April 4, 1947. It consists of two governing bodies, the assembly, which meets regularly and is made up of member states, and the council, which is a permanent body responsible to the assembly and is composed of twenty-one contracting states elected by the assembly for a three-year term. These governing bodies are served by an international civil service, a permanent secretariat which functions in relation to ICAO much as the secretariat of the United Nations functions in relation to that body; the head of the secretariat is the Secretary General of ICAO.

Among the aims of ICAO, as expressed in the Convention on International Civil Aviation, are "to develop the principles and techniques of international air navigation and to foster the planning and development of international air transport so as to insure the safe and orderly growth of international civil aviation throughout the world; encourage the arts of aircraft design and operation for peaceful purposes;... meet the needs of the peoples of the world for safe, regular, efficient and economical air transport. . . ." ICAO has the status of a specialized agency of the United Nations.

Prior to his appointment as Secretary General of ICAO, Ljungberg had been active in international aviation, representing his country on many occasions. In 1946 he was chairman of the technical commission of the Assembly of the Provisional International Civil Aviation Organization (PICAO), an interim body which preceded the actual establishment of ICAO. He had been Swedish delegate to many meetings of the international organization, and was elected chairman of the economic commission for the fourth session of the Assembly of ICAO in 1950.

On assuming the post of Secretary General on January 1, 1952, the Swedish air authority became chief executive officer for a five-year term of the international organization's secretariat. The secretariat has four main divisions: the air navigation bureau, the air transport bureau, the legal bureau and the administration and services bureau. It has a staff of about 400, and maintains field offices at Paris, Cairo, Lima and Melbourne in addition to the head office in Montreal. (There were reports in 1954 that ICAO might seek a new site for its headquarters as a result of taxation problems.) It is the task of the Secretary General to coordinate and direct this side of the work of the international organization.

On June 3, 1955 the council of the International Civil Aviation Organization reported that a record of 57,800,000 persons had traveled on scheduled airlines in 1954.

In 1927 Ljungberg married Lilian Murray. He is a Knight Commander of the Order of the North Star, Knight of the Order of the Sword, and holds the King Gustav V Jubilee Medal. His foreign decorations include Commander of the Order of Danebrog (Denmark), Commander of the Order of the White Rose (Finland) and Cross of Freedom with Sword (Finland).

References

U N Bul 11:441 D 1 '51

International Who's Who, 1954

Vem är det, 1951

LOCKER, JESSE D(WIGHT) May 31, 1891- United States Ambassador to Liberia; lawyer

Address: b. c/o American Embassy, Monrovia, Liberia; h. 934 Cleveland Ave., Cincinnati 29, Ohio

Bulletin: Jesse Locker died on April 10, 1955.

The United States Ambassador Extraordinary and Plenipotentiary to the Republic of Liberia since August 1953 has been Jesse D. Locker. Liberia, the only self-governing Negro republic in Africa, was founded in 1822 by freed slaves from the United States. Since the beginning of World War II the United States has been assisting Liberia in developing her rich mineral resources and industrial potential. On December 22, 1950 a five-year agreement for technical cooperation with the United States was signed. The agreement, which is being administered under a joint Liberian-American commission, was recently extended.

At the time of his appointment by President Dwight D. Eisenhower on July 17, 1953, Locker, a Negro attorney at law, was president pro tem of the Cincinnati city council. He succeeded Edward R. Dudley as Ambassador to Liberia.

Jesse Dwight Locker was born in College Hill (now Cincinnati), Ohio on May 31, 1891, one of the four children of the Reverend Laban S. Locker and the former Sarah Elizabeth Morgan. "My father was the first minister of color to be ordained in Ohio by the Christian (Disciples of Christ) Church . . . his father and grandfather were both Christian ministers," he wrote. The boy was not quite nine years old when his father died. His mother then worked variously as cook, housekeeper and laundress in order to make a home for her children.

Young Locker was graduated from College Hill High School in 1911 and was trained for the legal profession at Howard University School of Law in Washington, D.C., from which he received his LL.B. degree in 1915. In January 1917 Locker began practicing law in Cincinnati, where he became active in community and civic projects.

He is the president as well as co-founder of the Negro Sightless Society of Ohio and is on the board of the Catherine Booth Home and Hospital in Cincinnati and the Harriet Beecher Stowe Memorial Association. A member of the committee of management of the Walnut Hills branch of the Cincinnati Young Men's Christian Association, Locker has in the past served also on the Cincinnati Y.M.C.A.'s metropolitan board.

A Republican, Locker was selected in 1941 to the Cincinnati Council as a councilman at large. He was re-elected in 1943, 1945, 1947, and 1951 and was serving as president pro tem of the council when he resigned on August 31, 1953 to accept his appointment as Ambassador to Liberia.

The history of Liberia, a republic on the west African coast, dates from 1816 when the American Colonization Society received a char-

L. O. Rogers

JESSE D. LOCKER

ter from the U.S. Congress, authorizing it to send emancipated Negroes to Africa. The first settlers went to Liberia in 1822 and later in the same year Jehudi Ashmun arrived with a second group of freed slaves. With a handful of men he repulsed two native attacks and reorganized the colony. On July 26, 1847 independence was proclaimed and the first president was Joseph Jenkins Roberts, an ex-slave from Virginia.

Considerable progress has been made toward opening the interior since 1920, but the lack of transportation hampers development of the inland. Michael Clark has written: "For the most part in the interior the native chiefs continue to function according to tribal law and custom. But lately the process of fusion, encouraged by the present administration, has begun to make headway" (New York *Times*, December 27, 1953).

In 1926 the Liberian government approved the agreement to grant a concession for a ninety-nine year lease on 1,000,000 acres of land to the Firestone Plantations Company "for the production of rubber or other agricultural products" and gave the company special tax considerations. Today the plantation at Harbel is the largest in the world. It employs 25,000 workers and the annual harvest of dry rubber is nearly 80,000,000 pounds.

On May 4, 1943 William V. S. Tubman was elected president of Liberia. "He began," states Michael Clark (New York *Times*, December 27, 1953), "to build up his country. Loans, grants and technical assistance came from the United States. Ports, bridges, roads, railways, telephones and waterworks appeared where there were none before." (For further information concerning Liberia's present administration see biographical sketch on William V. S. Tubman in *Current Biography*, January 1955.)

LOCKER, JESSE D.—*Continued*

During World War II Liberia and the United States signed agreements for greater cooperation. On March 31, 1942 the United States obtained the right to construct airports in Liberia. Lend-Lease aid was extended to Liberia by the mutual aid agreement of June 8, 1943. As a result of the growing importance of American-Liberian relations, the U.S. diplomatic mission was raised in 1949 to Embassy status, and Edward R. Dudley, who was serving as Minister, became Ambassador.

Liberia signed a general agreement for technical cooperation with the United States on December 22, 1950 and embarked on a five-year economic and social development plan which cost about $30,000,000 with the Liberian government allocating 20 per cent of its annual revenue to the plan. The money has been used in part for building roads into the interior, establishing hospitals and schools for native tribesmen, developing public utilities and expanding government services.

The R. G. Le Tourneau Company leased 100,000 acres of land in Sinoe county in 1952. The company shipped into Liberia agricultural and construction machinery for commercial cultivation of rice, sugar, cocoa, coffee, lumber, and for the development of livestock and commercial fisheries. Liberia granted to Great Britain on July 30, 1953 the right to maintain military bases for twenty years in exchange for financial aid.

According to the Liberian Bureau of Census and Statistics (as reported in *Liberia Today,* October 1954) total imports into Liberia have more than quadrupled in the last ten years. Although 68 per cent of the imports came from the United States in 1953, American sales have not kept pace with expanding Liberian consumption. Relatively, the increase of sales of the United Kingdom, the Federal Republic of Germany, Canada, Sweden, Denmark, Norway, the Netherlands, Belgium and Italy to the Liberian market has exceeded the growth of sales of American products. Total imports for 1953 were $18,600,000. In the same year 74 per cent of Liberia's total exports went to the United States. The total exports were $49,000,000 and were in large part comprised of rubber, iron ore and piassava.

When Ambassador Dudley, a Democrat, resigned in July 1953, President Eisenhower nominated Jesse D. Locker on July 17 as Dudley's successor. His appointment was confirmed by the Senate on July 22, and on August 31 Locker was sworn into office.

On March 9, 1954 Liberia signed two agreements with the U.N. Technical Assistance Administration, one of which renews for another year a contract covering the assistance of an expert in reorganizing its civil service. The other agreement provides for U.N. technical aid as Liberia may request in organizing seminars, training programs or demonstration projects. It also makes Liberian citizens eligible for U.N. fellowships and scholarships.

Jesse D. Locker and Anna W. French were married on September 22, 1915. They are the parents of one son, Preston F., and four daughters, Mrs. Mary Hines, Mrs. Vivian Hall, Mrs. Bunny Leslie, and Mrs. Juanita Ivie. Ambassador Locker is a Mason and an Elk. His fraternity is the Kappa Alpha Psi. The envoy is five feet seven inches tall, weighs 200 pounds, has brown eyes, and black hair now turning gray.

References

N Y Times p5 Jl 18 '53; p8 S 1 '53

Who's Who in Colored America (1950)

LORENZ, KONRAD Z(ACHARIAS)
1903- Naturalist; author

Address: b. c/o Houghton Mifflin Co., 2 Park St., Boston 7, Mass.; c/o Max Planck Institute, Schloss Buldern bei Dülmen, Westphalia, Germany; h. Schloss Buldern bei Dülmen, Westphalia, Germany

The Austrian naturalist Konrad Z. Lorenz is inclined to accept as truth the venerable tale that King Solomon spake *to* the animals in their language. "I can do it myself," he said. In his long association with the fauna of his native country, Dr. Lorenz has also been able to understand the "signal code" of different species of social animals; this code is the "language" the animals "speak." *The Times* (London) has called Lorenz "one of the foremost authorities in the study of animal behavior."

In his widely-read books, *King Solomon's Ring* (Crowell, 1952) and *Man Meets Dog* (Houghton Mifflin, 1955), Lorenz tells of his observations of jackdaws, dogs, cats, shrews, sticklebacks, and cockatoos. He has taught at the University of Vienna and is now an assistant director with the Max Planck Society for the Advancement of Science in Westphalia, Germany and honorary professor of the University of Münster in Germany. His articles on comparative ethology have appeared in many scientific publications. During his recent trip to the United States he lectured at several universities and appeared on television.

Konrad Zacharias Lorenz was born in Vienna, Austria in 1903, the son of Adolf and Emma (Lecher) Lorenz. His father was a professor at the University of Vienna and was well known throughout the world for his work in orthopedic surgery. His brother, Albert Lorenz, is a teacher of orthopedic surgery at the University of Vienna.

Although brought up mostly in Vienna, it was at Altenberg, the family summer home in Austria, that Konrad Lorenz developed his interest in wildlife. As a boy he explored ponds with a home-made fishing net. He later wrote: "I caught, at the age of nine, the first Daphnia [small crustaceans] for my fishes, thereby discovering the wonder-world of the freshwater pond. . . . In the train of the fishing net came the magnifying glass; after this again a modest little microscope, and therewith my fate was sealed; for he who has once seen the intimate beauty of nature cannot tear himself away from it again. He must become either a poet or a naturalist . . . he may well become both" (*King Solomon's Ring*).

His interest in animals was tolerated by his family. "My parents," Lorenz has written, "only shook their heads or sighed resignedly when, as a schoolboy or young student, I once again brought home a new and probably yet more destructive pet." He has always allowed his animals to roam in his home, as a matter of principle. He has been rewarded for this, despite their destructiveness and their pranks, not only in terms of his scientific observations, but by the mutual affection that resulted.

Following his father's wish, Lorenz studied medicine at the University of Vienna; he also continued his work with animals. During this period he kept a female capuchin monkey named Gloria at his parents' home. Gloria was put in her cage one time when Lorenz went out. When he returned, he found the lights out and Gloria giggling from the curtain rod. The heavy bronze lamp had been dumped into the aquarium along with several medical tomes which Gloria had obtained by unlocking a bookcase. Lorenz later observed: "The interesting part . . . was the strict attention to detail with which the whole business had been performed. . . . Physically alone, this accomplishment was, for such a small animal, worthy of recognition; only rather expensive."

In 1922 he spent a year studying at Columbia University in the United States. He received the M.D. degree from the University of Vienna in 1928 and became an assistant to Professor F. Hochstetter at the anatomical institute there. He also studied zoology, was awarded the Ph.D. degree in 1933, and then devoted himself to his researches in animal behavior for several years. He began teaching comparative anatomy and animal psychology as a *Privatdozent* at the University of Vienna in 1937.

He received an appointment as professor of general psychology at the University of Königsberg, Germany in 1940. The following year he was called for service in World War II as a physician and soldier. From 1944 to 1948 he was a prisoner of war in the Soviet Union. After his return, he resumed his connection with the University of Vienna. The Austrian Academy of Science extended the institute which Lorenz had developed in Altenberg for the study of animals. Lorenz continued his work there, and also lectured in various international congresses as he had before the war. The Max Planck Society for the Advancement of Science invited Lorenz in 1950 to Germany, where he is assistant director of the Institute for the Physiology of Behavior.

Writing on the work of Lorenz, Julian Huxley commented: "It is to him more than any other single man, that we owe our knowledge of the existence of the strange biological phenomena of 'releaser' and 'imprinting' mechanisms." While rearing Jock, a jackdaw, from early infancy, Lorenz first observed imprinting. He describes this by stating that animals, reared away from their own kind "do not know which species they belong to; that is to say, [their] reactions . . . are directed toward those beings with whom they have spent certain impressionable phases of their youth." Jock, for example, was devoted to Lorenz' house-

KONRAD Z. LORENZ

maid and made numerous trips to see her when she had moved away to a nearby village.

In introducing an article by Dr. Lorenz published in *Auk* (July 1937), Francis H. Herrick wrote: "The doctrine of 'releasers' [is] herein set forth—as the 'keys' to 'unlock' or release those 'innate perceptory patterns,' characteristic of the species and the individual, and which result in instinctive reactions." For instance, certain attitudes or gestures on the part of fighting fish, whom Lorenz has closely watched, will act as releasers to promote or inhibit combat reactions in another individual of the species.

While observing another of his charges, Lorenz found, insofar as he knows, the only animal who "has ever spoken a human word to a man, in its right context." Lorenz was walking one day in a place which his raven Roah thought was dangerous; the bird came swooping down from the sky to urge Lorenz to fly up to safety with him. When a raven swoops on a fellow-raven with the same intent, he issues a call-note which has the effect of making the other birds follow him. Roah, however, did not issue this regular call-note, but instead "possessed a sort of insight that 'Roah' was [Lorenz'] call-note!" and said his own name, with human intonation.

When working on a film about greylag geese with Dr. Alfred Seitz, Lorenz decided to write his book, *King Solomon's Ring*, first published in German in 1949, and translated into English by Marjorie Kerr Wilson. The two men were trying to take pictures of the geese who were swimming in a small pond, but some mallard ducklings were in the way. Dr. Seitz called out, "Rangangangang, rangangangang—oh, sorry, I mean—quahg, gegegegeg, Quahg, gegegegeg!" He had wanted to call away the mallards, but by mistake, had used greylag language. "There was nobody," Lorenz wrote, "to appreciate the

LORENZ, KONRAD Z.—*Continued*

joke, Alfred being far too preoccupied with his work. I wanted to tell it to somebody and so it occurred to me to tell it to everybody."

In a chapter called "Morals and Weapons" in the book, Lorenz tells how the dove, while by reputation one of the most peaceful animals, is really one of the cruelest, and will mutilate and destroy members of its own species without a qualm. The wolf, on the other hand, will not finally kill another wolf in battle, if the enemy asks for clemency by baring its neck. In referring to the military tendencies of man, Lorenz wrote: "The day will come when two warring factions will be faced with the possibility of each wiping the other out completely. . . . Shall we then behave like doves or like wolves? The fate of mankind will be settled by the answer to this question. We may well be apprehensive."

During the winter of 1954-1955 Lorenz came to the United States and lectured at the Smithsonian Institution, Harvard University, Cornell University and other educational institutions. He appeared on *Adventure*, a television program of the Museum of Natural History in New York, and showed his film at the annual meeting of the New York Zoological Society, which awarded him its Gold Medal.

In *Man Meets Dog*, translated from the German by Marjorie Kerr Wilson, Lorenz described the behavior of dogs and cats. He discussed the characteristics of the two types of dogs descended from wolves and from jackals, offered his theory of how the "unique relationship" between man and dog arose in prehistoric times, and wrote about feline "play" and about cats' behavior toward their "masters." Writing on man and the domestic animals, the dog and cat, he stated: "I consider it the best test of genuine love and understanding of animals if a person has sympathies for both these creatures, and can appreciate in each its own special virtues."

Konrad Zacharias Lorenz married Margarethe Gebhardt, a doctor of medicine and a gynecologist, in June 1927. He has praised the patience of his wife who has "put up with" tame rats which ran free in the house and gnawed circular pieces out of sheets to build their nests, or with a cockatoo who bit off all the buttons from the washing which had been carefully hung up to dry in the garden. Dr. Lorenz and his wife have three children: Thomas, Agnes, and Dagmar. The scientist has gray eyes and gray hair. He is about six feet tall, and weighs 200 pounds. He smokes a pipe. He has illustrated both his technical papers and his books with his own drawings.

Dr. Lorenz enjoys reading, not only technical publications, but the literature of many languages, particularly the works of Rudyard Kipling (*The Jungle Book*) Rupert Brooke, Lewis Carroll, Goethe, Selma Lagerlöf (*Nils Holgersson*), Longfellow, and Shakespeare. He has, however, commented: "If I cast into one side of the balance all that I have learned from the books of the library and into the other everything that I have gleaned from the books in the running brooks, how surely would the latter turn the scales."

References

Time 59:58+ My 19 '52 por
Kürschners Deutscher Gelehrten Kalender, 1954
Lorenz, K. Z. King Solomon's Ring (1952); Man Meets Dog (1955)
Österreicher der Gegenwart (1951)
Who's Who in Austria (1955)

LOS ANGELES, VICTORIA DE *See* Angeles, Victoria de los

LYNCH, DANIEL F(RANCIS) June 16, 1902- Organization official; oral surgeon

Address: b. c/o American Dental Association, 222 E. Superior St., Chicago 11, Ill.; 1149 16th St., N.W., Washington 6, D.C.; h. 1678 Primrose Rd., N.W., Washington 12, D.C.

The American Dental Association's president for 1954-1955 is Daniel F. Lynch, who believes that dentists should actively engage in political and civic affairs. He has said: "Locally they should support such campaigns as those for fluoridation, nationally they should battle socialized medicine . . . they should even run for public office, for Congress, for mayor, and the like" (New York *World-Telegram and Sun*, December 7, 1954).

An active leader in the organization, Dr. Lynch served as the A.D.A. trustee from the fourth district from 1947 to 1953, secretary to the A.D.A. research commission (precursor of the council on dental research), chairman of the association's international relations committee (predecessor to the council on international relations) from 1940 to 1947, and president of the District of Columbia Dental Society (1940-1941). He was a representative at the International Dental Congresses in 1936, 1947, 1952 and served as vice-president of the Fédération Dentaire Internationale (1947-1953). Lynch has been an oral surgeon in Washington, D.C. since 1928. He was succeeded as head of the A.D.A. by Dr. B. C. Kingsbury in 1955.

Daniel Francis Lynch was born in Waterbury, Connecticut on June 16, 1902 to Daniel W. and Margaret (Hodges) Lynch. He attended Mulcahy Grammar School and Crosby High School in Waterbury. From the University of Maryland's School of Dentistry in Baltimore, he received the D.D.S. degree in 1925 and then interned at Fifth Avenue Hospital, New York City (1925-1926) and the Mayo Clinic, Rochester, Minnesota (1926-1928).

In Washington, D.C. Lynch began practicing oral surgery in 1928. In the same year he became a professor of anesthesia and associate professor of oral surgery at Georgetown University Dental School in Washington, D.C. Continuing his studies, Lynch attended George Washington University in Washington, D.C. (1928-1930) and Georgetown University (1930-1931). Lynch has also lectured at George Washington University, University of Pennsylvania in Philadelphia, Naval Dental School in Bethesda, Maryland, and Army Medical Center in Washington, D.C. He has conducted over seventy-five lectures and clinics in the United States before specialty societies, postgraduate groups, and other gatherings.

Clinics before the American Dental Society of Europe in Stockholm, Sweden (1938), Lausanne, Switzerland (1939), and London, England (1948, 1952) were held by Dr. Lynch. The oral surgeon was the official representative of U.S. Government at the ninth International Dental Congress in Vienna in 1936, delegate of the A.D.A. to the tenth congress in Boston in 1947, and delegate of the association at the eleventh congress in London, England in 1952. In 1941 he was a consultant to the U.S. coordinator of Inter-American Affairs.

During World War II Lynch served as a commander in the Dental Corps of the U.S. Navy from 1944 to 1946, and now holds a reserve commission. From 1949 to 1951 he was a member of the medical advisory committee to the Secretary of Defense, and a member of the reserve consultants board to the Surgeon General, U.S. Navy from 1948 to 1954. The dentist now serves as a consultant to the U.S. Air Force at Bolling Field, Washington, D.C., the Veterans' Administration, (Washington, D.C. regional office) and the U.S. Public Health Service.

On October 1, 1953 the A.D.A. selected Lynch as their president for the 1954-1955. At the ninety-fifth annual session, in November 1954, Lynch was inaugurated, succeeding Leslie M. FitzGerald. Dentists now comprise the third largest group of independent professional practitioners in the United States. Due to the immense volume of dental needs, it has been estimated that 153,000 dentists will be needed in 1960 (as compared with the present census of 93,726) to take care of the American population.

According to dental surveys, as reported in the *Journal of the American Dental Association,* considering fillings alone, it is necessary to insert 280,000,000 fillings to insure healthy mouths for every American child from six to eighteen years of age. There are about 38,000,000 new fillings needed in this age group each year. The estimated figures for adults, in the case of restoration, are 425,000,000 fillings. The establishment of new schools, use of preventive procedures and public education are needed to meet this problem.

In October 1953 the A.D.A. announced that it believes that fluoridation of community water supplies "is a direct responsibility of the local community, where leadership should be shared by the dental profession, official health agencies and appropriate civic groups" (New York *Herald Tribune*, October 2, 1953).

It is believed that a mixture of one part fluoride to 1,000,000 parts water will reduce dental cavities by about 60 per cent in persons who drink the fluoridated water from birth, and that such water is harmless. Fluoridation has been endorsed by the American Medical Association, American Association for the Advancement of Science, National Research Council, U.S. Public Service and American Hospital Association. In some communities, however, public officials believe that the safety of fluoridation has not yet been sufficiently demonsrated.

DANIEL F. LYNCH

The tenth anniversary of the beginning of fluoridation in Newburgh, New York was celebrated on April 21, 1955. It was announced that the teeth of Newburgh children were 60 per cent better than those in Kingston, New York, thirty-eight miles away, where the water had not been treated. Fluoridation had not adversely affected the health of the children.

Addressing the Greater New York Dental Meeting on December 6, 1954, Lynch stated that the A.D.A. is not in favor of the extension of the present dentist-physician draft act, which expires on June 30, 1955. (The Washington *Post and Times Herald* of May 4, 1955 reported that the A.M.A. also opposes continuation of the medical-dental draft.)

As reported by the New York *Times*, December 7, 1954 Lynch said that the association had decided that the armed forces have too many dentists now, and that they are not being used in the best way. In the armed forces there is one dentist for each 500 men. He compared this with civilian practice, where there is an average of one dentist for each 2,000 persons. He objected to taking dentists "away from their established civilian practices only to have them spend a great deal of time treating civilians."

Lynch also said that nothing had been done toward improving the military dental service in the last four years and felt that adequate administration would set the situation right without additional dentists (New York *World-Telegram and Sun*, December 7, 1954).

Among Lynch's articles are "Postoperative Roentgenograms" (*International Journal of Orthodontia, Oral Surgery and Radiography,* (February 1930); "Medical and Dental Relations" (*Medical Annals of the District of*

LYNCH, DANIEL F.—*Continued*

Columbia, March 1932); "Selecting the Anesthetic for Operation in Oral Surgery" (*International Journal of Orthodontia, Oral Surgery and Radiography,* 1936); and "Contribution of the Dental Profession to Continental Solidarity and Understanding" (*Journal of the American Dental Association,* December 1942).

The oral surgeon is a diplomate of the American Board of Oral Surgeons, a fellow of the Royal College of Surgeons (England), New York Academy of Dentistry, and a member of the American Society of Oral Surgeons, Pan-American Odontological Association (president, 1940-1942), Pan-American Medical Society, Mayo Foundation Alumni Association, American Academy of Oral Pathology, Gorgas Odontological Society, and Federación Odontologia Latino Americano. He is an honorary member of dental societies in Bolivia, Argentina, Colombia, Costa Rica, Chile, El Salvador, Cuba, Eduador, Mexico, Sweden, and Norway. His Greek letter societies include Sigma Xi, Omicron Kappa Upsilon, and Psi Omega; his clubs are the Rotary, University, Cosmos, and Waterbury.

Dr. Lynch, who is a bachelor, is tall and gray-haired. He has been decorated by the Republic of Ecuador. In order to help educate the public, he has said that dentists should explain to their patients what they are doing as they work.

References

Washington (D.C.) Post p18 O 2 '53
Who's Who in America (Sup. Ja '55)

MCCARTHY, EUGENE J(OSEPH) Mar. 29, 1916- United States Representative from Minnesota; educator

Address: b. House Office Bldg., Washington 25, D.C.; h. 1946 Selby St., St. Paul, Minn.

Minnesota's Fourth District is represented in the U.S. Congress by Eugene J. McCarthy, a former professor of sociology, farmer, writer, and a liberal Democrat. He was first elected to the House of Representatives in 1948 and has been returned to each succeeding Congress, most recently in November 1954. Currently, in the Eighty-fourth Congress, he is serving on the House Ways and Means Committee. He frequently receives letters and telegrams from people who have confused him with Senator Joseph R. McCarthy, Republican of Wisconsin.

Eugene Joseph McCarthy, who is of Irish descent, was born in Watkins, Minnesota on March 29, 1916, the son of Michael J. and Anna (Baden) McCarthy. Graduating from St. John's Preparatory School in 1932, "Gene" entered St. John's University in Collegeville, Minnesota, where he achieved a high scholastic record and in 1935 received the B.A. degree. He later attended the University of Minnesota, in Minneapolis, which granted him the M.A. degree in 1939.

For about four years, from 1936 to 1940, he taught social science in public high schools and from 1940 to 1942 was professor of economics and education at St. John's University. During 1944 he was engaged in civilian technical work with the military intelligence division of the U.S. War Department. Upon resuming his career in education, he taught in high school for a year and in 1946 was appointed acting chairman of the sociology department at the College of St. Thomas in St. Paul, Minnesota.

Elected chairman of the Democratic Farmer-Labor party of Ramsey county, Minnesota in June 1948, he attended the Democratic National Convention that year as a delegate at large. He became a candidate for a seat in the Eighty-first Congress and in November 1948 was elected to represent the Fourth District of Minnesota, comprising Ramsey county with a population (in 1950) of 355,332.

Representative McCarthy is known for his liberal voting record in the House. "The American Federation of Labor scores him 'right' (and Senator Joseph McCarthy 'wrong') on all of the twenty-five selected roll calls in which he has voted since entering Congress," John D. Morris reported (New York *Times Magazine,* August 8, 1954). In 1949 he supported extension of the trade agreements act (February) and of the rent control act (March), the long-range housing bill (June) and the anti-poll tax bill (July). He opposed repeal of Federal taxes on oleomargarine (April).

Generally favoring foreign assistance legislation, he voted in August 1949 against a 50 per cent cut in European arms aid and the following year approved Korea-Formosa economic aid (February) and the $2.7 billion Economic Cooperation Administration extension bill (March). On other 1950 roll call votes he supported the voluntary-compliance Fair Employment Practice Committee bill (February) and a $2 billion increase for farm price supports (June). He was against a $600,000,000 cut in Federal spending (May) and voted "yea" to canceling an economy cut in postal services (August).

During the Eighty-second Congress McCarthy again opposed a number of measures to reduce government spending: in 1951 voting against a decrease in government civil payrolls (April), a $10,000,000 cut for reclamation funds (May), a $350,000,000 cut for economic aid to Europe (August); and in 1952 against a $14,000,000 cut in Tennessee Valley Authority appropriations (March), a 10 per cent cut in Federal jobs (April) and a $615,000,000 reduction in European economic assistance (May).

On various domestic issues coming before the House during the Eighty-second Congress he favored in 1951 the draft extension-Universal Military Training bill (April) and opposed the tidelands oil bill (July). In 1952 he voted "nay" to limiting public housing to 5,000 units (March), to using the Taft-Hartley act to stop the steel strike (June), and to ending Federal rent controls in September 1952 (June). He approved retention of 90 per cent of parity farm price supports (June).

Legislative proposals which had McCarthy's endorsement during 1953 were retention of a nonpartisan tariff commission (June), a boost in Air Force funds (July) and admission of

217,000 refugees from Communism (July). In the last session of the Eighty-third Congress (1954) he approved raising the personal income tax exemption (March), an additional $17,000,000 for airline subsidies (March), a bill to make wire tap evidence admissable in certain types of cases (April), the St. Lawrence seaway authorization (May), and social security expansion (June).

Addressing the National Catholic Education Association in Cleveland, Ohio in March 1951, Representative McCarthy warned of the "danger of intrusion by the state into areas of culture and the social and private lives of its citizens." He said that interference by the state in matters of religion and morality is a greater threat to human freedom than interference at the material level. Although the state has duties in these areas, he noted, "this does not mean it has the right to make all decisions regarding every aspect of the lives of its citizens" (New York *Herald Tribune,* March 29, 1951).

In an article which appeared in the Catholic lay magazine, the *Commonweal* (December 14, 1951), he examined several causes of the present condition of political morality, pointing out that behavior in Government reflects the general level of morality in the United States. Among his suggestions for improvements was the recommendation: "We must take immediate action to develop in the United States a code of ethics for men in public office, and to lay the foundations upon which we can build a tradition of the high honor and responsibility of government office."

Another of McCarthy's articles for *Commonweal* (October 1, 1954), "The Christian in Politics," answered the question "What are the marks of a Christian politician?" The standard that the Minnesota Congressman set forth included holding fast to moral laws, shunning the devices of the demagogue, and speaking the truth. The Christian statesman, he also wrote, should show "alertness to protect and defend the rights of individuals, or religious institutions and other institutions from violation by the state or by other institutions, or by persons. He should be the first to detect and oppose a truly totalitarian threat or movement and the last to label every proposal for social reform 'socialistic.'"

McCarthy's "Election-Year Lessons for Our Children," which appeared in *Nationl Parent-Teacher* magazine (December 1954) expressed his concern for the influence of extreme partisan talk in election years upon the attitudes of children, who have become increasingly aware of political contests through television, radio and the newspaper. He particularly deplored cynicism, a tendency to look upon all politicians as corrupt.

He stated his conviction that "Truth will prove the best antidote for cynicism, which is an especially dangerous attitude when it prevails among young people. . . . Not only does it destroy confidence and hope, some of the most precious assets of youth, but it also eats away the will to attack difficult political problems—as it does problems in other fields."

Wide World

EUGENE J. MCCARTHY

In 1952 McCarthy, who has appeared on several radio and television discussion programs, took part with Senator Joseph R. McCarthy in a national television debate on foreign policy. He was said to have "definitely held his own" and to have "emerged unruffled and unscarred." John D. Morris further stated in his New York *Times Magazine* article, "The Other McCarthy," that "Representative McCarthy seldom discusses Senator McCarthy or McCarthyism, and then does so in positive terms, emphasizing the importance and desirability of fairness in the conduct of Congressional investigations."

The Congressman's voting record for 1955 indicates that he supported the bill increasing Congressional salaries (February), an 8.3 per cent (as against a 7.6 per cent) postal pay raise (April), restoring rigid farm price supports (May), raising the minimum wage to $1 an hour (July), and a $2.6 billion foreign aid grant (July). He opposed the Administration's highway bill (July) and the Natural Gas Act exemption (July).

McCarthy is a member of the American Association of University Professors and the Foresters. He married Abigail Quigley in 1945 and they have three children, Ellen Anne, Mary Abigail and Michael Benet. The "studious, reflective" legislator has graying black hair, is six feet two inches tall and weighs 180 pounds. A Roman Catholic, he belongs to the Knights of Columbus. McCarthy enjoys the writings of Sir Thomas More and Finley Peter Dunne's "Mr. Dooley."

References

N Y Times Mag p16 Ag 8 '54 por
American Catholic Who's Who, 1954-55
Congressional Directory (1955)
Who's Who in America, 1954-55
Who's Who in United States Politics (1952)

MCCARTHY, MARY (THERESE) June 21, 1912- Author

Address: b. c/o Harcourt Brace & Co., Inc., 383 Madison Ave., New York 17; h. RFD 2, Newport, R.I.

Reprinted from the *Wilson Library Bulletin* May 1955

"Life is a system of recurrent pains, the poison and the antidote being eternally packaged together by some considerate druggist," according to a passage in Mary McCarthy's collection of stories, *Cast a Cold Eye* (Harcourt, 1950). Of this book Lorine Pruette wrote in the New York *Herald Tribune Book Review* (September 24, 1950): "The McCarthy pictures have horror in them, and all her characters live in hell, but there is nothing depressing about reading her

MARY MCCARTHY

stories. There is an intellectual satisfaction to be found here, gratification in a style that is so perfect a tool for its purposes." Her latest book, *A Charmed Life,* was published by Harcourt in the fall of 1955.

Orphaned at six, Mary with her three younger brothers spent five years in Minneapolis "in the custody of a severe great-aunt" and uncle. While some of her relatives believe that she owes her literary successes, and her brother, Kevin McCarthy, his career as an actor, to their upbringing, she still refuses to "believe that artistic talent flowers necessarily from a wounding of the stem on which it grows."

Mary Therese McCarthy was born on June 21, 1912 in Seattle, Washington, the daughter of two students at the University of Washington, Roy Winfield McCarthy, whose Irish parents had made money in Minnesota grain elevators, and Therese (Preston) McCarthy, whose mother was "a lively Jewish beauty from San Francisco, where her parents were '49ers." The pair, "handsome, winning and romantic," died in the influenza epidemic of 1918, leaving four children.

With the aid of her mother's father, Harold Preston, a distinguished Seattle lawyer, and a later inheritance from her paternal grandfather, Mary acquired an excellent education at two boarding schools, Forest Ridge Convent in Seattle, and Annie Wright Seminary (Episcopalian), Tacoma, where she was valedictorian, and at Vassar College. She had already read Dickens, Tolstoy, Sienkiewicz, and Frank Stockton in her grandfather's library, and much poetry at school. "The discovery of Latin and, in college, of the Elizabethans provided two of those shocks of self-recognition that make us, in adolescence, elect what we are or shall be. Latin came to me very fluently. . . . Hence writing with a Latinate turn, compressed, analytic, and yet having a certain extravagance or oratorical flourish sounded in my ears like a natural, spoken language."

In 1933 Miss McCarthy was graduated from Vassar with a Phi Beta Kappa key, and married Harold Johnsrud, a playwright and actor. They separated in 1936. She had reviewed novels and biographies for the *Nation* and *New Republic,* and on returning from Reno to a one-room apartment in a crooked street in Greenwich Village, she also read manuscripts. Her outraged reaction to the Moscow trials alienated her from the fashionable Stalinist circles she had frequented. She decided that Marxism was "something you had to take up young, like ballet training," and was not for her. She "did not join the Trotskyist sect," she said, "but lived a bourgeois life."

After she became an editor and critic for *Partisan Review,* Miss McCarthy also wrote short stories, later "somewhat highhandedly brought together by the tenuous theme of lost personality" (according to one critic), in *The Company She Keeps* (Simon & Schuster, 1942). Though it seemed to the *Catholic World* (June 1942), "a studied attempt to be sophisticated and bawdy at the same time," Mason Wade in the *Commonweal* (June 19, 1942), regarded it as a brilliantly written book, "which evokes with a sometimes malicious accuracy of detail the life of one social group in the disordered 1930's."

She was married in 1938 to Edmund Wilson, the critic; they had one son, Reuel. She was later divorced from Wilson and in 1946 she married Bowden Broadwater.

In 1949 Random House published her book, *The Oasis,* which had first appeared in *Horizon.* L. A. G. Strong, in the *Spectator,* called this short novel about an intellectual group on a New England mountaintop "brilliant and a little chilly," and Brendan Gill, in the *New Yorker,* "an absolutely unmitigated triumph of wit and writing skill."

Before her third marriage, Miss McCarthy taught for a short time at Bard College and at Sarah Lawrence. This experience "awakened [her], slowly, to the fact that cleverness is not a substitute for knowledge," and led to the writing of *The Graves of Academic* (Harcourt, 1952), her best known novel. The New York

Times (February 24, 1952) called it "mortally entertaining," while the *United States Quarterly Book Review* (June 1952) thought that the author had an "acute eye for the absurdities and pretensions of the intellectual, be he modern scholar or poet."

Miss McCarthy has an easy, pleasant manner on the lecture platform. She and her husband live in the country, "close to a very sound library, and read with a certain gluttony which now and then overreaches itself." Her amusing "Confession" ("One Writer's Encounter with Communism") appeared in *The Reporter* for December 22, 1953, and January 5, 1954.

Reference

Who's Who in America (Sup. Mr '54)

MCCLEERY, ALBERT (KENNY) Dec. 30. 1911- Television producer; director

Address: b. c/o National Broadcasting Co., Hollywood 28, Calif.; h. 13275 Galewood Ave., Sherman Oaks, Calif.

"Faces are important in television," declares Albert McCleery, producer-director of the National Broadcasting Company. "Close-ups reveal people's souls. Audiences like to look at exciting faces." Since 1949 he has been adapting the technique of "theatre-in-the-round" or intimate staging to television and radio drama. Now, as one of six executive producers on the NBC staff, he presents and directs both the *Hall of Fame* telecasts, sponsored by Hallmark Cards, and the *Inheritance* radio series.

Among the oustanding productions directed by McCleery on the *Hall of Fame* program during 1953 and 1954 were two-hour versions of *King Richard II*, *Macbeth*, and *Hamlet*, and an hour-long excerpt from Thomas Wolfe's novel *Of Time and the River*. He won a Christopher Award in November 1954 for his radio production of "Proclaim Liberty" on the NBC *Inheritance* program.

As an undergraduate at Northwestern University in 1931, McCleery established the first arena stage in the Midwest. In 1939, as drama teacher at Fordham University, he founded the first theatre-in-the-round in the East.

Albert Kenny McCleery was born December 30, 1911 in Lawrence, Kansas. One of two sons of John Cass and Mary Margaret (Kenny) McCleery, he is of Scotch-Irish descent. Brought up in Kansas and Texas, Albert took part in dramatics, debating, and the Junior ROTC at Fort Worth's Central High School. For a time he attended Texas Christian University, also in Fort Worth, and in 1930 entered Northwestern University in Evanston, Illinois as a theatre arts major.

While an undergraduate, McCleery founded the Georgian Little Theatre at Evanston, Illinois in 1931. (Arena staging had been tried in 1914 by Azubah Latham at Teachers College, Columbia University; by T. Earl Pardoe in 1922 at Brigham Young University in Utah; the technique had been developed and achieved renown under the direction of Gilmor Brown at Pasadena, California in 1924, and of Glenn Hughes in 1932 at Seattle, Washington.) McCleery staged plays in the sunken lobby of a

ALBERT MCCLEERY

fashionable residential hotel and found it a perfect setting for arena production of brisk, gay drawingroom comedies.

Instead of completing his college course, McCleery went to California in 1932 where he served as assistant stage manager at the Pasadena Playhouse. McCleery has said that the two strongest influences upon his development were Gilmor Brown, of the Pasadena Playhouse, and Grant Wood, the artist. It was under Wood's sponsorship that in 1933 he staged Ibsen's *The Master Builder* on a long platform in the middle of a large hotel ballroom in Cedar Rapids, Iowa.

In the fall of 1934 McCleery went to New York, where his first job was as assistant stage manager for Guthrie McClintic, producer of *Romeo and Juliet*, in which Katharine Cornell was starred. For several years (1935-39), McCleery was on the reportorial side of show business as a member of the staff of *Stage* magazine. He edited *Prize Plays from Stage* (1936) and with Carl Glick, Springfield *Republican* columnist, wrote a 407-page report on community theaters in the United States, *Curtains Going Up!* (Pitman, 1939).

Albert McCleery had the experience of working with Ethel Barrymore during 1937 and 1938, when he adapted for radio presentation a series of thirty plays in which she was starred. Engaged as drama director of Fordham University, McCleery in 1939 persuaded the president, Father Robert Gannon, to let him remodel a penthouse into the first arena theater in the East.

Called to Hollywood by Columbia Pictures in 1940, he wrote, with James Edward, the script of *The Lady Is Willing* for Marlene Dietrich and Fred MacMurray. For Universal Pictures he worked on scripts starring Dietrich and John Wayne—*The Spoilers* and *Pittsburgh*. All three movies were released in 1942.

McCleery, who has been a member of New York's Seventh Regiment of the National Guard

MCCLEERY, ALBERT—*Continued*

since 1936, went on active duty in 1942. He was appointed aide-de-camp to Australian Prime Minister Joseph Curtin and British Marshall Sir Thomas Blamey during their state visits to the United States. He served at SHAEF in England as administrative officer, signal division, then in Paris and Berlin as photo officer of the First Allied Airborne Army (1941-45). He was decorated with the Silver Star and Bronze Star and attained the rank of lieutenant colonel. After hostilities ended, McCleery headed the Biarritz University Theatre and put on a G.I. production of William Saroyan's *The Time of Your Life*.

Returning to Fordham in 1946 as head of the drama department, McCleery directed productions in the theater that had been built in accordance with his ideas. The acting area was oval, for he had settled on the "cameo" shape as ideal for visibility. Among his "cameo" productions at Fordham were the American premieres of *Crown Colony*, *The Strong Are Lonely*, and *The Voice in Rama*, and the second production anywhere of Eugene O'Neill's *Lazarus Laughed*.

During the postwar expansion of television, McCleery joined the NBC staff as a TV director in 1949. According to Philip Minoff in *Cue*, he was "quite the fair-haired boy" and "increased his prestige with well-received productions (in arena style) of *Dark of the Moon* and *Romeo and Juliet*." Then came an unfortunate production of Raymond Chandler's *The Little Sister*, of which McCleery says, "Everything that could possibly have gone wrong, did. No one around NBC spoke to me for six weeks."

For months afterward, McCleery was limited to directing a little girl ventriloquist and her dummy, Judy Splinters. "I used *Judy Splinters* as my own TV school," he has said. "I twisted and turned those cameras every which way, until today I know all about cameras, where they can move, how fast they can get there, and how far they can see" (*Theatre Arts*, November 1951).

In the summer of 1950 McCleery launched his *Cameo Theatre*, introducing his technique of no scenery staging, with the cameras in the center and the actors very closely grouped around them. Close-ups are all-important in the McCleery style of directing, partly because he feels the small size of the TV screen makes them necessary and partly because of the feeling of intimacy he tries to produce. "When you get that close to another human, you care a lot about what happens to him," he says.

In place of scenery, McCleery used lighting, sound effects, and a few simple props like chairs and candlesticks McCleery says, "I can do a show with only a phone, a cigarette, and several out-of-view stools. Occasionally I show the back of a chair for its curving line, and sometimes for relief a desk, a bit of bunting back of a politician's head. But faces are the thing."

During the 1951-52 season director McCleery presented twelve-minute "cameo spots" on the weekly Kate Smith show. In the summer of 1953 he produced two weekly shows, *Cameo Theatre* and the summer version of *Fireside Theatre*. On *Cameo Theatre*, he presented such unusual material as Shirley Jackson's *The Lottery*. In casting, he cast faces. For *A Little Night Music*, he took great trouble to find two actors who could appear as a boy and as the same boy twenty years later. Those faces he used to spectacular effect in a close-up of a tear falling from the boy's eye, dissolving to a tear on the man's cheek.

Cameo Theatre carried on through the winter season, on Sunday nights, and achieved a comfortable viewership rating of twenty-one. In February-March 1952, McCleery presented *Peer Gynt*, starring Douglass Montgomery, and with decoration and costumes by Howard Bay. This was perhaps his most radical departure, in that the play was presented in three half-hour installments over as many weeks.

Presenting the *Hallmark Hall of Fame* series in 1953, McCleery worked out an agreement with his sponsor—"If I do four or five popular hits, then they'll let me do a serious show." Among the serious offerings were a two-hour *Hamlet* with Maurice Evans (which won McCleery a Christopher Award), Thomas Mitchell in a one-hour excerpt from Thomas Wolfe's *Of Time and the River*, the trial of Socrates, and Molière's *The Imaginary Invalid*.

In January 1954 he presented *King Richard II*, with Sarah Churchill and Maurice Evans. He departed from his usual style by using $175,000 worth of "production values"—rich scenery (including forty-foot castle battlements, horses, dogs, birds, ships, and a cast of thirty-seven). The costumes were from the 1937 stage version which first brought Evans fame. The two-hour production (cut down to that length by Evans) was described by *Life* as "by far TV's most successful Shakespeare to date."

The *Hall of Fame* two-hour production of *Macbeth* on November 28, 1954 was presented in compatible color and starred Judith Anderson and Maurice Evans. Harriet Van Horne in the New York *World-Telegram and Sun* commented: "Color was used with consummate taste throughout this Shakespearean tragedy . . . one of the finest aspects of this *Macbeth* was its imaginative camera work with its artful symbology."

In April 1954 McCleery began directing a Sunday evening radio series, *Inheritance*. Presented "in cooperation with the American Legion," the broadcasts dramatize important but little-known incidents in American history. The first showed George Washington's refusal to accept the kingship which the military leaders tried to give him. The second dealt with Dorothea Dix, the great nineteenth century reformer of prisons, and the care of the insane.

The producer-director is a member of the National Theatre Conference, ANTA, and American Educational Theatre Association, and often gives speeches before college drama departments, flying there and back the same day. Ohio State presented him with its award for the best cultural program of 1953, and in June 1950 he received an honorary Master of Theatre Arts degree from the Pasadena Playhouse College of the Theatre, which had earlier given him the Gilmor Brown Award. During the summer of 1953 he was recalled to active duty for forty-five days by the chief signal officer to advise the Army on its television productions, a task which won him a letter of commendation from Major General George I. Back.

The "kinetic, graying, Irish-eyed" producer commutes to Hollywood from his home in the San Fernando Valley. On January 1, 1938 he married Sanny Sue Bailey, formerly in the real estate business. He believes that color television "is the most exciting thing that has happened; color knocks ten years from the age of the average actress."

Two of McCleery's scripts, complete with his cue markings, are included in *Television Scripts for Staging and Study* (A. A. Wyn, 1953), edited by Rudy Bretz and Edward Stasheff.

References

Cue 20:13 Ag 25 '51 por
N Y World-Telegram p9 Ag 25 '51
Theatre Arts 34:48 O '50; 35:48 N '51 por
Time 55:48 Je 26 '50; 62:96 D 7 '53
Who's Who in America Monthly Supplement p227 S '50

MCCLINTOCK, ROBERT MILLS Aug. 30, 1909- United States Ambassador to Cambodia

Address: b. c/o United States Embassy, Pnompenh, Cambodia, Indochina

Department of State
ROBERT MILLS MCCLINTOCK

Cambodia's first resident Ambassador from the United States is Robert Mills McClintock, named by President Dwight D. Eisenhower on August 16, 1954. The new Embassy at Pnompenh was established in accordance with plans announced during the Geneva conference on the Indochinese war in July 1954. He had previously served in the triple capacity of Ambassador to Viet-Nam, Ambassador to Cambodia, and Minister to Laos.

A career foreign service officer, McClintock has filled posts in various parts of the world. He served in Finland during a period in World War II when relations between that country and the United States were strained. Later he was a political adviser to the U.S. delegation at the General Assembly of the United Nations and deputy chief of mission accredited to the Associated States of Indochina. He is well known in government circles as a writer and lecturer on diplomacy and naval affairs.

Robert Mills McClintock was born in Seattle, Washington on August 30, 1909, the son of John Mills and Christine (Chamberlain) McClintock. His twin brother, John Chamberlain McClintock, is a specialist in Inter-American problems and an executive with the United Fruit Company. The family moved to California and Robert attended the Pasadena High School.

In his article "The United Nations or World Government" (*Annals of the American Academy of Political and Social Science,* July 1949), he related that while in France when he was sixteen years old, he resolved to enter the foreign service. He regarded it as a career that would give him a chance "to do something in a small personal way to combat the terrible threat of war." He wrote that he had walked through a valley near Verdun, "where in six months 600,000 men had been killed," and later "saw the trench at Douaumont with the bayonets still sticking up above the earth where an entire French company had been buried alive."

Young McClintock entered Stanford University in California in 1927 and during the summer of 1929, studied at Geneva under Salvador de Madariaga y Rojo, Spanish author and diplomat. He attended sessions of the League of Nations and was concerned with the difficulties of the countries represented in reconciling their various views. He received his B.A. degree at Stanford in 1931 and in December of that year was accepted as a U.S. foreign service officer. His first classified appointment came on January 20, 1932 as vice-consul. He was sent to Panama City, Panama where he remained until recalled ten months later to enter the Department of State Foreign Service Officers' Training School in Washington.

He was sent to Kobe, Japan as vice-consul in March 1933. Reclassification as a third Embassy secretary came in December 1934 and he was assigned to Santiago, Chile. He was again reclassified in July 1937 and sent to Ciudad Trujillo, Dominican Republic as secretary of the Legation. Two years later, he was transferred to Helsinki, Finland. He became chargé d'affaires ad interim in December 1942, after H. F. Arthur Schoenfeld, U.S. Minister to Finland, was called to Washington for consultation.

Serious tension had developed between the United States and Finland after the Soviet Union had joined the Allies in World War II. The New York *Times* (April 24, 1943) related that the Department of State had closed American consulates in Finland and ordered the sus-

MCCLINTOCK, ROBERT MILLS— *Continued*

pension of Finnish consulates in the United States. Schoenfeld remained in Washington, and in April 1943 the American Legation staff in Helsinki was reduced to a single diplomatic official—Robert Mills McClintock—and a small clerical force. There were persistent rumors that the Legation would be closed and McClintock recalled; however, he remained at Helsinki until January 25, 1944, when he was assigned to the American Legation in Stockholm, Sweden. In June 1944 the United States broke off diplomatic relations with Finland; normal relations were re-established in 1945.

In April 1945 McClintock was designated a member of the International Secretariat for the U.N. Conference on International Organization held in San Francisco. He was secretary of Committee I (responsible for drafting the preamble, purposes and principles of the U.N. Charter) of Commission I (which dealt with the general provisions of the world organization) and a special assistant to the executive secretary of the conference. He then became an adviser to the U.S. delegation to the U.N. preparatory commission meeting in London in November and December 1945.

Subsequently McClintock served in the Department of State as special assistant to the director of the Office of Special Political Affairs. He was political adviser to the U.S. delegations at the U.N. General Assembly in 1946 and at the special General Assembly sessions in 1947 and 1948.

McClintock's next assignment (in 1949) was at the American Embassy in Brussels, Belgium, where he served as first secretary until selected to attend the National War College in Washington, D.C. He was graduated with the class of 1951-1952 and was sent to Egypt as deputy chief of mission and counselor of the U.S. Embassy at Cairo. In 1954 he was named deputy chief of mission accredited to the Associated States of Indochina. He also served as chairman of a committee composed of officials of the State and Defense departments, Foreign Operations Administration and the United States Information Service, whose function was part of a program to exert the material and moral influence of the United States to "win the peace" in Viet-Nam.

The New York *Times* (September 22, 1954) commented that Cambodia, and its neighboring Indochinese state Laos, had assumed new importance as barriers to further Communist penetration as a result of the Geneva armistice settlement in July 1954, which had awarded more than half of Viet-Nam to the Communist Vietminh. A resident minister was appointed for Laos and a U.S. Embassy was opened in Pnompenh, the capital of Cambodia. McClintock's appointment was confirmed by the Senate on August 17, 1954 and the following month the Ambassador sailed for Cambodia with his family.

On February 28, 1955 it was announced that a United States economic aid team in Cambodia planned to build a $4,000,000 highway through the Jungle Elephant chain of mountains which now cut off Pnompenh from its natural sea outlet on the Gulf of Siam. Ambassador McClintock said that he "welcomed the splendid cooperation of the French in volunteering to undertake construction of the port," and that both port and highway will mean that Cambodia will no longer have to channel its trade through Saigon (*Christian Science Monitor,* February 28, 1955).

His articles have appeared in government and other publications. In the *Annals of the American Academy of Political and Social Science* (July 1949), McClintock wrote: "I envision within the framework of the United Nations Charter, and carrying out the ideal of the Charter, a growing pattern of overlapping circles of mutual interest in keeping the peace on a regional basis, which will eventually blend into the grand harmony of some form of world order superior to national sovereignty."

Robert Mills McClintock was married on April 29, 1936 to Elena Barrios in Santiago, Chile. He has two sons—John Martin and Robert David. The Ambassador is a member of Phi Beta Kappa and Sigma Chi, of the Metropolitan and Chevy Chase clubs in Washington, D.C., and of the Edgartown Yacht Club, Martha's Vineyard. He is a life member of the United States Naval Institute, from which he received a gold medal in 1941. He has been described as tall and slim with brown hair and gray eyes.

In a lecture he gave in 1949, McClintock pointed out that the United States is trying "to keep the United Nations as a going concern which will keep the peace and . . . a United Nations which will keep an enduring peace based on freedom, and not mere absence of conditions where people are at each other's throats."

References

Ann Am Acad 264:26+ Jl '49
Who's Who in America, 1954-55

MCCLOSKEY, MARK A(LEXANDER) Oct. 21, 1891- Public official; social worker; educator

Address: b. New York State Youth Commission, 66 Beaver St., Albany, N.Y.; h. 145 E. 35th St., New York 16

The outlook for coping with juvenile delinquency is good, in the opinion of Mark A. McCloskey, who was appointed by Governor W. Averill Harriman on February 3, 1955 to head New York State's Youth Commission. His optimism is based, he says, on the fine men and women of today who were "the kids we grappled with years ago." But it will not be an easy or a speedy task, he warns. "No one, nor any agency, is deferred from working on this job, all the way from the neighborhood to the nation" (New York *Times*, May 1, 1955).

He brings to his new post experience as a social worker and administrator, sixteen years as associate head worker at the Hudson Guild Settlement House, director of the National Youth Administration of New York City for two years, and since 1938 director of the bureau of community education for the Board of Education of New York City. He has frequently been seen on national network television shows discussing youth problems with other experts.

Speaking at the United Neighborhood Houses annual meeting in May 1955, McCloskey called the use of whips to curb juvenile delinquents vigilante tactics. "The problem will be solved," he said, "not with whips and not with vigilantes." He urged an expansion of settlement house work to insure a better atmosphere for children living in over-crowded homes (New York *Times*, May 20, 1955).

Mark Alexander McCloskey was born on October 21, 1891 to John and Jane Ann (Bennett) McCloskey in the "Hell's Kitchen" district of New York City's West Side (between 30th and 42nd Streets). His father, a truck driver, always carried with him, his son testifies, the Bible, Shakespeare and Robert Burns' poems. Like his father, Mark soon found his chief relaxation and diversion in reading. (He was described by Albert Deutsch as "quoting Euripides and Homer with a Tenth Avenue accent" (*PM*, September 18, 1946).

Mark "fought" his way through the public school at Ninth Avenue and 35th Street (New York City) and worked his way through college. He put in seven years at the machinist's trade to save the money for his college education. He took his bachelor's degree at Princeton University, Princeton, New Jersey in 1918. (His alma mater subsequently made him a member of the advisory committee of its political department.) He served as a first lieutenant in the U.S. Army in World War I in the artillery.

He was graduated in 1922 from the New York School of Social Work at Columbia University. His orientation to social work as a career started when he came under the influence of Dr. John L. Elliott, founder of the Hudson Guild Settlement House on West 27th Street in Manhattan. He served from 1920 to 1936 as associate head worker at the Guild. He understood the problems of the clients because they had been his own problems.

He became director of the National Youth Administration for New York City, serving from 1936 to 1938, and has been director of the bureau of community education for New York City's Board of Education since 1938 (a post he relinquished when he accepted the State Youth Commission chairmanship). In his capacity as an educator he stated: "Children learn just as much when they play as when they go to schools. A happy childhood you can cart along with you the rest of your life" (New York *Times*, March 26, 1942).

McCloskey was summoned by President Truman in 1941 to become the director of recreation in the Federal Security Agency and then director of the Office of War Community Services from 1943 to 1945. He was a member of the Joint Army and Navy Committee on Welfare and Recreation in the Armed Forces during World War II, and a member of the President's Committee on Welfare in the Armed Forces. For these services, he was awarded the Presidential Medal for Merit in 1946. McCloskey also holds the New York City Adult Education Service Award, which he received in 1947.

MARK A. MCCLOSKEY

The State Youth Commission, which McCloskey now heads, was established in 1945 and was to have expired in 1956. However, recent concern with juvenile delinquency, especially gang warfare in the big cities, moved Governor Harriman to reactivate the commission which matches dollar for dollar the funds allocated for youth programs in the communities of New York State. It contributed $1,100,000 to such programs in New York City during 1954. The Governor hopes to increase State aid on a scale that would give New York City an additional sum of $450,000.

Frequently indicating his confidence in America's youth, McCloskey subscribes to the view expressed in a *Collier's* editorial, quoted in the *Reader's Digest* (May, 1955) that the negative side of youth problems has come in of late for more than its due share of public attention, forgetting that "non-delinquents still outnumber the delinquents by 50 to 1."

"We are working not only with the kids who already are in trouble," he emphasizes, "but to find out who's going to be in trouble, with 'difficult' kids. We work to help families keep their children from being what we call a 'drop-out,' a child who can't get on with others.

"The cohesive family is the greatest factor, and as I see it, the public agencies must not supplant but support the family" (New York *Post,* March 13, 1955).

His approach to his work is based on the premise that adolescents "want to be on their own but able to grab onto adults where necessary." He believes in a minimum of regimentation and a maximum of adroitly directed freedom. A strong supporter of teen-age clubs, he feels that these can be successful in proportion to the way young people take an active part in managing them.

"Because of his wide experience in many of the areas affecting child and community wel-

MCCLOSKEY, MARK A.—*Continued*

fare," Governor Harriman declared in announcing his appointment, "Mr. McCloskey is exceptionally fitted to head the Youth Commission at a time when its responsibilities are being widened." The work of the commission may well set a pattern for similar agencies in other states.

The Youth Commission's chairman believes that . . . "the family, as the core of our society, should assume its responsibilities in combating juvenile delinquency" (New York *Times,* April 15, 1955).

Regional institutes on law enforcement and crime, planned jointly by McCloskey as chairman of the State Youth Commission, and Attorney General Jacob K. Javits, were held in July 1955 at Syracuse, Buffalo and New York universities. They were attended by policemen, social workers, and prosecutors representing twenty-seven counties in New York state. Slum control, community planning, civic pride, recreation centers were some of the remedies suggested to curb juvenile delinquency.

"All the instruments of our society should pull together on this problem," McCloskey said. "Any public or private agency that attempts to 'go it alone' in this endeavor," he warned, "is licked before it starts."

McCloskey is a vice-president of the United Neighborhood Houses of New York City, a director of the Citizen's Housing and Planning Council and of the United Seamen's Service, and a member of the Advisory Committee to the Play Schools Association, Public Education Association and Citizen's Committee on Children of New York City. He has been a member of the board of the New York Adult Education Council and of the Public Education Association, and since 1946 a trustee of Vassar College.

He has lectured on social problems at Columbia University, New York University and the College of the City of New York. His writings include "What Will War Do to the Family?" (*Parents' Magazine,* June 1945); "Plan for Community Service" (*Journal of Educational Sociology,* January 1948); and "Learning for Millions" (*Adult Education,* November 1953).

He married his childhood sweetheart, Winifred Doherty on June 26, 1919. They now live at 145 East 35th Street, only a few blocks from the neighborhood where they were brought up. They have three daughters, Barbara Jean (Mrs. Donald G. MacDonald) Janet Ann and Winfred Doherty (Mrs. William H. Y. Hackett, Jr.) and several grandchildren. McCloskey is an Episcopalian and a Democrat.

For more than twenty years, the McCloskeys operated Camp Felicia, near Cornwall, New York. Here each summer 150 boys and girls from city streets worked and played together and discovered the joys of the country.

"There was a time when I wondered if we would ever have decent housing, whether there would ever be help for the families of men who lose their jobs, for the aged and the infirm. I have seen those problems become part of the public conscience," McCloskey told Nancy Seely (New York *Post,* March 13, 1955). "Many thousands . . . are deeply interested and are willing to help. . . . I refuse to believe those who talk about lost causes."

References

N Y Post Mag p2 Mr 13 '55 por
N Y Times p13 F 4 '55 por
Who's Who in America, 1954-55

MCCOMAS, O(LIVER) PARKER Sept. 1, 1895- Business executive

Address: b. c/o Philip Morris, Inc., 100 Park Ave., New York 17; h. 888 Park Ave., New York 21

In the highly competitive tobacco industry, which employs almost 1,000,000 people, which manufactures over 400 billion cigarettes a year, and which pays the U.S. Government $1.5 billion in taxes annually, Philip Morris, Inc., is the fourth largest company. Responsible for its operations is O. Parker McComas, who became its president in 1949 and its executive officer in 1954. He directs the manufacturing, distribution and promotion of numerous smoking tobacco blends (including Revelation, Bond Street, Lyon's Own) and six different brands of cigarettes (Philip Morris, Marlboro, Parliament, Dunhill, among others).

Under McComas's administration Philip Morris has expanded into a multi-brand company with international as well as national operations. During 1955 he introduced a king-size, filter-tip Marlboro in a new package which had been selected after seven years of experimentation, and a new red, white and gold jacket to replace the familiar Philip Morris brown package.

As chairman of the Tobacco Industry Research Committee during the spring of 1954, McComas faced up to the industry's most serious problem: the worrisome fears of smokers about the possible relationship between smoking and lung cancer. He also heads the Common Cold Foundation which during 1955 spent over $500,000 on research into the causes of colds. For eighteen years before joining Philip Morris as vice-president in 1946, McComas had been an executive with the Bankers' Trust Company.

Oliver Parker McComas was born in Baltimore, Maryland on September 1, 1895, the eldest of seven children of Oliver Parker and Elizabeth (McClymont) McComas. He is a descendant of Daniel McComas, who pioneered in raising tobacco near Chesapeake Bay in the latter part of the seventeenth century. Upon his graduation from Boys' Latin School of Baltimore in 1912, young McComas entered Princeton University, where he chose English as his major subject, and received the A.B. degree in 1916 and M.A. in 1917.

Enlisting in the U.S. Army shortly afterward, he fought during World War I in major campaigns in France as a first lieutenant and was awarded the Silver Star for gallantry. His first job was as a cable clerk in a brokerage house at a salary of $13 a week. After being employed as a foreign exchange trader at Sutro

Brothers & Company from 1919 to 1926 and as a bond trader at Cowen & Company from 1926 to 1928, he began working in the security department of the Bankers' Trust Company and lived for various periods in New York, London and Paris. During the next eighteen years he became a vice-president of the company in charge of the commercial banking and foreign departments and held the chief position in its Paris office.

When McComas accepted an offer from board chairman Alfred E. Lyon to become a vice president of Philip Morris in 1946, he knew little about cigarette manufacturing but he did have valuable experience with tobacco companies through the financial transactions that he had handled as a banker. In 1947 he was named executive vice-president, in April 1949 president and chief administrative officer, and in January 1954 chief executive officer.

The company was founded in 1847 by Philip Morris, a tobacconist, in Oxford, England whose customers—the students at Oxford University—liked his blend of tobacco and asked him to roll it into cigarettes. After they were graduated they continued to send him orders so that Morris was compelled to expand his business. The American company was incorporated in 1919 in the state of Virginia, by American stockholders who acquired the American business of the English Philip Morris & Company, Ltd.

With net sales in 1946 of $116,700,000 (as compared with $73,300,000 in 1939), Philip Morris had developed during World War II into one of the country's largest tobacco firms. McComas took an important part in modernizing some of the operations of the fast-growing company and encouraging a "big business" attitude while retaining a personal touch in its administration.

Philip Morris now has 4,325 employees who enjoy many benefits such as a surgical and in-hospital medical expense plan, retirement income at age sixty-five, and life insurance, as described in the firm's booklet, "The House That You Built." In a prefatory letter McComas wrote: "Philip Morris depends on the principle that people, not machines, are responsible for the success of our company."

By 1951 McComas could report an 80 per cent sales gain for Philip Morris in four years. Yearly earnings reached $16,600,000, with the firm acquiring 11 per cent of the cigarette market. "We built a network of communications, embracing employees, stockholders and the public," McComas said, "and we did it realistically," by making all three groups aware of benefits derived from the company's development (New York *World-Telegram and Sun*, August 18, 1951).

At the dedication of its $11,000,000 Louisville, Kentucky plant (which can produce more than 100,000,000 cigarettes on a single shift), McComas reviewed the company's achievements. He pointed out that the rise in wages and taxes was disproportionate to financial returns to stockholders and executive salaries, and stated that the function of management was to keep these "component parts of the modern

Myron Ehrenberg, Scope Associates, Inc.

O. PARKER MCCOMAS

corporation" in balance (New York *Herald Tribune*, May 16, 1952).

Discussing the subject of advertising in the tobacco industry, McComas said in July 1953, "Cigarettes are the most widely and intensively distributed products in our national economy. We are dealing with more than 1,300,000 retail sales outlets which sell more than 400 billion cigarettes a year to over 60,000,000 smokers... To reach this public, we must lay our primary emphasis on advertising, the lifeblood of [the] consumer packaged goods industry" (New York *World-Telegram and Sun*, July 16, 1953). From October 1951 until June 27, 1955 Philip Morris sponsored one of televisions most popular programs, *I Love Lucy*. It is currently presenting frequent spot announcements of its products on the major radio and television networks. Its new Philip Morris package is utilizing two-color full page newspaper advertisement.

Among company developments under McComas' presidency was the formation in March 1954 of Philip Morris (Australia), Ltd., and the construction of offices and a plant in Moorabbin, near Melbourne, where United-States style cigarettes are manufactured. McComas has also enlarged the operations of the company's subsidiary in England and in 1955 made arrangements for the manufacture and sale of Philip Morris cigarettes in the Philippine Islands by the La Suerte Cigar and Cigarette Factory.

In the domestic market Philip Morris expanded in February 1954 by acquiring the Parliament brand through the purchase of Benson & Hedges stock, thus becoming able to meet the increasing consumer demand for filter-tip and king-size cigarettes. Introduction of a "snap-open" packaging device for the Philip

MCCOMAS, O. PARKER—*Continued*

Morris brand in the spring of 1954 also boosted the company's sales.

The new king-size Marlboro filter cigarette in the "flip-top" crush-proof box was put on the market at popular prices by Philip Morris in 1955 after considerable laboratory research and experimentation. In developing the package, for example, Philip Morris designers made use of the candid-camera technique, among other devices, to determine what design and colors had most appeal for the customer.

The tobacco industry is concerned about the publicity resulting from studies on the possible effect of smoking on health. The U.S. Census Bureau reported in June 1955 that a million and a half people had given up smoking within a year and a half. Prominent in the industry's attempt to prove that smoking does not cause cancer, McComas served for three months during 1954 as chairman of the Tobacco Industry Research Committee, which appointed Dr. Clarence Cook Little (See *C.B.* 1944), eminent cancer investigator and director of the Jackson Memorial Laboratory at Bar Harbor, Maine, to head a scientific advisory board to make a study (independent of the cigarette manufacturers) of the possible connection between tobacco and lung cancer. The industry appropriated $1,000,000 for this study, the results of which have not yet been announced. (McComas, himself, is said to be a long-time cigarette smoker.)

McComas is chairman of the Common Cold Foundation, formed in 1950, in which some fifty leading bankers and industrialists join to sponsor research on the cause and cure for common colds. Since colds are very costly to industry (about 150,000,000 work days were lost in 1953), the foundation raises its funds among large corporations rather than through appeals for public contributions. In 1955 it initiated a plan to offer $500,000 for projects such as the application of the John F. Enders-Thomas H. Weller-Frederick Robbins tissue culture technique in research on colds.

Among public-benefit organizations with which McComas has been associated is the United Hospital Fund of New York; he served as chairman of the fund's 1950 drive. He is also a trustee of Lenox Hill Hospital in New York. He holds a directorship in Fairchild Engine and Airplane Corporation and belongs to the University Club in New York.

On February 1, 1929 McComas married Rhoda Stanley Drew, the daughter of a Pittsburgh, Pennsylvania judge. They have a son, Oliver Parker McComas, Jr., and a daughter, Rhonda Drew (Mrs. William Jacob). McComas, who is six feet one inch tall, has gray hair and blue eyes. Among his non-business interests are fishing, gardening and science. Of another hobby, cooking, he has said, "Cooking is like bridge. You should have a system, but know when not to follow it too literally" (New York *Post Magazine*). His favorite books include *Tom Jones, Alice in Wonderland,* and Boswell's *Life of Samuel Johnson.*

McComas has a summer home at Norfolk, Connecticut and after the flash flood of August 18 and 19, 1955 had inundated a large area in that section of the state, he sent Philip Morris's representative "Johnny" the bell-hop (John Roventini) to distribute some 20,000 cigarettes to flood victims.

References

Forbes 74:22 Jl 1 '54 por
N Y Post p2M N 5 '50 por
N Y World-Telegram p19 Ag 18 '51
Business Executives of America (1950)
Who's Who in America, 1954-55
Who's Who in Commerce and Industry (1953)

MCCORMICK, ROBERT R(UTHERFORD) July 30, 1880-Apr. 1, 1955 Editor; became publisher of Chicago *Tribune* in 1910 and New York *Daily News* (with Joseph M. Patterson) in 1919; was member of General John J. Pershing's staff in World War I with rank of colonel; became arch foe of the New Deal and President Franklin D. Roosevelt; an admitted isolationist; consistently opposed aid to Britain and China; made frequent broadcasts over the *Tribune*'s own radio station expounding his ideas on military strategy and America's foreign policy; champion of freedom of the press; author *Ulysses S. Grant, Freedom of the Press, The American Revolution and Its Effect on World Civilization* and other books on historical, military and political subjects. See *Current Biography* (Aug.) 1942.

Obituary

N Y Times p13 Ap 2 '55

MCDERMOTT, MICHAEL J(AMES) July 2, 1894-Aug. 5, 1955 Former United States Government official; Ambassador to El Salvador 1953-1955; for greater part of thirty years headed news division, Department of State; worked under eleven Secretaries of State, accompanying them to many international conferences as chief press officer; in 1950 received the State Department's second highest award for "notably outstanding contribution to the public service." See *Current Biography* (Feb.) 1951.

Obituary

N Y Times p73 Ag 6 '55

MCGINNIS, PATRICK B(ENEDICT) May 23, 1904- Railroad executive; investment broker

Address: b. 61 Broadway, New York 6; h. 30 Belair Rd., Staten Island 5, N.Y.

Elected president of the New York, New Haven and Hartford Railroad in April 1954, Patrick B. McGinnis succeeded Frederic C. Dumaine, Jr. He was also named head of another New England system, the Boston and Maine, in April 1955, through the election of a board of directors pledged to establish him as president of both railroads (subject to approval by the Interstate Commerce Commission.) He has been called by *Forbes* magazine "the most exciting railroading personality since Commodore Vanderbilt and old Dan'l Drew." During the summer of 1955 he was subject to sharp criticism by New Haven commuters because of a proposed parking fee for their cars at railroad stations.

McGinnis had previously headed his own New York investment brokerage concern and had specialized in railroad bonds since 1930, becoming a recognized authority on rail transportation financing and reorganization. Prior to becoming head of the New Haven, he had been director and chairman of the board of the Norfolk Southern and of the Central of Georgia railroads.

It has been said of Patrick Benedict McGinnis that he knows the railroad business "from roundhouse to board room" (*Time*). As a child he was thoroughly familiar with the rail yards in and around Palmyra, New York, where his father was employed as a floating gang foreman on the New York Central Lines. One of the four children of Patrick and Ann (Mulgannon) McGinnis, he was born in that Wayne County community on May 23, 1904, and attended the Palmyra High School. At St. Lawrence University in Canton, New York, he met his expenses by managing a motion picture theatre. He also managed the varsity football team and "occasionally tried his hand at amateur theatricals," thus "developing an easy, shot-sure public speaking delivery" (*Forbes*, April 1, 1955).

With the intention of becoming a chemical engineer, McGinnis majored in chemistry at St. Lawrence University, and received the B.S. degree with high honors in 1926. However, on graduation he accepted instead a position with a New York City brokerage firm offered by a wealthy St. Lawrence alumnus. While thus occupied, he took postgraduate courses at New York University and Columbia University. In 1930 McGinnis became the manager of the railroad bond department of Lehman Brothers in New York City, but in 1931 when the financial structures of the nation's railroads began to fall apart and Lehman Brothers closed its railroad-bond department, McGinnis was out of a job. During the next six years he was in and out of several investment firms until he joined the New York Stock Exchange firm of Pflugfelder, Bampton and Rust in 1937. He was in charge of the rail bond department there.

Special courses taken at Brooklyn Law School enabled him to serve as an expert witness in twenty-five out of thirty-six major railroad reorganizations, including that of the New Haven, which went into receivership in 1935. He also lectured at the New York Institute of Finance.

In 1938, Pflugfelder, Bampton & Rust issued the first book containing all the facts McGinnis had collected on the financial status of the thirty-six Class I railroads that were in bankruptcy proceedings.

During 1943 and 1944 he served as a consultant to the Office of Defense Transportation. His book *Guide to Railroad Reorganization Securities* is called "the best in the field" (*Time*, April 26, 1954). He became a partner of Pflugfelder, Bampton & Rust in 1943 and in 1946 following the dissolution of the firm, he

Wide World

PATRICK B. MCGINNIS

became the senior partner in the New York Stock Exchange firm of McGinnis, Bampton & Sellger. McGinnis & Company was organized in 1949.

Acquisition by McGinnis and a group of associates of a controlling interest in the Norfolk Southern Railway was followed in 1947 by his election as chairman of the board and director of both the Norfolk Southern Railway and the Norfolk Southern Bus Corporation.

He himself established the McGinnis Industrial Center, a Norfolk corporation, in 1948, and was elected chairman in 1949 of the board of the John L. Roper Lumber Company and the Roper Realization Company of Norfolk. McGinnis, Bampton and Sellger were, furthermore, the agents for the late Frederic C. Dumaine, Sr., who was elected in 1948, chairman of the board of the New York, New Haven and Hartford Railroad.

In 1952 the McGinnis group claimed that they had "brought the [Norfolk Southern] railroad from the brink of bankruptcy to a point where stock dividends were resumed" (*Time*, February 22, 1954). Nevertheless, in January 1952, the ICC "on its own motion ordered an investigation . . . into and concerning the management. . . ." As a result of the ICC report, McGinnis was fined $5,000 for "extravagance in handling the road's affairs" (*Forbes*, April 1, 1955). His reply to criticism was: "You have to spend money to make money! I put the road on its feet!"

Following his election as chairman of the board of the Central of Georgia Railway on January 16, 1953, McGinnis resigned from the Norfolk Southern, because of Federal regulations providing that no individual may occupy executive positions on two railroads without ICC approval. During his chairmanship of the Central of Georgia, McGinnis "pulled down its operating and transportation rates and boosted

MCGINNIS, PATRICK B.—*Continued*

its freight revenues, but . . . never did realize a dividend for the Central's long-patient stockholders" (*Forbes*).

Frederic C. Dumaine, Sr., died May 27, 1951 and was succeeded as president of the New York, New Haven and Hartford Railroad by his son, Frederic C. Dumaine, Jr. Under the Dumaines, father and son, the railroad (which furnishes almost all of New England's rail transportation south of Boston) was completely Dieselized, and new passenger cars were purchased (*Time,* April 5, 1954). McGinnis, who had personally "bought into" the New Haven in 1948, became dissatisfied with the modernization policy which had eaten into its operating capital to such an extent that dividends were being declared only on preferred shares.

Quietly increasing his holdings, McGinnis succeeded in electing four directors of his way of thinking to the New Haven board in April 1953. McGinnis charged, early in 1954, that although the New Haven had declared a profit each year since 1949, this profit came from the railroad's real estate holdings, and that as a carrier the railroad had actually lost over $4,000,000 under the Dumaines (*Time,* April 5, 1954).

With the support of certain other stockholders, McGinnis was able, by taking advantage of the New Haven's "cumulative voting" procedure, to elect on April 14, 1954 eleven directors as against ten favoring Dumaine, even though the McGinnis group actually owned only about 30 per cent of the stock. McGinnis was elected president and his friend John E. Slater, chairman of American Export Lines, chairman of the board.

With its main line (New York to Boston) only about 200 miles in length and with no continuous freight trackage, the New Haven is at a disadvantage in competing with highway transportation. McGinnis maintained, however, that "the New Haven . . . has the density to make passenger service really pay," and on May 6, 1954, shortly after he took office as president, the New Haven withdrew an application, previously filed by Dumaine with the ICC, for commutation fare increases of 24 to 30 per cent.

In two articles by Clarence Dean in the New York *Times* (August 1 and 2, 1955), the problems of the New Haven were discussed; the railroad's threats of parking fees set off charges by commuters of late trains, faulty equipment, inefficient air conditioning, narrow seats and other discomforts. McGinnis answered these charges, citing fiscal progress, obligation to stockholders to pay dividends, defended cutbacks in rebuilding the line to make it profitable, and pointed to increases in common and preferred stock since he took over the management.

In an address to the Greater Boston Chamber of Commerce on June 3, 1954, McGinnis predicted that within a year and a half the passenger-train running time between New York and Boston could be reduced to two and a half hours by use of low-slung aluminum trains of the Spanish "Talgo" type. He pointed out that the new talgo train could take curves at high speeds. On July 14, 1955, the Boston-bound Federal Express of the New York, New Haven and Hartford Railroad plunged off the rails on a sharp curve near Bridgeport, carrying the first eight cars and locomotive down a 40-foot embankment and killing the engineer and injuring about 24 passengers and crewmen. McGinnis said that the accident was not caused by faulty equipment but "seems to point up the need for the low-center-of-gravity trains which I have been advocating" (New York *World-Telegram and Sun,* July 14, 1955).

In December, 1954 it became known that three of McGinnis's friends had "acquired the largest single block of stock in the Boston and Maine Railroad." The prospect of having the New Haven railroad dominate the B&M caused consternation in certain Massachusetts circles. On March 7, 1955 the ICC, alerted by a group of New England Senators including Leverett Saltonstall and John Kennedy of Massachusetts, announced an inquiry into the purchase of B&M shares by interests "under the control of or friendly to" the New Haven management (New York *Times,* March 8, 1955).

At the B&M annual meeting held on April 13, 1955, the day after president Timothy J. Sughrue and chairman Edward S. French had resigned, the "slate" of directors favorable to McGinnis received 273,237 votes to 197,142 for the opposition, and control of the B&M passed to their hands.

The new board passed a resolution authorizing counsel to "take all necessary steps to obtain authority from the ICC to enable McGinnis to serve as president and director" (Boston *Globe*). Since action might not be forthcoming for as long as a year, an interim six-member executive board was set up and Lloyd J. Kiernan was elected executive vice-president.

On April 18 at the ICC hearings it was brought out that although McGinnis himself held no B&M stock, a sizeable block had been purchased for Mrs. McGinnis.

In a speech at Lawrence, Massachusetts, a city hard hit by retrenchments in the textile industry, McGinnis advised: "Never mind textiles—get something else. Have a little patience, and with the cooperation of the ICC I'll come to New England to help it."

McGinnis is a member of the New York Society of Security Analysts; his fraternity is Alpha Tau Omega and he belongs to the Princess Anne Country Club in Virginia and the Seaview Country Club in New Jersey. His faith is the Roman Catholic. "Pat" and Lucile Whitney were married on August 4, 1930 and have one son, Patrick Benedict, and one daughter, Carol Iveagh.

At the New Haven's meeting in 1955 McGinnis's control of that system was further strengthened, with nineteen McGinnis directors being elected, as against eleven in 1954.

References

Christian Sci Mon p2 Ap 16 '55
Fortune 51:146+ Ap '55 pors
Newsweek 43:73+ Ap 26 '54 por
Ry Age 134:51 Ja 26 '53 por
Who's Who in America, 1954-55

MCGRAW, ELOISE JARVIS Dec. 9, 1915- Author

Address: b. c/o Coward-McCann., Inc. 210 Madison Ave., New York 16; h. Route 2, Box 60, Sherwood, Ore.

Reprinted from the *Wilson Library Bulletin* April 1955

The author, an only child, was born in Houston, Texas, on December 9, 1915, to Genevieve Lucinda and Loy Hamilton Jarvis and she now lives on a filbert farm near Sherwood, Oregon. The forty years between are a story in themselves, full of activity and interest.

There is color and romance in the early history of Eloise Jarvis' forebears, all of them East Texans, though the origin of the Hamilton in her father's name can be traced back, through his mother's family, to Alexander Hamilton. Railroads and Indians, cotton plantations and slaves (who were started out with forty acres and a mule each when freedom came) merchandising and the cattle range, provided rich material for the stories told the little girl who decided at the age of eight that she wanted to be a writer and thereupon began, with a story called "The Cedar Pencil Boys." When Eloise was five the little family moved to Oklahoma City on account of her father's business interests.

In 1933 Eloise Jarvis was graduated from Classen High School in Oklahoma City and received an A.B. degree, *magna cum laude*, in 1937 from Principia College at Elsah, Illinois. Writing, painting, glee club, and hockey had been her active interests in school and two of her teachers, one in high school and one at Principia, encouraged her writing. She wrote poetry and received a literary award during her senior year in college.

From 1937 until 1940, Miss Jarvis won distinction as a painter in oils—portraits and murals—studied modern dance, and did radio and theatre work, broadcasting children's plays. There was also time for some graduate courses at the University of Oklahoma and Colorado University.

On January 29, 1940 Eloise Jarvis was married to William Corbin McGraw. He was a newspaper reporter and his work took them to Athens, Ohio, to Oklahoma City and finally, after his Navy duty, to San Diego with the *Tribune-Sun*. In 1950 they moved to Sherwood, Oregon. Mrs. McGraw says of that decision, "Our filbert farm is not a city block from the home of the cousin where I had the best times of my life during childhood summer visits. I finally lured my own family out here to live."

It was in San Diego that Mrs. McGraw turned again to writing. Some successful short stories for children preceded the writing of her first book, which was begun during a convalescence from a major operation. *Sawdust in His Shoes*, for ages twelve to sixteen, was published by Coward McCann in 1950 and became a Literary Guild selection. It was listed by the New York *Times* as one of the ten best juveniles of that year. The New York *Times* (April 30, 1950) review said, "Every character

ELOISE JARVIS MCGRAW

in this book is warm, true and different from the others. The language is racy with circus talk and farm talk. The action is fast, funny and often moving. Moreover, the author has respect for the honest facts of human living."

Crown Fire was published by Coward-McCann in 1951. The title is a logging term used to describe a fire which rages uncontrollably across the tops of trees. In the book the "fire" is the hero's temper. This was an honor book in the New York *Herald Tribune* Spring Book Festival that year. Margaret Scoggin wrote "This has everything a good story needs. The details of logging are colorful and authentic—not watered down. There is action to spare, with high-climbing, boxing, and fire-fighting. Chip's own French-Canadian buoyancy and explosiveness get into the style and the story surges along" (New York *Times*, May 20, 1951).

In 1952 *Moccasin Trail* (Coward-McCann) appeared, a story of a white boy who was early adopted by the Crow Indians. This book, like her first one, was a selection of the Junior Literary Guild. The *Library Journal* (October 15, 1952) said of it, "Despite a surfeit of historical books on the opening of the West, this should be a first purchase for any library. . . ."

These three books show the influence of the author's childhood experiences. A departure from that scene was *Mara, Daughter of the Nile* (Coward-McCann, 1953), written for older boys and girls. The heroine is a slave girl, living in the period when Thebes was a flourishing city. Virginia Kirkus said, "Some libraries may find the brutal beating of the heroine objectionable for teen-agers, but this reviewer recommends the book highly for older girls." The Denver *Post* (November 29, 1953) observed, "The book is destined for a wide audience. It will appear to those who demand danger and action on every page and those who

MCGRAW, ELOISE JARVIS—*Continued*
like to savor good writing and enjoy the pageantry of unfamiliar places and times."

Mrs. McGraw's own comment on her writing is succinct. She says, "I don't see how anybody writes without a writer-husband to read and criticize." A Portland paper describes them as a "unique husband and wife writing team. They work facing each other, where they can glare and pass the thesaurus back and forth. They began by working back to back but they said the lighting wasn't good."

The extracurricular interests of this dynamic writer are still as varied as they seem to have been all her life. She is active in the Parent Teachers Association now because of her son Peter, aged thirteen, and daughter Laurie, aged ten. She enjoys horseback riding, square dancing, and creative adventures in ceramics and metals.

Mrs. McGraw is a petite blonde, with greenish eyes. Her favorite reading ranges from *Huckleberry Finn* and *Alice in Wonderland* to Thomas Mann and Euripides. She is now at work on her first adult novel, as yet untitled, but it will be a further adventure into the heart of ancient Egypt.

MACKENZIE, GISELE Jan. 10, 1927-
Singer

Address: c/o MCA Artists, Ltd., 598 Madison Ave., New York 22

French-Canadian songstress Gisele MacKenzie is a regular entertainer on America's popular NBC-TV show, *Your Hit Parade*. She joined the program on September 19, 1953 after two years as a featured radio singer in Hollywood, first on Bob Crosby's *Club 15*, and then on *The Mario Lanzo Show*. Previously, for four years she starred as "Canada's First Lady of Song" in her own singing program, *Meet Gisele*, on the Canadian Broadcasting Corporation network. In the summer of 1955 she was a featured singer for one performance with the Denver Symphony Orchestra at the Red Rocks amphitheatre near Denver, Colorado. She also played Mary Martin's role in *South Pacific* in Dallas, Texas.

NBC
GISELE MACKENZIE

Miss MacKenzie, a skilled violinist, pianist, and comedienne, has never had a lesson in voice, and before she joined *Your Hit Parade* had not danced professionally. Since coming to the United States she has made radio and television appearances and toured with Jack Benny on road shows. She made her dramatic debut in April 1955 in the NBC-TV play *Now Where Was I?*

Marie Marguerite Louise Gisele La Fleche Mackenzie was born on January 10, 1927, in Winnipeg, Manitoba, Canada, the daughter of Dr. Georges MacKenzie La Fleche and the former Marietta Manseau. She shortened her name to Gisele MacKenzie in Hollywood in 1951. Besides French-Canadian ancestry, she claims "one-fifth Scotch" (New York *World-Telegram and Sun,* February 26, 1955). Her family includes two brothers and sisters, all musical. Gisele's father is a doctor of medicine, with a penchant for the violin, and her mother was a concert singer and pianist.

Gisele began her musical career at the age of three, receiving piano lessons from her mother. When she was seven, she started studying violin also, and gave her first public recital at the Royal Alexandra Hotel in Winnipeg when she was twelve. Two years later, she went to the Royal Conservatory of Music in Toronto to specialize in violin under the noted teacher, Kathleen Parlow. For the next six years she continued her conservatory studies, winning a scholarship in the graduate school.

During World War II, she played her violin and sometimes sang for service troops at camps and canteens. In the summer of 1946 Gisele was hired by Bob Shuttleworth (whom she had met when he was bandleader in the Royal Canadian Navy) as violinist-pianist-vocalist with his band at the Glenmount Hotel on the Lake of Bays, Ontario. He urged her to concentrate on developing her rich contralto singing voice. Contributing to her decision to follow his advice, was the theft of her $3,000 Ceruti violin.

Her voice and possession of absolute pitch drew the attention of Canadian Broadcasting Corporation officials, and on October 8, 1946 she began starring over the CBC radio network in her own quarter-hour singing program. She won immediate and favorable response to her unique song styling of popular and folk tunes, which she accompanied on the piano. Within a month, she was singing on three separate shows. During the next four years, her delivery of French ballads, rhythm tunes, blues songs, and novelty selections won her the title of "Canada's First Lady of Song."

Gisele signed a five-year Hollywood contract at $20,000 a year in the spring of 1951. After guest spots with Edgar Bergen and Morton Downey, she joined what she called "an informal gay little program" named *Club 15*, a radio broadcast with Bob Crosby and the Modernaires (*Saturday Night*, November 24, 1951). It was "one of the friendliest programs a radio performer could be on," she adds. She sang each week on Mondays, Wednesdays and Fridays, alternating with Jo Stafford who sang the other two nights, and was described in *Saturday Night* as "a simple, unaffected, quiet girl who reads a lot and plays bridge with the musicians between rehearsals."

In Hollywood, Gisele discovered that since the competition is very keen, an artist can never relax. As her fame grew, she found more time taken with interviews, photographs, recording sessions, benefits, previews, visits to disc-jockeys and autograph seekers. "It's most exciting of all to be recognized and asked for an autograph," she is quoted by *Saturday Night* as saying. "If anyone pretends this isn't a thrill, they're not telling the truth." For Capitol Records, she recorded song duets with Gordon Macrae.

Following her appearances on *Club 15*, Gisele was featured as a singer on *The Mario Lanza Show*. During the last five weeks, Lanza was absent from the radio broadcast, and the program was billed as *The Mario Lanza Show, Starring Gisele MacKenzie*. Invited to play in a violin duet with Jack Benny on his show, she was grateful for her early training as a concert violinist. Guest performances on *The Eddie Fisher Show* followed.

Gisele recalls her first reaction to television "was one of complete confusion; microphones, booms, props, cables, lights, cameras and people hanging from everything" (*Saturday Night*, November 24, 1951). Upon seeing the first kinescope of herself, she determined to streamline her hair style and to diet.

During the summers of 1952 and 1953, the singer went on tour with Jack Benny, who in the fall of 1953 recommended that Gisele fill the vacancy left by the singer June Valli on *Your Hit Parade*, the half-hour NBC-TV Saturday night song and dance show, dealing with the nation's seven most popular songs. Gisele got the job. Jon Whitcomb in *Cosmopolitan* (October 1954) called Gisele "a hot pianist, and an even hotter singer." For her comedienne acts, she "tries out her japes on the cast before polishing them for the television audience", (*Look*, May 3, 1955).

Gisele trouped again with Jack Benny in the summer of 1954, and in January 1955 appeared as guest on his CBS-TV program. "She played the violin and the piano with a master's touch, and did one of the best comedy sketches with Benny I've ever seen," wrote a commentator for the New York *World-Telegram and Sun* (February 4, 1955). In a comedy duet with Benny on "Getting to Know You," she interpolated on the violin, and in "gentle capers," she "beautifully complemented Mr. Benny's droll style of humor," Jack Gould commented in the New York *Times*, (January 26, 1955).

Established on *Your Hit Parade* as a songstress who "sings saucy or demure roles with equal ease," Gisele became ambitious for an acting role on television (*TV Guide*, January 8, 1955). Her "dramatic debut" came in April 1955 over NBC-TV network in the Kraft Theater play *Now Where Was I?*, "a precious, hollow comedy about the marital troubles of a composer," with Gisele playing the composer's former wife (New York *Times*, April 15, 1955).

On the NBC-TV *Justice* program, which dramatizes cases from the Legal Aid Society files, she was starred in *Hard to Get*, presented May 12, 1955. Gisele enacted a singer who is defrauded by her agent and introduced the blues song "Hard to Get," accompanied by a nineteen-piece orchestra. By popular request the NBC-TV *Justice* program repeated the play with the original cast on its program of June 9.

Early in June 1955 Gisele was a guest star on the premiere broadcast of the CBS radio musical program, *The Woolworth Hour*, featuring Percy Faith and his orchestra and chorus. Critic Jack Gould says of the songstress: ". . . she is no ordinary TV doll; she has talent" (New York *Times*, May 18, 1955).

The National Film Board of Canada includes among its *Canadian Talent Showcase* films those in which Gisele sings "Piper of Dundee," "J'ai Laissé Mon Cœur," "A Trout No Doubt," Black Is The Color of My True Love's Hair," and "Red Rosy Bush." The singer's current ambitions are: "a hit record, a movie, a Broadway show" (*Look*, May 3, 1955).

She is planning to become an American citizen. She is described by staff writer Weston Barclay of the New York *World-Telegram and Sun* (February 26, 1955) as "a very natural girl who wears no pancake makeup and chooses colorless nail polish," does not smoke, and drinks "only occasionally." Gisele is five feet six inches tall, weighs 120 pounds, and has brown hair and brown eyes. She also has brown dachshunds she enjoys taking out walking from her personally-decorated Park Avenue apartment, when she is not engaged in reading or her other favorite recreation, cooking. Her religion is Roman Catholic.

References

Cosmopolitan 137:77 O '54
Look 19:112+ My 3 '55
N Y Times p32 Ja 26 '55; p30 Ap 15 '55; II p11 My 1 '55; p40 My 12 '55; p63 My 18 '55
N Y World-Telegram Mag p3 F 26 '55 pors
San Francisco Chronicle p14 Mr 27 '55
Sat Night 67:45+ N 24 '51
Sunday News p9 II Jl 10 '55
TV Guide 3:17 Ja 8 '55

MACMILLAN, SIR ERNEST (CAMPBELL) Aug. 18, 1893- Orchestral and choral conductor

Address: b. 182 St. George St., Toronto 5, Ontario, Canada; h. 115 Park Rd., Toronto 5, Ontario, Canada

In the musical life of Canada, Sir Ernest MacMillan is one of the most notable personalities. He has been conductor of the country's best-known orchestra, the Toronto Symphony Orchestra, since 1931 and conductor of that city's Mendelssohn Choir since 1942. He is also

SIR ERNEST MACMILLAN

a composer and is president of the Composers, Authors and Publishers Association of Canada (CAPAC). He has received many honorary degrees in recognition of his contributions to music in Canada, and in 1935 he was knighted by His late Majesty King George V. He is an honorary member of the Royal Academy of Music.

With his orchestra, Sir Ernest appears frequently on Canadian Broadcasting Commission programs, heard in both Canada and the United States.

Ernest Campbell MacMillan was born on August 18, 1893 in Mimico, Ontario, Canada. His parents, the Reverend Alexander MacMillan and Wilhelmina (Ross) MacMillan were both of Scottish descent. He and his three sisters received their early schooling in the city of Toronto, where their father, a Presbyterian minister, held a succession of parishes. Ernest attended Rosedale School and for one year Jarvis Collegiate Institute. He then went to Scotland with his parents, his father having accepted a call to an Edinburgh church. For three years he attended Viewpark School in that city; he then returned with his family to Canada. Two years later he again spent a year studying in Edinburgh and then enrolled in the University of Toronto, from which he received a B.A. degree with honors in modern history.

From an early age the boy had shown an aptitude for music, especially for the organ; he learned to play that instrument by taking lessons from a local organist and became so proficient that he began to make public appearances at the age of ten. In Edinburgh, a year or so later, he studied the history of music, advanced harmony and counterpoint at the university and won a medal in advanced harmony. He studied under Frederick Niecks, Alfred Hollins and Dr. W. B. Ross, and at the age of thirteen he became an associate of the Royal College of Organists.

MacMillan became, at the age of seventeen, a fellow of the Royal College of Organists and won the Lafontaine prize. The same year he received the degree of Bachelor of Music from Oxford University. He filled the post of organist and choirmaster at Knox Church, Toronto from 1908 to 1910 and at St. Paul's Church, Hamilton, during 1911 and 1912. While attending the University of Toronto, he was organist and choirmaster for university services and compiled a university hymnal.

In the summer of 1914 MacMillan went to Paris to study, and on visiting Bayreuth for the Wagner festival, was retained there by the outbreak of World War I. He was interned at Ruhleben, near Berlin, and there he spent the war years. While participating in the musical activities of the camp, he gained his first experience as a conductor. During imprisonment he composed a musical setting to Algernon Swinburne's ode "England"; this work, after presentation to the Oxford authorities, earned him the degree of Doctor of Music in 1918.

On his return to Canada MacMillan undertook his first transcontinental tour, with a mixed program on which he gave an organ recital and lectured on the subject "My Four Years in a German Prison Camp." He was engaged as organist and choirmaster by one of Toronto's largest churches, Timothy Eaton Memorial, in 1920 and remained there until 1925. In this period, MacMillan was appointed to the staff of the Toronto Conservatory of Music of the University of Toronto.

In 1926 he was named principal of the conservatory and dean of the university's music faculty, thus becoming at thirty-three the administrative head of one of his country's foremost centers for the study of music. *Maclean's Magazine* stated on October 1, 1940: "The conservatory . . . is now the largest and most influential school of music in Canada. His founding of the conservatory choir of 200 voices was another stroke of MacMillan genius." In 1942 MacMillan resigned from the conservatory post. He remained dean of the university faculty of music until 1952.

Meanwhile, in 1931, MacMillan had been appointed conductor of the Toronto Symphony Orchestra, succeeding to the baton of the late Dr. Luigi von Kunits. Revived in the 1920's by von Kunits, the orchestra when MacMillan took over was still what has been described as "a group of hungry if dedicated afternoon players," and to Sir Ernest (as he became in 1935) is often ascribed a large part of the credit for raising it to professional status.

One of his first steps was to enlarge the size of the ensemble and to initiate a series of regular evening concerts. By 1953 the orchestra numbered eighty-three regular players and presented a twenty-six week season of some eighty concerts. In addition to the regular symphony evenings, the orchestra has since 1944 given a series of weekly "Pop" concerts, commercially sponsored and broadcast every Friday night during the season. (Assistant conductor Paul Scherman is usually on the podium for these.)

The broadcasting by the Canadian Broadcasting Commission of the regular symphony concerts and of the "Pop" concerts has been an important factor in making the orchestra and its conductor nationally celebrated. It has also helped to stabilize the financial situation of the orchestra, which draws the rest of its backing from subscribers, the city coffers, and individual contributors.

Since 1942 Sir Ernest has also been conductor of one of Canada's outstanding choral groups, the Toronto Mendelssohn Choir. The choir, which was formed about the turn of the century, has a tradition of giving annual performances in Toronto of Handel's *Messiah* and Bach's *The Passion according to St. Matthew.* In April 1954, under MacMillan's direction, it sang the two famous works in Carnegie Hall, New York. The choir of 170 voices, 105 female and 65 male, was accompanied by the Toronto Symphony Orchestra and featured outstanding Canadian soloists. Francis D. Perkins wrote in the New York *Herald Tribune* about the *Messiah:* "The general standard of the interpretation, vocally and instrumentally, was remarkably high.... There was thorough coordination; justness of balance, both in the chorus itself and in the contribution of the chorus and the orchestra. . . . One could imagine an interpretation of a less orthodox and more dramatic type, but . . . this was an eminently superior one of its kind."

Among the symphony orchestras that MacMillan has led as guest conductor are the Philadelphia, NBC (New York), Chicago, Los Angeles, Buffalo, Indianapolis, and the Washington, D.C. For eleven successive years he was guest conductor at "Les Concerts Symphoniques" in Montreal; in 1945 he toured Australia as a guest conductor; and in 1946 he wielded the baton at a series of concerts of the Symphony Orchestra of Brazil in Rio de Janeiro.

He has also given many recitals as a concert organist in the United States and Canada. Another facet of his talents is displayed on a weekly hour-long radio program *Sir Ernest Plays Favorites,* on which a selection of classical records is played with eight-minute commentaries by the conductor. As composer and arranger MacMillan has many published works to his credit, among them: "England"; four French-Canadian songs; three Indian songs; two carols for voice and string trio; two sketches for string quartet; and "A Song of Deliverance" for chorus and orchestra.

In 1953 he was a member of the CAPAC committee which chose the program for a concert of works by Canadian composers presented in Carnegie Hall. In an article for the New York *Herald Tribune* on October 11, 1953 he wrote of Canadian music: "Subject matter... has often a specifically Canadian slant yet the actual music remains as diversified as are the individual backgrounds of its composers.... No consistent pattern emerges. Nearly all Canadian music is of recent growth."

Citing the difficulties Canadian composers face in trying to get their works performed because of the limited domestic market and "the apathy and even antipathy of the public as a whole to what is loosely called 'modern' music," he went on to express a hope for the establishment of a federally subsidized arts council, as recommended by the government's Royal Commission on the Arts, Letters and Sciences (on which he had served), and pointed out that such a council "could coordinate isolated efforts and make possible many new ventures that seem at present financially risky."

Sir Ernest MacMillan has received honorary degrees from the University of British Columbia (Vancouver, 1936), Queen's University (Kingston, 1941), Laval University (Quebec 1947), McMaster University (Hamilton, 1948), and the University of Toronto (1953). He is a past president of the Canadian College of Organists, president of the Canadian Music Council, a vice-president of the Royal College of Organists, and a fellow of the Royal College of Music. In the music education field he is the author of *On the Preparation of Ear Tests* and of *Graded Piano Sight Reading Exercises* (in collaboration with organist Healey Willan), and joint author with Boris Berlin of *The Modern Piano Student, Our Piano Class,* and *Twenty Lessons in Ear-Training.*

In October 1955 it was announced that Walter Susskind will succeed Sir Ernest when he retires as head of the Toronto orchestra at the end of the present season.

MacMillan married Laura Elsie Keith on December 31, 1919 and has two sons, Keith Campbell and Ross Alexander. His wife was an occupational therapist before her marriage. The MacMillan home was planned by Sir Ernest; in it he has a study which is accoustically treated and which accommodates his books and scores, as well as a grand piano and a desk made of old carved church-stall panels acquired in Brittany. On the walls are autographed portraits of musical celebrities, and several caricatures of Sir Ernest by Canadian artists. The orchestra conductor is five feet nine inches tall, weighs 180 pounds, and has brown eyes and gray hair. His church affiliation is Presbyterian. He is a member of the Arts and Letters Club and the University Club, both in Toronto.

With a talent for mimicry, he enjoys a reputation as a raconteur, especially of Scottish dialect stories. Each year at the Toronto Symphony Orchestra's special Christmas performances he puts on "a tremendous one-man show," according to Leslie F. Hannon (*Mayfair,* February 1953). "He becomes a chortling Santa Claus, a workman who has just dropped in to fix the organ . . . a German professor explaining with very funny music the origin of *Good Night Irene;* he uses a solo typewriter to unravel Ravel." For recreation he likes to fish or swim and enjoys reading, book-binding, and collecting humorous phonograph records.

References

Thompson, O. ed. International Cyclopedia of Music and Musicians (1949)
Who's Who, 1954
Who's Who in America, 1954-55
Who's Who in Canada, 1953-54

MACMILLAN, (MAURICE) HAROLD
Feb. 10, 1894- British Foreign Secretary
Address: b. c/o Foreign Office, Downing Street, London S.W. 1, England; h. Birch Grove House, Chelwood Gate, Haywards Heath, Sussex, England

NOTE: This biography supersedes the article which appeared in *Current Biography* in 1943.

On April 7, 1955, soon after Sir Anthony Eden replaced Sir Winston Churchill as Prime Minister, Harold Macmillan assumed the post Eden had relinquished, that of Secretary of State for Foreign Affairs. The preceding year, when Macmillan was chosen on October 17, 1954 to succeed Earl Alexander of Tunis as Minister of Defense, he was "expected to bolster both the importance of that department and its ability to meet criticism in the House of Commons" (New York *Times,* October 18, 1954).

"It is probably as a diplomatic trouble shooter that Harold Macmillan has been of most service to Great Britain," stated the *World-Telegram and Sun,* November 27, 1954. Some Britons like his "enlightened Toryism," and call him "Happy Homemaker" because when he was Minister of Housing, over 350,000 new houses were built during 1953 and 1954.

Macmillan has been a member of Parliament for almost thirty years and has served as a diplomat, Privy Councilor, and Cabinet member. He is a grandson of the founder of the Macmillan publishing firm in London and a former director. He is the author of *The Middle Way* (1938) (a middle way between capitalism and socialism for the solution of Great Britain's economic problems) and other books on economics.

Maurice Harold Macmillan was born in London, England on February 10, 1894, the son of Maurice Crawford Macmillan, a Scotsman, and Helen Artie (Belles) Macmillan, who was born in the United States. He was reared in a "strongly religious background" (London *Observer,* May 19, 1946). His first language in the nursery was French. It is now said that Frenchmen talking with him almost forget he is not one of them.

After attending Eton he went to Balliol College, Oxford, where in 1919 he earned the B.A. degree in classics and mathematics. During World War I he served as an officer in the Special Reserve Grenadier Guards. While lying wounded in No Man's Land, he read a pocket edition of Homer in the original text.

He went to Canada in 1919 as aide-de-camp to the ninth Duke of Devonshire, then Governor-General of the Dominion. The following year he became a director of Macmillan & Company, Ltd., a position he held until 1940. In 1923 he made an unsuccessful attempt to represent Stockton on Tees in Parliament as a Conservative but in the next year he won this seat. He lost it in 1929 and did not regain it until 1931. He then represented Stockton on Tees continuously until 1945.

In the years before World War II his interest in social reform led him to become the center of a small "Northern Group" of Conservatives who thought that the party's weak leadership was undermining the principles of British Conservatism. During Prime Minister Ramsay MacDonald's coalition of Conservatives and Liberals, Macmillan called members of the Government's front bench "a row of misused slag heaps." He later referred to Baldwin and Chamberlain as "extinct volcanoes."

After the outbreak of the Italian-Ethiopian war, Macmillan stated that the League of Nations might fail, but "that is no reason that we should help to undermine [it]." He stated that it was hypocrisy to describe the Munich pact as peace by negotiation. He joined with Winston Churchill in urging that a Ministry of Supply be set up in November 1938, but the government refused. Older men in the Conservative party regarded him as a "prewar party rebel."

While Macmillan's independent spirit was displeasing to Stanley Baldwin and Neville Chamberlain, Winston Churchill saw him as "a man of fearless intelligence who, like himself, had violently criticized the rejoicings which followed Munich." When Churchill became Prime Minister and formed his coalition government in 1940, he appointed Macmillan parliamentary secretary to the Ministry of Supply. He was transferred in 1942 to the Colonial Office as Under Secretary of State and as such was spokesman on colonial affairs in the House of Commons.

He endeavored to increase production and shipping from the British colonies and at the same time to meet their need for certain commodities. "Englishmen would have to do without shirts so Africans could have cotton piece goods," he said.

At the end of 1942, following the landing of the Allied forces in Algeria, he was appointed to the newly created post of British Resident Minister at Allied Headquarters in Northwest Africa. Macmillan participated in negotiations towards a settlement between Generals Charles de Gaulle and Henri Honoré Giraud. He opposed the anti-Jewish laws, passed in 1940 and repealed in 1943, in North Africa. He was one of the key men at the Casablanca Conference in 1943. His knowledge of French language and culture brought him an appointment as Britain's representative to the French National Committee of Liberation after its recognition by the British government.

He was present when the Italian armistice was signed on September 3, 1943 and he accompanied the Allied headquarters to Italy. On November 22, 1943, in addition to his ministerial post, he was appointed British representative on the Advisory Council for Italy, with the title of United Kingdom High Commissioner. He became in November 1944 acting president of the Allied Commission in Italy. He helped to negotiate the peace pact between the Greek government and EAM (National Liberation Front). The pact was signed on February 12, 1945. It was said that he studied

Greek antiquities while being sniped at by partisans.

After his return to England from North Africa, Macmillan held the post of Air Minister in the "caretaker government" from May to July 1945. That July he lost his seat at the general election as parliamentary representative for Stockton on Tees, but in November won a by-election at Bromley, Kent, which he continues to represent as a Conservative member. He opened the debate on foreign affairs in February 1946, presenting a résumé of postwar European politics. By the spring of 1946 he was regarded as an important Opposition frontbencher.

Regarding the nationalization of industry, Macmillan said: "Let the government make the strategic plan; the tactical battle must be waged by industry itself" (London *Observer,* May 19, 1946). He expressed the view that nationalization of civil aviation "would impose unnecessary expenditure on the taxpayers and unnecessary restriction on the development of ingenuity and resourcefulness in aviation" (London *Times,* January 25, 1946).

When elected president for one year in March 1947 of the National Union of Conservative and Unionist Associations, Macmillan proposed a resolution, unanimously adopted, which condemned the government's "incompetent management of national affairs," and said the Conservative and Unionist party would sponsor any remedies required to re-establish the nation on a sound industrial and political economic basis.

In an article published in the London *Daily Mail* (May 28, 1948), Macmillan wrote: "In foreign affairs, we seem to have lost the old close cooperation with the United States which was the pivot of victory and the only guarantee of peace." From the first, he was a supporter of the European Movement. His "quiet, persuasive speeches" were called "the most soothing influence . . ." at the Congress of Europe on May 9, 1948, which led to the formation of the Council of Europe the following year. During 1948 he was founder and chairman of the Central and Eastern European Commission, largely comprised of leaders of countries behind the Iron Curtain, seeking to solve their problems and to plan for the time when they would be free of Russian domination.

Macmillan was deputy chairman of the Conservative party's subcommittee on trade and industry in 1949. He aided in preparing the Industrial Charter and was a vice-president of the executive committee of the British section of the Economic League of European Cooperation. As British delegate to the Consultative Assembly of the Council of Europe in Strasbourg, France in 1949, he represented the House of Commons Opposition front bench. As a delegate to the Council in 1950, he presented, together with David Eccles, the British Conservative party plan for the regulation and development in common of Europe's coal and steel industries. The Assembly selected Macmillan as chairman of a special committee formed to guard the interests of countries not

British Inf. Services

HAROLD MACMILLAN

represented in the Council, in cooperation with the Central and Eastern European Commission.

Macmillan attended the Conference of the European League for Economic Cooperation in Brussels in 1951 as head of Britain's delegation. The conference discussed problems of underdeveloped territories, gold, customs, and the European Payments Union. Macmillan was a delegate for the third time to the Consultative Assembly of the Council of Europe, held in Strasbourg in May 1951.

In the fall of 1951 he was appointed Britain's Minister of Housing and Local Government, a post he held for three years. In this position he helped local authorities hasten the building of private houses, decreasing the cost of public housing subsidies. He resigned in November 1951 his chairmanships of the Central and Eastern European Commission and of the Monotype Corporation and its subsidiaries.

In a Cabinet reshuffle announced by Sir Winston on October 17, 1954, Macmillan succeeded Earl Alexander of Tunis as Britain's Minister of Defense. As head of the Ministry of Defense, which was set up in January 1947, Macmillan was also deputy chairman of the Defense Committee, presided over by the Prime Minister and composed of Ministers concerned with problems of defense. The Defense Minister is responsible for carrying out the committee's decisions and policies in apportioning resources among the armed services.

Macmillan informed the House of Commons on December 1 that "drastic reductions" would soon be made in Britain's anti-aircraft organization, and that 50,000 men would be transferred to work on the newer and deadlier guided-missile methods of defense.

Among the books which Macmillan has written are *Reconstruction: A Plea for a National Policy* (1934), *The Middle Way; A Study of*

MACMILLAN, HAROLD—*Continued*

the Problem of Economic and Social Progress in a Free and Democratic Society (1938); and *Economic Aspects of Defense* (1939). These were published by Macmillan & Company, Ltd.

Harold Macmillan married Lady Dorothy Evelyn Cavendish, daughter of the ninth Duke of Devonshire in 1920. They have one son and three daughters. He is six feet tall, weighs about 165 pounds, and has brown eyes and dark hair. His clubs are the Carlton, Turf, Pratt's, and Beefsteak. Macmillan, in the words of the New York *Times* (October 19, 1954), "is lively, aggressive and tough-minded, and he is a first-rate administrator." Earlier, the *Sunday Times* of London (January 22, 1950) noted: "He has an Edwardian charm and courtesy, as well as an Edwardian mustache. He is a political philosopher, as well as a practical statesman. . . ." Tom A. Cullen, NEA writer in London, commented: "He may be the last of the suave, almost courtly British statesmen . . . who can turn up in Moscow wearing an astrakhan cap, or sit cross-legged talking oil with a Middle-Eastern sheik without loss of dignity."

References (See also references in 1943 biographical sketch)

London Daily Mail My 28 '48
London Observer My 19 '46
London Sunday Times Ja 22 '50
London Times Ja 25 '46; Mr 14 '47; My 10 '48; Je 3 '49; Ag 9 '50; Je 2 '51; F 19 '52
N Y Times p 1 O 18 '54
N Y World Telegram p7 N 27 '54
International Who's Who, 1954
Kelly's Handbook to the Titled, Landed and Official Classes, 1954
Who's Who, 1954
World Biography (1954)

MCNAIR, SIR ARNOLD D(UNCAN)

Mar. 4, 1885- President of the International Court of Justice; author

Address: b. c/o International Court of Justice, The Hague, the Netherlands; Gonville and Caius College, Cambridge, England; h. Dale Farm, Elsworth, Cambridge, England

When Sir Arnold D. McNair was elected president of the fifteen-member International Court of Justice on May 6, 1952 it marked the climax of a career in legal scholarship and international legal affairs. An associate of the Institute of International Law, fellow of the British Academy, and Queen's Counsel, Sir Arnold has been a judge of the International Court since its inception in 1946. He has also been the British member of the Permanent Court of Arbitration since 1945. Sir Arnold is the author of many books concerning international law and he has taught at the universities of Cambridge, Calcutta and London and The Hague Academy of International Law.

Sir Arnold informed the United Nations on September 3, 1954 that he would not be a candidate for re-election to the International Court when his term expired at the end of 1955. On February 10, 1955 he resigned the presidency of the Court and was succeeded by Judge Green H. Hackworth of the United States.

Born in London on March 4, 1885, Arnold Duncan McNair was the eldest son of John and Jeannie (Ballantyne) McNair. He was educated at Aldenham School and at Gonville and Caius College, Cambridge University where he was elected president of the Cambridge Union and received law tripos in 1908 and 1909. He was called to the bar at Gray's Inn. In 1913 McNair was made a fellow and law lecturer at Gonville and Caius College and in 1925 he received the LL.D. degree.

From 1926 to 1927 he was a reader of international law at the University of London. Representing the British Air Ministry, McNair attended a conference on air law in Chicago in 1930. His Tagore lectures at the University of Calcutta were published in 1932 as *The Law of the Air* (Butterworth). The *Journal of Air Law* (October 1932) made the comment, "Without doubt this book is the most valuable general textbook on British aeronautical law that has yet appeared."

McNair held the Whewell chair of international law at Cambridge University from 1935 to 1937. He was professor of The Hague Academy of International Law in 1928, 1933 and 1937. From 1937 to 1945 he was vice-chancellor of the University of Liverpool and in 1945 he was appointed professor of comparative law at Cambridge, a post he held for about one year.

In British public service McNair served as secretary of the Coal Controller's Advisory Board from 1917 to 1919. He was secretary of the Coal Industry (Sankey) Commission in 1919. In 1924 he wrote *The Problem of the Coal Mines.* From 1942 to 1944 he was chairman of the Committee on the Supply and Training of Teachers and Youth Leaders, the outcome of which was the McNair report which recommended creating a closer association between training colleges and universities.

In 1945 he was the chairman of the Palestine Jewish Education Commission. His services to his country have been officially recognized, in 1918 when he was made a Commander of the Order of the British Empire, and in 1943 when he was made a knight. Sir Arnold became a King's Counsel in 1945.

In international affairs he served as the British substitute member of the third session in 1926 of the committee of experts of the League of Nations Codification Committee. He was also a member of the International Labour Organization's commission of experts on the application of labor conventions, which contributes the international code of social justice in the field of industry and labor.

Despite the failure of the League of Nations, McNair did not give up hope of achieving the ideal of collective security. In 1940 he wrote: "It is unlikely in the extreme that international law will, if left to itself and unaccompanied by any kind of organization, ever develop satisfactory rules to ensure the just making and revision of treaties and to secure their observance. My hope is that at the end of the present war we shall begin where we left off in 1919, that we shall free a reformed Covenant of the League from connection with any particular group of treaties, that we shall endow the Permanent Court of International Justice with obligatory jurisdiction over all legal disputes amongst the states who belong to it."

On February 6, 1946 Sir Arnold was elected by the U.N. General Assembly and Security Council to a nine-year term on the International Court of Justice which had been created at the end of World War II by an international treaty, the Statute of the Court, which forms an integral part of the U.N. Charter. The new court had as a heritage the experience and traditions of the Permanent Court of International Justice created by the League of Nations. There was no break in the continuity of principles and system between the two courts. No state can be sued without its consent unless it has accepted compulsory jurisdiction of the court under the Statute of the Court, and then only with respect to specified classes of cases. As between parties to the statute, states which had accepted compulsory jurisdiction of the old court automatically accepted compulsory jurisdiction of the new court for the unexpired period of such acceptances.

The court decides cases in accordance with international law. It applies international conventions, international customs (as evidence of a general practice accepted as law), the general principles of law recognized by civilized nations, and it may look to judicial decisions and the teachings of highly qualified publicists, as subsidiary means for determining rules of law. At the request of the General Assembly or the Security Council, the court may give advisory opinions on legal questions.

The court elected Sir Arnold its president on May 6, 1952 for a three-year term. He succeeded Jules Basdevant of France. On the following July 22 the court in a 9 to 5 decision held that it had no jurisdiction in the British-Iranian dispute over oil nationalization. The decision was predicated upon the majority finding that the 1933 oil concession to the Anglo-Iranian Oil Company by Iran was a simple contract rather than an international agreement and that Britain could not invoke previous treaties because the Iranian declaration in 1932 accepting the court's compulsory jurisdiction excluded disputes involving prior agreements. Britain had protested Iran's breach of the concession of 1933 to the Anglo-Iranian Oil Company by unilateral nationalization of the company's property. The New York *Times* (July 23, 1952) noted: "Judge McNair's participation in the majority decision marked the first time in the history of the postwar court that a judge had voted against his own government."

Another important case was that of August 27, 1952 when the court found the French decree of December 30, 1948, imposing import regulations in Morocco, contrary to treaty rights of the United States, as set forth in the 1836 agreement and in the 1912 Act of Alge-

United Nations

SIR ARNOLD D. MCNAIR

ciras, but that U.S. citizens must pay Moroccan taxes and that, apart from certain civil and criminal cases when they may claim the right to be heard in U.S. consular courts, they are subject to Moroccan laws.

The court ruled on April 3, 1954 that Japan has a right to present disputes to the court. On June 15, 1954 the court ruled unanimously in favor of Italy's contention that the court was not competent to hear Italy's dispute with the United States, Great Britain and France over $2,600,000 in gold looted from Rome by the Germans. The court said it lacked jurisdiction because Albania, an essential party to the dispute, had not consented to the hearings.

By a 9 to 3 decision on July 13, 1954 the court found the U.N. General Assembly "has no rights on any ground" to cancel $179,420 in compensation to eleven U.S. citizens dismissed from U.N. jobs for refusal to answer questions of U.S. investigative bodies on alleged Communist connections. The court's ruling was advisory and the Assembly approved it.

The judge served as president of the Society of Public Teachers of Law in 1933, treasurer of Gray's Inn in 1947, and president of the Institute of International Law from 1948 to 1950. He was the recipient of the honorary LL.D. degree from the universities of Glasgow, Liverpool, and Birmingham; the D.C.L. from Oxford; and D.Litt. from the University of Reading. Among Sir Arnold's many books are *The Law of Treaties; British Practice and Opinions* (Oxford, 1938), *War and Treaties* (Oxford, 1940), *The Need for the Wider Teaching of International Law* (1944), and *Legal Effects of War* (Cambridge 1944).

Married to Marjorie Bailhache in 1912, Sir Arnold is the father of one son and three daughters. He is a member of the Athenæum Club. One of his interests is Dr. Samuel John-

MCNAIR, SIR ARNOLD D.—*Continued*

son and in 1948 he published *Dr. Johnson and the Law* (Cambridge). Norman Birkett (*Spectator,* January 21, 1949) commented: "The author . . . may well be assured that Johnson would have approved the use he has made of his leisure, for 'he has turned over half a library to make one book' and has enriched it with the fruits of his experience and his gifts of understanding and judgment."

References

U N Bul 12:410 My 15 '52 por
International Year Book and Statesmen's Who's Who, 1954
International Who's Who, 1954
Who's Who, 1954
Who's Who in the United Nations (1951)
World Biography (1954)

MCNAMARA, PATRICK V(INCENT)

Oct. 4, 1894- United States Senator from Michigan

Address: b. Senate Office Bldg., Washington, D.C.; h. 9708 Ward St., Detroit, Mich.

Senator Patrick V. McNamara who was victorious over the senior Senator from Michigan, Homer Ferguson, a Republican, in the election of November 1954 began on January 3, 1955 a six-year term in the United States Senate. A pipe fitter by trade, McNamara was president of Pipe Fitters Local 636 of the American Federation of Labor for twenty years. During the latter part of this period he was also the vice-president of a Michigan construction firm. He has described himself as a "conservative-liberal" Democrat. A member of the Detroit Board of Education at the time of his election, Senator McNamara considers Federal aid to education as one of the pressing issues of the day.

Eldest of the eight children of a couple who had migrated from Ireland to the United States, Patrick Vincent McNamara was born October 4, 1894 in North Weymouth, Massachusetts. He attended the local high school for two and a half years before transferring to the Fore River Apprentice School in Quincy, Massachusetts where he learned his trade as a pipe fitter. Young McNamara played some professional football before going to Detroit in 1920 to take a job as foreman of a construction gang. He continued his education by taking extension courses at the University of Michigan in Ann Arbor.

As a member of Pipe Fitters Local 636 of the AFL, he held a succession of unpaid minor offices, and was finally elected its president. He has occupied this unsalaried office for twenty of the past twenty-two years, although he left pipe fitting to become a customer contact man, head of labor relations, and vice-president in charge of sales with the Stanley-Carter Company, a mechanical contracting firm. During his tenure as a union president his local has been involved in no strikes.

From 1942 to 1945 he was area rent director of the Office of Price Administration in Detroit. He was elected to the ten-member common council of the city of Detroit in 1946, winning in twenty-one of the city's twenty-three wards. He did not seek re-election to the office of councilman, but instead became in 1949, a successful candidate for a six-year term on the Detroit Board of Education.

In the spring of 1954 former Senator Blair Moody (see *C.B.*, 1951) was slated to run as the Democratic candidate for Senator against Senator Homer Ferguson. Most political analysts expected it to be a close race, but predicted that the incumbent would be the victor. This belief was prevalent because of Michigan's tradition of sending Republican Senators to the legislature and Ferguson's strong position with the Eisenhower Administration, whereas Moody had the backing of both the CIO and Governor G. Mennen Williams (see *C.B.*, 1949). "Hardly anyone gave . . . McNamara a chance" (*Newsweek*, August 2, 1954), when he filed his application for the Democratic nomination against former Senator Blair Moody. However, following the sudden death of Moody on July 20, 1954 from pneumonia, ". . . the unknown McNamara, was the only Democratic candidate left in the field. Without enthusiasm, the machine backed him" (New York *Times,* January 4, 1955).

McNamara commenced his campaign "with commitments totaling only $12,000", which prompted the Detroit *Times* to call it "probably the most inexpensive senatorial effort in history." (Subsequently "the Democrats added to that sum," a truce between McNamara and Governor Williams having been arranged in the interest of party solidarity.) Although McNamara was (in the words of Foster Hailey) "no orator," at a monster rally in Detroit in October 1954, he "held a hall of 3,000 hot and tired listeners awaiting the arrival of Adlai Stevenson quieter that it had been all evening."

Those who campaigned with McNamara considered him "at his best" when he stopped his car in some little town and started down the street introducing himself to local citizens. In his visits to the normally Republican rural areas, McNamara stressed the allegedly adverse effect of the Administration's agricultural program on dairy farming, while in urban areas he emphasized statewide unemployment which reached a peak of 287,000 in September 1954. McNamara also called for repeal of the Taft-Hartley act, but without going "way back to the old Wagner act" and denounced the new atomic energy act as a "throw-away" of twelve billion dollars. He advocated Federal aid for schools, saying, "Let the United States build the schools where needed, then step out and let local school boards take over."

During the campaign, Ferguson and McNamara eschewed personal attacks, and "through an apparent 'gentlemen's agreement' neither . . . mentioned McCarthyism" (Ed Winge in the Detroit *Free Press*). McNamara won the election on November 2 by 1,088,550 votes to 1,049,420 for Ferguson.

Seated in the Eighty-fourth Congress on January 3, 1955, the new junior Senator from Michigan was assigned to the Senate's District of Columbia, Labor and Public Welfare, and

Public Works Committees. In a hearing held January 31 by the Labor and Public Welfare Committee, McNamara considered inadvisable appending an anti-segregation amendment to certain school construction bills, stating that he could see "no more of a segregation problem in building schools than in building roads."

With Senator Paul H. Douglas of Illinois, Senator McNamara became early in March one of the two dissenters to the Senate Labor Committee's approval of Theophil C. Kammholz to be general counsel of the National Labor Relations Board. They did not question the integrity or competence of the nominee, but felt that his appointment reflected a general policy of giving "key" NLRB posts to "employer-minded people."

In the first session of the Eighty-fourth Congress Senator McNamara voted against the President's atoms-for-peace ship, and the President's highway program. He also voted "nay" on dropping the twenty dollar income tax cut. McNamara supported the resolution for defense of Formosa, the Congressional pay raise to $22,500 and putting a $3.4 billion ceiling on foreign aid.

As a member of the Senate Labor Committee, McNamara was one of the seven Democrats to introduce a bill to provide free Salk antipoliomyelitis vaccine for children (New York *Times*, June 3, 1955). He supported an amendment made by Senator Richard L. Neuberger of Oregon to pay the prevailing wage to laborers engaged in work on highways built with Federal funds. When the motion was struck out of the bill, McNamara and Neuberger asked for a roll call vote to go on the record. This motion was also voted down.

During the fifty-four day Washington, D.C. streetcar and bus operator walkout the Washington *Post and Times Herald* of August 21, 1955 commented: "the District was fortunate at least to have former National War Labor Board member Senator Wayne Morse (Democrat-Oregon) and . . . labor 'pro' Senator Pat McNamara (Democrat-Michigan) maneuver a bill to hand the Commissioners enough power to deal with their own backyard scrap."

After the 1954 election, Senator-elect McNamara and Governor G. Mennen Williams, who had won a fourth term, pledged continued "mutual support and cooperation," with McNamara expressing himself as "happy . . . to be a member" of the Governor's "team." The Detroit *Times*, (November 4, 1954) reported local Democrats as asking "How long will it last?" since "McNamara's most striking characteristic is his independence."

Following the announcement in March 1955 of plans for a merger of the AFL and CIO, as a guest on the *Longines Wittnauer* television program of April 13, 1955, McNamara somewhat cautiously stated his belief that the merger would be "helpful" to Labor's bargaining power and that a guaranteed annual wage would have a "stabilizing effect" on industry; but he made it clear that he did not "speak for Labor." He also voiced the view that Federal aid to education was the "biggest issue," and strongly endorsed Senator Lister Hill's education bill. Regarding his relationship to the liberal and conservative wings of his party, McNamara refused to be pigeonholed. "I'm pro-people," he asserted. "I don't plead guilty to labels."

Wide World
PATRICK V. MCNAMARA

Senator McNamara was one of the 360 citizens who signed a petition demanding that the U.S. Supreme Court declare the Internal Security Act of 1950 unconstitutional. The petition was filed before the Supreme Court on September 16, 1955 as a "friend of the court" action in the first test of the act.

"He can charm a bird right down out of a tree," an admirer was quoted as saying of "Pat" McNamara in the Washington *Post and Times Herald* (November 6, 1954). Foster Hailey of the New York *Times* has commented on McNamara's "delightful sense of humor" and his sometimes "almost fanatical" integrity and has described him physically as having "a ruddy face of indubitable Irish contours, a broad smile and a man of snow-white hair." He carries "240 pounds on a 6-foot 2-inch frame" and in this regard contrasts strikingly with his wife, Mary, who is "only five feet tall and called 'Shorty' by her husband" (Stewart Didzun in the Detroit *News*). The McNamaras occupied in Detroit "a modest six-room brick house in a middle-income neighborhood." They have two children, Mrs. Mary Jane Ballard and Patrick V. McNamara, III, and eight grandchildren. Senator McNamara is a Roman Catholic.

References

Detroit News p14 O 24 '54
N Y Herald Tribune p10 N 4 '54
N Y Post Mag p4 N 21 '54 por
N Y Times p10 N 6 '54; p16 Ja 4 '55 por
Newsweek 46:19 Ag 2 '54
Time 64:23 N 15 '54
Washington (D.C.) Post p11 N 6 '54
Congressional Directory (1955)

MCNEIL, HECTOR Mar. 10, 1910-Oct. 11, 1955 Former British Government official; Member of Parliament (Labour) for Burgh of Greenock since 1941; Minister of State (1946-1950); Secretary of State for Scotland (1950-1951); headed British delegation to U.N. General Assembly (1946-1949); Vice-President, U.N. General Assembly (1947); a former editor of Scottish *Daily Express;* in U.N. was incisive debater for causes of United Kingdom and Western Powers. See *Current Biography* (Dec.) 1946.

Obituary

N Y Times p31 O 12 '55

MCNELLIS, MAGGI June 1, 1917- Radio and television commentator

Address: 1270 Ave. of the Americas, New York 20

One of the most active members of television's "glamour brigade," Maggi McNellis has had more than eleven years of experience as a radio commentator and interviewer, and about six years on television as a panelist, commentator, and innovator of magazine-of-the-air type of programs. Her name has appeared on the Fashion Academy list of the world's ten best-dressed women successively over a nine-year period. Her knowledge of fashions has brought her numerous speaking engagements, as well as the title of the country's top fashion show commentator. She is co-author, with Hubie Boscowitz, of the book *Party Games* (Prentice-Hall, 1949) which describes 793 games for adults and teen-agers, invented or played by celebrities.

MAGGI MCNELLIS

Her TV shows are on the Dumont Television Network, Monday-through-Friday afternoons, and at midnight (New York time.)

The radio critic for *Radio and Television Mirror* (April 1953) wrote: "Maggi McNellis is an artist when it comes to interviewing three or four people from widely separated fields of endeavor and somehow making the results sound like a discussion."

Maggi McNellis was born Margaret Eleanor Roche on June 1, 1917 in Chicago, Illinois, the daughter of George J. and Maude (McDonough) Roche. Her father is a contractor. She has a brother, George, in the oil drilling business. Margaret was educated in Chicago's local schools and then attended Marywood Academy High School in Evanston, Illinois. She received further education at Mundelein College, Chicago and studied at Rosemont College, Pennsylvania from 1936 to 1938. After completing her courses there, she married Richard Vincent McNellis, a member of the Chicago Board of Trade.

In 1939 Ernie Byfield, proprietor of the Pump Room of the Ambassador Hotel, Chicago, asked the young society matron to sing at his establishment and Mrs. McNellis agreed "just for the fun of it." John King Flynn in *American Weekly* (April 22, 1951) wrote that "what Maggi lacked in training and voice, she compensated for in poise and personality." Upon the suggestion of the late actress Gertrude Lawrence, Maggi assumed her present name, which Miss Lawrence called "chic, like you."

Following her singing debut Maggi received engagements at the Colony Club and the Blackstone Hotel in Chicago. In 1940 she went to New York City to sing for the next two years at various supper and entertainment clubs, including Monte Carlo, Armando's, Coq Rouge, Ambassador Hotel, and the Rainbow Room. She was divorced from Mr. McNellis in 1941.

Beginning her radio career in 1943 in a gossip and music program called the *Maggi McNellis Show,* she broadcast over the local New York station WINS three nights weekly for six months. In July 1944 she signed a five-year contract with NBC's station WEAF for a national network daytime program called *Maggi's Private Wire,* in which she interviewed celebrities.

She became an active participant in Martha Roundtree's original radio production of *Leave It to the Girls,* which came on the NBC network in May 1945 and which featured feminine opinion on how to deal with men. On March 21, 1946 she was selected by the Fashion Academy in New York City as one of the nation's best-dressed women.

With Herb Sheldon, Maggi McNellis became a principal in the radio show *Luncheon with Maggi and Herb,* broadcast from the club Latin Quarter, New York City over ABC's local WJZ station on weekdays from 2:00 to 2:30 P.M. This was an audience participation show in which studio visitors played various games on stage and received prizes. The program on Saturday was arranged for children. Radio critic Harriet Van Horne wrote in the New York *World-Telegram* (July 10, 1947): "The show is completely unoriginal in format." On Maggi and Herb Sheldon, the critic commented: "They deserve a far better showcase . . . for the principals are two of radio's nicest people."

Concurrently with her radio work, Maggi McNellis accepted engagements as a fashion commentator, earning from $500 to $1,500 for appearances at style shows.

Turning to the television medium in 1949, she appeared in a weekly program, *Maggi's Crystal Room,* over ABC's local New York station, WJZ. She interviewed outstanding people of the theatre in a night club setting, seated four or five around a table. In April 1949 she arranged with NBC's local New York station, WNBT, for the televising of Martha Roundtree's program *Leave It to the Girls,* with four girl panelists and one man, and herself as moderator of the program. It is claimed that this weekly one-half hour entertainment was the first panel show on television. It is described in *TV Guide* (April 16, 1954) as the "number one launcher of TV careers for women." One of the panelists, Dorothy Kilgallen, has said of her colleague, "Maggi is never in a bad mood."

For a program that dramatized Somerset Maugham's short stories during 1950 over the CBS television network, Maggi officiated as hostess. In January 1951 she became co-moderator with Bud Collyer of *Say It With Acting,* televised over NBC's New York station WNBT, bi-weekly on Saturdays from 6:30 to 7:00 P.M. The program consisted of two competing teams of actors, captained by the moderators and participating in a charade game that was based chiefly on song titles and familiar sayings. In August 1951 Maggi McNellis and Bud Collyer transferred their charade show to the ABC television network, featured on Friday evenings from 7:30 to 8:00.

In a cooperative enterprise between the film and television industries, in September 1951 Maggi appeared in *What's Playing,* televised by ABC's local WJZ station on Friday nights at 6:45. Brief screen clips from new films were shown on each program. *Variety* (September 5, 1951) called the show "an aid to the usual family squabble after dinner each night about what film they should go to see," and reported that "Miss McNellis, beauteously gowned as usual, did a brightly competent job . . . spotlighting human interest angles."

She began in August 1952, on Channel 7, the *Maggi McNellis Show,* a magazine-of-the-air type of program televised for one-half hour on Thursday evenings at 9:30. It was departmentalized into seven different fields and featured: "Maggi's Private Wire" (gossip about celebritics); "Fashion Spotlight"; "This Week in New York": "Motion Picture Page"; "The Theatre"; "Host of the Week" (a restaurant owner); and "Feature Page." Three guests were interviewed.

A later version of the *Maggi McNellis Show,* over ABC's television network Channel 7, began on September 21, 1953. Included are such features as "Young Ideas," games or interests pertaining to children or teen-agers; "Beauty Page," an interview with a beauty authority; "Feature Page," subjects of general interest are discussed; "Fashion Page" and "Decorating Page," interviews with decorators and designers; and "Open Wire," in which guests answer questions submitted by the audience. This program moved to the Dumont television network in the fall of 1955.

In the late fall of 1953 Maggi McNellis, while continuing her television work, returned to radio broadcasting with a half-hour program called *Maggi's Magazine,* over WABC at 12:30, Monday through Friday. This began at the Plaza Hotel, New York City and about a month later moved to the St. Moritz Hotel.

She won the Linguaphone diction award and the Imperial perfect-timing award in 1948. She is a member of the Musicians Emergency Fund for Hospitalized Veterans and of the American Federation of Radio Artists. She has black hair and blue eyes, stands five feet seven inches tall, and weighs 120 pounds.

She is the author of the articles "TV Now Doing the Impossible" (*Variety,* January 2, 1952) and "What Makes a Woman Attractive?" (*Cosmopolitan,* May 1953).

Maggi McNellis married Clyde M. Newhouse, of the Newhouse Galleries, Inc., New York City, on June 24, 1946. They have a daughter, Meg. The commentator has made cupids her personal signature; there are cupid decorations in her apartment, on her jewelry, and they are her favorite subject during her Sunday painting sessions. She answers her considerable fan mail herself, replying on a large card in her own handwriting. She receives about 150 questions each week, submitted for answer on her programs, and with the help of her "girl Friday," secretary Lillian de Gore, she makes selections.

Her taste in clothes runs to suits, and basic things mostly gray, navy, black or white. "Shoes and furs are my weaknesses," she admitted. She enjoys giving buffet suppers in her pink and gray apartment.

References

N Y Times p20 Ag 29 '52
N Y World-Telegram p22 Jl 10 '47
TV Guide 1:14 D 4 '53
Motion Picture and Television Almanac, 1953-54
Who's Who in the East (1953)

MCNUTT, PAUL V(ORIES) July 18, 1891-Mar. 24, 1955 Lawyer; former Governor of Indiana; dean of the Law School of the University of Indiana; American Legion Commander; held several New Deal posts including U.S. High Commissioner to the Philippine Islands, Federal Security Administrator, chairman of the War Manpower Commission; withdrew his name as possible Democratic candidate in 1940 when Franklin D. Roosevelt decided to run for a third term; upon retirement from public service became chairman of the board of the Philippine-American Life Insurance Company. See *Current Biography* (Jan.-Feb.) 1940

Obituary

N Y Times p23 Mr 25 '55

MAGALLANES, NICHOLAS (mä-jä-län'-ŭs) Nov. 27, 1919- Ballet dancer

Address: b. c/o New York City Ballet, City Center of Music & Drama, Inc., 130 W. 56th St., New York 19; h. 147-45 Coolidge Ave., Jamaica, Long Island, N.Y.

A dancer in the European classic ballet tradition whose training has been entirely American, Nicholas Magallanes is one of the well-known stars of the New York City Ballet. He has filled such roles as that of the Poet in *Illuminations* and the title role in *Orpheus*. He has been a partner for such celebrated ballerinas as Maria Tallchief, Melissa Hayden, Diana Adams and Tanaquil LeClercq. He has appeared with the company on its North American and European tours and has made a number of guest appearances on television. Prior to 1948 he danced in the Ballet Russe de Monte Carlo and in the Ballet Society, and in several Broadway musical productions including *Song of Norway*.

NICHOLAS MAGALLANES

According to an estimate made by Anatole Chujoy, dance historian, "Magallanes possesses a considerable technique, has a very fluid, romantic style of movement, and is an excellent partner, probably among the top half-dozen. He is handsome and well built and has a very winning stage personality."

Nicholas Magallanes, the son of Philip and Vicenta (Holquin) Magallanes, was born in Camargo, Chihuahua, Mexico on November 27, 1919. With his parents, he came to the United States when he was five. For a time the family lived in New Jersey; then it moved to New York City where young Magallanes received his public school education, graduating from De Witt Clinton High School.

When Magallanes was fifteen he saw his first ballet performance which fired his ambition to become a ballet dancer. Shortly after this, he met the artist Pavel Tchelitchew who introduced him to George Balanchine, the distinguished choreographer who, with Lincoln Kirstein and others, had started the School of American Ballet. Balanchine advised the young man to study at his school.

After three years' training, Magallanes entered upon his first professional engagement as a member of the ballet company which performed in the Ford Exhibit at the New York World's Fair in the summer of 1940. The idea for the ballet originated with Walter D. Teague, the industrial designer, and was carried out by Kirstein and the Ballet Caravan company. The group presented the ballet, *A Thousand Times Neigh!*, a sketch illustrating the fate of old dobbin when replaced by the automobile.

Magallanes' next engagement, following the closing of the Fair, was a brief one in which he toured with the Catherine Littlefield Ballet Company. He then joined the Balanchine-Kirstein American Ballet for its South American tour in 1941. Upon the return of the company to the United States, Magallanes was engaged for the Broadway production of *The Merry Widow*, for which Balanchine arranged the dances, and which enjoyed a successful run at the Majestic Theatre during the 1943-1944 season. The same season marked the beginning of the dancer's four-year association with the Ballet Russe de Monte Carlo, in which, beginning as a member of the *corps de ballet*, he worked his way up to such leading roles as that of Prince Siegfried in *Swan Lake*, the Poet in *Night Shadow*, and the Head Wrangler in *Rodeo*.

When Balanchine executed the choreography for *Song of Norway*, the entire Ballet Russe de Monte Carlo company was engaged for the production. Opening at the Imperial Theatre, New York City, in August 1944, the offering scored an immediate hit.

During an engagement of the Monte Carlo company at the New York City Center in 1945 Magallanes danced some of the principal roles. Walter Terry in the New York *Herald Tribune* (March 31, 1945) wrote: "He should be a good dancer and almost succeeds in being one, for he is a fine partner for the ballerina, and his solo actions indicate that he knows what ballet is about."

Magallanes filled a third Broadway engagement in the fall of 1947 when he was *premier danseur* in *Music in My Heart*, with choreography by Ruth Page, at the Adelphi Theatre. He next became a member of Ballet Society, the forerunner of the New York City Ballet, and in its third program on February 9, 1948 presented at the City Center, Magallanes portrayed the role of Bacchus in *The Triumph of Bacchus and Ariadne*. His performance, according to Anatole Chujoy (*The New York City Ballet*), was one to be remembered "with particular pleasure."

During his engagement with Ballet Society, he supported the distinguished ballerina, Maria Tallchief, in *Symphony in C*, and at the première of the Balanchine-Stravinsky-Noguchi ballet, *Orpheus*, Magallanes played the title role. Other principal dancers in the latter production were Miss Tallchief, Tanaquil LeClercq, Francisco Moncion and Herbert Bliss.

Ballet Society became the New York City Ballet in 1948. The first announcements listed Magallanes among the principal dancers, a position which he has continued to maintain, while his stature as a dancer has increased. The presentation of *Orpheus* in 1949 brought the following comment from John Martin of the New York *Times* (January 17, 1949): "This magnificent work received on this occasion quite the finest performance it has yet had. . . . The chief difference lay in the inspired playing of the title role by Nicholas Magallanes. He has always done it nicely in the past, but suddenly and inexplicably the projection of the character assumed a passion and a dramatic understanding that it has never even approximated heretofore."

In January 1949 Jerome Robbins' ballet, *The Guests,* with music by Marc Blitzstein, was presented for the first time, and although the New York *Times* critic considered the work on the whole "disappointing," his review (January 21, 1949) stated that the *pas de deux* danced by Maria Tallchief and Nicholas Magallanes was "far and away the best section." During the layoff following the first season of the new ballet company, Magallanes appeared as *premier danseur* in the Ballet Alicia Alonso, filling an engagement in Cuba. He was back with his own ballet organization for the following season, winning fresh tribute for his work.

Further acclaim came to the dancer with his creation of the role of the Poet in Frederick Ashton's ballet, *Illuminations.* Of Magallanes' work, Martin wrote on March 19, 1950, "It was a performance keyed high and with flashes of revelation. . . ." The New York City Ballet gave its première performance in London on July 10, 1950 and with the Sadler's Wells Company was entertained by the Arts Council of Great Britain. Magallanes was with the company for its London season and has appeared in its subsequent European tours.

Walter Terry commented (New York *Herald Tribune,* February 21, 1952) on the dancing of Magallanes when *Illuminations* was repeated. "He bettered his already eloquent portrayal. Not only were the peaks of emotion—fury and ecstasy, arrogance and despair, surrender and defiance—powerfully communicated, but the intermediate details of dramatic range were clearly expressed through movement, nuance, impulsive gesture, miming."

Première performances in which Magallanes appeared in the spring and fall seasons of 1952 were *Caracole,* to music of Mozart, and *Metamorphoses,* to music of Hindemith, both choreographed by Balanchine. *Valse Fantaisie* and *The Filly* were presented the following year, the first a Glinka-Balanchine arrangement, the second choreographed by Todd Bolender to the music of John Colman.

Tchaikovsky's famous ballet *The Nutcracker,* given a new presentation in 1954 with original choreography by Balanchine, was an immediate success and Magallanes shared in the triumph with his partner, Maria Tallchief. Magallanes "dances it better than he has danced anything in the classic style in a long time," commented John Martin (New York *Times,* February 3, 1954). Magallanes danced with Diana Adams, Herbert Bliss, Melissa Hayden and others in Balanchine's *Western Symphony* on February 27, 1955, which had very good reviews.

Magallanes believes that a ballet should unfold the suggestion of a story, rather than literally outline a plot. "The essence of a ballet, in addition to the patterns of movement and design it contains," he has said, "is to awaken feeling in an audience. It should touch you emotionally, perhaps each person in a different way, so that it provides identification, like something remembered. Through movement you are conveying an idea with gestures which are far more eloquent than words, and which create beauty and illusion for an audience. At least, that's how it is for me."

The dancer's favorite roles are those of Orpheus, in the ballet of the same name, and the Poet, in *Illuminations.* He has black hair and dark eyes, is five feet ten inches tall, and weighs 160 pounds. Recently, he obtained his first papers toward becoming an American citizen. Among his hobbies are photography and watching horse races.

References

Chujoy, A. Dance Encyclopedia (1949); The New York City Ballet (1953)

MANN, THOMAS June 6, 1875-Aug. 12, 1955 German-born author; received Nobel Prize for Literature in 1929; champion of democratic principles and fighter against totalitarianism; became U.S. citizen; moved to Switzerland in 1953; among his novels are *Buddenbrooks* (1900), *The Magic Mountain* (1924), *Joseph and His Brothers* (1933) which began the tetralogy of the Biblical story of Joseph, and *The Black Swan* (1954). See *Current Biography* (May) 1942.

Obituary

N Y Times p 1 + Ag 13 '55

MARSHALL, (SARAH) CATHERINE (WOOD) Sept. 27, 1914- Author

Address: b. c/o McGraw-Hill Book Co., Inc., 330 W. 42d St., New York 36; h. 4111 38th St., Washington 16, D.C.

Responsible for "two of the most popular books of nonfiction in recent times," Catherine Marshall won the Women's National Press Club award as "Woman of the Year" in 1953 in the field of literature. *A Man Called Peter,* her biography of her husband, Peter Marshall (chaplain of the United States Senate from 1947 until his death in 1949) has been on the non-fiction bestseller list since 1951. Over 1,000,000 copies have been sold, and the book was adapted for screen production in 1955 by Twentieth Century-Fox Film Corporation.

The collection of Dr. Marshall's sermons which his wife edited, entitled *Mr. Jones, Meet the Master,* attained the nonfiction bestseller list within six weeks after publication in 1949, and remained there for almost a year. Catherine Marshall also edited and wrote the

Chevy Chase Studio

CATHERINE MARSHALL

preface for *The Prayers of Peter Marshall*, published in the fall of 1954.

Sarah Catherine Wood Marshall was born in Johnson City, Tennessee, on September 27, 1914, the daughter of John Ambrose and Leonora Whitaker Wood. Her parents were of English and Scotch ancestry. She has a brother, Robert, and a sister, Mrs. Harlow Hoskins. The family lived for some years in Canton, Mississippi and Catherine went to school there until she was nine. Then they moved to Keyser, West Virginia, where her father became pastor of the Presbyterian Church.

Describing a childhood Christmas in "Christmas is for Children" (*Look*, December 29, 1953), she wrote: ". . . when I was eleven . . . I discovered for myself that giving actually is more fun than receiving, provided one gives oneself along with the gift."

Catherine graduated in 1932 from Keyser High School, where her extracurricular activities had included piano, debating, Girl Scout work, and church and youth group participation. In her book *A Man Called Peter* (McGraw-Hill, 1951), she wrote: "One of my youthful self-indulgences was a journal in which I poured out my hopes and dreams and let my poetic urge have full reign." She recalls writing in it: "I can never enjoy life until I learn *why* I am here and *where* I am going."

Miss Wood entered Agnes Scott College in Decatur, Georgia in 1932. Her major subject was history, and her outside interests included intercollegiate debating, writing for student publications, and the poetry society. The college awarded her a B. A. degree in 1936. Following graduation, she hoped to write books and to teach school in the West Virginia mountains. However, her meeting with Peter Marshall, a Scottish minister about twelve years her senior, then pastor of the Westminister Presbyterian Church, Atlanta, Georgia, changed her plans.

After their marriage in 1936 and a visit to England and Scotland, they settled in Washington, D.C., where Dr. Marshall was installed in 1937 as pastor of New York Avenue Presbyterian Church. She found opportunities for extensive service in the parish, and observes in *A Man Called Peter* that "to say that a pastor's helpmate was expected to be gracious, charming, poised, equal to every occasion, would be a gross understatement."

Catherine Marshall spent from March 1943 until the summer of 1945 in bed, ill with tuberculosis. It was a period of spiritual analysis for her, touching on mysticism, in which she concluded that the disease might be due to "spiritual as well as physical" malnutrition, and healing "came slowly, no doubt because my faith grew slowly" (*A Man Called Peter*, 1951).

Her husband died of a heart attack in January 1949, after serving two years as chaplain of the United States Senate. Mrs. Marshall wrote later: "My really valuable inheritance was two quite ordinary-looking cardboard filing boxes filled with sermon manuscripts" (*McCall's*, August, 1953).

Upon the suggestion of Fleming H. Revell Company, Inc., publishers, Catherine Marshall selected twelve of 600 of her husband's sermons and thirteen prayers. This collection, *Mr. Jones, Meet the Master*, to which she as editor contributed a seven-page sketch of Peter Marshall, was published in the fall of 1949. The book became a bestseller and stayed on the nonfiction list for nearly a year.

Mrs. Marshall received a letter from Edward C. Aswell, vice-president and editor-in-chief of McGraw-Hill Book Company, expressing an interest in seeing unpublished sermons of Dr. Marshall. "Out of my correspondence with Mr. Aswell," the author states, "grew the idea of *A Man Called Peter*." In the summer of 1950 at her Cape Cod cottage, she worked on the biography of her husband, and supplemented it with an eighty-page selection of his sermons and prayers. When the book appeared in October 1951, it reached the nonfiction bestseller list within ten days, remaining there for more than three years. This fulfilled one of the author's "deepest dreams," as she stated in "I Learned to Conquer Grief" (*Reader's Digest*, July 1953): "Through my writing I would like to make a contribution to my time and generation." The *Reader's Digest* published a condensation of her book in its September 1952 issue.

Clarence Seidenspinner, book review critic for the Chicago *Sunday Tribune* (October 7, 1951) commented on *A Man Called Peter*: "None of the novels concerning the ministry, written during the last few years, touches the heart and appeals to the mind in the same way that Catherine Marshall does in telling the story of her husband's life." The reviewer for the New York *Herald Tribune* (October 28, 1951) wrote: ". . . the sermons quoted appear somewhat less original and profound than they seem to the book's author."

In the New York *Times* (October 7, 1951) A. Powell Davies stated: "Catherine Marshall writes extremely well. Those who do not accept her religious viewpoint will nevertheless admit that she presents it with grace and charm."

Recordings for the blind have been made of *A Man Called Peter*, and, following negotiations begun in the autumn of 1953 between the author and Twentieth Century-Fox Film Corporation, the book was adapted for screen production starring Richard Todd and Jean Peters. "I thought and prayed hard before entrusting Peter's life to the movies, but I believe the great medium of the film—and all the entertainment media—are also meant for the Lord's work," Mrs. Marshall told a reporter for the Washington *Post and Times Herald* (May 25, 1954). She made two trips to Hollywood to aid in production plans. The film received very favorable reviews when it was released in 1955.

Catherine Marshall is also the author (with Peter Marshall) of *God Loves You: Our Family's Favorite Stories and Prayers* (McGraw-Hill, 1953). "This book will meet a real need, not only for family home use, but for ministers seeking illustrative material to use in Sunday Schools," commented Virginia Kirkus (March 15, 1953). N. L. Rathbun stated in *Library Journal* (May 1, 1953): "Nora Unwin's charming illustrations and a feeling of family warmth and intimacy keep the book from being didactic and sentimental." Mrs. Marshall wrote the introduction to, and edited *The Prayers of Peter Marshall*, a collection of 276 of her husband's pastoral and Senate prayers (McGraw-Hill Book, 1954).

Among the articles she has written for popular magazines is "What I've Learned at Gordon Cosby's Church" (*Reader's Digest*, December 1953), describing the progressive work of a young war veteran as minister of His Church of the Savior, Washington, D.C. "Both for her literary achievements and her contribution to the reawakening of national interest in spiritual welfare," Mrs. Marshall received the "Woman of the Year" award from the Women's National Press Club in 1953.

She is described by Richard L. Coe in the Washington *Post and Times Herald* (May 25, 1954) as being a "vivid" personality. "She speaks with a [Southern] accent and meets strangers with a grave graciousness that reflects a woman wholly at home with herself."

She was married to Peter Marshall on November 4, 1936, and their son is Peter John. Catherine Marshall is five feet six and one-half inches tall, weighs 138 pounds, and has blue eyes and brown hair. The book she enjoyed most in 1953 was the translation of the Gospels by J. B. Phillips.

Among her hobbies are painting and gardening. Her church affiliation is Presbyterian. In "I Learned to Conquer Grief" she wrote, ". . . the God I know is a realist and he expects us to be realists too."

References

Clear Horizons summer '54
McCall's 80:11 Ag '53
N Y Herald Tribune Book R p17 O 28 '51
N Y Times Book R p30 O 7 '51; p46 Ap 26 '53
Read Digest 63:19 Jl '53
Washington (D.C.) Post p32 O 7 '51
Marshall, S. C. W., A Man Called Peter (1951)

MARSHALL, MRS. PETER *See* Marshall, Catherine Wood

MARTINI, MRS. FRED *See* Martini, Helen

MARTINI, HELEN (FRANCES THERESA) June 6, 1912- Keeper of wild animal nursery

Address: b. c/o New York Zoological Society, 185th St. and Southern Blvd., New York 60; h. 1026 Old Kingsbridge Rd., New York 60

Known to thousands of zòo-enthusiasts as "the lady who raises wild animals in a Bronx apartment," Helen Martini is the author of *My Zoo Family* (Harper, 1955). It is the story of Mrs. Martini's career as foster mother to many young animals in the Bronx Zoo who need special care. The New York Zoological Society, founded in 1895, maintains in New York City, the Bronx Zoological Park, which is visited by nearly three million people each year (see Dr. Fairfield Osborn's sketch, C.B., September 1949).

Mrs. Martini's career began in 1942 when her husband, keeper of the Lion House at the Zoo, brought home a newborn lion cub—rejected by its mother—for her to take care of. Later, three tiger cubs found refuge in her apartment, then a black baby leopard. The neighbors complained when Bagheera, the black leopard, grew to full size and Mrs. Martini continued to bring him home at night. Thereafter, she had to leave him at the Zoo. It was largely through her efforts that the Nursery was established at the Zoo. Under her custodianship, the lives of many valuable animals have been saved. Her unusual occupation has been the subject of many magazine and newspaper articles. "Mother Was Human" (*Ladies Home Journal,* July 1953), her own account of early experiences with the baby animals, was condensed from her book.

Helen Frances Theresa Delaney, only daughter of Matthew and Alice (Fitzpatrick) Delaney, was born on June 6, 1912, in St. John's, Newfoundland. The Delaneys were of English-Irish ancestry. Matthew Delaney was a merchant seaman, an adventurous person with a love of the sea. Helen recalled that his home-comings were days of great festivity, with singing, storytelling, and reciting. Her mother

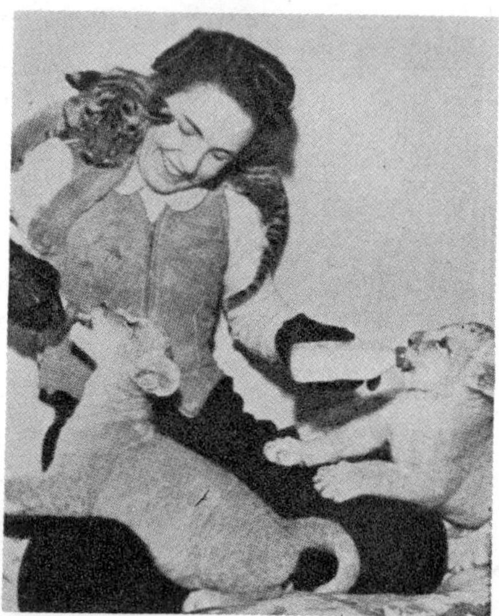

New York Zoological Society
HELEN MARTINI

made her home her hobby. Helen had two brothers.

She attended the Presentation Convent in St. John's and although in delicate health, walked several miles to school daily, and was rarely absent because of severe snow storms. Born with an eye affliction that Newfoundland doctors said would result in blindness, Helen refused to give up hope. After the death of her father, her mother brought her in 1925 to New York for a series of eye operations, which proved so successful that her vision became normal. She was able to continue her education at the Joan of Arc Junior High School in New York City.

Helen Delaney was married on August 6, 1932 to John Alfred ("Fred") Martini, and two years later prepared for the birth of a child. After the loss of her baby Mrs. Martini was told that she could never have another and was urged by her doctor to find a hobby. She concentrated on her home, then became interested in her husband's hobby—animals. Together they visited the Bronz Zoo every Saturday and Sunday. Her husband was a jeweler, but his love of animals was so great that he wanted to work among them.

Mrs. Martini encouraged him to apply for a job at the Zoo and he was hired in 1940 as a relief keeper and substituted for regular keepers in the various animal houses. Mrs. Martini has written that she found books in the library on various animal species which they studied in the evenings. A year later Martini was put in full charge of the Lion House.

Mrs. Martini's first apartment guest was a day-old lion, uncared for by its mother. There were no books on how to mother a baby lion, but Mrs. Martini treated it like a human infant. The cub weighed three pounds. Mrs. Martini named him Douglas MacArthur. He established his own feeding schedule of every three hours and slept in between. In five weeks he weighed seven pounds and was able to run and play. She was heartbroken when MacArthur was returned to the Zoo at the age of two months.

Her next visitors were tigers. The Bronx Zoo had never been able to rear a tiger born in captivity, and the general curator, Lee S. Crandall, asked Mrs. Martini to take a litter of three. Her husband brought them home one at a time—a day apart—two males and a female. She named them after cities in the province of Bengal—Raniganj, Rajpur and Dacca. Rajpur, the last to arrive, was so emaciated, weak and cold that he was placed on an electric heating pad. It took several hours of concentrated effort before Mrs. Martini could persuade him to take nourishment.

While she worked with Rajpur, the other two cried like human babies. Before the cubs were returned to the Zoo—after three months—they had the run of the apartment. The New York Zoological Society photographed them from their infancy to their maturity. Newsreels of Mrs. Martini and the three cubs at play were later shown.

A nursery at the Zoo became Mrs. Martini's ambition when the cubs left her apartment, and she discovered a large storeroom at one end of the Lion House that could be converted. The pink ceiling and soft blue walls of the Zoo Nursery were done by Mrs. Martini and she supplied much of the early equipment, which included a stove, white furniture, curtains for the windows, and toys. Baby scales, play pens and a large refrigerator were added later. She was put on the payroll in August 1944—the first and only woman keeper in the Bronz Zoo.

Her next charges were Ranee, a female baby tiger, two baby lionesses—Limpopo and Zambesi—, and Bagheera, a sickly baby black leopard, all of whom she cared for in her apartment. Bagheera remained after the others left and became her special pet. After he returned to the Zoo, she brought him home every night until he became so big and fierce looking that the neighbors complained. Mrs. Martini contended that he was "completely reliable."

The lion, tiger and leopard babies were not her only charges. She was soon caring for gorillas and marmosets, baby deer and antelope, squirrels and even frail skunks. *Pathfinder* (January 26, 1949) reported that preparing meals, feeding, keeping progress charts and weighing the animals were included in the nursery keeper's duties.

"Bringing Up Mambo" by Edmund Burke (*Collier's*, November 17, 1951) featured the baby gorilla imported from Central Africa in May 1951, to replace Makoko who was drowned in the moat of his play yard. Mambo enjoyed being pampered so much that he often went into a tantrum until Mrs. Martini picked him up. His toys included a rattle, a teddy bear and a large ball.

In 1948, Mrs. Martini became a foster grandmother to three baby tigers, children of Dacca and Rajpur. Dacca nursed her own brood and seemed happy over the event. It was not until Dacca had her seventh litter in March 1954, that one of her cubs needed special care. The cub was called Fer—Hindustani for tiger. In the north bay of the Lion House, for an hour each day of the July 4th holiday week-end, Mrs. Martini exhibited and publicly fed Fer along with Señor Lopez, Lolita and Rosita—the first jaguar cubs ever raised by the Bronx Zoo. The New York *Times* (July 2, 1954) reported that Fer was eight weeks old, but less well co-ordinated than the twelve-week-old jaguars, who occasionally "bashed him about" in a friendly spirit.

Fer was still in the Nursery at three months old and hadn't been weaned from the bottle. Mrs. Martini told Joy Miller (Washington *Post and Times Herald,* November 18, 1954) that he was more spoiled than any of the twenty-seven tigers she had raised. That Fer's parents remembered their foster mother was revealed when the 600-pound Bengal tigers flung themselves on the floor, rolled, purred and begged to be petted when Mrs. Martini approached their cage in the Lion House.

Bagheera, the black leopard, "streaked to the bars" and clutched her around the neck, as "the crowd gasped and fell back," then patted her cheeks with "desperate affection." She has often taken him for a walk on a leash, before she leaves the Zoo at night. "I know what they say about black leopards," Mrs. Martini once commented. "All I know anything about is Bagheera, whom I raised. But it must be the mother that teaches them to be ferocious—for their own protection. All Bagheera knows—and my lions and tigers, too—is the kitchen sink, pots and pans, and baby nursing bottles. And you see how they are."

Mrs. Martini, whose everyday wear is overalls and crepe-soled shoes, is four feet ten inches tall and weighs 100 pounds. She has brown hair and brown eyes. Before her husband became a keeper at the Zoo, she often went skiing and ice-skating. Charles Dickens is her favorite author, but since young animals became her major interest, she reads only books that help in her work. She became a citizen of the United States in 1940. Her religion is Roman Catholic. She looks upon her work generally as "fun," and has often said: "Every day is just like Christmas. Anything can happen."

References

Ladies Home J 70:36+ Jl '53 pors
Martini, H. My Zoo Family (1955)
Who's Who in America (Sup. O '44)

MATISSE, HENRI (EMILE BENOIT) Dec. 31, 1869-Nov. 3, 1954 One of the most famous 20th century French artists; leader of the "Fauves" art movement which began in 1905; won international fame as a colorist, decorative easel and mural painter, sculptor and book illustrator; his paintings hang in leading art museums and have been widely reproduced; foremost art critics note that through the years Matisse grew in stature, and never left his explorations, age only increased his daring and brilliance as a colorist; at eighty-three he donated 100 of his works—valued at up to $14,000,000—to his home town of Le Cateau; noted for his "odalisques"; the Philadelphia Museum of Art presented a retrospective show of his work (1948) and the Museum of Modern Art (1951); he designed and decorated a Dominican chapel at Vence, France. See *Current Biography* (June) 1953.

Obituary

N Y Times p 1+ N 5 '54

MATSKEVICH, VLADIMIR V(LADIMIROVICH) (mät'skĕ-vyĭch) 1910- U.S.S.R. government official; agronomist

Address: b. U.S.S.R. Ministry of Agriculture, Moscow, U.S.S.R.

The leader of the twelve-member delegation of U.S.S.R. agricultural officials who toured the United States and Canada during the summer of 1955 to study farming in those countries was Vladimir V. Matskevich, First Deputy Minister of Agriculture of the U.S.S.R. He was given much of the credit for the good impression made by the delegation. James K. Sparkman, the correspondent of the *Christian Science Monitor* (July 19, 1955) who covered their tour, commented on Matskevich's "ability both to avoid embarrassing situations, to present his own best case, and most of all, to keep tempers in check." The New York *Times* noted that the Russian officials were impressed with the increase in mechanization achieved on U. S. farms in the last fifteen years.

On March 1, 1955 Vladimir Matskevich became the senior official in the Soviet agricultural ministry. (At that time Ivan A. Benediktov was shifted from Minister of Agriculture to Minister of State Farms and no successor was named.) Later, on October 17, 1955, Matskevich was promoted to the post of Minister of Agriculture. For many years he has been a close associate of Nikita S. Khrushchev, First Secretary of the Communist party of the U.S.S.R.

Vladimir Vladimirovich Matskevich is a Ukrainian by birth and an agronomist by profession. He was born in 1910. For nine years he was the manager of a farm of 300 head of cattle, and then for six years before World War II was the director of the Zoo Technical Institute in Kharkov in the Ukraine. In 1946 he was named People's Commissar of Livestock in the Ukrainian republic, and in February 1947, he became the republic's Minister of Agriculture. At that time Khrushchev was the chairman of the Ukrainian republic's Council of Ministers.

Eventually Matskevich became the First Deputy Chairman of the Ukrainian Council of Ministers. However, he was relieved of this post without explanation in April 1952, at a time when the party leadership in the Ukraine was under severe criticism for its backwardness in spring planting and failure to eliminate "bourgeois nationalism."

In his present post as First Deputy Minister of Agriculture, Matskevich controls the 84,000 collective farms (*kolhoz*) of the Soviet Union. Most of the land of the collective is owned by the state and the heavy machinery is rented

Wide World
VLADIMIR V. MATSKEVICH

from machine tractor stations and serviced by workers of the tractor stations. However, on the collective, each member owns his own home and a small plot ranging in size from a half to one and a half acre. More than half of the Soviet Union's milk, fruit, and vegetables are produced on these privately-owned plots.

He is also in charge of the 5,000 state farms (where everything is owned by the state and the farm worker receives a wage), 10,000 machine tractor stations, the education of agronomists and zootechnicians, rural electrification, pest control and veterinary services, forest preserves, and land allocation.

Several months after Stalin's death Khrushchev became the First Secretary of the Communist party of the Soviet Union, and gradually brought about a shift in emphasis from the program of Georgi M. Malenkov to raise the production of consumer goods to a program concentrating on agricultural production. On January 25, 1955, Krushchev called for an eight-fold increase of corn production and the doubling of hog production. His objective was to spur meat supplies by concentrated growing of corn as feed, and he pointed to the corn-hog economy of Iowa as an example of what was needed. (On February 8, 1955 Malenkov resigned as Premier ostensibly because he had failed to increase consumer goods and was succeeded by Nikolai A. Bulganin, see *C.B.*, February 1955.)

The Des Moines (Iowa) *Register* immediately proposed in an editorial that the Soviet Union send a delegation to Iowa to study how a combination of corn and hogs had made it the second wealthiest farm state in the United States. Moscow welcomed the idea, and at length the U.S. Government agreed to the exchange of delegations.

A Soviet delegation was named that included Matskevich, a deputy chairman of the State Planning Commission, a deputy chairman of the Ukrainian Council of Ministers, a Deputy Minister of the Automobile, Tractor and Farm Machinery Ministry, a deputy Minister of State Farms of the Russian Soviet Federated Socialist Republic, as well as scientists and farm managers.

The members of the delegation arrived in New York by air on July 16, and the next day flew on to Des Moines, where they received a cheering welcome from 2,500 Iowans, who wondered if the delegation would be more interested in farming or propaganda. But as soon as they arrived they plunged into an exhaustive exploration of America's farm system.

During the next five weeks the Soviet group traveled 12,000 miles back and forth across the country by airplane and by chartered air-conditioned buses. They visited farms, universities, research stations, packing plants and farm implement factories. They clambered over farm machinery, trudged through fields, and sifted the rich soil with their fingers. Americans were impressed with their earnest, intelligent questions and their ready wit and fellowship.

Matskevich, a stocky man with twinkling eyes and a wide smile, charmed audiences and farm hosts alike. In Fort Worth, Texas he told an audience: "Texans are very sly people who don't brag nearly as much as they could." Members of the delegation attended Presbyterian church services in Iowa, played golf (an unknown game in Russia), sampled ice cream sundaes, and shopped. All along the way they passed out small green and gold medals from the All-Union Agricultural Exposition in Moscow and roses for the ladies. In California they made a pilgrimage to the grave of Luther Burbank, in Springfield, Illinois they visited the tomb of Abraham Lincoln, and they laid a wreath on the tomb of George Washington at Mount Vernon, Virginia.

The tour concluded in Washington, D.C. with a reception at the Soviet Embassy, a luncheon with Secretary of Agriculture Ezra Taft Benson, and an address by Matskevich at the National Press Club. In his Press Club talk Matskevich frankly admitted that American farm methods were more economical than Soviet, particularly in the use of labor. As a result of what had been learned on the tour, he said it was hoped the Soviet Union could improve the production of hybrid feed corn, expand production of hybrid poultry and hogs, increase the mechanization of small-scale processes, improve cattle feeding methods, and introduce better forage grasses, attempt to increase the efficiency of labor, and reorganize the production of processing hogs, beef and dairy products along assembly line techniques.

Matskevich had doubts as to the economic future of the 200 to 300-acre family farms in this country, and contended that the road to greater efficiency lay through larger units and greater specialization—"the transplanting of the Ford factory technique to the field" (New York *Times,* August 25, 1955). The Soviet official also called for increased trade and exchange of information between the United States and the Soviet Union.

"Perhaps the single factor," Harrison Salisbury wrote, "which time and time again the Russians have questioned and analyzed, is the way in which the one-man farm is operated by a single farmer with his labor-saving equipment" (New York *Times,* August 9, 1955). One of the Soviet delegates exclaimed: "By you one man—by us a hundred."

The Soviet Embassy requested that the *Voice of America* broadcast a speech by Matskevich to the Soviet Union. Although this request was granted, the broadcast was jammed, as usual, by the Russians. However, its text was printed in Soviet newspapers and broadcast throughout the U.S.S.R. on the Soviet radio. From a Texas ranch the group purchased for shipment to the U.S.S.R. sixty head of Santa Gertrudis cattle, a unique breed, and three Herefords. On August 25 the delegation flew to Canada for a 4,000-mile, week-and-a-half tour. From the beginning it was marred by the demonstrations of anti-Communist *émigrés.*

Matskevich, who shaves his head and is known for his good sense of humor, is married, and commented during the tour that his wife asked him to bring back information on American etiquette. His hobby is hunting and he enjoys performances of the ballet. In the Council of the Union of the Supreme Soviet of the U.S.S.R., he sits as a deputy from Novo-Ukrainka in the Kirovograd region of the Ukrainian republic.

References

N Y Times p14 Ag 25 '55
Time 66:13 S 5 '55

MAXIMOS, DEMETRIOS July 6, 1873-Oct. 15, 1955 Former Premier of Greece; head of Bank of Greece (1914-1923); member of Populist (Royalist) party; went into voluntary exile twice with King Constantine; Minister of Foreign Affairs (1933-1934); from January to August 1947 was Premier of a coalition government representing seven parties; won popular support when the U. S. Congress voted $300,000,000 for Greek aid.

See *Current Biography* (Mar.) 1948.

Obituary

N Y Times p27 O 17 '55

MAYS, WILLIE May 6, 1931- Baseball player

Address: b. c/o New York National League Baseball Club, 100 W. 42d St., New York 36

Voted by the Baseball Writers Association the Most Valuable Player in the National League during the 1954 season, centerfielder Willie Mays of the New York Giants had recorded the best batting average (.345) in either of the major leagues during the year, had scored forty-one home runs, had driven in 110 runs, and had fielded brilliantly. With Manager Leo Durocher and Pitcher Johnny Antonelli, Mays is generally accorded the major credit for bringing the Giants in 1954 their second league pennant since 1937 and their first world championship since 1933.

Mays had joined the Giants in May 1951; he was in the Army during most of 1952 and all of the 1953 baseball season; 1954 was his first full playing year in the major leagues. He is now one of the most popular and most publicized of the major league baseball stars. The popular song "Say Hey, Willie" was written about him by collaborators Dick Kleiner and Jane Douglas; numerous books (including his autobiography *Born to Play Ball,* Putnam, 1955) and articles have been published about his life and activities. The Negro centerfielder's "bread basket" catch is famous. His nicknames include "Buckduck," "Willie the Wallop," and "Amazing Mays."

Willie Howard Mays was born to William Howard and Ann Mays at Fairfield, Alabama, a suburb of Birmingham, Alabama on May 6, 1931. His grandfather Walter Mays had pitched for Negro amateur teams and his father was an outfielder with the Birmingham Black Barons of the Negro National League and was known as "Kitty Cat" because of his lithe grace; he also played with the amateur team of the steel mill at Fairfield where he was employed as a plumber's assistant. By the time Willie was three, "father and son were playing catch," stated *Time* (July 26, 1954).

The elder Mays and his wife were divorced when Willie was still a small child. He has two half brothers and eight half sisters, the children of his mother and her second husband, Frank McMorris. Willie's mother died in 1953 and his beloved aunt, Sarah Mays, who reared him at Fairfield after the separation of his parents, died in 1954.

At the Fairfield Industrial High School, where Willie took a special course in cleaning and pressing, there was no baseball team, but he played football and basketball. As a baseball player, Willie was good enough when he was fourteen years old to play with steel-mill clubs and independent semi-professionals, and when he was sixteen, his father "called up his old friend, Lorenzo ("Piper") Davis, manager of the Black Barons, and got the boy a tryout" (*Time*).

On July 4, 1948 Willie made his debut as a professional ball player, having been "taken on" by the Barons as a utility outfielder. "Mays stepped into a double-header, played both center field and left, hit two for four in the first game and one for three in the second," wrote Gilbert Millstein (New York *Times Magazine,* July 11, 1954). A few days later Willie was made the Barons' regular centerfielder.

During the school year, Willie played baseball only on Sundays and in the Birmingham area; during summer vacations he joined the Black Barons "on the road." In his two years under Manager "Piper" Davis he developed a good batting eye, hitting over .310. The Barons' second baseman, Willie has stated, helped him with his throwing technique and gave him some pointers on how to catch a ball.

At about this time, "A couple of hustling Giant scouts, Ed Montague and Bill Harris, came to Birmingham to take a look at the Barons' first baseman," wrote *Time* magazine.

WILLIE MAYS

"That night Montague telephoned New York. 'That first baseman won't do,' he reported. 'But I saw a young kid of an outfielder that I can't believe. . . . You've got to get this boy.' " The New York National League Club is said to have given the Black Barons $10,000 for Willie, while after his graduation from high school on June 20, 1950, the boy himself was offered $5,000 as a personal bonus.

Assigned by the Giants to their Class B Inter-State League "farm" team at Trenton, New Jersey, Willie played center field in eighty-one games during the balance of the 1950 baseball season and made a .353 batting average. Rewarded with promotion to the Giant-owned Minneapolis (Minnesota) Millers of the Triple A American Association, Mays was soon "working overtime" on hitting. "He collected pictures of his favorite ballplayer, Joe DiMaggio," *Time* noted. "He studied Joe's stance in the batter's box, patterned his swing after the Yankee Clipper's."

The result was that in the thirty-five games he played for Minneapolis in 1951, he amassed a high .477 batting average. He hit eight home runs. Leo Durocher, the Giants' manager, whose team in the first six weeks of the 1951 season lost eleven games in a row, soon summoned Willie to give the Giants what was described as "some sorely needed punch at the plate."

In his major league debut against the Phillies at Shibe Park, Philadelphia on May 25, 1951, the "preposterous rookie outfielder" failed to make a hit in five times at bat. During his first twenty-six times at the plate, he made only one hit, a home run at the Polo Grounds in New York. Despite his tendency to go after "bad" balls and the humiliation of "fanning" three consecutive times in one June game, he developed a good batting streak which persisted through August. A subsequent "slump" cut his season's batting average to .274, but he scored twenty home runs. He batted in sixty-eight runs and made nine errors.

His fielding was described as "phenomenal." *Time* magazine remarked: "Once, when he dove out from under his cap (Mays frequently loses his cap) to catch a sinking line drive, he reached back, caught his cap in one hand and the ball in the other." His cheery greeting of "Say, hey!," his hustle and his zest, made for a "personal bonfire" which "soon ignited all the Giants," with the result that the team went from a standing thirteen and a half games out of the lead on August 11 to a tie with Brooklyn for first place on the last day of the regular season, and to the winning of the National League pennant in the play-off with the Dodgers.

In the six ensuing World Series games against the New York Yankees of the American League, Mays hit four singles in twenty-two times at bat. The Giants lost the World Series. Mays was named the National League's 1951 rookie of the year by the Baseball Writers Association of America.

Since the winning of the 1951 National League pennant, "there has been a disposition around the club to believe that the Giants' fortunes are somehow bound up not only with Mays' technical ability but with his presence" (Gilbert Millstein). The Negro centerfielder's batting average actually dropped to .236 in the thirty-four games he played in 1952 before his induction into the Army in May; yet at that time the Giants were in first place in the National League race by two and a half games. "He hadn't been gone ten days," a Giants' official has been quoted as saying, "and we were in second place and that's where we finished the season." In 1953 the Giants were in fifth place in their league.

Willie spent almost two years in the Army at Fort Eustis, Virginia, where he was assigned to the physical training department. They had a baseball club there and he played about 180 games. After Willie was honorably discharged in March 1954, he rejoined the Giants and went to Arizona for spring conditioning. "When Mays showed up at the Giants' Phoenix base," *Newsweek* (April 5, 1954) stated, "a front-office official gloated: 'There's the pennant.' " That first day, Willie hit a home run and made several spectacular field plays.

The Giants won the National League pennant and World Series against the Cleveland (American League) Indians in four straight games. During the games Willie made four hits (one for two bases) in fourteen times at bat for an average of .286 and made ten "put-outs" in the course of errorless fielding. His back-to-the-plate catch of a 450-foot line drive by Vic Wertz is credited with having saved the first game of the series for the Giants (*Christian Science Monitor,* December 21, 1954).

In October 1954 Willie was named player of the year in his League by *Sporting News.* In December he was voted in the Associated Press poll of sportswriters and sportscasters as the male athlete of the year. In addition, Willie was the recipient of the 1954 B'nai B'rith sports award and of a diamond-studded belt valued at $10,000, presented to him as the professional athlete of the year by Ray and Allan Hickok in memory of their father.

In the fall of 1954, with the consent of the Giants' management, Mays joined the Santurce baseball club of the Puerto Rico Winter League. Following what *Time* (January 24, 1955) characterized as a "batting-practice scuffle" with his fellow Giant on that team, the pitcher Ruben Gomez, Willie stated that he would not again engage in winter competition. The Santurce Club gained the season's championship; Willie had the highest batting average (.395) within the league.

Willie Mays weighs about 175 pounds and is five feet eleven inches tall. *Time* (July 26, 1954) speaks of his playing "baseball with a boy's glee, a pro's sureness and a champion's flair." Until February 1955, when he moved to Englewood, New Jersey, Mays boarded, during the Giants' "homestands," in the apartment of Mrs. Anne Goosby in Harlem, where he often joined neighborhood children playing ball in the streets. Mays is a hearty eater, a collector of phonograph records and an extremely tidy dresser, with a leaning towards "monogrammed shirts, but very few ties" (*Time*). He is unmarried.

Gilbert Millstein has remarked on Willie's occasional excursions into mild practical joking, his "high-pitched laugh," his liking for comic books and Western films, his ability to sleep under any conditions, and his "great natural dignity." About one-third of his earnings is said to go to the support of his half brothers and half sisters. His salary from the Giants—believed to be around $17,500 a year—is augmented by income from radio and television appearances and merchandise endorsements.

But Willie Mays, considered a "natural-born ballplayer" by many of his fans, has written, "I'd play for nothing—I'd play ball even if they charged me."

References

N Y Times Mag p16+ Jl 11 '54 pors
Newsweek 38:63+ S 10 '51 pors; 44:74+ Jl 19 '54 pors
This Week p16+ S 12 '54 pors
Time 64:46+ Jl 26 '54 pors
Baseball Register (1954)
Mays, W. (as told to Einstein, C.) Born to Play Ball (1955)
Smith, K. The Willie Mays Story (1954)

MAZA (FERNÁNDEZ), JOSÉ Oct. 13, 1889- United Nations representative from Chile

Address: b. Ahumada 236, Santiago, Chile; United Nations, New York 17; h. Augustinas, 1291, Santiago, Chile

The system of geographical rotation practiced by the United Nations in selecting a diplomat each year to preside over the General Assembly gave, by general agreement, for 1955-1956 the office to a representative from Latin America. The delegates voted specifically for José Maza of Chile. He succeeded Eelco van Kleffens of the Netherlands to the office on

United Nations
JOSÉ MAZA

September 20, 1955. Maza was elected unanimously on the first ballot.

Señor Maza has headed the Chilean delegation at four sessions of the General Assembly. In Chile he has served as National Deputy and Senator for over thirty years, and has been his nation's Ambassador to several Latin American countries. He was co-author of Chile's Constitution drafted in 1925, and he helped to write laws on women's status.

As Chile's representative at the United Nations Conference on International Organization at San Francisco in 1945, he was a signer of the United Nations Charter. In June 1955 he was again in San Francisco as chairman of the Chilean delegation at the organization's tenth anniversary celebration. His writings include works on the United Nations and on political theory and he has had a special interest in the United Nations role in world economic development.

José Maza Fernández was born in Los Ángeles, Chile, on October 13, 1889, the son of Armando Maza and Josefina Fernández de Maza, and spent his boyhood in the city of Santiago. He attended the Liceo de Aplicación there and majored in literary subjects. During his school years he became a leader in students' organizations. He was graduated in 1908 and entered the Universidad de Chile in Santiago where he studied law and continued as a leader in student activities. He received the LL.B. degree in 1913.

His law career began in 1914 when he obtained a post as secretary to the court in Antofagasta, Chile. Political issues that embraced modern democratic ideals attracted him and he joined the Liberal party. In 1919, he was elected president of the Centro Liberal and a year later became the party's candidate for a seat in the National Chamber of Deputies. He was elected a National Deputy in 1921 and

MAZA, JOSÉ—*Continued*

the following year represented the Chamber of Deputies at the Brazilian Centenary celebration. In 1923 he was a delegate to the Red Cross Congress held in Buenos Aires, Argentina.

The "congressional dictatorship" which had blocked executive authority in Chile since 1891 was overthrown in 1925 and Maza was among the members of the Liberal Alliance who sought political and social reforms under President Arturo Alessandri, who took part in writing the new Constitution. He became Prime Minister and Minister of the Interior in 1924, and through these offices was instrumental in putting into effect decentralization of the national government, greater autonomy for the provinces and the separation of church and state. During the reorganization period he was elected national Senator from Santiago (1925), a post which he has held intermittently for twenty-six years. In 1936 and 1937 he was president of the Senate.

In order to make necessary adjustments in the Justice and Education Departments during government reorganization, Maza became Attorney General and Minister of Public Education in 1925. Because of his achievements in liberalizing the law, he was selected to attend the International Parliamentary Congress at Versailles, France in 1928 as Chile's senior representative.

Maza's diplomatic posts included the position of Ambassador to Uruguay and to Brazil in 1943 and Ambassador to the Dominican Republic, Haiti, Panama and Peru in 1944 and 1945. At San Francisco in 1945 he was the Chilean signatory to the United Nations Charter. Since then he has served as chairman of the Chilean Delegation at four sessions of the General Assembly.

In an article, "Spectacle of Social, Economic Injustice," (*United Nations Bulletin,* December 1, 1951) Maza voiced the opinion that small nations, because they are not responsible for direct action, can express their views objectively and thus come closer than great powers to interpreting the view of the man in the street. The League of Nations, in his opinion, was destroyed by new imperialisms which replaced those which the democracies had fought to destroy in World War I.

In connection with the work of the United Nations, Maza has deplored the slowness of progress in the economic field, particularly in the advancement of underdeveloped areas (*United Nations Bulletin,* October 1, 1953). He declared that too much needed economic improvement had been sacrificed in the interests of political gains, and unless success could be achieved in the economic field, the little that had been gained in other fields would be lost.

During a 1954 debate in the General Assembly, Maza complained that the underdeveloped nations had received "a generous amount of advice," and had been reminded of the "boundless importance of private enterprise and of the danger of the economic intervention of the state" (New York *Post,* October 3, 1954). He observed that "Latin American private enterprise . . . has no access to the international capital market." The international agencies in the field, he added, showed "a striking disproportion . . . between what is recommended to be done and what is actually being done."

In addition to his writings on the United Nations, Maza has produced many articles and studies, from the legal point of view, which were related to his work on the Chilean Constitution. He has also written a study on the U.N. Charter. "World public opinion," Maza has written, in reflection of his devotion to the United Nations, "wants nothing more than a feeling of security" (*U.N. Bulletin,* December 1, 1953).

The likelihood that Maza would be elected president of the United Nations General Assembly in September 1955 was assured as early as June, according to the New York *Times* (June 21, 1955), when many Latin-American delegates, as well as Indian, Turkish and Yugoslav representatives, had pledged to vote for him. Prime Minister Nehru was reported to be among those favoring him for the position.

On receiving the gavel from Dr. van Kleffens (see *C.B.,* 1947) on September 20, 1955, Maza told reporters: The Assembly was "opening in a different atmosphere." He attributed this to "the important conferences of statesmen at the highest level," and to "certain attitudes designed to relieve or eliminate sources of dissension and suspicion" (New York *Herald Tribune,* September 21, 1955).

José Maza Fernández was married to Raquel Lyon Vial in 1933. They have one daughter and one son, José Maza Lyon. Señor Maza is a Roman Catholic, a member of the Liberal party and a member of the Club de la Union and of the Club Liberal, both of Santiago. He is six feet one inch tall, weighs 180 pounds and has blue eyes and gray hair. "The Maza temperament," it has been said, ". . . is to try to be the conciliator, the arbitrator, the good will ambassador." Those who have known him during his long career as a Chilean Senator report that his interests have always been on the scholarly side.

References

N Y Times p7 Je 21 '55 por; p10 S 21 '55
N Y World-Telegram p7 S 16 '55
U N Bul 3:425 S 30 '47
International Who's Who, 1954
Who's Who in Latin America (1947)
World Biography (1954)

MERMAN, ETHEL Jan. 16, 1909- Singer; actress

Address: h. Cherry Hills, Denver, Colo.

NOTE: This biography supersedes the article which appeared in *Current Biography* in 1941.

Among Broadway's brightest luminaries is Ethel Merman, whose dynamic singing of "I Got Rhythm" in the musical comedy *Girl Crazy,* in 1930, so impressed audiences that she became a star overnight. Spectacular triumphs in twelve other musical comedies followed, including *Anything Goes, Panama Hattie, Annie Get*

Your Gun, and *Call Me Madam*. Described as "a doll from Astoria with a trumpet in her throat," Miss Merman has now said "good-bye" to the Broadway theatre and henceforth will appear in motion pictures and on television in order that she may live in Denver with her husband and children.

She has appeared in many motion pictures, including Irving Berlin's *There's No Business Like Show Business*, released in December 1954 by Twentieth Century-Fox Film Corporation. She appeared in March 1955 on the *Colgate Comedy Hour* television production of *Anything Goes*.

Her autobiography "as sung to Pete Martin," which ran serially in the *Saturday Evening Post* during February and March 1955 under the title, "That's the Kind of Dame I Am," was published by Doubleday & Company in June as *Who Could Ask For Anything More?*

Reviewing Miss Merman's television performance in *Panama Hattie*, performed in November 1954 on the Columbia Broadcasting System, Harriet Van Horne commented in the New York *World-Telegram and Sun*, November 11, 1954: "With her rowdy good spirits and her big, jubilant voice, Miss Merman was magnificent. . . . Her vitality lights up the screen."

Ethel Merman was born Ethel Agnes Zimmermann in Astoria, Long Island, New York on January 16, 1909, the daughter of Edward and Agnes Zimmermann. As a child she displayed vocal talents, sang in amateur shows. Ethel took the four-year commercial course at William Cullen Bryant High School in Long Island City, and after she was graduated she worked as a stenographer for the Boyce-ite Company on Queens Boulevard and later for the B. K. Vacuum Booster Brake Company in Long Island.

"In my teens," Miss Merman recalled in her autobiography (*Saturday Evening Post*, February 12-March 26, 1955), "when I was a secretary I was very happy to be a secretary. My mother and father are two of the happiest people I've ever known. Our family life is warm and friendly. . . . Pop always kept us in comfort. So where's the struggle? I didn't wear out a single shoe on sidewalks [going] from one casting office to another. Even when I was a tot I hoped to go on the stage some day and amount to something. I had a voice . . . I never had to study singing."

She persuaded her employer, Caleb Bragg, who knew many celebrities in the entertainment world, to give her a letter of introduction to his friend George White, theatrical producer. When she took the letter to White, he offered her a job in the chorus line of the *Scandals*, but Ethel turned it down. She wanted to sing. Returning to her typewriter, she supplemented her income by obtaining singing engagements after working hours, wherever an opportunity was available—at weddings, lodge meetings, or clambakes.

During a two-week engagement at Little Russia, a café on Fifty-seventh Street, Ethel caught the attention of theatrical agent Lou Irwin, with whom she signed a nine-year contract. He arranged an audition for her with Archie Mayo, a Warner Brothers' director at their Eastern studios. The result was a six-month contract for Ethel at $125 a week; upon achieving this she quit her office job. However, her only picture assignment was to wear a leopard skin in a jungle "short" at the Warner Avenue J studio in Brooklyn.

ETHEL MERMAN

Restless over her lack of opportunity to sing, Ethel requested permission to take outside singing jobs. In November 1929 she joined the team of Lou Clayton, Eddie Jackson and Jimmy Durante, to appear at Les Ambassadeurs. She next teamed with a piano player, Al Siegel, in vaudeville. "He gave me pointers on blues singing," she recalls. She shortened her name Zimmermann to Merman and sang in Long Island night clubs.

In the summer of 1930 theatrical producer Vinton Freedley heard her sing at the Paramount Theatre in Brooklyn and arranged for George Gershwin to hear her. She was hired for *Girl Crazy*, with music by George Gershwin and starring Ginger Rogers. During rehearsals Miss Merman also sang at the Palace Theatre in New York. When *Girl Crazy* opened at the Alvin Theatre in New York on October 14, 1930, Ethel Merman in Broadway parlance, "tied the show into a knot" by her rendition of "I Got Rhythm."

"As I went into the second chorus," she recalled, "I held a high C note for sixteen bars . . . the audience applauded through the whole chorus and I did several encores. . . . I was nobody before the show opened, and the next day everybody on Broadway knew about me." Gershwin advised her: "Don't ever let anybody give you a singing lesson. It'll ruin you." *Girl Crazy* ran for 272 performances. Miss Merman also sang after the show at the Central Park Casino.

(Continued next page)

MERMAN, ETHEL—*Continued*

Miss Merman's next stage performance was in 1932 in George White's *Scandals,* where she popularized such songs as "Life Is Just a Bowl of Cherries." The show ran for seven months. After a summer bill at the Palace Theatre, she appeared in the musical comedy *Take a Chance* by Laurence Schwab and Buddy De Sylva, which opened in November 1932. In his New York *Times* column Brooks Atkinson observed, "One of the most roistering items in the show is [Miss Merman's] half-burlesque, half-jubilee singing of the levee ballad, 'Eadie Was a Lady.'" The lyrics were by Roger Edens, now an M-G-M producer of musical shows, who still composes arrangements for her TV shows.

Paramount Pictures brought Ethel Merman to Hollywood in 1934 as a featured player in her first full-length picture, *We're Not Dressing,* starring Bing Crosby. Richard Watts, Jr., in the New York *Post* commented that she "hasn't enough opportunities for her singing, but she proves again that she is an exciting comedienne." For Samuel Goldwyn Productions Miss Merman appeared in the Eddie Cantor starring vehicle, *Kid Millions.*

Recalled to Broadway, Miss Merman continued her stage success in the musical comedy *Anything Goes* (1934), singing music and lyrics composed by Cole Porter. She was co-starred with William Gaxton and Victor Moore. The show included such hit tunes as "You're the Top," "I Get a Kick Out of You," and "Blow, Gabriel, Blow." In May 1935 Ethel Merman made her radio debut in her own weekly program broadcast over station WABC.

Miss Merman made several more motion pictures, the cinema version of *Anything Goes, The Big Broadcast* and *Strike Me Pink.* After a return to Broadway in the stage musical *Red, Hot and Blue,* she resumed her picture work with the films *Happy Landing, Alexander's Ragtime Band,* and *Straight, Place, and Show.* The theatre again commanded Miss Merman's career, offering a succession of stage musicals. "I love working with an audience," said Miss Merman, "and getting the response it gives." In 1939 Miss Merman co-starred with Jimmy Durante in the short-lived *Stars In Your Eyes.*

She opened in a new musical comedy *Du Barry Was A Lady* in December 1939, co-starred with Bert Lahr. In *Panama Hattie,* which opened in New York's 46th Street Theatre on October 30, 1940, Ethel Merman starred alone. This musical ran for 501 performances.

Miss Merman's next starring vehicles were *Something For the Boys* (1943) and *Annie Get Your Gun* (1946), which opened with an advance sale of $150,000. *Variety* praised her portrayal of the fabulous lady marksman Annie Oakley. Ward Morehouse in the New York *Sun* predicted that *Annie Get Your Gun* would be playing at the Imperial "until the exuberant Miss Merman gets tired of lifting her squirrel rifle to her shoulder." It ran for 1,147 performances.

When Howard Lindsay and Russel Crouse decided to write a musical play about Perle Mesta, U.S. Minister to Luxemburg, and asked Miss Merman to play the leading role, she telephoned to Madam Mesta, who said that she was charmed and couldn't think of anybody she'd rather have portraying her than Ethel Merman (Maurice Zolotow, *No People Like Show People*). Among the songs in *Call Me Madam* which became very popular was "The Hostess with the Mostes' on the Ball." The night she was invited to a dinner party to meet Mrs. Mesta she arrived very late because her son had come down with the measles. The first words Miss Merman said to Madam Mesta were, "Say, Perle, have you ever had the measles?" They became good friends.

Call Me Madam had a record-breaking advance sale of $1,000,000, when it opened at the Imperial Theatre on October 12, 1950. In the screen version of *Call Me Madam,* released in 1953, Miss Merman re-enacted her role of the ambassadress of a mythical country called Lichtenburg who "brushes aside rules like cobwebs."

On NBC's radio program *The Big Show* in 1950 Miss Merman made a guest appearance, parrying repartee with mistress of ceremonies Tallulah Bankhead. Other programs in which Miss Merman appeared include the Ford Motor Company's mammoth fiftieth anniversary television show on June 16, 1953, which, Jack Gould of the New York *Times* reported, "made national video darlings of Ethel Merman and Mary Martin." (Decca made a recording of their songs.)

In March 1953 Miss Merman married Robert F. Six, president of Continental Airlines. Her first marriage was in 1940 to Hollywood actors' agent William B. Smith, from whom she was divorced in 1941. She then married Robert D. Levitt, Hearst Publications executive, now publisher of the *American Weekly.* They have two children: Ethel, twelve, and Robert, nine. She and Levitt were divorced in 1952.

Miss Merman is five feet six inches tall and weighs 125 pounds. Her hair, black and luxuriant, is usually coiffured in curls piled high over her forehead. Her eyes are brown with a "saucer-like roundness" which conveys the "quixotic combination of a childlike and yet knowing expression" that delights audiences. She dresses with "elegant simplicity." When in New York Miss Merman maintained a duplex apartment on Central Park West with a terrace extending nearly a quarter of an acre and containing a waterfall and two wading pools. In recent years Miss Merman has become an enthusiastic art collector with a preference for the French impressionists; in her private gallery are Renoirs, Van Goghs, Picassos, and Dufys. Her favorite reading is "pulp stuff." She likes radio murder mysteries. She takes notes in shorthand at business conferences and types her own letters.

Selected References

Sat Eve Post 227:17+ F 12; 20+ F 19; 22+ F 26; 32+ Mr 5; 30+ Mr 12; 30+ Mr 19; 36+ Mr 26 '55 pors
Motion Picture and Television Almanac, 1953-54
Who's Who in America, 1954-55
Zolotow, M. No People Like Show People (1951)

MEYER, JEAN (mā"yâr) June 11, 1914-
French actor and director

Address: c/o Comédie Française, Salle Richelieu, Salle Luxembourg, Paris, France; h. 5, rue Jacques-Dulud, Neuilly-sur-Seine, France.

The Comédie Française, France's national theatre which was established in the seventeenth century by Molière, is making its first American and Canadian tour in the fall of 1955 by arrangement with the government of the French republic. The venerable company is presenting in its repertoire plays by Molière, Beaumarchais, Marivaux and Alfred de Musset. The première production, *Le Bourgeois Gentilhomme* by Molière, was directed by Jean Meyer, one of the company's foremost comedians and directors since 1942.

A former administrator of the Comédie Française, Pierre Aimé Touchard, wrote of Meyer as "living at the Comédie from morning till night, knowing its past and present history admirably, as well documented on administrative problems as on decorative . . . a great reader of manuscripts, possessing an unequalled dramatic, literary and technical culture, and endowed with a faultless memory."

Born in Paris June 11, 1914, Jean Meyer is the son of Leon Louis Meyer and Mathilde (Maguin) Meyer. Jean's initial training in dramatic technique was obtained under the tutorship of the late Louis Jouvet (see *C.B.*, 1949), an actor known to American audiences by his screen roles, and to French by his film and stage performances. Jouvet at that time was professor at the Conservatoire National d'Art Dramatique, where Meyer studied previous to his engagement by the Comédie Française in 1937.

As one of the *pensionnaires,* or apprentices, inscribed on the roles of the French national theater, Meyer found himself assigned to play the Abbé in *Il Ne Faut Jurer de Rien.* His versatility as a comedian, evident in the classic comic roles of valets in Molière, Marivaux, and Beaumarchais plays, was equally so in comedies drawn from the modern repertory. Meyer's comic creations ranged from Figaro, in *Le Mariage de Figaro,* and Géronte in *Le Légataire Universel,* Sganarelle in *Le Médecin Malgré Lui,* Don César de Bazan in *Ruy Blas,* and Navolski in *En Attendant l'Aurore* to outstanding interpretations in *Les Boulingrin, Un Client Sérieux, Les Fiancés du Havre, Le Roi,* and *L'Avare.* "His talent as an actor," declares a press release of the French Information Service, "alternately comic and mordant, caused him to be entrusted with very diverse roles," such as those of the police magistrate Mouzon in *La Robe Rouge,* Protos in Gide's *Les Caves du Vatican,* Sirelli in *Chacun Sa Vérité,* Floch in *Le Commissaire est Bon Enfant,* Vatelin in *Le Dindon,* Scapin in *Les Fourberies de Scapin,* Monsieur Loyal in *Le Tartufe,* Lemendin in *Donogoo,* Covielle in *Le Bourgeois Gentilhomme,* the director in *Six Personnages en Quête d'Auteur,* Bélin in *Monsieur le Trouhadec Saisi par la Débauche,* the Curé Lopez in *Curé Espagnol,* Claudio in *Les Caprices de Marianne,* and Bazile in *Le Barbier de Séville.*

Therese Le Prat

JEAN MEYER

At the annual election of members to the Comédie Française in 1942, Jean Meyer passed from the status of *pensionnaire* of the nationalized troupe to full membership in it, an honor accorded to one or two persons each year. The thirty full members, known as *sociétaires,* are engaged on a twenty-year contractual basis, which gives them a share in the net profits of the troupe and entitles them eventually to retirement and pension benefits.

The great personal successes of Jean Meyer, according to the *Dictionnaire Biographique Français Contemporain,* have not only been in the traditional classic comedy roles of the French repertory, but also in the farces and vaudevilles of Labiche, Courteline, and Feydeau. Pierre Aimé Touchard, in *Six Années de Comédie Française,* his reminiscences of the years he passed as administrator of the theater, estimates that Jean Meyer has directed more productions given there than any other contemporary, except perhaps Gaston Baty. Besides the traditional Molière comedies inevitably produced on the boards of the Salle Luxembourg or of the Salle Richelieu (the two theaters administered by the Comédie Française), Meyer has directed *Un Client Sérieux* (1947), *Les Jocrisses de l'Amour* (1947), *Un Mois à la Campagne* (1947), and *Les Espagnols en Danemark* (1948).

In his memoirs, Touchard has much to say about these productions, of which *Les Jocrisses de l'Amour,* for example, was a fiasco, hissed in the theater and "roasted" by the critics. Touchard recalls, "After the failure of *Les Jocrisses de l'Amour,* whose vaudeville air had seemed excessive, I suggested that Meyer practice on a more dramatic work and proposed that he put on *Un Mois à la Campagne,* in which his acute sense of the dramatic situation

MEYER, JEAN—*Continued*

enabled him to create about Yvonne Gaudeau and Jeanne Moreau a heavy and tense atmosphere, faithful to the spirit of the play. With *Les Espagnols,* he passed into a climate of fantasy, subtle and demanding infinite tact and precision. . . He was as charged with enthusiasm as an explosive, and I have always found him so for each new production: an incomparable, indefatigable animator. . . I liked his mettle, his probity, his passionate love for great works, his respect for talent and his devotion to the Comédie Française. . . It is difficult to imagine how anyone could find a more certain, more loyal and more fervent collaborator."

Subsequently Jean Meyer directed *L'Occasion* (1948), *Monsieur de Pourceaugnac* (1948), and *L'Avare* (1948). At the end of the 1948-1949 season, the last of these three productions was presented to Italian audiences during the Italian tour of the Comédie Française. *Jeanne La Folle,* in which Meyer directed Marie Bell in October 1949, met with little success. His other 1949 production was *Othello,* with sets by Cassandre. In 1950, Meyer was director of *La Robe Rouge* and *Les Caves du Vatican;* and in 1951, of *Le Dindon, Le Bourgeois Gentilhomme,* and *Donogoo.* For the 1952-53 season he directed *Don Juan, Les Fourberies de Scapin,* and *Monsieur le Trouhadec Saisi par la Débauche.* During the subsequent successful seasons Meyer directed *Les Amants Magnifiques* and Molière's *L'Ecole des Maris,* as well as Henry de Montherlant's controversial success, *Port Royal.*

For the first time in the history of the French National Theater, the Comédie Française was sent on an American and Canadian tour in October and November 1955. Seventeen of its actors, and eleven of its technicians were assigned to the overseas tour, in which it was planned to follow as closely as possible the traditional productions of the House of Molière. Traditionally, too, the curtain's rise would be signaled by six knocks, instead of the three used in other theaters.

The Comédie Française company presented its productions in Montreal, Quebec, Ottawa, and Toronto before arriving in New York for the opening in October, 1955 at the Broadway Theatre of Jean Meyer's production of *Le Bourgeois Gentilhomme.* In connection with the company's first visit to New York, the Metropolitan Musem of Art exhibited costumes and paintings selected by the Comédie Française from its collection in Paris, and augmented by the Museum's own paintings and prints.

Meyer was married to Pierette de Kerpezdrou on May 6, 1942; they have two children, Olivier Marie and Jean Baptiste.

Under the terms of his contract with the Comédie Française, Jean Meyer is occasionally free for film engagements. His first screen appearance was in 1941 in *Ne Bougez Plus.* This was followed by his role in *Huit Hommes dans un Château* in 1942, and in 1943, by his roles in *Coups de Feu dans la Nuit, Je Suis avec Toi,* and *Adieu Léonard.* Meyer played in *L'Insaisissable Frédéric* in 1945, and in *La Route du Bagne* and *Capitaine Blomet* in 1947. His 1948 screen appearance was in *Entre Onze Heures et Minuit.* Other motion pictures in which he has appeared are *Clara de Montargis* (1950), *Procès au Vatican* (1951), and *Le Plaisir* (1952).

References

Dictionnaire Biographique Français Contemporain (1954)
Who's Who in France (Paris), 1953-54

MEYNER, ROBERT B(AUMLE) (mīn'ẽr) July 3, 1908- Governor of New Jersey; lawyer

Address: b. State House, Trenton, N.J.; h. 372 Lincoln St., Phillipsburg, N.J.

The voters of New Jersey elected Robert B. Meyner, their first Democratic governor in thirteen years, on November 3, 1953 by a plurality of 153,919 votes. Meyner, who succeeded Alfred E. Driscoll, is the forty-third Governor of New Jersey and will serve until January 1958. A lawyer by profession, Meyner has been practicing in Phillipsburg, New Jersey since 1936. He was elected to the state Senate in 1947 and in 1950 served as minority leader.

In his inaugural address Meyner stated: ". . . we must ever be conscious that in government, as in life, nothing is ever permanently settled, nothing ever disposed of beyond the need for continuous study and action. It is a timeless process and an endless campaign against smug self-approval."

Robert Baumle Meyner was born on July 3, 1908 in Easton, Pennsylvania, the son of Gustave Herman Meyner, a loom-fixer and silk worker, and Mary Sophia (Baumle) Meyner. When Robert was eight, his family moved to Phillipsburg, where he attended public school. At the age of ten, he began working on a newspaper route in Paterson, New Jersey. (His family lived in Paterson for a short period.) At various times, to support himself through school, he worked as a grocery clerk, garage mechanic, foundry handy man and tutor.

After his family returned to Phillipsburg, Robert was graduated from Phillipsburg High School in 1926. He enrolled in Lafayette College in Easton, Pennsylvania and joined the debating team, dramatics group, and edited the school publication. In the 1928 Presidential campaign, he was president of the Young Democrats for Alfred E. Smith at Lafayette. After being graduated with the A.B. degree in 1930, he entered Columbia School of Law, where he received the LL.B. degree three years later.

Admitted to the New Jersey bar in 1934, he served as a law clerk with the firm of Walscheid & Rosenkranz in Union City and later in Jersey City. In 1936 he opened his own law office in Phillipsburg. The following year he became a counselor, and in 1940 he was admitted to practice before the United States Supreme Court.

In his first political contest, Meyner was defeated in the 1941 election for state Senator by fifty votes. In 1942 he entered the Navy with the rank of lieutenant (j.g.). For more than three years he served "as a commander of Naval gun crews on merchant vessels traveling the submarine-infested lanes of the Atlantic and Pacific" (Robert G. Spivack, New York *Post,* September 27, 1953). He was discharged as a lieutenant commander, a rank he retains in the Naval Reserve.

Following his return to civilian life, Meyner was the Democratic candidate for the U.S. Congress from the Seventh District in 1946. He was defeated by Republican J. Parnell Thomas. The next year he was successful in his second attempt for the state Senate against Wayne Dumont, Jr., a Republican. In the state Senate he introduced a bill providing for the investigation of gambling and official corruption in Bergen county. He favored the creation of a state crime commission and opposed the establishment of the New Jersey Turnpike Authority. Spivack (New York *Post*) wrote that Meyner's "objection to 'authorities,' aside from the fact that they are run mainly to profit their bondholders, is that they 'have become grossly irresponsive to the will and wishes of the people.' "

Meyner became minority leader in the state Senate in 1950 and permanent chairman of the Democratic state convention in 1951. He was defeated by Wayne Dumont, Jr., in his attempt to return to the state Senate in the latter year. In 1952 Meyner was an alternate delegate at large to the Democratic National Convention.

State Democratic leaders selected Meyner in March 1953 as "the organization's candidate for Governor." He won the primary, the first contest for a Democratic gubernatorial nomination in about thirty years, against Elmer H. Wene by approximately 1,500 votes. In the election for governor, Meyner was opposed by the Republican candidate Paul L. Troast, chairman of the board that planned the New Jersey Turnpike.

The program which Meyner advocated during his campaign included complete revision of the state tax structure, reorganization of the executive departments, increased aid to education, increased unemployment compensation benefits, and legislation of bingo and other games of chance operated for the benefit of welfare organizations and churches. Above all, he pledged strict enforcement of the laws. "New Jersey under Republican administration," he stated (New York *Post,* September 27, 1953), "has achieved an international reputation as a mecca for syndicated gambling and a haven for the underworld." On November 3, 1953 Meyner was elected by 959,669 to 805,750 votes.

In his inaugural address of January 19, 1954, Meyner declared: "I am a strong advocate of submitting important questions to the people on the ground that it makes for a livelier, more responsive and more responsible democracy. Without seeking to evade my own responsibilities as Governor, or to invade the province of the Legislature, I will consider recommending the submission of various matters of substance for popular decision, in the spirit of the old New England town meeting."

Wide World

ROBERT B. MEYNER

In March 1954 Meyner began a series of half-hour weekly TV-radio reports on the activities of the state administration. Later, members of the Legislature were granted equal time following the Governor's broadcasts to present nonpartisan informative broadcasts. The result, in the opinion of George Cable Wright (New York *Times,* June 20, 1954), was that "for the first time the general public" was receiving "a relatively true picture of the manner in which its state government functions."

Meyner suspended Harold G. Hoffman on March 18 as director of the division of employment security, pending an investigation of alleged "irregularities" in purchases of supplies made by the division. Hoffman, who had been Governor of New Jersey from 1935 to 1938, died of a heart attack in June 1954. An affidavit was released on June 14 disclosing that in a letter to his daughter, Mrs. Ada Leonard, Hoffman had confessed the embezzlement, over a period of years, of $300,000 from the South Amboy Trust Company, of which he had been president (*Saturday Evening Post,* October 23, 1954). However, the Legislature failed to act on Meyner's request for a $200,000 appropriation to finance a full-scale investigation.

On February 14, 1955 Meyner dismissed two of Hoffman's top aids in the division of employment security on charges of misconduct and neglect of duty (New York *Herald Tribune,* February 15, 1955).

Bingo and raffles were legalized on April 20, 1954 in the overwhelming majority of New Jersey's 567 communities in a special local option election. The voters of the state had approved on November 3, 1953 an amendment to the state constitution which would permit the games and the Legislature passed measures on February 15, 1954 enabling the local option election. On February 20, 1954 Meyner

MEYNER, ROBERT B.—*Continued*

had signed a bill establishing a Legalized Games of Chance Control Commission to prevent the operation of bingo and raffles by groups other than civic, charitable, religious, veterans and volunteer fire organizations.

The construction of a state medical and dental college and health center was endorsed by Governor Meyner, many state Republican leaders, and medical and dental societies. A referendum regarding a $25,000,000 bond issue for this project was defeated by the electorate on November 2, 1954.

During the 1954 Legislative session Meyner signed into law five bills for increased gasoline, corporate, and race track betting taxes to be used largely for education (June 30), three bills designed to improve educational facilities for physically handicapped and mentally retarded children (July 20), a bill increasing the salaries of legislators from $3,000 to $5,000 a year (July 29), a bill authorizing the division against discrimination of the department of education to enforce the state law against discrimination in housing built with public funds (July 29), a bill permitting municipalities to lease real property to private concerns for building parking facilities (August 4), a bill increasing the minimum yearly salary of teachers from $2,000 to $3,000 (December 13), and a bill extending rent controls to June 30, 1956 in sixty-five municipalities (December 22).

Of 344 bills adopted in 1954 by the Legislature, the Governor signed 230 into law, conditionally vetoed about forty-five, and vetoed about sixty outright. Several bills were passed over his veto, the first time in more than a decade that either house had passed a bill over the veto of the governor. (In the Senate there were seventeen Republicans and four Democrats; in the House of Assembly there were forty Republicans and twenty Democrats.)

The Governor's views on prison reform, expressed to the New Jersey Judicial Conference in June 1954, included suggestions for getting as many prisoners as possible "'out of their cells and into the sunshine,' improved and expanded parole and probation facilities, and a program to prevent crime by assisting young people who might tend toward delinquency."

At the annual Governors' Conference held in July 1954, considerable attention focused on Meyner, who "proved such good company," *Life* reported, "and so impressed people with his relaxed way of talking about serious issues that he suddenly began to look like a hot prospect for the Democratic Vice-Presidential nomination in 1956."

At the dedication of the war memorial library in Wood-Ridge, New Jersey on September 19, 1954, the Governor stated: "The freedom to read must be protected against those who would curtail it. . . . No reasonable person objects to selection of books for our public libraries. The mere selection of books is a form of censorship. When that selection is accomplished by competent, professionally trained people . . . and based on standards of selection acceptable to the community, we have the necessary safeguards for our way of life" (*Library Journal*, December 15, 1954).

In an address at the 101st annual convention of the New Jersey Education Association held in Atlantic City, Meyner said that "our teachers have been the victims of demagogues who, under the guise of fighting totalitarianism, are instilling totalitarian ideas in the minds of our people." If teachers fail to encourage students in the thoughtful consideration of issues besetting our civilization, he said, "we shall be raising a generation which is intellectually blind" (New York *Times,* November 12, 1954).

The appointment of a committee by Meyner to study the administration of Rutgers University was announced on January 25, 1955. The governor said "the board of a state university should be truly representative of the citizens." Thirty-nine of the fifty-four trustees of Rutgers, which became a state university in 1945, are known as "charter trustees" and are selected by a committee of members from that group (New York *Herald Tribune*, January 25, 1955).

Meyner is a member of the Warren, Hudson and American bar associations, is a trustee of the New Jersey Practicing Law Institute, and has served three terms as a trustee of the New Jersey Bar Association. He also belongs to the New Jersey State, Warren county, Pomona and Stewartsville granges, and to the Academy of Political and Social Science. He is a past president of the Phillipsburg Civic Association, and of the Phillipsburg branch of the Chamber of Commerce.

Other associations include the Elks, Eagles, Odd Fellows, Moose, Rotary, American Legion, Veterans of Foreign Wars, and Amvets. His fraternity is Alpha Chi Rho and his clubs are the Pomfert and Columbia University. The Governor has been awarded honorary doctorates by Lafayette College and Rutgers University. His religion is Protestant.

His principal forms of recreation are tennis and travel. He has brown hair and blue eyes, stands five feet ten inches tall and weighs 180 pounds. The New York *Times* has written that Meyner is "an effective speaker, has an excellent sense of humor, seldom loses his temper and possesses the gift of remembering names and faces." He is an admirer of Oliver Wendell Holmes.

References

N Y Herald Tribune p15 Ap 22 '53; p14 N 4 '53
N Y Times p33 Ap 23 '53; p17 N 4 '53
N Y World-Telegram p17 O 19 '53 por; p3 N 4 '53
N Y World-Telegram Mag p10 N 21 '53 pors
Who's Who in America, 1954-55
Who's Who in the East (1953)
Who's Who in United States Politics (1952)
World Biography (1954)

MIKOYAN, ANASTAS I(VANOVICH) (mē-kō-yän' ä-näs'täs) Nov. 25, 1895- U.S.S.R. government and Communist party official

Address: The Presidium of the Central Committee, Moscow, U.S.S.R.

For almost thirty years Anastas I. Mikoyan has been responsible for commerce in the Soviet Union. The domestic trade network over which he presides does a business of over $100 billion a year through 415,000 stores employing 3,000,000 persons and serving 210,000,000 customers. He is also responsible for some $6,000,000,000 worth of Soviet foreign trade, most of it with other Communist countries.

In March 1955 Mikoyan was promoted to First Deputy Premier, one of the five in the Council of Ministers including Viacheslav M. Molotov. He is also one of the nine members of the Presidium, or executive organ, of the Central Committee of the Communist Party of the Soviet Union, of which Nikita S. Krushchev is now the First Secretary.

Anastas Ivanovich Mikoyan was born on November 25, 1895, the son of a worker in the Armenian village of Sanain, near the Georgian border. He was graduated in 1915 from the Armenian Ecclesiastical Seminary at Tiflis, the Georgian capital, and in the same year joined the Bolshevik Party. After the 1917 revolution, when the Bolsheviks set up a local Soviet government at Baku, the capital of Azerbaidzhan, he became a member of the Baku party committee and the editor of the party newspaper and later the Soviet government newspaper.

During 1918 he fought with Bolshevik forces in the Baku area, occupied for a short time by the British, and became leader of the local Bolshevik organization. He was imprisoned three times during 1919 for his activities in strikes and partisan warfare, but each time he escaped. In that year he was named to the All-Russian Central Executive Committee, a body of local revolutionary leaders which was, in theory at least, the source of government power between sessions of the All-Russian Congress of Soviets.

In 1919 he was sent by the Caucasus Committee of the party across the enemy front to Moscow to confer with Lenin and the party's Central Committee on steps to reestablish Soviet power which he helped to do in Baku. For his civil war services he was awarded the Order of the Red Banner.

He was next ordered by the Central Committee to Nizhni-Novgorod (now Gorky), to take over the regional party organization. There he led the battle to oust the anarcho-syndical elements from the party, government and trade union organs.

Chosen a candidate member of the Central Committee in 1922, he was reassigned to Rostov-on-Don where he served as secretary of the southeast bureau of the Central Committee and later of the Northern Caucasus territory committee. During 1922-1923 he worked with Klementii Voroshilov, who was then commander of the North-Caucasus military district, in "purifying the party organizations" of opposition elements which supported Leon Trotsky. He was successful in lining up the majority of the party organizations in his area behind the policies of Stalin. At the Twelfth Party Congress in 1923 he was advanced to a full member of the party's Central Committee.

In August 1926 Mikoyan was called to Moscow as Peoples Commissar of Trade of the U.S.S.R. and a member of the Council of Labor and Defense. The latter, a commission of the Council of Peoples Commissars, was for the coordination of economic and defense matters. In the same year he was named a candidate member of the Central Committee's Political Bureau.

For the next eleven years Mikoyan had the task of ensuring agricultural supplies, creating a food industry, and organizing a trade network despite the economic disruptions of the drives for industrialization of manufacturing and collectivization of agriculture.

Mikoyan became the Peoples Commissar of Supply of the U.S.S.R. in 1930, and in 1934 the Peoples Commissar of the Food Supply Industry. He was advanced to a full member of the Political Bureau of the party's Central Committee in 1935, and in 1936 for overfulfilling the food supply plan he was awarded the Order of Lenin.

Mikoyan hired American experts to help in the expansion of the food industry. Announcing that "We must study America," he traveled to the United States in August 1936, for a three-month coast-to-coast tour to study methods of food production, processing and distribution. He subsequently introduced in the Soviet Union products like corn flakes, puffed wheat, tomato juice, grapefruit, eskimo pie and frozen corn on the cob.

In August 1937 Mikoyan became a deputy chairman of the Council of Peoples Commissars of the U.S.S.R., and in January 1938 he was transferred to the post of Peoples Commissar of Foreign Trade. During the years just after the Nazi-Soviet pact was signed (August 23, 1939) Mikoyan negotiated a series of trade agreements under which the Soviet Union acquired the machinery and production goods with which to build its war machine. A considerable amount of goods came from Germany. The Soviets, in turn, delivered grain and petroleum to Germany.

Following the Nazi attack on Russia in June 1941, the Soviet Union created a State Defense Committee of the Council of Peoples Commissars to direct the war effort. Mikoyan became one of its eight members and, in effect, chief quartermaster for the armed forces. He directed the conversion of consumer industry to war production, and the intricate operations of the multi-billion dollar war supply agreements with the United States and Great Britain. For his war services he was awarded in 1943 the title of Hero of Socialist Labor and the Hammer and Sickle Gold Medal.

After the end of the war in Europe in 1945, Mikoyan became a member of the Council of Peoples Commissars Committee for the Economic Rehabilitation of Liberated Areas headed by Malenkov. The two men reportedly clashed over the handling of German reparations—

Wide World

ANASTAS I. MIKOYAN

Malenkov holding that devastated areas could be rebuilt most rapidly by transporting what remained of German industry to the Soviet Union, Mikoyan contending that German industry should be left in place to produce goods to be brought to the Soviet Union. Mikoyan's view prevailed, for the most part.

In the postwar reorganization of the Soviet government when the former Peoples Commissariats became ministries, Mikoyan was named Minister of Foreign Trade as well as a deputy chairman of the Council of Ministers. In this capacity he negotiated a series of trade agreements with Hungary, Sweden, France, Outer Mongolia, Czechoslovakia, Great Britain and Uruguay. He also bid, unsuccessfully, for a $6 billion reconstruction loan from the United States and reportedly led an unsuccessful effort in the Political Bureau for Soviet participation in the Marshall Plan.

"When loans of such magnitude could not be obtained," wrote Harry Schwartz (New York *Times Magazine,* June 29, 1952) "Mikoyan turned to other sources. It was from the looting of Eastern Europe and Manchuria, instead, that Russia got its first big post-war start toward full recovery."

An economic conference of the East European satellites was called in Moscow in January 1949 and a Communist version of the Marshall Plan—a Council for Economic Mutual Assistance was established. Mikoyan was relieved as Minister of Foreign Trade and appointed Deputy Premier with policy supervision in both foreign and domestic trade.

In his report to the Nineteenth Party Congress in 1952 Mikoyan announced that the trade integration of Communist countries had reached the point that 80 per cent of Soviet trade was with the satellites, and that this trade and tripled since 1948, more than offsetting the decline in trade with the West.

When the government was reorganized after the death of Stalin in March 1953, Mikoyan was named as head of a combined Ministry of Domestic and Foreign Trade as well as a Deputy Premier. Within seven weeks after Stalin's death Mikoyan handled trade negotiations with Egypt, Sweden, Argentina and the Netherlands, as well as with Communist China, Hungary, Poland, Bulgaria and Albania. Negotiations with East Germany and India followed soon after.

The main task of the post-Stalin government was announced as the increased satisfaction of consumers' needs, and to enable Mikoyan to concentrate in this field, foreign trade affairs were placed in a separate Ministry of Foreign Trade on September 15, 1953. Mikoyan, as Minister of Domestic Trade, continued also to play a top-level role in foreign trade.

To launch the consumer drive, an All-Union Conference of Trade Workers was held in Moscow on October 17, 1953, at which Mikoyan called for sharp increases in the production of such items as refrigerators, vacuum cleaners and television sets. He also revealed that the Soviet Union planned to buy abroad about a billion dollars worth of food and consumer goods—the largest sum ever spent by the Soviet Union for such imports. Three government decrees called for wholesale expansion in the system of stores, peasant markets, warehousing and food transport. To support the extensive foreign purchases of consumer goods more than $100 million worth of Soviet gold was sold in Western Europe.

In April 1954 Mikoyan reported to the U.S.S.R. Supreme Soviet large increases in the production of meat, butter, fabrics and manufactured consumer goods and that the purchasing power of Soviet wage earners was up 30.5 per cent.

Mikoyan went to East Germany to the fourth congress of the Socialist Unity (Communist) Party in 1954 and was a member of a Soviet delegation to the fifth anniversary of the founding of the Chinese People's Republic at Peiping. In Germany and China he toured industrial centers, and on the return from China he inspected Siberian industrial cities. He then visited Helsinki to arrange for extending a $10 million loan to Finland made earlier in the year.

Mikoyan's resignation on January 24, 1955 as Minister of Domestic Trade was later seen by Western observers as having foreshadowed a government policy change putting stress on heavy industry rather than consumers' goods. This was the policy announced by the government of Nikolai A. Bulganin, who replaced Georgi M. Malenkov as Premier on February 8, 1955. In a cabinet reorganization on March 1, Bulganin appointed three Deputy Premiers to the post of First Deputy Premier: Mikoyan, Mikhail G. Pervukhin, and Maxim Z. Saburov. Mikoyan, presumably, is in charge of ministries handling foreign and domestic commerce.

There was speculation, commented the New York *Times* (March 1, 1955), that the promotions represented rewards to the three Premiers for having assented to Malenkov's demotion.

In the Soviet Cabinet system First Deputy Premiers and Deputy Premiers are normally in charge of a particular major department.

The All-Russian Central Executive Committee to which Mikoyan was named in 1919 became the All-Union Central Executive Committee after the formation of the U.S.S.R. in 1923, and the Supreme Soviet of the U.S.S.R. when the Stalin constitution went into effect in 1937. Through its successive changes Mikoyan remained a member and now represents the Stalin district of Yerevan, capital of the Armenian Soviet Socialist Republic, in the Council of Nationalities. A village in the Armenian republic has been named for him, as well as the Moscow ice cream trust and a Moscow bread factory.

Mikoyan is a dark, stocky man with a taste for well-tailored clothes. Walter Bedell Smith, former U.S. Ambassador to the U.S.S.R., has described him as an "intelligent and worldly wise little Armenian," and Joseph E. Davies, another former Ambassador, has called his mind "quick as a rapier."

While his contacts with Western political leaders have been open and congenial, those with Chinese leaders appear strained. Prime Minister Chou En-lai, for example, has made public criticism of him, apparently indicative of bitterness over bargaining in trade relations, and Mikoyan has been equally scornful of the Chinese leader (New York *Times*, January 2, 1954).

Mikoyan is married and has a son, Stepan, who won combat decorations during World War II. There have been reports that Mikoyan is a nephew of Stalin, but these have not been confirmed.

References

N Y Herald Tribune II p2 Mr 6 '55 por
N Y Times p1+ Ja 25 '55 por
N Y Times Mag p13 Je 29 '52 por
International Who's Who, 1954
World Biography (1954)

MILLES, CARL June 23, 1875-Sept. 19, 1955 Swedish sculptor; noted for his monumental sculptures and fountains throughout Sweden and United States; taught at Cranbrook Academy of Art, Bloomfield Hills, Michigan (1933-1951); among notable American commissions were monuments at Chicago Exposition (1933); New York World's Fair (1939—*Astronomer* and *Pony Express*); *Nature and Man* wood murals at Time & Life Building, New York (1941); *Peace Monument* and *Jonah* fountain in St. Paul, Minnesota; *Wedding of the Rivers* at St. Louis, Missouri; and *Fountain of Faith* comprising thirty-eight heroic figures at Falls Church, Virginia (completed in 1953); his figures symbolizing the arts will be installed at the Metropolitan Museum of Art's restaurant pool. See *Current Biography* (Dec.) 1952.

Obituary

N Y Times p31 S 20 '55

MIRANDA, CARMEN 1913-Aug. 5, 1955 Singer; dancer; actress; Brazil's "ambassadress of good will"; popularized Brazilian *samba* (a swing dance); developed a dynamic way of singing songs *con moviemento*, wearing a flamboyant Brazilian headdress and costume; performed extensively in motion pictures, night clubs, television and theatre, beginning in 1939 in *The Streets of Paris*, (a Broadway revue); her first film was *Down Argentine Way* (1940), and her last a film for television with Jimmy Durante, completed on the day of her death. See *Current Biography* (June) 1941.

Obituary

N Y Times p 15 Ag 6 '55

MITCHELL, JAMES P(AUL) Nov. 12, 1900- United States Secretary of Labor

Address: b. c/o United States Department of Labor, Washington, D.C.; h. Upland Terrace, N.W., Washington, D.C.; 214 S. Blvd., Spring Lake, N.J.

NOTE: The article on Secretary Mitchell which appeared in *Current Biography* in 1954 contained a misleading factual error. It is superseded by the present corrected biography.

Described as a personnel executive who "feels that trade unions are here to stay and that business should . . . view them as a challenge" (*Christian Science Monitor*, October 9, 1953), James P. Mitchell was sworn in as United States Secretary of Labor on October 9, 1953, succeeding Martin P. Durkin who resigned on the previous September 10. For four months prior to his appointment to the Cabinet post Mitchell was Assistant Secretary of the Army in charge of manpower and reserve forces affairs.

The Secretary has had more than twenty years' experience in personnel administration and in management-employee relations, both in private industry and government service. He is on leave of absence as vice-president of Bloomingdale Brothers department store in New York City, where he has been in charge of labor relations and operations since 1947. His views toward labor organizations are considered "middle-of-the-road" (New York *Times*, January 4, 1954).

James Paul Mitchell was born in Elizabeth, New Jersey, on November 12, 1900, the son of Peter J. and Anna C. (Driscoll) Mitchell. His uncle, Thomas Mitchell, the actor, was brought up with him. James attended St. Patrick's Parochial School and in the evenings and on Saturdays ran errands for a grocery store.

After his graduation from Battin High School in 1917, he went to work for fifteen dollars a week in this store. Within a year he was promoted to manager. Leaving his employer, he opened his own store in Rahway, New Jersey and in 1921 set up a second store in Elizabeth. Both failed in 1923. Mitchell recalls: "I was young and inexperienced, and vastly overextended myself" (New York *Post*, November 8, 1953).

(Continued next page)

JAMES P. MITCHELL

Following two years of employment as a truck driver and salesman, Mitchell in 1926 became an expediter in the Western Electric Company plant in Kearny, New Jersey, and was soon transferred to the personnel department. He secured a position in 1931 with the New Jersey relief administration to direct its program in Union county, and later returned to Western Electric.

Mitchell left that company in 1936 to take charge of labor relations in the New York City division of the Works Progress Administration, headed by the then Colonel Brehon Somervell. At a time when left-wing factions were attracting the unemployed, Mitchell found his task as "trouble-shooter" difficult, and says: "I have a recollection . . . of always having to cross a picket line to go to work in the morning" (New York *Post*, November 8, 1953).

When Somervell went to Washington, D.C., in 1940 to head the Army's construction program, he requested Mitchell to go with him as chief of the labor relations division. The next year, Mitchell became director of the civilian personnel division for the Services of Supply of the War Department. He was also a member of the National Building Trades Stabilization Board, the Joint Army-Navy Personnel Board, an alternate for the Under Secretary of War on the War Manpower Commission, and head of a program of special cooperation between the Army, War Manpower Commission and the War Production Board to supply workers where they were needed.

Mitchell supported preinduction training in the high schools ". . . to provide trained manpower that will not only produce the weapons for the Armed Forces, but provide them with men who know how to keep the weapons rolling and keep them fighting" (*Science News Letter*, November 14, 1942).

Returning to private industry in 1945, Mitchell became director of personnel and industrial relations for R. H. Macy and Company in New York City. The personnel expert helped to settle the strike at Macy's store in 1946, allowing full pay to employees who did not remain on the job and triple pay to those who did.

Mitchell became vice-president in charge of labor relations and operations at Bloomingdale Brothers in 1947. He is credited with stabilizing the store's "chaotic labor situation" by putting supervisory methods on a basis of "consent" and "communication" rather than authoritarian procedures (New York *Post*, November 8, 1953). A unionist remarked that Mitchell "never took a mechanical view of a contract, but was able to realize that it concerned human beings and not just commodities" (New York *World-Telegram and Sun*, October 12, 1953).

At the U.S. Army's request, Mitchell went to Germany in 1948 to study the military government's civilian employment program, and after the outbreak of the Korean War, he examined and reported on combat pay problems. After working on a research project for the Citizens Committee for the Hoover Report, the personnel manager headed a group of the Citizens Committee in 1951 to encourage public and Congressional recognition for the need of modernizing personnel policies.

President Dwight D. Eisenhower designated Mitchell in April 1953 as the Assistant Secretary of the Army, in charge of manpower and reserve forces affairs. On a leave of absence from Bloomingdale Brothers, Mitchell filled this position from May 4 until October 9, 1953. During this period he called the Administration's defense policy a "sensible long-range program" (New York *Times*, May 17, 1953).

Nominated as Secretary of Labor by President Eisenhower on October 8, 1953, Mitchell took office the following day. The President said his choice was based more upon Mitchell's "character and interest in other people than his broad experience in the labor relations field" (Washington *Post*, October 9, 1953). The appointment was unanimously confirmed by the Senate on January 19, 1954.

The Department of Labor was created March 4, 1913 and is charged with enforcing statutes "designed to advance the public interest by promoting the welfare of the wage earners of the United States, improving their working conditions, and advancing their opportunities for profitable employment." Included under its jurisdiction are the bureaus of standards, labor statistics, veterans' re-employment rights, employment security, wage and hour and public contracts division, and the women's bureau.

The New York *Times* (October 25, 1953) commented that "there are more Government functions and employes outside the department dealing with labor than there are in the department . . . the department has nothing to do with the Taft-Hartley Law except to receive union financial reports. It has nothing to do with the Railway Labor Act or with the mediation of labor-management disputes." Mitchell has said that he wants to see "the department strengthened and broadened."

On November 13, 1953, he told the National Council of Negro Women that he welcomed the banning of racial discrimination, effective November 16, 1953, in all contracts made with the District of Columbia government and that he was "particularly gratified" with progress toward ending racial segregation in the armed forces (New York *Times*, November 14, 1953).

Addressing the convention of the Congress of Industrial Organizations in Cleveland, Ohio, the Secretary recommended widening the national wage structure which leaves 63,000,000 working people without safeguard of a minimum wage and advocated "an increase in the present 75-cents-an-hour minimum" legal wage (New York *Times*, November 19, 1953).

Mitchell claimed that the Administration's policy "of leaving to labor and management the solution of their own labor relations problems" had resulted in a "smaller loss of man-hours" and led to "more genuine collective bargaining" (Washington *Post*, January 3, 1954).

In a speech before the New Jersey Republican Committee, Mitchell asserted: "Good industrial relations cannot be created by laws. At best, the Government can only provide the framework in which labor and management operate. Employers and employes themselves must develop better relationships at the plant level and settle their own differences without dictation from Washington. The Government's sole interest is that of protecting the public" (New York *Times*, January 14, 1954).

Secretary Mitchell urged the enactment of the fifteen revisions suggested by President Eisenhower to the Labor-Management Relations Act of 1947. One request of the Administration was for Federal polls of strikers. The other proposed changes included relaxation of the ban on the secondary boycott prohibition in certain instances, prohibiting of an election immediately after a strike called for economic reasons was effected, providing a union and an employer to make a contract before employees are hired and legalizing the right of such a contract to require employees to become union members in the construction, amusement and maritime industries, a non-Communist oath for employers until Congress adopted substitutes for dealing with Communist infiltration generally. (In August 1954 Congress passed a bill outlawing the Communist party.)

Secretary of Labor Mitchell conferred with George Meany, president of the American Federation of Labor on February 4, 1954 at the AFL executive council meeting in Miami, and discussed minimum wage law changes. Both men were agreed that the wage should be raised from its present 75-cents-an-hour level, but major disagreement was on the question of time. Mitchell said the changes should be made "at the appropriate time" and that "this is not the proper time". He said he looked for a rising trend in the national economy by the end of the year.

On August 26, 1954 President Eisenhower created the Committee on Migratory Labor, and named Mitchell chairman of the committee.

The Secretary of Labor has served as a special mediator of the New York State Board of Mediation, as chairman of the employee relations committee of the National Retail Dry Goods Association and of the executive committee of the Retail Labor Standards Association of New York, and has been a member of the executive committee of the National Civil Service League. He is a Republican and a Roman Catholic. Fordham University conferred the honorary doctor of laws degree on the Secretary of Labor in 1954.

Married to Isabelle Nulton of Roselle Park, New Jersey in 1923, Mitchell has one daughter, Elizabeth. He is six feet tall and weighs 196 pounds. *Time* describes him as a man with "deep-set blue eyes, . . . huge shoulders and bristling hair." Among his hobbies is deep-sea fishing.

References

N Y Times p10 Je 11 '51; p14 O 9 '53
N Y World-Telegram p22 O 12 '53
Time 62:27 O 19 '53
U S News 35:16 O 16 '53
Washington (D.C.) Post p2 N 8 '53
Who's Who in America, 1952-53

MITCHELL, WILLIAM D(E WITT) Sept. 9, 1874-Aug. 24, 1955 Former United States Attorney General; began his career as a lawyer in St. Paul, Minnesota in 1896; in Spanish-American war was acting judge advocate for the Second Army Corps; in World War I was a colonel in the Sixth Minnesota Infantry; in 1925 was appointed Solicitor General; was U.S. Attorney General from 1929 to 1933; was known as "a constitutional dry" and attempted to enforce the Eighteenth amendment; firmly upheld antitrust laws; member New York law firm, Taylor, Capron & Marsh; was chief counsel for Congressional Pearl Harbor investigating committee (1945). See *Current Biography* (Jan.) 1946.

Obituary

N Y Times p23 Ag 25 '55

MOISEIWITSCH, TANYA (moi-zā'ĕ-vĭch) Dec. 3, 1914- Scenic and costume designer

Address: b. c/o Stratford Shakespearean Festival, Stratford, Ontario, Canada; h. 169 Sloane St., London, S.W. I., England

Although she is never seen on stage, one of the shining lights of the Stratford Shakespearean Festival at Stratford, Ontario, Canada is Tanya Moiseiwitsch, who designed the apron stage and costumes for the productions during the past three summers. Considered one of England's foremost stage designers, she has worked at London's Old Vic Theatre, various West End productions, Stratford-on-Avon, and the Edinburgh Festival.

Broadway critics who journeyed to Stratford to see the Festival productions "seem to have formed a two-man cheerleading team for Tanya." Walter Kerr of the New York *Herald Tribune* has written that her designs are "breathtaking" and "achieve a near-sculptured effect" and Brooks Atkinson of the New York *Times* has called them "bold and beautiful" and

McKague, Toronto

TANYA MOISEIWITSCH

"stunning." The Festival company will make its debut on Broadway in late January 1956 in Christopher Marlowe's play, *Tamburlaine,* with costumes and settings by Miss Moiseiwitsch.

Her designs for Thornton Wilder's play, *A Life in the Sun,* which had its première at the Edinburgh Festival in the summer of 1955, "continue to be a joy," commented Henry Hewes in the *Saturday Review* (September 10, 1955), as they have been "for previous open-stage productions."

Tanya Moiseiwitsch was born on December 3, 1914 in London, England. She is the daughter of Benno Moiseiwitsch, the concert pianist, and Daisy Kennedy, the Australian violinist. While still very young Tanya learned to play the Irish harp and later the piano. After applying herself diligently to this instrument until the age of sixteen she came to realize she was not "concert material." By this time her parents were divorced and she was living with her mother and stepfather, John Drinkwater, the playwright, in Brampton, Huntingdonshire.

While attending various private schools she recalls that she disliked practically all of her studies except English, history and art. She states that her special hatred of geometry still gives her trouble when it comes to designing false perspective in stage sets.

Deciding to try art as a career, she enrolled at London's Central School of Arts and Crafts. She often attended the Old Vic and various other London theatres with Drinkwater and her mother. Halfway through her first year at art school, Tanya met the late Lillian Bayliss, manager of the Old Vic Theatre, who needed help in the making of hats for the opera *Snow Maiden.* She volunteered her services and developed an enthusiasm for theatre design.

Abiding by the advice of Ruth Keating, a teacher at the Central School of Arts and Crafts, Tanya applied at the Old Vic as an apprentice. Accepted as a scenic painting student, she learned to slap "size" on canvas, paint props, clean paint pots, how to take a design from a half-inch-to-one-foot scale drawing and paint it on a large "flat". The apprentices were also allowed to watch rehearsals, permitting Tanya to see the new director Tyrone Guthrie (see *C.B.,* 1954) in action.

After completing her apprenticeship with the Old Vic, Tanya became an assistant to Ruth Keating who had since been appointed designer at the Westminster Theatre where Hugh Hunt was directing. Tanya was asked to design the sets for two student productions. She created such a favorable impression that Hunt asked her to accompany him as designer when he went, in the summer of 1935, to direct the Abbey Theatre in Dublin, Ireland. They were offered a three-month trial period which was so successful that the team of Hunt and Moiseiwitsch stayed on for three more years. During that time she did the designing for fifty productions beginning with *The Deuce of Jacks.*

In 1939 Hunt left the Abbey for New York to produce an Irish play, while Miss Moiseiwitsch returned to London and obtained a job at the Q Theatre, near Kew Gardens. Her first West End show was Dennis Johnston's *The Golden Cuckoo.* Her next job was in 1941 at the Oxford Playhouse in London which, like the Abbey, produced a different play each week. The wartime restrictions on canvas, used in flats, and on clothing presented quite a problem. The flats were simply painted over and over again and eventually became as thick as regular walls. Since curtain material was unrationed, Miss Moiseiwitsch used this for many of the costumes.

In 1944 Tyrone Guthrie, who was then administrator at the Old Vic in London, offered her a job as designer with the Old Vic's Liverpool Playhouse company, thus beginning her long association with the Old Vic. During her stay with the Liverpool group (1944-1945) she costumed such plays as *Dr. Faustus, John Gabriel Borkman, The School for Scandal,* and *Point Valaine.*

She was still in Liverpool when Guthrie chose her for the show that was to place her among Britain's top theatrical designers. This was the Old Vic's memorable production of Anton Chekhov's *Uncle Vanya* which was directed by John Burrell and starred Sir Laurence Olivier, Sir Ralph Richardson, and Dame Sybil Thorndike. Miss Moiseiwitsch did careful research on the period for the costumes and settings, but she demonstrated a flexibility of treatment which has become the Moiseiwitsch trade-mark—imaginative designs perfectly related to each other and achieving a sort of "poetic realism".

The Guthrie-Moiseiwitsch collaboration which started with a production of Ben Jonson's *The Alchemist* at Liverpool, continued through some of the British theatre's notable postwar productions. There was an impressive *Cyrano de Bergerac* in 1946, *The Critic,* and the Covent Garden production of *Peter Grimes* in 1947.

Between 1946 and 1951 Miss Moiseiwitsch designed for *The Time of Your Life* at the Lyric in Hammersmith; for *Bless the Bride* at the Adelphi Theatre, a C. B. Cochrane production; for *The Beggar's Opera;* and at the New (Old Vic) Theatre *The Cherry Orchard* and *A Midsummer Night's Dream.*

In the summer of 1951 Tanya was part of a memorable season at Stratford-on-Avon. The company performed a history cycle including *Richard II, Henry IV,* Parts I and II, and *Henry V.* Director Anthony Quayle and Tanya Moiseiwitsch assisted by Alix Strand, made the productions even more unusual by pushing the action out past the proscenium arch onto an "apron" thrust forward into the audience. This was one of a long series of efforts to break out of the confines of the proscenium.

In 1952 she did the designs for *Timon of Athens* at the Old Vic (London) and during the winter of 1952-53 she designed, for the Stratford (Ontario) Shakespearean Festival, in collaboration with Guthrie and Cecil Clarke, the now-famous wedge-shaped or "apron" stage which projects into the center of a concrete amphitheatre. It is this stage which critic Brooks Atkinson of the New York *Times* has called "the most vital instrument in the production of Shakespeare that most of us have ever seen." It was put into operation in the summer of 1953 with the opening of the Festival in Ontario. This stage incorporates the basic principles of the Elizabethan stage. Seats are tiered up on three sides around it, and no spectators are more than fifty-five feet from the stage—thus insuring a closer relationship between audience and actors. The special lighting and movement techniques which replace the more common stage curtain effect a considerable saving in money which, combined with the saving afforded by the lack of scenery, permit the designer to create more effective and elaborate costumes.

During the first season in Stratford Tanya Moiseiwitsch designed costumes and settings for *Richard III* and *All's Well That Ends Well* which starred Alec Guinness and Irene Worth. She also worked for the Old Vic in London, designing costumes and sets for *Henry VIII.* Queen Elizabeth II attended the opening performance.

In 1954 she designed costumes for the Stratford-on-Avon production of *Othello,* the Edinburgh Festival production of *The Matchmaker,* and the Stratford productions of *Oedipus Rex, The Taming of the Shrew,* and *Measure for Measure.*

Oedipus Rex was one of Tanya Moiseiwitsch's most controversial efforts. It involved putting the actors into masks, standing them upon platform shoes and covering them with voluminous robes inspired by the ancient Greek theatre. Some critics thought that the masks inhibited the actors' performances unnecessarily while others thought they helped to produce one of the most exciting productions of *Oedipus Rex* ever seen. She designed the costumes for the 1955 productions of *Oedipus, Julius Caesar* and *The Merchant of Venice.* Tanya Moiseiwitsch "dressed all three productions with beauty and imagination" wrote the Canadian critic Robertson Davies in *Saturday Night* (July 23, 1955). More than 125,000 visitors attended the productions.

Tanya Moiseiwitsch has said that she considers Guthrie to be the greatest influence on her work and career. Guthrie says that for detail she is the best designer in the business. It could be said that her success lies in her use of "poetic realism" and the painstaking procedure of personally checking and rechecking her designs as they go from drawing board to completion.

While she was at the Oxford Theatre during the war she met Felix Krish on leave from the Royal Air Force. Soon afterwards he went to Canada for training and upon his return they were married. Only a few months later he was killed in a crash.

References

London (Ont.) Free Press Jl 31 '53
Mayfair p25 Je '55 por
Sat R 38:26 Je 4 '55
Who's Who, 1955
Who's Who in the Theatre (1952)

MOODY, RALPH (OWEN) Dec. 16, 1898-

Author; business executive

Address: b. c/o W. W. Norton, 101 5th Ave., New York 3; h. 1309 Castillo Ave., Burlingame, Calif.

Reprinted from the *Wilson Library Bulletin* January 1955

The literary history of Ralph Moody diverges somewhat from the familiar pattern of the lives of so many successful writers. There was no particular literary tradition in the long line of his Scotch-English forebears; no clearly-defined early urge to set his thoughts before the public; the story of occasional short pieces published amid a stream of rejection slips, culminating in final recognition, is not his story. His ancestors were New England educators and ministers for the most part. He never published a line anywhere prior to his first novel, but in his late maturity he realized that he had a story worth telling, and, not without some formal preparation, he wrote a series of straightforward autobiographical novels which have been uniformly successful.

Ralph Owen Moody was born on December 16, 1898, in Rochester, New Hampshire, to Mary Gould Moody and Charles Owen Moody. His father was a farmer whose affliction with tuberculosis forced the family to move to Colorado when Ralph was eight years old. Readers of Moody's first two novels will be familiar with the family's life in the new surroundings, a day-to-day account told from the point of view of the boy himself in *Little Britches* and *Man of the Family.*

Despite the ingenuity and resourcefulness of his father, the farm failed and the family moved into Littleton, Colorado, when Ralph was about eleven. Soon after, as the result of an accident, the elder Moody died, leaving Ralph, as the oldest boy, the man of the family. After a year or so, Mrs. Moody brought her three sons and three daughters back to Medford, Massachusetts, where Ralph completed his formal education through the eighth grade of grammar school, before joining his maternal

RALPH MOODY

grandfather on his farm in Maine—the period of the author's life covered in his latest novel, *The Fields of Home.*

In spite of his diversified farming experience and his mastery of farming techniques, Ralph Moody was not destined to be a farmer himself. He abandoned the land in 1921, he says, because his wife-to-be—Edna Lucille Hudgins, whom he married on January 25, 1922—was determined to raise her family (they now have three children—Charles, Edna, and Andrew) in the city. He completed his high school studies in the evening and continued his education in university extension classes.

Moody's original incentive to write was a result of his desire to emulate the expressive power of the authors from whose works his mother read to her family during his childhood. "When I was twenty-one," he stated, "I got a diary as a birthday present and I wrote in it that I was going to work as hard as I could, save fifty thousand dollars by the time I was fifty, and then start writing." True to his word, he did start writing on the night of his fiftieth birthday.

His intention was to collect a series of reminiscences of his youth as the basis of an article directed to the young people of our time. After three months of writing in spare moments, he showed the manuscript to a college professor for advice and criticism. The professor sent the copy to the W. W. Norton Company in New York who advised that the "article" might work out very nicely as a novel if its author could cut it down from 150,000 to 70,000 words. After six months of hard labor, the manuscript of *Little Britches* was ready for the press. It appeared in 1950.

An analysis of the reviews of Moody's first book suggests a classification of readers into three groups depending upon their attitudes toward rural life. Some may agree with the New York *Herald Tribune* (August 13, 1950) reviewer who tempers his admiration of *Little Britches* by noting that "the author's simplicity is sometimes precious and he pushes primitiveness pretty hard." Others may join the *Christian Science Monitor* (August 22, 1950) reviewer who found the novel "a gallant book from the first sentence to the last." The middle-roaders will probably align themselves with the *Saturday Review of Literature* (August 19, 1950), which wrote, "You can call this book regionalism or you can forget there is such a thing . . . either way you will get satisfaction."

With the publication by W. W. Norton of *Man of the Family* (1951) and *The Fields of Home* (1953), the reviewers generally turned their attention from the atmosphere of the stories to the stories themselves. The New York *Herald Tribune* found that in *Man of the Family* "Mr. Moody remembers, and can put on paper, the terrifying passion of a small boy's heart, where . . . every victory and every disappointment is . . . overwhelming." Concerning *The Fields of Home,* the San Francisco *Chronicle* (August 23, 1953) wrote, "the description of the boy and the old man, and how the two grew in understanding of each other, shows the author's gift for character portrayal."

Ralph Moody is an executive in a large chain of restaurants. In his office he has a "restaurant desk" and a "play desk"—the "play" one being his writing desk. Moody's first three books were chosen by book clubs. The popular response to his books is indicated by the ten thousand favorable letters he had received as of June 1954—and only four unfavorable ones. He has blue eyes and graying ash blond hair. He weighs 165 pounds and is about six feet tall. Moody's recreations are riding, golf, and sculpture; he is a Republican, and a Methodist. He is active in the San Francisco Union League Club, California Writers' Club, and California Authors' Guild. His favorite author is Shakespeare.

References

Newsweek 42:90+ S 7 '53

Moody, R. Little Britches (1950); Man of the Family (1951); The Fields of Home (1953)

Who's Who in America (Sup. N '50)

MOREHEAD, ALBERT H(ODGES) Aug. 7, 1909- Editor; writer; games expert

Address: b. c/o National Lexicographic Board, 846 7th Ave., New York 19; h. 171 W. 57th St., New York 19

Albert H. Morehead, an editor, games authority, author, newspaper columnist, lexicographer, businessman, translator, song composer, and amateur criminologist, leads a varied and interesting life. As president of the National Lexicographic Board in New York City, he has edited the *New American Dictionary,* the *Illustrated Encyclopedia of Knowledge,, 101 Best-Loved Hymns,* and *101 Best-Loved Songs.* Often referred to as "the modern Hoyle," he is a bridge columnist for the New York *Times,* games editor for the *Encyclopædia Britannica,* and author, co-author or editor of numerous books on games and game rules.

Albert Hodges Morehead was born on August 7, 1909 in Flintstone, Georgia, the son of Albert Hodges and Bianca (Noa) Hodges. His father, a choral conductor and musician, had earlier founded the Southern Conservatory of Music in Chattanooga, Tennessee and had met his future wife when she became a piano teacher there. Young Morehead's brother, James T. Morehead, is a musician.

Albert tried hard to follow in his parents' footsteps by taking piano lessons for seven years, but he showed no aptitude for the musical profession. He did learn something about cards, however; the Moreheads allowed the use of playing cards—called the "devil's tickets" by many Southern families—in the house for whist and other games.

The family lived at that time in Paris, Kentucky. After his father's death, they moved to Chattanooga, Tennessee. Albert went to the Baylor School there (from which he was graduated in 1925) and then to Harvard University to study English literature until 1927.

For two years he did considerably well selling cars and trucks for General Motors in New York, until the stock market crash in 1929. Writing had always been one of Morehead's interests; he had started newspaper work in 1922 and had been associated with the Lexington (Kentucky) *Herald*, the Chattanooga (Tennessee) *Times*, the Chicago *Daily News*, the Cleveland *Plain Dealer*, and the Newton (Massachusetts) *Town Crier* (a small weekly where he was managing editor).

In 1932 he got a job as a staff writer on Ely Culbertson's magazine, *Bridge World*. After two years he was made editor and in 1935 he became general manager of all Culbertson's bridge and business enterprises. He is still an editor of the Culbertson bridge books (*Point-Count Bidding*, 1952; *Contract Bridge Complete*, 1954) and conducts a monthly department in the magazine. He became a contributor of articles on bridge to the New York *Times* in 1935.

In business he was for four years (1934 to 1938) vice-president of Kem Playing Cards, Inc., and in 1946 was appointed a consultant on games to the United States Playing Card Company. From 1946 to 1948 he was associated with the John C. Winston Company, publishers, as a vice-president. He edited W. Somerset Maugham's series, The Greatest Novels of the World, as well as Fulton Oursler's best-seller, *The Greatest Story Ever Told.*

He was on the team which won the Charles M. Schwab Trophy in the international bridge competition in 1934. He served as both president (1943) and chairman of the board (1944 to 1945) of the American Contract Bridge League. He is still a director. He has been on the committees that control the official bridge laws and the Vanderbilt cup bridge tournament.

He was a staff writer for *Redbook* magazine from 1943 to 1945, for *Coronet* from 1945 to 1947; and from 1948 to 1952 he was with *Cosmopolitan*. His articles in these magazines appeared under several different names. He has been a consultant for *Esquire* and has written on games and related subjects for numerous other periodicals.

ALBERT H. MOREHEAD

In the *Annals of the American Academy of Political and Social Science* (May 1950) Morehead described professional gamblers and divided them into several categories: the "banker" (who owns or operates a gambling house); the percentage gambler (who does not bet unless he feels he has a better-than-even chance of winning because of his skill in a game); the cheater (the "cardsharp"); and the compulsive gambler.

Morehead points out that "professional gamblers are not necessarily of the underworld, although they tend to gravitate to underworld society . . . because their calling is not conventionally respectable and because their haunts bring them into contact with members of the underworld." He also notes that "professional gamblers are not necessarily dishonest, but there are few who can long resist the temptation to be so when offered the opportunity."

His article "Is it Chance? Is it Skill? Is it Gambling?" in the New York *Times Magazine* (November 29, 1953) describes the legal principle of gambling: "When chance predominates, a game or bet is gambling and so is illegal; when skill predominates, it is not gambling and is not illegal." He wrote that there has been little agreement in the courts in applying the principle, particularly in relation to card games and guessing games, for "here is where the individual opinion or prejudice of an individual jurist will outweigh the merits of the case." Poker has usually been held a game of chance, Morehead noted, and contract bridge a game of skill, but expert players are generally agreed that poker rewards skillful play even more than bridge does.

He is author, co-author or editor of about sixty-four books. He wrote *The Modern Hoyle*

MOREHEAD, ALBERT H.—*Continued*

(Winston, 1944), a collection of rules and instructions for popular games; it has been reprinted several times. Other books he has worked on have covered such subjects as games for two, crossword puzzles, and solitaire and patience games. He wrote a column on canasta for the King Features Syndicate from 1949 to 1953 and appeared on the Columbia Broadcasting System's television panel show, *I'll Buy That,* from June 1953 to July 1954.

Recently Morehead has been giving most of his time and effort to editing encyclopedias, a business which is rapidly growing. He attributes this growth largely to the modern educational system, which makes pupils responsible for many outside projects that need the aid of an encyclopedia. "Parental pride and desire for the next generation to have the best in cultural advantages makes encyclopedias almost a 'must' in many American homes," Morehead has said, "for 80 per cent of the buyers purchase encyclopedias, even those written for adults, for the sake of the children."

For relaxation he writes three or four songs or hymns a year. He is translating a play from the French and writing a juvenile novel. He occasionally translates French poetry and contributes articles on criminology to books on the subject.

Morehead is a member of the Cavendish Club, the Regency Club, the Friars Club, and the American Bridge Association. He has brown eyes and brown hair, is six feet four inches tall, and weighs 215 pounds. He is very affable —according to his office staff, he never has said "no" to anyone. He is a Presbyterian.

On January 21, 1939 Morehead married Loy Claudon, who came from Illinois. Mrs. Morehead is vice-president of the National Lexicographic Board. The Moreheads have two sons, Andrew Turner and Philip David. They live in mid-town Manhattan near Carnegie Hall, in a penthouse which has a front yard with three feet of soil, a fair-sized lawn, three trees, and a fountain.

References

Nation's Bsns 41:6+ Ag '53 por
Who's Who in America, 1954-55

MORROW, MRS. DWIGHT WHITNEY

See Morrow, E. C.

MORROW, ELIZABETH CUTTER

May 29, 1873-Jan. 23, 1955 Author; educator; civic leader; wife of Dwight W. Morrow (U.S. Senator and Ambassador to Mexico); wrote poetry (*Quatrains for My Daughter*) and children's books (*The Rabbit's Age*); was acting president of Smith College (1939-1940) and a trustee of several other educational institutions; active in community service (Englewood, New Jersey) and in national charitable organizations. See *Current Biography* (Apr.) 1943.

Obituary

N Y Times p23 Ja 24 '55

MORTIMER, CHARLES G(REENOUGH), JR.

July 26, 1900- Corporation executive

Address: b. c/o General Foods Corporation, Inc., 250 North St., White Plains, N.Y.; h. 17 Platt Pl., White Plains, N.Y.

Continued prosperity for the food industry was predicted by Charles G. Mortimer, president of the General Foods Corporation, "the largest processor of packaged foods in the United States," when he spoke over the American Broadcasting Company's television network on January 2, 1955. "With Americans continuing to eat better meals, and with our growing population," he said, "I think 1955 will be a good year . . . Time-saving 'convenience foods' are contributing, in one way or another, to a better life." Packaged foods, he believes, "mean more time for women to devote to their families and their communities . . .broadened and steadier markets for farm crops, fruits and vegetables . . . more and better jobs for a lot of people" (*Newsweek,* January 10, 1955).

For the fiscal year which ended in March 1955, Mortimer reported that General Foods had "achieved the highest earnings in its history" (New York *Times,* June 1, 1955), its sales volume being $824,837,506. The corporation processes more than sixty branded items, including such well-known products as Jell-O, Maxwell House Coffee, Swans Down Cake Flour, Post Toasties, Postum, Birds Eye Orange Juice, Baker's Chocolate, Minute Tapioca and Log Cabin Syrup. During 1955, under Mortimer's presidency, the company has added seven new products.

Mortimer was elected president of General Foods Corporation in April 1954, succeeding Austin S. Igleheart (see *CB,* 1950). He has been associated with the organization since 1928 when it was the Postum Company. Since 1935 he has been chiefly responsible for advertising and marketing, and in 1952 became the corporation's executive vice-president. Prior to 1928, Mortimer was an account executive for four years with George Batten Company, the advertising agency later known as Batten, Barton, Durstine and Osborn.

Charles Greenough Mortimer, Jr., was born in Brooklyn, New York on July 26, 1900, the son of Charles Greenough and Cecilia (Dessoir) Mortimer. The family later moved to New Jersey and young Mortimer was graduated from the East Orange High School. When he was eighteen, he enlisted in the U.S. Naval Reserve and was assigned to a course of training in submarine engineering at Stevens Institute of Technology in Hoboken, New Jersey. After the War he found employment as a clerk in the export department of the National Aniline and Chemical Company, and in 1921, he obtained a position in the sales department of the R. B. Davis Company, baking powder manufacturers. Within a short time he was sales manager.

Eager to find out how advertising made merchandise move, Mortimer joined the George Batten Company in 1924 where he was a contact executive for four years. He pioneered as head of a "team" that handled important accounts and during 1928 he handled the account of Sanka Coffee which had been purchased by the Postum Company, which in the same year hired him as merchandise manager.

In 1929 the Postum Company acquired Birds Eye Frosted Foods from Clarence Birdseye who had developed the process. Clarence Francis, (see *CB,* 1948) an executive of Postum and close friend of Birdseye, negotiated the transaction and the firm changed its name to General Foods Sales Company, Inc.

On March 6, 1930 the company introduced twenty-seven frozen food products in Springfield, Massachusets. The venture was a success, but difficulties arose when marketing was attempted on a national scale. Zero-degree storage cabinets which cost $1,500 each had to be installed in retail stores at the expense of General Foods. Later the problem was adjusted, the cost of cabinets reduced and put in on a rental basis.

General Foods added other packaged food products and Mortimer became merchandising manager for Calumet Baking Powder, Sanka Coffee, Log Cabin Syrup, Certo and Sure-Jell, and in 1935 was made a vice-president. He was named vice-president of the corporation in charge of advertising in 1943.

During World War II, Mortimer served on committees of the Adverising Council and as its chairman from 1947 to 1950. *Fortune* (September 1954) quoted his guiding doctrine as "The world won't be free if the United States is not economically sound; the United States won't be sound if its business organizations are not prosperous; the organizations will not be prosperous if they do not increase their inventiveness in moving goods."

As the demand for frozen food increased, new companies sprang up, and General Foods felt the competition. However, many were "opportunistic" packers, and as the war ended, the market slumped and many of the firms went out of business. GF turned over to Mortimer the responsibility for sales, advertising, consumer service and market research in 1947. In 1950 Mortimer was named operating vice-president for Birds Eye and a director of General Foods.

Elected executive vice-president in 1952, he served with Clarence Francis, chairman, and Austin S. Igleheart, president, on a three-man team responsible for the over-all management of the corporation. On April 7, 1954, Mortimer was made president of General Foods and chief executive officer. In the previous month the corporation had completed removal of its offices from midtown Manhattan to its new headquarters in White Plains, New York. Eighty-five per cent of some 1,200 headquarters employees decided to continue in their jobs at White Plains, and those who resigned received termination allowances.

General Foods operates 142 plants, warehouses and sales offices in the United States, as well as ten plants in Canada, England, Mexico and the Philippines. The company has received several citations for "intelligent personnel administration" of its approximately

Karsh, Ottawa

CHARLES G. MORTIMER, JR.

20,000 employees, and for "the progressive use of the best training methods and devices" in both its sales and plant training programs. Employees enjoy such benefits as retirement annuities, terminance allowances, and group insurance. Stock in GF is owned by some 68,000 stock-holders.

Mortimer had a hand in organizing a development division which examines promising new products. *Forbes* (August 15, 1955) reported that General Foods during the past year introduced a new flavor of Jell-O, an "instant" Postum, frozen turkey pies, fish "bites", canned dog food, a packaged salad dressing and "instant" cake mixes. Its expenditure on research reached $5,800,000 in 1954.

To keep ahead of the highly competitive package food industry, Mortimer believes that the firm with the best and newest products and promotion to-the-hilt—tops the market. The company's advertising budget rose from $43,000,000 in 1952 to $62,000,000 in 1954 and 1955. In the annual statement (March 31, 1955) Mortimer reported that a peak record had been set in net sales of $824,837,506, an increase of $42,000,000 or 5.4 percent over the previous year.

General Foods is known as one of the largest radio and television advertisers. Its twenty-fifth anniversary in 1954 was publicized by a Richard Rodgers and Oscar Hammerstein television and radio musical cavalcade presented on March 28. Four major networks carried the ninety-minute show over 245 stations.

Charles G. Mortimer, Jr., was married on November 10, 1927 to Elizabeth Kemply Atterbury. They have three sons, Charles III, John A., and Lee, a daughter Mary Cecil and two granddaughters. The family resided for many years in Glen Ridge, New Jersey. They moved to their new home in White Plains soon after General Foods transferred its head-

MORTIMER, CHARLES G., JR.—*Cont.*
quarters from 250 Park Avenue in New York City.

In Glen Ridge, Mortimer belonged to many civic organizations and served on the town's Board of Trustees. He is a member of Beta Theta Pi; of the board of governors of the Union League Club in New York and the Marketing Executive Society. He is a former chairman of the board of the Association of National Advertisers and was chairman of the board of the Advertising Club from 1947 to 1949.

Mortimer has dark hair and eyes, is medium tall and of average build. His week-ends are spent on his 400-acre farm in Montague, Sussex County, New Jersey, where he breeds pure-bred Holstein-Friesian and operates a dairy. His cows produce half a million pounds of milk a year, and show a neat profit. As a hobby, he rides, trains and breaks young Morgan horses.

References

Forbes 76:22 Ag 15 '55 por
Fortune 50:132+ S '54 por
Printers Ink 238:108 F 22 '52 por; 247:5 Ap 16 '54 por
Business Executives of America (1950)
Who's Who in America, 1954-55
Who's Who in Commerce and Industry (1953)
Who's Who in New York, 1952
World Biography (1954)

MORTON, JOHN JAMIESON, JR. May 19, 1886- Surgeon; university professor

Address: b. c/o Strong Memorial Hospital, Rochester 20, N.Y.; h. 1915 Westfall Rd., Rochester 18, N.Y.

As head of the U.S. Atomic Bomb Casualty Commission, an agency of the National Research Council, Dr. John Jamieson Morton, Jr., was called upon to examine the twenty-three Japanese fishermen from the sampan *Fukuryu Maru* who were hospitalized as the result of burns from ashes caused by the hydrogen bomb explosion off Bikini on March 1, 1954. An important part of the "long-range program" of the commission headed by Dr. Morton is the study of "possible delayed effects of radiation."

Dr. Morton was professor of surgery at the University of Rochester School of Medicine for more than twenty-five years, beginning in 1924, and is now professor emeritus and the acting director of the university's cancer research. Morton also serves as chief surgeon of the Strong Memorial and Rochester Municipal Hospitals. He was president of the American Society for the Control of Cancer (1938-1940). Morton was an assistant professor of surgery at Yale University Medical School and an assistant in orthopedics at Harvard Medical School. He is a fellow of the American College of Surgeons and has been a member of its board of governors since 1935.

Of Scotch-English ancestry, John Jamieson Morton, Jr., was born on May 19, 1886 in Holyoke, Massachusetts to John Jamieson and Nellie Augusta (Taylor) Morton. He is the third of five children. "Johnny" Morton attended Holyoke High School and was a member of the baseball and track teams. He also distinguished himself in track at Amherst College in Massachusetts, where he won his "letters" for track, relay racing, and gymnastics and was elected to the Phi Gamma Delta fraternity. He received his A.B. degree at Amherst in 1907 and an honorary D.Sc. degree just forty years later.

Among the persons named by Dr. Morton as having influenced his choice of a lifework are neurosurgeon Dr. Carl Wheeler Rand, who persuaded him to go to the Johns Hopkins Medical School in Baltimore, Maryland; Dr. Thomas Hunt Morgan, who had "previously arranged" for him to study biology at Columbia University in New York City; and Dr. Harvey Cushing, with whom he served in the U.S. Army Medical Corps.

Having received his M.D. degree—and also election to the Phi Beta Kappa honor fraternity—at Johns Hopkins in 1913, Dr. Morton served an internship in surgery at the Peter Bent Brigham Hospital, Boston, Massachusetts between June 1913 and the following summer. He was then awarded a fellowship in pathology at the Rockefeller Institute for Medical Research in New York City, where he concentrated his studies on radiant energy and cancer research.

A paper by James B. Murphy and Morton entitled "The Effects of Roentgen Rays on the Rate of Growth of Spontaneous Tumors in Mice" was published in the *Journal of Experimental Medicine* in 1915. Morton's "A Rapid Method for the Diagnosis of Renal Tuberculosis by Use of the X-Rayed Guinea Pig" appeared in the same periodical in the year following.

For two years beginning in September 1915, Morton was resident surgeon with the Massachusetts General Hospital Emergency Service in Boston; and from September 1916 to April 1917, when his World War I service began, he was an assistant resident physician at the Rockefeller Institute Hospital in New York City.

Commissioned a first lieutenant in the U.S. Army Medical Corps, Dr. Morton became a major before his discharge in April 1919. Associated in France with Base Hospital Number Five at Camiers (where he was "on loan" to the British Expeditionary Force) and at General Hospital Number Thirteen at Boulogne, Morton served continuously under Dr. Harvey Cushing. In Dr. Cushing's war diary *From a Surgeon's Journal* (Little, Brown, 1936) there are several mentions of "Johnny" Morton, who performed some deft bits of emergency surgery, and also "perpetrated" some "very clever skits in verse" at a 1917 Christmas celebration at Boulogne.

From 1919 to 1921 Dr. Morton practiced orthopedic surgery in Boston with Dr. Robert Lovett. He was also assistant attending surgeon in orthopedic surgery at Children's Hospital and assistant in orthopedics at the Harvard Medical School.

In 1921 he was asked by Dr. Samuel C. Harvey to help organize the surgical service at the Yale Medical School in New Haven, Connecticut, where he was to hold the position of assistant professor of surgery until 1924.

Scientific papers by Dr. Morton which were published during these years included (in collaboration with Drs. Elsa Hill and W. D. Witherbee) "Studies on . . . Direct Action of X-Rays on Transplantable Cancers in Mice" (*Journal of Experimental Medicine,* 1919); (by Morton alone) "The General Type of Osteitis Fibrosa Cystica, von Recklinghausen's Disease (*Archives of Surgery,* 1922); (with Dr. W. C. Duffy) "The Immediate Effect of Radium and X-Rays on Enzyme Action" (*American Journal of Roentgenology,* 1923); and "The Present Treatment of Cancer" (*Proceedings of the Connecticut Medical Society,* 1923).

Dr. Morton is a specialist in intestinal obstruction, circulatory disorders of the extremities, the sympathetic nervous system, and diseases of the bone as well as cancer research and radiant energy. He has from time to time published papers on all these subjects. Much of his eminence in these several fields was attained as professor of surgery and surgical chief of the School of Medicine and Dentistry of the University of Rochester, New York, to which he was appointed in 1924. He is now surgeon in chief of the Strong Memorial and Rochester Municipal Hospitals, a member of the consulting staff of the Highland, Rochester General and Monroe County Hospitals, and a member since 1939 of the board of scientific research of Yale University's Childs Memorial Foundation for Cancer Research.

Morton wrote an exhaustive study, "Cancer of the Skin" (*Archives of Surgery,* 1926) and a paper (in collaboration with Dr. G. Burroughs Mider) entitled "Production of Lymphomatosis in Mice of Known Genetic Constitution" (*Science,* April 8, 1938). Likewise of contemporary importance were his studies of acute pancreatitis in the *New York State Journal of Medicine* for February 15, 1940 and *Surgery* for April 1945. The entire November 1946 issue of *Surgery* was comprised of contributions from Dr. Morton's associates and was dedicated to him in honor of his sixtieth birthday.

Now a professor emeritus and the acting director of cancer research at the University of Rochester, Dr. Morton in 1953-1954 took a leave of absence to serve as head of the Atomic Bomb Casualty Commission, an agency of the National Research Council created under the sponsorship of the U.S. Atomic Energy Commission in 1947 to carry on the work of a Joint Army-Navy Commission appointed by General Douglas MacArthur to study survivors of the atomic bombing of Hiroshima and Nagasaki.

Dr. Morton examined the Japanese fishermen from the sampan *Fukuryu Maru* hospitalized at Tokyo and Yaizu as the result of burns from a fall of ashes from the hydrogen bomb explosion off Bikini on March 1, 1954. On

Kay Hart Studios, Inc.

DR. JOHN JAMIESON MORTON, JR.

March 20 Tokyo University's medical department revealed that two new drugs, the American-developed ethylenediamine tetraacetic acid and the university's iriloysin would be used in treating the men. The United States agreed in January 1955 to pay $2,000,000 for damages inflicted on the Japanese during the H-bomb tests.

He is a fellow of the American College of Surgeons, on the bone sarcoma committee of which he served for fifteen years beginning in 1925. He has been a member of the A.C.S. board of governors since 1935 and was on the legislative committee for New York State in 1935-1938. A member of the scientific committee of the American Medical Association since 1928, Dr. Morton has also served the Society of Clinical Surgery as treasurer in 1933-1935 and president in 1939-1940, and has been an executive committeeman of the American Society for the Control of Cancer since 1936. He was vice-president of the A.S.C.C. in 1937 and president in 1938-1940.

Scientific bodies other than those already mentioned to which Dr. Morton belongs include the American Surgical Association, the American Society for Clinical Investigation, the Johns Hopkins Surgical Society, the American Society for Experimental Pathology, the Robert Jones Orthopedic Society, the American Society for Cancer Research and the International Surgical Society. He is a member of the National Advisory Cancer Council of the United States Public Health Service. Dr. Morton is an honorary member of the Nu Sigma Nu medical fraternity and a member of Alpha Omega Alpha and Sigma Xi. His clubs are the Pithotomy in Baltimore and the Country in Rochester. The surgeon-scientist is a Republican and a Protestant.

(Continued next page)

MORTON, JOHN J., JR.—*Continued*

He married Nancy Barnard, a former nurse, on October 7, 1919; they have one son, John Henderson Morton. Dr. Morton is white-haired and brown-eyed, and is five feet eight inches in height and weighs 170 pounds. Golf, fishing, hunting, bird-watching and painting are his hobbies.

References

American Medical Directory (1950)
American Men of Science (1949)
Directory of Medical Specialists (1953)
International World Who's Who, 1948-49
Who's Important in Medicine (1952)
Who's Who in America, 1954-55
World Biography (1948)

MOSER, FRITZ (mō'zẽr) Jan. 18, 1908-
Librarian; author; editor

Address: b. c/o Amerika Gedenkbibliothek/Berliner Zentralbibliothek, Am Blücherplatz, Berlin S.W. 61, Germany; h. Paulsborner Strasse 65, Berlin-Grunewald, Germany

FRITZ MOSER

The American Memorial Library, a monument toward international friendship given to the city of Berlin by the United States Government, was completed in 1954 and is headed by Fritz Moser. An author and editor, Moser served in the Berlin government in various capacities after the end of World War II and assumed direction of the library as it was being constructed in 1952. It is an American-type free public library, which is staffed entirely by Germans and which now has about 100,000 books of interest to people of all professions and to children. The library, centrally located, is open to both West and East Berliners.

Fritz Moser was born in Berlin on January 18, 1908, the son of Alexander and Martha (Kleinau) Moser. His father was a stockbroker at the Berlin Stock Exchange. He had two brothers (his elder brother, an artist, is deceased; his younger brother is a general agent of the Stahl elevator company in Stuttgart) and a sister. He attended the Oberrealschule in Berlin-Steglitz and was graduated in 1926.

He then studied Germanic languages, the history of the arts and of the theatre, philosophy, psychology, and sociology at the University of Munich and the University of Berlin and received his Ph.D. degree from the latter in 1940. In that year his book *Die Anfänge des Hof- und Gesellschaftstheaters in Deutschland* (The Beginnings of Royal Court and Private Theaters in Germany) was published by the Otto Elsner-Verlag in Berlin. He worked as a free-lance writer and was persecuted by the Nazis.

At the end of World War II, Fritz Moser was appointed chief of the department of literature under the Magistrate of Greater Berlin (in February 1946). Later, in 1948, he became supervisor of the affairs of municipal libraries, publishers, authors, and booksellers for the Senate of West Berlin. He wrote *Die ungeweinten Tränen; Balladen vom gelben Stern* (The Unshed Tears; Ballads of the Yellow Stars) (Chronos Verlag) in 1947. He edited *Goethe in Berlin*, published by Wedding-Verlag in 1949, and *Luftbrücke Berlin* (Berlin Airlift), published by Arani-Verlag in 1949. His *Berliner Köpfe* (Berlin Heads), a calendar, appeared in 1949.

Remembering the heroism of the Berliners during the blockade in 1948 and 1949 and mindful that the U.S. occupation of Germany would soon be ending, John J. McCloy, then U.S. High Commissioner for Germany, asked the people of Berlin in 1950 what they wanted as a memorial which would serve as a constant reminder of the spirit of cooperation and mutual respect characterizing the relations between the Americans and Berliners during the years since 1945 (*Library Journal,* March 15, 1954). Many suggestions were made, but a group of prominent Germans decided that the proposal of Ernst Reuter, Mayor of Berlin, was the best. He had suggested as the memorial an American-type public library.

In Germany most of the libraries have been aimed toward satisfying the needs of scholars, and, therefore, books of general interest have not been readily available to the public. It was felt that an American-type public library, where every Berlin citizen would have access to the learning of all ages, would help produce the qualities necessary for effective self-government. In the library, most of the books would be on open shelves, a system untypical of German libraries as a whole.

In 1951 McCloy announced a grant to the city of Berlin of $1,250,000 from counterpart funds derived from the Marshall Plan for the erection of a public library; $1,000,000 was to be used for the actual construction of the building and $250,000 for buying books and periodicals. At the invitation of the U.S. Department of State two Americans, Charles M. Mohrhardt, associate director of the Public Library in Detroit, Michigan, and Francis Keally, an architect of New York City, arrived in Berlin to act as consultants for the American Memorial Library (*Wilson Library Bulletin*, December 1952).

They served on a jury with thirteen German librarians and architects and helped select the best entries in a contest among German architects for plans of the proposed building. From the winners were chosen those who would draw-up the final blueprint: the firm of Gerhardt Jobst, Willi Kreuer, and Hartmut Wille, and Fritz Bornemann.

Construction of the building began in 1952. In June U.S. Secretary of State Dean Acheson, Mayor Reuter, and Commissioner McCloy were present at the cornerstone-laying ceremonies. Moser was named director of the library in December 1952. While the building was being constructed, he was in charge of gathering a staff and obtaining and processing the books and other reading matter. Plans were made so that the contents of the new library would not duplicate the collections of existing scientific and technical libraries in Berlin, nor the library which the Ford Foundation had presented to the Free University of Berlin.

Approximately 40,000 books and the staff of the Wissenschaftliche Zentralbibliothek of Berlin were incorporated into the new library. The Library of Congress, which has "adopted" the American Memorial Library, appointed Edgar Breitenbach to act as its Berlin representative during the formative years of the library. His work in Berlin was made possible partly through a grant of the Ford Foundation.

The opening festivities of the library were held on September 17, 1954. Dr. James B. Conant, U.S. High Commissioner for Germany, attended as did Vice-Chancellor Franz Blücher of the Federal Republic of Germany. In the four weeks following the date (September 20, 1954) when the library was opened to the public, some 15,693 persons, including 2,800 children, used the library. In a single day (November 14) about 3,209 books were borrowed.

The library, located about one-third of a mile from the Soviet sector of Berlin, was built six stories high in order that the structure would be seen from all over the city. The public area is entirely on the main floor of the building. The other five stories are for offices, a library school, and stacks. On the main floor are the departments for belles-lettres, fine arts (theater, film, dance), humanities, reference, periodicals, social science, law and business, and science and technology. The music area has listening booths and a piano room. The children's department, in addition to books, has dolls, an aquarium, and plants, which provide a cheerful atmosphere. There is an auditorium with a seating capacity for 320 persons for lectures, film showings, discussions, and concerts.

Through an exchange program between librarians made possible by the U.S. Department of State, several German and American librarians have been able to give and receive information on American-type public libraries. Moser has visited the United States to inspect the libraries, as have other members of his staff. He has expressed his appreciation of the help received from the U.S. consultants who have recently visited the American Memorial Library. A gift of $1,300, to be used for whatever purpose the Berlin library staff considered wise, was donated by the staff of the Detroit Public Library.

Moser has written several articles on the American Memorial Library; these appeared in *Die Neue Zeitung* in June 1952 and on April 12, 1953 and in *Bücherei und Bildung* in July-August 1953. He belongs to the Association of German Librarians, the Association of German Public Librarians, and the Association of Berlin Authors.

Fritz Moser married Waltraut Hillmann on August 15, 1945. He has brown eyes and gray hair; he is almost six feet tall and weighs 160 pounds. He is a member of the Lutheran church. Among his recreations he includes fencing, boxing, and motor-car racing.

Reference

Wer ist Wer? (1955)

MOTRICO, JOSÉ MARÍA DE AREILZA, COUNT OF. *See* Areilza, José María de, Count of Motrico

MOTT, JOHN R(ALEIGH) May 25, 1865-Jan. 31, 1955 Evangelist; co-winner of Nobel Peace Prize (1946) for participation in five world church and missionary movements; at various times was executive head of the World's Alliance of the Young Men's Christian Association, International Missionary Council, American Christian Student Movement, Student Volunteer Movement, and World's Student Christian Federation; was decorated by many foreign governments; wrote numerous books and articles. See *Current Biography* (Jan.) 1947.

Obituary

N Y Times p29 F 1 '55

MUGGERIDGE, MALCOLM (THOMAS) Mar. 24, 1903- British editor; journalist

Address: b. c/o Punch, 10 Bouverie St., London E.C. 4; h. A 10 Albany, Piccadilly, London, W.1

The appointment of Malcolm Muggeridge as editor of *Punch*, the famous 114-year-old British humorous weekly periodical, in January 1953 caused "a lot of surprised and interested talk around Fleet Street, because for the first time, the magazine has gone outside the *Punch* office for its choice" (*New Yorker*, January 31, 1953). His career has been chiefly in the newspaper field, including two years on the editorial staff of the *Manchester Guardian* and a year as its correspondent in Russia, one year as assistant editor of the Calcutta *Statesman*, two on the editorial desk of the London *Evening Standard*, and Washington, D.C. correspondent for the London *Daily Telegraph* and its deputy editor (1950-52).

After one year at *Punch* he received from the London *Daily Mirror* (as reported in the London *World's Press News*, December 31, 1954) an accolade for injecting "new life and new bite into this famous weekly magazine,

Wide World

MALCOLM MUGGERIDGE

for courageously publishing some of the most controversial cartoons of the year." Muggeridge is the author of numerous books, including *Winter in Moscow* (1934), in which he was extremely critical of the Soviet regime and *A Study of Samuel Butler: the Earnest Atheist* (1937), a caustic treatment which was praised by the *American Review* as "a valuable antidote to the Butler worship of the day." He has become known to a wider circle than that of *Punch* readers by appearing during 1954 on a television interview feature called *Panorama,* and by filmed television he has also been seen and heard in America. He has been among the chief advocates of breaking the B.B.C.'s television monopoly by the establishment of commercial stations.

Malcolm Thomas Muggeridge (his "unbelievable name," as the New York *Post* calls it, is of Sussex origin), was born March 24, 1903 in Sanderstead, Surrey, just outside London, the son of Henry Thomas Muggeridge, a company secretary and later Labor Member of Parliament for Romford, Essex. His mother was born Annie Booler and came from the Yorkshire industrial city, Sheffield. Malcolm had four brothers, Stanley (deceased), Douglas, Eric, and Jack. He received a scholarship to Selhurst Grammar School, Croydon, Surrey, which he left in 1920 to enter Selwyn College, Cambridge, where he took the tripos (honors course) in natural science and English literature, earning his M.A. degree in 1923. Concerning the mixture of subjects he says: "I am afraid I didn't do very well in the natural science side, and so did not take a very good degree." His desire was to write, and in this ambition he was encouraged by Dr. Alec Vidler, Canon of Windsor, C.P. Scott, famous owner-editor of the *Manchester Guardian,* and the writer Hugh Kingsmill (Lunn).

Finding a temporary niche in the Egyptian Public Instruction Department, he lectured at the Egyptian University, Cairo from 1927 to 1930. While in Africa he became Cairo correspondent of the *Manchester Guardian* and in 1930 was appointed to the editorial staff, working in the Manchester office until 1932.

In that year he was sent to Russia by the *Manchester Guardian* as its Moscow correspondent. He came home in 1933 to write what he himself calls "a bitter book," *Winter in Moscow* (Little, Brown, 1934), in which he made no attempt to be dispassionate about the Russian experiment. He frankly expressed his dislike of the Soviet Union in a series of ironic sketches. "The characters are real people imaginatively described," he said. The *Saturday Review of Literature* commented: "It is refreshing to come across an intelligent observer who is just plain disgusted all through and doesn't give a hoot who knows it. . . . Outspoken and incisive in its destructive criticism of the Soviet." The London *Times* Literary Supplement wrote that Muggeridge "apparently regards the whole [Russian] thing as a fantastic show, equally monstrous and ridiculous, and devotes his considerable powers to deriding it." Lewis Gannett in the New York *Herald Tribune* called it "maliciously amusing . . . one of the wittiest attacks on Russia yet penned."

For a short time Muggeridge worked at Geneva with the International Labor Office, and then he went to India in 1934 to fill the post of assistant editor of the Calcutta *Statesman.* After a year he returned to London to join the *Evening Standard,* where he worked on the "Londoner's Diary," the daily gossip page. During the war he served from 1939 to 1945 in the Intelligence Corps in East Africa, Italy, and France, joining as a private and leaving as a major. He was awarded the Croix de Guerre (with palm) and the Médaille de la Reconnaissance Française, and was made a member of the Legion of Honor.

From a "light" Conservative paper he moved in 1946 to the Conservative *Daily Telegraph,* which has a circulation of over one million. He was sent out to the United States as Washington correspondent in 1947; on June 14, 1953 the New York *Post* printed an appreciative notice of his lighter reactions to the American scene. Returning to London, he did a great deal of reviewing and published a series on Malaya which he feels was one of his better efforts. In 1950 he became deputy editor of the *Daily Telegraph,* serving in that capacity until the end of 1952.

In October 1953, when a Bevanite Socialist member of Parliament attacked the United States foreign policy, Muggeridge defended America as "the mainstay of freedom," and "the imperfection of the instrument does not detract from the nobility of the aim." He pointed out in his article, "An Anatomy of Neutralism" in *Time,* November 2, 1953, that "American policy must be held responsible for the widespread proneness to neutralism on this side of the Atlantic, but not because, as [Tom] Driberg labors to demonstrate, American policy is brutal and power-seeking; rather the reverse —because it is sentimental and imprecise, because it so often seeks to evade the realities of power in favor of the abstractions of democratic theory."

His book, *The Thirties* (Hamilton, 1940) (American title: *The Sun Never Sets; the Story of England in the Nineteen-thirties,* Random House, 1940) received critical acclaim. The Boston *Transcript* commented: "The book crackles with wit, it outdoes earlier only-yesterday studies with its cutting, flashing style, its glittering satire. Its epigrams fairly cry for quotation." Geoffrey Bruun in the New York *Herald Tribune Books* wrote: "A more blistering indictment of British political leadership, Labor and Tory alike . . . would be difficult to find."

Critical opinion of his book, *A Study of Samuel Butler: the Earnest Atheist* (Putnam, 1937) (English title: *The Earnest Atheist*), (Eyre, 1936), was generally favorable. "There is an exquisite propriety in Muggeridge's treatment," commented the *Christian Science Monitor*'s reviewer; he has achieved "a portrait which is at once new, amusing, thought-provoking and truthful," said the *Manchester Guardian.* On the other hand, the New York *Herald Tribune Books* regarded the biography as "a thoroughly false and distorted view of Butler."

Muggeridge's other books include *Autumnal Face* (Putnam, 1931); *In a Valley of This Restless Mind* (1938); *Affairs of the Heart* (Hamilton, 1949); he edited an English edition of Count Galeazzo Ciano's diaries (Heineman, 1947), and was co-editor with Hesketh Pearson of the *Diplomatic Papers of G. Ciano* (Heineman, 1948). He was co-author, with Hugh Kingsmill (Lunn) of *Brave Old World: a Mirror for the Times* (Eyre, 1936), and with Hesketh Pearson edited *About Kingsmill* (letters) (Methuen, 1951). He translated from the French Maurice Bedel's *New Arcadia* (Cape, 1935). He is also the author of a play, *Three Flats,* produced in 1931 by the Stage Society, London (Putnam, 1931).

In 1952 Bradbury, Agnew and Company, proprietors of *Punch,* were on the lookout for an editor in chief to succeed Kenneth Bird ("Fougasse," the cartoonist), who was approaching the retiring age. They decided, for the first time in Mr. Punch's history, to go outside the office and find an experienced journalist who would contribute a new tang and fresh emphasis, and chose Muggeridge. "Nothing in his career seems to have led up to his arrival at the head of 'the table' on *Punch,*" commented the *New Yorker,* "which is exactly why so many people feel that the appointment may be highly stimulating for all concerned." It was not long before the *New Yorker* found itself wittily parodied in *Punch,* and reciprocated by parodying its British counterpart.

Muggeridge took over the *Punch* editorial chair on January 1, 1953. By September of that year he was immersed in the British controversy over the introduction of commercial television.

He spoke against the B.B.C. monopoly on several occasions. "Freedom, it seems to me," he said, "lies not so much in objectivity, which is largely beyond human realization, as in variety. . . . Those who appear regularly [on] B.B.C. . . . must be prepared to blow their trumpets or sound their cymbals or scratch their violins in accordance with the Corporation's baton. . . . Whether the music is good or bad, there is one orchestra with one conductor, following one score, and this state of affairs . . . is both unhealthy and dangerous. . ." (*Time,* August 3, 1953).

Now in his second year as editor, Muggeridge has carried on "in the great tradition of *Punch* cartoons," commented *Time* (March 29, 1954). "*Punch* boasts a stable of more than [seventy] artists [including Rowland Emett, Giovannetti, Brockbank, Sprod, Ffoulkes, David Langdon and Fougasse]. . . . Their efforts bring a freshness, verve and variety of cartoon humor to be found nowhere outside *Punch.*" Muggeridge's pungent editorials have been widely quoted in the United States. Under his editorship *Punch* is also becoming a literary magazine. "The signatures read like a Who's Who of modern English letters"; for example, Joyce Cary, Noel Coward, Lord Dunsany, J. B. Priestley, and Dorothy L. Sayers, write occasional pieces.

Punch's traditional cover by Richard Doyle showing the figure of Punch, used unchanged for nearly a century, now echoes the "renaissance that is taking place within." A recent one showed Punch celebrating the end of food rationing in England; another showed Punch studying the ticker tape while his dog has a pained expression. There also has been a typographical "streamlining." The type of humor has in some measure changed, being now more "charged with bite and satire than in the old jog-trot days." One feature, which has been running for months, is a series of parodies of various journals, imitating their typographical, illustrative and literary style. Another popular feature was a day's alleged program of the B.B.C., as seen in its weekly paper, the *Radio Times;* and still another was a four-page two-color inset of *Her,* an imaginary woman's magazine.

The idea for these brilliant parodies was Muggeridge's, and his anonymous contributors have ably supported him. When the new editor took over, *Punch*'s circulation was 133,742 (December 1952); it reached 145,276 by December 1954. The subscription price is $5.25.

Punch's editor has graying hair and is "tallish, spare, friendly, and of charming and modest manners." His hobby is walking, and his clubs are the Authors', the Garrick, and Pratt's. In 1927 he married Katherine Dobbs, and they have three sons and one daughter.

References

MacLeans Mag Ag 1 '54
N Y Post p3 Je 14 '53
New Yorker 28:70 Ja 31 '53
Time 60:47 D 8 '52
TV Mirror (London) Ja 1 '55
Who's Who, 1954

MURPHY, W(ILLIAM) B(EVERLY)
June 17, 1907- Business executive
Address: b. c/o Campbell Soup Co., 100 Market St., Camden, N.J.; h. Dodd's Lane, Gladwyne, Pa.

Vigorous and forward-looking, W. B. "Bev" Murphy, who was appointed president of the Campbell Soup Company on March 1, 1953, proved himself "a canny executive" when he engineered, in April 1955, "the food industry's biggest merger of the year" by purchasing the Omaha, Nebraska company of C. A. Swanson & Sons, producer of frozen food specialties. Murphy's job is keeping an old and successful company in step with the times—which nowadays means the frozen food business. In February 1955 Campbell introduced its own brand of eight frozen soups. Since Campbell's is the largest producer in the world of canned soups and spaghetti, and since Swanson sold over 80,000,000 frozen pies and 17,000,000 frozen dinners in 1954, Murphy heads a company which plays a large part in keeping America's farmers busy and families well-fed.

Fabian Bachrach
W. B. MURPHY

Murphy started his business career as a marketing analyst with the A. C. Nielsen Company, where he is credited with having invented the basic idea for the Nielsen Food and Drug Index. He joined the Campbell Soup Company in 1938 and has been with this firm ever since, except for a period during the war when he served on the War Production Board in Washington, D.C.

Born in Appleton, Wisconsin on June 17, 1907, William Beverly Murphy is the son of S. W. and Hilma (Anderson) Murphy. He grew up in Appleton and attended public schools there. After graduating from high school, Murphy studied at the University of Wisconsin where in 1928 he received the degree of B.S. in chemical engineering. His major extra-curricular activity during this period was track.

Immediately following graduation Murphy went to work for the A. C. Nielsen Company of Chicago. When he left this company as an executive vice president ten years later, his experience as a sales analyst stood him in good stead when he became assistant to the general manager of the Campbell Soup Company in Camden, New Jersey.

With the entrance of the United States in World War II, Murphy went to Washington for the War Production Board under Donald Nelson and was appointed director of the Facilities Division in February 1942. A year later he was named chairman of the Industrial Facility Committee and in August 1943 he was made deputy vice chairman for production. He held this position until September 1944. In January 1947 he was awarded a Civilian Medal for Merit for his services during this period.

One month prior to his resignation as deputy vice chairman for production, Murphy was appointed assistant general manager of the Campbell Soup Company. (His services to the War Production Board were of such a quality that he remained as consultant to that group from November 1944 through March 1945.)

With the end of the war, Murphy resumed his duties at the Campbell Soup Company in Camden and on June 27, 1946 was appointed director of Campbell Soup Company Limited [of Canada]. Promotions followed rapidly: he was made executive assistant to the president of the Campbell Soup Company on July 1, 1946 and executive vice president of the Campbell Soup Company Limited on April 24, 1947. The Campbell Soup Company appointed him executive vice president on August 15, 1949, and on July 25, 1950 made him a director of the company. He became president on March 1, 1953. On that date he also became president of the Campbell Soup Company Limited and director and chairman of the board of the Joseph Campbell Company. At this time he was forty-five years of age.

As president, Murphy is adhering closely to the "tried and true" formula of Dr. John T. Dorrance, creator of the Campbell condensed soup—which is to offer a good product at a competitive price, backed by strong advertising. Dorrance, a young chemist, joined the 28-year-old Joseph Campbell Preserve Company in 1897. In 1898 the varied line of more than 200 food products was dropped, and the company concentrated on a single product—heat-processed soup. The first Campbell advertising was a $4,600 trolley car-card campaign; in 1904 the "Campbell Kids" were first used in advertising; magazine advertising began in 1905. Dr. Dorrance headed the company from 1914 until his death in 1930 (see *Printers' Ink,* February 18, 1955 for a history of the company). Campbell now produces forty-eight kinds of heat-processed soups, pork and beans, spaghetti, tomato juice, ketchup, V-8 vegetable juice, and other products.

Murphy has added a few ideas of his own such as scientific marketing, continually improved standards of quality control and greater delegation of authority to his subordinates.

Recently Murphy stated: "You can advertise all you want. You can hire all the salesmen you want. But if you don't maintain the quality, you're helpless."

The original contribution of the Campbell Soup Company was to provide the housewife with a can of standardly good concentrated soup which would feed a small family. This saved the housewife from the laborious chore of making her own soup which would, of necessity, be made in large amounts. Murphy introduced the idea of providing the modern luxury-conscious housewife with quality foods (such as oyster and shrimp soup) which must be frozen or else their unique flavor would be lost. This led Murphy to the idea of providing the family not only with pre-prepared soups, but also with frozen foods to provide complete meals as well which prompted the purchase of C. A. Swanson & Sons frozen food company in 1955.

Campbell has some 13,500 permanent employees (and some 4,500 temporary employees in the peak tomato season), and has a personnel staff of twenty who work in cooperation with psychologists at the Industrial Relations Research Center of the University of Chicago to maintain good employee morale. Campbell provides an insured noncontributing pension plan, group life insurance, accident and health insurance. Campbell has nine food-processing plants in the United States and Canada, and in 1955 added C. A. Swanson & Sons' ten food-processing plants and 4,100 year-round employees.

The company's $11,094,157 advertising budget in 1953 was divided as follows: $3,867,542 for magazines; $1,052,020 for supplements; $521,245 for newspapers; $2,305,692 for radio; and $3,347,658 for television. Campbell total sales in 1954 were $339,000,000. In 1954 the company, for the first time since 1922, placed its stock on the market, at $39.25 a share; the 1,300,000 shares were sold to the public (as ordered by Murphy, "spread the stock thin from Portland Maine to Portland, Oregon" (*Forbes,* December 1, 1954).

In recognition of Murphy's achievements in both business and the war effort, Lawrence College in Murphy's home town of Appleton, Wisconsin presented him with the degree of Doctor of Laws *Honoris Cause* "for distinguished achievement . . . and imaginative business practice."

Murphy is a member of the Merion Golf Club in Ardmore, Pennsylvania, the Merion Cricket Club in Haverford, and Philadelphia's Racquet Club. He is also a member of Delta Upsilon, Tau Beta Pi and Iron Cross. In 1951 he was general chairman of the Camden County Community Chest. In 1933 he was made director of the American Radiator and Standard Sanitary Corporation in New York. During October 1954 Murphy was made the vice president of Keep America Beautiful and a member of the executive committee.

William B. Murphy married Helen Brennan on May 28, 1930. They have four children—Robert, Ann, John and Eric—and one grandchild. Murphy is a Republican and a Presbyterian. The Murphy family lives on a three and a quarter acre estate with a swimming pool and a greenhouse at Dodd's Lane in Gladwyne, a suburb of Philadelphia. Besides being an avid reader, Murphy plays tennis and grows orchids in his leisure hours. A big and forceful man, he moves about quickly and never seems to relax during business hours. He is himself a soup eater whose family has soup for dinner every evening. His own favorite is a mixture of Campbell's Chicken Noodle and Celery Soups. His ambition is to see every housewife in America serve soup three times a day—"including breakfast".

References

Forbes 74:23 D 1 '54 por
Fortune 51:78 Mr '55
N Y Times p39 Ap 4 '55
Printers Ink 250:24+ F 18 '55 por
Who's Who in America, 1954-55

MURVILLE, MAURICE COUVE DE *See* Couve de Murville, (Jacques) Maurice

MUSKIE, EDMUND S(IXTUS) Mar. 28, 1914- Governor of Maine; lawyer

Address: b. State House, Augusta, Me.; h. Blaine Mansion, Augusta, Me.

After eighteen years of Republican rule, the voters of Maine elected the Democratic candidate Edmund S. Muskie to the governorship on September 13, 1954. He attributed his victory over the incumbent Burton M. Cross to dissatisfaction with "the economic situation and the lack of progress in [Maine's] industrial development and education" (New York *Herald Tribune,* September 18, 1954). Muskie, who had practiced law for about ten years in Waterville, Maine, served in the Maine Legislature in 1947, 1949 and 1951 and was minority floor leader of the state House of Representatives in 1949. He has been a Democratic national committeeman since 1952.

Edmund Sixtus Muskie was born in Rumford, Maine on March 28, 1914, one of the six children of Stephen Marciszewski (who migrated from Poland) and his wife, Josephine Czarnecki. His father, who is a tailor, became a naturalized citizen and simplified his surname to Muskie. Edmund attended Virginia Primary School in Oxford county and the Stephens High School at Rumford, where he overcame his shyness and joined the debating team in his junior year.

Ed became "an enthusiastic fisherman, a good skier and a competent tracksman" (*Time,* September 27, 1954) and was "a high-scoring center" on the basketball team, as well as an "avid reader." He was valedictorian of the class of 1932 and received a $150 scholarship at Bates College, Lewiston, Maine.

Muskie majored in history and was president of his class for two years, a member of the debating team, politics club, and Delta Sigma Rho and was known as the "only Democrat on campus." He earned his meals by waiting on tables and during the summers washed dishes in a nearby hotel. He was elected

Wide World

EDMUND S. MUSKIE

to Phi Beta Kappa and received the B.A. degree in 1936.

A scholarship enabled Muskie to study at Cornell University Law School. He completed the requirements for the LL.B. degree in 1939. In that year he was admitted to the Massachusetts bar, in 1940 to the Maine bar, and in 1941 to practice before the U.S. District Court. Muskie began to practice law in Waterville, Maine in 1940. Two years later he volunteered in the Naval Reserve.

Discharged as a lieutenant (j.g.) in 1945, Muskie returned to Waterville to his law practice and began to participate in local politics. "His preliminary [political] training was obtained in a Waterville restaurant. There the future governor and Mayor Richard Dubord [of Waterville, Maine] were the only Democrats at a table daily occupied at luncheon by a group of vociferous Republicans" (New York *Times*, September 13, 1954). His debating skill was sharpened by the "thrusts and counter thrusts" of these midday arguments.

Muskie was elected in 1946 to the Maine House of Representatives. The Maine Legislature meets only in odd-numbered years, and after the conclusion of the 1947 session he ran for the mayoralty election in Waterville. He was defeated by the Republican candidate. In 1947 Muskie served as a member of the governor's budget advisory committee and chairman for Maine of the Citizens Committee for the Hoover Report. After his re-election to the state Legislature in 1948, he was made Democratic floor leader in the House of Representatives. While serving in the Legislature, Muskie gained a reputation of cooperating with the Republicans when the occasion required it. Although he was elected again to the lower chamber in 1951, he resigned during the session to join the Office of Price Stabilization as district director for Maine. In 1952 he retired from this post to become a Democratic national committeeman.

A serious injury incurred in 1953 compelled Muskie to spend four months in a hospital and to wear a brace afterwards. While doing some carpentry work in his attic he had fallen and crushed a vertebra. However, he was able to make the keynote address at the Maine state Democratic convention in March 1954 and to help in drafting a platform.

Muskie, who was unopposed in the gubernatorial primary, campaigned for the repeal of price fixing of milk above the producer level, a program to attract new industries to the state, improvement of highways and the harbor at Portland, progressive salary increases for teachers, and a minimum wage law for intrastate firms (Boston *Post,* September 26, 1954).

In the course of a campaign in which he traveled some 20,000 miles, Muskie turned the Republican 1948 presidential slogan, "Time for a Change," against the G.O.P.; "Maine Needs a Change" was his version. At the September 13, 1954 election, Muskie received 135,613 votes to 113,210 for Cross. However, the Republicans still control Maine's delegation to the U.S. Congress and hold 117 of 151 seats in the lower chamber of the state Legislature and twenty-seven of thirty-three seats in the upper chamber.

Commenting on the problems facing Muskie as governor, John H. Fenton of the New York *Times* (September 19, 1954) called attention to the political composition of the Legislature, which elects the seven-member executive council advising the governor. The Legislature also elects the state treasurer, attorney general, auditor, commissioner of agriculture, and secretary of state.

Time (September 27, 1954) noted that some of the local issues in determining the Maine election were the grievances of the Aroostook county potato growers who suffered from wet weather and were outraged by Governor Cross's stand against Federal price supports, and the problems of the textile workers who were worried about unemployment and disappointed over the failure of the Republican administration to attract new industries to the state. Muskie felt that another significant issue was that many young people were leaving the state.

After his election Muskie said that the voters "are awakening to their final power to hold politicians accountable for . . . [their] sins of commission and omission" (New York *Times,* October 23, 1954). Although he did not feel his victory indicated a national trend, he commented: "I think the results should be a psychological boost to the Democrats nationally" (New York *Post,* September 19, 1954).

As Maine's first Democratic governor-elect since Louis Jefferson Brann was re-elected in 1934, Muskie received much publicity. A series of articles about him appeared in the Boston *Post* and a nation-wide television audience became acquainted with him when he appeared on Dave Garroway's *Today* show on NBC several days after his election. He also made campaign addresses during the 1954 Congressional election campaign on behalf of Democratic candidates in various states.

Governor Muskie's two-year term began in January 1955. His annual salary is $10,000. Although he is the first Roman Catholic to be elected to the governorship of Maine, he is not actually Maine's first governor of that faith; Edward Kavanagh was appointed by Governor John Fairfield when the latter resigned to become a U.S. Senator in 1843.

The governor is a member of the Waterville, Kennebec county and Maine bar associations, and the Commercial Law League. In his home city of Waterville he has served on the zoning adjustment board and the advisory board of the Sisters Hospital. His club is the Lions. He was married to Jane Frances Gray on May 29, 1948. They are the parents of one boy, Stephen Oliver, and one girl, Ellen. Mrs. Muskie, who was a bookkeeper before her marriage, is now at twenty-seven believed to be the youngest "first lady" of any state.

Governor Muskie is six feet four inches in height, weighs 180 pounds, and carries his lanky frame with a slight stoop; his eyes are gray-blue and his curly hair is brown. He is addicted to bow ties. Nancy Seely (New York *Post,* September 19, 1954) wrote that the governor "has the homespun charm of a Will Rogers, combined with a hard core of practical political wisdom."

References

Boston Post p1+ S 19 pors; p1+ S 20; p1+ S 21 pors; p19 S 22 pors; p15 S 23 pors; p9 S 25 por; p30 S 26 '54 pors
Life 37:26+ S 27 '54 pors
N Y Herald Tribune p6 S 18 '54; II p3 S 19 '54 por
N Y Post Mag p2 S 19 '54 pors
N Y Times p24 S 15 '54 por
Newsweek 44:25+ S 27 '54 por
Time 54:15+ S 27 '54 por
U.S. News 37:16 S 24 '54
Who's Who in America, 1954-55
Who's Who in United States Politics (1952)

NADLER, MARCUS Aug. 29, 1895- University professor; financial consultant

Address: b. c/o New York University Graduate School of Business Administration, 90 Trinity Pl., New York 6; h. 180 Riverside Dr., New York 24

Noted economist and professor of finance at New York University's Graduate School of Business Administration, Dr. Marcus Nadler predicts that "the severe and prolonged depressions of the past will not recur in the United States." Evidence of this, Nadler pointed out in a recent pamphlet, "destroys the prop on which Communist propaganda rested, namely, that the capitalistic system is suffering from inherent contradictions which are bound to lead to depressions and large-scale unemployment."

For more than three decades Nadler, whose opinions are held in high respect on Wall Street, has been advising bankers and businessmen on economic policies and conditions. He began work as consulting economist for the Hanover Bank, New York City in 1936, and is currently also adviser to the Texas Company and a director of United Merchants & Manufacturers, Inc., textile combine. Besides teaching at N.Y.U., he has been since 1927 research director and assistant head of the university's Institute of International Finance.

Marcus Nadler was born in Campulung, Austria-Hungary on August 29, 1895 to Mayer Nadler, a Jewish farmer, and Leah (Javetz) Nadler. He entered the University of Vienna at the age of sixteen, but left at the end of one year to enter the Austrian army. During World War I he was wounded, and, following capture in the Ukraine, spent five years in a prison camp in Siberia. He moved to the United States in 1920 and learned English by memorizing a German-English dictionary.

The young Austrian immigrant enrolled in Columbia University and worked nights at various jobs to support himself for a year and a half while studying economics. He was awarded his B.S. degree by Columbia in 1922. With the help of Professor H. Parker Willis, author of the Federal Reserve Act, Nadler meanwhile secured a position as research assistant with the Federal Reserve Board, Washington, D.C. in 1921, which he retained until 1924. He undertook graduate study at George Washington University during 1923-1924 and then accepted a post as assistant economist of the National Bank of Commerce in New York for two years. Returning in 1926 to the Federal Reserve Board, he served for a year as chief of the foreign division.

New York University, which had granted Nadler a J.D. degree in 1926, engaged him as assistant professor of finance at its Graduate School of Business Administration in 1927 and soon promoted him to associate and then full professor. About 1,800 junior executives and 500 senior executives from investment, banking and brokerage houses currently attend classes here, the world's largest graduate business school. For two years, during 1928-1930, he lectured in the University Extension division of Columbia University.

Nadler's practice is never to repeat a lecture. "Nadler is no pedant," John Kord Lagemann wrote in *Nation's Business* (February 1952), ". . . he is committed to no particular theory or point of view. He reduces economics to the tactics and strategy of survival in a complex and competitive world." In his lectures he "has a way of diagnosing the money market with the assurance of a physician taking a blood count."

The Money Marketeers, very likely the only organization of its kind in the United States, was formed in Nadler's honor by his students, some of whom have attended his lectures for about twenty years. It is an outgrowth of a series of informal meetings of students to discuss with Nadler problems of finance. Over a period of years the group, which was formal-

MARCUS NADLER

ized in 1947, grew to comprise over 150 members, who dedicated their club to "good fellowship and high standards and just principles in business and social life."

Among the professional organizations that Nadler frequently addresses are the American Bankers Association, New York Bankers Association and New Jersey Bankers Association. He directs the faculty and curriculum for the "Investment Seminar," an annual one-day refresher course for banking executives which was started in 1950 by the New York Bankers Association in cooperation with the N.Y.U. business school.

In one of his early articles, on European currencies and the gold standard in the *Journal of Political Economy* (October 1924), Nadler stated: "Gold merely held in vaults of any central bank of issue is of no use or very little use in the restoration or stabilization of a currency, and so long as this gold is kept at home inactive, it has no effect on the exchange rates."

Reviewing President Roosevelt's plan to buy and sell gold abroad through the Reconstruction Finance Corporation, Nadler said in 1933 that the resulting depreciation of the United States dollar "would doubtless cause the abandonment of the gold standard by France and Great Britain." He recommended that the Administration instead "cooperate with other countries to avoid currency depreciation and world-wide financial chaos" (New York *Times,* November 5, 1933).

He favored the reciprocal trade treaty program of Secretary of State Cordell Hull in 1938 and proposed that part of the nation's $14 billion gold reserve be used to aid stabilization of Latin-American currencies and open new export markets. To correct domestic problems in the real estate investment and banking system, he advised the establishment of a state mortgage bank in 1935. Ten years later he again urged the Federal government to cooperate with private financial institutions in setting up a system of state mortgage banks to provide capital for small and medium-sized enterprises.

During the early part of World War II Nadler termed "unwarranted" a prediction that the U.S. rearmament program would create a commodity price inflation (New York *Times,* October 19, 1940). He urged life insurance companies in the nation to help prevent inflation by cooperating with the Government in its defense program, and so avoid "a rise in money rates" (New York *Times,* October 10, 1941).

Discussing the national debt problem, he said, "increasing the price of gold or instituting the 100 per cent Reserve banking system" was "unsound and obviously no solution" (New York *Times,* January 14, 1943). He expressed the conviction at the end of 1944 that the "catch-up" period of postwar industrial employment and reconversion would rest essentially on the "establishment of a sound system of taxation" and "labor legislation to make labor unions responsible," as well as "modification of laws passed which have not worked satisfactorily" (New York *Times,* December 2, 1944).

A five-point program proposed by Nadler in 1946 to stabilize the nation's economy included a reduction in Government spending, quick disposal of Government surplus materials in the consumer market, more sales of Government securities to the ultimate consumer, refund operations to decrease deposits and get Government obligations in the hands of investors, and maintenance of wage and price controls. With reference to price controls, he said: "It is better to maintain and improve them than to risk the danger of an inflationary explosion" (New York *Times,* May 7, 1946).

Nadler is convinced of the constant need for industry to raise risk capital, ordinarily accomplished through the sale of common stock, in order to prevent unemployment and a lower standard of living.

In Nadler's opinion, credit and debt management, as well as trust investment policies, should be geared to changing economic conditions in the United States. He also believes Federal Reserve System bank-reserve requirements demand "a general revision . . . based on geographical location of member banks" (New York *Herald Tribune,* November 12, 1954).

Early in January 1955 Nadler predicted that 1955 would be "a better year" than 1954. "The forces of inflation have run their course, and there are no signs of serious deflationary pressures," he told members of the American Bankers Association the following month. "The longer range outlook for the United States is favorable, indeed" (*Herald Tribune,* February 9, 1955).

Asked in March 1955 to give his views on the impact of the equity market on business activity, Nadler stated, "If the equity market declines, measures will be taken by the Administration to prevent it from exercising an adverse effect on the economy of the country as a whole. On the other hand, if the equity market continues to rise and to embroil more and more individuals in speculation, then measures will be taken to bring it to a halt. Hence, while the general outlook for business activity for the next few months is favorable, based primarily on the great momentum which has been gathered in the last few months, the outlook for the latter part of the year, irrespective of the movement of the equity market, is less favorable."

Nadler's books include a revision of C. A. Conant's *History of Modern Banks of Issue* (1927) and *Corporate Consolidations and Reorganizations* (1930). He is co-author of a number of others, including *International Money Markets* (with John T. Madden, Prentice-Hall, 1935), described as "a desk-book in the currency rehabilitation days to come," and *Money Market Primer* (with J. T. Madden and S. Heller, Ronald Press, 1948), a study of the institutions and operations of the New York money market. He is the author of a number of pamphlets published by the Hanover Bank, among them, in 1954 "Our Financial Strength" and "America's Economic Horizons." He has also written and edited pamphlets for the Institute of International Finance and has contributed to such periodicals as *Nation's Business* and *Annals of the American Academy of Political and Social Science.*

Organization memberships Nadler holds include the American Economic Association, the American Academy of Political Science, the American Finance Association (vice-president), the Arch and Square, and the Alpha Phi Sigma and Beta Gamma Sigma fraternities. He became a naturalized citizen in 1926, and married Cecilia Sachs on February 25, 1927. Their children are Eleanor Sachs and Paul Stephen. Marcus Nadler has been described by a colleague as "a lean, slightly stoop-shouldered man with . . . black hair," who is able to talk about economics in an exciting way and whose students are "dedicated to foster the ideas and ideals of Marcus Nadler" for whom they have great respect and affection.

References

N Y Times III p3 Ap 3 '55 por
Nations Bsns 40:61+ F '52 por
Newsweek 45:73 F 14 '55
Directory of American Scholars (1951)
Who's Who in America, 1954-55

NEILSON, FRANCES FULLERTON (JONES) Oct 21, 1912- Author

Address: h. 430 E. 57th St., New York 22; "Wood-Magic," Lloyd Neck, Huntington, N.Y.

Reprinted from the *Wilson Library Bulletin* Oct. 1955

By way of radio, Frances Fullerton Neilson entered the writing field. In the 1930's Mrs. Neilson was working with an amateur group, producing children's plays for settlement houses and hospitals. Station WINS asked the group for a children's program, but at the last minute the two writers assigned to create a sketch were unable to do it and Mrs. Neilson wrote one herself, between midnight and dawn. It concerned small invisible people called Orgets,

FRANCES FULLERTON NEILSON

who had been the author's imaginary playmates when she was a child. She continued to write children's stories for WINS and later her program went on the WEAF-Red network. In 1936 *Child Life* magazine accepted one of her Orgets stories and Mrs. Neilson's literary career was launched. She is the author of over ten books.

Born Frances Fullerton Jones on October 21, 1912, the daughter of William and Mary (Fullerton) Jones, Mrs. Neilson is of Irish and Scotch stock on her father's side—John Knox is one of her ancestors—and English on her mother's. Her great-grandfather, Sir William Fullerton, is buried in Westminster Abbey. Her father, who was a teacher, died when she was very young, and much of her girlhood was spent in her grandmother's house near Dorking, in Surrey, England. Frances Fullerton Jones was presented at the Court of St. James, and in 1928 was graduated from the Agnes Irwin School in Philadelphia, Pennsylvania. Two years later she married Winthrop Cunningham Neilson, Jr.

After her success with her WEAF *Orgets on the Air* program, which she narrated in addition to writing, Mrs. Neilson wrote other radio programs including *The Topaz Room, Alice in Wonderland, These Boys Became Presidents,* which won the Children's Radio Program Contest sponsored by the Association of the Junior Leagues of America, and women's daytime programs for a syndicate.

One summer Mrs. Neilson wrote a story for her two sons, Winthrop Cunningham, 3d, and John Fullerton, about a donkey called Longears. This was published as *The Donkey from Dorking* (Dutton, 1942) and for it she won the New York *Herald Tribune* Honor Award in 1942. The *Saturday Review of Literature* called it "very funny. . . . This is one to make you laugh."

(Continued next page)

NEILSON, FRANCES F.—*Continued*

The Neilsons have traveled extensively—the West Indies, South America, Canada, Scotland, France, and Switzerland—her second book, *Mocha the Djuka* (Dutton, 1943), grew out of an expedition into the jungles of Dutch Guiana. E. L. Buell of the New York *Times* (January 30, 1944) commented that although Mrs. Neilson's "pictures of primitive life do not leave one with sharp, first-hand impressions," her story of an American boy and a native lad whose "friendship surmounted differences of language and color" will be remembered.

The Adirondacks furnished the background for Mrs. Neilson's third book, *Giant Mountain* (Dutton, 1946), of a motherless mountain boy and his French-Canadian father. The *Library Journal* (September 15, 1946) remarked: "A well written story with good mountain atmosphere . . . will appeal to the nature-lover especially."

Turning from fiction to a book on the Bible, Mrs. Neilson wrote *The Ten Commandments in Today's World* (Nelson, 1946). The New York *Times* (December 22, 1946) said of the book: "Simply told . . . should prove helpful," while the *Horn Book* wrote: "Never more needed than at the present time. . . ."

With her husband, Mrs. Neilson wrote *Dusty for Speed!* (Dutton, 1947), followed by a series of three books about a boy, Bruce Benson, who goes deep-sea diving in the West Indies and hunting for snakes in British Guiana. The Neilsons' most ambitious book is a novel about Benjamin Franklin, *Edge of Greatness* (Putnam, 1951).

The *Christian Science Monitor* (July 30, 1951) said of it: "The buildup of local and historical background, streets, buildings, actual persons and weather . . . is done with fidelity. The style is sincere." The *Saturday Review of Literature* (May 19, 1951) commented: "We get a pleasant and frequently moving account of a thoughtful man of matured and modern wisdom handling with integrity complicated domestic and public problems. . . . He emerges from these pages as a very likable person." However, the New York *Times* (May 6, 1951) critic wrote: "The drama is not there . . . the book not only fails to bring a single character to life, but its tidbits of realism are dragged in."

During the war Mrs. Neilson served as a nurse's aide and on the Writers' War Board. She helped to establish libraries in service clubs and hospitals. For a number of years she was on the board of St. Johnland, and for two years was vice-president of Holiday House, both on Long Island.

Her most recent book, *Look to the New Moon* (Abelard, 1953), was a Junior Literary Guild selection. Two stories for younger children, "Nubbins of Marcy Mountain," and "Treasures from the Mountain," are now in preparation.

The Neilsons have a third child, a daughter, Mary Marcy. They divide their time between their home on Long Island in the summer and their New York apartment in the winter. When they can get away during the winter, they like to go to a small island in the Gulf of Mexico where they write all day, and sometimes well into the night. At present they are working on a novel and a play.

Hazel-eyed Frances Fullerton Neilson has brown hair, weighs 120 pounds and is five feet seven inches in height. She is an Episcopalian and generally votes the Republican ticket. For recreation she enjoys swimming, horseback riding, dancing, and growing wild orchids and ferns.

Reference

Who's Who in America (Sup. Je '42)

NEILSON, MRS. WINTHROP (CUNNINGHAM), JR. *See* Neilson, Frances Fullerton (Jones)

NEUBERGER, RICHARD L(EWIS) (nōō'bûr-gûr) Dec. 26, 1912- United States Senator from Oregon; journalist; author

Address: b. Senate Office Bldg., Washington, D.C.; h. 630 Alpine St. N.W., Portland, Ore.

The first Democrat in forty years to be sent to the United States Senate from the state of Oregon, Richard L. Neuberger was victorious over the incumbent Republican Senator Guy Cordon at the election on November 2, 1954 by a narrow margin. He had served in the Oregon Legislative Assembly since 1948 as senator representing the thirteenth district of Oregon. A journalist by profession, he has written nearly 300 magazine articles and is the author or co-author of six books. In his book *Adventures in Politics* (Oxford, 1954), he recommends that state constitutions be overhauled and that legislators be better paid so as to attract capable young men and women. His election to the U.S. Senate gives the control of the Eighty-fourth Congress, opening in 1955, to the Democrats by one vote. His wife, Maurine, was a representative in the Oregon legislature while he was a state senator, and together they comprised the first husband-and-wife team in American history ever elected simultaneously to both chambers of a state legislature.

Richard Lewis Neuberger was born to Isaac and Ruth (Lewis) Neuberger in Portland, Oregon, on December 26, 1912. His grandfather had come to the Pacific Northwest from southern Germany in 1870. Richard was reared in the Jewish faith. With his sister Jane he attended Portland grade and high schools. He earned his first dollar by carrying a golf bag for his grandfather, and later washed dishes in a restaurant run by his mother.

By 1928, when he was not yet sixteen, Dick Neuberger started to write articles for newspapers and magazines. While he was an undergraduate at the University of Oregon, the *Nation* published his article, "The New Germany." His first signed article in the New York *Times*, for which he later became the regular correspondent for the Pacific Northwest, appeared on September 23, 1934.

By 1940, the year in which he waged his first political campaign, Neuberger had made his name familiar to readers of the *New Republic, Harper's Magazine, Collier's*, the *Christian Century, Forum, Current History*, the *American Magazine, Reader's Digest* and other publications. His topics included Pacific Coast politics, the scenic beauties of the Northwest, power and salmon conservation problems in the Columbia River area, and Middle and Far Western celebrities such as Senators George W. Norris of Nebraska, Burton Wheeler of Montana, and Charles L. McNary of Oregon.

Although living in a preponderantly Republican state, Neuberger, who came of age in the depression, greatly admired President Franklin D. Roosevelt and welcomed New Deal development of public power, encouragement of unions through the Wagner act, agricultural supports and social security and pension policies.

He was shocked, however, by the way in which politicians kept alive the "Townsend Plan" for their own purposes. He considered it the "cruelest runaround" of his experience; and, in collaboration with Kelley Loe, he told the story in *An Army of the Aged* (Caxton Printers, 1936). This was the first book to carry the name of Richard L. Neuberger on its title page, the second being *Integrity; the Life of George W. Norris* (Vanguard, 1937), of which Stephen Bertram Kahn was co-author. *Our Promised Land* (Macmillan, 1938) was a collection of magazine articles by Neuberger concerning the Pacific Northwest.

During the latter part of the 1930's, Neuberger took several courses at the University of Oregon Law School at Eugene. Early in 1940 he was offered a job in New York "which would practically have doubled [his] income," he wrote in the *Saturday Evening Post*, December 16, 1950. But he decided to remain in Portland, where he had "a genuine sense of belonging" which he could feel "in no other place." In 1940 he accepted the nomination for representative in the Oregon Legislative Assembly in Salem. He was the "only Jew on the ballot" in November, when (in his words) he was elected "on President Roosevelt's coat-tails." Before his resignation (June 1942) to join the U.S. Army for World War II service, he sponsored a bill to regulate logging in the Oregon forests.

In the rank of captain, Neuberger was assigned as aide-de-camp to Brigadier General J. A. O'Connor, whose specific task was the construction of the Alcan Highway connecting and supplying U.S. airfields in Alaska. He served a year and a half at O'Connor's headquarters at Whitehorse in the Yukon Territory of Canada before being transferred to Washington, D.C.

He was married to Maurine Brown on December 20, 1945. The following April he was asked by the Democratic State Committee to run for the governorship of Oregon. He declined this opportunity to be "the youngest gubernatorial nominee in the history of the state," and ran instead for the Oregon Senate in the state's thirteenth district, going down to defeat by only about 3,000 votes.

Oregon "voted more preponderantly Republican than any state outside New England," wrote Neuberger, and the experience showed him that

Wide World

RICHARD L. NEUBERGER

"a local candidate often can be flotsam and jetsam when the currents are going against his party nationally." He was also made to "wonder whether people really care much at all about local government," as he found "no genuine interest" in such "home town" problems as the "pollution choking the salmon" in the Willamette River (*Harper's Magazine*, February 1947).

After his defeat at the polls he resumed writing for the New York *Times* and also became a feature writer on the Portland *Oregonian*, and wrote articles for many national magazines. (Since 1933 the *Reader's Guide to Periodical Literature* has listed nearly 300 titles under Neuberger's name.) In 1948 attempts were made to induce Neuberger to contest the re-election to the U.S. Senate of Guy Cordon.

"I was informed," Neuberger wrote in his article "It Costs Too Much to Run For Office" (New York *Times Magazine*, April 11, 1948), "that an adequate senatorial campaign . . . would require a minimum of $40,000." Since Neuberger and his wife had "saved barely enough to build a modest home," he declined the Federal candidacy, but did again seek the state senate seat at issue in the thirteenth district. He was not only successful, but "drew the biggest vote ever polled by any legislative candidate in Oregon" (*Holiday*, June, 1949).

Early in his first four-year term, he came to know what he calls "two-party blues" in a "one-party" state. "I began pioneering," he noted in a New York *Times* article, "for a constitutional convention to revise Oregon's outdated and cluttered basic charter. My bills could not get out of committee." (Two years later a Republican governor "endorsed the idea" and "designated a Republican to sponsor the bill" which Neuberger had drafted.) On the other hand, Neuberger denounced most of his fellow State Democrats "for backing a teachers'

NEUBERGER, RICHARD L.—*Continued*

loyalty oath and, conversely, gave credit for its defeat to an ex-Republican governor, Charles Sprague."

The pay of an Oregonian legislator was only $600 per annum plus a meager travel allowance; and, deprived of income as a writer for about three months each year, the Neubergers had their financial difficulties. ("We economize by pooling our groceries and cooking with the family of a young senator in an adjacent auto court," Neuberger wrote in 1949.) He believes with the Council of State Governors that salaries should be "adjusted to economic changes," and in the Oregon Senate he sponsored a bill to increase legislators' compensation to $1,200 a year.

As chairman of the Oregon State Senate's municipal affairs committee, Neuberger became much interested in the National Municipal League and the National Planning Conference. In August 1950 he delivered the keynote address of the conference at Los Angeles, California, in which he pointed out that most state legislatures were based on districting made in 1900, with the greater part of power coming from farm areas. This, he believed, explained why "such questions as juvenile delinquency, civic corruption, artificially curtailed milk supplies . . . often lack effective legislative answers."

In the 1950 campaign, in which for the first time there were more registered Democrats in the state than Republicans, Mrs. Neuberger was elected to the State House of Representatives. When the Neubergers were re-elected to new terms in their respective Houses in 1952 they were the only candidates on the Portland ballot to poll more votes than General Eisenhower did locally for the Presidency.

Convinced that 1954 was the time to seek a seat in the U.S. Senate, Neuberger accepted nomination by the Democrats to oppose a second full elective term for Guy Cordon, who led the G.O.P. fight in the Senate for the transfer of offshore oil resources to the states. Cordon endorsed the "partnership power program" of his fellow Oregon Republican, Secretary of the Interior Douglas McKay. The Secretary spoke for Cordon, as did President Eisenhower.

Adlai Stevenson spoke for Neuberger, as did Senator Wayne Morse. Neuberger, who made "conservation" of each state's natural resources a major campaign issue, unseated Cordon on November 2, 1954 by the narrow margin of about 2,400 votes. Neuberger, whose certification was signed by Oregon's Governor Paul Patterson, after the Senate Elections Committee had rejected an application for a recount, will serve until January 1961. He is the first Democrat to be elected to the Senate from Oregon since 1914.

To his list of published works Neuberger has added *The Lewis and Clark Expedition* (Random House, 1951) and *The Royal Canadian Mounted Police* (Random House, 1953), the first in the Landmark and the second in the World Landmark series of books for young people. *Adventures in Politics; We Go to the Legislature* (Oxford, 1954), discusses his and his wife's experiences in government. "More than a campaign document," commented the *Saturday Review*, "it expresses some worried thoughts on the weaknesses of states and their inability to carry out the responsibility President Eisenhower feels they should have."

The book contains an appendix entitled "Politics—And You" which offers suggestions to individuals interested in running for elective office. In it Neuberger states: "If you enter public life, you will have to decide when a compromise threatens your ideals and when it simply blends your own views with those of some other honest person."

Prior to her marriage in 1945, Maurine Brown Neuberger had been a teacher of English, physical education, and the modern dance. She is an expert swimmer and mountaineer. Senator Neuberger's own recreations include hiking, camping, gardening and golf; he is also "a cook of sorts, specializing in pot roast with plenty of potato pancakes" (*Holiday*, June, 1949). The Senator weighs somewhat over 200 pounds, has what he calls an "accompanying build" and is described in *Time* as "balding."

Neuberger is a director of the American Polar Society and a member of the Oregon State Grange; his service organizations are the Society of Military Engineers and Veterans of Foreign Wars. His fraternity is Pi Tau Pi and his clubs are the City and Tualitan Country in Portland.

References

Harper 194:153+ F '47
Holiday 5:32 Je '49 por
N Y Post Mag p5 N 21 '54 por
New Yorker 30:33 N 27 '54
Read Digest 54:99+ My '49
Sat Eve Post 223:30+ D 16 '50 por
Time 64:24 N 15 '54 por

Neuberger, R. L. Adventure in Politics; We Go to the Legislature (1954)
Who's Who in America, 1950-51

NEUMANN, JOHN VON *See* Von Neumann, John

NEWMAN, J(AMES) WILSON Nov. 3, 1909- Business executive

Address: b. c/o Dun & Bradstreet, 99 Church St., New York 7; h. 98 Highland Ave., Short Hills, N.J.

The world's oldest and largest international credit reporting agency, Dun & Bradstreet, Inc., is headed by J. Wilson Newman. He was elected to the presidency in November 1952, succeeding Arthur W. Whiteside, and thus at the age of forty-three became the chief executive of the company in which he had begun his career in 1931 as a credit reporter. His company has 150 offices in the United States and Canada and some seventy offices in countries throughout the world, and has built its reputation on giving correct business facts and appraisals. During 1954 its gross income was $56,626,735.

"Dun & Bradstreet," wrote Joseph Phillips in *Nation's Business,* August 1954 (*Reader's Digest,* February 1955) "makes over 6,000,000 investigations a year. . . . It knows the inside story of 3,000,000 businesses located in 53,000 cities and towns in the United States [and 7,000 in Canada]. Each day the credit agency checks into 6,000 changes in the commercial world: more than 2,000 new businesses start; nearly as many pass out of existence; many change hands. . . . Since there isn't enough cash in this country to do business for even one day, our $575-billion-a-year economy is geared to credit."

In its Reference Book, the "bible" of credit, the big question that D & B tries to answer is "*What kind of a person* is running the business?" Newman's prime objective is to bring buyer and seller together in an atmosphere of trust. "Business itself is increasingly aware," he said, "of the need for raising the level of our daily business relationships. Business itself is accepting a larger burden of responsibility in social welfare, and the spirit of rugged individualism has been supplanted by a nobler, if less spectacular, spirit of interdependence and cooperative effort, even among competitors" (From his address at the twenty-third annual meeting of the Controllers Institute of America, October 12, 1954).

Many of his speeches to management groups emphasize that in a mechanized age the machine must be kept the servant of man, that concern with mechanical advancement must not take precedence over interest in human welfare. Addressing the thirty-fifth anniversary meeting of the Conference of Apparel Credit Men in May 1953, Newman pointed out that the credit man's duties had broadened from the mere checking of customers' ability to meet their bills. "Statistics," he asserted, as reported by the New York *Times* (May 27, 1953), "are part of his kit of tools, but the appraisal of the human equation is still more important to the eye of the credit man than a column of figures."

James Wilson Newman was born in Clemson, South Carolina on November 3, 1909, the son of Charles Carter and Grace (Strode) Newman. His maternal grandfather, H. Aubrey Strode, was the first president of Clemson College; his father was professor of horticulture at the same institution for many years. This academic family background has had a lasting influence on Newman's outlook. According to a close associate, Newman subscribes to the view that while technical training is of course indispensable, the highest professional success—and personal satisfaction—is gained by the person who, in addition to such training, has a broad humanistic background and interests. As for his mother's influence, he stated recently: "Early in my life my mother gave me some very sound advice. She said, 'Wilson, you were born with two ears and one mouth. You will get along better in life if you use them in those proportions.'"

At Calhoun Clemson High School, from which he was graduated in 1927, Newman was active in athletics and debating. He next attended Clemson College, where he was on the track and intramural basketball teams, cadet colonel and corps commander, business manager of the yearbook, a member of Blue Key and Grey Friars, and vice-president of the senior class. After graduating with the B.S. degree in 1931 he attended the American Institute of Banking for two years and the New York University Graduate School of Business Administration for a year.

Fabian Bachrach

J. WILSON NEWMAN

Newman entered the employ of R. G. Dun and Company as a credit reporter in 1931, shortly before its merger with the J. M. Bradstreet Company in 1933. The organized system for checking credit risks traces its history back to the establishment of the Mercantile Agency in 1841 by Lewis Tappan, a silk merchant, one of whose Illinois correspondents was Abraham Lincoln. Dun & Bradstreet employs as its motto: "Credit-Man's Confidence in Man." In the words of *Fortune* (December 1953), it "gathers detailed credit information on practically every company in the U.S. and as many as it can abroad." This information, concerning some 3,000,000 U.S. manufacturers, wholesalers and retailers, is assembled by 2,000 credit reporters and 22,000 part-time correspondents, processed by a staff of 8,000 clerks, analysts and supervisors, and then made available to the agency's 80,000 subscribers.

Credit ratings, which are "designed to express an appraisal of the information and comments gathered from the concerns listed, from references, and from other pertinent sources," appear in the Dun & Bradstreet Reference Book, which is revised six times a year. They range from L5, meaning credit limited and strength under $1,000, to AaA1, meaning credit high and strength over $1,000,000.

While working as a credit reporter during the day, Newman took law courses at New

NEWMAN, J. WILSON—*Continued*

York University at night; he graduated with the degree of J.D. (Doctor of Laws) in 1937. As a result of his early credit reporting experience and his later legal training, he took a special interest in the management problems of American business, especially of small enterprises. Recently he wrote: "I like to talk with people, and I suppose the most rewarding years of my life were those spent as a Dun & Bradstreet reporter, talking with people . . . about business and its daily problems."

For several years he was a reporter in the company's analytical department and service manager of its fire insurance reporting department. During 1937 he left the company briefly to take a job with the Commercial Investment Trust of New York.

Returning to Dun & Bradstreet in 1938, he soon began to devote part of his time to the company's legal affairs. He was appointed assistant general counsel in 1943; the following year Arthur W. Whiteside, then president, chose him as his assistant; and in 1946 he became a vice-president. Among his various administrative assignments was the supervision of the construction of the company's new building on Church Street in downtown Manhattan. Previous offices were in the old New York *Sun* building at 280 Broadway. The new building has six floors of conveyor belts, sorting machines, drop-out slots and files, arranged in proximity to telephone operators and clerks so that subscribers can get credit information in a matter of minutes.

In November 1952 Newman succeeded Whiteside as president. He is frequently asked to speak at business and management meetings. Addressing the Society for Advancement of Management in October 1953 Newman discussed "Management and the Individual." He stressed three broad subjects: the importance of the individual, the significance of human values in management, and the responsibility of management in maintaining government and business on a high ethical and moral level. "Man, in his conquest of nature," he said in part, "has made phenomenal progress in our day, but there is a growing need to balance the material and physical gains with more evidence of moral and cultural advancement. The material progress is reflected in technology, but the humanist warns of the danger of man's subservience to the genii of science. With the humanist, we regard the rights of the individual as sacred."

A month later he observed to the Harvard Advanced Management Association: "Man, with a proper discipline over the greater power in his hands, has the opportunity of great service to his fellow man—in commerce and the professions. That discipline must be exercised in the way he governs himself, and in his relations with his neighbors. That applies to the individual political unit, the citizen and the composite citizen which is the state."

Newman is a member of the American Bar Association, the New York County Lawyers Association, the New York Credit Men's Association, Phi Delta Phi (legal fraternity), and the New York Southern Society. He belongs to the Down Town Association, Economic Club of New York and the Merchants Club. He is a trustee of the New York Institute of Credit and of the United States Council of the International Chamber of Commerce, Inc., and a director of the Commerce and Industry Association, Better Business Bureau and Home Life Insurance Company. He is an Episcopalian; politically, he is an independent voter. The business executive was married to Clara Cox Collier in July 1934: there are four children—Clare A., Mildred B., James Wilson, Jr., and Charles Carter. Newman's principal form of recreation is golf. He belongs to the Baltusrol Golf Club, Short Hills, New Jersey. He is five feet seven inches tall and weighs 160 pounds, has fair complexion, blue eyes and reddish hair. *Fortune* describes him as being "quick in ideas and easy in manner."

References

Fortune p134+ D '53 por
Who's Who in America, 1954-55
Who's Who in Commerce and Industry (1953)

NGO - DINH - DIEM (nō-dĭn-zĭm) 1901-
Premier of South Viet-Nam

Address: Dinh Doc Lap, Saigon, South Viet-Nam

On June 15, 1954 Viet-Nam's Chief of State, former Emperor Bao Dai, designated as Premier a scholar and ardent nationalist equally opposed to the French, who had been governing the country for nearly a century, and to the Communists, who had been waging war there for about seven and a half years. Ngo-dinh-Diem, who had spent the preceding four years in self-imposed exile and who had previously refused the premiership several times, assumed office at the end of the month and was charged with the task of rescuing the nation, as Associated Press writer John Roderick put it, "in its darkest hour."

During his tenure he has had to confront a host of problems, inherited and new, internal and external, and a continuing series of crises. Many of his most pressing problems resulted from the partitioning of Viet-Nam into two parts under the Geneva truce agreements of July 1954. Although generally respected for his personal integrity and the worthiness of his aims, he has been sharply criticized by many observers who have expressed doubts of his ability to unify the various factions within the southern territory he administers and to evolve and implement a program that would match the popular appeal of the one worked out by Ho Chi Minh in the north.

However, General J. Lawton Collins, President Eisenhower's special ambassador to Viet-Nam, gave "a moderately promising picture" of the situation as reported in the New York *Times* (January 28, 1955). The chief reason for "cautious optimism" was that Premier Ngo-dinh-Diem is emerging as a "sound and tenacious leader, and a true nationalist [whose] influence has been growing since he forced the former Army chief of staff, Nguyen-van-Hinh, to leave the country. . . . [The Premier] is believed by American officials to have as strong an appeal to the nationalist-minded people as any of the leaders of the Communist-dominated Vietminh in North Viet-Nam."

Ngo-dinh-Diem was born in 1901 in Quang Binh, Annam, the son of Ngo-dinh-Kha, Minister and Councillor to Emperor Thanh Thai, grandfather of Bao Dai. He has one sister and four brothers: Ngo-dinh-Khoi, Ngo-dinh-Thuc, Ngo-dinh-Nhu and Ngo-dinh-Luyen. Ngo-dinh-Thuc, now Bishop of Vinhlong, is the only Viet-Namese bishop to be ordained by the Pope. Ngo-dinh-Diem was trained at his country's school of administration in Hué, from which he was graduated first in his class. After passing his examinations for mandarin, he began his career in the civil service.

While still a young man, he was chairman of the Commission of Inquiry into Corruption of High Government Officials. He was chief of the province of Quangtri in 1930 and 1931. At the age of thirty-two he became Minister of the Interior. He fought against French encroachment on the domestic affairs of his country, urged modernizing reforms for Annam, and asked for genuine public participation in political affairs. Two months after taking office, he resigned, "decrying French hypocrisy and inefficiency," according to *Time*, and vowing to lead an ascetic life in protest against French colonialism.

During World War II he was associated with Frenchmen and with Viet-Namese nationalists, and was twice asked to be Premier during the Japanese occupation, but he maintained an independent position. After the war the state of Viet-Nam came into existence; it comprised Annam and other areas. Ngo-dinh-Diem was taken prisoner by the Vietminh (Communist) rebels, but through Catholic and nationalist intervention, he was released after six months. While a captive, he was invited to be Minister of the Interior in the government formed by Communist leader Ho Chi Minh, but he refused.

Ngo-dinh-Diem stated that the accords of March 8, 1949 establishing Viet-Nam as an associated state within the French Union were inadequate and would neither satisfy nationalist hopes nor offer a basis for a durable peace in Viet-Nam. In 1949 he was asked to join Bao Dai's government and again he refused, "insisting upon complete independence for Viet-Nam and a free hand for himself."

Ngo-dinh-Diem went into self-imposed exile in 1950, visiting Japan, Europe and the United States, where he lived for a time at the Maryknoll Seminary in Lakewood, New Jersey. In May 1953 Ngo-dinh-Diem entered a Benedictine monastery in Belgium as a lay member. He remained there less than a year.

While in exile, he reportedly received and declined four offers of the premiership. After the initialing of two treaties giving Viet-Nam complete political independence within the French Union in June 1954, he consented to become Premier in succession to Prince Buu Loc, a cousin of Bao Dai. He was asked to

Wide World

NGO-DINH-DIEM

form a government that would animate the population against the Communists. Bao Dai was said to have conferred "full powers" on him and promised him a free hand to initiate social and military reforms. *Time* (June 28, 1954) summarized the new Premier's assets as "the Asian fame of an ascetic, the ardor of an incorruptible nationalist, [and] a record of stubborn non-collaboration with the Communists and the French."

His program called for first, gaining greater (i.e., economic and military) independence from France; second, strengthening the Viet-Namese army as a condition for free elections; and third, preventing his country's partition. Since taking office, he has made progress toward the realization of his first aim and of his second, but circumstances beyond his control prevented the accomplishment of his third.

The cease-fire agreement signed at Geneva on July 21, 1954 raised several problems—problems so vast and complex that, according to John Roderick, "many observers expected the embittered Premier to resign." It provided for the partition of the country at the 17th parallel pending elections to be held by July 1956; it thus ceded to the Vietminh control of the north areas containing about 12,000,000 people (roughly half of the entire country's population) and highly valuable natural resources.

The agreement created a refugee problem of huge dimensions. Ngo-dinh-Diem's government had to work out a plan to provide for those who chose to move south rather than live under the Communist regime. France and the United States agreed to help with transportation costs and other aid, but the financial problem was overshadowed by the fact that the northern Viet-Namese came to be regarded as a propaganda prize. The Communists exerted every influence, Ngo-dinh-Diem told Jim Lucas of the Scripps-Howard staff, "to retain custody

NGO-DINH-DIEM—*Continued*

of as many as possible. If the Viet-Namese can persuade large numbers to flee, the Viet-Namese will win a tremendous psychological victory. If the Vietminh can persuade them to stay, the Reds win." (Some reports indicated that Ho Chi Minh wanted "northerners" to go south so that the economic burden of their presence would create "chaos" in South Viet-Nam.)

Addressing the "northerners" in an appeal for mass migration, Ngo-dinh-Diem declared: "I wish to say here solemnly that you have nothing to fear from the morrow. Your choice of liberty will not be a hazardous adventure. With the national government not only will you benefit from a free regime which you deserve, but you also will be helped materially and morally to build a new life." In addition to resettling more than 500,000 refugees who have moved south so far, he must deal with possible Communist infiltrators among them. Many Communists living in south Viet-Nam, who are supposed to go to the north under the truce terms, are remaining and present another threat to the southern government.

"Perhaps the most important problem facing Ngo-dinh-Diem's government," Henry R. Lieberman wrote in the New York *Times* (August 8, 1954), "is the problem of morale. This is related both to the question of Western support for the regime and what the regime can do for itself in the way of political, military and administrative reorganization." Western support was contingent on the establishment of a stable and representative government, capable of countering Communist propaganda

After Ngo-dinh-Diem had taken office, correspondent Tillman Durdin wrote from Hanoi that he had "no well-organized following. A shy 53-year-old Catholic recluse, he proved to have no flair for public life and fostered opposition to himself by political ineptness and rigidity" (New York *Times*, October 10, 1954). This rigidity manifested itself chiefly in his early refusal to take into his cabinet representatives of important local religious sects.

Some of his difficulties also arose from the fact that, as Roderick reported, "many ambitious men and groups in the south see no reason why they should be in his present nonpartisan government. He is bound to step on toes when he starts to eliminate the bribery, profit-making and dishonesty which have been the hallmarks of other governments."

In his own administration, Ngo-dinh-Diem's principal adversary was General Nguyen-van-Hinh, chief of staff of the national army. On September 11, 1954, the Premier, who suspected a plot to unseat him, dismissed the general and ordered him out of the country. When the general defied the order, Ngo-dinh-Diem issued it a second time. The order was repeated a third time, but far from obeying it, the general requested Bao Dai, who has been living on the French Riviera, to return to Viet-Nam and replace the government, on the ground that Ngo-dinh-Diem lacked the strength to withstand the Communists.

The contest between the two leaders precipitated a crisis in the course of which nine of Ngo-dinh-Diem's fifteen ministers offered their resignations. The Premier reorganized his Cabinet to include ministers from the Cao Dai and Hoa Hao sects. The Cao Dai sect, which embraces some 1,500,000 followers of a religion combining Christianity with Buddhism, Taoism, Confucianism and Hinduism, maintains its own military force of about 20,000 men. The Hoa Hao, a reform Buddhist movement numbering more than 1,000,000 adherents, also has its own military arm of 20,000 to 30,000 men. A third group, the Binh Xuyen, which has been termed "a vice and rackets syndicate," and which controls Saigon's police force, casinos and gambling dens, possesses a private militia of 2,000 to 4,000 men.

Early in November President Dwight D. Eisenhower sent General J. Lawton Collins as his special envoy to South Viet-Nam in order, as *Time* put it, "to try to resolve the feuding between [the Premier] and his generals, to coordinate and overhaul all U.S. aid to the tortured nation, to combat 'the dangerous forces threatening its independence and security,' to keep an eye on what the French are doing, and finally, to determine whether South Viet-Nam can be saved at all." Shortly after Collins' arrival, General Nguyen-van-Hinh left for Paris, indicating that he would ask Bao Dai to remove Ngo-dinh-Diem as Premier. The General was, however, dismissed as chief of staff.

According to the New York *Times* (January 19, 1955), the South Viet-Namese government is counting heavily on its land reform program to save the country from the Vietminh. Land areas previously owned by the government, by the French and by Bao Dai will be used by the peasants; Wolf Ladejinsky of the United States was assigned to administer the program. The government decreed drastic reductions in the price of farm rentals.

The land reform program is being carried out by the Premier "with a determination that is impressing observers. . . . Land is being made available to refugees from Communist-dominated areas; they will not be taxed the first year. In the second year the landlords will get one-fourth of the normal rent, and in the third year, one-half. The peasants will be allowed to acquire their land on a long-term basis" (New York *Times*, January 28, 1955).

In December 1954 South Viet-Nam and France signed agreements which gave the Indochinese state full financial and economic independence. The agreements transferred to local hands currency control and the bank of issue. With this national banking system, American aid now goes directly to the Viet-Namese government, instead of being routed through France.

France transferred command of the South Viet-Nam national army to the government of Ngo-dinh-Diem on February 11, 1955. By this action the French relinquished their last formal hold on the country. South Viet-Nam is still bound to France by private economic ties and is still a member of the French Union. French troops remain in the country as allies. According to previous agreements, American financial and technical aid will help to reorganize the national army with 100,000 regular soldiers and 150,000 men trained as reserves.

Further consolidation of Ngo-dinh-Diem's government was achieved when Nguyen-van-Hué, a leader of the Hoa Hao sect's private army, and 3,000 men under his command broke with the sect and offered their services to the national army. Trinh Minh, a leader of the Cao Dai sect, also joined the army with 5,000 men. In an initial effort to end vice and corruption in South Viet-Nam, the Premier ordered gambling casinos in Saigon closed. The Binh Xuyen leaders acquiesced in obeying this command.

In the first national vote ever taken in South Viet-Nam, Ngo-dinh-Diem replaced Bao Dai as Chief of State on October 23, 1955. Three days later South Viet-Nam was proclaimed a republic and Ngo-dinh-Diem became President under a provisional constitutional act. He also holds the post of Premier.

References

N Y World-Telegram p5 Jl 30 '54
Time 63:32 Je 28 '54 por; 64:36+ S 27 '54

NIZER, LOUIS (nī'zẽr) Feb. 6, 1902- Lawyer, author

Address: b. c/o Phillips, Nizer, Benjamin & Krim, 1501 Broadway, New York 36; h. 180 W. 58th St., New York 19

Major motion picture producing companies for over twenty years have retained the New York City attorney Louis Nizer. He is a recognized authority on contract, copyright, antitrust and plagiarism law and has represented numerous actors, actresses and writers in litigation. Nizer is well known as a witty after-dinner speaker and is the author of *Between You and Me* (Beechhurst Press, 1948), *The New Voice, A dramatic sketch* (1948), *What to do with Germany* (Ziff-Davis, 1944), *Thinking on Your Feet; Adventures in speaking* (Liveright, 1940), and *New Courts of Industry: Self-regulation under the Motion Picture Code* (Longacre, 1935). In the summer of 1954 Nizer represented the author Quentin Reynolds in his successful libel action against the columnist Westbrook Pegler.

Louis Nizer was born in London, England on February 6, 1902 to Joseph and Bella (Bialestock) Nizer. He was brought to the United States at the age of three and later attended Boys High School in Brooklyn, New York. During World War I the youth was awarded a special certificate by the U.S. Government for his successful Liberty Bond appeals before theatre audiences.

At Columbia University in New York City, where he received the A.B. degree in 1922, he was twice recipient of the Curtis Oratorical Prize. After he was graduated with the LL.B. degree from Columbia University School of Law, Nizer "went to work for a woman lawyer for $7 a week, serving summonses" (New York

LOUIS NIZER

Post, November 6, 1940). He was admitted to the New York bar in 1924 and became the clerk of Louis Phillips. In 1926 the law firm of Phillips, Nizer, Benjamin & Krim was formed; Nizer is presently the senior partner of the firm.

The young attorney attracted attention with one of his first cases, winning a suit against the City of New York when it reached the New York Court of Appeals. His arguments won praise from Benjamin Cardozo, then judge of the Court of Appeals and later Associate Justice of the U.S. Supreme Court. In 1928 Nizer was appointed executive secretary and attorney for the New York Film Board of Trade, an association of motion picture companies; he still holds these posts. Among his many clients of the entertainment field during the 1930's were Charlie Chaplin and Mae West. Nizer also obtained huge settlements in some famous divorce cases.

Greatly in demand as an after dinner speaker and toastmaster, Nizer is called upon to "introduce" innumerable celebrities. A publisher invited him to reconstruct his talks for a book. The result was *Thinking on Your Feet* in which he outlines the principles he has used as a toastmaster, gives sample introductions of well-known people, and comments on their addresses. The book also contains short speeches with explanations of the techniques used. It was a Book-of-the-Month Club "recommendation" in 1940 and in 1944 an inexpensive edition was published by the Garden City Publishing Company.

What to do with Germany, another book by Nizer, sold 30,000 copies immediately after publication. "A provocative blueprint for winning the peace after the conquest of Germany," the book revealed that Nizer advocated temporary surrender of German sovereignty, the trial of war criminals in national or international

NIZER, LOUIS—*Continued*

courts, return to rightful owners of stolen property, and an entire revision of the German educational system. Albert Salomon (*American Sociological Review,* October 1944) commented that the book is "written with a sense of responsibility and of self-control" and the New York *Herald Tribune Weekly Book Review* (December 31, 1944) critic remarked that the book "consults the interests of Germany at the same time that it consults our own—for the two cannot be separated."

On the other hand Edward Skillin, Jr. thought Nizer's "prescriptions . . . [were] more concerned with punishment than with reconstruction" (*Commonweal,* February 11, 1944). President Franklin D. Roosevelt read *What to do with Germany* and bought copies for his Cabinet members. General Dwight D. Eisenhower ordered 100,000 copies for his staff officers and others, requiring that each staff officer submit a report on the book.

In another book *Between You and Me* Nizer summed up the art of the jury trial, considering the problems of selection of a jury, examination of witnesses, and summation. He urged lawyers to pattern their style on their own personalities and emphasized that "the goal of an attorney is to submerge his talents in the interest of his case." The book also contains essays on various topics and over forty thumbnail biographies of prominent people whom Nizer has "introduced."

He also pointed out in the book that "the jury system is a magnificent system for determining the truth . . . [however] the responsibility imposed upon lawyers to aid the jury is a very heavy one."

Numerous articles by Nizer have appeared in legal journals and popular periodicals. His recollections of Rex Beach were published in *Reader's Digest* (January 1951) in its "The Most Unforgettable Character I've Met" series. The attorney has also written several legal textbooks and has lectured at New York and Columbia universities and at the Practicing Law Institute in New York.

In an article entitled "Our Founding Fathers at San Francisco" (New York *Times Magazine,* April 29, 1945), Nizer asserted that if our "founding fathers" could attend the United Nations Conference on International Organization, it is "clear from their words when faced with similar problems regarding thirteen sovereign states, they would urge us to accept the Dumbarton Oaks proposals" which outlined the general principles of a new world organization.

A frequent participant on radio forums, Nizer advocated, on the *American Forum* on August 13, 1946, an armed America; keeping the atomic bomb a U.S. secret; economic and other support to democratic groups in eastern Europe; a counter-propaganda invasion of the U.S.S.R.; abolishing the veto in the U.N. and if necessary, continuing the U.N. without the U.S.S.R.; and abolishing of the Communist party in the United States or requiring its members to register as foreign agents (New York *Post Magazine,* August 14, 1946). He later urged a four-point "drastic revision" of the American judicial procedure to insure that "Communists who come into court and defy the judicial system can be firmly dealt with" (New York *Times,* May 25, 1950).

During May and June of 1954 there came to trial in a Federal court in New York the $500,000 libel suit brought by journalist and author Quentin Reynolds, who was represented by Nizer, against the columnist Westbrook Pegler and two Hearst corporations for a column published on November 29, 1949. The trial was concluded on June 29 with a jury award of one dollar in compensatory damages for Reynolds and punitive damages of $100,000 against Pegler, $50,000 against the Hearst Corporation and $25,000 against the New York *Journal-American.* (Pegler's contract with Hearst was said to insure that he would not have to pay personally for libel claims against him.)

In a panel discussion at the Columbia School of Law on December 1, 1954, Nizer debated the issue "Fair Trial and Free Press" and defended the policy of New York County's District Attorney, Frank S. Hogan, of sometimes withholding from the newspapers information regarding pending prosecutions.

Nizer belongs to the Independent Order Of Odd Fellows, Association of the Bar of the City of New York, and American and New York state bar associations. He is director of the Motion Picture Charity Fund and *Film Daily* Relief Fund, and is an honorary member of the American Motion Picture Academy. Nizer has been active in the United Jewish Appeal, Federation of Jewish Philanthropies, National Foundation for Infantile Paralysis, and American Red Cross. He is chairman of the Algonquin Hotel Round Table, a daily luncheon meeting of literary luminaries.

In July 1939 Nizer married Mildred Mantel. They cooperate in making petit points for chairs of Gauguin's paintings, Nizer copies the painting on a canvas and Mrs. Nizer stitches the design into the fabric. He is known for his caricatures of people in court. Nizer also writes the words and lyrics of songs. The attorney is short, and has broad shoulders, curly hair, brown eyes and wears horn-rimmed glasses. He has been described as a "soft-voiced melancholy looking man," who "plans his speeches carefully but never memorizes them." *Esquire* (January 1955) commented: "Every time he . . . does something brilliant in court, it represents many sleepless work hours the night before."

References

Esquire 43:77+ Ja '55 por
N Y Post p12 N 6 '40 por

Martindale-Hubbell Law Directory, 1954
Motion Picture and Television Almanac, 1955
Who's Who in America, 1954-55
Who's Who in New York, 1952
Who's Who in World Jewry, 1955
World Biography (1954)

NUFER, ALBERT F. Oct. 21, 1894- United States Ambassador to Argentina

Address: b. c/o Dept. of State, Washington 25, D.C.; United States Embassy, Buenos Aires, Argentina

As United States Ambassador to Argentina, Albert F. Nufer played an important role during the last months of the Peron regime. On September 24, 1955 he informed the Argentine Foreign Ministry that the United States Government had recognized the revolutionary government of Argentina, of which Major General Eduardo Lonardi is the provisional President. Recognition came two days after Lonardi had replaced the evicted dictator, Juan D. Peron.

In 1953 Ambassador Nufer had been slated for transfer after one year in the post, but his popularity with American businessmen in Argentina as well as with the Government of Juan Perón led to the decision that he would remain in Buenos Aires—a decision that was announced after Dr. Milton S. Eisenhower, brother of the United States President, visited Argentina in July 1953 on his fact-finding tour of Latin America. In November 1954 Nufer headed the U.S. delegation to the general conference of the United Nations Educational, Scientific and Cultural Organization (UNESCO) which met in Montevideo, Uruguay.

Ambassador Nufer is a career diplomat who has specialized in Latin American affairs. He spent thirty-eight years in Mexico, Cuba, and Central and South America, part of the time as a private businessman. He was Ambassador to El Salvador for two years. Prior to his appointment as Ambassador to Argentina in April 1952, he was director of the U.S. State Department's Office of Middle American Affairs in the Bureau of Inter-American Affairs.

Albert F. Nufer was born in New York City on October 21, 1894, the son of Frank Xavier and Dorothy (Eypel) Nufer. He was educated at Buurmann's Institute in Bremen, Germany and also attended German business schools. In 1910 he became English correspondent in the office of the American Consulate for Bremen and neighboring Barmen, and vice-consul at Erfurt. Transferred to Cuba in 1917, he held the post of vice-consul at Cienfuegos. A year later he left the foreign service to become a partner and executive in business firms in Cienfuegos.

Nufer returned to Government service in July 1928 when he was made trade commercial attaché at Mexico City. The following November he became assistant commercial attaché at the United States Embassy in Mexico City. Two years later he returned to Cuba as commercial attaché at the Embassy in Havana. In 1937 he completed a two-year assignment as commercial attaché in Madrid, Spain and was transferred back to Havana as consul. While in this post he was made secretary in the Diplomatic Service, on November 16, 1939.

For nearly five years beginning in 1942, Nufer served as counselor for economic affairs at the Havana Embassy. Early in 1947 he was promoted to class I (career minister) in the foreign service. President Harry S. Truman appointed him Ambassador to El Salvador in March 1947 and he served there until 1949, when he returned to Washington. In 1951 he became director of the Office of Middle American Affairs. Among his important assignments was that of U.S. representative, with the rank of Ambassador, on the Inter-American Economic and Social Council.

Department of State

ALBERT F. NUFER

When Ambassador Ellsworth Bunker was transferred from Buenos Aires to Rome in March 1952, Albert F. Nufer was chosen to succeed him. Nufer arrived in Buenos Aires on July 16, 1952 at a time when "United States relations with Argentina had reached an all-time low," according to Drew Pearson (Washington *Post,* July 31, 1952). The low point referred to the bombing of the U.S. Information Service Abraham Lincoln Library in Buenos Aires on July 10. The Argentine Foreign Office had made no official acknowledgement to the U.S. protest over this incident and minor attacks against U.S. Embassy installations had also been ignored.

Businessmen in the North American colony were disturbed by these incidents and by the apparently casual manner with which the State Department had treated them. The too-frequent changes of Ambassadors—Nufer was to be the sixth since the war—was resented both by the colony and by the Perón Government. On arrival, the new Ambassador was asked by reporters if he had come with instructions to pursue a new policy. He suggested that they wait and see, but indicated that the State Department had not set a new line for him.

His first public address in Argentina, made before the University Women's Club in Buenos Aires in October 1952, was largely a plea for inter-American understanding. He pointed out that although more of the world today

NUFER, ALBERT F.—*Continued*

knew more about the United States than had ever been known about any country, many people had a distorted view of the principles and aspirations of the Government and its citizens. This he saw as a disturbing element because the future peace and prosperity of the world depended on the understanding that people of all nations had concerning the objectives of the United States. He stressed that the United States had no desire to dominate, but to help build a world where no nation, however powerful, could dominate another nation.

Nufer's effectiveness was evident in his success in obtaining the release of five U.S. businessmen who had been arrested on alleged charges during the economic crisis which had caused many political "incidents" in the winter and early spring of 1952-1953.

When President Perón attacked the three U.S. news services—the Associated Press, United Press and International News Service—in his speech to Congress in May 1953, he accused them of "openly engaging in an infamous campaign of lies against Argentina" (New York *Times,* May 2, 1953). Ambassador Nufer immediately conferred with Foreign Minister Jerónimo Remorino. Within an hour, mounted police were on guard outside the three news agencies and a police detail at the U.S. Embassy was strengthened.

"It was a time when a single new incident might have created a delicate situation," *Democracia,* the Perónista newspaper, commented on June 24, 1953 in praise of Ambassador Nufer. The occasion for this praise was the report from Washington, D.C. that a change of Ambassadors pended. Nufer was slated to go to Colombia and was to be replaced by Willard L. Beaulac, who was serving as Ambassador to Cuba. The Argentine press was unanimous in deploring the change after so many previous changes.

Democracia stated: "The stay of a United States Ambassador here is in inverse proportion to his efficiency in the task of achieving a greater *rapprochement* of our countries and a better understanding of our joint problems.... This rule would seem to be confirmed by the withdrawal of Mr. Nufer. . . . His abstention from our domestic affairs, his deep interest in the good neighbor policy, his equity in judging problems of common interest and his sincere belief that a better world can only be born of mutual respect, have given him the status of a man who ennobles the position with which he has been entrusted."

The Chamber of Commerce of the United States in Argentina cabled the State Department asking that due consideration be given to complications arising from frequent changes of Ambassadors and calling attention to the excellent representation that Nufer had given businessmen in Argentina representing firms in the United States.

In preparation for Dr. Milton S. Eisenhower's visit to Argentina on his Latin-American tour, Ambassador Nufer quietly paved the way, according to *Democracia* (July 22, 1953), by making statements of American policy that coordinated with the overtures made by the Perón Government and the Argentine press in their good-will endeavors. The reception given the Eisenhower mission on July 18 to 20 was enthusiastic.

"There were long and confidential conversations," the *Christian Science Monitor* (July 29, 1953) reported, "between General Perón and Dr. Eisenhower . . . and personal gestures which showed that opportunities were presenting themselves, and apparently being accepted, for a fresh post-war start."

The news reached Argentina on July 28 that Ambassador Nufer was to remain. No reason was given for this reversal of plan, but *Democracia* (July 28, 1953) hinted that Dr. Eisenhower had telephoned his brother, President Dwight D. Eisenhower, from Buenos Aires recommending that Nufer be retained in the Argentine post.

After a trip to Washington during September 1953 to consult with President Eisenhower and other officials, Ambassador Nufer returned to Buenos Aires and immediately called upon President Perón. In a subsequent statement to the press, the Ambassador said that a recent speech by President Perón to the effect that small differences between Argentina and the United States were "totally settled," had contributed toward good relations.

As evidence of the change, the New York *Times* was re-admitted to Argentina on October 10 and the end of the ban on other U.S. periodicals was announced. Also, the Alliance of Nationalist Liberators, a group of Argentina supra-nationalists which had repeatedly attacked the United States, changed its policy to conform with Perón's current good will. This change came after Ambassador Nufer had interviewed the chiefs of the Alliance.

Since Nufer became Ambassador, Argentina has made several other moves toward greater cordiality with the United States. A new law intended to encourage American investments was passed by Perón's Congress on August 26, 1953. "There is no doubt," wrote Sam Pope Brewer in the New York *Times* (December 15, 1953), "that relations are better than they have been for several years. Still the fear remains in the minds of experienced observers in Argentina that the pendulum may swing far in the opposite direction when it is found that the United States has not decided to drop all criticism of the strong-arm methods of the Perón regime and that United States capital is not flooding into Argentina." (The Peron regime was overthrown in September 1955.)

Ambassador Nufer is married and has two daughters, Hazel Vivian (Mrs. George Casares) and Miriam Frances (Mrs. Albert H. Norweb). His wife is the former Dolores Cabrera, whom he married on October 4, 1919 when he was a business executive in Cienfuegos, Cuba.

References

International Who's Who, 1954
International Year Book and Statesmen's Who's Who, 1954
Who's Who in America, 1954-55
World Biography (1954)

NURI AS-SAID (nö'rē äs-sä-ēd') 1888-
Premier of Iraq; statesman; army officer
Address: b. Office of the Premier, Baghdad, Iraq; h. Sharia El Malik Ali, Karredat Marriam, Baghdad, Iraq

Under the leadership of Premier Nuri as-Said, Iraq is the first Arab League nation to join a mutual defense pact with the West against Soviet aggression. By special agreement on April 4, 1955, Great Britain became a party to the Baghdad pact—which Iraq and Turkey had ratified on February 26, 1955—and with Pakistan, has formed a defense chain stretching from the North Atlantic Treaty Organization's eastern flank along Russia's lower border to Asia. Iraq still adheres "strongly" to the Arab League charter and to the Arab collective security pact; Iraq leaders stated that their country had signed the pact with Turkey because the Arab states themselves were not strong enough to meet Communist aggression.

Elder statesman General Nuri as-Said became Premier of Iraq on August 4, 1954, after having held this position and other government posts numerous times since 1930. *Newsweek* (January 17, 1955) called him "the Arab world's shrewdest politician." He was influential in the establishment of the League of Arab States.

He was chief of staff under British General E. H. H. Allenby of the Arab partisan forces revolting against the Turks during World War I, and in 1919 attended the Paris Peace Conference as military adviser to Emir Faisal, later King of Iraq.

Nuri as-Said was born in 1888 in Baghdad, then part of the Turkish Empire. He was the son of Said, a successful merchant. His early years were spent in a military school in Baghdad, and he later attended the Turkish Military College at Constantinople (now Istanbul) and was graduated in 1906. He became a junior officer in the Turkish Army and resigned in 1913. With other Arabs he became engaged in the Pan-Arab revolt.

For several years Nuri as-Said worked with Lawrence of Arabia. In his book *Seven Pillars of Wisdom*, Lawrence described the young soldier as a man whose "courage, authority and coolness" marked him as an ideal military leader.

In 1916, during World War I, Nuri as-Said joined the Shariffian Forces under General Allenby, and became chief of staff of Arab partisan forces during the Hejaz, Transjordan and Syrian operations. He was decorated for bravery and promoted to the rank of general by Emir Faisal, whom he accompanied to the Paris Peace Conference as military adviser in 1919. (Emir Faisal later became King Faisal I of Iraq under British mandate, after the French forced him off the Syrian throne.)

General Nuri as-Said became Army chief of staff of Iraq in 1920. Two years later he was made Acting Minister of Defense, and served as Minister of Defense from 1923 to 1930. From 1924 to 1933, he was a member of the Chamber of Deputies (lower house of Parliament) from Baghdad and in 1933 he was made Senator. Soon after his appointment as Premier

Wide World

NURI AS-SAID

in 1930, King Faisal I named him also as Iraq's representative to the League of Nations Assembly, although Iraq did not become a league member until 1932 when the British mandate was terminated. Nuri as-Said returned to the 1931 and 1932 sessions of the Assembly.

He resigned as Premier in October 1932 and, after a year, accepted the portfolio as Minister of Foreign Affairs. According to *Great Britain and the East* (September 17, 1936), "Iraq's Foreign Minister Nuri as-Said settled a prolonged dispute in Palestine" earlier that year by his insistence upon the termination of strikes and guerrilla warfare as a prelude to further parleys. He was exiled after the *coup d'état* of October 1936, but later was able to return and became Minister of Interior in 1938.

Becoming Premier again in February 1940, he broke off diplomatic relations with Nazi Germany. Through the influence of an anti-British Pan-Arab group, the Golden Square, he was asked to resign in April by the Regent for the young King Faisal II. Nuri as-Said took over the Ministry of Foreign Affairs to confer directly with the foreign ministers of the Allied nations during the beginning of World War II, at a time when the German menace to Iraq oil fields had become critical. He became Premier again in October 1941 and also Acting Minister of Defense. His country declared war on Germany in 1943.

The Pan-Arab movement, which had its inception in the 1890's and was revived by Lawrence of Arabia among others, held possibilities of unity which Nuri as-Said sought to develop in a book he published in 1942, later known as *The Blue Book*. He outlined a program for Arab unity, to be achieved by a union of Iraq with a Greater Syria. He worked with Egypt's Prime Minister Mustafa Nahas to influence other Arab states, and an agreement was finally signed on March 22, 1945. Egypt, Lebanon,

NURI AS-SAID—*Continued*

Syria, Jordan, Iraq, Saudi Arabia, Yemen, and Libya became members of the League of Arab States.

Nuri as-Said, who had resigned as Premier on June 10, 1944, returned to this position as well as that of Minister of the Interior in 1946, and 1947. He was elected president of the Senate in 1946 and again in 1947 and was Iraq's chief delegate to the U.N. General Assembly in 1947. The *United Nations Weekly Bulletin* (September 30, 1947) reported that he stressed that there was no quarrel between Arabs and Jews, but rather between Arabs and "political Zionists who want to dominate Palestine and other parts of the Arab world."

Demands made in Baghdad for a resumption of the Arab war against Israel brought General Nuri as-Said back as Premier and Minister of the Interior in January 1949. When activities abated he resigned, but again took over the reins of government in 1950 because of the oil crisis, after he had risked his public career as head of the Iraq petroleum delegation to London.

For the next two years, he was in and out of office depending upon where he could best work for a lasting settlement of Iraq's oil output. When his plan was put into operation and after the ceremonial opening of the second largest pipeline in the world by King Faisal II, Albion Ross (New York *Times*, December 7, 1952) wrote that riots in the streets of Baghdad broke out and that the mob was protesting against the man who had given the country "an excellent opportunity to become prosperous."

Nuri as-Said was responsible for the oil agreement which gave Iraq 50 per cent of profits before foreign taxes, the creation of a National Development Law and a board to implement the law. Mob hatred of British and Americans was extended to Nuri as-Said because of his policy of co-operation with the Occident. The riots turned into revolt, reportedly instigated by Communists who had built up strength under a mask of "partisans of peace." Martial law was proclaimed by the King's Regent, who ordered the Army chief of staff Mahmoud Nuriddin to take over the Premiership.

All political parties were dissolved under a new electoral law and a parliamentary election was called in January 1953. The New York *Times* (January 18, 1953) reported that in Iraq's first election by direct vote, the majority favored Nuri as-Said's party, Ittihad Al-Distouri (the Constitutional Union.) As the most powerful politician in the country, he could have been Premier, the *Times* (May 8, 1953) observed, but preferred the post of Defense Minister, which gave him an opportunity to improve the military organization.

Another election was held in June 1954. King Faisel II wanted Nuri as-Said to form a new Cabinet, but the "perennial Premier" was in London undergoing surgery, and the caretaker government remained in office until August 4, when Nuri as-Said again became Premier, and retained the post of Defense Minister.

To strengthen Middle Eastern security, the Premier visited Turkey, a member of NATO, to discuss Turkish-Iraqi collaboration with Premier Adnan Menderes in October 1954. The public announcement of a proposed defense pact, issued a month later, caused Egypt's Prime Minister, Gamal Abdel Nasser, to summon leaders of the Arab League nations to a conference in Cairo. The Egyptians argued that Arab countries were not ready for links with the West, or even with Turkey. Iraq's Premier did not attend because of ill health, but was emphatic in his decision to sign the pact. Several members of the Arab League were more agreeable to Iraq's action than Egypt had expected.

The Turkish-Iraqi pact, which pledges the two countries to cooperate in defense and security matters for five years, was signed in Baghdad on February 24, 1955 by the two Premiers and ratified two days later by the parliamentary governments of both nations. The New York *Times* (February 27, 1955) said that the pact was supported by Western powers as a step toward the Middle East defense system against Soviet aggression. Great Britain formally adhered to the Baghdad pact on April 4, 1955, and Pakistan reported acceptance on the same day. The United States is giving arms aid to Iraq.

The country's pro-Western course was further emphasized by Premier Nuri as-Said's "diplomatic trouble-shooter," Dr. Mohd Fadhel Jamali, who denounced Communism as a "new imperialistic colonialism far worse than the old colonialism" at the opening session of the Asian-African conference in Bandung, Indonesia on April 18, 1955.

From the sale of its oil, Iraq receives about $150,000,000 annually. These revenues are used in part for irrigation, flood control and electrification projects. The country supports a 50,000-man army, and thus is the second strongest Arab state (Egypt is first) from a military standpoint. Nuri as-Said recently announced a program of sweeping social reforms. He promised to reconsider tax laws to achieve social justice, to insure a maximum profit to the people in the use of the country's agricultural and mineral resources, to improve rural living conditions, to distribute government lands to deserving farmers, to raise trade and wage standards for industrial labor, and to make foodstuffs available at the cheapest prices to the people. Egon Kaskeline (*Christian Science Monitor*, September 22, 1954) wrote that because most of Iraq's Parliament is composed of landowners, who oppose land reform and social changes, little is expected to be done toward implementing this program.

Premier Nuri as-Said is married. His son is Sabah Nuri as-Said, who is director of Iraq Civil Airways. The Premier is reported to live in simple fashion and to have no wealth.

References

Christian Sci Mon p3 Je 13 '51
N Y Times p3 Ag 5 '54
U N Bul 3:424 S 30 '47 por

International Who's Who, 1954
New Century Cyclopedia of Names (1954)
World Biography (1954)

NUTTING, (HAROLD) ANTHONY Jan. 11, 1920- British Minister of State

Address: b. c/o United Kingdom Delegation to the United Nations, 350 5th Ave., New York 1; Foreign Office, London, S.W.1, England; h. 6 Chester Sq., S.W.1, London, England

Among the "brisk new talents" to be promoted in the recent reshuffling of the British government is the Right Honorable Anthony Nutting, whose appointment as Minister of State in the Foreign Office and Privy Councilor was announced on October 17, 1954. He succeeded Selwyn Lloyd whom he also replaced as head of the British delegation to the United Nations General Assembly on October 27, 1954.

For the past three years Nutting served as Under Secretary of State for Foreign Affairs, and in October 1954 signed the British-Egyptian treaty on the Suez Canal Zone. He accompanied Anthony Eden to the Berlin conference in 1954. From 1952 to 1954 he was a representative to the Consultative Assembly of the Council of Europe. Since 1945 Nutting has been the Conservative Member of Parliament for the Melton Division of Leicestershire. Speaking at the U.N. on November 16, 1954, Nutting announced Britain's allocation of forty-four pounds of fissionable material "as an initial contribution" to the projected international agency for use in experimental atomic reactors.

British Inf. Services

ANTHONY NUTTING

Harold Anthony Nutting was born on January 11, 1920, the youngest of three sons of Enid Hester Nina (Homan-Mulock) and Sir Harold Stansmore Nutting, 2d Bart., who is a lieutenant-colonel commanding the 6th Leicestershire Battalion. Anthony's two brothers died in military service.

After being educated at Eton and at Trinity College, Cambridge University, he joined the Leicestershire Yeomanry as a trooper in July 1939. He was invalided in France in 1940 and then served as an attaché to the British Embassy in Paris. Among the last of the Embassy staff to leave Paris, Nutting escaped in a small merchant ship that survived a torpedo attack in the Bay of Biscay.

Returning to London, he worked in the Foreign Office until November 1941, when he became attached to the British Embassy in Madrid as third secretary (local rank). In this post, he organized intelligence and escape lines in Spain for Allied personnel who had been captured by the Germans. Assigned to the British Foreign Office in 1942, he worked in the Scandinavian section of the Northern Department and also served as private secretary to Anthony Eden. He was transferred to the British Embassy in Rome in 1944, where he was third secretary for a year.

While on sick leave in England in 1945, Nutting was chosen as Conservative candidate for parliamentary representative of the Melton Division of Leicestershire. He won the seat in the general election of that year and continues to serve the Melton Division in Parliament.

During 1946 and 1947 Nutting was chairman of the Young Conservative and Unionist Movement, which doubled its membership at this time. In April 1950 he was appointed chairman of the National Union of Conservative and Unionist Associations. In a letter to the *The Times* of London on May 21, 1946, he stated: ". . . western Europe must have American backing if it is to have true strength. . . ."

He later said that Ernest Bevin, Foreign Secretary, should "press ahead" with the fusion of American and British zones in Germany and also extend the arrangement to the French zone and to Austria. In what was termed a "Conservative back-bench call," he said that the time was "overripe" for the organization of western Europe (*The Times,* London, January 23, 1948).

In May he warned Parliament that Britain had allowed the Soviet Union "to seize and hold the initiative" in the Far East, and declared the solution "was a program of economic and military aid to southeast Asia" (*The Times,* London, May 9, 1950). He was appointed British Under Secretary of State for Foreign Affairs in 1951.

Speaking at the European conference held in March 1952 for the organization of agricultural markets, Nutting said that "Britain obviously could not enter into new relationships with Europe which were incompatible with her Commonwealth relations. . . ." (*The Times,* London, March 26, 1952). The following May he stated that the North Atlantic Treaty Organization (NATO) "was not a closed association" and "must not be regarded as a power bloc" (*The Times,* London, May 3, 1952).

A delegate to the Consultative Assembly of the Council of Europe in 1952, 1953 and 1954, Nutting expounded the British proposal that the Council of Europe should "become the framework within which certain institutions of the European community operate" (New York *Times,* May 29, 1952), a proposal later clarified by Foreign Secretary Anthony Eden as a link-

NUTTING, ANTHONY—*Continued*

ing of the supranational associations of the states of western Europe "without impairing their independence" (New York *Times,* September 16, 1952).

In a speech on December 31, 1952 at Central Hall, Westminster, the Under Secretary stressed the development of "a new friendly relationship between France and Germany." He stated that this "more than any other factor" had resulted in "new thinking, new plans, and new organizations for reshaping and regrouping in western Europe" (*The Times,* London, December 31, 1952).

On behalf of the British government Nutting rejected proposals in the House of Commons on May 4, 1953 that another member of the United Nations, in addition to the United States, be represented at the Korean armistice talks, and that negotiations be handled by high-ranking politicians instead of military personnel.

Defending his country's Far East position, he said that Britain's trade in nonstrategic goods with Red China "is to the advantage of the free world." Nutting denied charges by U.S. Senator Joseph R. McCarthy of Wisconsin that British ships carried strategic materials and Chinese troops to Communist China (New York *Times,* June 18, 1953). He pointed out that Great Britain's recognition of Red China does not mean that it likes or condones its government.

On one occasion Nutting sought to conciliate Americans resentful of unjust criticism by the British people. For example, he commended three major American broadcasting stations for their film coverage of the Coronation of Elizabeth II, and he expressed regrets that his people had been told that crass commercialism and a lapse of good taste by some smaller stations was typical of American coverage of the event.

Nutting left England for Cairo in September 1954 to join British Ambassador Sir Ralph Stevenson in negotiations with Egypt's Premier, Gamal Abdel Nasser, and Mahmoud Fawzi, Egyptian Foreign Minister, on the Anglo-Egyptian treaty which was signed on October 19, 1954.

The agreement provides for withdrawal of British armed forces from the Suez Canal Zone during the following twenty months. Unless the two countries decide differently Egypt will assume complete control of Suez after seven years. Britain retained permission to reoccupy and operate its old Suez military base if an outside power attacked Egypt, Turkey, Iraq, Jordan, Libya, Lebanon, Syria, Saudi Arabia or Yemen during the next seven years. Permission was also granted to Britain to maintain a force of 1,200 civilian technicians (800 recruited outside Egypt, 400 in Egypt) as caretakers of essential defense installations in the canal zone. Nutting stated that the agreement could not "fairly give rise to anxiety" on Israel's part, as under the pact not any of the British arms in the Suez area would go to Egypt (New York *Times,* November 3, 1954).

Shortly after his appointment as Minister of State in Britain's Foreign Office on October 17, 1954 (replacing Selwyn Lloyd who became Minister of Supply), Nutting told the House of Commons he was convinced that the new Iranian oil pact would "bring prosperity to all concerned, particularly to the government and people of Iran" (New York *World-Telegram and Sun*).

On arrival in New York in November, he headed the British delegation at the ninth General Assembly of the United Nations. Among issues discussed by him at the Assembly's Political and Security Committee was the Greek proposal for a plebiscite in which citizens of Cyprus would decide between British and Greek rule. Nutting opposed this proposal, describing it as "an attempted territorial grab enthusiastically supported by the Communists." The General Assembly by a vote of 50 to 0, with 8 abstentions, decided on December 17 to take no action on the Greek proposal. (Cyprus has been administered by Great Britain since 1878.)

In an address before the Overseas Press Club in New York in November 1954 Nutting stated: "The imprisonment of the thirteen Americans on spy charges is very unfortunate and nothing less than outrageous. You can count on us allies and friends to do all in our power to mitigate this great grievous wrong" (New York *Herald Tribune,* November 25, 1954).

Harsh words about the Communists were used by Nutting during the U.N. debate on the charges of "espionage" against the American airmen. He commented on the Red claim that the Americans had "confessed." "That is the remarkable and sinister feature of Communist trials," he said. "The prisoner always confesses; the verdict is always 'guilty.' No doubt it is easier to invent the facts than to ascertain them. . . . But is it justice?" (*Time,* December 20, 1954).

The U.N. General Assembly passed, by an overwhelming majority, on December 10, 1954 a resolution declaring the imprisonment of U.S. Air Force men by Communist China a violation of the Korean armistice agreements and condemning "the trial and conviction of prisoners of war illegally detained" (New York *Herald Tribune,* December 11, 1954). (The eleven airmen were released on July 31, 1955 and some of the American civilians were later freed.)

Several interpretations were put upon Nutting's remarks during television interviews (on WRCA's program *Meet the Press,* December 12, and on CBS's *Longine Chronoscope* program, November 29) in which he stated that the rule of life is to back up one's friends, and that applies, in his opinion, to international affairs as well. Those who particularly objected to some of his statements were six Laborites who presented a motion in the House of Commons denying that Britain is committed to collective action in the event of a Chinese Communist attack on Formosa. Later, officials of the British Foreign Office assured both the House of Commons and the House of Lords that Nutting's statement that Britain would stand by its major ally, the United States, if the latter considered it essential to hold Formosa, did not involve Great Britain in any new commitment (New York *Herald Tribune*, December 21, 1954).

On September 15, 1955, Nutting was the British representative in the U.N. Disarmament Commission's five-nation subcommittee, where he described Prime Minister Sir Anthony Eden's plan to run a test of East-West arms inspection in Europe, a plan which had first been put forward at the Geneva summit conference in July.

Anthony Nutting married Gillian Leonora Strutt on August 6, 1941. Their children are John Grenfell, David Anthony and Zara Nina. Nutting is the author of several articles which have appeared in the *Spectator*. He enjoys hunting, racing and fishing, and lists Boodle's among his clubs.

References

N Y Herald Tribune p12 S 27 '54; p 1 N 8 '54; II p3 N 21 '54 por
N Y Times p2 S 29 '54; p10 N 8 '54
The Times (London) p4e My 2 '54
Burke's Peerage, Baronetage and Knightage (1953)
Who's Who, 1954

O'CONNOR, DONALD Aug. 28, 1925-

Comedian; singer; dancer

Address: b. c/o Paramount Studios, Hollywood, Calif.

NBC

DONALD O'CONNOR

Rated as the most versatile song-and-dance man in motion pictures and on television today, Donald O'Connor has appeared in some fifty films and headed the TV program, *Here Comes Donald,* on alternate Saturday evenings on the *Texaco Star Theatre,* National Broadcasting Company network. He was born into a circus and vaudeville family, and was trained from childhood in the "tough, knock-about school of the old-time trouper" to become "a one-man variety bill" (New York *Herald Tribune,* January 30, 1955).

The notably successful series of "Francis" films, in which O'Connor appeared with a trained mule, grossed millions at the box office. Among his outstanding roles was that of Cosmo Brown in the Gene Kelly picture *Singin' in the Rain* in 1952. He gave innumerable performances while in the Armed Services. In 1953 O'Connor was the winner of the Academy of Television Arts and Sciences Award as the TV star of the year.

Donald David Dixon Ronald O'Connor, the seventh child of John Edward and Effie Irene (Crane) O'Connor, was born in Chicago, Illinois on August 28, 1925. His father, known as "Chuck," a native of County Cork, Ireland, was a circus strong man, dancer, and comedian; his mother was a tight-rope walker, circus bareback rider, and dancer.

Both parents became vaudeville performers, and their children were members of "The O'Connor Family" act. When Donald was six months old his father and sister died. Mrs. O'Connor managed to keep the act together with the two older boys, Jack and Billy.

Donald was a little over a year old when he too became a member of the act. At the age of three he learned to dance and sing. He toured in the act, crossed the country seven times before he was able to talk and never attended public school. He received an elementary education from his mother, delivered backstage along with instruction in tap dancing, buck-and-wing, soft shoe, the double shuffle, handstands, and "cannon balls."

The 1930's brought hard times to the family. Vaudeville bookings declined. During layoffs, the O'Connors lived in the home of Donald's uncle and aunt in Danville, Illinois.

While appearing in a benefit performance at the Biltmore Hotel in Los Angeles in 1938 Donald, then thirteen, was seen by a talent scout and subsequently signed by Paramount Films for one year at a salary of $250 a week. During the year he appeared in bit parts in a dozen pictures, among them *Beau Geste* and *Tom Sawyer.* "I was everybody's son," he has said. In one film, *Sing, You Sinners,* he was cast in the role of Bing Crosby's brother. During this period he attended the studio school. Within twelve months he grew a foot taller and his voice changed. Since he was no longer suitable for boy parts, the studio did not renew his contract.

The O'Connor family act was again revived and took to the road, playing split-bookings and one-night engagements. In 1939 Donald's older brother Billy died of scarlet fever. Two years later, while the act was playing a date in Peru, Illinois, a wire came from Universal Studios summoning Donald to Hollywood, at a starting salary of $200 a week, and the family vaudeville act was disbanded.

(Continued next page)

O'CONNOR, DONALD—*Continued*

Among the pictures in which the young entertainer appeared during the next few years were *Mr. Big, Top Man, Chip Off the Old Block, Follow the Boys, This is the Life, The Merry Monahans, Bowery to Broadway,* and *Patrick the Great.* Of his work in *Mr. Big,* which was released in 1943, the New York *Times* critic wrote: "O'Connor, [Universal's] eighteen-year-old song-and-dance man . . . has come through with as fresh and delightful a performance as any jaded eye could care to see. . . . This lad out of a family of troupers has the poise and genuine ability to stir even old fogies from their crusts."

In reviewing *Chip Off the Old Block,* Alton Cook of the New York *World-Telegram* (March 16, 1944) wrote, "it makes Donald about the funniest young man around right now." *Variety* commented on *This is the Life* in the same year, "O'Connor continues to demonstrate his versatility as a screen entertainer in singing, dancing and acting."

A five-year contract between Universal and O'Connor was approved by the Hollywood Superior Court in 1944; in the same year he was inducted into the Army. During his two years and five months of service, he gave hundreds of shows. Upon his release, he returned to Hollywood for the making of *Something in the Wind,* released in 1947 by Universal-International, in which he was seen with Deanna Durbin. *Are You With It?* was released in 1948, *Yes, Sir, That's My Baby* in 1949. The first of the "Francis" pictures appeared in 1950. Alton Cook wrote that O'Connor's "precarious air of brashness and boyish ways are very funny, even though it did take the role of supporting actor to a mule to bring them out" (New York *World-Telegram,* March 16, 1950). In the same year, the entertainer toured five weeks in Great Britain at a $10,000-a-week fee.

Film presentations in 1951 in which O'Connor appeared were *The Milkman* (in which he co-starred with Jimmy Durante), *Double Crossbones,* and another "talking" mule episode, *Francis Goes to the Races.* In *Singin' in the Rain,* a Metro-Goldwyn-Mayer picture starring Gene Kelly, O'Connor's solo was acclaimed as "a wild, uproarious piece of slapstick," by Otis L. Guernsey, Jr. (New York *Herald Tribune* March 28, 1952). His next picture was *I Love Melvin,* with Debbie Reynolds, released in April 1953. Alton Cook commented, "Donald should be on his last legs as a juvenile. He decidedly is not." A new episode in the mule partnership, *Francis Covers the Big Town,* also appeared in 1953.

Universal-International released *Walking My Baby Back Home,* starring O'Connor, in January 1954. The picture was referred to by the New York *Times* critic as "one of those familiar budget musicals . . . impaled on an impossible and unbelievable story line." Later in the year, O'Connor became the fourteenth actor to be accepted for membership in the Screen Directors' Guild. At the end of 1954 he was signed by Paramount to co-star with Bing Crosby, Renée Jeanmaire and Mitzi Gaynor in a re-take of *Anything Goes,* the film version of Cole Porter's Broadway musical show of 1934.

Beginning in October 1951, as the star on the NBC-TV *Colgate Comedy Hour,* O'Connor received mixed notices; while the *World-Telegram* critic referred to his work as "first rate," *Variety* reported that, "he did well . . . but hasn't reached the status where he can perform for an hour and get away with it." The same authority, however, wrote a year later: "Donald O'Connor continues to develop as one of the brightest young all-round talents in show biz . . . there doesn't seem to be a limit to his ability to capture an audience and then hold them." In February 1954 O'Connor shared honors with Eve Arden, the two being named the best stars of TV for the year by the Television Academy of Arts and Sciences.

O'Connor left the *Colgate Comedy Hour* in 1954 to co-star with Durante on the TV *Texaco Star Theatre,* the two comedians alternating shows as part of the new NBC-TV lineup. Reporting on *Here Comes Donald,* John Crosby of the New York *Herald Tribune* wrote, ". . . a whizbang of a show . . . O'Connor is one of the greatest all around talents in show business—he can sing, dance, clown, act, anything." After making nineteen TV shows on film for Texaco, O'Connor announced on March 10, 1955 that he would drop out of television for a year and would devote his time exclusively to making movies in Hollywood.

Another "Francis" episode entitled *Francis in the Navy* had its première in August 1955, but the critics, while giving O'Connor credit for his comic characterization, generally agreed that "the talking mule gimmick is getting long in the tooth and should be pasturized" (New York *Times,* August 6, 1955). "And, more's the pity, Donald gets no chance to sing or dance, his real talents."

O'Connor married Gwendolyn Carter on February 6, 1944, in Tijuana, Mexico. They have a daughter, Donna. The marriage was terminated by divorce in July 1954. O'Connor is blue-eyed, brown-haired, five feet eight and a half inches in height, and weighs 138 pounds. He is known to show people as a "sweet guy," according to *Cue* (March 14, 1953), "which means he's only mildly temperamental, a good trouper, loyal and modest." He bought a house in San Fernando Valley for his mother, another house for his brother Jack, and one for himself. He has many hobbies, likes inventing things, and his favorite sports are golf and bowling. He plays the piano and "can do himself proud on the tambourine and trap drums." O'Connor has said that he would like to be a motion picture director.

References

Colliers 129:30 Ap 26 '52 pors
N Y Post Mag p11 S 11 '49 pors
N Y Herald Tribune IV p4 N 7 '54; IV p7 Ja 30 '55
N Y Sunday News Mag p5 Ap 11 '54
N Y Times p13 Je 14 '43
N Y World-Telegram p22 Mr 16 '50
Motion Picture and Television Almanac, 1953-54

OGBURN, CHARLTON Aug. 19, 1882-

Lawyer; author

Address: b. c/o 68 William St., New York 5; 1606 New Hampshire Ave., N.W., Washington 9, D.C.; h. 33 Washington Sq. W., New York 11

A "scholarly and monumental" contribution to the controversy regarding the authorship of the works traditionally attributed to William Shakespeare of Stratford-on-Avon is a 1,248-page volume entitled *This Star of England,* by Charlton Ogburn and his wife, Dorothy. In this book (Coward-McCann, 1952), which aroused vehement partisanship, both for and against their thesis, the Ogburns maintain that the real author of the greatest works in the English language was Edward de Vere, seventeenth Earl of Oxford, using a pseudonym "Shake-speare," and that William "Shaksper" of Stratford was an ignorant and hard-fisted grain dealer who could not conceivably have written them.

Thus the Ogburns accept and elaborate the theory first advanced in 1920 by J. Thomas Looney in his book, *Shakespeare Identified.* Those in accord with this unorthodox thesis include many scholars, writers, professors, and particularly lawyers who have praised the book in the *American Bar Association Journal* and other legal periodicals for "its logical marshaling of facts and convincing argument."

Ogburn is a lawyer who has represented numerous New York corporations. Since 1941 he has been general counsel of the National Planning Association. He is the author of several books on legal subjects, including *Government and Labor* and *The Lawyer and Democracy.* From 1949 until 1951 he was vice-chairman and counsel of the Interprofessional Commission on Marriage and Divorce Laws, organized by the American Bar Association. He is a vice-president of the Southeastern Law Center Foundation.

Charlton Ogburn was born in Butler, Georgia on August 19, 1882, the son of Charlton Greenwood Ogburn, a planter, and Irene (Wynne) Ogburn. His brother, who is four years his junior, is Dr. William Fielding Ogburn, the eminent sociologist. Charlton acquired his secondary education at Gainesville High School, from which he was graduated in 1898, and then entered Mercer University at Macon, Georgia, where he received his A.B. degree in 1902 and his LL.B. degree three years later.

Meanwhile, in 1902 and 1903, he taught mathematics at Georgia Military Academy and was the principal of Gainesville High School. From 1906 until 1907 he attended Harvard Law School; while at Harvard he took the course in Shakespeare offered by the late famous Professor George Lyman Kittredge. After being admitted to the Georgia bar, he practiced in Savannah until 1919.

From 1917 until 1919 Ogburn served as examiner of the National War Labor Board. During the next two years he made a nationwide investigation of the electric railway industry for the U.S. Government; at the same time he was counsel and executive secretary of the Federal Electric Railway Commission. Admitted to the New York bar in 1921, he has practiced in New York and also in Washington, D.C., since that date. In 1923 he opened a branch office in Paris to perform legal services for New York bankers in connection with European bond issues. This work occupied him until 1929.

Chase, Ltd.

CHARLTON OGBURN

The American Federation of Labor and its affiliated international unions retained Ogburn as general counsel from 1933 until 1938. In 1936 he began a seven-year association with the Reconstruction Finance Corporation, serving as the agency's special New York counsel from 1936 until 1942 and as its special counsel in railroad reorganizations from 1940 until 1943. Concurrently, from 1941 until 1942 he was legal consultant to the Board of Economic Warfare.

His book, *The Renaissance Man of England* (1947), has achieved a fifth edition. "The argument of this paper," Ogburn wrote, "is that the seventeenth Earl of Oxford was the foremost of the Renaissance poets, the author of the plays, sonnets and other poems published under the pen name of William Shakespeare. . . ." He maintains that many of the characters in the plays were modelled on eminent personages of the time, that Oxford portrayed himself in several characters, notably in Timon of Athens and Prince Hamlet, and that various events in the plays reflect episodes in Oxford's own life.

To the inevitable question, why the Earl of Oxford should conceal his authorship, Ogburn replies in part: "Oxford was prevented by Authority, against his wishes, from publishing works under his own name. In the sonnets he states clearly that he is anonymous and must remain so . . . so important was the state secret

OGBURN, CHARLTON—*Continued*

[his relationship with Queen Elizabeth] which had to be protected."

As for William Shakespeare of Stratford (or Shaksper, as Ogburn insists his name should be spelled), he was in Ogburn's opinion an "uncouth figure, the dummy in the show" who allowed his name to be used in return for generous payment.

In retrospect, Ogburn's first book on the subject may be viewed as merely a preliminary sketch for the monumental volume, *This Star of England: "William Shake-speare," Man of the Renaissance*, written in collaboration with his wife and published in 1952. The work involved prodigious research into Elizabethan sources. As might be expected, the book provoked a mixed response. Sidney S. Alderman, vice-president and general counsel of the Southern Railway, asserted: "This magnificent work sells me on the Oxford theory. It completely explains the devotion of [Oxford] to [the Earl of] Southampton, his son by Elizabeth, and all the riddles of the sonnets."

The *Virginia Quarterly Review* observed: "The authors maintain that Oxford throughout his life was writing straight autobiography—from the portrayal of his own fourteen-year-old bride (Juliet) and the devastating burlesque of his father-in-law, Lord Burleigh (Polonius), to the final tempests that swept around the head of the aged E-a-r-l (Lear). This point, illustrated in play after play, creates a cumulative effect which is persuasive." And the *Citizen-News* of Hollywood saluted the book as perhaps "the greatest mystery story of all time."

Dr. William Y. Elliott, professor of government at Harvard University, has said of the Ogburns' book, "*This Star of England* is one of the great books of our time." Robert H. Montgomery, an eminent Boston lawyer, wrote in the *Harvard Alumni Bulletin*: "It is a scholarly and monumental work, which may well be the most important piece of literary criticism of the century."

On the other hand, professional critics and Shakespeare authorities were for the most part unconvinced. Joseph Wood Krutch, for example, reviewing the book in the New York *Herald Tribune*, recommended it "to those who . . . believe that if you find the phrase 'blood and life' in both 'Antony and Cleopatra' and in a letter by the Earl then the Earl probably wrote the play. This gives a taste of its quality."

Oscar J. Campbell, professor of English at Columbia University, maintained the "orthodox," or Stratfordian view, and commented in the New York *Times*: "It is tempting to dismiss this fascinating exhibition of mental gymnastics and perverted ingenuity with ridicule. But that would ignore some questions of great human interest. . . . As one finishes this enormous tome, one asks in wonder what has impelled these authors, persons of some literary gifts, to devote countless hours of time and energy to this sleeveless enterprise."

Mercer University conferred an honorary LL.D. upon Ogburn in 1952. He is a member of the bar associations of New York State, New York County, and the District of Columbia, and also belongs to the Council on Foreign Relations and the American Political Science Association. His fraternity is Sigma Alpha Epsilon; his clubs are the Harvard, Downtown Association and Waccabuc Country Club, all of New York, and the Cosmos, of Washington, D.C. He is the only practicing American lawyer to be a member of the Grotius Society of London, a society for the advancement of international law.

In addition to the works mentioned, he has written *The Lawyer and Democracy* (1915), *The National Labor Relations Act—Its Constitutionality* (1935), and *Government and Labor* (1936), The lawyer-author married Dorothy Stevens, a former mystery story writer, on June 8, 1910; the Ogburns have a son, Charlton, Jr. Ogburn is a Democrat. Until recent years tennis was his hobby; now his favorite form of recreation is writing legal articles and book reviews, and studying Elizabethan history and literature.

References

Martindale-Hubbell Law Directory, 1954
Who's Who in America, 1954-55
Who's Who in New York, 1952

OGBURN, WILLIAM F(IELDING) (ŏg′ bûrn) June 29, 1886- University professor; sociologist

Address: b. c/o Florida State University, Tallahassee, Fla.; h. 1413 E. Randolph Circle, Tallahassee, Fla.

A sociologist who has attempted to apply findings in his field to the solution of some of society's problems created by technological advances is William F. Ogburn. He served on the faculty at the University of Chicago for twenty-four years until 1951. He held many government posts from 1927 to 1943 and is the author of numerous books and articles in professional journals. In 1952 and 1953 he was visiting professor of Nuffield College, Oxford University in England.

Professor Ogburn believes that a study of the basic principles of sociology should be of use to the individual regardless of his occupation. The individual has to know how to live intelligently in the modern world and how to deal with social problems that will press him during the course of his life. "It will," Ogburn has stated, be a benefit to people "to get a balanced perspective of social life and social issues. If they know how the social order came to be what it is, they will be better prepared to direct the social changes ahead."

William Fielding Ogburn was born in Butler, Georgia on June 29, 1886 to Charlton Greenwood and Irene Florence (Wynne) Ogburn. His brother Charlton Ogburn is an attorney practicing law in New York and Washington, D.C. After receiving the B.S. degree from Mercer University in Macon, Georgia in 1905, William F. Ogburn taught at the Morton School for Boys in 1905 and 1906. He served as assistant principal at the Darlington School in Rome, Georgia from 1906 to 1908.

A long and fruitful career in the academic world began while Ogburn was doing graduate work at Columbia University. It was during this period that he acquired an instructorship in economics, politics and history at Princeton University in New Jersey in 1911. After receiving the M.A. degree in 1909 and the Ph.D. degree in 1912 from Columbia he accepted a professorship at Reed College, Portland, Oregon, where he taught for five years. In that year his doctoral dissertation was published as *Progress and Uniformity in Child-Labor Legislation; A Study in Statistical Measurement* (Columbia University, 1912).

Ogburn held professorships at the University of Washington in Seattle in 1917 and 1918, Columbia University from 1919 to 1927, and the University of Chicago from 1927 to 1951. In 1933 he was appointed Chicago's Sewell L. Avery distinguished service professor of sociology. Columbia appointed him Stanford fellow in 1938. Presently Ogburn is teaching at Florida State University in Tallahassee.

Professor Ogburn had the opportunity to apply many of the findings of sociology when he served in various Federal posts. He was examiner and head of the cost of living department of the National War Labor Board in 1918 and 1919, special agent of the Bureau of Labor Statistics in 1919, and director of research for the President's Research Committee on Social Trends from 1930 to 1933.

In 1933 *Recent Social Trends in the United States; Report of the President's Committee on Social Trends* was published with a foreword by former President Herbert Hoover. The authors of *Recent Social Trends* stated: "The primary value of this report is to be found in the effort to interrelate the disjointed factors and elements in the social life of America."

Among their conclusions they mentioned that social phenomena are incessantly changing and that "not all parts of our social organization are changing at the same speed or at the same time. Some are rapidly moving forward and some are lagging." This unevenness in the rate of change is the cause of "social maladjustments." Owing to inventions and discoveries, the change, as a rule, takes place first and proceeds more speedily in the field of material culture (technology, economic phenomena) than in that of immaterial culture, where it lags. The practical solution of social maladjustments consists in "slowing up the changes which occur too rapidly and speeding up the changes which lag."

Pitirim A. Sorokin in analyzing the work stated: "Their main material, main evidence, main language and their 'truth' is the statistical table. . . . The first fundamental methodological principle of the work is the belief that a scientific study of social phenomena must be quantitative." Sorokin also stated: "It is easy to talk of the greater and lesser speed of change in various fields of cultural and social processes . . . most social processes are not so much quantitative as qualitative . . . most of the qualities are quite heterogeneous and irreducible to one another or to any common denominator" (*Journal of Political Economy,* April 1933).

Univ. of Chicago

WILLIAM F. OGBURN

Ogburn was director of the consumers advisory board, National [Industrial] Recovery Administration in 1933, special adviser of the Resettlement Administration in 1936, research consultant and member of the science committee of the National Resources Planning Board from 1935 to 1943, and chairman of the Census Advisory Committee in 1941.

In an article for the New York *Times Magazine* (April 16, 1933) Ogburn wrote: "While conservatives were insisting, as some still insist, that women's place was in the home, technological progress was eliminating some of the more important reasons for her presence there. The spindle, the loom, the candle mold and the soap vat have completely left the home. If their education is based on the old philosophy of women's place, as in many cases it still is, such women are in a serious predicament if left without male support, for they have neither the experience nor the training that would qualify them for jobs outside the home."

In the same article Ogburn stated that when inventions cause displacement in other parts of our civilization it appears that the "economic institutions are first affected, particularly those that make direct use of the new technology.... We must not only adapt ourselves to technological inventions after they are made but we must, if possible, look ahead along the line of technological advances and prepare for that advance."

"The South's recent appeal to states' rights," Professor Ogburn explained in a letter to the editor of the New York *Times* (April 22, 1949), "is a gesture for a letup in the continuing barrage of criticism from outsiders, that is, those not familiar with conditions in the South. . . . The critics seem to assume that what is feasible in their locality is feasible elsewhere. . . ."

(Continued next page)

OGBURN, WILLIAM F.—*Continued*

"The outlook for a higher plane of living for all of us here in the United States is very good . . ." wrote Ogburn in an article "Can Science Bring Us Happiness?" (New York *Times Magazine,* December 4, 1949). ". . . the standard of living of a people is the function of four factors—population, natural resources, inventions and social organization, all working together. The most important influences in raising the standard of living of modern times, and indeed all times, are scientific progress and the invention of mechanical devices . . . in the next fifty years [we] will see even more wonderful inventions . . . whatever they are, our standard of living will be enriched by them, and we shall be able to produce with fewer hours of work and with less expenditure of human energy. The effectiveness of measures to guard against [economic breakdown] depends somewhat on the knowledge of social science, but more on the application of this knowledge."

During the August 12, 1945 University of Chicago Round Table broadcast, Ogburn stated: ". . . the atomic bomb is the biggest challenge universities have ever faced . . . without liberal and spiritual education and training, it may become our master and our destroyer" (New York *Times,* August 13, 1945). He believes that "every major invention creates social problems and necessitates social adjustment" and he urged a cooperative study by physicists and social scientists of the social consequences following the utilization of atomic energy. At the Chicago Council of Foreign Relations, he predicted that the population will be compelled to adjust to the breaking up of cities into towns and villages in order to escape atom bomb attacks.

Among the many books which Ogburn has written are *Social Change with Respect to Culture and Original Nature* (Huebsch, 1922), *Living with Machines* (A.L.A., 1933), *You and Machines* (University of Chicago Press, 1935), *Social Characteristics of Cities, A Basis for New Interpretations of the Role of the City in American Life* (International City Managers' Association, 1937), *Sociology* (Houghton, 1940) with Meyer F. Nimkoff (which has been used as a standard text), and *The Social Effect of Aviation* (Houghton, 1946) with the assistance of Jean L. Adams and S. C. Gilfillan.

Professor Ogburn is a fellow of the American Statistical Association of which he served as president in 1931. He is a member of the International Statistical Institute, Population Association of America, American Sociological Society (president in 1929), Social Science Research Council (chairman from 1937 to 1939), and American Association for the Advancement of Science (vice-president in 1932). From 1920 to 1926 he served as editor of the *Journal of the American Statistical Association.* The sociologist was a lecturer at the University of Calcutta in 1952. He has served as associate editor of the *American Journal of Sociology* and *Social Forces.*

Rubyn Reynolds and William F. Ogburn were married in 1910. They had two children, Howard R., who is deceased, and William Fielding, Jr. Professor Ogburn received the honorary LL.D. degree from Mercer University in 1932 and the University of North Carolina in 1946. His clubs are the Sigma Alpha Epsilon, Quadrangle, Cosmos, and University. Professor Ogburn is over six feet tall, and has blue eyes and gray hair.

Upon his retirement from the University of Chicago, Ogburn said: "I want to spend three months seeing every athletic event in Chicago, then I want to go to all the movies. . . . I want to look at all the national parks, and I want to see some swamps. . . ." (*Time,* June 25, 1951).

Professor Ogburn predicted that the future will see a much more highly organized society than we have ever had before—some kind of union of government and industry is to be expected, and both are expanding more and more elaborately. The tremendous organizations in prospect for the future lay a heavy burden on democracy, if we define democracy as government by the people (New York *Times Magazine,* December 4, 1949).

References

Time 57:43 Je 25 '51 por

American Men of Science (1949)
Directory of American Scholars (1951)
Who's Who in America, 1954-55
Who's Who in American Education. 1933-34

O'KONSKI, ALVIN E(DWARD) (ō-kŏn' skĭ) May 26, 1904- U.S. Representative from Wisconsin; educator

Address: b. House Office Bldg., Washington 25, D.C.; h. Mercer, Wis.

Now in his seventh consecutive term in the United States House of Representatives, Alvin E. O'Konski was first elected to Congress from Wisconsin's Tenth District on the Republican ticket in 1942. "I'm a New Deal Democrat domestically and a rabid conservative internationally," he has said regarding a voting record that shows him in favor of such domestic legislation as high farm price supports and against foreign economic aid (*Life,* June 21, 1954).

Because of his vigorous opposition to Communism and frequent criticism of the U.S.S.R., O'Konski has been denounced in the Soviet paper *Pravda* and other Communist organs. He is a former speech teacher and has won national and international public speaking honors.

Of Polish ancestry, Alvin Edward O'Konski was born to Frank and Antonia (Paska) O'Konski on May 26, 1904 on a farm at Kewaunee, Wisconsin. He was graduated from Kewaunee High School in 1922 and later entered Oshkosh State Teachers College in Oshkosh, Wisconsin, where he was twice elected president of the student body. Active in public speaking, he won the Vilas Forensic Medal of the Big Ten Championship. He majored in history and speech, and received the Ed. B. degree in 1927.

In postgraduate study at the University of Wisconsin in Madison, for which he was granted the Ph.M. degree in 1932, and at the University of Iowa in Iowa City, O'Konski also specialized in speech. Meanwhile, in 1927, he had begun work in education as a speech instructor in high schools in Omro and Oconto, Wisconsin. After a year or two he became professor of speech at Oregon State College in Corvallis, where he remained until 1931.

O'Konski served as superintendent of schools in Pulaski, Wisconsin from 1933 to 1935, as dean of Itasca Junior College in Coleraine, Minnesota in 1935-1936, and as head of the speech department at the University of Detroit, Michigan from 1936 to 1938. His book, *Speech Practice,* was published in 1937.

Influenced by biographies of statesmen like Thaddeus Kosciusko, Casimir Pulaski and Patrick Henry, O'Konski became interested in a career in politics and government. From 1938 to 1940 he was engaged in public relations work for the Republican National Committee. During the next two years he gave much of his time to publishing and editing a weekly paper, the *Montreal River Miner,* at Hurley, Wisconsin, which he had bought in 1940.

When O'Konski campaigned successfully in 1942 as a Republican candidate for a seat in the House of Representatives of the Seventy-eighth Congress, he was already known to many Wisconsin voters because of the lectures against Communism that he had been making for some years throughout the state. Wisconsin's Tenth District, which he has represented since that election, comprises fourteen counties with a population of 249,654 (in 1950) which is largely Scandinavian-American.

During his first term in the House, O'Konski voted independently of party policy on a number of issues. He supported retention of President Franklin D. Roosevelt's $25,000 limit on wartime salaries and the President's veto of the anti-subsidy bill. He also went on record as opposing anti-labor legislation.

O'Konski early proved himself an outspoken critic of the U.S.S.R. and a champion of the rights of small nations when in the spring of 1945 he condemned the partition of Poland made at the Yalta Conference "as the most ghastly crime of all ages known to man or beast" (New York *Herald Tribune,* February 23, 1945). Assailed by *Pravda* as a Fascist, he replied, "I despise Fascists and Nazis with my whole soul but when *Pravda* calls me a Fascist I am not worried because they call anyone that who does not agree with the Russian position on anything" (New York *Times,* February 19, 1945).

Later in the year he urged at a July meeting of Polish-Americans in Buffalo, New York that U.S. Government representatives insist on a free election in Poland. "I want to see freedom preserved," he said, as reported in the New York *Times* (July 15, 1945), "not because of my Polish ancestors, but because if freedom dies in Poland it will die in Europe. And don't let yourself be fooled that, if that happens, it will survive in America." He announced in September the formation of the World Bill of Rights Association, of which

Wide World

ALVIN E. O'KONSKI

he was president and which had as its objective the extension of the Bill of Rights throughout the world, including the Baltic and Balkan countries under Soviet influence.

In Congress during 1945 he voted "yea" to a permanent Committee on Un-American Activities (January), the anti-poll tax bill (June), and anti-trust exemption for railroads (October). The following year he opposed the Case strike control bill (February), extension of the draft to 1947 (May), $400,000,000 housing subsidies (May), and the $3¾ billion loan to Great Britain (July); and supported the President's strike control bill (May).

Succeeding former governor of Pennsylvania George H. Earle, O'Konski became president of the American Anti-Communist Association in February 1947 and led that organization the following June in its efforts to deny Henry A. Wallace the use of the Washington, D.C. Water Gate amphitheatre to make a speech. The Wisconsin legislator also served as director of the World League to Stop Communism in 1947-1948.

On the floor of the House in February 1947 Representative O'Konski attacked the State Department's attitude toward Argentina, stating that the people of the United States wanted friendly relaions with Argentina and that Argentina had been "the victim of the most outrageous smear campaign during the last six years" (New York *Herald Tribune,* February 25, 1947). In July of that year it President of Argentina, Juan D. Perón, was announced that at the invitation of the O'Konski would pay a two-week visit in Buenos Aires.

With Republican assumption of leadership in the Eightieth Congress, which opened in January 1947, O'Konski was named chairman of the House Veterans Affairs Committee. His

O'KONSKI, ALVIN E.—*Continued*

voting record in 1947 shows him favoring a two-year limit for the Presidency (February), and opposing restoration of cuts in reclamation funds (April), rent-control extension (May), and the Greek-Turkish aid bill (May). In 1948 he supported the Republican tax reduction bill (February), the tidelands oil bill (April), the subversive activities control bill (May) and the displaced persons bill (June). He voted against repeal of Federal taxes on oleomargarine (May).

Among the measures which he introduced in the House in 1948 were a resolution in March to establish an American Foreign Legion made up of displaced soldiers in Europe and a bill in July to provide a $5,000,000 fund to relieve livestock farmers in drought-stricken areas of the West and Mid-West.

The House acted favorably in March 1948 on his controversial amendment to the foreign aid bill to include Spain tentatively in the nations to be given Marshall Plan aid, but this provision was later excluded from the bill by Senate-House conferees. O'Konski voted in April 1949 against extending the Marshall Plan and also opposed in February of that year extension of the trade agreements act. In August he approved a 50 per cent cut in European arms aid; on later foreign aid proposals he was against the Korea-Formosa economic assistance bill (February 1950) and in favor of a $615,000,000 cut in aid for Europe (May 1952).

Bills on domestic issues that he supported were a provision for a Fair Employment Practice Commission (February 1950), a $600,000,000 cut in Federal spending (May 1950), raising farm price supports (June 1950), a cut in government civil payrolls (April 1951), and retention of 90 per cent farm price supports (June 1952). He opposed a $10,000,000 cut in reclamation funds (May 1951) and the use of the Taft-Hartley Act to end the steel strike (June 1952).

In mid-1949 O'Konski refused to join a House expenditures subcommittee on a forty-day fact-finding tour of Asia, explaining, as quoted by the United Press, "I think Congress spends too much time worrying about other countries and not enough time on the welfare of our own people." However, he did go to Europe in April 1952 as a member of a special House committee to conduct hearings on the Kaytyn Forest massacre of World War II in which thousands of Polish soldiers were murdered near Smolensk, presumably by either German or Russian troops.

During the fall of 1953 O'Konski wrote a letter to Republic of Korea President Syngman Rhee urging him to release anti-communist North Korean and Chinese prisoners of war who were being held in accordance with terms of the armistice that ended the fighting in Korea. This request, as pointed out by James Reston of the New York *Times* (October 20, 1953) and other news analysts, was contrary to the Republican Administration policy of encouraging both Communists and South Koreans to abide by the armistice.

In the first session of the Eighty-third Congress (1953) O'Konski voted for statehood for Hawaii (March); and against a proposal to keep a nonpartisan tariff commission (June), a boost in Air Force funds (July), a $4.4 billion foreign aid appropriation (July) and admission of 217,000 refugees from Communism (July). In 1954 he supported the St. Lawrence seaway (May), social security expansion (June), the President's housing bill (April), a wire tapping bill making wire tap evidence admissible in court cases involving treason, espionage and sabotage (April), and a bill making Communist party membership in the United States a crime (July).

He went on record in 1955 as disapproving the foreign trade bill without restriction of Presidential powers (February) and a bill raising the salaries of Congressmen and Federal judges (February). The House Armed Services Committee, of which O'Konski is a member, voted in March 1955 to give career men in the services a salary increase. O'Konski favored the dropping of the proposed $20 income tax cut (February), restoring rigid farm price props (May), and raising the minimum wage to $1 an hour (July) and opposed shelving the Hawaii-Alaska statehood bill (May).

Representative O'Konski also voted in 1955 against a $2.6 billion foreign aid grant (July), the conference report of the military reserve bill (July), and exempting independent gas producers from Federal regulation of prices charged in the field.

Frequently called upon to address anti-Communist groups, O'Konski has given a number of speeches before the Polish American Congress, and at a rally in May 1953 in New York he proposed the formation of an anti-Communist Polish Freedom Army in Western Europe, financed by the United States, to serve with similar units under NATO command. On a television program in May 1954 he suggested that since, in his opinion, the United States would eventually have to break diplomatic ties with the U.S.S.R., it begin by severing relations with the Soviet satellite countries.

The Foreign Language Press voted Representative O'Konski the Most Distinguished American for 1945 for his anti-Communist activities. He also holds the Polonia Restitucia, the highest medal of Free Poland. Since 1947 he has been owner and operator of two Wisconsin radio stations, WLIN in Merrill and WOSA in Wausau, and he is president of WOSA-TV, Inc.

O'Konski married Veronica Hemming on August 26, 1935. He has blue eyes and black hair, is five feet ten inches tall and weighs about 165 pounds. His church affiliation is Catholic. He belongs to the Eagles and the Moose organizations, and makes the study of history one of his recreations.

References

Biographical Directory of the American Congress, 1774-1949 (1950)
Congressional Directory (1955)
Who's Who in America, 1954-55
Who's Who in United States Politics (1950)

OLSON, HARRY F(ERDINAND) Dec. 28, 1902- Acoustical engineer

Address: b. c/o David Sarnoff Research Center, Radio Corporation of America, Princeton, N.J.; h. 71 Palmer Sq. W., Princeton, N.J.

Scientists and musicians alike expressed considerable interest, recently, when a complex machine called the "electronic music synthesizer" developed by Dr. Harry F. Olson was publicly revealed at the annual meeting of the American Institute of Electrical Engineers, held in New York City in February 1955. The electronic music synthesizer is able to imitate sounds produced by any human voice or musical instrument, singly or in combination. Moreover, tones as yet unheard by the human ear may be conceived by manipulating the unit's more than 300 electronic circuits. "It can explore unpredictable areas of sound," wrote Howard Taubman (New York *Times*, February 6, 1955).

Associated with the Radio Corporation of America since 1928, Dr. Olson is now the director of its acoustical and electromechanical research laboratory, which is carried on at RCA's David Sarnoff Research Center in Princeton, New Jersey. He holds more than sixty patents for acoustical developments; his contributions include pioneering developments in loudspeakers, sound motion pictures, public address systems, high fidelity recording equipment, and underwater sound instruments.

Harry Ferdinand Olson, the son of Frans O. and Nelly (Benson) Olson, was born in Mt. Pleasant, Iowa on December 28, 1902. He was educated at the State University of Iowa where he received the B.S. degree in 1924, and the M.S. degree the following year. In 1928, he completed his doctorate thesis on "Acoustics" and was awarded the Ph.D. degree. Four years later, he received the E.E. degree.

His association with RCA began in 1928, when he was employed in the research department. Two years later, he joined the engineering department of RCA Photophone, and in 1932 was transferred to the RCA Manufacturing Company in Camden, New Jersey to direct acoustical research. In 1942 Dr. Olson was appointed to his present position as director of acoustical research of RCA.

Early contributions of Olson include the development of various highly sensitive microphones designed for radio and motion picture application. The velocity microphone, which he designed in the early 1930's, became standard for broadcasting use. A later development in this field was the directional microphone, designed by Dr. Olson in 1949. This device is a highly sensitive instrument capable of picking up sounds in narrowly defined areas without interference from undesired sounds. In recent years, the directional microphone has found wide acceptance in television broadcasting and sound motion picture application.

An ultra-sensitive stethoscope for medical research was developed by Dr. Olson in 1943. This unique acoustical instrument consists of

RCA

HARRY F. OLSON

a pickup device having a relatively high impedance coupled by a tubular acoustical line to a detector with an extremely low impedance, thereby permitting amplification of sounds ranging from forty to 4,000 cycles (New York *Times*, December 1, 1945).

Dr. Olson has also done outstanding work in the field of high fidelity sound recording and reproduction. On March 12, 1948 it was announced in the New York *Times* that he had devised a vacuum tube phonograph pickup which was the forerunner of the modern "Hi-Fi" pickups. The device consists of a miniature vacuum tube with a jeweled pickup point extending from it. As the jeweled tip rides in the groove of the phonograph record, it relays vibratory signals to the tube, which in turn transfers them into electrical impulses for subsequent amplification.

The electronic musical synthesizer, introduced by RCA in January 1955, can produce any musical sound that man has heard. It has matched the timbre of the tuba and piccolo, and it can also combine many instruments to build up a 100-piece "synthetic" orchestra. However, commented one critic, "the rhythms have a robot-like tread" and are "no substitute for human error, warmth of sympathy."

After listening to the music synthesizer, Alfred Wallenstein, conductor of the Los Angeles Philharmonic Orchestra, commented: "In its present state, the electronic system of synthesized music is not at a point where it can replace or personalize live artists or orchestras. However, further development of this system, when realized, should make it possible not only to expand the boundaries of music as we know them today, but also to achieve musical results that can now be achieved only through human hands and voices and with existing

OLSON, HARRY F.—*Continued*

musical instruments" (Kansas City *Times,* July 6, 1955).

In response to many letters of inquiry about the RCA synthesizer, a Victor record was issued in June 1955 entitled "The Sounds and Music of the RCA Electronic Musical Synthesizer." Reviewing the record in the New York *Herald Tribune* (July 17, 1955), John D. Molleson wrote: "The disk shows what Dr. Harry F. Olson . . . has wrought. Judging from this sampling the present quality of the synthesizer's manufactured music is not likely to throw any nonelectronic musicians out of a job. The different instruments are suggestive of an electric organ."

Among the synthesizer's accomplishments are parts of Chopin's A-flat *Polonaise* and Debussy's "Clair de Lune" and Irving Berlin's "Blue Skies."

Another RCA laboratories invention developed by Dr. Olson and his associates was demonstrated at the dedication of the Minnesota Mining and Manufacturing Company's new research center at St. Paul, Minnesota. It was the first tape-recorded color TV program ever transmitted over network facilities. The tape-recorded telecast was installed for field testing at the NBC studios in New York, and was transmitted over a closed-circuit to Minnesota. The magnetic tape was hailed by David Sarnoff, chairman of RCA, as a "historical occasion" (New York *World-Telegram and Sun,* May 12, 1955).

Honors presented to Olson include the Modern Pioneer Award of the National Association of Manufacturers and the Audio Engineering Society's John H. Potts Medal "for outstanding accomplishment in the field of audio engineering." Dr. Olson's fraternal associations include Tau Beta Pi, Sigma Xi, and Gamma Alpha. He is a fellow of the Institute of Radio Engineers, American Physical Society, Audio Engineering Society, and Acoustical Society of America (president, 1952).

Other activities of Dr. Olson have included four years of lecturing on acoustical engineering at Columbia University in New York, from 1939 to 1942. He is also the author of over seventy articles and papers which have appeared in professional journals. His books include *Dynamical Analogies* (Van Nostrand, 1943), *Elements of Acoustical Engineering* (Van Nostrand, 1940, 1947), and *Musical Engineering* (McGraw-Hill, 1952).

Dr. Olson presently resides in Princeton, New Jersey. His wife is the former Lorene E. Johnson, whom he married on June 11, 1935. Olson is five feet seven inches tall, weighs 160 pounds and has brown hair and hazel eyes.

References

Fortune 50:112+ N '54
N Y Times p28 D 1 '45; p8 My 10 '47; p21 O 29 '49
American Men of Science (1955)
Who's Who in America, 1954-55
Who's Who in Engineering, 1948
World Biography (1954)

O'NEIL, THOMAS F(RANCIS) Apr. 18, 1915- Business executive; organization official

Address: b. 1440 Broadway, New York 18, N.Y., h. Meadow Wood Drive, Belle Haven, Greenwich, Conn.

Known as "a new giant in the field of entertainment," industrialist Thomas F. O'Neil is a "Mr. Big" in motion pictures, television and radio (New York *Journal-American,* August 14, 1955). Vice president and director of General Tire & Rubber Company, he is also president of its major subsidiary, General Teleradio, which owns and operates five television and seven radio stations, and controls the Mutual Broadcasting System, the world's largest radio network. He is responsible for the $25,000,000 purchase by Teleradio on July 18, 1955 of RKO Radio Pictures, of which he is board chairman.

Thomas Francis O'Neil was born in Kansas City, Missouri, on April 18, 1915, the son of William and Grace Agnes (Savage) O'Neil. His father is founder, chairman of the board and president of General Tire & Rubber Company, Akron, Ohio, a rubber—radio—rocket empire (*Business Week,* August 27, 1955). Young O'Neil has three brothers, Michael Gerald, John and William.

After receiving the A.B. degree in 1937 from the College of the Holy Cross, Worcester, Massachusetts where he played football, he joined his father's firm and specialized in sales and production. During 1940 and 1941 he was manager of the company's office in Washington, D.C. His business career was then interrupted by World War II, and in the next five years he rose from a petty officer with the U.S. Coast Guard to the rank of lieutenant. His services included being skipper of an LST at Leyte in the Philippine Islands and at Mindoro in 1944.

Returning to the General Tire & Rubber Company after the war, O'Neil was sent to Boston, Massachusetts. He says: "I was sent to Boston to run the tire setup there, and they told me to 'take a look at the broadcasting thing we've got there.'" The "thing" was the Yankee Radio Network of New England, purchased by General Tire & Rubber Company in 1942, then a twenty-five station chain.

This launched O'Neil on his career in the broadcasting business, and in December 1947 he became vice president and director of the Yankee Network. In February 1948 he was elected a director of the Mutual Broadcasting System, and during that year the network increased its outlets to 519 and added 100 stations. Mutual named O'Neil a vice chairman of the board on May 1, 1949.

He was made a director of General Tire & Rubber Company on December 12, 1948 and on June 5, 1950 a vice president, in charge of radio and television. At the end of that year his company acquired the Don Lee Broadcasting System, the West Coast's largest radio chain, with forty-five stations, and the western outlet of the Mutual Broadcasting System. The purchase doubled the stock interest of General Tire in Mutual to 38 per cent from the 19½ per cent previously represented by its control of the Yankee Network.

In 1951 Thomas O'Neil became president and director of Thomas S. Lee Enterprises, Los Angeles, California, which comprised both the Don Lee and the Yankee networks. In June 1952, these enterprises obtained WOR-TV and WOR of New York, (of which R. H. Macy & Company owned about 10 per cent) and raised General Tire & Rubber Company's stock control in MBS to 58 per cent. To allow for this majority control of Mutual stock, the network abolished its bylaw prohibiting one entity from voting more than 30 per cent of stock. O'Neil's Lee Enterprises at that time changed its name to General Teleradio, Inc.

After naming O'Neil chairman of the board in April 1951, the Mutual Broadcasting System elected him president of the network in June 1952, to succeed Frank White, (see *C.B.*, 1950) whose resignation became effective on May 31, 1952. O'Neil announced his intention to continue Mutual "as a network predominantly composed of a large number of relatively small stations, mostly in non-metropolitan markets, with emphasis on acceptability and flexibility" (*Broadcasting-Telecasting*, September 27, 1954).

Under his guidance the Network signed an agreement with Metro-Goldwyn-Mayer which brought it Hollywood names for stars. *Newsweek* (April 28, 1952) observed: "O'Neil has big plans for Mutual," and mentioned television as one, explaining that "so far" O'Neil "has just been sitting back . . . observing the mistakes of other TV networks."

His first innovation on television was in April 1952 when WOR-TV began a twenty-six week series of dramatic shows each of which ran for five successive nights. The plays included such former Broadway hits as *The Trial of Mary Dugan* and *Three Men on a Horse*. *Newsweek* (April 28, 1952) credited O'Neil as "the man who had the idea" for *Broadway TV Theater*.

When more than a hundred engineers of stations WOR and WOR-TV went on strike from August 18 to September 28, 1953, forcing WOR television outlets to shut down temporarily, O'Neil denied rumors that the station was for sale. The union claimed that management was demanding workers "double in brass," instead of filling a single job, and station executives accused the union of "featherbedding" (New York *Herald Tribune*, September 29, 1953). Labor troubles again plagued WOR in March 1954, when the local section of American Federation of Musicians, AFL, picketed it, following dismissal of forty musicians. Asked by the union to debate the issue on radio and television, O'Neil declined on March 29, 1954, on the ground that the dispute was in the courts.

Under O'Neil's guidance, General Teleradio bought the radio-television rights to Phillips H. Lord's programs in December 1953, and the following spring began the highly successful venture of filming *Gangbusters* for production on television under the title of *Captured*. O'Neil's interest in acquiring films for TV also led in March 1954 to Teleradio's purchase of thirty major studio feature films from the Bank of America, which had not previously been shown on TV. They included such well-

THOMAS F. O'NEIL

known motion pictures as *One Touch of Venus*, *Arch of Triumph*, *Double Life* and *Body and Soul*. In the fall of 1954, Teleradio acquired a series of twenty-six films depicting history-making exploits of the United States Marine Corps.

Replying to a *Newsweek* poll of several broadcasting stations in March 1954, asking whether radio and television ought to editorialize, O'Neil said that ". . . any attempt to prevent individual commentators from expressing their interpretation of local, national, or international events would be a disservice to the public. . . ."

When O'Neil spoke early in September 1954 on "What's the Future for Radio Networks?" on Mutual's program *State of the Nation* he was optimistic. "Despite the inroads of TV on the nation's listening habits," he said, "there will always be a place for radio and a need for radio networks to serve the American public."

In a statement honoring the twentieth anniversary of the Mutual Broadcasting System in October 1954, he commented, as a result of a Mutual audience study, "we are learning the exact nature and scope of such factors as out-of-home listening, family composition, and program tastes—in and out of TV areas" (*Broadcasting-Telecasting*, September 27, 1954).

His influence was extended to motion pictures as well as radio and television in July 1955, when he purchased RKO Radio Pictures for General Teleradio, from Howard Hughes. This brought Teleradio control of approximately 600 feature films, and movie-producing facilities in Hollywood and Culver City, California, besides more than 100 domestic and foreign motion picture exchanges operated by RKO, and use of RKO Pathe, Inc., and RKO Television, Inc. It now controls not only these interests, in addition to the Mutual national network and the two regional networks—Yankee and Don Lee—but television stations WNAC-TV (Boston),

O'NEIL, THOMAS F.—*Continued*

WOR-TV (New York), WHBQ-TV (Memphis), KHJ-TV (Los Angeles), and WEAT-TV (West Palm Beach), and radio stations WNAC, WOR, WGTH, WHBQ, KHJ, KFRC, and WEAT.

Long interested in making films for TV, O'Neil stated, "... the tendency of the future will be the filming of dramatic shows. Film, because of the nature of its production, is better equipped to handle the dramatic show than is 'live' television" (New York *Journal-American*, August 14, 1955). "Live" TV is more suitable for spot news and sports, some types of panel shows, and "possibly" variety programs.

Variety (August 31, 1955) describes O'Neil as one who has "seen already that shrewd investment, low budgets and high-geared merchandising can pay big dividends." And James L. Kilgallen calls him "a quiet unassuming man with a warm Irish smile" (New York *Journal-American*, August 14, 1955).

Since April 1955 O'Neil has been chairman of the executive committee of the Brand Names Foundation, and he is a member of the board of directors of the Advertising Council. On June 15, 1946, he married Claire M. McCahey, and their children are Shane, Eileen, Mark, Conn and Claire. The six-feet-four-inches tall broadcasting executive makes golf his recreation.

References

Bsns W p23 O 20 '51
Forbes 76:23 Ag 15 '55
N Y Journal-American p37L Ag 14 '55
Newsweek 39:93+ Ap 28 '52
Time 66:54+ Ag 1 '55
U S News 39:14+ Jl 29 '55
Who's Who in America, 1954-55
Who's Who in Commerce and Industry (1953)
World Biography (1954)

ORTON, HELEN FULLER Nov. 1, 1872-Feb. 16, 1955 Author; her over thirty-five books for children included stories based on the American colonial period and mysteries; the total sale of her books, including foreign editions, was over a million copies. See *Current Biography* (Jan.) 1941.

Obituary

N Y Times p27 F 17 '55

PAPAGOS, ALEXANDER Dec. 9, 1883-Oct. 4, 1955 Premier of Greece; led Greek forces which repelled Italian invaders in 1941; as Supreme Commander of Greek Army directed successful campaign against Communist rebels in 1949; was imprisoned in German concentration camps during World War II; a founder of Greek Rally party (1951); became Greek Premier in 1952; veteran of Balkan War and World War I; received rank of field marshal in 1949. See *Current Biography* (Nov.) 1951.

Obituary

N Y Times p35 O 5 '55

PARKER, BUDDY Dec. 16, 1913- Professional football coach

Address: b. c/o Detroit Lions Football Club, 1401 Michigan Ave., Detroit, Mich.; h. 23051 Lodge Lane, Dearborn, Mich.

The "quiet perseverance" of Coach Raymond "Buddy" Parker has been a factor in leading the professional football team, Detroit Lions, to three Western Conference championships. Head coach since 1951, Parker reorganized a team which had been split by internal strife, and unified its many talents with the result that the Lions won the world championship playoff in 1952 and 1953, and Detroit stockholders received their first financial return in many years. From 1944 to 1949 Parker was a coach of the Chicago Cardinals professional team.

Sports Illustrated has called Parker "the top football coach in America," and states that his simplicity of method and his thoroughness will probably keep his team winning. The games in which the Detroit Lions play each week are also seen by nation-wide television audiences during the season.

On December 16, 1913 in Kemp, Texas, a small town outside of Dallas, Raymond Klein Parker was born into a family of very moderate means. His father operated a small lumber yard. Buddy has an older brother. He played baseball, basketball, and football in Kemp High School. There was no money in the family to send him to college, but his athletic prowess won him a scholarship to North Texas, a junior college. After finishing there in 1931 with an excellent sports record in three fields, he received bids from several southwestern senior colleges such as the University of Texas.

Although his hitting in baseball impressed the college coach, he preferred to play football. He joined his brother Bob at Centenary College of Louisiana in Shreveport. He received financial aid, aside from his scholarship, from local boosters while going to school. In his senior year, 1934, he ranked among the leading collegiate ground gainers in the country.

Many professional offers were made to him on graduation, but he was advised by a friend, Cal Hubbard, to go with George Clark, coach of the Detroit Lions. He received $1,200 for his first season and was part of the Lions team that won the conference championship in 1935. Parker had served as substitute fullback and blocking halfback and was one of the more potent factors which led to the Lions' winning the world championship that season. This was the only year Detroit won either conference or "World" title until 1952 when Parker was again with the club.

In 1937 Parker was traded to the Chicago Cardinals, at that time a very unsuccessful club. He retired from the active playing list relatively unknown in 1943, but turned up the next year as assistant coach with the Cardinals under Jimmy Conzelman. Parker coached the backfield during the years 1947 (when they won the world championship) and 1948 (when they won the conference title but lost the world championship playoffs). When Conzelman left the Cardinals in 1949 Parker was appointed co-coach with Phil Handler. At mid-season Handler was diverted to other duties and Parker was made head coach for the remaining seven games.

Deciding to leave Chicago at the end of the season, Parker in 1950 began as assistant to Alvin (Bo) McMillin, head coach and general manager of the Detroit Lions. A heavy deficit existed because of the poor won and lost record of the team and the resultant low attendance. The year 1950 was no better, with attendance at only 151,600 (this was increased to 370,186 in 1953).

According to Stanley Frank's article in the *Saturday Evening Post* (November 13, 1954), McMillin was a strict disciplinarian and the many talents in the club were discontent and consequently not performing well. Parker was appointed head coach in 1951 and in his first season lost the Western Conference title by losing their final game to the San Francisco Forty-Niners in the last four minutes. The next year Parker's team won the Conference title and went on in the playoff against the eternally strong Cleveland Browns to win the championship. Against the same team in 1953 they repeated the feat, but were turned back fifty-six to ten in 1954. Until the fall 1955 season, Parker's record was thirty victories, eleven defeats, and one tie.

During this period a deficit of $221,000 was turned into a net profit of $66,287 for the 136 stockholders. Football's increasing nation-wide popularity has also helped Parker's team. In 1951 he received a salary of $12,000. According to *Sports Illustrated* (November 15, 1954), "For winning, Parker draws approximately $40,000 a year. He works on a one-year contract with bonuses based on home attendance and team performance. The Lions drew 370,186 for seven games in 1953" as compared with a seven home game total attendance of 237,161 in 1951.

To solve the personal tensions and discontentments that had occurred among the team's members, Parker formed a players' executive committee of five (selected by the players themselves), which gives a voice to the players' disagreements with management and gives the squad a "self-policing unit." Parker "figures you're grown up and he treats you that way," said Leon Hart in *Sports Illustrated* (November 15, 1954), voicing the entire team's satisfaction with Parker's personal method.

"The quarterbacks are the bread-and-butter guys of a winning team," Parker says, speaking of his training method. He spends extra hours with Bobby Layne, but gives him a good deal of freedom while on the field. "That 'play messenger' stuff is the bunk; what's so mysterious about football," says Parker, who often gives his quarterback the choice of the play, avoiding the constant substitutions between plays which Paul Brown of Cleveland has found so successful. Parker has only twenty basic plays, believing too many add to the confusion, while many teams have plays numbering in the hundreds.

Each Sunday's game is reviewed by Parker, using films and the blackboard before the entire team and its several coaches. George Wilson, Aldo Forte, Garrard Ramsey and Paul Christman are Parker's assistants. To avoid injuries Parker does not allow his players to use body contact in practice sessions.

Wide World

BUDDY PARKER

Important coaching successes of Parker's are Bobby Layne, who was bought from New York, Doak Walker, who was stagnant under McMillin, Bob Hoernschemeyer, and Leon Hart. "What's the use of kidding ourselves?" coach Parker asks. "You got to get the players." Detroit spends $20,000 a year on scouting. Bob Nussbaumer is the main scout, and other part-time scouts are scattered throughout the country.

The first professional football team to be recognized as such played in the township of Latrobe, in Westmoreland County, Pennsylvania in August 1895. Soon other professional teams began to appear and in December 1902 Syracuse played the Philadelphia Nationals in Madison Square Garden, New York. The American Professional Football Association, predecessor of the National Football League, was formed in 1904 in Ohio. On September 17, 1920, the National Football League was founded with Jim Thorpe as president. In subsequent years teams such as the Green Bay Packers, New York Giants, and the Chicago Bears were formed, and by 1933, professional football was firmly established as a major league sport. It was in this year that the league split off into two divisions—East and West—and thereby established a championship playoff. It also began to form an apparatus to keep official statistical records and, generally, came of age.

Weighing 200 pounds and standing six feet tall, Buddy Parker has the look of a man who has spent almost thirty years of his life on the playing field. He has dark hair, his skin is leathery, and his face lined. His Southwestern drawl contains a nasal twang. "After [losing], there's a deep silence around the house until Tuesday," Mrs. Parker relates (*Saturday*

PARKER, BUDDY—*Continued*

Evening Post, November 13, 1954), and attests in the same article to his superstition. The writer, Stanley Frank, says, "he kowtows to superstition like a witch doctor in the deepest jungle." Tommy Devine in *Sports Illustrated* (November 15, 1954) says, "After a losing game, [Parker's] . . . friends keep strictly away from him."

Buddy and Jane Parker's son, Bobby, is eight years old. Parker has few interests outside of football, but he does bet ardently on horse races. About the game for which he "lives" or "dies" he says, "There's no tomorrow for a football coach."

References

Sat Eve Post 227:25 N 13 '54 por
Sports Ill 1:28 N 15 '54 por

Treat, R. L. Official National Football League Football Encyclopedia (1952)

PARKER, JOHN J(OHNSTON) Nov. 20, 1885- Judge; lawyer

Address: b. c/o U. S. Circuit Court, Federal Bldg., Charlotte, N.C.; h. 135 Queens Rd., Charlotte, N.C.

For the past thirty years a judge of the U. S. Court of Appeals, Fourth Circuit, John J. Parker of North Carolina is regarded as an eminent authority on both state and Federal constitutional law, on improvement of the judicial system, and on international law. He was the Republican nominee for Governor of North Carolina in 1920 and was named by President Herbert C. Hoover to the U. S. Supreme Court in 1930, but failed to receive Senate confirmation. On two other occasions Parker was considered for appointment to the nation's highest bench—in 1943, when James F. Byrnes resigned, and in 1945, when Owen J. Roberts retired. Judge Parker served in 1945-1946 as alternate U. S. judge at the Nuremberg war criminal trials.

Wide World

JUDGE JOHN J. PARKER

Following the Supreme Court's pronouncement on May 17, 1954 that segregation of public school children is unconstitutional, Judge Parker headed the three-member board of judges which issued the first lower court injunction (in the Summerton, South Carolina school case) implementing the Supreme Court's ruling. "Whatever may have been the views of this court as to the law when the case was originally before us," Judge Parker stated at the opening of the proceedings, "it is our duty now to accept the law as declared by the Supreme Court" (New York *Times*, July 16, 1955).

Born to John Daniel and Frances Ann (Johnston) Parker on November 20, 1885, John Johnston Parker is a native of Monroe, North Carolina, where his father was a merchant. (His mother was a daughter of Dr. Samuel Iredell Johnston, an Episcopal clergyman.) John attended local public schools in Union County and worked his way through the University of North Carolina at Chapel Hill.

He was president of his class in both the freshman and senior years, won prizes for Greek, economics and oratory, and was elected to Omicron Delta Kappa and Phi Beta Kappa. After graduating in 1907 with the A.B. degree he studied at the Law School for the LL. B. degree (awarded in 1908) and was a fellow of the university faculty in the department of Greek. (He is a member of the Phi Delta Phi law fraternity, the Golden Fleece, and the Order of the Coif.)

Parker gained much practical political experience by serving in 1908 as secretary of the G.O.P. campaign committee for the Fifth North Carolina District, a hitherto strongly Democratic area which in that year elected the Republican candidate, John M. Morehead, to the U.S. House of Representatives.

Admitted to the North Carolina bar in 1908, Parker worked for one year in a Greensboro, North Carolina law office and then returned to Monroe, where in 1910, at the age of twenty-four, he received the Republican nomination for U.S. Representative from the Seventh North Carolina District. He was defeated by the Democratic candidate, Robert N. Page, in the November election, polling 11,000 votes to his opponent's 13,000.

Also in 1910 he formed with Amos M. Stack (later a Superior Court Justice) the Monroe law partnership of Stack & Parker, which nine years later became Stack, Parker & Craig. Parker was the Republican nominee for Attorney General of North Carolina in 1916. Although Parker lost the election for Governor in 1920 he received 43 per cent of the ballots, his 230,000 votes being 6,000 more than any member of the G.O.P. had ever before polled for that office.

Moving to Charlotte in 1922, he became the head of the law firm of Parker, Stewart, Mc-

Rae & Bobbitt. He served as special assistant to the Attorney General of the United States in 1923 and 1924.

Serving on the Republican National Committee in 1924, Parker was a delegate-at-large from North Carolina to the G.O.P. national convention. On October 3, 1925 President Calvin Coolidge appointed him a judge of the Fourth Circuit Court of the United States, covering Maryland, Virginia, West Virginia, North Carolina and South Carolina. During the next four and a half years, Judge Parker rendered some 125 decisions. The most celebrated was made in 1927 when he heard an appeal by the United Mine Workers against an injunction which had been granted to the Red Jacket Consolidated Coal and Coke Company restraining the union from "efforts to persuade nonunion members to break so-called 'Yellow-dog' contracts" under which, as a condition of employment, the worker agreed not to join a union (*American Bar Association Journal*, December 1946). Judge Parker wrote the 2 to 1 majority opinion, continuing the injunction on the authority of a Supreme Court decision in a similar case, which had held such contracts valid.

According to the New York *Times* (March 22, 1930), this decision and the hostility of a leading Negro organization were to be key reasons for the rejection by the U. S. Senate of the appointment of Judge Parker as an Associate Justice of the Supreme Court after President Hoover had named him on March 21, 1930 to fill the vacancy created by the death of Justice Edward T. Sanford of Tennessee. Although a Republican, Parker had received Democratic endorsement when named to the Circuit Court; and he was recommended for the Supreme Court appointment by ten Southern Senators and seven Democratic governors as well as by eminent fellow judges and lawyers. However, his appointment was protested by President William Green of the A.F.L., by the "liberal" weeklies and the National Association for the Advancement of Colored People.

On April 21 the Senate Judiciary Committee reported adversely on the appointment by 10 to 6; and on May 7 Judge Parker was rejected by the full Senate by a vote of 41 to 39. (Owen J. Roberts of Philadelphia was subsequently appointed.) Two weeks later the Supreme Court upheld a Circuit Court decision by Judge Parker in favor of a Negro who had been threatened by the municipality of Richmond, Virginia with criminal prosecution for purchasing a home in a "white" neighborhood.

In 1931 Judge Parker served as member of a commission to draft a new constitution for North Carolina and in the years that followed he frequently contributed articles to legal periodicals on the relation of the bar and judiciary to the Federal and the state constitutions, on international law and other subjects. (See *Index to Legal Periodicals.*)

A member of the American Bar Association since 1914, Parker became a vice-president and the chairman of the judiciary section in 1937. On April 9, 1939 he became the Senior Circuit Judge of the Fourth Circuit. His William H. White Foundation lectures at the University of Virginia were collected in his book, *Democracy in Government* (Michie, 1940).

The Supreme Court had ruled in 1940 that a certain Pennsylvania school board had been within its rights in requiring two children who were members of the Jehovah's Witnesses sect to salute the flag. About two years later, in a similar case involving three West Virginia children, Judge Parker wrote a majority opinion declaring that forcing the salute "upon one who has conscientious scruples against giving it is petty tyranny unworthy of the spirit of this Republic."

In 1943 Parker was again mentioned as a possibility for Supreme Court membership following the resignation of James F. Byrnes. He was the recipient on August 25 of that year of the American Bar Association Gold Medal annually awarded for "conspicuous service to the cause of American jurisprudence." Since 1940 he had served as chairman of the Association's special committee on improving the administration of justice. He was appointed to the advisory board on just compensation of the War Shipping Administration in 1943. In 1945 he was a delegate to the national study conference on a just and durable peace, instituted by the Federal Council of Churches.

His acceptance of an appointment by President Harry S. Truman on September 12, 1945 as alternate United States judge to former Attorney General Francis S. Biddle on the International Military Tribunal to try Axis war criminals at Nuremberg, Germany, removed him from a third consideration for Supreme Court appointment, in succession to Justice Roberts, who was retiring. Judge Parker served on the tribunal for about one year, his resignation then being accepted by President Truman with praise for his "learning, integrity and conscience and judicial temperament" (New York *Times*, October 13, 1946). In 1949 he was judicial adviser to the U. S. High Commission to Germany.

Having returned to the Fourth Circuit, Judge Parker, as a member of a special three-judge Federal court, wrote in June 1951 a majority opinion affirming the right of Clarendon County School District Number One at Summerton, South Carolina to maintain separate schools for white and colored pupils, provided that equal facilities were afforded. At a Senate subcommittee's hearings on the proposed Bricker amendment to limit the President's treaty-making powers, Judge Parker testified on March 27, 1953 in opposition. Addressing the Governors' Conference held at Boca Raton, Florida in November 1954, he characterized as "vital" the doctrine of a state's right to preserve local government, but also stressed that "a man must not be prejudiced by race or color or creed in his standing before the law."

Following the U. S. Supreme Court ruling of May 17, 1954 that segregation of public school pupils is unconstitutional, Judge Parker presided at a three-judge reconsideration of the Summerton, South Carolina school case and on July 15, 1955 recommended that the law as declared by the Supreme Court be enforced. The Fourth Circuit Court's ensuing order to

PARKER, JOHN J.—*Continued*

the trustees of the Summerton schools enjoined them from "refusing because of race to admit any child to any school in their jurisdiction." The injunction, however, was not to become operative until "necessary arrangements" on "a nondiscriminatory basis" had been made (New York *Times*, July 16, 1955).

Honorary LL.D. degrees have been conferred on Judge Parker by the University of North Carolina and four other universities. He is a council member of the American Law Institute and vice-president of the American Judicature Society as well as a member of the American and North Carolina bar associations, the American Society for International Law and the American Academy of Political and Social Science. He was elected Honorary Master of the Bench by the Inner Temple, London, in 1946. Judge Parker is an Episcopalian. He is a Mason and a member of the Kiwanis and of the Charlotte Country Club.

He married Maria Burgwin Maffitt on November 23, 1910. Their elder son, John Johnston, Jr., was killed in an automobile accident while a student at the University of North Carolina; their surviving children are a daughter; Sara Burgwin (Mrs. Rufus M. Ward), and a younger son, Francis Iredell. Judge Parker is six feet tall; his eyes are gray. In a biographical article in the *American Bar Association Journal* (December 1946) he was characterized as "a true liberal with a heart and a head, but with his feet on the ground. . . He reads much and widely, plays no golf, but walks considerably."

References

N Y Times p3 Mr 22 '30 por
Directory of American Judges, 1955
International Year Book and Statesmen's Who's Who, 1955
National Cyclopædia of American Biography current vol G (1946)
Who's Who in America, 1954-55
World Biography (1954)

PARKER, RAYMOND K(LEIN) *See* Parker, Buddy

PARRISH, MRS. WAYNE WILLIAM *See* Knight, Frances G(ladys)

PARTRIDGE, EARLE E(VERARD) July 7, 1900- United States Air Force officer

Address: b. c/o Continental Air Defense Command, Ent Air Force Base, Colorado Springs, Colo.

An Army private in World War I who became a combat air general in World War II, General Earle E. Partridge never lost his love for flying as he rose to top command. On April 25, 1955 he was chosen as head of the U.S. Continental Air Defense Command, succeeding General Benjamin W. Chidlaw who retired. The command is charged with defending the North American continent against thermonuclear attack, and works in conjunction with the Royal Canadian Air Command.

General Partridge had headed the U.S. Air Force's Far East Command from April 1, 1954 to April 1955, with authority over non-Naval American fighter and pursuit aircraft in that area. He has had over 11,000 hours of flying time in aircraft ranging from the World War I "Jenny" to the latest jets. During a large part of the Korean war he commanded the Fifth Air Force and was officially credited with the development of "new tactics and theory in the new era" of jet warfare. Previously General Partridge had made an impressive combat and command record in Africa and Europe during World War II.

On February 4, 1955 General Partridge said that the United States has enough strength in the Far East to handle any aggressive move by Communist China against Formosa and the offshore islands. "The enemy is capable of starting a war. We have to be able to fight a war once it starts. We are maintaining combat readiness."

Earle Everard Partridge was born to William Henry and Mary Jane (Dempsey) Partridge in Winchendon, Massachusetts on July 7, 1900. In 1918 he enlisted in the Army and was assigned to the Fifth Engineer Training Regiment at Camp Humphreys, Virginia. He was sent overseas in August 1918 and served with the 79th Division during the Argonne offensive. After his discharge in June 1919, he spent one year at Norwich University in Northfield, Vermont.

Re-enlisting in the Army in June 1920, Partridge was assigned to the Army Service Detachment at West Point, New York for service as an enlisted man. He entered the U.S. Military Academy in September 1920. Partridge, an honor student, received the B.S. degree on June 12, 1924 and was commissioned a second lieutenant in the Air Service of the Regular Army.

After pursuing courses at the Advanced Flying School, Kelly Field, Texas he became an instructor at the school for three years. He won the Distinguished Aerial Gunner's Medal at three annual matches at Langley Field, Virginia.

For one year beginning September 1929 he was an instructor in mathematics at West Point. Later he served at France Field, Panama Canal Zone, with the Seventh Observation Squadron. Transferred to Selfridge Field, Michigan in 1932, he served successively with the 94th and 27th Pursuit Squadrons and at post headquarters.

The young officer was promoted to the rank of captain (permanent) in 1935 and sent to the Air Corps Tactical School, Maxwell Field, Alabama, from which he was graduated in 1937. After studying at the Command and General Staff School at Fort Leavenworth, Kansas, he returned to Maxwell Field as an instructor in the pursuit section of the Tactical School. Transferred to the Southeast Air Corps training command in June 1940, Partridge organized the first advanced single-engine flying schools in the southeastern states, at Barksdale Air Force Base, Shreveport, Louisiana and at Dothan, Alabama, on which subsequent schools of this type were modelled.

When the War Department was reorganized in March 1942, he was advanced to the rank of colonel (temporary) and named a member of the War Department General Staff and a member of the Joint Strategic Committee, Joint Chiefs of Staff. In December 1942 he became a brigadier general (temporary). After assuming command of the New York Air Defense Wing in January 1943, Partridge described this unit as "a highly integrated striking force, working as a team containing fighter or pursuit aircraft and antiaircraft artillery."

From this assignment he joined the Northwest African Air Force as operations officer and chief of staff of the 12th Bomber Command. He was later reassigned as chief of staff and deputy commander of General James (Jimmy) H. Doolittle's Fifteenth Air Force. When Doolittle was named head of the Eighth Air Force in January 1944, Partridge became deputy commander and was promoted to the rank of major general (temporary). In the following June he succeeded General Curtis E. LeMay as commander of the Third Bombardment Division (later redesignated the Third Air Division). Following the end of the war in Europe, Partridge assisted in the reorganization of the Eighth Air Force and its movement to Okinawa.

For his service in World War II Partridge was awarded the Distinguished Service Medal (for "directing strategic bombing operations against the Nazis"), Distinguished Flying Cross (for combat missions over Sicily, Italy and Austria), Legion of Merit, Bronze Star Medal, and Air Medal with three oak-leaf clusters. His foreign decorations include the French Legion of Honor and Croix de Guerre with two palms, Polish Order of Polonia Restituta, British honorary Companion of the Order of the Bath (military division), and Belgian Croix de Guerre.

In January 1946 he was assigned to Washington, D.C. as Assistant Chief of Air Staff for Operations. After the Air Force was established as an executive department by the National Security Act of 1947, General Partridge was appointed director of training and requirements in the office of the Deputy Chief of Staff for Operations. He attained on June 11, 1948 the permanent rank of major general dated as of February 29, 1944. In August 1948 he was reassigned to the Fifth Air Force at Nagoya, Japan, and in October became its commander.

After the North Korean Communists had invaded South Korea in June 1950, Partridge and the Fifth Air Force were ordered to Korea. During the Korean conflict, the United States for the first time employed jet aircraft on a large scale in combat. General Partridge "instituted a new system of rapid movement of jet tactical units and established a rear echelon maintenance system which enhanced U.S. air supremacy" (*Generals of the Army and the Air Force,* March 1954).

U. S. Air Force

GEN. EARLE E. PARTRIDGE

The New York *Herald Tribune* (July 30, 1950) praised the general's "ability to plan such details as keeping planes up at night to hammer North Korean truck convoys and equipping them by day to drop 500-pound bombs by parachute on . . . bridges." Jim G. Lucas called Partridge one of the "ablest" of air officers and said "he has never had an adequate reserve. But only once—in six months—have his planes been grounded for as long as forty-eight hours" (New York *World-Telegram and Sun,* January 29, 1951).

The general received the Distinguished Service Cross on October 7, 1950 with a citation referring to "flights at personal risk of life from Communist ground fire and air patrols in unarmed planes." Other awards with which he was decorated for his service in Korea include an oak-leaf cluster to his Distinguished Flying Cross, another Bronze Star Medal, and the Silver Cross of the Korean Order of Military Merit.

Partridge became a lieutenant general (temporary) in April 1951 and in July he was named commanding general of the Air Research and Development Command at Wright-Patterson Air Force Base (which had moved from Dayton, Ohio to Baltimore, Maryland). This command is charged with developing qualitatively superior technical means by which the Air Force can further national security. In June 1953 the general was appointed Deputy Chief of Staff for Operations at Air Force headquarters.

On April 1, 1954 Partridge assumed command of the Far East Air Forces and received the temporary rank of "full" general. After arriving at his Tokyo headquarters, Partridge visited French air bases in Indochina in connection with the beleaguered garrison of Dienbienphu. The general announced on June 18 that the Far East Air Forces Bomber Command

PARTRIDGE, EARLE E.—*Continued*

was being deactivated and replaced by the Strategic Air Command's Third Air Division at Andersen Air Force Base, Guam.

An Associated Press dispatch explained that this would accomplish "a double objective. First the long-range bombers on Guam are protected by a vast radar screen against any surprise attack. Second, the removal of the atomic-bomb carriers from Japan relieves the Japanese of the worry of being the target of retaliatory bombings should a major war come to Asia" (New York *Times,* June 18, 1954).

U.S. air strength in the Far East, as estimated by Partridge, totals about 2,400 bombers, fighters, reconnaissance and transport planes. He also said that the Communists have an "armada" of approximately 7,500 warplanes in the Far East. Nevertheless, "our first objective," Partridge stated, "would be to gain control of the air" (New York *Times,* July 17, 1954).

Prior to the evacuation of the Tachen Islands by the Chinese Nationalists, Partridge announced on January 27, 1955 that one wing (the Eighteenth Fighter Bomber Wing) of F-86 Sabrejets had already begun moving from Okinawa to "temporary duty bases" on Formosa, and other offensive units within his command were being "redeployed to forward bases."

According to Greg MacGregor (New York *Times,* February 27, 1955), General Partridge estimated that the Chinese Communists have about 2,000 planes of types similar to those under his command. He believes the U.S. Air Force is superior technically and operationally while the Communists have numerical superiority.

Katherine Louise Holder and Partridge were married on January 28, 1928; they have two daughters, Patricia Earle and Kay Blythe. The general is a member of the Army and Navy Country Club in Washington. His Air Force ratings are command pilot, combat observer and aircraft observer. He has been described as "tall, lean, perfectly poised, with quiet eyes and an easy smile." The general's nickname is "Pat."

References

Gen Army 2:21+ Mr '54 por
N Y Herald Tribune II p 1 Jl 30 '50 por; p 1 My 24 '51
N Y Times p4 Ag 8 '44; p6 Ja 27 '45; p19 S 20 '50; p3 O 8 '50; p10 F 9 '54
N Y World-Telegram p4 Ja 29 '51
Newsweek 36:16+ Jl 24 '50 por
Who's Who in America, 1954-55

PASQUEL, JORGE 1907(?)-Mar. 7, 1955
Mexican businessman; sportsman; former baseball executive who led the "raid" on U.S. baseball talent in 1946; was at one time president of *Novedades,* a Mexico City newspaper; his business interests included an oil distributing company, banks, real estate, and shipping. See *Current Biography* (July) 1946.

Obituary

N Y Times p56 Mr 9 '55

PATTERSON, ALICIA Oct. 15, 1906-
Editor; publisher

Address: b. c/o Newsday, Garden City, N.Y.; h. Port Washington, Long Island, N.Y.

The founder, editor and publisher of Long Island's tabloid *Newsday,* Alicia Patterson, is the only surviving member now engaged in newspaper publishing of the famed Patterson-McCormick dynasty, which made the New York *Daily News* and the Chicago *Tribune* two of the country's leading newspapers. With a circulation of more than 200,000 fifteen years after its founding in 1940, *Newsday* is, according to *Time,* "the fastest-growing and most profitable big daily paper started in the United States in the last twenty years."

Newsday, whose development has kept pace with Long Island's rapid postwar economic expansion and population increase, has been described by Alicia Patterson as a "big-city paper that just happens to be published in the suburbs." Notable for its reporting of local news in a community where subscribers generally also read Manhattan newspapers, *Newsday* won the Pulitzer Prize in 1954 for exposing corruption and graft at Long Island's trotting tracks. It has also received awards for excellence in typography.

The second of three daughters of Captain Joseph Medill Patterson and Alice (Higinbotham) Patterson, Alicia Patterson was born in Chicago, Illinois on October 15, 1906. She is the great granddaughter of Joseph Medill, who directed the Chicago *Tribune* from 1855, seven years after its establishment, until his death in 1899. Her father and her cousin, Colonel Robert R. McCormick, took control of the paper in 1911, and in 1919 founded the New York *Daily News* (then the *Illustrated Daily News*), later guided by Patterson, who has been called "the father of tabloid journalism in America." When McCormick died in 1955, nine years after the death of Patterson, the combined circulation of the two papers was about 3,000,000, with a Sunday circulation of more than 5,000,000.

Another prominent member of the publishing family was Alicia Patterson's aunt, Eleanor Medill (Cissy) Patterson, publisher of the Washington *Times-Herald.* She died in 1948 and six years later that paper was sold to the Washington *Post* (now the Washington *Post and Times Herald*). Alicia Patterson's sisters are Elinor (Mrs. Donald Baker) and Josephine (Mrs. Ivan Albright), who writes a column for *Newsday.*

Growing up "amidst a family turmoil and intellectual ferment that never subsided," as *Time* (September 13, 1954) has pictured it, Alicia spent much of her childhood in Chicago and on a farm in Libertyville, Illinois, where she learned riding and swimming. She was formally educated at private schools in the United States (principally Foxcroft School in Middleburg, Virginia) and in Europe. After her debut in Chicago society in 1925, she went to New York City to be with her father, who then was giving his full attention to the affairs of the *Daily News.*

Captain Patterson exerted a strong influence on his daughter's lifework. "The best thing about him," *Time* quotes Alicia Patterson as saying, "was his wonderful curiosity and interest. He taught me to see things and be curious." In 1927-1928 she worked as a cub reporter for the New York *Daily News*, leaving, it is told, after a confusion in names in one of her stories on a divorce case led to a libel suit. About a year later she joined the staff of the family-owned *Liberty* magazine. For one of her assignments, to write a series of articles entitled "How to Get a Job Without Experience," she worked as a theatre cashier, sold magazines, and was a store detective, using the name Agnes Homberg.

Following a suggestion of her father, who was interested in flying, Alicia Patterson became a transport pilot in 1931 and held several records for women flyers. She also wrote a number of articles on flying, among them, "Flying for Fun" for *Vogue* and "Joy Ride—A Story of Love and Wings" for *Liberty*. She returned to the New York *Daily News* in 1932 as literary critic and reviewed books for that paper until 1943.

For some time Alicia Patterson had been interested in publishing her own newspaper, an ambition in which her family reportedly gave her little encouragement. In 1939 Harry F. Guggenheim, "a mining scion" whom she had married in July of that year, learned of a newspaper for sale in Hempstead, Long Island. It was the *Nassau County Journal*, which had ceased publication after nine days. The press and Linotype machines that he bought had been set up in a Hempstead garage, *Newsday's* first home. (It moved to nearby Garden City in 1949.) During the next six years Guggenheim, who continues to control the paper's financial affairs, invested about $750,000 before *Newsday* began to show a profit. He owns 51 per cent of the stock; Alicia Patterson owns 49 per cent.

Publisher Patterson ignored her father's advice: "Don't try a tabloid. Country folks are too accustomed to standard-sized newspapers" (*Newsweek*, March 28, 1949). The first issue of *Newsday* (11,000 copies) came off the press on September 9, 1940. Less than two years later it surpassed the 32,000 circulation of its twenty-year-old Republican competitor, the *Nassau Review-Star*, which became defunct in 1953.

By 1954 *Newsday*'s circulation had risen to 213,813. It is largely home-delivered and appears in four different editions to provide local news for various parts of Long Island. Politically independent, *Newsday* has supported every Republican Presidential candidate since 1944, but it often crosses party lines and in local politics it sometimes backs Democratic candidates.

"*Newsday* looks like no other U.S. daily," *Time* (September 13, 1954) stated. "It has only three columns instead of the usual five-column tabloid format, and the first and last pages have only two wide columns, usually filled with national and international news. ('We try to make it read as easily as a magazine,' says Alicia.) In between is a whopping filling of local news, features, comic, first-rate picture spreads, and page after page of solid advertisements." In 1948 *Newsday* reported that it ran more advertisements than any competing afternoon paper in New York and more than any tabloid in the country, except the New York *Daily News*.

ALICIA PATTERSON

Unlike the isolationist publishers of the Chicago *Tribune* and the New York *Daily News*, Alicia Patterson is an internationalist. At the time of McCormick's death in 1955, she wrote a tribute to him in *Newsday* which took note of the fact that "many disagreed with his editorial policy, including *Newsday*." On community affairs, *Newsday* is editorially concerned "with needling the Long Island Rail Road, stumping for a stronger Nassau county government, and poking into similar cracker-barrel issues" (*Newsweek*, March 28, 1949). Typical of this concern was a number of articles published in April 1955 on the need for a community low-tuition college for Nassau and Suffolk counties. One of Miss Patterson's many successful campaigns was helping to raise funds to purchase Walt Whitman's birthplace at Huntington, Long Island in 1951 as a memorial to the poet.

It was on a local issue that *Newsday* in May 1954 won the Pulitzer Prize "for disinterested and meritorious public service." Since 1950 the paper, with Alan Hathway as managing editor, had been exposing graft at New York's trotting tracks, charging that William DeKoning, leader of Long Island's building trade union, was guilty of "shaking down" contractors and workers at Roosevelt Raceway in Westbury. *Newsday*'s exposé was in large part responsible for eventual state inquiry which brought corrective legislation and for the extortion conviction of DeKoning.

Judged the best-looking tabloid-sized newspaper in the United States, *Newsday* in 1952 and 1955 won the award in its category in the annual contest held by N. W. Ayer & Son, the advertising agency, to honor newspapers for

PATTERSON, ALICIA—*Continued*

excellence in typography, makeup and printing. It was also given recognition in 1941, 1943, 1953 and 1954 when it was a finalist in the tabloid class. Its 1955 award, announced on April 22, was accorded on the basis of "clear printing and ease of reading, balance and harmony of different elements on a page, the use of a limited number of points of top interest on front pages, good selection and reproduction of photos, and the treatment of pages as a unit of design" (*Newsday*, April 22, 1955).

In a speech at the annual convention of the New York State Publishers Association in Lake Placid in September 1954, Alicia Patterson pointed out that opportunities for increasing circulation and advertising volume were greater than before because of the current shift in population from cities to suburban areas. She suggested that publishers could offset the competition in advertising from television by giving more attention to community stories.

She assigned a reporter, Virginia Pasley, to write a series of articles about the twenty-one GI's who in January 1954 chose to stay in Red China. Mrs. Pasley's articles (published in 1955 under the title *Twenty-One Who Stayed*) were obtained by interviewing the families, friends and neighbors of the young men. Mrs. Pasley received favorable reviews for her careful documentation of their case histories, and Miss Patterson was acclaimed for her contribution to good journalism.

Alicia Patterson is a director of the New York *Daily News*, vice-president of the Harry F. Guggenheim Foundation, and a trustee of Hofstra College in Hempstead and of the Solomon R. Guggenheim Museum. She belongs to the American Newspaper Publishers Association, the American Society of Newspaper Editors, the International Press Institute, the Women's National Press Club and the River Club. Her church is the Episcopal.

Harry F. Guggenheim is Alicia Patterson's third husband. In the late 1920's she married James Simpson, Jr., who later became a director of Marshall Field & Company in Chicago. The marriage was terminated after about a year. On December 23, 1931 she married Joseph W. Brooks, from whom she was divorced in 1939. She married Guggenheim on July 1, 1939.

The brown-eyed publisher is five feet three inches tall and weighs 115 pounds. Her favorite sports are shooting and fishing. She has a vacation home in Georgia.

Kenneth Stewart and John Tebbel wrote of Alicia Patterson in *Makers of Modern Journalism* (1952) as "an able, imaginative woman" who may "prove to be the best-balanced and eventually the most successful member, everything considered, of a dynasty that has been one of the most powerful journalistic voices of the last hundred years."

References

Newsweek 33:61+ Mr 28 '49
Sat Eve Post 223:36+ My 12 '51 pors
Who's Who in America, 1954-55
World Biography (1954)

PATTON, FRANCES GRAY Mar. 19, 1906- Author

Address: b. c/o Russell & Volkening, Inc., 522 5th Ave., New York 36; h. 614 Swift Ave., Durham, N.C.

Reprinted from the *Wilson Library Bulletin* Nov. 1955

The author of many short stories and a best-selling novel, *Good Morning, Miss Dove* (Dodd, 1954), Frances Gray Patton, began her writing career by way of the theatre. While attending the University of North Carolina in Chapel Hill, she was active in the Carolina Playmakers there. She wrote the opening play for the Playmaker Theater, dedicated in 1925, but did not think highly of it, saying she wrote a better one later, published in the Playmakers' second book of folk plays, alongside of what is regarded as Thomas Wolfe's first published work. She later joined the Stuart Walker stock company in Cincinnati, Ohio.

Frances Gray was born on March 19, 1906 in Raleigh, North Carolina. Her parents, Robert Lilly Gray and Mary S. (MacRae) Gray, as well as her grandparents and most of her great-grandparents were natives of North Carolina. Many of her forbears came from Scotland; others crossed the Atlantic on the *Mayflower*, settling in New England and later moving to the South.

Miss Gray's father was a newspaperman and held editorial positions in North Carolina, Virginia, Maryland, Washington, D.C., and New York. Both of her brothers are newspapermen, and her mother, who was the first coed at the University of North Carolina, contributed to the *St. Nicholas Magazine* and *Youth's Companion.*

Since childhood, writing has been Frances Gray's abiding interest. After studying at a Newport News, Virginia high school, where she went in for cheerleading, orating, debating and writing for the paper, she atended Trinity College (now Duke University) in Durham, North Carolina for a year. She transferred to the University of North Carolina, where she held a playwriting fellowship. Shortly after college, in 1927, she married Lewis Patton, a member of the English department of the faculty of the University of North Carolina. They have a six-foot son, Robert Gray, and twin daughters, Mary MacRae and Susannah (Mrs. Karl A. Zener).

The *O. Henry Memorial Award Prize Stories of 1945* included Mrs. Patton's first published story, "A Piece of Bread." It had originally appeared in the *Kenyon Review,* and was about the impact of a chain gang on a little Southern white girl. In a recent letter Mrs. Patton wrote of that distinction: "I cannot tell you what that meant to me. It gave me a great feeling of happiness and optimism and really kept me writing through discouraging times. Incidentally, though I've written a lot since then, that little tale will always have a place in my heart like a first-born child and a lucky one."

Stories by Mrs. Patton began to appear in the *New Yorker, Collier's, Harper's, McCall's Ladies' Home Journal,* and *Charm.* Her first book, *The Finer Things of Life* (Dodd, 1951), was a collection of short stories, four of which concerned a family in a small Southern town, with a college-professor father, and his Northern wife struggling gaily with "the finer things of life." The New York *Herald Tribune Book Review* (December 9, 1951) critic wrote that the book "introduces a new writer of genuine talent." The *Christian Science Monitor* (January 3, 1952) applauded its "subtle storytelling," and the late Joseph Henry Jackson wrote in the San Francisco *Chronicle* (November 8, 1951), "If [Mrs. Patton] is sometimes ironic, her irony is invariably gentle." One of the collection, "A Nice Name," was awarded a prize from the Society for Intercultural Education. Another story was "The Terrible Miss Dove" which later became an episode in *Good Morning, Miss Dove.*

Good Morning, Miss Dove, a novel, was published by Dodd, Mead in 1954. It has been published in twelve editions in England by Victor Gollancz and appeared in the *Ladies' Home Journal* (November 1954). It was a Book-of-the-Month Club selection for April 1955 and Twentieth Century Fox is producing a movie based on it, in which Jennifer Jones plays the terrible Miss Dove. As in England, *Good Morning, Miss Dove* was enthusiastically received by the reviewers.

The *Atlantic* (October 1954) observed that Mrs. Patton used the relativity Thornton Wilder applied successfully in *Our Town,* and "makes us see education for the dedicated task it is." Two critics compared the book with James Hilton's *Goodbye, Mr. Chips,* and Dan Wickenden, writing in the New York *Herald Tribune Book Review* (October 31, 1954) said that it might become a minor classic: "It is just about flawless and completely enchanting."

Mrs. Patton is slender, five feet six and a half inches tall, and has gray eyes and light brown hair. She speaks occasionally at writers' conferences, and enjoys traveling. During the summer of 1955 she visited England, Scotland and the Continent. Her third book, *A Piece of Luck"* (Dodd, 1955) contains her first story, "A Piece of Bread." The New York *Herald Tribune Book Review* (October 2, 1955) captioned its review, "Thirteen Remarkable Tales," and noted that Mrs. Patton has "the infallible eye and ear, the acute sympathies of a born storyteller," and that the stories showed "superbly her sage grasp of the human scene and the excellence of her narration."

Rosemary Benét in *Book-of-the-Month Club News* (October 1955) wrote: The stories are varied in situation and character and age-range. Mrs. Patton is unusually acute about domestic frictions. She knows adolescence." Charles Lee in the New York *Times Book Review* (October 16, 1955) thought that the stories in *A Piece of Luck* were "poised in style, psychologically searching in manner. . . Their mood is dominantly ironic and comic, but the tender touch is rarely absent."

The quality I most admire in writing," Mrs. Patton has said, "is the quality of illumination—the mysterious moment that has shaken all of us when, pursuing a printed page, we have suddenly felt that we have glimpsed the vein-structure of human life. I hope that some day that quality will be in something I write, if only in the tag end of a solitary sentence."

PATTON, FRANCES GRAY

References

N Y Herald Tribune Bk R p3 O 24 '54
North Carolina Writers (a University of North Carolina Library Extension Publication, 1952)

PATTON, MRS. LEWIS *See* Patton, Frances Gray

PENFIELD, WILDER GRAVES Jan. 26, 1891- Neurosurgeon; author

Address: b. c/o Montreal Neurological Institute, 380 University St., Montreal, Canada; h. 4302 Montrose Ave., Westmount, Quebec, Canada

For advancing man's knowledge of the regions of the brain and for his researches in epilepsy, Dr. Wilder Graves Penfield, director of the Montreal Neurological Institute and former neurology professor at McGill University, has been honored by universities and medical societies in Canada, England and the United States. His work has made epilepsy less frightening to afflicted individuals and their families and his researches have shed light on the causes of the disease, which can now be considerably controlled. Since 1928 he has been neurosurgeon at the Royal Victoria and Montreal General Hospitals in Montreal.

In addition to books on neurology, Dr. Penfield has also written a novel concerning Abraham and the Hebrew people before their jour-

DR. WILDER GRAVES PENFIELD

ney to Canaan entitled *No Other Gods* (Little, 1954). *The* (London) *Times Literary Supplement* (June 3, 1955) praised it as a work of "solid scholarship" and "great understanding."

Wilder Graves Penfield was born in Spokane, Washington, on January 26, 1891, the son of Dr. Charles Samuel Penfield and the former Jean Jefferson. Following his early education in local schools, young Penfield attended Princeton University in New Jersey where he excelled as a student and football star. He was also active in starting one of the first Wilson-for-President clubs on the Princeton campus. He was graduated in 1913 with a Bachelor of Literature degree.

As a Rhodes Scholar, he studied medicine at Oxford University, England, from which he received a Bachelor of Arts degree in 1916. Interrupting his studies, Penfield served in France in the latter part of 1916 as a dresser in l'Hôpital V. R. 76, Ris Orangis. He was wounded severely in 1917 while at sea on the S.S. *Sussex*. After recuperating he returned to active service as a surgeon at No. 2 American Red Cross Hospital in Paris.

After completing his military duties, Penfield returned to the United States to resume his medical training at the Johns Hopkins University where he was awarded the M.D. degree in 1918. Returning to Oxford University on another Rhodes Scholarship, he received the Master of Arts and Bachelor of Science degrees in 1920. Penfield did post-graduate work in neurology at medical centers in Germany and Spain. He also studied at Harvard University Medical School in Cambridge, Massachusetts.

In 1921 Dr. Penfield was appointed an associate in surgery at Columbia University in New York and in 1926 he was made an assistant professor. During the years 1921-1928 he was a junior attending surgeon at the Presbyterian Hospital and the New York Neurological Institute, and from 1924 to 1928 he was an assistant neurologist at the Vanderbilt Clinic. In 1924 he founded the Neuro-cytology Laboratory at Columbia-Presbyterian Hospital, for the study of nerve cells.

The brilliant young surgeon was appointed to the staffs of the Royal Victoria and Montreal General Hospitals in 1928, as well as a professor of neurology and neurosurgery at McGill University.

When the Rockefeller Foundation donated $1,232,652 to McGill University to establish a neurological center to be "second to none on this continent", it was understood that Dr. Penfield would be at its head. Although many American and Canadian medical centers had vied for the gift, it was Penfield's researches in brain surgery which had influenced the trustees to select the Canadian university (New York *Times,* April 20, 1932). The Institute has attracted students from Europe, Canada, and the United States. Trained as specialists in neurology, these men establish their own hospital units upon returning to their native countries.

In 1933 Dr. Penfield announced to a conference of the American College of Physicians that his studies of the human brain, while observing epileptic seizures, proved that it was possible to cure some sufferers by operating to remove "the scar that causes the disease by pressing on the brain and the system of arterial nerves around it which produce the bodily movements of an epileptic attack" (New York *Times,* February 10, 1933).

By studying the flow of blood through the brain, Penfield learned that he could produce headache pains by stimulating the large surface veins that drain the brain of blood. He found that other sections of the brain, on the other hand, which were not near the large blood vessel, did not show the same response upon stimulation. This report aroused a great deal of enthusiasm from delegates to the 1934 meeting of the Association for Research in Nervous and Mental Diseases (New York *Times,* December 29, 1934). By 1937, Penfield's observations led him to conclude that epilepsy was a result of alterations in the blood flow through the brain, and that a cure might be effected by stabilizing the circulation.

During World War II Dr. Penfield interrupted his researches on epilepsy temporarily to work with Dr. C. H. Best, on a cure for seasickness. According to a report in the New York *Herald Tribune* (November 21, 1943), the "pink pill" developed could be used as a preventive if taken a few hours before embarking, as well as a curative after the disturbances had started.

Delivering the Thayer Lectures to neurologists at the Johns Hopkins University in 1950, Dr. Penfield explained his concept of the brain as composed of a master nerve in the central section functioning as the over-all control switch, to coordinate all sensory and motor impulses, and guiding conscious activity. But as concerns the individuality of the human mind, Dr. Penfield has stated: "Perhaps we will always be forced to visualize a spiritual element or different essence, . . . a spiritual element that is capable of controlling the mechanism" (*Christian Science Monitor,* March 28, 1950).

In the same lecture series, Dr. Penfield reported that he had been able to awaken memories which patients had stored in their subconscious, by stimulating specific areas of the cortex with electrodes in operations using local anesthesia. Although his primary purpose in conducting these experiments was to examine the various centers of the brain and their specific functions, he saw this method of turning memories "on and off" as an important advance in psychology "provided we can interpret the facts properly" (New York *World-Telegram and Sun,* March 24, 1950). He showed that an electrical impulse applied to an area caused the same reaction every time. He indicated that there is "some mechanism of the brain that inhibits—presses back—other memory patterns in the same area as the one being 'used' at the time."

By 1951 Dr. Penfield was using surgery successfully in cases of epilepsy which had been caused by brain damage. At the 14th International Congress of Psychology held in 1954, he discussed further developments in experiments conducted with patients on the "reliving" of past experiences. He specifically located the temporal lobes on each side of the ears as the nerve center storing memories. (See New York *Times,* June 10, 1954 and *Fortune,* January 1955, "New Light on the Brain" by Francis Bell.)

Dr. Penfield has served on the National Research Council of Canada and of the United States. In the latter group, he has been active in the committee on neurobiology and the committee on medical research. During World War II he was a colonel in the Royal Canadian Army Medical Corps.

His contributions to journals on neurological questions have been extensive. (See *Index Medicus* for detailed listings of topics.) He has also lectured frequently before medical societies in Canada, the United States and England. He wrote *Epilepsy and Cerebral Localizations,* with T. C. Erickson, (Thomas, 1941); *The Cerebral Cortex of Man,* with T. B. Rasmussen (Macmillan, 1950); *Epileptic Seizure Patterns,* with Kristian Kristiansen (Thomas, 1950) and *Epilepsy and the Functional Anatomy of the Human Brain,* with Herbert H. Jasper (Little, Brown, 1954). Penfield was the editor of *Cytology and Cellular Pathology of the Nervous System* (Hoeber, 1932) and the *Manual of Military Neurosurgery* (Government Printing Bureau, Ottawa, 1941) which was used as a treatise during World War II. War II.

Turning to the literary field, Dr. Penfield wrote *No Other Gods* (Little, 1954), a fictionalized version of Abraham's search for a monotheistic religion, and his leadership of the Hebrew people on the journey to Canaan and a new destiny. The book received mixed reviews from the critics. *Library Journal* (February 15, 1954) recommended it highly, but the New York *Times* thought that Penfield had not made adequate use of his material, calling the finished product "unconvincing" (March 21, 1954). *The Times* (London) *Literary Supplement* (June 3, 1955), however, said the book "was a fascinating study of the origins of the Hebrew nation." Harold Ribalow suggested that "Dr. Penfield is not an experienced enough novelist to bring to realization all of his ambitions. The novel does, however, have virtues. It is sometimes exciting and Dr. Penfield frequently captures the tensions of the times. There is plenty of action and Abraham is occasionally a thrilling figure" (New York *Herald Tribune,* March 7, 1954).

The novel was inspired by a visit to excavations in Ur in Mesopotamia, and by his mother's manuscript concerning the life of Sarah, wife of Abraham.

Honors which the neurologist has received include the Flavelle Medal of the Royal Society of Canada (1951), the Jacoby Award of the American Neurological Association (1953), the Order of St. Michael and St. George (1943), the United States Medal of Freedom with silver palms (1948), Chevalier of the Legion of Honor (1950), and the Order of Merit (1953), conferred by Queen Elizabeth II, and limited to just twenty-four members.

In 1954 he was elected to membership in the Athenaeum Club (London), reserved exclusively for men of great accomplishments in the arts and sciences.

Among the numerous societies which have elected Dr. Penfield to membership are the Royal Society of London, the Royal College of Physicians and Surgeons (Canada) of which he was president in 1940 and 1941. He is an Honorary Fellow of the Royal College of Surgeons (England) and the American Academy of Arts and Sciences. Organizations in which he has been active include the Association for Research in Nervous and Mental Diseases (president, 1936), the International Neurological Association (vice-president, 1937, 1949), the American Surgical Association (first vice-president, 1948-9), Canadian Neurological Association (president, 1948-9), and the American Neurological Association (president, 1950-51). He has received honorary degrees from several American and foreign universities.

Dr. Penfield was married to Helen Katherine Kermott, a doctor's daughter, on June 6, 1917. The couple has two sons, Wilder Graves, Jr. and Amos Jefferson, and two daughters, Ruth Mary and Priscilla. Known everywhere as an excellent speaker, Dr. Penfield finds a great deal of his time now is spent in traveling to speak before medical groups.

When he is relaxing, he is usually to be found with his family at his farm near Magog, Quebec. He also enjoys skiing, sailing and tennis. His social fraternity is Nu Sigma Nu, and his clubs include the University and Faculty in Montreal and the Century in New York. He became a naturalized Canadian citizen in 1934. His religion is Presbyterian.

The president of Princeton University, in conferring an honorary degree on her distinguished son, described him as "a strong and gentle man, with extraordinary dexterity he penetrates the recesses of the human brain

PENFIELD, WILDER GRAVES—*Cont.*

and restores to lives of usefulness and happiness those who had been facing the future without a single ray of hope" (New York *Times,* June 21, 1939).

References

N Y Times 71:4 Mr 26 '50
Canadian Who's Who, 1952-54
Who's Who, 1955
Who's Who in America, 1954-55
Who's Who in British Science, 1953
Who's Who in Canada, 1953-54

PERKINS, C(HARLES) H(ARVIE) Aug. 9, 1889- Nurseryman

Address: b. c/o Jackson & Perkins Co., South Main St., Newark, N.Y.; h. 502 West Maple St., Newark, N.Y.

During its annual June Rose Festival about 2,000,000 blooms grace the seventeen acres of gardens of the Jackson & Perkins Company in Newark, New York of which C. H. Perkins is the president. Some 400,000 visitors who see the festival also learn about rose culture and flower arranging. The eighty-three-year-old company, which is recognized as the largest

Jackson & Perkins Co., R. E. Briggs

C. H. PERKINS

rose grower in the world, also sells trees, shrubs and perennials. Perkins is the nephew and namesake of a founder of the firm.

Charles Harvie Perkins was born in Grand Rapids, Michigan on August 9, 1889, the son of Herbert D. Perkins and Nellie (Guild) Perkins. His father and his grandparents were farmers. Charles has six brothers and two sisters. He was reared in Grand Rapids and in Newark, New York.

Perkins began his career as a farmer. His uncle, Charles Harvie Perkins, was a lawyer who gradually became more interested in growing plants than in the law. In 1872 he established with his father-in-law, A. E. Jackson, a firm which began by selling general nursery stock to retail nursery concerns and to large farmers. Jackson soon left the firm and Perkins became its head. He had taken his nephew and namesake into the employ of the company in 1902. Young Perkins became president of the firm in 1929.

The firm's test gardens were located near downtown Newark in upstate New York and many townspeople began to want to buy directly from the firm. During the New York World's Fair (1939-1940), the company had an exhibit rose garden and many viewers also wanted to buy the rose plants from the firm. The Jackson & Perkins Company then decided to begin retail selling. It found a large mail order market and at present 65 per cent of its business goes through the mail.

Each year the rose gardens are visited by about 600,000 persons, 400,000 of whom come during the festival. The gardens were opened in 1945 and have been maintained for the public ever since. There are about 36,000 rose plants, which are exhibited against a background of shrubs and shade trees. There are about 200 different kinds of hybrid tea, floribunda, and climbing roses. Visitors come to enjoy the flowers, to note what they would like to buy later, and to learn about rose culture (they see the way the beds are cultivated and the way various sprays and fertilizers should be used).

During the three-week celebration of the annual Rose Festival, a rose princess—selected from the kindergartens and first grades of the Wayne county schools—is crowned. There are floats, leading American flower arrangers give lectures, and rose experts advise gardeners on their problems.

The firm has branch nurseries at Shiloh, New Jersey, at Pleasanton, California, and at Richmond, Indiana. Three of Perkins' brothers now work with the firm: Clarence is a vice-president and the West Coast manager; Ralph is general manager and treasurer; and Carroll, Eastern sales manager. The research and development of the firm's plants is directly supervised by Eugene S. Boerner, who holds a record for the number of roses patented in his name. He is research director and secretary of the Jackson & Perkins Company.

In 1938 a group of leading American rose growers and originators sought a way to help rose buyers to choose wisely from the several thousand kinds of roses on the market each year. They established the All-America Rose Selections as a guide. Plants of any new rose may be entered and tested for two years in twenty official trial grounds in the United States. It is then scored for fifteen vital qualifications and if the score meets an established standard, the rose is allowed to be represented as an All-America Rose Selection (AARS) and is promoted by all members of the group. (*American Home* magazine, February 1951).

Since the first awards were made in 1940, only forty-odd varieties of roses have qualified. No rose was found worthy in 1951, so judges decided to select the ten which they considered best and which the public liked best of the AARS in the 1940-1950 decade. Those which the Jackson & Perkins Company had developed were the Rubaiyat and the Katherine T. Marshall. Other All-America Rose Selections developed by the firm include the Mary Margaret McBride (1943), Diamond Jubilee (1948), Vogue (1952), and Ma Perkins (1953).

The company grows hybrid teas, floribundas, common roses, climbers, and tree roses. Its shrubs include lilacs and magnolias. Its chrysanthemums, such as cockatoo, ruffed grouse, desert quail, and cedar waxwing are well known. The other perennials it offers include coreopsis, delphinium, shasta daisies, bleeding heart, and campanula. Dusters, sprayers, watering tools, trowels, pruning shears, and gardening gloves are among the accessories listed in its catalogue.

One of the Jackson & Perkins 1955 offerings is the everblooming Blaze, a red climbing rose. This variety was developed from one particular plant which outbloomed and outperformed all others in the nursery. During July, August and September it continued to bloom and so it was isolated, carefully nurtured, and used as a stock plant from which to multiply the new strain. The firm propagates all its rose bushes by budding (inserting the bud of a specified, desired variety into an opening in the bark of a different, vigorous understock).

About 1,500,000 catalogs are sent out by the company each year. The largest market at present, as Genevieve Smith reported in *Printers' Ink* (December 3, 1954), is the suburban home owner—the population in the suburbs has increased 43 per cent in the years since the end of World War II.

The rose gardens have often been photographed for use other than for the Jackson & Perkins catalogue. In the Flower Grower magazine, many of the pictures of roses and gardening effects using roses have been taken in the Newark gardens. A 16mm. film in color, *The Story of Modern Roses,* shows close-ups of well-known varieties and views of the Jackson & Perkins gardens (see *Educational Film Guide,* 1953, page 656).

In 1906 Perkins married Grace Willower, who died in 1942. They had two children, James W. Perkins and Charles Harvie Perkins, Jr. His marriage to Mabelle Atkins, a secretary, took place on January 28, 1946. He has blue eyes and gray brown hair. He is five feet eleven inches tall and weighs 175 pounds. He belongs to the Masons and the Elks and is a member of the Republican party. For recreation he enjoys spectator sports, fishing, reading, and gardening. Perkins has said, "Rose growing is like most any other business. We have our successes and failures. We enjoy progress."

Reference

Printers' Ink 249:46+ D 3 '54 pors

PERLMAN, ALFRED E(DWARD) Nov. 22, 1902- Railroad president

Address: b. c/o New York Central System, 230 Park Ave., New York 17; h. Premium Point, Mamaroneck, N.Y.

One of the first official acts of the new board of directors of the New York Central System was to elect Alfred E. Perlman as president and chief executive officer on June 14, 1954. He was the choice of financier Robert R. Young, who won his long battle for the 10,713-mile New York Central by an overwhelming vote of the company's stockholders. The second largest railroad in the nation (Pennsylvania Railroad is the first), the New York Central System combines the old New York Central and Hudson River Railroad with the Michigan Central, the West Shore, the Cleveland, Cincinnati, Chicago and St. Louis, and other lines.

Six months after taking office Perlman announced that the New York Central's net profits were "substantially in excess of $5,000,000, and gross operating revenues were about $710,000,000." He credited the good results to the new management's program of cost-control (New York *Times,* January 7, 1955). He also disclosed that the New York Central and the New York, New Haven & Hartford Railroad Company were studying suggestions to redevelop the Grand Central Terminal, retaining the concourse, but erecting an immense theatre, television studio and office building over it.

Perlman, who had advised on railroad problems in Korea in 1949 and in Israel in 1950, formerly served as executive vice-president of the Denver & Rio Grande Western Railroad Company, with which he had been associated since 1936. He held positions of increasing responsibility with the Northern Pacific Railway Company from 1923 to 1934. He has introduced many measures for modernizing railroad equipment and service. Since assuming his new post, he has traveled about 3,000 miles on Central's tracks in an especially equipped automobile.

A native of St. Paul, Minnesota, Perlman was born on November 22, 1902, the son of Louis H. and Leah (Levin) Perlman. His interest in railroading began when he went to work in 1918 cleaning day coaches. Planning to follow in his father's footsteps by becoming a civil engineer, Alfred attended the Massachusetts Institute of Technology in Cambridge and received the S.B. degree in civil engineering in 1923. He then worked as a construction draftsman for the Northern Pacific in Forsyth, Montana.

After a year behind a drawing board, Perlman decided to learn the railroad business from the bottom and spent eight months as a track laborer. In early 1925 he served as assistant engineer for Foley Brothers, St. Paul, Minnesota. He was appointed in April 1925 inspector of icing facilities in St. Paul by the Northern Pacific and one year later became assistant supervisor of bridges and buildings in Glendive, Montana. He then served successively

Jafay

ALFRED E. PERLMAN

as roadmaster at Carrington, North Dakota (1927-1929); Sandpoint, Idaho (1929-1930); and Staples, Minnesota (1930-1934).

The Northern Pacific sent Perlman to the Harvard Graduate School of Business Administration in 1930. In 1934 Perlman became an assistant to the vice-president in charge of operations. In that year he made a study for the railway division of the Reconstruction Finance Corporation on the New York, New Haven & Hartford. Later for the Denver & Rio Grande Western Railroad Company he helped formulate a five-year reconstruction plan. Perlman worked for a year (1935-1936) as assistant maintenance of way engineer for the Chicago, Burlington & Quincy Railroad Company in charge of reconstruction of the Colorado, Nebraska and Kansas lines after the flood of 1935.

On May 1, 1936 he was appointed maintenance of way engineer of the Denver & Rio Grande, with headquarters in Denver. By 1941 he was the railroad's chief engineer, and by 1948 its general manager. In 1952 he became executive vice-president. During World War II he served as engineering consultant for the Defense Plant Corporation in Las Vegas, Nevada.

When Perlman joined the Denver & Rio Grande, it was in bankruptcy and had a net annual deficit of $4,000,000. By 1947 his reorganization plan was completed and the line was able to pay a dividend for the first time in seventy-six years. Its net income for 1953 was $9,800,000 and it paid six dollars plus a 50 per cent stock dividend on earnings of $14.79 a share.

Innovations made by the Denver & Rio Grande which have been attributed to Perlman's leadership include the dieselizing of its equipment, installing vista dome cars and train-radio communications, and instituting a junior board of bright young employees to check all operations. Perlman saved the Denver & Rio Grande and Western $1,000,000 a year by a scientific check on fuels and oil. Many of these techniques were adopted by other roads.

On June 14, 1954 it was announced that Robert R. Young, chairman of the board of the Alleghany Corporation, had won control of the Central by 1,067,273 votes. Less than an hour later the new board, including the first woman member, Mrs. Lila Bell Acheson Wallace, met and elected Young as one-dollar-a-year chairman of the board and Perlman president and chief executive officer. The new directors own or control 17.4 per cent of shares of stock outstanding. At this time Central had a $6,700,000 deficit. The contest which brought control of Central to Young and ousted William White, now president of the Delaware & Hudson Railroad Corporation, was one of the most expensive proxy battles in history.

The New York Central officially came into existence on July 7, 1853 when ten small railroads in mid-state New York were consolidated, although its first predecessor company received a charter in 1826. This was the seventeen-mile Mohawk and Hudson Rail Road linking Albany and Schenectady. The fact that the ten railroads advertised themselves as "the central route" is considered to be the origin of the name "Central."

In 1869 Commodore Cornelius Vanderbilt, who had acquired control of the Hudson River Railroad, consolidated it with the Central and called the new company the New York Central and Hudson River Railroad. Vanderbilt secured control of the Lake Shore and Michigan Southern Railroad by 1873, and the New York-Chicago route, which became the Central's main route, was established. In 1914 the name became the New York Central Railroad when the Central, the Lake Shore and Michigan Southern, and nine subsidiaries were consolidated. Altogether, the Central has approximately 560 predecessor companies. It now operates in eleven states and two provinces of Canada.

During his first six months as president of Central, Perlman decreased operating expenses by $40,000,000 by such measures as closing two of Central's Diesel shops, removing 15,000 employees from the pay roll, and "eliminating 1,000,000 passenger-train miles yearly by cutting deadwood out of schedules" (*Business Week,* October 30, 1954). He announced that a new lightweight train was on order by Central. Perlman also introduced a fast, through Chicago-New York freight service as Central's answer to the "piggy-back" system of hauling truck trailers; the initial run was completed in twenty-three hours and fourteen minutes. With this new service, Central is the only road which has freight entering Manhattan.

After realty operator William Zeckendorf proposed in 1954 to redevelop the Grand Central Terminal and construct a huge television and office building and theatre over it, 220 members of the architectural and planning professions signed an open letter (published by *Architectural Forum,* November 1954) to Perlman and Patrick B. McGinnis, president of the New York, New Haven & Hartford, urging that the lofty, dramatic concourse be preserved.

Central announced on October 29, 1954 that it had granted Perlman the right to purchase 32,000 shares of its stock at $19.87½ a share over a ten-year period. In return, Perlman agreed to remain in the company's employ for at least two years. The plan for these purchases is subject to the approval of the Interstate Commerce Commission.

On February 14, 1955 Perlman petitioned the New Jersey Board of Public Utilities Commissioners outlining reasons for discontinuing Central's passenger service on the West Shore division and Weehawken Ferry, which has operated since 1885. He pointed out in an announcement in the New York *Times* that 85 per cent of the regular commuters had discontinued using the service, and that it represented a loss of more than $2,500,000 a year for the company's shareholders. At the hearing it was agreed to continue operations of the West Shore division until June 30 while its 4,000 commuters could retain legal counsel and file a protest. The New Jersey Public Utility Commission on November 4 directed the New York Central Railroad to continue service on its West Shore Division, although such service could be reduced.

Perlman has served as president of the Denver Union Terminal Railway Company and the Rio Grande Land Company; vice-president of the Denver Market and Produce Terminal, Inc.; and director of the Rio Grande Motor Way, Inc., and the Yellow Cab Company of Denver. He was recently made a director of Central and of the Association of American Railroads. He belongs to the Colorado Society of Engineers, Newcomen Society of England and Rotary International. His clubs are the St. Paul Athletic, the Press in Denver, and the Economic and Cloud in New York. He has contributed to professional journals.

Married to Adele Sylvia Emrich on June 15, 1937, Perlman is the father of Constance G., Lee Alfred, and Michael Louis. He is five feet eight inches tall and slender of build. He is known as a quiet, modest and thoughtful man, but he is also regarded as a "dynamo of human energy." Railroading is his career and hobby; Saturdays, Sundays and holidays do not interfere with work to be done. He has said: "After you've done a thing the same way for two years, look it over carefully. After five years, look at it with suspicion. And after ten years, throw it away and start all over."

References

Bsns W p70 O 30 '54
Christian Sci Mon p11 Je 16 '54 por; p14 N 23 '54
N Y Times p57 Je 12 '54; p46 Je 15 '54; p51 S 15 '54; p37 O 22 '54; p24 O 30 '54; p21 N 29 '54; p51 D 9 '54
Time 63:92 Je 21 '54
Who's Who in America, 1954-55
Who's Who in Engineering, 1954

PETHERBRIDGE, MARGARET *See* Farrar, Margaret (Petherbridge)

PEURIFOY, JOHN E(MIL) Aug. 9 1907-Aug. 12, 1955 United States Ambassador to Thailand; was a leading "trouble-shooter" for U.S. Department of State in critical areas; as Ambassador to Greece (1950-1953) advised Greek government to take certain steps which aided them to survive the aftermath of civil war with the Communists; as Ambassador to Guatemala (1953-1954) forced agreement between two anti-communist factions resulting in the overthrow of the Communist-influenced regime; was credited for his work in reorganizing the State Department. See *Current Biography* (Jan.) 1949.

Obituary

N Y Times p 1+ Ag 13 '55

PFLIMLIN, PIERRE (EUGÈNE JEAN) Feb. 5, 1907- French Minister of Finance and Economic Affairs; economist

Address: b. Palais Bourbon, Paris 7ᵉ, France; h. 54 rue Poussin, Paris 16ᵉ, France; 7 rue des Pontonniers, Strasbourg, France

The French Minister of Finance and Economic Affairs is Pierre Pflimlin, a lawyer and economist, who has been a member of fourteen of the twenty Cabinets France has had since World War II. Besides holding the Agriculture portfolio, he has been Under Secretary for Health, Minister for National Economy, Minister of Commerce and Foreign Economic Relations, Minister of State in charge of relations with the Council of Europe, and Minister of France Overseas Territories.

Pflimlin's agricultural policy was aimed at increasing French exports to restore the balance of trade. As Minister of Finance and Economic Affairs he set up a national planning committee in June 1955 to advise the government on ways to make the French economy best serve the changing educational, housing and employment needs of the people. Pflimlin is known as the "young rising star" of the Popular Republican Movement (M.R.P.). He represents the moderate political tendencies of his party, and favors a planned economy for Europe and for France.

Pierre Eugène Jean Pflimlin was born in Roubaix (Nord) on February 5, 1907, of Alsatian parents, Jules and Leonie (Schwartz) Pflimlin. After attending the Lycée de Mulhouse, he studied at the Faculty of Law of the Catholic Institute of Paris and concluded his legal education at Strasbourg University where he was awarded the Doctor of Laws degree. From 1933, when he was admitted to the bar, until 1939, he practised law in Strasbourg. Mobilized in 1939 as a lieutenant interpreter, Pflimlin participated in the campaigns in Belgium and in France. During the German occupation, he took refuge at Thonon-les-Bains.

His political career began after the war with his election in May 1945 as municipal councillor of Strasbourg. He took office September 30, 1945, and has served continuously since then. As a member of the M.R.P. he was elected a deputy from Bas-Rhin to both Constituent Assemblies (1945-1946). In November

French Embassy Press & Inf. Division

PIERRE PFLIMLIN

1946 he won the election as deputy to the National Assembly and was re-elected in June 1951. During 1945-1946 he served as president of the Commission on Economic Affairs, Customs and Commercial Conventions. In 1945 he was elected general councillor of Haguenau, a position he still holds. Since 1951 he has served as president of the general council of the department of Bas-Rhin.

Pflimlin's first Cabinet post came in February 1946 when he was appointed Under Secretary of State for Public Health and Population. In Georges Bidault's Cabinet (June-December, 1946), Pflimlin held the post of Under Secretary of State for National Economy. He became Minister of Agriculture in November 1947 in the Robert Schuman Cabinet and held this post in seven successive Cabinets. In developing a national agricultural policy, Pflimlin asserted that agriculture "must be treated as a basic industry and given the means to accomplish specific results." His aim, he said, was not the favoring of farmers, but the attainment of national economic objectives.

In the fall of 1948, when he journeyed to Washington, D.C. for Marshall plan conferences, he declared that in order for France to survive, Marshall plan aid was needed until French agriculture could begin to export its products. "By the time Marshall plan aid ends in 1952, our agriculture must be able to assure France a sufficient revenue to buy our necessary imports" he stated.

In 1949 the French Council of Ministers voted to fix the price of sugar beets at a rate lower than previously set. In protest, Pflimlin resigned on December 1, saying the action threatened the entire policy of a guaranteed minimum price for agricultural products—a policy aimed at stimulating export trade to maintain a balance of currency abroad for imports. On the day following his resignation, he received the Agricultural Cross of Merit.

When Bidault's government fell in June 1950, Pflimlin was appointed Minister of Agriculture in the government of Henri Queuille, which lasted a month. He was retained in the same post in two succeeding governments. He proposed in September 1950, the creation of a European agricultural pool providing a unified market for wheat, sugar, wine and dairy products for member countries of the Coal and Steel Community.

In August 1951 Pflimlin was appointed Minister of Commerce and Foreign Economic Relations by René Pleven. Pflimlin introduced a proposal for reducing world trade barriers at a Geneva, Switzerland conference on tariffs and trade in September 1951. The proposal called for a reduction over a three-year period of 30 per cent, not in all tariff duties but in the "weighted average level of duties afforded to each main branch of economic activity." Under Edgar Faure (January-February 1952), Pflimlin served as Minister of State in charge of relations with the Council of Europe, and under Antoine Pinay (March-December, 1952) as Minister of France Overseas Territories.

Presiding over a conference of representatives of sixteen European nations who met at France's invitation on March 25, 1952, Pflimlin again proposed a "green pool" of agricultural products. "For us the creation of a European agricultural community would be an important step in the difficult but necessary road toward European integration, which is the duty and requirement of our generation," Pflimlin declared. The conference approved the idea and decided to hold further conferences to formalize a European agricultural community.

A candidate for the presidency of the National Assembly, Pflimlin was defeated for that post in January 1954, when the Communists threw their decisive ninety-six votes to André Le Troquer, a Socialist, who polled 300 votes to Pflimlin's 251. The Communists described Pflimlin as a "rabid" friend of a European Defense Community and German rearmament.

Shortly after the fall of Pierre Mendès-France's government in February 1955, President René Coty asked Pflimlin to try to form a Cabinet. If he succeeded, Pflimlin said, he would stress economic reforms similar to those already framed by Mendès-France, including reconversion of old-fashioned French factories and farms to modern methods and improvements in wages for workers. He further said he favored Mendès-France's policy in North Africa as well as ratification of the Paris agreements. However, he was unable to produce a coalition and on February 14, 1955, withdrew as a candidate for the Premiership. He was appointed Minister of Finance and Economic Affairs by Edgar Faure who succeeded in forming a Cabinet on February 22.

One of Pflimlin's first actions in his new post was to support limitation of pay rises for government workers on the grounds that this group had had sufficient wage increases. He pointed out, in April 1955, that France would have to increase taxes if its deficit, standing at about $1,142,000,000, went any higher. When small businessmen demonstrated their protest of a bill that provided for inspection of accounts and penalties for merchants who resisted such inspection, Pflimlin said the government could not drop all sanctions against tax evasions, but would do all possible to end fiscal injustice.

Tax reforms were announced on April 29, simplifying the system and reducing indirect levies. For small businessmen with annual receipts of less than 15,000,000 francs, a single tax on business turnover was substituted for inspection of accounts. The cost of these reforms, according to Pflimlin, could amount to more than $290,000,000, but might be offset by increases in corporation taxes.

Pflimlin supported the appropriation of $290,-000,000 for a three-year atomic research plan to enable France to "become an atomic power" through the development of nonmilitary atomic projects. Adoption of this plan, fiscal reforms and the fixing of military credits brought the state's overall deficit to more than $2,570,000,000, and occasioned another warning from Pflimlin who said: "It is no longer possible to increase expenditures without finding new receipts."

When the French stock market, which had been booming since the end of 1953, suddenly dropped 25 to 30 per cent early in May 1955, Pflimlin described the slump as an inevitable "correction" and maintained it would have no lasting effect on "reasonable investments" since the French economy was sound. Before the end of May, the market had recovered its former level.

Although Pflimlin and three other Popular Republicans in Faure's Cabinet urged the government on May 22 to extend the power of the European Coal and Steel Community and retain Jean Monnet as its chairman, the French government, faced with de Gaullist opposition, voted against retaining Monnet and avoided committing itself on extending the Community.

When the issue of a return to convertibility of currencies was raised in June 1955 at the meeting of the Organization for European Economic Cooperation, Pflimlin warned Europeans and Americans that making all their currencies freely exchangeable with the U.S. dollar might be a technical success but a "political failure." He urged the eventual return to full convertibility, but by moderate stages, so that countries like France with an excess of imports from the U.S. over exports, could continue to enjoy the protection of the European Payments Union, a system for clearing intra-European debts. "Any monetary technique should be judged by its aptitude for raising living standards and developing peaceful cooperation among nations," he declared. The OEEC seemed to favor moving in the direction of full convertibility by continuing with modifications the present protections of the European Payments Union.

Addressing the annual Strasbourg Fair on September 3, 1955, Pflimlin reported that French production had increased by 11 per cent in the last year and by 40 per cent from 1950 to 1955. Purchasing power rose by 29 per cent since 1949. He noted that the recent increases in workers' incomes had been accomplished without price increases, and he warned both business and labor that the government intended to continue to block price rises and told them to keep this in mind when new wage contracts are negotiated. The workers, he said, would be the first victims of a new wage-price inflationary spiral.

Pflimlin recommended the establishment of a "European Adaptation Fund" to enable European countries to overcome the economic difficulties of a common market. He urged that participating nations bring their social services up to the French level to equalize competitive conditions, and mentioned in particular salaries for women, the length of the work week, and family allocations (New York *Herald Tribune,* September 6, 1955).

As aids to industrial expansion, the Minister announced, the reduction of interest rates from 7 to 6.5 per cent on long-term loans made by the government's credit office; the abolition of government authorization heretofore required of companies wishing to float stocks and bonds; and help by the public treasury in guaranteeing loans made by the credit office, (New York *Times,* September 5, 1955). Pflimlin has also been concerned about the decrease in U.S. orders for defense materials in France, which could lead to the closing of factories and loss of jobs for thousands of workers within a year or two.

The Minister has written a number of books on the French economy. He was awarded the Croix de Guerre. Pflimlin is a captain in the Reserves, and during 1946 served as head of the Red Cross and Aid to Foreign Countries. His marriage to Marie Odile Heinrich took place on November 25, 1939; they have a son, Etiènne, and two daughters, Antoinette and Odile.

The Finance Minister has a reputation for forceful speaking, incisive action and hard work. In favoring a planned economy, he comes close to the Socialists on many issues, but as a Catholic he opposes them fiercely in their fight against state subsidies for Roman Catholic schools.

References

N Y Herald Tribune pl F 11 '55 por
N Y Times pl F 11 '55
Dictionnaire Biographique Français Contemporain (1955)
International Who's Who, 1954
World Biography (1954)

PFOST, GRACIE (BOWERS) (pōst)

Mar. 12, 1906- United States Representative from Idaho

Address: b. House Office Bldg., Washington, D.C.; h. 200 C. St., S.E., Washington, D.C.; 1611 Central Ave., Nampa, Idaho

Idaho's first Congresswoman is Mrs. Gracie Pfost, who was elected to the U.S. House of Representatives in 1952 and re-elected in 1954 on the Democratic ticket. Her initial victory was outstanding in a year when her Idaho First District went to Republican Presidential candidate General Dwight D. Eisenhower, by 25,000 votes.

(Continued next page)

Chase

GRACIE PFOST

Her 1952 campaign slogan was "Tie Your Vote to a Solid Post—Gracie Pfost, for Congress," which puns on her name and indicates its pronunciation. Her slogan in the 1954 campaign was "One Good Term Deserves Another." Presently she serves on the House Interior and Insular Affairs Committee and the Post Office and Civil Service Committee.

Mrs. Pfost prepared for her Government position by an apprenticeship in public office of nearly twenty years, as deputy county clerk, auditor and recorder for Canyon county, Idaho from 1929 to 1939 and as county treasurer from 1941 to 1950. Through her own business as a real-estate broker, she acquired a knowledge of the problems of the small businessman in whose interest she has worked in Congress. She also has become known for her minority report as a member of the House committee to investigate alleged subversion in tax-exempt foundations. With Democrat Representative Wayne L. Hays of Ohio, Mrs. Pfost dissented from the Republican report.

Mrs. Gracie Bowers Pfost was born in Harrison, Arkansas, on March 12, 1906, one of five children of William Lafayette and Lily Elizabeth (Wood) Bowers, who were then living in a log house on an Ozark farm. At an early age, she moved with her family to a farm in Boise Valley, Idaho.

After attending local public schools, Gracie Bowers received her secondary education at Meridian High School, Meridian, Idaho. She then entered Links Business University in Boise, the State capital, where she obtained high grades. She was married at the age of seventeen to John Walter Pfost.

Following her graduation from business school in 1926, she took a position as chemical analyst for a milk products company. As quoted by Georgette Ross Howard (*Christian Science Monitor*, September 17, 1954), Mrs. Pfost has recalled that she "didn't know a thing about chemistry" when she started, but in ten days she was able to "analyze the raw product as well as the finished milk in the can."

At the age of twenty-three she began her career in public service with an appointment as deputy county clerk, auditor and recorder of Canyon county, in 1929. She held this position until 1939 and later was treasurer of the county. Her work brought her into contact with many people and with State conditions.

She took an active interest in the Idaho Young Democratic State Organization, for which she filled two terms as secretary and treasurer, and one term as vice-president. She was a delegate to the Democratic national conventions in 1944, 1948 and 1952, acting as a member of the platform and resolutions committee at all three meetings, and in 1944 serving as secretary to the Idaho delegation. An unsuccessful candidate from Idaho's First District for a seat in the U.S. House of Representatives in 1950, she was defeated by 783 votes by her Republican opponent Dr. John T. Wood.

Completing her service as Canyon county treasurer in 1950, the following year Mrs. Pfost started her own business as a real-estate broker in Nampa, Idaho, which she operated until 1952. That year, encouraged by her husband, she again became a Democratic candidate for the U.S. House of Representatives from Idaho's First District, having won over three men in the primary election. Her district includes nineteen counties, an area over 500 miles long and 200 miles wide. Among the issues which she supported were Fair Deal legislation, repeal of the Taft-Hartley act, higher minimum wage, broader Social Security coverage, Federal aid to education, and Government construction of a high dam at Hell's Canyon on the Idaho-Oregon border.

In the November 4, 1952 election, Mrs. Pfost defeated incumbent Republican Representative John T. Wood "by almost the same narrow margin by which he had beaten her two years before" (*Independent Woman*, February 1953). Dr. Wood challenged her 591-vote margin and asked a House committee to recount the votes. The committee on December 16, 1952 refused to grant his request.

During her first month in the Eighty-third Congress, Gracie Pfost requested and obtained an appointment to the House Committee on Interior and Insular Affairs. With a seat on its subcommittees on irrigation and reclamation, mines and mining, and public lands, as well as on a special subcommittee to study water resources, she was in a position to promote the chief interests of her district.

At a dinner given at the Hotel Statler in Boston in January 1953 honoring newly elected Congresswomen, Mrs. Pfost declared: "I am going to support President-elect Eisenhower in his recommendations, both on foreign and domestic affairs, when I am convinced they are for the best interests of the people. . . . I for one want to see our people keep the gains they have made in the past 20 years" (*Congressional Record*). In the first session of the Eighty-third Congress, she was chairman of new

House Democratic members, organized as the Democratic Eighty-third Club, which held breakfast meetings for exchange of views on pending legislation.

In her maiden speech on the floor of the House on April 16, 1953, Congresswoman Pfost introduced a bill to authorize the construction by the Federal Government of Hell's Canyon dam in Snake River. She stated: "Hell's Canyon power will be low-cost power. . . . Power sales would repay the Government almost 90 per cent of the cost of building the dam" (*Congressional Record*). She opposed as "high-cost power" the Idaho Power Company's application to construct a less multiple-purpose dam, and said the Federal dam would make surrounding lands useful for agriculture, permit economic extraction of "60 per cent of the nation's phosphate rocks" in the region, and "add 1,124,000 kilowatts of prime power to existing Federal plants."

Her strong support of the Federal Hell's Canyon dam project won Mrs. Pfost the nickname "Hell's Belle," and considerable opposition from private power interests. "I do not intend to be bluffed, bullied or frightened by the private monopolies," she told her colleagues in the House. She voted in April for recommitment of the Interior Department appropriations bill for amendment in accordance with the Sam Rayburn (Texas) motion to restore $120,000 for the Idaho Panhandle construction of electric public power services. The bill failed to receive recommitment and was passed without the amendment.

In a speech to the House on June 16, 1953, Mrs. Pfost supported the Simpson bill, later defeated, to set up a "sliding scale" tariff on lead and zinc which would stabilize domestic prices of these metals. She pointed out: "No quotas are involved, and the bill would not block needed imports. It merely would keep the largest part of our lead and zinc industry in a healthy condition" (*Congressional Record*).

Maintaining that the country's lead and zinc industry was in "one of the gravest crises in its history," Mrs. Pfost introduced a bill to the House on July 30, 1953, which called for "an incentive payment plan" for encouraging "exploration, production and conservation of domestic critical and strategic ores, minerals and metals" (*Congressional Record*). "This is not a price-support bill in any sense of the word," she said. During the same month she presented a bill asking for free marketing of newly mined gold. Concerning amendment of the Trade Agreements Extension Act of 1951, she told the House on July 23, 1953, ". . . it just doesn't make sense to me to build up Peru, or any other foreign nation at the expense of our own western mining areas" (*Congressional Record*).

Congresswoman Pfost was appointed on August 3, 1953, to a five-member special committee to conduct an investigation and study of educational and philanthropic foundations. Mrs. Pfost and her minority Democratic supporter, Wayne L. Hays of Ohio, were accused by majority members of the committee, headed by B. Carroll Reece of Tennessee, of "frustrating orderly procedure," when they objected to "name-dropping" and demanded closed committee sessions.

After their request was defeated, they walked out, forcing the majority members to discontinue public hearings. The split committee filed separate reports on December 19, 1954. Mrs. Pfost stated that the "foundations have been indicted and convicted under procedures which can only be characterized as barbaric" (New York *Herald Tribune*, December 20, 1954) without due process of law.

Mrs. Pfost's voting record during 1953 showed her in favor of statehood for Hawaii (March), continuing the public housing program (April), increased funds for public power (April), and extending the excess profits tax (July). She opposed the quitclaim bill (April), the King amendment to the Department of Agriculture appropriations bill for 1954 to reduce conservation program funds (May), and private development of Niagara power (July).

On domestic issues coming before the House during 1954 she voted "yea" on a bill providing an increase of $17,000,000 for airline subsidies (March), the Eisenhower housing bill to stimulate home building through various Government aids (April), the St. Lawrence seaway authorization (May) and Social Security expansion (June).

In campaigning for re-election to Congress in 1954, she made the Equal Rights Amendment a plank in her platform and also favored support of the United Nations. She had no primary opposition for the nomination, and on securing re-election from Idaho's First District in November 1954, defeated her Republican opponent, Erwin Schwiebert, by nearly 9,000 votes.

Early in the Eighty-fourth Congress (1955) she voted with the majority of the House for a bill authorizing the establishment of a U.S. Air Force Academy (January) and for continuation of the reciprocal trade program, without restricting Presidential powers (February). Mrs. Pfost opposed a $10,000 pay increase for members of Congress (February).

On March 28, 1955 she announced a new set of rules for visitors to the House gallery admonishing them not to smoke, applaud, read, take notes, or hang their coats over the railings.

Mrs. Pfost is a member of the National Association of Real Estate Brokers and of the Idaho State and Nampa real-estate boards. She has served on the Girl Scouts council. Her clubs include the Idaho Federation of Women's Clubs, the Soroptimists, and the Business and Professional Women's Club (president, Southwestern district, 1942). She is a Methodist. An acquaintance has said, "She goes all-out in everything she does." Mrs. Pfost told a writer for the *Christian Science Monitor*, "people stimulate me—and I love to meet new people—all kinds." She dislikes household chores.

The Congresswoman married John Walter Pfost, a master mechanic, on August 4, 1923. She has brown eyes and auburn hair, weighs 115 pounds, and is five feet three inches tall. Her hobbies include reading, fishing, hunting,

PFOST, GRACIE—*Continued*

riding and watching football games. Mrs. Pfost observed that a woman running for Congress "must be willing to have her every motive challenged, her every move criticized" (Washington *Post*, March 23, 1953).

References

Christian Sci Mon S 17 '54
Ind Woman 32:34+ F '53; 34:23 Ja '55
N Y Times p20 Ap 16 '54
Washington (D.C.) Post p17 Mr 23 '53
Who's Who in America, 1954-55

PHILLIPS, LENA MADESIN 1881-May 20, 1955 Founder and former president of the International Federation of Business and Professional Women's Clubs; lawyer; lecturer; author; organized in New York the Business and Professional Women's Club, and was president of the national federation of these clubs (1926-1929); practiced law in New York City and was an associate editor of *Pictorial Review* (1935-1939). See *Current Biography* (Apr.) 1946.

Obituary

N Y Times p88 My 22 '55

PICK, VERNON J. Oct. 1903- Businessman

Address: b. c/o Atlas Corp., Grand Junction, Colo.; h. Grand Junction, Colo.

Among the new crop of "overnight" millionaires is Vernon J. Pick, who discovered a bonanza of uranium near Hanksville, Utah and sold his mine in August 1954 to Floyd Odlum of the Atlas Corporation for nearly $10,000,000. The story of Pick's rich "strike" is as dramatic as any prospector's story ever told. After a fire in 1951 had destroyed his small flourishing electrical goods factory near Royalton, Minnesota, Pick used the insurance money to purchase a house trailer and truck. He spent nearly all of his funds prospecting for uranium but without success until, after climbing inaccessible cliffs, fording rivers, enduring hunger, thirst and other hardships, he found uranium ore near Muddy River Creek, Utah in mid-June 1952, and filed his claim.

With some of his fortune he established, in 1955, the Pick Foundation to make grants of scholarship aid, many of them to graduate students in the humanities, for Pick is an avid reader of the classics and is concerned that too much attention is paid to technology in the colleges. Pick is now in charge of operations of Delta Mines, Inc., which is working the mine he discovered.

Vernon J. Pick was born in October 1903, on a farm in southern Wisconsin, the son of staunchly Methodist parents. He was the eldest of three boys and a girl. The family moved to a farm near Redwood Falls, Minnesota, when he was about eight, and again to a farm near Warroad, in the far northwestern part of the state, when he was fifteen.

His formal education ended with the first year of high school, but he was always a great reader and student, familiarizing himself with the classics and delving into psychology, history, statistics, writing, and Greek. George Rice, who spent three days visiting with Pick at Grand Junction, gives the following account in the Washington *Post and Times Herald* (November 14, 1954) of his early years: "He left the farm at seventeen and tried a little of everything. He worked for General Electric in the East, for a firm making radios in St. Louis, Missouri. He joined the Marines for three years and became an expert rifle shot. In 1927, Pick got a job as an electrician with the Hudson Bay Mining and Smelting Company at Flin Flon, Canada. Three years later, with money saved from this job, he headed back to the United States, with the idea of setting up a motor rewinding shop. He stopped in Minneapolis." Although it was 1930 and the depression was just getting under way, Pick became successful. Owners of electrical equipment who, in better days, would have thrown away their old motors sent them to Pick to be rewound.

About 1940, Pick thought of developing his own self-sustaining community, "without socialistic trimmings." A conservative in his economic thinking, according to George Rice, Pick is convinced that all the state owes anyone is an equal opportunity and from that a man should make his own way. He found what he wanted on the Two Rivers, near Royalton, Minnesota, an abandoned flour mill and a dam, in need of repair, a generous parcel of land and three old houses. "He rebuilt the dam, installed generators, fixed up one of the houses for living quarters, and in 1946 he moved in."

Soon he was doing a substantial mail order trade in rewound motors and auto generators, according to Robert Coughlan's article, "Vernon Pick's $10 Million Ordeal" (*Life,* November 1, 1954). He also built a woodworking shop producing maple and birch furniture, while in another sector his daughter, Virginia (by his first marriage), ran a job-printing plant. His wife, who entered into "self-sustenance" wholeheartedly, canned vegetables and fruits from the gardens and orchards. By 1951 Pick was employing half a dozen neighborhood farm boys as help. He was independent, he had leisure to read and he was making a living; he had no other material ambitions. This was the enterprise which was destroyed by fire on May 9, 1951.

The loss of the plant was total, and the insurance covered a scant third of its value. Pick lacked the heart to rebuild, and he and his wife decided to travel, while the daughter took a secretarial position in Minneapolis. About half of the $6,000 of their $13,500 insurance went for a panel truck and house trailer. They made their way leisurely to Colorado Springs, where the idea of uranium prospecting began to interest him.

Pick quietly studied all the information available from every source he could find and bought equipment carefully. His wife settled in a trailer camp at Grand Junction, Colorado and Pick began his trips, searching the uninhabited canyons, washes and deserts around Hanksville, Utah. From the end of 1951 until June 1952 he located only a problematical claim for which he had none of the capital needed to explore it adequately. His funds had dwindled to $300. He planned to take one more trip, and if it failed, he would leave for California and look for a job there. This was in June 1952.

His custom was to drive his truck as far as possible then walk. He had to carry his pack, which weighed over fifty pounds, as well as the Scintillometer (roughly defined as a "souped-up" Geiger counter) which had cost him $986 and which weighed nearly fifteen pounds and could pick up radioactivity several hundred feet away. On this last trip he wanted to reach the San Rafael Swell. Beyond its huge outer reef, a tilted mass of jagged rocks, geological reports gave him a good chance of encountering a Shinarump layer. He drove to the edge of the wash and plodded up one canyon after another, finding all impassable. At last only one possibility remained, the Muddy River. Old-timers had told him to stay away from it. Still it offered his only chance.

The terrain proved rougher than he had expected, but he managed to reach its banks by moonlight. He had ultimately to cross and recross its strong currents, sullied with sediments, twenty-seven times, holding his Scintillometer high over his head to protect it. His feet blistered from the sand that worked into his shoes, and after a few days the arsenic in the water which he drank poisoned him.

His sufferings were great, but as Robert Coughlan put it, it had become conceivable to Pick that he might die but not that he could turn back. The first erratic registerings on the meter he thought were failure of mechanism, but soon he realized the source in the speckled gold in rocks around him, which had fallen from a formation 400 feet above. Climbing up, forgetting his pain and fatigue, he pried out a chunk all incredibly yellow.

He made a painful desperate trip back to his truck and to Hanksville, recorded his claim at the county seat, rested briefly, made arrangements for supplies by pack animals, and returned to occupy the claim for the required thirty days. Later he mortgaged his trailer and began to mine the ore. He was finally able to build roads and to buy equipment and hire a skilled crew. It had become evident that his was one of the biggest uranium finds ever made.

He had taken out some $1,000,000 in ore before he decided, in August 1954, to sell the mine to industrialist Floyd Odlum (see C.B. 1940), who paid him a reported $9,370,000 in cash, plus Atlas Corporation stock, and a $250,000 twin-engine flying laboratory. Moreover, Pick receives a salary as president of Delta Mines, Inc., which became a subsidiary of Atlas Corporation with Pick in charge of operations.

In 1947, at Royalton, a little more than ten years after he and his first wife were divorced, Pick married Ruth Johnson, a grade school teacher from Grand Rapids, Minnesota. There is a daughter, Virginia, from the first marriage.

The Picks now live in a six-room ranch-style house in Grand Junction, Colorado, Pick commuting to the mine 170 miles southwest by private plane. At the time he started prospecting, he had a strong 200-pound body and rugged health. On the return from the trip that gave him the Delta, his figure had become "weak, thin, battered." He is slightly stoop-shouldered, with a receding hairline and alert eyes. Pick has logged over 1,000 hours of flying.

Wide World

VERNON J. PICK

According to an interview reported by the Denver *Post,* January 25, 1955, Pick is now busy with plans to make use of the laboratory plane in long range exploration, starting with South America. The plane is amphibious, with a 3,000 mile range, and can carry a good-sized crew and provisions for a month to sustain them in inaccessible areas. Pick believes that the same reasoning and planning that led him to his first strike may help him to find more rich uranium in all parts of the world.

References

Denver Post Ja 29 '54; Ag 30 '54; Ja 25 '55
Life 37:112 N 8 '54 por
N Y Herald Tribune II pl S 5 '54 por
Washington (D.C.) Post p3B N 14 '54 por

PIERRE, ABBÉ Aug. 5, 1910- French priest

Address: 38, ave. Paul-Doumer, Neuilly-Plaisance, Seine-et-Oise, France

American lecture audiences in April and May 1955 heard a first-hand account of a grassroots movement in France to shelter and feed the homeless and hungry sponsored by Abbé Pierre —the more familiar name of Father Henri Antoine Grouès. He reported in person on the accomplishments of his Companions of Emmaus, a group which in the harsh winter of 1953-1954

Agence Diffusion Presse

ABBÉ PIERRE

had come to grips with a major French problem.

As the Abbé declared in an interview with President Eisenhower, "today the military war is over but we need to go on fighting the misery of the world." A World War II hero, the Abbé served on two fronts before engaging in Resistance activities during the occupation of France. After the liberation of France in 1945, he entered politics, and was elected both to the Constituent and National Assemblies.

Fifth of a family of eight children, Henri Antoine Grouès was born on August 5, 1910 in Lyon, France where his well-to-do father was engaged in silk manufacturing. As a child, he sometimes accompanied his father on the charitable missions to the poor of the city to which the elder Grouès devoted his Sundays. A visit to Italy during his youth made him sure of his vocation. He recalls: "All night long I roamed Assisi, the *Life of St. Francis* under my arm. When morning came, I knew I wanted to be a priest." To prepare for the ministry he studied at the Collège des Jésuites in Lyon. At the age of eighteen, he entered a Capuchin monastery and demanding his patrimony from his father, distributed the entire sum to the poor. Subsequently, he studied at the Capuchin seminary in Crest (Drôme) and at the Faculté de Théologie de Lyon.

Eight years of monastic life proved to be too harsh for Father Grouès, and his superiors assigned him to the post of secular priest at the St. Joseph Basilica in Grenoble, where it was hoped that the mountain air would relieve his tuberculosis. During World War II, he served on the Alsatian and Alpine fronts. He became Vicar of the Cathedral in Grenoble after the defeat of France. In July 1942 he entered into resistance activities against Italian occupation troops in that region, assuming the name of Abbé Pierre and helping Jews and other victims of occupation policies. To do this, he crossed the frontier—over the Alps and the Pyrenees—a number of times. One of these escapees was Jacques de Gaulle, the paralyzed brother of General Charles de Gaulle, whom the small Abbé had to carry for a good part of the distance. At his home in Grenoble, the Abbé started another clandestine enterprise: the manufacture of false identity papers. He also founded Maquis groups in the Chartreuse and Vercors regions and participated in raids on German and Italian barracks. He was captured but managed to escape and then took to the underground, concealing himself at Lyon, where he established a newspaper, *L'Union Patriotique Indépendante,* and organized the distribution of a review, *Cahiers du Témoignage Chrétien.*

He became one of the principal aides to Commandant Descour, a well known Resistance leader. Returning from a mission to Spain, the Abbé was captured by the Gestapo, escaped and offered his services to the Provisional Government of General de Gaulle. Appointed chaplain of the French Navy at Casablanca in August 1944 and of the whole Free French Navy in January 1945, he was sent on a number of intelligence missions by the Ministry of Information: to France, North Africa, and the expeditionary forces. His return to France was with the Army of Liberation.

Prevailed upon to enter politics, Abbé Pierre ran as an independent candidate from Meurthe-et-Moselle for the first Constituent Assembly of the Fourth French Republic, and was elected. He entered the next election as a candidate of the Mouvement Républicain Populaire (MRP), and was elected to the Second Constituent Assembly. In November 1946, he was re-elected on the MRP ticket to the National Assembly. His disagreement with MRP policies led him to become affiliated with the Gauche Indépendante Socialiste in 1950. In the following year he ran as an independent candidate but was defeated in the June elections.

With the aid of friends, the Abbé Pierre acquired a run-down house at Neuilly-Plaisance, near Paris. Boris Simon in his book, *Abbé Pierre and the Ragpickers of Emmaus* (Kenedy, 1955) wrote: "He purchased, on the installment plan, the empty huts of the prisoners' camps at Saint-Denis, had them brought to Emmaus." He named the place Emmaus in memory of the village in which Christ appeared to His disciples after His resurrection. He was aided by an ex-convict from the French penal colony at French Guiana, the first of many unfortunates who found their way to Emmaus.

Heading a band of outcasts, the homeless and the hopeless, whom the Abbé rounded up under the bridges and from the park benches, he established a squatters' colony on the outskirts of Paris and "after various brushes with the public authorities was finally allowed to found a permanent cooperative community on some vacant lots he had purchased for a nominal sum," wrote Edmond Taylor in the *Reporter* (March 30, 1954).

About this time, the Abbé came up for re-election to the executive committee of a world federalist movement at a meeting in London. There, his eloquence, and his description of himself as a "delegate of misery," and "one of a community of miserable people," made such an impression on the audience that Lord Beveridge declared, "I am voting for the Abbé because he speaks a French that every man can understand."

With the cessation of his deputy's salary in 1951, the Abbé was obliged to beg for funds in Paris cafés. Wearing all his medals, Simon recalls, the Abbé found that "in the extreme poverty of his station, his seven decorations constituted his sole protection against the hostility of the order he dared to trouble." After one of his companions contributed a thousand francs earned by ragpicking to the community fund, the Abbé organized fifty of his recruits, sent them forth with sacks to collect junk, which was then sorted and sold. He appeared on a French radio quiz program, *Quitte ou Double*, correctly answered the questions and with the money earned purchased a truck. Within a year, the Companions of Emmaus owned a fleet of trucks, and had begun the repair and resale of various objects and the manufacture of cement building blocks.

The activities of the Companions of Emmaus were suddenly augmented by the unprecedentedly cold winter of 1953-1954. The deaths of more than ninety homeless people, and particularly, of a baby frozen to death in a slum, caused the Abbé to take drastic action. He used the baby's funeral as a means of compelling the government's attention, and invited the Minister of Reconstruction, Maurice Lemaire, to be present. He addressed an open letter to the newspaper, *Le Figaro*, and appealed on radio, television and on street corners. Within two days clothes, furniture, money, and food were brought to collection points throughout Paris. *Time* (February 15, 1954) reported: "The Ministry of Health doled out 4,000,000 francs. From another ministry came blankets. The army contributed trucks to move supplies, hospitals established dormitories, and municipal buildings were turned into soup kitchens and sleeping halls. The Métro turned over three unused subway stations . . . for shelters against the cold." The police restored the medieval right of sanctuary to the homeless and promised that no one would be asked for identity papers. From other sources came 20,000 blankets (the Abbé had asked for 5,000), more than $1,285,715 in cash, 15,000 overcoats, and over a thousand pairs of shoes.

In February 1954 Abbé Pierre, during a personal interview with Premier Joseph Laniel, obtained the services of a liaison officer. The government, which had turned down the Abbé's plan for emergency housing, approved a measure allotting twelve times the sum he had asked—thirty million dollars. Besides an emergency type shelter to be built for $2,000 and rented at $5 a month as envisioned by the Abbé (of which 3,000 were already under construction by the Companions of Emmaus for 1954 occupancy in the Paris region) the French Government planned to build 12,000 more emergency dwellings. The Abbé declared: "The people have discovered that soluble problems can be solved. The wave of enthusiasm has had the character of an insurrection—an insurrection of benevolence" (*Reporter*, March 30, 1954).

Jubilee magazine in April 1955 sponsored the Abbé Pierre's visit to the United States, on an invitation extended by a nonsectarian committee headed by Jacques Maritain. (The first American visit of the Abbé had been made as a parliamentarian, six years before.) Arriving in New York on April 25, the "Ragpicker Priest" lectured in major cities and showed a film of his work. In an interview reported by the New York *Times* (April 27, 1955), the Abbé said that there was a grave need today to make those who "have" understand the misery and need of those who "have not." He suggested the formation of movements similar to that of the Companions of Emmaus.

Accompanied by French Ambassador Maurice Couve de Murville, the Abbé Pierre visited the White House in Washington, D.C. on May 3, when he told President Eisenhower of the world's need for a voluntary army against poverty. He also presented the President with the book *Abbé Pierre and the Ragpickers of Emmaus* by Boris Simon (Kenedy, 1955). Activities of the Emmaus group are recorded in their publication, *Faim et Soif*.

Extremely interested in world cooperation, Abbé Pierre in 1947 was elected vice-president of the executive committee of the Universal Movement for a World Confederation and he was subsequently vice-president of the International Liaison Committee of Peace Organizations, and member of the executive committee of the Peoples' World Constituent Assembly.

The Abbé is a Chevalier of the Legion of Honor, holds the Croix de Guerre with two citations, the Médaille de la Résistance, the Médaille des Evadés, the Médaille des Combattants Volontaires; and the Médaille des Maquis de Belgique. He has a "brown beard, which combines with rather large limpid eyes to lend him an appearance of asceticism," Harry Gabbett has written (Washington *Post and Times Herald*, May 3, 1955).

References

Commonweal 60:219+ Je 4 '54
Life 36:53+ F 22 '54
Newsweek 43:42+ F 15 '54
Read Digest 65:91+ O '54
Reporter 10:23+ Mr 30 '54
Time 63:49+ F 15 '54
Dictionnaire Biographique Français Contemporain (1954)
Simon, B. Abbé Pierre and the Ragpickers of Emmaus (1955)

PLA Y DENIEL, ENRIQUE, CARDINAL (plà ē dĕ-nyĕl) Dec. 19, 1876- Roman Catholic prelate

Address: Placto Arzobispal, Toledo, Spain

His Eminence Enrique Pla y Deniel, Cardinal Archbishop of Toledo, Primate of Spain, is influential in determining the relationship between the Spanish Catholic church and the government of Francisco Franco. *Ecclesia*, official organ of the Spanish episcopacy, published his assurance on November 1, 1953 that

Rodriquez, Toledo

ENRIQUE CARDINAL PLA Y DENIEL

the church would not oppose the military and economic collaboration between Spain and the United States.

He was proclaimed Cardinal by Pope Pius XII at the Consistory in February 1946. His pastoral letters on Catholic values, religious history and philosophy have been collected for book publication. Through his activities in Acción Católica Española, he has instituted many welfare benefits.

Enrique Pla y Deniel was born in Barcelona, Spain, on December 19, 1876. He attended the Instituto de Segunda Enseñanza in Barcelona and received a civil bachelor's degree before entering the Seminario de Barcelona to begin his studies for the priesthood. He continued at the Spanish Pontifical College of St. Joseph in Rome, and at the Academy of St. Thomas Aquinas, Gregorian University, Rome, where he won honors and received a doctorate in philosophy, theology and canon law. He was ordained in Rome on July 15, 1900 and was appointed a professor at the Seminario de Barcelona. *Crítica de la Escuela Histórica según los Principios de Santo Tomás sobre la Mutabilidad de las Leyes* (1900) was one of many articles he wrote during the nine years of his professorship.

Dr. Pla y Deniel was made a Canon in the Cathedral of Barcelona in 1912, in charge of visiting schools of the diocese, and distinguished himself by defending Catholic educational methods. He became director of the magazine *Reseña Eclesiástica,* and president of the Church Association of Popular Apostleship.

He was proclaimed Bishop of Avila on December 4, 1918 by Pope Benedict XV and was consecrated in the Cathedral of Barcelona on June 8, 1919. During his sixteen years in the diocese of Avila, he directed the repair and reconstruction of many churches, established a Catholic Action chapter and founded Casa Social Católica for which he set aside a part of his own residence. He revived the commemorative fiestas celebrating the Canonization of Santa Teresa de Jesús and of San Juan de la Cruz.

During the dictatorship of Miguel Primo de Rivera, Bishop Pla y Deniel attracted widespread Catholic interest by his pastoral letters, particularly a circular concerning the obligations of Catholic citizens in which he predicted that a change in government would result in the separation of church and state. (Under the Republican Constitution of 1931, Spain was declared to have no official religion.)

Pope Pius XI proclaimed Bishop Pla y Deniel as Bishop of Salamanca and he assumed his new duties on May 26, 1935. Most of the church property in the diocese had been destroyed during anticlerical demonstrations. His pastoral letter, "Las dos Ciudades" ("The Two Cities"), was a powerful appeal to the bishops of all Spain to join in the crusade to expound the doctrine of laws for God and country. With the end of the Civil War in 1939, Bishop Pla y Deniel issued a pastoral entitled "El Triunfo de la Ciudad—de Dios y la resurrección de España," an historical review of the happenings during the Civil War. (Under the new Franco regime, Catholicism was declared to be the state religion.)

The restoration of the Pontifical Ecclesiatic University of Salamanca was completed in 1940, largely through the efforts of Bishop Pla y Deniel, who recruited competent teachers and secured the authority of Pope Pius XII for the inaugural on November 6, 1940. Bishop Pla y Deniel was made president of the Council of Bishops and charged with the "protection" of the university.

Pope Pius XII named Pla y Deniel in October 1941 Archbishop of Toledo, the Primatial See of all Spain. The archdiocese had suffered almost total destruction during the Civil War. Three hundred priests and a hundred monks and nuns had been assassinated. Taking office on March 25, 1942, he outlined a program of complete reconstruction, patterned after the restoration of Salamanca. The plan, detailed in a pastoral letter April 15, 1943, was carried out.

Cordial relations were established with the Franco government, through Archbishop Pla y Deniel's intervention and without condescending to government pressure. In two pastoral letters dated September 2, and May 8, 1945 the Archbishop endorsed the Francisco Franco regime, but denied that the church favored totalitarianism and solemnly declared that the Catholic church in Spain had remained neutral. He also defended the position of the church against the attacks of the anticlericals.

Archbishop Pla y Deniel was created and proclaimed Cardinal at the Consistory on February 18, 1946 by Pope Pius XII. As Primate of Spain, he gained leadership of a national character by the development of welfare activities and the founding of the Brotherhood of Catholic Action for the consolidation and protection of workers.

Cardinal Pla y Deniel's review of Church laws, his pastorals to bishops and all of his earlier writings have been compiled by the technical division of Acción Católica Española. A first volume was published in celebration of the twenty-fifth anniversary of the Consecration of Spanish Bishops to the Sacred Heart of Jesus.

Sam Pope Brewer reported (New York *Times,* June 25, 1950) that Enrique Cardinal Pla y Deniel in a pastoral letter dated June 16 urged the Spanish people to put their faith in Catholic censorship: "... if a Catholic state like ours ought to prohibit that which is gravely immoral, a civil censorship cannot be as exacting as a censorship of religious character dedicated to orienting the faithful."

After the bilateral agreements to grant the United States use of air and naval bases in return for support of Spanish armament were signed on September 26, 1953, Cardinal Pla y Deniel declared that Catholic unity and loyalty to God were "not obstacles to advantageous collaboration" with powerful non-Catholic nations (*Ecclesia,* November 1, 1953). This was regarded as acceptance by the Church. The Primate pointed out that on August 27, 1953, Spain and the Holy See had signed a concordat that officially re-established Roman Catholicism as the state religion of Spain.

Time (May 31, 1954) reported that the Reverend Jesus Iribarren, editor of *Ecclesia,* wrote after attending the 1954 International Convention of the Catholic Press: "Newspaper men from other countries have a spirit of initiative and personal decision, compared to [our country], where the press is directed. We can write only what is ordered. . . . In Spain public opinion is disregarded, and anybody who wants to read the news has to look anywhere except in newspapers."

Ecclesia announced on November 13, 1954 that Cardinal Pla y Deniel had "accepted the resignation" of Father Iribarren. Camille M. Cianfarra (New York *Times,* November 9, 1954) had reported that Father Iribarren had been dismissed for "failure to submit an article on press censorship to his immediate superior, Enrique Cardinal Pla y Deniel, Spanish Primate, before publishing it."

"The religious and civil societies are both perfect and independent in their respective field," stated Cardinal Pla y Deniel on June 26, 1954. "This means that the church, even though it may collaborate cordially [with the state] is not tied to any regime." Therefore, it is the government that must be credited with the "glory for its successes and the responsibility for its possible errors" (New York *Times,* July 2, 1954).

Cardinal Pla y Deniel is president of the central committee of Acción Católica Española; Conferencia de Metropolitanos Españolas; Unión Misional del Clero; and commissioner general of Bula de Cruzada. He was awarded the Collar of Isabel la Católica; Cruz Meritisma de S. Raimundo and the Grand Cross Alfonso el Sabio.

Since General Franco came to power, the ancient city of Toledo, the seat of Church authority, has been regarded as the second capitol of Spain. As evidence of the Primate's political independence, *Life* (April 4, 1949) quoted his statement: "Any change of regime is up to the people—the church would not interfere except to prevent the rise of a communist government."

References

International Who's Who, 1953
World Biography (1954)

PRINCE RAINIER III *See* Rainier III, Prince of Monaco

PULITZER, JOSEPH, 2d Mar. 21, 1885-Mar. 30, 1955 Publisher; editor; as owner of politically independent St. Louis *Post-Dispatch,* carried on policy of militant journalism of his father Joseph Pulitzer; noted for his crusades against crime and injustice; began newspaper career in 1906 with *The World*; became president of the Pulitzer Publishing Company in 1912 and a member of the advisory board on Pulitzer Prizes of the Graduate School of Journalism at Columbia University; his newspaper won five of the awards. See *Current Biography* (Dec.) 1954.

Obituary

N Y Times p27 Ap 1 '55

PYLE, (JOHN) HOWARD Mar. 25, 1906- United States Government official; former Governor of Arizona

Address: b. The White House, Washington 25, D.C.; h. 1120 Ash Ave., Tempe, Ariz.

Active in the Governors' Conference in trying to establish "guide posts in the twilight zone of Federal and state responsibility," Howard Pyle is using his experience as a former Republican Governor of traditionally Democratic Arizona in his present post as President Eisenhower's deputy assistant in charge of liaison with the states. Since joining the White House staff on February 1, 1955 he has helped to build up a "partnership" with the states, which proved useful during the flood disaster in the Northeastern states during August. He had previously been a radio announcer and program director of a large network in the Southwest.

Pyle's job is the outgrowth of President Eisenhower's appointment of a Commission on Inter-Governmental Relations. A report by that commission, under the chairmanship of Meyer Kestnbaum (see *C.B.*, 1953), is likely, in Pyle's opinion, to result in the return to the states of some of the functions and obligations assumed by the Federal Government under the New Deal and the Fair Deal.

John Howard Pyle was born on March 25, 1906 at Sheridan, Wyoming. His father, Thomas Miller Pyle, was a structural steelworker in the railroad yards. His mother was the former Marie Anderson. He is related to the late Ernie Pyle. Thomas Pyle had a talent for composing conflicts between men. Better to employ this talent, he took his family to Waco, Texas, and enrolled as a divinity student at

Wide World

HOWARD PYLE

Baylor University. He is now pastor of the Community Church at Buckeye, Arizona. As a youth, Howard Pyle held different jobs to help his family financially. In this period he decided upon a singing career. His first radio engagement was at Lincoln, Nebraska.

When Howard was nineteen the family moved to Tempe, Arizona. He entered the Atwater Kent radio tryouts for musical talent, reaching the semi-finals at San Francisco, California. Later he turned to selling real estate, managing the Tempe Chamber of Commerce and writing and selling advertising for the Arizona *Republic* of Phoenix.

Entering the field of radio, Pyle appeared on two regular KTAR programs—*Arizona Highlights,* in which he presented Arizonians in every walk of life, and *Poetry Exchange.* His voice "schooled to do a shivery whisper or a resounding roll," thrilled thousands. In 1930 he became program director for KTAR and later vice-president of the Arizona Broadcasting Company, which owns KTAR and other stations. His favorite assignment was broadcasting the Easter morning sunrise service in Grand Canyon, at which his father preached in 1951. During World War II Pyle interviewed Arizona soldiers in the Pacific for a radio program.

At a Young Republican meeting, after the war, Pyle stated that he would give the group any assistance they needed. When the group asked him to run for the governorship in 1950, he kept his promise. At that time Arizona had 279,533 registered voters, 225,114 enrolled as Democrats and only 50,191 as Republicans. There had been only two Republican Governors in the state's history. Pyle was unopposed for the Republican nomination.

His opponent was State Treasurer Ana Collins Frohmiller, described as "good-looking, popular and smart at the Arizona Democratic brand of politics" (*Saturday Evening Post,* June 16, 1951). She was the first woman to run for the governorship in Arizona. As a candidate, Pyle traveled more than 26,000 miles, largely in a plane owned and piloted by his campaign manager, Barry M. Goldwater, now U.S. Senator from Arizona. Pyle also spoke at the Navaho Indian reservation (the Navahos had been given the vote in Arizona elections in 1948).

On November 7, 1950 the voters gave Pyle 99,109 ballots and Mrs. Frohmiller 96,118. Democrats took all other state-wide and national offices, all nineteen seats in the state Senate and sixty-one of the seventy-two in the House.

Pyle was inaugurated on January 1, 1951. As Governor, Pyle had harmonious relations with the Legislature. During his first three months in office, he signed seventy-six measures and vetoed none.

At the 1952 Republican National Convention in Chicago, Pyle deplored the "vast number of voters" who have the attitude of "you'll have to give more than that if you expect to get my vote." "The sad, sad thing about this point of view," he said, "is that it has created a kind of competition for favor that is slowly but surely burying the right answers to what is right for America" (New York *Herald Tribune,* July 9, 1952). He was re-elected as Governor in 1952, carrying the state by a margin larger than Eisenhower's. In November 1954 he was defeated in his bid for re-election by former U.S. Senator Ernest W. McFarland.

On January 22, 1955 Pyle was appointed an administrative assistant to the President and was later promoted to the post of deputy assistant. To this work he brings executive experience with state problems, and a political philosophy which is similar to the President's. The White House staff comprises 250 Presidential aides, clerks and stenographers with an annual payroll of $1,500,000. (During Herbert Hoover's Presidency the staff included three secretaries and about forty clerks.)

One of Pyle's jobs is editing a mimeographed "newsletter," issued several times a week, summarizing in a few terse paragraphs the Administration viewpoint on every public issue. It goes to some 1,000 top Department executives, Republican leaders in Congress and Republican Governors.

On the subject of Federal versus state financing and taxation, Pyle told reporters interviewing him on NBC's *Meet the Press* radio and television program (August 21, 1955): "I still believe that if the states will follow through the Kestnbaum [report] suggestion of a thorough-going analysis of their own ability to pay, they are going to discover that they have more financing ability than they have exercised . . . what is to keep the states from moving into the areas of taxation [for schools, highways, etc.] . . . no longer collected at the federal level?

On August 9, 1930 Pyle was married to Lucile Hanna; they have two daughters, Mary Lou and Virginia Ann. They keep as their permanent home a one-story, two-bedroom white brick house in Tempe. Pyle's personality has been described as warmly magnetic. He can and does quote the Scriptures. His hobby is horses, three of which are corralled in the backyard of the Tempe home. He does not smoke, drink or dance, but he does not "act as if the fires were lit for those who do."

Pyle is a Baptist. He holds the honorary LL.D. degree from the University of Redlands (1950). His eyes are brown and his hair dark. His garb as a public official is conservative, but when the occasion permits, he likes wearing slacks or Western ranch clothes.

A political opponent, speaking from the same platform with Pyle, once said that the reason the Republican Governor got along so well with the Democratic legislature was that "for years he has been bossed by a Democrat"—Mrs. Pyle.

"It takes more than laws, however well written and justified, to make men and nations responsible," Pyle told the Los Angeles Bar Association on November 19, 1953. "Beyond them we must build in men a desire to keep the law because it is right that they should, right as David believed it to be right when he added these words to the Psalms—'I delight to do Thy will, O God, because Thy law is within my heart.'"

References

Christian Sci Mon p14 N 12 '51
N Y Herald Tribune p11 N 10 '50; p4 Jl 9 '52; p2 Je 19 '55
N Y Times p22 N 10 '50; p70 N 1 '53; p56 My 9 '54; p26 Ja 22 '55
Sat Eve Post 223:29+ Je 16 '51
Time 57:26 Mr 26 '51; 62:12+ Ag 17 '53
Washington (D.C.) Post p12 N 3 '53
Who's Who in America, 1954-55

QUARLES, DONALD A(UBREY) July 30, 1894- United States Secretary of the Air Force; engineer

Address: b. c/o Department of the Air Force, Washingotn 25, D.C.; h. 3041 Porter St., N.W., Washington, D.C.

In a widely praised appointment Donald A. Quarles, an expert in the field of weapons development, was selected in August 1955 to succeed Harold E. Talbott as U.S. Secretary of the Air Force. Secretary of Defense Charles E. Wilson, who had recommended Quarles to President Dwight D. Eisenhower, had earlier said that the man needed to fill the exacting position was one "with technical and administrative experience, the kind of character that would permit him to sit at God's right hand, and the kind of past that would insure confirmation by the Senate" (New York *Herald Tribune*, August 22, 1955). Quarles was sworn into office on August 15, but his appointment cannot be confirmed until January 1956 when Congress reconvenes.

Secretary Quarles was interviewed on the Columbia Broadcasting System program *Face the Nation* on September 11, during which he said that "by and large" the Air Force intended to stick to its planned goals—specifically in-

U. S. Air Force
DONALD A. QUARLES

creased production of B-52 jet bombers, hydrogen bomb carriers, and supersonic fighter planes, but would "comb over" its spending in an effort "to find every possible economy to help balance the Federal budget without injuring the military program" (New York *Times*, September 12, 1955).

A research engineer and business administrator, Quarles had spent most of his adult life in the laboratories and executive offices of the Western Electric Company and Bell Telephone Laboratories. He was Republican Mayor of Englewood, New Jersey for two years. Entering Federal Government service in 1953, he became Assistant Secretary of Defense for Research and Development. Among the projects which he was concerned with in this office were atom-powered planes and the planned earth satellite.

Donald Aubrey Quarles, the son of Robert Warren and Minnie (Hynes) Quarles, was born in Van Buren, Arkansas on July 30, 1894. During the Civil War his grandfather, a Confederate soldier, died in a Union prison camp and the family plantation in Mississippi was destroyed by Northern troops. His father afterward moved to Arkansas, where he practiced dentistry for fifty years.

At the age of fifteen young Quarles was graduated from Van Buren High School with the highest scholastic rating in his class. For three summers (1910-1912) he took courses at the University of Missouri Summer School in Columbia and in intervening sessions returned to his home town to teach high school mathematics.

Quarles entered Yale University in 1912, majored in mathematics and physics, was elected to Phi Beta Kappa, and received the A.B. degree in 1916. Enlisting in the Army, he attended an officers candidate school and later served with

QUARLES, DONALD A.—*Continued*

the Rainbow Division. After two years in France and Germany, he was discharged in 1919 with the rank of captain in the field artillery.

While working at the Western Electric Company (later the Bell Telephone Laboratories) in New York City, he pursued graduate courses at Columbia University during 1920 and 1921. His first position at Western Electric was in the engineering department, where he specialized in transmission engineering research. From 1924 to 1928 he was in charge of apparatus inspection engineering and from 1929 to 1940 in charge of the outside plant development department of Bell Telephone Laboratories. His work here involved the study of existing telephone materials and design, the development of new equipment, and research on open-wire insulators and coaxial cable structures. Papers which he wrote in this period appear in the *Bell System Technical Journal.*

During World War II Quarles directed the transmission department and thus had charge of Bell Laboratories' radar program. He was also concerned with research in broad-band telephone and television systems and voice frequency transmission systems. One of his technical papers, "Radar Systems Considerations," was published in *Electrical Engineering* (April 1946).

As director of apparatus development from 1944 to 1948, Quarles was responsible for developments in telephone apparatus for both military and commercial purposes. In August 1946 he was named one of the first members of the Joint Research and Development Board's (later called the Research and Development Board) committee on electronics, of which he became chairman in January 1949. He was made a vice-president of Bell Telephone Laboratories in 1948.

Quarles at this time was living in Englewood, New Jersey, where he took an active part in civic affairs. After serving as a member and then president of the common council from 1940 to 1946, he was elected mayor of Englewood on the Republican "good government" ticket and held that office from 1946 to 1948. Later appointed chairman of the Bergen County Sewer Authority, he directed without salary a $13,000,000 sewer project.

In March 1952 he became a vice-president of Western Electric Company and president of Sandia Corporation, a subsidiary of Western Electric which operates the Sandia atomic weapons research laboratory in Albuquerque, New Mexico for the Atomic Energy Commission. He lived in New Mexico for about a year, until being called to Washnigton, D.C. to direct the government's vast military research program.

The office of Assistant Secretary of Defense for Research and Development, which Quarles assumed on September 1, 1953, was a newly created post replacing the Research and Development Board. He was directly responsible for research involving expenditures of more than a billion dollars a year and including such projects as intercontinental ballistic missiles and the military aspects of the earth-circling satellite that the United States expects to send into space in 1957 or 1958. In an interview in August 1955 for *U.S. News & World Report,* Quarles explained that information gained from the flight of the satellite would be made available to scientists of all nations, but that "it will be necessary for some of the equipment and technical details for launching the satellite to remain classified."

During his first two years in the Pentagon, Quarles, on several occasions, expressed publicly his concern over the shortage of scientific and technical manpower in the United States. An excerpt from his address "Need of Scientific Manpower" was printed in *Science News Letter* (March 5, 1955). In an earlier address, before members of the American Institute of Chemical Engineers in March 1954, he estimated that the U.S.S.R. was training twice as many engineers as the United States.

In June 1954 he stated: "We must conclude that on balance our technical position vis-à-vis the Soviets is less favorable than it was a year ago. Our margin of advantage has been narrowed and we must face the sober inferences to be drawn from these facts" (New York *Times* June 20, 1954). "My own appraisal," he stated in September, "is that we are in a race where our best is none too good" (New York *Times* October 1, 1954).

In an article for *Scientific Monthly* (June 1955) he stated the "theorem": "that scientific and technical manpower is our most precious commodity, our real critical resource, that our competitor is very smart in fostering and conserving his stock of this precious commodity, and that we must sharpen our own practices all along this line."

When Quarles was named Secretary of the Air Force on August 11, 1955, his appointment was praised in leading American newspapers. Quarles told reporters that he would divest himself of any stock holdings that might imply a "conflict of interest," but that he would retain his annual $10,000 "irrevocable" pension from the Western Electric Company. He was sworn into office as Secretary of the Air Force, at a salary of $18,000 a year, on August 15, 1955. However, Quarles' appointment must await confirmation by the Senate when it meets in January 1956.

After taking office, Secretary Quarles received considerable attention when he cleared Airman 3/c Stephen Branzovich of security charges based on allegations that his father was a Communist. Quarles, who made a personal review of the charges, was commended in a *Washington Post and Times Herald* editorial (August 29, 1955): "The Secretary lifted the case out of the hands of a hearing board for the obvious purpose of laying down a policy that would extend beyond this individual case. His decision is a pointed direction to Air Force security officers that they should not hereafter bring charges based on nothing more substantial than 'guilt by kinship.' "

Secretary Quarles stated in September 1955 that "neither the United States nor the free world is interested in an arms race with anyone. The balance we seek is not between free world air power and that of any potential opponent. We seek, instead, a balance between our air power and any opponent's temptation to aggression." (New York *Times*, September 6, 1955). On September 11, 1955 it was announced that a new pinch-waisted design in military aircraft had produced increases up to 25 per cent in supersonic speeds. The new fuselage shape had been developed several years ago by Richard T. Whitcomb.

Quarles announced on October 25 that an eight-year study of "flying saucer" reports showed that "none of them were aircraft of foreign origin." He also told of the new Avro plane which resembles a saucer, now being developed by the U.S. Air Force.

Quarles is a director of United Engineering Trustees and a fellow of the American Physical Society and American Institute of Electrical Engineers (president, 1952-1953). He also belongs to the American Institute of Radio Engineers, American Association for the Advancement of Science, Telephone Pioneers of America, Yale Engineering Society, and Sigma Xi. His clubs are the Englewood, Knickerbocker Country (Tenafly, New Jersey), Baltusrol Golf (Springfield, New Jersey) and Engineers (New York City). Other Government positions that Quarles has held are first chairman of the reorganized Air Navigation Development Board; and member of the National Advisory Committee for Aeronautics. He has honorary degrees from the University of Arkansas (1953) and New York University (1955).

Quarles married Rosina Cotton on October 27, 1939. By a previous marriage he has two daughters and a son, Carolyn Anne, Elizabeth Whittemore (Mrs. Stanley C. Lewis) and Donald Aubrey, Jr. The slim, graying blue-eyed Air Secretary has a quiet manner and a dry sense of humor. *Time* (August 22, 1955) reports that he is so "scrupulous about the ethics of high office, he never lets his wife take his government-furnished limousine for her own use." He plays the guitar, enjoys classical music, chess, bridge, tennis and golf. He also mentions dishwashing as a pastime. His pet, a three-year-old dachshund, is named Zeppy (short for Graf Zeppelin).

References

Chem & Eng N 31:3760 D 14 '53 por
N Y Herald Tribune p1+ Ag 12 '55 por; II p2 Ag 14 '55 por
N Y Times p1+, p6 Ag 12 '55
Time 66:19 Ag 22 '55
Washington (D.C.) Post p1+ Ag 12 '55
Who's Who in America, 1954-55
Who's Who in Engineering, 1948
World Biography (1954)

QUEEN ELIZABETH II *See* Elizabeth II, Queen of Great Britain

QUEEN FREDERIKA *See* Frederika, Consort of Paul I, King of the Hellenes

QUEEN JULIANA *See* Juliana, Queen of the Netherlands

RAINIER III, PRINCE OF MONACO

May 31, 1923-

Address: Palais Princier, Monaco

The thirty-first hereditary ruler of the principality of Monaco, a tiny, hilly wedge driven into the French Mediterranean coast, is Prince Rainier III. He succeeded his grandfather, Prince Louis II in 1949. Famous for its gambling casino, Monte Carlo—one of three communes in the realm—a symbol of gaiety and excitement for nearly a century, faced in the summer of 1955 its first real crisis since 1871.

In normal times, the casino grossed $10,000,000 yearly. After World War II the daily intake per visitor dropped from fifty to fifteen dollars (*Newsweek*, May 23, 1949). In June 1955 it was discovered that the president of Monaco's biggest bank — the Société Montégasque de Banque et de Métaux Précieux (Monaco Banking and Precious Metal Company), where most of the casino funds were deposited—had invested and had lost some of the bank's money in a commercial television station. A run on the bank resulted. Prince Rainier made up the deficits with state funds, and on the advice of the eighteen-member National Council dismissed his top four financial advisers. Subsequent investigation revealed a shortage of $8,625,000 and the bank was closed. The New York *Times* (August 30, 1955) stated that France had offered to reopen the bank on condition that a Frenchman take charge of Monaco's financial affairs.

Monaco is an independent principality of eight square miles on the Mediterranean Sea near the French-Italian border. It has approximately 24,000 inhabitants and about 2,300 are citizens of Monaco. The capital of this small country is also called Monaco and is located on a rocky headland projecting into the Mediterranean Sea and has a famous oceanographical museum which was opened in 1910. The Genoese Grimaldi dynasty has controlled Monaco since the tenth century.

Rainier Louis Henri Maxence Bertrand de Grimaldi was born in Monaco on May 31, 1923, the only son of Pierre de Polignac and Princess Charlotte of Monaco. Among his twenty-four legal titles are the Duc de Valentinios, Marquis des Baux, Baron de Saint Lô, and the Compte de Carlades.

His education began in England where he attended Summer Fields, Hastings and the Stowe School. He continued at Rosey, Switzerland and the University of Montpellier in France. During World War II he enlisted in the French Army and served with the Seventh Regiment of Tirailleurs Algeriéns as Lieutenant Grimaldi. In combat during the Alsatian campaign, Rainier was cited for bravery several times and offered a colonelship, which he refused. After the war, he completed his education in Sciences Politiques at the University of Paris.

Princess Charlotte renounced her rights to succession in 1944 in favor of her son and on May 5, 1949, her father, Prince Louis II, who had reigned for twenty-seven years and had

Monaco Inf. Center
PRINCE RAINIER III OF MONACO

been in ill health for months, relinquished his rule to Prince Rainier. A week later, Prince Louis died.

In an article entitled "Monte Carlo" (*Holiday*, November 1953) Sam Boal related that the first gambling concession was given by Charles III in 1850 and operated in a private home. Ten years later, it was purchased by a Franco-German promoter—François Blanc—for $34,000 and reorganized as the Société des Bains de Mer et du Cercle des Étrangers à Monaco (Sea Bathing and Foreigners' Club of Monaco). Blanc named the location Mount Charles, but Italians who flocked there, called it Monte Carlo. Within five years the club was a success. The present casino was started in 1880 and enlarged five times. The legend of "the man who broke the bank at Monte Carlo" was founded on the story of an Englishman, Charles Wells, who "broke one table" and it was draped in black until funds came from the bank. In 1953 control of Monaco's casinos was purchased for $1,000,000 by Greek shipping magnate, Aristotle Socrates Onassis.

Residents of Monaco pay no income or inheritance taxes. The principality derives its income from these sources: it receives a percentage on French customs; thirty-five per cent of the Casino profits; the tourist trade; the sale of regular and commemorative postage stamps, and hotel taxes. The country has its own police courts, judges, school system, an army of ninety men — used for ceremonies — and Radio Monte Carlo, which unlike most European radio stations, accepts advertising.

Prince Rainier is said to take his responsibilities seriously, and is deeply concerned about the decrease in revenue from the tourist trade and the casino. He was further disturbed in June 1955 when he learned that Constantin Liambey (a wealthy Greek), president of the Société Montégasque de Banque et de Métaux Précieux (Monaco's biggest bank) had invested some of the bank's resources (535 million francs) in 40 per cent of the stock of Images et Son (Pictures and Sound), according to *Barron's* (August 22, 1955), a promising new local enterprise.

Images et Son had been incorporated in 1949 by Charles Michelson, a former manager of a Tangier radio station, and Armand Worms, owner of a French radio and television equipment manufacturing firm. Since commercial television is banned throughout France, as explained in *Barron's,* Michelson obtained from Radio Monte Carlo a contract giving him the right to operate a commercial television station—Tele Monte Carlo—in the principality. Michelson planned to build a chain of TV stations at strategic points near the French border and "invade" France with attractive sponsored shows and advertising.

According to *Barron's,* a "concerted attack against the Michelson group, believed to have been inspired at least partly by competitive interests, was launched in the French National Assembly . . . led by Pierre Henri Teitgen who charged that the national interests of France had been neglected. Since 80 per cent of the stock of Radio Monte Carlo belongs to a government owned French company (Société Financière de Radiodiffusion "Sofirad"), the French Parliament in a tempestuous session in January 1955, ordered the cancellation of all the arrangements between Michelson and Radio Monte Carlo, and the stock of Images et Son was barred from the Paris Stock Exchange.

A run on the Monaco Banking and Precious Metal Company resulted. The National Council agreed with Prince Rainier's decision to make up the bank's deficit on condition that he dismiss certain members of his Cabinet and also replace certain bank officials. A large initial deposit of state funds (700 million francs), according to *Barron's* (August 22, 1955), was made in June. The government eventually invested about one and a half billion francs, the equivalent of a full year's budget in the principality. Although Liambey's bank was not strictly a state institution, a large part of the principality's funds were invested in it.

After the bank was closed by court order, three international finance groups offered to reopen it and assume the deficit (over $8,000,000), the New York *Times* noted (June 30, 1955), and added that the French government's offer was unlikely to be refused. France has largely governed Monaco's diplomatic and custom services and French currency is interchangeable in the realm.

The Monégasques are worried because their Prince is a bachelor. He is not a woman-hater and there are persistent rumors that he will visit the United States "in search of a wife." So far, the only woman's name publicly linked with his was that of a French actress—Gisele Pascal—but "publicity had frightened him." The romance ended before his African cruise in 1954.

The American motion picture star, Grace Kelly paid a courtesy call on the prince while she was in Monaco making a film. The Prince, according to Art Buchwald (New York *Herald Tribune*, September 25, 1955), "ardently hoped to meet the young actress again."

Rainier's subjects fear that the principality might become a French protectorate subject to French taxes, should Rainier die without issue. Morton Sontheimer explained in *McCall's* that "in the darkest hours of World War I," a German prince had claimed succession to the throne, and Prince Albert I had signed a treaty with France that should a vacancy occur because of no direct heir, Monaco would become a protectorate under France. The Prince's father is not a hereditary heir and his mother no longer lives in Monaco. Although there is no precedent for his sister, Princess Antoinette, to succeed Prince Rainier, there is much talk of pushing through legislation in Monaco's National Council making her the heiress-apparent. She is married and has several children.

Prince Rainier occupies a five-room apartment, which he has modernized on a luxurious scale, in one wing of the 300-room ancient palace. The handsome Prince is athletically built, he has blue eyes and brown wavy hair, usually combed to conceal a white forelock, and he wears a neatly-trimmed mustache.

He prefers to wear lounge suits. His dress uniforms and neckties are invariably blue. He speaks excellent English, while his French—the official language of Monaco—has an English accent. His religion is Roman Catholic and his adviser and court chaplain, Father Francis Tucker, is American-born.

In an average day at the palace, Prince Rainier attends to his mail, plays a game of tennis, lunches with his Cabinet, and devotes the afternoon to audiences with his subjects and visitors. He gives elaborate parties at which his sister, Princess Antoinette, two years his senior, usually acts as hostess.

Much of Prince Rainier's time is devoted to sports. He skis in Switzerland, races cars in France and owns eight motor cycles. Crowds cheered his return to Monaco in October 1954 after a seventy-one day African cruise on his eighty-foot motor yacht *Deo Juvante II*. *Time* (November 8, 1954) said that he brought back cages of live animals, which he had purchased and were destined for a new national zoo. His adventures included spearfishing in the shark-infested waters off Dakar, a 1,200-mile trek through French Guinea and shooting pictures under water during an Atlantic storm.

Popular with the French because of his brilliant war record, Rainier was decorated by the French as a Grand Master of the Order of St. Charles and with the Grand Cross of the Legion of Honor. He also received the Grand Cross of the Royal Order of George I of Greece, the Grand-Cordon of the Order of Leopold of Belgium, and many other honors.

The Prince once said that the casino and hotel companies should have younger people, and clarified: "We need young ideas." Art Buchwald (New York *Herald Tribune*, January 3, 1954) said that the Prince told him that he had no interest in gambling, not even on horse races. Rainier heads the Red Cross in his country.

References

France Illus 6:395-7 Ap 20 '50 por
Le Monde (Paris) pl D 3 '54
McCalls 82:36+ F '55 por
N Y Herald Tribune II p5 Ja 3 '54
Time 67:37 N 8 '54 por
New Century Cyclopedia of Names (1954)
World Biography (1954)

RANKIN, K(ARL) L(OTT) Sept. 4, 1898-

United States Ambassador to Nationalist China

Address: b. c/o American Embassy, Taipei, Formosa; h. South Bridgton, Me.

The U.S. Senate's unanimous confirmation of the appointment of K. L. Rankin as Ambassador Extraordinary and Plenipotentiary to Nationalist China in Formosa in February 1953, satisfied both American and Chinese advocates of "a more positive policy to combat Communism in the Far East." His assignment is considered "one of the most delicate diplomatic posts in the world" where the situation is explosive and unpredictable.

Just prior to the successful evacuation of civilians and Chinese Nationalist military forces from the Tachen Islands in February 1955 by the U.S. Seventh Fleet, Ambassador Rankin expressed the view that a firm stand by the United States in the midst of Communist threats to "liberate" Formosa worked in favor of peace instead of war. "The stronger the line we take without being provocative—and we won't be—the less likelihood there is of any important conflict breaking out" (New York *Times*, January 29, 1955). "Continued firmness," he stated, "would cause the Communists to alter their 'liberation' timetable."

A career diplomat since 1927, Ambassador Rankin has served in the Middle East, the Balkans and the Far East. Since August 8, 1950 he had been minister and chargé d'affaires in Taipei, occupying the top position because Ambassador J. Leighton Stuart's ill health kept him away in the United States. In urging the confirmation of Rankin's nomination as Ambassador, Senator Alexander Wiley of Wisconsin stated that the diplomat "understands the Chinese problem. He has been close to the Nationalist government at its headquarters in Formosa. He knows the very complicated and difficult issues which the United States confronts in China. I think I speak for the committee [the Committee on Foreign Relations] when I say that the President has selected a very able representative to perform a very difficult mission."

Senator H. Alexander Smith of New Jersey praised Rankin for having "established, not only among the Chinese Nationalist people there but also among the Formosans themselves, a high degree of confidence in the United States and its purpose of helping the people in that area."

(Continued next page)

U. S. Inf. Services

K. L. RANKIN

Karl Lott Rankin was born on September 4, 1898 in Manitowoc, Wisconsin, the only son of Emmet Woollen and Alberta (Lott) Rankin. His father later became well known in Maine, serving as a clergyman in New Gloucester (1928-1930) and in South Bridgton (1930-1940). He then went into politics as a Republican member of the Maine Legislature (1941-1949).

The family lived in Topeka, Kansas from 1906 to 1915, the year when Karl was graduated from the Topeka High School. The following year he studied at Mercersburg Academy in Pennsylvania. He subsequently attended Cornell University, Columbia University, the California Institute of Technology (1917-1919), Federal Polytechnic Institute in Zurich (1920-1921), and Heidelberg University in Germany. In 1922 he received a degree in civil engineering from Princeton University.

After serving in the U.S. Navy in 1918 (he became a lieutenant commander in the Naval Reserve in 1937), Rankin began his career as a field engineer in 1919. He was employed in Smyrna, Turkey in 1920 and then held the post of construction superintendent of Near East Relief in the Russian Caucasus from 1922 to 1925. For the next two years he managed a real estate development company in Linden, New Jersey.

Rankin entered the United States foreign service in 1927, and his first assignment was as assistant trade commissioner in Prague, where two years later he became commercial attaché. In 1932 he was named commercial attaché in Athens and Tirana (Albania). He served as delegate to the twenty-third session of the International Institute of Statistics in Athens in 1936.

Following his appointment is commercial attaché in Brussels and Luxembourg in 1939, he became consul and secretary in the diplomatic service. Then in 1940 came service as commercial attaché and consul in Belgrade. Rankin's next assignment was as commercial attaché in Cairo in 1941; but before going to Egypt he made a trip to Manila, was interned by the Japanese and remained in prison from January 1942 to October 1943.

He was reassigned as commercial attaché to Cairo in 1944. Briefly during that year he was counselor of the Embassy for economic affairs to the government of Greece established in Egypt, also with supervision over economic relations with Albania and Yugoslavia. In October he was transferred to Athens as counselor of the Embassy for economic affairs and two years later (1946) was made counselor of the Legation for economic affairs at Vienna. Senator Margaret Chase Smith read into the *Congressional Record* (February 27, 1953) praise for his "excellent work" in Austria, which she had seen firsthand.

In 1947 he became counselor of the Embassy at Athens. His service during those crucial times "when the Communist guerrillas were most active" was "exceptionally fine and competent," according to Senator Wiley. In both Greece and Vienna, he had opportunities to observe the Communists in action, an experience which was to serve him in good stead later in the Far East. Rankin's Far Eastern duties began in 1949 with his appointment as consul general at Canton and then at Hong Kong and Macau. During his stay in Hong Kong he transformed the consulate general into "a highly efficient listening post." He was chargé d'affaires ad interim at Taipei as well as consul general and minister from August 1950 until February 1953, when he became Ambassador.

The Chinese Nationalist government had moved its capital to Formosa in late 1949, after the defeat of Chiang Kai-shek's army by the Chinese Reds. While Great Britain and some other countries transferred diplomatic recognition to the Communist People's Republic, the United States continued to recognize the Nationalist regime as the *de jure* government of China. American military and economic aid to Formosa was estimated in early 1953 to be $300,000,000 a year.

While still minister in Formosa, on May 11, 1952, Rankin revealed his confidence in Formosa's future, which he based on accomplishments of the Nationalist government and the people in agriculture, industry and defense. On April 3, 1953, Ambassador Rankin told a news conference that armistice in Korea would not be followed by a betrayal of Nationalist China and that there could be no breaking of faith by the United States Government.

A mutual defense treaty with the Chiang Kai-shek government was ratified by the U.S. Senate on February 9, 1955, by a vote of 64 to 6, and a resolution was adopted by Congress on February 8 granting authority to President Eisenhower to take action in emergencies and if military necessity requires such action to protect Formosa and the Pescadores from Communist attack. The offshore islands remain outside the scope of the treaty, and it will be one of Ambassador Rankin's tasks "to work toward a solution which shall meet the realities, strategic and political, in the Formosa region" (New York *Herald Tribune,* February 14, 1955).

Ambassador Rankin has made numerous contributions to government publications. He is an associate member of the American Society of Civil Engineers and a member of the Cosmos Club in Washington, D.C. He also belongs to Phi Kappa Sigma (Cornell) and Dial Lodge (Princeton).

The Ambassador and his wife, Pauline Jordan Rankin, whom he married on October 3, 1925, live in a charming, unpretentious Japanese house on Grass Mountain, a few miles outside of Taipei, and not far from Generalissimo Chiang Kai-shek's residence. He has gray eyes and graying brown hair, is five feet eleven inches tall and weighs 190 pounds. He is a Congregationalist. Hunting and reading are his favorite recreations.

References

Christian Sci Mon p9 Ap 9 '53
Portland (Maine) Telegram p 1+ Mr 8 '53
Congressional Record p1545+ F 27 '53
International Year Book and Statesmen's Who's Who, 1954
Who's Who in America, 1954-55
World Biography (1954)

RESHEVSKY, SAMUEL Nov. 26, 1911-
Grand Master of Chess

Address: b. c/o Manhattan Chess Club, 100 Central Park S., New York 19; h. 20 Funston Ave., Spring Valley, N.Y.

Since Samuel Reshevsky was eight years old, master chess players have been predicting that some day he would become the chess champion of the world. So far he has not reached that goal, but in advancing resolutely in that direction he has six times, beginning in 1936, captured the chess championship of the United States and "is generally conceded to be the best chess player in the free world" (New York *World-Telegram and Sun,* June 26, 1954.)

Early in 1954 arrangements were made by the U.S. Chess Federation to bring a team of eight Soviet chess players to the United States for a match, and the State Department gave assurances that the restrictions proposed in 1953 would not be repeated. For the match, which began on June 16 and ended on June 24, Reshevsky held down the No. 1 board. The Russians won the tournament (20-12), which was played at the Hotel Roosevelt in New York City and which attracted more than 1,000 spectators at each session. Reshevsky tied with Vassily Smyslov. Reshevsky won the Lessing J. Rosenwald trophy tournament at the Marshall Chess Club on December 31, 1954 and headed the team which was sent to Moscow in May 1955 for a return series of matches with the Russians. The American team lost (25-7) but Reshevsky won from the Russian Grand Master, Mikhail Botvinnik by 2½ to 1½ games.

Wide World
SAMUEL RESHEVSKY

In 1950 Reshevsky went on a coast-to-coast tour of some thirty United States and Canadian cities, taking on all comers in simultaneous play for $2 a head. This tour proved so successful financially that he was able to quit his accountant's job and has become the first full-time professional chess player in the United States.

Samuel Reshevsky was born November 26, 1911 in the Polish town of Ozorków, and when he was five years old learned the moves of the chess pieces from his father. At six he appeared in his first public competition in Vienna, Austria, and after that went on an exhibition tour performing remarkable feats of simultaneous play against the chess masters of Berlin, London, Paris and other major cities.

In October 1920, his parents brought him to the United States and within a week he had proved his ability by defeating nineteen of West Point's best chess players in simultaneous play. The nine-year-old boy created a sensation in exhibition matches in New York, Philadelphia, Chicago, St. Louis, Los Angeles and San Francisco.

His family moved to Detroit in 1922 where Samuel attended high school and pitched on the school baseball team. With the financial help of the philanthropist Julius Rosenwald, he studied at the University of Chicago. His record was good in mathematics, but was otherwise average. After his graduation he returned to New York, took a job as an accountant and settled down to devote all his spare time to chess.

During his school days Reshevsky had appeared occasionally in tournaments, finishing fifth in the western tournament at Detroit in 1924 and in a triple tie for third in the national tournament of 1927. In 1931 he won both the championships of the National Chess

RESHEVSKY, SAMUEL—*Continued*

Congress and of the Western Chess Federation. In August 1934 he won first prize in the international tournament of the New York Chess Association at Syracuse, New York.

He entered the international chess arena in April 1935 at the eastern congress of the Kent County Chess Association in Margate, England, where he defeated the former world champion, José R. Capablanca of Havana, and won the tournament without losing a game. In July he won first prize in the open tournament of the British Chess Federation at Great Yarmouth, England. Returning to the United States, he triumphed over fifteen rivals in the spring of 1936 to win the U.S. chess championship which had been held since 1909 by Frank Marshall.

In the ensuing two years he played in tournaments in England, Latvia and Sweden and led the U.S. chess team in a successful defense of the Hamilton-Russell trophy. In the spring of 1938 he defended his United States championship, and in the fall returned to Europe for an international chess masters tournament at Amsterdam in which he ended in a fourth-place tie. From there, in early 1939, he went to the Soviet Union for a similar tournament in which he placed second.

During World War II international chess was dormant. Reshevsky successfully defended his U.S. title first in tournament play in 1940 and in a match with Israel A. Horowitz in 1941. In the 1942 tournament, however, he ended in a tie with Isaac I. Kashdan. In the match playoff that followed, Reshevsky lost for the first time in seventy-four games for the U.S. championship, but retained the title. He did not take part in the 1944 tournament for the U.S. championship, and his title passed to Arnold S. Denker. However, he played for, and won, the open championship of the U.S. Chess Federation.

International play resumed with the end of the war in 1945, and in August of that year Reshevsky won first place in a Pan American Chess Masters tournament held in Hollywood, California. Later the same month he held down the second board for the United States in a radio match with the Soviet Union. Reshevsky lost both his games to Vassily Smyslov, and the American team was defeated.

The U.S. team immediately challenged for a return match. When this was held in Moscow in September 1946, Reshevsky played the first board, opposite Mikhail Botvinnik. He drew one game, lost the other, and the Americans again lost the match. As soon as he returned home Reshevsky entered the tournament for the U.S. chess championship and regained his title. A year later, in the fall of 1947, he captained the U.S. team that went down to unexpected defeat in a match with Argentina.

Early in 1948 Reshevsky faced his first chance to win the world chess championship. The world titleholder, Dr. Alexander A. Alekhine, had died in Lisbon early in 1946, and a world tourney to decide his successor was arranged. Opposing Reshevsky in the tournament, held partly in Amsterdam and partly in Moscow, were Dr. Max Euwe of Amsterdam, and Mikhail Botvinnik, Vassily Smyslov, and Paul Keres of the Soviet Union. The tournament was won by Botvinnik. Reshevsky tied with Keres for third place.

Reshevsky announced his temporary retirement from active play, and did not contend for the U.S. title in the tournament in the fall of 1948 nor for the international tournament in Budapest in 1950. However, in February 1950 he played the first board in a radio match between U.S. and Yugoslav teams, which was won by the Yugoslavs. In August he went to Dubrovnik, Yugoslavia with the U.S. team to play for the Hamilton-Russell trophy in the first postwar chess Olympics. The United States ended up fourth.

Entering the international masters tournament at Amsterdam, Holland in November 1950, Reshevsky ended second to Miguel Najdorf, a former Polish player who had moved to Buenos Aires. In June 1951, in an international tournament held in New York, their positions were reversed.

He competed in 1951 for the U.S. championship but lost to Larry Evans. In February 1952 he competed in an international tourney in Havana, Cuba, where he ended in a tie with Najdorf. A match was then arranged between the two for the unofficial title of "chess champion of the non-communist world," and Reshevsky won by a score of 11 to 7.

Another victory in match play was won by Reshevsky in June 1952 against the Yugoslav star Svetozar Gligoric. Two months later he flew to Helsinki to head the U.S. team in competition for the Hamilton-Russell trophy. The Russian team won the cup, the U.S. team ending in fifth place although it tied its match with the Soviet players.

During the meeting in Helsinki the Russians were sounded out about a return match with the U.S. team in New York. This was accepted and Reshevsky was named to head the American team, but the Russians turned back after reaching Paris, objecting to the travel restrictions which the U.S State Department proposed to impose upon them in this country.

Another chance at the world championship came to Reshevsky in September 1953, at the challengers' tournament in Switzerland. But he ended in a triple tie for second place with David Bronstein and Paul Keres of the Soviet Union. Vassily Smyslov, who won the tournament but lost his challenge match with Botvinnik, said that Reshevsky was "the greatest player of the west—a tough little man full of brilliant ideas" (*Time*, November 2, 1953).

At the chess board, Reshevsky plays with a "glacial calm and lethal poise." "He acts as though he can save any game no matter how hopeless the position," an opponent has said.

Reshevsky was married in 1941 to Norma Mindick of Roxbury, Massachusetts. They have two children, a daughter, Sylvia, and a son, Joel. He is five feet two inches in height, and has dark balding hair. He is an orthodox Jew. He reads a good deal, relaxes with ice skating, bridge and table tennis, spends hours listening to classical music, and avidly follows baseball and basketball. He likes to sing duets with his wife. He is co-author, with Fred Reinfeld, of *Learn Chess Fast!* (McKay, 1947) and author of *On Chess; the U.S. Champion Tells How He Wins* (McKay, 1948).

In his article "Chess Is Another Soviet Gambit" in the New York *Times Magazine*, June 13, 1954, Reshevsky advanced his reasons why the Russian chess players have won all the international competitions since the end of World War II. "The Russian players do not have any more of the natural qualifications than the American players," he wrote, "but the Soviet regime, by giving its chess players professional status, by providing the climate in which chess players get paid well and enjoy social prestige, also makes it possible for them to devote all their time to study and play. But the motives behind the Russian system would not be acceptable to the American chess player. We play it as a challenging, exciting, frequently beautiful game and not, as the Russians would have it, as a diplomatic game . . . as standard bearers of Soviet culture."

References

N Y World Telegram Mag p7 Ag 1 '53 por
Time 60:47 O 20 '52 por

REYNOLDS, R(ICHARD) S(AMUEL), SR., Aug. 15, 1881-July 29, 1955 Business executive; chairman of the board of the Reynolds Metal Company since 1948; founded the metal foil business in 1918 in Louisville, Kentucky for use as wrappers for candy, cigarettes, chewing gum; expanded his manufacturing interests to develop aluminum-bauxite, and as president of Reynolds (1928-1948) aided the U.S. World War II effort by producing foil-lined wrappers for ammunition and aluminum for weapons; was known as the "poet-industrialist"; author of two volumes of poetry. See *Current Biography* (Feb.) 1953.

Obituary

N Y Times p17 Jl 30 '55

RIBICOFF, ABRAHAM A. Apr. 9, 1910- Governor of Connecticut; lawyer

Address: b. State Capitol, Hartford, Conn., c/o Ribicoff & Ribicoff, 50 State St., Hartford, Conn., h. Executive Residence, West Hartford, Conn., 59 Bloomfield Ave., Hartford, Conn.

"Divided elections contain a mandate to cooperate," declared Governor Abraham A. Ribicoff of Connecticut in his inaugural message to a joint session of the General Assembly on January 5, 1955, "to search for areas of common agreement, to share credit—in short, to understand and practice what I should like to call the integrity of compromise." Generally regarded as a "middle-of-the-road" Democrat, Ribicoff defeated the Republican incumbent, John Davis Lodge, in the election on November 2, 1954 by a narrow margin.

A lawyer by profession, Governor Ribicoff was a Hartford police court judge and a member of the Connecticut legislature before going to Washington, D.C. in 1949. He served two terms as member for the First Connecticut District in the U.S. House of Representatives in which he did important work upon the Foreign Affairs Committee.

Wide World

ABRAHAM A. RIBICOFF

Born in a tenement on Star Street in New Britain, Connecticut on April 9, 1910, Abraham A. Ribicoff came of Polish-Jewish stock; his immigrant parents were Samuel and Rose (Sable) Ribicoff. "My father was a factory worker and we were really poor," Ribicoff told T. E. Murphy who interviewed him for the *Saturday Evening Post* (June 21, 1952). "But everything I earned peddling papers and working in stores, he made me put aside for education."

Many of his New Britain neighbors recall "Abe" (who began his education in the Smalley Elementary School), who ran errands and was an eager sandlot baseball player. During one vacation from the New Britain High School, where he played tackle on the football team, he worked with a road construction gang. For one year after graduation from high school, "Abe" worked in the slide-fastener factory of the G. E. Prentice Company at New Britain in order to meet future expenses at New York University, where he enrolled in 1928.

In 1929, when he was only nineteen, he accepted an offer from the Prentice Company of $70 a week to take charge of its Chicago office. He moved to Chicago and attended late afternoon classes at the University of Chicago. He was permitted to enter the Law School, despite the lack of a baccalaureate degree. Elected to the staff of the *University of Chicago Law Review,* Ribicoff became editor in his third and final year at the law school. He received the LL.B. degree *cum laude* in 1933, and was elected to the Order of the Coif.

(Continued next page)

RIBICOFF, ABRAHAM A.—*Continued*

Ribicoff's impressive record in law school and his paper published in the *University of Chicago Law Review* (May 1933) on the jurisdiction of the Supreme Court in hearing appeals from state courts in certain categories, was noted by executives in Federal departments. He was offered a $3,800-a-year position with the Treasury Department, but preferred to return to Connecticut, where he was admitted to the state bar and went to work in the office of a Hartford lawyer.

When offered a $4,800-a-year position with the Tennessee Valley Authority he declined it, telling himself that he was a "small-town lawyer" at heart. Shortly afterward he set up a practice in Kensington, Connecticut and later in Hartford. In November 1938, he was elected as a Democrat to the first of two terms in the lower house of his state's General Assembly. In a poll of political reporters he was voted the legislature's "most promising freshman" and in his second term was called the "most able representative."

He became a member in 1941 of the American Arbitration Association's Motion Picture Panel, and was appointed in the same year as judge of the Hartford Police Court. He was chairman of the Connecticut Assembly of Municipal Court Judges in 1941-1942, and in 1943 served as chairman of a special state committee for the study of alcoholism and crime. He was reappointed to the Hartford bench by Republican Governor Raymond Baldwin.

Ribicoff was a member (1945-1947) of the bi-partisan Hartford Charter Revision Commission, whose recommendations brought the city-council and city-manager type of municipal government to the Connecticut capital. In 1947-1948 Ribicoff served as the hearing examiner authorized under the Connecticut Fair Employment Practices Act.

In November 1948 he defeated U.S. Representative William J. Miller, the Republican incumbent for the First Connecticut District, by about 25,000 votes, and the Democratic turnout he attracted in Hartford county was widely said to have swept the Democratic candidate for Governor, Chester Bowles, to victory.

On most major domestic issues in the Eighty-first Congress, he concurred with the Truman Administration. Measures he supported in the 1949 session included the housing bill (June) and the Brannan farm plan (July), and in July 1950 he recorded a "nay" on the Lodge-Gossett amendment. On the other hand, he favored a reduction in Federal spending (May) and passage of the Communist control bill over President Truman's veto (September).

When representatives of the Connecticut valley shade tobacco-growing interests called on him to sponsor an amendment to the Farm bill putting shade tobacco under the parity program, Ribicoff agreed to introduce the bill, but made it clear that he would not support it. During the 1950 session of the Eighty-first Congress he surprised old-line politicians by opposing the appropriation of $32,000,000 in Federal funds for the construction of a dam at Enfield on the Connecticut River. "We have fixed charges which must be met before we can even begin to discuss appropriations for such projects," he explained to his constituents. "The security of our nation, as represented in military and foreign aid commitments, is now primary."

During his two terms in Washington, Ribicoff was assigned only to the House Foreign Affairs Committee, to which senior and experienced legislators are ordinarily appointed. He represented the Administration in foreign policy debates on television and radio. In March 1949 Ribicoff sponsored and saw adopted by the Foreign Affairs Committee an amendment to the bill appropriating $5,580,000,000 for the second year of the Marshall Plan which would earmark $300,000,000 for guaranteeing American investors abroad against "loss through seizure, confiscation or destruction by riot, revolution or war."

In the autumn of 1949 Ribicoff went to Europe with Representative Thurmond Chatham of North Carolina to survey conditions for the Foreign Affairs Committee, and on his return characterized as "dangerous" the wishful thinking that we could soon withdraw from our world responsibilities and reduce taxes. "It looks to me more like a task of ten more years calling for an additional outlay of $25 billion . . ." he said. "We must look upon the cost of keeping Europe free as a cost of keeping ourselves in business."

In the November 1950 election which made Republican John Davis Lodge Governor of Connecticut, Ribicoff was returned to his First District seat at Washington with a majority increased to about 38,000. Re-assigned to the Foreign Affairs Committee in the Eighty-second Congress, Ribicoff was one in a bi-partisan group of eight members of the House of Representatives sponsored in January 1951 a bill favoring a Pacific pact. With Representative Jacob K. Javits of New York he sponsored "a resolution favoring a Far Eastern recovery program implemented by an organization for Far Eastern economic cooperation" (New York *Herald Tribune,* January 30, 1951).

With the late Senator Brien McMahon he authored and introduced to the House a resolution affirming that the "American people deeply regret the artificial barriers which separate them from the peoples of the Union of Soviet Socialist Republics" and calling on the Soviet people "to cooperate in a spirit of friendship." After adoption by the Senate, the resolution passed the House on June 26 by a roll call vote of 349 to 6, and on July 7 was transmitted to President N. M. Shvernik of the Soviet Union Presidium by letter from President Truman.

Named an "additional delegate" to the signing of the peace treaty with Japan at San Francisco in September 1951, Ribicoff was empowered "to act as an alternate" for Representative "Mike" Mansfield of Montana, who could not attend. Ribicoff's group was instructed to work on the United States-Australia-New Zealand mutual defense pact and the Philippine Security Treaty.

Ribicoff ran against Republican Prescott S. Bush as candidate to fill out the remaining four years of the Senatorial term of Brien McMahon, who died on July 28, 1952. In the campaign, Ribicoff stressed international relations and the conditions of "national survival" in speeches which Don Ross of the New York *Herald Tribune* characterized as containing "a minimum of . . . folksiness and promises" and as sounding "more like university lectures." He lost to Bush in November by less than 30,000 votes out of over 1,000,000 cast.

Resuming his partnership with Irving S. Ribicoff in the Hartford law firm of Ribicoff & Ribicoff, he handled corporation, real estate, labor and probate cases. On June 25, 1954 Ribicoff was nominated "by acclamation" at the Democratic State Convention to run against Governor Lodge, who was seeking reelection in November.

Pledging a campaign that would be "positive, constructive and free from personalities," Ribicoff said: "If we cannot win decently, I do not want to win at all." Governor Lodge also preferred the "statesmanlike level," with the result that the "Connecticut campaign, while hard fought, was among the cleanest in the nation" (New York *Herald Tribune,* November 5, 1954).

"There are some [men in politics] who are retailers for votes and others who are wholesalers," said Ribicoff: "The retailers . . . get votes, one by one, individually, by favors given or patronage distributed. I am a wholesaler. I go after whole blocks of votes—by the thousands, by following principles I believe in and know other people not in politics also believe in" (*Saturday Evening Post,* June 21, 1952).

Local issues stressed by Ribicoff included the need to abolish county government, to provide better highways, schools and institutions for mental patients, and to establish a state department of commerce. In the final week of the campaign, during an address to an Italian-American audience, he told his listeners that "nowhere except in the Democratic party could a boy named Abe Ribicoff be nominated for governor of this state" and that the "American dream" would be fulfilled by his election.

The November balloting brought defeat to Lodge by the narrow margin of 3,115 votes. He was the only Democrat elected on the state administrative ticket. The Republicans also control the House of Representatives in the new General Assembly by 186 to 93. The composition of the Connecticut Senate in the 1955 session is twenty-six Democrats and sixteen Republicans.

Governor Ribicoff is a member of the American and Hartford County bar associations. He married Ruth Siegel on June 28, 1931 and they have two children, Peter and Jane. He is five feet eleven inches in height and 180 pounds in weight, and has black hair and dark eyes. He keeps in shape by taking long walks. In an article in the Hartford *Courant,* Keith Schonrock has commented on his "keen sense of humor."

References

Hartford (Conn.) Courant O 20 '54 por; p 1+ N 4 '54
N Y Times p59 S 7 '52 por; p34 Je 27 '54; p 1+ N 3 '54 por
N Y World Telegram p23 N 3 '54 por; p6 N 4 '54; Mag p6+ N 20 '54 pors
Newsweek 44:28 S 15 '52 por
Sat Eve Post 224:30+ Je 21 '52 por
Time 64:27 N 15 '54 por
Washington (D.C.) Post p5B F 26 '50
Congressional Directory (1952)
Martindale-Hubbell Law Directory, 1952
Who's Who in America, 1954-55

RICH, DANIEL CATTON Apr. 16, 1904-
Art museum director

Address: b. Art Institute of Chicago, Chicago 3, Ill.; h. 1620 Tower Rd., Winnetka, Ill.

A leading defender of contemporary art, Daniel Catton Rich, director of the Art Institute of Chicago, has introduced exhibitions of abstract and surrealist art to Chicago which have attracted national attention. One such exhibit, denounced by most Chicago critics, provoked the remark by President Harry S. Truman that "modern art is merely the vaporings of half-baked, lazy people" (New York *Herald Tribune,* March 28, 1948). In numerous articles and several books Rich has interpreted modern art, pointing out that "far from being a minority movement largely in the hands of foreign-born artists, today hundreds of painters in all parts of the nation have adopted abstract techniques, and three out of four of them are native-born Americans" (New York *Herald Tribune,* March 28, 1948).

He joined the Art Institute in 1927 as editor of its bulletin, became curator of painting and sculpture in 1938, and since 1945 has been its director. The Institute, which was established in 1879, has an average annual attendance of about 1,250,000. It maintains an extensive library and the School of the Art Institute of Chicago and the School of Drama.

Under Rich's supervision will be the organization of the American exhibit for the Venice (Italy) Biennale Exhibition of International Art in 1956. He has been appointed the Commissioner for the United States and will act as a member of the international jury to award the prizes underwritten by the Italian government.

Daniel Catton Rich was born in South Bend, Indiana, on April 16, 1904, the son of Daniel Rich and Martha (Catton) Rich. He attended the University of Chicago, where he majored in English, graduating in 1926 as a Bachelor of Philosophy. For one year, 1926-27, he was a student at Harvard, continuing the study of English while attending the fine arts museum course at Fogg Museum. When thus working toward a master's degree in fine arts, Rich was offered a job at the Art Institute of Chicago as editor of the *Bulletin,* and he accepted in

Wide World

DANIEL CATTON RICH

1927. He has never done painting or sculpture of his own, and has never aspired to be an artist.

Rich remained editor of the *Bulletin* from 1927 to 1939. He was assistant curator of painting and sculpture from 1929 to 1931, associate curator from 1931 to 1938, and curator from 1938; between 1938 and 1945 he also carried the title of director of fine arts. Since 1945 he has been director of the Art Institute.

When Rich was in the post of associate curator in 1936, the famous Chicago episode of the Logan Prize took place. The judges awarded the prize of $500 for the painting *Thanksgiving Dinner* by Doris Lee (see *C.B.*, 1954) and while this painting of a scene in a kitchen is not now regarded as extreme modern technique, it was denounced by Mrs. Frank G. Logan (the donor of the award and a patron of the Art Institute of Chicago) as "insane" modern art. Mrs. Logan founded a group called Sanity in Art Movement to fight against this contemporary tendency, but Rich and the Institute trustees stood firm and the controversy helped to establish Doris Lee's reputation as a painter.

In 1947, after Rich assumed the directorship, the Institute's American Show (one of the largest of its kind in the country) created a sensation with a display of abstract and surrealist art. Members of Rich's staff, sent on a 24,000 mile trip around the United States, had returned with the conviction that abstractionism is "the prevailing mode for most artists under thirty" (*Time,* November 17, 1947). Rich said the attendance at the exhibition was higher than any other in recent years, with a heavy turn-out of younger art enthusiasts despite the Chicago critics' protests. "There can be no doubt," he said, "that a very substantial number of American painters and sculptors have departed from the broadly realistic tradition of our art and have commenced to develop more personal forms of painting" (New York *Herald Tribune,* March 28, 1948).

Rich has made many trips to Europe and its art centers. In 1943 he was sent to South America by the committee on Inter-American Artistic and Intellectual Relations. He is convinced that "nationalist labels mean less and less to art. There is certainly not enough 'American' character in what is being produced to identify it as national." (*Magazine of Art,* March 1949).

In Rich's article, "Romanticism in Chicago" (*Atlantic Monthly,* April 1951), he wrote: "Wealthy Chicagoans travel New Yorkward and in the leisure and stimulation of a large art market pick up what pleases them. Now and again they come back from Manhattan with a painting by some Chicago artist—an experience which always amazes everyone. . . . There are many excellent artists in the city, and during the hectic, developing days of the WPA Art Project, Chicago's painting and printmaking were perhaps the most vital in the country." However, he wrote, "when government subsidy stopped, private patronage made no attempt to fill the void, and many of the most gifted [artists] left for the East or West Coast."

In June 1955 the Institute was involved in a controversy over the use of funds donated by an art-loving Chicago lumber merchant, Benjamin F. Ferguson, for "the erection and maintenance of enduring statuary and monuments." The Institute decided in 1955 to use the money to finance a new Art Institute office building. The Artists Equity protested this and brought the case to court. However, the court upheld a previous ruling that "monuments" could be interpreted to mean "buildings." Rich commented: "We want to build a building . . . which will be in memory of Benjamin Ferguson."

The American exhibit for 1956 in the Venice (Italy) Biennale Exhibition of International Art, regarded as the most important exhibition of contemporary art in Europe, if not in the world, will be organized by the Art Institute of Chicago. The Museum of Modern Art, which owns the United States pavilion in Venice, prepared the American exhibit in 1954, but decided to ask other leading art institutions to assist in organizing future shows. The first invitation has been made to the Art Institute, as "an outstanding museum from another part of the country."

Rich is the author of articles on art, past and present, and of short books or booklets, often extended catalogue introductions. Among his books are: *Seurat and the Evolution of La Grande Jatte* (University of Chicago Press, 1935), *Henri Rousseau* (Museum of Modern Art, 1942) and *Edgar Hilaire Germaine Degas* (Abrams, 1951). Some of his poetry has appeared in *Poetry* (Chicago), of which he has been president since 1952. He has frequently been a member of art juries across the nation, and was co-founder of Film-Art, Inc. in Chicago. He served as a member of the patrons committee of the Federal Art Project of Illinois and as the Illinois chairman of the selection committee for the exhibition of American Art at the New York World's Fair in 1939. He is now a member of the advisory committee on art of the Department of State, a member of the board of trustees of the Chicago Educational TV Council and a trustee of Marlboro College, Vermont.

Among his many clubs are the Cliff Dwellers (of which he is the director), Arts, The Wayfarers, Art Directors (honorary life), Chicago and the Tavern. The recipient of many honors, Rich is a Chevalier of the Légion d'Honneur, an Officer of the Order of Orange of Nassau and a member of Phi Beta Kappa. He is a member of La Société des Rosettes et Rubans de France and the International Council of Museums, Paris. In politics he is a Democrat.

Rich married a poet, Bertha Ten Eyck James, on September 23, 1927. They have four children, Michael James, Stephen Ten Eyck, Penelope, and Anthony Catton. Rich and his family moved in May 1955, into a new modern home in the Chicago suburb of Winnetka. His hobby is gardening.

References

Who's Who in America, 1954-55
Who's Who in Art (1954)
Who's Who in the Midwest (1954)

RICHARDS, JOHN S(TEWART) Feb. 16, 1892- Librarian; library association official
Address: b. c/o American Library Association, 50 E. Huron St., Chicago 11, Ill.; Seattle Public Library, Seattle 4, Wash.; h. 6841 49th Ave., N.E., Seattle 15, Wash.

Forde

JOHN S. RICHARDS

A mail ballot in June 1954 among more than 20,000 members of the American Library Association in the United States, Canada, Alaska, and Hawaii brought John S. Richards election as first vice-president and president-elect for a year's term. Richards, who became president automatically at A.L.A.'s July 1955 convention in Philadelphia, Pennsylvania, succeeded L. Quincy Mumford, Librarian of Congress.

As director of the Seattle (Washington) Public Library since 1942, Richards has been especially interested in public libraries' work in presenting informal adult educational programs. He has for some years recognized the educational possibilities of television and is a member of the advisory board of Seattle's educational TV station KCTS, operated under the sponsorship of King county educational institutions and the public library.

John Stewart Richards, the elder of two sons of Milton Nash and Minnie Cunningham (Stewart) Richards, was born in Chicago, Illinois on February 16, 1892. He is of Scotch-Irish and Welsh descent. His father was a farmer who pioneered in the Yakima Valley, Washington under the first irrigation project in 1896.

Through early use of a small Carnegie library serving the Yakima Valley, Richards became interested in the library profession, and after graduating from Yakima High School in 1911 he studied at the University of Washington School of Librarianship in Seattle. He received the B.A. degree in 1916 and began his career as librarian of the public library in Marshfield, a small community in southwest Oregon.

Two years later he became librarian at Camp Fremont, California for the American Library Association War Service. In 1918-1919 he served also as agent of the A.L.A. dispatch office and library organizer for camp libraries, at San Francisco, in charge of overseas shipments to Siberia. After a year (1919-1920) of study at the New York State Library School in Albany, he accepted the post of librarian at Idaho Technical Institute in Pocatello. He worked there until 1923 when he was appointed librarian at the Washington State Normal School in Ellenburg.

Moving to Berkeley in 1926, he served as superintendent of circulation at the University of California Library until 1929 and as assistant librarian from 1929 to 1934. Meanwhile, in 1932, the university's School of Librarianship awarded him the M.A. degree. He was executive assistant at the University of Washington Library from 1934 to 1941, associate librarian in 1941-1942, and lecturer in the School of Librarianship from 1938 to 1942.

The Seattle Public Library, of which Richards was made librarian in June 1942 upon the retirement of Judson T. Jennings, currently owns some 867,221 volumes and has a yearly circulation of about 3,000,000 volumes. In 1954 almost a quarter of a million people borrowed books. In his article "After Thirty-three Years" (*Library Journal,* May 1, 1954), Richards described three new branches of the library, which was founded in 1891 and which had constructed no new buildings since 1921. Its main building and seven of its eight city-owned branches had been constructed with Carnegie funds. In a 1950 election the library lost a bond issue for new buildings, as Richards has

RICHARDS, JOHN S.—*Continued*

related in "On Losing a Bond Issue" (*Library Journal,* February 15, 1951); but in 1953 the city appropriated funds to begin the long-retarded expansion program.

Active in adult education circles in Seattle, Richards is particularly interested in discussion technique. The Seattle Public Library is currently sponsoring four different types of discussion programs, one of which uses television for half-hour weekly discussions of new books.

Since joining the American Library Association in 1920, Richards has held many varied positions in the organization, including membership on the subcommittee of the board on personnel administration on budgets, compensation and schemes of service for libraries connected with universities, colleges, and teacher training institutions (1939-1943), and chairmanship of the committee on public library-public school relationships and committee on annuities, pensions and life insurance (1946-1947).

He was a member of the A.L.A. council from 1941 to 1945 and a member of the executive board from 1945 to 1949. Before he became president of the A.L.A. public libraries division for 1949-1950, Richards had been chairman of the division's committee on constitution, by-laws and organization (1947) and the planning committee (1948-1949).

Richard's election as first vice-president and president-elect was announced at A.L.A.'s annual conference, in Minneapolis, Minnesota, in June 1954. The theme of the conference, "Knowledge—A Free People's Surest Strength," was in keeping with A.L.A.'s practice in recent years of reaffirming the principle of the freedom to read. It has opposed banning books from public libraries for political reasons and has objected to the removal of certain books from the U.S. Information Service libraries overseas.

In 1954 and 1955 A.L.A. supported a library service bill, introduced in Congress both years, calling for appropriation of $7,500,000 a year to bring library facilities to rural communities. During 1955 A.L.A. cooperated with the U.S. Department of State in sponsoring a five-month tour of the United States by librarians from eleven countries, including Ceylon, Greece, Finland, Guatemala, and Argentina.

When Richards assumes the presidency in July 1955 at A.L.A.'s seventy-fourth convention, in Philadelphia, he will be the third librarian from the Northwest to hold that position. Ernest C. Richardson of Portland, Oregon was president in 1904-1905, and Richards' predecessor in the Seattle Public Library, Jennings, was president in 1923-1924.

Other professional organizations in which Richards has been active are the California Library Association (president of the first district in 1932-1933), the Pacific Northwest Library Association (vice-president, 1935-1936; president, 1937-1938), and the Washington Library Association.

Since 1948 Richards has been a member of the board of directors of the Great Books Foundation and had an important part in bringing the program into the Pacific Northwest. He edited and wrote an introduction to *Joaquin Miller: His California Diary Beginning in 1855 and Ending in 1857* (Dogwood Press, 1936). In collaboration with John A. Lowe, he wrote: "Report of a Survey of the Vancouver (British Columbia) Public Library to the Board of the Vancouver Public Library" (1949), on behalf of the A.L.A.

Among the many articles that he has contributed to professional journals are "Dilemma of the University Library" (*School and Society,* December 3, 1938), "In-service Training at Work" (*Wilson Library Bulletin,* April 1940), "National Plan for Public Library Service" (*American Library Association Bulletin,* September 1, 1947). He has also written a number of reviews of books on library science.

Richards is active in the Health and Welfare Council of Seattle and King county, and was chairman in 1953-1954 of the city government section of the United Good Neighbor fund. His clubs are the Seattle College, Municipal League, and Rotary. He attends the Congregational Church.

He married Irene Fry on April 14, 1919 and has two children, Robert Milton and Lynn Stewart. The librarian weighs 160 pounds, stands five feet ten inches tall, and has dark-brown eyes and dark-brown graying hair. In his leisure hours he travels, reads, attends the theatre, and listens to music.

References

A.L.A. Bul 48:404 Jl '54 por
Library News Bul 21:1 Ja-F '54; 21:45 My-Je '54 por
Who's Who in America, 1954-55
Who's Who in Library Service (1943) (1955)
Who's Who in the West (1954)

RIESMAN, DAVID, (JR.) Sept. 22, 1909- University professor; social scientist; author

Address: b. c/o University of Chicago, Chicago 37, Ill.; h. 5621 University Ave., Chicago 37, Ill.

Author of *The Lonely Crowd; A Study of the Changing American Character,* David Riesman claims to be no mantled prophet with the last word or the definitive system of social behavior. He has brought to his work in the social sciences his experiences in the worlds of business and law, and in his teaching and writing he endeavors to help the individual attain his independence in contemporary society. He has been a professor at the University of Chicago since 1946, and in 1953 headed its Kansas City Study of Middle-Age and Aging of the Committee on Human Development.

In recognition of his studies in sociology, Dr. Riesman was one of fifteen writers, artists and composers to be awarded grants of $1,000 each on May 26, 1954 by the American Academy and National Institute of Arts and Letters. A paper-back edition of *The Lonely Crowd,* published by Anchor Books (Doubleday, 1953), has sold more than 70,000 copies. Riesman is "a man with a wide-swinging imagination," commented *Time* (September, 1954), "a scientist's disciplined mind and a burning curiosity about people as they are."

David Riesman, Jr., was born in Philadelphia on September 22, 1909 to Dr. David and Eleanor L. (Fleisher) Riesman. His father had come to the United States from Germany and after obtaining an M.D. degree at the medical school of the University of Pennsylvania in 1892 practiced medicine and was a professor at his alma mater. Young Riesman attended the William Penn Charter School in Philadelphia. After his graduation in 1926 he enrolled at Harvard University, majoring in the biochemical sciences and receiving his A.B. degree in 1931. He was awarded a John Harvard scholarship and was elected to Phi Beta Kappa. He also served as assistant managing editor of the *Harvard Crimson.*

After studying for three years at Harvard Law School, where he served as editor of the *Harvard Law Review,* Riesman received an LL.B. degree in 1934 and a fellowship for the following year. At Harvard, Professor Carl J. Friedrich and Felix Frankfurter, then a professor of the Law School, encouraged Riesman to follow an academic career.

Riesman was admitted to the Massachusetts and District of Columbia bars in 1935 and the New York bar in 1939. In 1935 and 1936 he served as a clerk to Associate Justice Louis Brandeis of the U.S. Supreme Court. Later he practiced law in Boston. From 1937 to 1941 he was a professor of law at the University of Buffalo. During this period he was also executive secretary of the American Committee for the Guidance of Professional Personnel, an organization which helped refugees in the professions on arrival in the United States. In 1941 Riesman was granted a visiting research fellowship at the Columbia University Law School, where he wrote "Civil Liberties in a Period of Transition" and "Democracy and Defamation." Riesman's work *The American Constitution and International Labour Legislation* (1941) was published by the International Labour Review.

In 1942 and 1943 Riesman served as deputy assistant district attorney of New York county. For the next three years he was assistant to the treasurer and war contract termination director of the Sperry Gyroscope Company on Long Island, New York. In 1946 Riesman became a visiting associate professor of social sciences at the University of Chicago, and the following year joined the university's faculty as a professor of social sciences.

Professor Riesman was granted leave from the university to direct a research project on mass communications for the Yale University Committee on National Policy during 1948. This project resulted in the publication in 1950 of *The Lonely Crowd; A Study of the Changing American Character.* Collaborating with Riesman in this work were Reuel Denney and Nathan Glazer. A subsequent volume was *Faces in the Crowd; Individual Studies in Character and Politics* (1952) written by Riesman and Glazer. In 1953 Riesman, again on leave from Chicago, was visiting professor at the University of Kansas City in Missouri, and co-director of the Kansas City Study of Middle-Age and Aging, a project of the University of Chicago Committee on Human Development.

Robert McCullough

DAVID RIESMAN

Seeking a relationship between socio-economic eras and character modes in *The Lonely Crowd,* Riesman identifies the three fundamental periods as those with a high population growth potential (for example, the Middle Ages or areas of the contemporary world untouched by industrialization), those of transitional population growth (as the Renaissance-Reformation period), and those in which an incipient decline appears (the highly industrialized areas of the present).

A typical social type is then related to each of these socio-economic eras. The first of these periods produces a character which is "tradition-directed" because the conformity of the individual "tends to be dictated to a very large degree by power relations among the various age and sex groups, the clans, castes, professions . . . relations which have endured for centuries and are modified but slightly, if at all, by successive generations." In the second of these periods Riesman calls the typical individual "inner-directed." His source of direction "is implanted early in life by the elders and directed toward generalized but nonetheless inescapable destined goals"; that is, "inner-direction" is the principal mode of securing conformity. Riesman utilizes the analogy of the gyroscope to suggest the psychological mechanism of such individuals; the gyroscope replacing the situational controls of the primary group.

In the third period individuals are described as becoming "other-directed." Their sources of direction are what Riesman calls their "peer-groups," contemporary individuals of comparable class, status, age, etc. These sources are "internalized" in the sense that "dependence on

RIESMAN, DAVID—*Continued*

it for guidance in life is implanted early. The goals toward which the other-directed person strives shift with that guidance; it is only the process of striving itself and the process of paying close attention to the signals from others that remain unaltered throughout life." To be aware of the signals an elaborate equipment like radar, instead of a gyroscope, is needed.

Riesman further develops a series of concepts by which individuals may be characterized as "adjusted" (passive to the psychological forces that play upon them), "anomic" (incapable of adjustment), or "autonomous" (capable of selecting among elements of prevailing or surviving modes).

Russell Amos Kirk in *A Program For Conservatives* (Regnery, 1954) takes issue with some of Professor Riesman's assumptions, claiming that "this facile analysis of social change is interesting; but it is undemonstrable, and one is almost astonished that [Riesman] should venture to build the elaborate structure of *The Lonely Crowd* upon it."

Faces in the Crowd includes twenty-one interviews with students, housewives, a business executive, and a variety of other American types. The author notes in the preface: "the profiles . . . may indicate the possible usefulness of my typology in the understanding of individual character in its social setting."

The social scientist has also contributed to *Public Opinion Quarterly, International Journal of Opinion and Attitude Research, Psychiatry, Saturday Review, American Journal of Sociology,* and *Child Care.* His fantasy depicting an "all-out bombing of the Soviet Union with consumer goods" as a campaign in the "cold war," was reprinted in *Christian Century* (May 2, 1951). He was selected by the editors of *Commentary,* organ of the American Jewish Committee, to introduce their anthology, *Commentary on the American Scene.*

His third major work, *Thorstein Veblen, A Critical Interpretation* (Scribner), appeared in 1953. It is an analysis and evaluation of the work and influence of Veblen. "Riesman on Veblen is very rich fare," commented *Yale Review* (winter 1954). "Much of the charm of both is their speculative fancy; Riesman imaginatively interprets an imaginative interpreter." The New York *Times* (September 27, 1953) also agreed that Riesman's ideas "may be debatable, but they are never dull."

Riesman is a member of the editorial board of *American Scholar* and a contributing editor of *American Quarterly.* He belongs to the American Anthropological Society, American Sociological Society, Society for Applied Anthropology, and American Association of Public Opinion Research. Riesman married Evelyn Hastings Thompson, a writer and art critic, on July 15, 1936; their children are Paul, Jennie, Lucy and Michael. The sociologist, who is five feet nine inches in height, weighs 160 pounds, and has green eyes and black hair. He enjoys a game of tennis and relaxes during the summer on his farm near Brattleboro, Vermont. He belongs to the Arts Club of Chicago, and is affiliated with the Republican party. He enjoys movies but not "message" movies, because the movies' proper message is the "enrichment of fantasy."

In *Individualism Reconsidered, and Other Essays* (Free Press, 1954) Riesman writes: "What is feared as failure in American society is, above all, aloneness. And aloneness is terrifying because it means that there is no one, no group, no approved cause to submit to. Even success . . . often becomes impossible to bear when it is not socially approved or even known." To counterbalance this, Riesman proposes the "nerve to be oneself when that self is not approved of by the dominant ethic of a society."

References

Time 64:24+ S 27 '54 por
Directory of American Scholars (1951)
Who's Who in America, 1954-55

RITER, HENRY G., 3d Oct. 6, 1892- Industrialist; organization official

Address: b. 51 Lakeside Ave., West Orange, N.J.; h. 36 Stonebridge Rd., Montclair, N.J.

When the National Association of Manufacturers elected Henry G. Riter, 3d, as president for the year 1955, it chose a businessman with over thirty-five years of experience. He has been president of Thomas A. Edison, Incorporated, since 1950 and had previously been engaged in investment banking. He was associated with Dillon, Read & Company, Incorporated, from 1919 until 1933. He organized his own company in 1933, and, as an underwriter, participated in the financing of numerous corporations. He serves the NAM for a one-year term ending in December 1955.

Upon assuming the presidency of the organization, Riter urged his fellow industrialists to participate actively in city and state government. "If there is to be an end to the increasing domination in our lives by the Federal Government, we must develop strong, intelligent local government," he declared. "Until a businessman actually becomes involved in the affairs of his own town, he cannot hope to understand the needs of the community or the manner in which his tax monies are being spent" (New York *Times,* December 4, 1954).

As spokesman for some 20,000 NAM members, Riter was asked to comment on the guaranteed "annual wage," as advocated by Walter Reuther and other union officials. "If industry gives in to labor's demands for a 'guaranteed annual wage,' even in principle," Riter warned, "it could have seriously damaging effects on the American economy, perhaps leading to a socialistic state . . . such as England has experienced. . . . Evolution rather than revolution is what made this country great" (*Newsweek,* June 20, 1955).

However, the NAM president has urged more effective action by management in stabilizing employment by using "time tested" techniques available for achieving this objective.

Announcing the publication of a study entitled "Toward Steadier Work and Pay," Riter said that "giant strides" in this direction had been made by industry "long before the unions came out for the so-called guaranteed annual wage" (New York *Times,* July 11, 1955).

Henry G. Riter, 3d, was born in Philadelphia, Pennsylvania on October 6, 1892, the son of Henry G. Riter, Jr., and Mary L. (Cram) Riter. He entered Germantown Academy in 1901 and was graduated in 1908. When he was sixteen, according to Robert E. Bedingfield, he entered the brokerage business because "the only relative who ever made or had any money was a stock broker" (New York *Times,* July 18, 1954). He obtained his first position with the Philadelphia brokerage house of Chandler Brothers & Company, and continued to work until 1919 for local investment firms.

In 1919 Riter became associated with Dillon, Read & Company, as a member of its Philadelphia staff. In 1927 he was appointed a member of the firm and, at the request of the late James V. Forrestal, then an officer of the company, transferred his activities to the New York office. He left Dillon, Read in 1933 to organize his own investment firm, Riter & Company. As president of the company he enlarged his reputation for "effective financing programs and management of stock offerings in the industrial field" (*Newsweek,* December 13, 1954). It was in this capacity that his attention was first drawn to the affairs of Thomas A. Edison, Incorporated.

The Edison company was formed some seventy-five years ago to consolidate the inventor's various enterprises and to manufacture his inventions. It does not, contrary to the general belief, produce electric lamps. "Its principal products," according to the *NAM News* (December 1954), "are in the field of office dictation equipment, batteries, aeronautical instruments and fire detection equipment, precision electronic test equipment, medical gases, and nursery and juvenile furniture." It has plants in West Orange, Bloomfield, and Boonton in New Jersey, at Stuyvesant Falls, New York, and New London, Wisconsin.

Riter first became interested in the company's financial position in 1944. Two years later he persuaded Charles Edison, son of the inventor and former Governor of New Jersey, to offer the company's stock publicly as the first step toward "rejuvenation" and expansion. Riter & Company marketed 110,000 shares of a total issue of 150,000 shares of non-voting stock, and Riter was invited to become a director of the firm. On January 1, 1949 he became chairman of the executive committee; in 1950 the board elected him president. In that year the company's annual sales were $30,000,000; in 1953, after Riter had instituted an expansion program including basic research, they totaled $41,500,000.

Elected to the board of directors of the NAM in 1951, Riter served on the association's committees on finance and industrial problems in 1953 and 1954. In December 1954 he was elected at its fifty-ninth annual meeting to succeed Harold C. McClellan (see *C.B.,* 1954) as

HENRY G. RITER, 3d

the association's president for 1955. At his first press conference in his new post he expressed optimism about the country's economic prospects, forecasting "higher employment, higher take-home pay for the average worker, a substantial increase in national income and an increase of about 5 per cent in the nation's business."

At the time of his election *Newsweek* predicted that his "special concern" during his tenure would probably be the NAM's efforts to limit income taxes to 35 per cent. "We won't be able to absorb the coming increases in the labor market," he stated, "unless individuals have more tax incentive to save and invest in capital." In February 1955 he filed a statement with the Joint Congressional Economic Committee asserting that because of an undesirable tax structure profits had been "stagnating" for seven years. His statement also objected to President Eisenhower's recommendations for the expansion of the Federal Social Security and unemployment compensation programs.

After opposition was expressed concerning "right to work" laws in several states outlawing compulsory union membership in December 1954, Riter declared: "The charge . . . that state right-to-work laws 'do more harm than good' is astounding in that it is contrary to President Eisenhower's announced intention to respect the sovereign rights of states. . . . At this time industry wants to pledge its continued support to the President in his desire to vest more authority in the states" (New York *Herald Tribune,* December 9, 1954).

Asked to comment on the merger of the AFL and the CIO, he asserted: "There is no such thing as a good monopoly. Monopoly is always at the expense of the consuming public, and labor monopoly should be tolerated no more than business monopoly. . . . Industry has for many years asked for legislation to make or-

RITER, HENRY G, 3d—*Continued*

ganized labor subject to the same antitrust statutes which are now applicable to every other segment of the economy. Labor unions should no longer be permitted to engage in conduct amounting to restraint of trade" (*Newsweek*, February 21, 1955).

At the end of March 1955 Riter engaged in a dispute with Walter Reuther (see *C.B.* 1949), president of the CIO, on union proposals for a guaranteed annual wage. The exchange was precipitated in a letter to Riter denouncing what was described as the NAM's effort to raise a $30,000,000, "propaganda fund" against the U.A.W.'s guaranteed wage fight. Reuther asserted that it was "nothing more than an attempt to buy public opinion without regard for public welfare" (New York *Herald Tribune*, April 1, 1955). Riter denied that the NAM was seeking to raise $30,000,000 to block the guaranteed annual wage drive, as Reuther had charged, and accused Reuther, in turn, of using the "big lie" technique in making the allegation (New York *Times*, April 2, 1955).

Addressing a meeting of Women-Investors-in-America in April 1955, Riter attacked what he termed the "growing power and arrogance of labor union leaders" (New York *Times*, April 26, 1955). Earlier he had written on the issue: "The words 'guaranteed annual wage' have a strong emotional appeal to employees, for to many they symbolize the answer to a fundamental human desire for economic security. But what these words actually do is to create an illusion of security—an illusion because nobody can foretell future business developments nor how the rigid financial liability of a guaranteed wage agreement might threaten the very solvency of a business." At the NAM's twenty-seventh Institute of Industrial Relations held in April 1955, Riter delivered the keynote address.

The NAM policy on the proposed Federal policing of "over the counter" trading in stocks was in opposition to that of the New York Stock Exchange. Riter called the proposal far too tough already, "entirely unnecessary" and a measure which would impose burdens and new risks on small business enterprises (Washington *Post and Times Herald*, July 1, 1955).

In addition to his major professional activities, Riter is also chairman of the board of the Copperweld Steel Company, and a limited partner in Riter & Company. He is vice president, director and a member of the executive committee of the New Jersey State Chamber of Commerce, a member of the Investment Bankers Association of America, of which he was governor in 1947, a member and past chairman of the board of governors of the National Association of Securities Dealers, and former president of the Bond Club.

From 1937 until 1947 he was president of the Montclair, New Jersey, YMCA; since 1947 he has been chairman of the board of trustees. He is a member of the Newcomen Society of North America and of the Pilgrims of the United States. His clubs are the Bond and the Lunch, both of New York; Edison Pioneers, Montclair Golf, the Union League, the New York Yacht, and the Bay Head Yacht. He is a Republican. A Congregationalist, he has been a trustee of the First Congregational Church of Montclair since 1948.

He married Margaret A. Chase on October 9, 1913; the Riters have three children—Margaret (Mrs. David T. Agens), Henry G., 4th, and Maryl (Mrs. John Y. G. Walker, Jr.). The industrialist has been described as a "tall, gray-haired man, who looks like a scholar. . . . He has a family that includes ten grandchildren, a busy schedule that allows only occasional trips in Barnegat Bay aboard his 36-foot Chris-Craft cabin cruiser, *Eight Bells*."

References

N Y Herald Tribune II p 1 D 5 '54 por
N Y Times III p3 Jl 18 '54
Newsweek 44:75+ D 13 '54
Time 64:92 D 13 '54
Who's Who in America, 1954-55
Who's Who in Commerce and Industry (1953)
World Biography (1954)

ROBBINS, FREDERICK C. *See* Enders, John F(ranklin)

ROBERTS, OWEN J(OSEPHUS) May 2, 1875-May 17, 1955 Former Associate Justice of the U.S. Supreme Court; practiced law in Philadelphia; prosecutor in connection with the Teapot Dome scandal; retired from Supreme Court after fifteen years service and became dean of the University of Pennsylvania Law School; on the Court sometimes cast the vote which upheld New Deal legislation, including the Wagner Labor Relations Act; headed the commission which investigated the Pearl Harbor attack in 1941; leading figure in many educational and civic causes; from 1948 he was president of the Atlantic Union Committee and devoted the closing years of his life to the concept of federal union. See *Current Biography* (Oct.) 1941.

Obituary

N Y Times p 1+ My 18 '55

ROBERTS, (WILLIAM) GOODRIDGE Sept. 24, 1904- Artist

Address: b. c/o Dominion Gallery, 1438 Sherbrooke St. W., Montreal, Quebec, Canada; h. 1600 Selkirk, Montreal, Quebec, Canada

"A quality of sustained and sober reflection marks the work of Goodridge Roberts, the Canadian artist," wrote Donald W. Buchanan in his book *The Growth of Canadian Painting*. Roberts, whose landscapes and figure and still-life studies hang in his country's main galleries and in private collections in Canada, the United States and Europe, has had over twenty one-man exhibitions. In 1953 his *Port au Persil* was presented to Queen Elizabeth II by the Royal Canadian Air Force Association.

He has been represented in all the group shows sent by Canada within the last seventeen years to important international exhibitions such as the New York World's Fair (1939), the UNESCO exhibition in Paris (1946), and the Venice Biennale (1952).

William Goodridge Roberts was born on September 24, 1904, to Theodore Goodridge and Frances Seymour (Allen) Roberts, Canadians then residing in Barbados, British West Indies. He has two sisters. His father, a journalist, poet and novelist, was related to Ralph Waldo Emerson.

Goodridge, whose family left the West Indies when he was one year old, spent his childhood in Canada, England and France and attended several schools in the course of his family's frequent moves. He received his high school education at the Fredericton (New Brunswick) High School and the Ottawa (Ontario) Collegiate Institute. After his graduation from the latter in 1923, he studied art at the École des Beaux-Arts in Montreal for two years.

From about the age of ten Roberts had done occasional paintings and drawings. He remembers being strongly impressed by some reproductions of J. M. W. Turner water colors at the age of twelve and finding the "very essence of landscape" in some Japanese prints. Later he was particularly impressed by the work of Puvis de Chavannes and of James Wilson Morrice, an outstanding Canadian painter.

Moving to New York, he attended the Art Students League where he studied figure drawing under John Sloan and Boardman Robinson, and the painting of still life and the human figure under Max Weber. His capacity as a draftsman was attested to in 1928 by Sloan in a letter of recommendation in which he wrote that Roberts' drawings were "of the highest order."

Returning to Canada in 1929 Roberts took a position with the New Brunswick forestry service. In Ottawa in 1931 he became an instructor at the Ottawa Art Association. During the summers of 1931, 1932, and 1933 he concentrated on painting landscapes. He was named resident artist in 1933 at Queen's University in Kingston, where he taught classes and organized exhibitions. Roberts filled the post, which was financed by a Carnegie grant, for three years and then moved to Montreal.

A show of his water colors—a medium he had chosen for economic reasons—at the Arts Club in Montreal in 1931 brought the young landscape painter to the attention of John Lyman, an established Canadian artist. He wrote to Roberts, "I knew by my elation that I had seen some real stuff. I like your work immensely for its terse characterization in drawing and particularly for your rare ability to *see* colour, not merely use it illustratively or as a schematic ornament."

In Montreal Roberts met a number of artists who in 1938 at Lyman's suggestion formed an exhibiting organization called the Eastern Group, and he became a member of the Contemporary Arts Society when it was founded in 1939 under Lyman's presidency. The latter association aimed to create an interest in painting by holding exhibitions of locally owned work from other countries, particularly France, by arranging lectures and presenting exhibitions of the work of its artist members. "It was a stimulating atmosphere," Roberts has remarked. "Montreal in earlier days had had its good painters, but never had there been such widespread interest on the part of so large a group of painters in real pictorial problems as then."

GOODRIDGE ROBERTS

While his frequent exhibitions drew favorable comment, the artist in these years did not earn a living by the sale of his work. At first he joined with another artist, Ernst Neumann, in giving classes and lecture courses and then in 1939 he took a post as an instructor in the art school of the Montreal Museum of Fine Arts. During the summer months he produced many landscapes, both water colors and oils, painted mainly in the Laurentian country north of Montreal. The artist has indicated in an article "From This Point I Looked Out" in *Queen's Quarterly* (Autumn 1953) that his best creative periods have been in the summers when he was free from giving lessons.

In 1943 Roberts became an official artist with the Royal Canadian Air Force. He was posted to England and spent about a year there. He produced a number of drawings and water colors of airfields and a series of drawings of members of a fighter squadron. Toward the end of 1944 he returned to Canada and received his discharge soon thereafter. During this interlude his reputation as an artist had been growing in Canada.

A retrospective exhibition of his works, arranged by critic Maurice Gagnon in 1943, was his first real financial success. It drew him his first notices in the French-language press. A monograph on him by the French Canadian artist Jacques G. de Tonnancour, a former pupil, appeared in 1944. A traveling exhibition of his water colors was seen in the western provinces.

(Continued next page)

ROBERTS, GOODRIDGE—*Continued*

He resumed teaching in Montreal and after several years was able to give it up and live on the proceeds of his painting, being assured an annual show at one of Montreal's leading commercial galleries. His paintings have been seen in such Canadian group shows held outside the country as at Yale University (1944), the Carnegie International Exhibition of Paintings, Pittsburgh (1952) and the biennials in Saõ Paulo, Brazil (1951 and 1953). The permanent collections of the Montreal Museum of Fine Arts, the National Gallery of Canada, the Quebec Museum and the Art Gallery of Toronto have examples of his work. Among the awards he has won are two from the Montreal Museum of Fine Arts and one from the Provincial Government of Quebec. In 1953 he received a Canadian government fellowship for a year of painting in France.

In "A Report from Canada Fellowship Holders" (*Canadian Art,* Summer 1955), Roberts wrote: "I am conscious of having come to a fuller awareness, through my extended stay in Paris and my limited travels in a few European countries, of such wider implications as art's close identification with history, the shortness of the individual's life, and the deathlessness of man's spirit. . . . There must always be this transmutation into forms of art."

In the section devoted to Roberts in *The Growth of Canadian Painting* (1950), Donald W. Buchanan, Canadian critic, commented on the "interplay of color and texture" in Roberts' work. "Trees, human figures, flowers, hills—all these rest in equilibrium." He quoted the artist as having said, "I like to paint people sitting, standing, or reclining, quite static, serene, and impersonal. . . ." Jacques G. de Tonnancour, analyzing this sense of detachment in Roberts' work, suggests it may be traced to his childhood with its lack of attachment to one place, and a resulting necessity to withdraw from the transitory aspect of things into an inner synthesis. He contrasts Roberts' approach to landscape painting with that of the famous school of Canadian landscape painters, the Group of Seven, pointing out that where they emphasized the dramatic, the evanescent, Roberts stresses the calm, enduring qualities.

Roberts is a member of the Canadian Group of Painters, the Canadian Society of Painters in Water Colour, and the Canadian Society of Graphic Art, and is an Associate of the Royal Canadian Academy of Arts. In 1933 he married; the marriage terminated in divorce. The artist is six feet two inches tall and weighs 185 pounds. His hair is graying and his eyes are blue. His favorite recreations are camping and boating; he also enjoys reading and occasionally writes poetry.

References

Queens Q 60:316 Autumn '53

Buchanan, D. W. The Growth of Canadian Painting (1950)

Canadian Who's Who (1952-54)

Who's Who in Art (1952)

ROBERTSON, REUBEN B(UCK), JR.

June 27, 1908- U. S. Deputy Secretary of Defense; businessman

Address: b. The Pentagon, Washington 25, D.C.; h. 9974 McKelvey Rd., Cincinnati 15, Ohio; 2424 Wyoming Ave., N.W., Washington, D.C.

Deputy Secretary of Defense Reuben B. Robertson, Jr., holds the second highest civilian post in what has been called "the biggest business operation in the world." When he was named in July 1955 as deputy to Secretary Charles E. Wilson, who directs the wide-ranging functions of the Department of Defense, *U. S. News & World Report* (July 22, 1955) referred to him as "a business leader who seems to have talked himself into the job by being critical of the way in which it was being run."

Over a period of thirteen years Robertson has taken time from his work as president of the Champion Paper and Fibre Company to serve the U. S. Government in several capacities. Shortly before receiving his present appointment he had participated in a study of the business activities of the Department of Defense for the second Hoover Commission on government reorganization. In one of his earliest important public statements after taking office, Deputy Secretary Robertson discussed the intention of his department to trim $1 billion during the coming year from its $35 billion budget without impairing the defense program.

A native North Carolinian, Reuben Buck Robertson, Jr., was born in Asheville on June 27, 1908 to Reuben Buck Robertson, a paper manufacturer, and Hope (Thomson) Robertson. The other children in the family were Hope (now Mrs. Russell Norburn), Laura Thomson (deceased) and Logan Thomson. Reuben obtained his early education at a grammar school in Asheville and then prepared for college at the Asheville School for Boys. In 1930 he was graduated from Yale University's Sheffield Scientific School with a B.S. degree in chemical engineering.

Joining the Champion Paper and Fibre Company of Hamilton, Ohio in 1930, Robertson rose to assistant general manager of the Canton, Ohio division four years later. From 1936 to 1938 he was in charge of personnel relations at this division and subsequently extended his personnel work to other divisions of the company as well as holding the position of general production manager. The aim of Champion's personnel policies, Robertson has said, is to preserve "a small shop" atmosphere (*Business Week,* August 1, 1953).

Robertson accepted the first of a number of government assignments in 1942 when he went to Washington, D.C. as a member of the War Production Board. The following year he was commissioned a captain in the Army and served as control officer or supply officer in Washington and in Atlanta, Georgia until his discharge in the rank of lieutenant colonel in November 1945. He returned to government service in November 1950 after President Harry S. Truman appointed him an industry member of the Wage Stabilization Board.

At the Champion Paper and Fibre Company, in the meantime, Robertson was named executive vice-president in 1946 and president in 1950. The company, which owns some 500,000 acres of forest land in the Carolinas, Georgia, Texas and Tennessee, is one of the largest paper manufacturers in the United States. It is also a fast-growing organization, with sales for the fiscal year which ended in March 1953 reaching about $118,500,000 as compared with $43,000,000 ten years earlier. Among the customers for Champion's daily output of 1,500 tons of paper (in 1953) are *Life* magazine and the American Can Company, which produces milk containers.

As part of its personnel and public relations program Champion released three motion pictures in the autumn of 1953 describing the entire paper manufacturing operations of the company, its timberland work and its methods of doing business. The films were made, at a cost of over $200,000, to be shown to employees and management and then to audiences in communities where the company maintains plants and mills. (See *Educational Film Guide*, 1954.)

Business Week (August 1, 1953) pointed out in an article about Champion Paper and Fibre Company that while many business concerns have been "diversifying their product lines," Champion under Robertson's presidency has been following the reverse policy of eliminating subsidies not directly connected with paper manufacturing and has put its efforts into strengthening the over-all paper making organization from the source to the consumer. "Today you must invest more in a tree than you ever dreamed of, to end up with a piece of paper," Robertson was quoted as explaining. "Now, we're acquiring interests in paper distributors and in some converting operations to balance our inlets with our outlets."

After the inauguration of President Dwight D. Eisenhower in January 1953, Robertson, who is a Republican, began to spend more of his time in government offices. Early in that year he was chosen by the President and by Director of Mutual Security Harold E. Stassen as head of a sixteen-member group of businessmen who went to Europe to evaluate the U. S. Mutual Security Program. He was also named in 1953 to the post of vice-chairman of the Business Advisory Council to the Secretary of Commerce.

Robertson's next appointment was as vice-chairman of the Committee on Business Organization of the Department of Defense, a task force of the Commission on Organization of the Executive Branch of the Government, which was set up in 1953 under former President Herbert Hoover to make a two-year study of governmental practices. The committee's report, of which Robertson was the chief author, noted that maintaining national defense costs about $35 billion a year and required the employment of more than 4,000,000 people. It recommended fourteen major changes in policies and administration to achieve "a more efficient, economical and businesslike defense organization" (quoted in *U. S. News & World Report*, July 22, 1955).

U. S. Army

REUBEN B. ROBERTSON, JR.

Nominated Deputy Secretary of Defense by President Eisenhower on July 12, 1955 (following the resignation of Robert B. Anderson), Robertson was sworn into office on August 5. The Senate had confirmed his appointment on July 22, after he had acceded to the request of the Committee on Armed Services that he divest himself of stock holdings in B. F. Goodrich Company and Proctor & Gamble Company, in conformity with Senate policy that a Defense Department official should not maintain an interest in a company engaged in business with the Pentagon. Robertson volunteered also to resign his directorate in the Cincinnati and Suburban Bell Telephone Company.

Since the Champion Paper and Fibre Company had no direct business with the Defense Department, although it had sold paper to other government agencies in 1954, the Senate committee saw no "conflict of interest" in Robertson's remaining a director of the firm. He also was allowed to keep a directorate in the related Dairypak, Inc. He resigned as president of Champion in July and was succeeded in that office by his father, who had held the presidency prior to 1950 and who is also chairman of the board of directors.

Several observers of the Washington political scene expressed the view that the selection of Robertson as Deputy Secretary of Defense was indicative of the Eisenhower Administration's intention to put into effect some of the recommendations of the Hoover commission. In August Secretary of Defense Wilson announced that his department would close fourteen commercial-type operations which were competing with private business. These military service plants were located in several states and included coffee roasting, rope making, dry cleaning and paint manufacturing facilities.

In answer to two Democratic Senators who had criticized reported new military spending

ROBERTSON, REUBEN B., JR.—*Cont.*

cutbacks as "dangerous and unjustified," Robertson denied in September 1955 that the Department of Defense intended to make drastic reductions as a means of balancing the Federal budget within a year. He explained that the department would continue its efforts to cut expenses by eliminating duplication and cutting down excess supplies and unnecessary manpower, but added that "no steps will be taken" that will "adversely affect the attainment of approved force objectives and military readiness goals" (New York *Herald Tribune*, September 8, 1955).

Among Robertson's business affiliations is the Employers Labor Relations Information Committee, Inc., of which he has served as president. This organization, which is registered as a lobbyist but states that it does not engage in lobbying, seeks to improve human relations in industry by furthering understanding as to how the interests of employees, employers and the public can best be served. He has also been a member of the Committee for Southern Conference on Human Relations in Industry, a vice-president of the American Paper and Pulp Association, director of Wachvia Bank and Trust Company in Asheville, a trustee of the National Industrial Conference Board and a member of the American Institute of Chemical Engineers.

A leader in civic activities in Ohio and North Carolina, Robertson has served as director of the Ohio Foundation of Independent Colleges and the Cincinnati Community Chest and as a trustee of the Asheville School for Boys. He maintains membership in the Commercial Club and the Commonwealth Club in Cincinnati, the Chamber of Commerce and Industrial Council in Hamilton, the Ohio State Chamber of Commerce, the national committee for industrial service of the Young Men's Christian Association, the North Carolina State Planning Board and the North Carolina State Board of Vocational Education. He is a Mason and a Protestant.

When Robertson took his oath of office at the White House in August, Secretary Wilson commented to President Eisenhower that Robertson had "no conflict of interests except his family." The new Deputy Defense Secretary was accompanied to the ceremony by his wife, the former Margaret Watkins of Charleston, South Carolina, whom he married on December 17, 1938, and by his six children ranging in age from one to fifteen years. They are Reuben Buck 3d, Daniel Huger, Peter Thomson, Margaret Laurens, Louisa Hope and George Watkins.

Robertson is six feet tall and weighs 210 pounds.

References

Bsns W p94+ Ag 1 '53 por; p28 Jl 16 '55 por
N Y Herald Tribune p8 Jl 13 '55 por
U S News 39:14 Jl 22 '55
Washington (D.C.) Post p31 Ag 24 '55
Who's Who in America, 1954-55
Who's Who in Commerce and Industry (1953)

ROBINSON, ELMER E(DWIN) Oct. 3, 1894- Mayor of San Francisco; lawyer
Address: City Hall, San Francisco, Calif.

When the tenth anniversary of the signing of the United Nations Charter was celebrated at San Francisco in June 1955, the visiting dignitaries were officially the guests of the California municipality and its mayor, Elmer E. Robinson. A lawyer who had served as both a San Francisco Municipal Court and California Superior Court Judge before election in November 1947 to his first four-year term, Mayor Robinson was re-elected in November 1951. He was president of the United States Conference of Mayors from November 1953 to May 1955, and presided over the May 1955 meeting of the conference which was held in New York City.

Elmer Edwin Robinson was born in San Francisco on October 3, 1894 to Ralph Sidney and Edyth Alice (Rahlves) Robinson. He was educated in the public schools and at the Kent Law College. Admitted to the California bar in 1915, he began the general practice of law in his native city. In 1917 and again in 1919, he was on the staff of the District Attorney of San Francisco, and in the latter year was admitted to the Arizona bar.

He was again attached to the San Francisco District Attorney's office when in 1921 he sought election, as a Republican, to the California Senate. Unsuccessful in this bid for legislative office, Robinson resumed private law practice until January 1935, when he was appointed judge of the San Francisco Municipal Court. (He also served as secretary of the Republican State Central Committee in 1934-35). Appointed in September 1935 to the Superior Court, he was elected in November 1936 to a regular six-year term as a judge of the Superior Court of the State of California, to "serve in and for the City and County of San Francisco."

President Franklin D. Roosevelt named the California jurist in 1938 to be chairman of the Reviewing Board to Adjust Compensation for World War I veterans, and in December of the same year Judge Robinson was appointed to membership in the Judicial Council of California. He was elected president of the Conference of California Judges in September 1940.

In the spring of 1947 when the Mayor of San Francisco, Roger D. Lapham, decided not to seek a second term, three candidates sought the "non-partisan" office. One was the realtor Chester R. MacPhee, a Republican who had the endorsement of the Scripps-Howard newspapers; another was State Representative Franck R. Havenner, a Democrat backed by the Congress of Industrial Organizations. The third was Judge Robinson, who had the support of the Hearst newspapers and "a substantial segment of the financial district" (New York *Times*). In the November municipal balloting, Judge Robinson defeated Representative Havenner by 116,937 votes to 101,498. (MacPhee ran third). A $57,000,000 bond issue for rehabilitation of the transit system, and retention of San Francisco's picturesque cable tram cars, won approval.

One point on which Mayor Robinson differed from his predecessor was that of engaging a special "Washington public relations counsel" to take over from the Chamber of Commerce the city's lobbying in the nation's capital. Soon after Robinson was installed in office in January 1948, he selected Francis V. Keesling, Jr., an attorney, for this duty which he performed until early 1955. In July 1949, a U.S. Senate subcommittee held hearings on a proposal to construct a second bridge across San Francisco Bay, about 300 feet distant from the existing span from San Francisco to Oakland. The proposal was sponsored by Senator William F. Knowland, a resident of Oakland, and opposed by Mayor Robinson, who wanted the new bridge located much farther to the south. Keesling presented the mayor's viewpoint, and succeeded in blocking Knowland's proposal. Two years later when the bridge matter was revived, priority was given to the site advocated by Robinson.

Mayor Robinson has since credited Keesling's lobbying with having "aided immeasurably in obtaining an $8,000,000 addition to the city's Hetch Hetchy water project and in getting $5,200,000 in Federal aid for San Francisco's International Airport" as well as "contracts for the San Francisco naval shipyard" (New York *Times,* February 6, 1955). In October 1950, Robinson and Keesling joined in inducing the Board on Geographic Names not to change "San Francisco Peninsula" to "Santa Cruz Peninsula."

The eleventh largest city in the United States, San Francisco had in 1950 a population of 775,357 occupying an area of 44.6 square miles, with water on three sides. As the country's major Pacific seaport, and a principal naval and military center, it would doubtless be a primary target for enemy air attack in the event of war. In 1950, accordingly, Mayor Robinson took a lead in prodding the Federal Government to assume responsibility for defense against the atom and hydrogen bomb.

At an April 3 hearing by the Congressional Joint Committee on Atomic Energy he complained of delays by top Federal agencies; and in May in an address to the U.S. Conference of Mayors, he charged the Government with intolerable "indecision, inaction and sleepwalking" (New York *Times,* May 13, 1950). He urged his fellow mayors to endorse a three point program calling for "immediate liaison" between the Department of Defense and state and local governments to supply officials with a "steady flow" of information; a "sweeping general information program" and "assignment by the military commander of each primary target-area of a trained expert to sit in with local officials in planning civilian defense measures" (New York *Times,* May 13, 1950).

Before the National Security Board's Office of Civil Defense published a "master blueprint" in September 1950 Mayor Robinson reported that San Francisco already had in effect an "interim" defense plan. ("The broad basis of our planning is dispersal," Robinson explained. "We hope to make each district of the city as near a self-contained damage control unit as we can"). He later stated that civil defense

Wide World

ELMER E. ROBINSON

preparations in San Francisco were being delayed because of doubts as to the extent of Federal responsibility and the amount of financial aid to be given to communities. (This was to be settled by the Civil Defense Act of January 1951).

San Francisco celebrated the centenary of its city charter and the admission of California to the Union in 1950 with an elaborate pageant. In the summer of 1951 Mayor Robinson and the city were hosts to the Japanese Peace Treaty conference.

Having won a second four-year term as mayor at the municipal election of November 6, 1951, Robinson in the following month visited New York City to confer with Board of Transportation chairman Sidney H. Bingham on plans for a San Francisco subway. In November 1953, Robinson became president of the U.S. Conference of Mayors. In the fall of 1954 he was one of eighty-five civic leaders to visit Germany and other countries to inspect operations of Radio Free Europe.

Noteworthy in Robinson's second mayoral term was his attempt, through the California Public Utilities Commission, to induce the Federal Government in January 1954 to declare the San Francisco airport a "free zone" so that "articles sent in by foreign shippers may be left in customs there until there is a market for the produce" (New York *Times*); he said that there were already free trade zones at various seaports, and that such a zone at the airport would "attract airlines and get customers."

In January 1955 Mayor Robinson gave his support to a bill introduced by Democratic Assemblyman John O'Connor to the California Legislature to transfer to the city the administrative control of San Francisco's harbor, vested in the state since 1863.

(Continued next page)

ROBINSON, ELMER E.—*Continued*

With the authority of the city's board of supervisors, which appropriated $150,000 for the purpose, Mayor Robinson invited the United Nations to return to San Francisco in June 1955 to participate in a tenth anniversary observance of the signing of the Charter there on June 26, 1945. The invitation was accepted by the U.N., and a six-day celebration (June 20-26) was observed, culminating with a speech by President Eisenhower on "Charter Day."

At New York City on May 21, 1955, Robinson was succeeded as president of the U.S. Conference of Mayors by Mayor John B. Hynes of Boston, Massachusetts. His second term as mayor of San Francisco expires in January 1956, at which time he intends to retire to private life (New York *Times*, June 17, 1955). His successor, Republican George Christopher, was elected on November 8, 1955.

Mayor Robinson was married to the former Doris Gould in June, 1917. She is now deceased. He has two daughters; Elizabeth Jane (Mrs. Vincent Price Bolton), and Rosemarie Kerr. He is a Mason (Knight Templar, Shriner and Jester) an Eagle, a Moose and a Knight of Pythias; he is also a Native Son of the Golden West. His religious affiliation is with the Episcopal Church. The "silver-haired" mayor is an avid reader and a collector of Americana.

References

Time 50:24+ N 17 '47
Who's Who in America, 1954-55
Who's Who in the West (1954)

RORIMER, JAMES J. Sept. 7, 1905- Museum director

Address: b. c/o The Metropolitan Museum of Art, Fifth Ave. at 82nd St., New York 28; h. 1000 Park Ave., New York

"A connoisseur, a scholar, an enthusiast, a man who profoundly loves art and has a real flair for showmanship"—in this manner the New York *Times* described James J. Rorimer at the time of his appointment as director of the Metropolitan Museum of Art. Chosen in August 1955 to succeed Francis Henry Taylor, who resigned, Rorimer heads a New York institution which since 1870 has served the art-loving public, and has extensive collections of American and European paintings, Egyptian, Asiatic and Classical art, costumes, textiles, and decorative arts which are seen by over 2,000,000 visitors annually.

Rorimer has been a member of the museum staff since 1927 and was largely responsible for the Cloisters, the branch of the Metropolitan Museum devoted to medieval art. He pioneered in the use of ultraviolet rays in examining art objects to determine their authenticity.

During his military service in World War II, he headed the Monuments, Fine Arts and Archives Section of the Seventh United States Army, Western Military District, and was concerned with the preservation and protection of art treasures of Europe. He and his staff discovered many art caches hidden by Nazi generals in castles and salt mines. He is the author of several books, including *Survival; The Salvage and Protection of Art in War* (Abelard, 1950). *Cue* (July 22, 1950) commented on the book: "This taut fast-moving account of his tracking down of looted European art during the war, proves pipe-smoking, scholarly Mr. Rorimer a man Agatha Christie's Hercule Poirot might grudgingly admire."

James J. Rorimer, the son of Louis and Edith (Joseph) Rorimer, was born in Cleveland, Ohio, on September 7, 1905. His father, a noted interior decorator and designer, was a founder and vice-president of the American Institute of Decorators, a teacher at the Cleveland School of Art for eighteen years and a member of the advisory board of the Cleveland Museum of Art.

At the age of seven, young Rorimer entered the University School in Cleveland. "I was a wood carver before I was a Boy Scout," he recalled to a *Time* (August 8, 1955) interviewer. "At nine I took a course in arms and armor. I got two years off from prep school to visit the art centers of Europe." He received instruction in drawing and design, architectural planning, and metalworking, and began to collect medieval candlesticks. While in Europe he attended the École Gory in Paris.

Returning to the University School in 1922, Rorimer completed his work there, and entered Harvard University the following year. He was graduated *cum laude* in 1927. Joining the staff of the Metropolitan Museum in New York shortly after his graduation, Rorimer began as an assistant in the department of decorative arts. Two years later, he was named assistant curator of the Metropolitan, a post he held from 1929 to 1932, when he was promoted to associate curator. From 1930 to 1933 he was associated with Joseph Breck, curator of decorative arts, in the planning of the Cloisters. Named curator of the Metropolitan's department of medieval art in 1934, Rorimer served in that capacity until 1938, when he became curator of the Cloisters as well.

The nucleus of the medieval collection out of which the Cloisters developed, was in the documents, sculpture, and other objects collected in Europe by the late George Gray Barnard, the sculptor, which was purchased for $600,000 in 1925 by John D. Rockefeller, Jr., and presented by him to the Metropolitan Museum of Art.

From time to time, donations by Rockefeller permitted the enlargement of the collection, until, in 1930, the need for a permanent building to house it became evident, and led to Rockefeller's gift of a large tract of land in northern Manhattan—fifty-six acres for Fort Tryon Park, to the City of New York, and four acres to the Metropolitan, for the Cloisters. Working in collaboration with architect Charles Collens, Rorimer saw through the completion of the $2,500,000 building, which was opened to the public on May 10, 1938.

With funds supplied by Rockefeller (who in 1952 added $10,000,000 in securities to his gifts to the museum) Rorimer gathered together the major acquisitions upon which the distinction of the Cloisters rests: these included the Unicorn series and Nine Heroes tapestries, the Pontaut Chapter House, the tomb of Armengol VII, frescoes, paintings, sculptures, and furniture. By a process of scholarly detection, Rorimer in 1941 determined that the Unicorn tapestries had been made for Anne of Brittany in celebration of her marriage to Louis XII in 1499.

Obtaining a leave of absence from the museum in 1943, Rorimer entered the United States Army as a private in the infantry. Subsequently he held the ranks of lieutenant and captain, detailed as a monuments, fine arts, and archives officer, in Normandy, Paris, and Germany. As chief of the Monuments, Fine Arts, and Archives Section of the Seventh Army in the Western Military District, he was responsible, *Newsweek* (May 28, 1945) reported, for finding the art objects hidden by Nazi propagandist Alfred Rosenberg at Neuschwanstein Castle.

In *Cue* (July 22, 1950) Rorimer recalled his Army experiences: "It was really two jobs in one—we started out to preserve and protect art in wartime, and ended up catching international thieves and their loot. I followed Goering all the way from Normandy to Austria." He tracked down Goering, Goebbels, and Rosenberg . . . discovered their invaluable caches in castles, salt mines and underground tunnels. Rorimer expressed his bitterness over G.I. vandalism and appealed "for more education and military training on the subject of respecting historic art." Returning to the Cloisters in 1946, Rorimer arranged a photographic display of the damage wrought to Europe's medieval buildings. He had taken a number of the photographs himself.

When named director of the Cloisters in 1949, Rorimer told a New York *Times* interviewer about the meticulous selection of elements for the Cloisters, their subjection to analysis by ultraviolet ray, the removal of any restored parts, and their careful installation. Students came to the Cloisters to study Rorimer's methods of identifying fakeries and restorations. His book, *Ultra-Violet Rays and Their Use in the Examination of Works of Art* (published by the Metropolitan Museum in 1931), remains a landmark in its field.

"The ability to establish the date and place of a work of medieval art becomes a sort of sixth sense," Rorimer said. "Applying it to contemporary records and characteristics of objects of the same period, you arrive at an answer." It was through such a process that Rorimer, over a period of twenty-nine years, identified the three sections of a medieval tapestry, of which one belonged to the Metropolitan, another to the Walters Art Gallery in Baltimore, and a third to a private dealer, as being a wedding gift to Charles VIII from his father-in-law on the occasion of his marriage. "Brought together, the three sections matched perfectly in design, color and thread count," reported *Time* (June 14, 1954). "Carefully cleaned and put together again, the tapestry turned out to be one of the most beautiful works of its kind ever brought to the United States." The Cloisters director admitted in

Halsman

JAMES J. RORIMER

the *New Yorker* (July 3, 1954), "The most difficult part of the whole experience was not being able to tell anyone about it. If I'd told and been proved wrong, I'd have looked a fool. If I'd told and been proved right, the various arrangements that were necessary to bring the three pieces together might have been queered forever."

As curator of medieval art for the Metropolitan, Rorimer was also responsible for a number of additions to the medieval collections of the museum's main building, among them the Burgos, Trojan War, and Annunciation tapestries, a monumental wood sculpture of St. James the Less, statues of the Virgin and Child from Saint Chéron and Poligny, and sculptures attributed to Claus Sluter. A three-year reconstruction of the Metropolitan's medieval galleries was carried out under Rorimer's direction and opened in February 1954. His *Cloisters Handbook* is the museum's most popular publication; since the first edition in 1938, 166,000 copies have been printed.

The resignation of Francis Henry Taylor as director of the Metropolitan Museum in December 1954 started eight months of speculation on the choice of his probable successor, which was not dispelled until a special meeting of the museum's board of trustees in August 1955 unanimously elected James J. Rorimer to be the institution's sixth director. Rorimer, as a member of the staff policy committee and as chairman of the architectural committee, had worked closely with Taylor on the renovation of the museum.

Two considerations uppermost in his mind, the new director told Aline B. Saarinen of the New York *Times* (August 14, 1955) would be humanization and scholarship. One way to accomplish this, he said, would be by creating "thumbnail sketches of background" and another, by making "the objects self-explanatory." "We have an opportunity to enrich the whole

RORIMER, JAMES J.—*Continued*

museum field through training younger people in apprenticeships and internships." Rorimer then announced a policy of buying only the best for the museum, in preference to a multitude of "secondary objects which belong in study collections."

His book *Survival; The Salvage and Protection of Art in War* (Abelard, 1950) was reviewed by *Art Digest* (November 1, 1950): ". . . adventures of Rorimer in Normandy, Paris and Germany make good if often sad-to-horrifying reading . . . a long documented account of the Einsatstab Reichleiter Rosenberg, the Nazi looting agency, forms an absorbing chapter."

Decorations which Rorimer has received include the Bronze Star, the European Theatre Ribbon, with four battle stars, the Croix de Guerre, and the Legion of Honor, with the rank of chevalier. Rorimer's professional memberships are the following: the American Association of Museums (chairman in 1948 of the technical art section); the American Federation of Arts; the American Institute of Decorators (honorary member); the Archaeological Institute of America; the Art and Antique Dealers League (honorary member); the Association of Art Museum Directors; the Cleveland Institute of Art (adviser); the College Art Association of America; the International Institute of Conservation; the Medieval Academy of America (councillor, 1955).

He also belongs to the American Academy of Political and Social Sciences; the American Geographical Society (fellow); the France-America Society; the French Institute in the United States; the Pierpont Morgan Library (fellow); the Swedish Royal Academy of Letters, History, and Antiquities (foreign corresponding member). Rorimer, who allowed only herbs known in the Middle Ages to be planted in the Cloisters herb beds, is also a member of the Botanical Society of New York.

The Metropolitan Museum has also played another role in Rorimer's life: for it was there that he made the acquaintance of art researcher Katherine Newton Serrell, to whom he was married in 1942. The Rorimers have two children, a daughter, Anne Newton, and a son, Louis. Their New York home is a Park Avenue apartment not far from the museum, and their second home is a farm at Chagrin Falls, Ohio, not far from Cleveland. Rorimer is known as a capable cook, and a somewhat less capable farmhand—at the time of his election to the directorship of the Metropolitan, he was on crutches, owing to a farm accident. Dark, stocky, and pipe-smoking, Rorimer has expressed his appreciation of the smoking lounges recently installed in the Metropolitan.

On September 19, 1955 Rorimer was elected a trustee of the Metropolitan Museum of Art.

References

Cue 19:12 Jl 22 '50
New Yorker 31:19 S 3 '55
Sat Eve Post 228:32+ O 29 '55
Time 66:56 Ag 8 '55 por
Who's Who in America, 1954-55
Who's Who in American Art (1953)

RUSSELL, CHARLES H(INTON) Dec. 27, 1903- Governor of Nevada

Address: b. Capitol Bldg., Carson City, Nev.; h. Governor's Mansion, Carson City, Nev.

A strong advocate of economy and low taxes in state administration, Governor Charles H. Russell was elected the first Republican Governor of Nevada in sixteen years in November 1950 and was re-elected in 1954. He defeated former Democratic Governor Vail Pittman in both contests and attained the leadership of a state with no sales tax, inheritance tax or state income tax, and with legalized gambling.

Russell served as agent for the strategic and critical materials division of the Joint Congressional Committee on Foreign Economic Cooperation from January 1949 to June 1950 and as Congressman-at-large to the Eightieth Congress of the United States from 1947 to 1949. His previous political experience included service as senator in the Nevada State Legislature from 1941 to 1946 and as assemblyman from 1935 to 1940. Before entering politics Russell was the publisher and editor of the Ely *Record* in Ely, Nevada.

Charles Hinton Russell was born in Lovelock, Nevada, on December 27, 1903, the son of Robert James and Ellen Daisy (Ernst) Russell. His father was a rancher and a stockman. Charles attended public schools in Elko, Nevada, and was graduated from Elko County High School. He entered the University of Nevada and received the A.B. degree in 1926. The following year, he taught at Ruby Valley School in Elko County.

Turning from teaching to the mining industry in 1928, Russell was a timekeeper with the Nevada Consolidated Copper Company in Ruth, Nevada for a year. This experience gave him an insight into some of the problems and difficulties of the mining business. When an opportunity opened in 1929 in the newspaper field, Russell became part owner and managing editor of the weekly Ely *Record*, in Ely, Nevada, retaining these publishing and editorial posts until 1946.

He began his political career when he was elected in 1934 as a Republican from White Pine County to the Nevada Assembly. Reelected for two more terms he served as assemblyman until 1940. Russell was elected to the Nevada Senate in 1940 and again in 1944 and was president pro tempore of the Senate during its 1943 and 1945 sessions. He resigned from this body in 1946 to become a candidate for the U. S. House of Representatives.

Elected in 1946 as Congressman-at-large (by voters of the whole state), Russell served during the Eightieth Congress from January 1947 to January 1949 as a Republican member. During the first session of the Eightieth Congress (1947) he favored a bill to reduce individual income tax rates (March), the rent control extension bill (May), and continuance of the Commodity Credit Corporation as an agency of the United States to provide support for wool (June) which he urged to help prevent the serious decrease in sheep population in Western states.

During the second session of the Eightieth Congress (1948) Russell favored aid to Europe and China in the form of the Marshall plan (March), the tidelands oil bill (April), and the Mundt bill to protect the United States against subversive activities (May). In May 1948 he introduced to the House Committee on Public Lands a bill to stimulate the production and conservation of strategic and critical ores, minerals and metals, and to establish within the U. S. Department of the Interior a mine incentive payments division.

Speaking before the House of Representatives on April 20, 1948, Russell called "mass mining" the most efficient method of ore extraction, and stated that the "exploration of new ores" had lagged in the United States "since the late 1920's." However, the House Rules Committee postponed indefinitely in June 1948 the mine subsidy bill Congressman Russell sponsored.

After he was defeated for re-election in 1948 to the House of Representatives, Russell was appointed by Senator Styles Bridges an agent for the strategic and critical materials division of the Joint Congressional Committee on Foreign Economic Cooperation. In this post he traveled throughout the countries in Europe and Africa which were included in the Economic Cooperation Administration. Two years later he resigned from E.C.A. to seek the Republican nomination for Governor of Nevada.

Basing his gubernatorial campaign on a proposed economic reorganization of state administration, Russell was elected Governor of Nevada for a four-year term on November 7, 1950, over his Democratic opponent, Vail Pittman. In the Nevada legislature in 1951 he had the support of a Republican majority in the Senate with a slight Democratic edge in the Assembly.

During the first year of Governor Russell's administration, Nevada became the thirty-sixth and last state required to ratify the proposed Twenty-second Amendment to the U. S. Constitution limiting the President's tenure of office to two terms. Russell improved state finances by arranging disposal negotiations for the sale of the state-owned inactive Basic Magnesium Plant at Henderson, Nevada. The sale price was reported to have been over $150,000,000. Its sale laid the groundwork for future development of a large chemical center in southern Nevada.

In accordance with his emphasis on economy in state government, Russell inaugurated in Nevada during 1951 a central purchasing department for major state institutions and a budget control system extending to all state agencies. His concern with the development of general agriculture and with mine production contributed to Nevada's thriving livestock and mining industries. Together with these industries, Russell classed the promotion of tourist business in Nevada as "fundamental to the state's economy and welfare" (New York *Times,* January 1, 1951).

During the initial state campaign for a "right to work" open shop law, Russell stated that he would follow a "hands-off policy"

Harris & Ewing

CHARLES H. RUSSELL

(New York *Times,* January 1, 1951). He also affirmed his belief that "with proper economies and its substantial revenue from gambling, property and excise taxes, Nevada can remain a state with 'no sales tax—no inheritance tax—no state income tax.'" His support of women in political office in Nevada resulted in the state's receiving a gold medallion from the Women's International Exposition on November 8, 1951 "for having done the most to further the interests of its women by appointments and legislation" (New York *Times,* November 9, 1951).

In a letter to the U. S. Congress in April 1952, Russell urged that the Atomic Energy Act of 1946 be changed to remove the immunity from state taxes allowed to private contractors working on atomic energy projects. He wrote that it was expensive for Nevada to provide atomic energy facilities for the Atomic Energy Commission testing grounds, as the state "needed tax revenues" (New York *Times,* April 25, 1952).

A special session of the Nevada legislature was called in December 1953 by Governor Russell, who recommended "immediate legislative action . . . to remedy the growing school emergency" (New York *Times,* December 16, 1953), which had been aggravated by Nevada's 30 per cent rise in population since 1950 (*Collier's,* March 18, 1955).

Russell was re-elected as Governor in November 1954, campaigning on his past record of economy, and not taking a stand on the most controversial matter in the election—the proposed repeal of the state's "right to work" (compulsory open shop) law. His Democratic opponent, former Governor Vail Pittman, was backed by Senator Pat McCarran.

After the death of Senator McCarran on September 28, 1954, Russell appointed a Republican attorney, Ernest S. Brown to fill the

RUSSELL, CHARLES H.—*Continued*

vacancy in the U. S. Senate. However, when the Democrats contested this, the Nevada Supreme Court ruled that the voters must choose a successor in the November 1954 general election. Brown (Russell's appointee) ran against the Democratic candidate Alan Bible, and was defeated.

In March 1955, Albert Deutsch wrote an article for *Collier's* entitled "The Sorry State of Nevada" which was sharply critical of the health and welfare program in Nevada. He wrote that Nevada depends on the Federal Government to a greater degree than any other state to provide health and welfare services. Deutsch described the inadequate facilities of the schools, relief centers, and the prisons. He also revealed that the state had no Aid to Dependent Children program. "Governor Russell strongly favors an ADC program, having introduced a bill to that end unsuccessfully several times when he served in the state Senate. He failed to put it through during his first term as governor. The governor hopes it . . . will be adopted by the 1955 legislature" (*Collier's* March 18, 1955). Some three weeks after the *Collier's* article appeared on the newsstands the Nevada legislature passed the Aid to Dependent Children program.

Nevada, the smallest state in population, has an area of 110,540 square miles. It was made famous by the discovery of the Comstock Lode in 1859, and has lived mainly on income from its mines. Reno became "the divorce capital of the nation" when it created an easy divorce law in 1931.

In July 1955 prisoners at the Nevada State Prison staged a sit-down strike demanding, primarily, a conference with Governor Russell. The strike ended without violence but the governor ignored their demand. "Russell said he would take 'whatever action [he deemed] necessary.' But that consisted only in keeping in constant touch with [warden] Bernard" (New York *Herald Tribune,* July 20, 1955).

During 1955 the Nevada Library Association's plan to provide bookmobiles failed to pass the Nevada Assembly. The library budget was reduced by Governor Russell from $271,071 to $131,066. The legislature's finance committees cut this to $123,759, but this still represents an increase in appropriations for library facilities in the state over the past four years (*Library Journal,* October 1, 1955).

Russell is an honorary president of the Nevada area council of the Boy Scouts of America. He is a past president of the Lions Club of Ely, Nevada, and a past vice president of the White Pines (Nevada) Chamber of Mines and Commerce. He is a member of the Masonic Order (Royal Arch, Scottish Rite, Shrine), Elks Club, Variety Club of Las Vegas, Nevada, and the University Club of Washington, D.C. His religious affiliation is Episcopalian.

Governor Russell married Marjorie Ann Guild, a teacher, on March 19, 1939. Their children are Clark George, Virginia Ellen, Craig Robert, Charles David, and James Todd. The Governor likes to cook and enjoys watching sports events.

References

Biographical Directory of the American Congress, 1774-1949 (1950)
National Cyclopedia of American Biography current vol H (1952)
Who's Who in America, 1954-55
Who's Who in United States Politics (1952)
World Biography (1954)

RYAN, PATRICK J(AMES), RT. REV. MSGR. Dec. 3, 1902- United States Army chaplain

Address: b. c/o Office of the Chief of Chaplains, Department of the Army, Washington 25, D.C.; h. 3839 Massachusetts Ave., N.W., Washington 16, D.C.

The Right Reverend Monsignor Patrick J. Ryan, who began a four-year appointment as the U.S. Army's Chief of Chaplains in May 1954, holds the rank of Major General. He has been an officer of the Chaplains Corps continuously for over twenty-six years. In World War II he was chaplain of the Third Infantry Division and chief chaplain of the Fifth Army in North Africa, Sicily and Italy. He was awarded the Legion of Merit and many other American and foreign decorations for the distinguished performance of perilous duties under heavy fire.

While serving as Deputy Chief of Chaplains at Army headquarters in 1947, he was elevated by Pope Pius XII to the rank of domestic prelate, with the title of Right Reverend Monsignor. General Ryan is the first Roman Catholic to become Army Chief of Chaplains since the 1937-1945 tenure of that office by the present Most Reverend Bishop William R. Arnold. The intervening Chiefs of Chaplains, Generals Luther Miller, Roy H. Parker and Ivan L. Bennett, belonged to Protestant denominations. Since General George Washington appealed for a corps of chaplains to correct "the mean and low vice" of swearing in the Continental Army, and Congress made provision on July 29, 1775 for the payment of chaplains, the post of Army chief of chaplains has most often been held by a Protestant minister.

Patrick James Ryan was born December 3, 1902 in the village of Manannah, near Litchfield, Minnesota. He attended St. Thomas Military Academy in St. Paul, and was graduated in 1919. He enrolled at the College of St. Thomas, the Roman Catholic institution chartered in 1865 as the St. Thomas Seminary. After receiving his A.B. degree in 1923, he prepared for the priesthood at the St. Paul Seminary, and on taking his degree of Bachelor of Sacred Theology in 1927, was ordained.

For one year following his ordination, Father Ryan served as a civilian priest in St. Helena's Parish in Minneapolis. He joined the Reserve Corps of the U.S. Army on April 27, 1928, serving as a reserve officer at Fort Snelling,

Minnesota. On November 2 of the same year he was commissioned a first lieutenant in the Corps of Chaplains.

Assigned in December to the Chaplains' Training School at Fort Leavenworth, Kansas, Lieutenant Ryan was stationed there until the following February, when he was transferred to Fort Riley, Kansas to assume the duties of assistant chaplain at the Cavalry School and to take the equitation course, which he completed in 1930. At Fort Shafter, Hawaii where he was sent in January 1932, he was occupied as chaplain of the 64th Coast Artillery Regiment when promoted to captain on October 5, 1933.

In August 1935 Captain Ryan returned to the continental United States to assume a chaplain's duties at the Army Medical Center (Walter Reed Hospital) in Washington, D.C.; in October 1939 he resumed his duties as regimental chaplain to the 64th Coast Artillery at Fort Shafter and also officiated as post chaplain at the Tripler General Hospital at Fort Kamehameha in Hawaii. He was advanced to the rank of major on October 6, 1940.

Major Ryan was reassigned in November 1941 as chaplain of the Third Infantry Division, which trained for World War II overseas service successively at Fort Lewis in Washington, Fort Ord in California and Camp Pickett in Virginia. He was promoted to lieutenant colonel (temporary) on February 1, 1942.

The following October he went to North Africa with his division, which came immediately under fire and "suffered one of the heaviest casualty rates of the war." *Newsweek* (March 29, 1954) further stated that "he landed with his men at Fedala in French Morocco and received the Legion of Merit for his work in burying the many dead." In February 1943 Lieutenant Colonel Ryan was appointed chief chaplain to General Mark Clark's Fifth Army, with which he served in combat first in Sicily and later in Italy, and participated in the Salerno landings. He was promoted to colonel (temporary) on December 25, 1943.

In addition to the Legion of Merit, Colonel Ryan received such American awards as the Bronze Star Medal and the Army Commendation Ribbon, and such foreign decorations as the Order of the British Empire, Brazil's Medalha de Guerra, Italy's Bronze Medal of Valor with Star, and the Italian Order of the Crown.

Recalled to the United States in July 1945, Ryan assumed new duties in the office of the chief of chaplains in Washington, D.C., where he became director of plans and training under Major General Luther D. Miller, and in 1946 became Deputy Chief of Chaplains. In June 1947 he was elevated by Pope Pius XII to the rank of domestic prelate, with the title of Right Reverend Monsignor.

In September 1948 Colonel Ryan became chaplain to the Sixth Army and was stationed at the Presidio, San Francisco. He was recalled to Washington in July 1952 to become Acting Deputy Chief of Chaplains; on August

U. S. Army

RT. REV. MSGR. PATRICK J. RYAN

21 he was named Deputy Chief; and on March 6, 1953 he was advanced to brigadier general (temporary). President Dwight D. Eisenhower nominated Monsignor Ryan to take over the position of Army chief of chaplains from Major General Ivan L. Bennett, when the Baptist minister retired on April 30. Monsignor Ryan was promoted to major general (temporary) on May 1, 1954. His permanent Army rank, dating from March 11, 1948, is colonel.

"The Chief of Chaplains," states the *U.S. Government Organization Manual*, "advises the Secretary of the Army and the Chief of Staff on moral and religious matters and formulates plans for, and supervises, moral training and religious ministration in the Army." In the *Army Almanac* it is further stated that he "is charged with the responsibility for procuring equipment" and "supervises chaplain training" which in recent years has been centered in the Chaplain School at Carlisle Barracks, Pennsylvania. The Chaplains Corps reached its peak strength of 8,171 on July 31, 1945, but is now reduced to less than 1,500.

Service organizations of which Ryan is a member are the Military Chaplains Association, Inc., and the Military Order of the World Wars; his clubs are the Army and Navy and the Columbia Country in Washington. He has been described as "short, plump, and brown-eyed." "Monsignor Ryan is called a 'lace-curtain Irishman' by his colleagues." He is "known for his fine social graces, his constant stream of Irish jokes and his elegant dinners," but in his office at the Pentagon is "all business" (*Newsweek*, March 29, 1954). His "constant companion" is a German police dog named Duke, which he "liberated" in Italy while with the Fifth Army.

"Monsignor Ryan," according to *Newsweek*, "is famous for his insistence that chaplains emphasize their spiritual duties and avoid the

RYAN, PATRICK J.—*Continued*

'miscellaneous' activities commanders often impose upon them—such as running the baseball team."

Citations for spiritual stewardship and service in interfaith goodwill were presented on February 5, 1955 to Major General Patrick J. Ryan (Army), Major General Charles I. Carpenter (Air Force), and Rear Admiral Edward P. Harp, Jr. (Navy) by the Alexander D. Goode Lodge of B'nai B'rith.

References

N Y Herald Tribune p17 Mr 19 '54 por; p24 My 2 '54
N Y Times p3 Jl 19 '47; p9 Mr 19 '54 por; p31 My 2 '54
Newsweek 43:80+ Mr 29 '54
Washington (D.C.) Post p2 Mr 19 '54 por
American Catholic Who's Who, 1954-55

SAID, NURI AS- *See* Nuri as-Said

SAINT, EVA MARIE July 4, 1924- Actress

Address: b. c/o Columbia Pictures Corp., 729 Seventh Ave., New York 19; h. 51 Fifth Ave., New York 3

Hollywood acknowledged its debt to television by awarding its "Oscar" for the best supporting actress of 1954 to TV alumna Eva Marie Saint, for her performance of the convent-reared girl in *On the Waterfront.* "Her essential characteristic is serenity," *Mademoiselle,* which had also bestowed a merit award on her for 1954, commented. This quality has been evident in her many TV roles, in the Broadway play, *The Trip to Bountiful,* as well as in *Waterfront,* her first film, for which she also received a *Look* magazine award.

Previous to working before the television and motion picture cameras, Miss Saint had modeled and acted in radio serials. "Her slender blondness is not easily forgotten," *Newsweek* remarked. "She moves and speaks with plainness, but with implications of depth that avoids either dreariness or harshness."

The younger daughter of Eva and John Merle Saint, Eva Marie Saint was born July 4, 1924, in Newark, New Jersey. Her elder sister, Adelaide, was a research chemist prior to her marriage. Their father, a district manager for the Goodrich Rubber Company, is now a resident of Bryn Mawr, Pennsylvania. In the years that the girls were growing up, the family home was in Delmar, New York, near the State capital of Albany, and it was in Delmar that Eva Marie received most of her schooling, up through the high school.

Planning to become a teacher—of third grade, as her mother had been before her marriage—Eva Marie Saint entered Bowling Green State University in Bowling Green, Ohio, where it soon became evident that her best abilities lay in the fields of art, English and speech. With the encouragement of a friend, she tried out for a college play, in which she was given the leading role—the first of three she was to have before graduating in 1946. Other campus honors were given to her: the freshman class named her its "Dream Girl," and she was also "Sweater Queen," the "feminine half of the Moonlight Couple," and May Queen. Between her sophomore and junior years, she spent the summer working as an $87-a-month guide at the National Broadcasting Company radio station in New York.

With her Bachelor of Arts degree in hand, Eva Marie Saint returned to New York and lived with her family in Flushing, Long Island. One year of haunting radio producers' offices made her so familiar to them that one finally assumed she was an experienced radio performer, and gave her an eighteen-word part as a telephone operator. Parts in radio serials followed: *Rosemary, Young Doctor Malone,* and for two and a half years, she was familiar to radio audiences as Claudia in *One Man's Family.* "With me," she told Oscar Godbout, of the New York *Times* (August 1, 1954) "there were years of doing small things, soap operas, ads, modeling, then the snowball just seemed to grow." In 1948 she began attending Actors Studio classes regularly.

Miss Saint made her debut before the television camera, in a show called *Camp Hoop-La.* More and more, she came to be known to television viewers for her roles in *Robert Montgomery Presents, Studio One, Philco Playhouse, The Web,* and *The ABC Album.* She won the Sylvania award in 1954 as "the best dramatic actress in television." Her performance in a TV adaptation of Sidney Howard's play *Yellow Jack* in January 1955 for NBC's *Producer's Showcase* was praised by Harriet Van Horne in the New York *World-Telegram and Sun.*

One of the television plays in which she appeared, *The Trip to Bountiful,* by Horton Foote, was adapted for the theatre in 1953 and produced by the Theatre Guild and Fred Coe, with Lillian Gish as the star. Miss Saint's previous Broadway experience had been as understudy to Jocelyn Brando in the role of the Navy nurse in *Mister Roberts.* Originally hired for the part, she was told after a week by director Joshua Logan that she was too inexperienced and would be replaced by someone more familiar with the stage. "I went into a dark corner and cried," Miss Saint recalled. "I understudied Jocelyn Brando for six months, but she never got sick once, and I never got to play the part. So I quit" (New York *World-Telegram and Sun,* October 16, 1954).

The Trip to Bountiful brought her praise from New York's critics for her "warm and sympathetic", "touching and sensitively beautiful" performance. William Hawkins of the *World-Telegram and Sun* thought her "lovely and composed as the traveling companion to the mother," while Brooks Atkinson of the New York *Times* considered hers "a sweet characterization." Commenting on her approach to the role, Walter F. Kerr of the New York *Herald Tribune* observed that "she just nudges the role into existence, working softly, placidly, and with infinite attractiveness."

While she was appearing in *Bountiful,* Miss Saint was offered the feminine lead in *On the Waterfront,* to which she was signed by producer Sam Spiegel and director Elia Kazan in November 1953. Filmed entirely on the docks in Hoboken, New Jersey, with Marlon Brando as its star, the motion picture was adapted by Budd Schulberg from the exposé of racketeering on the New York docks by Malcolm Johnson. "For Eva Marie Saint," predicted *Collier's,* "this low-key setting holds more promise than a glamor-gutted Hollywood lot . . . She plays a convent-bred youngster whose menfolk work on the docks."

When the picture opened in July 1954, the New York *Times* critic referred to Miss Saint as "a pretty and blond artisan who does not have to depend on these attributes. Amid scenes of carnage, she gives tenderness and sensitivity to genuine romance." A. H. Weiler of the same newspaper found that "Kazan's choice of Eva Marie Saint is inspired. She is sweet, intelligent, and appealing in the role . . . poignant, tender, and moving." The *Christian Science Monitor* reviewer described Miss Saint as "a compassionate actress who possesses beauty and something much more."

At the end of 1954, a poll of film critics throughout the United States by *Film Daily* resulted in her being chosen "find" of the year. On March 30, when the twenty-seventh annual Oscar awards of the Academy of Motion Picture Arts and Sciences were announced, *On the Waterfront* garnered seven of the prize statuettes. One of these was awarded to Eva Marie Saint as the best supporting actress of 1954, and was announced over a television hook-up from the Century Theatre in New York to the Pantages Theatre in Hollywood.

Miss Saint has received fan letters saying, "You're my favorite movie star. P.S. Your husband is very handsome." Her husband, Jeffrey Hayden to whom she was married on October 27, 1951, is a television director and producer. Their son, born four days after receiving her academy award, has been named Darrell. They are residents of New York's Greenwich Village. The Haydens spend their leisure time aboard their cruiser, an acquisition that was something Miss Saint "always wanted." Tennis, water skiing, fishing, and skiing are her other recreations. Her husband says that she is an excellent cook.

Her six years of violin study as a child have left her with a taste for classical music. For reading, she turns to the plays of Sean O'Casey, Arthur Miller or Anton Chekhov, or to the works of Sherwood Anderson, William Faulkner, and Thomas Wolfe. Miss Saint is five feet, five and a half inches tall and weighs 115 pounds. She has what one biographer has described as "honey-colored" hair. Biographers differ on the color of her eyes, one calling them "willow-plate blue" and another calling them "green." Television will probably remain her preferred medium, she told Aline Mosby of the New York *World-Telegram and Sun:* "Doing good scripts on TV puts you ahead much more than one mediocre movie. . . . Besides, I'm too old to be a starlet."

EVA MARIE SAINT

Television director Fred Coe and playwright Sumner Locke Elliott say that she is a "joy to work with because she finds nuances in a part the writer himself might not previously have suspected."

"It's all concentration," says Miss Saint. "With three cameras on you simultaneously—you *must* concentrate" (*Cosmopolitan,* March 1955).

References

Cosmop 138:58+ Mr '55 pors
Mademoiselle 40:63 Ja '55
N Y Sunday Mirror Mag p4 D 20 '53
N Y Times II p5 Ag 1 '54
N Y World-Telegram p11 Je 29 '53; p8 O 16 '54
Newsweek 44:78 Ag 2 '54

SALISBURY, HARRISON E(VANS)

Nov. 14, 1908- Journalist

Address: b. c/o The New York Times, 229 W. 43d St., New York 36

The winner of the 1955 Pulitzer Prize for international reporting was Harrison E. Salisbury, who from 1949 to 1954 was the New York *Times* correspondent in the Soviet Union. In his quarter century as a newspaperman, Salisbury has also been a reporter, bureau manager and foreign news editor of the United Press.

During 1954 he made a 12,000-mile trip through the Soviet North and Siberia, "probably the most extensive survey of this . . . region by an American since the 1880's." He found it "incredibly harsh and grim . . . an empire-within-an-empire, the slave state of prison labor and forced-residence workers . . . men and women going blankly about their jobs under the eyes of armed MVD agents." From what Salisbury saw in Russia since Stalin's

New York Times

HARRISON E. SALISBURY

death, he is convinced that no "era of sweetness and light has suddenly descended. . . . What is new . . . is that Russia has passed into the hands of a group of men who are displaying striking flexibility . . . in their handling of domestic and foreign problems." These men have "a large measure of confidence as a result of possession of the hydrogen and atomic fission bombs . . . and jet aircraft."

In the summer of 1954 he returned to New York to accept an assignment on the *Times* city staff. His series of articles, "Russia Re-Viewed," was published in the *Times* in September and October 1954 and was expanded into a book, *American in Russia,* published by Harper & Brothers in 1955. For this series he was awarded the Pulitzer Prize for international reporting, announced in May 1955. His first book on the Soviet Union, *Russia on the Way,* was published by the Macmillan Company in 1946.

"Among colleagues at home and abroad," the New York *Times* wrote of Salisbury after he won the Pulitzer award, "he built a reputation for energy, curiosity and objectivity whether covering local stories in his home city of Minneapolis, war news for the United Press in London, or the Russian scene on the challenging assignment as head of the *Times* bureau in Moscow."

The son of Percy Pritchard and Georgiana (Evans) Salisbury, Harrison Evans Salisbury was born in Minneapolis, Minnesota on November 14, 1908. While still a college student at the University of Minnesota, he became a reporter for the Minneapolis *Journal,* which employed him from 1928 until 1929. He became a correspondent for the United Press in St. Paul in 1930, the year in which he received his B.A. degree. After graduation he worked for the U.P. in Chicago and Washington, D.C., then moved to its foreign desk in New York City. In 1943 he became manager of the London office, and the next year, in October 1944, the association's foreign news editor. In this capacity he made a 50,000-mile tour of all war theaters, including an unexpectedly lengthy survey of Russia.

Salisbury was in Algiers late in 1943 when the U.P. sent him to Cairo "where the news of the Teheran conference was breaking, and then on to Moscow to relieve Henry Shapiro." He left Cairo on December 16, 1943; reached Stalingrad, after a series of misadventures, on January 14, 1944; and Moscow shortly thereafter. "I came to Russia," he wrote later, "for a six weeks' look, a quick survey—in and out—and the summit of my ambition was a trip to the Red Army front. Instead, I stayed eight months and saw the battlefields of the Ukraine and the Crimea, the secret arsenals that kept Russia going when the West was overrun, the beginnings of Russo-American military collaboration, the inner workings of Soviet recesses I had never expected to penetrate—and the Russian people." He traveled with Eric Johnston on his tour of the Soviet Union.

Shortly after his return to the United States in 1944, he published a series of articles on his Russian observations in *Collier's* (September 2, November 18, December 23, 1944). Salisbury expanded his articles into his first book, *Russia on the Way* (1946). It was in the main descriptive, an objective report of his observations, but his conclusion ventured some political forecasting. "Speculation often arises in the West as to what will happen in Russia when Stalin dies," he noted. "Stalin's death will bring far less change to Russia than Roosevelt's did to America. . . . It is safe to prophesy that the death of Stalin will cause no major change in Russian policy, foreign or domestic. Nor is Stalin's death likely to precipitate such a struggle for power as resulted when Lenin died." On the future course of Russo-American relations he remarked that "it is bound to be marked by wrangling and disputes, growing out of the basic differences in our philosophy and point of view."

J. S. Curtiss, writing in the *Political Science Quarterly* (September 1946), referred to *Russia on the Way* as on the whole, "one of the most informative of the Russian war correspondent books, and, thanks to an easy style and numerous illustrations from his own experiences, very entertaining." Maurice Hindus commented in the *Saturday Review of Literature* (July 20, 1946) that Salisbury's book was "interpolated with lucid, unpretentious, thought-provoking interpretations."

In January 1949 Salisbury joined the New York *Times* as its Moscow correspondent. The *Times* had had no correspondent in the Russian capital since the spring of 1947, when Drew Middleton left for a vacation and was refused re-entry. Salisbury held this post until September 1954, when, at his own request, he was replaced; his successor is Clifton Daniel. In his more than five years as "the *Times* man" in the Soviet Union, Salisbury wrote several series of widely read and frequently controversial dispatches.

In the fall of 1950 he took a vacation in the United States, and after his return to Moscow, wrote one such series. The *Times* prefaced his reports with the cautionary note: "As is the case with all news dispatches from Moscow, these articles were subject to Soviet censorship and were written with that fact in mind." Salisbury was both praised for his objectivity and criticized for "glorifying" the Soviet regime. However, after Salisbury's uncensored articles were published in the New York *Times* (in September and October 1954), his critics remarked on the contrast between these and his earlier reports.

During May and June 1954 Salisbury made a 12,000-mile trip through Siberia. Some of the impressions gathered on this journey were incorporated in a widely discussed series of fourteen articles entitled "Russia Re-Viewed," which appeared in the New York *Times* after Salisbury's return to the United States. *Time* magazine commented that his series was "not only a well-written, fresh, firsthand report on Russian Communists, but it also vividly demonstrated how misleading many of his censored *Times* stories were." Salisbury explained: "This is the real story, not the emasculated one that was all that fearful censors permitted correspondents to cable."

Perhaps Salisbury's most startling statement concerned the manner of Stalin's death: "It is by no means impossible that Stalin was murdered on or about March 5, 1953, by the group of his close associates who now run Russia." If Stalin "just happened to be struck down by a ruptured artery on March 2 [1953]," he wrote, "it must be recorded as one of the most fortuitous occurrences in history. It saved the lives of some thousands of Russians." Just before his death Stalin was preparing for a purge. He had already touched off a widespread campaign of violent anti-Semitism with the "doctors' plot" (*Time*, October 4, 1954).

On the basis of these articles Salisbury wrote his second book, *American in Russia*. Leslie C. Stevens wrote in the *Saturday Review* (February 26, 1955), "It is as a reporter of scenes, moods, and atmosphere that Salisbury excels, rather than as an interpreter of ultimate meanings and a predictor of the future." E. S. Pisko, reviewing the book in the *Christian Science Monitor* (February 17, 1955), wrote: "There are many statements and conclusions . . . which one would like to argue about. But it would be an argument that only future events can settle. Until then, the author would have the better of the argument because he was 'there'; he watched and listened—and he has woven his observations into a colorful account." J. N. Hazard commented in the New York *Herald Tribune Book Review* (February 13, 1955): "Salisbury's insights into Russian life ring true to those who have lived among the Russians. He got to the roots of that life. Whether he has guessed right on the reasons for Stalin's and Beria's deaths would be hard to say."

Salisbury stated in his book that he was not returning to the United States after nearly six years in Russia "as a pessimist. Nor as an optimist." But he hoped, "as something of a realist." He regarded people who think that the threat of war could be banished as "surely the greatest idealists of all time. Never in man's history had it been banished and who were we so overweening in our pride to think we had the key to Paradise?" He urged that America maintain its position of strength, "for to be second best in a nuclear world was unthinkable folly." Nor does he lean toward the "gloom-mongers, the 'let's drop the A-bomb now' school. . . ." He advocated patience and Yankee common sense and applying a little "honey as well as vinegar to the critical joints" of the Communist machine, since the United States and Russia "must go on living under the same roof or perish."

Speaking at the New York *Times* Youth Forum in November 1954, Salisbury expressed the view that a scheme of coexistence with Russia was feasible. "It is difficult and will require great effort and forbearance on both sides," he pointed out. "But I believe it can be accomplished if there is courage and good will by both parties." He has since addressed other groups on his Russian experiences.

Among the stories which Salisbury has written since his return from Moscow were a series on economic changes in the city of Yonkers due to the closing down of factories; the litter problem on New York City streets; the United Steelworkers union bargaining with the United States Steel Corporation in Pittsburgh; and an article in the New York *Times Magazine* on January 23, 1955 entitled "Clues to the News About Russia." "The Soviet censorship is the world's strictest," he wrote. "Not one word about political prisoners, forced labor, prison camps, political exiles, deportation of populations, or any of the other terrible abuses of the Soviet system may be transmitted from Moscow."

Salisbury is a member of Theta Delta Chi and of Sigma Delta Chi fraternities. He married Mary Hollis on April 1, 1933; the Salisburys had two sons, Michael and Stephen. The marriage ended in divorce. The journalist, who speaks Russian, has been described as "tall, thin, professional-looking" (*Newsweek*, September 27, 1954).

References

N Y Times p5 Ja 22 '49; p28 My 3 '55 por

Who's Who in America, 1954-55

World Biography (1954)

SALIT, NORMAN, RABBI (sal'ĭt) June 8, 1896- Lawyer; organization official

Address: b. 320 Broadway, New York 7; h. 160 Wildacre Ave., Lawrence, N.Y.

The first American Jewish leader to visit Germany at the invitation of the German government in twenty years was Dr. Norman Salit, president of the Synagogue Council of America, who conferred with officials at Bonn in 1953 on the problem of anti-Semitism in present-day Germany. During 1952 he made a first-hand study of the religious life of Euro-

RABBI NORMAN SALIT

pean and Israeli Jews. A rabbi and attorney, he has long been actively associated with religious and professional groups and with patriotic and cultural organizations. He was elected president of the Synagogue Council of America in 1953 and re-elected in 1954.

After serving as rabbi in synagogues in New York and Pennsylvania, he began the practice of law in New York City in 1929. During World War II he was executive director of the Wartime Emergency Commission for Conservative Judaism. Freedom Foundation, of which he is a director, has twice conferred awards upon him.

Norman Salit was born in New York City on June 8, 1896, the son of Michael and Rachel Ethel (Altschul) Salit. His father, a descendant of Rabbi Samuel Strashun, a Lithuanian commentator on the Talmud, was a liquor merchant who was treasurer of the Federation of American Zionists, the forerunner of the Zionist Organization of America.

Norman received his secondary education at Townsend Harris Hall in New York, from which he was graduated in 1912. He attended the College of the City of New York, with philosophy his major subject, and won the board of trustees' Original Oration Prize, an achievement that did much to give direction to his career. Participating in numerous extracurricular activities, he was a member of the swimming team and assistant manager of the tennis team, was president of his class in his sophomore year and secretary and vice-president of the Student Council, served on the junior prom committee, belonged to the Phrenocosmia Literary Society and the Menorah Society, and played violin in the college orchestra.

After graduating with the B.A. degree in 1916, Salit entered the Law School of New York University where he won honors in his second year. He was awarded the degree of J.D. (Doctor of Jurisprudence) in 1919 and was admitted to the New York bar in the following year. He was ordained a rabbi in 1920 at the Jewish Theological Seminary of America, where he won the Lehman Public Speaking Prize. He was granted the M.A. degree from Columbia University in 1922; his thesis was entitled "The Law of Torts in the Pentateuch, as Compared with the Code of Hammurabi and the Twelve Tables of Rome."

In 1917 he became assistant rabbi to the congregation Beth Israel Anshei Emes in Brooklyn, New York. The next year he occupied the pulpit of the Tree of Life congregation in Oil City, Pennsylvania. Another of his duties in 1918 was to represent the Jewish Welfare Board at Fort Riley and Camp Funston in Kansas. From 1919 until 1924 he was rabbi of Temple Adath Israel in the Bronx. For four years (1920-1924) he was president of the Intercollegiate Zionist Association. His last pulpit was in Far Rockaway, Long Island, where he served as rabbi of congregation Shaaray Tefila from 1924 until 1929 when he gave up his ministry and began to practice law in New York City.

The Queens County Bar Association named Salit as head of its committee on legislation and law reform, a post he held from 1933 until 1937; from 1933 until 1939 he was also a member of the association's committee on discipline. He became associate counsel of the New York State Home Owners' Loan Corporation in 1934, retaining that office until 1937. That year he was admitted to practice before the bar of the United States Supreme Court. He has also been admitted to the bar of the Treasury Department and of the Federal courts of the southern and eastern districts of New York.

During World War II Salit served as executive director of the Wartime Emergency Commission for Conservative Judaism from the date of the commission's formation in August 1944 until its dissolution in December 1946. The object of the commission, which represented the Chaplaincy Availability Board, the Jewish Theological Seminary of America, the Placement Committee, the Rabbinical Assembly of America, and the United Synagogue of America, was to aid congregations whose rabbis had entered military service. For his work on the commission the Jewish Theological Seminary presented him with a scroll in 1946 in recognition of his "faithful and distinguished service to faith and country."

Salit was unsuccessful candidate on the Democratic ticket for presiding supervisor of Nassau County in 1947 and for children's court judge of Nassau County two years later. In 1951 he was honored jointly with Erwin D. Canham, editor of the *Christian Science Monitor*, by Freedom Foundation, of which he is a director. He was similarly honored in 1952. On March 21, 1952 he began a ten-week tour of Europe and Israel to investigate the religious life of the Jews in those areas. Upon his return he reported his discovery of a strong religious spirit among Israeli Jews, and the urgent need of more American rabbis in Israel.

Salit became president of the Synagogue Council of America in June 1953. He was re-elected to a second term in June 1954. The Council, which represents all branches of Judaism in the United States, comprises the Rabbinical Council of America and the Union of Orthodox Jewish Congregations; the Rabbinical Assembly of America and the United Synagogue of America (Conservative); the Central Conference of American Rabbis and the Union of American Hebrew Congregations (Reform). Shortly after assuming the Council presidency Salit announced the formation of a 100-member national advisory committee to draw up plans to foster "the primacy of the synagogue in all aspects of Jewish life in the United States."

On September 20, 1953 the Synagogue Council announced that the West German government had invited nine American religious leaders, including Salit, for a month-long inspection trip of West Germany. Salit would be, the Council pointed out, "the first Jew to visit Germany on an official German government invitation since the rise of Hitler twenty years ago." Through conferences early in his trip with Dr. Hermann Ehlers, president of the Bundestag, and other high government officials, Salit gained "the impression that the West German government is thoroughly ashamed of the Nazi and anti-Semitic excesses of the past."

Later he conferred with President Theodor Heuss and Chancellor Konrad Adenauer. Upon his return to the United States, he voiced "great disappointment" over the failure of the West German government to do all it could "to wipe out anti-Semitism and Nazism," and urged the American government to "exert every effort to influence the West German government to strengthen its fight against any resurgence of bigotry and totalitarianism." He noted that German leaders recognized that their country must accept responsibility for Hitler, but added that the same could not be said of the German people.

"Anti-Semitism in Germany is too deeply rooted," he remarked on another occasion, "to yield to anything but the most thorough campaign of extirpation. A deeply intrenched disease cannot be cured by a surface-scratching remedy; the therapy must be in proportion to the malady. The devil of hate must be exorcised from the soul of Germany before that country can take its place with the civilized nations of the world." On February 7, 1954, representing the Jewish faith, Salit appeared on the American Legion's *Back to God* program with President Dwight D. Eisenhower, Rev. Dr. Norman Vincent Peale and Bishop Fulton Sheen.

Salit is a member of the American Academy for Jewish Research, B'nai Brith, the Rabbinical Assembly of America (of which he is counsel), the New York Board of Rabbis (of which he has been secretary, treasurer and vice-president), the Zionist Organization of America, the United Synagogue of Long Island, and the Long Island Jewish American Congress. He is on the Board of Overseers of the Jewish Theological Seminary, the Board of Directors of the Jewish Educational Committee, and vice-president of the American Biblical Encyclopedia Society. Salit was succeeded by Dr. Abraham J. Feldman as president of the Synagogue Council of America on June 8, 1955.

In 1950 Salit, who is also a member of the New York County Lawyers Association, served on the committee on professional ethics of the Nassau County Bar Association. He is on the national council of the Boy Scouts of America and on the executive of the Nassau County Council of the Boy Scouts. His fraternities are Kappa (of C.C.N.Y.) and Theta Sigma Lambda (of the N.Y.U. Law School).

Among the more recent of his numerous articles are "The Jew in Germany Today" for the U. S. Information Service, 1953; and "Amidst the Ruins" in *The Jewish Horizon*, February 1954. In 1943 and 1944 he conducted a weekly column under the title "The Bible's Message" in *The Jewish Examiner*. The Jewish Theological Seminary awarded him the degree of M.H.L. in 1949.

He married the former Ruth Levy on July 1, 1928; they had two daughters, Naomi Hannah and Miriam Rachel; the latter died in 1949. The attorney's favorite forms of recreation are reading, traveling, swimming and golf. He is five feet nine inches tall and weighs 164 pounds; his eyes and hair are brown.

In a Rosh ha-Shanah message on September 27, 1954 Salit urged Americans to strengthen religious values abroad instead of offering only material assistance. He said, "We must create a spiritual Point Four program in the present crucial world struggle."

References

Who's Who in America, 1954-55
Who's Who in American Jewry, 1938-39
Who's Who in New York, 1952
Who's Who in the East (1953)

SAMUEL, HERBERT (LOUIS) SAMUEL, 1ST VISCOUNT Nov. 6, 1870- British statesman; Liberal party leader

Address: h. 32 Porchester Ter., London W. 2, England

One of the oldest of contemporary British statesmen is the first Viscount Samuel, the leader of the Liberal party in the House of Lords. Herbert Samuel, who served in the House of Commons for twenty-two years before being elevated to the peerage in 1937, was Secretary of State for Home Affairs in Cabinets under Prime Ministers Herbert Asquith and Ramsay MacDonald. He was the first British High Commissioner for Palestine (1920-1925). Lord Samuel is the author of an autobiography and of several books on politics, philosophy and science, including *Essays in Physics: With a Letter from Albert Einstein* (Harcourt, 1952).

On June 8, 1955 Lord Samuel announced that he had relinquished the leadership of the Liberal party, a position he held in the House of Lords for fourteen years.

Herbert Louis Samuel, the youngest child of Edwin Louis and Clara (Yates) Samuel, was born on November 6, 1870 in Liverpool, England where his father was a prominent banker. Herbert's eldest brother, Stuart Montagu, be-

British Inf. Services

LORD SAMUEL

came a Member of Parliament and was created a baronet; the second, Dennis Edwin, was a banker; the third, Gilbert Ellis, a solicitor; his sister, Mabel Henrietta (Spielmann), wrote books for children. The family later moved to London where Herbert's father was a senior partner in the banking firm now known as Samuel Montagu & Company, Ltd. When Herbert was six years old, his father died.

His mother's and father's families were orthodox Jews and Herbert received a thorough grounding in Hebrew. He attended the undenominational University College School in London from 1883 to 1888 and matriculated at Balliol College, Oxford University, in 1889.

Before that date, however, much had occurred which was to have a decisive bearing on Herbert's future. His uncle and guardian (who later became Lord Swaythling) had joined the Liberal party and was the Member of Parliament for the Tower Hamlets constituency of London, including Whitechapel, a slum district. When Herbert's brother, Stuart Montagu became the Progressive candidate for the Whitechapel seat in the London County Council, Herbert assisted him in door-to-door canvassing.

Samuel later stated in his autobiography that he was "appalled" by what he saw of squalid home life and sweatshop working conditions and was deeply moved by the plight of the London dock workers who went on strike to secure sixpence an hour. "From that early date," he wrote, "the House of Commons became my objective, and to take part in social legislation, my aim" (*Grooves of Change*, Bobbs, 1946; English edition, *Memoirs*, Cresset, 1945).

At Oxford, Samuel took his B.A. degree in history with First Class Honors in 1893 and the M.A. degree in 1897. He was elected president of the radical Russell Club as well as secretary of the Social Science Club, and was on close and friendly terms with the leaders of the Fabian movement, although he himself never accepted doctrines of socialism.

He made some political addresses in Oxfordshire with such success that he was adopted as the Liberal candidate in 1895 for the House of Commons in the South Oxfordshire District. He was defeated by only 361 votes and when he ran again in the same district in 1900, he lost by only 172 votes.

In the interim he had been made honorary secretary of both the Home Counties Liberal Federation and the Land Law Reform Association and was instrumental in starting the excellent but short-lived *Progressive Review*. He also began work on his first book, *Liberalism* (Richards, 1902), shortly before an important by-election in the Cleveland Division of North Riding, Yorkshire. Local Liberals invited Samuel to be their candidate and in November 1902, he was elected to Parliament by a 2,000 vote majority. He represented the Cleveland Division for the next sixteen years.

Believing that every Member of Parliament should "be well informed on . . . some province of Empire questions," Samuel specialized on African problems. He made a personal tour of the Uganda Protectorate in 1902 and spoke in favor of the construction of the Uganda railway. In May 1903 he introduced into the House of Commons a resolution concerning administrative abuses in the Congo Free State which prompted both Belgian and British inquiries and led to the establishment of a more progressive government. He also brought attention to the maltreatment of Chinese laborers in South Africa.

When the Liberal party returned to power under Sir Henry Campbell-Bannerman in 1905, Samuel was appointed Parliamentary Under-Secretary in the Home Department and during the next several years he promoted much important social legislation. Samuel was made a Privy Councillor (P.C.) in 1908 and after Herbert Asquith became Prime Minister, he was called to the Cabinet as Chancellor of the Duchy of Lancaster in 1909. He has always been proud, he has said, that he was the first "member of the Jewish community" to attain Cabinet rank (Prime Minister Benjamin Disraeli had been "withdrawn" at an early age from the Jewish community by his father).

As Postmaster-General (1910-1914), Samuel negotiated the first contract between the British government and Marconi's Wireless Telegraph Company, Ltd., and also the acquisition by the post office department of the telephone business in Britain. In 1914 he was appointed head of the Local Government Board, subsequently expanded to become the Ministry of Health.

In 1916 Herbert Samuel was Asquith's Secretary of State for Home Affairs. When David Lloyd George succeeded Asquith as Prime Minister in December 1916, Samuel told him that he "greatly disliked the way the change had come about" (*Grooves of Change*) and declined to take office under him. Samuel continued to be active in the House of Commons, however, and helped to pass a bill making women eligible for Parliament.

When the "khaki election" was held in 1918 the coalition of Conservatives and Lloyd George Liberals was overwhelmingly victorious, and Samuel was defeated with Asquith and all the other members of the Liberal Cabinet who had not followed Lloyd George.

Out of Parliament for the next eleven years, he was appointed president of the British branch of the Anglo-Belgian Union and British Special Commissioner to Belgium (1919) and helped with the post-war rehabilitation of that country. He was knighted in 1920 and appointed High Commissioner for Palestine. He concurred in the Balfour Declaration and favored the creation of a "Jewish homeland" rather than of a Jewish state. Under his five-year administration, Palestine made remarkable economic progress.

In 1925 Prime Minister Stanley Baldwin asked him to take the chairmanship of a Royal Commission "to inquire into and report upon the economic position of the coal industry." The commission's recommendations in the following spring were praised and Samuel entered into negotiations with the strike committee to end the general strike of 1926. He was created a Knight Grand Cross of the Order of the Bath in the same year.

Re-elected to Parliament by the Darwen Division of Lancashire in 1929, he was named deputy leader of the Liberal parliamentary party in the House of Commons. He took over the party's formal leadership in 1931 and became Secretary of State for Home Affairs under Prime Minister Ramsay MacDonald. As a lifelong "free trader" Samuel was, however, unable to accept the Ottawa tariff agreements concluded in 1932 and he resigned from the Cabinet with the other ministers who were representing the Liberal party. Samuel continued to be Liberal party leader in the House of Commons, however, until his defeat in the general election of 1935.

In his autobiography Samuel has stated that the loss of his seat at Darwen—which ended his career in the House of Commons—gave him leisure to resume what he describes as his "exploration into fundamentals." He had become president of the British Institute for Philosophical Studies (later renamed the Royal Institute of Philosophy) in 1931. One of his institute lectures was published as *Philosophy and the Ordinary Man* (Routledge, 1932) and another as *The Tree of Good and Evil* (Davies, 1933). During the middle 1930's he traveled widely in Europe and the United States (on one occasion in connection with seeking aid for persecuted Jews in Germany).

He also paid a long visit to India, returning to concentrate in 1936-1937 on the completion of his principal work on faith and conduct, *Belief and Action* (Bobbs, 1937). This book was favorably reviewed in *Nature, Christian Century,* and other publications.

The London *Times Literary Supplement* (October 16, 1937) commented: "If politics had not claimed him Lord Samuel might have given new distinction to the English and common-sense school of philosophy. Even as it is, in a book whose eminently practical aim is indicated by its title, he makes no small contribution to thought."

He was raised to the peerage in June 1937 by King George VI and took the title "Viscount Samuel of Mount Carmel, and of Toxteth in the City of Liverpool." In the House of Lords he became deputy leader of the Liberal party in 1941 and leader in December 1944.

Since elevated to the peerage, Lord Samuel has written such books as *Liberty: Principles and Practice* (Longmans, 1940), *Democracy, Its Failings & Its Future* (Oxford University Press, 1941), and *Creative Man, and Other Addresses* (Cresset, 1949). His political speeches are not frequent, but he participated in the 1951 general elections. In a talk before the upper chamber of the British Parliament in November 1952, he attacked as "irrational" the hereditary principle as a method of choosing legislators and warned the House of Lords against "falling into the senility of an asylum for octogenarians."

Lord Samuel, who holds an honorary D.C.L. degree from Oxford University and honorary LL.D. degrees from Cambridge and Liverpool universities, was made an honorary fellow of his own Balliol College in 1935 and a "Visitor" in 1946. He was the chairman of the Palestine Electric Corporation, Ltd., from 1937 to 1954. He was president of the Royal Asiatic Society of Great Britain and Ireland from 1940 to 1943 and of the English Association in 1941. His clubs are the Reform and National Liberal.

Lady Samuel is the former Beatrice Miriam Franklin, to whom he was married on November 17, 1897. They have three sons, Edwin Herbert (now principal of the Institute of Public Administration at Tel-Aviv, Israel), Philip Ellis Herbert and Godfrey Herbert, and a daughter, Nancy Adelaide. Lord Samuel, who has been characterized in the New York *Times* as "a quiet man of precise and orderly mentality," likes to read poetry and to take long walks in the country.

References

N Y Times p3 N 6 '31 por; p13 My 11 '37 por

Burke's Peerage, Baronetage, and Knightage (1953)

Jewish Year Book, 1950-52

Samuel, H. L. S., 1st Viscount, Grooves of Change (1946)

Who's Who, 1954

SARASIN, POTE (să-ră-sēn') Mar. 25, 1905- Thailand Ambassador to the United States; Representative to the United Nations

Address: b. c/o Embassy of Thailand, 2300 Kalorama Rd., N.W., Washington, D.C.; Thailand Delegation to the United Nations, 20 E. 82d St., New York 28

"When a threat to peace begins to appear [in any part of the world]," stated Pote Sarasin, "it is the duty of [U.N.] members to call the attention of the [U.N.] organization to the existence of such a threat, [which] should not be considered as a problem particular to a cer-

POTE SARASIN

tain country or group of countries, for no one can say for certain how such a threat will develop . . ." (New York *Times,* June 4, 1954). Sarasin, who has been the Thai Ambassador to the United States since 1952, has represented his nation at the United Nations General Assembly during the Third, Seventh, Eighth and Ninth Sessions. He is presently attending the Tenth Session.

He was a member of the Thai delegation at the Southeast Asia defense treaty conference held in Manila, Philippines in September 1954 which drafted the SEATO pact, and attended the Bandoeng conference in Indonesia in April 1955. Sarasin, who is a lawyer, was on the U.N. Commission for the Unification and Rehabilitation of Korea established in October 1950, and was chairman of the Fifth (Administrative and Budgetary) Committee of the U.N. in 1954. The diplomat held the post of Minister of Foreign Affairs from 1949 to 1950.

Pote Sarasin was born in Siam on March 25, 1905. He was educated at the Wilbraham Academy, near Springfield, Massachusetts and is a member of Middle Temple, London, England. Between 1932 and 1945 he practiced in the courts of law of his country. He occupied a seat in the Senate from 1948 to 1950. In 1948 he was also Deputy Minister of Foreign Affairs, and was chosen as a representative from Siam during the Third General Assembly of the United Nations.

The Thai diplomat resigned from his post as Deputy Minister of Foreign Affairs on November 25, 1948, after the government was reorganized by Premier Luang Pibul Songgram (see *C.B.,* 1951). The following year, Sarasin became Thailand's Minister of Foreign Affairs, and led the Cabinet opposition to the recognition of the Vietnam government of Bao Dai. When Premier Pibul decided to grant this recognition, Sarasin resigned as Foreign Minister on February 28, 1950.

In the fall of 1950 the U.N. Commission for the Unification and Rehabilitation of Korea was set up to replace the U.N. Commission on Korea. On the new commission, Thailand was represented by Sarasin. Other member nations were Australia, Chile, the Netherlands, Pakistan, the Philippines, and Turkey. The commission was established for the purpose of creating "a unified, independent and democratic government of all Korea" through elections supervised by the United Nations (*The Americana Annual,* 1951). In its report on October 19, 1951, to the General Assembly, the Commission advised that "the people of North Korea lived in the heavy atmosphere of a police state" (*The Americana Annual,* 1952). The commission also reported that $58,119,266 had been spent by the U.N. for relief to Korean civilians; the United States had contributed $41,859,551.

Following his appointment as Ambassador to the United States, succeeding Prince Wan (see *C.B.,* 1954), Sarasin declared in June 1952 that his government and people held "cordial ties of friendship and mutual understanding" with the United States, and wanted to reinforce these bonds (New York *Times,* June 13, 1952). Sarasin represented Thailand at both the Seventh and Eighth Sessions of the General Assembly.

At the annual Far East Conference sponsored by the Far East-America Council of Commerce and Industry, and held in New York City on October 8, 1953, Sarasin said that the progress of a peace agreement on Korea has been marked by lack of a desire for peace on the Communist side (New York *Times,* October 9, 1953). Commenting upon the funds provided by the United States for economic developments in the Far East, including Thailand, he declared he was gratified by these plans to assist areas still threatened by Communist aggression.

After Vietminh troops moved for the first time against the Kingdom of Cambodia (the southeast neighbor of Thailand) in April 1954, Sarasin conferred with U.S. Secretary of State John Foster Dulles and asked for an increase in American arms shipments to Thailand, under an agreement signed in October 1950, to give more protection to his country against possible Communist invasion. He declared that if the situation calls for it, Thailand will order immediate mobilization (*Christian Science Monitor,* May 6, 1953).

Following the fall of Dienbienphu in Vietnam, Sarasin went to Bangkok, the capital of Thailand, in May 1954 to discuss the situation with other government officials. Upon his return to the United States, he formally requested on May 29 that the Security Council establish "a subcommission of the Peace Observation Commission . . . with the authority to dispatch observers to any part of the general area of Thailand on the request of any state . . . concerned" (New York *Times,* June 4, 1954).

"Recent events have made it clear," he said, "that the situation is becoming worse, and that the Vietminh forces have the intention of overthrowing the legal governments of Cambodia and Laos." He added: "Thailand considers itself to be directly threatened by these developments," and the provision of impartial observation will have the salutary effect of preventing the situation from deteriorating. With ten votes in favor, and only the U.S.S.R. opposed, the Council on June 3 put the Thai request on its agenda (United Nations *Bulletin,* June 15, 1954). However, actual debate was postponed indefinitely to give the Geneva Conference on Asian Affairs a chance to run their full course on the cease-fire question.

On June 16, 1954 Pote Sarasin modified his original request for a subcommission of the Peace Observation Commission empowered to go to the "general area of Thailand." He now asked that a subcommission be sent "as soon as possible" to Thailand alone, "to make such reports and recommendations as it deems necessary" (New York *Herald Tribune,* June 17, 1954). The U.S.S.R. vetoed such a project on June 18. The seven-and-a-half-year war in Indochina was halted on July 21 when armistice agreements were reached at the Geneva Conference.

On behalf of the Thai government Sarasin protested to the U.S. State Department on June 4, 1954 against the omission of Thailand from the five-power conversations in Washington, D.C. of military leaders of Britain, France, Australia, New Zealand and the United States in early June on the security of Southeast Asia. He claimed that Thailand was "directly involved" and it was "only logical" that it should be invited to participate in the discussions (New York *Times,* June 6, 1954). His complaint accompanied a similar one from the Philippines. The envoys of both countries suggested that the Communists would make propaganda of the absence of two Asian nations from talks concerning their own defense (New York *Times,* June 5, 1954).

In July 1954 Sarasin commented on U.S. Department of Defense approval for increased military aid to Thailand and the construction of a $3,000,000 highway, saying it was important to strengthen the troops so that they could contribute to a proposed Southeast Asian alliance (New York *Times,* July 14, 1954).

Early in September 1954, Pote Sarasin served as a member of the Thai delegation to the Southeast Asia defense treaty conference held in Manila. At the conference eight nations, Australia, Great Britain, France, New Zealand, Pakistan, the Philippines, Thailand, and the United States, signed a treaty, protocol and "Pacific Charter" pledging joint action against aggressive threats to any member nation, cooperation in economic and technical-aid programs, and "practical measures to insure conditions favorable" to self-determination by colonial peoples.

The treaty became effective on February 19, 1955. Thailand had been the first ratifying nation, on September 22, 1954. In February 1955 Premier Pibul indicated that the Southeast Asia Treaty Organization (SEATO) must do something about the puppet "Free Thailand" regime (established in 1953) in the Chinese Yunnan province, which is menacing Thailand.

The Thai diplomat was elected as chairman of the Fifth (Administrative and Budgetary) Committee of the Ninth General Assembly of the U.N. on September 21, 1954 by a vote of 46 to 10. His opponent was Henryk Birecki of Poland, who had been nominated by the Soviet bloc. As chairman of the Fifth Committee, Sarasin is a member of the General Assembly's steering committee.

As a member of the Thai delegation headed by Prince Wan, Minister of Foreign Affairs, Sarasin attended the conference of twenty-nine Asian and African countries in Bandoeng, Indonesia held in April 1955. At the meeting Thailand and other pro-Western nations challenged the Red and neutralist Asian nations on the issue of condemning Red colonialism. In a communiqué issued by the conference on April 24 it was stated that the "existence of colonialism in many parts of Asia and Africa . . . not only prevents cultural cooperation but also surpresses the natural cultures of the peoples," and it was declared that "all states should cooperate, especially through the U.N., in bringing about the reduction of armaments and the elimination of nuclear weapons under effective international control."

Into the "troublesome picture" facing Thailand has come new hope, wrote Harriet La Barre (*Cosmopolitan,* November 1955). "The United States is helping to train Thailand's armed forces; it has sent millions to bolster the country's faltering economy. . . . Most important: SEATO . . . gives Thailand the moral backing of the United States and four other powerful overseas nations."

The Ambassador is short in stature, adheres to no political party, and is a Buddhist. He has been a lecturer at Chulalongkorn University in Bangkok, and has served as director and honorary treasurer of the Thai Red Cross. Sarasin is married and has several children.

Reference

Vogue 124:200 S 1 '54 por

SAUNDERS, ROBERT (HOOD) May 30, 1903-Jan. 16, 1955 Chairman of the Hydroelectric Power Commission of Ontario; a leading supporter of the St. Lawrence Seaway project; as Mayor of Toronto during four terms, known for his slum-clearing and housing projects and for his concern for the good public relations of the city government. See *Current Biography* (Dec.) 1951.

Obituary

N Y Times p5 Ja 17 '55

SCHNEIDER, HANNES 1890-Apr. 26, 1955 Ski meister; Austrian-born ski instructor who introduced the Arlberg (now widely adopted) technique based on the snowplow, stem and stem-christiania turns; he is credited with helping to develop skiing in the United States; established school in 1939 at Eastern Slopes Inn, North Conway, New Hampshire. See *Current Biography* (Mar.) 1941.

Obituary

N Y Times p31 Ap 27 '55

SCHNEIRLA, T(HEODORE) C(HRISTIAN) July 23, 1902- Animal psychologist
Address: b. American Museum of Natural History, Central Park West & 79th St., New York, 24; h. 418 Central Park West, New York, 25

Studying ants to discover behavior patterns which may help explain oddities of human conduct and actions of other animals has been for more than thirty years the chief professional interest of T. C. Schneirla, curator of the department of animal behavior in the Museum of Natural History in New York City. He is also visiting professor in animal psychology at New York University.

Since 1932 his principal field work has been with the Eciton (army) ants in Barro Colorado Island, Panama Canal Zone, and he has also explored the habits of ants in Mexico and Trinidad. By observing large numbers of ants in the jungle and the laboratory, he has been able to report, among other findings, that there are differences in the abilities of species and in individuals within species.

Theodore Christian Schneirla was born in Bay City, Michigan, on July 23, 1902, one of eight children (four boys and four girls) of Christian and Mary Emily (Badger) Schneirla. His paternal grandfather came to the United States from Nuremberg, Germany and settled as a farmer in Clinton, Michigan. His "Scotch-Irish" maternal grandfather migrated to Canada from Northern Ireland and became a merchant, first in Ontario then in Saskatchewan.

Reared in his native city, Schneirla attended the local elementary schools and Western High School, where he took part in the boys' club activities and played in local bands and orchestras. His attention was first "attracted to scholarly interests," he states, "by an excellent high school faculty." At the University of Michigan, which he entered in 1920, he developed a liking for philosophy and psychology. His interest in animal psychology was aroused by Professor John F. Shepard, who convinced his pupil of the value of studying ants. Shepard arranged to have a large room over the science library turned over to the young scientist, who often worked through the night watching the Formica, or common mound-builder ant, attempt to go through a maze. For recreation, he played a trumpet in the university band and took part in the Alpha Nu debating society.

Schneirla received the B.S. degree in 1924 and the M.S. degree in 1925 from the University of Michigan. While continuing his graduate studies of insect behavior. he held a teaching fellowship in psychology (1925-1927). His doctoral thesis, *Learning and Orientation in Ants* (1929), discussed his experiments with the Formica ants and their ability to learn new or varied maze patterns. The University of Michigan awarded him a Sc.D. degree in 1928.

During 1928-1929 Schneirla taught general psychology at New York University and the following year carried on psychological research as a fellow of the National Research Council.

New York University promoted Dr. Schneirla to the rank of assistant professor in animal psychology in 1931, a position he retained for the next ten years. Under a grant of the National Research Council in 1932, he made his first of eight approximately six-month field trips to the Barro Colorado Island, Panama Canal Zone to examine behavior patterns in army ants. The island, situated in Gatun Lake and covered with thick jungle, has been set aside for scientific research under the supervision of the Institute for Research in Tropical America. Early experiencing the horror of being lost in the jungle, Schneirla said, "My problem was to be out at night and not be distracted by irrelevant things . . . it was a process of emotional adjustment" (*Saturday Evening Post,* May 16, 1953). He discarded his laboratory coat for what resembled a pirate's dress, carried a heavy machete and no gun, and made it a rule never to run in the jungle.

In "Studies on Army Ants in Panama," in the *Journal of Comparative Psychology* (April 1933), Schneirla reported some of his early findings on Eciton, or army ant species. He discovered that these ants travel and rest in definite cycles, alternating a nomadic existence of sixteen days with a twenty-day "statary" phase. The queen, he stated, is the pacesetter of the colony, and during each thirty-six-day cycle produces from 20,000 to 30,000 eggs that yield female workers. Dr. Schneirla discovered that once a year in the dry season she produces a brood of about 1,500 males and twelve queens.

At a meeting in May 1934 of the National Academy of Sciences, Schneirla presented a paper entitled "Raiding and Other Outstanding Phenomena in Behavior of Army Ants." He noted that "a small group of ants, the pushing party, heads the advance into new territory, behind which ants move in a narrow column." The Eciton raids, he said, typically show "two peaks of activity," one in the morning and the other in the afternoon—their bursts of activity "appearing to be related to meteorological changes" (*National Academy of Sciences Proceedings,* May 1934). In a report before a meeting of the American Philosophical Society in May 1944, he exploded the idea that army ant raiding is stimulated by a scarcity of prey in a given area and pointed out that "the critical factor appears to be the internal condition threshold of excitability of the colony" (*American Philosophical Society Proceedings,* No. 5, 1944).

Dr. Schneirla was one of a council of directors conducting a study of social issues for the Society of Psychology from 1937 to 1941. A research grant from the National Academy of Sciences Bache Fund in 1938 helped him carry on his insect studies. New York University made him associate professor of animal psychology and of the psychology of thinking in 1942, and the following year he was appointed associate curator of animal behavior at the American Museum of Natural History.

As a fellow of the John Simon Guggenheim Memorial Foundation, Schneirla studied army ants in Southern Mexico in the winter of 1944-1945. The next year he resigned from his associate professorship at New York University, but agreed to act as a visiting professor for a graduate course in animal psychology. He was made curator of the department of animal behavior at the American Museum of Natural

History in 1947 and soon afterward led a group of museum scientists to Panama in an expedition supported by the American Philosophical Society, the National Research Council, and the United States Office of Naval Research.

After observing two groups of army ants for about five months moving in the jungle nearly 500 yards each day, he brought back to the museum around 20,000 marauding ants, the first to enter the United States. In a public demonstration, he showed how these ants, mostly blind and quite stupid, remain together in their movements by following a chemical exudate deposited by their leaders. An individual ant, removed from this chemical trail, is helpless, he has stated. As quoted by the New York *Times* (March 31, 1948), Schneirla characterizes ant behavior as a "very complicated social order . . . with no leanings toward either communism or socialism."

With Dr. Max Renner and other scientists, Schneirla took part in an unusual experiment begun in June 1955 to determine whether bees remember time intervals. The bees, trained to a strict feeding schedule, were flown from Paris to New York in an attempt to discover whether geographical change would affect their observance of routine. Schneirla commented that the results of the experiment (which showed that bees have a time sense independent of their position on earth) may throw light on the behavior of other animals.

Schneirla is the author of *Principles of Animal Psychology*, in collaboration with N. R. F. Maier (McGraw-Hill, 1935), and *Recent Experiments in Psychology*, in collaboration with L. C. Crafts (McGraw-Hill, 1938). In the latter book he discusses such topics as the behavior of the newborn infant, cooperation and competition, duplicity theory of vision, judgment of vocational aptitude, and the maze as an instrument in the study of learning. He contributed to the *Encyclopædia Britannica* in 1946 and 1954 and wrote "Ant Learning as a Problem in Psychology" in *Twentieth Century Psychology* (edited by Philip L. Harriman and others, 1946) and the chapter "Levels in the Psychological Capacities of Animals" in *Philosophy for the Future* (edited by R. W. Sellars and others, 1949).

Among the numerous articles Dr. Schneirla has written for scientific journals is one entitled "Carpenter Ants" (*Natural History*, May 1951), in which he described how anyone can construct an artificial nest in which to maintain and study these ants. He has contributed to such magazines as *Psychological Review, Biological Bulletin, Scientific American, Journal of Comparative Psychology*, and *Psychological Bulletin*.

Schneirla is a fellow of the American Psychological Association and is chairman of the North American branch of the International Union for the Study of Social Insects. Other professional organizations to which he belongs are the American Society of Naturalists, the American Association for the Advancement of Science, the American Society of Zoologists, and the New York Entomological Society (president, 1950). He is a member of the Explorers Club of New York, and his fraternities are Sigma Xi, Phi Sigma (biological), Gamma Alpha, and Psi Chi (psychological). He is a Democrat.

Fabian Bachrach

T. C. SCHNEIRLA

In the *Saturday Evening Post* (May 16, 1953) John O'Reilly describes Schneirla as "a mild-mannered man" with "calm outlook," whose "eyes are always alert" and who talks about ants "in a rich mixture of military and scientific terminology." He has blue eyes and brown hair, is five feet seven and a half inches tall and weighs 155 pounds. The psychologist married Leone Margaretta Warner on June 13, 1925. Their children are Lois Janet and Donn Richard. Schneirla considers his "present professional activities" also his hobby, and in addition enjoys music and literature.

References

Sat Eve Post 225:36+ My 16 '53 por
American Men of Science (1949)
Leaders in Education (1948)
Who's Who in New York, 1952
Who's Who in the East (1955)

SCHNURER, CAROLYN (GOLDSAND)

Jan. 5, 1908- Fashion designer

Address: b. 575 8th Ave., New York 18; h. Rte. 6N, Mahopac Falls, N.Y.

"A leading designer in the casual and sports field, and an indefatigable globe-trotter" is the way a New York newspaper described Carolyn Schnurer, a former teacher who turned to fashion designing in 1940. She produces 600 designs a year for a $7,000,000 business of which she is the only designer and her husband is the director.

Mrs. Schnurer likes what she calls "the Fords of Fashion"—those clothes which become widely popular because of their functional qualities and reasonable prices. She believes

CAROLYN SCHNURER

that a designer should be so close to the consumer that she gets the feeling of a local dressmaker.

The recipient of a number of awards, she won the New Orleans Fashion Group Award in 1950 and the Citation for American Fashion Critics Award in 1945.

Carolyn Goldsand was born in the Yorkville section of New York City on January 5, 1908 to Henry and Rebecca (Bronner) Goldsand. She has one sister. Educated in the New York school system, she attended Wadleigh High School and New York Training School for Teachers. In 1941, while she was building her early reputation as a sportswear designer, she took courses at New York University to get her B.S. degree. At present she is continuing her studies for a master's degree and hopes to find the time eventually to achieve a doctorate. She feels that the additional education is helpful to her career and also says, "Once a student always a student," adding that she would find it very hard to stop studying.

On July 30, 1930 she married Harold Teller Schnurer, a bathing suit manufacturer. She taught music and art in the New York public schools for ten years before becoming actively engaged in designing. After the birth of her son, Anthony Teller, in 1939, she returned to school at her husband's suggestion to study pattern design and in 1940 became the designer for her husband's manufacturing business. Her creations for women's casual and sports wear were immediately popular and in 1946 the firm's name was changed from Bert Schnurer to Carolyn Schnurer, Inc., since the line of clothing had become closely identified in the mind of the public with her name.

Carolyn Schnurer put her efforts into designing informal wear because she and her family are devoted to outdoor life and because she is a firm believer in American design and feels that sportswear is the field in which American designers retain their identity. When asked what qualities she thought made a designer's clothes popular, she voiced the opinion that the designer must understand the purpose for which the clothes are designed.

According to Mrs. Schnurer, understanding the consumer and timing new creations with the consumer's demands are important factors in the popularity of a designer's work. To this end, she visits the places where women may be expected to wear her styles and frequents the stores which carry her line. She talks to customers, fits them, and gets their reactions. It was in this way that she learned that women wanted pockets in their casual clothes. "Pockets do for women what cigarettes do for smokers," she says. "They give them something to do with their hands." In 1953 she put pockets in her bathing suits.

Carolyn Schnurer's designs are inspired frequently by the indigenous customs and clothing of other countries. She started her fashion travels in 1944 during World War II when she went to the Andes Mountains in South America. From this trip she returned with her now-famous Cholo coat, a loose-fitting, high-necked, hip-length jacket or shirt worn by native shepherds. A little boy's jacket picked up in a South African market place inspired the design for a sports jacket to go with beach clothes. From Japan a judo wrestler's dressing gown was adapted to become a terry cloth coat. Ideas for a pullover sweater were borrowed from the fishermen of Brittany.

Some of her best ideas, she believes, came from Ireland. To a *Time* magazine interviewer she said: "I decided just to relax when I got there and go to the races. The first thing I saw were the most gorgeous satin jockey coats in the most wonderful colors you've ever seen. I adopted them. Then I went to the pawn shops. I got some of the most marvelous heavy cableknit sweaters there and even some underwear. When I got back to New York I remembered the beautiful blue, blue Irish sky and the fresh green grass, so I combined the colors in my fashions" (January 11, 1954).

Her first trip to South America was made under the auspices of Franklin Simon and Company of New York City and three other department stores, which engaged her to look for new fabrics and designs. Other stores have helped to pay the cost of subsequent trips to countries outside the United States. In 1954 she made "a voyage of fashion discovery" to Norway. She has also visited Turkey (1953), Africa's Gold Coast (1952), Japan (1951), India (1950), Greece (1949), Portugal (1948), Ireland (1947), and Brittany and Normandy (1946).

It is Mrs. Schnurer's designing procedure each year to first choose a country on whose native costume she will plan her forthcoming collection. Then she consults the books and experts of the Brooklyn Museum and the costume division of the Metropolitan Museum of Art. Here she develops and correlates her theme, studying the costumes, background and native habits of the country she has selected.

She then goes, usually by plane, to see the country and its people for herself.

The clothes which she then creates are simply designed and produced so that they can sell at popular prices. Although she does not sew, she can tell her cutters how to make anything.

"Fashions from Mrs. Schnurer's expeditions are never of the costumy variety," commented the New York *Times* (June 1, 1953). "There is a foreign influence but it is subtly expressed . . . she also invents novel techniques in fashioning—for example—knot and twist wrapped belts on bathing suits and casual dresses."

One of the distinctive things about Mrs. Schnurer's designs is the fabric used in their manufacture. She works closely with the fabric houses, principally Dan River, to produce fabrics of her own design. Thus the materials used are exclusive with her own collection. Carolyn Schnurer was the innovator of a wrinkle-resistant cotton tweed, inspired by her trip to Ireland. This started a trend in the fashion world toward cotton tweeds. Another fabric which received wide popularity was a Portugal-inspired cotton of rich deep red with bright yellow and blue spots and dark-green vertical stripes. A recent resort collection featured fabrics based on Byzantine embroideries, carpet designs, ceramics, religious themes, flowers, iron grillworks and the like in every type of lounging and beach costume.

One of Mrs. Schnurer's major contributions to the fashion field was made several years ago in the cotton bathing suit. The big dressmaker skirts that had enjoyed favor for a number of years gave way in her workshops to a more soft but form-fitting one-piece design with shorts. Her 1954 interpretation of her own innovation was the bathing suit with the "bloomer bottoms and fitted tops that look poured-in but can be lived-in." To this she added a straight middy-type jacket.

When introducing dresses and other garments to her line, Carolyn Schnurer applies what she has learned in making bathing suits. She says: "We got used to working with the body that way and so we make our garments the way the girdle- and brassière-makers do. They fit so well it's not necessary to wear a brassière" (*Time*, January 11, 1954).

Mrs. Schnurer is outspoken in her opinions on the controversies of fashion. In reply to the statement of the late French designer, Jacques Fath, that women are bad designers and design only for themselves, she said: "Creative people are creative people, irrespective of sex. And it would certainly be foolish for you to confine your designs to yourself. There aren't that many people in the world like you" (New York *World-Telegram and Sun*, January 18, 1954).

Mrs. Schnurer, who occasionally lectures at various colleges and schools of design, is a consultant for the Parsons School of Design and the Rhode Island School of Design. She is a sponsor of "The Party of the Year," a benefit for the costume division of the Metropolitan Museum of Art. She studies languages which will help her in her travels. She is interested in dramatics and enjoys playing the piano. Her religion is Jewish.

The designer is a vivacious brunette with, in the words of the Miami *Daily News*, "friendly dark eyes that peep out from behind stylish black-rimmed glasses." Five feet seven inches in height and 130 pounds in weight, she wears size-fourteen clothes.

References

Miami Daily News p1B Ja 12 '54
N Y Times p20 Je 1 '53 por
Time 63:71+ Ja 11 '54 por

SCHNURER, MRS. HAROLD T(ELLER)

See Schnurer, Carolyn

SCHREIBER, JEAN-JACQUES SERVAN-

See Servan-Schreiber, J.-J.

SCHWARZKOPF, ELISABETH December 9, 1915- Singer

Address: b. c/o Teatro Alla Scala, Milan, Italy

Before October 25, 1953 when Elisabeth Schwarzkopf made a highly successful concert debut in America, she had been known to Americans only through her recordings. But for over a decade the German singer had earned a reputation in Europe and in England as an operatic and concert soprano of the first order. She has sung in a wide variety of roles in the Vienna State Opera House, in the Royal Opera, Covent Garden, in London, and at La Scala in Milan. As a leading soloist, she has appeared at the Bayreuth, Salzburg, Perugia, Lucerne and Florence Festivals. Her numerous lieder recitals have evoked praise from audiences and critics alike, and have led to frequent comparisons between Miss Schwarzkopf and Lotte Lehmann.

Born on December 9, 1915 in Jarotschin (in English, Jarocin), a town in the province of Poznań in West Poland, Elisabeth Schwarzkopf is the only daughter of Friedrich and Elisabeth (Fröhlich) Schwarzkopf. The family moved to Berlin, where the daughter went to school.

At the Berlin High School for Music, Elisabeth was an outstanding student, winning prizes in musical theory, harmony, and history, as well as in piano, viola, and singing. Singing lessons in school were supplemented by private instructions from a Dr. Egenolf, who trained her for operatic work. While she was still a student, Miss Schwarzkopf won a League of Nations scholarship that enabled her to study in Leicester, England and to learn English.

Miss Schwarzkopf's first professional operatic engagement (1938) was in the Deutsches Opernhaus in Charlottenburg, a suburb of Berlin. On thirty-six hours notice she learned, in an emergency, the part of the first flower-maiden, second group, in Wagner's *Parsifal.* During her first year at the Deutsches Opernhaus, she sang almost twenty minor parts in such diverse operas as *Tannhäuser, Siegfried,*

ELISABETH SCHWARZKOPF

The Merry Widow, Rigoletto, The Magic Flute, and *The Bartered Bride.* While still in high school in 1937 she made her recording debut as a member of the chorus in the Mozart Opera Society's edition of *The Magic Flute.*

By 1941 Miss Schwarzkopf had sung in the Deutsches Opernhaus such prominent parts as Oscar in *Un Ballo in Maschera* and Zerbinetta in *Ariadne auf Naxos.*

It was her singing in the role of Zerbinetta that attracted the attention of the famous Hungarian soprano, Maria Ivogün. When Richard Strauss composed *Ariadne auf Naxos,* he personally selected Miss Ivogün for the part of Zerbinetta; she later heard Miss Schwartzkopf sing this role and was so impressed that she took her as a private pupil. With her husband, Michael Raucheisen, an accompanist and coach, Maria Ivogün trained her pupil to sing lieder, thus adding a new dimension to Miss Schwarzkopf's vocal attainments. This period of training in the art song culminated in a successful lieder recital in Vienna (November, 1942); and, shortly afterwards, Miss Schwarzkopf was engaged as coloratura soprano at the Vienna Opera House.

A severe illness forced her to retire from the operatic stage for a short time (1943-1944) to rest and recuperate. But in the years that followed she sang with the Vienna State Opera Company in many roles, including Rosina (*The Barber of Seville*), Gilda (*Rigoletto*), and the familiar Zerbinetta. After the end of World War II, Miss Schwarzkopf's European reputation grew rapidly. She sang lyric soprano solo parts at the Salzburg Festival in 1947 and again in the summer of 1948; and three years later she sang at the Bayreuth Festival.

When the world première of Stravinsky's *The Rake's Progress* was given in Venice (September 11, 1951), she had a leading role in the performance, as she did in the production of the opera at La Scala in Milan, that winter. Walter Legge wrote, in an article on Elisabeth Schwarzkopf (*Opera*), "Only those who have heard and seen [Miss] Schwarzkopf in these performances . . . can take full measure of her abilities as an operatic artist." Arturo Toscanini is reported to have greeted Miss Schwarzkopf in London with: "You sang the *Missa Solemnis* at La Scala. *Molto bène!* I never had the soprano so good."

After Miss Schwarzkopf's first appearance in London with the Vienna State Opera Company at Covent Garden (September, 1947), she was so well received that she appeared regularly as a guest artist there for three years. Singing always in English, in accordance with the policy of Covent Garden, she undertook many varied roles, including Pamina (*The Magic Flute*), Sophie (*Der Rosenkavalier*), Mimi (*La Bohème*), Eva (*Die Meistersinger*), and Marzelline (*Fidelio*). Besides her operatic repertoire in England, she gave recitals of lieder, singing songs by Schubert, Wolf and Bach.

Her American concert debut was delayed until October 1953, when Miss Schwarzkopf was enthusiastically received. Irving Kolodin, wrote in the *Saturday Review* (November 7, 1953) that she would have been welcomed here long ago (certainly the Met would have used her) had she not a wartime record of association with the Nazis. *Time* (November 9, 1953) commented: "As a nineteen-year-old music student . . . she became a leader in the Nazi *Studentenbund* . . . throughout the war she was a favorite of German audiences."

Appearing at a debut recital in Town Hall, New York City (October 25, 1953), under the auspices of the Concert Society of New York, for a single performance, she sang lieder to a completely sold-out house, and utterly captivated the critics. Describing her as "a beautiful woman with a superb stage presence" (New York *Times,* October 26, 1953), the critics agreed that she was "a lieder singer worthy of the tradition of German song" (*Christian Science Monitor,* November 7, 1953).

This single performance was followed by a tour (October to December 1954) of the principal American cities, where most of the critics seemed to be competing with each other in their eulogies of Miss Schwarzkopf's vocal artistry. Back at Town Hall (November 28, 1954), she was hailed as "the reigning queen of German song" by a critic in the New York *World-Telegram and Sun.* Another critic, in *Musical America,* wrote that "her singing displayed the exquisite finish, technical mastery, and interpretative felicity that had marked her debut recital here last season." However, he complained that in some songs she "treated passages more in the manner of a *diseuse* than in traditional lieder style" (December 15, 1954). Such complaints were but a small minority in the general critical applause for her performances.

When Miss Schwarzkopf made her operatic debut in America with the San Francisco Opera Company in October 1955 in *Der Rosenkavalier,* Mildred Norton wrote in the *Saturday Review* (October 15) that a capacity audience saluted "a memorable new Princess Werdenberg in the blonde and beautiful person of Elisabeth Schwarzkopf . . . a poised and vibrant new personality with a vocal radiance and a personal grace."

Since her minor part in the recording of *The Magic Flute* (1937), she has made many recordings such as Eva (*Die Meistersinger*) and Countess Almaviva (*The Marriage of Figaro*) for Columbia and sang the title role in a recording devoted wholly to Bach in 1954. Referring to Miss Schwarzkopf's performance in the latter recording, Irving Kolodin described her as "first and foremost a technician of solid attainments" (*Saturday Review*, January 29, 1954). In 1955 she sang the part of Fiordiligi in the Angel recording of *Così Fan Tutte* and Rosalinde in *Die Fledermaus*.

In March of 1954 a small but heated controversy was created among music lovers by the revelation that she had contributed two high C's to a recording, by Kirsten Flagstad, of Wagner's *Tristan und Isolde*. While some listeners argued that this was but a legitimate exploitation of advanced recording techniques, others contended bitterly that such a substitution presaged the degeneration of music as an art form to mere technical juggling.

On October 2, 1955 Miss Schwarzkopf was among the first recipients of a new musical prize to be presented annually in Mantua, Italy. A golden "Orfeo" (depicting the mythical poet Orpheus singing and valued at more than $1,000) was presented to her by Maestro Arturo Toscanini.

Miss Schwarzkopf is the wife of Walter Legge, a recording director of Electric & Musical Industries (EMI), producers of "Angel" records. He is the founder of the Philharmonia Orchestra. When she is not on tour, she lives with her husband in London. She is a striking blonde, statuesque and poised, with grey eyes and expressive features. Her hobbies are skiing, mountain climbing, and cooking.

References

Mus Am 75:4 S 15 '55
Opera 4:396+ Jl '53 pors
Time 62:49+ N 9 '53 por
Vogue 124:116 N 15 '54 por

Blom, E. ed. Grove's Dictionary of Music and Musicians (1955)
Söhlmans Musiklexikon (1952)
Who's Who, 1955

SEGNI, ANTONIO (sä'nyė) Feb. 2, 1891-

Premier of Italy; university professor; lawyer

Address: b. Camera dei Deputati, Rome, Italy; h. Via Sallustiana 15, Rome, Italy

The new Premier of Italy, Antonio Segni, is expected to "steer Italy along a course of firm alliance with the West and close ties with the United States." Segni, a Christian Democrat and a member of the Italian Chamber of Deputies, was able to create a government in July 1955 without enlisting the support of leftist parties. He is continuing the moderate course in national and international affairs, set for Italy by the late Alcide de Gasperi after World War II. Segni's Cabinet differs little in policy or personnel from that of his predecessor, Mario Scelba, also a Christian Democrat.

While he was Minister of Agriculture and Forestry from 1946 to 1951, Segni was responsible for the passage of Italy's land reform bills which have already given over 1,200,000 acres of land to the Italian peasants. Under his program, some 250 acres of his estate in his native Sardinia have been divided among poor farmers. Segni, an anti-Communist and anti-Fascist, is a lawyer by profession and has taught law at the universities of Perugia, Cagliari, Pavia, Sassari and Rome. His skill in bringing together all elements of the Christian Democratic party caused one commentator to remark, "In Segni, the party may have discovered a personality who can play the same unifying role so ably performed by de Gasperi."

Antonio Segni is the scion of an old Sardinian family of landowners and lawyers. He was born on February 2, 1891 in Sassari on the island of Sardinia in Italy and is the son of Anna (Campus) and Celestino Segni. He studied at the University of Rome where he specialized in commercial and agrarian law. He was graduated in 1913 and began his career as a lawyer. After serving in World War I in the Italian Army as a sergeant in the artillery, he became a professor of civil procedure at the University of Perugia in 1920. Five years later he went to the University of Cagliari as a professor and as president of its law faculty.

In 1929 he was appointed professor at the University of Pavia and in 1931 he returned to his home in Sassari and became a professor of commercial law at the university there. He was appointed commissioner of the university in 1943 and in the following year was made rector. In 1954 he began to teach as a professor of civil procedure at the University of Rome. In addition to teaching, Segni has written numerous scholarly books about law (listed in *Chi è?*).

His participation in politics began in 1919 when he became active in the Popolari (the Popular party), founded by Don Luigi Sturzo in that year and a forerunner of the present Christian Democratic party. After Benito Mussolini came to power in 1922, Segni became an exponent of a Popular party faction which opposed any compromise with Fascism. He was made national councillor of the party in 1924 just prior to its dissolution by the Fascist dictator.

Segni continued with his teaching during the years of Mussolini's government and in 1942, during World War II, he became a member of the Sardinian Clandestine Committee of Liberation, an anti-Fascist, anti-Nazi organization working toward the liberation of Italy from these two forces. After the surrender of Italy to the Allied powers in 1943, Segni was made a member of the First Regional Council of Sardinia. He helped to found the Christian Democratic party on his native island.

In the second anti-Fascist national government of Ivanoe Bonomi, Segni became in December 1944 the undersecretary of state for

Wide World

ANTONIO SEGNI

agriculture and forestry. He was renamed to this post by Premier Ferruccio Parri in June 1945 and again in December of that year when Alcide de Gasperi became Premier. Segni's home district elected him on June 2, 1946 a member of the Constituent Assembly, which framed the constitution for the new Italian republic. Alcide de Gasperi appointed Segni to his second Cabinet as Minister of Agriculture and Forestry later in the same year. Segni held this position from 1946 to 1951 through five successive cabinets formed by de Gasperi. He became a member of the Chamber of Deputies in 1948.

During a trip to the United States in 1948, Segni spoke on a broadcast and conveyed "the heartfelt thanks" of the Italian people for the Marshall Plan aid they had received after World War II. Without this help, Segni said, millions of Italians would have fallen victim to "destitution, despair, and the ensuing evils of communism." In his own office, as agriculture minister, Segni did much toward preventing the spread of communism, particularly with his land reform program, which was designed to relieve social and economic distress in southern Italy, to develop the country's agricultural resources, and to create a new middle class of small landowners who would support a democratic form of government.

Of several land reform bills written by Segni, two were passed by the Italian Parliament in 1950. They provided for the splitting up of large estates to make land available to about 200,000 peasants and for improving agricultural techniques and working conditions on farms. When announcing the plans, Segni stated that about 8,000 big landowners would be forced to sell some 3,112,700 excess acres to the government, which would reimburse them with twenty-five year government bonds bearing 5 per cent interest. Acreage belonging to large companies and 370,000 acres of public lands were also to be distributed. The total cost of the ten-year program was estimated to be $1 billion, including about $240,000,000 of Marshall Plan funds (New York *Times*, March 24, 1950).

When his reform bills were being discussed in Parliament, Segni caused the defeat of an amendment proposed by the Communists that would have saved model farms such as his own from being split up. Subsequently 250 acres of his and his wife's olive groves and vineyards in northern Sardinia were expropriated and turned over to the peasants. As the report goes, Segni gave his wife a present of a bottle of perfume to console her.

The lands bought by the government are being resold to the peasants on long-term, low-cost loans. Peasants draw the land by lot (this means that some get no land) and receive farms ranging from twelve to thirty-eight acres. The assessed value of the land will be paid to the government by each new owner over a period of thirty years, with 3 per cent interest. While realizing in 1950 that this program would not offer a direct help to most of the 2,000,000 persons then unemployed in Italy, Segni hoped that secondary advantages would accrue to the unemployed through increased needs for fertilizer, for transportation for the new agricultural goods produced, and for outlets for the produce.

Under Segni's program 1,222,337 acres of farm land had been taken from the landlords and given to 93,247 peasants by July 1955. Most of the first part of the program (redistribution) is expected to be completed by the end of 1955, when 100,000 more families will receive land for farms. In the next five years (1955 to 1960) the government plans to help develop these land areas by spending $650,000,000 for aid and advice to the owners.

When de Gasperi formed his seventh Cabinet, in 1951, Segni became Minister of Public Instruction. In this position, according to the New York *World-Telegram and Sun* (July 2, 1955), he "instituted far-reaching school reform which was left unfinished with the fall of de Gasperi in 1953." He was reappointed to this post in 1953 when Giuseppe Pella formed his government, but did not participate in the succeeding governments of Amintore Fanfani and Mario Scelba.

The Cabinet formed by Scelba, which was supported in Parliament by his Christian Democratic party (holding 40 per cent of the seats in the Chamber of Deputies) and by three Center parties (the Liberals, the Republicans, and the right-wing Social Democrats), fell on June 22, 1955. Four days later Segni was called on by Italian President Giovanni Gronchi (see *C.B.,* October 1955) to explore the possibility of setting up a new government. Gronchi did not exclude the possibility of an "opening to the left" to end the government stalemate, that is, getting support from the left-wing Social Democrats (allied with the Communists) headed by Pietro Nenni.

The *Christian Science Monitor* (June 27, 1955), however, stated that Segni's "first moves are reportedly directed toward exploring the possibilities of reviving the four-party center coalition which . . . collapsed under Prime

Minister Mario Scelba." After long negotiations, Segni was able to present his Cabinet on July 6; he had succeeded in getting three of the four center parties to participate in this government. The fourth, the Republican party, decided to remain outside the Cabinet (it does not approve of Segni's land reform program), but promised to support his government in Parliament.

On July 6 Segni and his Cabinet ministers were sworn into office. Out of twenty-one ministers in his government, twelve had served under Scelba. Except for Premier and Minister of Interior, all key positions were held by the same persons as in the previous Cabinet. The Italian Chamber of Deputies confirmed Segni's government on July 18, 1955 by a confidence vote of 293 to 265 with twelve abstentions. The Senate voted its confidence in Segni and his Cabinet on July 22, 1955 by a count of 121 to 100, with three abstentions.

"The Atlantic Pact and Western European Union are the cardinal points of our foreign policy," Premier Segni stated. Peace, he continued, is not guaranteed without security, which is based on the maintenance and strengthening of the Atlantic alliance and Western solidarity. Segni said that Italy desires "a truly united Europe and believes that the current steps toward economic integration may pave the way for the more difficult political union" (New York *Herald Tribune*, July 14, 1955).

Segni's government has also promised to implement the ten-year plan for eliminating unemployment known as the (Ezio) Vanoni Plan. Segni has stated that his coalition is ready to "open the gates to private investment from abroad and particularly the United States, speed Italy's oil development, and press the land reform program." The plans revolve around the coordination of private enterprise and state enterprise.

In November 1955, however, Segni's Cabinet recommended to Parliament that the exploitation of Italy's recently discovered oil deposits in the Po Valley be left to E.N.I., the state monopoly, thus discouraging U.S. and other oil companies from competing on an equal basis, as in Saudi Arabia and Venezuela.

On January 22, 1921 Antonio Segni was married to Laura Carta, who now helps him in his work by serving as his confidential secretary. They have four sons. Segni has been described as a slim, gray-haired man who is "scholarly, rigidly honest, enlightened and moderate" and who has a pungent wit. According to a report in the New York *Times* (July 6, 1955), the last time Mrs. Segni took her husband away from his work and his books and Beethoven records, he "picked the film to see: Walt Disney's *The Living Desert*."

References

N Y Herald Tribune II p5 Jl 10 '55 por
N Y Times p4 Jl 6 '55 por
N Y World-Telegram p5 Jl 2 '55 por
Chi è? (1948)
International Who's Who, 1954
World Biography (1954)

SEIF-UL-ISLAM ABDULLAH, PRINCE 1912-Apr. 14, 1955 Yemen government official; diplomat; became Minister of Education, later governor of the Touhama district of Yemen; represented his late father, the King of Yemen, at various Arab conferences; was chairman of Yemen's delegation to the United Nations in 1947; became Foreign Minister; rumored to have replaced his brother as King of Yemen briefly in 1955 after a *coup d'état* and was reportedly hung after return of brother to throne. See *Current Biography* (Dec.) 1947.

Obituary

N Y Times p3 Ap 22 '55

SELINKO, ANNEMARIE Sept. 1, 1914-
Author

Address: b. c/o William Morrow, 425 4th Ave., New York 16

An historical novel, *Désirée*, by Viennese author Annemarie Selinko, has sold over a million copies in the United States since it was published by William Morrow in January 1953. It was a Literary Guild selection and it has also been published in Austrian, British, Danish, Dutch, Finnish, French, Italian, German and Spanish editions.

The book, told in diary form about a Marseilles silk merchant's daughter who was engaged to Napoleon Bonaparte and who became a Queen of Sweden, is Miss Selinko's fourth novel and her second to be published in the United States. A motion picture dramatization in CinemaScope by Twentieth Century-Fox Film Corporation starring Jean Simmons in the title role, opened at the Roxy Theatre in New York City on November 17, 1954.

Miss Selinko was regarded as one of the most promising young novelists in Europe and she had also gained a reputation as a journalist before the Nazis entered Austria.

She spent years on the research and writing of *Désirée* while she herself was living through the tragedy and turmoil of Europe's war and post-war years. Her book is dedicated to her sister Liselotte, who was murdered by the Nazis.

Annemarie Selinko was born in Vienna, Austria on September 1, 1914. Her father, Felix Selinko, was an industrialist and former adjutant of Emperor Charles. She attended the University of Vienna, where her favorite studies were languages and history. She began her career as a writer while still at the university, reporting local events for several Vienna newspapers. At the age of eighteen, and on the day she received her degree from the university, she obtained a staff job on one of Vienna's leading daily papers.

A year later Miss Selinko attracted considerable attention by posing as a page boy in one of Vienna's fashionable hotels. She revealed her experiences in what the newspaper's editor, Hans Habe, later recalled as "a remarkable piece of adult [reporting]" (Los Angeles *News*, March 22, 1953).

(Continued next page)

Politikens Presse Foto.
ANNEMARIE SELINKO

Annemarie Selinko's first novel, *I Was An Ugly Girl,* was published in Vienna in 1937 and surprised everyone by becoming a best-seller in Austria and twelve other countries. It was unusual for a young Viennese girl to win fame as an author. The story was serialized in several magazines and sold to motion picture companies. She continued as a journalist and became a political writer and the Viennese correspondent for the French *L'Intransigeant.*

Miss Selinko's second book, another novel with a Viennese background, was published in seventeen languages and was made into a film in Holland. It was published in the United States under the title *Tomorrow is Another Day* (Alliance, 1939). "It is a blithe and incredible story set down with rippling charm," wrote Lisle Bell in New York *Herald Tribune Books* (October 8, 1939) while Charlotte Dean in the New York *Times* (October 15) commented that the leading character, Toni, a timid little typist in Vienna, "is made genuinely appealing despite her lack of brains."

At a student's conference in Czechoslovakia in 1937 Miss Selinko met Erling Kristiansen; they became engaged and were married in the spring of 1938. Her husband is now a member of the Danish foreign office.

For several years after Miss Selinko went to Denmark, she was active in the Danish underground. During this period, she wrote her third novel *My Husband Marries Today.* The book—with a Danish background—was published in Denmark and several other countries and was later made into a Swedish movie.

For a short time in 1943 Miss Selinko was interned by the Gestapo in Nazi-occupied Denmark, but managed to escape and with her husband sailed for Sweden in an open fishing boat. Subsequently, her husband was sent to the Danish Embassy in Washington, D.C., and Miss Selinko—alone in Stockholm—obtained work with a Scandinavian news agency and managed to support herself.

The war and Miss Selinko's experiences had an effect on her writing. She was no longer interested in the contemporary type of fiction that had brought her fame. She had read some of the books that had been written about Jean Baptiste Bernadotte, marshal of France under Napoleon, whom the Swedish Riksdag elected as their Crown Prince. There was very little written about his wife Désirée, but it was mentioned in one of the books that as a young girl Désirée had been engaged to Napoleon, and deserted by him for Joséphine de Beauharnais.

Giving serious thought to the life of this unknown figure of history, Miss Selinko began the long, slow process of collecting the material for her book. She decided to write in diary form the story of Bernardine Eugénie Désirée Clary, daughter of a Marseilles silk merchant, who became Sweden's first Queen of the House of Bernadotte.

Further inspiration for the story came through a descendant of her heroine, the late Count Folke Bernadotte. Miss Selinko joined the Swedish Red Cross as an interpreter and worked with some of the 30,000 prisoners who had been liberated from Ravensbrueck and other extermination camps through Count Bernadotte's efforts.

Soon after Miss Selinko had rejoined her husband in Denmark in July 1945, she accompanied him to London to the Danish Embassy. Despite official diplomatic parties and household duties made difficult by rationing, she found time for research at the British Museum, where her knowledge of languages helped her to discover additional material about the period when Désirée lived.

She made the acquaintance of Joyce Weiner, an English literary agent, who was enthusiastic about her book. Since the story of Désirée was in the public domain, Miss Weiner was eager for Miss Selinko to finish the book before another writer used the idea. However, before much headway could be made, her husband was recalled to Denmark.

Work on the book continued at a slow pace after their son, Michael, was born in 1948. The family spent two years in Paris, where Kristiansen was head of the Danish delegation of the Organization for European Economic Cooperation, and economic advisor to the Danish Embassy, and Miss Selinko welcomed the opportunity to do active research in France. She visited Marseilles and also historic places in Paris where events in Désirée's life had occurred.

During the years of research and writing of *Désirée,* Miss Selinko contributed to Danish newspapers and occasionally wrote short stories. Her public had not forgotten her, and when *Désirée* was published it was hailed as an immediate success. It was written in German, but appeared simultaneously in Danish, Swedish, Norwegian and Dutch editions. It was later published in Finland and by Heinemann in England and William Morrow in the United States. The Literary Guild of America made it the selection for February

1953. Miss Selinko felt that it was "quite a miracle" for a European author to have a book selected by a major American book club. The book became a best-seller and continued to be among the first ten during the early months of 1954. Twentieth Century-Fox purchased the American movie rights.

E. J. Fitzgerald in *Saturday Review* (January 17, 1953) said that an artless appearance was achieved because the story was told in diary form and praised the craft with which Miss Selinko combined a tale of high court, pomp and circumstances with "opportunities for the entrapped housewife to identify with the heroine." F. H. Bullock of the New York *Herald Tribune* (January 18, 1953) found *Désirée* "a fascinating, well-devised, well-written novel about a fascinating period of history."

The *Christian Science Monitor* described it as "a story of unusual vigor and charm," while the *New Yorker* (January 17, 1953) commented: "Miss Selinko has a sprightly hand, and she seems to have a good deal of gossipy knowledge of the court of Napoleon, but her characters are thin and the book is far too long." The *Library Journal* (June 15, 1953) found it "one of the few best-selling historical novels that can be recommended for young people."

One of the important themes in *Désirée* concerns the fundamental rights of man. Miss Selinko believes that General Bernadotte was an inspired Republican who was elected to the throne of Sweden and became the liberator of Europe, and she thinks that the success of her book has been partly due to the new meaning she has given to the old message of human rights.

With her husband and son Miss Selinko now lives in Copenhagen. She has been described by her agent Joyce Weiner, according to Alice Dixon Bond (Boston *Traveler,* January 14, 1953), as "bubbling with enthusiasm" and having "an endearing quality . . . for wholehearted friendship."

Reference

Los Angeles Sunday News p37 Mr 22 '53

SERVAN-SCHREIBER, J(EAN)-J(ACQUES) Feb. 13, 1924- Journalist; publisher

Address: b. c/o L'Express, 37 av. des Champs-Elysées, Paris 8e, France

During the Premiership of Pierre Mendès-France of France (June 1954-February 1955) an adviser in his "brain trust" was J.-J. Servan-Schreiber, co-publisher and managing editor of *L'Express,* a weekly political review that has brought fresh life to French journalism. Scion of a newspaper family, Servan-Schreiber began his journalistic career by writing political articles which caught the attention of the editor of *Le Monde.* On October 13, 1955 *L'Express* was replaced by a daily newspaper of the same name, under Servan-Schreiber's editorship and with a regular column by the former Premier.

J.-J. SERVAN-SCHREIBER

He has been on the staff of *Le Monde* and *Paris-Presse* and has contributed articles to the New York *Herald Tribune, Time* and the *Reporter.* Having recently appeared on Edward R. Murrow's CBS-TV programs, *Person to Person* and *See It Now,* he has become known to American television audiences. He has been heard by radio listeners on Radiodiffusion Française, the British Broadcasting Corporation, and the Columbia Broadcasting System. A graduate engineer, Servan-Schreiber has the lucid, incisive mind that the French are accustomed to attribute to *Polytechniciens* or graduates of the École Polytechnique, at which he studied. Servan-Schreiber, a supporter of the Mendès-France "New Deal," believes that "France may still be saved by young men convinced of their mission, whose personal lives are austere and dedicated to work."

Jean-Jacques Servan-Schreiber was born in the fashionable sixteenth *arrondissement* in Paris on February 13, 1924, a son of Emile and Denise (Bresard) Servan-Schreiber. He passed his childhood in the atmosphere of the journalistic dynasty created by his father and his uncle, Robert, the sons of an exporter, and co-founders in 1908 of *Les Echos,* the first French newspaper to specialize solely in financial, economic, and industrial news. Emile Servan-Schreiber, an international reporter for *L'Illustration* at one time and a former lecturer for the Alliance Française, was an economics expert in the French delegation to the San Francisco conference in 1945.

J.-J. Servan-Schreiber received specialized training as an engineer and holds a diploma from the École Polytechnique, an institution of higher learning noted for the precision of its training and its contribution of outstanding technicians to France. After the Nazi occupation of France in World War II, Servan-Schreiber succeeded in escaping from the country and reaching the United States, where he

SERVAN-SCHREIBER, J.-J.—*Continued*

was trained as a fighter pilot with the Ninth Air Force for service with the Free French Forces, with which he saw action in Europe until the end of the war.

His contributions as a free-lance writer to the French press after the liberation of France brought him to the attention of several editors. At the invitation of Hubert Beuve-Méry, he joined the staff of *Le Monde* in October 1947 as a reporter on foreign politics; he continued to write for that newspaper until February 1951. He was a writer on foreign affairs for *Paris-Presse* from May 1951 to December 1952. During this period, he was also a contributor to various South American newspapers. Servan-Schreiber resumed his connection with *Le Monde* in January 1953 in the capacity of diplomatic editor.

For a while he was closely associated with Georges Bidault in helping to make specific Bidault's proposals for an "Atlantic High Council" which would coordinate the defense, economic and political policies of the North Atlantic Treaty nations (after a reorganization within NATO in May 1950, such a coordinating body, the North Atlantic Council, came into existence).

In 1949 Servan-Schreiber had become a European correspondent for the *Reporter* magazine. In a contribution to the May 23, 1950 issue of the *Reporter,* he wrote about the study tours which he often takes through Europe: "On these trips, sometimes simply as a newspaperman, but sometimes on a more personal and intimate basis, I have met and talked to statesmen as well as businessmen and plain citizens."

From these interviews he obtained an impression of current opinions which he described in such articles as "How it Looks from Europe" *(Reporter,* June 6, 1950) on European and particularly French reactions to American policies: "The man in the street is the most confused.... [The intellectuals] feel that they are being personally attacked when the new anti-intellectual attitude of big political groups in the United States is reported to them. . . . The policy makers are uneasy about what will happen in the future because that depends on the tenure of the people they are accustomed to work with [in the United States] and this in turn seems to them completely uncontrollable and unpredictable."

Analyzing Russian policy for the *Reporter* in 1951 (March 20), Servan-Schreiber queried, "Is Russia Ready to Appease?" and pointed out the factors of friction—German rearmament and the Indochinese war—which would have to be settled in order to secure a less harsh Soviet policy. Listing the Communist objectives in the cold war (*Reporter,* April 17, 1951), he observed: "If they attain these objectives, the Atlantic alliance will be annulled in abjection and defeat, the political war ended—and lost. But the Communists will fail at this level too, if the West develops the weapons—political and economic, and not only military—with which to resist."

With the help of his father, J.-J. Servan-Schreiber in 1953 established *L'Express,* a weekly which he has attempted to make "a cross between *Time* and the London *Economist.*" He is co-publisher with Françoise Giroud; Pierre Viansson-Ponté is editor in chief. The *Express,* one of the few French newspapers which receives no sort of hidden subsidy either from the government or private interests, has achieved a circulation of 125,000. One factor contributing to its circulation rise was its publication of a secret defense report on Indochina. As a result of this, the offices of *L'Express* were temporarily closed by the police in June 1954. However, in view of the publicity, observed Servan-Schreiber, "the government really did us the best turn they possibly could" (*Time,* June 14, 1954).

After Mendès-France (a Radical Socialist) had failed by thirteen votes to become the French Premier in June 1953, Servan-Schreiber, in order to "organize and kindle new enthusiasm" for him, began a series of informal *dîners du travail* to which members of other political parties were also invited. These occasions provided "a sounding board" for Mendès-France and gave him an opportunity to learn "how to work in a team" (*Time,* July 12, 1954).

Mendès-France became Premier in June 1954 and resigned in February 1955. *L'Express* served as an organ of explanation for his government. It was *L'Express* which launched the style of referring to the Premier by his initials alone, and this repetition of "PMF" reminds the French people of those other familiar initials, "FDR," and of the New Deal associated with President Franklin D. Roosevelt.

In order to devote more time to his role of unofficial adviser to Mendès-France, Servan-Schreiber took a leave of absence from *L'Express.* The editor, who is considered "the most articulate" of the Premier's young braintrusters, described the program of the new government in an article for *Time* (September 27, 1954): "The first part of the Mendès plan consisted of deflating illusions and facing facts. This is the story of Indochina and the story of the European Defense Community. . . ."

"The second stage opens with Mendès' economic plan. Two of its aims have top priority: wrest away from the Communist party the grip it holds today on 5,000,000 Frenchmen by giving back to the French people the long-forgotten feeling of social and material progress... [and] put back Franco-American relations on a healthy basis. This can only be achieved if France ceases to stand like a beggar in the U.S. bread line. When the old regimes decided to rely on American charity, they committed an unpardonable crime against Franco-American friendship, which can only be based upon mutual respect. The Atlantic alliance should not rely on satellites.

"The essential aim of the Mendès-France revolution is to break the crust which weighs upon the French economy and hinders its free development. This crust is made up of layers of protections, subsidies and financial subterfuges. . . . [Mendès-France] decided to plunge

French economy into international competition as quickly as possible by reducing customs tariffs and opening the frontiers. . . . When a business has to face the necessity of reconversion, it may apply to the state. The government will provide both plans and credit, and it will assume responsibility for unemployed workers who will need readaptation to new jobs."

The publisher-editor returned to his desk in September 1954. The outbreak of the (Jean) Dides scandal, which had revealed the filtration of reports on the secret proceedings of the Committee of National Defense into Communist hands, menaced the security of the Mendès-France government. In its October 12, 1954 issue, *L'Express* charged that a renascent neo-Fascist group of interests, stemming from the Cagoulards of the 1930's and the Vichy collaborationists of the 1940's, had conspired to discredit the Mendès-France Cabinet by constructing a spurious relationship between it and the Communist party.

The by-lines of foremost French and foreign figures, such as François Mauriac and Aneurin Bevan, are to be found heading articles in *L'Express.* Its features include a "Forum," in which outstanding figures in French life answer readers' questions, and a "Côte"—or current market quote—on the political value of certain politicians. A third is "The March of Ideas," which includes philosophical studies in the arts, the theatre, literature, and the cinema.

In September 1947 J.-J. Servan-Schreiber married Madeleine Chapsel. He has blue eyes and light-brown hair, is five feet six inches tall, and weighs about 150 pounds. He is particularly devoted to swimming and playing basketball and tennis, and requires his ten-man staff to share his interest in gymnastics as well —their day at the office is rounded off by an hour's work-out in a gymnasium across the street on the Champs-Elysées. The editor often gets up early in the morning and puts in a four-hour stint of work at home before going to his office at eight. He has been described by his colleagues as a "dynamic and calm" person and as a "leader able to deal with people."

Reference

Time 63:93+ Je 14 '54 por

SHAFIK, DORIA (AHMAD) (shä'fĭk)

Dec. 14, 1919- Feminist leader; journalist

Address: b. c/o Bent el Nil 48, Kasr el Nil, Cairo, Egypt; h. 6, Salah el Din, Famalck St., Cairo, Egypt

As president of the Bent el Nil union (Daughters of the Nile), which she founded in 1948, Doria Shafik is campaigning not only for women's suffrage in Egypt but also to eliminate illiteracy among the women of her country and to abolish polygamy. She made her first visit to the United States in the fall of 1954 under the auspices of the American Friends of the Middle East, and spent six weeks of an eighty-day world tour lecturing from coast to coast.

Paul Cordes

DORIA SHAFIK

Mme. Shafik, who holds a Ph.D. degree from the Jean Jacques Rousseau Institute of Philosophy, is the editor and publisher of three Egyptian magazines and the author of several books. She led 1,000 Bent el Nil women in storming the Egyptian Parliament in 1951. A hunger strike, which she conducted in March 1954, resulted in the inclusion of an equal-rights-for-women provision in the new Egyptian constitution then being drafted.

Doria Ahmad Shafik was born in Tanta, Egypt on December 14, 1919, the daughter of Ahmad and Ratiba (Nassif) Shafik. According to *Holiday* (January 1955), Doria Shafik remembers her mother as a "gentle, lovely woman who spent her entire life in typical Moslem seclusion and whose husband kept a harem. The men in Doria's family were both wealthy and intellectual." She attended Notre Dame des Apôtres, a French religious school in Tanta and completed her secondary education in Alexandria, at the top of her class, when sixteen years old.

The late Madame Hoda Charaoui, who was known as Egypt's Susan B. Anthony, urged Doria to continue her studies in France. Doria's family believed that she would lose her chance of marriage, but Doria chose a career and left for France in 1934. In Paris, she studied journalism, Greek, Latin and modern languages at the Sorbonne. The history of Egyptian art in its early religious phases interested her, and her first book, *L'Art pour l'Art dans L'Egypte Antique*, was later published (1940). She continued her studies at the Jean Jacques Rousseau Institute and majored in philosophy. The thesis for her doctorate, granted in 1942, *La Femme et le Droit Religieux en Egypte* (Woman and Her Religious Rights in Egypt), was based on the study of complex religious laws that affected all Moslem women and showed that Islam did not oppose the emancipation of women.

(Continued next page)

SHAFIK, DORIA—*Continued*

Upon her return to Egypt in 1942, Dr. Shafik applied for a teaching position at the University of Cairo and was told that she was "too young and elegant" to be a professor for men. For a brief period she worked for the Ministry of Education. Her articles on living conditions for Egyptian women and possibilities for improvements led her into journalism, and in 1944 she became editor of *La Femme Nouvelle* (The New Woman), a fashion magazine published in French. She purchased the magazine in 1945 and a year later started *Bent el Nil* in Arabic, which soon became the leading woman's magazine in the Middle East. *Katkout* (Chick), a magazine in Arabic for children, was launched in 1947.

A feature of *Bent el Nil* was a housekeeper's forum—a letters-to-the-editor column. As reported by *Pathfinder* (May 16, 1951), Dr. Shafik found that most of the letters were complaints about the inferior social status of women, polygamy, and repudiation (the right of Egyptian men to obtain divorce and void legal and moral obligations). The veil, she believed, was the symbol of woman's slavery. To combat the two ancient Moslem institutions, polygamy and repudiation, and to encourage women to take part in the government, she organized the Bent el Nil union in 1948.

The organization's first major protest was made in February 1951, when Doria Shafik with 1,000 other women besieged Parliament. "We used cunning rather than arms," she told Ruth Shumaker (Washington *Post and Times Herald*, November 11, 1954). *Pathfinder* reported that they carried banners and shouted: "Down with Parliament without women." Mme. Shafik made a keynote speech declaring that Parliament could not represent the nation until women were allowed to take their rightful place. "Overwhelmed by the feminine invasion," the legislators promised cooperation. The next day King Farouk forbade consideration of the women's petition, and Mme. Shafik was warned that another demonstration would mean jail.

As the agitation increased, it was expected that the government would modify voting qualifications to include all literates. The possibility caused a flood of anti-feminist pronouncements from religious circles. The New York *Times* (May 3, 1952) said that Dr. Shafik countered by citing a contrary opinion given by the president of the Association of Ulemas of Pakistan, largest of all Islamic states. She was rebuked by the Grand Mufti of Egypt, Hassanein Mohammed Makhlouf, who proclaimed that Islam had built barriers to protect women from being abused. Several Moslem associations endorsed the Mufti's declaration.

The Cairo newspaper *Al Ahram* stated on June 13, 1952 that the Cabinet, obeying Moslem authority, based its decision to reject women's suffrage on an article in the Egyptian Constitution which made Islam the "religion of state." An article written by Mme. Shafik in June demanded that the government explain its real reason for denying women's rights "instead of taking cover behind religion."

While the elders of Islam proclaimed Dr. Shafik an "infidel" and her life was threatened by young Moslem zealots, a special group of the Constitutional Committee recommended an end to political discrimination against women (*Newsweek*, June 22, 1953). Although the recommendation was shelved, Bent el Nil was recognized as a political party, but its list of candidates failed to get on the ballot.

Following the government's announcement that women would not be allowed to run for public office or vote in the July 1954 elections, a strike that "electrified all Egypt" was organized (*Holiday*, January 1955). With eight other women, Mme. Shafik moved mattresses into the Press Syndicate Building in Cairo and for "seven days and four hours lived on lemonade, glucose tablets and nerves, in an atmosphere of constant turmoil." Mme. Shafik poured coffee for visitors and made speeches. She was rewarded by a message from President Major General Mohammed Naguib, who agreed to relay her claims to a Committee of the Constituent Assembly, which would consider admitting literate women to suffrage.

Bent el Nil is affiliated with the International Council of Women and the International Alliance of Women. Dr. Shafik attended the UNESCO Congress in 1949, and at the 1951 meeting of the General Assembly of the International Council of Women, held in Athens, her report on the fight against illiteracy of adult women was said to be the "best achievement of the assembly."

One of Dr. Shafik's topics during her lecture tour in the United States in the fall of 1954 was "The Fight for Literacy in the Near East." She explained that her campaign for educating women included social and hygienic subjects as well as cultural literacy, and estimated that more than 1,000 women a year received sufficient education to understand women's responsibility in government. She stated that seventy instruction centers had been set up in Cairo, Alexandria and the provinces.

Impressed with the educational possibilities of television, Mme. Shafik told the New York *Herald Tribune* (November 29, 1954) that she had discussed the construction of stations in Egypt's six major cities with American television engineers. She was sure the government would finance the project, as it would also benefit the poor peasants who had recently been given land. Reading and writing instructions could be broadcast for an hour a day and received in social centers where people meet.

On a brief visit to Karachi, Pakistan Dr. Shafik announced that 7,000 members of Bent el Nil had started a campaign throughout the Islamic world of 400,000,000 to "convince men that polygamy was frowned upon by women" (New York *Times*, January 10, 1955). She quoted the Koran: "You may have two, three or four wives on the condition that all are treated equally; but you cannot do it, however hard you may try."

While studying in Paris, Doria Ahmad Shafik met Nour el-Din Ragai, an Egyptian law student. They were married in 1938 and returned to Egypt after they had completed their studies. They have two daughters, Aziza and Gehan. Ragai is a prominent lawyer and professor of law at the University of Cairo.

He has supplied legal advice to Bent el Nil and is financially interested in his wife's publications. A new magazine *Bent el Nil Politique,* aimed at the political education of Egyptian women, will soon be added to the list. Dr. Shafik is the author of *La Bonne Aventure,* a collection of short poems, and an historical novel with a strong feminist slant, *L'Esclave Sultane.* Her next book, *The Egyptian Women,* will be published in English and Arabic.

Mme. Shafik is a member of the Gezine and Cairo Automobile clubs. She spends her leisure moments reading and likes to play tennis. Tall and slender, with black hair, brown eyes and a light complexion, she was described in *Newsweek* as "ultra fashionable . . . a beauty concealing an Arab warrior's spirit." Since her school days in Alexandria, she has said of herself: "Every day of my life is a storm."

References

Holiday 17:52+ Ja '55 pors
Pathfinder 58:26 My 16 '51 por

SHEPILOV, DMITRI TROFIMOVITCH

(shē-pē-lŏv', d-mē'trē trŏ-fēm-ō-vētch) Editor; Soviet Government and Communist Party official

Address: *Pravda,* Moscow, U.S.S.R.

When a Soviet delegation journeyed to Yugoslavia in May 1955 to try to repair relations with that country, one of the Soviet Union's most powerful figures stepped from the shadow of the iron curtain into the spotlight of the free world. He was Dmitri Trofimovitch Shepilov, editor in chief of *Pravda* since December 1952, and chairman of the foreign affairs commission of the Supreme Soviet's Council of Nationalities.

His unexpected presence on a major foreign mission inspired reports that he was acting for Foreign Minister Viacheslav M. Molotov, and might even succeed Molotov at the Foreign Ministry. In Washington and London, at least, it was believed that Shepilov was the most logical person to succeed Molotov when he retired. It was clear that Shepilov—one of the leading specialists in the Soviet Union on Communist theory, or ideology, and an economist of some note—was a rapidly rising man in the Communist hierarchy. This impression was confirmed in July 1955 when the Central Committee of the party named him as one of its secretaries.

Since *Pravda,* as the voice of the Central Committee, is the chief source of national news and ideological guidance for the party workers throughout the Soviet Union, its editor holds one of the most important positions in that country. Stalin was its founder and Mikhail A. Suslor was Shepilov's immediate predecessor.

Pravda, which goes to all parts of the country and is the model for republic, provincial and local party newspapers, has a daily circulation of 4,900,000. To meet the enormous demand *Pravda* prints more than 2,000,000 copies daily in Moscow and flies page matrices to twelve other major cities for printing.

Sovphoto

DMITRI TROFIMOVITCH SHEPILOV

In March, 1949, Shepilov was named director of the Propaganda and Agitation Department of the Central Committee of the Communist Party of the Soviet Union, whose "tentacles" reach into the furthest corner of the Soviet Union. This department is charged with organizing and mobilizing public opinion in support of party policies. In addition, it keeps the party leaders informed on the attitudes of the public toward party policies.

The department has general supervision over all aspects of the Soviet press, radio, television, motion pictures, education, the arts, and the sciences—in short, every form of public information. It is responsible for organizing all propaganda drives, and for the training and assignment of the propaganda personnel who carry out such drives.

For many years Andrei A. Zhdanov, a powerful member of the Central Committee's Political Bureau, was in charge of this department. In 1947, however, Georgi F. Aleksandrov, a philosopher and political scientist whom Zhdanov had made director of the department, was accused of bourgeois leanings and replaced by Suslov. This was believed to be part of a move by a Politburo faction headed by Georgi M. Malenkov to undermine Zhdanov.

Soon after Shepilov had relieved Suslov in the post in 1949, the party's Central Committee passed a decree condemning errors in ideology in a book by the economist Nikolai A. Voznesensky entitled *The Economy of the U.S.S.R. During World War II.* The decree sharply criticized the party's ideological journal, *Bolshevik,* for publicizing Voznesensky's views. And Shepilov was criticized for tolerating the magazine's errors.

Voznesensky, a member of the Central Committee's Political Bureau, was removed as head of the State Planning Committee and disappeared from the Soviet political scene. His disappearance was believed to be another victory

SHEPILOV, DMITRI TROFIMOVITCH
—Continued

of the Malenkov faction, since Voznesensky had been closely associated with Zhdanov in the Leningrad party apparatus.

Shortly after Voznesensky's disappearance, Shepilov's department launched in August, 1949, through the Communist Party organ *Culture and Life,* a series of attacks on Konstantin V. Ostrovityanov, a leading economist and director of the Institute of Economics of the Soviet Academy of Sciences. Western observers noted that in this case, also, Dr. Ostrovityanov had been closely associated with Zhdanov.

At the Nineteenth Congress of the Soviet Communist Party in October 1952, Shepilov was elected a full member of the party's Central Committee. In December of that year he was named the chief editor of *Pravda,* the national newspaper published by the Central Committee. He succeeded Leonid F. Ilichev, who had held the post since 1951.

Under Shepilov's administration there were several changes in the makeup and news emphasis of *Pravda.* Much greater frequence and prominence was given to political cartoons, particularly those drawn by the Kukryniksi, a trio of collaborating cartoonists. More full and critical reviewing of plays and films was begun. And even greater publicity, including page one pictures and stories, was given to the leading production workers in industry and agriculture. Another innovation was the tieing-in of the traditional page one editorial with a bold-faced news dispatch appearing on the inner or back pages of the newspaper.

In March 1954, Shepilov was elected to the Supreme Soviet's Council of Nationalities by the Krasnodar district of the Russian republic. This could be an indication that his early career was in some way associated with that area in south European Russia on the Sea of Azov and the Black Sea.

The Council of Nationalities subsequently named him as chairman of its Foreign Affairs Commission, a body through which the Supreme Soviet, in theory at least, exercises its legal control over the foreign relations of the Soviet Union. It was apparently in this capacity that Shepilov in September of 1954 accompanied a government and party delegation headed by Khrushchev that visited Communist China.

It was perhaps indicative of Shepilov's importance as the editor of *Pravda* that it fell to him, as the author of a signed full-page article in the newspaper on January 24, 1955, to announce the impending shift of Soviet economic policy from emphasis on consumer goods production to heavy industry.

An editorial along this line had been published, unsigned, in *Pravda* on December 21—in apparent conflict with the editorial of that day in the government newspaper *Izvestia.* Shepilov's article appeared just two weeks prior to the meeting of the highest government body, the Supreme Soviet, which enacted the economic policy shift into law and replaced Malenkov as Premier.

Shepilov's article was ostensibly aimed at economists who, he claimed, had been advocating increasing consumer goods production at the expense of heavy industry. Articles appearing in the journals *Questions of Economics* and *Questions of Philosophy* were cited as examples.

"In practice," Shepilov argued in his article, "this would mean that the development of our heavy industry, which is the backbone of our Socialist economy, would be reduced to a lower level. That would lead to the withering away of all branches of our national economy and not to a rise, but to a decline in the standard of living of the workers and to an undermining of the economic power of the Soviet motherland and its defense capacity."

In May 1955, when Shepilov accompanied the Soviet delegation to Yugoslavia, he also accompanied it on stopovers in the other Soviet satellite countries. These visits were believed to be connected with the plans for unification of Communist armed forces in Eastern Europe and a closer integration of economic efforts.

Shepilov branded the reports of his possible succession to Foreign Minister Molotov's post as "nonsense" and "irresponsible speculation" (New York *Herald Tribune,* June 1, 1955). And Nikita S. Krushchev, First Secretary of the Communist Party of the Soviet Union and chief of the delegation to Belgrade, told Marshal Tito that Shepilov was there primarily to deal with ideological differences between the parties in the two countries.

When Shepilov visited Cairo on July 22, 1955 to attend Egypt's Liberation Day celebration, the New York *Times* interpreted this as an indication of the Soviet Union's increasing interest in the Moslem world, particularly Egypt. Subsequently the Soviets offered to sell arms to Egypt.

Shortly after the Geneva conference, there was a marked reversal in editorial policy seen in *Pravda* regarding its news coverage and general attitude toward the West. Readers were able to see "front-page pictures of top Soviet leaders engaged in intimate friendly conversation with . . . Western figures." The New York *Times* (August 9, 1955) commented on *Pravda*'s reports of a country party given for Moscow diplomats by Premier Nicolai A. Bulganin: ". . . that solemn and doctrinaire journal, the pontifical voice of the Soviet Communist Party, printed the gayest article that probably has ever appeared on its front page."

However the usual aggressive tone of *Pravda* was resumed in October when, as reported by Marguerite Higgins in the New York *Herald Tribune* on October 13 and 14, 1955, an article in *Pravda* was bluntly critical of Secretary of State John Foster Dulles for a prediction he had made in a speech at the American Legion convention in Miami, Florida on October 10 in which he predicted that world opinion would force the Soviet Union to relax its grip on the satellites of Eastern Europe. The U.S.S.R., wrote Miss Higgins, "took the most hostile and critical line toward the United States and other Western Powers that has appeared since the conference of the Big Four at Geneva."

Pravda also denounced Iran for its decision to join Iraq and Turkey in a Middle East defense pact. *Pravda* accused the United States, Great Britain and France of using the spirit of Geneva as a "propaganda decoy" to hide "the hard realities which consists of the Western powers' putting together new aggressive military alignments and drawing other countries into them."

Representatives of *Pravda* and *Izvestia* were in the first group of Russian editors and reporters to visit the United States since the start of the cold war. They arrived in October 1955 for a thirty-day tour of the United States.

Shepilov was interviewed in Moscow in June 1955, by Stewart Alsop, an American newspaper columnist. Alsop described him as "a big, handsome man with a tired middle-aged face, copious grey hair and an authoritative manner of speaking." But the comments of this "coming man in the younger generation of Soviet leaders" were, Alsop wrote, "straight down the party line" (New York *Herald Tribune,* July 1, 1955).

Reference

N Y Herald Tribune Jl 1 '55 p 12

SHERMAN, HENRY C(LAPP) Oct. 16, 1875-Oct. 7, 1955 Biochemist; in 1899 joined faculty of chemistry department, Columbia University, became Mitchill professor in 1924; chief, bureau of human nutrition and home economics, Department of Agriculture (1943-1944); member, food and nutrition board, National Research Council (1940-1945); did pioneer work in determining functions of vitamins; "debunked" value of spinach; among his books is *The Science of Nutrition* (1943). See *Current Biography* (Jan.) 1949.

Obituary

N Y Times p19 O 8 '55

SHOEMAKER, SAMUEL M(OOR) Dec. 27, 1893- Clergyman; author

Address: b. c/o Calvary Episcopal Church, Shady Ave., Pittsburgh 6, Pa.; h. 400 Shady Ave., Pittsburgh 6, Pa.

Business men, steel workers, the "golf club crowd," and the H-Y-P Club (Harvard, Yale and Princeton) of Pittsburgh are being influenced by Dr. Samuel M. Shoemaker, rector of Calvary Episcopal Church, to attend church, conduct Sunday School classes, and to meet for weekly Bible study.

During his thirty-five-year ministry he has been "in the vanguard of the church's concern for men's souls," and his evangelism and personal counseling work has spanned all sectarian divisions. For twenty-six years he was rector of Calvary Episcopal Church in New York City, and since 1952 has held his present pastorate in Pittsburgh, a parish with over 1,900 communicants. He is the author of more than twenty-five books and is frequently heard on the Mutual Broadcasting System's *Radio Chapel* and *Faith in our Time* radio programs. He also broadcast regularly over the American Broadcasting System, Station WJZ, *Gems for Thought* program from 1946 to 1952. Among his recent books are: *How To Become A Christian* (1953) and *By the Power of God* (1954), published by Harper & Brothers.

Carlyle Studios, Inc.

REV. DR. SAMUEL M. SHOEMAKER

The son of Samuel Moor and Ellen Ward (Whitridge) Shoemaker, Samuel Moor Shoemaker was born December 27, 1893, in Baltimore, Maryland. He received his education at St. George's School, in Newport, Rhode Island, from which he was graduated in 1912, and from Princeton University, where he was granted the B.A. degree in 1916.

From 1917 to 1919 he served as Y.M.C.A. secretary in Pekin (Peiping), China, and returned to Princeton, where for a year he was secretary of the Philadelphia Society and its general secretary until 1924. He studied theology and related subjects at the General Theological Seminary and at Union Theological Seminary in New York City. He received his D.D. degree from Virginia Theological Seminary and his S.T.D. degree from Berkeley Divinity School in 1948.

He was ordained a deacon in the Protestant Episcopal Church in 1920. At the age of thirty-one, in 1925, he became rector of Calvary Church. Two years later plans for a new parish house were proposed, but were voted down by the vestry as being impractical. Nevertheless, the rector requested the Parish House Committee to meet with him and the architect. At this meeting the junior warden became convinced that, although the venture was a risk, it was a good risk. Once persuaded, the junior warden convinced others, and the members of the vestry reversed their decision. The result was "the house that faith built"—the eight-story Calvary House, overlooking Gramercy Park.

Dr. Shoemaker spoke once a week for four months during 1945 over Station WJZ in connection with the Federal Council of Churches of Christ in America, on *Your Life Today*, and in 1945-1946 twice a week over a network of 120 stations of the American Broadcasting Company.

(Continued next page)

SHOEMAKER, SAMUEL M.—*Continued*

In 1945, as an outgrowth of his years of counseling, Dr. Shoemaker conducted a lecture course, "How to Help People," which drew hundreds from outside his parish and included representatives of twenty-three denominations. Material used in this course formed the basis of his book, *How You Can Help Other People*, which was published in January 1946 and chosen by the Religious Book-of-the-Month Club as one of its selections. The obliteration of denominational lines which characterized Shoemaker's lectures was also evident in the *Evangel*, a monthly magazine published by Calvary Church of New York, which has a circulation of more than 7,000.

Among his books are: *Realizing Religion* (1921), *A Young Man's View of the Ministry* (1923), *Children of the Second Birth* (1927), *Religion That Works* (1928), *Twice Born Ministers* (1929), *If I Be Lifted Up* (1931), *The Conversion of the Church* (1932), *Confident Faith* (1932), *Christ's Words from the Cross* (1933), *The Gospel According to You* (1934), *Christ and This Crisis* (1943), *How You Can Help Other People* (1946), *How You Can Find Happiness* (1947), *Living Your Life Today* (1947), *Freedom and Faith* (1949), *The Church Alive* (1950), *They're On the Way* (Dutton, 1951), *How To Become A Christian* (Harper, 1953), and *By the Power of God* (Harper, 1954).

In the fall of 1945, under the leadership of Dr. Shoemaker, the Reverend Canon Quinton Warner of London, Ontario, and the Reverend Ernest W. Churchill, first Protestant chaplain of Rockland State Hospital, the Calvary Clergy School was opened. Those who attended the 1945-1946 session were newly ordained clergymen serving a pastoral "interneship"; others were older men seeking a "refresher course"; and still others were returning servicemen who had found their vocation in the ministry. Of these last, Shoemaker said, "It is very natural that men who have risked everything in war will make an investment in a different kind of world, and the basis must be Christian."

Dr. Shoemaker founded Peace Builders, an organization launched formally on March 9, 1946, at the centennial of Calvary Church. The mission of the group is to carry the spirit of peace from person to person in the manner of a positive "chain reaction." Following the theory that the negative, destructive force which tears apart the individual, causing breakdown and unhappiness, is the same force which on a larger scale results in divorce, class and racial tensions, and wars, the group investigates the basic causes of the problems by setting right the individual and the community, and by working outward from these to greater objectives.

His enthusiasm for transplanting Christian practices into everyday life was first kindled by his experience with Frank Buchman's Oxford Group (see *Current Biography*, October 1940). According to *Fortune* (October 1953) Shoemaker "recoiled from Buchman's Moral Re-Armament twelve years ago, when he concluded that the movement had become a 'plain dictatorship,' and in respect to 'the historic church . . . divisive'. He has, however, lost none of his evangelical enthusiasm, and he goes armed with his special audacity."

When called to Calvary Church, Pittsburgh in March 1952 he told the vestry that he felt committed to his work on university campuses, and the vestry said that he could take time from parish duties to continue this work. He has held student conferences on the campuses of Yale, Harvard, Princeton, Lehigh, Lafayette, University of Pittsburgh and Pennsylvania College for Women. His sermons are mimeographed each week and subscribed to by many people across the United States. Some of them have been published in the *Christian Century*, *Christian Herald*, *Evangel* and *Reader's Digest*.

In Pittsburgh he began thinking in terms of how he could get the steel industry figuratively "down on its knees in prayer." He offered no blueprint, but was strongly convinced that "God is the one answer. . . . You cannot forge together two bars of cold iron: but if you heat them first, you can forge them together." Both groups (management and labor) have come through something of "a spiritual fire" under Dr. Shoemaker's guidance.

Among Dr. Shoemaker's parishioners is a young man, David Griffith, a war veteran, now employed at U.S. Steel's plant in Homestead, Pennsylvania. Convinced that only through a mutuality of faith could labor and management live in peace, he asked permission to hold weekly prayer meetings in the power-and-fuel department. The meetings are amplified over a public-address system so that others can hear them. "The singing of hymns out at Homestead is an unusual sound on that old and bloody ground" commented *Fortune* (October 1953). Griffith was inspired to get CIO steelworkers together for prayer by one of Dr. Shoemaker's sermons in which the clergyman urged listeners in their places of business to "make friends with as many individuals as you can, open up on God and human relations and see what you find." Parishioners like David Griffith and Admiral Ben Moreel (chairman of the board of Jones & Laughlin) agree that Dr. Shoemaker has showed them the efficacy of prayer, and that both boss and employee can be "in tune with God."

He also won over the "golf club crowd" (their own phrase). He conducted a series of lectures on "How to Become A Christian" at the Pittsburgh Golf Club. From fifty to seventy young married couples attended. Most of the husbands had seen service in World War II, were university graduates, and had excellent positions and family prestige. "None of us had any particular problem that would cause us to turn to religion," said one young executive. "But we found that (after praying and attending church) we got along better with people."

In 1953 Dr. Shoemaker's book *How to Become A Christian* was published by Harper & Brothers. "In clear, forceful language he presents a challenge to all Christians everywhere," wrote the reviewer in *Presbyterian Life*. *The Christian Advocate* commented: "Readable, stimulating and very urgent." The Religious Book Club news stated: "This is not a book of theory but one of practical action. It is dealing with the 'how' or the 'what' of the Christian life."

On April 26, 1930 Dr. Shoemaker married Helen Dominick Smith, daughter of Senator and Mrs. H. Alexander Smith of Princeton, New Jersey. They have two daughters, Sally Falls and Helen Dominick. Dr. Shoemaker is a Democrat, and his clubs are the Society of the Cincinnati, Ivy Club (Princeton), and the Union League Club. In the Diocese of Pittsburgh he is a member of the Diocesan Council and the Department of Missions. He is editorial assistant of the *Pulpit* magazine and a member of the board of trustees of the Koinonia Foundation.

He is five feet ten inches tall, and stocky in build, has blue eyes and graying blond hair. He is a firm believer in the recreative value of working with one's hands and so finds relaxation in carpentry and gardening.

Sam Shoemaker believes that prayer is something that can be shared by everyone, from boss to laborer. "The preponderant factor in freedom as Americans know it is our inherited Christianity," he has said, and has pointed out the relation between freedom and faith in a democracy. "Christians are 'the salt of the earth' . . . and the light of the world. They are not atavistic, out-dated relics: if they are real Christians they are the vanguard of the future. . . . The real place to begin it is not to show the error of Communism, but to show the reality of Jesus."

References

Fortune 48:140+ O '53
Pittsburgh Press p8 N 8 '53 por
Read Digest 65:7 O '54
Shoemaker, S. M. By the Power of God (1954)
Who's Who in America, 1954-55

SHULMAN, HARRY Mar. 14, 1903-Mar. 20, 1955 Dean of the Yale University Law School; professor of law since 1930; one of America's leading authorities on labor law; noted as an arbitrator in labor-management disputes; since 1943 was umpire between the Ford Motor Company and the United Auto Workers, C.I.O.; was author and editor of several books on law and labor. See *Current Biography* (Apr.) 1952.

Obituary

N Y Times p25 Mr 21 '55

SIEPI, CESARE (sē-ĕ'pē, chä'zä-rā) 1922(?)- Singer

Address: b. c/o Rasponi Associates, Inc., 667 Madison Ave., New York 21

One of the leading bassos of the New York Metropolitan Opera Association is Cesare Siepi, who made his American debut on the opening night of the Metropolitan's 1950-1951 season. He won enthusiastic recognition for his performance. Subsequent appearances with the Metropolitan, in concerts, with other musical organizations, and in televised and radio broadcasts have confirmed his initial reception. The range, beauty, richness, and power of his voice, his sincerity and dignity, his characterizations of his roles, and his musicianship, have all been the subject of critical acclaim. He has sung at La Scala in Milan and at the Edinburgh and Salzburg festivals, in addition to making appearances at various opera houses in Europe and under the baton of Arturo Toscanini, Bruno Walter, and other conductors.

Bruno of Hollywood

CESARE SIEPI

Cesare Siepi was born in Milan, Italy in 1922(?). He originally aspired to be a boxer, but he never fought professionally and finally gave up his amateur bouts because his mother grieved so much over his cut and bruised features. He had done his first singing in his school chorus, but did not decide to become a singer until he was eighteen, when his school friend, Giuseppe di Stefano (now a Met tenor), urged him to enter a competition in Florence. Although he knew only two arias, Siepi won the competition. He made his operatic debut two months later in Venice in a presentation of *Rigoletto*.

The opera *Il Nabucco* introduced him to Milan and after his first appearance at La Scala he became one of the leading singers at that historic opera house. Guest appearances in all of Italy's principal opera houses followed, and the young basso's reputation spread, taking him further afield. Concert and operatic appearances in Spain, Switzerland, Scandinavia, England, and Mexico resulted. Siepi was engaged for the Edinburgh Festival, where he was heard in Mozart's *Requiem* and Verdi's *Requiem*; he repeated the latter work in Albert Hall in London. Under the direction of Maestro Arturo Toscanini in 1948 he was again at La Scala, singing in *Mefistofele* and in *Nerone*.

The singer's American debut was made in November 1950 at the Metropolitan Opera

SIEPI, CESARE—*Continued*

House in New York, the presentation being Verdi's *Don Carlos*, with Siepi in the role of King Philip II. Acclaim was immediate. "An admirable bass of the most accomplished mastery," wrote Olin Downes in the New York *Times*. "Clearly a fine musician and an artist," Virgil Thomson of the New York *Herald Tribune* commented. "His rich bass voice, moreover, is both vibrant and warm. It is a beautiful voice and seems to be thoroughly schooled. Mr. Siepi's dramatic performance was no less distinguished than his vocal work." The New York *World-Telegram* critic, Robert Bagar, hailed the singer as "the vocal star of the night," and went on to say, "And what a presence, what a fine, assured singing actor he is!"

In *The Barber of Seville* at the Metropolitan in December of the same year Siepi sang the role of Don Basilio. His "brilliant bass singing and pantomime of the highest comic potency united to make an effect that dominated the whole evening's entertainment," wrote Virgil Thomson, while the critic of the New York *Post* spoke of the fulfillment of the role as "a masterpiece of characterization." *Newsweek* reported, "For a full two minutes the audience exploded with applause and bravos for a young man . . . who had played the grotesque and unscrupulous singing master with all the polish and nuance of a veteran singing actor."

Again under the direction of Toscanini—and selected by him—Siepi took the part of soloist in a presentation of Verdi's *Requiem* in the Verdi Memorial Concert at Carnegie Hall on January 27, 1951. He was chosen also by the conductor Bruno Walter for the performances of Mozart's *Requiem* given by the Chicago Symphony Orchestra in March of the same year.

Siepi was heard in a concert recital at the Hunter College Auditorium in New York City in March 1952, his program including airs by Mozart and Verdi, and songs by Durante, Caldara, Schumann, Strauss, Fauré, Ravel and Tchaikovsky. The New York *Herald Tribune* critic thought that "as a recital instrument," Siepi's voice was "somewhat inflexible," but that "the power and beauty of his bass, managed to overcome any objections one had to the similarity of approach which he brought to bear on differing style, sentiment, and period."

Don Carlos was again in the repertoire of the Metropolitan Opera Company in the spring of 1952. On this occasion, the production was staged by Margaret Webster, and Fritz Stiedry conducted. The New York *Times* reported that Siepi "stopped the show every time he finished an aria, for his portrayal of the ill-starred King Philip was a human experience. His singing, always a joy, has rarely surpassed the heights of richness and eloquence it reached last night."

Mozart's *Don Giovanni* was presented at the Metropolitan in the fall of 1952, with Fritz Reiner conducting and Siepi taking the title role for the first time in his career. Olin Downes thought that he "sang both the music and the text beautifully and skillfully throughout," but he was less satisfied with the characterization Siepi gave to the role, which was "youthful to the point of adolescence" (New York *Times*, November 27, 1952).

Returning to Hunter College Auditorium for another concert appearance in February 1953, Siepi was again heard in a widely varied program comprising offerings in Italian, German, French, and English. "Sincerity, dignity and expert musicianship were marked characteristics of the Italian vocalist's work," the New York *Times* critic stated; "although Mr. Siepi could infuse his interpretations with tender lyricism, he was most successful in music demanding intensity of emotion."

Boris Godunoff in Mussorgsky's original version was presented at the Metropolitan in March, with Siepi heard in the role of Boris for the first time. "Not only because of his superb voice, dark colored and well suited to this role, but also by reason of the sincerity and the dignity of his conception, Mr. Siepi now has a meritorious accomplishment to his credit; potentially, it is a great one" (New York *Times*, March 10, 1953).

In the summer of 1953 Siepi was in Salzburg, the birthplace of Mozart, singing the title role in *Don Giovanni*. Returning to the Metropolitan Opera Company in the fall, he took part in the televised presentation of excerpts from *Boris Godunoff*, TV's salute to the seventieth anniversary of the Metropolitan. The motion picture and television critic of the New York *World-Telegram*, Harriet Van Horne, wrote: "Cesare Siepi sang with great dignity and feeling, but no Boris ever took that death fall with such a thud. Down the steps he rolled, and it looked to this reviewer as if he knocked his wig off in the process. A most gallant death, theatrically speaking" (November 9, 1953).

The Marriage of Figaro, La Bohème, La Forza del Destino, Aïda, offered by the Metropolitan in 1954, all served to advance Siepi's mounting reputation, while the critics still found fresh praise for roles in which he had been seen and heard previously. Of his Figaro, Howard Taubman in the New York *Times* wrote that Siepi was "a light-footed, supple Figaro, and his singing of the role has taken on an easy, delightful flexibility." As Colline in *La Bohème*, Siepi "sang impressively" (New York *Times*, February 2, 1954). His role in *La Forza del Destino* was "ideally tailored to fit the warmth and singular spaciousness of his large range and vivid resources of dramatic projection" (New York *Herald Tribune*, February 3, 1954). His Basilio in *The Barber of Seville* was "a figure full of humor" (New York *Times*, November 13, 1954).

The San Francisco Opera Company engaged Siepi for its thirty-second season, and in October of 1954 the basso appeared in *La Forza del Destino* with the company. A review in *Musical America* (October 1954) by Marjory M. Fisher remarked that "Cesare Siepi's beautiful bass voice was heard for the first time here. . . . One could have wished at times for more variety of tone and more dramatic characterization."

Back with the New York company for the 1954-1955 season, Siepi participated in the Metropolitan Opera broadcasts over the ABC television network, presented by the Texas Company, singing in *The Marriage of Figaro, Don Giovanni* and *The Barber of Seville.* In January he appeared in a concert presentation of *La Somnambula* by Bellini, offered by the American Opera Society at Town Hall, New York. Taubman in the New York *Times* (January 26, 1955) reported that Siepi "sang with poise and authority, and in the *cavatina 'Vi ravviso,'* he evoked a nostalgic mood with a sustained legato and a musician's taste."

The *New Yorker* (March 19, 1955), commenting on Siepi's portrayal of Don Giovanni during the 1954-1955 opera season, said: "There is the wholly intuitive, tasteful, and engaging interpretation by Mr. Cesare Siepi." He appeared as the guest artist at a concert in Town Hall, New York given by the John Harms chorus on May 1, 1955. In the fall of 1955 Siepi was again engaged to sing with the San Francisco Opera Company. He plans to return to the Metropolitan in February 1956 for the remainder of the New York opera season.

Cesare Siepi, who has been described as "one of the Metropolitan's handsomest stage figures," is over six feet in height. One of his hobbies is social dancing. In an interview with Myles Fellowes, published in *Etude* (June 1952), Siepi is quoted on the subject of singing: "Once you are sure of a relaxed throat free of all tension or forcing, forget about it. . . . In the last analysis, it is just this ability to forget self and serve the meaning of the music with complete love and faith, which is the essence of the artist. It is delightful to sing around the house, but art is something different!"

References

Newsweek 42:96 N 30 '53
Time 57:92+ Mr 19 '51 por

SIMONETTA Apr. 10, 1922- Italian dress designer

Address: b. Via Gregoriana 5, Rome, Italy; h. Via Metelli 55, Rome, Italy

The distinction of Italian design, which has influenced style and mode since the Renaissance, is still vital and appealing today, thanks to such designers as Simonetta who have made the fashionable world conscious of their native talents. One of the first of the postwar Italian *couturières* to launch a collection, Simonetta has brought to current fashion a quality of youth and wearability which particularly attracts the American woman.

Simonetta's "elegantly textured clothes" and comfortable sports outfits were brought to the attention of *Vogue's* editors shortly after World War II, with the result that her collections are closely watched by both commercial and private buyers in search of sophisticated and yet practical models.

In September 1955 Simonetta brought to New York City her newest collection which she personally presented in fashion showings in fifteen major cities in the United States and

SIMONETTA

Canada and introduced her perfume, "Incanto" (enchantment), a blend of many ingredients including jasmine, wood oil, rose and mignonette from Sicily and Northern Italy and packaged like a Roman column. She revived the Empire look in her latest collection, the high-waisted style being carried into play clothes for resort wear as well as in evening dresses.

A descendant of the Sicilian branch of the Colonna family, Simonetta Colonna di Cesarò was born in Rome on April 10, 1922 to Duke Giovanni Colonna, and his Duchess, the former Barbara Antonelli. The political tradition of the family was at that time being continued by her father, who was then Minister of Posts and Telegraphs, a post from which he was subsequently dismissed by the Fascist government, under a penalty preventing him from leaving Italy with his family.

Reared in Rome and educated at Italian government schools, Simonetta Colonna brought complaints from her teachers for her lack of studiousness and her refusal to interest herself in anything but her favorite occupation: designing clothes for her dolls. While she was still a teen-ager, she thought of opening a custom dress shop, inspired by the insistence of friends who kept urging her to make "new, amusing, smart" models for them.

At the age of nineteen she was interned for nine months by the Mussolini government for her anti-Fascist activities; three years later, in 1944, she was again sentenced to a two-month jail term on a similar charge. After the war she was married to Count Galeazzo Visconti di Modrone, and in 1946 she used her married name, Simonetta Visconti, for the presentation of her first collection.

An Italian press release stated of her first postwar show: "To understand how difficult it was to open a *maison de couture* and have a show with fourteen models just after the liberation of Rome by the Allies, one must

SIMONETTA—*Continued*

remember the general situation at that time. Materials and trimmings were very scarce. The most surprising and common materials had to be used to make the extraordinary collection—dish cloths, gardeners' aprons, butler's uniforms, strings and ribbons, and everything that could be found on the market."

With international interest in Italian design stimulated by the success not only of Simonetta's work, but that of the other Roman and Milanese houses of *haute couture,* which offered a severe challenge to the French lead in the field, the fashion world was alerted to Italian developments. The American *Vogue* sent its fashion editor and a photographer to Rome to prepare a double-page spread on Simonetta's contributions, which appeared in the January 1, 1947 issue of the magazine.

American interest in her designs was aroused, and the first American private customers began to arrive at her *atelier.* Simonetta costumes are to be found in the wardrobes of film actresses Teresa Wright, Dorothy McGuire, Jennifer Jones, Lauren Bacall, and Evelyn Keyes, as well as in those of Mrs. Douglas Fairbanks, Jr., and of *Look* editor Fleur Cowles. Italian screen stars Eleonora Rossi Drago, Silvana Pampanini, and Silvana Mangano also own originals by Simonetta.

Vogue's introduction of Simonetta to the American public met with interest chiefly because of the "wearable" quality of her designs, which met the requirements of American taste and living more than many European *couturières.* Bergdorf Goodman in New York and Marshall Field in Chicago began to import Simonetta models. For Bergdorf Goodman's golden anniversary in 1951, Simonetta was asked by Andrew Goodman to design an exclusive collection which had its première in the Bergdorf Goodman custom salons without a previous unveiling before Italian viewers.

After showing her collection in New York, Simonetta went to Montreal, where she signed a two-year contract with Holt, Renfrew and Company for the exclusive use of her designs and label in Canada. This 1951 visit established a tradition for Simonetta, who has since paid two visits each year to the United States and Canada. She has also granted rights to her designs to shops in England, Denmark, Sweden, Germany, Switzerland, and Argentina.

"Petite and coquette Simonetta makes clothes admirably suited to her type. Skirts were bouffant below trimly molded hips and saucily short," wrote Virginia Pope in the New York *Times* (July 24, 1954), reporting her showing in Rome. "Simonetta likes to design sportswear," remarked Eugenia Sheppard in the New York *Herald Tribune* of the Italian designer's August 1954 collection. "[She] dislikes the discipline of coats and suits." Winter flower prints and long-torsoed cocktail dresses, fanning into fullness below a low waistline, were the distinguishing characteristics of this collection, shown in Florence in collaboration with the Giorgini group of designers. By the following month copies of Simonetta designs appeared at Ohrbach's and Macy's stores in New York. Her boutique accessory fashions were singled out by the New York *Times'* shopper.

When the Italian designer brought out her 1955 winter models in January of that year, the New York *Herald Tribune* correspondent reported that "Simonetta's collection was top couture designing. Her balloon or slightly cocoon skirts turned the long torso and mock low waistline theme into a silhouette particularly her own." Virginia Pope was impressed by the "youthful sophistication" of Simonetta's models, the "consistency of thought" devoted to the new line, and the "lovely color expressions" of the coats, with their peplum-length beltlines and lantern skirts. The Simonetta styles introduced with those of other European *couturières* in March by Bergdorf Goodman showed "dresses . . . almost knee-high with bouncy, flounced skirts."

Simonetta's collection, shown in Florence in July 1955, featured "the Empire silhouette, the coquettish Watteau look, the apron silhouette, all with a kind of court richness," as reported by Eugenia Sheppard (New York *Herald Tribune,* July 25, 1955).

Donna Simonetta is sole owner and proprietor of the *atelier* where she creates her styles, which are shown and marketed under the label of "Simonetta." Her marriage to Count Visconti was terminated in 1949. On December 2, 1953 she married Alberto Fabiani. Although the Fabianis are both designers, they make and show their collections independently. Fabiani is known to the trade as "the surgeon of suits and coats," whose clean, conservative tailoring dispenses with cluttering detail, observed Nan Robertson in the New York *Times,* October 19, 1955. "Simonetta's forte is young, ultrafeminine sports and cocktail clothes." They do not intend to merge their respective fashion concerns. "Fashion design is a mad business," Simonetta explained to Hope Johnson (New York *World-Telegram and Sun,* September 22, 1955). "While I'm doing a collection, I work until three in the morning for days on end. If my husband were a lawyer, he would not understand this. But, you see, he's doing the same thing. . . . My husband is known for his style and I for mine. We discuss our plans and that's all."

Simonetta, who spends each day at her Via Gregoriana workshop, relaxes in the evening at her home on the Via Metelli with her daughter by her first marriage, Verde Visconti, and her small son, Bardo Andrew Fabiani (his middle name is in honor of Andrew Goodman, of Bergdorf Goodman). She enjoys dancing and collecting antiques. She has been described as a "pretty woman with a slender figure." (She is five feet four inches tall and weighs 121 pounds.) Her dark hair above her youthful face has streaks of white, a coiffure created by Georgel of Paris, who regularly visits Rome, according to *Vogue.* Simonetta likes American designs and purchases inexpensive sports wardrobes for her personal use.

References

N Y Herald Tribune p6 My 31 '54
N Y Times p37 O 19 '55
N Y World-Telegram p20 S 22 '55

SINGER, S(IEGFRIED) FRED Sept. 27, 1924- University professor; physicist
Address: University of Maryland, College Park, Md.

An announcement of far-reaching significance was made at the White House on July 29, 1955: "Within three and one half years the United States will launch an earth satellite." This event will herald "not a bloody conflict but peaceful and constructive collaboration on an international scale in the exploration of extraterrestrial space" (*Jet Propulsion*, August 1955).

The proposed unmanned satellite is similar to the plans designed by Dr. S. Fred Singer of the University of Maryland's physics department. In a paper read before a symposium on space travel at the Hayden Planetarium in New York in 1954, Dr. Singer revealed the plans for his satellite, MOUSE (Minimum Orbital Unmanned Satellite of Earth), which is expected to travel in outer space at a rate of 18,000 miles per hour.

He estimates that his satellite could be launched at a cost of $1,000,000 (one bomber costs $15,000,000). Dr. Singer has also experimented on such problems as cosmic rays, meteorites and the exploration of the upper atmosphere with small rockets.

The project to launch the satellite has been called the beginning of the "space age," and a leading U.S. Navy rocket researcher, Dr. Homer E. Newell, Jr. (see *C.B.*, 1954), has proclaimed it "one of the greatest . . . philosophical and scientific achievements of mankind."

Dr. Siegfried Fred Singer, born on September 27, 1924 in Vienna, Austria, was reared and educated in the United States. After receiving the B.E.E. degree in 1943 from Ohio State University in Columbus, he continued his postgraduate studies at Princeton University in New Jersey. While working on his M.A. degree, which he was awarded in 1944, he was an instructor in the physics department at Princeton.

During World War II Singer served with the U.S. Navy and did research in the fields of mine warfare and mine design. At the Naval Ordnance Laboratory, he developed the arithmetic element for an electronic digital computer. These computers or calculators (also known as "electronic brains") are of value in performing mathematical problems (see John Von Neumann, *C.B.*, 1955). Singer also devised a coding system for a floating decimal point and circuits to control its operations.

Upon his discharge from the Navy in 1946, Singer joined the staff of the applied physics laboratory of Johns Hopkins University, Silver Spring. He received his Ph.D. degree in physics from Princeton University in 1948; his thesis was entitled "Extensive Airshowers of Cosmic Rays." At Johns Hopkins University he was engaged in research on primary cosmic rays, sea level cosmic radiation, the ionosphere, and cosmic ray balloon measurements. He joined in a Naval operation to the Arctic and shipboard rocket launchings at the equator.

S. FRED SINGER

In 1950 Dr. Singer served in the Office of Naval Research as a scientific liaison officer, attached to the U.S. Embassy in London. His functions were to study European research programs in cosmic radiation and elementary particle physics, upper atmosphere physics, radioastronomy and astrophysics. Upon his return to the United States in 1953, Singer was appointed associate professor of physics at the University of Maryland in College Park.

In 1953 Professor Singer suggested a new method of launching a rocket into space. Instead of using a balloon to raise the rocket above the air's resistance, he proposed that it be fired by a high-flying plane, either piloted or pilotless. He found that this device simplifies the range-safety problem because balloons are subject to wind conditions, and this method is cheaper. Singer stated: "It would, in fact, put rocket research on much the same basis as weather balloon soundings or ionosphere radio soundings" (*Nature*, June 20, 1953).

On August 17, 1955 when the Navy launched its first Rockairs it was carrying out this idea proposed by Dr. Singer. The venture consists of launching rockets vertically upward from high-flying aircraft in order to overcome the drag effects of the lower atmosphere and achieve great altitudes for purposes of upper atmosphere research. Into the nose of the rocket were placed a Geiger counter to measure cosmic rays, a power supply and a radio transmitter to broadcast the data back to ground. The rocket is inexpensive, costing about $50, and thus makes more frequent measurements feasible. This project is being supervised by Singer, who is also engaged on a project to take instrumental samples of the very high atmosphere from aircraft-launched rockets.

The possibility of shooting artificial satellites into space has been a foregone conclusion among astrophysicists since World War II. However, the problems inherent in such an ambitious

SINGER, S. FRED—*Continued*

undertaking were manifold. Dr. Singer's plans were the first to concern themselves with concrete problems, such as the structure and composition of the satellite, and the collection of scientific data by instruments housed inside the mechanism.

His satellite, MOUSE, is similar in size to a basketball. The satellite will travel 200 to 300 miles above the earth's surface, circling the earth every ninety minutes. Dr. Singer suggested that the satellite would be most useful if it circled the earth over the North and South Poles along a plane perpendicular to a line connecting the earth and the sun. Thus the satellite could always point directly to the sun. The earth would turn under the satellite orbit (see Andrew G. Haley, *C.B.,* 1955). Because of air friction the satellite will disintegrate in a few days, but the information collected by this earth-circling device will be invaluable.

Packed within the body of the satellite will be instruments to record scientific data, which will be transmitted to earth at forty-five minute intervals, as the satellite passes each Pole. The broadcast would be made by solar-powered transistor devices, triggered by a radar beam from an airplane circling below. (See *Life,* January 24, 1955.) Meteorologists will undoubtedly gain from information collected on solar radiation, which affects the atmosphere and weather conditions; communications specialists will gain from data collected on the electrified layers of the ionosphere, which make possible wireless transmissions; geodetics will be advanced by information on the size and shape of the earth, and the fluctuations in the earth's gravitational field. (See *Jet Propulsion,* February 1955.)

The satellite will be launched during the International Geophysical Year, 1957-1958, which is being sponsored by the National Science Foundation and the National Academy of Sciences. The U.S. Department of Defense will provide the launching rockets, the firing and observations sites and will handle all aspects of the launchings. About seven satellites will be launched and 600 rockets will blast off. Scientific representatives to the Conference of the International Geophysical Year, 1957-1958, were promised that the U.S. Government intended to cooperate with other countries participating in satellite experiments (New York *Times,* September 10, 1955).

At a meeting before the American Rocket Society in April 1955, Singer reported that a larger satellite carrying television cameras, telescopes, and spectrographs would be much more valuable, but "the larger satellite vehicle seems far removed from the standpoint of feasibility" (New York *Times,* July 30, 1955). Nevertheless, he did say that the launching of an artificial satellite "would pave the way for flights into interplanetary space" (New York *Times,* January 9, 1955).

Addressing a meeting of the International Astronautical Federation in August 1955, Singer said that in explorations of the moon, radioactivity from cosmic ray bombardment would be too small in amount to cause any damage to humans. He also noted that primary cosmic rays themselves might have serious effects on man, but "shields" containing kerosene, paraffin or water might give protection against them (*Christian Science Monitor,* August 5, 1955).

Dr. Singer is a naturalized U.S. citizen. He is affiliated with several professional organizations: the American Physical Society, American Rocket Society, American Geophysical Union, Washington Philosophical Society, Washington Academy of Sciences, and American Association of University Professors. He is a member also of the British Interplanetary Society and Royal Astronomical Society. He is a member of the technical panel on rockets and the technical panel on cosmic rays of the U.S. National Committee for the International Geophysical Year.

Fred Singer's accomplishments belie his youth. Only thirty-one years old, he is the picture of an earnest and serious young man working towards new and limitless goals. He has dark curly hair and dark eyes.

Reference

American Men of Science (1955)

SLEZAK, WALTER May 3, 1902- Actor; singer

Address: b. Majestic Theatre, 245 W. 44th St., New York 36

Co-starred with Ezio Pinza in the musical play *Fanny* during the 1954-1955 Broadway theatrical season is the Austrian-born actor and singer, Walter Slezak, whose career on the American stage and screen dates back to 1930. Prior to his New York debut in the musical show *Meet My Sister,* Slezak had been prominent in the Berlin theatre and in German motion pictures.

His subsequent Broadway successes included the musical comedies *Music in the Air* (1934) and *I Married an Angel* (1938). From 1942 through 1952, Slezak was occupied with film work in Hollywood, most frequently in sinister roles such as that of the Nazi submarine commander in *Lifeboat* (1944). An outstanding personal triumph in the stage comedy *My 3 Angels* (1953-1954) preceded his engagement in *Fanny.*

The son of the late Leo Slezak and Else (Wertheim) Slezak, Walter Slezak was born in Vienna, Austria on May 3, 1902. His paternal forebears were millers in Moravia (now a part of Czechoslovakia), where the elder Slezak had worked as a blacksmith before becoming a celebrated operatic tenor at the Vienna Opera House. Walter was early taught to accompany his father on the piano. He paid his first brief visit to New York at the age of seven, the occasion being Leo Slezak's first appearance (November 17, 1909) at the Metropolitan Opera House in the title role of Verdi's opera *Otello.*

Educated somewhat irregularly in various European schools, young Slezak was more interested in tennis, boxing and other sports than in scholarly attainments. He eventually enrolled at the University of Vienna for the study of chemistry and medicine but after a

WALTER SLEZAK

year and a half he left the university to work in a bank in his native city. "I thought a bank would lead to the international life I wanted," he later told Murray Schumach in an interview for the New York *Times*, April 19, 1953. "My job was to sweep up the floor."

Walter Slezak had already mastered several languages, and had made a debut as a concert pianist, when he was observed in a Viennese beer garden by the Continental film director Michael Kerteze (known to American moviegoers as Michael Curtiz) who thought the big, blond, smilingly boisterous young man ideal for a role in *Sodom and Gomorrah* and offered him a contract. Being under twenty-one, Walter had to get his father's signature. He overcame his father's objections and went to Berlin for the filming of *Sodom and Gomorrah*.

During the Berlin run of Jean Gilbert's operetta *Dorine und der Zufall*, the star, Harold Paulson, was forced by illness to retire from the cast. Young Slezak, engaged as Paulson's successor, learned the part (including songs and dances) in a single day, and played three months in Berlin and went on tour through the Netherlands and Austria. This led to a three-year contract with the German film concern UFA, and to several roles on the Berlin stage.

By 1929 Walter Slezak had been seen in Berlin in Oscar Straus's operetta *Hochzeit in Hollywood*; in a revival of Sigmund Romberg's *The Student Prince*; in the German production of Vicki Baum's *Grand Hotel*; as Lord Fancourt Babberly in Brandon Thomas' farce *Charley's Aunt;* and in leading roles in Offenbach's *La Vie Parisienne* and Franz Lehar's 1928 operetta *Frederika*.

An outstanding novelty of the German and Austrian stage in the season 1929-1930 was the chorusless musical comedy, with score by Ralph Benatzky, later known to American audiences as *Meet My Sister*. The American manager Lee Shubert saw this piece with Oscar Karlweis in the leading role, and later sent his brother Jacob to Europe to secure the American rights, along with the "male lead" for appearance on Broadway.

By that time, however, Walter Slezak had succeeded Karlweis in the leading role and was duly "signed up" by J. J. Shubert. Lee Shubert promptly denounced the young man as an "imposter" on his arrival in the United States; but the contract held, and it was accordingly in Harry Wagstaffe Gribble's adaptation of *Meet My Sister* that Walter Slezak made his New York debut at the Shubert Theatre on December 30, 1930.

His "delightful personality and a Maurice Chevalier touch to his method of putting over his principal song" (which he rendered in English, French and German) resulted, wrote one critic, in "a pronounced hit." Since then, Slezak's professional activity has been confined entirely to the United States.

Slezak next appeared as Karl Reder in the Oscar Hammerstein-Jerome Kern musical comedy *Music in the Air*, which ran in New York for 231 performances at the Alvin Theatre beginning on November 8, 1932, and in which he scored a hit with the song "I've Told Every Little Star." In March 1934 the Actors Equity Association modified its alien-artist regulations to permit Slezak to participate in spring dramatic festivals at Milwaukee (Wisconsin) and Ann Arbor (Michigan), where he re-enacted his role of Eric Molinar, the psychology student, in *Meet My Sister* and portrayed the character of the Hessian soldier in Lawrence Langner's and Armina Marshall's comedy *The Pursuit of Happiness*.

He made his first New York appearance in a non-musical role at the Lyceum on December 21, 1934 in Sidney Howard's *Ode to Liberty*, starring Ina Claire. Brooks Atkinson of the New York *Times* found Slezak's portrayal of an amorously involved policeman "quiet and pleasant and . . . completely winning."

He attained star billing at the St. James Theatre in New York on December 6, 1935, when he played and sang the leading role of a bashful pedagogue in the Frank Mandel-Sigmund Romberg operetta *May Wine* with a "modest, half-shy, cheerful style" which proved "completely charming" (Brooks Atkinson). His next New York appearance (May 11, 1938) was in a comedy role in the Lorenz Hart-Richard Rodgers musical play *I Married an Angel*, which ran for 338 performances at the Shubert Theatre. Beginning on November 16, 1941 Slezak was seen at the John Golden Theatre in *Little Dark Horse*, a comedy adapted by Theresa Helburn from the French of André Birabeau. Despite what Brooks Atkinson characterized as his "genuinely comic performance," this piece was a quick failure.

Early in 1942 Slezak was called to Hollywood by producer Leo McCarey to support Cary Grant and Ginger Rogers in the motion picture *Once Upon a Honeymoon*. He was "tremendously impressive as the Nazi weasel" in this film, according to Bosley Crowther in the New York *Times*. Slezak was occupied with screen work for the next ten years. He was a Gestapo officer in the Jean Renoir-Dudley

SLEZAK, WALTER—*Continued*

Nichols picture *This Land Is Mine* and a crippled Norwegian scientist in *The Fallen Sparrow* (1943). (Slezak has identified Dr. Skaas in the latter film as his favorite screen role.)

As the "fat, greasy, conceited" German submarine commander in John Steinbeck's *Lifeboat* (released in January 1944), Slezak "came through with a terrific delineation" (*Variety*). The following October, Slezak's elderly father, then still singing Wagnerian roles in Vienna, was fined 100,000 marks by the Nazi authorities because of his son's appearances in anti-German Hollywood films.

The film *The Spanish Main* (1945) gave Slezak scope to "luxuriate in the role of a fat and villainous governor of Cartagena in the seventeenth century" (Archer Winsten in the New York *Post*). In *Cornered* (1945), a film about Nazi machinations in Argentina, he made "a real character, clever, sordid, droll" out of a venal tourists' guide and was so effective that his part became "more interesting than that of the star" (Eileen Creelman in the New York *Sun*).

Supporting Douglas Fairbanks, Jr. in *Sinbad the Sailor* (1947), Slezak was again "the foulest villain . . . a greedy, murderous, ship's barber" (Irene Thirer in the New York *Post*). *Sinbad* was followed by *Born to Kill, Riffraff* and *The Pirate.*

In the screen version of Nikolai Gogol's classic comedy *The Inspector General* (1949), Slezak was "coldly effective" as a crooked showman. Subsequent screen characterizations by Slezak were in the Red Skelton comedy *The Yellow Cab Man* (1950) and in *Bedtime for Bonzo* and *People Will Talk* (1951).

Returning to the legitimate theatre after an absence of over eleven years, Selzak scored a personal triumph at the Morosco Theatre, New York on March 11, 1953 in *My 3 Angels,* a comedy by Sam and Bella Spewack based on the French play *La Cuisine des Anges* by Albert Husson. In this piece, dealing hilariously with three convicts escaped from Devil's Island, Slezak portrayed Joseph, "a monklike soul with a tidy talent for embezzlement," according to the New York *Herald Tribune* critic Walter Kerr, who found "irresistibly comic" the actor's "little lesson in irregular economics." The play ran for 342 performances in New York, largely on the strength of Slezak's performance.

During the run of this play he found time for several television appearances: in May 1953 as the Bulgarian major, Petkoff, in the *Omnibus* presentation of Bernard Shaw's *Arms and the Man*; and in February 1954 as the Pennsylvania Dutch father in the U.S. Steel Hour presentation of Patterson Greene's comedy *Papa Is All.*

At the Majestic Theatre, New York, beginning November 4, 1954, Ezio Pinza and Walter Slezak were co-starred in *Fanny*, a musical play with score by Harold Rome and book by S. N. Behrman and Joshua Logan, based on Marcel Pagnol's French film trilogy, *Marius, Fanny* and *Cesar.* Slezak as Panisse, a wealthy Marseilles waterfront storekeeper, "has never been so charming," commented Brooks Atkinson. "Nor has he ever sung a love song more ingratiating than 'To My Wife.' "

Walter Slezak and Johanna van Rijn were married in Beverly Hills, California on October 10, 1943; his Netherlands-born wife was formerly on the operatic stage. The Slezaks are the parents of two girls, Erica and Ingrid, and one boy, Leo Lauritz Walter, who is a godson of the Wagnerian tenor Lauritz Melchior. Slezak collects original Bach scores, plays chess like a master, flies his own airplane, and is an accomplished amateur painter, sculptor and cook. He is also fond of reading and hunting; a talented mimic, he can burlesque an opera singer in either bass or tenor voice. He is six feet tall and has bright blue eyes. His weight varies between 190 and 280 pounds, depending on when he adheres to or goes off his diet.

References

Etude 72:17+ Mr '54 por
N Y Herald Tribune VI p3 N 8 '42; IV p3 O 4 '53
N Y Times II p3 Ap 19 '53 por; III p8 Ja 11 '31
N Y World-Telegram p19 Ag 1 '53 por
N Y World-Telegram Mag p10 D 4 '54 por
Motion Picture and Television Almanac, 1953-54
Who's Who in Central and Eastern Europe, 1935-36

SLOAN, GEORGE A(RTHUR) May 30, 1893-May 20, 1955 Industrialist; his career bridged the worlds of business and music; chairman of the board of the Metropolitan Opera Association (1946-1955) and director of its fund appeals; director, U.S. Steel Corporation, Goodyear Tire and Rubber Company and other corporations; chairman, since 1950, of the United States Council of the International Chamber of Commerce, which elected him president in May 1955; president of the Nutrition Foundation and the Blue Ridge Mutual Fund. See *Current Biography* (Jan.) 1952.

Obituary

N Y Times p 1+ My 21 '55

SLONIMSKY, NICOLAS Apr. 27, 1894- Musicologist; composer; conductor
Address: h. 295 Beacon St., Boston, Mass.

The "jovial, knowledgeable and encyclopedic-minded" Russian-born composer, conductor and critic, Nicolas Slonimsky is editor or co-editor of recent editions of standard music dictionaries and encyclopedias, including Oscar Thompson's *International Cyclopedia of Music and Musicians* (Dodd, 1952). He has been a citizen of the United States since 1931, and has pioneered for the recognition of the younger school of American composers. His books, *Music Since 1900* (1937; 3rd edition, 1953), *Music in Latin America* (1945; 1951) and *Thesaurus of Scales and Melodic Patterns* (1937), are regarded as standard works. Slonimsky's own compositions include *Studies in Black and White for Piano* (1929), *My Toy Balloon* (1942), *Gravestones* (1945) and *Yellowstone Park Suite* (1950). He has lectured on music at Colorado College and Simmons College and has taught Russian literature at Harvard University.

His most recent book, *Lexicon of Musical Invective* (Coleman-Ross, 1953), has provoked much comment as it brings together "an extensive record entertainingly and informatively compiled . . . of obtuseness, insensitivity, incomprehension and slander uttered against leading composers of Europe and America since Beethoven's time" (Alfred Frankenstein, San Francisco *Chronicle*, January 10, 1954), showing that in each age there has been unfavorable contemporary response to new music. "This survey of devastating critiques," commented Jay S. Harrison in the New York *Herald Tribune* (January 3, 1954), "is a treasury of roasted composers . . . that no musical Scrooge can afford to be without."

Nicolas Slonimsky (in Polish, Slonimski) was born in St. Petersburg (now Leningrad), Russia on April 27, 1894 to Leonid Slonimski and the former Faina Wengeroff (in Polish, Vengerova). His elder brother Alexander is a leading Russian literary critic and authority on Pushkin; his younger brother Mikhail is a novelist; his sister Julia Sazonova is a writer on Russian literature and the dance. Haim Selig Slonimsky, the Warsaw astronomer and scholar was his paternal grandfather. His father was an economist and political writer; he wrote the first (says his son) "somewhat critical" Russian study of Karl Marx. His mother's sister, Isabella Vengerova (who later taught at the Curtis Institute of Music in Philadelphia) gave him his first piano lessons at the age of six following the "startling discovery" that he "possessed absolute pitch."

At the age of ten Nicolas began to improvise his own music. After graduating from the St. Petersburg High School in 1912, he studied at the University of St. Petersburg for four years (1912-1916). He was also a student (1913-1918) at the St. Petersburg Conservatory of Music (after receiving the highest mark in the entrance examination) and learned music theory and composition from Maxmilian Steinberg, who later taught Dmitri Shostakovitch, and from Vassily Kalafati, the teacher of both Stravinsky and Prokofieff.

As a concert pianist, Slonimsky toured Turkey, the Balkan countries, Italy, Germany, and France between 1921 and 1923. He arrived in the United States in 1923, where he was first engaged to coach opera at the Eastman School of Music in Rochester, New York. Slonimsky has made his home in this country ever since and was naturalized in 1931.

Slonimsky perfected himself in English by studying the libretti of the Gilbert and Sullivan operas and the advertising in the *Saturday Evening Post.* During his two years (1923-1925) at the Eastman School, Slonimsky assisted Vladimir Rosing in organizing the American Opera Company's coast-to-coast tours and also provided the score of the ballet *The Prince Goes A-Hunting* (1924), with libretto

John Brooks
NICOLAS SLONIMSKY

by Paul Horgan, which was produced at Rochester in 1925 under the direction of Rouben Mamoulian. The conductor of the Boston Symphony Orchestra, Serge Koussevitzky, heard Slonimsky at Rochester and in 1925 invited him to move to Boston as his secretary and companion.

During his two years (1925-1927) with Koussevitzky, Slonimsky published two collections of songs, *Fifteen Russian Melodies* (1925) and *Impressions* (1927), the latter to texts of Oscar Wilde. From 1928 to 1930 he conducted the Pierian Sodality (Harvard University's orchestra) and organized the Chamber Orchestra of Boston, whose concerts he conducted for seven years. In 1927 he began to contribute articles to the Boston *Transcript*, which he continued to do until the newspaper's demise in 1941. In 1928 he composed the song "My Little Pool," which has only twelve bars and which calls for only black keys in the left hand and white keys in the right. It has been sung frequently by Roland Hayes.

His *Studies in Black and White* (New Music, 1929) is based on the principle of counterpoint in consonant intervals, treated with atonal and polytonal effects. This technique of "mutually exclusive counterpoint," commented critic Isaac Goldberg, "is a style that Slonimsky developed out of his fondness for stunts . . . he admired P. T. Barnum and believes that in every public entertainer there is a trace of that showman's blood." The titles of the individual numbers such as *Typographical Errors* (which uses a portable typewriter with a woodwind ensemble and percussion instruments), and *Anatomy of Melancholy* (which suggests using a live cat "with tail manipulated" to induce a meow) are examples of Slonimsky's propensity for the "dadaistic."

By 1930 Slonimsky had acquired a reputation in musical circles as a champion of "ultra-modern" music. He had expressed his point of

SLONIMSKY, NICOLAS—*Continued*

view in lectures and demonstrations at the Boston Public Library and in his essay "The Plurality of Melodic and Harmonic Systems" (1930). Between 1930 and 1932 he made numerous appearances as pianist or conductor in Havana, San Francisco, Paris, New York, Prague and Budapest. In Paris, he was the guest conductor of the Orchestre Symphonique de Paris in two concerts in February 1932 featuring the piano concerto of Béla Bartók, with the composer as soloist, and in Germany he conducted the Berlin Philharmonic on March 5 and 10 in programs of modern American music. Some of the compositions offered were received by hisses, but the critic Alfred Einstein praised the conductor. He appeared as guest conductor with the Orquestra Filharmónica of Havana and the Los Angeles Symphony in 1933 and conducted his own *Overture on an Ancient Greek Theme* in the Hollywood Bowl (this work for orchestra uses the Greek enharmonic scale).

His *Music Since 1900*, comprising a chronology of almost 2,000 musical events and biographies of twentieth century musicians, was first published in 1937 and was characterized in the *Saturday Review of Literature* as "a landmark of the new American musical scholarship" (it was revised in 1949 and 1953). In 1938 Slonimsky conducted the Orquestra Nacional de Bogotá (Colombia) in a Pan-American music festival, and in the following year composed his *Moto Perpetue for Violin and Piano*, which became a part of the repertory of Jascha Heifetz.

After tours of South America (1938, 1941, 1942) he was made an honorary professor of the Conservatory of Brazil in Rio de Janeiro. He composed *My Toy Balloon*, variations on a Brazilian folk tune. It uses toy balloons exploded by hatpins at the climax and has been performed at many children's concerts by the New York Philharmonic, Boston "Pops" and other orchestras. A piano version is entitled "Variations on a Kindergarten Tune" (1942). An outgrowth of his tours was his book *Music of Latin America* (1945; 1951).

In 1943 he had contributed the introductory chapter "Modern Music: Its Style, Its Techniques" to David Ewen's *The Book of Modern Composers*. Following the death of Oscar Thompson in 1945, he was made editor in chief of the *International Cyclopedia of Music and Musicians* and supervised the fourth, fifth and sixth editions, published in 1946, 1949 and 1952).

Gravestones (a cycle of voice and piano to texts from authentic tombstone inscriptions) was composed in 1945, *Silhouettes ibériennes* in 1948 and *Yellowstone Park Suite* in 1950. Slonimsky translated and edited the collection *Fifty Russian Art Songs from Glinka to Shostakovitch* (1951). For the children's page of the *Christian Science Monitor* Slonimsky wrote the music appreciation articles for young readers which were collected in book form in 1947 under the title *The Road to Music*, a Book-of-the-Month Club alternate selection.

In 1947 his *Thesaurus of Scales and Musical Patterns*, "a reference book of more than 2,000 melodic and harmonic progressions for composers in search of new materials," was published. His *A Thing or Two About Music* (a collection of musical anecdotes and other matter culled from periodicals dating back to 1784) appeared in 1948. Slonimsky was the compiler of the 1949 supplement to *Baker's Biographical Dictionary of Musicians*; he has been the author since 1951 of annual music surveys in the *Britannica Book of the Year*, wrote the 1952 music survey for the *People's Encyclopedia*, and is the American editor of the forthcoming fifth edition of the *Oxford Companion to Music*. He is co-author with David Ewen of *Fun With Musical Games and Quizzes* (1952). He translated from the Russian Gretchaninoff's *My Life* (1952).

Quoting Samuel Butler's remark, "The only things we really hate are unfamiliar things," Slonimsky in his preface to *Lexicon of Musical Invective* (1953) pointed out that music is an art in progress, and that objections leveled at every musical innovator are all derived from the same psychological inhibition, which may be described as Non-Acceptance of the Unfamiliar. . . . Music critics whose ears are still attuned to the aural comforts of nineteenth-century harmonies . . . are unanimously in favor of melody . . . [yet they may be] as much inspired by the desire to write a readable article as by any just indignation."

Slonimsky has conducted the column "Musical Oddities" in *Etude* since 1950, has been associate editor of *New Music Quarterly* since 1938, and has been over a period of years a contributor to other publications including the *Saturday Review*, *Musical America*, the *Musical Quarterly*, and the Mexican review *Nuestra Música*. He has recorded for Columbia an album of South American chamber music, also several modern works including the *Ionisation* of Edgar Varese.

Organizations to which Nicolas Slonimsky belongs include the American Musicological Society and American Society of Composers, Authors and Publishers (ASCAP). His favorite recreations are languages, chess, and traveling by air. Slonimsky has been married since July 30, 1931 to the former Dorothy Adlow, art critic and lecturer. The couple have one daughter, Electra. He is five feet six inches in height and weighs around 150 pounds; his eyes are black and his hair a graying black. Of his personality Isaac Goldberg once wrote that Slonimsky had "a needle-point wit rather than a deep sense of humor." Olin Downes referred to Slonimsky as "one of the two musicians in the entire nation who can play from an [Charles] Ives score."

References

Disques 3:199+ Jl '32 por
Etude 53:575 O '35
Ewen, D. ed. Living Musicians (1940); American Composers Today (1949)
Saleski, G. Famous Musicians of Jewish Origin (1949)
Who is Who in Music (1951)
Who's Who in America, 1954-55
World Biography (1948)

SMITH, BRUCE May 23, 1892-Sept. 18, 1955 Police administrator; criminologist; author; director of the Institute of Public Administration; advised on police matters in major cities in the United States, Canada and Europe; author *The State Police; Organization and Administration* (1925) and *Rural Crime Control* (1933) among others; also wrote articles for encyclopedias and criminology journals. See *Current Biography* (Feb.) 1953.

Obituary

N Y Times p25 S 19 '55

SMITH, CECIL WOODHAM *See* Woodham-Smith, Cecil (WLB) Yrbk 55

SMITH, SIDNEY (EARLE) Mar. 8, 1897- University president; lawyer

Address: b. c/o University of Toronto, Toronto, Ont., Canada; h. 86 Queen's Park, Toronto, Ont., Canada

"The test of an educated person is what he can do, not with his hands, but with his mind," said Dr. Sidney Smith, president of the University of Toronto, one of Canada's oldest and largest institutions of learning, which has a student enrollment of nearly 10,000 and a faculty of nearly 1,500.

Dr. Smith began his career as a lawyer and earned distinction as a King's Counsel and author of law books. He was the youngest university president in Canada in 1934 when he became president of the University of Manitoba, a post he held for ten years. In 1945 he assumed his present position; he has won a reputation in educational circles as one who believes that a university should develop intellectual and moral power, should teach its students how to live and think as well as how to earn a living. This point of view has marked his approach to such problems in education as the current trend from cultural to vocational subjects.

"I have long advocated that the 'core curriculum' should include the basic disciplines of words and numbers, such as English, French and mathematics," Dr. Smith declared in an address at the Canadian Education Association's 1952 conference. "The curriculum should also make the student deeply aware of his cultural heritage and his physical and social environment by the study of literature, history and geography. This would assure at least a modicum of education to all, and thus enable them to take an intelligent part in the great controversies that affect our social, economic, political, national and international affairs. . . . In a democracy, where all have a voice in their own government, all the people need education. . . . If we want free competition of ideas, it must be our endeavor to give our youth the widest opportunity to formulate, develop and express ideas and this means not only schooling, but education."

A Nova Scotian of Scottish, English and Irish descent, Sidney Earle Smith was born

SIDNEY SMITH

on March 9, 1897 in Port Hood, a small town on the west coast of Cape Breton Island in the Canadian maritime province. His father, John Parker Smith, a farmer, and his mother, Margaret Jane (Etheridge) Smith, a schoolteacher, had another son, Frank and two daughters, Myrtle and Maude.

Of his boyhood years when he attended the Port Hood Academy for his secondary school education, Sidney Smith "remembers that he liked to fish, swim and sail but most of all that he was terribly serious and worked hard, entered King's College [Halifax, Nova Scotia] at the immature age of fourteen" (*Maclean's Magazine*, January 1, 1945). He majored in English and French at King's College and was granted his B.A. degree in 1915.

During World War I he fought overseas as a gunner in the 9th Canadian Seige Battery from 1916 to 1918 and as a cadet in the Royal Flying Corps in 1918-1919. He returned to King's College in 1919 for his M.A. degree and the following year fulfilled requirements at Dalhousie University in Halifax for his LL.B. degree. He completed his formal training in law with a year's study (1920-1921) in the United States at Harvard University Law School.

The young lawyer, who was called to the bar of Nova Scotia in 1921, entered the field of education also in that year when he joined the faculty of Dalhousie Law School as lecturer. His promotion to assistant professor on trusts, wills and mortgages came in 1922. After four years, from 1925 to 1929, as a lecturer at Osgoode Hall Law School in Toronto, Smith accepted the appointment of dean of Dalhousie Law School. During this early period he wrote three law books: *Selection of Cases on the Law of Trusts* (Canada Law Book, 1928); with J. D. Falconbridge, *Manual of Canadian Business Law* (Pitman, 1930);

SMITH, SIDNEY—*Continued*

and with H. E. Read, *Selection of Cases on Equity* (Burroughs & Company, 1931).

In the early years of his career, when he was occupied with law as well as education, Smith served from 1925 to 1934 as assistant editor of *Canadian Bar Review* and from 1929 to 1934 as secretary of Commissioners on Uniformity of Law in Canada. During part of his tenure as dean of Dalhousie Law School, he was on the board of governors of Halifax Ladies' College (1930-1934).

Leaving Dalhousie Law School in 1934, Smith spent the next ten years in Winnipeg as president of the University of Manitoba. At the time of his appointment he was thirty-seven years old, "the youngest university president in Canada, facing one of the most difficult college situations in the country" (*Maclean's Magazine*, January 1, 1945). He was called to the bar of Manitoba in 1935. He was made King's Counsel of Manitoba in 1939 and of Nova Scotia in 1941.

His association with the University of Toronto dates from 1944, with his being named principal of University College. A year later the university chose him to be its president. Established in 1827, the University of Toronto currently has a student enrollment of 9,811 and a faculty of 1,446. (Canada, with a population of nearly 15,000,000, has twenty-nine universities and colleges, not including its agricultural, technical and theological colleges.)

Smith has made his views on education known through a number of articles in Canadian periodicals. He wrote "The Liberal Arts: an Experiment," which appeared in the 1944 spring issue of *Queen's Quarterly*. He noted a change in emphasis in education from arts to sciences and suggested that if a stronger general arts course were not encouraged, "Canada will get from the university, from year to year, expert practitioners and skilled recruits for industry and commerce who know little of the economic, social and moral issues which are vexing society. . . ."

Certain problems of Canadian education were discussed by Dr. Smith in *Saturday Night*: "Will It Be Schooling or Education?" (October 11, 1952) and "Pressure of Numbers on Universities" (January 30, 1954).

During a speech in October 1953 the president urged newcomers to the University of Toronto to develop a greater degree of individuality. While not "praising eccentricity for its own sake," he considered it the function of the university to produce "the man or woman who has the capacity for dissent, who sets up a resistance to mass movements and mass ideas" (*Saturday Night*, October 7, 1953).

A research grant of $40,000 from the Ford Foundation enabled a five-department team at the University of Toronto to make a survey of the comparative values of television, radio, lectures, and textbooks in teaching. The results of the study, announced on March 4, 1954, revealed that students who watched a television "lesson" scored higher grades when tested on what they had learned, than those who heard the same subject discussed on the radio, and than those who read mimeographed copies of the lecture. The university expects to adopt television as a standard method of conducting extension courses.

Dr. Smith has had a prominent part in the work of several national organizations: National Film Society of Canada (president, 1937-1945), National Council of Young Men's Christian Associations in Canada (president, 1938-1942), Canadian Association for Adult Education (president, 1941-1944), National Conference of Canadian Universities (president, 1942-1944), Canadian Youth Commission (chairman, 1943-1945) and United Nations Associations in Canada (president, 1948-1950).

Smith became a fellow of the Royal Society of Canada in 1950; he holds honorary LL.D. degrees from Queen's University (1937), University of Manitoba (1945), University of Ottawa (1947), Laval University (1947), Dalhousie University (1948), University of Cambridge (1948), University of Western Ontario (1953) and University of Aberdeen (1954). Honorary D.C.L. degrees have been conferred on him by King's College (1939), Acadia University (1940), Bishop's University (1942), Mount Allison University (1947) and McGill University (1948).

Smith and his wife, the former Margaret Jane Etheridge, who were married on June 29, 1926, are the parents of three daughters: Sheila Rand, Moyra Jean and Heather Margaret. The educator attends the United Church of Canada; in politics he is an "independent." He has blue eyes and gray hair, weighs 194 pounds and stands five feet eleven inches in height. With fishing as his favorite sport, he belongs to the Caledon Mountain and Trout Club and to the Echo Beach Fishing Club. His other clubs are the Toronto Club and the York Club in Toronto. An article in *Maclean's Magazine* (January 1, 1945) describes him as having an "almost supernatural memory" for names and faces.

References

Maclean's Mag 58:13+ Ja 1 '45 por
Nat Home Mo 47:22+ Je '46 por
Who's Who in America, 1954-55
Who's Who in Canada, 1951-52
World Biography (1954)

SNYDER, HOWARD MCC(RUM) Feb. 7, 1881- United States Army officer; physician

Address: b. The White House, Washington, D.C.; h. 2101 Connecticut Ave., N.W., Washington, D.C.

Major General Howard McC. Snyder was recalled from the U.S. Army's retired list to assume the post of physician to his long-time friend, President Dwight D. Eisenhower, in January 1953. An officer of the Army Medical Corps since 1908, Snyder served in World War I as a medical training school commandant and in World War II as assistant to the inspector general.

While General Eisenhower was president of Columbia University, General Snyder served as adviser on two important study projects conducted by the university, and was subsequently attached to SHAPE headquarters at Paris as special adviser to Eisenhower.

Born in Cheyenne, Wyoming on February 7, 1881, Howard McCrum Snyder is the son of Albert Campbell and Priscilla McClelland (McCrum) Snyder. He attended the University of Colorado from 1899 to 1901, received his M.D. degree at Jefferson Medical College in Philadelphia in 1905, and during the following year interned at Philadelphia's Presbyterian Hospital. About two years after he was licensed to practice medicine, he became a contract surgeon, in July 1907, at Fort Douglas in Utah; he liked the service so well that when his contract expired in September he had resolved on a military-medical career. He was graduated from the Army Medical School in Washington, D.C., in June 1908 with the highest honors and was simultaneously commissioned a first lieutenant in the Medical Corps of the regular Army.

Snyder's first regular military assignment was to the Philippine Islands, where he was stationed for about two years with the Research Board of Tropical Medicine. He was returned to the continental United States in 1911 and sent to Fort D. A. Russell (now Fort Francis E. Warren) in Wyoming, where he remained until 1915. He then went to Douglas, Arizona for duty on the Mexican border.

Subsequently, Snyder served briefly at the Walter Reed General Hospital at Washington, D.C. before being returned in the late fall of 1916 to border service, this time at Llano Grande in Texas, where he was stationed when the United States entered World War I. The following year Snyder was reassigned as adjutant and instructor at the training camp for medical officers established at Fort Benjamin Harrison in Indiana. In November he was moved to Kansas for similar duty at Fort Riley and in July 1918 he was ordered to Camp Greenleaf in Georgia to assume command of a Medical Corps school for noncommissioned officers. From October 1918 to February 1919, when he was transferred to the Army's General Hospital No. 41 on Long Island, New York, Snyder was the commandant at Camp Crane, Pennsylvania.

After the war, in early 1920, Snyder was transferred to Fort Leavenworth, Kansas. During part of 1924 he studied at the Mayo Clinic, Minnesota. In August he took up his duties on the staff of the U.S. Military Academy at West Point, New York. For slightly over two years, beginning in June 1929, Snyder was assigned to the School of Tropical Medicine in San Juan, Puerto Rico; he was relieved of his Caribbean duty in September 1932 in order that he might proceed to Carlisle Barracks, Pennsylvania for an advanced course at the Medical Field Service School. He completed this course in December and was then appointed an instructor with the 102d Medical Regiment and all Medical Detachments of the New York National Guard. While in New York in 1934

U. S. Army
MAJ. GEN. HOWARD MCC. SNYDER

he took courses at New York University and Bellevue Hospital. Snyder was ordered in September 1936 to Washington, D.C. for what proved to be four years of duty with the National Guard Bureau as medical adviser.

In October 1940 Snyder, who had risen through the ranks to brigadier general, was transferred to the office of the inspector general in Washington. He became assistant to the inspector general in December 1940 and was so serving when just about one year later the United States entered World War II. "In addition to duties in the United States," notes a Defense Department press release, "he visited all theaters of operation overseas." These theaters included North Africa, where in 1943 General Snyder was awarded the decoration of Grand Commander, Order of Ouissam Alouite, by the Sultan of Morocco. He has also been decorated by the late President Getúlio Vargas of Brazil with the Brazilian War Medal and, in the rank of Grand Commander, with the Order of the Southern Cross.

Promoted to major general (temporary) on November 3, 1943, Snyder became in the latter months of World War II the close personal friend of General Dwight D. Eisenhower, then Supreme Allied Commander in Europe. For his service as assistant to the inspector general from October 1940 to June 1945, General Snyder was awarded (October 1945) the Distinguished Service Medal. "Through his skillful and energetic approach to a wide variety of problems," stated the accompanying citation, "General Snyder was largely responsible for the success of many important military functions. His was a material contribution to the war effort."

Technically "retired for age" on March 1, 1945, Major General Snyder had been "continued on active duty" in Europe as General Eisenhower's personal physician until after the

SNYDER, HOWARD MCC.—*Continued*

German surrender. In November of the same year, when Mrs. Eisenhower had pneumonia, he flew to Boone, Iowa to attend her. In May 1946, six months after General Eisenhower had become Army Chief of Staff, he was appointed to the latter's medical advisory group. He held this assignment until June 30, 1948, when he reverted to retired status. General Eisenhower himself had meanwhile been placed on the inactive list and had accepted the presidency of Columbia University in New York City.

Dr. Snyder, too, moved to New York City, where he was appointed medical consultant to the New York State Hospital Study of Columbia University. He also became associated with the Conservation of Human Resources Project and Manpower Council. This project, scheduled to operate for five years on an annual budget of $100,000, was instituted by General Eisenhower in 1950 to find ways and means to correct the alarming manpower wastage found in World War II. Snyder was named senior adviser of the project, of which the first important study to reach publication was *The Uneducated* (Columbia University Press, 1953). This work by Doctors Eli Ginzberg and Douglas W. Bray is dedicated to Dr. Snyder.

Following the recall of General Eisenhower to active service in December 1950 as commander of the North Atlantic Treaty Organization forces in Europe, General Snyder went back on the active list and was assigned to the U.S. Army element of SHAPE (Supreme Headquarters, Allied Powers in Europe) at Paris beginning January 1951. Shortly afterward he was made special adviser to General Eisenhower and continued as such until September 1952, when he was again retired. He had meanwhile accompanied Eisenhower back to the United States. Marquis Childs has noted in one of his newspaper columns that "during virtually the entire campaign. . . Snyder rode the campaign train and was at the side of his friend."

After the Presidential inauguration on January 20, 1953, General Snyder returned to active status as physician to the President and member of the White House staff. As such he has made periodic reports on the President's health. In November 1953 he counteracted rumors that Eisenhower was suffering from cardiac trouble. Shortly before the President's 64th birthday (October 14, 1954) Dr. Snyder issued a report stating that he appears to be maintaining an excellent state of health. "All the laboratory findings were within the normal range," he announced. He also encouraged Eisenhower to take up the hobby of painting. "It's a great diversion for him," Dr. Snyder said. "He can become so interested in his art problem he forgets his worldly troubles." He recommended that the President continue to play golf for exercise and relaxation.

Among the professional organizations with which Dr. Snyder is affiliated are the American College of Surgeons (fellow), American Medical Association, and Association of Military Surgeons of the United States. He belongs also to the New York Society of Military and Naval Officers of World Wars and the Military Order of Carabao. In 1946 he was a member of the committee to the President on integration and improvement of U.S. medical and hospital services. General Snyder married Alice Elizabeth Concklin on July 12, 1910. They have two sons, Richard Concklin and Howard McCrum Snyder, Jr., the latter a colonel in the U.S. Army.

References

Gen Army 1:22 Je '53 por
U S News 35:14 O 23 '53 por
Washington (D.C.) Post p6S D 21 '52; p19 O 15 '53
Who's Who in America, 1954-55

SOBELOFF, SIMON E(RNEST) Dec. 3, 1894- Solicitor General of the United States

Address: b. c/o Department of Justice, Washington 25, D.C.; h. 4545 Connecticut Ave., N.W., Washington 8, D.C.

Simon E. Sobeloff took the oath of office as Solicitor General of the United States in February 1954, after having served about two years as Chief Judge of the Maryland Court of Appeals. Known as a "liberal" Republican, he was the adviser and confidant of Governor Theodore R. McKeldin, and chairman in 1952-1953 of the Commission on Administrative Reorganization of the State of Maryland. Earlier he had been United States district attorney for Maryland (1931-1934) and city solicitor of Baltimore (1943-1947).

In accepting an award for public service from Yeshiva University (New York City) in November 1954, Sobeloff spoke of a way out of spiritual confusion in the atomic age. "We are not driven to a choice between irreligion on the one hand and pseudo-religious obscurantism on the other," he said. "Rather, the truly religious and enlightened modern man perceives an essential harmony between faith and knowledge."

One of the seven children (five boys and two girls) of Jacob Harry and Mary Hilda (Kaplan) Sobeloff, both emigrants from Russia, Simon Ernest Sobeloff was born December 3, 1894 in Baltimore, Maryland. During the summer of 1907, when he was twelve, he worked for two lawyers, receiving from each the weekly wage of seventy-five cents. "The following summer I got a better paying job," he recalls. "There were then three men in the office in which I worked" (*Jewish Criterion*, December 12, 1952).

By this time he had already dabbled in politics, delivering in the course of Baltimore's mayoral campaign (1907) a speech that aroused the interest of Congressman John Kronmiller, who was later to secure for the boy orator an appointment as a page in the House of Representatives in Washington. This was in 1910-1911, after young Sobeloff had completed a year's attendance at the Baltimore City College.

In the fall of 1911 Sobeloff entered Loyola College in Baltimore. He transferred in 1912 to the law school of the University of Maryland in College Park and during the next two years met expenses by working as a clerk in the office of the United States Attorney in his home city. In 1914, the year before his graduation from the University of Maryland Law School, he became a secretary in the office of Chief Judge Morris A. Soper of the Baltimore Supreme Bench.

Awarded his LL.B. in 1915 and admitted to the bar, Sobeloff engaged in private law practice while continuing as a secretary to Judge Soper until 1917. After four years (1920-1924) as assistant city solicitor of Baltimore, Sobeloff resumed private practice, and was so engaged when Baltimore's Mayor William F. Broening appointed him temporary deputy city solicitor (1927) and later deputy city solicitor (1928). In 1930 he was recommended by Judge Soper for the post of U.S. attorney for the Maryland District and then nominated to that office by President Herbert Hoover. Sworn in on February 12, 1931, he served until his resignation in March 1934.

As a Federal district attorney, Sobeloff forced customs officials to release copies of the *Lysistrata* of Aristophanes and *Wise Parenthood* by Dr. Marie Stopes, which had been seized as "obscene" matter. On the other hand, he prosecuted the publishers of *Baltimore Brevities*, described as "specializing in crude sex stories and blackmail." Late in 1933 Sobeloff went before the Senate Judiciary Committee to plead for a Federal anti-lynching bill. As a "militant supporter of civil and human rights, he . . . consistently opposed segregation in a city with a partially Southern heritage" (American Jewish Congress *Record*, January 1953).

Having resumed private practice, Sobeloff served in 1934-1935 as an arbitrator for the men's clothing industry. About two years later, as a court-appointed investigating attorney, he rendered a report on the Baltimore Trust Company bankruptcy.

When the Republican Theodore R. McKeldin became mayor of normally Democratic Baltimore in 1943, he named Sobeloff as his city solicitor. "Throughout the administration," wrote Odell Smith (Baltimore *Sun*, June 26, 1952), "the Mayor relied on him for advice on nearly every significant decision." In 1947 McKeldin's successor, a Democrat, retained Sobeloff in the newly created position of special counsel to the city on labor affairs. Under the same mayor, Sobeloff served as general counsel of the Baltimore City Housing Commission.

During McKeldin's four years at the head of Baltimore's municipal government, Sobeloff had "imparted substance and form" to "speeches and mayoral pronouncements" which he composed in collaboration with Galen L. Tait (Odell Smith). The "team" performed similar duties for McKeldin in his successful campaign for the governorship of Maryland in 1950.

Early in his administration, Governor McKeldin named Sobeloff to the chairmanship of a twelve-member Commission on Administrative Reorganization of the State of Maryland, which "set about reorganizing the governor's

Wide World

SIMON E. SOBELOFF

office, the state budget, the department of public works and buildings, the state personnel set-up, the educational administration, the health and welfare administration, and other aspects of state government" (Henry W. Levy in the *Jewish Criterion*).

Addressing the National Conference of Christians and Jews in Washington in November 1952, McKeldin confirmed a prediction made earlier in the year that he would appoint Sobeloff as Chief Judge of the five-member Maryland Court of Appeals. Sobeloff, who took office as such on December 16, 1952, was the first Jew ever to sit on this "highest court of the Free State" and only the "fifth in the history of the United States to head a state's highest tribunal" (Henry W. Levy). The governor and Sobeloff had visited Israel together earlier in 1952 and in the following year were to confer with President Dwight D. Eisenhower on matters pertaining to the Zionist republic.

In August 1952 Philip B. Perlman, the Baltimore Democrat who had been Solicitor General of the United States under President Truman since 1947, resigned this post. Work of the office was being carried on by Acting Solicitor General Robert L. Stern when, in October 1953, it became known that Judge Sobeloff was the choice of President Eisenhower and Attorney General Herbert Brownell, Jr., for Solicitor General. The nomination was made in January 1954 and on February 25 Sobeloff was sworn into his $17,000-a-year office.

The Solicitor General, who ranks second to the Attorney General in the Department of Justice, "has special charge of the business of, and appears for and represents, the Government in the Supreme Court." He may "argue any case in which the United States is interested, in any court in the United States," and "no appeal

SOBELOFF, SIMON E.—*Continued*

is taken by the United States to any appellate court" without his authorization (*U.S. Government Organization Manual*, 1954-55).

Presented to the Supreme Court on March 8, 1954, Sobeloff made his first official appearance there as Solicitor General two days later, when the bench considered an appeal by the Franklin National Bank of Long Island against a New York state law prohibiting national banks from using the word "savings" in soliciting or receiving deposits. The Solicitor General maintained that the "sole issue" was the precedence of a Federal over a state law, and that inasmuch as a 1927 amendment to the Federal Reserve act had authorized national banks "to continue . . . as heretofore" to receive savings deposits, this implied the right to use the word "savings" in advertising. When the Supreme Court took under advisement the question of whether the Federal Power Commission has jurisdiction to regulate natural gas sales by independent producers to interstate pipeline companies, he argued that inasmuch as the Natural Gas Act of 1938 had not specifically authorized such regulation, it had been the clear intention of Congress "to leave to the states the regulation of gas producer sales to pipeline concerns" (New York *Times*, April 8, 1954). The court, however decided that it is the commission which has such regulatory power.

"It has been very impressive to me," Solicitor General Sobeloff said in an address at the seventy-seventh annual convention of the American Bar Association in Chicago on August 16, 1954, "that the law is so solicitous of the defendant in safeguarding his rights at every stage of the trial before the verdict, and yet leaves him completely without protection when he stands before the judge to be sentenced." He accordingly urged the criminal law section to study the desirability of providing for appellate review of sentences.

Speaking on September 16 at the ninth National Conference on Citizenship, Sobeloff lauded the Supreme Court's anti-segregation ruling of May 17. He also warned against "averting national dangers by surrendering some of our liberties" to save the rest. "The constitutional protections asserted by a Communist or a gangster today," he pointed out, "may tomorrow be the necessary shield of an honest and responsible man."

Sobeloff is a member of the Har Sinai Congregation in Baltimore, a board member and the legal counsel of the Associated Jewish Charities, and a past president of both the Baltimore Board of Jewish Education and the Baltimore Jewish Council. He is also national vice-president of the American Jewish Congress and a member of the Urban League. Professional organizations to which he belongs are the American Bar Association, the Maryland Bar Association, and the Bar Association of the City of Baltimore. His clubs are the Suburban and Phoenix in Baltimore.

Mrs. Sobeloff, the former Irene Ehrlich, is an authority on child welfare and has long been active in Baltimore civic and Jewish movements. The Sobeloffs, who were married on May 19, 1918, have two daughters, Mrs. Evva S. Goldstrom and Mrs. Ruth S. Mayer. "Scholarly" and "urbane" are adjectives applied by Odell Smith of the Baltimore *Sun* to Simon E. Sobeloff. "His good sense, which is perhaps his greatest asset," Henry W. Levy remarked, "has been combined with a literate simplicity that has given style and substance to whatever he has written—speeches, briefs or opinions."

References

Am Jewish Cong Rec 6:2 Ja '53 por
Baltimore Sun Je 26 '52 por
Jewish Criterion p46-7+ D 12 '52 por
N Y Times p1 O 30 '53; p50 Ja 22 '54
Time 63:14 F 1 '54
U S News 36:14 F 5 '54
Washington (D.C.) Post p8 Ja 23 '54
Martindale-Hubbell Law Directory, 1950
Who's Who in America, 1954-55
Who's Who in American Jewry, 1938-39

SOBOLEV, ARKADY A(LEKSANDROVICH) (sô-bô-lĕv′ är-kä′dē â-lĕk-săn′drô-vēch) 1903- Soviet diplomat

Address: b. c/o U.S.S.R. Delegation to the United Nations, 680 Park Ave., New York 21

Since the death of Andreĭ Vishinskiĭ on November 22, 1954, the supervision of the Soviet Union's permanent delegation at the United Nations has been the responsibility of Arkady A. Sobolev, who has been a long-term delegate. He was appointed permanent representative on March 3, 1955 and holds the rank of Ambassador. A former electrical engineer turned diplomat, he is regarded as one of the ablest members of the diplomatic corps. His association with the U.N. dates from the conferences that preceded its founding, and he was one of its first Assistant Secretary Generals.

Arkady Aleksandrovich Sobolev was born in 1903 in St. Petersburg (now Leningrad) and was graduated in electrical engineering from the Electrotechnical Institute of Leningrad in 1930. For the next nine years (1930-1939) he was engaged in research work in connection with the development of power plant equipment, and in 1936 he was a member of the Soviet delegation to the Third World Power Conference in Washington, D.C.

In 1939 he entered the diplomatic service, and at the end of that year was appointed Secretary-General of the Peoples Commissariat for Foreign Affairs in Moscow. Sobolev was rushed to Bulgaria in November 1940 when it appeared that Adolf Hitler was pushing that country toward war with Turkey. His intervention was credited with ironing out the differences between Bulgaria and Turkey and temporarily keeping Bulgaria out of the German sphere of influence in the Balkans.

In May and June 1942 Sobolev accompanied Soviet Foreign Minister Vîâcheslav Molotov on a diplomatic visit to London, where a twenty-year friendship treaty was signed, and to Washington, where military aid for the Soviet

Union was arranged. In December of that year he was named counselor to the London Embassy, with the rank of minister.

While holding that post, he served in March 1944 as one of the Soviet delegates to the meeting of the European Advisory Commission in London, which discussed proposed armistice terms for Germany. In July of that year he came to the United States as a delegate to the Bretton Woods Conference, which set up the International Bank, and the Dumbarton Oaks Conference, which laid the basis for organizing the U.N.

He was also a delegate to the San Francisco Conference in May-June 1945, where the United Nations charter was drafted and signed. Before the signing, however, he was recalled to Moscow and transferred from London to Berlin, where he became chief of the political section of the Soviet military mission headed by Marshal Georgi K. Zhukov.

In Berlin he also served as head of the Soviet delegation to the Allied Reparations Commission and as a member of the delegation to the Potsdam Conference.

When the U.N. preparatory commission met in London in November 1945 to organize the staff of the new world body, Sobolev was a Soviet delegate. It was agreed that each of the Big Five powers should have one post among the Assistant Secretary Generals, and on February 17, 1946 Sobolev was named to the post allotted to the U.S.S.R.—Assistant Secretary General in charge of the political and security department.

This department, one of eight, was among the smallest but most important at the U.N. Arkady Sobolev had constant duties as secretary for the Security Council, the Atomic Energy Commission and the Commission for Conventional Armaments. In addition, he assigned staff members to the various U.N. commissions sent to Greece, Indonesia, Palestine, and Korea.

As an international civil servant, Sobolev, like other U.N. employes, was supposed to be impartial in the service of all nations. He was credited with considerable success at this objectivity, but was not immune from criticism. When he selected his personal assistant, a Ukrainian, as head of the staff for the U.N. investigation commission sent to Greece, the British delegation protested that a Russian could scarcely be objective in a dispute between Yugoslavia and Greece. Secretary General Trygve Lie heard the case and named a Norwegian to the top staff post (New York *Times*, February 27, 1947).

A charge that he had discriminated against an aide because he was a former British intelligence officer was, however, declared by the person concerned to be "mischievous and incorrect." Charges that Sobolev "exercised a reign of terror on the personnel" of the U.N., made before a Senate subcommittee, were called by Byron Price, the Assistant Secretary General from the United States, "the nuttiest story I have heard yet" (New York *Times*, July 24, 1949).

At the end of January 1949 Sobolev left New York to return to Moscow on a leave of absence because of illness in his family. He resigned from the United Nations, for the same reason, on March 28, 1949, and was praised as "a man who ran his department in the United Nations with complete efficiency, as a man who did his job well and was completely dependable in his job" (New York *Herald Tribune*, April 28, 1949).

United Nations

ARKADY A. SOBOLEV

Sobolev acted as an adviser to the Ministry of Foreign Affairs in Moscow until March 1, 1951, when he was named Soviet Ambassador to Poland. While still holding that post, he went to Paris in November of that year as a member of the Soviet delegation to the General Assembly of the United Nations. As an official of the U.N. Sobolev had appeared to be a mild-spoken man, but in Paris as the spokesman of his government he made one of the harshest speeches ever heard in the U.N. In replying to the Yugoslav charges of Soviet pressure against Tito's government he accused the Yugoslavs, almost in one breath, of being "Fascist liars, foul slanderers, master spies, saboteurs, and an American colony." In January 1952, still in Paris, he accused Trygve Lie of being an "obedient servant of the United States" and submitting a United Nations report that was "crude mockery" and "shameless hypocrisy."

From October to December 1952 Sobolev was in New York as a member of the Soviet delegation to the first half of the seventh session of the U.N. General Assembly. He was relieved as Ambassador to Poland on June 21, 1953, and became a division head in the Foreign Ministry in Moscow as well as a member of the collegium of the Foreign Ministry.

Sobolev was a member of the Soviet delegations at the Big Four Foreign Ministers Conference in Berlin in January 1954 and at the Geneva Conference that devised the Indochina settlement later in that year. On September

SOBOLEV, ARKADY A.—*Continued*

15 it was announced that he had been named deputy permanent representative of the U.S.S.R. to the U.N., replacing Semyon K. Tsarapkin as number two man on the Soviet delegation. After the death of Vishinskiĭ, chief Soviet representative to the U.N., on November 22, 1954, Sobolev took over his duties, and on March 3, 1955 was named permanently to the post.

During the U.N. Security Council's efforts in early 1955 to ease the tension in the Far East over Formosa, Sobolev made propaganda speeches in which he charged U.S. aggression against Red China and U.S. interference in China's internal affairs. He opposed New Zealand's proposal for a cease-fire between the two Chinese governments as "nothing but a clumsy maneuver" to deny Red China its "sovereign rights" to certain islands and "to perpetuate the illegal seizure of these islands by the United States" (New York *Times,* February 1, 1955).

As the leader of the Soviet delegation, Vishinskiĭ was considered more colorful both in personality and speeches. Sobolev, by contrast, is more reserved, more businesslike. He has a fluent knowledge of English and is said to have a far better grasp of Western thinking than his predecessor had. He is married and has a son.

References

N Y Herald Tribune p16 Ja 1 '48
N Y Times p3 F 1 '55
U N Bul 6:476 My 15 '49; 2:75 Ja 28 '47
International Who's Who, 1953
World Biography, 1948

SOMERVELL, BREHON (BURKE) May 9, 1892-Feb. 13, 1955 President and chairman of the board of Koppers Company; retired U.S. Army officer; as commanding general of Army Services of Supply (later Army Service Forces) during World War II spent $172,000,-000,000; in 1925 studied navigation conditions on the Rhine and Danube rivers for League of Nations; Works Progress Administrator for New York (1936-40). See *Current Biography* (Aug.) 1942.

Obituary

N Y Times p19 F 14 '55

SOMES, MICHAEL (GEORGE) Sept. 28, 1917- Ballet dancer

Address: b. c/o The Royal Opera House, Covent Garden, Ltd., London; h. 4 Archery Fields House, Lloyd Sq., London, W.C. 1, England

Recognized for his qualities as a partner and *danseur-noble,* Michael Somes has performed major roles in practically the entire repertory of the Sadler's Wells Ballet, ranging from *Le Lac des Cygnes* to *Daphnis and Chloe* and *Rinaldo and Armida.* In the title role of *Tiresias*—shared with Violetta Elvin—which had its New York première at the Metropolitan Opera House on September 16, 1955, Somes (according to John Martin of the New York *Times*) made a "dramatically admirable" Tiresias with "a wealth of eloquence in his every restrained gesture." Critics have warmly praised his dancing in the role of the Prince in the company's most popular ballet, *The Sleeping Beauty.*

A member of the Sadler's Wells Ballet company for over two decades, Somes was introduced to American audiences when the troupe filled its first New York engagement in 1949, and returned with the company for its 1950, 1953 and 1955 seasons. Walter Terry (New York *Herald Tribune,* September 26, 1953) hailed Somes' role of Daphnis in the Frederick Ashton version of *Daphnis and Chloe* as his most rewarding part when it was presented at the Metropolitan Opera House.

Michael George Somes was born in Horsely, Gloucestershire, England on September 28, 1917, the son of Edwin Joseph and Ethel Mary (Pridham) Somes. From his father, who was a musician, young Michael acquired his love of music, and he showed an inclination to dance at the age of four. He was given dancing lessons when he entered Huish's Grammar School at Taunton, Somersetshire, and at the time of graduation, had already passed the preliminary examinations of the Royal Academy of Dancing.

He continued to study dancing with Katharine Blott of Weston super Mare and at fifteen won the first boy scholarship for the Sadler's Wells Ballet School. He was graduated in 1935. During his years at the school and later training, he had such famous teachers as Ninette de Valois, Judith Espinosa, Idzekovsky, Phyllis Bedells and Margaret Craske.

Somes first appeared with the Sadler's Wells *corps de ballet* in *Casse Noisette, Les Rendez-Vous, Job* and other incidental dance sequences provided for the repertories of the Vic-Wells Theatre and the opera at the Sadler's Wells Theatre. He was given small, and later leading roles in *Checkmate, Le Carnaval, Les Sylphides* and *Pomona* and in 1937 danced the Bluebird *divertissement* from *The Sleeping Beauty* and the *pas de huit* from *Les Patineurs.*

Hugh Fisher in *The Story of the Sadler's Wells Ballet* (1949) noted that Somes had emerged as one of the most promising English male dancers during the company's 1937-1938 London season through his interpretation of the Young Man in Frederick Ashton's *Horoscope.* This role suited his particular style and temperament and brought wide acclaim. He appeared in *The Wise Virgins* (as the Bridegroom) and *Dante Sonata*—also Ashton's work—in 1940, and in Tchaikovsky's *Le Lac des Cygnes* the same year. His career was interrupted by World War II during which he served from 1941 to 1945 in the British Army.

After this long absence from the ballet, Gladys Davidson noted in *Ballet Biographies* (1952), that Somes quickly developed as a more "reliable dance partner" and in a short time attracted much favorable attention from the critics. The London *Observer* (December 17, 1946) commented that Somes—partnered with Margot Fonteyn—in the Ashton version of *The Fairy Queen,* had practically flown from one end of the enormous Covent Garden stage to the other in a "dazzling *pas de deux*" which received a "thunderous ovation."

Other critics considered Somes' role in *Symphonic Variations,* first performed in April 1946, his most outstanding success. In this he appeared with Brian Shaw, Harry Danton, and the three leading ballerinas—Margot Fonteyn, Moira Shearer and Pamela May. All six were chosen for their "musical sensitivity" and ability to fit their individual techniques into a synchronized pattern. The group later appeared on May 23, 1947 in a BBC-TV program with equal success.

Examples of Somes' versatility were expressed in his serious dramatic role of the Stranger in *Miracle of Gorbals* and the comic Caricaturist in *Mam'zelle Angot.* Other ballets in which he played a leading role were *Giselle, Scènes de Ballets, Hamlet,* and *Les Sirènes.*

When the Sadler's Wells Ballet made its first tour of the United States and Canada in 1949, Somes was among the principal male dancers. For his "skillful partnering of the ballerina" in *Cinderella*—Ashton's first full-length ballet, which had its première in the spring of 1949—and his "splendid technique" as Prince Siegfried in *Le Lac des Cygnes* (better known in the United States as *Swan Lake*), Somes received excellent notices in New York and other cities.

His first choreographic effort, *Summer Interlude,* in which Somes appeared on March 28, 1950 at the Sadler's Wells Theatre, was hailed by London audiences. On April 3, 1950 his role in George Balanchine's production of *Ballet Imperial* was also well received. He danced in the first performances of Ashton's *Daphnis and Chloe* (at Covent Garden, April 5, 1951) and *Rinaldo and Armida* (at Covent Garden, December 18, 1952).

A second American tour of the company brought Somes back to the United States and Canada in the fall of 1950. On the third tour a critic in the New York *Times* (October 18, 1953) commented that Somes was "everything a first dancer should be" and danced far better than formerly.

Of the company's opening presentation, *Swan Lake,* on September 13, 1953, Walter Terry (New York *Herald Tribune*) wrote that Somes as the Prince gave the star ballerina "impeccable support" and "mimed his role pleasantly." The New York *Post* (September 27, 1953) commenting on the *Daphnis and Chloe* New York debut, observed that Somes was more appealing in the simple pastoral role of a goatherder than in his princely classical roles. In the opinion of Margaret Lloyd (*Christian Science Monitor,* October 3, 1953), *Sylvia* was the more exciting ballet, with Somes as Aminta. And John Martin (New York *Times,* September 17, 1953) lauded *The Sleeping Beauty* as a "glowing performance" and referred to Michael Somes as "handsome and gracious."

The Sadler's Wells Ballet opened its fourth New York season on September 11, 1955 with *The Sleeping Beauty. Time* (September 26, 1955) praised Somes as a "self-effacing partner," who had developed into a *"danseur-noble."* Although some of the critics found *Tiresias* (with musical score by the late Constant Lambert and choreography by Frederick Ashton) "pretentious" and lacking in magic, John Martin (New York *Times*) called it "superb" and noted that Somes "unfalteringly sustained a vivid transformation" in the continuity of the "provocative" role. On the 1955 tour the company also visited Boston, Philadelphia, Washington, San Francisco, Los Angeles, Detroit, and Toronto.

MICHAEL SOMES

In *Ballet Biographies* Gladys Davidson described Somes as having a "splendid physique and a build reminiscent of the youth of ancient Greece." When he has a choice he prefers to dance to "complicated modern rhythm" rather than in the classical roles. He has dark hair and dark eyes and has been called "handsome" by many of the critics. His recreations are music and motoring.

References

Chujoy, A. ed. Dance Encyclopedia (1949)
Davidson, G. Ballet Biographies (1952)
Who's Who, 1954
Who's Who in the Theatre (1952)

STANLEY, KIM Feb. 11, 1925- Actress

Address: b. c/o Lucy Kroll, 119 W. 57th St., New York 19; h. Laurel Dr., Centerport, Long Island, N.Y.

Stardom came to Kim Stanley during 1954 when she portrayed the leading role in Horton Foote's play, *The Traveling Lady,* which marked her fifth Broadway engagement in five years. In her sixth appearance, *Bus Stop,* by William Inge, which opened in March 1955, Miss Stanley asked to be billed along with the other actors, but critics generally agreed that she is the real star of the show. She received the Drama Critics' Award in 1953 for her

KIM STANLEY

acting as a supporting member of the cast of Inge's Pulitzer Prize-winning play, *Picnic,* and also the Donaldson Award. In March 1955 she won the New York Newspaper Guild's annual Page One award, shared with Albert Salmi, for acting.

Seventy-five television appearances have added considerably to Miss Stanley's reputation. She was seen as Cleopatra and Joan of Arc in *You Are There,* in N. Richard Nash's *The Brownstone,* in Horton Foote's *A Young Lady of Property,* and in *The Bridge.* Other TV programs in which she has been seen are *Danger, Omnibus,* and *Big Story.*

Kim Stanley is the stage name of Patricia Reid, born to Ann Miller Reid and Dr. J. T. Reid in Tularosa, New Mexico on February 11, 1925. Patricia was raised in Texas, where she received her elementary education and also attended the state university, majored in psychology and was graduated in 1946. She then took a general arts course at the University of New Mexico, where her father is a professor.

A director from the Pasadena Playhouse saw her perform in one of the college plays and urged her to become an actress. Her first engagement was with a winter stock company in Louisville, Kentucky, and because there had been another Pat Reid in her drama class, she took the name Kim Stanley. Following the Kentucky engagement, she went to New York. The year was 1947. She arrived on a bus in the rain with $21.00 in her pocket, rented a furnished room in the West Thirties, and started job hunting. She told Earl Wilson (New York *Post,* March 13, 1955), "The first producer I saw was Russel Crouse, who ordered me to go back to Texas. I don't blame him. I sat everybody down and made them listen to me do Shakespeare—very badly."

She found work with a summer stock company in Pompton Lakes, New Jersey, but when the season came to an end, no other opening presented itself. For two years she could obtain no employment on the stage and supported herself by working as a fashion model and a waitress at the Sheraton.

Resuming her study of dramatics, she became a member of the Actors Studio under the tutelage of Elia Kazan and Lee Strasberg, both at one time associated with the Group Theatre. In the same year with the money she had saved, the young actress was able to join an off Broadway group, the Interplayers, working without salary. Miss Stanley appeared in such avant-garde offerings as *The Dog Beneath the Skin,* by W. H. Auden and Christopher Isherwood, at the Carnegie Recital Hall beginning on December 25, 1948. She also played in *him,* by e. e. cummings, presented at the Provincetown Playhouse in New York's Greenwich Village.

A similar engagement followed in the same year at another Greenwich Village theatre, the Cherry Lane, where, under the auspices of Off Broadway, Inc., Miss Stanley had one of the leading parts in the Gertrude Stein play, *Yes Is For a Very Young Man.* The New York *Herald Tribune* critic, Howard Barnes, while reporting unfavorably on the play, described Miss Stanley's work as "splendid"; Brooks Atkinson of the New York *Times* said that she was "a talented actress with temperament, craft, and, if there is any justice on Broadway, a future."

Seen next in the Equity Library Theatre presentation of *St. Joan,* in which she had the stellar part, Miss Stanley was offered her first Broadway engagement by producer Kermit Bloomgarden who engaged her to replace Julie Harris in the cast of *Montserrat,* the play by Lillian Hellman which had opened at the Fulton Theatre on October 29, 1949.

Miss Stanley's second Broadway engagement was in *The House of Bernarda Alba,* a pastoral drama by the Spanish poet and playwright, García Lorca, presented at the ANTA Playhouse on January 7, 1951. Miss Stanley had the part of one of the five daughters of Bernarda (played by Katina Paxinou). She was seen by the wife of Horton Foote, the playwright, who became an ardent "rooter" for her, with the result that her next engagement was in Foote's *The Chase,* presented by José Ferrer at the Playhouse on April 15, 1952.

Although the play ran for only thirty-one performances, Miss Stanley's acting of the wife of a hunted Texas killer furthered her standing in the theatre. Richard Watts, Jr., stated in the New York *Herald Tribune* (April 17, 1952) that "in the small role of the killer's dull, frightened and unfaithful wife, Miss Stanley is particularly believable and understanding." William Hawkins wrote in the New York *World-Telegram and Sun* that "she projects all the drab pathos" of the part.

The following year Miss Stanley was again on Broadway, this time in *Picnic,* a play by William Inge about ordinary people in a small Kansas town, presented at the Music Box by the Theatre Guild and Joshua Logan on February 19, 1953. "As a tom-boy sister with brains and artistic gifts, Kim Stanley gives a penetrating performance that conveys the distinction as well as the gaucheries of a disarming young lady," Brooks Atkinson wrote.

Walter F. Kerr in the New York *Herald Tribune* (February 20, 1953) appraised her acting: "Miss Stanley seems to me to be one of the most promising performers on Broadway and she has a wonderfully lyric moment in *Picnic* as she tries out her wings, to the tune of a banging piano, when no one is around to watch. But her assumption of the nervous-tic mannerisms, the lolling tongue, and the singsong rhythms, cuts across and falsifies the independent vision of her performance; it also makes her seem more a cretin than a class intellectual." But to William Hawkins of the *World-Telegram and Sun,* "one of the rare, deeply moving moments" was provided by Kim Stanley.

The play received the Pulitzer Prize and ran for 477 performances, and for her work in it, the actress was given the New York Drama Critics' Award for having rendered the best supporting performance of the year. In May, Miss Stanley, who in private life is Mrs. Curt Conway, left the cast of *Picnic* because of approaching motherhood.

Back in the profession the following year, Miss Stanley made her debut as a leading lady under the management of The Playwrights' Company in Horton Foote's drama, *The Traveling Lady,* which opened at the Playhouse on October 27, 1954. At a special meeting of The Playwrights' Company two days after the opening, the decision was made to elevate Kim Stanley to stardom.

She played the part of Georgette Thomas, a commonplace young woman whose husband has deserted her and her child. She "retains the drab facts of the character—the flat vocal tones, the embarrassed hesitation, the awkward posture, the daze and indecision. But by the time Miss Stanley gets through with her, Georgette is a glowing beauty with a valiant spirit and heroic strength. . . . This is a stunning piece of acting. . . Miss Stanley is magnificent" (Brooks Atkinson, New York *Times,* October 28, 1954). Maurice Zolotow wrote in *Theatre Arts* (January 1955): "Miss Stanley is on her way to being a very great actress. She has a quality that cannot be taught at dramatic schools or learned in summer stock. When she makes an entrance she lights up a stage."

Other reviewers were equally impressed but did not view the play itself with the same favor, and *The Traveling Lady* closed after thirty performances.

Her dramatic work in *The Bridge* in January 1955 on *The Elgin Hour* television program was highly praised by Harriet Van Horne in the New York *World-Telegram and Sun,* January 12. "Her technique must have its roots in a deep understanding of human emotions." Miss Stanley also gave a dramatic performance of Theodore Herzl's wife in *The Great Dreamer,* opposite Dana Andrews, in a play by Norman Rosten at the Hanukkah Festival for Israel at Madison Square Garden on December 23, 1954.

When William Inge's play *Bus Stop* opened at the Music Box Theater in March 1955, Miss Stanley was warmly praised for her portrayal of Cherie, the Ozark girl who became a night club singer. Brooks Atkinson (New York *Times,* March 3, 1955) wrote, "She gives a glowing performance that is full of amusing detail . . . radiant with personality." Walter F. Kerr in the New York *Herald Tribune* commented, "When she walks on the stage, the set changes color. When she drawls out a simple 'Well, really!' in her long, low, and magnificently adenoidal tones, the English language acquires . . . comic and pathetic overtones."

Her parody of a night club chanteuse singing "That Old Black Magic" "stops" the show at each performance. Miss Stanley explained that she was virtually tone deaf, but modeled her singing on that of a vapid singer whom she saw in a honky-tonk.

She finds television the most relaxing medium for acting. "I never think anybody's watching," she said (New York *World-Telegram and Sun,* October 23, 1954) "until I go home to Texas, and find out they see everything."

Miss Stanley is married to the actor-director Curt Conway whom she met at the Cherry Lane Theatre. They have two children, Lisa, a three-year old girl, and a son Jamison, fifteen months old, and live in their own house near Huntington, Long Island. She has dark blonde hair and hazel eyes, and is five feet five and a half inches in height. Miss Stanley has described herself as "the outdoor type." She enjoys sketching and skiing.

References

N Y Post Mag p3 Mr 13 '55
N Y Times II p1+ Ap 3 '55 por
N Y World-Telegram p9 O 23 '54 por

STANLEY, THOMAS B(AHNSON) July 16, 1890- Governor of Virginia; businessman

Address: b. State Capitol, Richmond, Va.; h. Stanleytown, Va.

Successful in business and farming as well as in a political career, Virginia's Democratic Governor Thomas B. Stanley is the president and treasurer of the Stanley Furniture Company, Stanleytown, Virginia, which he founded in 1924. He is also president of the Ferrum Veneer Corporation and is the owner of two purebred Hereford and dairy Holstein farms in Stanleytown.

Elected sixty-third Governor of Virginia in November 1953, after a campaign supported by Senator Harry F. Byrd's Democratic organization, Stanley took office on January 20, 1954. In the U.S. Congress, where he represented Virginia's Fifth District from 1946 to 1953, he became known as a strong advocate of the "pay-as-you-go" system. He had previously been a member of the Virginia House of Delegates for sixteen years and three times its speaker. Stanley is serving a four-year term.

Thomas Bahnson Stanley was born on a small tobacco farm in Spencer, Henry county, Virginia, on July 16, 1890, the youngest son of

Wide World

THOMAS B. STANLEY

Crockett and Susan Matildah (Walker) Stanley. His father was a farmer and millwright. With his three brothers and three sisters, Thomas grew accustomed to farm chores at an early age. From his parents, he states, he received ethical and religious training that taught him to have the "utmost respect for other people . . . to let his Christian training be a guide for his conscience" (*Virginia and the Virginia Record,* January 1954).

Thomas began his education in a one-room school house in Henry county and was graduated at seventeen from the local high school, where he was catcher on the baseball team. For a short time he worked in the coal mines of the North Folk Coal and Coke Company, Maybeury, West Virginia, and then prepared for a business career. After attending the Eastman Business College in Poughkeepsie, New York and obtaining a degree in accounting, he became a bookkeeper with the R. J. Reynolds Tobacco Company in Winston-Salem, North Carolina.

In 1913 he was a clerk for one year in the Bank of Ridgeway in Virginia. He worked as clerk-bookkeeper at the First National Bank of Martinsville in 1914 and 1915 and as cashier at the First National Bank of Rural Retreat from 1916 to 1920. Then he helped to organize his father-in-law's furniture manufacturing firm, Vaughan-Bassett Furniture Company at Galax, and in 1921 was made vice-president. Three years later he established his own plant, the Stanley Furniture Company in Stanleytown, of which he became president and treasurer.

From the start of his legislative career Stanley found his accounting experience invaluable. During his first year in the Virginia House of Delegates, in 1930, he was appointed to the appropriations committee, where he had the task of balancing the biennial state budget. During the fourteen years he served on the Governor's advisory board, he was concerned with costs and operation of Virginia's highway, education, health and welfare, agriculture, labor and prison systems.

Upon his election to speaker of the Virginia House in 1942, he became chairman of the rules committee. Stanley worked for improved highways, education and agriculture, and obtained the initial funds for building and maintaining state department of agriculture diagnostic laboratories.

As Representative from Virginia's Fifth District, comprising nine counties in the southern part of the state, he won election to the U.S. Seventy-ninth Congress on November 5, 1946, to fill the unexpired term of Thomas G. Burch and to serve in the subsequent Eightieth Congress. He was re-elected to the Eighty-first, Eighty-second and Eighty-third Congresses.

In the first session of the Eightieth Congress (1947) Stanley favored overriding President Truman's veto of the Taft-Hartley labor management relations bill (June), and opposed the rent control extension bill (May), the Greek-Turkish aid bill (May) and the anti-poll tax bill (July). In the second session (1948), he voted "yea" for the G.O.P. tax reduction bill (February), for the $6 billion foreign aid authorization (March), and for the repeal of Federal taxes on oleomargarine (April). He opposed the displaced persons bill (June).

Congressman Stanley was not in favor of a large part of the Fair Deal program submitted by President Truman to the Eighty-first Congress. During 1949 he voted against the long range housing bill (June) and for the coalition (as opposed to the Truman) minimum-wage bill (August). In the area of foreign affairs, he supported the trade agreements act extension (February) and the Marshall Plan extension (April).

During the second session (1950) he opposed the Korea-Formosa economic aid bill (February) and the voluntary compliance Fair Employment Practice Commission bill (February). He favored a $600,000,000 cut in Federal spending under the omnibus appropriation bill (May), as well as overriding the communist-subversive control bill veto (September).

Stanley voted "yea" in 1951 on the draft extention–U.M.T. bill (April) and "nay" on the $7.5 billion foreign aid bill (August). On domestic issues, he favored the tidelands oil bill (July) and the $5.7 billion tax increase (October). His 1952 votes supported a $46 billion military ceiling in 1953 (April) and a $615,000,000 cut in economic aid for Western Europe (May). He approved limiting public housing to 5,000 units (March), cutting Federal jobs 10 per cent (April) and keeping 90 per cent farm price supports (June).

While in Congress, Stanley served on the House Administration Committee (chairman in the Eighty-second Congress), and on the Interstate and Foreign Commerce Committee. His record brought him praise from the majority leader of the House as "a stalwart warrior in our battle for economy" (*Congressional Record,* 1953).

On a number of occasions since 1941 Stanley had been mentioned as a possible gubernatorial candidate. Having gained the backing of Senator Byrd's political organization, he resigned from Congress in February 1953 to begin his campaign for Governor. In spite of the Republicans making "their greatest bid for a major office" in Virginia, Stanley defeated their candidate, state senator Theodore R. Dalton, for the governorship by a five to four vote ratio in the November 1953 election (New York *Herald Tribune,* November 5, 1953). He based his campaign largely on a continuation of the poll tax, a "pay-as-you-go" balanced state budget, a debt-free highway system and adherence to Byrd organization conservative policies—a program, he said, that would "advance the Virginia economy" (Washington *Post,* July 12, 1953).

In his inaugural address on January 20, 1954, Governor Stanley recommended a raise in teachers' salaries and proposed a tax increase of one cent-a-gallon on gasoline to raise state highway funds (later rejected by the state legislature). The following April he signed a bill tightening restrictions on roadside advertising, and in December 1954 expressed himself in favor of Federal aid for maintenance of interstate roads.

He was among the governors of nine coal-producing states who formed a resolution on July 12, 1954, asking the U.S. Congress to restrict imports of residual oil and natural gas into this country.

After the U.S. Supreme Court on May 17, 1954 ruled segregation illegal in public schools (a decision also affecting state parks) Governor Stanley stated that he would "work toward a plan which will be acceptable to our citizens and in keeping with the edict of the court" (Washington *Post and Times Herald*). On June 25, 1954, however, he announced, "I shall use every legal means at my command to continue segregated schools in Virginia," and urged repeal of the constitutional provision that requires the state to maintain a public school system (New York *Times,* June 26, 1954).

At the Southern Governors Conference in November 1954, Stanley was among seven governors signing a joint statement agreeing to try "by constitutional methods to preserve the right of the states to administer their public school systems to the best interest of all of our people" (Washington *Post and Times Herald,* November 14, 1954). The following June 1955 he called a "practical and reasonable approach" the Gray Commission recommendation that Virginia operate its public schools on a segregated basis in 1955 and 1956, and, with the State Board of Education, accepted this policy. In October 1955 the State Board of Education asked for a record appropriation of almost $147,000,000 to operate Virginia's public schools in fiscal 1956-1958, an increase of over $33,500,000 (Washington *Post and Times Herald,* October 6, 1955).

An increase in the educational budget is necessary, in part, because the state expects the daily pupil attendance to rise from 638,532 in 1954-1955 to 701,135 in 1956-1957 and 734,427 in 1957-1958.

The Governor has been called "a big man with a friendly smile" and "calm, cooperative, instinctively optimistic." The governors of the American Furniture Mart named him the industry's Man of the Year in 1954. He is a director of the Stanley Land and Lumber Company, the First National Bank of Bassett, Virginia and Forests, Inc. He is a trustee of Ferrum Junior College, Randolph-Macon College, and the Virginia Museum of Fine Arts, and is also a co-sponsor of the proposed Graduate School of Business Administration at the University of Virginia. He is a member of the Virginia Chamber of Commerce, and the Virginia Manufacturers Association.

Stanley married Anne Pocahontas Bassett on October 24, 1918, and their children are Anne (Mrs. Hugh H. Chatham), Thomas Bahnson, and John David. Virginia's chief executive is six feet two inches tall and has broad shoulders and blue eyes. He is a Thirty-second degree Mason, a Shriner, an Elk, and a member of Omicron Delta Kappa fraternity. Among his hobbies are hunting, fishing and golf. His religion is Methodist.

References

N Y Herald Tribune p12 N 4 '54
N Y Times p14 Jl 16 '53; p34 Ja 21 '54
Virginia and the Virginia Record 76:13+ Ja '54
Washington (D.C.) Post p6B Ap 2 '50; p17 O 25 '53; p2B My 23 '54
Biographical Directory of the American Congress, 1774-1949 (1950)
Congressional Directory (1952)
Who's Who in America, 1954-55
World Biography (1954)

STARR, CECILE July 14, 1921- Film critic

Address: b. c/o The Saturday Review, 25 W. 45th St., New York 36; h. 311 E. 72d St., New York 21

As a specialist in 16mm. motion pictures, Cecile Starr is rendering a service which makes it possible for schools and adult groups to keep well informed on the latest noncommercial films. She has "firmly established herself as the foremost critic and authority on 16mm. production in this country" (*Glamour,* February 1954). Since 1949 Miss Starr has been the 16mm. film editor of the *Saturday Review* and since 1953 the home movies editor of *House Beautiful.* She is also a part-time instructor in the development and history of motion pictures, at Hunter College, New York City.

She is currently on the editorial board of the Film Council of America, and at various times has been engaged in special film projects and research studies. In the past she had worked for March of Time Forum films and had served for two years as associate editor of the former *Film Forum Review.* The film critic edited *Ideas on Film* (Funk, 1951).

Cecile Starr, of Hungarian and Russian descent, was born on July 14, 1921 in Nashville, Tennessee to Jacob and Carrie (Lightman)

CECILE STARR

Starr. Her father died while she was in grade school. Cecile was reared in New Orleans and was graduated from Eleanor McMain High School in New Orleans in 1937. She majored in Romance languages at Louisiana State University and Agricultural and Mechanical College in Baton Rouge, receiving the B.A. degree in 1941.

"A number of people in my family," she says, "uncles, cousins, and for a while my brother, have worked in motion picture exhibition as theatre owners and managers.

"As a family we were always devotees of the movies," she recalls. "My brother and I thought it natural to see a film over and over again, if we really liked it. Six or seven different times would mean we really thought it was great." Upon meeting the director Rouben Mamoulian in the summer of 1954 she had the opportunity to tell him that "his wonderful movies of the 1930's such as *Gay Desperado* and *Love Me Tonight* were not only great entertainment, but . . . were the focal point of many happy family memories."

Miss Starr came to New York City in 1941 to pursue graduate work in the French language, in preparation for a teaching career. During the war, she worked for the Australian News and Information Bureau. She has said that here she learned "bits and snatches about public relations and news services to magazines, radio, movie theatres, and news sources, and educational services to schools, churches, and clubs."

In 1945 and 1946 Miss Starr worked in the promotion department of March of Time Forum films. She recalls ". . . at this time the Museum of Modern Art ran a six-month show of documentary films—and this was my first chance to see the extensive and thrilling use of reality in movies."

She attended Teachers College, Columbia University, from 1947 to 1948 on a part-time basis, taking courses in adult education and receiving her M.A. degree in 1952. While at Teachers College, Cecile Starr was a research assistant and scholar in the Institute of Adult Education and associate editor of the Institute's *Film Forum Review.* This quarterly magazine, published from 1946 to 1948, contained articles and reviews of 16mm. films, with particular reference to the use of films by adult discussion groups.

After working for the New York office of the Princeton Film Center, Miss Starr was appointed reviewer of 16mm. films in 1949 for the *Saturday Review of Literature* and editor of its "Ideas on Film" department.

First used in 1923, 16mm. film acquired sound in the early 1930's and developed rapidly during World War II when thousands of films were used to train and inform both servicemen and civilians. By 1954 more than 14,000 different titles were available for use on the 200,000 16mm. projectors owned by schools, universities, public libraries, film societies, factories, churches, and civic organizations.

Sometimes referred to as "documentaries" or "educational films," 16mm. pictures are made for a wide variety of purposes. Their scope includes films for training employees, "sponsored" films intended to sell a product or build good will, those for entertainment or recreation (for example, the many films on sports and travel), and "experimental" films by artists who use the motion picture for creative expression.

Miss Starr's reviews of new films appear each month under the heading "The Film Forum—The *Saturday Review*'s Guide to Selected 16mm. Sound Films." The accompanying "Ideas on Film" department presents a major article on some phase of 16mm. films and their use. This article is usually by Miss Starr, but it is occasionally written by a contributor who is a specialist in his field. Contributors have included Willard Van Dyke, Julien Bryan, Frances Flaherty (the widow of Robert Joseph Flaherty), and Pearl Buck (describing the film programs she arranged for children on her Pennsylvania farm).

In reviewing *Educational Film Guide* (eleventh edition), H. W. Wilson Company, 1953, Miss Starr commented: "It includes over 11,000 films currently available on 16mm. All the vital statistics (running time, date, rental and sales prices, source, etc.) are given for each film, and there is a high degree of accuracy. Also included are helpful references to all the full-length film reviews that have appeared in *Educational Screen, Film News* and the *Saturday Review*" (*Saturday Review,* September 12, 1953).

In her *Saturday Review* columns, Miss Starr says she is not interested in merely giving her own opinion of a film. Instead she tries to describe a film so effectively that "each reader can decide for himself whether it is a film that he would like to see or use." Miss Starr receives correspondence from people throughout the United States who seek assistance in locating and showing films. She personally answers these requests, often indicating where additional information can be obtained in the writer's own community.

Richard Griffith, curator of the film library at the Museum of Modern Art, stated that the *Saturday Review*, through its "Film Forum" and "Ideas on Film" departments, has made itself "the leading American authority on nontheatrical film, its uses, and the ideals and aspiration of its makers."

With the assistance of Cecile Starr, Gloria Waldron wrote *The Information Film* (1949). The chapters on films in public libraries were based upon the reports of Miss Starr's visits to the various libraries. She has also contributed to *Films in Review, Consumer Reports, This Generation, Pastoral Psychology*, and the New York *Herald Tribune*.

Ideas on Film, edited by Miss Starr, is a collection of articles from the *Saturday Review of Literature's* column, reviews by Miss Starr and Raymond Spottiswoode, and a listing of 16mm. films and where they can be purchased in the United States.

In 1953 Miss Starr was named home movies editor of *House Beautiful* and was appointed instructor of a course in the history and development of the motion picture at Hunter College, New York City. In this year she also began serving on the editorial board of the Film Council of America, an organization which operates under a grant from the Ford Foundation's Fund for Adult Education.

A pamphlet, "How to Obtain and Screen Films for Community Use," was written by Miss Starr in 1949 for the council. In 1954 the council published "A Guide to Film Services of National Associations," for which Cecile Starr conducted sample interviews and prepared the materials. At various times Miss Starr has been engaged in special film projects for nonprofit organizations such as the National Association for Mental Health, Medical Film Institute, New York Society for Mental Health, and World Health Organization.

Cecile Starr is five feet, six inches in height, has brown hair and brown eyes, and weighs 130 pounds. From her parents and grandparents she inherited "a feeling of belonging to the Jewish faith and to the Democratic party—despite the lack of formal affiliations in either." She likes foreign languages and music, and studying trees and flowers.

"Public libraries are another hobby, resulting from my six months tour in 1949," she has said. "Whenever I'm in a new town I stop in to inspect the library, particularly the film services." Most important, Miss Starr has written, is that "everyone have an opportunity to see the films he wants to see, that film makers be confident of having larger and more varied audiences, and that films become a more integrated part of recreation and of work in as many different situations as possible" (*Ideas on Film*).

References

Glamour 17:128 F '54
Starr, C. ed. Ideas on Film (1951)

STEINHAUS, EDWARD A(RTHUR)

Nov. 7, 1914- Insect pathologist; microbiologist

Address: b. 207 Agriculture Hall, University of California, Berkeley 4, Calif.; h. 2388 Westcliff Lane, Walnut Creek, Calif.

Since Edward A. Steinhaus became director of the University of California's Laboratory of Insect Pathology in 1945, he has pioneered in much important research in insect diseases (such as the classification of insect viruses) and in the practical application of new knowledge. With insects doing an estimated four billion dollars of damage annually to U.S. crops and with farmers spending about four hundred million dollars every year to purchase and apply insecticides, agriculture is expected to benefit substantially by the laboratory's achievements in controlling destructive insects by spreading artificial epidemic among the pests. Professor Steinhaus has been a member of the University of California faculty since 1944 and he had previously worked in the U.S. Public Health Service as assistant bacteriologist.

Edward Arthur Steinhaus was born on November 7, 1914, in Max, North Dakota, to Arthur Alfred and Alice (Rhinehart) Steinhaus. He has three younger brothers, Ralph Quentin, John R., and James F. His father is a merchant and farmer of German descent, and his mother's forebears came to America from England on the Mayflower. Edward was graduated in 1932 from Max Public High School, where he had participated in the activities of the dramatic and debating societies, in addition to playing football and basketball. He majored in bacteriology at North Dakota Agricultural College in Fargo, advised and encouraged by bacteriologists Dr. C. I. Nelson and Miss Delaphine Rosa, and took his B.S. degree in 1936. While an undergraduate, he competed in intramural athletics, became a member of Alpha Gamma Rho fraternity and other student societies and worked as a laboratory assistant in the bacteriology department.

In 1939 Steinhaus received the degree of Ph.D. in bacteriology and entomology from Ohio State University. His combined interests in microbiology and entomology were rather unusual, and, with the encouragement of Dr. Alvah Peterson, professor of entomology at Ohio State, he decided to pursue both fields, and obtained the Muellhaupt Fellowship for 1939-1940 for postdoctorate work in insect microbiology.

As assistant bacteriologist and later as associate bacteriologist for the U.S. Public Health Service in Hamilton, Montana, Steinhaus was engaged from 1940 to 1944 in the study of rickettsial diseases and other diseases transmitted by insects. He spent 1943-1944 as a member of the U.S. Army Bullis Fever Commission, while still employed by the U.S.P.H.S. Dr. Steinhaus had been unsuccessful in six attempts to enlist for military service in World War II because of failure to pass the physical examination. He joined the faculty of the University of California in Berkeley as lecturer in bacteriology in 1944, was promoted to

Acalanes-Bray Studio

EDWARD A. STEINHAUS

assistant professor, associate professor and finally professor of insect pathology.

For some time before World War II, Professor Harry S. Smith, chairman of the division of biological control in the College of Agriculture at the University of California, had hoped for a unit to study the diseases of insects and their use in destructive insect control. His project was realized as the Laboratory of Insect Pathology, set up on the Berkeley campus in 1945 with Steinhaus as director. The work of the laboratory falls into five main divisions. The first of these is the basic research done on insect diseases and the organisms, or microorganisms, which cause them. Laboratory diagnosticians have isolated several hundreds of these diseases, which have been or will be subjected to intensive study. Although the insect has been found to be vulnerable to the same types of organisms that cause many of the illnesses of man and other higher animals, the insect has its own peculiar set of bacteria, viruses, fungi, nematodes, and protozoa. This fact makes it possible to infect crop pests with fatal diseases which will be harmless to the farmer and livestock.

The second phase of the laboratory's work is an attempt to profit by nature's own system of insect control. Some diseases appear in cycles, alternately killing off all of the insects in the affected area and then allowing them to rebuild their populations. Study of these cycles and their causes will enable the scientist to benefit by the assistance of nature in protecting crops from their destroyers.

Since nature's reduction of the size of insect populations is too spasmodic to have the desired effect, this process is supplemented by the third phase of the laboratory's work. Once a lethal organism is isolated, the laboratory staff seeks means of preparing and disseminating it. Success results in artificially induced epidemics (or, the insect equivalent, epizootics) which can be delivered to the right place at the right time to destroy hordes of insects before they can set about their own work of destruction. An outstanding example of the application of this technique is the now classic case of the alfalfa caterpillar. As Steinhaus tells the story (*Americas*, June 1954), "A farmer brought in a dead caterpillar. We diagnosed the virus disease and two years of experiments followed. Finally we were able to get the poisonous virus simply by grinding up sick caterpillars. The more we spread the disease, the easier it became to prepare the virus solution. You can see how microbial control can be an inexpensive method."

The laboratory's fourth function is its diagnostic service. Insects from all over the United States and from many other parts of the world arrive at the clinic by mail. Sick insects are bedded down in individual glass containers stocked with their favorite foods. The course of their disease is watched and their charts are kept up to date. Dead specimens go into deep freeze storage until they can be autopsied or tested. When the cause of their illness or death has been determined (either by dissection of the insect or by microscopic examination of cultures prepared from crushed insects), a report is sent to the shipper of the insects, sometimes with instructions for cultivating more of the organisms for the infection of more insects.

Not all of the applicants for this service want to destroy insects, however. Healthy insects are needed by the insectaries—"stock farms" that raise millions of insects which can be set free to prey upon various crop destroyers at times when they are needed. Many ailing troops are sent to the clinic to have their illnesses treated. Equally well cared for are insects like bees and those used as test specimens by insecticide manufacturers.

Besides being occupied with laboratory work, the pathologists at Berkeley are engaged in training men to carry on their work. This fifth phase of their program includes a lecture and laboratory course in insect pathology, as well as graduate instruction and seminar sessions in the subject. The graduate work leads to the M.Sc. and Ph.D. degrees, and the undergraduate courses can be taken by students majoring in entomology in universities where this specialized training is not available.

While Steinhaus agrees with other scientists working with insect diseases that microbial control will not completely replace the use of insecticides and other forms of control, he is confident of continued progress in the application of insect pathology to agricultural problems. "Enough has been done to indicate that the use of microorganisms in the control of noxious insects holds considerable promise in spite of several well-known abortive attempts in the past," he has written. "Indeed, one of the primary reasons for certain of the past failures has been the fact that the work was not done by men trained or experienced in the fundamentals of insect pathology." Steinhaus would like to see "entomologists trained in insect pathology . . . included on every staff of biologists engaged in an extensive ecological study of insects." He also believes that "those whose interests compel them to be insect pathologists, regardless of whether or not there are to be great practical applications of the field, are probably destined to be among the happiest and most satisfied of biological scientists" (*Canadian Entomologist*, March 1949).

He is the author of more than sixty articles in his field and a contributor to *Bergey's Manual of Determinative Bacteriology* (sixth edition, Williams and Wilkins, 1948). Steinhaus' own books are *Catalogue of Bacteria Associated Extracellularly with Insects and Ticks* (Burgess, 1942), *Insect Microbiology* (Comstock, 1946), and *Principles of Insect Pathology* (McGraw-Hill, 1949). He is a member of numerous professional organizations including the American Society of Tropical Medicine, Entomological Society of America, Society of Parasitologists and the Society for the Study of Evolution.

Edward A. Steinhaus was married on June 14, 1940 to Mabry Clark, who taught bacteriology at North Dakota State College. They have a son named Timothy Clark and a daughter, Margaret Ann. Steinhaus has brown hair and dark-brown eyes, is six feet three inches tall, and weighs 198 pounds. Politically nonpartisan, he votes for both Republican and Democratic candidates. He is affiliated with the Congregational Church. He enjoys reading and is interested in fine books and fine printing. Other hobbies are gardening and philately. He has a complete collection of stamps picturing insects, and his article, "Insects on Stamps," appeared in *Weekly Philatelic Gossip* in 1954.

References

American Men of Science (1955)
Who Knows—and What (1954)

STEPHANOPOULOS, STEPHANOS

(stě -fä-nŏp'ô-lôs stě'fä-nôs) 1898- Greek Member of Parliament; author

Address: b. c/o Parliament of Greece, Athens, Greece

A distinguished economist and diplomat is Stephanos Stephanopoulos, who has served in responsible posts of the Greek Cabinet since the liberation of his country from Axis occupation in 1944. As the Minister of Transport from 1944 to 1946, he helped to restore the war-ravaged communications of Greece; as Minister of Economic Coordination from 1946 to 1950 he played a key role in the distribution of United States economic aid, and as Foreign Minister from 1952 to October 1955, he was one of the architects of the twenty-year pact between Greece, Turkey and Yugoslavia which was signed on August 9, 1954.

After the death of Premier Alexander Papagos on October 4, 1955, King Paul I asked Constantin Karamanlis to form a new Cabinet, which was sworn in on October 6. At that time Stephanopoulos was replaced by Minister of Foreign Affairs Spyros Theotokis, who also replaced Stephanopoulos as Greece's representative to the North Atlantic Council. Stephanopoulos continues as a member of the Greek Parliament.

STEPHANOS STEPHANOPOULOS

Under the chairmanship of Stephanopoulos the North Atlantic Council met in ministerial session in Paris in May 1955 and welcomed the accession of the Federal Republic of Germany to the North Atlantic Treaty, hailed the Western proposal for "Big Four" talks, and hoped for a "cessation of hostilities in the Far East."

A wealthy royalist, Stephanopoulos has long been associated with the National Bank of Greece and was one of the leaders of the Populist party. Later, in 1951 he joined the Greek Rally of the present Premier, Field Marshal Alexander Papagos. Stephanopoulos is the author of a number of books on economics.

Stephanos Stephanopoulos was born in Pyrgos, department of Achaea and Elis, Greece in 1898, the son of Christos and Phane (Vakalopoulou) Stephanopoulos. He attended the University of Athens, which awarded him the LL.D. degree. He also received the LL.D. degree from the University of Paris in 1929, after writing a dissertation on the character of the metallic reserve of the Greek bank of issue.

His political career began in 1930, as soon as he returned to Greece, when he was elected a Populist, or conservative royalist, party deputy. He was re-elected in the subsequent elections of 1932, 1933, 1935 and 1936, when elections were suspended until after World War II.

When the first Populist government took office in October 1932, Stephanopoulos was named under secretary of state in the Ministry of Economy and Labor, and in the second Populist government he was Minister of National Economy. During the Axis occupation of his country Stephanopoulos remained in Greece and took an active part in the resistance movement.

(Continued next page)

STEPHANOPOULOS, STEPHANOS —*Continued*

After his country was liberated in October 1944 Stephanopoulos was named Minister of Transport in the first National government. During the national elections of 1946, the first since before the war, Stephanopoulos was one of the four members of the Populist party's election campaign committee. After the election, which returned the Populists to power, he became Minister of Economic Coordination.

In the second half of 1946 he served briefly as Deputy Foreign Minister, filling in many times for Constantin Tsaldaris, who was both Premier and Foreign Minister. At the time, Greece was embroiled in stormy border relations with Yugoslavia, Bulgaria and Albania as well as with Russia. In November 1946, Stephanopoulos returned to his former position of Minister of Economic Coordination.

After President Harry S. Truman's program of economic aid for Greece and Turkey began, Stephanopoulos met frequently with U.S. relief representatives, who were often critical of the way in which the Greek government handled the program. More than $500,000,000 of American assistance was given during 1947 and 1948 to help bolster the Greek economy.

Stephanopoulos was of great help to Dwight P. Griswold (see *C.B.,* December 1947), director of the American Mission for Aid to Greece, when Griswold sought in 1947 to lessen the political dominance of the Populist party. Griswold particularly sought to oust the right-wing leader Napoleon Zervas from the Cabinet and to bring the Liberal, Themistokles Sophoulis, into the government. The effort led to a Cabinet crisis. Griswold won the support of Stephanopoulos, and finally a Populist-Liberal Cabinet was installed, with Sophoulis as Premier. Stephanopoulos remained as Minister of Economic Coordination.

He continued to hold that post until March 1950 when, after a bitter Cabinet crisis, a new Liberal government, with Sophocles Venizelos as Premier, was formed. Stephanopoulos was dropped from the government, until September, when he became Minister of Economic Coordination for a short time.

Toward the end of 1950 Stephanopoulos broke completely with Tsaldaris and led a group of twenty-seven deputies out of the Populist party. In January 1951 his group combined with the six deputies of the National Unionist party, led by Panayotis Canellopoulos, to form the new Unionist-Populist party, which briefly held the balance of power in Parliament.

When in 1951 Papagos, Commander in Chief of the Greek Army in its long desperate war against Communist rebels, decided to run for election, the Unionist-Populist party agreed to disband, and Stephanopoulos joined Marshal Papagos' Greek Rally which won four-fifths of the seats in Parliament in the 1952 election. On November 19, 1952, when Papagos took over as Premier, Stephanopoulos became his Foreign Minister. Spyros B. Markessinis, the former leader of the New party, was installed as Minister of Economic Coordination.

Beginning his new term in the Cabinet, Stephanopoulos stated that Greece's foreign policy would remain unchanged under the Papagos government. He reaffirmed Greece's intention "to adhere firmly to the North Atlantic Treaty Organization (NATO) and her friendship with Turkey" and he added: "The Greek government watches with pleasure the gradual development of the country's relations with our other neighbor, Yugoslavia, looking forward to their future . . . tightening of bonds" (New York *Times,* November 23, 1952).

On December 29, 1952 it was announced that Yugoslavia and Greece were raising their diplomatic representatives to the rank of Ambassador. This, diplomatic circles said, was a step on the road toward a treaty between Turkey, Greece and Yugoslavia providing for military cooperation to check any possible aggression from the Soviet bloc.

A treaty of friendship and collaboration was finally concluded by the three Balkan countries and signed by Stephanopoulos, Fuat Köprülü (see *C.B.,* June 1953), Foreign Minister of Turkey, and the Yugoslav Foreign Minister, Koca Popovic, in Ankara on February 28, 1953. It expressed the resolution of the three governments to unite their efforts in the organization of defense against possible aggression. On the same day, February 28, a commercial treaty was signed by Greece and Yugoslavia in Athens.

The signing of the friendship pact was followed by a visit to Athens by John Foster Dulles, U.S. Secretary of State, and U.S. Mutual Security Director Harold E. Stassen. On October 12, 1953 the U.S. Department of State announced that the U.S. Ambassador to Greece, Cavendish Cannon, had signed an agreement with Greece giving the United States the right to use several Greek air and naval bases. The agreement, which will be effective until 1969, also permits the United States to construct roads and railways and to improve the facilities of the bases.

Stephanopoulos returned the visit of Dulles and Stassen later in 1953, when he accompanied King Paul I and Queen Frederika of the Hellenes on their tour of the United States. Upon his return to Athens, Stephanopoulos stated that he and Dulles had reached "full comprehension and coincidence of views . . . on the line of our common policy" (New York *Herald Tribune,* November 24, 1953).

In April 1954 the Greek government was again shaken up, and Markessinis was dropped as head of the Ministry of Economic Coordination. Eleven ministers were replaced; however, Stephanopoulos remained in his post of Foreign Minister. This was followed by a Cabinet reshuffle in December, when Stephanopolous became Deputy Premier while retaining the portfolio of foreign affairs.

The "friendship and cooperation" treaty of February 28, 1953 became a full-fledged military alliance on August 9, 1954. At that time a twenty-year pact pledging immediate military aid to each other was signed by Yugoslavia, Greece, and Turkey. The signing took place at Bled, Yugoslavia, and the signees for their governments were Foreign Ministers Stephanopolous, Köprülü, and Popovic of Yugoslavia. "The pact, for alliance, political cooperation and mutual assistance, linked three well-trained armies with a total potential exceeding seventy divisions in one of the most sensitive sectors of the Western defensive system. Greece and Turkey are members of NATO; Yugoslavia is not" (New York *Times,* August 10, 1954).

In terms almost identical with those used in the North Atlantic Treaty articles, the Balkan treaty says that the signatories are agreed that an aggression against one or more of them, in no matter which part of their territory, will be considered an aggression against them all. By provision of the 1954 treaty, a permanent Balkan secretariat was established in Ankara. It is conducting studies to foster closer economic, military, cultural and political cooperation among the three signatory nations.

One of the problems confronting the present Greek government is the repatriation of Greek children, who had been abducted by the Communist nations during the civil war. These hostages are being returned and, according to Associated Press reporter William L. Ryan, many of them have undergone thorough indoctrination courses and are ardent Communists (Washington *Post and Times Herald,* April 17, 1955). Earthquakes during 1954 and 1955 in Greece resulted in wide-spread destruction.

Another difficulty facing the Greek government is the Greek-Turkish dispute caused by Greece's submission to the United Nations of the question of self-determination for the island of Cyprus. Greece announced in April 1955 plans to seek again U.N. action on the Cyprus dispute (the U.N. Political and Security Committee voted to defer this issue on December 15, 1954). Cyprus has been under British rule since 1878 and is about 80 per cent Greek in population. Cyprian leaders and the Greek Orthodox church are pressing for self-determination and *enosis* (union with Greece). The Turkish minority on Cyprus is generally opposed to *enosis.* The government of Great Britain believes that Cyprus is needed as a military base for Britain and NATO, now that British forces are being withdrawn from the Suez Canal area.

The Anti-Rally Coalition defeated in November 1954 government and liberal opposition candidates in major urban centers including Athens, Piraeus and Salonika. The *Christian Science Monitor* (May 13, 1955) reported that the Anti-Rally Coalition is composed of remnants of the Progressive party (EPEK) and the Socialist party and is supported by the Union of the Democratic Left (EDA), regarded as the legal cover for the proscribed Greek Communist party.

Among the more important books written by Stephanopoulos are *Money and Exchange Crisis* (1930), *Social Insurance* (1932), *Economic and Social Studies* (1935), and *Philosophy and Social Systems* (1936). He also is the author of an article published after World War II in the *Encyclopaedia Ilios* on "Reconstruction in Greece."

Reference

World Biography (1948)

STEVENS, ROGER L(ACEY) Mar. 12, 1910- Theatrical producer; realtor

Address: b. c/o Playwrights' Company, 1545 Broadway, New York 36

A real estate broker who turned his interest in the theatre into one of the most successful theatrical producing enterprises, Roger L. Stevens conducts two high-pressure careers. His real estate holdings in recent years have included vast properties in Seattle, Miami, Boston, and New York. In 1951 he negotiated the purchase of the tallest building in the world, the Empire State Building in New York City. In that same year he was elected a member of The Playwrights' Company, through which he has been involved in the production of such Broadway successes as *The Fourposter, Tea and Sympathy, Sabrina Fair, Ondine, The Bad Seed,* and *Cat on a Hot Tin Roof.* As co-producer with Robert Whitehead he brought *Bus Stop* to Broadway in 1955. For ANTA (American National Theatre and Academy) he has financed a number of productions during the past five years.

Roger Lacey Stevens, the son of Stanley and Florence (Jackson) Stevens, was born in Detroit, Michigan, on March 12, 1910 and was raised in nearby Ann Arbor. His father was in the real estate business. Young Stevens was educated at the Choate School in Wallingford, Connecticut from 1925 to 1928. He prepared to enter Harvard, but the financial reverses suffered by his father in 1928 made it necessary for him to return to Ann Arbor. After studying for one year at the University of Michigan Roger left college and in 1930 went to Detroit, where for the next five years he worked on the assembly line at the Ford Motor Company and later as an attendant in a gas station. "I had a lot of time to read," he recalls, "and somehow found myself reading mostly plays." In a *New Yorker* profile of Stevens in 1954, E. J. Kahn quoted him: "Of all the things that can make a person happy, I'd put literature first. Many people need other people around them, but I don't if I [have] books."

Joining the staff of Hannan Real Estate Company, a large Detroit firm, Stevens was soon able to earn a good living as a broker, largely (as James S. Keat described his career in the New York *Herald Tribune,* February 15, 1953) by "finding likely sites, locating investors to buy them, accepting an interest in the property as part of his fee, taking a profit when the property was resold and starting the cycle again with another deal." By 1938, Kahn reported in the *New Yorker,* he had amassed some $50,000 from his real estate activities.

During World War II Stevens was commissioned a lieutenant in the U.S. Navy and spent two years at a naval air station in Miami, Florida. "During leave while in the East I saw a good deal of theatre and gave much thought to it," he has said. "As war neared its end I decided that I wanted to do something in and for the theatre. But I didn't know what. I simply realized that it would take some money and that I'd have to make it."

(Continued next page)

ROGER L. STEVENS

Upon his return to civilian life, Stevens invested in a number of hotel buildings in Cleveland and in Miami. In 1949 he formed a real estate corporation in New York and acquired (and later sold) interests in the Brooklyn Paramount Theatre, the Hotel Taft, the Squibb Building, and other New York properties. In the same year Stevens financed several artistic, although not commercial, successes for the Detroit Theatre Guild among them, Molnar's *The Play's the Thing* and Pirandello's *Right You Are If You Think You Are.*

In the spring of 1949 Stevens helped provide the financial backing for a revival of the Ann Arbor Drama Festival, which had been suspended during the war. Its most successful production was Shakespeare's *Twelfth Night* which Stevens brought to Broadway. He retained most of the cast of the Ann Arbor production—Arnold Moss as Malvolio, Frances Reid as Viola, and Carl Benton Reid as Sir Toby—and Nina Foch joined the company in New York to play Olivia.

Twelfth Night opened in New York in October 1949 and ran for forty-eight performances. In order to keep the price of admission very low, the actors agreed to work for lower salaries than the prevailing scale. The New York critics were not enthusiastic about the production, but Stevens, who had not expected it to be financially profitable, was not discouraged. It was announced in *Variety* (October 12, 1949) that he planned "to commute henceforth between New York and Detroit, continuing his real estate activities in both cities."

Stevens' next venture in the theatre was as co-producer with Peter Lawrence of the revival of Sir James M. Barrie's *Peter Pan,* which co-starred Jean Arthur and Boris Karloff and had a musical score by Leonard Bernstein. *Peter Pan* opened in New York in April 1950 and ran for 320 performances.

Although most of the productions with which Stevens has subsequently been associated have been Broadway successes, he insists that financial reward has not been his aim, and he has not hesitated to invest in enterprises which offer esthetic rather than financial returns. He became interested in the Congress-chartered ANTA, which had been founded in 1935 "to promote the development of the living theatre in all parts of the nation." In April 1950 he provided the backing for ANTA's revival of Bernard Shaw's *Getting Married,* with Sir Cedric Hardwicke directing and acting in the play. The play was sent on a tour to the West Coast, making a stop first at the Ann Arbor Festival.

ANTA productions that Stevens backed again in 1950-1951 were Lorca's *The House of Bernarda Alba* and Paul Green's adaptation of Ibsen's *Peer Gynt.* A member of ANTA's board of governors, Stevens headed a committee in 1951 which studied and effected the reorganization of ANTA "along more democratic lines" (New York *Times,* January 2, 1953). At the second National Theatre Assembly, which met in Cincinnati in January 1953, Stevens, as co-chairman, stated that theatre interest throughout the United States was high and that if all the 250,000 amateur producing groups in the country gave even a small amount to support ANTA, it would have sufficient funds to establish its goal of a national theatre.

Through Stevens' real estate connections ANTA was able to open its own playhouse—the redecorated old Guild Theatre on West 52d Street in New York City—in December 1954. (The mortgage on the theatre building was purchased from the Shubert theatrical interests and Stevens himself donated $25,000 to the project.)

On April 25, 1951 Stevens was elected to membership in The Playwrights' Company, which had been organized in 1938 and included among its founders Maxwell Anderson, Elmer Rice, and Robert E. Sherwood. The election of Stevens as a production executive was, the group reported, "in line with a contemplated expansion program that would include the more frequent production of plays by outside authors."

Stevens commented on his affiliation with The Playwrights' Company: "I wanted to back the best in the theatre . . . the top craftsmen. I am looking for quality when I invest, and I think I have found it." The first production of the group after Stevens joined it was Jan de Hartog's *The Fourposter,* which ran for 632 performances.

Independently of The Playwrights' Company, Stevens has co-produced with Alfred de Liagre, Jr., the off-Broadway Phoenix Theatre's musical comedy *The Golden Apple.* He also financed the new production firm of Lyn Austin and Thomas Noyes in *Take a Giant Step* and *The Frogs of Spring.* As co-producer with Katharine Cornell, Stevens brought to Broadway Christopher Fry's *The Dark Is Light Enough,* and with Robert Whitehead he produced *Bus Stop.*

In 1953 Stevens joined in the organization of The Producers' Theatre with Robert W. Dowling, head of the City Investing Company (a large real estate company), Robert Whitehead, the director and producer and former managing director of ANTA, and The Playwrights' Company, the latter retaining its independent corporate existence. The Producers' Theatre, with a capital estimated at $1,000,000, has an interest in three Broadway theatres, the Fulton, the Morosco, and the Coronet.

The plans of The Producers' Theatre were outlined by Stevens in *Theatre Arts,* April 1955. The main idea behind it, he wrote, "was our conviction that sound internal financing and long-term continuity of operation were bases on which we could erect an organization flexible enough to encompass a variety of tastes in play production, and strong enough to stand behind those tastes without involving outside investors." Producers' Theatre, Stevens continued, intends to apply to the theatre various methods used in modern business—profit-sharing plans, provisions for pensions, and "plans whereby playwrights could be assured of consistent income during 'dry' periods, in lieu of the feast-or-famine existence most of the better ones now face."

Productions of The Producers' Theatre include *The Remarkable Mr. Pennypacker,* T. S. Eliot's *The Confidential Clerk,* a touring company production of Shaw's *Saint Joan,* Clifford Odets' *The Flowering Peach,* and William Archibald's dramatization of Henry James' novel *Portrait of a Lady.*

In October 1955 Stevens brought to New York the British company of the Jean Giraudoux-Christopher Fry drama *Tiger at the Gates,* starring Michael Redgrave. One of his future projects is to import the Shakespeare Memorial Theatre Group from Stratford, England, to play in the American Shakespeare Festival Theatre at Stratford, Connecticut, of which he is the treasurer. He also plans for The Producers' Theatre to bring to New York one production of the Stratford, Ontario, Shakespeare Festival Foundation in early 1956, Christopher Marlowe's *Tamburlaine the Great.*

In July 1955 he succeeded Howard Lindsay as president of the New Dramatists' Committee, a group founded in 1949 by the Dramatists' Guild, "to serve as a sort of postgraduate school for deserving young playwrights" (New York *Times,* July 1, 1955). As a further encouragement to young talent, Stevens joined with Lyn Austin and others from the off-Broadway Phoenix Theatre in September 1955 in a plan to give young directors an opportunity to direct plays of their own choosing.

Long concerned about the inefficiency and inconvenience connected with purchasing theatre tickets, Stevens announced in September 1955 his plan to establish a Broadway information center in order to help people obtain tickets by telephone or in person.

Since 1949, when he moved most of his business interests to New York, Stevens has divided his time between real estate and the theatre. In April 1951, he headed a syndicate which purchased the Empire State Building for $51,-600,000, the highest price paid for a single building. Stevens sold out his interest in 1954. Other important real estate transactions in which he has played a prominent part include the leasing of a ten-acre area of downtown Seattle and the purchase, in February 1953, of a twenty-eight acre site in Boston from the New York Central Railroad for $4,500,000.

Stevens has a house in Ann Arbor and an apartment in New York City. His wife, whom he married in 1938, is the former Christine Gesell, daughter of the physiologist Robert Gesell and niece of Dr. Arnold Gesell, the child psychologist. They have one daughter. Stevens has been described as tall, balding, and "casually dressed." In the 1952 American Presidential campaign he served as chairman of the finance committee of the National Volunteers for Adlai Stevenson.

References

N Y Herald Tribune V p 1 O 2 '49; II p7 F 15 '53
N Y Times II p 1 O 2 '49
New Yorker 39:37+ F 13 '54; 29:30+ F 20 '54; 29:28 O 9 '54
Time 57:89 Je 4 '51

STREIBERT, THEODORE C(UYLER)

Aug. 29, 1899- United States Government official

Address: b. c/o United States Information Agency, 1778 Pennsylvania Ave. N.W., Washington 25, D.C.; h. Locust Valley, N.Y.

When Theodore C. Streibert became director of the U.S. Information Agency on July 30, 1953, he stepped into one of the most challenging posts in the Federal government. His primary assignment was to supervise all the overseas information services which "explain to peoples everywhere the policies and objectives of the United States." His task also was to convince Congress and the public of the value of the work despite Senatorial attacks, and to restore and maintain morale in an organization badly shaken by budget cuts, policy changes, firings and resignations.

The information operations directed by Streibert include the radio broadcasting division known as the Voice of America, which beams more than seventy-five daily programs in thirty-eight languages to both sides of the Iron Curtain; the press, photographic and film services; and the maintenance of U.S. libraries overseas.

Following a Presidential directive, Streibert completed the agency's reorganization, and revised its operation in its 216 posts located in seventy-seven countries. Increased responsibility and authority were placed in its public affairs officers who regularly consult with American diplomatic missions abroad. The agency uses many communication media to explain the benefits of free enterprise and free labor versus the Soviet system of state ownership and slave labor, and to expose international communism as Red colonialism.

Streibert, who succeeded Dr. Robert L. Johnson in the post of director, brought to his multifaceted task broad experience acquired in business and broadcasting, as a member of the

Wide World

THEODORE C. STREIBERT

Radio Advisory Committee on Information, as president of WOR, Bamberger Broadcasting Service since 1945, as chairman of the board of the Mutual Broadcasting System (1949-1951), as chairman of the executive committee of Ward Baking Company, and as consultant to Ambassador James B. Conant, High Commissioner for West Germany.

Theodore Cuyler Streibert was born on August 29, 1899 in Albany, New York, the son of Henry and Catherine (Kaiser) Streibert. He attended schools in Albany and was graduated in 1921 from Wesleyan University and was awarded the Phi Beta Kappa key. He received an M.B.A. degree at the Harvard Business School, graduating in 1923.

In that same year he became a member of the research staff of the Bureau of Business Research at Harvard Business School. From 1926 to 1928 he was an official in New York of FBO Pictures Corporation (which later became RKO), an executive of Cinema Credits Corporation of New York and a member of the board of directors of Pathé Exchange. He became assistant to the executive vice-president of Pathé Exchange of New York in 1928, leaving this post in 1929 to take the position of assistant dean of Harvard Business School.

In 1933 he joined station WOR as assistant to Alfred J. McCosker, then president, and in 1935 was elected a member of the station's board of directors. A year later Streibert was appointed executive vice-president and general manager, a post he held until January 1, 1945, when he succeeded to the presidency. He actively participated in the founding of the Mutual Broadcasting System, of which WOR is the New York key station. He was a member of the board of directors of Mutual and was chairman of the board from 1949 to 1951.

He served as a director of the National Association of Broadcasters, of Broadcast Music, Inc., and as a member of the board of directors of the Broadcast Advertising Bureau. He has been trustee of the Brooklyn Institute of Arts and Sciences (since 1948) and a member of the board of the Visiting Nurse Service of New York, of the New York City Better Business Bureau, and of the Legal Aid Society of New York.

For a short time in 1953 he was a consultant to Robert L. Johnson, then administrator of the U.S. information program and on June 17 was appointed by President Dwight D. Eisenhower as consultant on public affairs to James B. Conant, the High Commissioner in West Germany. In July he was recalled to replace Johnson in Washington, D.C.

The organization headed by Streibert was formed early in 1942 as the Office of War Information, directed by Elmer Davis. After the war it was taken over by the U.S. Department of State, in August 1945, and was called by various names and organized and reorganized a number of times. The Republican Administration put most of its functions—except the exchange of students and teachers—under a separate direction. The U.S. Information Agency is subject to foreign policy guidance by the State Department.

President Eisenhower, when he appointed Streibert director on July 30, 1953, issued the following statement: "Our overseas information service never carried a heavier responsibility than it does now. The service must clearly and factually present to the world the policies and objectives of the United States. It is not enough for us to have sound policies, dedicated to goals of universal peace, freedom and progress. These policies must be made known to and understood by all peoples throughout the world. That is now the responsibility of the new U.S. Information Agency" (New York *Herald Tribune*, July 31, 1953).

On October 22, 1953 President Eisenhower directed the U.S.I.A. to "unmask and counter hostile attempts to distort U.S. policies and objectives . . . to project abroad those aspects of the life and culture of the American people which will facilitate understanding of U.S. policies and objectives."

In a speech in St. Louis on November 14 before the Sigma Delta Chi journalistic fraternity, Streibert said that the agency's primary job was to combat the "enormous resources" of the Communist propaganda machine and that it would concentrate on straight factual reporting (New York *Times*, November 15, 1953).

As tension in Indochina mounted, information programs were increased. Streibert made a twenty-day tour of the Far East, to determine the needs for that area. When the President made known his plan for peaceful international use of nuclear energy, the U.S.I.A., largely through the Voice of America, announced that program to the world

Early in 1954 the agency received both criticism and praise. On January 23 the Senate Permanent Subcommittee on Investigations, headed by Senator Joseph R. McCarthy, stated that an "anti-American content" had marked some Voice of America broadcasts (New York *Times*, January 24). On February

3 the President's Advisory Commission on Information urged that the agency be "spared" from further special Congressional investigations and "lashed out," according to the New York *Herald Tribune* (February 4), at the inquiry conducted in 1953 by the McCarthy group.

In the U.S.I.A.'s second review of operations (January-June 1954) it was reported that the agency "used every means of communication" to give peoples overseas "a true picture of the peaceful nature of the U.S. atomic energy policy. . . . The Supreme Court decision outlawing segregation in U.S. public schools, one of the severest blows to Communist propaganda, was flashed around the world by U.S.I.A. media within minutes after its announcement."

On his return from a tour of Asia in June 1954, Streibert said that Communist propaganda in that part of the world "constantly paints the United States as an imperialistic colonial power. This propaganda has been and still is effective with many Asians." The U.S.I.A., he emphasized, "must set the record straight. Our own national life began in a successful resistance to colonialism. Our relations with the Philippines give the lie to the charge that we today are colony-minded."

On June 30, 1954 the total number of the agency's full-time employees was 9,539; of these, 3,235 were Americans, 2,207 employed in the United States and 1,028 overseas, and 6,304 were citizens of foreign nations, all employed overseas. This represents a reduction of 2,291. The fiscal 1954 operation funds totaled $84,200,000 (compared with $122,700,000 in 1953). Its budget request for fiscal 1955 was $89,000,000, but Congress voted the Agency $77,100,000.

The U.S.I.A.'s book program was strengthened during 1954 and additional funds were used to stimulate book translations. Examples of anti-Communist translations made possible by the Agency's assistance are *Exiled to Siberia* and *Red Prison*, written by North Korean refugees and published by Korean publishers. U.S. book publishers were encouraged to issue paperback overseas print runs of useful books that compete pricewise with the heavily subsidized Communist publications on sale throughout the Near and Far East. The use of bookmobiles and book lockers (foot lockers converted to portable bookcases) and cooperation with local libraries increased.

The U.S.I.A.'s "Atoms for Peace" exhibit was displayed at Hunter College in New York City in early December 1954 prior to being sent overseas for showing in India and Pakistan. Similar mobile exhibits on the peaceful uses of the atom were opened during 1954 in Brazil, West Germany, Italy and Belgium. The Voice of America moved to its new headquarters in the Health-Education-Welfare Building in Washington, D.C. on December 1.

Because of a "critical shortage" of propaganda specialists for overseas work, the U.S.I.A. ordered all employes in its Washington, D.C. headquarters to drop their regular work on Monday, November 1, 1954 to recruit qualified persons for these assignments. Streibert said that his Agency had greatly increased its staff in the Far East and in Latin America. His aim is to "blunt the Soviet Union's propaganda campaign in Asia" by exposing Communism as "Red colonialism."

Anti-Communist films produced to explain U.S. policies and objectives, and released through commercial distributors in the Far and Near East, included *Atomic Power for Peace*, and *The Korea Story* (which emphasized the successful checking of Communist aggression by U.N. action), and *Falcón Dam* (concerning a water conservation and power development on the Rio Grande jointly undertaken by the United States and Mexico).

The U.S.I.A. has increased its film audience to over 200,000,000 persons weekly, Streibert announced on August 2, 1954. "The marked expansion of prospective viewers of documentaries explaining United States objectives has been possible," he said, "by releasing the Agency's films through the overseas commercial channels of the American motion picture industry."

On a recent trip to South America Streibert reported that despite the fact that thirteen of the twenty republics have outlawed the Communist party, there are over 200,000 well-financed and well-organized Communists at work in that area, this total based on official estimates. He compared the public relations methods of the Soviet Union to those of an unprincipled company seeking to destroy its competitor. While our "company" has no legal redress against such tactics, he said, it can refute the charges. The Soviet Union uses propaganda "to distort, divide and corrupt," and spends millions each year (New York *Times*, November 30, 1954).

Streibert is a member of Alpha Delta Phi, the Racquet and Tennis Club, the Harvard Club (New York) and the Piping Rock Club. He is an Episcopalian. His wife is the former Margaret Grout, whom he married on March 6, 1935; there are three children, Catherine, Marshall and Theodore.

References

N Y Herald Tribune p4 Jl 31 '53 por
Who's Who in America, 1954-55
Who's Who in Commerce and Industry (1951)
World Biography (1948)

SUHR, OTTO (ERNST HEINRICH HERMANN) (zōōr) Aug. 17, 1894- Mayor of West Berlin; economist

Address: b. Rudolph-Wilde-Platz, Berlin-Schöneberg, Germany; h. Hüninger Strasse 4, Berlin-Zehlendorf, Germany

"It is a life-and-death question of world political significance how many more years Berlin and—what is even more important—the people in the Soviet zone can stand up to the pressure of the cold war," Otto Suhr, the Mayor of West Berlin, wrote recently. "In this question there is hope and danger at the same time; in it lies Berlin's obligation and the duty of the Western world."

(Continued next page)

Wide World

OTTO SUHR

Suhr, a Social Democrat who was elected to his position in January 1955 (succeeding Walther Schreiber), is well acquainted with the problems of the divided city for he has held important positions in the Berlin government since World War II. Before Adolf Hitler's rise to power, Suhr was prominent in the German trade union movement and later he wrote books on economics and contributed articles to the Frankfurter *Zeitung.* In February 1955 he was also elected vice-president of the Bundesrat (the upper house) in the Parliament of the Federal Republic of Germany. Suhr once said to an American foreign correspondent: "I can assure you that no part of Germany will ever go Communist. We have seen too much."

Otto Ernst Heinrich Hermann Suhr was born on August 17, 1894 in Oldenburg, Germany, the son of Hermann-Heinrich and Klara (Runge) Suhr. His father was a government official; his brother is a writer. He was brought up in Oldenburg, Osnabrück and Leipzig. During World War I he served in the Army and was decorated. After the war he studied at the University of Leipzig, from which he received a Ph.D. degree in 1923.

From 1920 to 1922 he had been a press officer in Kassel. In 1922 he became secretary of the Allgemeiner Deutscher Gewerkschaftsbund (federation of free trade unions) in that city. While there he also taught at several schools. Moving to Berlin, he became in 1925 manager of the economic department of the "white-collar" workers' unions. He taught at the Deutsche Hochschule für Politik in Berlin and was a guest lecturer at other schools. After the Reichstag voted Hitler dictatorial powers in March 1933, all existing trade unions were abolished and Suhr was without work. In 1935 he began writing on economics for the Frankfurter *Zeitung.*

At the end of World War II he was for seven months chief department head of the German Industrial Administration in the Soviet zone of occupation. He resisted the efforts of the Soviets to merge the Social Democrat and Socialist Unity (Communist) parties. When municipal elections were held throughout Berlin in October 1946, the non-Communist parties received about 80 per cent of the votes and the Socialist Unity party about 20 per cent. Suhr was elected president of the City Assembly.

Commenting on the results of the 1946 assembly election, Suhr has written that "the Soviets never got over this overwhelming defeat of their Communist satellites" and that "their disappointment intensified the cold war in Berlin and their acts of violence, which culminated in the division [of the city], were particularly against that parliament as the last manifestation of Western democracy."

In June 1948 all ground communication between the Western zones of occupation in Germany and Berlin was stopped by the Soviet zone authorities. To counteract this blockade the United States and Great Britain established the "Berlin airlift." In July the Soviet Union withdrew as a member of the Kommandatura (quadripartite Allied military council in Berlin) and a completely separate municipal government was established in the Eastern sector of the city.

When Soviet attempts were made during the blockade to persuade West Berlin to stop depending on Western supplies and to use West German marks, Suhr declared that "80 to 90 per cent of the West Berlin population would prefer the hardships of the present Soviet blockade to permitting the Russians to take over sole control of the city."

When Berlin Communists raided the City Hall in the Soviet sector to prevent the City Assembly from meeting, Suhr demanded on August 27, 1948 that the Soviet Union guarantee the assembly's safety from interruptions. Almost two months later, the Russians announced that a Soviet military court had convicted Suhr and five other anti-Communist Berlin leaders as "Fascist war-mongerers." City Assembly president Suhr was re-elected in January 1949, at the same time as Mayor Ernst Reuter, also a Social Democrat.

After the Soviets and the Allies began to free Berlin from the blockade and counter-blockade in May 1949, the West Berlin government refused to negotiate with the East Berlin government, because, according to Suhr, to do so would be to recognize the "rump" government of the Soviet sector. He rejected an offer from the Socialist Unity party for joint talks to restore normal life in Berlin and said that free elections should be held throughout the city as a basis for organizing a new city administration (New York *Times,* May 11, 1949).

Meanwhile Suhr had become a member of the Parliamentary Council which had worked out the Basic Law for West Germany. This constitution came into force in the three Western occupation zones on May 23, 1949 (Berlin was named a state of the Republic but was not formally incorporated in it). Suhr became a delegate, without vote, to the Bundestag (lower house of Parliament). When the German Democratic Republic was established in the Soviet zone in October 1949, Suhr addressed a meeting of 60,000 persons in West Berlin and declared: "We want no part of the Soviet protectorate." Emphasizing West Berlin demands that the city be allowed formally to join the West German republic, he stated that the morale of West Berliners "requires that they feel themselves an integral part of the West German regime" (New York *Times*, October 9, 1949).

The West Berlin government faced increasing economic difficulties, and when Suhr presented the annual budget to the City Assembly in July 1950, he said that there was no hope of balancing the budget unless funds were supplied by the Bonn government. The deficit of $156,000,000 was caused by the burden imposed on the treasury by the blockade, aid for refugees, help for the unemployed (about 270,000 out of about 2,000,000 persons in West Berlin), and other emergency expenditures. This crisis was met with funds mainly from the German Federal Republic and the United States, which through the Economic Cooperation Administration, by October 1951 had given $95,000,000 in direct aid and $80,000,000 in long-term investment funds.

Acceptance of more economic responsibility for West Berlin by the Bonn government was indicated when the West German Bundestag passed a law in December 1951 which drew the city into the Federal Republic financially. Suhr praised the Bonn government for its "intelligent cooperation" and said that the law had been made possible by a "true compromise between all the authorities involved." By 1953 the West German government was providing the city with about $250,000,000 annually.

Under the Berlin Constitution of October 1, 1950, a House of Representatives with 200 seats was established; it elects the mayor who heads the Senate, the executive branch of the government. "The Berlin House of Representatives became one of the most peculiar parliaments in the world," Suhr wrote. "Since the Berlin Constitution does not differentiate between East and West Berlin, some representatives from the East have been elected in the West, courageous men and women who still live and work in the East sector, but who have identified themselves with the freedom of the West. . . . The Berlin House of Representatives has made allowance for the population of East Berlin to be represented in the city parliament [seventy-three seats are reserved]. The house, therefore, can still claim to be the mouthpiece for the population of Berlin as a whole, with special emphasis on its function as a forum for freedom" (Washington *Post and Times Herald*, December 26, 1954).

After the December 1950 elections, in which the Social Democrats gained 45 per cent of the votes, the House of Representatives made Suhr its president. When Ernst Reuter, the mayor and leader of West Berlin, died on September 29, 1953, Suhur was nominated by the Social Democrats as their candidate for mayor. The right-wing parties, the Christian Democrats and the Free Democrats, formed a coalition, however, and elected Walther Schreiber, a Christian Democrat, as mayor by a slight majority on October 22, 1953. Suhr remained president of the House.

In an interview with the late Anne O'Hare McCormick (New York *Times*, September 2, 1953), Suhr said that "the morale of the Berliners reached an all-time high following the June 1953 risings in the East zone." While the spirit of resistance was strong in 1948 and 1949 during the air-lift, it sagged in 1952 and then rose in 1953. This was in spite of the fact that West Berlin then had 230,000 unemployed and 400,000 (including the old, sick and impoverished pensioners) on the relief rolls. By October 1955 unemployment had dropped to 115,000.

In the 1954 elections, the Socialists won a majority of the votes in the city parliament. Suhr was elected on January 11, 1955 by 104 to 18 votes as Mayor of Berlin. The Social Democrats and the Christian Democrats had agreed to run the city government on a coalition basis in order to present a united front to the Communist regime in East Berlin. The Senate is composed of six Social Democrat and five Christian Democrat councilors.

During reports of "despondency" in West Berlin and of a visit there by Theodor Heuss, president of the Federal Republic of Germany, to raise morale, Suhr started in February 1955 a campaign to reduce the number of persons unemployed (about 185,000). By getting the Bonn government to rule that 3 to 4 per cent of all business arising out of public contracts must be handled in West Berlin, he believes that serious unemployment can be prevented. Certain Bonn measures already help the city—tax relief of various kinds, government loans and capital investments on terms considered too risky elsewhere, and the financing of work relief projects. The U.S. Foreign Operations Administration plans to provide about $57,000,000 in counterpart funds for West Berlin in 1955.

Suhr has been a director of the Deutsches Institut für Wirtschaftsforschung and was the director of the Deutsche Hochschule für Politik in Berlin from 1948 until 1955. He is an honorary professor at the Freie Universität Berlin. He belongs to numerous educational and political organizations. The Federal Republic of Germany decorated him in 1954 for his political work.

He is the author of several books on economics and the position of workers, including *Die Organisation der Unternehmer* (Berlin, 1924), *Die Welt der Wirtschaft vom Standort des Arbeiters* (Jena, 1925), *Die Lebenshaltung der Angestellten* (Berlin, 1928), *Die Angestellten in der Wirtschaft* (with others; Berlin, 1928), and *Die Tarifverträge der Angestellten* (Berlin, 1928). His articles have appeared in numerous newspapers and in the German encyclopedia, *Der Grosse Brockhaus*. He edited *Die Sozialistische Jahrhundert*, a newspaper, after World War II.

(Continued next page)

SUHR, OTTO—*Continued*

He married Susanne Pavel, a librarian and editor, in 1921. Mayor Suhr has gray eyes and blond hair. He weighs 175 pounds and is five feet ten inches tall. His favorite recreation is collecting books and engravings on old Berlin. He has a pet dachshund.

References

N Y Times p14 O 13 '53
International Who's Who, 1954
Wer ist Wer? (1955)

SULLIVAN, FRANCIS L(OFTUS) Jan. 6, 1903- Actor

Address: b. c/o Henry Miller Theatre, 124 W. 43d St., New York 36; c/o J. F. Sullivan, 29 The Chase, Clapham Common, London S.W. 4, England

Having portrayed some seventy characters on the screen and many stage roles in his native London, Francis L. Sullivan has in recent years become known to American audiences as the lawyer Jaggers in the Hollywood film version of Dickens' *Great Expectations* and as Mr. Bumble in *Oliver Twist.* On the New York stage he won the Antoinette Perry ("Tony") award for best featured performance (announced March 27, 1955) in the role of Sir Wilfrid Robarts, Queen's Counsel, in Agatha Christie's melodrama *Witness for the Prosecution,* which opened in December 1954 and is playing to capacity audiences at the Henry Miller Theatre. The actor, who is above-average in height and weight, is also familiar to television viewers.

Francis Loftus Sullivan was born to Michael and Gertrude (Wilson) Sullivan in London, England on January 6, 1903. He was educated at Neuchâtel in Switzerland and at Stonyhurst College, a Jesuit boys' school in Lancashire. In 1920 he spent six months preparing for a career as a civil engineer before he turned, with his parents' consent, to the stage.

Shortly after he was eighteen years old he appeared at the Royal Victoria Hall ("Old Vic") in London on April 16, 1921 as the Pursuivant and Messenger in Shakespeare's *Richard III.* He continued to act subsidiary roles in the classic repertory company, directed by Robert Atkins, until June 1922, when he joined Charles Doran's Shakespearean troupe. He later understudied Matheson Lang, and in 1924, as Major Crespin in William Archer's *The Green Goddess,* toured Great Britain.

Even in his early twenties Sullivan had become "massive in girth and imposing in height," a size which rendered him effective in the role of Great Big Little Panther in the Yuletide revival of J. M. Barrie's *Peter Pan* in December 1924 at the Adelphi Theatre, London. With Sybil Thorndike he toured during 1925 in Bernard Shaw's *Saint Joan,* appearing as Warwick. For a year he was a member of the Charles Macdona company at the Regent Theatre, London, acting in a succession of Bernard Shaw plays. This was followed by a season at the Manchester Repertory Theatre, where he played leading roles; in Shaw repertory at the Little Theatre, London in 1927: as Sempronius in Shakespeare's *Timon of Athens* at the Stratford-on-Avon Memorial Theatre in 1928; and as successor to Charles Laughton in Agatha Christie's *Alibi* for a year on tour.

Sullivan made his American stage debut at the Maxine Elliott Theatre, New York on September 25, 1929 as Stanley Rosel in Monckton Hoffe's play *Many Waters,* which ran for 109 performances. "Notably good," was the comment of Brooks Atkinson in the New York *Times* on Sullivan's portrayal of the "brutal business partner" of the leading character.

Returning to London, Sullivan played the role of Thésée in Racine's *Phèdre,* presented in French at the Arts Theatre. In September 1930 he joined the repertory company at the Embassy Theatre Swiss Cottage, London, where he acted as Frederic in Somerset Maugham's play *Home and Beauty,* Mester Johannes in *The Witch* (adapted by John Masefield from the Danish of H. Wiers-Jenssen), and Hercule Poirot in Agatha Christie's *Black Coffee.* His performance in the latter play, when it moved to St. Martin's Theatre on April 9, 1931, was described by *The Times* (London) as "engrossing," played with "zest and versatility." In June he played in Louis Weitzenkorn's American newspaper drama *Five Star Final* (English title, *Late Night Final*).

"After that," Sullivan later remarked to a writer for *Theatre World* (March 1935), "unctious villains came my way." In 1931 he made his motion picture debut as the villain in the Twickenham film *The Missing Rembrandt* (based on one of the Sherlock Holmes stories). Not in the "unctious villain" category, however, was his portrayal of the great lexicographer Dr. Samuel Johnson in G. K. Chesterton's play, *The Judgment of Dr. Johnson,* at the Arts Theatre on January 20, 1932.

His King Henry VIII in *Fire,* a play by Ernita Lascelles presented at the Fortune Theatre, London on March 2, 1932 was a "facetious" rather than a sinister monarch (*The Times,* London.) At the Embassy Theatre on November 21, 1932, Sullivan as Canon Ronder shared acting honors with Baliol Holloway in *The Cathedral,* Hugh Walpole's dramatization of his novel of "petty intrigues and ecclesiastical jealousies." During 1933 and in early 1934 Sullivan was seen in three other London productions, all short-lived.

Called to Hollywood in 1934, he made his American film debut as Jaggers in the Universal Pictures production of Dickens' *Great Expectations.* That year he also acted in the Gaumont-British film version of Lion Feuchtwanger's novel *Jud Süss.* Among other pre-World War II British films in which Sullivan appeared were *Red Wagon, Chu Chin Chow, The Return of Bulldog Drummond,* and A. J. Cronin's *The Citadel.*

Subsequent roles played on the London stage by Sullivan were as Gorotchenko in Jacques Deval's comedy *Tovarich* (1935); Claudius in Shakespeare's *Hamlet* (1937) at the Old Vic; as Oscar Wilde in Leslie and Sewell Stokes' play (1938); as Hercule Poirot in Agatha Christie's *Peril at End House* (1940); as Bottom the Weaver in *A Midsummer Night's Dream* (1940), and as the bewigged Mr. Crispin in *The Man With Red Hair* (1942).

In the Gabriel Pascal filming of Bernard Shaw's *Caesar and Cleopatra* (1946), Sullivan was cast as Pothinus. Bosley Crowther (New York *Times*) found that he portrayed this scheming courtier "with shrewd finesse." The actor's second screen portrayal of the lawyer Jaggers in *Great Expectations* was first viewed in London, and then in New York in May 1947, when Howard Barnes (New York *Herald Tribune*) commented on the "rotund malevolence" of this Jaggers.

Sullivan was next seen in the British film *The Man Within,* based on the novel by Graham Greene and released in April 1947. In the Cineguild version of Dickens' *Oliver Twist,* Sullivan was Mr. Bumble. The film was shown in England in 1948 and in the United States on July 30, 1951. Bosley Crowther thought Sullivan "tremendous as . . . the workhouse warden who is full of stupidity and greed."

Duet for Two Hands, the melodrama by Mary Hayley Bell in which Sullivan made his second New York stage appearance, at the Booth Theatre on October 7, 1947, was a quick failure despite his deft characterization of a surgeon with a twisted mentality. The British actor then went to Hollywood, where he portrayed the "fat, corrupt" Bishop of Beauvais in the Ingrid Bergman film *Joan of Arc* (1948), the "flamboyant" tenor Perami in *Broken Journey* (1949), and Colonel Omicron in *The Red Danube,* in which he "shines magnificently." He portrayed Phil Mosseross, a night club proprietor, in *Night and the City* (1950), filmed in London for Twentieth Century-Fox. In London Sullivan was also seen as the barrister, Sir Robert Morton, in the British film version of Terence Rattigan's *The Winslow Boy.*

With the advent of television the British actor came into demand in both the United States and England. For the New York *Times,* May 22, 1949, he wrote an informative article on the differences of technique in TV drama in the two countries. When Nicholas Joy retired from the role of Pothinus in the Sir Cedric Hardwicke-Lilli Palmer revival of *Caesar and Cleopatra* at the National Theatre, New York in March 1950, Sullivan succeeded him briefly. Films in which Sullivan was seen between 1951 and 1954 include *Behave Yourself, My Favorite Spy, Sangaree, Plunder in the Sun, Drums of Tahiti,* and *Caribbean.* Among his later films are *The Prodigal* and *Hell's Island.*

Returning to the New York stage on December 16, 1954 in *Witness for the Prosecution,* he gave a performance "in the grand manner" as Sir Wilfrid Robarts, Q.C., "swinging his vast bulk . . . with the lazy good humor that masks a shrewd operator" (William Hawkins in the New York *World-Telegram and Sun*). Walter F. Kerr of the New York *Herald Tribune* found his "sighs,, grunts, mumbles and snorts . . . delectable," while to Brooks Atkinson of the New York *Times,* "Francis L. Sullivan, corpulent, bland, Mephistophelean" was "a show in his own right."

Bender

FRANCIS L. SULLIVAN

In 1935 Sullivan married Frances Joan Perkins, the daughter of a Yorkshire solicitor. His wife is a designer, known professionally as Danaë Gaylen. The actor, whose once jet-black hair is now graying and thinning, stands six feet two inches tall and weighs around 260 pounds. Criminology has long been one of his hobbies. Swimming is mentioned as his favorite physical recreation. Both the Sullivans are animal-lovers, and wherever they have lived, they have kept dogs (especially Welsh corgis). On December 27, 1954 Sullivan became a naturalized U.S. citizen.

References

N Y Herald Tribune IV p 1 D 12 '54
N Y Sunday News p92+ My 8 '55 pors
N Y Times II p7 My 11 '47; II p3 Je 4 '50
N Y World-Telegram p20 Mr 4 '55 pors
Motion Picture and Television Almanac, 1953-54
Who's Who, 1954
Who's Who in the Theatre (1952)

SUMAC, YMA (ē'mä) Sept. 10, 1927- Singer

Address: b. c/o Yma Sumac Enterprises, 3065 McConnell Dr., W., Los Angeles 64, Calif.

Probably no other singer before the public today has received more flamboyant publicity than Yma Sumac, who specializes in Peruvian songs. She has been described as a Brooklynite who spelled her name Amy Camus backwards, and as an Inca princess directly descended from Atahualpa, the last emperor of the Inca Empire. Imaginative publicity writers have

YMA SUMAC

shrouded her past in mystery, have set her aside as one of the chosen "Golden Virgins," a Sun worshiper, and marked her singing as the work of Indian sorcerers evoking from her throat the spirits of birds and jaguars. Her good looks and dignity, her use of heavy Peruvian silver and gold jewelry of ancient design, and, most of all, her remarkable vocal range from deep contralto to coloratura high C's have brought her world renown.

She has sung in night clubs, the Hollywood Bowl, concert halls in South America and Europe, in Washington, D.C. at Constitution Hall, and in New York at Carnegie Hall and the Lewisohn Stadium. Her concert in Carnegie Hall in February 1954 was acclaimed by Virgil Thomson, who wrote in the New York *Herald Tribune* (February 18, 1954): "The Peruvian vocalist (all at the same time a female baritone, a lyric soprano and a high coloratura)" has a voice of "great beauty, and her vocal technique is impeccable. She sings very low and warm, very high and bird-like; and her middle range is no less lovely than the extremes of her scale. That scale is very close to four octaves, but it is in no way inhuman or outlandish in sound."

Capitol Records has sold well over a million of her albums (4,000,000 records), the first of which, *Voice of Xtabay*, was released in 1950, *Mambo*, in 1953 and *Legend of the Sun Virgins*, in 1954. In the fall of 1955 she appeared for a six-week engagement at the Hotel Pierre in New York City.

A Peruvian, of Indian and Spanish forebears, Yma Sumac is a native of the little highland village of Ichocan, some 12,000 feet up the side of Mt. Cumbemayta, in the Department of Cajamarca. She was born Emperatriz Chavarri on September 10, 1927, the last and sixth child of Imma (Sumack Emilia Atahualpa) Chavarri her full-blooded Indian mother, and Sixto Chavarri, her mixed Indian and Spanish father. She was brought up as a Quechuan and she participated in Indian festivals from early childhood. The Andes abound in colorful religious and secular celebrations, many of them dating back to Inca times. The most famous of these was the Inti Raymi, held in June at the time of the winter solstice. An article in Lima's *La Cronica*, states that it was at such a festival that Yma was heard by a government employee. He passed news of her voice along to the Ministry of Education, which eventually brought the family to Lima. Yma was presented in a concert and entered in the Instituto de Santa Teresa, a Catholic school for girls.

A year before Yma's arrival in Lima, Moises Vivanco, musician, composer, and director of the Peruvian National Board of Broadcasting, had formed the Compañia Peruana de Arte, a group of forty-six Indian dancers, singers and musicians. On hearing the young girl sing, he invited her to join his company, but her mother would not consent. Yma, however, was interested. On the pretext of attending night classes with an older sister, Yma rehearsed regularly with the Moises' Compañia and with them made her radio debut early in 1942. Her family then permitted her to go to Buenos Aires as star of the Compañia when it appeared there in April over Radio Belgrano.

Vivanco and Miss Sumac were married on June 6, 1942 in a civil ceremony in the city of Arequipa, at the foot of El Misti, famed Andean peak. After the wedding, the troupe played in theatres, night clubs, concert halls, and over radio networks in Rio de Janeiro, Buenos Aires and Mexico City. They arrived in New York in January 1946, the company reduced to three members, Moises, Yma, and her cousin Cholita Rivero, and sought engagements as the Inca Taky Trio.

At the start, the group found North America cold to their folk art and indifferent to the music of ancient Peru. From 1946 through 1949 there were spot engagements in night clubs such as New York's Blue Angel, a concert at the Peruvian Embassy in Washington, D.C., on radio's *We the People*, and twice on Arthur Godfrey's TV show, where Yma's and Cholita's costumes showed to fine advantage. In going to New York, Miss Sumac had counted on the sponsorship of opera singer Grace Moore, who, stopping over in Lima on a concert tour in 1941, had heard Yma sing and offered to assist her in the United States. Miss Moore's death in an airplane crash shortly after Yma's arrival in New York, cancelled this invaluable backing. Instead, the group discovered the famous "Borscht Circuit" in the Catskill resort area of New York state for a welcome eight-week booking.

It was during these lean years that Yma bore her son, Papuchka ("Charlie"), on February 7, 1949, and Vivanco gave up his art to go into the fish business. He abandoned this work when bookings came through for Montreal and Havana, which led at last to the Hollywood Bowl.

She attained recognition in the United States as the immediate result of a single record album made by Capitol Records. In order to market an album by an unknown singer with a vocal span of four octaves, imitating birds and kettle drums, singing ancient Peruvian melodies in the tongue-twisting Quechua Indian language, Capital decided to title it *Voice of Xtabay* (there is no such word in Quechua or any other language) and to feature a story about the mysterious Inca princess. With no advertising other than a three-inch item in an obscure journal, the album sold 500,000 copies "overnight." The issuance of the album preceded Miss Sumac's notable performance at the Hollywood Bowl, where she was heard by a huge audience including many representatives of the film industry, invited by N. Peter Rathvon, head of RKO production. (Rathvon had her in mind for the lead in a film version of Hudson's *Green Mansions*, which was never produced.)

Other eminent singers have had ranges equal to Yma Sumac's. Since there is but a limited repertoire for the four voice range, these performers usually confine themselves to the single range in which they feel most at home. Yma, however, uses all ranges, gliding from one to the other with apparent ease. Her repertoire is composed for her by her husband and is derived from ancient Andean folk themes, rich in their abundance and variety. Among these compositions are *Accla Taqui* (Dance of the Chosen Maidens), *Choladas* (Dance of the Moon Festival), *Tumpá* (The Earthquake). Rather than authentic Inca music, this is music in modern form reminiscent of the days of Peruvian pomp and splendor.

Subsequent to her Hollywood Bowl success, Yma appeared in a Broadway musical *Flahooley* as an Arabian sorceress, on radio and TV shows, at Las Vegas nightclubs, at New York's Roxy Theatre with featured billing under Danny Kaye, and in concerts in London, Paris, and other major cities of three continents.

She would like to sing at the "Met" but she told Art Buchwald (New York *Herald Tribune*, April 22, 1954), "I want to show the world what I can do with my voice. Why not opera? But if you only appear three or four times a year, how can you live? I'd have to sing popular songs . . . on television in order to pay the rent." She has sung *The Magic Flute, Lakmé* and *La Traviata* in South American concerts and includes arias in her regular programs. In Naples the Italian audiences liked her operatic work so much that they applauded for twenty minutes.

Of her appearance in the Paramount motion picture *Secret of the Incas*, released on May 30, 1954, the Washington *Post and Times Herald* reviewer wrote: "Wherever she was born, Yma Sumac behaves righteously as a faithful Inca princess. This allows the sound track to pick up some of her notorious thrusts at the sound barrier." The *Christian Science Monitor*'s movie critic observed: "One striking figure emerges, that of Yma Sumac, the Peruvian singer . . . both the upper and lower reaches [of her voice] are exploited here, along with her darkly dramatic appearance."

Virgil Thomson described her as "a pretty young woman with a very, very fine voice, a pleasing personality and a perfect ear. . . . If her mental capacities are even reasonably comparable to her musical gifts, she belongs in the great houses of opera" (New York *Herald Tribune*, February 18, 1954).

She became an American citizen in July 1955. She has dark hair and stands five feet three inches tall.

References

Colliers 127:18+ Ap 14 '51 pors
Los Angeles Times IV p1+ D 16 '51
Time 56:58 Ag 28 '50 por

SUMNER, JAMES B(ATCHELLER)

Nov. 19, 1887-Aug. 12, 1955 Biochemist; shared Nobel Prize in chemistry in 1946 for isolating the first enzyme "urease", in 1926 at Cornell University where he was an assistant professor for fifteen years; promoted to full professor in 1929; retired on July 1, 1955; author of many articles on enzymes in the *Journal of Biological Chemistry* and several textbooks. See *Current Biography* (Jan.) 1947.

Obituary

N Y Times p13 Ag 13 '55

SUTHERLAND, GRAHAM (VIVIAN)

Aug. 24, 1903- English painter
Address: White House, Trottiscliffe, West Malling, Kent, England

When Parliament decided to present Sir Winston Churchill with his portrait in honor of his eightieth birthday, the House of Commons commissioned Graham Sutherland, considered by art critic Sir Kenneth Clark "the outstanding British painter of his generation," to do the painting. Another English art critic, Sir Herbert Read, characterizes Sutherland as "the first English painter since Turner to take up an independent position and maintain it with conviction. . ."

Essentially a painter of "thorny" landscapes, he has more recently turned to portraiture. His portrait of W. Somerset Maugham in 1949 and of Lord Beaverbrook in 1950 were widely praised. The selection of Sutherland to do Sir Winston's portrait was acclaimed by art critics not only as "a triumph for the kind of imaginative painting that Sutherland stands for; it was also a remarkable index of a swing in taste in a strong-hold of tradition" (Eric Newton, New York *Times*, December 5, 1954).

When the portrait was presented to the Prime Minister on November 30, 1954 at Westminster Hall, it provoked strong reactions, both for and against Sutherland's interpretation. A Conservative member of the House of Commons found the portrait "ill-mannered and terrible." A Socialist member of Parliament, on the other hand, called it "a splendid legacy to posterity." Sir Winston himself publicly called it a great example of modern art, and at a private viewing before the public unveiling, remarked: "It makes me look half-witted, which I ain't."

(Continued next page)

British Inf. Service

GRAHAM SUTHERLAND

In the storm of controversy that ensued, the artist stood his ground. "The portrait is my idea of Churchill—he who stopped the enemy," declared Graham Sutherland. "He is sitting in a chair in what I think is a typically Churchillian pose—bull-dogged, you know. I painted what I saw. I don't paint pretty pictures just to win applause." When criticized because the feet were omitted from the portrait, the artist said that the feet once were in the painting, but he thought that they destroyed the balance of the head and hands and so he painted them out. Leading London art critics such as Eric Newton praised the portrait as "a masterpiece."

For his own fiftieth birthday, in 1953, Sutherland was honored by three large retrospective shows—at the Tate Gallery in London, the Curt Valentin Gallery in New York, and the Boston Institute of Contemporary Art. These forty-nine canvases, showing his preoccupation with organic forms and semi-abstract landscapes, were subsequently exhibited in major cities of the United States.

The son of G. H. V. Sutherland, a civil servant and lawyer, and of his wife, Elsie, Graham Vivian Sutherland was born in London August 24, 1903. "Raised in middle-class comfort," according to *Time*, he lived until he was nine either in Surrey, at Merton Park, or in Sussex, at Rustington. Edward Sackville-West, writing on the painter for the Penguin Modern Painters Series (1943), reports that the boy was placed in boarding school at Sutton when he was twelve, passing his vacations at Swanage, "from which time he dates that mysterious intimacy with nature which has since developed into the basis of his art."

That period also revealed Sutherland's aptitude for Greek and Latin, just as a subsequent period at Epsom College, to which he was sent at the age of fourteen, revealed his incapacity for scientific study, on which the curriculum emphasis was placed. For four years there, wrote Sackville-West, the boy was "miserable," so miserable that he began to draw for consolation, with the result that by the time he was seventeen, he had had several landscapes put on exhibition at the Royal Academy. He was apprenticed to the engineering department of the Midland Railway Works in Derby, where a year of mechanical drafting convinced him of his true vocation.

Enrolling at Goldsmiths' School of Art, a branch of the University of London in New Cross, he studied art from 1919 to 1925. From this developed Sutherland's fourteen-year excursion into the graphic arts. Sales of his etchings started in 1925 when his first one-man show at the Twenty-one Gallery was held. He was encouraged to establish himself independently in London, where he taught evening classes in Kingston. From 1927 until the beginning of World War II, he was on the staff of the Chelsea School of Art, producing his etchings in academic style. Of those which he exhibited with the London Group and the Salon d'Automne between 1930 and 1934, Sackville-West singles out particularly *Pastoral*, as displaying "clearly some elements of his mature vision and method." He gradually made the transition from etcher to painter.

In 1935 he began to teach book illustration at the Chelsea School and to branch out into commercial art, designing posters for the Shell-Mex Company, the Orient Line, and the London Transport Company, as well as ceramics, china, designs for wallpapers, rugs and fabrics for other concerns.

The four years from 1936, when he contributed to the International Surrealist Exhibition, to 1940 resulted in the canvases *Red Tree, Rocky Landscape with Cairn, Green Tree Form, Black Landscape, Gorse on the Seawall,* painted at Trottiscliffe (near Maidstone), where he had moved in 1937. Some of these were shown at the Memes, Rosenberg, and Helft galleries, London, in 1938.

Sackville-West discerned in Sutherland's paintings the influence of William Blake and "a quality unique in modern landscape painting —an expression of doom and foreboding."

Bombed Wales supplied Sutherland with the subject matter of the big devastation pictures shown at the Leicester Galleries in 1940, "terrible in their accurate and ruthless virtuosity." He became a salaried artist with the War Artists Advisory Committee in 1941. His work was exhibited in a three-man show, with Henry Moore's and John Piper's, at the Leicester Galleries in 1943. His first postwar shows were held in London at the Reid, Lefevre, Redfern galleries.

His first one-man exhibition in the United States was held at New York's Buchholz Gallery in March 1946. While praising Sutherland as a colorist, the New York *Herald Tribune* critic wished he had been less original and more communicative. The New York *Times* critic also had serious reservations about the thirty pictures shown, and expressed himself as "gravely disappointed." Henry McBride of the New York *Sun*, on the other hand, found that Sutherland "built his eye-music as steadily as Bach might have done." His second Buchholz show, held in November 1948, of canvases produced during his sojourns in the south of France, also received praise from McBride.

Other critics dissented, Sam Hunter of the New York *Times* noting "a gratuitous morbidity," and the *Art News* critic expressing a sentiment that Sutherland had "lost his bearings in a clash of emotion and intellect." During that year, too, some of the same paintings were shown at the Hanover Gallery in London, the Galerie Drouin in Paris, and at the Museum of Modern Art in Brussels.

In the meantime, Sutherland had completed one of his major works, the *Crucifixion*, commissioned for St. Matthew's Church in Northampton, England, and unveiled on November 16, 1946. In his monograph, *Graham Sutherland* (1950), Robert Melville wrote: "Sutherland alone has found an appropriate iconographical conception into which to cast his sense of the fearful things done by man to man . . . and his crucified Christ contains the eloquent protest of a man who has examined with wonderment and pity the photos of Buchenwald, Auschwitz, and Belsen."

Ever wider international recognition came to Sutherland in the ensuing years: with other British painters he exhibited at the Stedelijk Museum in Amsterdam (1949) and in an individual retrospective show there (1953); another retrospective show was held at the Institute of Contemporary Arts in London (1950) and the same year at the Hanover Gallery there, while two more retrospectives honored him in 1952, one at the Musée National d'Art Moderne in Paris and another at the Venice Biennale that year, at which an international jury awarded him the acquisition prize contributed by the Museum of Modern Art in São Paulo, Brazil.

Other work dating from this period were tapestries for the Edinburgh Tapestry Company (1949) and for the reconstructed cathedral at Coventry (in work, 1952-present). Another commission was for the large painting *Land*, shown at the Festival of Britain in 1951 and later acquired by the Tate Gallery.

Forty-nine of his paintings were exhibited at the Curt Valentin Gallery in New York in 1953 and jointly with a group of Henry Moore's sculptures at the Boston Institute of Contemporary Art. Commenting on the recurrent thorn tree motif in his work, Dorothy Adlow, in the *Christian Science Monitor*, praised his "exhilarating" color and his "boldly assertive style." Aline B. Louchheim of the New York *Times* observed "a drier, more literary, thinner" quality. The same group of paintings was shown at the Tate Gallery under the auspices of the Arts Council of Great Britain.

His capabilities as a portraitist were evident in his portrait in 1949 of W. Somerset Maugham "looking like some hieratic, sophisticated dinosaur" and described by the novelist himself as "magnificent," and in his portrait in 1950 of Lord Beaverbrook, "impishly grinning." In 1954 a group of members of Parliament commissioned him to do the presentation portrait in honor of Sir Winston Churchill's eightieth birthday. Sutherland consented rather hesitantly, according to Eric Newton, British art historian and art critic for *Time & Tide* (London), in an article devoted to the portrait in the New York *Times Magazine* (December 5, 1954). The first of eight sittings took place in August 1954.

Unveiled on November 30, the "life-sized, seated figure on a canvas fifty-seven inches high and forty-eight and a half inches wide," showed the Prime Minister upright in his chair, "liable at any moment to rise to his feet." Churchill, wearing his customary Parliamentary clothes of black jacket and striped trousers, against a plain greenish-yellow background, presents the dual aspect of "a bulldog and a cherub."

Newton observes, "The portrait is certainly a masterpiece. . . . It has what all great portraits should have . . . a sense of timelessness together with a sense of immediacy. Here, one feels, is an unusually complex character summed up. . . . The attitude is casual, but the effect is monumental."

Commenting on the omission of the feet in the Churchill portrait, G. S. Whittet in *Studio* (April 1955) wrote: "It makes a distraction . . . but the portrait must rank as a strong and outstanding study of character."

A striking example of Sutherland's designs in crystal was included in an exhibition in April 1954 at Steuben Glass, 718 Fifth Avenue, New York City, of a collection of the work of twenty British artists. A pear-shaped vase of clear crystal, with Sutherland's drawing of a praying mantis engraved on it, attracted much attention.

Paintings by Sutherland belong to the permanent exhibitions of the Tate Gallery (of which he was a trustee from 1949 to 1954), the British Museum, the Victoria and Albert Museum, the Exeter New Museum, the Aberystwyth Museum, and the Museum of Modern Art in New York. In 1942 he supplied the illustrations for David Gascoyne's *Poems*.

While a student at Goldsmiths', Graham Sutherland met Kathleen Frances Barry whom he married in 1928. He "divides his time," reports *Time*, "between the sun-swept luxury of the Riviera and the box-hedged comfort of his home in Kent." Lean and elegant, Sutherland strikes *Vogue* as being "a rather sunny man, intelligent, well-dressed, and somewhat extroverted." The main effect of Sutherland's art can be summed up in his own description of his thorn trees: "A sort of paraphrase of the Crucifixion—the cruelty."

References

Time 62:46 Ag 3 '53

Melville, R. Graham Sutherland (1950)

Sackville-West, E. Graham Sutherland (1943)

Who's Who (1954)

SWEENEY, JAMES JOHNSON May 30, 1900- Art museum director; author

Address: b. c/o Solomon R. Guggenheim Museum, 1071 Fifth Ave., New York 28; h. 120 East End Ave., New York 28

Since James Johnson Sweeney took over the directorship of the Solomon R. Guggenheim Museum in New York City in 1952, this museum has become, in the opinion of *Time*, "one of the . . . best showcases of modern art." The museum, formerly known as the Museum of Non-Objective Painting, has, under Sweeney's guidance, embarked upon an ambitious new program to broaden its activities beyond the exclusive preoccupation with "non-objective" art. "We want to present an inspirational stimulant by showing the high points of what is going on in the world of modern art," Sweeney has explained.

Described by one museum director as "the most respected American authority on the art of the avant-garde," Sweeney has organized many exhibitions of modern art both in the United States and abroad. He is the author of a number of books and articles, and has lectured widely at universities and museums. From 1945 to 1946 he was director of the Museum of Modern Art's department of painting and sculpture.

Born in Brooklyn, New York on May 30, 1900, James Johnson Sweeney is the son of Patrick M. and Mary (Johnson) Sweeney. The family originally came from Donegal, Ireland. His father was the founder and head of a large rug, lace, and textile importing firm. His mother was deeply interested in art. "I grew up regarding painting . . . as a normal, natural activity," Sweeney has explained in *Catholic Authors*. "While I never aspired to be a painter myself I always drew for my own pleasure and was always interested in how painters produced their work."

At the end of World War I, Sweeney was attending the Field Artillery Officers' Training School at Camp Zachary Taylor, in Louisville, Kentucky. Four years later he received his B.A. degree from Georgetown University in Washington, D.C. From 1922 to 1924 he did graduate work in literature at Jesus College, Cambridge University. He played guard on the football team at Georgetown and on the Rugby team for Jesus College; as shot putter he established undergraduate records at both institutions. In 1925 he studied at the Sorbonne in Paris, and the following year he spent at the University of Siena in Italy.

During this period Sweeney wrote verse, some of which was published by the poet Æ (George Russell) in the *Irish Statesman*. At Cambridge, Sweeney met I. A. Richards, from whom he learned "a great deal about criticism and aesthetics." Later, from 1935 to 1938, he served as associate editor of the avant-garde Paris magazine *Transition*, which published part of James Joyce's *Finnegans Wake* serially. In this connection, Sweeney read Joyce's manuscript back to him and wrote in Joyce's additions and corrections.

While Sweeney was attending Cambridge University, he became interested in Matisse and Picasso. His professor introduced him to Roger Fry, the foremost British art critic of that time. His copious reading, plus personal contact with many of the leading modern artists in Paris, served to quicken Sweeney's perceptions concerning art. His article praising modern painting was published in the *Irish Statesman* and his defense of Modigliani and of Rouault appeared in the Sunday art page of the New York *Times*, whose art critic, Edward Alden Jewell, introduced him to other editors.

He was soon writing art criticism for a number of periodicals, including the Chicago *Evening Post*, from 1931 to 1932. He arranged exhibitions of twentieth century painting and sculpture for the Renaissance Society of the University of Chicago in 1933 and 1934. These lectures were published in book form under the title, *Plastic Redirections in 20th Century Painting*. According to one critic, this work "set a new standard of scholarly precision and critical penetration."

Between 1935 and 1940 Sweeney was visiting lecturer at the Institute of Fine Arts at New York University. He spent about half of his time abroad, some of it in Ireland, where he rented a castle in the summer. These trips were undertaken primarily in the interest of his father's business.

On January 29, 1945 Sweeney was appointed director of the department of painting and sculpture at the Museum of Modern Art in New York. As a member of the museum's advisory committee, he had directed three of its exhibitions: "African Negro Art" (1935), the Joan Miró retrospective (1941), and "Alexander Calder: Sculpture and Constructions" (1943). At the time of his appointment, he was preparing the museum's memorial exhibition of the works of Piet Mondriaan. He organized the museum's exhibitions of work by Stuart Davis (1945), Marc Chagall (1946), and Henry Moore (1946).

When a coordination committee composed of five staff members was named in September 1946 to take administrative responsibility for the major divisions of the museum's activities, Sweeney maintained that it was impossible to function as director within the framework of the new setup, and submitted his resignation, which was formally announced, "with regret," by the president of the museum on November 1, 1946.

In 1947 Sweeney directed the "Alfred Stieglitz Exhibition: Photographic Work and Collection" for the Museum of Modern Art, organized an exhibition of Picasso's work for the Art Gallery of Toronto in 1949 and a show of Calder's sculpture at the Massachusetts Institute of Technology in 1950. He served as one-man jury and director of the Virginia Museum of Fine Arts' biennial survey of contemporary American painting in 1950 and as visiting scholar for the Richmond Area University Center he lectured on this controversial show in various parts of the state. From 1950 to 1951 he was a resident scholar in the art department of the University of Georgia.

During the summers of 1947 and 1948 Sweeney went abroad as visiting lecturer at the Harvard Seminar on American Studies, in Salzburg, Austria. In 1950-51 he gave a fortnightly radio broadcast on art, literature, and the theatre over Radio Eireann, in Dublin. He was responsible for the "Masterpieces of the 20th Century" exhibition, which was shown at the Musée National d'Art Moderne in Paris and the Tate Gallery in London in 1952, and later in the same year he selected an exhibition of Calder's sculpture for the United States Pavilion at the Venice Biennial Exposition. In December 1953 he was a member of the nine-man prize award jury for the second biennial International Exhibition of Modern Art held by the Museum of Modern Art in São Paulo, Brazil.

It was announced on October 14, 1952 that Sweeney had been appointed director of the Solomon R. Guggenheim Museum, formerly the Museum of Non-Objective Painting. It is operated by the Solomon R. Guggenheim Foundation, which had been set up in June 1937 for "the promotion and encouragement of art and education in art and the enlightenment of the public, especially in the field of art" and specifically concerning the branch of abstract art called "non-objective," which altogether dispenses with any attempt to reproduce objects from nature.

A noted philanthropist and mining executive, Solomon R. Guggenheim had become interested in "non-objective" art in the late 1920's, and by 1939 had acquired nearly 800 paintings. His art adviser in assembling this collection was Baroness Hilla Rebay, herself a painter of the "non-objective" school. She served as director of the Museum of Non-Objective Painting, which housed part of Guggenheim's collection, from its opening in June 1939 until her resignation in March 1952. During his lifetime, Guggenheim gave the foundation more than $3,000,000. When he died in 1949, he bequeathed to it his entire collection (by then numbering some 1,400 works of art), a fund of $6,000,000 to serve as an endowment, the Fifth Avenue site where the museum has its present headquarters in an old mansion, and an additional sum of $2,000,000 for the construction on this site of a seven-story, spiral-shaped museum designed by Frank Lloyd Wright.

According to *Time,* when Sweeney became the museum's director, it was "a cultist temple of non-objective art," with emphasis placed largely on the work of Kandinsky, Rudolph Bauer, and Baroness Rebay. In the opinion of Aline B. Saarinen (New York *Times*), Sweeney "symbolically as well as literally swept the place clean." The walls of the museum were painted white, all paintings were removed from distracting frames, and "second-rate paintings" were replaced by "master-works, long hidden in storage or the Guggenheim suite."

Since Sweeney assumed the directorship of the museum, there have been four exhibitions devoted to showing selections from the Guggenheim collection of chiefly representational works by pioneer figures in the modern movement. In the fall of 1953 the museum played host to a

Herbert Matter

JAMES JOHNSON SWEENEY

large retrospective show of Frank Lloyd Wright's work, and a full-scale model dwelling to illustrate Wright's residential style. The Wright exhibition attracted over 80,000 visitors in fifty-two days.

Sweeney devoted one exhibition to thirty-nine "Younger European Painters" (December 1953—April 1954), and another to fifty-four "Younger American Painters" (May—December 1954). His criteria for selection was "soundness of composition, quality of workmanship, and individuality of expression." The works finally chosen for the American exhibition were selected from over 1,000 pictures submitted by 284 artists. This show was described by Aline B. Saarinen in the New York *Times* as having provoked "more heated talk, more ardent praise, and more irate antagonism" than any other exhibition of the season. In December 1954 the museum opened the first major retrospective show of the work of Robert Delaunay ever to be held in this country.

In addition to Cézanne's *The Clock Maker,* for which $110,000 was reportedly paid, and Picasso's *Mandolin and Guitar,* the museum has recently purchased examples of work by Brancusi, Arp, Pevsner, Feininger, Malevich, and many younger artists. It has sent out paintings from its collection for extended loans to various educational institutions. Sweeney himself installed a loan exhibition of modern masters from the Guggenheim collection at the Art Gallery of Toronto in April 1954. Other current or forthcoming activities include an ambitious publications program, an art film laboratory, a library, a conservation department, and allocation of the director's time to serious consideration of the work submitted by any artist. Sweeney's desire is to maintain an intimate museum with never more than 150 paintings on view.

(Continued next page)

SWEENEY, JAMES JOHNSON—*Cont.*

In connection with the exhibitions he directed for the Museum of Modern Art, Sweeney wrote the catalogues on *Joan Miró* (1941), *Alexander Calder* (1943, revised in 1951), *Stuart Davis* (1945), *Piet Mondriaan* (1945), *Marc Chagall* (1946), and *Henry Moore* (1946). He has edited *African Negro Art* (1935) and Calder's *Three Young Rats* (1944). Together with Paul Radin, he helped prepare *African Folk Tales and Sculpture* (1952), and in collaboration with José-Luis Sert he is the author of the forthcoming book, *Antoni Gaudí.* He has been an advisory editor of *Partisan Review* since 1948, and a director of the *Burlington Magazine* since 1951, and served as a contributing critic to the *New Republic* from 1952 to 1953. In addition, he has provided the commentary for two art films, *Henry Moore* (1948) and *Images Médiévales* (1952).

Since 1948 Sweeney has been vice-president of the International Art Critics Association in Paris. He has held the posts of director (1950-1951) and vice-president (1952-1953) of the Edward MacDowell Association. Among the many organizations in which he holds membership are the Association of Art Museum Directors and the International Council of Museums. He is a fellow of the Royal Society of Antiquaries of Ireland (Dublin). His clubs are the Grolier, Century, and Players in New York and the Ccsmos in Washington, D.C.

He was married on May 17, 1927 to Laura Harden, and they have five children—Ann, Sean, Siadhal, Tadhg, and Ciannait. His church is the Roman Catholic. He has been described as a "big, powerful-looking man with large features and a deep resonant voice," and his speech is illuminated by flashing Irish wit.

His home has been called "one of the most distinguished modern apartments in New York." The furniture was designed by Mies van der Rohe and Le Corbusier; Aztec, African, and Calder sculptures, and paintings by Picasso, Léger, Miró, Klee, and Mondriaan, are arranged against a background of white walls.

References

N Y Post Mag p41 N 18 '46 por
N Y Times Mag p16 My 30 '54
New Yorker 17:20+ D 13 '41
Newsweek 25:91+ F 12 '45
Saturday Night 69:4 Ap 17 '54 por
American Catholic Who's Who, 1954-55
Directory of American Scholars (1951)
Who's Who in America, 1954-55
Who's Who in American Art (1953)

SYMES, JAMES M(ILLER) (sĭmz) July 8, 1895- Railroad president

Address: b. c/o Pennsylvania Railroad, 1617 Pennsylvania Blvd., Philadelphia 4, Pa.; h. 311 Brentford Rd., Haverford, Pa.

The Pennsylvania Railroad, fourth largest rail system in route mileage in the United States and the world's biggest carrier of freight tonnage, is headed by James M. Symes. In June 1954 he became the railroad's thirteenth president, succeeding Walter S. Franklin, in the company's 109 years of existence. During World War II Symes was in charge of the Pennsylvania's western division and after the war became vice-president in charge of operations, and executive vice-president in 1952.

Symes and his predecessor have been given much credit for the Pennsylvania's billion-dollar postwar program of modernization and rehabilitation. The Pennsylvania, with some 10,000 miles of routes, operates westward from New York through Philadelphia and Pittsburgh to Chicago and St. Louis, northward as far as the tip of Michigan, and southward into Virginia.

In September 1955 Symes announced plans for a far-flung managerial streamlining of the Pennsylvania's organization, effective November 1. He stated that the system's three regions, and eighteen divisions would be replaced by nine regions, each autonomous in operation except for top coordination and authority. Each region, he said, will be about the size of a smaller railroad. "The plan is somewhat revolutionary in the railroad industry, but is similar in many ways to the new line and staff plans of organization which some of our leading manufacturing companies have adopted in recent years" (New York *Herald Tribune,* September 29, 1955).

Born in Glen Osborne, Pennsylvania, on July 8, 1895, James Miller Symes is the son of a Pennsylvania Railroad baggage master, Frank H. Symes, and Clara (Heckert) Symes. "As a child," *Newsweek* has observed, "his heroes were the engineers who sent 'Pennsy' trains hurtling by his home," and his father, who "helped build the boy's ambitions to be a railroad man." After graduation from the high school in Sewickley near Pittsburgh in 1914, James studied for a while at the Carnegie Institute of Technology, but by 1916 had entered the Pennsylvania Railroad's trainmaster's office in Pittsburgh, where for the next four years he was occupied as a clerk or car-tracer. "Now that I look back on it," Symes recalls, "I think that the four years I spent under those old, tough railroad men did me more good than if I had spent four years in college" (*Forbes,* August 1, 1954). His next job, beginning in 1920, was as a clerk in the "Pennsy's" general superintendent's office at Cleveland, Ohio. He was transferred back to Pittsburgh in 1923 to become freight movement director in the office of the local superintendent of freight transportation, then during 1927 and 1928 he was chief clerk to the general manager of the Chicago office.

Continuing his advancement, Symes was promoted in 1928 to the post of superintendent of passenger transportation for the Pennsylvania's western region. Then in 1929 he was transferred from Chicago to the road's headquarters in Philadelphia to occupy a similar position in the eastern division. For one year beginning in 1934, Symes was chief of freight transportation in Philadelphia.

Leaving the Pennsylvania in 1935, Symes became vice-president of the Association of American Railroads in charge of operation and maintenance. (The A.A.R., established in

Washington, D.C. in 1934, now has a membership of 131 lines, and has acted as a correlating agency for railroad interests throughout the country.) Symes's responsibilities with the then young organization have been characterized as "extensive." In an address to the association's mechanical division on June 16, 1937 he asserted that "more real progress has been made in improving transportation in the last ten years than in any previous period of twice that length," and cited as evidence a 53 per cent increase in the speed of freight trains as well as the introduction of streamlined passenger trains, air conditioned services and improved signaling systems.

Symes returned to the "Pennsy" in 1939, after approval by the Interstate Commerce Commission (in March of that year) of his appointment as general manager of the railroad's western region "in addition to holding office with various Pennsylvania subsidiaries." While serving as general manager of the western region he was promoted (1942) to a vice-presidency.

Looking forward to postwar problems he told the Association of American Railway Engineers on March 15, 1944 that "to achieve better transportation the roads will have to adopt a program of rehabilitation," and pointed out that "our engineering thinking will have to be just as modern as the service we shall have to provide." He also advocated a "sound national transportation policy based upon equity to all forms of transportation, with special favors to none."

Announcement was made on March 26, 1946 of the recall of Symes to Philadelphia to become deputy vice president in charge of operations. It followed by one week the news of an agreement whereby two major eastern roads, the Pennsylvania and the New York Central, and four western systems, would route Atlantic-Pacific passenger trains through the Chicago railyards instead of subjecting passengers to the inconvenience of a taxi trip from one Chicago terminal to another.

Expanding from the short Philadelphia to Harrisburg line, opened in 1846, to a post World War II routage of more than 10,000 miles in fourteen states, the Pennsylvania Railroad was for one hundred years regarded as a gilt-edge security enterprise, and had a record of not missing a quarterly dividend since 1848. Nevertheless, after having done what E. Frederick Uhrbrock called in *Barron's* (December 3, 1931) "an outstanding transportation job" during the war, the carrier in 1946 "for the first time in its history . . . failed to earn its fixed charges."

The confirmation of Symes as vice president in charge of operation in October 1946 was viewed as one preliminary to the top-level reorganization which took place in April 1947 and which brought Walter S. Franklin to the post of executive vice-president under president Martin W. Clement. The new executive vice-president, with Symes as his head operation subordinate, launched a modernization program under which, by the summer of 1951, the Pennsylvania was "spending $587 million for new and renovated equipment, more than any

Alfred A. DeLardi

JAMES M. SYMES

other railroad in the U.S." (*Time*, July 2, 1951). When Clement became chairman of the board in 1949, Franklin succeeded him as president. In June 1952 Symes was installed as executive vice-president and Franklin gave him "full responsibility for clearing the site and adopting a development plan" for the Penn Center realty project to occupy the rail approaches to, and edifice of, the now-demolished old Broad Street passenger terminal in Philadelphia (*Business Week*, September 25, 1954).

During Symes's two years as executive vice-president the Pennsylvania's expenditure for modernization rose to over $1 billion. Nearly a third of this amount was spent to make the road 96 per cent dieselized; $19,000,000 went into expanded signal facilities; $34,000,000 went for building and repairing bridges, trestles and culverts, and $14,000,000 for improved yards and sidings (*Forbes*, August 1, 1954). Symes announced in July 1955 an expenditure of $46,000,000 for new freight cars to be delivered in 1955 or early 1956.

Walter Franklin resigned as president as of June 1, 1954, at which time Symes was chosen president by the board of directors. A company announcement noted that he had been "active in studies and considerations . . . on the introduction of trailer-truck-service, popularly known as 'piggy-back.'" The railroad had placed orders for 200 extra-long 75-foot flatcars capable of carrying two trailers each, and in July 1954 became one of the first railroads in the country to place the "piggy-back" in service.

Regarding passenger transportation, Symes stated that "where there is no hope, we will continue to eliminate" but "where there is, we will modernize." An innovation in this respect has been the ordering by the Pennsylvania of new-type long-haul passenger trains with low-slung lightweight tubular-shaped cars—an adap-

SYMES, JAMES M.—*Continued*

tation of the Spanish "Talgo" train—which are expected to be ready for delivery some time in early 1956 (*Business Week*, March 26, 1955).

During the first year of the Symes presidency the Pennsylvania applied for higher commutation rates in the New Jersey area. On the matter of governmental support, direct or indirect, of rival means of freight haulage, Symes has been outspoken. In an address at Philadelphia on June 23, 1954 he referred to the recently authorized St. Lawrence seaway as a "subsidized competitive transportation route that will deprive the railroad of tonnage they have been built to handle" and warned that the rail carriers would be unable to duplicate their excellent World War I and II national service record "if much of the normal traffic is diverted to subsidized competition in peace time."

Symes is a director of the Association of American Railroads and a director or officer of various Pennsylvania subsidiaries and affiliates including the Pennsylvania Company for Banking and Trusts (director), the Pennsylvania-Reading Seashore Lines (president), and the Norfolk and Western, the Wabash, the Detroit, Toledo and Ironton, and the Long Island railroads (director). The Pennsylvania's "retarded stepchild" (as *Forbes* has called the Long Island Rail Road) was reorganized in 1954 under a plan calling for higher fares, lower taxes, and an advance by the Pennsylvania of $5,500,000 toward modernization. In April 1955 it announced that it had since "operated in the black."

In his first annual report to Pennsylvania Railroad stockholders a month earlier, President Symes had been able to note a reduction in the road's passenger deficit by $12,900,000 in the fiscal year then concluding, as well as a reduction of more than $52,000,000 in system debt; and although operating revenues were the lowest since 1949 and freight revenues showed a 20 per cent decline, he felt "more optimistic going into 1955 than at any time in the past eight years." He cited among other reasons the "near-completion of the company's billion-dollar improvement program" and the outlook for the "piggy-back" truck-train service which had just been placed on a daily run basis between Chicago and the Atlantic. Net income of the Pennsylvania Railroad in the first eight months of 1955 was $28,505,285 against $8,604,629 in the 1954 period.

In June 1955 the Pennsylvania Railroad signed a one-year option with Webb & Knapp, Inc., in connection with the real estate company's plan to build a $100,000,000 "Palace of Progress" atop the Pennsylvania Station in New York City. If the project is carried out, the railroad will receive $30,000,000, of which about $13,000,000 (Symes has said) will be spent to modernize the station.

In behalf of the Pennsylvania Railroad, Symes accepted the gold "Oscar of Industry" trophy for the best annual report in 1955 in all industry, presented by the *Financial World* magazine on October 24.

Symes was awarded an honorary LL.D. degree in 1948 by Waynesburg College in Pennsylvania; he is a trustee of Temple University in Philadelphia and is a member of the Newcomen Society of England as well as of the American Railway Engineers Association. In Chicago his clubs are the Commercial and the Chicago, and in Philadelphia the Philadelphia Country, the Racquet, the Rittenhouse and the Union League; he also belongs to the Merion Cricket Club, and golf is his favorite outdoor recreation. Symes has been married since September 27, 1919 to the former Fern Elizabeth Dick; they have one daughter, Jeanne.

References

Bsns W p62+ S 25 '54 por
Forbes 74:15 Ag 1 '54 pors
N Y Herald Tribune p29 My 12 '54
N Y Times p46 Mr 27 '47; p47 My 12 '54 por; III p3 My 30 '54 por
N Y World-Telegram p41 My 12 '54
Newsweek 38:54 D 24 '51; 43:70 My 24 '54 por
Time 63:96+ My 24 '54 por
Poor's Register of Directors and Executives (1955)
Who's Who in America, 1954-55
World Biography (1954)

SZENT-GYÖRGYI, ALBERT (VON NAGYRAPOLT) (sänt-jôrj) Sept. 16, 1893- Biochemist

Address: b. c/o Institute for Muscle Research, Marine Biological Laboratory, Woods Hole, Mass.; h. Penzance Rd., Woods Hole, Mass.

Hungarian-born Dr. Albert Szent-Györgyi, biochemist and Nobel Prize winner, is fascinated by the mystery and the miracle of muscles. "That a soft jelly should suddenly . . . change its shape and lift a thousand times its own weight," he has said, " is little short of miraculous." He has found a key in chemistry to the mystery of muscular contraction and relaxation, and out of his laboratories, at first in the University of Szeged, Hungary and since 1947 at the Institute for Muscle Research, Marine Biological Laboratory, Woods Hole, Massachusetts, has come the first workable theory of muscular physiology.

He has duplicated muscle fibers synthetically in his laboratory out of their chemical constituents, actin and myosin. Through his researches Szent-Györgyi, one of the eminent scientists to come to the United States from a Soviet satellite country, hopes to reach a better understanding of the inner working of muscle which may lead to the easing of much human suffering from such afflictions as lumbago, heart disease, high blood pressure, and muscular dystrophy.

He won the Nobel Prize in 1937 "for his discoveries in connection with the biological combustion processes, with especial reference to vitamin C [in paprika] and the catalysis of fumaric acid." He has also done important work in the development of Vitamin P (useful in counteracting the effects of radiation from atomic weapons and from prolonged radium therapy on cancer patients). He himself attaches greater importance to his studies of muscular structure and function. He received the 1954 Albert Lasker $1,000 award of the American Heart Association for the contributions of his muscle research in the fields of cardiovascular diseases and the basic physiology of the heart.

Albert von Nagyrapolt Szent-Györgyi was born in Budapest, Hungary, on September 16, 1893. His father, Nicholas, was a landowner and his mother, the former Josephine Lenhossek, came from a family of scientists; her father and uncle were professors of anatomy at the University of Budapest. Albert completed his early education in Budapest and then entered the medical school at the university in 1911, starting research in his uncle's laboratory during his freshman year. By the time he had reached his third year, he had published a series of histological papers with special reference to the structure of the vitreous body. His studies were interrupted by the war, during which he saw service in the Austro-Hungarian Army on the Russian and Italian fronts. He was decorated for bravery and after being wounded, he returned to Budapest to complete work for his M.D. degree in 1917.

After the war Szent-Györgyi began his career as an anatomist, and found it dull. He turned to biochemistry and undertook a "grand tour" of professional appointments, studies, and laboratory research in universities in Prague, Berlin, Hamburg, Leiden, Liége, Groningen, Budapest, Minnesota (the Mayo Clinic), and finally Szeged. In Berlin, he was deeply influenced by Leonor Michaelis and then during his postgraduate studies in Cambridge University, he worked with Sir Frederick Gowland Hopkins. During Dr. Szent-Györgyi's tour of the universities, he observed that experiments with animals whose adrenal glands had been removed suggested that the adrenal cortex is in some way involved in biological oxidation. While at the Physiological Institute of Groningen, Holland, he discovered the reducing agent, which he tentatively named hexuronic acid. This turned out to be the same acid found in fruit juices and was potent in reducing human and experimental scurvy.

He received aid from three American foundations (Rockefeller, Mayo and Josiah Macy) to pursue his researches. "From the beginning," Szent-Györgyi wrote, "I suspected the substance to be identical with Vitamin C [discovered in 1907 by A. Holst and T. Frölich]."

He discovered that paprika—Hungarian red pepper—was an unbelievably rich source of hexuronic acid, and with the help of young Dr. J. L. Svirbely, an American in Szeged, prepared a full pound of pure white acid crystals and shared it with Dr. Walter N. Haworth and other chemists.

In 1932 Dr. Szent-Györgyi was appointed to the chair of medical chemistry in the University of Szeged, Hungary in the modern river town rebuilt upon the wreckage of Old Szeged, leveled in the 1879 Danube-Tisa River flood.

With an abundance of hexuronic acid crystals for laboratory study, Dr. Szent-Györgyi could determine the molecular structure and

ALBERT SZENT-GYORGYI

proved that the antiscorbutic factor was intrinsic and not due to the contamination of foreign matter. With this in mind, Dr. Szent-Györgyi suggested changing the name to antiscorbutic acid. The final name was ascorbic acid. His work made possible the synthesization of Vitamin C by Walter N. Haworth and Paul Karrer, who won the Nobel Prize in chemistry in 1937, the same year in which Szent-Györgyi won the Prize in medicine.

In 1939 Dr. Szent-Györgyi assembled in Szeged his first team of muscle research scientists. After World War II began he found his work an ideal cover for anti-Nazi underground guerilla warfare. He went to Turkey and other neutral countries to deliver important political and scientific papers to the British Legations in spite of the Nazi surveillance. By 1941 members of the Gestapo were closing in on Dr. Szent-Györgyi, and he was compelled to hide and to disguise himself as an old man with a beard and spectacles.

Most important to him was the preservation of the Szeged experiments so that if the worst happened to him, others would be able to carry on where he left off. Accordingly, he wrote a report and turned it over to the Swedish Legation to transmit to the editor of *Acta Physiologica Scandinavica* in Sweden. Not realizing that Dr. Szent-Györgyi was wanted by the Nazis and that his hiding place in the Swedish Legation was unknown to the Gestapo, the editor cabled an answer in care of the Legation. The Nazis intercepted the wire and prepared to enter the Legation. Immediately the King of Sweden conferred citizenship upon Szent-Györgyi, who then escaped into the underground movement.

Following World War II Szent-Györgyi became professor of biochemistry in the University of Budapest. Thinking that it would be possible to work with the Russians and build a democratic and peaceful world, he

SZENT-GYORGYI, ALBERT—*Continued*

plunged into political activity and accepted election to the Hungarian Parliament. He was quickly disillusioned, however, and left Hungary.

Reassembling his Szeged team, he established the Institute for Muscle Research at the Marine Biological Laboratory, Woods Hole, Massachusetts in 1947. Economic difficulties beset the little group, however, and one by one the scientists left the Institute. Finally Armour & Company came to the rescue, financing Dr. Szent-Györgyi's research in the hope that his work in muscle tissue might help the meat packers to improve the color and taste of their products, most of which are the muscles of animals. By this time only two of the original Szeged group were left, Dr. Andrew Szent-Györgyi, nephew of Dr. Albert Szent-Györgyi, and Dr. Stephen Hajdu. With these two, and others who have since joined him, he has continued his research in muscle physiology.

In 1940 Dr. Szent-Györgyi had isolated two kinds of muscle protein from the substance myosin, which until that time had been thought to be the single basic component of muscle tissue. One of these substances was composed of rod-shaped particles and the other was in the form of minute globular beads. The rod-shaped components retained the name myosin, and the globular components he named actin. Dr. Szent-Györgyi renamed the combined compound actomyosin. When the compound, adenosine triphosphate, ATP for short, is added, a change takes place in the relationship between the two components of the muscle protein which results in the contraction of the fiber. Dr. Szent-Györgyi has recently announced the discovery of another compound, ATP-CP, which causes the muscle to relax.

In a recent statement concerning his work, he said, "We now know that actin and myosin come together and ATP makes the muscle contract, but still we are only describing the machine. We must still learn how the engine is all put together, then we will know how it works. Only then can we really understand the muscle in health and in disease, and perhaps learn how to overcome disease." In attempting to obtain the answers to such questions, Dr. Szent-Györgyi and his associates and others in the field are experimenting with extracted actomyosin, examination of muscle fibers through the electron microscope and spectrographic analysis of the muscle tissues.

Acting on Szent-Györgyi's suggestion that the synthetic "muscle" might be cured of its "listlessness" if only the stringy actomyosin molecules could be oriented properly—in long sheaves as in natural muscle, Professor Teru Hayashi of Columbia University succeeded in forming muscle fibers strong enough to do actual work, but they have not yet proved so strong nor so fast-acting as natural muscle (*Newsweek*, June 4, 1951).

The physiology of muscle is one of the least understood aspects of life. In his book, *Chemistry of Muscular Contraction* (Academic Press, 1951), Dr. Szent-Györgyi states, "Human happiness and efficiency are dependent to a great extent on the good working order of our muscles, and no end of suffering is due to their dysfunction. . . . We begin life enclosed in a strong bag of muscle, the womb, which is inactive for nine months and then goes into strong contraction to bring us out into the world. And life is terminated, for more than half of us, by the failure of another muscle, the heart. Diseases of this organ take a toll in the United States of about one life per minute."

During the late 1940's Dr. Szent-Györgyi made further investigations into the chemistry of citrus fruits, the principle sources of Vitamin C, and succeeded in extracting the so-called Vitamin P from lemon peel. Vitamin P is a complex compound of three flavonoids (from the class name for plants pigments), and it is valuable in reducing the fragility of blood capillaries. Since the breakdown of these tiny blood vessels is a frequent result of prolonged radiation therapy of cancer patients, Vitamin P has been a boon to patients undergoing this form of treatment. It is also important to scientists studying means of counteracting the effects of atom-bomb radiation which, like prolonged X ray or radium therapy, causes a breakdown of blood capillaries.

The Muscular Dystrophy Associations of America, the American Heart Association, and the Association for the Aid of Crippled Children joined with Armour & Company and several other industrial firms, as well as public contributions, in making it possible for Dr. Szent-Györgyi and his staff of six scientists and four technicians to continue their work at the Institute for Muscle Research.

His books include *On Oxidation, Fermentation, Vitamins, Health and Disease,* published by Williams & Wilkins in 1939 and three publications of Academic Press: *Chemistry of Muscular Contraction* (1947, 1951), *Nature of Life* (1948) and *Chemical Physiology of Contraction in Body and Heart Muscle* (1953). His articles have appeared in *Nature, Science* and *Science Illustrated.*

Dr. Szent-Györgyi is five feet eight inches tall and weighs 175 pounds. His eyes are blue and his hair is white. He acknowledges no church or political affiliation. He married in 1949 Martha Borbiro, who is now associated with him in his work. He has one daughter, Cornelia, by a previous marriage, now Mrs. Geoffrey Pollitt. His hobbies are sailing, fishing, and swimming.

In a recent interview he was asked what great or useful things might come from solving the puzzles of the muscle engine. He replied, "Benjamin Franklin flew a kite to learn some basic facts about electricity long before anyone dreamed of electric lights. When someone asked him what good the new knowledge was, Franklin replied: 'What good is a baby?' Who can say what we will learn? It is not possible yet to make any promises."

"Research is four things," he emphasized: "Brain with which to think. Eyes with which to see. Machines with which to measure. And fourth, money. It is brains and eyes which are most important. You can have too many machines, so many that you fail to use your brains and eyes" (Washington *Post*, September 22, 1954). His students and colleagues say that in discussing the scientific aspects of his work he is "witty, articulate and highly convincing . . . and has a masterly command of the English language" (*Newsweek*, March 22, 1954).

References

Collier's 133:90 My 28 '54
N Y Herald Tribune p21 D 3 '51
N Y Times IV p11 D 9 '51; p8 Mr 15 '54
Newsweek 43:94 Mr 22 '54 por
Sat Eve Post 224:34 My 8 '52
Time 54:42 Jl 4 '49
International Who's Who, 1954
MacCallum, T. W. & Taylor, S., The Nobel Prize-Winners, 1901-1937 (1938)
Stevenson, L. G. Nobel Prize Winners in Medicine and Physiology, 1901-1950
Who's Who, 1954
Who's Who in America, 1954-55
World Biography (1954)

TAFFIN DE GIVENCHY, HUBERT *See* Givenchy, Hubert (James Taffin) de

TEBALDI, RENATA Jan. 2, 1922- Singer
Address: b. c/o Columbia Artists Management, Inc., 113 W. 57th St., New York 19; h. I Piazza Guastalla, Milan, Italy

"There is no question that Renata Tebaldi is one of the really great sopranos of the day; an uncommonly fine artist and a good artist," commented the New York *Herald Tribune* music critic, Paul Henry Lang, on February 10, 1955, after hearing the tall, statuesque Italian soprano sing the role of Mimi in Puccini's *La Bohème* at the Metropolitan Opera House in New York. She made her debut at La Scala in 1946 at the reopening of the Milan opera house after the war for a concert conducted by Maestro Arturo Toscanini. Her New York debut was at the Metropolitan on January 31, 1955 in the role of Desdemona in Verdi's *Otello*. Each subsequent opera in which she has appeared at the "Met" has attracted capacity audiences. "They are beginning to compare her with Kirsten Flagstad," wrote Howard Taubman (New York *Times*, February 20, 1955) "because the new soprano from Italy has become an instantaneous magnet at the Metropolitan Opera House."

The lyric soprano, who made her American debut at the San Francisco Opera House in October 1950 in the title role of Verdi's *Aïda*, has become well known to record collectors for her "many striking performances on disks." Her London Records album of Verdi's *La Traviata*, in which she sings the role of Violetta, was released in January 1955 and was considered by Paul Hume in the *Saturday Review* to be "the best *Traviata* on records . . . that it will be surpassed is problematic."

RENATA TEBALDI

Renata Tebaldi was born in Pesaro, Italy on January 2, 1922, the only child of Teobaldo Tebaldi and Giuseppina (Barbieri) Tebaldi. Her father was a cellist; he still plays in orchestras in Pesaro and Parma opera houses. In her childhood Renata studied the piano for six years. When it was discovered that she had a good voice a family council was held, and it was decided that she should have her voice trained. She continued her musical studies at the Arrigo Boito Conservatory in Pesaro and at the Gioacchino Rossini Conservatory in Parma, and at eighteen became a pupil of Carmen Melis, operatic soprano. She later studied with Giuseppe Pais.

Her professional debut was made at Rovigo in May 1944, as Elena in Boito's *Mefistofele*, and in December 1945 she sang the role of Desdemona in Verdi's *Otello*. A scout from La Scala heard her and signed her for the Milan opera house. When Toscanini came from the United States in the spring of 1946 he auditioned the most promising younger singers.

"I sang 'La mamma morta' from *Andrea Chénier*," Miss Tebaldi recalled (when interviewed by Victor Seroff for the *Saturday Review*, February 26, 1955), "and then Maestro let me sing the whole last act of *Otello*. Toscanini said 'Brava, brava' and told his son Walter to take my name and address." Among the six artists chosen for the concert at La Scala, Tebaldi was the only "new" one. She was heard in excerpts from Rossini's *Moïse*.

Since then she has sung in triumph at the opera houses of Naples, Rome, Venice, Pompeii, Turin, Cesana, Modena, Bologna and Florence. Fully established as a favorite with Italian opera-goers, she toured England, France, Spain and South America. Her debut in *Aïda* with the San Francisco Opera Company, singing opposite Mario del Monaco (with whom she sang in her New York debut in *Otello* on

TEBALDI, RENATA—*Continued*

January 31, 1955) was "the biggest sensation in California opera in twenty-eight years." "Tall and expressive," reported *Time* (October 9, 1950), "she made a big impression both physically and vocally. Her flexible and powerful voice, known in the U.S. only on records, brought down the house in her first-act 'Ritorna vincitor' and third-act 'O patria mia' arias."

Her first collection of arias became one of London Records' most popular vocal recordings, and her singing in the FFRR complete sets of *La Bohème, Madame Butterfly, Tosca* and *Aïda* received warm praise from the critics. She "lent her voice" to a film, *Colonna Sonora* (*Lohengrin*), made in Venice in 1946, and her voice was also "dubbed in" to a film version of *Aïda* (released in the United States in 1954).

Because of her appearance in leading opera houses of Europe, her debut in Verdi's *Otello* at the Metropolitan Opera House in New York City aroused more than the usual amount of anticipation. Although some critics commented on her nervousness, they generally admitted that she has "a beautiful voice and a commanding stage presence." Miles Kastendieck (*Christian Science Monitor*, February 5, 1955) also remarked on her "musicianship, her artistic sense and her communicative power" particularly in the fourth act when she sang the "Willow Song" and the "Ave Maria," which "fitted her kind of lyric production."

"By comparing her with the most distinguished Desdemonas I have ever heard," wrote Winthrop Sargeant in the *New Yorker* (February 12, 1955), ". . . Miss Tebaldi's Desdemona was not a great one. But it had a pleasingly lush and impassioned quality, nevertheless. . . . She is an extremely handsome woman with a large voice of rich emotional power, and hence a very valuable addition to the Metropolitan's roster."

Her subsequent debut as Mimi in Puccini's *La Bohème* on February 9, 1955 at the "Met" attracted a capacity audience and pleased most of the critics. Olin Downes wrote in the New York *Times* (February 10, 1955), "We have heard no Mimi who moved us so much by the sincerity and the gripping emotion that she gave the part. One could even say that Miss Tebaldi, whose height is something that can easily be embarrassing to her partners on the stage, and whose stature gives her a more imposing effect than one naturally associates with the figure of the little seamstress Mimi, makes the character in a manner proportionate to her height and a greater and more dramatic figure than one imagines the girl of Puccini and Murger to be."

Many opera lovers went to the opera house on February 16 to hear Miss Tebaldi in *Aïda*, but the performance was canceled because the soprano was suffering from an ear infection, and *Tosca*, featuring another new singer, Zinka Milanov, was substituted. Miss Tebaldi returned on February 23 to sing her first Maddalena in Giordano's *Andrea Chénier*. "Her impersonation was, as everything she has done up to now," commented the New York *Times* (February 24, 1955), "artistically and sensitively sung. There is no doubt that her voice does thin out a trifle in the upper register, but that is unimportant in view of the color she brings to her singing. Her mezzo-piano singing is a delight to hear. With no effort at all it fills the house, emerging with a sheer velvet quality."

She credits the operatic soprano Carmen Melis with teaching her dramatic roles. Other stage directors from whom she learned a great deal were Herbert Graf, at the Roman amphitheatre production in Pompeii in *Julius Caesar*; Roberto Rossellini, who directed her in *Otello* in Naples; Pierre Bertin of the Comédie Française, who staged *Andrea Chénier*. Critics have remarked how she moves across a stage "with uncommon grace and agility" (Jay S. Harrison in the New York *Herald Tribune*, February 24, 1955) and have praised her "inherent artistic consciousness and capacity to communicate emotion" (Olin Downes in the New York *Times*, February 1, 1955).

In her large repertory of roles she has no favorite. "They all are like my children," she said. Tebaldi has dark-brown hair and blue eyes, is five feet ten inches tall and gives her weight as "variable." She candidly admits she is "too tall" (for most tenors) and "tròppo robùsta," but she thinks dieting might hurt her voice. Among her hobbies are crossword puzzles. She also likes to drive. "I like New York," she told Victor Seroff (*Saturday Review*, February 26, 1955). "New York is very impressive. . . . At first it frightened me. I felt like an ant . . . I like the American ways." The efficiency and the discipline at the "Met" please her, and the orchestra, she said, is "bellissima." Her religion is Roman Catholic. She can speak a little French and English, but uses an interpreter when interviewed. After the "Met" season closes she sings in Rome and Florence, and each August she reserves to study new roles. She told Howard Taubman (New York *Times*, February 20, 1955) that the equable behavior of American audiences is very pleasant. Next season, she will sing in San Francisco and Chicago before rejoining the Metropolitan Opera.

References

N Y Times II p9 F 20 '55 por
Newsweek 45:56 F 14 '55 por
Saturday R 38:42 F 26 '55 pors
Time 56:44 O 9 '50 por; 65:54 F 14 '55 por

THARP, LOUISE (MARSHALL) HALL

June 19, 1898- Author; lecturer

Address: b. c/o Little, Brown and Co., 34 Beacon St., Boston 6, Mass.; h. South Trail, Darien, Conn.

Reprinted from the *Wilson Library Bulletin* January 1955

After her career as an author of juveniles was firmly established, Louise Hall Tharp applied her literary talent, with notable success, to the writing of adult biographies. *The Peabody Sisters of Salem* attracted wide popular and critical attention in 1950 and received the

Educator's Award of $1,000 granted biennially by the professional education sorority Delta Kappa Gamma for "the most significant contribution to education by a woman." *Until Victory: Horace Mann and Mary Peabody* brought new laurels: the National Education Association's citation as "the most important book of 1953," one "that will remain a classic for generations."

Born on June 19, 1898, in Oneonta, New York, Louise Marshall Hall is a New Englander by heritage, thoroughly at home in the background depicted in her books. Her father, the Reverend Newton Marshall Hall, a Congregational minister and writer of religious works, was of New Hampshire birth and ancestry; her mother, Louise Buffum (Varney) Hall, a Quaker, from Maine, was of Salem ancestry. Mrs. Hall died young and Louise, an only child, was brought up in Springfield, Massachusetts, in her father's quiet home—"a writer's workshop." Her formal schooling at the Springfield Classical High School and the Boston School of Fine Arts was followed by two years of study and travel in Europe.

On August 13, 1925 Louise Marshall Hall married Carey Edwin Tharp, a Texan. As a wife and mother—the Tharps have two sons, Carey Edwin, Jr. and Marshall Allen—she gave up art as a profession. "My original intention," she says, "was to be an illustrator, but I found I could combine homemaking with writing, while art remains an avocation." She started writing as a magazine editor and columnist for the Girl Scouts, an organization she has served in many capacities over the years.

Discovering that her small sons could not find enough reading matter they liked, Mrs. Tharp proceeded to write books for them. Her first efforts, published by Crowell, were novels set in early Connecticut: *Lords and Gentlemen* (1940), a boy's adventures (including capture by Indians) as a New England pioneer; *Tory Hole* (1940), a story of the Revolution; and *Six-pence for Luck* (1941), a tale about a captain's children involving smugglers and buried treasure.

Subsequent books appealed to more mature readers. *Down to the Sea* (McBride, 1942), subtitled "A Young People's Life of Nathaniel Bowditch, the Great American Navigator," tells of the author of the "seaman's bible" of navigation. *Champlain, Northwest Voyager* (Little Brown, 1944) is a biographical novel. *A Sounding Trumpet* (McBride, 1944) is the biography of the author of "The Battle Hymn of the Republic," Julia Ward Howe. *Company of Adventures* (Little Brown, 1946) gives an account of the Hudson's Bay Company and its place in Canadian history. These books have been welcomed not only by young readers but by librarians and teachers for their swift action, readable style, and sound historical foundation. Also in the juvenile field, Mrs. Tharp has published stories in *Target* and *Child Life*.

For her first adult book Mrs. Tharp chose as her subject the sisters who aroused her curiosity when she found references to them in Van Wyck Brooks' *The Flowering of New England*.

LOUISE HALL THARP

Finding little in print about them, she undertook the necessary research and wrote the book herself. *The Peabody Sisters of Salem* (Little Brown, 1950) chronicles the lives of Elizabeth, who figured so prominently in the educational, intellectual, and literary currents of nineteenth century America; of Mary, who became the second wife of the educator Horace Mann; and of Sophia, who married Nathaniel Hawthorne. A 1950 Book-of-the-Month Club selection, the biography was praised for its scholarship, literary charm, and psychological insight.

In her research on the Peabody family, Mrs. Tharp was touched by the warmth and humanity of Horace Mann as revealed in his letters. Using a mass of previously unpublished documents, she wrote *Until Victory: Horace Mann and Mary Peabody* (Little Brown, 1953), the story of the personal life and illustrious career of the champion of public schools. Mrs. Tharp's style and her evocation of character and locale received the general approbation of critics, among them M. A. De Wolfe Howe, who found, as he stated in the New York *Times* (September 13, 1953) that she had shed "fresh light upon . . . [Mann's] time" and had "delved deep and fruitfully into unexplored sources." The book was selected in 1953 by the Christian Herald Book Club and the Atlantic Monthly Book Club and was listed as one of the fifty notable books of the year by the Public Libraries Division of the American Library Association.

Mrs. Tharp, whose husband is an insurance executive, lives in Darien, Connecticut. She has brown eyes and brown hair; she is five feet five inches tall and weighs 130 pounds. She is a Congregationalist, a Republican, an active participant in civic and community life, a member of several historical organizations, and an honorary member of Delta Kappa Gamma and

THARP, LOUISE HALL—*Continued*

the national journalism sorority, Theta Sigma Phi. Besides writing books she enjoys lecturing and writing about her adventures in unearthing primary sources—the manuscripts hidden in libraries or prized as family treasures by her biographees' descendants. As outdoor recreations she likes swimming, motor trips, and sketching. Her favorite books are the novels of Marquand, the biographies of André Maurois, and appropriately, *The Flowering of New England.*

References

N Y Herald Tribune Bk R p2 Ja 15 '50 por

Sat R Lit 33:8 Ja 7 '50 por

Who's Who in America, 1954-55

THURMAN, HOWARD, REV. DR. Nov. 18, 1900- Clergyman; university professor; author

Address: b. Marsh Chapel, Boston University, 300 Bay State Rd., Boston 15, Mass.; h. 184 Bay State Rd., Boston 15, Mass.

Now in his third year as dean of the Chapel and professor of spiritual resources and disciplines at the Boston University School of Theology, Dr. Howard Thurman was appointed to his present duties in March 1953. He is the first member of the Negro race to become a full-time member of the Boston University faculty. For nine years he was co-pastor of the Church for the Fellowship of All Peoples, founded in San Francisco in 1943 for common worship by members of the white, yellow and black races.

Dr. Thurman, who had previously taught Christian theology at Howard University, has been described in *Life* as one of the "great preachers" of the present time. He is the author of several books including *Jesus and the Disinherited* (1949), *Deep Is the Hunger* (1951) and *Meditations of the Heart* (1953).

Born to Saul Solomon and Alice (Ambrose) Thurman at Daytona Beach, Florida, on November 18, 1900, Howard Thurman was brought up in a poor home in the colored section of Daytona Beach. "During much of my boyhood," he has stated in his book *Jesus and the Disinherited,* "I was cared for by my grandmother, who was born a slave . . . she could neither read nor write. Two or three times a week I read the Bible aloud to her." His father died when he was seven.

The boy attended a public elementary school at Daytona Beach, where he was coached by a friendly principal and became "the first Negro child in the town to receive an eighth grade certificate."

A few months after he attained this distinction Thurman entered the Florida Baptist Academy, then located at Jacksonville (later moved to St. Augustine). He met expenses by summer work in a bookstore or as a janitor or shoeblack. He also became active in Y.M.C.A. work. Dr. Channing H. Tobias, in his article "Some Outstanding Negro Christians" in the *Missionary Review of the World,* June 1936, recalled Thurman as "the chief promoter of voluntary religious activities at the [Baptist] Academy and a debater of more than ordinary ability." He attended Florida Normal School and in his senior year was licensed to preach.

In the chapter on Thurman in her book *Twelve Negro Americans* (Friendship Press, 1936), Mary Jenness has told of a while benefactor whose financial assistance made it possible for him to attend Morehouse College, the Baptist institution for Negroes at Atlanta, Georgia. Here he ranked first in scholarship in three different years, majored in economics, was sophomore and senior class president, and valedictorian, even though he worked thirty-six hours a week to earn expenses. He played leading Shakespearean roles in college theatricals, was editor-in-chief of his class yearbook, varsity debater, and as a senior was president of both the college Y.M.C.A. and the inter-racial Atlantic Student Council.

The winning of both the Edgar Allan Poe short story prize and the Chamberlain prize for scripture history in his junior year made it possible for him to spend a summer at Columbia University in New York City, where he took courses in philosophy and for the first time attended classes with white students. "It was here," Jean Burden quotes him, "that I made the precious discovery that a brain is a brain and the package doesn't count."

Graduated from Morehouse College in 1923 with the B.A. degree, Thurman spent the next three years at the Colgate-Rochester Divinity School, Rochester, New York, where he was greatly influenced by Dr. Henry Robins and Dr. George Cross. Upon graduation in 1926 with the Bachelor of Divinity degree, he accepted a call to the Mount Zion Church at Oberlin, Ohio. Following his marriage to Katie Kelley on June 6, 1926, he moved to the South (because of his wife's failing health) and became professor of theology at Morehouse College and its affiliated Spelman College for Women in Atlanta, Georgia. His wife died on December 21, 1930, leaving a baby daughter, Olive Katharine.

Deciding to devote a year to meditation and study, Thurman applied for and was granted a Charles Fisher Kent fellowship by the National Council on Religion in Higher Education. He studied the history of mysticism with the eminent Quaker teacher, Dr. Rufus Jones, at Haverford College, Haverford, Pennsylvania. He preached in Scotland the following summer.

Returning to Atlanta, he taught and preached at Morehouse and Spelman Colleges until 1932, when he was called by Dr. Mordecai Johnson to Howard University, Washington, D.C. to become assistant professor of Christian theology and chairman of the university committee on religious life.

Taking a leave of absence from the Howard faculty in 1935, Professor Thurman was chairman of a "Pilgrimage of Friendship," sponsored by the World Student Christian Federation, to India, Burma and Ceylon. On this "evangelical tour" he spoke in forty-five educational centers. He met Mohandas Gandhi and other leaders who criticized Christianity for "fostering segregation." These conversations started Thurman on a study of the teachings of Jesus with reference to "the disinherited and the under-privileged."

The idea of an "inter-racial church" came to Thurman while visiting the Khyber Pass. He decided to stay in the Christian tradition and "to make it live for the weak as well as the strong—for all peoples, whatever their color, whatever their caste" (*Atlantic*, October 1953). His address on this subject at the Boston University School of Theology was published in the Summer 1935 number of *Religion in Life* under the title "Good News for the Disinherited."

On his return to the United States Thurman was appointed dean of the Chapel at Howard University and promoted to full professor. He contributed to such periodicals as the *Christian Century, World Tomorrow,* the *Southern Workman, Christendom,* and the *Journal of Religion,* and published papers on "The Modern Significance of Jesus" in 1937 and "Religious Ideas in Negro Spirituals" in 1939.

"The idea . . . of a church which would be a *religious* fellowship, not another settlement house, nagged at Howard Thurman's mind" (Jean Burden). He took a leave of absence from Howard in July 1944 to become co-pastor, with the Reverend Alfred Fisk, of San Francisco's newly formed Church for the Fellowship of all Peoples. (The Church, which during its first two years was aided by the Presbyterian Board of Missions, had been established in a former Japanese district which had been largely occupied by Negroes, and aimed to bring together Caucasians, Africans and Orientals in common worship and fraternity.)

Dr. Thurman was co-pastor for the next nine years, sharing duties with a succession of white associates and a Japanese-American Methodist. He built up church membership from thirty to about 300 by 1951. By outside preaching he helped to finance the purchase in 1949 of the present Fellowship Church building on Vallejo and Larkin Streets. He organized the "Friends of the Fellowship Church," an auxiliary of about 1,000 members-at-large, which includes such figures as author Alan Paton, Dr. Channing Tobias, and singer Todd Duncan. Dr. Thurman now serves as minister-at-large of the church.

Frequently expressing his devotional thoughts in verse, Dr. Thurman published his "poetic meditations" in 1944 under the title *The Greatest of These.* In 1945 Eucalyptus Press published his *Deep River: An Interpretation of Negro Spirituals.* Invited by the Harvard University Divinity School at Cambridge, Massachusetts to deliver on April 14, 1947 the annual Ingersoll Lecture on the Immortality of Man, Dr. Thurman chose as his subject "The Negro Spiritual Speaks of Life and Death." (This address was issued by Harper in book form in 1948.)

"In this brief lecture," wrote *Library Journal,* "Professor Thurman . . . concludes that the slave singers can rightfully take their place alongside the great creative religious thinkers because they succeeded in making 'a worthless life worth living.'"

REV. DR. HOWARD THURMAN

The Fellowship Church published in 1947 *Meditations for Apostles of Sensitiveness,* a sermon preached by Dr. Thurman at the Cathedral of St. John the Divine in New York City on February 10, 1946. His book *Jesus and the Disinherited* (Abingdon-Cokesbury, 1949), was a series of Mary L. Smith Memorial Lectures delivered at Samuel Huston College, Austin, Texas in April 1948. A greatly amplified edition of *Meditations for Apostles of Sensitiveness* was published by Harper in 1951 under the title *Deep Is the Hunger.* Virginia Kirkus described it as "one of the best devotional books of the year" and as dealing with "problems we all face today: on keeping one's nerve, on taking a stand, on finding serenity in the midst of confusion."

Reviewing a companion work, *Meditations of the Heart* (Harper Brothers, 1953), a critic on the San Francisco *Chronicle* was particularly impressed by the chapters on prayer which (he wrote) "give not only a philosophy of prayer, but also practical suggestions for strengthening the prayer habit." *The Creative Encounter* was published by Harper in 1954 and *Deep River* is scheduled for publication in November 1955.

Appointment of Dr. Thurman as dean of the Daniel L. Marsh Chapel and professor of spiritual resources and disciplines in the School of Theology of Boston University, Boston, Massachusetts, was announced by President Harold C. Case on March 21, 1953. Dr. Thurman was photographed in *Life* (April 6) as one of twelve "Great Preachers" of this century. Also in 1953 he was elected to the board of trustees of the National Association for Mental Health. Dr. Thurman gave two courses on spiritual resources and disciplines (including

THURMAN, HOWARD, REV. DR.—*Cont.*
methods of personal and group devotion) at Boston University in the academic years 1953-54 and 1954-55.

Dr. Thurman and Sue E. Bailey, formerly a national student secretary of the national Y.W.C.A., were married on June 12, 1932. He has two daughters, Olive Katharine by his first marriage, and Anne Spencer, by his second. Mrs. Thurman, a trained musician, has assisted her husband in his study of Negro spirituals and while in San Francisco organized the forum and lectures held in the hall of the Fellowship Church.

He belongs to the Book Club of California in San Francisco and to the Authors Guild and the Schoolmasters Club of Boston. He is five feet ten inches in height and weighs 205 pounds. In politics he is a "New Deal Democrat," and his church affiliation is Baptist. "In repose his face is sad," wrote Jean Burden in *Atlantic* (October 1953), ". . . his humor is as famous as his eloquence—the unselfconscious grin, the rollicking laughter, particularly at himself. His favorite distraction . . . is the detective story." *Time* has commented on his rich baritone voice and his expressive hands. His hobby is oil painting.

He holds honorary degrees from Colgate-Rochester (D.D., 1935); Morehouse College (D.D., 1935); Wesleyan University (D.D., 1946); Ohio Wesleyan University (H.H.D., 1954); Lincoln University (D.D., 1954); and Washington University (LL.D., 1955).

References

Atlantic 192:39+ O '53
Christian Cent 68:1040+ S 12 '51
Life 34:128 Ap 6 '53 por
N Y Times p79 Mr 22 '53 por
Religious Leaders of America, 1941-42
Thurman, H. Jesus and the Disinherited (1949)
Who's Who in America, 1954-55

TICE, MERTON B(AIRD) Dec. 7, 1909-
Veterans organization official; lawyer

Address: b. V.F.W. Bldg., Broadway at 34th St., Kansas City 11, Mo.; h. 204 E. Fifth Ave., Mitchell, S.D.

As commander in chief for 1954-1955 of the Veterans of Foreign Wars of the United States, Merton Baird Tice heads the second largest veterans organization in the country and the oldest of the major veterans groups. (The American Legion is the world's largest veterans organization; see C.B. April 1955, Seaborn P. Collins, national commander.)

The V.F.W., which was founded in 1899 and has a current membership of nearly 1,300,000 combat overseas veterans, maintains nation-wide programs for "fraternal, patriotic, historical and educational" purposes.

Since his discharge from the Army after World War II, Tice has from year to year held offices of increasing responsibility in the V.F.W. He is a lawyer by profession, with a general practice in Mitchell, South Dakota.

Merton Baird Tice was born to Charles E. and Grace Tice in Chicago, Illinois on December 7, 1909. His parents, homesteaders in South Dakota, settled in Mitchell, where Merton attended local schools. In high school, from which he was graduated in 1929, he was voted the member of his class "most likely to succeed." He studied law at the University of South Dakota in Vermillion, receiving his LL.B. degree in 1935.

Prominent in athletics, Tice was a member of the all-state and all-conference basketball and football teams in both high school and college and earned his letters in tennis. He also took part in boxing at the university, edited the school's newspaper, and was president of Phi Delta Theta fraternity.

For six years, after leaving the university, Tice was employed by the U.S. Treasury Department in Washington, D.C, New York, and Chicago. His legal services included work as a trial lawyer and judge in administrative hearings, investigating black market income tax evasion cases, and acting as special legal representative of the department in its penal division.

Shortly before the United States entered World War II, Tice joined the Army. He served from October 3, 1941 to January 26, 1946, rising in rank from first lieutenant to lieutenant colonel of infantry. As a glider with the 18th Airborne Corps in Europe, he engaged in combat with airborne troops in the Netherlands, the Battle of the Bulge, the Ruhr pocket "cleanup," and the crossing of the Rhine and the Elbe rivers. He was also for a time on the staff of General Matthew B. Ridgway in the G-3 section.

Tice had a part in a unit citation, received four battle stars and two general commendations, and is entitled to wear the American Defense, European Theater of Operations, Victory, and Pre-Pearl Harbor ribbons. Since his separation from the service in 1946 he has been engaged in the general practice of law in Mitchell, where he was elected judge of the municipal court in 1953.

He joined the Veterans of Foreign Wars in his home town, Corn Palace City Post, number 2750, and in 1947-1948 was commander of the department of South Dakota. Soon receiving recognition in the national organization of V.F.W., he became chief of staff for 1948-1949 and judge advocate general for 1951-1952. He was elected junior vice-commander in chief in 1952 and senior vice-commander in chief in 1953. While in the latter office Tice, who has traveled in every section of the country to address V.F.W. members, gave a Memorial Day (1954) speech in which he outlined a three-point program for strengthening the United States: "Strive for unity among your own people, work to maintain a unity that embraces free people everywhere, and live and teach Americanism."

V.F.W. delegates at the fifty-fifth national encampment, in Philadelphia, Pennsylvania on August 6, 1954, chose Tice by acclamation to succeed Wayne E. Richards of Kansas City, Kansas as national commander in chief. In his acceptance speech Tice pledged to work for more aid to disabled veterans and veterans' dependents, a vigorous drive for new members, and increased community service projects. He emphasized his organization's advocacy of universal military training and of building up an "armed might superior in all respects to Russia." Another V.F.W. conviction, he said, is "that no country should be permitted to blast itself into the United Nations as Red China is at this time attempting to do" (New York *Times,* August 7, 1954).

Among the resolutions passed at the 1954 convention was one opposing the trial of U.S. servicemen by foreign (rather than U.S.) courts for crimes committed on foreign soil. The delegates also voted to urge that Federal aid be withheld from educational institutions employing teachers who refuse to give information concerning their communist activity when being questioned by members of Congressional committees.

The 1,300,000 members in V.F.W.'s 8,500 local posts are exclusively campaign medal service veterans of the U.S. Army, Navy, Marine Corps and Coast Guard. "The aims and activities of the organization, crystallized in the phrase 'To honor the dead by helping the living,' are constantly keyed to these threefold objectives: 1) the welfare of disabled veterans and their dependents; 2) care of the widows and orphans of veterans; 3) preservation of the basic principles of Americanism as expressed in the Bill of Rights" (*Encyclopædia Britannica*). Besides endeavoring to secure legislation to benefit the ex-servicemen, V.F.W. provides for veterans' widows and orphans at the V.F.W. National Home, Eaton Rapids, Michigan, which it has maintained since 1925.

In a Veterans Day address made on November 10, 1954 over the American Broadcasting Company network, Tice said: "In the modern concept of a war for survival, there will be no time for specialized training" and called for immediate adoption of a system of military training in advanced scientific skills. He gave a talk over the Columbia Broadcasting System on December 7, 1954—the thirteenth anniversary of the Pearl Harbor attack—in which he discussed the threat of world Communism and the U.S. need for greater military preparedness, including civil defense.

A problem of much concern to Tice was the plight of the eleven U.S. airmen and two civilians imprisoned by the Chinese Communists on charges of espionage. Tice expressed his view in a speech in December 1954 that "it's time for the United States to do some fist-doubling and nose-punching" to obtain the release of the Americans (New York *Herald Tribune,* December 12, 1954). The following March he said that the United States "should run the risk of war" by blockading China in an effort to have the captives freed—although he did not believe that a blockade would result in war (New York *Times,* March 22, 1955). The airmen were freed in July 1955.

Tice and his wife, the former Elfrieda Freeman of Norfolk, Virginia, have three children: Charles C., Merton B., and Virginia. He is a

MERTON B. TICE

trustee of the Mitchell Presbyterian Church, a 32d degree Mason and a member of the Odd Fellows, Toastmasters, United Commercial Travelers, Elks, American Legion and South Dakota Bar Association. Among his civic interests is the Mitchell community chest campaign, of which he has been chairman. The V.F.W. leader is said to be "a speaker of eloquence and force." Tice was succeeded in September 1955 by Timothy J. Murphy as commander in chief.

TITO May 25, 1892- President of Yugoslavia; Yugoslav Communist party leader
Address: Belgrade, Yugoslavia

> NOTE: This biography supersedes the article which appeared in *Current Biography* in 1943.

The survival of civilization, Yugoslavia's President Tito believes, depends upon the promotion of peaceful coexistence of nations with differing political and economic systems. As head of a government of some 16,000,000 Yugoslavs which is the first, and thus far only, Communist state to free itself of Cominform domination and turn to the West for support, Tito may be regarded as "the man in the middle" of the conflict between the "free world" and the U.S.S.R. and its satellites.

The leader of the Partisan army which effectively resisted fascist invasion during World War II, Marshal Tito became in 1945 Prime Minister (later President) of the Federal People's Republic of Yugoslavia. He is also Secretary General of the Federation of Yugoslav Communists, which controls that government. His role in the 1948 break between Yugoslavia and the Soviet Union has been described by Hamilton Fish Armstrong (author

Wide World

MARSHAL TITO

of *Tito and Goliath,* 1951) as politically and strategically "world shaking" in its importance because it "impaired [the] physical strength" of the Communist alliance.

Following Stalin's death in 1953, Tito responded to U.S.S.R. initiative in establishing a "normalization" of diplomatic relations between the two countries. In late 1954 while encouraging a growing *rapprochement* with the Soviet Union, he joined Harold E. Stassen, U.S. Foreign Operations Administrator, in discussing wider economic and military ties between Yugoslavia and the West. During his visit to India and Burma in the winter of 1954-1955, Tito denied any attempt to set up a "third bloc" which would stand aside from the East-West conflict. "Such a bloc," he said in a statement issued jointly with India's Prime Minister Jawaharlal Nehru, "would involve [Yugoslavia and India] in the very system of alignments which they regard as undesirable" (New York *Times,* December 24, 1954).

Tito was born Josip Broz on May 25, 1892 in the Croatian village of Kumrovec, then part of the Austro-Hungarian Empire. He was the seventh of fifteen children (seven of whom survived infancy) of a Croat father, Franjo Broz, and a Slovene mother, Marija (Javeršek) Broz. "My childhood was difficult," Tito has said. Beginning at the age of seven he worked on his father's farm, but despite family poverty he was allowed to attend elementary school from the age of seven to twelve. (Tito has made known much information about himself in "Tito Speaks," a series of articles appearing in *Life* magazine from April 21 to May 12, 1952, written with the assistance of Vladimir Dedijer. These articles form the basis of Dedijer's biography, *Tito,* 1953.)

At fifteen he went to Sisak to learn the locksmith trade, a craft that appealed to him because of his family tradition of blacksmithing. Attending the apprentice school in the evening, he was taught geography, history and languages, among other subjects. After a three-year apprenticeship he went to Zagreb to practice his trade, later to Ljubljana, Trieste and other nearby cities. During 1912 Josip Broz traveled in Bohemia, Germany and Austria-Hungary, taking jobs in metal-working factories.

In 1913, having reached the age of twenty-one, he began his compulsory two-year military service in the army of the Austro-Hungarian Empire. During World War I, as a private in the army, he was captured by the Russians and detained in prisoner-of-war camps in Russia. After the outbreak of the Bolshevik Revolution, he joined the Red International Guard and was active in behalf of the revolutionists until leaving Russia in September 1920.

On his return home, Broz found employment in Zagreb in a mechanic's workshop, applied for trade-union membership, and joined the Yugoslav Communist party. He later worked in a flour mill in Veliko Trojstvo and in the shipyards of Kraljevica, where he organized a trade-union branch and took part in Communist party affairs. In 1927 he was appointed secretary of the Metal Workers Trade Union in Zagreb and secretary of the local Communist party committee.

Broz was several times jailed for his part in strikes and in demonstrations against the regime of King Alexander, head of the new kingdom of South Slavs, called the Serb-Croat-Slovene State (named Yugoslavia in 1929), which was created after the collapse of Austria-Hungary in World War I. Following his trial in November 1928 on charges of carrying out Communist propaganda as a member of the illegal Communist party, he was sentenced to five years' imprisonment at Lepoglava and Maribor.

Unwilling upon his release to abide by the restriction that he remain in his native village, he found it necessary to change his name so that he might travel about more freely. He had earlier used a number of assumed names in his work for the Communist party. In 1934 he adopted the name "Tito" and used it exclusively after 1937. "Why did I take this name 'Tito' and has it special significance? . . . the name is frequent in my native district," Tito has explained. "The best-known Zagorje writer of the late eighteenth century was called Tito Brezovăcki. . . . The father of Ksaver Šandor Gjalski, one of the greatest Croatian writers, was also called Tito" (*Tito*).

Appointed in 1934 to membership in the Politburo of the Yugoslav Communist party, Tito was sent to Moscow to work on Yugoslav affairs in the Balkan Secretariat of the Comintern. During this stay in the Soviet Union he was known as Walter. When he returned to his country toward the end of 1936, he undertook the task of organizing the mobilization of Yugoslav volunteers to fight in the International Brigade in the Spanish Civil War.

Tito became Secretary General of the Communist party of Yugoslavia in 1937. He began at once a reorganization of party leadership, which for many years had been suffering from factional dispute. "We created a leadership of new men," he said, "of young revolutionaries hardened directly in the field in the process of the struggle" (*Tito*). Many of the men that were appointed to top positions in the party, such as Edvard Kardelj and Aleksandar Ranković, have since remained in office.

After the invasion of Yugoslavia by Germany and Italy in 1941, Tito organized a guerrilla force to fight the Axis. His army, the National Liberation Partisan Detachments, was popularly known as the Partisans. "Tito's successes in the face of Axis military strength were almost miraculous. As the territory he controlled and the number following him grew, he began to become an almost legendary hero" (*New Century Cyclopedia of Names,* 1954).

In the early part of the war the identity and activities of Tito, however, received less attention in the Western press than those of Drăza Mihailović, leader of another underground movement, which had the backing of the Yugoslav government in exile. After May 1943 the Allies gave their support to the resistance effort headed by Tito, who in the course of the war became President of the National Committee and Commissioner of Defense of the Anti-Fascist Council of National Liberation, and Marshal and Supreme Commander in Chief of the National Liberation Army. The National Committee served as executive organ or temporary cabinet for the Partisans until March 1945. At that time, some months after the defeat of the Axis in Yugoslavia, Tito merged his government with the royalist government to form in Belgrade a provisional government in which he retained his high positions.

The victory of the Communist party in the election of autumn 1945 resulted in the abdication of King Peter II (successor of King Alexander) and the proclamation of the Federal People's Republic of Yugoslavia. As Prime Minister, Minister of Defense and Secretary General of the Yugoslav Communist party, Marshal Tito set up a Communist-dominated government that speedily eliminated all opposition. Mihailović was tried and executed on charges of Nazi collaboration. Convicted on similar alleged war crimes, Archbishop Alojzije Stepinac was sentenced to sixteen years' imprisonment (he was released in 1951).

From the end of the war until 1948 Tito visited the U.S.S.R. each year. At home the dictator introduced, among other Soviet methods, nationalization of industry, collectivization of farms, and a secret police. Cooperating with the Soviet Union in foreign affairs, he encouraged the Pan-Slavic movement and fostered anti-American propaganda. A quarrel arising from Tito's refusal to be subservient to Cominform policies brought to an end in June 1948 Yugoslavia's satelliteship within the orbit of Eastern European Kremlin-dominated countries. At the time of his break with the U.S.S.R., many Western observers predicted Tito's immediate loss of power. Tito, however, backed by Yugoslav nationalist spirit and by a well-organized and unified party apparatus, retained his control of the government in the face of Cominform denunciation of him as a fascist and henchman of Western imperialism.

According to Neal Stanford of the *Christian Science Monitor* (December 3, 1954), Washington officials came to regard Tito's quarrel with the Cominform as "the West's biggest victory since VE-Day." Convinced of the genuineness of Yugoslavia's proclaimed independence of the U.S.S.R., several Western democracies made an effort to better their relations with the new Communist state. Millions of dollars in economic aid granted to Yugoslavia by the United States made it possible for Tito's government to survive a number of seasons of crop failures and the economic blockade of Cominform countries.

Tito has rejected membership for Yugoslavia in the North Atlantic Treaty Organization because of what he considers its anti-Communist ideology, but in August 1954 he signed a Balkan accord which aligns his country with two NATO states, Greece and Turkey. The "link" that Yugoslavia thus represents between NATO's Western and Middle Eastern members is seen to have been strengthened by Tito's settlement of Yugoslavia's dispute with Italy, another NATO country, over the Adriatic seaport of Trieste. The compromise agreement concluded in October 1954 terminated the nine-year-old quarrel between the two nations and prepared the way for talks on economic and military collaboration.

In the past few years while pursuing a policy of friendship with the West, Tito has sought to renew normal diplomatic trade, cultural and political relations with the U.S.S.R. and Soviet-bloc countries. After the death of Joseph Stalin in March 1953, Tito came to believe that the new Soviet government under Georgi M. Malenkov, which sent an ambassador to Yugoslavia the following summer, had adopted a nonaggressive foreign policy. In a speech on November 21, 1954 Tito said that the U.S.S.R. now regards Yugoslavia as an "independent and sovereign country, which Stalin refused to do" (Washington *Post and Times Herald,* November 22, 1954). On January 5, 1955 the two nations signed a $20,000,000 trade pact, a barter agreement to run for one year.

The principle of peaceful coexistence, which is now the keynote of Yugoslavia's foreign policy, was the chief topic of discussion among government leaders during Tito's visit to India and Burma in late 1954 and early 1955. He was the first non-Asian head of state to pay an official call to the independent state of India.

Tito's title is President of the Federal People's Republic of Yugoslavia, a position which he assumed at the time of the reorganization of governmental structure in January 1953 and to which he was re-elected in January 1954. He is also Secretary General and a member of the Executive Committee of the Federation of Yugoslav Communists. Among his other more important positions are President of the Socialist Federation of Working People of Yugoslavia (formerly the People's Front), to which he was elected in February 1953.

(Continued next page)

TITO—*Continued*

During Tito's stay in Russia in World War I he married a sixteen-year-old Russian girl named Pelaghia Belousnova, with whom he returned to Yugoslavia and who died in 1938. They had a son, Žarko. In 1940 Tito married Berta Has, a Slovene, whom he divorced after World War II. Their son was named Miško. His third wife, Jovanka Budisavljevic, a Serbian woman, whom he married in 1952, had taken part in the war as a member of Partisan units.

The Western press has frequently pictured Tito as a power-mad dictator, shrewd, knowledgeable, and ruthless in his suppression of opposition. Away from work he likes to play chess, tennis and billiards, and enjoys fishing. He is tall and heavy-set, often appearing in a bemedaled uniform. "Tito has a knack of surviving in a profession where all actuarial tables are against him," *Christian Science Monitor*'s Neal Stanford recently observed. "Anyone who can outwit or outstay Stalin should not be underrated."

References

International Who's Who, 1954
Robinson, D. The 100 Most Important People in the World Today (1952)
White, L. Balkan Caesar; Tito Versus Stalin (1951)
World Biography (1954)

TODD, MICHAEL *See* Todd, Mike

TODD, MIKE June 22, 1909- Theatrical producer

Address: b. 1700 Broadway, New York 19; Michael Todd Productions, Hollywood, Calif.

Theatrical impresario Mike Todd will produce anything the public will buy tickets to see. "The most colorful producer since Florenz Ziegfeld and Morris Gest," Todd is described by John Chapman (*Collier's*, May 12, 1945) as having "the soul of a carnival pitchman and the ambition of a Napoleon."

Todd's productions have ranged from a Flame Dance at the Chicago World's Fair in 1933 to a Johann Strauss operetta, *A Night in Venice* at Jones Beach in 1952 and 1953, which featured gondoliers, a water ballet and a revolving stage on an island. Between these he has produced many musical comedies such as *Up in Central Park*, which grossed more than $2,000,000 (despite discouraging reviews by Broadway critics), *The Hot Mikado*, and a streamlined *Hamlet* with Maurice Evans, which also prospered at the box office. When Todd found Shakespeare lucrative, he commented, "This is a new kind of show business."

With Lowell Thomas, Todd was one of the founders of the company that produced the three-dimensional film process called Cinerama, but he gave up his share in the partnership before the first show was presented. Recently Todd has devoted his energies to the new Todd-AO process, which uses one camera and a single projector, and gets its multi-dimensional effect by means of a 65mm. film and a full-stage curved screen. The first film to be produced in this process is *Oklahoma!*, under the supervision of Richard Rodgers and Oscar Hammerstein, which opened at the Rivoli Theatre in New York on October 10, 1955. Todd had suggested the one-camera idea to the American Optical Company whose scientists, headed by Dr. Brian O'Brien, developed the Todd-AO process. The name is derived from a combination of the name of Todd and the initials of the American Optical Company.

On November 2, 1955 it was announced that Todd had sold his holdings in the Magna Theatre Corporation which controls the Todd-AO wide-screen process.

Michael Todd was born Avrom Hirsch Goldbogen in Minneapolis on June 22, 1909 and grew up in the nearby town of Bloomington, Minnesota, where his father, an impoverished rabbi, ran a crossroads general store. Mike began his career in show business at the early age of nine. He was hired by a carnival "pitchman" to work a device that prevented customers from throwing three balls into a bucket and winning a live duck.

When Mike was twelve, his family moved to Chicago, where he became the youngest apprentice pharmacist in Illinois. At the age of fourteen he started as a promoter, arranging "lost our lease" and "must vacate" sales for small merchants, and later opened a College of Bricklaying.

While attending Tuley High School in Chicago, he founded the Michael Todd Ready-Made Home Company. He placed "modernize your home" ads in small foreign language newspapers, and sold the contracts he gained to building concerns. He was soon engaged in building apartment houses, at which he is reputed to have made a million dollars.

With the beginning of talking pictures in 1927, Todd went to Hollywood to sell himself to the motion picture companies as an expert on soundproofing. He built some of the first soundproof stages there, making and losing another fortune before he was twenty. Returning to Chicago, he wrote radio skits for the comedy team of Olsen and Johnson. He created his own sixty-minute vaudeville revue called *Bring on the Dames*, starring "Pete, the Personality Penguin."

Todd's flair for showmanship found its first full-fledged expression at the Chicago World's Fair in 1933. There he created the Flame Dance, in which a girl representing a moth had her clothes gradually singed off by a real flame. He also invented a gadget called Kute Kris Kringle which was successful in department stores.

With the money gained from these two ventures he went to Broadway in 1937 to produce his first musical comedy, *Call Me Ziggy*. It was so bad a failure that George Jean Nathan reviewed Todd's resplendent dress suit instead of the show. His second production, *The Man from Cairo*, was a similar fiasco in 1938.

However, he more than recouped his losses with the production of *The Hot Mikado*, starring dancer Bill Robinson in 1939. In Chicago he had briefly presented a straight version of Gilbert and Sullivan's *The Mikado* with an opera singer; it had been unsuccessful. After changing the original into a jazz version, he received enthusiastic notices from the New York critics. When he moved *The Hot Mikado* to the New York World's Fair it became as great a money-maker as the other three attractions he had there; these were Gypsy Rose Lee's revue, *Streets of Paris, Gay New Orleans,* and the *Dancing Campus* which attracted "10, 000 jitterbugs" (New York *Times,* May 9, 1943).

His first big-time Broadway venture was the musical *Star and Garter* with Gypsy Rose Lee in 1942, which brought him the capital to finance his second lavish musical, *Something for the Boys,* starring Ethel Merman in 1943. In the same year he presented *The Naked Genius,* written by Miss Lee and directed by George S. Kaufman. Todd withdrew the play although it was doing well at the box office, because a poll revealed that only 44 per cent of the audiences liked the show.

In 1944, after another successful musical, *Mexican Hayride,* with songs by Cole Porter, Todd turned to serious social drama with *Pick-up Girl,* a play about female juvenile delinquents. The play was produced in London and was well received. Also in 1944 he presented Mae West in *Catherine Was Great* which ran for 191 performances.

The impresario's relationship with the critics on the one hand and the public on the other is best represented by his biggest money-maker, *Up in Central Park.* Opening on Broadway at the Century Theatre in January 1945, it received unfavorable notices but grossed more than $2,000,000 and ran for 504 performances. Moreover, Todd had produced it successfully at the Hollywood Bowl and had sold it to Universal Pictures for $100,000. It had also had a great success as a USO Camp Show, one of the first full-scale musical comedies to tour Army bases.

As civilian consultant to the Special Services Division of the U. S. Army, Todd was sent to Europe in 1945 to provide entertainment to improve the morale of the troops. He organized entertainment using talent recruited from the ranks. When Todd brought Maurice Evans' "streamlined G.I. *Hamlet*" from the Army camps to Broadway, Burton Rascoe wrote in the New York *World-Telegram,* "It was unlike anything I've ever seen or expect to see," and called it a "bizarre theatrical experience" (December 14, 1945). It was presented in nineteenth century costume and ran for 131 performances.

A further cultural tinge was added to Todd's production schedule with his presentation of comedian Bobby Clark's version of Molière's *The Would-Be Gentleman* early in 1946, followed by *January Thaw,* a straight play which the critics found "implausible" and "dull." With *Up in Central Park* and *Hamlet,* he then had four productions running on Broadway at one time.

Todd's *As the Girls Go* (1948) ran for 420 performances. In June 1950 he produced *Peep Show,* which ran for 276 performances. A Garson Kanin comedy, *The Live Wire,* presented by Todd in August 1950, closed after 28 performances.

Wide World

MIKE TODD

A Night in Venice was produced by Todd at the Jones Beach $4,000,000 Marine Stadium in the summers of 1952 and 1953. With a company of 300, including Metropolitan Opera singers, Todd presented the show, set to Johann Strauss music, across a 90-foot stretch of Zachs Bay from a 104-foot island stage with a revolving center. The production, which reportedly cost $380,000, was called "a strange parlay between culture and carnival excitement . . . between Strauss and a hot dog." Todd's son, Michael, was his production assistant and also supervised the Marine Circus produced there in the afternoons.

The new Todd-AO film process was introduced in *Oklahoma!* in October 1955, directed by Fred Zinnemann and distributed by Magna Theatre Corporation which Todd organized in 1953 with Joseph M. Schenck. It imparts width of perception and depth of focus comparable to that in Cinerama's wide-screen process. The projector is operated from the standard booth in the rear of the movie theatre. It also may be used to project regular 35mm. motion pictures. Bosley Crowther's review of *Oklahoma!* was very favorable, but he had reservations about the new process, and criticized "the distortion of the images when the picture is viewed from the seats on the sides." However he praised the fine sense of depth in the outdoor scenes (New York *Times,* October 11, 1955). William K. Zinsser in the New York *Herald Tribune* wrote: "In the new film process . . . the figures are tremendous, and the close-ups are so sharp in detail that the texture of skin and clothing, the sheen of a girl's hair, are almost real enough to touch. . . . The landscape curves, depending on where you

TODD, MIKE—*Continued*

sit. The colors are vivid." The image on the curved screen is fifty feet wide and twenty-five feet high. After the première of *Oklahoma!* Todd insisted that the process was "great" but that the print used was "scratchy and covered with snow. And the sound was muffled by the closed curtain" (New York *World-Telegram and Sun*, October 15, 1955).

Todd has blue eyes and black hair; he stands five feet eight inches tall and weighs 160 pounds. His first wife, Bertha Freshman, whom he married in 1926, died in 1946. On July 4, 1947 he married actress Joan Blondell, from whom he was divorced in 1950. His son, Michael, Jr., by his first wife, was born on October 8, 1929. Todd was a member of the Theatrical and Motion Picture Industry Committee for Roosevelt, Truman and Wagner in 1944. Todd does most of his business by telephone, getting and making as many as 400 calls a day. He smokes 65-cent cigars, but otherwise has simple tastes. He enjoys watching baseball and prize fights. Most of his reading is confined to books that offer possibilities for shows. He is planning two pictures in the Todd-AO process: *War and Peace* in Yugoslavia, "where there are lots of cavalry and the countryside isn't full of telegraph poles", and *Around the World in 80 Days.*

References

N Y Times II pl My 9 '43
N Y Times Mag p17 My 13 '45 por
New Yorker 30:20 Ja 15 '55
Sat Eve Post 223:32 Je 9 '51
Theatre Arts 37:80 Jl '53
Who's Who in the Theatre (1952)

TODD, RICHARD June 11, 1919- Actor

Address: b. c/o Associated British Picture Corporation, Ltd., Elstree Studios, Boreham Wood, London, England

First acclaimed for his convincing Scottish burr in the leading role in Warner Brothers' motion picture, *The Hasty Heart,* Irish actor Richard Todd has since 1950 appeared in over a dozen English and American films, ranging from moody psychological melodramas to swashbuckling romances.

In *A Man Called Peter* (1954), Todd was praised by critics for his warm and sympathetic portrayal of Dr. Peter Marshall, the evangelical Scottish preacher. He also received favorable reviews of his role as Sir Walter Raleigh opposite Bette Davis in Twentieth Century-Fox Film Corporation's production of *The Virgin Queen,* which opened at the Roxy Theatre in New York on August 5, 1955. In London he was acclaimed for his characterization of the Royal Air Force pilot Guy Gibson, V.C., in *The Dam Busters,* an Associated British production.

Richard Todd, whose full name is Richard Andrew Palethorpe-Todd, was born in Dublin, Ireland on June 11, 1919, the son of Major A. W. and Marville Palethorpe-Todd. When Major Palethorpe-Todd was transferred to India for two years (1921-1923), he took his wife and son with him. During the next two years, the family was back in Ireland, where they frequently spent their vacations on a beautiful estate owned by Todd's grandfather. In 1925 the family moved to Devon, England, and remained there while the boy began his education.

After receiving private lessons from a tutor, Todd was sent to a preparatory school not far from Exeter. While there he was seriously ill with rheumatic fever, but a careful regimen including outdoor exercise finally restored him to health. From the preparatory school, he went to Shrewsbury Public School, founded in 1551 by Edward VI.

Deciding to become a playwright, Todd looked for practical theatre experience and enrolled in the Italia Conti School in London. Since 1911 this school had trained many fine actors and actresses, among whom were Noel Coward, Gertrude Lawrence, Brian Aherne, and Margaret Lockwood. After six months Todd left the school and played in repertory and stock companies in several small towns in England and Scotland. He appeared in many roles including Danny in Emlyn Williams' melodrama, *Night Must Fall,* and George in John Steinbeck's play, *Of Mice and Men* (New York *Times,* April 17, 1955).

In the late 1930's many theatrical companies were forming in Scotland and in December 1939, Todd helped to found a repertory company in the town of Dundee. He soon found that he enjoyed acting so much that he relinquished his plan of becoming a playwright.

The war interrupted Todd's acting career. Volunteering for duty, he served as a staff officer in the British Army for six years, in the Infantry, the Commandos, the Armored Cavalry, and the Airbourne. While he was with the Commandos, he trained for an entire winter in Iceland. One of the first paratroop officers to be dropped into Normandy the day before the invasion, he fought through the European campaign and later served in Palestine until he was honorably discharged in June 1946.

After the war, Todd returned to the Dundee Repertory Company and played the male lead in *Claudia.* He became engaged to the young leading lady, Catherine Grant-Bogle. He played the part of Yank in the play *The Hasty Heart* by John Patrick, and incidentally learned from a Scotch actor how to speak with a Scottish burr, which later proved useful in his acting career.

Seeking more financial security than the Dundee theatre could offer, Todd went to London in 1948 to find work in motion pictures, and casting director Robert Lennard gave him a contract with Associated British Picture Corporation, Ltd. His first picture was *For Them That Trespass* (1948), a melodrama in which he played a young man punished for a murder he did not commit. The consensus of critical opinion was that the young star's acting was almost the sole redeeming feature in the picture. When the film appeared in American theatres,

Alton Cook observed in the New York *World-Telegram and Sun* that Todd "already was a matured and effective actor."

When director Vincent Sherman of Warner Brothers was looking for an actor to play the role of Lachie, the young Scotsman in *The Hasty Heart,* he heard of Todd's convincing Scottish burr and offered him the part. *The Hasty Heart,* in which Ronald Reagan and Patricia Neal also appeared, was highly praised after its release in 1949.

"Much of the credit for this success," wrote the London *Times* critic, "belongs to Mr. Richard Todd." In America Todd was hailed as "a vivid and vigorous actor" (New York *World-Telegram and Sun*) whose performance was "star calibre in every facet" (*Variety*) and "combined lofty stature with deep feeling, attracting enormous sympathy without an ounce of sentiment" (New York *Herald Tribune*). Warner Brothers promptly announced that Todd was a definite contender for an "Oscar" Academy of Motion Pictures Arts and Sciences award.

But the further development of Todd's reputation was hampered for a while by poor material. After *The Hasty Heart* he appeared with Valerie Hobson in *Interrupted Journey* (1949). Bosley Crowther complained that "an excellent British cast has been put to playing this nonsense with a serious and determined will" (New York *Times*). A starring role in Alfred Hitchcock's melodrama *Stage Fright* (1949), with Jane Wyman, Marlene Dietrich, and Michael Wilding, did not enhance Todd's reputation. Nor was his next picture, *A Portrait of Claire* (1949), an improvement. As a critic in *Variety* complained, "Todd is most inadequately served in what is, to all intents and purposes, a minor role."

On December 26, 1949, Todd came for the first time to the United States to make *Lightning Strikes Twice,* but again his talents were wasted upon what the critics called mediocre material. They made similar comments on the British pictures *Flesh and Blood* (1950), in which Todd appeared with Glynis Johns and Joan Greenwood, *Affair in Monte Carlo* (1952), in which he played opposite Merle Oberon, and *The Assassin* (1952), costarring Eva Bartok.

More suited to Todd's abilities were the three motion pictures he made in England for Walt Disney. As the romantic outlaw in Disney's live-action production of *Robin Hood* (1951), Todd gave a vivacious and appealing performance. He next played opposite Glynis Johns as the hero of *The Sword and the Rose* (1953), a story set in the time of Henry VIII and based on Charles Major's popular novel, *When Knighthood was in Flower.* During the filming of this picture, on November 24, 1952, Todd was thrown from a horse and fractured several ribs. The third picture he made for Disney was *Rob Roy* (1953), also costarring Glynis Johns. A critic described him in this picture as being "among the best of adventure heroes, virile and sympathetic" (*Photoplay*).

When the picture opened in February 1954 at the Criterion Theatre Otis L. Guernsey, Jr., commented in the New York *Herald Tribune*

RICHARD TODD

(February 4, 1954): "Rob Roy, the Highland Rogue, is unmatched for boldness and resolve; that is as it should be, and as it is played by Richard Todd, in a red beard." Bosley Crowther in the New York *Times* described Todd as "handsome as the kilted and bonneted Rob [but] simply a splendid idealization of the hero in Highland costume. Don't look for history or plausible fiction in this film."

Recognition came to Todd for his memorable performance in Twentieth Century-Fox Film Corporation's *A Man Called Peter,* based on the best-selling novel of the same title by Catherine Marshall. A critic for the New York *Daily News* wrote: "Richard Todd's performance of the man Peter is an inspired one. It would be difficult to name another actor who could have given so vital and impressive a characterization of the popular minister as Todd gives." Todd had listened to recordings of Peter Marshall's sermons, and Mrs. Marshall was quoted in an interview as saying that he "was just about the only film actor whose Scottish syllables would have met her husband's standards" (New York *Herald Tribune*).

Todd's next picture, also made for Twentieth Century-Fox, was *The Virgin Queen* (1955), in which he played the role of Sir Walter Raleigh. Bosley Crowther praised his performance as "fine and aggressive" . . . [he] makes reasonable the interest and the confidence Elizabeth had in him" (New York *Times,* August 6, 1955).

For his outstanding performance in *The Hasty Heart,* Todd won the annual award of the London *Daily Express* and on May 24, 1950 the "Silver Star," Britain's national film award. He was voted one of the top ten British box-office attractions in the *Motion Picture Herald-Fame* Poll (1952). *Rob Roy* was selected as the Command Performance Film in England for 1953.

(Continued next page)

TODD, RICHARD—*Continued*

Richard Todd married Catherine (Kitty) Grant-Bogle in August 1949. A son, Peter, was born on June 30, 1952. Todd is five feet ten inches in height and has hazel eyes and dark-brown hair. His hobbies are riding, fishing, shooting, and farming. He says that he is saving his money to purchase a farm and, perhaps, to reclaim his grandfather's estate in Ireland.

References

N Y Herald Tribune V p5 Ja 15 '50
N Y Post My 14 '50
N Y Post Mag p11 Ap 9 '50 pors
N Y World-Telegram Ap 29 '50
Motion Picture and Television Almanac, 1955

TOUSSAINT, JEANNE (tōō' săn zhăn)

Jewelry designer

Address: b. 13 rue de la Paix, Paris 2, France; h. 1 Place d'Iéna, Paris 16, France

For thirty years, as "directrice-artistique" for Cartier's, Jeanne Toussaint has been a leader in the field of jewelry design. Under her direction heirloom jewels have been reset and new creations have been produced that have influenced fashions around the world. Trained by Louis Cartier, she has not only provided ideas for resetting the diamonds, rubies and emeralds of the wealthy, but has also created many costume jewelry designs in semi-precious stones. "No one," wrote Cecil Beaton, "is more revered among the initiates for her extraordinary taste than the talented Jeanne Toussaint." She has been honored for her artistic achievement by the French Government.

Jeanne Toussaint was born before the turn of the twentieth century in France in Vaucouleurs, Lorraine, to Édouard Victor and Marie-Louise (Elegeer) Toussaint. Her mother was Flemish; her father's family can be traced back to the Hauvettes and other neighbors of Jeanne d'Arc in Domremy. Jeanne was reared in Lorraine, where she attended Catholic schools. From her father, who was in the cloth industry, she acquired her deep love of precious materials. At thirteen, in revolt against country life, the girl left home to live with her elder sister in Paris. There she began her artistic development, coming under the influence of the antiquarian Charles Michel and of such artists as Helleu, Boldini, Sem, Iribé, Vertès, and Christian Bérard. Combining her intelligence and training with the sound values of her Lorraine background, the country girl began to take her place among the leaders of good taste and fashion in Paris.

Mademoiselle Toussaint started her career by designing women's handbags whose novelty met with great success. Her work attracted the attention of Louis Cartier, grandson of Louis-François Cartier, who had founded the famous French jewelry house in 1853. Louis Cartier had entered the family business in 1898 when his father, Alfred Cartier, opened the shop at 13 rue de la Paix. Together, father and son became world-famous as jewelers to royalty. In 1902 they opened their house in London and in 1907 in New York. Recognizing flawless taste in the work of Jeanne Toussaint, Louis Cartier in the early 1920's introduced her to the field of jewelry design in the workshops of his firm. A master craftsman himself, he advised the young woman not to learn to draw, warning: "If you do so, you are lost!" Although Mlle. Toussaint retained a keen interest in the work of contemporary artists and draftsmen in every field, she followed Cartier's advice and never learned to draw. "It is this inability to draw," she explains, "which enables me to criticize the work of others."

As "directrice-artistique" for Cartier's, she has provided the ideas for resetting the gems of royalty and of some of the world's wealthiest people. Also, as a result of her "love for strange settings and stones, unique jewelry never before seen has made its appearance in the world of fashion." Her work, according to Cecil Beaton in *The Glass of Fashion,* has a fresh approach yet is "bounded by the classical. Her sense of equilibrium and proportion is so strong that anything she creates represents safely good taste."

With her it is not the stone itself that is important, but the way in which the stone lends its color, brilliance and shape to the whole design. She enjoys working with less expensive stones as well as with those of fabulous value, creating color combinations with yellow sapphires, tourmalines, amethysts, coral and aquamarines that rival the jewels of India. Using platinum settings—first introduced by Louis Cartier—she has removed the stones from heavy First Empire tiaras, bracelets and brooches and has created parures of filigree lightness. She particularly likes the style of

JEANNE TOUSSAINT

eighteenth century brooches with bunches of diamond flowers trembling on taut wires and "has made diamonds flexible, hanging them in little fringes, stalactites or tassels, creating chains of diamonds that are as supple as the beads of a rosary."

Although her jewel-maker's touch is light, her "gift springs from an unswerving, granite-hard instinct, allied with irrevocable powers of decision," wrote Beaton. "She knows exactly what she wants and, if she is convinced that one of her ideas is good, can never be influenced by any opposition nor swayed by any theory of public taste. This extraordinary independence insures the originality that is eventually acclaimed by the public."

Jeanne Toussaint's ideas come from "everywhere and from everything—from flowers and animals, from statuary and architecture," reported Jane Barry in the *Christian Science Monitor*. "Each one seeks to interpret some shape or form hitherto unseen in the field of jewelry." The designer has no preference for any particular period of art or for any special country, her tastes ranging from the antique to the most modern, from Egyptian, Chinese and Indian art to all periods of French design. Although she has an exquisite touch with diamonds, she particularly enjoys creating sprays of flowers made of carved coral and ivory, tasseled lapel ornaments of rubies or sapphires, bright jewelled birds in tiny gold cages. These express the designer's belief that jewelry settings should be decorative in themselves and not merely a background for precious stones.

One of her favorite creations is a jewelled clip in the shape of a leopard mounted on a large sapphire "rock." Sculpturally perfect, the animal's platinum body is spotted with hundreds of tiny sapphires. To match this clip, she has designed a bracelet with a leopard springing, his body shaped to encircle the wrist. So fond is she of these two pieces that she has kept them in her private collection of jewels.

Pierre Claudel summed up the professional position of Jeanne Toussaint when he wrote: "In her designs one finds the origin of all that has given French jewelry its outstanding position in this field. Beginning her career at a time when Paris was at the height of its brilliance and prosperity, Jeanne Toussaint helped guide styles in jewelry through several decades of change and adaptation without ever sacrificing good taste to purely commercial or popular interests. Today she continues to give herself to her work with the enthusiasm and freshness of imagination that have characterized her activities throughout her long and brilliant career."

By her daily contact with the most exacting international clientele, she has subtly influenced fashion and good taste, while her close association with the leaders of French design and decoration—Christian Dior, Schiaparelli, Balenciaga—gives evidence of the high place she holds in the world of elegance and style. The French Government paid homage to the artistic talents of Jeanne Toussaint by presenting her with the Cross of the Chevalier of the Legion of Honor.

Mlle. Toussaint's apartment at one Place d'Iéna has been described by Cecil Beaton and others as a model of perfection and good taste. Combining rare eighteenth century pieces, fragments of Greek sculpture, the head of a Buddha and other priceless objects of art, she has created rooms that are simple and modern in spirit. There is no noisy color scheme—only a discreet use of white and champagne-colored fabrics. Skilled in the "allied arts of living," she has won praise as a gourmet for the "superb quality of the wine and food over which she presides."

She has been described by Beaton as "a birdlike little woman with a beak of a nose, an exquisitely pretty mouth that hints of her sensitivity and with chinchilla-colored hair worn in the bobbed wisps of the twenties." Jeanne Toussaint is five feet four inches tall, weighs 127 pounds, has blue eyes and a low voice. She told *Current Biography*'s Paris correspondent that she believes jewels are the best investment in a troubled world because one can always carry them along in case of war. She also believes that expensive jewelry gives a woman confidence.

References

Christian Sci Mon II p10 My 17 '51 por
Jardin des Modes O '48

Beaton, C. W. H., The Glass of Fashion (1954)

TOWERS, J(OHN) H(ENRY) Jan. 30, 1885-Apr. 30, 1955 U.S. Naval officer; pioneer naval airman; early in career began fight to build up naval aviation; won wings in 1911; participated in famous NC trans-Atlantic flight (1919); one of his flying accidents led to development of safety belt; became chief of Navy's Bureau of Aeronautics (1939); chief aviation adviser to Fleet Admiral Chester W. Nimitz in Pacific Ocean (1944) and then commander in chief in the Pacific (1945); after retirement as Admiral in 1947 became vice-president of Pan American World Airways; death by cancer. See *Current Biography* (Oct.) 1941.

Obituary

N Y Times p88 My 1 '55

TRIPPE, JUAN T(ERRY) (trĭp wän) June 27, 1899- Airline executive

Address: b. c/o Pan American World Airways, Chrysler Bldg., 135 E. 42d St., New York 17; h. Mead's Lane, Greenwich, Conn.

NOTE: This biography supersedes the article which appeared in *Current Biography* in 1942.

Maintaining that the United States must continue to hold the lead in "atomic weapons, in military air power, and in guided missiles," Juan T. Trippe, president of Pan American World Airways, is also convinced that the American aviation industry must help "the

Pan American World Airways
JUAN T. TRIPPE

uncommitted nations of the world . . . with its capital and know-how, in partnership with local investors, to develop transportation systems so that these countries may enter directly into the age of flight." He expressed these thoughts in a speech before the Aero Club of Washington, D.C. on December 18, 1954 in which he credited American aviation with having played "a major role in helping to avert a shooting war and with an even greater part to play in the current fight of the free world to win the cold war" (New York *World Telegram and Sun*, December 18, 1954).

Trippe, who is one of America's foremost pioneers in international commercial aviation, directs the global operations of "the world's longest airline." Pan-American, which now has offices in eighty-four countries and colonies, was established by Trippe and two air-minded friends in 1927, when it bid successfully for the first U.S. international airmail contract. Pan American's "clippers" and other aircraft flew a new record of 2,015,000 passenger miles in 1953, more than any competitor, domestic or foreign, engaged in international air transport. Its Tokyo to Honolulu flight, which makes use of the Pacific jet stream, is the longest non-stop regularly scheduled run of any commercial airline. (The jet stream is an air current which runs over the Pacific Ocean at an altitude of about five miles; airliners use the eastbound winds to speed them from Tokyo to Honolulu.)

On May 1, 1954 Pan American World Airways inaugurated its sale of round-the-world trips and other overseas flights on the installment plan, with passengers making down payments of 10 per cent of the cost of a ticket, the balance payable over a period of twenty months. The traveling public has welcomed the new ticket-purchasing plan, and payment collections have presented no bothersome problems to the airline. Repayment was 100% at the end of the plan's first year.

The International Air Transport Association, a seventy-airline organization known as "the congress of the world's airlines," elected Trippe president at its tenth annual meeting in September 1954 for a one-year term beginning in 1955.

Juan Terry Trippe was born to Charles White and Lucy Adeline (Terry) Trippe at Seabright, New Jersey on June 27, 1899; he was named Juan in memory of Juanita Terry, the Venezuelan wife of his great-uncle. His mother's ancestors had taken part in the colonization of South America. The Trippes are of English origin, descendants of Henry Trippe, who migrated from Kent to eastern Maryland in 1698. Juan's father was in the investment banking and brokerage business in New York City.

Most of Juan's childhood was spent in New York, where he attended the Bovea School. By the time he was ten years old he was making a hobby of building model airplanes propelled by elastic bands, and flying them in Central Park. At the Hill School, Pottstown, Pennsylvania, where he prepared for college, and played football, Juan Trippe was so modest and quiet that he was nicknamed "The Mummy" by his classmates. He entered Yale University in 1917 and took private flying lessons with the result that he was accepted in the Naval Flying Service. He qualified for night flying at the Pensacola Florida Naval Air Station and received his ensign's commission but the Armistice prevented his being assigned overseas.

Returning to Yale, he was active in collegiate swimming, rowing and football. He was founder and president of the Yale Flying Club and in his senior year was chairman of the college pictorial, the *Yale Graphic*. He was elected to St. Anthony Hall, the Delta Psi fraternity and the Mohican, and was one of seven seniors elected to the Aurelian Honor Society. He received his Ph. B. with the class of 1921.

On graduation from Yale in 1921, Trippe became a bond salesman with the banking firm of Lee, Higginson and Company, intending at the time eventually to enter the family business of Trippe and Company. Early in 1923, however, he learned from a trade publication that the Navy was offering nine surplus planes for sale, and with former members of the Yale Flying Club, he purchased seven of these "boats" for $500. He organized Long Island Airways, Inc., at Rockaway Beach, where passengers were taken up for sightseeing flights. Charter service was furnished, and occasional contract work was done for motion picture companies. In 1924 he interested a group of Boston bankers in supplying the bulk of the capital needed to start the Colonial Air Transport Company, which undertook a New York and Boston service under the first United States airmail contract ever awarded.

He served as managing director of Colonial until 1926, when he proposed extending Colonial's route from New York to Miami and Havana. His argument that by so doing, Colonial could "corner" the Atlantic Coast airways and later branch out into the West Indies and South America did not convince Colonial's conservative-minded stockholders, who voted him down. His association with Colonial having then been ended, Trippe and two wealthy friends, Cornelius Vanderbilt Whitney and John T. Hambleton, formed a new corporation capitalized at $300,000, which acquired a single Fokker three-engine monoplane and bid successfully for the first U.S. international airmail contract in 1927 between Florida and Cuba, and also started a mail service in Alaska.

A rival group, Pan American Airways, Inc., merged with the Trippe-Whitney-Hambleton concern, and a holding company eventually named Pan American Airways Corporation was formed with Whitney as chairman of the board and Trippe as president and general manager. Airmail contracts to Puerto Rico, the Canal Zone, and elsewhere followed, with the result that by the end of 1929, Pan American had 11,000 miles of routes.

The company engaged Colonel Charles A. Lindbergh as a consultant, and in the early 1930's he explored possible commercial air-routes across the Atlantic and over the polar regions to Asia. Island bases on Pacific islands were also established, a service to the Philippines being inaugurated in 1936.

By 1940, despite attempts in 1938 and 1940 by members of Pan Am's board to wrest some of the executive power from Trippe, he had maintained his one-man authority and had increased the airline's route mileage to 72,000, and its net profit exceeded $2,250,000 (most of which was plowed back into the company). A New York to Lisbon service was inaugurated in 1939.

At the invitation of the Royal Aeronautical Society Trippe delivered the twenty-ninth Wilbur Wright Memorial Lecture in 1941 and revealed that 3,000 horsepower airplane engines were "in prospect" and predicted that in another two years the passenger service between New York and London could be restored with a flying time of only twelve hours.

In South America during World War II the company's previous so-called "air conquest" of the continent made it possible for Pan American to "freeze out" rival German and Italian airlines and to plan and put into operation a vast system of air fields and bases for use in the ferrying of personnel and matériel. After the Japanese attack on Pearl Harbor the company's fleet was largely occupied as a contract carrier for the U.S. government. Trippe was decorated by Secretary of War Robert P. Patterson with the Medal of Merit "for organizing and operating the world-wide network of routes that supported our fighting forces from December 7, 1941 to victory in the fall of 1945."

In the postwar period Trippe, who in 1946 became acting chairman of the board and chairman of the executive committee as well as president, has championed two principles: the consolidation of U.S. flying interests to meet foreign subsidized competition, and the establishment of low-cost air travel at tourist class rates. As early as 1943, in a speech before the National Institute of Social Sciences, he had said that air transport had "a very clear choice—of becoming a luxury service to carry the well-to-do at high prices—or to carry the average man at what he can afford to pay."

Trippe's much-discussed article "Now You Can Take That Trip Abroad" appeared in the December 1948 issue of *United Nations World* (a condensation was published in the *Reader's Digest,* January 1949). He pointed out that "a beginning is being made in low-cost travel to Europe," the cost of a round-trip ticket between New York and London having dropped to well under $500. By 1952 the principle of two classes of air service (first and tourist) had found acceptance by all "major operators" on international routes.

The name Pan American World Airways dates from the end of 1949, when the holding and operating companies were merged. In 1953 it had a record net income of $10,802,644, as compared with $6,673,265 earned in 1952, despite taxes that were more than double the year before (New York *Times*, April 20, 1954). During 1953 the company carried a record of 1,657,000 passengers in overseas service, a gain of 16 per cent over the previous year. In 1954 it recorded the largest volume of business in its history—passenger revenue increased 9 per cent and cargo revenue 14 per cent, compared with 1953.

A pioneer in the use of upper-air jet streams in regularly scheduled commercial flights, Pan American began in November 1954 its third season of non-stop 3,870-mile flights from Tokyo to Honolulu. For its transPacific jet-stream operation it was awarded the Frye Airline Performance Trophy. Among many earlier notable awards in aviation that Trippe has won are the Robert Collier Trophy in 1937 and the Harmon Aviation Trophy in 1947.

Other business enterprises with which Trippe is associated include the Metropolitan Life Insurance Company, the Chrysler Corporation, the Waldorf Astoria Corporation and the Fidelity and Deposit Company of Maryland, of all of which he is a director.

Trippe holds honorary degrees from a number of universities. Foreign honors have been conferred on him by the Dominican Republic and by Panama, Colombia, and Honduras (1939), Brazil, Portugal and Belgium (1946), the Netherlands (1949), France and Colombia (1951), Germany, Lebanon and Liberia (1952), (1954). He is a trustee of the Public Health Research Institute of New York City, Carnegie Institute of Washington, D.C., National Geographic Society, National Safety Council, and the National Foundation for the Prevention of Infantile Paralysis. He is also a director of the New York Chapter of the American Red Cross and a member of the executive committee of the Business Advisory Council of the U.S. Department of Commerce and is president of the Economic Club of New York.

TRIPPE, JUAN T.—*Continued*

He belongs to the Wings Club, the Society of Colonial Wars, and Aviation Post of the American Legion in New York.

He married Elizabeth Stettinius, a sister of former Secretary of State Edward Stettinius, Jr, on June 16, 1928. They are the parents of one daughter, Betty, and three sons, Charles, John and Edward. "Trippe is a relaxed and placid parent . . . who likes to hear all about his four children's day in school," stated *Time*. He enjoys swimming and surf-fishing and in winter skiing with his entire family.

Determined to keep ahead of British jet leadership. Trippe "has placed firm orders with de Havilland for three yet unbuilt Comet III's, despite the fact that he spent $40,000,000 for Boeing Stratocruisers . . . the giant double-deckers [which proved] excessively expensive to operate" (*Forbes*, November 1, 1954).

References (see also references listed in 1942 biographical sketch)

Air Transportation p26+ Ap '43 por
Colliers 100:16+ Ag 14 '47 por
Coronet 33:104+ D '52 por
N Y Times VII p16+ Je 4 '44; p16 S 28 '46
Scholastic 41:31 O 4 '43 por
Time 48:75+ Jl 29 '46 por; 53:84+ Mr 28 '49 pors
Holland, M. and Smith, T. M., Architects of Aviation (1951)
National Cyclopædia of American Biography, Current vol F, 1939-42
Poor's Register of Directors and Executives, 1952
Who's Who in America, 1954-55
World Biography (1954)

TUBMAN, WILLIAM V(ACANARAT) S(HADRACH) Nov. 29, 1895- President of Liberia; lawyer

Address: Executive Mansion, Ashmun St., Monrovia, Liberia

The Chief Executive of Liberia for over eleven years, William V. S. Tubman has worked to modernize his country, an independent African republic, through a series of educational and economic reforms. "Bodor Shad" (i.e., Brother Shadrach), as Tubman is known among his people, has given voting rights to the back-country tribesmen and also to women and introduced the secret ballot.

In the fall of 1954 President Tubman made an official visit to the United States at the invitation of President Dwight D. Eisenhower. Tubman had previously served as an Associate Justice of Liberia's Supreme Court from 1937 to 1943 and as a Senator from 1923 to 1931 and 1934 to 1937.

Liberia (which means "land of freedom") has an area of 43,000 square miles along the coast of western Africa between British Sierra Leone and the French Ivory Coast. Its Constitution is patterned after that of the United States. English, the official language, is spoken in the cities, while some thirty native dialects are spoken in the interior, which is largely covered with tropical forests. Only "Negroes or persons of Negro descent" may vote or hold office. The land, purchased from six native tribal kings, was settled in 1822 by American freed slaves under the auspices of the American Colonization Society and Jehudi Ashmun. The colony became a self-governing republic on July 26, 1847 and received U.S. recognition in 1862.

William Vacanarat Shadrach Tubman was born at Harper, Liberia on November 29, 1895. His father, the Reverend Alexander Tubman, was descended from settlers who migrated from Augusta, Georgia in 1834; his mother, *née* Elizabeth Barnes, moved to Liberia from Atlanta, Georgia in 1872. William attended the Cape Palmas Seminary and Cuttington College and Divinity School.

Admitted to the bar in 1917, he began to practice law in Harper. From 1919 to 1922 he served as collector of internal revenue for Maryland county. For a short period he taught school and then served with the Liberian militia, rising in grade from private to colonel. A candidate on the True Whig ticket (the party in power since 1878), Tubman was elected in 1923 to the Liberian Senate for a term of six years. He was re-elected in 1929. Tubman, who had become a distinguished lay preacher, was selected in 1928 to represent Liberia at the Quadrennial Conference of the Methodist Church meeting at Kansas City, Missouri.

In 1930 a League of Nations commission found Liberia, a member of the League, guilty of selling her own people into slavery to cocoa planters on the Spanish island of Fernando Poo. The President of Liberia, Charles D. B. King, and the Vice-President, Allen N. Yancy, resigned. Tubman, who had been Yancy's legal adviser, withdrew from the Senate in 1931. (A full discussion of the episode may be found in Arthur I. Hayman and Harold Preece's *Lighting up Liberia* [1943] and Ernest Jerome Yancy's *Historical Light of Liberia's Yesterday and Today* [1934].)

Tubman returned to the Senate in 1934 but resigned in 1937 to accept an appointment as Associate Justice of the Liberian Supreme Court, a post he held until 1943. The nominee of the True Whig party, Tubman was elected President of the republic on May 4, 1943. In the spring of 1943 Liberia's President Edwin Barclay visited the United States, accompanied by President-elect Tubman. Barclay had been invited by President Franklin D. Roosevelt, who had stopped at Monrovia on his return trip from the Casablanca conference. Barclay and Tubman were the first Negro guests to spend a night in the White House and the first to be entertained there since Booker T. Washington lunched with President Theodore Roosevelt in 1901 (*Time*, June 7, 1943).

During World War II Liberia cooperated with the United States. On March 31, 1942 an agreement was signed by the two countries giving the United States the right to construct, operate and defend airports in Liberia for the duration of the war. A mutual aid agreement was concluded on June 8, 1943 whereby the United States extended Lend-Lease aid to Liberia for defense. One of Tubman's first acts as President, after taking office on January 3, 1944, was to declare war on Germany and Japan.

In the period following his inauguration, President Tubman's efforts resulted in the enactment of civil service and income tax laws. He drafted an amendment to the Constitution which was approved on December 11, 1945 and resulted in the extension of the suffrage to women. "We collect hut taxes from [the aborigines] and I will not tolerate taxation without representation," he told Earl Parker Hanson (*Harper's Magazine,* February 1947). Aboriginal membership in the House of Representatives, as provided by a Constitutional amendment adopted in 1946, is on the basis of one representative to each of the three provinces. Since that time the number of native representatives has been increased to eight.

The first President of Liberia to travel extensively in the interior, Tubman toured the Western Province in 1945 and the Central and Eastern Provinces in March 1946, holding councils with chiefs of the aboriginal tribes and listening to complaints. At the councils he reaffirmed his earlier decree that "no man is to be called for forced labor on government projects during the planting season." He also discharged several district commissioners and members of the Frontier Force for "malfeasance, misfeasance and unfeasance."

During Tubman's Administration economic and technical progress has been made in Liberia, which is almost completely undeveloped. Until World War II the only important foreign concession was a grant of 1,000,000 acres in 1926 to the Firestone Plantations Company for the cultivation of rubber. In 1945 Liberia granted iron mining rights in the Bomi Hills to the Liberia Mining Company (a subsidiary of Republic Steel Corporation), which built Liberia's first railroad. Since 1949 production has been 1,000,000 tons of high-grade iron a year, bringing Liberia $2,000,000 a year in royalties. Regular air service has been scheduled from Roberts Field, now operated by Pan American World Airways. On April 25, 1952 a new airport, the James Spriggs Payne Field, at Sinkor, was opened.

On December 22, 1950 an agreement was signed by the United States and Liberia for a development program costing $30,000,000 under Point IV, to be implemented under control of a joint Liberian-American Commission. The U.S. health and economic missions that had been sent in 1944 have been merged in this new organization. Point IV (now called Technical Cooperation Administration) projects in Liberia include demonstration farms, malaria control centers, school improvement and teacher training, surveying of mineral resources, and the organization of a bureau of statistics. The Export-Import Bank also granted Liberia about $6,000,000 for a loan to be used in constructing roads and building public water and sewerage systems in Monrovia.

Wide World

WILLIAM V. S. TUBMAN

The Port of Monrovia (named for U.S. President James Monroe), constructed with Lend-Lease funds at a cost of approximately $20,000,000, was opened July 26, 1948 and will become the property of Liberia when the original cost has been met. (The first payment of $150,000 was made in December 1952.) At present, the port is operated by the Monrovia Port Management Company, Ltd., of New York.

In 1954 negotiations were concluded with the African Fruit Company of Hamburg, Germany for an eighty-year concession by which the company will grow tropical products on a 600,000-acre area in southern Liberia. Recently, Liberia has attained a balanced budget, a condition made possible largely by foreign investments and American aid.

A constitutional amendment was passed in 1949 which provided that a President may succeed himself for a four-year term. (The initial term is for eight years.) Tubman then announced his candidacy to succeed himself. As the election of May 1, 1951 approached, a new Reformation party was formed. Its candidate for the Presidency was Didwe Twe, a native who had also opposed Tubman in 1943. President Tubman provided police protection for his opponent during the campaign. Oden and Olivia Meeker stated (*New Yorker,* November 29, 1952) that just before the election a technicality was found to disqualify Twe from the ballot.

"A number of observers think the True Whig party made a serious mistake in not letting Twe run . . . " commented the Meekers, since Tubman was the obvious choice because of "the country's growing prosperity and his personal popularity."

During his four-week visit to the United States, beginning on October 16, 1954, Tubman spent the night of October 18 at the White

TUBMAN, WILLIAM V. S.—*Continued*

House and the next evening entertained President and Mrs. Eisenhower at the Liberian Embassy in Washington. In New York City on October 28 he was presented with the city's Medal of Honor. He received an honorary degree from Lafayette College in Easton, Pennsylvania and from eight other colleges.

On October 29, 1954 President Tubman in an address to the United Nations General Assembly stated that if member states retained their national powers, the ability of the U.N. to resolve world problems would be limited. He further stated: ". . . those islands of agreement which already exist between us must be developed. We must continue the search for fresher evidences of a unity of purposes" (New York *Times,* October 30, 1954).

William V. S. Tubman has been married three times, first to the former Ariminta Dent. By his marriage to Martha A. R. Pratt in November 1935, he has five children, one of whom, William Tubman, Jr., is an undergraduate at Harvard University. In September 1948 he married Antoinette Padmore, a granddaughter of former President Arthur Barclay.

President Tubman is of medium build, soft-spoken and dapper in attire. He enjoys dancing, singing in barber-shop quartets and entertaining at the Saturday Afternoon Club in Monrovia. He likes people and is easily accessible. He named the most beautiful street in Monrovia "UN Drive." He appointed a traveling teacher to go about the country giving lectures on the United Nations (New York *Post,* November 28, 1954).

Earl Parker Hanson has written: "No one sees more clearly than Tubman the hard fact that a nation with a ruling class of 15,000 and a subject people one hundred times as large is headed for disaster in the modern economic world . . ." (*Harper's Magazine,* February 1947).

Symbolic of the distance separating Liberia's ruling oligarchy (disdainful of manual labor) from the native tribesmen is the Sunday procession to church with the Americo-Liberian gentry in long-tailed coats, carrying canes, followed by poorly clad boys carrying their hymn books. President Tubman is well aware of the tribesmen's resentment and is doing all he can to narrow the gap (New York *Post,* November 28, 1954).

References

Christian Sci Mon p 1 O 18 '54 por
Liberia Today 1:2+ F '52 pors; 1:2+ N '52 por
N Y Herald Tribune II p3 O 24 '54
N Y Times IV p6 Jl 1 '51; p7 Ja 9 '52
New Yorker 28:104+ N 29 '52
Scholastic 65:9 N 10 '54 por
U N Review 1:16 D '54
U S News 37:54+ Ag 6 '54 por
Anderson, R. E., Liberia, America's African Friend (1952)
Hayman, A. I. and Preece, H., Lighting Up Liberia (1943)
World Biography (1954)

USTINOV, PETER (ALEXANDER) Apr. 16, 1921- British actor; playwright; producer

Address: b. c/o M.C.A. (England) Ltd., 139, Piccadilly, London, W. 1., England; h. 215 King's Road, London, S.W. 3., England

"Of the films I have had the pleasure of making . . . this was the one which gave me the most pleasure, and the one which I wished could have gone on for longer," said British actor Peter Ustinov of Paramount Picture's *We're No Angels* (1955). In less than sixteen years he has reached the front rank of international entertainment in motion pictures and the theatre.

His career consists of three separate activities: acting, playwriting and producing. Acting was Ustinov's first choice, and he has appeared in at least a dozen plays and films. Writing is almost as strong an interest and he has turned out a play nearly every year since he was twenty, and the pleasure of production is one which he has indulged ever since his *School for Secrets* (1946).

Peter Alexander Ustinov was born in London on April 16, 1921. His father, descended from a Liberal Lutheran family which left Russia in 1868, is Iona Ustinov, a celebrated journalist known professionally as "Klop." Nadia Benois, his mother, is a distinguished artist who held an exhibition of her works at the Matthiesen Gallery in 1953.

In childhood Ustinov showed signs of that gift for mimicry that is so powerfully aided by an unusually flexible upper lip and a choral society's range of vocal chords. His faithful reproduction of the voices and characteristics of his parents' guests was excelled later by the perfection with which he imitated his schoolmasters. Ustinov's attendance at Westminster school was otherwise undistinguished. At sixteen he studied acting under Michel Saint-Denis at the London Theatre Studio and also experimented with playwriting.

The young actor delighted habitués of the Players' Theatre Club in 1939 with his inventions of larger-than-life characters, the Bishop of Limpopoland and Madame Lise Lotte Beethoven-Finck, the Wagnerian primadonna (*Radio Times,* May 8, 1953).

As a playwright Ustinov began with *House of Regrets* (1940), which depicted an exiled community living in London amid dreams of a Czarist restoration. James Agate, foremost critic of the day, hailed it as a masterpiece. The following year Ustinov proved his versatility by producing *Squaring the Circle* by Katayev.

Joining the British Army, Peter Ustinov found himself batman for a short while to actor David Niven. From 1942 to 1946 he served in the Royal Sussex Regiment and Royal Army Ordnance Corps. In 1942 *House of Regrets* was presented at the Arts Theatre, with sets designed by Ustinov's mother. Very soon afterward his second play, *Blow your own Trumpet,* a portrait of the phantasies and delusions of some South London café frequenters, was showing at the Old Vic (1943).

During his next four years in the army Ustinov wrote and acted in the film *The Way Ahead* (1943-1944), directed by Sir Carol

Reed, and was also author of *The Banbury Nose,* a penetrating study of family traditions with Roger Livesey starring at its production at Wyndham's (1944). After his release from military service in 1946 Ustinov was commissioned by the Air Ministry to write, direct and produce *School for Secrets,* a film about radar in which (Sir) Ralph Richardson starred. It was in this year that Ustinov played opposite (Sir) John Gielgud in *Crime and Punishment.* He adapted and produced *Vice-Versa* in 1947.

From time to time Ustinov has been given severe criticism, as in T. C. Worsley's *New Statesman and Nation* review (December 1, 1951) of *The Moment of Truth,* his interpretation of the tragedy of Marshal Pétain: "It is apparently no use any longer for us to urge Mr. Ustinov to concentrate his talent and try to produce one satisfactory play instead of three or four near-misses. If he won't stop to polish and shape, and above all to cut, that is because, we must now presume, he can't."

Ustinov sets himself high standards: "Literature cannot cheat as history can," he wrote in the London *Daily Telegraph* (August 23, 1952), and his attention to detail extends to such efforts as taking singing lessons at the Rome Opera House to prepare for his rôle of Nero in *Quo Vadis?* "I believe," said Ustinov to Art Buchwald (New York *Herald Tribune,* December 10, 1953), "the whole business of a dramatist is to ask questions, not to answer them"—a point which may explain the public's varying reception of his works. Thus *The Indifferent Shepherd,* a Chekhovian portrayal of two clergymen of differing ideals, had a successful run at the Criterion in 1948 while *No Sign of the Dove,* a modern morality play about Noah in a large rococo house, lacked popularity at the Savoy in 1953.

Ustinov's military service, he has said, enabled him "to appreciate to the full the limited magnificence of colonels, those exalted beings who need only reserve their politer smiles for generals, but who can lavish their frowns on the drab little worlds they rule." He rejoices in the fact that his play *The Love of Four Colonels* (1951) has been performed in fourteen European countries, and his part of the Wicked Fairy in this satire on national concepts of the ideal woman is a pleasant "leg-pull" of the officers he must have plagued.

Although not so successful in the United States as in Britain—the 141 Broadway performances (at the Broadhurst Theatre starring Rex Harrison and Lilli Palmer) were more than quadrupled in London—the play found the American press generally appreciative. Richard Watts, Jr., expressed a prevalent view in the New York *Post* (February 1, 1953): "I wish Ustinov would pull himself together and try to organize his unruly talents, but, if he did, some of that wild, free imagination might depart from him, and, while I am aware of his defects, I think he deserves the audience salute he is receiving for what is fresh and delightful in his work."

Ustinov's film acting—he made his screen debut in the British picture *Mein Kampf, My Crimes* in 1941—has been widely discussed.

Paramount Pictures Corp.

PETER USTINOV

He himself is severely critical: "Movies are awfully like the army. There are the in-trays, the out-trays, the orders of the day, and the last inch of responsibility is thrown about with the speed of a football in a professional game. . . . The making of a happy film, a gentle and charming film under these quasi-military conditions [in Hollywood] is far more difficult than to spill passion and violence onto the screen" (New York *Herald Tribune,* July 10, 1955). In 1950 he appeared in *Odette* and *Hotel Sahara.* The spectacular film *Quo Vadis?* showed Ustinov at his best. When this "box-office blockbuster" (as *Variety* called it) had its première in New York in 1951 Alton Cook (New York *World-Telegram and Sun,* November 9, 1951) gave "the real acting medal . . . to Ustinov for his strutting weakling, Emperor Nero." On the other hand, *Variety* (November 14, 1951) criticized Ustinov's "sybarite" conception of Nero as "out of focus. . . . It wasn't necessary to pile it on . . . the producer and director might have curbed some of the fiddlin' around."

Although M-G-M's film *Beau Brummel* (1954) received the signal honor of a Royal Performance, most British newspapers thought it in bad taste. American papers were more generous: most of them had a good, but not over-enthusiastic, word for Ustinov's portrayal of the lonely, pompous Prince of Wales.

In *The Egyptian* (1954), Darryl F. Zanuck's film version of Mika Waltari's novel, Ustinov brought "a fine bravado to [Kaptah], this waggish but amiable rogue" (New York *Herald Tribune,* August 25, 1954). "So efficiently does he leer with his single eye," commented Richard L. Coe, "that he becomes, evidently, the audience's favourite character" (Washington *Post and Times Herald,* September 21, 1954).

In the motion picture *We're No Angels,* which opened in July 1955, Ustinov played the role of

USTINOV, PETER—*Continued*

Joseph, "a monk-like soul with a tidy talent for embezzlement," which had been portrayed by Walter Slezak in the Broadway play. Both play and movie were based on *La Cuisine des Anges* by Albert Husson. The New York *Herald Tribune* (July 8, 1955) commented: "Ustinov is an urbane Britisher who can cajole any lock to open. He is also the most agile farceur in the cast, and it is easy to see how casually—almost carelessly—he delivers his dry and witty comments."

An intimate side to his work has only been glimpsed by the public so far. Always avoiding large parties, Ustinov is at his best in friendly gatherings of half-a-dozen people where he indulges his gift for mimicry. "People just being themselves can be very funny, you know," he says; and recently in a series of somewhat highbrow but popular BBC broadcasts entitled *In all Directions,* he has held a slightly distorted but amusing and understanding mirror to contemporary civilization, in collaboration with actor-dramatist Peter Jones.

In these broadcasts he often introduces American types such as tourists in Europe, politicians, and after-lunch speakers, and although his interpretation is invariably entertaining, it is deftly sympathetic. He also does many of the sound effects in these programs, and in his one phonograph recording "Mock Mozart" (No.R3612 made by Parlophone Company, Ltd.), he imitates a male quartet and a full orchestra.

Ustinov is six feet tall, weighs 195 pounds and has green eyes and light brown hair. He was described as "a tubby character with the affable, slouchy, sulky exterior of a Giant Panda" (*New Statesman and Nation,* March 27, 1954). He flaunts extravagant waistcoats with impeccable Savile Row suits worn with effective carelessness. His clubs are Queen's, Royal Automobile, Arts Theatre, Garrick, and Savage.

By his first marriage, to Isolde Denham in 1940, Ustinov has a daughter, Tamara. He is now married to Suzanne Cloutier, the French Canadian actress. Their daughter, Pavla, was born in Los Angeles in 1954. In the studio of the fine Queen Anne House in Chelsea where Ellen Terry once lived, the signs of his many interests and hobbies lie scattered in profusion: tape recorders, phonograph records, music, pictures, books, scripts, sketches. He plays tennis and squash, writes to the press, takes part in the work of the Arts Council and the British Drama League, and reads books and papers in several languages. Someone gave him a conductor's baton: "Now," says Ustinov, "I spend hours in front of the gramophone conducting."

References

Everybody's (London) p24+ O 22 '55
New Statesm 47:407+ Mr 27 '54 por
Motion Picture and Television Almanac, 1955
Noble, P. Profiles and Personalities (1946)
Who's Who, 1955
Who's Who in the Theatre (1952)

VAN BEINUM, EDUARD See Beinum, Eduard (Alexander) van

VAN VOLKENBURG, J(ACK) L(AMONT) Dec. 6, 1903- Television executive

Address: b. c/o CBS Television, 485 Madison Ave., New York 22; h. Compo Parkway, Westport, Conn.

The president of CBS Television, J. L. Van Volkenburg, is trying to "increase the creative quality and entertainment value of its programs." He joined the Columbia Broadcasting System in 1932 and became president of the television division in 1951. He brought into operation Columbia's Hollywood "Television City" in 1952 and supervised the telecasting of Columbia's first major TV program in color, Ed Sullivan's *Toast of the Town,* in August 1954.

In that month CBS announced that CBS-Columbia, its manufacturing division, had begun mass production of large-screen television color sets. Its regular color television shows are the *Best of Broadway* and *Shower of Stars;* other programs appear in color from time to time. CBS is credited with having "led all networks in revenue from television broadcasting" in 1953 (New York *Times,* January 10, 1954).

From Sioux City, Iowa, where he was born to Earl L. and Mildred Madge (Dunham) Van Volkenburg on December 6, 1903, Jack Lamont Van Volkenburg was taken in childhood to Minnesota, where he attended public grade and high schools and subsequently the University of Minnesota. In 1928 he joined the account department of the Chicago office of Batten, Barton, Durstine & Osborn, Inc., an advertising agency with headquarters in New York City. Soon afterward he organized and headed its radio department.

This was at about the time (September 1928) of the acquisition by William S. Paley, a Pennsylvania cigar manufacturing executive, of United Independent Broadcasters, Inc., a small chain of Eastern radio stations. Paley changed the name of the network to Columbia Broadcasting System, became its president, and expanded the chain so that it included seventy stations in the United States in 1930.

Among the outlets owned by CBS was Station KMOX in St. Louis, Missouri, and it was as sales manager of this station that Van Volkenburg began in 1932 his association with Columbia. He was advanced to president and general manager of KMOX in April 1933, and three years later (1936) was transferred to the CBS central division at Chicago, where he became assistant to vice-president H. Leslie Atlass as well as assistant manager of Station WBBM. During the next nine years Van Volkenburg undertook various Chicago civic responsibilities, including the chairmanship of the advertising division of the Community Fund in 1940 and of the Red Cross drive in 1942.

When President Paley returned from two years of World War II service in 1945, Frank Stanton (who had joined CBS in 1935) was appointed general manager of the company, and Van Volkenburg was called to the New York headquarters to become general manager of CBS radio sales. In January 1946 Paley, turning over the presidency of the Columbia network to Stanton, became chairman of the board. Two years later (January 1948) Van Volkenburg assumed supervision of all Columbia-owned stations with the title of director of station administration.

In February 1948 President Stanton of CBS announced that his network, which had closed down its New York television studio, was about to convert 700,000 cubic feet of space into "the nation's largest television-studio plant." This decision was interpreted as meaning that "CBS was finally climbing all the way up on the video bandwagon" and that "the trade could sit back and watch" a "supremacy struggle" between Columbia and NBC (*Newsweek*, March 1, 1948).

Van Volkenburg was named vice-president and director of CBS television operations in May 1948; at the end of the year Columbia "launched a full-scale talent raid on NBC and captured such . . . entertainers as Jack Benny, Amos 'n' Andy, George Burns and Gracie Allen, Edgar Bergen, Red Skelton" (*Time*, December 4, 1950). However, in 1948 a Federal Communications Commission order halting the construction of new television stations, caught CBS "still scrambling to build its black-and-white TV network," with the result that by the end of 1950, according to *Time* (December 4, 1950), there were "still no CBS-owned stations in the big markets of the Midwest." (In April 1952 TV station construction was "unfrozen" by the FCC, and by 1954 CBS owned one television station in Chicago and was affiliated with many others.)

In January 1950 Van Volkenburg was appointed CBS vice-president in charge of network sales. On July 15, 1951 CBS created three new "separate autonomous" divisions to cover operations in radio, television, and laboratory and development work. "Each will have its own department for programs, sales, sales promotion, company-owned station operation, station services, research, press information operations, business and legal affairs, and accounting," the announcement disclosed. Van Volkenburg was formally named president of the CBS television division the next day.

Van Volkenburg was elected on August 6, 1952 to the CBS board of directors. The Columbia system was able to report for 1952 a net income of $6,445,506, the highest in its twenty-four years of existence, and to record that the television network had expanded to seventy-four stations as compared with sixty-two in 1951.

After the first transcontinental television network was inaugurated, when the coaxial cable linked the East and West coasts of the United States, on September 4, 1951, Van Volkenburg concentrated his efforts on bringing into operation Columbia's much-publicized Television City at Hollywood, California. Here four studios were erected on a fifteen-acre tract at an investment of $12,000,000, and an additional ten acres was kept available for expansion. Television City was described as "a self-contained production center, even to its Diesel-generated electric power" (New York *Times*, November 14, 1952).

CBS-TV

J. L. VAN VOLKENBURG

CBS engineers had been experimenting with color television in the late 1930's, and a method of three-color television had been demonstrated by CBS on September 4, 1940, but World War II priorities interrupted further research. During 1946, however, improved color images were developed by CBS, and in that year Columbia petitioned the FCC for permission to use commercially its "field sequential" color system. NBC meanwhile had been working on the perfection of a "simultaneous" technique for color television. In March 1947 the FCC decided that further development of both systems was necessary, and denied the CBS petition.

In October 1950 CBS scored what *Time* characterized as a "major victory" over NBC through a "5-2 decision by the FCC in favor of CBS's color TV over the rival systems of RCA and California's Color Television." In a quick countermove NBC obtained a Federal injunction suspending the FCC decision until a board of three judges could study and report on the CBS and NBC systems. The chief objection to Columbia's "noncompatible" system was that owners of black-and-white sets could not receive programs broadcast in color on their sets. The NBC system provided "convertors." After subsequent improvements, the present "compatible" methods of color telecasts were adopted, and approved by the FCC on December 17, 1953. (Details of the NBC and CBS color systems are described on page 68 in *Life*, January 4, 1954.)

(Continued next page)

VAN VOLKENBURG, J. L.—*Continued*

In December 1953 Van Volkenburg announced that CBS had leased the RKO-Keith 81st Street Theatre in New York City for conversion by CBS engineers into "one of the world's largest studios for color television program productions." It was from this "veritable electronic fairyland," named "Studio 72," that the first CBS color production, Ed Sullivan's *Toast of the Town,* originated on August 22, 1954. More than twenty other color shows are now telecast from CBS Television City, Hollywood, three or more each week, and are all receivable on black-and-white or color sets.

Following a broadcast on CBS-TV by Edward R. Murrow on his *See It Now* program, March 9, 1954, in which he criticized Wisconsin Senator Joseph R. McCarthy for "stepping over the line between investigating and persecuting," equal time was offered to Senator McCarthy for reply on April 6.

Jack Lamont Van Volkenburg and Kathryn L. Hurst were married on December 13, 1930; they have two children, Jack, Jr., and Margaret Jane. The television executive, whose hobbies are hunting and fishing, is a member of the Michigan North Woods Club at Ishpeming, Michigan and the Weston Gun Club in Connecticut, as well as of the Radio Executives Club. His fraternity is the Phi Kappa Sigma. He is a director of the Advertising Foundation of America.

References

N Y Post Mag p33 Ag 16 '49 por
Business Executives of America (1950)
Who's Who in America, 1954-55
World Biography (1954)

VISHINSKIĬ, ANDREĬ (ĬANUAR'EVICH) Dec. 10, 1883-Nov. 22, 1954 Chief United Nations Representative from Soviet Union; received J.D. degree from Kiev University (1913); taught criminal law procedure, First Moscow University (1923-25); joined Red Army and Communist party (1920); prosecutor of "purge" trials of Soviet officials accused of treason in the 1930's; First Deputy Minister for Foreign Affairs (1940-46); supervised "plebiscites" forcibly incorporating Latvia and Estonia into U.S.R.R.; Foreign Minister (1949-53); since 1946 made many vituperative speeches at U.N. meetings to discredit the United States (e.g., falsely accused the U.S. and the U.N. of being "aggressors" after U.N. forces had repelled the invasion of North Korean troops into South Korea, June 1950); named a candidate member of central committee praesidium (1952); First Deputy Foreign Minister (1953); received Order of Lenin four times; awarded Stalin Prize (1947) for his book *Theory of Evidence in Soviet Jurisprudence*; was co-editor of Soviet Diplomatic Dictionary. See *Current Biography* (May) 1944.

Obituary

N Y Times p1+ N 23 '54

VON BRENTANO, HEINRICH *See* Brentano (di Tremezzo), Heinrich von

VON KÁRMÁN, THEODORE May 11, 1881- Aerodynamicist

Address: h. 1501 S. Marengo Ave., Pasadena, Calif.

One of the world's leading aerodynamicists, Dr. Theodore von Kármán, is regarded as the man who has had the greatest influence on the development of high-speed aircraft in the United States. His pioneer investigations and theories dealing with the phenomena associated with objects in flight paved the way for many of the spectacular achievements in the air age such as supersonic aircraft and guided missiles. The Kármán Vortex Trail, formulated in 1935, is accepted as the first theory of supersonic drag.

He now holds two key posts in the western world's air defense system: chairmanship of the aeronautical research and development group of the North Atlantic Treaty Organization (since 1951) and chairmanship of the U.S. Air Force's scientific advisory board (since 1944). The highly coveted Wright Brothers Memorial Trophy for 1954 was awarded to von Kármán for his many contributions to the science of aeronautics.

Under von Kármán's leadership in the years 1912-1930 the Aeronautics Institute of the University of Aachen in Germany became one of Europe's outstanding research centers in aeronautics; and when von Kármán settled permanently in the United States in 1930, he achieved a similarly high reputation for the aeronautics center at the California Institute of Technology at Pasadena, which he directed from 1930 to 1949.

As a multilingual teacher, von Kármán has traveled over most of the globe to spread theories, ideas and information that blazed the trail for the coming air age. He has written and edited well over a hundred articles, books and papers in a wide variety of fields touched by his specialized knowledge of applied mathematics, mechanics and physics such as aerodynamics, hydrodynamics, thermodynamics, and supersonic wind tunnels.

Theodore von Kármán was born in Budapest, Hungary on May 11, 1881, the son of Professor Maurice and Helene (Konn) von Kármán. His father was professor of philosophy and education at the University of Budapest and was one of the most eminent teachers and philosophers of the Austro-Hungarian Empire in the late nineteenth century. Young Theodore's interests from the beginning were directed toward science and technology. He was graduated with highest honors and the M.E. degree from the Budapest Royal Technical University in 1902. After a year of military service, he returned to this school as an assistant professor, but left in 1904 to accept a mechanical engineering position with the Ganz Company, manufacturers of machinery. His interest in practical engineering problems which he developed during his two years in this company deeply influenced the later course of his life.

Deciding to resume technical studies, von Kármán enrolled as an advanced student at the University of Göttingen in Berlin, Germany in 1906. He received the Ph.D. degree in 1908, and remained as an associate professor at the university from 1909 to 1912. In 1912 came one of the most significant opportunities in von Kármán's career: an offer to become director of the newly established Aeronautics Institute and professor of aeronautics and mechanics at the University of Aachen, Germany. His work here was soon interrupted by the outbreak of World War I, and von Kármán left to serve as a lieutenant in the Austro-Hungarian Aviation Corps. While directing one of the corps' research departments, he invented a helicopter with two counter-rotating propellers, which he maintains will eventually prove its superiority over the ones made today.

In the decade following World War I, Dr. von Kármán returned to the University of Aachen, and under his guidance the Aeronautics Institute evolved into one of Europe's foremost aeronautical research centers. During this period he was also a consultant to such leading airplane companies as Junkers, Zeppelin and others. Under the auspices of the Guggenheim fund for the promotion of aeronautics, he came to the United States in 1926 on a lecture tour. He then made a trip around the world, which took him to the lecture halls of universities in Japan, China and India. One result of the trip was von Kármán's appointment as an adviser to the Kawanishi Airplane Works of Japan in 1927. He helped build the first wind tunnel in Japan and introduced into that country the all-metal propeller.

The drift toward a closer identification of von Kármán's activities with the aeronautics movement in the United States became clearly defined when he accepted the post of research associate at the California Institute of Technology (C.I.T.) in Pasadena in 1928. He divided his time between the University of Aachen and C.I.T. from 1928 until 1930, when he settled permanently in California and became head of the Guggenheim Aeronautical Laboratory, C.I.T. and director of research at the Guggenheim Airship Institute, Akron, Ohio. Dr. von Kármán became an American citizen in 1936.

As a delegate from the United States, von Kármán attended the Fifth Volta Congress, held in Italy in 1935, and presented the first theory of the air resistance of bodies moving with supersonic speed—now known as the Kármán Vortex Trail. He lectured at the Sorbonne in Paris, at the Central Aero-Hydrodynamical Institution in Moscow, and at the National Tsing Hua University in Peiping. In 1937 he was Rouse Ball lecturer at Cambridge University in England and Wilbur Wright lecturer at the Royal Aeronautical Society in London; in 1939 he was Gibbs lecturer at the American Mathematics Society.

When Europe became enveloped in World War II, Dr. von Kármán devoted his research more and more toward military objectives. He

U. S. Air Force

THEODORE VON KÁRMÁN

undertook leadership of the Army Air Forces first jet propulsion and rocket motor program at C.I.T. in 1938, and in the following year was appointed a consultant to the Army Air Forces and a special adviser at Wright-Patterson Air Force Base in Dayton, Ohio.

Dr. von Kármán's ideas were instrumental in starting research on the Bell X-1, which later became the first plane to break the sound barrier. Charles E. Yeager was the Air Force test pilot of the research plane (See *Current Biography* Yearbook 1954).

Von Kármán's association with the Ordnance Department dates from 1938 when he presented the first memorandum concerning the possibilities of utilizing supersonic wind tunnels in ballistic research. From 1940 to 1942 he developed a model supersonic wind tunnel at C.I.T. which became the pioneer installation for the design and operation of the wind tunnel at the Aberdeen (Maryland) Proving Ground. He has been a member of the scientific advisory committee of the Ballistic Research Laboratory at Aberdeen since 1940.

After an unsuccessful attempt to interest the American corporations to manufacture rockets, von Kármán and four associates formed the Aerojet Engineering Corporation at Azusa, California, which was selling JATO (jet-assisted take-off) rockets to the Air Forces and Navy within eighteen months. The company, which also has a plant near Sacramento, is today a major producer of guided missiles, and although von Kármán is no longer its president, he still serves as Aerojet's chief scientific consultant. Later the Government set up the "ORDCIT," the Ordnance Department's program for rocket and jet propulsion development at C.I.T.

The Air Forces named von Kármán director of its scientific advisory group and a special consultant to General Henry H. ("Hap") Arnold

VON KÁRMÁN, THEODORE—*Continued*
in 1944, and in the following year he headed an important mission abroad engaged in the study and evaluation of technical developments in Germany and Japan, and also in England and Switzerland. One of his most important posts in 1955 is chairman of NATO's aeronautical research group, which serves a key role in developing military aviation for the Western European nations. Von Kármán resigned his position at C.I.T. in 1949 and has since held the title of professor emeritus.

The Convair Division of the General Dynamics Corporation, which is responsible to the armed forces for development of certain types of military aircraft and missile systems, engaged von Kármán as a consultant in March 1955. He was one of fourteen world authorities selected by the company to give advice on guided missiles and nuclear research.

Dr. von Kármán's work has been concentrated on the mathematical analyses of complex phenomena in the fields of aerodynamics, hydrodynamics, strength of materials, thermodynamics, elasticity and vibration phenomena. His ability to create simplified formulae and then to carry on to practical applications is recognized as a significant contribution to the achievement of supersonic flight and the development of guided missiles. Some of the theories and principles which bear his name, the Kármán double-modulus theory of columns, the Kármán Vortex Trail, the Kármán similarity theory of turbulence represent milestones in the progress of flight beyond the sound barrier.

Among the many awards bestowed on him in addition to the Wright Brothers Memorial Trophy for 1954 have been the American Society of Mechanical Engineers Medal, 1941; the Sylvanus Reed Award of the Institute of Aeronautical Sciences, 1941; the Medal for Merit, 1946; the John Fritz Medal, 1948; the Kelvin Gold Medal, 1950; the Legion of Honor, 1947; and thirteen honorary degrees from American and European universities. He was named an honorary professor of mechanical engineering at Columbia University in 1948.

Of the many books and articles he has edited in English and German, the most recent example is *Aerodynamics* (Cornell University Press, 1954). Some of von Kármán's other books are *General Aero-dynamic Theory*, a two-volume study written in collaboration with J. M. Burgers in 1924, and *Mathematical Methods in Engineering*, written with M. A. Biot (McGraw, 1940).

Dr. von Kármán is currently a member of the Academy of Sciences, Paris; Royal Academy of Sciences, Torino, Italy; American Society of Mechanical Engineers; National Academy of Science; American Philosophical Society; American Society of Chemical Engineers; and the Spanish Academy of Sciences. He holds honorary memberships in the Institute of Aeronautical Sciences and the Royal Aeronautical Society, and a foreign membership in the Royal Society of London. He is also a member of the Athenæum Club and of Tau Beta Pi society. His hobbies are collecting antique furniture and making color movies.

Some of the committees on which von Kármán has served, *Newsweek* (December 20, 1954) reported, were "to study municipal water pumping in Los Angeles, to design hydrodynamics systems for the Grand Coulee Dam. . . . He was called in to find out why the Tacoma Bridge crumpled in the wind in 1941. The trouble here, it turned out, was that the bridge builder had neglected to allow for the Kármán Vortex Trail."

Dr. von Kármán, who is a bachelor, has been described in the following terms by one of his colleagues. "Those of us who have had the privilege of knowing and working with him intimately will always cherish the memory of evenings in his home when, surrounded by cultural objects collected in his travels over the world, the conversation turns to art, philosophy, politics and other human affairs, and all are given a fresher and more profound significance. All of his colleagues know well the keenness of intellect, depth of understanding, humor and sympathy which make any contact with him so delightful."

On April 16, 1955 von Kármán was named to the Pontifical Academy of Science by Pope Pius XII.

References

Mech Eng 71:82 Ja '49
Newsweek 44:80+ D 20 '54 por
American Men of Science (1955)
Robinson, D. The 100 Most Important People (1952)
Who Knows—and What (1954)
Who's Who in America, 1954-55
World Biography (1954)

VON KLEIST, PAUL LUDWIG *See* Kleist, Paul Ludwig (Ewald) von

VON NEUMANN, JOHN (fôn noi'män)
Dec. 28, 1903- United States Government official; mathematician

Address: b. c/o U.S. Atomic Energy Commission, Washington 25, D.C.; h. 26 Westcott Rd., Princeton, N.J.; 1529 29th St. N.W. Georgetown, Washington, D.C.

The appointment of one of the world's leading mathematicians, John Von Neumann, to the U.S. Atomic Energy Commission by President Dwight D. Eisenhower in October 1954, has been regarded with approval by scientists, laymen, and the press. He brings to the commission a broad knowledge of atomic energy problems, gained as a member of the General Advisory Committee of the AEC since 1952 and as a consultant on U.S. Government military and scientific projects since 1940. The AEC, established after World War II, has responsibility for developing and producing nuclear weapons and for regulating the use of atomic power in industry in the United States.

A New York *Times* editorial (October 25, 1955) stated that Von Neumann's work on computers (such as MANIAC) "played an essential role in permitting the creation of the hydrogen weapon." Von Neumann is also an expert on games of strategy. His monumental book, *Theory of Games and Economic Behavior* (1944), was written in collaboration with Dr. Oskar Morgenstern. Von Neumann has been a research professor of mathematics at the Institute for Advanced Study, Princeton, New Jersey, since 1933.

In a statement made shortly after his appointment, he said that "all scientists whose work has made them familiar with atomic energy matters have an obligation to take a turn in shouldering the administrative responsibilities" (*Scientific American*, December 1954).

Born on December 28, 1903 in Budapest, Hungary, Johann (later changed to John) Von Neumann is the son of Max Von Neumann and the former Margaret Kann. He and his family were purposely away from Hungary during most of the time when the Communists held power there in 1919. As a young student eager for training in science, Von Neumann studied chemistry at the University of Berlin from 1921 to 1923. Two years later he received a diploma in chemical engineering from the Technische Hochschule in Zurich, Switzerland, and in 1926 he was granted the Ph.D. degree in mathematics from the University of Budapest. As a Rockefeller Fellow in 1926 and 1927 at the University of Göttingen, he became acquainted with a fellow student, J. Robert Oppenheimer, with whom he has maintained a long professional and personal friendship.

Dr. Von Neumann's first teaching assignment in 1927 brought him back to the University of Berlin as *Privatdozent* in mathematics. In 1929 he took a similar position at the University of Hamburg. The next year he came to the United States as a guest lecturer at Princeton University in New Jersey and in 1931, was appointed a professor of mathematical physics there. He became associated with the Institute for Advanced Study, a research center in Princeton not connected with the university, in 1933.

He is known for his contributions to the point-set theory, theory of continuous groups, quantum mechanics, the operator theory, and mathematical logic. While still teaching in Germany, Von Neumann became intrigued with the mathematical theory of games. Nonstrategical games could be scientifically described in terms of probability. But for games requiring strategy, mathematicians had no accepted formula. "A strategical game, like poker," wrote *Time* (November 1, 1954), "where the player has a choice, and where winning or losing may depend on finding out what is in an opponent's mind and concealing what is in one's own, is far more difficult to cope with theoretically. Von Neumann gets at the heart of the strategic conflict through the concept of 'Minimax.'" (For further details see John McDonald's articles in *Fortune*, March 1948 and June 1949, and his book *Strategy in Poker, Business and War* [1950], with its bibliography on the theory of games and economic behavior.)

Professor Von Neumann has worked for a number of years on his theory of games. A treatise devoted to the theory was published in the *Annals of Mathematics* during 1928. In America, the mathematician worked with Dr. Oskar Morgenstern, professor of economics at Princeton University; together, they applied the theory of games to economic structures in a book published in 1944, *Theory of Games and Economic Behavior* (Princeton University Press; third edition, published 1953). This union of mathematics and economics demonstrated "that the typical problems of economic behavior become strictly identical with the mathematical notions of suitable games of strategy." The theory is also considered of value for the study of government and sociology, and is being applied to problems of military strategy by the U.S. armed forces.

Wide World

JOHN VON NEUMANN

Von Neumann shouldered many governmental responsibilities during World War II. He has been a member or consultant to various armed forces' committees since 1940. He became a consultant to the Los Alamos Laboratory in New Mexico in 1943 and was associated with the development of the atomic bomb. He has also worked with the Office of Scientific Research and Development.

During World War II Dr. Von Neumann's experiments advanced the development of high speed calculators, now being used in science and industry. His belief is that these computers offer remarkable advantages, since "problems which seem interesting to scientists, but which formerly were impossible for practical reasons, can now be undertaken with this new tool, thus widening the range of scientific investigation" (New York *Herald Tribune*, June 11, 1952). Von Neumann developed much of the theory behind such computers as ENIAC and UNIVAC, which television viewers saw at work on the 1954 election returns. These machines are also useful to the armed forces for ballistics research.

(Continued next page)

VON NEUMANN, JOHN—*Continued*

Continued experimentation led to the development of the MANIAC (mathematical analyzer, numerical integrator and computer). His design of high speed calculators made (he modestly admits) an "important difference" in the success of the hydrogen bomb program. A job that ordinarily might take several years can be completed by these machines in an hour. The time element cannot usually be cut by employing more people on a project, since each part of a problem must be accomplished in sequence.

Fundamental work carried out by Von Neumann led to the construction of ORDVAC (ordnance variable automatic computer), which was formally unveiled in 1952. Two machines were constructed, one at the University of Illinois in Urbana and one at the Institute for Advanced Study. With it, Professor Von Neumann tested the theory of E. E. Kummer, a nineteenth-century German mathematician, with a million equations in several hours. Contemporary questions are also being submitted to the calculator for analysis. Professor Oskar Morgenstern is using the machine to clarify problems concerning the impact of a military budget on the U.S. economy (New York *Times*, June 15, 1952).

A new calculator, NORC (naval ordnance research computer), can do a twenty-four-hour weather prediction in a few minutes. According to Von Neumann, the Navy, which was the chief sponsor of the machine, can use the NORC to: 1) compute the tidal motions of the entire Atlantic and Pacific oceans; 2) throw new light on the core of the earth, believed to be liquid, by computing the turbulent motion at the center; and 3) help the armed forces plan the movement of men and matériel by mathematically simulating logistical problems (New York *Herald Tribune*, December 3, 1954).

Von Neumann was appointed a member of the General Advisory Committee of the AEC in 1952. He has also served as a consultant to the Central Intelligence Agency and worked with the Rand Corporation. In June 1954, when he was called before a subcommittee of the Government Operations Committee of the U.S. House of Representatives, he testified on the serious state of government relations with the scientific community. Stating that "there is grave danger of confusing a technical opinion with a political intention," he explained to the legislators that being discharged for security causes could for the "average person" be a "professional catastrophe" (*Christian Science Monitor*, October 19, 1954). He has suggested using judicial procedures for security cases.

On October 23, 1954 President Eisenhower honored Von Neumann with an appointment to the five-man Atomic Energy Commission, to succeed Eugene M. Zuckert. The New York *Times* commented that "President Eisenhower appears to have made a useful gesture of conciliation toward a large group of scientists who have been unhappy about the [J. Robert] Oppenheimer verdict" (October 25, 1954). Von Neumann's appointment for a five-year term was confirmed by the Senate on March 14, 1955. He will take a leave of absence from the institute.

Von Neumann and Oppenheimer differed in their opinions on the advisability of advancing the hydrogen-bomb project (Von Neumann advocated an accelerated program) but Von Neumann has stated his belief in the latter's loyalty and integrity. At the hearings of the Personnel Security Board of the AEC in the spring of 1954 on whether to grant Oppenheimer security clearance for his work on the AEC General Advisory Committee, Von Neumann said that he did not consider Oppenheimer a "security risk" and testified that Oppenheimer had accepted President Truman's decision to create the new weapon "with very good grace" and "cooperated" (New York *Times*, October 24, 1954). He later said that the verdict of the AEC in withdrawing Oppenheimer's clearance had been "properly reached" (New York *Herald Tribune*, March 9, 1955).

The mathematician was awarded the Medal for Merit and the Distinguished Civilian Service Award in 1946 for his outstanding contributions during World War II. Honorary degrees conferred upon Dr. Von Neumann include those from Princeton (1947), Harvard University (1949), Istanbul University, Turkey (1952), University of Munich, Germany (1953), and Columbia University in their bi-centennial celebration (1954).

Other books Dr. Von Neumann has written include *Mathematische Grundlagen der Quantenmechanik* (Springer, 1932; and Dover Publications, 1944); *Charakterisierung des Spektrums eines integraloperators* (Hermann, 1935); and *Functional Operators* (Princeton University Press, 1950), for the studies of the *Annals of Mathematics*. Some of his lectures appear in *Continuous Geometry* (Institute for Advance Study, 1936-1937). His articles have been published in numerous mathematical and philosophical journals. He has been editor of *Annals of Mathematics* and co-editor of *Compositio Mathematica*.

Professor Von Neumann is a member of the American Mathematical Society (of which he was president in 1950-1951), the National Academy of Sciences (since 1937), American Philosophical Society, Mathematical Association of America, and the American Academy of Arts and Sciences, and is a fellow of the American Physical Society. He has been honored with memberships in foreign professional societies of the Netherlands, Italy, and Peru. He belongs also to Sigma Xi.

By his marriage to Mariette Kovesi on January 1, 1930, Von Neumann is the father of a daughter, Marina Von Neumann. This marriage ended in divorce in 1937. On December 18, 1938 he married Klara Dan. He has a large brown dog, Inverse. The mathematician enjoys eating sweets, driving his Cadillac, and reading medieval history. He is an independent politically. He became a naturalized U.S. citizen in 1937.

Von Neumann can converse in French, German, Hungarian and English. He is an extremely warm and affable person. Commenting on his appointment, *Time* reported: "People who should know say that Von Neumann is eminently qualified to sit across the atomic table from the Russians in the greatest game in the world."

References

N Y Times p4 O 24 '54
Newsweek 45:63 Mr 21 '55 por
Time 64:20 N 1 '54 por
U S News 37:16 N 5 '54 por
Washington (D.C.) Post p7E Je 5 '55 por

American Men of Science (1955)
International Who's Who, 1954
Who's Who in America, 1954-55
World Biography (1954)

VON SZENT-GYÖRGYI, ALBERT *See* Szent-Györgyi, A. (von N.)

VYSHINSKY, ANDREĬ Y. *See* Vishinskiĭ, Andreĭ (I͡Anuar'evich)

WAURINE WALKER

WALKER, WAURINE (ELIZABETH) June 30, 1911- Teacher; education association official

Address: b. c/o National Education Association, 1201 16th St., Washington 6, D.C.; Texas Education Agency, Austin, Tex.; h. 1712 Enfield Rd., Austin Tex.

The National Education Association, representing about 90 per cent of the teaching profession in the United States, has as its president Waurine Walker, who was elected for the 1954-55 term at the organization's ninety-second annual convention in New York City in July 1954. A specialist in teacher education and professional standards, Miss Walker has been director since 1950 of the division of teacher relations and certification of the Texas Education Agency.

As president of NEA she attended the second conference of the World Confederation of Organizations of the Teaching Profession, held in Oslo, Norway in the summer of 1954. Addressing educators from all over the world on the subject of teacher training, Miss Walker expressed her view that "the best teacher was he who succeeded in educating his pupils to meet the central problems of life." Stressing the importance of the teaching profession, she pointed out that "in a modern world neither free speech, a free press, nor a popular government could last long without a well-educated, free and constantly renewed staff of teachers" (*Christian Science Monitor*, August 14, 1954).

"Teaching is more challenging and rewarding than any other profession," said Miss Walker. Her long record of service in educational groups includes top executive posts on a number of important state and national committees.

The only child of Lon Singleton and Minnie Lee (Rogers) Walker, Waurine Elizabeth Walker was born in Tyler, Texas on June 30, 1911. Her father worked as manager of the freight division for the St. Louis Southwestern Railway. Reared in Waco, Texas, Waurine attended the local high school, where her main extrascholastic interests were debate, declamation and drama.

At Baylor University in Waco she chose education and social studies as her major subjects, while her recreation centered around the activities of the Little Theatre and Pi Gamma Mu and Kappa Delta Pi societies. Her B.A. degree was awarded *magna cum laude* in 1930. She also holds the M.A. degree in speech, conferred in 1939 by Columbia University.

Meanwhile, after graduation from Baylor, Miss Walker had begun her career in education as a teacher of English and speech at Mineral Wells (Texas) High School. She left Mineral Wells in 1934 to teach speech and English at South Junior High School in Waco. The following year (1935) she joined the staff of the Waco High School, where she taught social studies until 1950.

As a public school teacher in Waco, Miss Walker began to take part in the work of several local, state and national educational organizations. Vice-president of the Waco Classroom Teachers Association in 1945, she became president in 1946, to hold office until 1948. In the Texas Classroom Teachers Association she filled the position of vice-president in 1946 and of president in 1947, serving also during that time as a member of the executive board (1945-48).

After two years in executive posts in the central Texas division of the Texas State Teachers Association (vice-president, 1947; president, 1948), Miss Walker was elected state vice-president of that organization (1948-49) and then president (1949-50). She has held membership in four of its committees: organizational affairs (1947-48), executive (1948-51), legislative (1949) and improving educational services (since 1941).

(Continued next page)

WALKER, WAURINE—*Continued*

Miss Walker was a member of the National Commission on Teacher Education and Professional Standards from 1948 to 1954, when she reached the limit of two three-year terms. As the commission's chairman, to which office she was elected in 1951 following a year as vice-chairman, she visited almost every state in the nation. Making on the average of two out-of-state trips a month, she counseled and addressed many professional groups on teacher problems at all levels of education, community as well as countrywide.

Since giving up her classroom work at the Waco schools in 1950, Miss Walker has been director of teacher relations and certification of the Texas Education Agency in Austin. One of her objectives is to improve requirements for teacher accreditation, preparing recommendations for presentation to the state legislature. As Margaret T. Bleil has pointed out in the April 1954 issue of the *Texas Outlook*, an official organ of the Texas State Teachers Association, 96 per cent of Texas' teachers are college graduates, but it is possible for a person to teach in either elementary or secondary schools without a college education. After first raising the standard to make the bachelor's degree a prerequisite for teaching in any grade, Miss Walker would like to see accreditation eventually dependent upon five years of college training.

Her work in teacher relations for the educational agency has made her concerned with the fact that every year over 10 per cent of the teachers in the United States leave the profession. She has called attention to the need for a comprehensive survey to discover the underlying causes of this problem and to alleviate it. Among other undertakings reported by the *Texas Outlook* has been her attempt "to get local school systems to make classroom teachers conscious of selecting good possibilities for future teachers and encouraging them to enter the profession."

Her many years of participation in the work of the National Education Association has also broadened her experience in the various aspects of the teaching field One of the country's most influential educational organizations, the NEA, with its affiliated groups, has a membership of more than 950,000 teachers. It was established in 1857 "to promote the welfare of pupils and teachers, to advance the science and practice of education, and to build strong school-community relationships." Miss Walker has represented the association on the Council on Cooperation in Teacher Education. She is a member also of NEA's board of directors and executive committee and served as national first vice-president in 1953-54.

At NEA's 1954 meeting in New York, Miss Walker, nominated without opposition for the presidency, was elected on July 2 for the year 1954-55. The 4,500 voting delegates of the five-day convention, which for the first time in twelve years was open to all members as well as to the delegates, also passed a resolution asking that Federal funds be used to assist states in raising teachers' salaries. As an adequate salary scale they recommended an annual minimum of $4,000 for beginning college graduates and of $9,000 for teachers with a master's degree and fifteen years' experience.

Among other resolutions adopted at the convention was support of the Supreme Court decision which rejected racial segregation, the delegates asserting that "all problems of integration in our schools are capable of solution by citizens of intelligence, saneness and reasonableness working together in the interests of national unity for the common good of all" (New York *Times*, July 4, 1954). They also called for preservation of "freedom of thought and expression and access to the thoughts of others" and for a revision of methods of Congressional inquiry. Miss Walker was succeeded by John Lester Buford as NEA president in July 1955.

With other members of an NEA delegation, Miss Walker went to Washington, D.C., in July 1954 to urge passage of Congressional bills for an emergency school building program authorizing $250,000,000 yearly during a two-year period. "We are not asking for a long-range, but for an emergency program," she was quoted in the New York *Times* (July 20, 1954) as explaining.

A frequent contributor to professional journals, Miss Walker has written a number of articles for the *Texas Outlook*. Among her other papers are "Building Morale from the Teacher's Viewpoint" (*School Executive*, July 1951), "How Professional Am I?" (*National Business Education Quarterly*, December 1951) and "Power We Forget" (*American Association of Colleges for Teacher Education Yearbook*, 1952).

In "A Life's Work," which appeared in the October 1950 issue of the *NEA Journal*, she discussed the efforts being made by educators themselves to stabilize their profession, "the profound, intense movement among teachers in every state to transform teaching from an in-and-out profession to a lifelong career." Her most recent contribution to the *NEA Journal* is "To the New Teacher, Welcome!" (September 1954).

Miss Walker is affiliated with the American Association of University Women, the Alpha Chapter of Delta Kappa Gamma, the Youth Welfare Council, the Texas Council on Teacher Education, the Texas Congress of Parents and Teachers, and the State Youth Development Council. In 1948 she was a member of the state-wide advisory committee on textbooks, curriculum and certification to the Gilmer-Aikin legislative committee in Texas and in 1950 a state sponsor of Future Teachers of America. She is also a member of the National Association of State Directors of Teacher Education and Certification, of the executive committee of the American Association of Colleges and Teacher Education, and of the temporary committee of the National Council for the Accreditation of Teacher Education.

Waurine Walker stands five feet five inches tall and weighs 128 pounds. She is a former member of the Waco Little Theatre group.

She enjoys swimming, square dancing and reading. Among her hobbies are collecting antique glassware and china, with satin glass and Dresden as her favorite items. She attends the Methodist Church and votes the Democratic ticket.

References

Life 37:85+ Jl 12 '54 pors
Texas Outlook 38:12+ Ap '54 pors

WARREN, AVRA M(ILVIN) Aug. 26, 1893- United States Ambassador to Turkey

Address: b. c/o American Embassy, Ankara, Turkey; c/o Department of State, Washington 25, D.C.; h. 5322 Cedar Springs, Dallas, Tex.

The American Ambassador to Turkey since September 1953, Avra M. Warren, heads both the diplomatic and economic aid missions of the United States to a country that has recently become of major importance to the maintenance of security in the Middle East.

A treaty of friendship signed in the spring of 1954 by Turkey and Pakistan has been described by William Clark in the *Reporter* (June 8, 1954) as "one of the most revolutionary occurrences in the Middle East since the end of the war." Stating that the pact is considered "an expression of American policy," Clark named Ambassador Warren as the man most responsible for it. "Warren realized some years ago that Pakistan was a new state looking for friends, and the policy of American aid to Pakistan and of the alliance with Turkey flows directly from that realization."

During more than thirty years in the foreign service Warren has represented the U.S. Government in many areas including Kenya, New Zealand, Finland, Argentina and Pakistan. He is a specialist on Latin American affairs who in 1945 held the post of director of the Office of American Republic Affairs in the Department of State.

Avra Milvin Warren, the son of Frederick and Mary Jane (Myers) Warren, was born in Ilchester, Maryland on August 26, 1893. On graduating from Catonsville High School, he entered Johns Hopkins University, where he took his B.A. degree in 1915. During the next year he was engaged in forestry work.

After serving in the Officers' Training Camp at Fort Myer, Virginia in 1917, Warren was commissioned a second lieutenant in the 310th infantry machine gun company of the Army's 78th division and was sent overseas. Transferring to the Air Corps, he served until August 1919. For several months after his military discharge he was employed by a grain exporting and importing company.

Warren entered the foreign service in 1920, receiving his first assignment as consul at Cap Haitien, Haiti. In the same capacity he served in Karachi, India (1921-24), Nairobi, Kenya Colony (1924-25), St. John's, Newfoundland (1926-30) and Buenos Aires, Argentina (1930-35). He also attended the Pan American Commercial Conference, held in Buenos Aires in 1935, as adviser to the United States delegation.

Department of State
AVRA M. WARREN

Assigned to the Department of State in Washington, D.C. in December 1935, Warren occupied the post of foreign service inspector until January 1938 when he was named chief of the Department's visa division. During the critical early years of World War II his division had the task of ruling upon admission to the United States of anti-Fascist refugees from Europe.

In March 1942 Warren was appointed Minister (later Ambassador) to the Dominican Republic, where he remained until being named Ambassador to Panama in 1944. Before presenting his credentials in Panama City, the diplomat in May 1944 undertook a fact-finding mission to Bolivia to study the situation in that country under the revolutionary Villaroel regime. The United States and a large number of Latin American countries that had broken off diplomatic relations with Bolivia made use of Warren's report in reconsidering the question of recognizing the new government.

When Warren left the American Embassy in Panama in December 1944, he returned to Washington to become director of the Office of American Republic Affairs in the Department of State. In this post he was considered the "No. 1 deputy" to Nelson A. Rockefeller, then Assistant Secretary of State for Latin-American Affairs.

Following the resumption of normal diplomatic relations between the United States and Argentina, which had deteriorated earlier in World War II, Warren in April 1945 headed a mission to Buenos Aires to discuss mutual problems between the two nations as co-belligerents against Germany and Japan. In addition to reaching agreement on economic and military cooperation, Warren's mission had

WARREN, AVRA M.—*Continued*

a part in paving the way for Argentina's being invited to the United Nations Conference on International Organization at San Francisco.

Warren's next assignments in the diplomatic corps took him first to New Zealand as Minister at the American Legation from 1945 to December 1947 and then to Finland as Minister from 1947 to 1949. The appointment of Warren, one of "Washington's ablest diplomats," (New York *Times*, February 5, 1950), as Ambassador to Pakistan was indicative of the United States' diplomatic interest in Asia.

One of the Ambassador's objectives in Pakistan was to help that newly formed country settle its dispute with India over control of Kashmir. Finding that war was imminent, he flew from Karachi to New Delhi to consult with American Ambassador Loy Henderson and to urge that compromise talks be started. The resulting discussions between the Prime Ministers of India and Pakistan succeeded in preventing the outbreak of full-scale fighting (New York *Times*, April 12, 1950).

As chief of the U.S. delegation Warren attended the fourth conference of the Colombo Plan's Consultative Committee, which met in Karachi in March 1952. The Colombo Plan, a six-year program of assistance to Southeast Asia, began as a British Commonwealth undertaking but later included other countries of the Far East. Warren stated at the Karachi meeting that the United States, a cooperating member of the Plan, had provided about $500,000,000 for economic aid to nations associated with the project.

On a visit to Washington, D.C. in June 1952 the Ambassador gave an address before the Middle East Institute in which he discussed Pakistan's political and economic development and its role in international relations. He consulted with government officials on Pakistan's economic needs and the Kashmir crisis. It was announced in August that Pakistan, earlier expected to receive $20,000,000 in United States aid, would be granted $14,000,000 for the 1952 fiscal year.

After three years at the Embassy in Karachi Warren returned to the United States and in July 1953 he was nominated by President Dwight D. Eisenhower to succeed George C. McGhee as Ambassador to Turkey. He was also made chief of the American Aid Mission to Turkey, a program which he regards as having helped to make that Middle East nation an "enthusiastic member of the North Atlantic Treaty Organization." Upon arrival in Turkey in September 1953 Ambassador Warren said, "My countrymen are impressed with the steady rate of expansion of the Turkish economy, and they share the common feeling of sacrifice from our experiences in fighting in Korea" (New York *Times*, September 9, 1953).

Encouraged by the United States, on April 2, 1954 leaders of Turkey and Pakistan signed a treaty of friendly collaboration by which they laid the foundations for negotiations on a Middle East collective security system. In another United States effort to maintain stability in the Middle East, Warren participated with a number of State Department officials and American envoys to Middle East countries at a four-day conference in Istanbul in May 1954. The discussions were primarily concerned with the Israeli-Arab conflict and with means of preventing aggression on both sides of the dispute.

Warren and his wife, the former Mary N. Newman, to whom he was married on April 7, 1924, have two children: Geoffrey Spencer and Anna Maria Lloyd. The diplomat is a Mason (Knight Templar) and his clubs are the Sind (Karachi) and the Metropolitan (Washington).

References

American Men in Government (1949)
International Who's Who, 1954
Who's Who in America, 1954-55
World Biography (1954)
World Diplomatic Directory, 1951

WASHBURN, GORDON BAILEY Nov. 7, 1904- Art museum director

Address: b. Carnegie Institute, 4400 Forbes St., Pittsburgh 13, Pa.; h. 420 Coventry Rd., Pittsburgh 13, Pa.

Compatibility rather than geography determines the position of the over 300 paintings which Gordon Bailey Washburn, director of the Department of Fine Arts at the Carnegie Institute in Pittsburgh, Pennsylvania, exhibits in each year's International Exhibition of Contemporary Painting. "By playing down national characteristics," wrote Belle Krasne in *Art Digest,* "Washburn presents a better show, one which properly establishes universal art criteria, one in which the only borders to cross are esthetic borders." Washburn's career as a museum director culminated in his appointment in 1950 to the Carnegie Institute. He had previously spent eighteen years in the art museum field, starting at the age of twenty-six as director of the Albright Art Gallery in Buffalo, New York.

Of New England stock on both sides, Gordon Bailey Washburn was one of three children of Frederic B. Washburn and Jessica (Bailey) Washburn. He was born on November 7, 1904 at Wellesley Hills, Massachusetts and lived most of his boyhood life in Worcester, Massachusetts, where he attended the North High School. Later he attended Deerfield Academy, Deerfield, Massachusetts, from which he graduated in 1924. Special interests at this time were writing and theatricals. Later he entered Williams College, Williamstown, Massachusetts, graduating in 1928 with the A.B. degree, having majored in art and English. He was a member of Phi Beta Kappa and Kappa Alpha.

Immediately following graduation young Washburn took his first trip to Europe and later moved to New York to seek a career in publishing. While unsuccessfully trying to find a place in this business, he spent his free time in museums and art galleries. He soon realized that this was work he would like to devote his life to—that art and the museum field meant far more to him than the book business. As a result he did postgraduate work at Fogg Art Museum, Harvard University which he completed in 1930 and was offered, at the age of twenty-six, the directorship of the Albright Art Gallery in Buffalo, New York.

After eleven years at the Albright Art Gallery (1931-1942), where he made a number of innovations and brought the gallery closer to the life of the community, Washburn was appointed, in 1942, director of the Museum of Art, Rhode Island School of Design in Providence. He felt, in his new position, that his primary duties were to bring the riches of the museum into more active use in the community and to bring the museum and school into a closer relationship. Washburn commented, "In the one case the general public, and in the other, those students specializing in art within our own institution, stand at too great a distance from us." A gallery canteen initiated by him attracted almost a quarter of a million service men in three years. Chamber music concerts held in the museum became so popular that they were moved to large quarters in the School of Design.

Following Washburn's appointment as director of the Department of Fine Arts at the Carnegie Institute, he went to Europe, accompanied by his predecessor, Homer Saint-Gaudens (who retired in 1950). Washburn selected 305 paintings for the International Exhibition, which was held in Pittsburgh in October 1952. The paintings represented twenty-four nationalities, but Washburn hung them according to compatability, color and form, rather than by countries, as in former Internationals.

In general the art world as well as the residents of Pittsburgh felt that Washburn's first International leaned too far in the direction of the abstract, but he explained that he could not find equal strength in the conservative field of art when he was collecting paintings for this important exhibition. He strongly feels that there is an underlying urge on the part of the public for abstract art. Belle Krasne in *Art Digest* (November 1, 1952) wrote: "It is Washburn's first and an auspicious first, indeed—from the catalogue cover to the installation (festive, effective and sagacious) to the pictures themselves (on the whole provocative and lively)—almost every aspect is up to date. Perhaps it is because Washburn has broken a number of tired precedents that this show is an exciting one to see."

Washburn believes that the Carnegie Museum, and all museums, should serve the individual community first, and secondly art as a whole or on an international scale. An example of such a relationship is the creative art programs offered children on Saturdays by the Division of Education of Carnegie Institute. More than 1200 children between ten and fifteen years of age, chosen on the basis of art ability by the schools of Pittsburgh and Allegheny county, attend these "Tam O'Shanter" and "Palette" art classes weekly during the school year. In the same department, art and craft classes are also offered adults while art students carry on their art classes with well-known artists in the College of Fine Arts.

GORDON BAILEY WASHBURN

The permanent collection at the Carnegie Museum represents the work of artists since the first International in 1898. One of the purposes of the International was that such an exhibition would be a source for purchasing a permanent collection. It was Andrew Carnegie, the founder, who suggested that the Institute purchase only current paintings which he indicated might become the "Old Masters of tomorrow."

While other great museums throughout the United States developed collections of Rubens, Rembrandt, Titian, and other masters, Pittsburgh—famous for its industrial prowess—concentrated on contemporary art, taking its keynote from Carnegie's words in 1896: "Let us hope that the pictures exhibited here from time to time will be of all schools and reach both extremes—the highest artist and the humblest citizen. . . .If art has its periods of decadence and revival it is proper that a historical record should show this, fairly."

"Everyone recognizes that judgments in the field of contemporary art must be tentative and open to correction." With this in mind, wrote Washburn, a new, independent Gallery of Contemporary Art was opened in the Carnegie Museum in the spring of 1953 with a nucleus of paintings purchased from the 1952 International by the Museum. They included the French artists, Jean Bazaine, Alfred Manessier and Jacques Villon; the Italian artists Leonardo Cremonini and Mario Sironi; the German artist Fritz Winter and the American artist Samuel Rosenberg. In addition, paintings by an Italian, a Belgian and two Americans were bought and donated to this new gallery. About twenty other paintings were on loan.

In writing about this new gallery in the *Carnegie Magazine* (May 1953) Washburn commented, "Contemporary art needs to be seen and studied over a longer period of time than temporary exhibitions allow. Such work,

WASHBURN, GORDON BAILEY—*Cont.*

which is sometimes startling at first, needs to be lived with and pondered over before we are capable of judging its permanent worth. In the meantime, the visiting public is offered ample opportunity to become intimately acquainted with the current trends in art and to study individual examples of the best that is being created in our time. . . .It is the intention to change the contents as new material is borrowed or acquired." (Washburn had inaugurated a similar plan when he was director of the Albright Art Gallery.

Belle Krasne in *Art Digest* (November 1, 1952) praised Washburn for "including no hoary chestnuts, no academic portraits, no very still still lifes" in his first International exhibition of 305 paintings. In Washburn's International in 1955, which exhibited 328 paintings from twenty-three countries of Europe, the Western Hemisphere, and the Orient, Howard Devree in the New York *Times* (October 16, 1955) found it disturbing that much of the work was "dead-level . . . too many of the paintings are too much alike . . . clichés have developed within this international style. This is not a criticism of Gordon Washburn, director, who spent six months assembling the show . . . and who has brought together to the best of his ability what he finds to be representative of the work being done in twenty-three countries. . . .I cannot believe that so many artists are really so much alike." First prize ($2,000) went to Alfred Manessier of France for his abstract *Crown of Thorns;* second ($1,000) to Rufino Tamayo (see *C.B.,* March '53) for his figure composition *Fruit Vendors.* The other prizes (totaling $5,100) were all awarded for abstract paintings in Carnegie's fortieth International. It remains on view through December 18, 1955. The international jury making the awards included Rene Huyghe, Perry T. Rathbone, David Thompson, Ben Shahn and Afro.

On June 14, 1933 Washburn married Ruth Ballard Goodell, a former teacher. They have two children, Frederic Baldwin and Frances Lambard Washburn. Both Washburn and his wife enjoy gardening and travel. He is a Republican and a Protestant and is a member of the College Art Association, Association of Art Museum Directors of America and the American Association of Museums. Washburn is five feet eleven inches in height, weighs 160 pounds, and has brown hair and blue eyes. He holds an honorary M.F.A. degree from Williams College. The French government made him a Chevalier of the Legion of Honor in 1952.

In the *Art Digest* (November 1, 1952) Washburn wrote: "No one need imagine that he can successfully disparage the entire history of great painting to convince us of the virtues of the non-objective approach. We must still be shown a single non-objective work of power equal to the greatest representational works of earlier times."

References

Art Digest 27:7+ N 1 '52
Carnegie Mag 37:153 My '53
Who's Who in America, 1954-55
World Biography (1954)

WAUGH, SAMUEL C(LARK) (wô) Apr. 28, 1890- U. S. Government official; banker
Address: b. c/o Export-Import Bank, 811 Vermont Ave., N.W., Washington 25, D.C.; h. 3419 Prospect Ave., N.W., Washington 2, D.C.

The president and chairman of the board of directors of the Export-Import Bank of Washington, D.C., is Samuel C. Waugh, former president of the First Trust Company of Lincoln, Nebraska. The Export-Import Bank, which has a "lending authority" of $5 billion, is a U. S. Government agency for the financing and facilitation of foreign trade. Waugh succeeded Major General Glen E. Edgerton in October 1955 after serving two years in the U. S. State Department, first as Assistant Secretary for Economic Affairs and later as Deputy Under Secretary.

Samuel Clark Waugh was born in Plattsmouth, Nebraska on April 28, 1890. His father, Samuel Waugh, a Princeton graduate and a country banker, was for three years a vice-consul in the U. S. State Department. His mother was the former Flora Rawlins. Following his graduation in 1907 from the Lincoln (Nebraska) High School, young Sam Waugh worked at various clerical jobs in a railroad and an insurance office for two years. After studying law for one year (1911-1912) at the University of Nebraska he began in July 1913 his forty-year association with the First Trust Company of Lincoln.

Starting as an insurance solicitor, he later "went through all branches" of the trust business. In 1930 he administered an estate which had been left to make annual purchases for the art collection of the University of Nebraska. During the next decade articles and speeches by Waugh on various phases of the trust business appeared in financial periodicals. (See *International Index to Periodicals.*) He also became active in the American Bankers Association and served as president of the trust division in 1939. He was president of the Lincoln Chamber of Commerce during much of World War II.

Elected president of the First Trust Company of Lincoln as well as a director in 1946, Samuel Waugh also served in the course of the next seven years as a director of the Citizens State Bank of Lincoln, the Dempster Mill Manufacturing Company of Beatrice (Nebraska), and the Searle and Chapin Lumber Company of Lincoln. He was the recipient in 1951 of the Distinguished Service Award conferred by the Board of Regents and the Alumni Association of the University of Nebraska, of which he is now a trustee. He is also a trustee of Doane College in Crete, Nebraska, of the Cooper Foundation, a charitable trust, and of the Nebraska Art Association. He has also served on committees of the U. S. Chamber of Commerce and the American Bankers Association.

"I was not far from retirement at the bank and my wife and I had never dreamed of pulling up stakes after forty years in Lincoln. But my father taught me that an American should serve his country when called upon to do so, as part of his duties as a citizen." Thus was

Waugh (who is a Republican) quoted when his appointment was announced by President Eisenhower on May 25, 1953 to the post of Assistant Secretary of State for Economic Affairs to succeed Willard Thorp. The Assistant Secretary of State for Economic Affairs is "responsible for the development of basic economic aspects of over-all United States foreign policy" and has under his authority the offices of international trade policy, financial and development policy and transport and communications policy (*U. S. Government Organization Manual*).

Resigning his industrial directorates and the presidency of the First Trust Company of Lincoln, Waugh took leave of absence from the company's board of directors and was sworn in as Assistant Secretary on June 5. He agreed generally with "the announced policy of the U. S. Chamber of Commerce of more trade with other countries and a certain amount of aid" (New York *Times*), and on July 13, before a subcommittee of the Senate Foreign Relations Committee, he urged approval of treaties of friendship, commerce and navigation negotiated by the United States with eight foreign countries, including Japan.

On July 30 Waugh was appointed alternate U. S. governor of both the International Monetary Fund and the International Bank for Reconstruction and Development (popularly known as the "World Bank") for a five-year term beginning August 4, without relinquishing his State Department post. At the eighth session of the contracting parties of the General Agreement on Tariffs and Trade (GATT) held in Geneva, Switzerland beginning September 14, 1953 Waugh supported an application by Japan for provisional admission to GATT. He attended conferences in New Delhi, India, on the Colombo Plan for the economic development of southeastern Asia.

During the tenth Inter-American Conference, held in Caracas, Venezuela in March 1954, Assistant Secretary of State Waugh, as a U. S. delegate spoke before the economic committee and gave assurance that this country was "prepared to undertake bilateral treaties to alleviate double taxation" or (in other words) "payment of foreign capital abroad on accrued profits and also in the United States" (Paul D. Kennedy in the New York *Times*, March 10, 1954).

Waugh was named in July 1954 to a special U. S. interdepartmental committee set up under Arthur S. Flemming to study the soft coal industry in relation to national defense. The following September Waugh went to Ottawa as the chief U. S. delegate to the sixth Colombo Plan conference. He urged the Asiatic members of the Colombo Plan consultative committee to make greater use of the Agricultural Trade Development and Assistance Act, which was passed by the U. S. Congress in June and which, he explained, "had the net effect of enabling underdeveloped countries to get long-term loans for the purchase of consumer goods" (New York *Times*, October 7, 1954).

As chairman of the U. S. delegation to the ninth annual session of GATT opening in Geneva in late October, Waugh urged that the United States' "chief partners in world trade" give exports from the United States the equal treatment to which they are, by agreement, entitled (New York *Times*, November 11, 1954). He promised that the United States would consider how its international commitments could be made more consistent with its domestic agricultural policies. Later in November 1954 Waugh was a member of the U. S. delegation to a special Inter-American Economic Conference meeting at Petrópolis in Brazil.

Department of State
SAMUEL C. WAUGH

In Paris at the ministerial meetings of the Organization for European Economic Cooperation Waugh was a delegate. On March 21, 1955 in Geneva he became, on behalf of the United States, the first signatory of the "documents necessary for . . . adherence to the revised General Agreement on Tariffs and Trade" and "the continuation, at least until December 31, 1957, of the world tariff truce" (New York *Times*).

In testimony before a subcommittee of the House of Representatives Appropriations Committee Waugh affirmed the State Department "position" that it "would sell perishable material, agricultural commodities to Russia for any needed strategic materials we could get in exchange" (New York *Times*, April 6, 1955).

At Geneva on June 8, 1955, on behalf of the United States, he cast the first vote in favor of admitting Japan to GATT, an admission confirmed on August 11. (Numerous policy statements and speeches by Waugh are recorded in the U. S. Department of State bulletins and in *Vital Speeches*, 1953-1955.)

President Eisenhower announced in August 1955 that Waugh had been chosen to succeed Glen E. Edgerton, who resigned as president of the Export-Import bank. The appointment to the $17,500-a-year position became effective

WAUGH, SAMUEL C.—*Continued*

in October. After receiving an interim promotion to Deputy Under Secretary of State for Economic Affairs, Waugh attended the International Monetary Fund and World Bank conferences in Istanbul, Turkey in September, and later in the month participated with Treasury Secretary George M. Humphrey in international economics discussions in Paris.

The Export-Import Bank of Washington, the management of which Waugh assumed on October 4, 1955, was first organized as a District of Columbia corporation in 1934. It "finances foreign purchases of United States products, helps United States firms which want to sell their goods abroad, and also lends to foreign nations and companies for development projects for which private capital is not available (Washington *Post and Times Herald*, September 18, 1955). The Bank is authorized to have a capital stock of $1 billion, can borrow from the U. S. Treasury on its own obligations, and has a "lending authority" of $5 billion. In the fiscal year ending June 30, 1955, the Bank authorized credits of $628,000,000, an all-time record, its yearly average having been around $400,000,000.

Since his student days when he played baseball, basket ball and football, Waugh, has maintained his interest in amateur athletics. For five terms he was general manager of the National Amateur Athletic Union which staged track and field try-outs in Lincoln for the Olympics. He has attended Olympiads in Germany and Finland. His religious affiliation is with the Presbyterian Church. His fraternity is the Delta Upsilon; his clubs are the County and University in Lincoln, and the Chevy Chase in Washington, where he enjoys an occasional game of golf. He is a collector of paintings and sculptures, particularly of rising young American artists.

By his marriage to Ruby Barns on May 1, 1913 Waugh has one daughter, Elizabeth, now Mrs. John T. Brownlee. Mrs. Waugh died in 1934, and on April 11, 1942, he married the former Mrs. Della Ladd Romans, whose children are Mrs. Carl H. Gibke and Major Warren L. Romans. Waugh stands at five feet ten inches, weighs around 200 pounds, and has blue eyes and reddish-brown hair. A Washington *Post and Times Herald* writer has described him as "genial" and "stocky," with "a smile as expansive as a corn field in Nebraska."

References

N Y Herald Tribune p2 Ag 12 '55 por
N Y Times p11 My 26 '53; p20 Ag 21 '55
Washington (D.C.) Post p4 Ag 21 '55; p11C S 18 '55 por
Department of State Biographic Register (1954)
Poor's Register of Directors and Executives, 1955
Who's Who in America (Sup. Je '55)
World Biography (1954)

WEAVER, SYLVESTER L(AFLIN), JR.

Dec. 21, 1908- Radio and television executive
Address: b. c/o National Broadcasting Co., 30 Rockefeller Plaza, New York 20

"The grand design of television," wrote Sylvester L. Weaver, Jr., president of the National Broadcasting Company from 1953 to 1955, "is to create an aristocracy of the people . . . to make the average man the uncommon man." Known in network circles as NBC's "thinker-in-chief," he is credited with putting on television's first big daytime shows (*Today* and *Home*), starting the "Faces of the Age" series, developing the "magazine concept" of television programming and advertising, bringing top comedy stars to television on the rotation system, and allowing irregular programming and multiple sponsorship.

In 1955 he introduced RCA's *Monitor,* the 48-hour weekend radio program of news and special events.

He was in charge of plans for NBC's introduction of the "compatible" color television process in 1953. The network now has one regular weekly color television program, the *Ford Theatre;* other color programs, such as the "spectaculars" and the televised operas, are broadcast from time to time. In October 1954 the call letters of NBC stations in New York, Los Angeles and Washington, D.C. were changed to the suffix RCA (NBC is a subsidiary of the Radio Corporation of America).

The coverage of the November 2, 1954 election by NBC was applauded by Vice-President Richard M. Nixon, by Senator Paul Douglas and by many others "as a model of fairness." The new "split-screen" technique made it possible for four NBC reporters from as many cities to talk to each other and to the TV-viewers at the same time. Harriet Van Horne in her radio-TV column in the New York *World-Telegram and Sun* described the method as "technical legerdemain that had engineers holding their breath."

Sylvester Laflin Weaver, Jr. (also known as "Pat" Weaver), the oldest of the four children of Sylvester Laflin and Annabel (Dixon) Weaver was born on December 21, 1908 in Los Angeles, California, where the Weaver family was in the roofing manufacturing business. Pat's younger brother is "Doodles" Weaver, a comedian. Pat attended public schools and was graduated from the Los Angeles High School. He entered Dartmouth College in 1926, majored in philosophy, and in his third year, was admitted to Phi Beta Kappa. He was graduated from Dartmouth *magna cum laude* in 1930.

His ambition was to become a fiction writer, and he began writing while traveling in Europe and Egypt. Unable to sell his stories, he returned to Los Angeles and worked for Young & MacCallister, an advertising and printing firm. In 1932 he obtained a job with Station KHJ, the Don Lee radio outlet in Los Angeles, as a combination announcer, writer, producer, director, actor, and salesman.

KFRC, San Francisco's Don Lee radio station, offered Weaver the job of program manager, and he spent a year there. In 1935 he went to New York, where he first worked for NBC on a weekly musical show, *Evening in Paris,* and for the United Cigar Company. Later that year he joined Young & Rubicam, Inc., an advertising agency, where one of his first ventures was the planning and production of the Fred Allen radio show. In 1937 he was made supervisor of all the programs for the agency's radio division.

The American Tobacco Company, then under the direction of the late George Washington Hill, was impressed with Weaver's growing reputation and hired him in 1938. While still under thirty, Weaver was made advertising manager and a member of the company's top management group. In 1941, he took a leave of absence to become associate director of communications for the Office of the Coordinator of Inter-American Affairs. In this position he organized the broadcasting of anti-Fascist radio programs to South America.

After the United States had entered World War II, Weaver went into the Navy where he spent two years in command of an escort vessel and had time to write a mystery story and a novel which he called "The Journal of John Jason James." Neither manuscript has been published.

During the last nine months of the war, Weaver produced the well-known radio show, *Command Performance,* for the armed forces overseas. After the war, he went back to the American Tobacco Company, but in 1947, returned to Young & Rubicam as vice-president in charge of radio and television. He served as a member of the plans board and executive committee.

About 2,000,000 television sets had been sold by August 1949, when Weaver went to NBC as vice-president in charge of the new medium. According to *Cue* (December 2, 1950), television from then on became Weaver's dominant interest as he became convinced that it helped to clarify contemporary civilization for viewers. "For the first time," he said, "the average man [finds] himself a participant in the world of his own time."

Newsweek (April 7, 1952) commented that Weaver—convinced of television's potentialities —was afraid it "would become just a toy if there wasn't anyone to whip it into shape . . . and he was the boy to do the whipping." He determined to force the sale of sets by providing good shows and top talent that would attract profitable sponsorship and large audiences. Others in the field criticized him for pushing the medium before it was ready, but he was backed by his network and many of his early shows made history. *Your Show of Shows,* starring Sid Caesar and Imogene Coca, became the big Saturday night attraction for several years (February 24, 1950-June 5, 1954).

The Colgate Comedy Hour began its Sunday evening series in the fall of 1950 with Eddie Cantor. The plan, as inaugurated by Weaver, called for a series of star comedians to appear on a rotation basis, a system which gave the comedians and their writers a chance to develop

NBC
SYLVESTER L. WEAVER, JR.

fresh material, offered the viewers a wider variety of shows, and the sponsors a large range of audience. Eddie Cantor, Bob Hope, Bud Abbott and Lou Costello and others made their television debuts on the *Comedy Hour.* Weaver also secured opera singers, Broadway and Hollywood stars, top recording artists, and comedians from other television shows as guest stars.

The first afternoon extravaganza was introduced by Weaver on television with Kate Smith and Ted Collins; during 1951 NBC-TV grossed $8,000,000 from the show. His next "brain child" (*Newsweek,* January 28, 1952) was *Today,* in which Dave Garroway appeared. This was the first big early morning network program on television, which Weaver hoped would "change the listening habits of the nation" (the *New Yorker* reported on October 23, 1954 that *Today* was NBC's "most profitable program"). Other popular shows inspired by Weaver have been the *All Star Revue* and *Tonight,* the latter starring Steve Allen. Following out his "Faces of the Age" concept, several programs in which such distinguished persons as Bertrand Russell, Robert Frost, and Wanda Landowska talked about their work, have been televised, and more are scheduled.

Another Weaver innovation in television management was the "magazine concept"—the network controls the programs and sells time on them, just as a magazine sells space to advertisers. This arrangement allows multiple sponsorship of a television program and gives small as well as large advertisers the opportunity to promote their products on the most popular shows.

During the three years that Weaver was in charge of NBC television, the number of sets in American homes increased from 2,000,000 to nearly 20,000,000. In June 1952 the organization coordinated the activities of radio and

WEAVER, SYLVESTER L., JR.—*Cont.*

television, with Weaver as vice-president in charge of both networks. He was given in December 1952 the responsibility of planning and supervising NBC's introduction of the RCA color television system and was elected vice-chairman of the board of directors.

Under a special temporary authorization from the FCC, Weaver conducted several colorcast experiments during the summer of 1953. After FCC approval of the "compatible" color TV system (i.e., receivable also on black and white sets) in late December 1953, NBC produced its first commercial colorcast, *Amahl and the Night Visitors* (an opera by Gian-Carlo Menotti). Since then, a number of the network's programs have been televised in color (the color receivers cost from $800 to $1100; there are about 10,000 of them in the United States and about 33,000,000 black-and-white sets).

When Weaver was elected the president of NBC on December 4, 1953, Robert W. Sarnoff was named executive vice-president. Sarnoff—son of Brigadier General David Sarnoff, chairman of the board of RCA and NBC—had served as Weaver's executive officer and had "carried out" the Weaver ideas. Weaver succeeded David Sarnoff as president. Then in December 1955 it was announced that Weaver had been elected chairman of the board and Robert Sarnoff became NBC's president.

In an interview with John Brooks (*This Week,* May 3, 1953), Weaver called himself an "information optimist," one who believes his "social responsibility . . . is to see that every opportunity is used to expose people to things in which they have expressed no interest, but in which . . . they would have expressed interest if they *had* been exposed to them." In exposing children to a "pluralistic world," he said, television would enable them to lose their subservience to "the We-Group formula," or "provincial conformity."

"Every writer, every director, every producer is having an influence upon upwards of ten million people when he goes on the air for NBC," Weaver wrote recently. "It is therefore more than just his self-interest as a creative artist that is challenged in this day. It is his self-interest as a member of the human race. For he can do something personally that will increase the vitality of a medium that can increase the individual's ability to meet and decide his own future" (*New Yorker,* October 16, 1954).

The marriage of Weaver and Elizabeth Inglis took place on January 23, 1942. Mrs. Weaver is British and had been on the stage in New York prior to her marriage. Their children are Trajan Victor Charles and Susan Alexandra. The family lives in Manhattan, not far from Rockefeller Plaza, and has a summer home at Sands Point, Long Island. Weaver is a member of the University, Dartmouth and Bath clubs. He is a director and member of the executive committee of the American Heart Association and of the Foreign Policy Association.

Before television began to govern Weaver's life, he was a ski enthusiast in winter and took an active interest in yachting and tennis in summer. Now his recreation is reading history and philosophy. He is six feet four inches tall, and has reddish brown hair and blue eyes. His conversational style, according to Thomas Whiteside in the *New Yorker* (October 16, 1954) is "a dialectical fugue of parasociological phraseology, Madison Avenue advertising talk, Broadway chatter, merchandising argot, and oblique philosophical references, all flowing together in brisk counterpoint."

References

Cue 19:18+ D 2 '50 por
N Y Herald Tribune p24 N 26 '51 por
N Y Times III p3 Ap 15 '51 por
New Yorker 30:37+ O 16 '54 por; 30:43+ O 23 '54 por
This Week p13 My 3 '53
Who's Who in America, 1954-55

WEBB, JACK (RANDOLPH) Apr. 2, 1920- Actor; director

Address: c/o National Broadcasting Company, Los Angeles, Calif.; c/o Walt Disney Studio, Burbank, Calif.

Widely imitated and often parodied, Jack Webb's *Dragnet,* as a radio and television series and a motion picture, has a record of popularity unmatched by any other production of its kind. The "low-keyed" documentary-type crime drama, in which Webb stars as Sergeant Joe Friday and of which he is director, producer and story editor, first appeared on radio in 1949 and on TV in 1951. It retains in 1955 its place among the top shows of both media. The Academy of Television Arts and Sciences awarded *Dragnet* its "Emmy" statuette as the best program for 1953 in the mystery, action or adventure category.

In his efforts to achieve a realistic presentation of crime detection, Webb makes use of technical advice supplied by the Los Angeles Police Department, from whose files *Dragnet* stories are taken. "We try to make cops human beings," he has explained, "doing a job for low pay, but we're trying to get away from the 'dumb-cop' idea. . . . We try to combine the best qualities of the men I've seen downtown (at the police station) . . . try to incorporate their way of speaking, make a composite" (*Saturday Evening Post,* September 26, 1953).

Before reaching motion picture stardom in the 1954 screen version of *Dragnet,* Webb had played minor roles in a dozen Hollywood films. Like *Dragnet,* his 1955 movie, *Pete Kelly's Blues,* originated as a radio series. Webb was master of ceremonies on February 12, 1955, when for the first time the Motion Picture Academy of Arts and Sciences telecast the announcements of persons and movies nominated for the "Oscars" to be awarded March 30.

The only son of Samuel and Margaret (Smith) Webb, Jack Randolph Webb was born in Santa Monica, California on April 2, 1920.

His father was Jewish and his mother, the daughter of a surveyor for the Santa Fe Rail Road, was Catholic. Since his parents were separated when the boy was about two years old and he was taken to live with his mother and grandmother, he remembers nothing of his father. Jack grew up in a downtown section of Los Angeles, spending his boyhood in "poverty and slime," as he has described it (*Time,* March 15, 1954).

While a pupil at Belmont High School in Los Angeles, where he was president of his class in his senior year, Jack Webb became interested in dramatics and often took part in school shows. In his studies, he excelled in art and after graduation in February 1938, he was offered an art scholarship by the University of Southern California. The need to help support himself and his mother made him decide to take a job in a men's clothing store instead of entering college. During the next four years as a clerk, salesman and store manager, he found time away from work to appear on various radio programs over local stations.

Jack Webb joined the Army Air Forces as an aviation cadet in 1943. At Camp St. Cloud in Minnesota, where he took preflight training, he wrote, directed and acted as master of ceremonies for two U.S.O. variety shows. For a short time he piloted B-26 bombers before being granted a dependency discharge from the Army.

Leaving Laughlin Field at Del Rio, Texas in 1945, Webb went to San Francisco to seek a career in radio broadcasting. He was employed by the American Broadcasting Company's station KGO as an announcer for programs covering the United Nations conference which was then meeting in San Francisco. He spent much of his time learning about the technical aspects of radio. Interested in jazz records, he "disc-jockeyed" an early morning show called *The Coffee Club.* For twenty-six weeks he played the role of a tough detective in *Pat Novak for Hire,* a story about waterfront crime written by Richard Breen and broadcast over ABC's West Coast stations.

After his return to Hollywood in about 1947, he was heard in a number of radio programs, among them, the *Johnny Modero Show, The Whistler,* and *This Is Your FBI.* When not on the radio, Webb appeared in motion pictures, some twelve films in all, including Eagle Lion's *Hollow Triumph* (1948); Paramount's *Sunset Boulevard* (1950), *Dark City* (1950), and *Appointment with Danger* (1951); and Twentieth Century-Fox's *Halls of Montezuma* (1951) and *You're in the Navy Now* (1951). His performance in United Artists' *The Men* (1950), a drama about paraplegic war veterans starring Marlon Brando, was commended by critics Bosley Crowther of the New York *Times* and Otis L. Guernsey, Jr., of the New York *Herald Tribune.*

Another movie in which he had a part was *He Walks by Night* (released by Eagle Lion in 1949), a semi-documentary play based on a case from the Los Angeles Police Department files. During the filming of the story, Webb, playing Lieutenant Lee, met Sergeant Marty

NBC-TV

JACK WEBB

Wynn, who had been assigned by the police department to give technical advice for the picture. Wynn's suggestion that someone should develop a radio program of documentary stories adapted from actual police cases gave Webb the idea for *Dragnet.*

With the cooperation of the Los Angeles Police Department, Webb began to study police procedures, techniques, terminology; accompanied two detectives on their police calls; and attended classes at the police academy to learn about criminal law. He took the plots and characters for his program from the department files, preparing stories that would authentically describe the work of the police and its routine, usually unspectacular, manner of investigating crime.

Dragnet made its debut on radio as a summer replacement over NBC in Los Angeles on June 3, 1949. Webb, who directed the production, played the role of a hard-working police detective, Sergeant Joe Friday. Collaborating with script writer Jim Moser, he gradually developed the terse, clipped dialogue and quality of understatement that were to become *Dragnet*'s trademark. Within two years it was radio's most popular show (*Time,* March 15, 1954). Harriet Van Horne of the New York *World-Telegram and Sun* (December 17, 1951) called it "one of radio's more intelligent (and less bloody) crime programs." She pointed out its "constructive" feature of putting "the emphasis on the people who enforce the law rather than on those who break it."

The winner of many awards for entertainment, the radio *Dragnet* has also been recognized for its public service achievements. One of its stories, on the television repair racket, "was instrumental in obtaining legislation in California and Pennsylvania for the examination and licensing of TV repair men. RCA

WEBB, JACK—*Continued*

Service Company, Inc., also used the script for indoctrination of its employees" (New York *Herald Tribune,* December 16, 1951).

The filmed *Dragnet* had its première on NBC-TV on December 16, 1951 with a story called "The Human Bomb," a preview of the regularly televised Thursday night program, which was to begin on January 3, 1952. It is filmed at the Walt Disney Studio in Burbank, California, where in keeping with his concern for realism and factual detail, Webb has had constructed a replica of the lower floor of the Los Angeles Police Department. "On the screen, as before the microphone," commented Jack Gould (New York *Times,* December 19, 1951), "he displays a complete disdain for the clichés of the conventional crime show."

The program's total audience was further enlarged when old *Dragnet* films were rerun as *Badge 714.* Among the awards that Jack Webb has won are the *Look* TV awards in 1953 and 1954 for best director, given to "the individual who most effectively utilized the skills of actors and technicians in television presentations." In *Billboard*'s 1954 competition he was named by television, film and advertising executives as the best actor and *Dragnet* was voted the best television show. Webb's contracts with the Music Corporation of America, which owns the program, call for TV films that will carry *Dragnet* into 1956.

The feature-length motion picture version of *Dragnet,* with screen play by Richard Breen, was released in the summer of 1954 as a Stanley Meyer production for Warner Brothers. In directing the picture, which was filmed in natural color on a wide screen, Webb employed many of the techniques of his television show, such as the use of very little theatrical make-up, emphasis upon close-ups, and reliance on the teleprompter (a device which gives actors their lines in large letters just off camera so that they do not have to memorize each word). The partner of Webb's Joe Friday was played by Ben Alexander, who appears in the same role, Officer Frank Smith, on radio and TV.

In early 1955 Webb directed a second motion picture for Warner Brothers, *Pete Kelly's Blues,* in which he has the role of a Dixieland band leader of the 1920's. He is also planning a television series under the same title. Originally a sustaining radio show over NBC, *Pete Kelly's Blues* ran for thirteen weeks in 1951 with Webb as its star.

Jack Webb married Dorothy Towne on January 11, 1955. By a previous marriage, to actress Julie London in 1947, from whom he was divorced in 1954, he is the father of two children: Stacy, born in 1950, and Lisa, born in 1952. The black-haired, brown-eyed actor is six feet tall and weighs 165 pounds.

Almost all magazine and newspaper feature articles on Webb call attention to his penchant for long working hours. "Since *Dragnet* began," *Time* reported in March 1954, "Webb has produced the equivalent of thirty-five full-length motion pictures—more than the output of many a major studio. For months, recently driving for extra time, he turned out two films and two taped radio shows a week." His leisure pursuits are collecting jazz records and projecting 16mm. movies. A member of the executive board of the United Cerebral Palsy Fund, Webb has conducted a number of radio telethons for that organization in Los Angeles and San Francisco.

References

Am Weekly p4+ S 12, p16+ S 19, p26+ S 26, p26+ O 3 '54 pors
McCall's 80:26+ S '53 pors
N Y Post Mag p2 D 20 '53 pors; p5 Jl 11 '54 por
TV Guide 1:5+ Ap 10 '53 pors
Motion Picture and Television Almanac, 1953-54

WECHSBERG, JOSEPH (wĕks'bûrg)

Aug. 29, 1907- Author; journalist

Address: b. c/o Paul R. Reynolds & Son, 599 5th Ave., New York 17; h. Sunset Hill, Redding, Conn.

Author Joseph Wechsberg settled in the United States in 1938 after varied experiences in Europe as an itinerant fiddler, soldier, photographer, lawyer, and malt salesman. Subsequently naturalized, he was a technical sergeant in the U.S. Army during World War II and was still in the service when his first book in English, *Looking for a Bluebird,* was published in 1945.

This collection of gracefully written recollections of his European wanderings was followed in 1946 by *Homecoming,* in 1948 by *Sweet and Sour* and *The Continental Touch,* in 1953 by *Blue Trout and Black Truffles,* and in 1955 by *The Self-betrayed.* He is now a roving correspondent for the *New Yorker;* for his article in that magazine on August 29, 1953 about the East German uprisings against the Communists, he received the annual magazine award of the Sidney Hillman Foundation.

Josef (Joseph) Wechsberg, the son of Siegfried and Hermine (Krieger) Wechsberg, was born on August 29, 1907 in Moravská Ostrava, in what was then part of the Austrian province of Silesia. His father was a banker; members of his mother's family were merchants. He has one brother, Max, an executive who now lives in the United States. Joseph was eleven years old when Czechoslovakia was proclaimed an independent republic in 1918 and was living in his home town (which became part of the new republic) with his widowed mother and brother in an apartment above the business premises of his paternal grandfather.

In *Sweet and Sour,* Wechsberg recalls that as a child he was little interested in such things as toy trains, chemistry sets and stamp collecting; but his musical talent was early developed by an uncle who taught him the violin and he became the regular second violinist in his uncle's amateur chamber music quartet.

Upon graduation from the local Gymnasium in 1925, Wechsberg registered at the law school of Prague University. He later studied at the

Hochschule für Welthandel in Vienna and at the Conservatory of Music. While there he joined the "claque" at the Staatsoper in order to gain free admission to the performances. His recollections of the "claque" provided the substance of several chapters in his books.

In the fall of 1926 he went to Paris to study at the Sorbonne, but eventually returned to Prague, where he continued to study law. "My family thought that I should win an academic degree," he explained in *Sweet and Sour,* "and the study of law gave me a legitimate excuse for doing a great many things, such as fiddling, traveling, writing, loafing, which I preferred to the dismal vagaries of jurisprudence." On taking his doctorate in law in 1930, *summa cum laude,* at Prague University, he began with a leading Prague law firm the apprenticeship necessary before he could set up practice. During 1935 he also served briefly as secretary to a member of the Czechoslovakian Chamber of Deputies.

He soon wearied of his law work, however. "As a lawyer I was a mess," Wechsberg told Lewis Nichols in an interview (New York *Times Book Review,* June 7, 1953). "I did everything wrong. . . I was terrible. All this time I was writing newspaper pieces. . . I've been a newspaper man at heart ever since."

Meanwhile he had been traveling and doing many of the things which later provided material for his articles and books. On his early trip to Paris he had joined the string section of a theatre orchestra augmented for the Paris engagement of the American Negro revue *Blackbirds.* In the summer of 1928 he signed on as second violinist with the orchestra aboard *La Bourdonnais,* a boat belonging to the Compagnie Générale Transatlantique (French Line), and saw New York for the first time in July.

After other engagements aboard French Line vessels he transferred to the Messageries Maritimes fleet operating out of Marseilles. As orchestra leader aboard the *Porthos,* he made the first of his voyages to the Orient in 1929. Later in Paris, he played in night clubs and cabarets.

After finally abandoning his legal career, Wechsberg became a free-lance journalist, covering a wide area of Europe and Asia. He was "detained by the Italian secret police, and thrown into jail by the Japanese 'Thought Police,'" stated a publisher's release, which added that "he lived through an earthquake in the Philippines and a typhoon in Hong Kong." He "worked on a Malay rubber plantation" and "between journalistic forays, filmed the siege of Shanghai . . . and lectured in most major European cities, 'sometimes on such unpopular subjects as 'democracy.'"

In 1929 Wechsberg had returned to Czechoslovakia for eighteen months' military training in an officers' candidate school. Later, as a lieutenant in the army, he commanded a machine gun company on the Polish frontier at the time of the May 1938 mobilization. In September he revisited the United States as secretary of a parliamentary commission sent

JOSEPH WECHSBERG

to discuss the Sudeten crisis and decided to make this country his permanent home.

His travel book *Die grosse Mauer* (The Great Wall) was published in 1938. This volume and other of Wechsberg's writings were later suppressed by the Nazis and the author himself was arrested by the Gestapo.

"In 1939," he told Lewis Nichols, "I went to California. I spoke a little pidgin English. I knew about enough to study out the headlines in the newspapers. I determined not only to read it but to write it." (His articles "Case Against Japan" and "War in the Suez Canal," which had appeared in *Living Age* in 1934 and 1935, had been translated from the German.) He wrote a series of articles for *Travel* magazine in 1941 and in the following year the *Menorah Journal* published two of his short stories; there were, however, "literally hundreds of rejection slips" he has said, before the *New Yorker* bought "a piece" from him in 1943.

After Wechsberg became a naturalized American citizen, he enlisted in the U.S. Army and was in training for overseas duty when in February 1944, the Houghton Mifflin Company of Boston announced the award to him of a $1,500 "literary fellowship" for the completion of a work of nonfiction.

Wechsberg was "in a place too close to the enemy line to be comfortable," when his "fellowship" book, *Looking for a Bluebird,* appeared in the spring of 1945. This collection of *New Yorker* sketches was received by the reviewers with high favor. "To such notable purveyors of Danubian charm as Ferenc Molnár and Ludwig Bemelmans a new name must now be added, that of Joseph Wechsberg," wrote Orville Prescott in the New York *Times* (February 13, 1945).

After crossing Germany with the invasion forces, Wechsberg had the distinction of being one of the first Americans to reach Prague.

WECHSBERG, JOSEPH—*Continued*

There the Czechoslovakian government awarded him the Order of the White Lion. As a technical sergeant assigned to the U.S. Army's psychological warfare division, Wechsberg edited at Cologne the Allied-sponsored newspaper *Kölnischer Kurier* for a period during 1945. Wechsberg's book, *Homecoming*, much of which had appeared in the *New Yorker* prior to publication in book form by Alfred A. Knopf in 1946, had none of the gaiety of *Looking for a Bluebird.* "He meets nine people in his home town, out of a thousand he had known," observed May Lamberton Becker in the New York *Herald Tribune Weekly Book Review*, July 21, 1946. "There are eighty Jews left; there were 8,000." Mrs. Becker thought the book a "memorable record."

After his discharge from the Army, Wechsberg continued to write for such periodicals as the *New Yorker*, *Esquire*, the *Atlantic Monthly*, the *Saturday Evening Post*, *This Week*, *Town and Country*, and *Holiday*. A collection of these sketches, a number of which dealt humorously with music and musicians, was published by Houghton Mifflin in 1948 under the title *Sweet and Sour.* The composer Richard Rodgers, who reviewed the book for the New York *Herald Tribune Weekly Book Review* (October 31, 1948), found it "charming."

Quite different—at least in certain respects—was the picture of life in Europe and America presented in Wechsberg's first novel in English, *The Continental Touch* (Houghton Mifflin, 1948). R. E. Kingery observed that this novel "strongly recalls Briffault's *Europa* in its concern with moral rottenness" (*Library Journal*); F. H. Bullock thought the work "rather on the cheap side" (New York *Herald Tribune Book Review*).

In an article in *This Week Magazine* (December 19, 1948) entitled "I'm Not Going Back," Wechsberg gave a number of reasons for choosing America for his permanent home. This article, later reprinted in the *Reader's Digest* as "Why I Live in America," is in the form of an open letter to a onetime Czech friend who became a Communist. "I have scores of reasons," Wechsberg wrote: "Because you can live for years without ever getting in touch with authorities and officials. . . . Because families don't break up for being members of different parties. Because for every American who beats up a man or calls him a dirty name, two others stand up against the aggressor. . . ."

"He is never too busy to travel hundreds of miles and to cross international boundaries just to have lunch at one of his favorite restaurants," his New York publishers have observed. One outcome of his "enthusiastic encounters with *la haute cuisine*" was a series of articles which first appeared in the *New Yorker*, *Holiday* and *Gourmet*. These pieces, with additions, form the substance of Wechsberg's book, *Blue Trout and Black Truffles; The Peregrinations of an Epicure* (Knopf).

Rex Stout wrote in the New York *Times* (May 24, 1953) it is "for delight, not instruction—the delight of meeting the greatest practitioners of the oldest art in the world." Lucius Beebe found it "a charming book" with "overtones of melancholy" because "so many of the wonderments the author remembers have now passed from the world, never to be replaced" (*Saturday Review*, August 1, 1953).

Joseph Wechsberg's latest novel, *The Self-betrayed* (Knopf) is written in a more serious vein and concerns the rise and fall of a Red despot. Frederic Morton (*Saturday Review*, February 12, 1955) referred to this novel as "a wobbly patchwork of nostalgia and politics."

On the other hand, Gouverneur Paulding in the New York *Herald Tribune Book Review* (February 13, 1955) praised Wechsberg's book. "In *The Self-betrayed* there is the excitement and suspense of Jacques Willert's [the naturalized American journalist] hazardous pursuit of the truth Bruno Stern [the dictator] refuses him. But it is Willert's memories, so ably fused by Wechsberg with the narrative, that give this book its quality."

Joseph Wechsberg married Jo-Ann Novak, a designer and "an accomplished lady chef," on March 24, 1934. They have a four-year-old daughter, Josephine Hermine. He is five feet eleven inches tall, weighs 175 pounds, and has dark hair and brown eyes.

"For relaxation," stated Lewis Nichols, "he plays chamber music once a week. . . . For exercise, his desires fail to go beyond 'a brisk sit in a chair.'" ("Don't forget," Wechsberg told his interviewer, "that I walked in two armies.") Wechsberg states that his prominent dislikes are telephones, automobiles, crowds and noise.

References

N Y Times Book R p19 Je 7 '53 por

Author's and Writer's Who's Who (1948-49)

Wechsberg, J. Looking for a Bluebird (1945); Homecoming (1946); Sweet and Sour (1948); Blue Trout and Black Truffles (1953)

WELKER, HERMAN Dec. 11, 1906- United States Senator from Idaho; lawyer

Address: b. Senate Office Bldg., Washington 25, D.C.; h. Payette, Idaho

Idaho voters elected Herman Welker, Republican, to the United States Senate on November 7, 1950 by the largest majority polled in the state's Senatorial elections since 1936 when William E. Borah won his final term in Congress. Previous to this, Welker was unknown on the national scene. His only other public offices came in 1929 when he was appointed prosecuting attorney of Washington county, Idaho and in 1948 when he was elected to the Idaho state Senate.

Since entering the U.S. Congress Senator Welker has frequently spoken about the threat of Communism both in the United States and abroad. During the November and December 1954 censure debate on charges brought against

Senator Joseph R. McCarthy by his Senate colleagues, Welker served as the Wisconsin Republican's "floor manager." Early in the hearings Welker presented an "exhaustive defense" (New York *Times,* November 17, 1954) of Senator McCarthy that took two days to complete and called the Senator "one of the greatest living foes of Communist slavery."

Speaking on the Senate floor against the recognition of Red China, Welker has argued that "nothing—not one single act or deed—can be pointed to which would afford the least indication that the government of Red China will alter its course of hatred for the United States and the free world. . . ." (*U.S. News & World Report,* January 29, 1954).

Herman Welker was born on December 11, 1906 in Cambridge, a small rural community in Idaho, to John Thornton and Ann Zella (Shepherd) Welker. He is the youngest of eight boys, three of whom still live at the family home in Cambridge. After attending high school in Weiser—the Washington county seat about thirty miles south of Cambridge—he entered the University of Idaho at Moscow, where he worked his way through law school. He received the LL.B. degree in 1929.

While still at the university, he was appointed prosecuting attorney of Washington county, a job he held until 1935. In 1936 he moved to Los Angeles, California, where he established a general law practice. While living on the West coast, he made many friends among Hollywood's movie colony. He served with the U.S. Army Air Forces as an enlisted man from 1943 to 1944. After his military service, he returned to Idaho and went into private practice—primarily as a trial attorney—in the town of Payette. He also became a farmer and raised livestock.

He was elected to the Idaho state Senate from Payette county in 1948 and served through one regular and one special session. Politically unknown at the time of his election, he quickly became prominent and although he was only a freshman legislator, he was soon considered a power in the Senate (New York *Herald Tribune,* November 26, 1950).

In the Republican primary for the U.S. Senate, he defeated Charles A. Robins, then Governor of Idaho, and John Sanborn, then Representative to Congress, thus enabling him to enter the race for the seat occupied by Glen H. Taylor, Democrat. (Taylor lost the Democratic primary to the former Senator D. Worth Clark.) During the election campaign, Welker was considered by far the best orator and showman running for office. Bing Crosby, Hollywood actor and singer and one of Welker's pheasant-hunting companions, spoke in his behalf. Welker defeated Clark in the election by a 45,000 vote majority.

When Welker took office in January 1951, he was appointed to the U.S. Senate's District of Columbia and Post Office and Civil Service committees. As a result of the death of Senator Kenneth S. Wherry, Republican of Nebraska, there was a shift in committee assignments early in January 1952. Senator Welker

Wide World

HERMAN WELKER

was taken off the Post Office and Civil Service Committee and was given a seat on the Rules and Administration Committee.

He was assigned to its subcommittee on privileges and elections, which was at that time investigating charges made by Senator William Benton, Democrat, of Connecticut, regarding McCarthy's activities in support of the successful Maryland Senate campaign of John Marshall Butler, and other of McCarthy's activities since his election to the Senate. In September 1952 Senator Welker resigned from the subcommittee because he felt the group was being "prejudicially unfair" to Senator McCarthy.

In the summer of 1951 Senator Welker, along with Senator Harry P. Cain, Republican, of Washington, introduced a resolution calling for an investigation by the Senate Judiciary Committee of the International Boxing Club. Welker contended that the I.B.C. was operating as a monopoly and that many able fighters were unable to get title bouts unless they signed contracts with it.

After a nation-wide Federal Grand Jury investigation of professional boxing, the Department of Justice filed a civil anti-trust suit in Federal court charging the I.B.C. of New York and Illinois with conspiring to monopolize the professional championship boxing business. The suit was dismissed because of the U.S. Supreme Court decision that baseball was a sport, not a business (thus outside the scope of laws restricting monopolies), was applicable to boxing.

Senator Welker's voting record on domestic issues in the two sessions of the Eighty-second Congress showed him in favor of cutting government civil payrolls by 10 per cent (June, 1951), ending wage-price controls on June 30, 1952 (May, 1952), and cutting the TVA appropriation, soil conservation payments and

WELKER, HERMAN—*Continued*

river-harbor appropriations (all three in June, 1952). He also favored bills opposing the merit selection of city postmasters and U.S. marshals (June, 1952). He opposed the draft extension-universal military training bill (March, 1951), government operation of defense plants (June, 1951), a $5.5 billion tax increase (September, 1951), and giving President Harry S. Truman the power to seize steel plants (June, 1952).

With Senator Homer Ferguson of Michigan and Richard M. Nixon, then a Senator from California, Welker introduced a bill supporting President Truman's proposed revisions of the Defense Production Act. Although the bill was never passed, Senator Welker stated at the time it was introduced: "We have asked just what the President asked . . . the ball is in your [Democrats] corner and I hope it works" (New York *Times,* August 24, 1951).

On bills concerning foreign affairs that were voted on in the Eighty-second Congress, Welker favored lending India money to buy U.S. surplus wheat instead of giving it half the wheat as a gift (May, 1951), an absolute ban on Allied trade with the Soviet bloc (August, 1951), and reinstating the "cheese embargo amendment"—restricting dairy imports—into the Defense Production Act (June, 1952). He voted against a troops-for-Europe resolution as our contribution to an international army (April, 1951) and against an amendment liberalizing the omnibus immigration bill (May, 1952). When President Truman vetoed the whole immigration act, Welker voted to override the veto.

Herman Welker has favored bills cutting the amount of money appropriated for foreign aid. In August 1951 he favored a $500,000,000 cut for economic aid to Europe, and in the spring of 1952 he led eleven Republicans in sponsoring two amendments proposing drastic deductions. These were defeated.

When the Senate convened for the beginning of the Eighty-third Congress, Welker was appointed to the Agriculture and Forestry Committee and the Judiciary Committee. When the emergency immigration bill, designed to admit 214,000 aliens to the United States (many of them Iron Curtain refugees), was considered by that committee in the spring of 1953, he opposed it. Senator Welker also serves on the Senate internal security subcommittee.

Legislation which he favored in the 1953 session of Congress included the offshore oil bill (May), an amendment to the NATO agreement forbidding the trial of American soldiers in foreign courts (July), a bill for selling government-owned rubber plants (July), and a provision for using foreign aid to cut farm surpluses (July). He opposed confirming Charles E. Bohlen as Ambassador to the Soviet Union (March).

His voting record in the second session of the Eighty-third Congress (1954) indicates that he favored the John W. Bricker constitutional amendment limiting the President's power to negotiate foreign treaties (February). He voted against the St. Lawrence seaway proposal (January), a bill giving statehood to Alaska and Hawaii (April), and a bill extending the Reciprocal Trade Agreements Act three years instead of just one (June).

When the Arthur V. Watkins committee report was made public in September 1954 advising that Senator Joseph R. McCarthy be censured on certain counts, Welker was one of the few Senators to immediately announce that he disagreed with the findings. In the Senate debate on the censure issue that took place two months later, he was one of McCarthy's staunchest supporters. McCarthy was censured by the Senate by a vote of 67-22.

Welker married Gladys Pence on September 20, 1930. They have one daughter, Nancy. He belongs to the Episcopal Church and is a member of the Masonic Lodge (El Korah Shrine), Elks, Knights of Pythias, American Legion, Idaho and California bar associations, Sigma Chi and Phi Alpha Delta fraternities, and the Cattlemen's Association.

He has been a part-time baseball scout for the Pittsburgh Pirates, partly owned by his friend Bing Crosby. When Welker shot a hole-in-one (the distance was 150 yards) while playing golf on a vacation in 1953, he sent a wire to President Eisenhower advising him to brush up on his golf.

References

Christian Sci Mon p7 O 16 '50
N Y Herald Tribune p22 N 26 '50
Congressional Directory (1954)
Who's Who in America, 1954-55
World Biography (1954)

WELLER, THOMAS H. *See* Enders, John F(ranklin)

WELLMAN, MANLY WADE May 21, 1903- Author

Address: b. c/o University of North Carolina Press, Box 510, Chapel Hill, N.C.; h. Box 744, Chapel Hill, N.C.

Reprinted from the *Wilson* Library Bulletin April 1955

Manly Wade Wellman is a child of two continents—Africa and North America. Born in Africa, where his father was a medical officer for a mission board, he was brought to the United States as a child, and grew up in the Middle and Far West. "For years," he says, with a distant look in his eyes, "I wanted to return to Africa and explore, but somehow I never got there." Instead, he became the author of over half a dozen books for teenagers, numerous murder mysteries, and a biography. He has also sold more than five hundred stories and articles to national magazines on adventure, fantasy, mystery, and folklore; has been a newspaper reporter, feature writer, and book reviewer; has written plays, radio scripts, and TV dramas. His stories have appeared in a dozen anthologies and have been translated into four foreign languages.

Manly Wade Wellman was born on May 21, 1903, in Kamundongo, a village in Angola, Portuguese West Africa, below the Belgian Congo. Through his father, Frederick Creighton Wellman, he is descended from Devonshire colonists who came to Jamestown, Virginia, about 1630. His mother (the former Lydia Jeanette Isely) was Swiss-French. He learned to speak the native African dialect along with English. "My chidhood in a savage and exotic country," he remarks, "may have had something to do with stimulating my imagination. That, and all the reading I did." Wellman says he owes much, too, to his oldest brother, Paul, the novelist. "We started trying to write together. We had a sense of facing a whole world determined to shunt us into some other activity. His help to me, and perhaps mine to him, may have been chiefly, comradeship—a rare thing with writers, who are usually alone."

During high school and college Manly Wellman worked on local newspapers, as well as in the harvest fields and, briefly, as floor manager for a dance hall. After his graduation in 1926 from Fairmount College (now the Municipal University of Wichita), he went on to earn another degree (B.Lit., 1927) at Columbia University. Then he became a reporter for the Wichita *Beacon,* later for the Wichita *Eagle.* When the depression deprived him of his newspaper job in 1934, Wellman decided to try New York as a free-lance writer. The years which followed were lean ones, but in 1946 his luck turned. He won the $2,000 prize in the first Ellery Queen awards with his story, "A Star for a Warrior."

The next year his book-length murder mystery, *Find My Killer* (Farrar, Straus), was serialized in a New York newspaper, syndicated by the Associated Press, published in England, translated into the Scandinavian and French, and appeared in soft covers. "I made more money at that than anything I ever wrote," the author comments. The award enabled him to turn to a pet project—the life of Civil War General Wade Hampton. When *Giant in Gray* was published in 1949 by Scribner's, it received high praise. The *Nation* (November 5, 1949) called it "an excellent and voluminously documented biography." The *Saturday Review of Literature* (November 26, 1949) wrote: "Mr. Wellman combines the two essentials of a successful historical work, he knows how to write and he knows what he is writing about. The result is an excellent biography."

Simultaneously, Wellman embarked on quite a different sort of writing. "I had always thought that someday, when I was old and mellow," he says, "I would write books for boys. Irving Crump, then editor of *Boys' Life,* asked me to write stories for the Boy Scout magazine. From them grew my first juvenile, *The Sleuth Patrol* (Nelson, 1947), about a Scout patrol which unravels a mystery." This book was a selection of the Junior Literary Guild. The *Library Journal* (September 15, 1947) found it "full of action and suspense."

His second book for boys, *The Mystery of Lost Valley* (Nelson, 1948), also was a choice of the Junior Guild. Four other boys' books followed—*The Raiders of Beaver Lake* (Nelson, 1950), *The Haunts of Drowning Creek* (Holiday, 1951), *Wild Dogs of Drowning Creek* (Holiday, 1952), and *The Last Mammoth* (Holiday, 1953). This last title was another Junior Guild choice. The *Saturday Review* classed it among informative history books for children, calling it "ingenious . . . so real that one can take it as history." Two more juveniles were published in the fall of 1954—*Gray Riders,* in Aladdin's American Heritage Series, the story of Jeb Stuart and his men, and *Rebel Mail Runner* (Holiday), another Confederate story. In January 1955 *Dead and Gone,* a collection of stories about historical crimes of North Carolina, was published by the University of North Carolina Press. Currently Wellman is at work on a novel of the Kansas frontier.

MANLY WADE WELLMAN

Wellman writes in a tiny study in the library of the University of North Carolina. He is a strapping six-footer, with brown eyes and graying hair. An entertaining talker, he is also a popular lecturer. He manages to be outdoors a great deal, and his favorite recreation, aside from playing the guitar, is going up into the mountains and talking to the mountain folk. He can quote poetry by the yard, and has written a lot of it. He works in civic affairs, taking a modest part in local politics (he is a Democrat). He belongs to the Episcopal Church. His passionate hobby is American history, and he is a member of the North Carolina Society of Local Historians. He is also a member of the Baker Street Irregulars and the North Carolina Folklore Society.

On June 14, 1930 Wellman married Frances Obrist. They have one son, Wade. The Wellmans moved to North Carolina in 1947, and to Chapel Hill in 1951.

Reference

North Carolina Authors (1952)

WHITE, HUGH L(AWSON) Aug. 19, 1881- Governor of Mississippi; businessman
Address: b. Executive Dept., New Capitol, Jackson, Miss.; h. Columbia, Miss.

When Hugh L. White was elected Governor of Mississippi in November 1951, he became, with the exception of the late Theodore Bilbo, the only chief executive since 1889 to serve two terms in the gubernatorial office at Jackson. Prior to his first term (1936-1940) he had been mayor of Columbia, Mississippi for six years, at which time he evolved the "Balance Agriculture With Industry" plan which was put into statewide operation during his first administration. During his second administration, which expires in January 1956, Governor White attracted national attention through his endeavors to adjust Mississippi's segregated public school system to successive U. S. Supreme Court rulings.

Youngest of the seven children of John James White, a pioneer in the lumber business in Mississippi, and Helen Elizabeth (Tyre) White, Hugh Lawson White was born on August 19, 1881 in McComb, Mississippi. For three years (1898-1901) he studied at the University of Mississippi in Oxford and played tackle on the varsity football team.

At about the age of twenty-five, White took over the management of his family's timberlands and sawmill at Columbia in Marion County.

Several years after White became president of the J. J. White Lumber Company he realized that the hundreds of acres of pine stumps meant that the local timber supply was approaching exhaustion. "I vowed that I would work to restore, in part at least," he said, "the wealth that I and my brethren of the lumber industry of the South had taken from the soil." With other Marion County citizens, White urged clearance of the former timberlands for farming.

Following his election in the fall of 1929 to the first of three consecutive two-year terms as mayor of Columbia, a movement with the slogan "Balance Agriculture With Industry" was launched to attract manufacturing to the town. This resulted in Marion County raising $85,000 to construct a building for the manufacture of men's clothing; factories were subsequently opened which hired former sawmill employees to make boxes and can pickles. Other industries were soon attracted to the area.

Success of the B.A.W.I. movement having attracted statewide interest, White sought in 1935 the Democratic nomination (tantamount to election in a "Deep South" state) for the governorship of Mississippi. In the August 7 primary he led a list of candidates, and in a run-off on August 28 he defeated Judge Paul Johnson of Hattiesburg by about 10,000 votes. (White was supported by both outgoing Governor Martin Sennett Conner and Mississippi's U. S. Senator Theodore G. Bilbo.)

Elected without Republican opposition in November 1935, White was inaugurated at Jackson in the following January as Mississippi's forty-ninth chief executive. He continued to be concerned about the state's under-industrialized condition, and at a special session during 1936 the legislature enacted what White characterized as "a law to enable county and municipal governments to issue bonds, proceeds from the sale of which might be used in the construction and operation of industrial plants." A three-member Industrial Commission and a Mississippi Advertising Commission were set up to publicize the state's resources.

Before the end of his 1936-1940 administration Governor White suffered a heart attack which confined him to bed for a full year. Barred by the state constitution from a second consecutive elective term, he left office in January 1940, and resumed the presidency of his various Mississippi business enterprises, which today include White's Lumber Yard at Jackson, White's Lumber and Supply Company at Meridian, the H. L. White Lumber Yard at Yazoo City, and White's Box Company and the J. J. White Lumber Company at Columbia. The B.A.W.I. statute lapsed in his successor's administration, but when Thomas L. Bailey won the campaign for governor in 1943, White was elected to the legislature. Thereafter he helped put the law back in operation (in 1946) and to set up the Mississippi Agricultural and Industrial Board for its administration (*Manufacturers' Record,* December, 1948). In April 1947 he proposed the formation of a Mississippi Export-Import Commission to build up a world market for the state's industrial products.

At the Democratic National Convention of 1948 White led the walk-out of the Mississippi delegation after the adoption of the civil rights platform plank. Subsequently he was active in forming the Southern States' Rights Democratic ("Dixiecrat") party, which nominated Fielding L. Wright, Bailey's successor as Governor of Mississippi, as its candidate for the vice-presidency.

Three years later (summer of 1951), with Wright's support, White sought for the second time the Democratic gubernatorial nomination, and at the primary on August 8 topped Paul Burney Johnson (the son of his former gubernatorial opponent) by some 8,500 votes. He did not, however, secure a majority of all votes, and a run-off primary on August 28 became necessary. White then defeated Johnson by a narrow margin. Unopposed in the November election, White again took office as governor on January 20, 1952.

"The state has neglected, to a large extent, to sufficiently encourage the owners of some 250,000 farms so that they might produce more and better grades of livestock, poultry, and eggs, and thereby encourage the location of stockyards, meat-packing, cheese and dairy processing and fertilizer plants in this state." Thus in a message to the 1952 legislature Governor White introduced a proposal, adopted with comparative ease, to create a $2,000,000 state fund to underwrite private loans to farmers. (By this time the re-enacted B.A.W.I. statute had brought seventy new industries to Mississippi and created some 16,000 jobs.)

Ordinarily the Mississippi legislature meets only in even-numbered years, and its regular 1952 session ended well before the Democratic

National Convention, at which Governor White headed an anti-Trumanism delegation. But on November 3, 1953 it met in special session to consider a $49,000,000 per annum appropriation endorsed by the Governor and adopted late in December, for the equalization of educational facilities in the state's schools for white and colored pupils, this being necessitated as the result of a Supreme Court decision earlier in the year. During the 1954 session in February, Mississippi became the fifteenth state to outlaw the "closed shop."

On May 17, 1954 the U. S. Supreme Court, by unanimous decision, declared racial segregation in public schools to be unconstitutional, thus setting aside the "doctrine of 'separate but equal' facilities" handed down in 1896. Governor White, as chief executive of a state in which educational segregation is stipulated by law, immediately urged a "go slow" attitude on the part of officials. "We're going to work our problem out, and we're going to keep segregation," he was later quoted (*Christian Science Monitor,* August 11, 1954). A twenty-five member advisory committee of lawyers and educators was assigned to study the situation and presented the draft of a state constitutional amendment which would "permit the legislature to abolish all public schools 'as a last resort' by two-thirds vote; allow individual localities to abolish public schools as they choose; and sell, rent or lease school property to private individuals, then pay each 'educable' child's tuition to what would then be private, segregated schools" (*Time,* September 20, 1954).

The legislature, called into special session in September, approved the amendment, which was submitted to the voters at a special referendum held December 21, and endorsed by a two to one majority; and on April 5, 1955, during another special legislative session, Governor White signed an act providing fines and possible jail sentences for whites who attended state-supported schools with Negroes.

The alleged kidnapping at Money, Mississippi on August 28, 1955 of Emmett Till, a fourteen-year-old Negro boy who was said to have "whistled" at a white woman and whose body was subsequently found in the Tallahatchie River, again focussed national attention on the race problem in the state. Two white men indicted by the Tallahatchie County grand jury were placed on trial for murder in the circuit court at Sumner on September 19, and five days later were acquitted by the jury. They were then transferred to the custody of law officers of another county to await trial for the kidnapping and were subsequently acquitted.

Meanwhile, on August 29, a special committee met for the first time to study "methods of cutting down the number of Negro voters" in Mississippi, where according to chairman Tom Tubb of the state Democratic Committee, they had "perhaps played too large a part" in the primary and run-off primary of August 2 and 23, when John P. Coleman was nominated as the Democratic gubernatorial candidate. (Coleman was elected Governor the following November.)

Hugh Lawson White and Judith Wier Sugg were married June 14, 1905. The Governor of Mississippi favors the continuance of prohibition in one of the country's two "dry" states. He is a Presbyterian, a Mason (Knight Templar and Shriner), a Rotarian, and a member of the Delta Psi fraternity. Southwestern College in Memphis awarded him an honorary LL.D. degree in 1934. Massively built and weighing over 260 pounds, he has been described as "robust" for his seventy-four years. White is said to have few hobbies. "A lot of fellows think I'm kidding when I say it," he stated many years ago, ". . . but what I would rather do than anything else is to sit on the fence and listen to a little pig there munch old crack corn. That's fun."

Wide World

HUGH L. WHITE

References

Coronet 26:78+ My '49
N Y Times p62 Ag 12 '51; p17 Ag 30 '51 por
Newsweek 13:15+ Je 26 '39 por
Time 31:22 Ja 17 '38 por
U S News 37:16 S 17 '54 por
American Guide Series: Mississippi (1946)
Who's Who in America, 1954-55

WHITE, PAUL DUDLEY June 6, 1886-

Physician

Address: b. 264 Beacon St., Boston, Mass.; h. 200 Marsh St., Belmont, Mass.

One of the world's leading authorities on heart disease, Dr. Paul Dudley White was called into consultation by Army doctors treating President Dwight D. Eisenhower following his collapse from coronary thrombosis in September 1955. A cardiac specialist since 1913 and a pioneer of electrocardiography, Dr. White has been a teacher and trainer of doctors at the Harvard Medical School and the head

Wide World

DR. PAUL DUDLEY WHITE

of the heart clinic at the Massachusetts General Hospital. He is the author of the standard work *Heart Disease,* in its fourth revised edition in 1951, and is author or co-author of other works on electrocardiography and heart ailments. In the course of forty years of practice he has treated some 12,000 heart cases.

Born to Herbert Warren and Elizabeth A. (Dudley) White at Roxbury, Massachusetts on June 6, 1886, Paul Dudley White was brought up in that section of greater Boston, where his father was in practice as a family physician. He was graduated from the Roxbury Latin School and from Harvard College, where he received the A.B. degree in 1908. Already determined on the medical profession, he studied for the next three years at the Harvard Medical School, acquiring the M.D. degree in 1911.

Two years as an intern at the Massachusetts General Hospital in Boston followed, and it was during this period that Dr. White prepared with Dr. R. I. Lee "Clinical Study in the Coagulation Time of Blood," which was published in 1913 in the *American Journal of Medical Science.*

The death of a sister from rheumatic fever had prompted young Dr. White to take special interest in cardiovascular disease. The grant by Harvard in 1913 of a one-year Sheldon traveling fellowship enabled him to pursue this subject at the University College Hospital Medical School in London, and to meet Sir Thomas Lewis and Sir James Mackenzie, two "leaders in the field" from whom he "received great stimulation and helpful training" (Foreword to his book, *Heart Disease,* 1931).

He collaborated with Sir Thomas Lewis on two papers, "The Susceptible Region in A-V Conduction" and "The Effects of Premature Contractions in Vagotomised Dogs, with Especial Reference to Atrio Ventricular Rays," which appeared in the London periodical *Heart* during 1914. While in England Dr. White acquired for the Massachusetts General Hospital that institution's first electrocardiograph.

Joining the Harvard Medical School in 1914 as a teaching fellow, Dr. White was engaged thereafter in research, practice and teaching, especially in the field of heart disease. His work as resident in medicine at the Massachusetts General Hospital in 1914 was interrupted in 1916 when he went to France with the World War I British Expeditionary Force as a medical officer. Commissioned a captain in the U.S. Army Medical Corps in 1917, he remained with the American Expeditionary Force for the duration of the war. Then in 1919, as a medical officer of the American Red Cross, he went to Macedonia to fight a typhus epidemic for which he won a decoration from the Greek government. He wrote an account of this mission, "Public Health in Macedonia," in the *American Journal of Public Health,* January 1920.

After resuming his appointment as resident in medicine at the Massachusetts General Hospital later in 1919, Dr. White was advanced to assistant to the physician in charge of consultative medicine, in 1920, and was eventually placed in charge of the hospital's cardiac clinic and laboratory. One of his patients during the 1920's was the elderly father of President Calvin Coolidge.

Dr. White was one of the founders of the American Heart Association in 1922 and served from 1921 to 1924 as secretary of the section of pharmacology and therapeutics of the American Medical Association. A Moseley traveling fellowship made it possible for him to travel to London, Paris and Vienna in 1928 and obtain additional data for his book *Heart Disease.* First published by Macmillan in 1931, it was revised and reissued in 1932, 1937, 1944 and 1951. Prior to the first appearance of *Heart Disease,* which is still regarded as the standard text on the subject, Dr. White had observed some 4,000 cardiac cases in private practice.

In the course of a long-range study to "show that in human patients the 'normal' range of heartbeats as measured by EKG (electrocardiograph) time intervals must be widened to allow for the difference in the size of the heart" (*Time*), Dr. White established in 1932 that an infant's heart beats twice as fast as an adult's ("Heart of a Child," *Hygeia,* February 1933). In 1936, as part of his study of heartbeat range, he established that the pulse rate of an elephant is thirty-five to forty beats a minute. His shorter book, *Heart Disease in General Practice* (National Medical Book Company), was published in 1937.

He was vice-president of the American Heart Association in 1940 and in the same year delivered the annual Hermann Biggs lecture before the New York Academy of Medicine and began six years as chairman of the subcommittee on cardiovascular diseases of the National Research Council. *Electrocardiography in Practice* (W. B. Saunders Company), a standard work of charts and comment compiled by Dr. Ashton Graybiel and Dr. White, was first published in 1941. Subsequent editions appeared in 1946 and 1952. He served as president of the American Heart Association from 1942 to 1944 and was chairman of a special A.M.A. committee that presented a comprehensive exhibit on heart disease at Philadelphia in 1945. An honorary member of the Czechoslovak Cardiological Society since 1938, Dr. White headed the American Unitarian medical teaching mission to Czechoslovakia in the summer of 1946.

"What we need mainly to do now is to concentrate on the study of the three most common causes of heart disease, rheumatic fever, hypertension and pre-senile obstruction. . . . We do not yet know the causes of any of these three vital factors; together they are responsible for at least 90 per cent of the cases of heart disease in this country." So stated Dr. White in February 1947 at a New York Academy of Medicine meeting to launch a campaign for a $500,000 heart research fund. In the following year he was made executive director of the newly created National Advisory Heart Council.

In April 1948 Charles University in Prague, Czechoslovakia awarded Dr. White a degree *honoris causa*. He has also received honorary degrees from Athens and Salonika universities (awarded in 1948 when he headed an American teaching mission to Greece and Italy) and from Harvard University (awarded in 1950).

At the First World Cardiological Congress held in Paris in 1950 Dr. White urged a study of racial, climatic and diet links to heart disease. At the Second International Gerontological Congress meeting in St. Louis, Missouri, he joined with Dr. Menard Max Gertler in reporting that "short, thick-chested, and wide-bodied, muscular men" are the most susceptible to coronary heart disease. (They further found that "children of those afflicted with coronary heart disease are more likely to have heart-muscle trouble" than others, thus suggesting an hereditary factor.) In 1952 Dr. White was a member of a Point IV mission to Pakistan, India and Israel.

Soon after receiving the A.M.A. Distinguished Service Medal in 1952, Dr. White sailed to the coast of Alaska to extend the data on heartbeat range in the animal kingdom by recording for the first time the heart beats of the white whale. Harpoons were used as electrodes to obtain the electrocardiographs of a one-ton, twelve-foot specimen, which recorded fifteen beats a minute.

On February 2, 1953 Dr. White became the first heart specialist to receive the annual Albert Lasker award. In his speech of acceptance he said that "in this push-button age man is overeating and pampering himself" and that "the life of Riley . . . leads to a lot of early coronary disease, high blood pressure and diabetes" (as reported in *Time,* February 9, 1953).

He became vice-president of the International Society of Cardiology following the First Cardiological Congress in 1950, and at the Second World Congress on Cardiology at Washington, D.C. in September 1954 he was elected president of the International Society in succession to Dr. Charles Laubry of France. Dr. White, who is now retired from his Harvard Medical School professorship, is the co-author with Dr. Menard Max Gertler of *Coronary Heart Disease in Young Adults: A Multidisciplinary Study* (Harvard University Press, 1954). His *Clues in Diagnosis and Treatment of Heart Disease* (C. C. Thomas, 1955) is in the "American Lectures in Circulation" series.

Following the collapse of President Eisenhower from coronary thrombosis on September 24, 1955 Dr. White was called to Fitzsimons Army Hospital at Denver, Colorado as a consultant to Major General Howard McC. Snyder and other Army doctors in the treatment of the President.

He became their spokesman, and, at a press conference which Waldemar Kaempffert of the New York *Times* described as "a model of medical candor," not only did much to relieve the national anxiety but "thoroughly reviewed what is and what is not known about coronary thrombosis."

He found the Chief Executive's chances of recovery "reasonably good" and did not believe that addiction to golf had precipitated the attack. At a subsequent press conference (October 9) Dr. White recommended that the President be allowed to make decisions in matters of national emergency and to have conferences with his Cabinet and other officials. However, he stated that at that time it was impossible to say whether Eisenhower would be physically able to run for a second term.

Dr. White is a trustee of Anatolia College and a councilor of Smith College. He belongs to numerous organizations including the American Academy of Arts and Sciences, the Royal Society of Medicine, the Cardiac Society of Great Britain and Ireland, the National Academy of Medicine of France, and the French, Mexican, Brazilian and Argentine cardiac societies. His social clubs are the Harvard, St. Botolph and Saturday in Boston. Dr. White's church affiliation is the Baptist.

Dr. White and Ina Reid were married June 28, 1924 and have one daughter, Penelope Dudley, and one son, Alexander Warren. They make their home in the Boston suburb of Belmont, where he still mows his own lawn in summer, and in winter puts up the storm windows. Imitating his father, who "sometimes cycled 100 miles a day," Dr. White "still clicks off a brisk five or 10 miles whenever he can" (*Life*). "The Boston heart specialist is a wiry, little man with thinning gray hair, gray eyebrows and a gray mustache," the New York *Times* has observed. He has blue eyes.

References

Am Med Assn J 149:765 Je 21 '50 por
Life 39:156-7 O 10 '55 pors
N Y Times p14 Je 18 '40; p17 Je 10 '52 por; p11 F 3 '53 por; p14 F 7 '53; p20 O 10 '55
N Y World Telegram p4 O 1 '55 por
Newsweek 43:53 Ja 25 '54
Sci N L 63:84 F 7 '53
Time 61:46 F 9 '53 por; 66:28 O 10 '55
American Men of Science (1955)
Directory of Medical Specialists (1953)
Who's Who in America, 1954-55
World Biography (1954)

WHITE, PAUL W. June 9, 1902-July 9, 1955 Radio executive; founder of the Columbia Broadcasting System's news bureau; news director of KFMB-TV, San Diego, California (1948-1955); reporter for United Press (1924-1930); covered Charles A. Lindbergh's trans-Atlantic flight in 1927; became associated with CBS in 1930; vice-president and general manager in charge of news (1933-1946); received the Peabody Award (1945) for outstanding news coverage; wrote radio textbook *News on the Air* (1947); was an assistant professor of journalism (1939-1946) at his alma mater, Columbia Graduate School of Journalism; recognized as "pioneer in electronic journalism." See *Current Biography* (Mar.) 1940.

Obituary

N Y Times p72 Jl 10 '55

WHITE, THEODORE H(AROLD) May 6, 1915- Journalist; author

Address: b. c/o Collier's, 640 5th Ave., New York 19; h. 239 Central Park W., New York 24

A foreign correspondent with sixteen years of experience on the news fronts of Europe and Asia, Theodore H. White is the author of the best-selling book *Fire in the Ashes: Europe in Mid-Century*, a Book-of-the-Month Club selection for November 1953. His controversial *Thunder Out of China*, written with Annalee Jacoby, was a Book-of-the-Month choice in November 1946. Earlier, he had been chief of *Time* magazine's bureau in China. He was senior editor of the *New Republic* in 1947. From 1950 to 1953 he was European correspondent of the *Reporter* and then became its national correspondent. He resigned in 1955 to write for *Collier's* magazine. It was announced on March 31, 1954 that White had received the annual nonfiction award of the Sidney Hillman Foundation for *Fire In the Ashes*, his study of postwar Europe.

Two articles by White in the *Reporter* (September 14 and 23, 1954) entitled "U.S. Science: The Troubled Quest" provoked much comment. He wrote that centers of intellectual life were troubled by recent government actions concerning scientists.

The son of David White, a lawyer, and Mary (Winkeller) White, Theodore Harold White was born in Boston, Massachusetts on May 6, 1915. He was raised in Boston with his two brothers and one sister, and he describes his early years as "a normal Boston boyhood—placid, penurious, hopeful." After being graduated from Boston Latin School in 1932, White entered Harvard University on a newsboy's scholarship and received the B.A. degree in history, *summa cum laude*, in 1938.

In that year White won a Sheldon Traveling Fellowship and went to England in the critical months preceding the outbreak of World War II. By 1939 White's fellowship had taken him as far as China. Having acquired a knowledge of Chinese while at college, White obtained a job with the Chinese Ministry of Information. In July 1939 he joined the staff of *Time* magazine as Far Eastern correspondent.

White was a firsthand observer of the Chinese defense against Japanese troops, the Honan famine, the opening of the Burma Road, the politics in the Chungking government, and the signing of the Japanese surrender agreement in Tokyo Bay aboard the U.S.S. *Missouri*. He traveled about 200,000 miles in the course of his work. The first white man in fifteen years to penetrate (and return from) remote parts of the Chinese province of Shansi, White reported on the routing of the Japanese in the Chung Tiao Shan Mountains.

In 1943 White spent several months with the American pilots in China under command of Claire Chennault. He went on numerous bombing missions with them and was the only newsman who flew on the raid on the airdrome of Shinchiku, Formosa. White accompanied the 14th Air Force on the "hump" route over the Himalayas from India to China. By this time he was recognized as the "dean of the Chungking correspondents." For his services he received the Air Medal in 1944.

White's reporting from China was distinguished for its informative qualities and its insight. Reporting on a trip through Sinkiang he recognized the complexity of Chinese-Soviet relations: "In the heart of Asia these two powers must live side-by-side, sharing the rich resources, promoting a common trade, developing common irrigation, and controlling undisciplined nomadic tribes. Only mature and wise statesmen can solve these problems" (*Time*, October 25, 1943).

After resigning from his post as chief of the China bureau of *Time*, White returned to the United States in the spring of 1946. In the fall he and another former *Time* correspondent, Mrs. Annalee Jacoby, completed *Thunder Out of China* (Sloane, 1946), a book which John K. Fairbank (New York *Times Book Review*, October 27, 1946) described as "the first full-length portrait of Kuomintang China since the war began in Asia."

Richard Watts, Jr., (New York *Herald Tribune Book Review*, October 27, 1946) found it "the clearest, frankest and most combatively readable key to an understanding of that great and tormented country's current tragedy." Charles Poore (New York *Times*, October 24, 1946) wrote that it is not "a dispassionate book but," he continued, "it is animated by a profound belief in the Chinese people." *Newsweek* praised it as "some of the best and most perceptive reporting to come out of Asia in recent years."

Since the book was critical of the National Government of China it inevitably drew sharp criticism as well as praise. In December 1948 the sale of the book—which had been translated into Chinese——was banned in China by the Ministry of the Interior.

White has written on Asia and Europe since 1947 for a number of American periodicals—among them *Harper's Magazine*, the *Saturday Review of Literature*, and the New York *Times Magazine*. In the first half of 1947 he was senior editor of the *New Republic*. He resigned from the magazine to work for a year as a free-lance writer. During this period he edited *The Stilwell Papers* (Sloane, 1948), the diaries and private papers of the late General Joseph W. Stilwell.

In June 1948 White went to Europe as chief correspondent of the Overseas News Agency. In 1950 he became European correspondent of the *Reporter* magazine. It was in the course of this work that he acquired much of the background and information for *Fire in the Ashes* (Sloane, 1953).

When the book was completed in July 1953, White returned to the United States. ("You can't stay away, the roots tug irresistibly and the home call can't be denied," he wrote in the New York *Herald Tribune Book Review*, October 11, 1953). *Fire in the Ashes* appeared on the best-seller lists early in 1954. Charles J. Rolo described this book (*Atlantic Monthly*, November 1953) as "the best book of the year in the field of foreign correspondence . . . [and] the sanest and most specific appraisal . . . of the plus and minuses of United States postwar policies toward Europe."

Essentially the book deals with the regeneration of Western Europe and the responsibilities America must undertake in the free world. J. G. Harrison commented in the *Christian Science Monitor* (October 29, 1953): "He is able to see the great promise which still lies hidden—like 'fire in the ashes'—beneath the present disarray of life in Western Europe. Yet, equally, he is unsparingly and factually frank in his analysis of the continent's deep and dangerous weaknesses."

White surveys the accomplishments of American economic aid to Europe, the various movements toward European integration, and warns of the continuing Communist threat. Percy Knauth wrote in the *Saturday Review* (October 31, 1953) that it is a hopeful book, one which showed human wisdom and historical perspective, and that it was written "in a manner we have not seen from a reporter since Vincent Sheean made journalistic writing a living art with *Personal History*."

"It is [our] faith in the opportunity of tomorrow," White wrote in *Fire in the Ashes*, "more than anything else, which has kept America from any infection of Communism. And it is this faith, totally lacking in some countries of Europe or unable to express itself effectively in others, which we have been trying, without realizing, to spread in Europe by the injection of techniques and 'expertise.'"

Fire in the Ashes was discussed on the Dumont TV network's *The Author Meets the Critics* on February 7, 1954. In answer to critic Henry J. Taylor's comment that he devoted too much of the book to Europe, White replied: "I wanted the American people to know that they got their money's worth from the U.S. Government's investing nearly 20 billion dollars in Europe. I saw Europe rise from the ruins. When I first went there at the end of World War II the food ration was one-quarter of a pound a day. Now—we have an Army—and our Allies, 300,000 troops of greater strength than the Russian's, and we have modern weapons. We have rebuilt a continent—and now we can decide how to go forward in the future. America is a fluid society. I agree that the Russian's sweet talk and peace offensive is more dangerous than its cold war."

THÉODORE H. WHITE

White wrote in the *Reporter* (May 26, 1953): "A continuation of present Soviet economic expansion and present European stagnation offers the Soviets an almost ironclad guarantee of ultimate superiority. The basic strategy of the Atlantic alliance and NATO needs, therefore, total rethinking at once so that we can make use of the decade or two of economic advantage that remain."

Of the Congressional investigations of the Army, White wrote: "If now officers must deviate from the ordained laws and regulations of the Army in order to temper their actions to outside political whimsy or passion, or if they are to be invited to vent their frustrations to receptive ears in Congress . . . then the integrity of the Army is shaken to the roots" (*Reporter*, March 30, 1954).

White was married to Nancy Ariana Van Der Heyden Bean, a journalist, on March 29, 1947. They have a daughter, Ariana Van Der Heyden, and a son, David Fairbank. White has brown hair and brown eyes, is five feet five and one-half inches tall, and weighs 150 pounds.

In "A Letter from the Publisher" for June 21, 1943, *Time* said of White: "He has short legs, a freckled face, a cocky walk, an indomitable spirit, a compassion for suffering people and a curiosity which would cost a cat all nine of its lives in no time."

White is a Democrat. His memberships include the Overseas Press Club of America, Anglo-American Press Club of Paris and Harvard Club of New York. He received the Page One Award of the Newspaper Guild in

WHITE, THEODORE H.—*Continued*

1947. An avid reader, he has said: "I read practically anything," and confesses, "I can spend more money more quickly in a bookstore than anywhere else I know." His other hobbies are "household tinkering and mechanics," swimming, hiking and painting. His nickname is "Teddy."

He plans, for the present at least, to focus his reporting on America—"America is so much the energizing center of the world today that the whole frame of foreign correspondence has changed. The place to cover the world now is from America" (*Saturday Review*, October 31, 1953).

References

N Y Herald Tribune Book R p14 O 11 '53
New Repub 116:45 Ja 20 '47
Who's Who in America, 1954-55

WHITE, WALTER (FRANCIS) July 1, 1893-Mar. 21, 1955 Executive secretary of the National Association for the Advancement of Colored People since 1931; author; lecturer; leader in the fight for civil rights for Negroes; urged passage of Federal anti-lynching, anti-poll-tax, and anti-segregation laws; his books include *A Rising Wind* (1945) and *A Man Called White* (1948); active as U.S. government adviser on the United Nations and Virgin Islands. See *Current Biography* (Apr.) 1942.

Obituary

N Y Times p31 Mr 22 '55

WHITE, WILLIAM S(MITH) May 20, 1906- Journalist

Address: b. c/o New York Times Bureau, 1701 K St., N.W., Washington, D.C.; h. 5223 Reno Rd., N.W., Washington, D.C.

The Pulitzer Prize for biography in 1955 was awarded to William S. White for his book *The Taft Story* (Harper, 1954). As a Capitol Hill reporter for the New York *Times* Washington bureau since 1945, White came to know the late Senator Robert A. Taft of Ohio, and followed his career at close range. Prior to 1945 White worked for the Associated Press as a war correspondent, editor and reporter. *The Taft Story* is an account of the career of the late Senator from Ohio and an analysis of his contributions to the American political scene. It won wide critical acclaim.

William Smith White was born May 20, 1906, at De Leon, Texas, the son of John W. VanDyke and Lucia Alberta (Smith) White and the grandson of Archibald Wade White, 3d, a major in the Confederate army. His ancestors came from England and settled in North Carolina about 1720. William was educated in Texas public schools and at the University of Texas in Austin. While still a student at the university, White worked as a reporter on the Austin *Statesman*. When he was twenty he joined the Associated Press bureau in Austin as a legislative correspondent.

In 1933 White was transferred by the Associated Press to its Washington bureau, where he served on the feature and general assignment staff. He went to New York three years later as news editor of the Associated Press photo service, and later general night editor there.

When World War II broke out in 1939, White was assigned to the Associated Press foreign service with the title of war editor. Shortly after Pearl Harbor, however, he took a leave of absence to volunteer for the U.S. Army. He was accepted as an officer candidate in the infantry in June 1942. While on field maneuvers at Camp Joseph T. Robinson, Arkansas, he was afflicted with spinal meningitis and in November 1942 received a medical discharge.

After regaining his health, White returned to the Associated Press bureau in New York, and in the spring of 1943 was sent overseas as a war correspondent. After a year in Britain, during which he was injured when struck by a British army truck, he crossed the English Channel with assault troops on D-Day. That night he came back across the Channel to file his story.

As an assault correspondent, White entered Caen in Normandy with the first British attack wave and entered Paris on "Liberation Day" with the French troops of General Jacques-Philippe Leclerc. After the fall of Paris he joined the Third Armored Division of the First U.S. Army in the breakthrough across Belgium, and was with the task force of that division when it entered Germany. While accompanying an American infantry company fighting in Aachen, Germany, White wrote: "This infantry company is moving forward only ten feet at a time in an attack which in more that two hours has carried us only two blocks through one ravaged street" (New York *Times*, October 10, 1944).

At the end of 1944 White returned to the United States, and in February 1945 he joined the staff of the New York *Times*. He has been assigned to the Washington bureau of that newspaper since that time, covering a series of major assignments on Capitol Hill.

One of the first major stories he wrote for the *Times* was a series, after a thirteen-day tour of the Tennessee Valley, on the controversy over the reappointment of David E. Lilienthal as chairman of the Tennessee Valley Authority. Later in 1945 White was sent by the *Times* to cover revolutions in Venezuela and Brazil. White wrote the lead stories for the *Times* on the Republican national convention of 1948, in 1951 covered the (Millard E.) Tydings hearings and the (Douglas) MacArthur hearings, and all major foreign policy debates in the Senate.

In the spring of 1952 he was sent to Africa for two months. From there he reported on the constitutional-racial struggle in the Union of South Africa, and also wrote a series of political articles from the Belgian Congo, British Central Africa, and the Gold Coast. Later in 1952 he wrote stories on the Congressional campaign of that year, and in 1953 he had frequent dispatches on controversial Congressional investigations.

A few days after Senator Taft died in the summer of 1953, Harper & Brothers, publishers, turned to White for an objective appraisal of "Mr. Republican's" life and stormy career. White had first met Taft in 1945, and last saw him in the Senator's private office a few days before he went to the hospital in his last illness. In the intervening years he had been in close association with Taft, and grew to admire him as a statesman, politician and man. Taking a two-month leave of absence from the *Times,* White wrote the biography from his own knowledge of the Senator, but filling this out with extensive interviews with others who had known Taft well; these ranged from a trusted family servant to a former President.

In February 1954, just prior to the publication of the book, White gave a memorial lecture at The Taft School in Watertown, Connecticut, a preparatory school founded by Senator Taft's uncle, Dr. Horace D. Taft. In the lecture he declared that the Ohio Senator was "utterly without hypocrisy, too big for small gestures." He said Taft was "accepted as a leader, even when he was most tactless, for the simple reason that he was a leader and nobody could take that from him."

On May 2, 1955 it was announced by the trustees of Columbia University that White's book had been awarded the Pulitzer Prize for "a distinguished American biography or autobiography teaching patriotic and unselfish services to the people, illustrated by eminent example."

In his review of the book, Jack Steele (*Saturday Review,* April 24, 1954) commented: "It is obvious that White watched the Senator's activities with utter fascination, with much admiration for his integrity and forthrightness, and with fairly constant disapproval of his basic viewpoints and important decisions. . . . Almost every page contains a sharply tailored vignette, a revealing anecdote, or a previously unreportable aside—all of which give new clues to the Senator's motives. . . . All this is done in the clean, lucid style which has made the author the envy of his colleagues."

The *New Yorker* (June 5, 1954) reviewer, Richard H. Rovere, wrote that "the book is warm and perceptive and not infrequently brilliant. . . . White's contention is open to criticism from several points of view, but he does conclusively demonstrate Taft's intelligence, his decency and his courage, all of which were of rare quality, though immeasurable."

In an article for the August 1954 issue of *Harper's Magazine,* White wrote that "the Republicans are more fundamentally divided, and in more ways, than the Democrats—more divided, even, than the Democrats were in the long years of minor civil war between the Roosevelt-Trumanites and their intra-party opponents."

Some of the important stories covered by White in 1954 for the *Times* centered around the controversy over the (John W.) Bricker amendment to restrict the President's treaty-making powers. In April 1955 at a course for teachers given by the New York *Times,* he declared that the area of "genuine political dispute" between the political parties in Congress was growing smaller. Shortly after the award of the Pulitzer Prize it was announced that White was at work on an anecdotal book about the U.S. Senate for Harper.

WILLIAM S. WHITE

White's newspaper colleagues described him as "handsome, smooth and polished," with a youthful appearance that belies his long years of experience. But that the experience is there is attested by his ability to remain calm and effective under the tremendous pressures of his work. The journalist is married to the former June McConnell of Boston. They have two daughters, Lucia Stanton and Ann Victoria. He is a member of the National Press and Overseas clubs.

References

Harpers 209:17 Ag '54
N Y Times p28 My 3 '55 por

WILLIAMS, ESTHER Aug. 8, 1923- Motion picture actress

Address: b. c/o Metro-Goldwyn-Mayer Studios, Hollywood, Calif.; h. Brentwood, Calif.

Amphibious Esther Williams, who can make "a mint of money with equal ease under water and on dry land," has been in motion pictures for the past twelve years and has recently signed a ten-year contract with Metro-Goldwyn-Mayer. Formerly a champion swimmer, she turned professional in 1940 and became the star of Billy Rose's Aquacade in San Francisco. In all her pictures, many of which are in Technicolor, her talents as a swimmer are featured (she also water-skis).

(Continued next page)

Metro-Goldwyn-Mayer

ESTHER WILLIAMS

Among her recent pictures have been *Easy to Love* (filmed in Cypress Gardens, Florida in 1953) and *Jupiter's Darling* (filmed in CinemaScope at Catalina, California in 1954).

Her ability for making profits in a variety of business enterprises ranging from machine shops to restaurants has placed her among the ten top money-making stars in Hollywood. "I can't sing, I can't dance, I can't act," she admits cheerfully, but her fans continue to like her "wholesome charms and youthful smile." Her picture appears on at least fifteen magazine covers a year, and only one of her films has made less than a half a million dollars profit for her studio.

As popular abroad as she is in America, she has been called India's favorite pin-up girl, and draws large audiences in the Middle East as well as in South America and Europe.

The youngest of five children (three sisters and two brothers), Esther Jane Williams was born in Inglewood, a suburb of Los Angeles, on August 8, 1923. Her father, Lou Williams, a descendant of Rhode Island Welsh and Virginia Scotch-Irish pioneers, was a master sign painter and commercial artist. Her mother, Bula Williams, came of a family of Dutch English stock in Pennsylvania. Mrs. Williams was a school teacher and at one time a counselor for Dr. Paul Popenoe's Institute of Family Relations and also was certified by the Los Angeles Board of Education to hold classes for parents on parent-child relations. In 1950 she started her own non-profit counseling service on parent-child problems.

Taken frequently to the beach by her family, young Esther was taught to swim by her sister, Maureen. When she was eight a playground swimming pool opened across the street from her home (her civic-minded mother had campaigned for the playground). Esther took a job counting locker room towels at the pool to earn swimming time, one hour's swimming for every hundred towels. Guards at the pool coached the youngster, and when she was fifteen the swimming team of the Los Angeles Athletic Club asked her to join. The club's athletic director and swimming coach, Aileen Allen, told her that if she worked hard she would be a champion in four years.

Two years later, at the Women's Outdoor Nationals at Des Moines in 1939, she anticipated the prediction, won all her races and broke a record. She won the 100-meter free style, was a member of the relay teams that won the 300-meter relay championship, the 800-yard relay title, and the 300-yard relay, and set a record for the 100-meter breast stroke. She later won titles in Seattle and Miami.

"She wanted to win because it was fun," her mother wrote in an article in *Parents' Magazine* describing the part Esther's happy temperament and "even disposition" played in her success. Slated to go to Finland as a member of the American Olympics team the following May, Esther lost her chance to compete internationally when the outbreak of war cancelled the Olympics. Instead, the young champion took a position modeling sportswear at Magnin's, a Los Angeles department store.

Esther attended the Los Angeles public schools, was graduated from high school and from the Los Angeles City College, and also attended the University of Southern California. A future in show business, which she had never imagined, opened up to her in 1940. She turned professional when she tried for and won the star role in Billy Rose's Aquacade at the Golden Gate International Exposition in San Francisco. Co-starred with Johnny Weissmuller, for eight months she swam in the show four times a day and five times a day on weekends.

Hollywood scouts who saw her in the Aquacade offered her movie contracts, but when the Billy Rose show closed she went back to Magnin's store to model, not convinced that she had any ability for acting. A year later, however, Louis B. Mayer of Metro-Goldwyn-Mayer offered her a contract which assured her six months of study and preparation. Because, according to her mother, she thought learning to act "would be fun," she accepted the offer and began a regimen of training in speech and dramatics, singing and dancing.

After six months of training Miss Williams made a test with Clark Gable, and during 1942 was given small parts with Mickey Rooney in *Andy Hardy Steps Out* and in *Andy Hardy's Double Life.* The Hardy pictures were considered "Metro's showcase for new girls." She next danced briefly with Van Johnson in *A Guy Named Joe* (1943), a picture starring Spencer Tracy and Irene Dunne. Her first starring role was in *Bathing Beauty* (1944), in which she played opposite Red Skelton. That picture began pulling in fan mail. For *Ziegfeld Follies* in 1944 she swam in an underwater ballet. In 1945 came *Thrill of a Romance* with Van Johnson.

By the time *Easy to Wed* appeared (in 1946), Archer Winston of the New York *Post* was able to conclude: "Miss Williams has enough physical and facial charm to cover her deficiencies as an actress. To tell the truth, she is improving rapidly. At her present rate she ought to be able to dispense with swimming in about a year." The film, a light comedy, which also starred Van Johnson, was generally thought to be "easy to enjoy" (New York *Times*), and Miss Williams was consistently described in reviews as "attractive." Most of the same critics agreed that *The Hoodlum Saint* (1946), a film with a religious theme in which she played a newspaper woman and starred opposite William Powell, was a mistake—the story was "in bad taste" (New York *Sun*) and "implausible" (*Christian Science Monitor*).

Her next release, *Fiesta,* (1947) introduced Miss Williams as a "beautiful if somewhat improbable matador" (New York *Times*). Miss Williams got better notices than the "lame and weary plot." The 1948 musical *On An Island With You* was generally agreed to be a "pleasantly simple romance" (New York *Post*) with Miss Williams appearing in becoming bathing suits and swimming in a jazz water ballet to make up for what the New York *Times* called "the tedium of the plot."

The star played the lady owner of a baseball team in *Take Me out to the Ball Game,* which also featured Gene Kelly and Frank Sinatra (1949). This one was "bright . . . gay . . . romantic" but also "corny," according to the New York *Post.* As for "the beautiful Miss Williams," the New York *Times* concluded, "you can watch her with pleasure." In the musical *Neptune's Daughter* (1949) she returned to the bathing suit. "Miss Williams is no actress," commented the New York *Herald Tribune,* "but she is extraordinarily graceful when she gets in the drink."

The 1950 *Duchess of Idaho,* set in Sun Valley, cast her as a swimming star in a "routine" story (New York *Times*). For *Pagan Love Song,* released the same year, she went to Hawaii where she performed in underwater swimming scenes in a manner described as "wonderfully graceful" by one critic. For her performance in *Texas Carnival,* in which Red Skelton played a carnival barker, she won this comment from the New York *Herald Tribune:* "Miss Williams, easy on the eyes in a one-piece bathing suit, gets a fair chance to show she has possibilities as a comedienne." In *Skirts Ahoy* (1952) the star played a Wave in a light musical comedy described as "flimsy and incredible" in story, but "fair entertainment" nonetheless (New York *World-Telegram and Sun*).

A role that "fit her to perfection" (New York *Herald Tribune*) came in the 1952 *Million Dollar Mermaid:* she played Annette Kellerman, the onetime champion swimmer from Australia who "pioneered the one-piece bathing suit." Her "spectacular" water performances in Cypress Gardens, Florida, in *Easy to Love* (1953) resulted in what the critics considered refreshing entertainment, though the script, as usual, was "fairly standard stuff" (*New Yorker*).

Life magazine dubbed Miss Williams "The Mermaid Tycoon" in an April 1951 article, pointing out that she had invested her earnings in successful business enterprises, including a service station, the Trails restaurant, a metal products plant, and real estate holdings, and had a business connection with Fred Cole of California bathing suits. But the busy actress finds time to teach swimming to blind and partly blind children.

In her bathing suit the actress, who is five feet seven inches tall, weighs 123 pounds. Her hair is brown, her eyes are hazel.

Early in her career Miss Williams married a young medical interne, Dr. Leonard Kovner. That marriage ended in divorce. In 1945 she was married to Ben Gage, radio announcer and singer. They live in an Early American farmhouse in Brentwood. Their children are Benjamin Stanton, born in 1949, Kimball Austin, born in 1950, and Susan Tenney, born in 1953. They were baptized in the Congregational Church, with Governor Walter Kohler of Wisconsin as one of the godparents. Miss Williams likes decorating her home, which is full of antiques and potted plants, and enjoys a swimming pool where she swims every morning. She and her husband like to entertain friends at small dinner parties, and they prefer home life to night clubs.

References

Am Mag 142:54+ Jl '46 por
Life 14:53+ Ap 19 '43; 30:139+ Ap 16 '51 pors
Look 17:38+ Ap 21 '53 pors
N Y Herald Tribune VIII p34 O 5 '47
N Y Times II p4 Mr 28 '43; II p5 N 14 '54
N Y World-Telegram p15 D 12 '44
Photoplay 36:36+ S '49; 45:43 Ja '54
Washington (D.C.) Post p15 Mr 28 '54
Motion Picture and Television Almanac, 1953-54
Winchester's Screen Encyclopedia (1948)

WILLIAMS, JAY May 31, 1914- Author
Address: b. c/o Little, Brown & Co., 34 Beacon St., Boston 6, Mass.; h. Fox Run Rd., R.F.D. #1, West Redding, Conn.

Reprinted from the *Wilson Library Bulletin* Oct. 1955

The evolution of an historical novelist has not yet been charted by the literary anthropologists. In Jay Williams' case it is a devious path—camp counsellor, press agent, actor, writer of juveniles, research scholar, and finally, historical novelist. "The fact is, becoming a writer," he observes, "is like an egg becoming a chicken: it is rarely a matter of conscious choice."

In 1955, with the success of his first nonfiction book *Fall of the Sparrow* (Oxford University Press, 1951) only a few years behind

C. Wilcox

JAY WILLIAMS

him and a solidly established reputation as the author of historical novels for boys, Williams published what many reviewers hailed as one of the best historical novels of the season, *The Siege*. A vigorous and carefully documented story of the Albigensian Crusade of the thirteenth century, *The Siege*, as Orville Prescott wrote in the New York *Times* (April 19, 1955), shows that Williams "really knows the period of which he writes," and "cares about subtleties of characterization."

Jay Williams, the son of Max and Lillian (Weinstein) Jacobson, was born in Buffalo, New York on May 31, 1914. He spent his childhood in Buffalo and in Rochester. His most vivid early memories—and the first source of his books for boys of teen age—are of "the imaginative games I played as a boy in the woods of Rochester and in and about the Barge Canal, which became, by turns, Sherwood Forest, Caerleon, the African jungles, or the Amazon River." Williams attended DeWitt Clinton High School in New York City.

At the University of Pennsylvania (1931-1932) and Columbia University (1933-1934), he majored in English and took part in amateur theatricals. He emerged from college into the depression of the 1930's and drifted around in odd jobs. For a while he studied art; then he worked as a comedian in night clubs and summer camps on the "Borscht circuit" (in the Catskill Mountains, New York), and for two years was general stage manager for the Federal Theatre Project. From 1936 to 1941 he was a theatrical press agent for the Group Theatre, Dwight Deere Wiman, Jed Harris, and the Hollywood Theatre Alliance. Even today Williams maintains a lively interest in all things theatrical. In 1953 he played a featured role in the prize-winning movie *Little Fugitive*.

Williams' first published work was an historical-mystery novel for boys from twelve to fourteen, *The Stolen Oracle* (Oxford University Press, 1943), set in Rome in the Augustan era. Success did not come easily—Williams confesses that he rewrote the first chapter "no fewer than seven times." The book was well received and praised especially for its authentic background. When Williams returned from military service in 1945 (with a Purple Heart won in Germany), he settled down to full-time writing.

His books for boys—*The Counterfeit African* (Oxford University Press, 1944), *The Sword and the Scythe* (Oxford University Press, 1946), *The Roman Moon Mystery* (Oxford University Press, 1948), *The Magic Gate* (Oxford University Press, 1949), and *Octavius Augustus* (Row Peterson, 1949)—were uniformly praised for their lively pace and their vivid settings. "Jay Williams," wrote the New York *Times* in its review of *The Roman Moon Mystery,* "has a remarkable talent for tearing away the romantic glamor of remote historical periods and getting down to the bedrock human emotions and motives that change very little over the centuries." *Eagle Jake and Indian Pete* (Rinehart, 1947) was written for small children.

In 1948 Williams completed his first adult historical novel, *The Good Yeoman* (Appleton, 1948) a fresh and original interpretation of the Robin Hood legend. (Robin Hood is seen as a "conservative" bandit leader while Little John is the true fighter for the oppressed peasantry of England.) A year later, financed by a Guggenheim fellowship, Williams made a trip to Europe to gather material for new historical novels. *The Rogue from Padua* (Little, 1952) a story of the German peasant rebellion of the sixteenth century, was a lusty romance, "several cuts above the standard costume drama," wrote the *Saturday Review,* full of humor, reflecting in some measure the writer whom Williams considers his master, François Rabelais, "a man of spirit who loved life."

The most ambitious of his novels to date is *The Siege* (Little, 1955), the result of arduous research into the medieval tradition of courtly love and the religious wars of the period. His aim in the book, Williams writes, is to create "a more comprehensible picture of the true mind of the Middle Ages." The critical consensus was that he was generally successful in this.

His only work of adult nonfiction is the popular *Fall of the Sparrow* (with a preface by Stanley Edgar Hyman and some startling illustrations by Richard Taylor). The book was a brief survey of extinct animal species ranging from the sicklebill, the dodo, and the basilisk, through the great auk and the American bison. Written with wry humor, the book was actually a sharp warning of the terrible consequences of man's destructiveness. The New York *Times* called it "a cautionary tale," and observed that "a light manner masks a deep purpose, a cheerful and entertaining style is put to admirable uses in the service of humanity."

Stories and articles by Williams have appeared in the *Saturday Evening Post, Esquire, Women's Day*, several Canadian and British magazines, and *Cross Section, 1944* and *Cross Section, 1945.*

Williams married Barbara Girsdansky on June 3, 1941. They have a son, Christopher, and a daughter, Victoria, and live in West Redding, Connecticut, where Williams is very active in community life—Cub Scoutmaster, PTA, the Grange, and volunteer fireman. He says: "I believe passionately that writers should be accepted as responsible professional citizens with special problems. And also that the historical novel is a serious art form and should be approached seriously and written seriously."

Williams has blue eyes, brown hair, is five feet ten inches in height and weighs 135 pounds. He is a member of the Nautical Research Guild, Patrons of Husbandry, American Folklore Society, and Association for American Indian Affairs. He enjoys travel, especially in England, where his work has been well received.

Reference

Smith's Trade News p29 F 6 '54 por

WILSON, RUFUS H(AROLD) Sept. 14, 1925- Veterans organization official

Address: b. c/o Amvets National Hdqrs., 1710 Rhode Island Ave., N.W., Washington 6, D.C.; h. 11110 Waycross Way, Kensington, Md.

Fabian Bachrach

RUFUS H. WILSON

Having joined the American Veterans of World War II soon after its founding, national commander Rufus H. Wilson is one of Amvets' oldest members. At the same time he is the youngest national commander of any veterans group in the United States. He was elected to office for one year in August 1954 at Amvets' tenth anniversary convention. The largest of the organizations for ex-servicemen of World War II, Amvets, which since 1950 has also included veterans of the Korean conflict, has a membership of about 125,000.

Rufus Harold Wilson, born in Sweetwater, Tennessee on September 14, 1925 is a son of James S. Wilson, an automobile worker, and Jessie Mae (Marshall) Wilson. He has a sister, Celena Jane Clinesmith, and three brothers, Oscar Thomas, Robert Samuel, and Benjamin Joseph Wilson. Reared in Clinton, Tennessee and later Detroit, Michigan, Rufus attended public schools in both states and was graduated from Highland Park (Michigan) High School in 1943. He played baseball and basketball at school, took part in track sports, and was a member of the student council.

A liberal arts student, Wilson for a time attended Wayne University in Detroit, where he became manager of the university baseball team. Later, in Washington, D.C., he studied at American University, which granted him a special degree in 1946, and at the Washington College of Law.

During World War II Wilson entered the U.S. Marine Corps in the rank of private. After his discharge as a corporal he joined Amvets and in 1946 became the first full-time national service officer of that organization. In this post, which he held for two years, he established the Michigan service department, now the largest in the country.

When he left Michigan in 1948, he went to Amvets' national headquarters in Washington, D.C. to become the first assistant national service director. In 1950 he was made acting national legislative director and as such handled representation of World War II veterans before Congress and other government organizations. He was national service and legislative director of Amvets from 1952 until early 1954, when he took the position of confidential assistant in the office of Veterans Administrator Harvey V. Higley.

Amvets was established on December 10, 1944 through a merger of a number of independent groups of discharged World War II servicemen and held its first convention as a national organization in Chicago, Illinois in 1945. Two years later, on July 23, 1947, it was granted a Federal charter, the only organization exclusively of World War II veterans to receive such a charter.

When President Harry S. Truman signed the bill for the charter, he said: "Were I a veteran of this war, I would prefer to have a veteran of World War II looking after my affairs than a veteran of some other war." At Amvets' request Congress amended the charter in 1950 to admit veterans of the Korean war to membership.

As part of its effort to secure benefits for veterans and dependents, Amvet handles through its national service officers about 100,000 cases a year involving hospitalization, disability compensation, educational benefits and similar considerations. It has given much attention to the Veterans Administration medical program, and

WILSON, RUFUS H.—*Continued*

while careful to safeguard that program, in 1953 it showed its realistic attitude toward budget problems by advocating certain curtailments of the Veterans Administration service. Amvets has also played an important part in the development and enactment of legislation that has become known as the Korean GI Bill of Rights.

At Amvets' tenth national convention, held in Miami Beach, Florida, Wilson was elected on August 29, 1954, to succeed Henry J. Mahady of Pennsylvania as national commander. Wilson is also chairman of Amvets savings bond drive. He represented his organization in Vienna, Austria in December 1954 at the fifth general assembly of the World Veterans Federation, which is dedicated to opposition to communism and rehabilitation of disabled veterans. (Secretary of State John Foster Dulles recently congratulated the leaders and members of Amvets on their role in supporting and helping to organize the World Veterans Federation.)

Later in the month the new commander presented two awards in behalf of Amvets: on December 10, a silver steel helmet to General George C. Marshall for his wartime service; and on December 22, a bronze plaque to Dr. Howard A. Rusk for his accomplishments in medical rehabilitation.

In a letter to *Look* (August 9, 1955) Wilson wrote that the Amvets are "vitally concerned in the treatment accorded by the various military services to ex-prisoners of war accused of collaboration with the Communist enemy during and after the Korean conflict."

On September 11, 1955 Wilson was succeeded by Rudolph G. Pesata as national commander of Amvets.

Wilson, who is the author of technical manuals on veterans affairs, has served as confidential assistant of the Federal advisory council, Department of Labor; official adviser to the veterans re-employment rights division, Department of Labor; and a member of the President's Committee on Employment of the Physically Handicapped. He has been commended by the Commission on Organization of the Executive Branch of the Government (the first Hoover commission), to whose work the Amvets contributed substantially.

Other organizations to which Wilson belongs are the Disabled American Veterans, the Fourth Marine Division Association, and the Military Order of the Purple Heart. In 1954 he was nominated as Junior Chamber of Commerce Outstanding Young Man of the Year.

On November 26, 1949 Wilson married Florence Carol Mieczkowski, a secretary. They have two sons. The blue-eyed, blond-haired veterans leader is five feet nine inches tall and weighs 138 pounds. His church is the Baptist. In politics he is an independent. For recreation he turns to reading or watching sports events.

WOHL, LOUIS DE *See* De Wohl, Louis

WOODHAM-SMITH, CECIL 1896- Author

Address: b. McGraw-Hill Book Co., 330 W. 42d St., New York 36; h. 48 Cadogan Pl., London, S.W.1, England

Reprinted from the *Wilson Library Bulletin* March 1955

In the spring of 1954 the television program *Author Meets the Critics* was obliged to cancel plans for a discussion of Cecil Woodham-Smith's *The Reason Why* when it was discovered, after an extensive search, that no critic could be found to take the "anti-" position and attack the book. No one, it appeared, had anything but praise for it. *The Reason Why,* a study of one of the most egregious blunders in modern history, the disastrous Charge of the Light Brigade in the Crimean War, was Mrs. Woodham-Smith's second venture into the field of historical writing. Her first had been her book about Florence Nightingale (1950), hailed as the definitive Nightingale biography and awarded the James Tait Black Memorial Prize in England . "The reason why" for the success of these books is at least partly suggested in an essay she wrote on the writing of history (published in the New York *Times Book Review,* July 1, 1954): "The historian's task is to make the past live again, to find out the truth and make it real. He does not need the assistance of novelty to attract his readers, he needs historical imagination, the capacity so to live in the past that it becomes as actual at the present."

Mrs. Woodham-Smith did not become a historian until middle life, but her early background peculiarly suited her for this work. Cecil Blanche FitzGerald was born in 1896 in Tenby, Wales, the daughter of Colonel James and Blanche Elizabeth (Philipps) FitzGerald.

CECIL WOODHAM-SMITH

Her father, a descendant of the old Irish family, the FitzGeralds of Leinster, had served with his regiment for many years in India. His stories of army life stirred her interest even in childhood. It was many years before she began work on her Nightingale biography, but in all that time she read nineteenth century history eagerly and—without actually knowing to what purpose she would put her knowledge—prepared herself as an authority in the field.

After completing her education at St. Hilda's College, Oxford University, where she read English literature, Cecil FitzGerald worked in an advertising agency until her marriage to George Ivon Woodham-Smith, a London solicitor, on April 3, 1928. Managing a Regency house in Cadogan Place, London, and a small country house, and raising two children kept her sufficiently occupied, but she also found time to write a number of articles, short stories, and plays. None of these had any particular success, but three books were published (under a pseudonym, Janet Gordon): *April Sky* (Hutchinson, 1938), *Tennis Star* (Hutchinson, 1939) and *Just Off Bond Street* (Hurst, 1940).

In 1942, with her children old enough for school, Mrs. Woodham-Smith almost accidentally stumbled upon the subject of her first historical book. In a dinner table conversation with Michael Sadleir, the bibliophile and publisher, she revealed such special knowledge of Florence Nightingale that Sadleir suggested that she write a biography of her. Mrs. Woodham-Smith set about consulting the formidable collection of materials—letters, documents, state records, family papers—on Miss Nightingale. Her job was enormously complicated by World War II., papers were scattered all over England and transportation and normal channels of information were blocked. She did most of her research at the British Museum, sometimes climbing over bomb debris in the streets to get there, and once nearly becoming part of that debris herself when a flying bomb fell within a few yards of the North Library of the British Museum where she was working.

Florence Nightingale, 1820-1910 (published by Constable in 1950 and McGraw-Hill in 1951) proved to be worth the more than six years that Mrs. Woodham-Smith put into it. Based on contemporary records and family papers never before made public, it was informative, sympathetic yet scrupulously fair, and gracefully written. Its picture of hospital conditions, both in military and civilian life, in mid-nineteenth century England, made it, as Morton Dauwen Zabel observed in the *Nation* (May 5, 1951), "a distinguished social document, not only beautifully readable but a revelation of much more than its specific subject." Iin 1951 Mrs. Woodham-Smith prepared an abridged edition for young people, *Lonely Crusader: The Life of Florence Nightingale, 1820-1910* (published by McGraw-Hill).

Her research into the Crimean War for the Nightingale biography led Mrs. Woodham-Smith to her study of the slaughter of the Light Cavalry Brigade in the Battle of Balaclava in 1854. *The Reason Why* (Constable, 1953; McGraw-Hill, 1954) is an examination of the historical events involved: an absorbing and revealing portrait of the two men most closely involved in the disaster, Lord Lucan, who ordered the charge, and Lord Cardigan, who led it, and of the hopelessly corrupt and decadent military system in which it took place.

"The story she relates will take its place as one of the most electrifying and dramatic exposés ever written on the history of the Victorian age," Geoffrey Bruun wrote in the New York *Herald Tribune Book Review* (May 2, 1954). This book, along with *Florence Nightingale,* commented the London *Times Literary Supplement* (November 6, 1953), "must establish the author as a leading authority for the middle reaches of the ever-receding nineteenth century."

Mrs. Woodham-Smith lives in the Cadogan Square house in London, where she has now converted the nursery into a workroom crowded with nineteenth century books and her collection of nineteenth century Staffordshire portrait figures. Her children are grown—her daughter, Eliabeth Sarah (now Mrs. B. B. W. Goodden), was presented at Court and her son, Charles James, is in military service.

References

N Y Herald Tribune Bk R p2 My 9 '54 por
N Y Times Bk R p18 Mr 4 '51 por
Who's Who, 1955
Who's Who in America, 1954-55

WRIGHT, BENJAMIN F(LETCHER)

Feb. 8, 1900- Educator; author

Address: b. College Hall, Smith College, Northampton, Mass.; h. President's House, Smith College, Northampton, Mass.

"We need a much clearer and altogether more sharply defined conception of the aims and the nature of higher education in America than any now available," stated Benjamin F. Wright, president of Smith College, recently. "We have relied too much upon inherited platitudes and have been remiss in the formulation of an adequate philosophy of higher education."

He was chosen in 1949 fifth president of Smith, a woman's private liberal arts college in Northampton, Massachusetts, with an enrollment of over 2,200. Previously he had been influential in educational circles as a professor of American constitutional history and political theory at Harvard University, as an author, and as a member of the twelve-man committee which wrote the comprehensive study, *General Education in a Free Society* (1945). President Wright had some pertinent things to say about academic freedom in the *Saturday Review* (September 29, 1953), in which he stated his belief that teachers who sincerely believe in democratic institutions should cooperate in answering questions about their former associations when queried by governmental investigating committees.

Benjamin Fletcher Wright, the son of Benjamin Fletcher and Mary (Blandford) Wright

Eric Stahlberg

BENJAMIN F. WRIGHT

was born in Austin, Texas on February 8, 1900. He is descended from early Texas pioneers. He received his early education in the public schools in his native city and served as a private in the infantry of the U.S. Army in 1918 during World War I.

He attended the University of Texas, from which he received both the A.B. and M.A. degrees and then went to Harvard University where he was awarded the Ph.D. degree in 1925. He had taught at the University of Texas as an instructor in government from 1922 to 1924, and he returned there for the 1925-1926 academic year as an adjunct professor. From 1926 to 1928 he was an instructor in government at Harvard and in 1928 became an assistant professor. After twelve years he became an associate professor, and in 1945 he was made a full professor at the university. He was chairman of the department of government from 1942 to 1946.

At Harvard Dr. Wright took part in the establishment and administration of what is believed to be the first program for the graduate study of American civilization, inaugurated in 1937. Several years later, in 1943, President James B. Conant of Harvard appointed Wright a member of the Committee on the Objectives of a General Education in a Free Society. After two years work, the twelve-man committee presented its report, "General Education in a Free Society" (later published by the Harvard University Press), which dealt with the question: "What is the right relationship between specialistic training on the one hand, aiming at any one of a thousand different destinies, and education in a common heritage and toward a common citizenship on the other?"

The committee advocated that high school students be required to take at least eight and preferably eleven courses out of the sixteen needed for graduation in general subjects: English, science and mathematics, and history, government and related social studies. Of the sixteen courses required for the B.A. degree at Harvard College, the committee recommended that six be compulsory in the humanities, sciences and social sciences. To implement this requirement, the committee asked for a number of survey courses.

The Harvard faculty approved the report, and Professor Wright was named chairman of the Committee on General Education, which established in 1949, after several years of experimentation, the new undergraduate program based on the report. This program made compulsory for all Harvard undergraduates general courses in the humanities, social sciences and the natural sciences.

In 1947 Professor Wright delivered the Lowell Institute lectures in Boston; he spoke on the topic, "The Political Philosophy of the Federalist Papers." In that year and again in 1949 he was a member of the faculty of the Salzburg (Austria) Seminar, a summer session designed to give European students, especially those who plan to teach or enter public life, an understanding of American society. Wright was described by *Higher Education* (May 1, 1950) as a "leader in the development of the seminar."

When Herbert J. Davis resigned in 1949 as president of Smith College, the trustees of the college selected Benjamin F. Wright to succeed him. Wright, giving his inaugural speech in John M. Greene Hall in October 1949, considered the purpose of education for women. A liberal education was all right as far as it went, he said, but something more needed to be added: "We must constantly bear in mind . . . that the majority of women who attend college will marry and have children, and that for most of them their home will be the focus of their lives." This responsibility, he said, should not be carried lightly, for "the American home is not so satisfactory a place as it might be and should be." He has also pointed out that there is "need for improvement in education for the days before marriage, and also for preparing for the life of the post-graduate mother—when the children have grown up and left."

In 1950 Smith College celebrated the seventy-fifth anniversary of its founding by Sophia Smith, an American philanthropist. Speaking at one assembly in honor of this anniversary, Wright stated: "Smith is known as a college which has aspired to and has in fact attained the scholarly standards of a university, and as one which has adapted its curriculum to the changing demands of a new and troubled century. . . . This college, and others like it, are both products of our civilization and contributions to its shaping. . . . We can and must determine our own destiny, not for ourselves alone, but because we have been placed in a position where the hopes of freedom depend largely upon our success or failure."

"A liberal education should equip a person for a varied life," President Wright said in New York at the Smith Club in 1950. "We still supply the girls with a broad liberal education but it is not limited in scope to the traditional concepts." He pointed out that certain courses in Smith's curriculum had integrated a broad traditional liberal education with elements of a practical value such as those in gardening (given by the botany department), in household finance (economics department), and practical courses in art, music and the drama (New York *Times*, April 2, 1950).

During the winter of 1952-1953 President Wright visited the Smith College groups in Italy, France, Switzerland, and Spain. Students in these groups spend their junior years studying in foreign universities, learning the languages and customs of their respective countries. The President has encouraged many students to take advantage of the honors program, which was established in 1944 and allows qualified students to spend more of their time doing seminar rather than course work and to write theses in their senior year. He has also supported a compulsory half-semester course for seniors which tries to integrate for each senior the work done in the last three and a half years in her major field of interest.

The Smith faculty numbers 225 persons, of whom 108 are men and 117 women. The William Allan Neilson Library contains 390,000 volumes; the Smith College Museum of Art specializes in French, English and American paintings of the last 200 years, particularly nineteenth-century French. The Alfred Einstein Music Collection contains about 8,000 hand-written copies of sixteenth and seventeenth century Italian music.

The Elisabeth Morrow Morgan Nursery School and the Smith College Day School offer opportunities for students to observe children and to do practice teaching. In January 1952 the Carnegie Foundation gave Smith College a grant of $50,000 for a period of five years to increase the number of interdepartmental courses offered by the college. In these courses, one subject, such as Africa, is taught by professors from several different departments, such as those of history, government and sociology.

The college offers graduate degrees in the arts and sciences, and in physical education. The Smith College School for Social Work, a graduate school which celebrated its thirty-fifth anniversary in 1953, has summer class work for its students on the Northampton campus, and in the winter it sends its students to do casework in social agencies throughout the country. Encouragement of continued education for Smith alumnae is given through the Alumnae College, held each year at Commencement time.

Although independent colleges in the United States are having increasing difficulty in meeting their financial obligations, President Wright was able to report in 1954 that for the fifth successive year, Smith emerged with a surplus. He stated in his annual report for 1953-1954 that while faculty salaries on the average are 30 per cent higher than in 1950-1951, student tuition fees are only 12½ per cent higher. The endowment is $14,358,572. A student pays 79 per cent of the cost of her education, the rest is met from other sources, including that of the annual gifts from over 29,000 Smith alumnae. A bequest of $1,200,000 from Mrs. Thomas W. Lamont was received by the college in August 1953.

One of the most important problems facing the colleges today is the question of academic freedom. In a guest editorial for the *Saturday Review* (September 29, 1953), President Wright asked the questions: "Should one who is called before a Congressional committee testify about his present and past membership and activities in the Communist party?" and "Should a witness give the names of persons whom he knew to be engaged in such activities?"

"In my opinion," he wrote, "the answer to both these questions is 'yes'. . . . It is an essential precept of popular government that the citizen must cooperate with its agencies, even though he disapproves of their objectives, criticizes them, and seeks to bring about a change. . . . It is difficult to see how the citizen who believes in democratic institutions can reconcile the refusal to give information with the responsibilities of citizenship in a free society, how the teacher can reconcile that attitude with respect for the candid and open statement of the truth which is an essential element of academic freedom."

The books which Wright has written include: *The Merit System in the American States* (University of Texas, 1923), *American Interpretations of Natural Law* (Harvard University Press, 1931), *The Contract Clause of the Constitution* (Harvard University Press, 1938), and *The Growth of American Constitutional Law* (Houghton Mifflin, 1942). He edited *A Source Book of American Political Theory* (Macmillan, 1929) and was the general editor of *The Major Foreign Powers: The Governments of Great Britain, France, the Soviet Union and China* (Harcourt Brace, 1949), written by John C. Ranney and Gwendolen M. Carter. Wright's articles have appeared in numerous periodicals.

President Wright is a trustee of Connecticut College in New London; The Winsor School in Boston, Massachusetts; the Clarke School for the Deaf in Northampton, Massachusetts; the Woodrow Wilson Foundation; and the Carnegie Foundation for the Advancement of Teaching. He is a member of the American Academy of Arts and Sciences, the American Political Science Association, and the American Association of University Professors. He was awarded an honorary LL.D. degree by Amherst College in Massachusetts in 1950.

Benjamin F. Wright married Alexa Foote Rhea in 1926 and is the father of two children, David and Janet. He smokes a pipe. He enjoys listening to recordings of Mozart and reading novels—"anything but detective stories." For outdoor recreation he prefers swimming and playing golf.

References

N Y Times p29 Mr 16 '49 por
Newsweek 33:86+ Mr 21 '49 por
Time 53:49+ Mr 21 '49 por
Who's Who in America, 1954-55
World Biography (1954)

WRIGHT, JERAULD June 4, 1898-
United States Navy officer
Address: b. c/o Headquarters, Commander in Chief, U.S. Atlantic Fleet, Norfolk 11, Va.; h. Missouri House, U.S. Naval Base, Norfolk 11, Va.

The United States Navy's leading specialist in amphibious and joint operational warfare is Admiral Jerauld Wright, who took over the dual duties in April 1954 of Commander in Chief of the U.S. Atlantic Fleet and Supreme Allied Commander, Atlantic (SACLANT), the latter an agency of the North Atlantic Treaty Organization. "The responsibility of SACLANT," asserted Admiral Wright, is to "make the Atlantic Ocean from the North Pole to the Tropic of Cancer and between Europe and North America, a NATO lake, a protected body of water on which shipping can move with safety" (New York *Herald Tribune*, April 19, 1954).

As the principal speaker at the Navy League's fifty-second annual dinner on November 23, 1954, Admiral Wright warned that Soviet sea power is the greatest military threat to the free world. He said that Russia's "feverish activity" in the construction of a modern navy is aimed at the sea lanes of the NATO countries. He estimated that Russia has invested more than $33 billion in her navy since 1945 and has 200,000 more men than the U.S. Navy (New York *Times*, November 24, 1954).

Prior to receiving his present appointments, Admiral Wright was Commander in Chief of U.S. Naval Forces in both the Eastern Atlantic and the Mediterranean. He holds the Distinguished Service Medal, the Bronze, Gold and Silver Stars, Navy and Victory medals and Legion of Merit for meritorious service during World War II in connection with landings in North Africa and amphibious assaults on Pacific islands.

Jerauld Wright was born in Amherst, Massachusetts on June 4, 1898 to General William Mason Wright, U.S. Army, and Marjorie R. (Jerauld) Wright. His elder brother, William Mason, Jr., followed their father in choosing an Army career and is now retired in the rank of colonel. Their sister, Marjorie, is the wife of Assistant Secretary of State David McKay Key.

Most of Jerauld's boyhood was spent in his father's native city of Newark, New Jersey; and it was through the Congressman for the Tenth New Jersey District that he received his appointment to the U.S. Naval Academy at Annapolis, Maryland in 1914. Commissioned in June 1917, Ensign Wright joined the U.S.S. *Castine*, a destroyer based on Gibraltar on convoy and patrol duty. For his 1917-1918 service, he was awarded the World War I Victory Medal with Fleet Clasp. His temporary promotions to lieutenant, junior grade, and full lieutenant, conferred during the war, were made permanent in 1920.

After some three additional years in Mediterranean waters aboard the destroyers *Dyer* and *Reid*, Lieutenant Wright was ordered to the Asiatic station, where he served successively in the destroyers *Breese* and *John D. Ford*. Returning to the United States in August 1924, he reported for duty on the U.S.S. *Mayflower*, Presidential yacht, with additional responsibility as Naval Aide at the White House to President Calvin Coolidge.

He then served in the U.S.S. *Maryland* and was aboard that battleship when she took President Herbert Hoover and his party on a goodwill tour to South American ports in 1928. He had assignments in connection with the development of anti-aircraft control equipment in the Bureau of Ordnance, Navy Department, Washington, D.C. from August 1929 until August 1931 with additional duty as Naval Aide at the White House to President Hoover. He was promoted to lieutenant commander in January 1931.

Following nearly three years service aboard the cruiser *Salt Lake City* as her first lieutenant and (later) her gunnery officer, Lieutenant Commander Wright was assigned in 1934 to the executive staff of the Naval Academy at Annapolis. He began a year's assignment in Washington in June 1935 as aide to Assistant Secretary of the Navy Henry Latrobe Roosevelt. After returning to the Bureau of Ordnance for another tour of duty, Lieutenant Commander Wright was placed in charge of the fitting out of the U.S.S. *Blue* at the Norfolk, Virginia yard, and took command of that destroyer when she was commissioned in August 1937.

In the rank of commander, Wright returned to the executive staff of the Naval Academy for twenty-two months beginning May 1939. In March 1941 he went back to sea as executive officer of the U.S.S. *Mississippi*, and following the Pearl Harbor attack on December 7, 1941, sailed in this battleship to the Pacific.

Promoted to captain in 1942, he was recalled to Washington to serve on the staff of Admiral E. J. King, Commander in Chief of the U.S. Fleet and Chief of Naval Operations, and was particularly concerned with plans for amphibious operations. Later, as a Naval member of the staff of General Dwight D. Eisenhower, commanding the Allied Expeditionary Force, he helped to plan Operation TORCH, the joint landing of Allied forces in North Africa. He also negotiated with French army, navy and air officers to effect General Mark Clark's landing in French North Africa. (For this he later received the Army Legion of Merit.)

In November 1942 Captain Wright was placed in temporary command of the British submarine H.M.S. *Seraph*, which evacuated General Henri Giraud from La Fosette in southern France. The general, his son and two staff officers were picked up from a rowboat and transferred to an airplane, using collapsible boats launched on a choppy sea. "We delivered Giraud to Eisenhower," concluded Captain Wright's official account of this exploit.

General Eisenhower in January 1943 named Wright to a committee created "to coordinate and plan the rearmament of the French forces . . . with American equipment." He also served on the combined staff of British Admiral of the Fleet Sir Andrew B. Cunningham, then Commander in Chief of the Allied Naval Forces in the Mediterranean. On March 23, 1943 he was in Washington to receive from President Franklin D. Roosevelt the Distinguished Service Medal for his "exceptionally meritorious service . . . immediately before the occupation of French North Africa."

Appointed in the same month as Assistant Chief of Staff to Admiral Henry K. Hewitt, Commander of U.S. Naval Forces in Northwest African Waters, Captain Wright was "intimately concerned in the planning and execution of the Tunisian, Sicily and Salerno invasions," and was awarded a Gold Star in lieu of a second Legion of Merit.

When he was transferred in December 1943 to the Pacific Theater, Captain Wright took command of the heavy cruiser U.S.S. *Santa Fe.* As a unit of the Fast Carrier Task Forces under Admirals Raymond A. Spruance and William F. Halsey, the cruiser participated in carrier strikes and amphibious assaults . . . at Kwajalein and in the Caroline Islands, the seizure of Saipan, the first Battle of the Philippine Sea, and strikes against Formosa and the Japanese mainland. He received the Commendation Ribbon for "distinguished service" in the Marianas and a Silver Star for "conspicuous gallantry and intrepidity" in the Battle of the Philippines.

He was promoted to commodore (temporary) in October 1944 and to Rear Admiral in November. He then commanded Amphibious Group 5, winning the Bronze Star Medal for his "meritorious service in connection with... the planning, staging and execution" of the conquest of Okinawa. His final World War II duty, beginning August 1945, was as commander of Cruiser Division 6 of the Pacific Fleet.

Honors, other than those previously mentioned, conferred on the Admiral for his World War II services include the Victory Medal (Patrol Clasp), the Army Commendation Ribbon, the American Defense Service Medal (Fleet Clasp), the European-African-Middle Eastern Campaign Medal, the World War II Victory Medal, the National Defense Service Medal, and the French Legion of Honor with rank of chevalier.

Official announcement was made in November 1946 that Rear Admiral Wright, then with the Operational Readiness Section of the office of the Chief of Naval Operations, would be "given responsibility . . . for the formulation of fleet requirements for new developments, except those pertaining to aircraft, atomic energy and guided missiles." After taking over command of Amphibious Forces, U.S. Atlantic Fleet from retiring Rear Admiral Ralph O. Davis in November 1948, he "revised tactical and strategic concepts of amphibious assaults and directed the training of Army, Navy and Air Force units."

In the New York *Times,* March 14, 1950, Hanson W. Baldwin credited Rear Admiral Wright's "command and staff" with being the "brain and nerve center" of Operation Portrex off Puerto Rico, described officially as "the first large scale amphibious operation in which atomic bombs were assumed to be employed."

Official SACLANT Photograph
ADM. JERAULD WRIGHT

Wright was advanced to Vice-Admiral on September 1, 1950 and was named Deputy United States Representative to the Military Standing Group of NATO. He worked with the service representatives of other participating nations on "the formulation of plans and policies on the concepts of NATO military operations," and participated in NATO conferences abroad.

At NATO headquarters in London on April 3, 1952 Vice-Admiral Wright took over from Rear Admiral Walter F. Boone the command of U.S. Naval Forces, Eastern Atlantic, and at Naples, Italy on June 14 succeeded Admiral Robert B. Carney as Commander in Chief of U.S. Naval Forces in the Mediterranean as well as the Eastern Atlantic. "This command," states a Navy release, "included all U.S. Navy ships, aircraft and personnel in the Eastern Atlantic, Mediterranean, Middle East and Indian Ocean (north of the equator). Its major component was the U.S. Sixth Fleet, in the Mediterranean."

President Eisenhower announced on February 17, 1954 that he had nominated Vice-Admiral Wright to relieve Admiral Lynde D. McCormick (subsequently assigned to the presidency of the Naval War College) as both Commander in Chief of the U.S. Atlantic Fleet (CINCLANTFLT) and Supreme Allied Commander, Atlantic (SACLANT). The latter (NATO) command, with headquarters at Norfolk in Virginia, had been established in April 1952. Wright was promoted to full Admiral on April 6, 1954.

Addressing the New York State convention of the American Legion on July 29, 1954, Admiral Wright spoke of his responsibility for the defense of the Atlantic Ocean area as "parallel" to that of General Alfred M. Gruenther "for the defense of Europe," and in the same speech warned that "Soviet naval strength

WRIGHT, JERAULD—*Continued*

today, and what they plan for the future, is a clear indication that they are making a bold challenge to the traditional superiority of Western nations for the control of the seas."

The Admiral noted that with "375-400 U-boats already," the Soviets were "far outbuilding the United States" in submarines, and that they had "on active duty" more high-speed modern cruisers capable of raids on shipping than any single member nation of NATO. "There is," Admiral Wright continued, "a rather widespread notion . . . to the effect that Soviet ships are poor in quality, like much of their consumer goods. I can assure you that NATO's military planners hold to no such view."

Jerauld Wright and the journalist Phyllis B. Thompson were married on July 23, 1938. They have two children, Marion and William Mason. Washington, or its environs, is their usual place of residence.

References

N Y Herald Tribune p5 D 21 '42 por; p5 F 18 '54 por; p3 Ap 15 '54
N Y Times p7 D 21 '42 por; p4 Mr 24 '43; p6 Ap 4 '52; p5 F 18 '54
Who's Who in America, 1954-55
World Biography (1954)

WRIGHT, LOYD (EARL) Dec. 24, 1892-
Lawyer; organization official

Address: b. c/o American Bar Association, 1140 N. Dearborn St., Chicago 10, Ill.; c/o Wright, Wright, Green and Wright, 111 W. 7th St., Los Angeles 14, Calif.; h. 336 S. Hudson Ave., Los Angeles 5, Calif.

In many of his speeches since he was elected president of the American Bar Association in August 1954 for a one-year term, Loyd Wright has deplored "paternalistic tendencies" in government and has urged that the integrity of the individual be maintained and that "the quest for security" be replaced by "the search for opportunity." Wright, a practicing attorney in California for forty years and a corporation director, has been a member of the ABA's board of governors, and from 1940 to 1953 was a member of its house of delegates. The association has a membership of over 54,000, and through affiliated organizations represents about 135,000 attorneys.

A native of San Jacinto, California, Loyd Earl Wright was born on December 24, 1892 to Lucius A. Wright, a physician and a pharmacist, and Naamah Pauline (Hank) Wright, who was also a pharmacist. He had two brothers and one sister. Wright received his secondary education at Hemet Union High School, in Hemet, California, from which he was graduated in 1910. At the University of Southern California in Los Angeles he played baseball, basketball and football, and was active in debating societies. He received the LL.B. degree from the university's Law School in 1915. During World War I, from 1917 until 1919, he served overseas as a first lieutenant in the 8th Infantry in command of Company D. He was influenced in his choice of a career by his older brother, Arthur, and by Judge William J. Hunsaker of Los Angeles.

Admitted to the California bar in 1915, he has maintained a general civil practice, including representation of a number of corporations, in Los Angeles since that time. His present law firm is Wright, Wright, Green and Wright. From 1921 until 1926 he lectured on corporate practice at the University of Southern California Law School. He served as president of the Los Angeles Bar Association in 1938 and 1939, and helped to start its lawyer reference service, the first to be established by a local bar association.

From 1940 until 1941 he was president of the state bar of California, and in that capacity was instrumental in carrying out a state bar crime prevention study and an investigation of the operations of administrative agencies and bureaus which led to the adoption of California's Administrative Practice Act. It was during his tenure, also, that the association's public relations program was initiated and that a special committee was established to investigate California's court system. The work of this committee paved the way for legislation overhauling the state's entire system of inferior courts.

During World War II Wright attended the Command and General Staff School at Fort Leavenworth, Kansas, and was graduated in January 1943. By appointment of the Department of Justice, he served as a member of the Attorney General's board of appeals for enemy alien hearings. Wright returned to his law practice in Los Angeles. He is a member of the boards of directors of Trans World Airlines, Inc., and Cole of California, Inc., and of the United States Spring & Bumper, Southern Pipe & Casing, Reserve Oil and Gas, McClintock Manufacturing, Cohn-Goldwater Manufacturing, and Roscoe Moss companies. Since 1944 he has been chairman of the California Horse Racing Board; he is also a member and past president of the National Association of State Racing Commissioners; and he has been affiliated with the Society of Independent Motion Picture Producers.

In September 1953 Wright was appointed by Vice-President Richard M. Nixon to a commission to study Congressional and judicial salaries.

On March 9, 1954, at the annual midwinter meeting of the House of Delegates of the American Bar Association, Wright was nominated to be president of the association for a one-year term to succeed William J. Jameson (see C.B., July 1954). In August, at the organization's seventy-seventh annual meeting, he was elected and formally inducted into office. Since assuming his post, he has expressed his views on legal, political and economic issues in public addresses delivered on various occasions.

On September 13, 1954 addressing the National Institute of Municipal Law Officers in San Francisco, he decried "paternalism" in government as destructive of "individual incentive and of one of the great building blocks of

America—risk capital." He warned that "some of the things we must watch are those companions to the heavy, progressive, graduated income tax which have the same ultimate ends of destruction of constitutional government and freedom of individuals." On January 12, 1955 he announced the establishment by the ABA of a special committee headed by former Assistant Attorney General James H. McInerney "to give free legal assistance," as the New York *Times* reported on January 13, "to government workers who might be involved in security cases."

Wright addressed the American Bankers Association on February 8, 1955 on the theme "Our Common Responsibility." He asserted that "although there are those who would install the Federal Government as all-powerful and beneficent, 165 years' experience of constitutional government in which integrity of the individual is emphasized more than in any other government in the history of the world, has proven that our sacrifice of alleged material advantage to the somewhat idealistic belief that a man has a right to chart his own course, to realize his potentialities in his own way, to follow his own conscience—in short, the right to be a man and not a number—is a sound concept of government." He criticized with particular sharpness government intervention in economic affairs: "I fear that we have departed further from our basic principles, and are closer to the welfare state, than most of our citizens realize."

Under Wright's presidency, the ABA has organized a seven-man legal committee, headed by Major General William J. Donovan (see C.B., September 1954), former director of the Office of Strategic Services, to undertake "the first complete study" in the country's history "of criminal justice administration" on a nationwide scale. According to an editorial in New York *Times* (February 7, 1955), "attention will be focused on four major areas of our criminal justice system: the police function, the prosecution and defense of crimes, the criminal courts and probation, sentence and parole." The association has also drafted a new disciplinary code, "designed to promote a more uniform observance of the ethics of the legal profession in the United States." On February 21, 1955 the organization's board of governors recommended that lawyers be included in the social security system on an individual and voluntary basis.

Wright was succeeded as ABA president by E. Smythe Gambrell on August 22, 1955.

Wright is a Fellow of the University of Southern California, a past member of its board of trustees, and a member of its General Alumni Association. He has been a director of the American Judicature Society, a member of the board of governors of the National Legal Aid Society, and a director of the ABA endowment since 1937.

He belongs to the Order of the Coif and Phi Delta Phi, a legal fraternity. He is a Republican and serves on the party's central committee in California. He is a member of the First Congregational Church of Los Angeles. His clubs are the California and the Los Angeles Country. He is a 32nd degree Mason.

Bullock's Portrait Studio

LOYD WRIGHT

He married Julia Martha Kingsbury on September 7, 1918; they have four children—Loyd, Jr., Pauline (Mrs. Long Ellis), Clarissa Jane, and Dudley K. Wright. The lawyer is five feet eight inches tall and weighs 175 pounds; he has blue eyes and gray hair. His favorite forms of recreation are hunting, and—as a spectator—baseball, basketball and football.

References

Martindale-Hubbell Law Directory, 1952
Who's Who in America, 1954-55
Who's Who in the West (1954)

WRIGHT, MARTHA Mar. 23, 1926-
Singer

Address: c/o Columbia Broadcasting System, 485 Madison Ave., New York 22

An estimated 500,000 people saw the Broadway musical *South Pacific*, in which Martha Wright succeeded Mary Martin in the role of Ensign Nellie Forbush. Miss Wright played the part 1,080 times—the longest run ever recorded for any Broadway performer. Starting in April 1954 she was seen Sunday nights on the ABC television network for a fifteen-minute program in which she was starred with trumpeter Bobby Hackett and the Norman Paris Trio. In December she began a daily radio morning program on Station WCBS which during 1955 has continued to be popular.

From the chorus part in *Up in Central Park* which brought her to Broadway, Miss Wright quickly came to prominence in her own radio show and as leading singer in the musical productions *Music in My Heart* and *Great to be Alive*.

Duval, Washington, is the farming town to which Martha Wright's family moved four years after her birth in Seattle on March 23,

Bruno of Hollywood
MARTHA WRIGHT

1926. There the Wiederrecht family (Martha has used her mother's maiden name of Wright for stage purposes) rejoined her maternal grandparents; her grandfather was Duval's justice of the peace as well as a lawyer and farmer, and her grandmother, Mrs. Cora C. Wright, a graduate of the Boston Conservatory of Music, was the local music teacher. Besides being musically influenced by her parents, who belonged to a local Gilbert and Sullivan repertory group, Martha also credited her grandmother with encouraging her. When Martha was not studying voice and piano she helped with the farm chores.

After the family returned to Seattle, where Martha studied at the Franklin High School, she continued her music studies, and also began to sing from time to time on local radio stations KJR and KOMO. At the age of sixteen she entered the University of Washington, where she remained only until her sophomore year, when an offer to do an early morning radio program conflicted with her morning classes. She chose to sign the radio contract. Her spare time was given to the Seattle Repertory Playhouse, at which in 1946 she sang in Mozart's *Abduction from the Seraglio* and later, in *The Magic Flute.* During this period she also won a Bob Hope radio contest and a Don McNeil contest, which brought her an appearance on his *Breakfast Club* program in Chicago.

When the touring company of *Up in Central Park* visited Seattle in the summer of 1947, one of the chorus members dropped out. As a result of this, Martha Wright auditioned for Sammy Lambert, the general stage manager, and was brought into the show as replacement, remaining with it until it returned to New York for a brief second run. When the musical closed, she began to make the rounds of the New York agents and casting offices. She auditioned for the Mutual Broadcasting System's station WOR, which signed her to appear each Sunday in a full network show.

This minor success gave her the courage to continue the rounds of the agents, in the hope of getting stage work once again. Eventually she was hired to understudy Florence George in *Music in My Heart*, an operetta dealing with the composer Peter Ilych Tchaikowsky. While the play was still in the tryout stage at Philadelphia's Schubert Theater, she was called to replace Miss George, who had fallen ill. "That night," said Michel Mok of the New York *Post*, "Martha did no mere understudy job. She made a hit." The show opened on Broadway at the Adelphi Theatre on October 2, 1947, with Martha Wright playing the role of the French singer, Desiree Artot, and ran for 125 performances.

Miss Wright then made the supper club circuit—the Bagatelle in London, the No 1. Club, the Blue Angel, and the St. Regis Maisonette in New York, the Mayflower in Washington, and the Empire Room at the Palmer House in Chicago. Several times during this period she was heard by Rodgers and Hammerstein: the composer himself accompanied her in a Rodgers and Hammerstein concert in the Yale Bowl at New Haven.

She played the ingenue lead of Carol in the musical comedy *Great To Be Alive,* produced by Vinton Freedley, which opened on March 23, 1950 at the Winter Garden and ran for fifty-two performances.

Nevertheless, she was astonished when she was offered the job of replacing Mary Martin in the Ensign Nellie Forbush role in *South Pacific.* For a while, she went through a conflict of choosing between that and a role in *A Tree Grows in Brooklyn,* before deciding that she preferred the *South Pacific* offer.

When she stepped into the part in June 1951, she was tense, she recalls. "The first night I went on for Miss Martin . . . I felt like a puppet." Most of the critics, however, thought that she had brought her own style to the part and her own evaluation of the character. "Martha Wright," said the New York *Times*, July 10, 1951, "is quite at home in the part by this time. She sings pleasantly and is endowed with other properties that make her something special to see." Brooks Atkinson added later, "Miss Wright is a pretty young lady . . . who has a pleasant voice and a charming personality. She does very well by the part. If Miss Martin had never been in it, every one probably would be very happy about Miss Wright's cheerful singing and sunny performing." By the time *South Pacific* closed on January 16, 1954, Martha Wright had sung the role of Nellie Forbush 1,080 times, 180 times more than Mary Martin). She expressed her attachment to the musical, in which she had co-starred with Goger Rico and later with George Britton, in *Cue*: "These past two years have been absolutely wonderful. Among other things, I think they have helped me to grow up as a performer."

Television was the next step for Miss Wright, who began a fifteen-minute Sunday program over the ABC network in April 1954. Harriet

Van Horne of the New York *World-Telegram and Sun* observed that "Miss Wright has a bouncy, almost hoydenish charm. At the same time, she is a perfect lady. And she sings very nicely." Richard Kleiner of the same newspaper commented that Miss Wright "is that rare bird—a beautiful gal with a beautiful voice. She's a versatile singer, too. She's studied and sung opera, pop, and musical comedy, and she wants to do all of them on TV, too." Simultaneously, Miss Wright sang in the Empire Room of the Waldorf Astoria.

She commutes from her home in Connecticut to New York. Her marriage to Teddy Baumfeld, her manager, ended in divorce. In 1953 she was theatrical chairman of the New York March of Dimes campaign. Much interested in outdoor life and still fond of the skills she learned as a child on the Duvall farm, she sees to it that her friends get baskets of the fruits she raises in her own orchard. "I love to climb mountains," she told one interviewer after a summer's vacation in Maine, "but I go mad if I have to walk three blocks on Manhattan's pavements." The blue-eyed, strawberry-blond singer is pleased that her career has developed so favorably, but says, "I have only one regret —I wish Gramma could be here to see me."

After her record run in *South Pacific*, Miss Wright admits that she still likes to play records of the musical at her home. Although she enjoys radio and television, she hopes to get back to Broadway soon. "If you've ever been on the stage you want to go back—any ham will tell you that," she said (New York *Herald Tribune*, May 16, 1954).

References

Cue 20:16 Je 2 '51
N Y Herald Tribune IV p2 Je 3 '51
N Y World-Telegram Mag p2 Jl 1 '51; p3 Ag 15 '53 por
Washington (D.C.) Post p4B F 21 '51

WYETH, ANDREW (NEWELL) (wī'ĕth) July 12, 1917- Artist

Address: b. c/o Knoedler Art Galleries, 14 E. 57th St., New York 22; h. Chadds Ford, Pa.; Cushing, Me.

Wide World

ANDREW WYETH

"If there is such a thing as a purely American tradition in art, it is represented at its best in the straightforward canvases of Andrew Wyeth," commented *Life* (May 17, 1948). He is admired by critics and public alike for his intimate and loving portrayals of the land and people of Maine and Pennsylvania. His water colors and temperas are exhibited in a number of major museums and his work is purchased by collectors as well as the general public.

Andrew Newell Wyeth is one of the five children of the noted illustrator and mural painter, Newell Convers Wyeth, and was born on July 12, 1917 at Chadds Ford, Pennsylvania. His sisters Henriette (Mrs. Peter Hurd) and Carolyn are painters; another sister, Ann (Mrs. John McCoy), is a musician and composer. His brother, Nathaniel Convers, is an engineer. Of his mother, the former Carolyn Brenneman Bockius, Andrew Wyeth has said, her "love and energy have, over the years, supplied a rich background of domestic completeness incalculable to an artistic family."

Because of sickness during his childhood, Andrew Wyeth received most of his schooling at home under tutors. He constructed a toy theatre, which greatly impressed his father, who began to give him art lessons. Wyeth recalls, "My father didn't teach [me] his method, just kept at me to try to express an object as clearly as possible." At fifteen, he contributed a water color to a show in Wilmington, Delaware.

For a number of years, the Wyeth family spent its summers at Port Clyde, Maine, where young Wyeth found the subjects of the landscapes and seascapes exhibited in October 1937 at his first "sell-out" show at the William Macbeth gallery in New York City. Of the twenty-year-old painter, the New York *World-Telegram* remarked, "He has a complete understanding and mastery of his medium and its potentialities. *Early Morning,* with its dynamic strength, its stark forms, its brilliant tonal harmonies, and extreme simplicity is perhaps the most memorable of the exhibition."

Following the success of this show, Wyeth once said, "a feeling came over me . . . that I'd gotten by with these water colors on only a rather clever brilliance, and I came back and went to my father's lower studio and drew and drew." Sometime later he began experimenting in the tempera technique, which his brother-in-law, Peter Hurd, had also begun to use. By the time he gave his second show at the Macbeth gallery in 1939, *Art Digest* could comment, "A deeper, richer color appears in the latest works and the percentage of ephemeral effects that 'come off' remains magically high. . . . The artist's technique defies formula." A re-

WYETH, ANDREW—*Continued*

turn exhibition at the Macbeth gallery in the fall of 1941 brought Wyeth equally enthusiastic notices.

In 1943 he was among the painters invited to contribute to the Museum of Modern Art's American Realists and Magic Realists show. He exhibited in the latter category, wrote *Art News* (November 15-30, 1943), because "he stepped forward and clean out of the popular water-colorist class . . . almost overnight." The same publication found that his group at the show gave evidence of a technique that was "polished without glossiness, meticulous but highly selective, factual, and at the same time poetic."

From among the works in Wyeth's 1943 show at the Macbeth galleries, *Art Digest* selected *Blackberry Picker* as "the dazzle painting of the show, for it is a remarkable achievement in paint, showing depth, control, love of weather, [and] a sensitive use of color. . . ." On the other hand, the New York *Herald Tribune* discerned a "certain hardness of effect" in the temperas. The New York *Times* critic considered the dry-brush drawings to be "in the nature of a *tour de force*."

At the 1945 exhibition of the American Watercolor Society, Wyeth's entry received not only the Obrig prize but unqualified praise from the reviewers. "*The Skaters* is wonderfully free," wrote Emily Genauer of the New York *World-Telegram,* "a water color with all the action and airy grace of the skaters themselves, and with details of landscape subordinated to its gray, cold atmosphere."

During his next one-man show at the Macbeth gallery, the New York *Herald Tribune* (November 4, 1945) noted "his exceptional skill and taste" and "the brevity and directness of his style," while the New York *Times* lauded his steady development, "beautiful brushwork and lighting," and "lyric imagination."

The American Academy of Arts and Letters awarded Wyeth its Merit Medal in 1947 and its $1,000 prize, given only once every five years to a painter (in other years it goes to a writer, sculptor, or other practitioner of the arts). In 1947 Wyeth was one of the participants in the annual exhibit of the Whitney Museum of American Art. Henry McBride of the New York *Sun* found him among the best of the conventional painters represented, "in spite of his evident pleasure in mere dexterity."

When the same critic visited the Whitney's water color show in 1948, he rated Wyeth's *Spool Bed* as one of "the two most impressive examples" of that medium on exhibition. *Art News,* reviewing Wyeth's show at the Macbeth gallery in November 1948, observed, "In his most recent paintings and water colors, the principal gain is in depth of feeling. . . . All is spacious clarity from the dazzling net-like design of the minutely delineated blades of grass to the distant gray skies."

Analyzing the paintings shown by Wyeth in 1950 at the Macbeth gallery, *Time* (December 18, 1950) commented that his "best make him a candidate for the mantle of the great Pennsylvania realist Thomas Eakins. . . ." During the summer of 1951 the Currier Gallery of Art at Manchester, New Hampshire, presented an exhibition of his paintings for the ten-year period, 1941-1951. This show was subsequently presented at the Farnsworth Art Museum in Rockland, Maine, near the countryside, wrote Stuart Preston of the New York *Times* (August 26, 1951), "that has his spellbound." Preston considered Wyeth's technique "flawless, without there being anything flashy or irritating about its verisimilitude. . . ."

At the American Watercolor Society's eighty-fifth annual show in February 1952, the gold medal went to Wyeth for what Carlyle Burrows of the New York *Herald Tribune* described as his "somber, two-tone farmscape, *March*." On the occasion of the artist's one-man show at the Knoedler Art Galleries in the fall of 1953, an art critic of the same newspaper made a "minority report," which paid tribute to the painter's technical virtuosity, but found him on the whole without "spontaneity or freshness." The New York *Times* critic wrote, "It is only the rigorous discipline of his craftsmanship that keeps the lid on pessimism and on a sort of wild nostalgia for the lost and for the displaced."

Technical notes on Wyeth's method appeared in the *American Artist* in September 1942 and were reprinted in Ernest W. Watson's *Color and Method in Painting* (1942). For water color, Wyeth works on medium rough paper with numbers five, ten, and fifteen sable brushes. For tempera he works on Masonite, which has been sized with whiting and casein glue and sandpapered. He then applies dry pigments mixed on his palette, as he works, with distilled water and egg yolk. In tempera painting, he uses only one, very fine sable brush. Of his approach to painting, Wyeth told Watson: "I believe the artist should . . . be indigenous to the country which he paints. This, I know, is contrary to the practice of many present-day painters who dash about to sketch here and there."

Other exhibitions at which Wyeth's work has been shown are the Philadelphia Art Alliance (1936), Cornell University (1938), Art Institute of Chicago (1941), and at various times, in one-man shows at the Doll & Richards gallery in Boston. He has received awards from the Butler Art Institute (Youngstown, Ohio) and the Wilmington (Delaware) Society of the Fine Arts.

His work is represented in the Art Institute of Chicago, University of Nebraska, Boston Museum of Fine Arts, Metropolitan Museum of Art, Butler Art Institute, Dallas and Toledo museums, New Britain (Connecticut) Institute, and Lincoln museum in England. Wyeth has illustrated *The Brandywine* (Farrar, 1941), and *Arthur Pendragon of Britain* (Putnam, 1943), as well as children's books. He is a director of the Chester County Art Association, of the Audubon Artists Group, and of the Philadelphia, Washington, and Baltimore water color clubs. He is a member of the National Institute of Arts and Letters and an academician of the National Academy of Design. He served as a one-man jury in judging the 1,247 paintings submitted to the Corcoran Gallery, Washington, D.C., in January 1955.

Mrs. Wyeth is the former Betsy Merle James, whom the painter married on May 15, 1940. Their two sons are Nicholas and James Browning. *Life* once reported that Wyeth likes to "box, fence, and pilot an airplane." The Waldorf Astoria's *Promenade* described him as "sporting a crew haircut and a gridiron physique." Wyeth has said, "Painting is living to me. If I had to stop painting, I'd just as leave die."

References

N Y Times Mag p28 O 25 '53 por
Time 52:48 N 29 '48; 58:72+ Jl 16 '51 por
Watson, E. W. Color and Method in Painting (1942)
Who's Who in America, 1954-55
Who's Who in American Art (1953)
World Biography (1948)

YU HUNG-CHUN *See* Yui, O. K.

YUI, O. K. (yü) 1896(?)- Premier of Nationalist China

Address: Taipei, Formosa

Wide World

O. K. YUI

The Premier of Nationalist China is O. K. Yui, who was appointed in May 1954 by President Chiang Kai-shek. Throughout a public career of nearly thirty years he has enjoyed a reputation for ability, personal integrity and courage. He has been a journalist, a municipal official, and a financial expert. Premier Yui was the mayor of Greater Shanghai in 1937 during its resistance to Japanese attack.

Between 1937 and 1953, when he became Governor of Formosa, Yui was director of China's Central Trust, governor of the Central Bank, Vice-Minister of Finance, Minister of Finance in the Kuomintang government at Chungking, and Taipei, Formosa. His predecessor as Premier was General Chen Cheng.

Premier Yui told the Legislative Yuan (Parliament) meeting at Taipei that the Nationalists would defend the Quemoy and Matsu islands from the Communists "as part of the defense chain of the free world in the Western Pacific" (New York *Times,* March 16, 1955).

The given name of the Premier of Nationalist China is Yu Hung-chun, but he has preferred to be known as O. K. Yui. He was born at Hsingsui in China's Kwantung Province in 1896 (according to most press dispatches and articles), or 1898 (according to recent Chinese English-language reference works). Yui completed his formal education at St. John's University in Shanghai, where, after receiving his B.A. degree, he became "the star reporter and staff writer" of the *Evening Star* in that city (*China Weekly Review,* July 31, 1937).

Eventually entering government service, Yui was briefly occupied as secretary to the Ministry of Foreign Affairs of the "liberal" Wuhan Nationalist government established in December 1926. Following its dissolution in April 1927, Yui joined the municipal government of Greater Shanghai as a secretary, and was later named a senior counselor and acting commissioner of finance. For seven years beginning in 1930, Yui was the secretary general of the Great Shanghai municipality. This period marked the inception of "government-owned trust companies" in China through the establishment of the Shanghai Development and Trust Company in 1932 and the organization of the Central Trust of China at Shanghai in 1935 (*China Handbook*). Yui was, furthermore, the secretary general of the municipality when in 1932 the Japanese, having seized Manchuria from China in the previous year, landed troops in the city's International Settlement.

When the mayor of Greater Shanghai, General Wu, left the city in March 1937 for military duties elsewhere, O. K. Yui became acting mayor. On July 27, 1937 the Executive Yuan of the Chinese Nationalist Government announced the permanent appointment of Yui as mayor of Shanghai. The choice of this "veteran at handling difficulties with the Japanese" was (the dispatch to the New York *Times* declared) "widely popular in the area." Three weeks afterward (August 11), when the Japanese massed thirty-two warships at Shanghai and landed sailors, Mayor Yui served what was virtually the first clear notice of Chinese determination to resist by refusing a Japanese demand for the withdrawal of all Peace Preservation Corps "gendarmes" from the city.

Following the evacuation of Shanghai and the removal, later in November 1937, of the Chinese Nationalist Government from Nanking to Chungking, Yui was named deputy director of the Central Trust and early in 1938 became managing director of the Trust, which through

YUI, O. K.—*Continued*

the remainder of the Sino-Japanese conflict and the entirety of World War II, was in charge of government bond issues as well as currency and insurance (*China Handbook*).

When Dr. H. H. Kung, Madame Chiang Kai-shek's brother-in-law, was China's Minister of Finance, Yui was appointed in 1941 his political Vice-Minister. He served in this post until November 1944. Then, "with China's military position becoming more critical," President Chiang yielded to "popular clamor" for a shake-up of the Cabinet, and Dr. Kung was supplanted by Yui as Finance Minister (New York *Times*). Bertram D. Hulet soon afterward commented in the New York *Times* (November 26, 1944) that Yui was "a man of recognized integrity." A few days previously it had been stressed in the New York *Times* that the new Finance Minister was "regarded as a 'Kung Man'" and would be faced with "a tremendous problem in attempting to straighten out China's inflationary currency and sky-rocketing prices."

Dr. Kung remained governor of the Central Bank of China until July 1945, when he resigned this post also, his duties being taken over by Finance Minister Yui. At the same time the brother of Madame Chiang Kai-shek, T. V. Soong, who had recently become head of the Executive Yuan (Premier), succeeded Kung as vice-chairman of the joint administrative office of China's government banks.

Yui continued to grapple with his country's increasingly vexing fiscal and economic problems, and in January 1947 refused to change the official exchange rate for Chinese currency (3,350 Chinese dollars to one United States dollar), although the bank market rate was already 6,500 to one. Increase in the official rate, Yui declared, "would stimulate high prices," while "the only way to balance the government budget was to try to bring the black market within reasonable limits."

Reporting to the People's Political Council in May, he stated that the government was "trying to collect more taxes from the wealthy" and was "attempting to get a census of property to institute a property tax" (New York *Times*, May 24, 1947). He disclosed that in the previous twelve months "more than three hundred employees accused of graft had been ousted or held for trial."

Meanwhile, Yui had yielded the governorship of the Central Bank to Chang Kai-ngau, but when on May 21, 1948 Chang resigned, he resumed the bank governorship, which he retained after the withdrawal of the Nationalist government to Formosa on December 8, 1949. He was reappointed governor (or president) of the bank, now the Central Bank of Taiwan (Formosa) when the Nationalist Cabinet was again reorganized on January 26, 1950. He was chairman of the board of directors of the Bank of Communications in 1950 and chairman and president of the Philippine Bank of Communications in 1951.

On April 10, 1953 the Executive Yuan named Yui to the governorship of Formosa in succession to Dr. K. C. Wu, who had resigned after much friction with President Chiang Kai-shek and his son, Lieutenant General Chiang Ching-kuo. Yui then brought what the New York *Times* called his "great skill in finance" to bear upon the "manifold and complex" problems.

At this time the Premier (head of the Executive Yuan) was General Chen Cheng, who in the spring of 1954, as the inauguration of President Chiang Kai-shek for a new six-year term approached, declined reappointment. The President then named Governor Yui to succeed Chen—subject to the concurrence of the Legislative Yuan, which approved Yui as Premier on May 25 by a vote of 360 to 87.

The old Cabinet had meanwhile resigned en bloc, and when the composition of the new Yui government was announced, it was found to contain no member of Chen Cheng's wing of the Kuomintang and no professional soldier. Foreign Minister George K. C. Yeh was the only "holdover" in the Cabinet.

Upon his confirmation by the Executive Yuan, and prior to taking office as Premier on June 1, 1954, Yui had promised that his government would "be ready at all times . . . to promote the collective security of Asia and the world as a whole, and any united action that may be taken to resist the forces of totalitarianism."

When the United States defense pact with Nationalist China, pledging American protection for Formosa and the Pescadores, was signed in Washington on December 2, 1954, Premier Yui said the pact had reinforced the Nationalists' determination to carry out "the sacred task of restoring freedom to mainland China," and hailed the treaty as a vital link in the defense system against Communist aggression in the Western Pacific (New York *Times,* December 4, 1954).

Addressing a gathering at Taipei on Christmas Day in 1954, he reiterated the determination of Nationalist China to become "strong enough" to invade the mainland, and stated that the Nationalist Army divisions were already "about one-third stronger, division for division, than the Chinese Red divisions used in the Korean War" (New York *Herald Tribune*).

The English-language *China News* quoted Yui as declaring that his government was "firmly opposed" to evacuation of the Tachen Islands. Even after Chiang Kai-shek had (according to reports) "agreed in principle" to the evacuation of those islands, Nationalist officials continued "to express opposition to a United Nations cease-fire effort" such as had been suggested by President Eisenhower to end the Formosa Straits fighting (Henry R. Lieberman in the New York *Times*, January 28, 1955). (The Tachen Islands were evacuated on February 6, 1955.)

When O. K. Yui became Governor of Formosa, a New York *Times* editorial (April 13, 1953) mentioned his reputation "for great courage and high integrity" and noted that he was "admired as a genuinely 'liberal' scholar."

References

N Y Times p8 Jl 26 '37; IV p4 N 26 '44; p26 Ap 13 '53
China Handbook, 1954-55
Who's Who in Modern China (1954)

ZABACH, FLORIAN Aug. 15, 1921- Violinist; television personality

Address: c/o Guild Films Co., Inc., 460 Park Ave., New York 22

Telecasts of the violinist Florian ZaBach can be seen from Maine to Hawaii (syndicated by Guild Films Company) over 120 television stations including WPIX in New York. His repertoire ranges from the classics to jazz and folk music. The music department of the Board of Education for the City of New York formally accepted a ZaBach film on September 21, 1955 for use as part of the music curriculum of the New York School system to stimulate students' interest in stringed instruments.

Hal Humphrey, Los Angeles *Mirror* (July 15, 1954), said that ZaBach was hailed in certain quarters as "the Liberace of the violin." *Radio TV Mirror* (August 1953) commented that his success as a violin soloist was "something of a phenomenon" when he was featured on the *Club Embassy Show* over WNBC-TV. He was a winner on *Arthur Godfrey's Talent Scouts* show in 1950; his first record, "The Hot Canary" and "Jalousie" (Decca, 1951), sold over 1,000,000 copies and helped to establish ZaBach in the field of popular music.

Florian ZaBach was born in Chicago on August 15, 1921, the only child of Florian ZaBach, Sr., and Anna (Morganfort) ZaBach. An accident had halted the elder ZaBach's career as clarinetist as he was about to win recognition in his native Austria. In Chicago he was employed as superintendent of an apartment house. Determined to develop his son's talent, he bought Florian a violin when the boy was nine years old, taught him the technique of music and—through long hours of practice—stressed perfection. Three years later, Florian made his debut playing Beethoven's Concerto in D for violin and orchestra with the Chicago Symphony Orchestra at the Auditorium Concert Hall.

While Florian attended Senn High School, he studied at the Chicago Conservatory of Music and in 1935 performed at the Chicago World's Fair. The following year his parents sent him to Europe to broaden his training. His introduction of a newly discovered Mozart violin concerto brought him to the attention of outstanding European symphony orchestras and he appeared as guest artist before diplomats and royalty, and on European radio networks. Later, he studied at a conservatory of music in Prague, Czechoslovakia.

Returning to the United States, young ZaBach toured as concert violinist and soloist. He became interested in popular music and spent two years on Chicago's NBC radio station as staff artist and soloist with band leaders Roy Shields, Henry Weber, and Percy Faith.

During World War II ZaBach spent two and a half years with the United States Army Medical Corps, first at Camp Grant, Illinois and later in Alaska. His interest in popular music grew as he observed the preferences of most of his fellow G.I.'s. In his spare time he composed various themes, which he used later on his television shows.

FLORIAN ZABACH

After completing his military service ZaBach toured the country for a season as musical director and band leader for the extravaganza *Holiday on Ice*. Upon his return to Chicago he formed his own society orchestra and played for two years at the LaSalle Hotel. In 1949 he filled engagements at other hotels, including the Plaza in New York, the Mayflower in Washington, D.C., the Palmer House in Chicago. He developed a talent for showmanship, displayed a good sense of humor, sang, whistled, and did magic tricks.

It was at the Mayflower Hotel that he met Helen McCollomb, who urged him to try a solo violin act. After a year's courtship they were married, and shortly afterward, ZaBach disbanded his orchestra and moved to New York. He found a definite prejudice against violinists in the popular music field. ZaBach found it difficult to get bookings and even had to pawn all but one of his dozen violins.

"Being in the right place at the right time with the right act," was how ZaBach explained his change of luck (New York *World-Telegram and Sun,* May 23, 1953). An appearance on *Arthur Godfrey's Talent Scouts* show—January 13, 1950—resulted in five performances on the Godfrey morning show and secured a two-week engagement at New York's Strand Theatre for him. The engagement was lengthened to a thirty-three week run and followed by an engagement at New York's Roxy Theatre. Originally booked for three weeks, ZaBach made such a hit at the Roxy that he was held over at that theatre for an additional three weeks.

He filled hotel engagements, appeared on TV shows and secured twenty-six weeks as featured entertainer on a CBS-TV late Saturday night show. A Decca recording of "The Hot Canary," made on February 26, 1951, was an immediate hit. By the end of 1951. ZaBach had appeared at leading clubs and hotels across the country

ZABACH, FLORIAN—*Continued*

and wound up at the Flamingo in Las Vegas, Nevada and the Ambassador Hotel's Coconut Grove in Los Angeles, California.

Several engagements on the East Coast were filled in 1952. *Variety* (May 7, 1952) called his Washington, D.C. performance "one of the best to hit the Capitol stage in recent months," and added that ZaBach opened with the semi-classical "Hora Starcato," ended with Leroy Anderson's "Waltzing Cat," and proved that he could "pack a punch with the masses as well as the classes." Another spot at the Roxy Theatre in New York followed and *Variety* (June 4, 1952) commented that he knew how to make his violin "pay off applausewise." Forty-one weeks as a featured player on the Steve Allen CBS-TV daytime show followed.

Before he appeared on WNBC-TV Embassy Club early in 1953, he purchased a genuine Guarnerius from his friend Rembert Wurlitzer —member of the famed music family—for $75,000 (payable over a twenty-year period). According to the New York *World-Telegram and Sun* (May 23, 1953), the violin was made in 1732 and was once played by Paganini. ZaBach reported he liked it better than a Stradivarius because of its "robust tone."

The president of Guild Films was impressed by the young artist's talents and early in 1954 put ZaBach under contract for a series of half-hour TV programs and sent him to Hollywood. While the films were being made, ZaBach made personal appearances at smart night clubs on the West Coast, including Hollywood's Mocambo, and gave his time for a number of benefit performances. When the films were released in September 1954, thirty-five TV stations were under contract. These contracts have since been renewed and with the addition of new stations the number more than tripled within a year.

During July 1955, ZaBach was featured with the Denver Symphony Orchestra at the Red Rocks Music Festival in Denver. Late in August he gave a performance at the annual music festival at Soldiers Field in Chicago. On his return to New York he appeared on the Steve Allen RCA-TV program *Tonight* on September 22, 1955 and told the story of the film donated by Guild Films the previous day to the Board of Education music department. The best from his telefilm series of classical and popular music were combined on a single film. ZaBach had earned the distinction of being the first musician to have examples of his work on film circulated in New York's public schools.

An album of ZaBach's classical and semi-classical records was recently assembled by Decca. Single recordings include "Jazz Legato," "Jazz Pizzicato," "The Gypsy Fiddler," "The Happy Whistler," "Cold Turkey," "Tea For Two," "Running Off the Rails," "The Waltzing Cat," and "The Whistler and his Dog."

Florian ZaBach and his wife have a new home in Pound Ridge, Westchester County, New York. Mrs. ZaBach has a daughter, Julia, by a previous marriage. ZaBach has blond wavy hair and blue eyes. He is six feet tall and slim, with broad shoulders, and says that he keeps in condition by swimming, that in 1936 he won the Chicago all-scholastic backstroke championship. Other hobbies are fishing, practicing magic tricks, collecting pipes, neckties, and books.

In his double violin case, ZaBach carries a $500 prop instrument with his Guarnerius—as a safeguard against mishaps during a performance. He said that his biggest "thrill" is seeing children take an interest in the violin.

References

Radio TV Mirror 40:21 Ag '53 por
TV Guide 3:22 Ap 30 '55 por

ZERNIKE, FRITS July 16, 1888- Physicist; university professor

Address: b. c/o Rijksuniversiteit te Groningen, Groningen, the Netherlands; h. van Ketwich, Verschuurlaan 5, the Netherlands

Now, for the first time, scientists can study usually indistinguishable details of living tissue, thanks to the "phase contrast" microscope developed by Professor Frits Zernike, the 1953 Nobel Prize winner in physics. Although it was proposed in 1932, Zernicke's microscope was not widely used until after World War II. It eliminates the use of coloring substances, and provides a closer view of minute living cells than had been obtainable before. It has proved of particular value in the field of cancer research.

Known and used in laboratories all over the world are the Zernike galvanometer and, in astronomy, the Zernike phase contrast test for imperfections in curved mirrors, and the Zernike polynomials in which such imperfections are expressed. Their inventor has spent his entire career at the University of Groningen in Holland where he has done much work in statistical mechanics and thermodynamics.

Frits Zernike, son of C. F. A. and Anne (Dieperink) Zernike, was born on July 16, 1888 in Amsterdam, the Netherlands. According to Henry S. Van Klooster in a letter to *Chemical and Engineering News,* the future physicist started as a chemistry student. At the age of nineteen he won a gold medal for his answer to a mathematical problem proposed by the science faculty of the University of Groningen.

Four years later, in 1912, he won the Dutch Society for Sciences (Haarlem) gold medal for his answer to a problem concerning the scattering of light by pure substances and by mixtures at their critical points. Zernike pursued this topic in "Critical Opalescence, Theoretical and Experimental," the dissertation for his doctorate which he submitted to the science faculty of the University of Amsterdam in April 1915 and which established the twenty-seven-year-old Netherlander as a leading authority in the field. Today, over forty years later, Frits Zernike's early work on opalescence is still quoted in textbooks of thermodynamics and statistical mechanics.

Dr. Zernike's entire career has been spent at the University of Groningen. In 1913 he became an assistant in the astronomical laboratory of Professor J. C. Kapteyn (1851-1922), an authority on the structure of the Milky Way. After earning his Sc.D., he was appointed a lecturer on theoretical physics, and five years later, in 1920, was made professor (*Hoogleraar*) of theoretical and technical physics and theoretical mechanics.

Among the journals which have printed his papers are the Dutch *Physica, Tijsdschrifte,* and *Transactions of the Royal Netherlands Academy of Science;* the German *Zeitschrift für Physik, Zeitschrift für technische Physik,* and *Chemische Weekblatt;* the journals of the Optical Society of America and the British Royal Astronomical Society. He was selected to contribute the article on statistics to the authoritative German scientific encyclopedia, *Handbuch der Physik* (1928).

Among Zernike's earlier contributions are a series of papers written with L. S. Ornstein on the kinetics of matter. He also did some work in spectroscopy. His interest in establishing the limits of possible observation led to the development of the Zernike galvanometer, now in use all over the world. In 1926 his paper, "The Natural Observation Limits of Current Strength," explained the mysterious fluctuations in the most sensitive galvanometers used to measure tiny electric currents. Six years later, the Dutch professor presented methods of making the most accurate measurements possible in the face of the deflection of measuring instruments by the impact of molecules in their normal Brownian motions.

The phase contrast method of detecting irregularities in the surfaces of curved mirrors was first published by Zernike in March 1934. Pointing out that even the smallest aberration in the mirror surface would give rise to an image out of phase with the central image, he proposed the use of a phase plate. Looking through a phase plate, the experimenter can see the out-of-phase spots clearly indicated. This is a method of great sensitivity, which enables deviations as slight as one-sixtieth of a wavelength to be detected. A German-language article by Zernike in *Physica* in June 1934 presented a theory of functions suitable for expressing the errors in the mirror. The equations which he called "orthogonal circle polynomials" are now widely known as the "Zernike polynomials."

The inventor of phase contrast soon turned from the astronomical to the microscopic use of the method, with "Das Phasenkontrastverfahren bei der Mikroskopischen Beobachtung," published in 1935. Three years earlier, Professor Zernike had gone to the great Carl Zeiss optical plant in Jena, Germany to ask its collaboration in applying his theory and making such a microscope commercially practical. But the Zeiss scientists were not interested, Zernike recalls—"They said if it were practical they would already have developed it." Nevertheless, in 1941 the Zeiss researchers Köhler and Loos showed several practical applications of phase contrast microscopy, which inspired some others to work on it independently. The method did not become widely known until after World War II, however.

Netherlands Inf. Services
FRITS ZERNIKE

The British journal *Nature* commented in 1953 on Professor Zernike's "other contributions to optics, his work and that of his pupils on the diffraction theory of aberrations, the experimental study of these effects, the use of the method of 'coherent background' in diffraction, and the theory of 'partial coherence,' equally constitute an outstanding contribution to our present knowledge of optics."

A continued interest in chemistry is shown by Zernike's publication of "Phase Rule and Allotropy" in *Chemische Weekblatt,* 1939. He also made a series of contributions on the subject of the thermodynamics of alloys, under such titles as "Propagation of Order in Cooperative Phenomena" (1941).

When American troops arrived at Jena in 1945, they found photomicrographs taken by the Zernike method, and the two phase contrast microscopes which they brought back aroused great attention in the scientific world. There has been a flood of literature on phase microscopy ever since. The great advantage of the method is that it makes possible the observing of transparent objects. Under an ordinary light microscope, the many specimens that are transparent cannot be seen unless they are stained, a procedure which usually kills a living specimen.

Moreover, it often happens that the process of staining tissue results in the production of artefacts in the tissue (as a result of a reaction between the stain and the living matter) which may be mistaken for original structures. The phase contrast system not only makes it possible to study living organisms in greater detail than was formerly possible, it also enables the researcher to check on the accuracy of the staining techniques in use.

(Continued next page)

ZERNIKE, FRITS—*Continued*

A phase contrast microscope is a standard microscope modified by the addition of a light controlling diaphragm and a diffraction plate. The diaphragm, mounted in the substage condenser is used to concentrate the light into a narrow cone which is carefully focussed on the detail to be studied to give an even background illumination. The diffraction plate is a ring of glass coated with a transparent material and mounted between the lenses of the microscope objective. It is capable of changing the speed of the light that passes through it if the light has been diffracted by the object under the microscope, while the background illumination remains unchanged. This selective change is manifested to the observer by the appearance of a marked contrast in tone between the areas through which the two phases of light are transmitted.

When the system is properly adjusted, the ordinarily transparent detail of the object appears either dark against a light background or light against a dark background. Of course this can take place only if there is a difference between the refractive indices of the two contiguous areas. It is the usual practice to illuminate the object with a monochrome light provided by a green filter over the light source.

In 1948, while Professor Zernicke was visiting professor of physics at the Johns Hopkins University in Baltimore, he first discussed the possibility of using white light and producing colored images by a new technique of phase contrast. His theoretical calculations had indicated that the optical characteristics of the diffraction plate for this process were such that no single substance possessed them. After extensive experimentation with combinations of plastics, he succeeded in accomplishing color phase microscopy, and, together with two colleagues in his work, presented his findings at a meeting of the Optical Society of America in Buffalo in October, 1949. While the results obtained showed an improvement in the precise rendition of details, the system has not yet been fully perfected, and is not yet available through commercial sources.

Zernike, who is a member of the Royal Netherlands Academy of Sciences, was elected to honorary membership in the Royal Microscopical Society of London in 1950. Two years later the medical faculty of his alma mater gave him an honorary M.D. In presenting to Zernike the Rumford Medal of the British Royal Society in 1952, Dr. E. D. Adrian, 1932 Nobel laureate in medicine and physiology, said: "Phase contrast microscopes are now in daily use . . . throughout the world. Science is also indebted to Zernike for many valuable contributions to the underlying mathematical theory. Zernike's work has also acted as a great stimulus to the study of diffraction phenomena and has led indirectly to other important advances in the field of interferometry."

On December 1953 the Nobel Prize in physics, which included a money grant of about $33,840, was awarded to Dr. Zernike by the Swedish Academy of Science in Stockholm.

They physicist has been described by colleagues as earnest and methodical. He married Dora van Bommel van Vloten, and they have two children.

References

Chem & Eng N 32:466 F 8 '54
Nature 170:946 D 6 '52; 172:938 N 21 '53
Newsweek 42:86 N 16 '53 por
Time 62:67 N 16 '53 por
Wie is dat? (1948)
World Biography (1954)

ZHUKOV, GEORGI K(ONSTANTINOVICH) (zhōō'kôf) 1895- U.S.S.R. Minister of Defense; Army officer; Communist party leader

Address: c/o Ministry of Defense, Moscow, U.S.S.R.

NOTE: This biography supersedes the article which appeared in *Current Biography* in 1942.

Marshal Georgi K. Zhukov's appointment as Minister of Defense in February 1955 was part of a Soviet government shake-up which brought increased political power to leaders of the Red Army. In succeeding Marshal Nikolai A. Bulganin, who replaced Georgi M. Malenkov in the Premiership, Zhukov became head of the entire Soviet military establishment, including the army, navy, and air force, with authority also in the armament industry.

One of the U.S.S.R.'s most brilliant and popular generals of World War II, he was three times given the title of Hero of the Soviet Union. "No other . . . General" said *Time*, "can match his experience in the maneuvering of so many millions of men over so many thousands of square miles, in the simultaneous use of massed tanks, artillery and tactical aviation." Zhukov, who has been called "a dedicated Communist," has been a member of the Communist party since 1919 and an alternate member of its Central Committee since 1941 and a full member since 1953. He is also a member of the Supreme Soviet of the U.S.S.R.

Georgi Konstantinovich Zhukov (his last name means "of the beetles") was born to peasant parents in 1895 in Strelkovka, a small village in Kaluga Province of Central Russia, some sixty miles from Moscow. When he was about eleven years old, the family moved to Moscow, where the boy, who had very little schooling, was apprenticed to a leather dresser and furrier. Drafted into the army of the Czar in 1915, he fought as a non-commissioned officer in the Novgorod Dragoons and was twice awarded the Cross of St. George for bravery.

Joining the Red Army soon after the revolution of 1917 and the Communist party in 1919, Zhukov took part in the civil war as a cavalry officer and was decorated with the Order of Lenin. He went to Germany in the 1920's to study armor; then in 1932 he entered Frunze Military Academy for Soviet officers and became a specialist in mechanized warfare.

Stalin sent him to Spain in 1936 as one of the U.S.S.R.'s chief military observers in the civil war. He also had an opportunity there to test Soviet tank tactics in actual combat. Away from Moscow in 1937, he was able to survive the great Army purge, and he later rose rapidly with other junior officers by assuming the rank and duties of those who had been liquidated or exiled. In 1938 and 1939 he commanded the Soviet forces sent to Outer Mongolia (Mongolian People's Republic) to fight against Japanese troops that were testing Soviet defenses. He adapted cavalry tactics to armored warfare and defeated the Sixth Japanese Army in battles along the Mongolian-Manchurian border.

Zhukov fought in the Russo-Finnish War (1939-1940) on the staff of Semyon K. Timoshenko and was promoted to general in June 1940 when that title was restored in the Red Army soon after that campaign. Earlier, in May 1940, he had been assigned to command the Kiev military district. It was during his stay in Kiev that he gave a public talk in which he warned that Germany might be a threat to the U.S.S.R., despite the Soviet-Nazi non-aggression pact. "It is possible, indeed probable," according to Hanson W. Baldwin in *Collier's* (January 12, 1952), "that this talk by Zhukov was previously approved by Timoshenko, then Commissar of Defense, and by Stalin, and was intended as a 'tip-off' for the future, for Zhukov had been close to the dictator prior to his assignment to Kiev."

As chief of the general staff and Vice-Commissar of Defense, to which he was appointed in February 1941, Zhukov was especially interested in reorganizing and strengthening the Soviet Army, introducing stricter standards of competence and discipline among the officers. A few months after he had undertaken this task, Germany invaded the U.S.S.R.; and as the Wehrmacht approached Moscow, Zhukov in October 1941 was made commander in chief of the defense of the Soviet capital. His skillful use of reserve troops saved Moscow from capture and forced the Germans to retreat.

During the winter of 1941-1942 Zhukov led the Soviet offensive as commander in chief of the western front. In August 1942 he was named First Deputy Commissar for Defense. At that time Stalingrad was under attack by the German forces, which engaged in house-to-house and street-to-street fighting in an unsuccessful effort to capture the city. The Nazis continued their march westward, however, until Zhukov's counteroffensive before the end of the year brought military disaster to the invaders and drove them from the Don-Volga area.

With Marshal Klementii Voroshilov, he was responsible for breaking the siege of Leningrad in January 1943. Immediately after that battle he was promoted to Marshal of the Soviet Union. During 1944-1945 he commanded the First Byelorussian Front and in January 1945 his troops liberated Warsaw, a little more than five years after the Nazis had taken the Polish city. He then returned briefly to Moscow to complete plans for the drive into Germany. "Zhukov's military apogee was the Battle of Berlin [in the spring of 1945]. He launched 4,000 tanks, supported by 5,000 planes and 22,000 guns, into a 50-mile-wide front" (*Time*, February 21, 1955).

Wide World

MARSHAL GEORGI K. ZHUKOV

This series of victories made Zhukov the foremost Soviet general of the war, and especially well liked and trusted by his soldiers despite his policy of sacrificing lives to gain time. He once told General Eisenhower that it was his practice to have his infantry attack through a mine field because the loss in personnel would be no greater than if the enemy had defended the area. Eisenhower stated in *Crusade in Europe* (1948) that Zhukov showed little interest in measures used by U.S. commanders to protect individual soldiers and little concern for such methods of maintaining morale as providing recreational facilities. "The Russians clearly understood the value of morale," Eisenhower wrote, "but for its development and maintenance they apparently depended upon over-all success and upon patriotism, possibly fanaticism."

A month after the fall of Berlin in April 1945, Zhukov signed the German unconditional surrender document for the U.S.S.R. in Berlin. As Soviet military administrator in Germany during 1945, he represented the U.S.S.R. on the Allied Control Commission. During this period he became acquainted with General Eisenhower, then commander of the U.S. occupation forces in Germany, who made the statement at about that time, "To no man do the United Nations owe a greater debt than to Marshal Zhukov." At Zhukov's suggestion the Soviet government invited Eisenhower to Moscow in August 1945. Eisenhower accepted and Zhukov acted as host. Preparations were made and then canceled for Zhukov to visit the United States.

Recalled to Moscow in March 1946, Zhukov was appointed to the Supreme Soviet Presidium and named commander in chief of all Soviet

ZHUKOV, GEORGI K.—*Continued*

ground forces. Then in July, in a move which many observers attribute to Stalin's fear of Zhukov as a potential rival, the popular war hero was demoted to commander of the Odessa military district on the Black Sea. A few years later he became commander of the northern Urals military district. In 1948 he headed the Soviet military mission in Poland, and in October 1952 at the Communist party's nineteenth congress he was renamed an alternate member of the Central Committee. Otherwise, during the rest of Stalin's life, he remained in comparative obscurity.

Following Stalin's death in March 1953, Zhukov became First Deputy Minister of Defense in the government of the new Premier, Georgi M. Malenkov. This appointment, it is thought, had the purpose of insuring the loyalty of the armed forces, since Zhukov was leader of an important clique of top army officers. When Deputy Premier Lavrenti P. Beria, head of the secret police, was arrested for treason in the summer of 1953, Zhukov, who gave the support of the army to the ousting, took his place as a member of the Central Committee of the Communist party.

Zhukov succeeded Bulganin as Minister of Defense on February 9, 1955, just after Bulganin took the place of Malenkov as Premier. On the preceding day in an interview with William Randolph Hearst, Jr. (American newspaper publisher), Zhukov had spoken of his earlier friendly meetings with Eisenhower and of his "dream" of some day visiting the United States. Several comments in the American press were optimistic toward Zhukov's appointment. Marquis Childs wrote (Washington *Post and Times Herald,* February 15, 1955), "Zhukov has a more realistic knowledge of the industrial and military power of the United States than any other high Russian official." *Newsweek* (February 21, 1955) described the marshal as "less doctrinaire regarding relations with the West than other Soviet leaders."

Two weeks after becoming Defense Minister, however, on the thirty-seventh anniversary of the Soviet Army and Navy, Zhukov issued an order of the day in which he accused "the aggressive forces of the imperialist countries headed by United States monopolists" of "openly preparing a new war against the Soviet Union" (New York *Times,* February 23, 1955). In his first television speech, made later in the day, he stated, "The pacific policy of the U.S.S.R. has not raised any favorable echoes on the part of the capitalist countries, notably the United States, which is carrying out a policy of propaganda and preparation for war" (New York *Herald Tribune,* February 23, 1955).

Among some twenty-six decorations awarded to Zhukov are the Order of Suvorov, the Order of Victory, Virtuti Military (first class), and Gruenwald Star (first class). He speaks French, German and Spanish, as well as his native language, and is an expert on the history of war. He has a stocky build, close-cropped gray hair, and brown eyes. He is married and has two daughters.

In an interview for *U.S. News & World Report* (March 4, 1955) General Walter Bedell Smith, former U.S. Ambassador to the U.S.S.R., said that he had been impressed by Zhukov's personality when he met him just after the war. "He was a man of dignity and character," Smith stated, "and in those days he seemed to express himself with more frankness and freedom than most." General Georges Catroux, former French Ambassador to the U.S.S.R., found that Zhukov had a "less-narrowminded viewpoint in world affairs than most of his fellow citizens." He added, "It would be an error to believe that Marshal Zhukov is not faithful to the Communist doctrine or that he is not a loyal member of the Communist Central Committee. But he can see the other person's point of view."

President Eisenhower gave his impression of Zhukov in a press interview in February 1955, "When I knew Marshal Zhukov . . . he was a competent soldier. A man could not have conducted the campaigns he did, could not have explained them so lucidly and in terms of his own strength and his own weaknesses and so on, except that he was a well-trained, splendid military leader." Eisenhower and Zhukov met again at the Geneva Conference in July 1955.

References

Bsns W p130+ F 19 '55 por
Collier's 129:9+ Ja 12 '52 pors
N Y Herald Tribune p6 F 10 '55
N Y Times p 1+ F 10 '55 por
Newsweek 42:32+ S 7 '53; 45:34 F 21 '55 por
Time 65:18+ F 21 '55 por
Washington (D.C.) Post p7 F 10 '55
International Who's Who, 1954
Robinson, D. The 100 Most Important People in the World Today (1952)
World Biography (1954)
10 Eventful Years 4:789 (1947)

ZINN, WALTER H(ENRY) Dec. 10, 1906-
Physicist; educator

Address: b. Argonne National Laboratory, Box 299, Lemont, Ill.

A key member of the University of Chicago group of scientists who designed and constructed the first atomic pile, Dr. Walter H. Zinn, a physicist, has been concerned with the behavior of atoms since 1933. It has been said that only a "handful of men can match his knowledge of how to build atomic reactors." Since 1946, as director of the Argonne National Laboratory near Chicago, he has been supervising research on reactors which will eventually generate electricity as cheaply as conventional fuels.

At the United Nations First International Conference on Peaceful Uses of Atomic Energy, meeting in Geneva, Switzerland in August 1955, Zinn gave reports on fast power reactor development and discussed experiments with a new "water boiler" reactor which makes steam to produce electricity. Models of four nuclear reactors of the Argonne National Laboratory were exhibited at the Palace of Nations during the conference, along with photographs of new U.S. atomic furnaces. Zinn was elected in June 1955 as president of the American Nuclear Society, composed of scientists and engineers who work full time on atomic energy projects.

The son of John and Maria Anna (Stoskopf) Zinn, Walter H(enry) Zinn was born in Kitchener, Ontario, Canada on December 10, 1906. An honor student at Queen's University in Kingston, Ontario, Zinn received the B.A. degree in 1927 and the M.A. degree in 1930. In 1927-1928 he taught at Queen's University and in 1928-1929 he was bursar of the National Research Council of Canada.

Specializing in the study of X-rays and nuclear physics, Zinn received the Ph.D. degree from Columbia University in 1934. Dr. Zinn also taught at Columbia in 1931-1932. Between 1932 and 1941, when he returned to Columbia for a year as research associate, Zinn was a faculty member of the City College of New York. He was appointed physicist at the Metallurgical Laboratory of the University of Chicago in 1942 and had a part in the so-called "Manhattan Project."

Working under Dr. Enrico Fermi, members of the deliberately misnamed Metallurgical Laboratory built the first atomic pile—in a squash court under the university's Stagg Field. On December 2, 1942 "on a signal from Fermi, Zinn yanked out one of the control rods from its place between the bars of pure uranium, and thus released the first flow of atomic energy ever induced by man" (*Pathfinder*, April 21, 1948). Zinn later had charge of building another pile.

He also supervised the dismantling of the first chain reaction atom pile in 1944 and its removal from the University of Chicago to the Argonne National Laboratory, established by the Army in 1942 as part of its Manhattan District atom bomb project. Argonne, which became a laboratory of the Atomic Energy Commission, is operated, under contract from the AEC, by the University of Chicago and other regional universities and serves as a research center of the Midwest. As director of Argonne since 1946, Zinn has supervised the research of hundreds of scientists engaged in work in such fields as applied medicine, genetics, chemical engineering and instrument development, as well as reactor improvement.

By experimenting with neutrons which, when shot through a crystal produced a "diffraction pattern," Zinn demonstrated that the neutrons were really waves and confirmed the wave mechanics theory in 1946. As the discoverer of this phenomenon, Zinn stated that the neutrons could very likely be used like X-rays to examine the structure of molecules. He also said neutrons could be used to study organic molecules such as viruses. In December of the same year he expressed his belief that atomic energy for commercial and industrial use is "still some time away." "Nobody wants governmental control of research," he said, "but peace-time de-

Argonne National Laboratory

WALTER H. ZINN

velopment of atomic energy is too costly for any private individual or corporation. To carry on this work, we need governmental support and the taxpayers' money" (New York *Herald Tribune*, December 3, 1946).

Early in 1947 the need for scientists to work on remote control devices at the Argonne Laboratory became so acute that Zinn inserted "help wanted" ads in Chicago newspapers. Under Zinn's direction, the laboratory expanded its work on both wartime and peacetime applications of atomic power, and the Atomic Energy Commission centralized its atomic power plant projects at Argonne. Zinn commented in 1948: "I don't know how far away power is. The only way to find out these things is by work. If you don't work on it, it gets even farther away" (*Time*, August 23, 1948).

The Atomic Energy Commission disclosed in December 1951 that its "breeder reactor" had been "tamed down" to generate, by means of a steam turbine, enough electricity for the lights of the building which housed the pile. Under the supervision of Zinn and H. V. Lichtenberger, the experiment was performed at the National Reactor Testing Station operated by Argonne at Arco, Idaho. An AEC official quoted Zinn as explaining, "No comparisons should be made of the cost of producing electric power from this reactor with power from conventional sources. The technical information gained, however, may be useful in the design of future reactors aimed at generating electricity at a competitive cost" (New York *Times*, December 30, 1951). The next goal would be an atomic power plant.

Looking at the experimental breeder reactor a year later in 1952, Zinn continued in his view that commercial atomic power was technically possible but commercially impractical. When finished "playing" with the experimental breeder reactor, scientists should have a plant

ZINN, WALTER H.—*Continued*

to produce 269 times the electricity of a conventional power plant for the same amount of money. He explained that the system was still full of problems, such as the cost of building a power plant. Private producers of atom power, he suggested, could realize a profit by selling surplus plutonium to the government (*Newsweek*, September 15, 1952).

The breeder reactor at Arco, Idaho produces "power only" by burning its own by-product, plutonium, to breed more uranium. Zinn has said that commercial development of atomic power may well depend on cheap and efficient chemical processes, that is, claiming unused uranium from the atomic pile.

In June 1953 Gordon Dean of the AEC announced a new atomic plant that could manufacture new fuel as fast as fuel is consumed in operation of the plant. It was essentially the same as the reactor producing atomic power in 1951; however, it was now consuming uranium-235 and changing nonfissionable uranium into fissionable plutonium at a rate about equal to the rate uranium-235 was being used. Dean said of this successful demonstration of the principle of breeding, "Dr. Zinn and his colleagues are to be congratulated for bringing us to another important milestone in the development of atomic energy" (New York *Times*, June 5, 1953).

"Many times . . . cost has been sacrificed for speed or for a guaranteed performance by a certain date," Zinn told the Joint Congressional Committee on Atomic Energy in Washington, D.C., in July 1953. "What is needed now is experience in getting results in an area where cost is paramount. This experience the private utility companies have," he explained. He further advised building a power reactor that could produce from 75,000 to 100,000 kilowatts of electricity as the minimum size from which private industry could learn the most (New York *Times*, July 7, 1953).

Dr. Zinn also had an important share in the construction of the atomic-powered U.S. Navy submarine *Nautilus*, serving as chief scientific adviser on this project. He has written a number of papers on atomic reactor development and other aspects of nuclear physics. He is a fellow of the American Physical Society and belongs to the Institute of Chemical Engineers, American Association for the Advancement of Science, and Sigma Xi.

The "guiding spirit of Argonne" is tall, slim, blond-haired with bushy brows, youthful and friendly. He married Jennie A. Smith on March 4, 1933; they have two sons, John Eric and Robert James. Zinn became a naturalized American citizen in 1938.

References

Pathfinder p20 Ap 21 '48 por
American Men of Science (1955)
Who's Who in America, 1954-55

BIOGRAPHICAL REFERENCES

Consulted by the research staff of CURRENT BIOGRAPHY.

American Catholic Who's Who, 1954-55
American Medical Directory, 1950
American Men in Government (1949)
American Men of Science vol 1-2 (1955)
American Women, 1939-40
America's Young Men, 1938-39
ASCAP Biographical Dictionary of Composers, Authors, and Publishers (1952)
Author's & Writer's Who's Who (1948-49)

Baker, T. ed. Biographical Dictionary of Musicians (1940)
Baseball Register (1955)
Bénézit, E. ed. Dictionnaire Peintres, Sculptures, Dessinateurs et Graveurs (1948-55)
Biographical Directory of the American Congress, 1774-1949 (1950)
Blom, E. ed. Grove's Dictionary of Music and Musicians (1955)
Blue Book of American Aviation, 1942
British Film Annual, 1949
Burke's Landed Gentry (1952)
Burke's Peerage, Baronetage, and Knightage (1953)
Business Executives of America (1950)

Canadian Who's Who, 1952-54
Catholic Who's Who, 1952
Chemical Who's Who, 1951
Chi è? (1948)
Chujoy, A. ed. Dance Encyclopedia (1949)
Congressional Directory (1955)

Dictionnaire Biographique des Artistes Contemporains, 1910-30
Dictionnaire Biographique Français Contemporain (1954)
Dictionnaire de Biographie Française (1933-)
Dictionnaire National des Contemporains (1936)
Directory of American Judges (1955)
Directory of American Scholars (1951)
Directory of Medical Specialists (1951)
Directory of Medical Women, 1949
Directory of the American Political Science Association, 1953

Ewen, D. ed. Composers of Today (1936); Living Musicians (1940); Men and Women Who Make Music (1949); European Composers Today (1954)

Hindustan Year-Book & Who's Who, 1954
Hoehn, M. A. ed. Catholic Authors (1952)
Hvem er Hvem? 1950

Indian and Pakistan Year Book and Who's Who, 1948
International Press Who's Who; New Zealand, 1938
International Who's Who, 1954
International Who's Who in World Medicine, 1947
International World Who's Who (1949)
International Year Book and Statesmen's Who's Who, 1954
Italian-American Who's Who (1946)

Japan Who's Who, 1950-51

Kelly's Handbook to the Titled, Landed and Official Classes, 1951
Kraks Blaa Bog, 1954
Kunitz, S. J., and Haycraft, H. eds. Junior Book of Authors (1951)
Kürschners Deutscher Gelehrten-Kalender, 1954

Leaders in Education (1948)

Martindale-Hubbell Law Directory, 1952
Motion Picture and Television Almanac, 1955
Musicians' International Directory and Biographical Record (1949-50)

Nalanda Year-Book and Who's Who in India and Pakistan, 1951-53
National Cyclopædia of American Biography current vol A-H (1926-52)
Near and Middle East Who's Who, 1945-46
New Century Cyclopedia of Names (1954)

Österreicher der Gegenwart (1951)

Prominent Personalities in American Methodism (1945)

Quem é Alguém (1947)

Religious Leaders of America 1941-42

Salter, J. T. ed. Public Men and Out of Office (1946)
Slavonic Encyclopaedia (1949)
South African Who's Who, 1952

Thompson, O. ed. International Cyclopedia of Music and Musicians (1949)
Turkin, H., and Thompson, S. C. Official Encyclopedia of Baseball (1951)
Twentieth Century Authors (1942, First Supplement, 1955)

Universal Jewish Encyclopedia (1948)

Vem är Det, 1949
Vem och Vad, 1948

Warfel, H. R. American Novelists of Today (1951)
Webster's Biographical Dictionary (1953)
Wer ist Wer? (1955)
Who is Who in Music (1951)
Who Knows—and What (1954)
Who's Important in Medicine, 1945
Who's Who, 1955
Who's Who in Alaska, 1947

Who's Who in America, 1954-55
Who's Who in American Art (1953)
Who's Who in American Education (1953-54)
Who's Who in American Jewry, 1938-39
Who's Who in Art (1952)
Who's Who in Australia, 1950
Who's Who in Aviation, 1942-43
Who's Who in British Science, 1953
Who's Who in Canada, 1953-54
Who's Who in Central and East-Europe, 1935-36
Who's Who in Chicago and Illinois (1950)
Who's Who in Colored America, 1950
Who's Who in Commerce and Industry (1955)
Who's Who in Egypt and the Near East, 1953
Who's Who in Engineering, 1954
Who's Who in France, 1955-56
Who's Who in France (Paris), 1953-54
Who's Who in Government (1932-33)
Who's Who in Insurance (1955)
Who's Who (in) Israel, 1952
Who's Who in Japan, 1940-41
Who's Who in Labor (1946)
Who's Who in Latin America Pts 1-7 (1946-51)
Who's Who in Law, 1937
Who's Who in Library Service (1955)
Who's Who in Modern China (1954)
Who's Who in New England (1949)
Who's Who in New York, 1952
Who's Who in New Zealand (1951)
Who's Who in Philosophy (1952)
Who's Who in Railroading, 1946
Who's Who in Switzerland, 1950-51
Who's Who in the East (1955)
Who's Who in the Midwest (1954)
Who's Who in the Nation's Capital, 1938-39
Who's Who in the South and Southwest (1954)
Who's Who in the Theatre (1952)
Who's Who in the United Nations (1951)
Who's Who in the West (1954)
Who's Who in United States Politics (1952)
Who's Who in World Aviation (1955)
Who's Who in World Jewry (1955)
Who's Who of the Allied Governments, 1943
Wie is Dat? (1948)
Wier, A. E. ed. Macmillan Encyclopedia of Music and Musicians (1938)
Winchester's Screen Encyclopedia (1948)
Women of Achievement (1940)
World Biography (1954)
World Diplomatic Directory, 1951

Yost, E. American Women of Science (1943)

PERIODICALS AND NEWSPAPERS CONSULTED

including abbreviations used

NOTE: Most, but not all, of the publications below are listed in Wilson Company periodical indexes found in most libraries. For addresses, subscription price, etc., consult your librarian.

A. L. A. Bul—American Library Association Bulletin
Adult Ed—Adult Education
Formerly Adult Education Journal
Adv Agency—Advertising Agency
Am Artist—American Artist
Am Assn Univ Women J—Journal of the American Association of University Women
Am Bar Assn J—American Bar Association Journal
Am Collector—American Collector (discontinued)
Am Federationist—American Federationist
Am Hist R—American Historical Review
Am Home—American Home
Am Mag—American Magazine
Am Mercury—American Mercury
Am Phot—American Photography. See Photography
Am Pol Sci R—American Political Science Review
Am Scand R—American Scandinavian Review
Am Scholar—American Scholar
Am Sociol R—American Sociological Review
America—America
Américas—Américas
Ann Am Acad—Annals of the American Academy of Political and Social Science
Apollo—Apollo, the Magazine of the Arts for the Connoisseurs and Collectors
Arch Forum—Architectural Forum, the Magazine of Building
Arch Rec—Architectural Record
Archaeology—Archaeology: A Magazine Dealing with the Antiquity of the World
Art Bul—College Art Association of America. Art Bulletin
Art N—Art News
Arts & Arch—Arts & Architecture
Arts Digest—Arts Digest
Asian R—Asian Review
Atlan—Atlantic Monthly
Automotive Ind—Automotive Industries
Aviation W—Aviation Week

Banking—Banking
Barrons—Barron's
Bet Hom & Gard—Better Homes & Gardens
Book-of-the-Month Club N—Book-of-the-Month Club News
Books Abroad—Books Abroad
Bronx Home News—See N Y Post
Bsns W—Business Week
Bul Atomic Sci—Bulletin of the Atomic Scientists
Bul Bibliog—Bulletin of Bibliography and Dramatic Index
Bul Pan Am Union. See Américas

Can Forum—Canadian Forum
Can Hist R—Canadian Historical Review
Cath Lib World—Catholic Library World
Cath N—Catholic News
Cath Sch J—Catholic School Journal
Chem & Eng N—Chemical and Engineering News

Christian Cent—Christian Century
Christian Sci Mon—Christian Science Monitor
Christian Sci Mon Mag—Christian Science Monitor Weekly Magazine Section (discontinued)
Civil Eng—Civil Engineering, the Magazine of Engineered Construction
Col Engl—College English
Colliers—Collier's
Commonweal—Commonweal
Cong Digest—Congressional Digest
Connoisseur—The Connoisseur
Contemp R—Contemporary Review
Coronet—Coronet
Cosmop—Cosmopolitan
Cue—Cue (Manhattan edition)
Cur Hist—Current History

Dance Mag—Dance Magazine
Design—Design
Dublin R—Dublin Review

Ed—Education
Ed & Pub—Editor & Publisher
El Engl—Elementary English
Engl J—English Journal
Esquire—Esquire
Etude—Etude

Facts on File—Facts on File
Far East S—Far Eastern Survey
Finance—Finance
Flying—Flying Magazine
For Affairs—Foreign Affairs
For Policy Bul—Foreign Policy Bulletin
Forbes—Forbes Magazine
Fortnightly—Fortnightly
Fortune—Fortune

Gen Army—Generals of the Army and the Air Force and Admirals of the Navy
Good H—Good Housekeeping

Harper—Harper's Magazine
Harpers Bazaar—Harper's Bazaar
Holiday—Holiday
Horn Bk—Horn Book
House & Gard—House & Garden
House B—House Beautiful

Illus London N—Illustrated London News
Ind Woman—Independent Woman
Inland Ptr—Inland Printer
Inter-American—Inter-American

J Am Med Assn—Journal of the American Medical Association
J Home Econ—Journal of Home Economics
J Negro Hist—Journal of Negro History
Jet Propulsion—Jet Propulsion, Journal of the American Rocket Society

PERIODICALS AND NEWSPAPERS CONSULTED

Knickerbocker—"The Knickerbocker"—The Netherlands Magazine

Ladies Home J—Ladies' Home Journal
Library J—Library Journal
Life—Life
Look—Look

McCalls—McCall's
Macleans Mag—Maclean's Magazine
Mag Art—Magazine of Art (discontinued)
Mag of Wall St—Magazine of Wall Street and Business Analyst
Mlle—Mademoiselle
Mo Labor R—Monthly Labor Review
Motion Pict—Motion Picture and Television Magazine
Mus Am—Musical America
Mus Courier—Musical Courier
Mus Mod Art—Museum of Modern Art Bulletin
Mus Q—Musical Quarterly
Musician—Musician

N Y Herald Tribune—New York Herald Tribune
N Y Herald Tribune Bk R—New York Herald Tribune Book Review
N Y Post—New York Post
Bronx Home News consolidated with N Y Post February 16, 1948.
N Y State Ed—New York State Education
N Y Sun—New York Sun. See N Y World-Telegram and Sun
N Y Times—New York Times
N Y Times Bk R—New York Times Book Review
N Y Times Index—New York Times Index
N Y Times Mag—New York Times Magazine
N Y World-Telegram—New York World-Telegram and Sun
Nat & Engl R—National and English Review
Nat Ed Assn J—Journal of the National Education Association
Nat Geog Mag—National Geographic Magazine
Nation—The Nation
Nations Bsns—Nation's Business
Natur Hist—Natural History
Nature—Nature
Nature Mag—Nature Magazine
New Engl Q—New England Quarterly
New Repub—New Republic
New Statesm—New Statesman and Nation
New Yorker—New Yorker
Newsweek—Newsweek

Opera N—Opera News

Parents Mag—Parents' Magazine
Pathfinder—See The Town Journal, Pathfinder
Phot—Photography. Continued as Popular Photography beginning February 1955
Photoplay—Photoplay
Poetry—Poetry
Pol Sci Q—Political Science Quarterly
Pop Mech—Popular Mechanics Magazine
Pop Phot—Popular Photography
Pop Sci—Popular Science Monthly
Progres Ed—Progressive Education
Pub W—Publishers' Weekly

Q R—Quarterly Review
Queen's Q—Queen's Quarterly

Read Digest—Reader's Digest
Ref Shelf—The Reference Shelf
Reporter—The Reporter
Rotarian—Rotarian

Sales Management—Sales Management
Sat Eve Post—Saturday Evening Post
Sat Night—Saturday Night
Sat R—Saturday Review
Sch & Soc—School and Society
Sch R—School Review
Scholastic—Senior Scholastic
Sci Am—Scientific American
Sci Mo—Scientific Monthly
Sci N L—Science News Letter
Science—Science
Sign—The Sign
So Atlan Q—South Atlantic Quarterly
Spec—Spectator
Sport—Sport
Sport Illus—Sports, Illustrated
Sporting N—Sporting News
Studio—Studio; An Illustrated Magazine of Fine and Applied Art
Sunset Mag—Sunset Magazine
Survey—Survey (discontinued)

Theatre Arts—Theatre Arts
This Week—This Week Magazine
Time—Time
Town and Country—Town and Country
Town J—The Town Journal, Pathfinder
Name changed from Pathfinder April 1953.
Travel—Travel

U N Bul—United Nations Bulletin. See United Nations Review
U N R—United Nations Review
U S Bur Labor. See Monthly Labor Review
U S Bur Labor Statistics Bul—United States Bureau of Labor Statistics. Bulletins.
U S News—U. S. News & World Report
U S Office Educ Bul—United States Office of Education. Bulletins.

Va Q R—Virginia Quarterly Review
Variety—Variety
Vital Speeches—Vital Speeches
Vogue—Vogue

Washington (D.C.) Post—Washington Post and Times Herald
Wilson Lib Bul—Wilson Library Bulletin
Womans Home C—Woman's Home Companion
Writer—Writer

Yale R—Yale Review

NECROLOGY

This is a list of biographees' obituaries which are in this Yearbook, including those of late 1954. Deaths which occurred in late 1955 are recorded in the early 1956 issues of CURRENT BIOGRAPHY.

Aswell, James (biog WLB 1951)

Bailey, L. H. (biog 1948)
Barrymore, Lionel (biog 1943)
Beardsley, William S. (biog 1950)
Bethune, Mary McLeod (biog 1942)
Blakeslee, A. F. (biog 1941)
Bliss, Henry E. (biog 1953)
Bryan, Ernest R. (biog 1950)

Carnegie, Dale (biog 1955)
Castillo Nájera, Francisco (biog 1946)
Chase, Harry Woodburn (biog 1948)
Coffin, Henry Sloane, Rev. Dr. (biog 1944)
Collier, Constance (biog 1954)
Corbett, Jim (biog 1946)

Davis, John W. (biog 1953)
Deakin, Arthur (biog 1948)
Déat, Marcel (biog 1942)
Deviny, John J. (biog 1948)
Doughton, Robert L. (biog 1942)
Downes, Olin (biog 1943)

Einstein, Albert (biog 1953)
Emery, DeWitt (biog 1946)

Fatemi, Hossein (biog 1953)
Fath, Jacques (biog 1951)
Fermi, Enrico (biog 1945)
Fleming, Sir Alexander (biog 1944)

Gibson, Hugh (biog 1953)
Golden, John (biog 1944)
Gorman, Herbert Sherman (biog 1940)
Graziani, Rodolfo (biog 1941)

Hampden, Walter (biog 1953)
Harrison, Earl G. (biog 1943)
Hartman, Grace (biog 1942)
Hays, Arthur Garfield (biog 1942)
Hedtoft, Hans (biog 1949)
Hilton, James (biog 1942)
Hooper, C. E. (biog 1947)
Horder, Thomas J. Horder, 1st Baron (biog 1944)
Hull, Cordell (biog 1940)

Jarman, Sanderford (biog 1942)
Johnson, Nelson T. (biog 1940)
Jones, Robert Edmond (biog 1946)

Kasner, Edward (biog 1943)
Keenan, Joseph B. (biog 1946)
Kleist, Paul Ludwig von (biog 1943)
Knoll, Hans G. (biog 1955)
Kress, Samuel H. (biog 1955)

Léger, Fernand (biog 1943)
Lentaigne, Walter D. A. (biog 1944)
Locker, Jesse D. (biog 1955)

McCormick, Robert R. (biog 1942)
McDermott, Michael J. (biog 1951)
McNeil, Hector (biog 1946)
McNutt, Paul V. (biog 1940)
Mann, Thomas (biog 1942)
Matisse, Henri (biog 1953)
Maximos, Demetrios (biog 1948)
Milles, Carl (biog 1952)
Miranda, Carmen (biog 1941)
Mitchell, William D. (biog 1946)
Morrow, Elizabeth Cutter (biog 1943)
Mott, John R. (biog 1947)

Orton, Helen Fuller (biog 1941)

Papagos, Alexander (biog 1951)
Pasquel, Jorge (biog 1946)
Peurifoy, John E. (biog 1949)
Phillips, Lena Madesin (biog 1946)
Pulitzer, Joseph, 2d (biog 1954)

Reynolds, R. S., Sr. (biog 1953)
Roberts, Owen J. (biog 1941)

Saunders, Robert (biog 1951)
Schneider, Hannes (biog 1941)
Seif-ul-Islam Abdullah, Prince (biog 1947)
Sherman, Henry C. (biog 1949)
Shulman, Harry (biog 1952)
Sloan, George A. (biog 1952)
Smith, Bruce (biog 1953)
Somervell, Brehon (biog 1942)
Sumner, James B. (biog 1947)

Towers, J. H. (biog 1941)

Vishinskiĭ, Andreĭ (biog 1944)

White, Paul W. (biog 1940)
White, Walter (biog 1942)

CLASSIFICATION BY PROFESSION—1955

Agriculture

Arnon, Daniel I.
Burpee, David
Byrd, Harry F.
Clements, Earle C.
Johnston, Clem D.
Lambert, W. V.
Matskevich, Vladimir V.
Perkins, C. H.
Steinhaus, Edward A.

Archaeology

Albright, William F.
Coon, Carleton S.
Field, Henry

Architecture

Aronin, Jeffrey Ellis
Callender, John Hancock

Art

Bohrod, Aaron
Brancusi, Constantin
Callery, Mary
Carroll, John
Chase, Joseph Cummings
De Kooning, Willem
Der Harootian, Koren
Feininger, Lyonel
Guptill, Arthur L.
Halpert, Edith Gregor
Kress, Samuel H.
Rich, Daniel Catton
Roberts, Goodridge
Rorimer, James J.
Sutherland, Graham
Sweeney, James Johnson
Washburn, Gordon Bailey
Wyeth, Andrew

Aviation

Chidlaw, Benjamin W.
Davis, Benjamin O., Jr.
Foss, Joseph Jacob
Horner, H. Mansfield
Hurley, Roy T.
Ljungberg, Ernst Carl
Partridge, Earle E.
Quarles, Donald A.
Trippe, Juan T.
Von Kármán, Theodore

Business

Alexander, Archie A.
Antoine
Blough, Roger M.
Breech, Ernest R.
Brownson, Charles B.
Burpee, David
Childs, Richard S.
Cisler, Walker
Clark, Paul F.
Collins, Seaborn P.
Cullen, Hugh Roy
Davis, Edward W.
Dreyfus, Camille
Goldwater, Barry M.
Halpert, Edith Gregor
Holifield, Chet
Horner, H. Mansfield
Hurley, Roy T.
Johnson, Arnold M.
Johnston, Clem D.
Johnston, Eric A.
Knoll, Hans G.
Kress, Samuel H.
Krupp, Alfred
Lelong, Lucien
McComas, O. Parker
McGinnis, Patrick B.
Moody, Ralph (WLB)
Mortimer, Charles G., Jr.
Murphy, W. B.
Newman, J. Wilson
O'Neil, Thomas F.
Perkins, C. H.
Perlman, Alfred E.
Pfost, Gracie
Pick, Vernon J.
Riter, Henry G., 3d
Robertson, Reuben B., Jr.
Simonetta
Stanley, Thomas B.
Stevens, Roger L.
Symes, James M.
Trippe, Juan T.
Waugh, Samuel C.
White, Hugh L.

Dance

Alonso, Alicia
Butler, John
Hayden, Melissa
Magallanes, Nicholas
Somes, Michael

Diplomacy

Areilza, José María de, Count of Motrico
Brosio, Manlio
Couve de Murville, Maurice
Johnson, U. Alexis
Kotelawala, Sir John
Locker, Jesse D.
McClintock, Robert Mills
Maza, José
Nufer, Albert F.
Rankin, K. L.
Sarasin, Pote
Sobolev, Arkady A.
Warren, Avra M.

Education

Adrian, E. D. Adrian, 1st Baron
Albright, William F.
Anderson, Howard
Arnon, Daniel I.
Babb, James T.
Baxter, Frank C.
Bohrod, Aaron
Born, Max
Bothe, Walther
Bridgman, P. W.
Broglie, Louis, Prince de
Brown, Harrison
Buck, Paul H.
Carnegie, Dale
Carnegie, Dorothy
Carroll, John
Chase, Joseph Cummings
Coon, Carleton S.
Davis, Edward W.
Dickey, John Sloan
Dunnock, Mildred
Emrich, Duncan
Enders, John F.
Feynman, R. P.
Gold, Herbert (WLB)
Hatcher, Harlan
Hesburgh, Theodore M., Rev.
Hildebrand, Joel H.
Hilleboe, Herman E.
Jordan, W. K.
Kelly, E. Lowell
Lambert, W. V.
Livingston, M. Stanley
McCloskey, Mark A.
Morton, John Jamieson, Jr.
Nadler, Marcus
Ogburn, William F.
Penfield, Wilder Graves
Riesman, David
Robbins, Frederick C.
Schneirla, T. C.
Segni, Antonio
Singer, S. Fred
Smith, Sidney
Starr, Cecile
Steinhaus, Edward A.
Suhr, Otto
Thurman, Howard, Rev. Dr.
Von Kármán, Theodore
Von Neumann, John
Walker, Waurine
Weller, Thomas H.
Wright, Benjamin F.
Zernike, Frits
Zinn, Walter H.

Engineering

Alexander, Archie A.
Alexanderson, Ernst F. W.
Barnes, Henry A.
Davis, Edward W.
Dexheimer, W. A.
Heinlein, Robert A.
Krupp, Alfred
Olson, Harry F.
Perlman, Alfred E.
Quarles, Donald A.

Fashion

Antoine
Givenchy, Hubert de
Lelong, Lucien
McNellis, Maggi
Schnurer, Carolyn
Simonetta
Toussaint, Jeanne

Finance

Clark, Paul F.
Coyne, James E.
Harris, Walter
Livingston, Homer J.
McGinnis, Patrick B.
Nadler, Marcus
Pflimlin, Pierre
Riter, Henry G., 3d
Waugh, Samuel C.
Yui, O. K.

Government—Foreign

Areilza, José María de, Count of Motrico
Brentano, Heinrich von
Brosio, Manlio
Bulganin, Nikolai A.
Burns, E. L. M.
Café Filho, Joao
Campney, Ralph Osborne
Castillo Armas, Carlos
Couve de Murville, Maurice
Coyne, James E.
Dehler, Thomas
Dhebar, U. N.
Elizabeth II, Queen of Great Britain
Feisal II, King of Iraq
Gregg, Milton F.
Gronchi, Giovanni
Harris, Walter
Hatoyama, Ichiro
Hussein I, King of Hashemite Jordan
Juliana, Queen of the Netherlands
Kaganovich, Lazar M.
Kaur, Rajkumari Amrit
Kotelawala, Sir John
Macmillan, Harold
Matskevich, Vladimir V.
Maza, José
Mikoyan, Anastas I.
Ngo-dinh-Diem
Nuri as-Said
Nutting, Anthony
Pflimlin, Pierre
Rainier III, Prince of Monaco
Samuel, Herbert Samuel, 1st Viscount
Segni, Antonio
Shepilov, Dmitri Trofimovitch
Sobolev, Arkady A.
Stephanopoulos, Stephanos
Suhr, Otto
Tito
Tubman, William V. S.
Yui, O. K.
Zhukov, Georgi K.

Government—United States

Alexander, Archie A.
Allott, Gordon
Beall, J. Glenn
Brownson, Charles B.
Brucker, Wilber M.
Byrd, Harry F.
Case, Clifford P.
Clement, Frank G.
Clements, Earle C.
Cooper, Jere
Daley, Richard J.
De Sapio, Carmine G.
Dexheimer, W. A.
Ervin, Samuel J., Jr.
Farmer, Guy
Farrington, Elizabeth Pruett
Foss, Joseph Jacob
Fulbright, J. William
Gary, Raymond
George, Walter F.
Goldwater, Barry M.
Griffiths, Martha W.
Hall, Fred
Harlan, John Marshall
Hill, William S.
Holifield, Chet
Hollister, John B.
Johnson, U. Alexis
Johnston, Eric A.
Knight, Frances G.
Knight, Goodwin
Lehman, Herbert H.
Leopold, Alice K.
Locker, Jesse D.
McCarthy, Eugene J.
McNamara, Patrick V.
Meyner, Robert B.
Mitchell, James P.
Morton, John Jamieson, Jr.
Muskie, Edmund S.
Neuberger, Richard L.
Nufer, Albert F.
O'Konski, Alvin E.
Parker, John J.
Pfost, Gracie
Pyle, Howard
Quarles, Donald A.
Ribicoff, Abraham A.
Robertson, Reuben B., Jr.
Robinson, Elmer E.
Russell, Charles H.
Sobeloff, Simon E.
Stanley, Thomas B.
Streibert, Theodore C.
Von Neumann, John
Waugh, Samuel C.
Welker, Herman
White, Hugh L.

Industry

Blough, Roger M.
Breech, Ernest R.
Cisler, Walker
Davis, Roy H.
Grebe, John J.
Hurley, Roy T.
Johnston, Eric A.
Krupp, Alfred
McComas, O. Parker
Mortimer, Charles G., Jr.
Murphy, W. B.

International Relations

Areilza, José María de, Count of Motrico
Brosio, Manlio
Burns, E. L. M.
Couve de Murville, Maurice
Johnson, U. Alexis
Kotelawala, Sir John
Ljungberg, Ernst Carl
Locker, Jesse D.
McClintock, Robert Mills
Macmillan, Harold
McNair, Sir Arnold D.
Maza, José
Nufer, Albert F.
Nutting, Anthony
Rankin, K. L.
Sarasin, Pote
Sobolev, Arkady A.
Stephanopoulos, Stephanos
Warren, Avra M.
Waugh, Samuel C.
Wright, Jerauld

Journalism

Areilza, José María de, Count of Motrico
Café Filho, Joao
Cassidy, Claudia
Darrell, R. D.
Fadiman, Clifton
Hearst, William Randolph, Jr.
Lapp, Ralph E.
Lewis, Anthony
Muggeridge, Malcolm
Neuberger, Richard L.
Patterson, Alicia

Labor

Law

Library Service

Literature

Medicine

Military

Motion Pictures

Music

Naval

Nonfiction

Angle, Paul M.
Areilza, José María de, Count of Motrico
Aronin, Jeffrey Ellis
Bannister, Constance
Born, Max
Bridgman, P. W.
Broglie, Louis, Prince de
Brown, Harrison
Buck, Paul H.
Carnegie, Dale
Chase, Joseph Cummings
Clayton, P. B., Rev.
Coon, Carleton S.
Darrell, R. D.
Emrich, Duncan
Fadiman, Clifton
Farrar, Margaret
Field, Henry
Funk, Wilfred
Gordon, Dorothy
Guptill, Arthur L.
Hass, Hans
Hatcher, Harlan
Hauser, Gayelord
Johnstone, Margaret Blair, Rev.
Jordan, W. K.
Kazantzakis, Nikos
Le Gallienne, Eva
Lorenz, Konrad Z.
McNair, Sir Arnold D.
McNellis, Maggi
Marshall, Catherine
Martini, Helen
Moody, Ralph (WLB)
Morehead, Albert H.
Moser, Fritz
Muggeridge, Malcolm
Neuberger, Richard L.
Nizer, Louis
Ogburn, Charlton
Ogburn, William F.
Rich, Daniel Catton
Riesman, David
Rorimer, James J.
Salisbury, Harrison E.
Samuel, Herbert Samuel, 1st Viscount
Schneirla, T. C.
Shoemaker, Samuel M., Rev. Dr.
Slonimsky, Nicolas
Smith, Sidney
Steinhaus, Edward A.
Suhr, Otto
Sweeney, James Johnson
Thurman, Howard, Rev. Dr.
Wechsberg, Joseph
White, Theodore H.
White, William S.
Woodham-Smith, Cecil (WLB)
Wright, Benjamin F.

Organizations

Angle, Paul M.
Blake, Eugene Carson, Rev. Dr.
Chapman, Mrs. Theodore S.
Childs, Richard S.
Cisler, Walker
Collins, Seaborn P.
Haley, Andrew G.
Hildebrand, Joel H.
Johnston, Clem D.
Johnston, Eric A.
Kelly, E. Lowell
Kumm, Henry W.
Livingston, Homer J.
Lynch, Daniel F.
Richards, John S.
Riter, Henry G., 3d
Shafik, Doria
Tice, Merton B.
Walker, Waurine
Wilson, Rufus H.
Wright, Loyd

Politics—Foreign

Bourguiba, Habib ben Ali
Brentano, Heinrich von
Bulganin, Nikolai A.
Café Filho, Joao
Castillo Armas, Carlos
Dehler, Thomas
Dhebar, U. N.
Gregg, Milton F.
Gronchi, Giovanni
Harris, Walter
Hatoyama, Ichiro
Kaganovich, Lazar M.
Kotelawala, Sir John
Macmillan, Harold
Matskevich, Vladimir V.
Maza, José
Mikoyan, Anastas I.
Ngo-dinh-Diem
Nuri as-Said
Nutting, Anthony
Pflimlin, Pierre
Samuel, Herbert Samuel, 1st Viscount
Segni, Antonio
Shepilov, Dmitri Trofimovitch
Stephanopoulos, Stephanos
Suhr, Otto
Tito
Tubman, William V. S.
Yui, O. K.
Zhukov, Georgi K.

Politics—United States

Allott, Gordon
Beall, J. Glenn
Brownson, Charles B.
Brucker, Wilber M.
Butler, Paul M.
Byrd, Harry F.
Case, Clifford P.
Clement, Frank G.
Clements, Earle C.
Cooper, Jere
Daley, Richard J.
De Sapio, Carmine G.
Ervin, Samuel J., Jr.
Farrington, Elizabeth Pruett
Foss, Joseph Jacob
Fulbright, J. William
Gary, Raymond
George, Walter F.
Goldwater, Barry M.
Griffiths, Martha W.
Hall, Fred
Hill, William S.
Holifield, Chet
Knight, Goodwin
Lehman, Herbert H.
Leopold, Alice K.
McCarthy, Eugene J.
McNamara, Patrick V.
Meyner, Robert B.
Muskie, Edmund S.
Neuberger, Richard L.
O'Konski, Alvin E.
Pfost, Gracie
Pyle, Howard
Ribicoff, Abraham A.
Robinson, Elmer E.
Russell, Charles H.
Stanley, Thomas B.
Welker, Herman
White, Hugh L.

Publishing

Angoff, Charles (WLB)
Byrd, Harry F.
Fadiman, Clifton
Funk, Wilfred
Guptill, Arthur L.
Hearst, William Randolph, Jr.
Lippincott, Joseph Wharton
Morehead, Albert H.
Muggeridge, Malcolm
Patterson, Alicia
Servan-Schreiber, J.-J.

Radio

Alexanderson, Ernst F. W.
Angoff, Charles (WLB)
Fadiman, Clifton
Gordon, Dorothy
Kelly, Nancy
McCleery, Albert
McNellis, Maggi
Merman, Ethel
O'Neil, Thomas F.
Saint, Eva Marie
Streibert, Theodore C.
Weaver, Sylvester L., Jr.
Webb, Jack
Wright, Martha

Religion

Blake, Eugene Carson, Rev. Dr.
Clayton, P. B., Rev.
Hesburgh, Theodore M., Rev.
Johnstone, Margaret Blair, Rev.
Marshall, Catherine
Pierre, Abbé

Science

Social Science

Social Service

Sports

Technology

Television

Theatre

Other Classifications

BIOGRAPHIES OF WOMEN—1955

Alberghetti, Anna Maria
Alonso, Alicia
Angeles, Victoria de los

Bailey, Pearl
Bannister, Constance

Callery, Mary
Carnegie, Dorothy
Cassidy, Claudia
Chapman, Mrs. Theodore S.
Churchill, Sarah
Conner, Nadine
Cottrell, Dorothy (WLB)

Dobbs, Mattiwilda
Dunnock, Mildred

Elizabeth II, Queen of Great Britain
Eustis, Helen (WLB)

Farrar, Margaret
Farrington, Elizabeth Pruett
Fergusson, Erna (WLB)
Frederika, Consort of Paul I, King of the Hellenes

Garbo, Greta
Gordon, Dorothy
Griffiths, Martha W.
Gueden, Hilde

Halpert, Edith Gregor
Hayden, Melissa

Johnstone, Margaret Blair, Rev.
Juliana, Queen of the Netherlands

Kaur, Rajkumari Amrit
Kelly, Grace
Kelly, Nancy
Kitt, Eartha
Knight, Frances G.
Knight, Ruth Adams (WLB)

Le Gallienne, Eva
Leopold, Alice K.
Lindfors, Viveca

McCarthy, Mary (WLB)
McGraw, Eloise Jarvis (WLB)
MacKenzie, Gisele
McNellis, Maggi

Marshall, Catherine
Martini, Helen
Merman, Ethel
Moiseiwitsch, Tanya

Neilson, Frances Fullerton (WLB)

Patterson, Alicia
Patton, Frances Gray (WLB)
Pfost, Gracie

Saint, Eva Marie
Schnurer, Carolyn
Schwarzkopf, Elisabeth
Selinko, Annemarie
Shafik, Doria
Simonetta
Stanley, Kim
Starr, Cecile
Sumac, Yma

Tebaldi, Renata
Tharp, Louise Hall (WLB)
Toussaint, Jeanne

Walker, Waurine
Williams, Esther
Woodham-Smith, Cecil (WLB)
Wright, Martha

CUMULATED INDEX—1951-1955

This is a five-year cumulation of all names which have appeared in CURRENT BIOGRAPHY from 1951 through 1955. The dates after names indicate monthly issues and/or Yearbooks in which biographies and obituaries are contained.

For the index to 1940-1950 biographies, see CURRENT BIOGRAPHY 1950 Yearbook.

(5846)